THEOLOGICAL DICTIONARY
OF THE
OLD TESTAMENT

THEOLOGICAL DICTIONARY

OF THE

OLD TESTAMENT

EDITED BY

G. JOHANNES BOTTERWECK,

HELMER RINGGREN,

AND

HEINZ-JOSEF FABRY

Translated by

DAVID E. GREEN

Volume IX

נָשָׂה - מָרַד

māraḏ – nāqâ

WILLIAM B. EERDMANS PUBLISHING COMPANY

GRAND RAPIDS, MICHIGAN / CAMBRIDGE, U.K.

THEOLOGICAL DICTIONARY OF THE OLD TESTAMENT
Volume IX
Translated from
THEOLOGISCHES WÖRTERBUCH ZUM ALTEN TESTAMENT
Band V, Lieferungen 1-5
Published 1984-1986 by
Verlag W. Kohlhammer GmbH, Stuttgart, Germany

255 Jefferson Ave. S.E., Grand Rapids, Michigan 49503 /
P.O. Box 163, Cambridge CB3 9PU U.K.

Printed in the United States of America

03 02 01 00 99 7 6 5 4 3 2

Library of Congress Cataloging-in-Publication Data

Botterweck, G. Johannes
Theological dictionary of the Old Testament
Translation of Theologisches Wörterbuch zum Alten Testament.
Translated by David E. Green and Douglas W. Stott
Includes rev. ed. of v. 1-2.
Includes bibliographical references.
1. Bible. O.T. — Dictionaries — Hebrew. 2. Hebrew language — Dictionaries — English.
I. Ringgren, Helmer, 1917 — joint author. II. Fabry, Heinz-Josef — joint author.
III. Title.

ISBN 0-8028-2338-6 (set)

Volume IX ISBN 0-8028-2333-5

CONSULTING EDITORS

George W. Anderson
Henri Cazelles
David Noel Freedman
Shemaryahu Talmon
Gerhard Wallis

CONTRIBUTORS

G. W. Anderson, Edinburgh
†C. Barth, Basel
K.-M. Beyse, Halle am Saale
H. Cazelles, Paris
J. Conrad, Leipzig
C. Dohmen, Bonn
†H. Eising, Münster
H.-J. Fabry, Bonn (Editor)
D. N. Freedman, Ann Arbor / San Diego
H. F. Fuhs, Würzburg
F. Garcia-López, Salamanca
H. Gross, Regensburg
W. Gross, Tübingen
L. Harper, Pinole
†G. F. Hasel, Berrien Springs
F. J. Helfmeyer, Cologne
F. L. Hossfeld, Bonn
B. Johnson, Lund
M. Z. Kaddari, Ramat Gan
O. Kaiser, Marburg-Cappel
B. Kalthoff, Bergisch Gladbach
†A. S. Kapelrud, Oslo
B. Kedar-Kopfstein, Haifa
†D. Kellermann, Tübingen
K. Koch, Hamburg
T. Kronholm, Madla
B. Lang, Paderborn
E. Lipiński, Louvain
J. Lundbom, Cambridge
H. Madl, Graz
†P. Maiberger, Mainz
J. Marböck, Graz
G. Mayer, Zornheim
J. Milgrom, Berkeley
H.-P. Müller, Münster
†M. J. Mulder, Badhoevedorp
†H. D. Preuss, Neuendettelsau
†J. Reindl, Erfurt
H. Ringgren, Uppsala (Editor)
L. Ruppert, Freiburg im Breisgau
J. Scharbert, Munich
L. Schwienhorst, Münster
H. Seebass, Bonn
K. Seybold, Basel
H. Simian-Yofre, Rome
L. A. Snijders, Huizen
S. Wagner, Leipzig
G. Warmuth, Kiel
B. E. Willoughby, Ann Arbor
D. P. Wright, Provo
H.-J. Zobel, Greifswald

CONTENTS

ABBREVIATIONS

AAH	*Acta Antiqua Academiae Scientiarum Hungaricae,* Budapest
AANLR	*Atti dell' Academia Nazionale dei Lincei, Rendiconti,* Rome
AASOR	*Annual of the American Schools of Oriental Research,* New Haven, Ann Arbor, Philadelphia
AAWLM	*Abhandlungen der Akademie der Wissenschaften und der Literatur in Mainz*
AB	*The Anchor Bible,* ed. W. F. Albright and D. N. Freedman, Garden City, N.Y.
ABAW	*Abhandlungen der bayerischen Akademie der Wissenschaften,* Munich
ABBU	*Altbabylonische Briefe in Umschrift und Übersetzung,* Leiden, 1964ff.
ABL	R. F. Harper, *Assyrian and Babylonian Letters,* 14 vols. (Chicago, 1892-1914)
ABR	*Australian Biblical Review,* Melbourne
abs.	absolute
AC	*L'Antiquité classique,* Brussels
acc.	accusative
ACLing-SémCham	*Actes du premier congrès internationale de linguistique sémitique et chamito-sémitique,* Paris, 16-19 July, 1969. *Janua linguarum,* 159 (The Hague, 1974)
AcOr	*Acta orientalia,* Copenhagen, Leiden
act.	active
ADAI.Ä	*Abhandlungen des Deutschen Archäologischen Instituts in Kairo.* Ägyptologische Reihe, Glückstadt
ADAW	*Abhandlungen des Deutschen Akademie der Wissenschaften,* Berlin
adj.	adjective
ADPV	*Abhandlungen des deutschen Palästinavereins,* Wiesbaden
adv.	adverb
ÄF	*Ägyptologische Forschungen,* Glückstadt
AFNW	*Arbeitsgemeinschaft für Forschung des Landes Nordrhein-Westfalen,* Cologne
AfO	*Archiv für Orientforschung,* Graz
ÄgAbh	*Ägyptologische Abhandlungen,* Wiesbaden
AGSU	*Arbeiten zur Geschichte des Spätjudentums und Urchristentums,* Leiden
AGWG	*Abhandlungen der Gesellschaft der Wissenschaften zu Göttingen,* Berlin
AHw	W. von Soden, *Akkadisches Handwörterbuch,* 3 vols. (Wiesbaden, 1965-81)
AION	*Annali dell'Istituto Universitario Orientali di Napoli*
AIPH	*Annuaire de l'Institut de Philologie et d'Histoire Orientales et Slaves,* Brussels
AJBA	*Australian Journal of Biblical Archaeology,* Sydney
AJBI	*Annual of the Japanese Biblical Institute* (*Seísho-gaku ronshī*), Tokyo
AJP	*American Journal of Philology,* Baltimore
AJSL	*The American Journal of Semitic Languages and Literatures,* Chicago
AJT	*American Journal of Theology,* Chicago
AKGW	*Abhandlungen der Königlichen Gesellschaft des Wissenschaften zu Göttingen*
Akk.	Akkadian
AKM	*Abhandlungen für die Kunde des Morgenlandes,* Leipzig, Wiesbaden, Hildesheim
Amhar.	Amharic
Amor.	Amorite
AN	J. J. Stamm, *Die akkadische Namengebung. MVÄG,* 44 (1939, ^{2}1968)
AnAcScFen	*Annales Academiae Scientarum Fennicae,* ser. B, Helsinki

AnBibl	*Analecta biblica,* Rome
AncIsr	R. de Vaux, *Ancient Israel: Its Life and Institutions* (Eng. trans., New York, 1961, repr. 1965)
ANEP	*The Ancient Near East in Pictures,* ed. J. B. Pritchard (Princeton, 1954, ^{2}1969)
ANET	*Ancient Near Eastern Texts Relating to the OT,* ed. J. B. Pritchard (Princeton, ^{2}1955, ^{3}1969)
ANH	G. Dalman, *Aramäisch-Neuhebräisches Handwörterbuch,* Göttingen, ^{3}1938
AnOr	*Analecta orientalia,* Rome
AnSt	*Anatolian Studies,* Leiden
ANVAO	*Avhandlinger utgitt av det Norske Videnskaps-Akademi i Oslo*
AO	*Der Alte Orient,* Leipzig
AOAT	*Alter Orient und AT,* Kevelaer, Neukirchen-Vluyn
AOB	*Altorientalische Bilder zum AT,* ed. H. Gressmann (Berlin, ^{2}1927)
AO Beiheft	*Beiheft zum AO,* Leipzig
AOS	*American Oriental Series,* New Haven
AOT	*Altorientalische Texte zum AT,* ed. H. Gressmann (Berlin, ^{2}1926, repr. 1953)
AP	A. E. Cowley, *Aramaic Papyri of the Fifth Century B.C.* (1923, repr. Osnabruck, 1976)
APN	K. Tallqvist, *Assyrian Personal Names. ASSF,* 43/1 (1914, repr. 1966)
APNM	H. B. Huffmon, *Amorite Personal Names in the Mari Texts* (Baltimore, 1965)
Arab.	Arabic
ARAB	D. D. Luckenbill, *Ancient Records of Assyria and Babylonia,* 2 vols. (Chicago, 1926-27)
Aram.	Aramaic
ARM	*Archives royales de Mari. Textes cunéiformes,* Paris
ARM.T	———. *Transcriptions et traductions,* Paris
ArOr	*Archiv orientální,* Prague
ARW	*Archiv für Religionswissenschaft,* Freiburg, Leipzig, Berlin
AS	*Assyriological Studies,* Chicago
ASAE	*Annales du Service des Antiquités de l'Égypte,* Cairo
Ash.	Tablet in the Ashmolean Museum
ASOR	American Schools of Oriental Research
ASORDS	*ASOR Dissertation Series,* Missoula, Chico, Atlanta
ASSF	*Acta Societatis Scientiarum Fennicae,* Helsinki
Assyr.	Assyrian
ASTI	*Annual of the Swedish Theological Institute in Jerusalem,* Leiden
AT	Altes Testament, Ancien Testament, etc.
ATA	*Alttestamentliche Abhandlungen,* Münster
ATANT	*Abhandlungen zur Theologie des Alten und Neuen Testaments,* Zurich
ATD	*Das AT Deutsch,* ed. V. Herntrich and A. Weiser, Göttingen
ATR	*Anglican Theological Review,* Evanston
ATS	*Arbeiten zu Text und Sprache im AT,* St. Ottilien, Munich
Aug.	*Augustinianum,* Rome
AUM	*Andrews University Monographs,* Berrien Springs
AuS	G. Dalman, *Arbeit und Sitte in Palästina,* 7 vols. (1928-42, repr. Hildesheim, 1964)
AUSS	*Andrews University Seminary Studies,* Berrien Springs
AUU	*Acta universitatis upsaliensis,* Uppsala
AzT	*Arbeiten zur Theologie,* Stuttgart
BA	*The Biblical Archaeologist,* New Haven, Ann Arbor, Philadelphia, Atlanta
Bab.	Babylonian, Babylonian Talmud
BAfO	*Beiheft zur AfO*

BAr	*Bulletin archéologique du comité des travaux historiques et scientifiques,* Paris
BAR	*Biblical Archaeology Review,* Washington
BA Reader	*Biblical Archaeologist Reader,* ed. D. N. Freedman, et al., 3 vols. (1961-70, repr. Winona Lake, 1975), vol. 4 (Sheffield, 1983)
BASOR	*Bulletin of the American Schools of Oriental Research,* New Haven, Ann Arbor, Philadelphia, Baltimore
BASS	*Beiträge zur Assyriologie und semitischen Sprachwissenschaft,* Leipzig, Baltimore
BBB	*Bonner biblische Beiträge*
BBET	*Beiträge zur biblischen Exegese und Theologie,* Frankfurt, Las Vegas
BBLAK	*Beiträge zur biblischen Landes- und Altertumskunde. ZDPV,* 68 (1949-51)
BBR	*H. Zimmern, Beiträge zur Kenntnis der babylonischen Religion. Assyriologische Bibliothek,* 12 (Leipzig, 1901)
BCPE	*Bulletin du Centre Protestant d'Études,* Geneva
BDB	F. Brown, S. R. Driver, and C. A. Briggs, *A Hebrew and English Lexicon of the OT* (Oxford, 1907; Peabody, Mass., ^{2}1979)
BDBAT	*Beiheft zur Dielheimer Blätter zum AT*
Beeston	A. F. L. Beeston, *Sabaic Dictionary* (Louvain-la-Neuve, 1982)
Benz	F. L. Benz, *Personal Names in the Phoenician and Punic Inscriptions. StPohl,* 8 (1972)
BeO	*Bibbia e oriente,* Milan
BethM	*Beth Miqra,* Jerusalem
BETL	*Bibliotheca ephemeridum theologicarum Lovaniensium,* Paris, Gembloux
BEvT	*Beiträge zur evangelische Theologie,* Munich
BFCT	*Beiträge zur Förderung christliches Theologie,* Gütersloh
BHHW	*Biblisch-historisches Handwörterbuch,* ed. L. Rost and B. Reicke, 4 vols. (Göttingen, 1962-66; index and maps, 1979)
BHK	*Biblia hebraica,* ed. R. Kittel (Stuttgart, ^{3}1929)
BHS	*Biblia hebraica stuttgartensia,* ed. K. Elliger and W. Rudolph (Stuttgart, 1966-77)
BHT	*Beiträge zur historischen Theologie,* Tübingen
BibB	*Biblische Beiträge,* Fribourg
Bibl	*Biblica,* Rome
bibliog.	bibliography
Biella	J. Biella, *Dictionary of Old South Arabic, Sabaean Dialect. HSS,* 25 (1982)
BIES	*Bulletin of the Israel Exploration Society,* Jerusalem (= *Yediot*)
BietOr	*Biblica et orientalia,* Rome
BiLe	*Bibel und Leben,* Düsseldorf
BiLi	*Bibel und Liturgie,* Klosterneuberg
BIN	*Babylonian Inscriptions in the Collection of James B. Nies* (New Haven, 1918–)
BiOr	*Bibliotheca orientalia,* Leiden
BJRL	*Bulletin of the John Rylands Library,* Manchester
BK	*Biblischer Kommentar AT,* ed. M. Noth and H. W. Wolff, Neukirchen-Vluyn
BL	*Bibel-Lexikon,* ed. H. Haag (Einsiedeln, 1951, ^{2}1968)
BLe	H. Bauer and P. Leander, *Historische Grammatik der hebräischen Sprache des ATs* (1918-22, repr. Hildesheim, 1991)
BM	Tablet in the collections of the British Museum
BMAP	E. G. Kraeling, *The Brooklyn Museum Aramaic Papyri* (New Haven, 1953)
BMB	*Bulletin du musée de Beyrouth*
BN	*Biblische Notizien,* Bamberg
BOT	*De Boeken van het OT,* Roermond en Maaseik
BR	*Biblical Research,* Chicago

BRA	*Beiträge zur Religionsgeschichte des Altertums,* Halle
BRL	K. Galling, *Biblisches Reallexikon. HAT* (1937, ^{2}1977)
BS	*Bibliotheca sacra,* Dallas
BSAW	*Berichte über die Verhandlungen der Sächsischen Akademie der Wissenschaften zu Leipzig*
BSOAS	*Bulletin of the School of Oriental and African Studies,* London
BT	*The Bible Translator,* London
BTB	*Biblical Theology Bulletin,* Rome
BuA	B. Meissner, *Babylonien und Assyrien,* 2 vols. (Heidelberg, 1920-25)
BVC	*Bible et vie chrétienne,* Paris
BWA(N)T	*Beiträge zur Wissenschaft vom Alten (und Neuen) Testament,* Leipzig, Stuttgart
BWL	W. G. Lambert, *Babylonian Wisdom Literature* (Oxford, 1960)
BZ	*Biblische Zeitschrift,* Paderborn
BZAW	*Beihefte zur ZAW,* Berlin
BZNW	*Beihefte zur ZNW,* Berlin
ca.	circa, about
CAD	*The Assyrian Dictionary of the Oriental Institute of the University of Chicago* (1956–)
CAH^3	*Cambridge Ancient History,* ed. I. E. S. Edwards, et al. (Cambridge, 1970–)
CahRB	*Cahiers de la RB,* Paris
CahTh	*Cahiers théologiques,* Neuchâtel
Can.	Canaanite
CAT	*Commentaire de l'AT,* Neuchâtel
CB	*Coniectanea biblica,* OT Series, Lund
CBC	*Cambridge Bible Commentary on the New English Bible,* Cambridge
CBQ	*Catholic Biblical Quarterly,* Washington
CBQMS	*Catholic Biblical Quarterly Monograph Series*
CD A,B	Damascus document, manuscript A, B
cf.	compare, see
ch(s).	chapter(s)
CH	Code of Hammurabi
CHAL	W. L. Holladay, *A Concise Hebrew and Aramaic Lexicon of the OT* (Leiden, Grand Rapids, 1971)
ChrÉg	*Chronique d'Égypte,* Brussels
ChW	J. Levy, *Chaldäisches Wörterbuch über die Targumim und einen grossen Theil des rabbinischen Schriftthums,* 2 vols. (Leipzig, 1867-68, repr. 1959)
CIH	*Corpus inscriptionum himyariticarum* (= *CIS,* IV)
CIJ	*Corpus inscriptionum judaicarum* (Vatican, 1936–)
CIL	*Corpus inscriptionum latinarum* (Berlin, 1862–)
CIS	*Corpus inscriptionum semiticarum* (Paris, 1881–)
CJT	*Canadian Journal of Theology,* Toronto
CML	G. R. Driver, *Canaanite Myths and Legends* (Edinburgh, 1956; ^{2}1977, ed. J. C. L. Gibson)
col.	column
comm(s).	commentary(ies)
ComViat	*Communio viatorum,* Prague
conj.	conjecture
const.	construct
ContiRossini	K. Conti Rossini, *Chrestomathia arabica meridionalis ephigraphica* (Rome, 1931)
Copt.	Coptic
COT	*Commentaar op het OT,* Kampen

CRAI	*Comptes rendus des séances de l'Academie des Inscriptions et Belles Lettres,* Paris
CSD	R. Payne Smith, *A Compendious Syriac Dictionary* (Oxford, 1903, repr. 1976)
CTA	A. Herdner, *Corpus des tablettes en cunéiformes alphabétiques découvertes à Ras Shamra-Ugarit,* 2 vols. (Paris, 1963)
CThM	*Calwer theologische Monographien,* Stuttgart
CTM	*Concordia Theological Monthly,* St. Louis
D	D (doubling) stem
DAWB	*Deutsch Akademie der Wissenschaft zu Berlin. Schriften der Sektion für Altertumswissenschaft*
DAWW	*Denschriften der (kaiserlichen) Akademie der Wissenschaften in Wien*
DB	*Dictionnaire de la Bible,* ed. F. Vigouroux (Paris, 1895-1912)
DBS	*Dictionnaire de la Bible, Supplement,* ed. L. Pirot, et al. (Paris, 1926–)
DISO	J. F. Jean and J. Hoftijzer, *Dictionnaire des inscriptions sémitiques de l'ouest* (Leiden, 1965)
diss.	dissertation
DJD	*Discoveries in the Judean Desert* (Oxford, 1955–)
DLZ	*Deutsche Literaturzeitung,* Berlin
DMOA	*Documenta et monumenta orientis antiqui,* Leiden
DN	Deity name
DtrN	nomistic Deuteronomistic source
DtrP	prophetic Deuteronomistic redactor
DTT	*Dansk teologisk Tidsskrift,* Copenhagen
E	Elohistic source
EA	Tell el-Amarna tablets
EAEHL	*Encyclopedia of Archaeological Excavations in the Holy Land,* ed. M. Avi-Yonah and E. Stern, 4 vols. (Englewood Cliffs, N.J., 1975-78)
Eb.	Eblaite
EB	*Die Heilige Schrift in deutscher Übersetzung. Echter-Bibel,* Würzburg
ÉBib	*Études bibliques,* Paris
ed.	edition, editor
EdF	*Erträge der Forschung,* Darmstadt
EDNT	*Exegetical Dictionary of the NT,* ed. H. Balz and G. Schneider, 3 vols. (Eng. trans., Grand Rapids, 1990-93)
Egyp.	Egyptian
EH	*Europäische Hochschulschriften,* Frankfurt; Bern
EHAT	*Exegetisches Handbuch zum AT,* Münster
EMiqr	*Enṣiqlōpedyā miqrāʾit (Encyclopedia Biblica)* (Jerusalem, 1950–)
emph.	emphatic(us)
EncBib	*Encyclopaedia Biblica,* ed. T. K. Cheyne, 4 vols. (London, 1900-1903, repr. 1958)
EncJud	*Encyclopaedia judaica,* 16 vols. (Jerusalem, New York, 1971-72)
EnEl	Enuma Elish
Eng.	English
ERE	*Encyclopedia of Religion and Ethics,* ed. J. Hastings, 13 vols. (New York, 1913-27)
Erg.	Ergänzungsheft, Ergänzungsreihe
ErIsr	*Eretz-Israel,* Jerusalem
ErJb	*Eranos-Jahrbuch,* Zurich
esp.	especially
EstBíb	*Estudios bíblicos,* Madrid
EstEcl	*Estudios ecclesiásticos,* Madrid

Eth.	Ethiopic
ETL	*Ephemerides theologicae lovanienses,* Louvain
ETR	*Études théologiques et religieuses,* Montpellier
ETS	*Erfurter theologische Studien,* Leipzig
EÜ	Einheitsübersetzung der Heilige Schrift (Stuttgart, 1974-80)
EvQ	*Evangelical Quarterly,* London
EvT	*Evangelische Theologie,* Munich
ExpT	*Expository Times,* Edinburgh
fem.	feminine
fig(s).	figure(s)
fr.	fragment
FRLANT	*Forschungen zur Religion und Literatur des Alten und Neuen Testaments,* Göttingen
FuF	*Forschungen und Fortschritte,* Berlin
FzB	*Forschung zur Bibel,* Würzburg
GaG	W. von Soden, *Grundriss der akkadischen Grammatik. AnOr,* 33 (1952, ²1969 [with Erg., *AnOr,* 47])
Ger.	German
GesB	W. Gesenius and F. Buhl, *Hebräisches und aramäisches Handwörterbuch über das AT* (Berlin, ¹⁷1921, ¹⁸1987–)
GesTh	W. Gesenius, *Thesaurus philologicus criticus linguae hebraecae et chaldaeae Veteris Testamenti,* 3 vols. (Leipzig, 1829-58)
Gilg.	Gilgamesh epic
Gk.	Greek
GK	W. Gesenius and E. Kautsch, *Hebräische Grammatik* (Halle, ²⁸1909) (= Kautsch and A. E. Cowley, *Gesenius' Hebrew Grammar* [Oxford, ²1910])
GLECS	*Comptes rendus du Groupe Linguistique d'Études Chamito-Sémitiques,* Paris
GSAT	*Gesammelte Studien zum AT,* Munich
GTT	*Gereformeerd theologisch Tijdschrift,* Aalten, Kampen
GTTOT	J. J. Simons, *The Geographical and Topographical Texts of the OT. SFS,* 2 (1959)
Guillaume	A. Guillaume, *Hebrew and Arabic Lexicography* (repr. Leiden, 1965)
GUOST	*Glasgow University Oriental Society Transactions,* Glasgow
H	Holiness Code
Habil.	Habilitationschrift
HAL	L. Koehler, W. Baumgartner, et al., *The Hebrew and Aramaic Lexicon of the OT,* 5 vols. plus Sup (Eng. trans., Leiden, 1967-96)
HAT	*Handbuch zum AT,* ser. 1, ed. O. Eissfeldt, Tübingen
HAW	*Handbuch der Altertumswissenschaft,* ed. W. Otto (Munich, 1923–)
HDB	*Dictionary of the Bible,* ed. J. Hastings, 4 vols. (Edinburgh, 1898-1902; *Sup,* 1904; New York, ²1963)
Heb.	Hebrew
Herm	*Hermeneia,* Philadelphia, Minneapolis
HeyJ	*Heythrop Journal,* Oxford
Hitt.	Hittite
HKAT	*Handkommentar zum AT,* ed. W. Nowack, Göttingen
HO	*Handbuch der Orientalistik,* Leiden
HP	E. Jenni, *Das hebräische Piʿel* (Zurich, 1968)
HS	*Die Heilige Schrift des ATs,* ed. F. Feldermann and H. Herkenne, 8 vols. (Bonn, 1930-31)
HSAT	*Die Heilige Schrift des ATs,* ed. E. Kautsch and A. Bertholet, 4 vols. (Tübingen, ⁴1922-23)

HSM	Harvard Semitic Monographs, Cambridge, Mass.
HSS	*Harvard Semitic Studies,* Missoula, Chico, Atlanta
HTC	*Herders Theological Commentary on the NT,* New York
HTR	*Harvard Theological Review,* Cambridge, Mass.
HUCA	*Hebrew Union College Annual,* Cincinnati
Hurr.	Hurrian
IB	*The Interpreter's Bible,* ed. G. A. Buttrick, 12 vols. (Nashville, 1952-57)
ICC	*The International Critical Commentary,* Edinburgh
IDB	*The Interpreter's Dictionary of the Bible,* ed. G. A. Buttrick, 4 vols. (Nashville, 1962); *Sup,* ed. K. Crim (Nashville, 1976)
IEJ	*Israel Exploration Journal,* Jerusalem
IKZ	*Internationale kirchliche Zeitschrift,* Bern
ILC	J. Pedersen, *Israel: Its Life and Culture,* 4 vols. in 2 (Eng. trans., Oxford, 1926-40, ^{5}1963)
ILR	*Israel Law Review,* Jerusalem
impf.	imperfect
impv.	imperative
inf.	infinitive
in loc.	on this passage
Int	*Interpretation,* Richmond
Intro(s).	Introduction(s) (to the)
IPN	M. Noth, *Die israelitischen Personennamen im Rahmen der gemeinsemitischen Namengebung. BWANT,* 46[3/10] (1928, repr. 1980)
J	Yahwist source (J^1, earliest Yahwist source)
JA	*Journal asiatique,* Paris
JAC	*Jahrbuch für Antike und Christentum,* Münster
JANES	*Journal of the Ancient Near Eastern Society of Columbia University,* New York
JAOS	*Journal of the American Oriental Society,* Baltimore, Boston, New Haven
JARCE	*Journal of the American Research Center in Egypt,* Boston
JARG	*Jahrbuch für Anthropologie und Religionsgeschichte,* Saarbrücken
Jastrow	M. Jastrow, *A Dictionary of the Targumim, the Talmud Babli and Yerushalmi, and the Midrashic Literature* (1903; repr. 2 vols. in 1, Brooklyn, 1975)
JB	Jerusalem Bible (Garden City, N.Y., 1966)
JBL	*Journal of Biblical Literature,* Philadelphia, Missoula, Chico, Atlanta
JBLMS	*JBL Monograph Series,* Philadelphia, Missoula, Chico, Atlanta
JBR	*Journal of Bible and Religion,* Boston
JCS	*Journal of Cuneiform Studies,* New Haven, Cambridge, Mass., Philadelphia, Baltimore
JDAI	*Jahrbuch des Deutschen Archäologischen Instituts,* Berlin
JDAISup	———, *Supplement,* Berlin
JE	Yahwist-Elohist source
JE	*The Jewish Encyclopedia,* ed. I. Singer, 12 vols. (New York, 1916)
JEA	*Journal of Egyptian Archaeology,* London
JEOL	*Jaarbericht van het Vooraziatisch-Egyptisch Genootschap 'Ex Oriente Lux,'* Leiden
Jer.	Jerusalem (Palestinian) Talmud
JES	*Journal of Ecumenical Studies,* Pittsburgh, Philadelphia
JHS	*Journal of Hellenic Studies,* London
JJS	*Journal of Jewish Studies,* London
JLA	*Jewish Law Annual,* Leiden
JM	P. Joüon and T. Muraoka, *A Grammar of Biblical Hebrew. Subsidia biblica,* 14/I-II (Eng. trans. 1991)

JMOS	*Journal of the Manchester Oriental Society,* Manchester
JNES	*Journal of Near Eastern Studies,* Chicago
JNSL	*Journal of Northwest Semitic Languages,* Stellenbosch
JOS	*Journal of Oriental Studies*
JPOS	*Journal of the Palestine Oriental Society,* Jerusalem
JQR	*Jewish Quarterly Review,* Philadelphia
JRAS	*Journal of the Royal Asiatic Society,* London
JSHRZ	*Jüdische Schriften aus hellenistisch-römischer Zeit,* Gütersloh
JSJ	*Journal for the Study of Judaism in the Persian, Hellenistic and Roman Period,* Leiden
JSOT	*Journal for the Study of the OT,* Sheffield
JSS	*Journal of Semitic Studies,* Manchester
JTS	*Journal of Theological Studies,* Oxford
Jud	*Judaica,* Zurich
K	*Kethibh*
KAI	H. Donner and W. Röllig, *Kanaanäische und aramäische Inschriften,* 3 vols. (Wiesbaden, ^{2}1966-69, ^{3}1971-76)
KAT	*Kommentar zum AT,* ed. E. Sellin and J. Herrmann, Leipzig, Gütersloh
KBL	L. Koehler and W. Baumgartner, *Lexicon in Veteris Testamenti Libros* (Leiden, ^{1}1953, ^{2}1958, ^{3}1967–)
KBo	*Keilschrifttexte aus Boghazköy. WVDOG* (1916–)
KD	C. F. Keil and F. Delitzsch, *Comm. on the OT,* 10 vols. (Eng. trans., repr. Grand Rapids, 1954)
KEHAT	*Kurzgefasstes exegetisches Handbuch zum AT,* ed. O. F. Fridelin (Leipzig, 1812-96)
KHC	*Kurzer Hand-Commentar zum AT,* ed. K. Marti, Tübingen, Leipzig
KHS	*Kleinkommentar zur Heiligen Schrift,* Düsseldorf
KJV	King James Version
KlPauly	*Der Kleine Pauly. Lexikon der Antike,* ed. K. Ziegler and W. Sontheimer, 5 vols. (Stuttgart, 1962-75)
KlSchr	*Kleine Schriften* (A. Alt [Munich, 1953-59, ^{3}1964]; O. Eissfeldt [Tübingen, 1962-79]; K. Elliger [*ThB,* 32 (1966)]; E. Meyer [Halle, 1910-24])
KTU	*Die keilalphabetischen Texte aus Ugarit,* I, ed. M. Dietrich, O. Loretz, and J. Sanmartín. *AOAT,* 24 (1976)
KUB	*Keilschrifturkunde aus Boghazköi,* Berlin
KuD	*Kerygma und Dogma,* Göttingen
Kuhn	K. G. Kuhn, *Konkordanz zu den Qumrantexten* (Göttingen, 1960); Nachträge, *RevQ,* 4 (1963-64), 163-234
l(l).	line(s)
Lane	E. W. Lane, *An Arabic-English Lexicon,* 8 vols. (London, 1863-93, repr. 1968)
LAPO	*Littératures anciennes du Proche-Orient,* Paris
LÄS	*Leipziger ägyptische Studien,* Glückstadt
Lat.	Latin
LB	*Linguistica biblica,* Bonn
LCL	*Loeb Classical Library,* Cambridge, Mass., and London
LCP	*Latinitas Christianorum primaeva,* Utrecht
LD	*Lectio divina,* Paris
Leslau, *Contributions*	W. Leslau, *Ethiopic and South Arabic Contributions to the Hebrew Lexicon* (Los Angeles, 1958)
Leš	*Lešonénu,* Jerusalem
LexÄg	W. Helck and E. Otto, eds., *Lexikon der Ägyptologie* (Wiesbaden, 1975–)

LexHebAram	F. Zorrell, *Lexicon hebraicum et aramaicum Veteris Testamenti* (Rome, 1958, repr. 1968)
LexLingAeth	A. Dillmann, *Lexicon linguae aethiopicae* (Leipzig, 1865)
LexLingAram	E. Vogt, *Lexicon linguae aramaicae Veteris Testamenti documentis antiquis illustratum* (Rome, 1971)
LexSyr	C. Brockelmann, *Lexicon syriacum* (Halle, 1928, ^{2}1968)
LidzEph	M. Lidzbarski, *Ephemeris für semitische Epigraphik* (Giessen, 1900-1915)
Lisowsky	G. Lisowsky, *Konkordanz zum hebräischen AT* (Stuttgart, 1958, ^{2}1966)
lit.	literally
LSJ	H. G. Liddell, R. Scott, and H. S. Jones, *A Greek-English Lexicon* (Oxford, ^{9}1940)
LUÅ	*Lunds Universitets Årsskrift*
LXX	Septuagint (LXX^{A}, Codex Alexandrinus; LXX^{B}, Codex Vaticanus; LXX^{Or}, Origen; LXX^{R}, Lucianic recension; LXX$^{S[1,2]}$, Codex Sinaiticus, correctors 1, 2, etc.)
MAD	*Materials for the Assyrian Dictionary,* Chicago
Mand.	Mandaic
Mandelkern	S. Mandelkern, *Veteris Testamenti Concordantiae* (Tel Aviv, 1971)
MAOG	*Mitteilungen der Altorientalistischen Gesellschaft,* Leipzig
MarTS	*Marburger theologische Studien,* Marburg
MÄS	*Münchener Ägyptologische Studien,* Berlin
masc.	masculine
MDAI.K	*Mitteilungen des Deutschen Archäologischen Instituts. Abteilung Kairo,* Munich
MdD	E. S. Drower and R. Macuch, *Mandaic Dictionary* (Oxford, 1963)
MEE	*Materiali Epigrafica di Ebla,* ser. maior, Naples
Meyer	R. Meyer, *Hebräische Grammatik,* 4 vols. (Berlin, ^{3}1966-72)
mg.	margin
MGWJ	*Monatsschrift für Geschichte und Wissenschaft des Judentums,* Breslau
Midr.	Midrash
MIO	*Mitteilungen des Instituts für Orientforschung,* Berlin
MKAW	*Mededelingen der Koninklijke Nederlandse Akademie van Wetenschapen,* Amsterdam
Moab.	Moabite
MPG	J. P. Migne, *Patrologia graeca,* 167 vols. (Paris, 1857-66); index, 2 vols. (1928-36)
MPL	J. P. Migne, *Patrologia latina,* 221 vols. (Paris, 1841-64); Sup, 5 vols. (1958-70)
MRS	*Mission de Ras Shamra,* Paris
MS(S).	manuscript(s)
MSL	*Materialen zum sumerischen Lexikon,* Rome
MT	Masoretic Text
MTS	*Münchener theologische Studien,* Munich
Mur	Wadi Murabbaʿat text(s)
Mus	*Muséon,* Louvain
MUSJ	*Mélanges de l'Université St.-Joseph,* Beirut
MVÄG	*Mitteilungen der Vorderasiatisch-Ägyptischen Gesellschaft* Berlin, Leipzig
n(n).	note(s)
N	name
Nab.	Nabatean
NBSS	T. Nöldeke, *Neue Beiträge zur semitischen Sprachwissenschaft* (Strassburg, 1910)
NEAJT	*Northeast Asia Journal of Theology,* Tokyo
NEB	*Die Neue Echter-Bibel,* Würzburg

NedGTT	*Nederduitse gereformeerde teologiese Tydskrif,* Kaapstad
NERT	*Near Eastern Religious Texts Relating to the OT,* ed. W. Beyerlin. *OTL* (Eng. trans. 1978)
NGWG	*Nachrichten von der Gesellschaft der Wissenschaften zu Göttingen,* Berlin
NICOT	*The New International Commentary on the OT,* Grand Rapids
NJB	The New Jerusalem Bible (New York, 1985)
NJPS	The New Jewish Publication Society of America Translations of the Holy Scriptures (Philadelphia, 1962-78)
NKZ	*Neue kirkliche Zeitschrift,* Erlangen, Leipzig
no(s).	number(s)
NovTSup	*Novum Testamentum, Supplements,* Leiden
NRSV	New Revised Standard Version (New York, 1989)
NRT	*Nouvelle revue théologique,* Louvain, Paris
N.S.	new series
NSS	J. Barth, *Die Nominalbildung in den semitischen Sprachen* ([2]1894, repr. Hildesheim, 1967)
NT	New Testament, Neues Testament, etc.
NTS	*New Testament Studies,* Cambridge
NTT	*Norsk teologisk Tidsskrift,* Oslo
obj.	object
OBO	*Orbis biblicus et orientalis,* Fribourg, Göttingen
OBT	*Overtures to Biblical Theology,* Philadelphia, Minneapolis
obv.	obverse of a papyrus or tablet
OIP	*Oriental Institute Publications,* Chicago
OLZ	*Orientalistische Literaturzeitung,* Leipzig, Berlin
Or	*Orientalia,* Rome
OrAnt	*Oriens antiquus,* Rome
OrBibLov	*Orientalia et biblica Lovaniensia,* Louvain
OSA	Old South Arabic
OT	Old Testament, Oude Testament, etc.
OTL	*The Old Testament Library,* Philadelphia, Louisville
OTS	*Oudtestamentische Studiën,* Leiden
OTWSA	*Ou testamentiese werkgemeenskap in Suid-Afrika,* Pretoria
p(p).	page(s)
P	Priestly source (P^G, Priestly *Grundschrift* ["basic material"]; P^S, secondary Priestly source)
Palmyr.	Palmyrene
par.	parallel / and parallel passages
pass.	passive
PEQ	*Palestine Exploration Quarterly,* London
perf.	perfect
Pes.	Pesiqta
Phil.-hist. Kl.	Philosophische-historische Klasse
Phoen.	Phoenician
PJ	*Palästinajahrbuch,* Berlin
pl(s).	plate(s)
pl.	plural
PLO	*Porta linguarum orientalium,* Wiesbaden
PN	Personal name
PNPI	J. K. Stark, *Personal Names in Palmyrene Inscriptions* (Oxford, 1971)
PNU	F. Grondähl, *Die Personennamen der Texte aus Ugarit. StPohl,* 1 (1967)
POS	*Pretoria Oriental Series,* Leiden

POT	*De Prediking van het OT,* Nijkerk
prep.	preposition
PRU	*Le Palais royal d'Ugarit,* ed. C. F.-A. Schaeffer and J. Nougayrol. *MRS*
ptcp.	participle
Pun.	Punic
PW	A. Pauly and G. Wissowa, *Real-Encyclopädie der classischen Altertumswissenschaft,* 6 vols. (Stuttgart, 1839-52); Sup, 11 vols. (1903-56); ser. 2, 10 vols. (1914-48)
Q	Qumran scroll (preceded by arabic numeral designating cave)
Q	*Qere*
R	Redactor (R^D, Deuteronomistic; R^P, Priestly)
R (preceded by roman numeral)	text in H. C. Rawlinson, *The Cuneiform Inscriptions of Western Asia,* 5 vols. (London, 1861-84)
R.	Rabbi
RA	*Revue d'assyriologie et d'archéologie orientale,* Paris
RAC	*Reallexikon für Antike und Christentum,* ed. T. Klauser (Stuttgart, 1950–)
RÄR	H. Bonnet, *Reallexikon der ägyptischen Religionsgeschichte* (Berlin, 1952, ^{2}1971)
RB	*Revue biblique,* Paris
RE	*Real-Enzyklopädie für protestantische Theologie und Kirche,* ed. A. Hauck, 24 vols. (Leipzig, 1896-1913)
RechBib	*Recherches bibliques,* Paris
REJ	*Revue des études juives,* Paris
repr.	reprint, reprinted
Répr. géogr.	*Répertoires géograpique des textes cunéiformes,* ed. W. Röllig. *TAVO Beihefte,* B, 7 (1974–)
RES	*Répertoire d'épigraphie sémitique* (Paris, 1900–) (with number of text)
RÉS	*Revue des études sémitiques,* Paris
rev.	revised, revision
RevBíbl	*Revista bíblica,* Buenos Aires
RevExp	*Review and Expositor,* Louisville
RevQ	*Revue de Qumrân,* Paris
RGG	*Die Religion in Geschichte und Gegenwart* (Tübingen, ^{2}1927-31, ed. H. Gunkel and L. Zscharnack, 5 vols.; ^{3}1957-65, ed. K.Galling, 6 vols.)
RHPR	*Revue d'histoire et de philosophie religieuses,* Strasbourg, Paris
RHR	*Revue de l'histoire des religions,* Paris
RivBibl	*Rivista biblica,* Rome
RLA	*Reallexikon der Assyriologie,* ed. E. Ebeling and B. Meissner (Berlin, 1932–)
RoB	*Religion och Bibel,* Stockholm
RS	Ras Shamra text
RSO	*Rivista degli studi orientali,* Rome
RSP	*Ras Shamra Parallels: The Texts from Ugarit and the Hebrew Bible,* ed. L. R. Fisher, et al., I, *AnOr,* 49 (1972); II, *AnOr,* 50 (1975); III, *AnOr,* 51 (1981)
RSPT	*Revue des sciences philosophiques et théologiques,* Paris
RSR	*Recherches de science religieuse,* Paris
RSV	Revised Standard Version (New York, 1946, 1952)
RT	*Receuil de travaux relatifs à la philologie et à l'archéologie égyptiennes et assyriennes,* Paris
rto.	recto, on the obverse of a papyrus or tablet
RyNP	G. Ryckmans, *Les noms propres sud-sémitiques,* 3 vols. *Bibliothèque de muséon,* 2 (Louvain, 1934-35)

Sab.	Sabaic
Saf.	Safaitic
SAHG	A. Falkenstein and W. von Soden, *Sumerische und akkadische Hymnen und Gebeten* (Zurich, 1953)
Sam.	Samaritan
SANT	*Studien zum Alten und Neuen Testament,* Munich
SAOC	*Studies in Ancient Oriental Civilization,* Chicago
SAT	*Die Schriften des ATs im Auswald,* ed. H. Gunkel and H. Gressmann, 7 vols. (Göttingen, ^{2}1920-22)
SAW	*Sitzungsberichte der Óesterreichischen Akademie der Wissenschaften in Wien,* Vienna
SB	*Sources bibliques,* Paris
SBFLA	*Studii biblici franciscani liber annus,* Jerusalem
SBL	Society of Biblical Literature
SBLDS	*SBL Dissertation Series,* Missoula, Chico, Atlanta
SBLMS	*SBL Monograph Series,* Missoula, Chico, Atlanta
SBLSBS	*SBL Sources for Biblical Study,* Chico, Atlanta
SBLSCS	*SBL Septuagint and Cognate Studies,* Missoula, Chico, Atlanta
SBM	*Stuttgarter biblische Monographien*
SBOT	*Sacred Books of the OT,* ed. P. Haupt (London, 1893)
SBS	*Stuttgarter Bibel-Studien*
SBT	*Studies in Biblical Theology,* London, Naperville
ScrHier	*Scripta hierosolymitana,* Jerusalem
SDAW	*Sitzungsberichte der Deutschen Akademie der Wissenschaften zu Berlin*
SEÅ	*Svensk exegetisk Åarsbok,* Lund
Sem.	Semitic
Sem	*Semitica,* Paris
ser.	series
Seux	J. M. Seux, *Epithètes royales akkadiens et sumériennes* (Paris, 1967)
SFS	*Studia Francisci Scholten memoriae dicata,* Leiden
sg.	singular
SGKA	*Studien zur Geschichte und Kultur des Altertums,* Paderborn
SHAW	*Sitzungsberichte der Heidelberger Akademie der Wissenschaften*
ShnatMikr	*Shnaton le-mikra ule-ḥeker ha-mizraḥ ha-kadum (Shnationian Annual for Biblical and Ancient Near Eastern Studies),* Jerusalem
SJLA	*Studies in Judaism in Late Antiquity,* Leiden
SJT	*Scottish Journal of Theology,* Edinburgh
SKG.G	*Schriften der Königsberger Gelehrten Gesellschaft,* Geisteswissenschaftliche Klasse, Halle
ŠL	A. Deimel, *Šumerisches Lexikon* (Rome, 1925-37, repr. 1961)
SNumen	*Sup to Numen,* Leiden
SNVAO	*Skrifter utgitt av det Norske Videnskaps-Akademi i Oslo*
Sond	Sonderband, Sonderheft
Soq.	Soqoṭri
SOTS	Society for Old Testament Studies, Cambridge
SPAW	*Sitzungsberichte der Preussischen Akademie der Wissenschaften,* Berlin
SPIB	*Scripta Pontificii Instituti Biblici,* Rome
SR	*Studies in Religion / Sciences religieuses,* Toronto
SSAW	*Sitzungsberichte der Sächsischen Akademie der Wissenschaften zu Leipzig,* Phil.-hist. Kl.
SSN	*Studia semitica neerlandica,* Assen
st.	status

ST	*Studia theologica,* Lund, Århus
St.-B.	H. L. Strack and P. Billerbeck, *Kommentar zum NT aus Talmud und Midrasch,* 6 vols. (Munich, 1922-61)
STDJ	*Studies on the Texts of the Desert of Judah,* Leiden, Grand Rapids
StOr	*Studia orientalia,* Helsinki
StPb	*Studia Postbiblica,* Leiden
StPohl	*Studia Pohl,* Rome
StSem	*Studi semitici,* Rome
subj.	subject
subst.	substantive
suf.	suffix
Sum.	Sumerian
SUNT	*Studien zur Umwelt des NTs,* Göttingen
Sup	Supplement(s) (to)
s.v.	*sub voce* (*vocibus*), under the word(s)
SVT	*Supplements to VT,* Leiden
syn.	synonym(ous)
Synt	C. Brockelmann, *Hebräische Syntax* (Neukirchen-Vluyn, 1956)
Syr.	Syriac
Syr	*Syria. Revue d'art oriental et d'archéologie,* Paris
Tanḥ.B	*Tanḥuma* (ed. Buber)
Targ.	Targum; Targ.[f], Targ. Jonathan from Codex Reuchlinianus
TAVO	*Tübinger Atlas des Vorderen Orients,* Wiesbaden
TCL	*Textes cunéiformes du Musée du Louvre,* 31 vols. (Paris, 1910-67)
TCS	*Texts from Cuneiform Sources,* Locust Valley, N.Y.
TDNT	*Theological Dictionary of the NT,* ed. G. Kittel and G. Friedrich, 9 vols. plus index vol. (Eng. trans., Grand Rapids, 1964-76)
TDOT	*Theological Dictionary of the OT,* ed. G. J. Botterweck, H. Ringgren, and H.-J. Fabry (Eng. trans., Grand Rapids, 1974–)
TGI	K. Galling, *Textbuch zur Geschichte Israels* (Tübingen, 1950, ^{2}1968, ^{3}1979)
TGl	*Theologie und Glaube,* Paderborn
Tham.	Thamudic
ThB	*Theologische Bücherei,* Munich
ThS	*Theologische Studien,* Zurich
Tigr.	Tigriña
TLOT	*Theological Lexicon of the OT,* ed. E. Jenni and C. Westermann, 3 vols. (Eng. trans., Peabody, Mass., 1997)
TLZ	*Theologische Literaturzeitung,* Leipzig, Berlin
TM	Tell Mardikh-Ebla tablets
TOTC	*Tyndale Old Testament Commentaries,* London, Downers Grove
TP	*Theologie und Philosophie,* Freiburg im Breisgau
TQ	*Theologische Quartalschrift,* Tübingen, Stuttgart
trans.	translation, translated by
TRE	*Theologische Realenzyklopädie,* ed. G. Krause, G. Müller, and H. R. Balz, 22 vols. (Berlin, 1977-92)
TRu	*Theologische Rundschau,* Tübingen
TSK	*Theologische Studien und Kritiken,* Hamburg, Gotha, Leipzig
TSSI	J. C. L. Gibson, *Textbook of Syrian Semitic Inscriptions,* 3 vols. (Oxford, 1975-82)
TTQ	*Tübinger theologisches Quartalschrift,* Tübingen
TTS	*Trierer theologische Studien*
TU	*Texte und Untersuchungen der altchristlichen Literatur,* Leipzig, Berlin

TUAT	*Texte aus der Umwelt des ATs,* Gütersloh
TW	*Theologische Wissenschaft,* Stuttgart
TWNT	*Theologisches Wörterbuch zum NT,* ed. G. Kittel and G. Friedrich, 10 vols. plus index (Stuttgart, 1933-79)
TZ	*Theologische Zeitschrift,* Basel
UF	*Ugarit-Forschungen,* Neukirchen-Vluyn
Ugar.	Ugaritic
UM	C. H. Gordon, *Ugaritic Manual. AnOr,* 35 (1955)
Univ.	University
UT	C. H. Gordon, *Ugaritic Textbook. AnOr,* 38 (1965, ^{2}1967)
UUÅ	*Uppsala universitets årsskrift*
v(v).	verse(s)
VAB	*Vorderasiatische Bibliothek,* 7 vols. (Leipzig, 1907-16)
VAS	*Vorderasiatische Schriftdenkmäler der königlichen Museen,* Berlin
VD	*Verbum domini,* Rome
VF	*Verkündigung und Forschung,* Munich
VG	C. Brockelmann, *Grundriss der vergleichenden Grammatik der semitischen Sprachen,* 2 vols. (1908-13, repr. Hildesheim, 1961)
vo.	verso, on the reverse of a papyrus or tablet
VT	*Vetus Testamentum,* Leiden
Vulg.	Vulgate
VVAW.L	*Verhandelingen van de Koninklijke Vlaamse Academie voor Wetenschappen, Letteren en Schone Kunsten van België,* Klasse der letteren, Brussels
WbÄS	A. Erman and H. Grapow, *Wörterbuch der ägyptischen Sprache,* 6 vols. (Leipzig, 1926-31, repr. 1963)
WbMyth	*Wörterbuch der Mythologie,* ed. H. W. Haussig (Stuttgart, 1965–)
WbTigr	E. Littmann and M. Höfner, *Wörterbuch der Tigre Sprache* (Wiesbaden, 1962)
WdF	*Wege der Forschung,* Darmstadt
Wehr	H. Wehr, *A Dictionary of Modern Written Arabic,* ed. J. M. Cowan (Ithaca, 1961, ^{3}1971, ^{4}1979)
Whitaker	R. E. Whitaker, *A Concordance of the Ugaritic Language* (Cambridge, Mass., 1972)
WMANT	*Wissenschaftliche Monographien zum Alten und Neuen Testament,* Neukirchen-Vluyn
WO	*Die Welt des Orients,* Göttingen
WTJ	*Westminster Theological Journal,* Philadelphia
WTM	J. Levy, *Wörterbuch über die Talmudim und Midraschim,* 4 vols. (Leipzig, ^{2}1924, repr. 1963)
WuD	*Wort und Dienst,* Bielefeld
WUNT	*Wissenschaftliche Untersuchungen zum NT,* Tübingen
WUS	J. Aistleitner, *Wörterbuch der ugaritischen Sprache. BSAW,* Phil.-hist. Kl., 106/3 (1963, ^{4}1974)
WVDOG	*Wissenschaftliche Veröffentlichungen der deutschen Orient-Gesellschaft,* Leipzig
WZ Halle	*Wissenschaftliche Zeitschrift der Martin-Luther-Universität Halle-Wittenberg,* Halle
WZKM	*Wiener Zeitschrift für die Kunde des Morgenlandes,* Vienna
YNER	*Yale Near Eastern Researches,* New Haven
YOSBT	*Yale Oriental Series: Babylonian Texts,* New Haven
YOSR	*Yale Oriental Series: Researches,* New Haven
ZA	*Zeitschrift für Assyriologie,* Leipzig, Berlin
ZÄS	*Zeitschrift für ägyptische Sprache und Altertumskunde,* Leipzig, Berlin

ZAW	*Zeitschrift für die alttestamentliche Wissenschaft,* Giessen, Berlin
ZBK	*Zürcher Bibelkommentare,* Zurich, Stuttgart
ZDMG	*Zeitschrift der Deutschen Morgenländischen Gesellschaft,* Leipzig, Wiesbaden
ZDPV	*Zeitschrift des Deutschen Palästina-Vereins,* Leipzig, Stuttgart, Wiesbaden
ZEE	*Zeitschrift für evangelische Ethik,* Gütersloh
ZKT	*Zeitschrift für katholische Theologie,* Innsbruck
ZMR	*Zeitschrift für Missionskunde und Religionswissenschaft,* Berlin
ZNW	*Zeitschrift für die neutestamentliche Wissenschaft,* Giessen, Berlin
ZRGG	*Zeitschrift für Religions- und Geistesgeschichte,* Cologne
ZS	*Zeitschrift für Semitistik und verwandte Gebiete,* Leipzig
ZTK	*Zeitschrift für Theologie und Kirche,* Tübingen
→	cross-reference within this Dictionary
<	derived from
>	whence derived, to
*	theoretical form

TRANSLITERATION

VOWELS

◌ַ	a
◌ֲ	^{a}
◌ָ	ā
◌ָה	â
◌ָיו	āw
◌ַי	ay
◌ָי	āy
◌ֶ	e
◌ֱ	^{e}
◌ֶי	ey
◌ֵ	ē
◌ֵי	ê
◌ְ	^{e}
◌ִ	i
◌ִי	î
◌ִיּ	iyy
◌ָ	o
◌ֳ	^{o}
◌ֹ	ō
וֹ	ô
◌ֻ	u, ū
וּ	û

CONSONANTS

א	ʼ
בּ	b
ב	ḇ
גּ	g
ג	ḡ
דּ	d
ד	ḏ
ה, הּ	h
ו	w
ז	z
ח	ḥ
ט	ṭ
י	y
כּ, ךּ	k
כ, ך	ḵ
ל	l
מ, ם	m
נ, ן	n
ס	s
ע	ʻ
פּ	p
פ, ף	p̄
צ, ץ	ṣ
ק	q
ר	r
שׂ	ś
שׁ	š
תּ	t
ת	ṯ

מָרַד mārad̲; מֶרֶד mered̲; מַרְדוּת mardûṯ

Contents: I. Etymology. II. Occurrences. III. Usage. IV. Meaning: 1. Political; 2. Theological. V. Summary. VI. LXX and Dead Sea Scrolls.

I. Etymology. The root *mrd,* "rebel," is attested in Egyptian Aramaic, Jewish Aramaic, Christian Palestinian Aramaic, Mandaic, Arabic, and Safaitic, as well as in Hebrew and Biblical Aramaic. In Ethiopic the noun *mĕrād* means "rebellion"; in Lihyanian it means "rebel"; in Old South Arabic the root appears as a proper name.[1] The noun that appears as *mered̲* in Biblical Hebrew and as *m^erad̲* in Biblical Aramaic ("rebellion") occurs as *mirdā'* in the Jewish Aramaic of the Targums, as *merdā* in Syriac, and as *mirda* in Mandaic.[2] Biblical Heb. *mardûṯ* is cognate with Mand. *marda/mardita* 2, "rebellion."[3] The root *mrd* also appears in the Hebrew PN *mered̲* (1 Ch. 4:17,18).[4]

II. Occurrences. The verb *mrd* occurs 25 times in the OT (only in the qal): 5 in Josh. 22, 4 each in 2 Kings and Ezekiel, 3 in Nehemiah, 2 each in 2 Chronicles and Dnl. 9, and 1 each in Genesis, Numbers, Isaiah, Jeremiah, and Job. The nouns *mered̲* (Josh. 22:22) and *mardûṯ* (1 S. 20:30) occur once each. In the Aramaic section, the noun *m^erad̲* occurs once (Ezr. 4:19) and the adj. *mārād̲* twice in the feminine (Ezr. 4:12,15).

The text of Josh. 22:19b is difficult: the qal of *mrd* is preceded by an accusative object. Martin Noth and *BHS* read the hiphil of *mrd.*[5] It is probably better to follow the Targ., reading *ûḇānû* instead of *w^e'ōṯānû* and retaining the qal of *mrd.*

III. Usage. In most cases, the verb *mrd* is used with the prep. *b^e* (18 times). Twice it is used with *'al* (Neh. 2:19; 2 Ch. 13:6), and 4 times it is used in the absolute (Gen. 14:4; Ezk. 2:3; Neh. 6:6; Dnl. 9:5). Once it appears in the construct (Job 24:13). Ten times the object of *mrd* is a king, 9 times Yahweh/God, once the nine and a half tribes (Josh. 22:19), and once it occurs in a construct relationship with "light" (Job 24:13). Two different usages of *mrd* may be distinguished: political and theological.

---

mārad̲. R. Knierim, "מרד *mrd* 'to rebel,' " *TLOT,* II, 684-86; *idem,* "פשׁע *paéša'* 'crime," *TLOT,* II, 1033-37; I. Plein, "Erwägungen zur Überlieferung von I Reg 11,26–14,20," *ZAW,* 78 (1966), 8-24; I. Riesener, *Der Stamm* עבד *im AT. BZAW,* 149 (1979); C. Schäfer-Lichtenberger, *Stadt und Eidgenossenschaft im AT. BZAW,* 156 (1983).

1. See, respectively, *LexLingAeth,* 169; *HAL,* II, 632; ContiRossini, 181a.
2. *HAL,* II, 632.
3. *MdD,* 253; cf. M. Wagner, *Die lexikalischen und grammatikalischen Aramaismen im alttestamentlichen Hebräisch. BZAW,* 96 (1966), no. 179.
4. Cf. *IPN,* 250.
5. *Das Buch Josua. HAT,* VII (^{3}1971), 130.

IV. Meaning.

1. *Political.* In political contexts *mārad̲* denotes the attempt to escape from political dependency with the goal of achieving or regaining political independence (Gen. 14:4; 2 K. 18:7; 18:20 par. Isa. 36:5; 2 K. 24:1; 24:20 par. Jer. 52:3; Ezk. 17:15; Neh. 2:19; 6:6; 2 Ch. 13:6; 36:13). In most cases, a vassal refuses to acknowledge vassal status. Hezekiah escapes from the suzerainty of the Assyrian king that had been accepted by his predecessor Ahaz by refusing to pay tribute (2 K. 18:7f.). This act is described as *mārad̲ bᵉ* and *lō' ʿᵃb̲ād̲ô,* "he would not serve him" (v. 7). From the Assyrian perspective this act is also described as *mārad̲* (v. 20 par. Isa. 36:5). The rejections of vassalage to the Babylonian king Nebuchadnezzar by Jehoiachim (2 K. 24:1) and Zedekiah (24:20 par. Jer. 52:3; 2 Ch. 36:13) are also designated *mārad̲.* Ezk. 17:15 alludes to Zedekiah's rebellion reported in 2 K. 24:20.

As synonyms for *mārad̲,* 2 Ch. 13:6 uses → קום *qûm,* "rise up," and Ezk. 17:14 uses → נשׂא *nś'* (hithpael), "rise up." The only antonym found in a political context is → עבד *ʿāb̲ad̲,* "serve" (Gen. 14:4; 2 K. 18:7) or *hāyâ ʿeb̲ed̲,* "be slave/servant" (2 K. 24:1). In 2 K. 24:1 the opposition between "be someone's servant" and *mārad̲* is underlined by → שׁוב *šûb̲,* here used adverbially, "expresses a movement opposite to one mentioned previously."[6] In these passages, the expressions *ʿāb̲ad̲* and *hāyâ ʿeb̲ed̲* denote a vassal's dependence on his suzerain, which finds concrete expression in tribute (→ מנחה *minḥâ*); cf. 2 S. 8:2,6; Jgs. 3:15,17f.; 1 K. 5:1 (Eng. 4:21); 2 K. 17:3; Hos. 10:6; 2 Chr. 17:11; 26:8.[7] The vassal relationship is established by oath in the presence of God and by treaty (2 Ch. 36:13; Ezk. 17:13-18). Politically, such apostasy consists in refusing to give tribute and joining foreign coalitions (2 K. 17:4; 18:20ff.; Ezk. 17:15). In international law, it represents breach of treaty (Ezk. 17:13-18; → ברית *bᵉrît̲*).

In political contexts, therefore, *mārad̲* has a meaning similar to that of the verb → פשׁע *pšʿ* when it appears in political contexts. There are differences, however: only twice is a king the subject of *pšʿ* (2 K. 3:5,7); 9 times the subject is a land (1 K. 12:19; 2 K. 1:1; 8:20,22a; 2 Ch. 10:19; 21:8,10aα) or city (2 K. 8:22b; 2 Ch. 21:10aβ). By contrast, the subject of *mārad̲* is always a person or group of persons, 10 times one or more kings (Gen. 14:4; 2 K. 18:7,20; 24:1,20; Isa. 36:5; Jer. 52:3; Ezk. 17:15; 2 Ch. 13:6; 36:13), twice a nation and its governor (Neh. 2:19; 6:6). In political contexts the only prepositional objects of *mārad̲* are kings, whereas the prepositional objects (with *bᵉ* or *mittaḥat̲ yad̲*) of *pšʿ* include the names of countries (2 K. 1:1; 8:20,22; 2 Ch. 21:8,10) and dynasties ("house of David": 1 K. 12:19; 2 Ch. 10:19). The antonyms found with *mārad̲* (*ʿāb̲ad̲,* "serve," and *hāyâ ʿeb̲ed̲,* "be slave/servant," in Gen. 14:4; 2 K. 18:7; 24:1) are not found with *pšʿ*. It is true, though, that 2 K. 3:4 also refers to a dependency relationship involving tribute, against which the king of Moab rebels (*pšʿ;* 2 K. 3:5). *pšʿ* probably always has negative connotations,[8] whereas the valuation

6. JM, §177b (1).
7. Riesener, 142f.
8. Plein, 10.

of an act denoted by *mārad* may vary according to the political and theological standpoint of the author: it can be positive (2 K. 18:7,20ff.), negative (2 K. 24:1,10; Ezk. 17:15; 2 Ch. 36:13), or neutral (Gen. 14:4).

The verb *pš'* points historically to the small-scale altercations of the tenth and ninth centuries B.C. among the "fraternal nations" of Judah, Israel, Moab, and Edom, which were politically about equal in strength. Here *pš'* denotes the usually successful "dropping out" of a country or city from the sovereignty of an adjacent or surrounding country or from a political alliance based on personal union. In the passages cited here, it should be translated "secede."

The verb *mārad,* however, points historically to the period of Assyria's expansion as a major power in the eighth and seventh centuries (exceptions: Gen. 14:4; 2 Ch. 13:6). It denotes the usually unsuccessful attempts of the kings of Judah, robbed of their political independence, to rebel against the king of the power to which they were subject. Besides the meaning "secede, desert," *mārad* thus has the sense of "rise up, rebel." This semantic distinction between *pš'* and *mārad* is also preserved in Chronicles. In 2 Ch. 10:19 the Chronicler uses *pš' b^e* to denote the separation of the northern from the southern kingdom ("so Israel seceded from the house of David"); in 2 Ch. 13:6, however, he uses *mārad 'al,* best translated "rebel against," as the context (vv. 7-20) suggests: "And Jeroboam . . . rose up *(qûm)* and rebelled against his lord [= Rehoboam]."

The verb *mārad* can also denote the attempt of a governor to achieve autonomy. Nehemiah is accused of seeking political separation from the Persian king by rebuilding the walls of Jerusalem and reorganizing the Judahite community, with the goal of himself becoming king of the Jews (Neh. 2:19; 6:6). The accusation addressed to Artaxerxes, the Persian king, by those who opposed rebuilding the temple (Ezr. 4:7-16; preserved in Aramaic) calls Jerusalem a rebellious *(mārāḏtā')* and wicked *(bi'yštā')* city (v. 12; cf. v. 15: *qiryā' mārāḏā').* The document conjures up the danger that the Persian king will no longer receive tribute, custom, or toll from the Jews (vv. 13,16). The reply of the Persian king includes the statement: "This city has risen *(miṯnaśś^e'â)* against kings from long ago; rebellion *(m^eraḏ)* and sedition *('eštaddûr)* have been made in it" (v. 19).

The noun *mardûṯ* is found only in 1 S. 20:30, in the expression *ben-na'^awaṯ hammardûṯ,* probably a colloquial term of abuse. The double construct and the niphal participle of *'āwâ* (cf. Prov. 12:8: *na'^awēh-lēḇ[9]*) make the expression hard to translate ("you son of perversion and rebellion"?). As 1 S. 20:30b-31 shows, it is emphatically political: from Saul's perspective, Jonathan's loyalty to David represents rebellion against Saul and his kingdom.

2. *Theological.* The meaning "secede, turn away," found in political contexts, is still clearly present in Josh. 22, a text that may reflect an ancient tradition, now probably the product of Priestly redaction.[10] The nine and a half tribes accuse the Reubenites,

---

9. H. J. Stoebe, *Das erste Buch Samuelis. KAT,* VIII/1 (1973), 378f.
10. For the most recent discussion see Schäfer-Lichtenberger, 338f.

Gadites, and the half-tribe of Manasseh of having rebelled against Yahweh (*mārad̠ b*ᵉ*YHWH:* vv. 16,18,19,29) because they have built a second altar by the Jordan (vv. 19,23,29) outside the land of the children of Israel (v. 11) in addition to the one altar (in Jerusalem). As synonyms of *mārad̠* we find here the phrases *šûb̠ mē'aḥ*ᵃ*rê YHWH* (→ שׁוּב, *šûb̠*), "turn away from Yahweh" (vv. 16,18,23,29), and *mā'al b*ᵉ*YHWH/ bē'lōhê yiśrā'ēl,* "break faith with Yahweh/the God of Israel" (vv. 16,20). V. 22 describes this breach of faith with the nouns *mered̠* (a hapax legomenon) and *ma'al,* here appearing in disjunction. As an antonym of *mārad̠,* v. 27 uses the root *'bd* in *figura etymologica: '*ᵃ*b̠ōd̠ 'et̠-'*ᵃ*b̠ōd̠at̠ YHWH,* "perform the service of Yahweh."

In the characteristic complaint narratives of the desert tradition (Ex. 15:22-25a; 16; 17:1-7; Nu. 12–14; 16; 17; 20), *mārad̠* occurs only in Nu. 14:9 (JE), and then not as a description of Israel's complaints in the narrative context (for which 14:2 uses → לוּן *lûn*), but as a warning (vetitive of *mārad̠*) by Joshua and Caleb not to let apostasy frustrate the occupation of Canaan made possible and guaranteed by Yahweh. Here *mārad̠* has the political connotations described above,[11] insofar as the text reflects the conception (typical of J) that the relationship between Yahweh and Israel is based on royal law, a conception that probably arose to counter the royal ideology of Assyria.

Two Ezekiel passages exhibit an extended meaning of *mārad̠.* In the prophet's commission, Ezk. 2:3 uses *mārad̠* as a participle in apposition to "people of Israel,"[12] followed by a relative clause in *figura etymologica.* Here the verb no longer describes an individual act but rather the total conduct of the house of Israel in the past as permanent apostasy from Yahweh. Directly in parallel with *mārad̠* the text uses *pš' b*ᵉ, "break with." The context goes on to describe the people of Israel as having a "hard heart" and a "stubborn face" (v. 4). They are called a "rebellious house" (*bêt̠ m*ᵉ*rî;* vv. 5-8). In Ezk. 20:38 the plural participles of *mārad̠* and *pš'* appear in parallel: the rebels *(hammōr*ᵉ*d̠îm)* and transgressors *(happôš*ᵉ*'îm)* will be purged by Yahweh and not allowed to enter the land of Israel.

This extension of meaning continues in the theological use of the word in the postexilic books of Nehemiah, Daniel, and Job. In the historical retrospect of Nehemiah's confession, *mārad̠* parallels → מרה *mārâ,* "be disobedient" and "reject Yahweh's law" (Neh. 9:26). In Daniel's confession (formulated in the pl.), *mārad̠* parallels → חטא *ḥṭ',* "sin," → עוה *'āwâ,* "do wrong," → רשׁע *rš',* "act wickedly," "turn aside (→ סוד *sôd̠*) from your commandments and ordinances," "not listen (→ שׁמע *šāma'*) to your servants the prophets" (Dan. 9:5f.), and "not obey *(šāma')* the voice of Yahweh our God by following his laws" (9:9f.). In these passages *mārad̠* is one of many terms for "sin." In a similar vein, Job 24:13 describes the wicked as "those who rebel against the light" *(mōr*ᵉ*d̠ê-'ôr).*

V. Summary. The verb *mārad̠* presupposes an asymmetrical relationship. A king's political, economic, or military weakness forces him into willing or unwilling depen-

11. See IV.1 above.
12. On the text see W. Zimmerli, *Ezekiel 1. Herm* (Eng. trans. 1979), 89f., n. c.

dence on another king. He is obligated to political loyalty. Our verb denotes the attempt of the subordinate to escape from this dependent relationship. The relationship between Israel and Yahweh is an asymmetrical relationship. The exodus and gift of the land enable and require that Israel serve *(ʿāḇaḏ)* Yahweh alone. Now *māraḏ* denotes Israel's attempt to escape from this relationship of loyalty. This attempt is always doomed to fail.

VI. LXX and Dead Sea Scrolls. The LXX translates *māraḏ* 9 times with *aphistánai* (politically and theologically: Gen. 14:4; Josh. 22:18,19,29; Ezk. 17:15; Dnl. 9:5,9; Neh. 9:26; 2 Ch. 13:6), 5 times with *atheteín* (only politically: 2 K. 18:7,20; 24:1,20; 2 Ch. 36:13), 3 times with *apostátēs gínesthai* (only theologically: Nu. 14:9; Josh. 22:16,19), twice each with *apostateín* (politically: Neh. 2:19; 6:6) and *parapikraínein* (theologically: Ezk. 2:3), and once each with *apeitheín* (Isa. 36:5) and *asebḗs* (Ezk. 20:38).

In the Dead Sea Scrolls *māraḏ* occurs 5 times. In 1QpHab 8:11 the Wicked Priest is said to have "robbed and taken wealth from men of violence who rebelled against God *(ʾašer mārᵉḏû bᵉʾēl).*" In l. 16 the Wicked Priest is described in a relative clause with *māraḏ;* the rest of the text is damaged. CD 8:4 uses *māraḏ* absolutely, describing all the princes *(śārîm)* of Judah as apostates or rebels *(môrᵉḏîm).* In 4Q181 fr. 1 2, *māraḏ* in parallel with *pšʿ* describes apostasy from *(min)* the community. The context of 4Q509 233:2 is too damaged to reconstruct.

Schwienhorst

מָרָה *mārâ;* מְרִי *mᵉrî*

Contents: I. Etymology. II. Occurrences. III. Usage. IV. Meaning: 1. Basic Meaning; 2. Preexilic Prophets; 3. Ezekiel; 4. Deuteronomistic History; 5. P[G]; 6. Other Exilic and Postexilic Literature. V. LXX and Dead Sea Scrolls.

I. Etymology. Heb. *mārâ,* "be disobedient," is etymologically related to Jewish Aram. (Bab.) *mry* (aphel), "make angry, be disobedent," Syr. *mry* (pael), "contend, provoke," and Arab. *mry,* "goad," III "oppose."[1]

---

mārâ. W. Dietrich, *Prophetie und Geschichte. FRLANT,* 108 (1972); F. Hossfeld, *Untersuchungen zu Komposition und Theologie des Ezechielbuches. FzB,* 20 (²1983); R. Knierim, "מרה *mrh* 'to be obstinate,' " *TLOT,* II, 687-88; H. D. Preuss, *Deuteronomium. EdF,* 164 (1982); J. J. Stamm, *Beiträge zur hebräischen und altorientalischen Namenkunde. OBO,* 30 (1980); T. Veijola, *Die ewige Dynastie. AnAcScFen,* 193 (1975); *idem, Das Königtum in der Beurteilung der deuteronomistischen Historiographie. AnAcScFen,* 198 (1977); E. Zenger, *Gottes Bogen in den Wolken. SBS,* 112 (1983); *idem, Die Sinaitheophanie. FzB,* 3 (1971).

1. *GesB,* 459f.; *HAL,* II, 632; Knierim, 687.

The masc. PNs *m*

The masc. PNs *mᵉrāyâ* and *mᵉrāyôṯ,* "obstinate," probably derive from the root *mry.*[2] Four etymologies have been suggested for the name *miryām:*[3] (1) "stubborn" *(mrh),* (2) "fatty" *(mr'),* (3) "beloved" (Egyp. *mryt*), and (4) "gift (of God)" (Akk. *rym*). J. J. Stamm considers the derivation of the name from *mrh* unlikely.[4] The interpretation "gift" is most appropriate, both linguistically and semantically. The name *yimrâ* in 1 Ch. 7:36 should probably be emended to *yimnā'* (cf. v. 35).[5]

The phrase *'ereṣ mᵉrāṯayim* reflects Akk. *nār marratu,* which denotes only the territory around the mouth of the Tigris and Euphrates.[6] Its use in Jer. 50:21 to refer to the entire land of Babylonia is probably a deliberate play on *mᵉrî,* "disobedience, rebelliousness," formed after the pattern of *miṣrayim* or *'ᵃram-nahᵃrayim.*[7]

II. Occurrences. The verb *mārâ* occurs 45 times in the OT: 22 in the qal (4 in Lamentations; 3 each in Numbers, Isaiah, and Psalms; twice each in Deuteronomy, 1 Kings, and Jeremiah; and once each in 1 Samuel and Hosea; the root *mr'* in Zeph. 3:1 is probably a by-form). It occurs 22 times in the reflexively transitive hiphil with roughly the same meaning as the qal[8] (7 in Psalms, 6 in Deuteronomy, 4 in Ezekiel, once each in Joshua, 1 Samuel, Isaiah, Job, and Nehemiah). The noun *mᵉrî* occurs 23 times (16 in Ezekiel, once each in Numbers, Deuteronomy, 1 Samuel, Isaiah, Job, Proverbs, and Nehemiah). This list assumes three readings that vary from the MT: 2 K. 14:26, *hammar* (from → מרר *mrr)* instead of *mōreh;* Ex. 23:21, *temer* (hiphil of *mārâ*) instead of *tammēr* (from *mrr*);[9] and Neh. 9:17, *bᵉmiṣrāyim* (following the LXX) instead of *bᵉmiryām.*

The earliest occurrences are Dt. 21:18,20; Hos. 14:1 (Eng. 13:16); Isa. 1:20; 3:8; Jer. 4:17; 5:23; possibly Prov. 17:11; all are qal, except for Isa. 3:8. Both *mārâ* and *mᵉrî* are common in the Deuteronomistic history (13 occurrences): Ex. 23:21;[10] Dt. 1:26,43; 9:7,23,24 (probably DtrN[11]); 31:27; Josh. 1:18; 1 S. 12:14f. (DtrN[12]); 15:23 (probably DtrP[13]); 1 K. 13:21,26 (DtrN[14]). Isa. 30:9 probably also belongs to a stratum reflecting exilic redaction.[15] In P^G *mārâ* occurs 3 times (Nu. 20:10,14; 27:14).

---

2. W. Rudolph, *Esra und Nehemia. HAT,* XX (1949), 66f.; cf. *IPN,* 250b.
3. *HAL,* II, 635f.
4. *Namenkunde,* 129.
5. *IPN,* 246; W. Rudolph, *Chronikbücher. HAT,* XXI (^{3}1968), 74.
6. *AHw,* II, 612b.
7. W. Rudolph, *Jeremia. HAT,* XII (^{3}1968), 303; *HAL,* II, 639.
8. W. Gesenius and G. Bergsträsser, *Hebräische Grammatik,* II (^{29}1926, repr. Hildesheim, 1962), §19d; *GK,* §53.2.
9. Cf. *BHS; GesB,* 460, 463; *HAL,* II, 639.
10. Cf. Zenger, *Sinaitheophanie,* 70f., 165.
11. Dietrich, 96.
12. Veijola, *Königtum,* 83-91.
13. Veijola, *Ewige Dynastie,* 102, n. 156.
14. Dietrich, 120, n. 44.
15. O. Kaiser, *Isaiah 13–39. OTL* (Eng. trans. 1974), 292f.

III. Usage. With two exceptions (Ex. 23:21; Josh. 1:18), the object of *mārâ* is restricted to Yahweh, God, other divine epithets (e.g., the Most High), or Yahweh's ordinances or words. Yahweh, God, or the Most High is the object of *mārâ* in 26 texts, 10 of which use the expression *mārâ 'eṯ-pî* (7 Deuteronomistic, 2 P^G, Lam. 1:18), 6 the prep. b^e, 3 the prep. *'im* preceded by a participle (Deuteronomistic), 3 the accusative particle *'eṯ*, 3 no connective (Isa. 3:8; Ps. 78:17; 106:7 [reading *'elyôn* instead of *'al-yām*]), and once a pronominal suffix (Ps. 78:40). In 3 texts the object of *mārâ* is God's ordinances (Ezk. 5:6) or words (Ps. 105:28; 107:11). Once Yahweh's messenger is the object (Ex. 23:21, with b^e), and once Joshua is the object (Josh. 1:18). The verb is used absolutely 14 times, 6 of these as a participle.

In most cases, the subject is the people or house of Israel, "our fathers," or some other collective entity such as Jerusalem, Samaria, or the land of Israel. Twice Moses and Aaron are the subject (Nu. 20:24; 27:14 [P^G]), twice a man of God from Judah (1 K. 13:21,26), twice in a 1st person singular lament "virgin Zion" (Lam. 1:18,20), once each the Egyptians (Ps. 105:28, probably to be understood with the MT as a rhetorical question[16]), the enemies of the individual in a lament (Ps. 5:11[10]), Job's friends (Job 17:2), and the "servant of Yahweh" in the 1st person singular, negated (Isa. 50:5).

IV. Meaning.

1. *Basic Meaning.* Dt. 21:18-21, which probably belongs to the early nucleus of Deuteronomy,[17] is a good passage for determining a basic meaning for *mārâ.* In this text *mārâ,* together with *sārar,* is an attributive participle modifying *bēn;* it denotes the willful and constant disobedience of a son toward his parents. Such a "stubborn and rebellious son" *(bēn sôrēr ûmôreh)* does not listen to the voice of his father and the voice of his mother (*'ênennû šōmēa' b^eqôl,* vv. 18,20), and must therefore be stoned. With this text as our point of departure, and taking into account the other occurrences of the verb in the OT, we may outline the meaning of *mārâ* as follows: the subject is always someone obligated to obey another by virtue of natural inferiority (son/parents; Israel/Yahweh). A deliberate, willful decision to disobey is always present. This decision is totally at variance with what one would expect. It is a reaction of rebellion. It is always condemned and results in punishment and/or change of heart and confession coupled with a plea to be forgiven. Thus *mārâ* is a word of negative import denoting willful, fundamental, and rebellious disobedience.

2. *Preexilic Prophets.* The preexilic prophets (Hosea, Isaiah, and Jeremiah) often attribute predicted or actual disaster to rebellious conduct on the part of those afflicted (Hos. 14:1[13:16]: "Samaria shall suffer her punishment, because she has rebelled against [*mār^eṯâ b^e*] her God"; Isa. 3:8; Jer. 4:17). In the style of a preacher presenting

---

16. Meyer, III, 87; for a different view see H.-J. Kraus, *Psalms 60–150* (Eng. trans., Minneapolis, 1989), 308.

17. Preuss, 56.

an alternative, Isa. 1:19f. says: "If you are willing (→ אבה *'ābhāh*) and listen (→ שׁמע *šāma'*) . . . , but if you refuse (→ מאן *mē'ēn*) and rebel (*mārâ*). . . ." Rebelliousness is here conscious and freely willed refusal to listen obediently, with death as its consequence. Jer. 5:23 charges the people with having a "stubborn and rebellious heart" *(lēḇ sōrēr ûmôreh)*. In parallel we find *sārû wayyēlēḵû,* "they have turned aside and gone away." The context (v. 21) lends the phrase "stubborn and rebellious heart" overtones of obdurate impenitence.

3. *Ezekiel.* In Ezekiel rebelliousness is the outstanding characteristic of the house of Israel. The noun *m^e^rî,* "rebelliousness," occurs 16 times in Ezekiel (out of a total of 23 in the OT), all but once in conjunction with *bayiṯ.* In 8 of these occurrences, it is an undetermined predicate in a noun clause introduced by *kî* (*kî bêṯ m^e^rî hēmmâ:* Ezk. 2:5,6,7 [LXX, Syr., Targ.]; 3:9,26,27; 12:2b,3); in 7 it is determined (*bêṯ hammerî:* 2:8; 12:2a,9,25; 17:12; 24:3; 44:6 [LXX]). In 12:9 *bêṯ hammerî* stands in apposition to *bêṯ yiśrā'ēl;* in 44:6 the relationship is reversed. In Ezekiel, therefore, the phrase "house of rebelliousness," after the analogy of "house of Israel," has become a kind of second name for Israel.[18] Israel's rebelliousness finds expression in total incomprehension of the prophet's message, which therefore needs "unraveling" (17:12ff.) and outrageous symbolic action (12:2f.). In Ezekiel the people's rebelliousness tends toward obduracy. Ezk. 12:2 expands on the phrase *bêṯ hamm^e^rî* with a relative clause: "They have eyes to see but do not see, ears to hear but do not hear." It then adds in summary: "For they are a rebellious house."

This rebelliousness is directed not least against the prophet himself. It can so terrify him that he himself opposes the message of Yahweh. This theme is sounded in Ezekiel's call (2:1–3:15): "Hear what I say to you! Do not be rebellious [*m^e^rî;* abstract for concrete] like that rebellious house. Open your mouth" (2:8).

The experience of the prophetic call articulated here (cf. Jer. 1:6ff.) appears also to lie behind Isa. 50:5, where the "servant of Yahweh" speaks of himself in the third Servant Song: "The Lord Yahweh has opened my ear, and I was not rebellious (*lō' mārîṯî*), I did not turn backward."

Ezk. 20 is an invective in the form of a theological review of Israel's history. Three times a description of Israel's disobedience is introduced by the recurring formula *wayyamrû-ḇî,* "but they rebelled against me" (vv. 8,13,21). Here Israel's rebelliousness consists in its refusal to accept Yahweh's life-giving instruction. Parallel to *mārâ* we find in v. 8 "and they would not listen to me," in vv. 13,21 "they did not observe my statutes but my ordinances they rejected *(mā'as)*/were not careful to observe *(lō'-šāmar)*."

4. *Deuteronomistic History.* The Deuteronomistic history uses *mārâ* primarily in two phrases: *mārâ 'eṯ-pî YHWH* (7 occurrences: Dt. 1:26,43; 9:23 [DtrN?]; 1 S. 12:14,15 [DtrN]; 1 K. 13:21,26 [DtrN]) and *mamrîm h^e^yîṯem 'im-YHWH* (3 times: Dt. 9:7,24 [DtrN]; 31:27). Neither phrase occurs earlier.

---

18. W. Zimmerli, *Ezekiel 1. Herm* (Eng. trans. 1979), 134; Hossfeld, 75; cf. Isa. 30:9.

In the Deuteronomistic history *mārâ* appears primarily in historical retrospects. In the phrase *mārâ 'eṯ-pî YHWH,* it refers to the people's refusal to go up to the land given them by Yahweh (Dt. 1:26) to possess it (9:23) or to independent occupation of the land without Yahweh's help (1:43; cf. Nu. 14:39-45). In the phrase *mamrîm hᵉyîṯem ʿim-YHWH,* it refers to the continual rebelliousness of the people against Yahweh from the exodus to "today" (Dt. 9:7,24; 31:27). In its typical plerophoric style, this literature uses many synonyms for *mārâ:* infinitive with *lō' 'āḇâ,* "be unwilling" (Dt. 1:26); *lō' šāmaʿ (bᵉqôl YHWH),* "not listen" (1:43; 9:23); *lō' he'ᵉmîn lᵉYHWH,* "not trust Yahweh" (9:23); *rgn* niphal, "complain" (1:27); *zyd* hiphil, "act presumptuously" (1:43).

Thus in the Deuteronomistic history *mārâ* (esp. in the phrase *mārâ 'eṯ-pî YHWH*) takes on a clear nomistic nuance: Israel's rebelliousness consists in not listening to the "mouth," word, voice, or commandments of Yahweh. This development continues especially in DtrN (1 S. 12:14f.; 1 K. 13:21,26; cf. also Isa. 30:9).

5. *P*ᴳ. The typical use of *mārâ* as a term for the *people's* rebelliousness, established by preexilic prophecy and Deuteronomistic theology, is adopted by Pᴳ but turned *against* the tradition. It is not the people — even though so addressed by their spiritual and political leaders (Moses and Aaron: "Listen, you rebels. . . ," Nu. 20:10) — but the leaders themselves who were rebellious "against the mouth of Yahweh" (20:24; 27:14). They failed because they did not trust in Yahweh (20:12).[19]

6. *Other Exilic and Postexilic Literature.* In the postexilic period *mārâ* appears primarily (7 times) in Ps. 78 and 106, didactic historical psalms standing in the tradition of Deuteronomistic historiography, and in the confession in Neh. 9. There it denotes the rebellious conduct of the patriarchal generation (Ps. 78:8: *dôr sôrēr ûmōreh*) during the wilderness period (78:17,40; 106:7,33) and the occupation (78:56; 106:43; Neh. 9:26). Here *mārâ* appears with many synonyms; besides those of Deuteronomistic origin, we find expressions from the language of wisdom and the general terminology of sin: *ḥṭ',* "sin" (Ps. 78:17); *nissâ-'ēl (bᵉlēḇ),* "test God (in one's heart)" (78:18,41,56); *dibber bē'lōhîm,* "speak against God" (78:19); *ʿāṣaḇ (YHWH),* "grieve (Yahweh)" (78:40); *twh* hiphil, "provoke" (78:41); *lō' šāmar ʿēḏûṯ (YHWH),* "not observe (Yahweh's) instruction" (78:56); *swg* niphal, "turn away" (78:57); *bāgaḏ,* "be faithless" (78:57); *bṭ'* piel, "speak rashly" (106:33); *māraḏ,* "rise up, rebel" (Neh. 9:26).

The meaning of *mārâ* is extended until it becomes one of the many words for sin. In Lam. 3:42 it parallels *pšʿ* (cf. Ps. 5:11[10]). In Lam. 1:18 "virgin Zion" in her lamentation describes her past misconduct in a single sentence: "He, Yahweh, is in the right, for I have rebelled against his mouth/word" (cf. v. 20).

V. LXX and Dead Sea Scrolls. In most cases the LXX translates *mrh/mry* with *parapikraínein* (26 times) or *apetheín/apeithḗs* (11 times).

---

19. Zenger, *Gottes Bogen,* 47.

In the Dead Sea Scrolls *mārâ* appears 11 times. In the phrase *mārâ ('eṯ) pî,* the object is once "his neighbor" (1QS 6:26), twice God (1QH 14:14; 4QDibHam[a] [4Q504] fr. 1f. 2:8). In the scrolls, however, *mārâ* means primarily rebellion against the Torah (4QOrd[a] [4Q159] fr. 2-4 5; 4Q185 fr. 1f. 2:3; 4QDibHam[a] fr. 7 14) and against repentance as the basic condition for membership in the community (4QpPs[a] [4Q171] 2:2,3 par. *mē'ēn,* "refuse"). The *byt hmrh* of the Copper Scroll (3Q15 2:3) is, as the context shows, an obscure toponym, which cannot be identified with the OT *bêṯ hamm[e]rî.*

Schwienhorst

מַרְזֵחַ *marzēaḥ*

Contents: I. Etymology. II. Extrabiblical Occurrences: 1. Ugaritic; 2. Aramaic; 3. Phoenician; 4. Nabatean; 5. Palmyrene. III. OT. IV. Rabbinic Literature.

I. Etymology. The etymology of *marzēaḥ* is obscure. The earliest occurrence is from Ebla. The noun itself is a *maqṭil* form of an otherwise unattested root *rzḥ.*[1]

Wilhelm Gesenius proposed a root *rzḥ,* "cry aloud,"[2] for the word in the OT, the only occurrences known at the time, despite the "strange" LXX translation *thíasos* in Jer. 16:5. For the extrabiblical occurrences, Otto Eissfeldt claims a root *rzḥ* II, "join

---

marzēaḥ. D. B. Bryan, "Texts Relating to the Marzeah" (diss., Johns Hopkins, 1973); M. Dahood, "Additional Notes on the *MRZḤ* Text," *The Claremont Ras Shamra Tablets,* ed. L. R. Fisher. *AnOr,* 48 (1972), 51-54; M. Dietrich and O. Loretz, "Der Vertrag eines *MRZḤ*-Klubs in Ugarit," *UF,* 14 (1982), 71-76; *idem* and J. Sanmartín, "Zur ugaritischen Lexikographie, XIII," *UF,* 7 (1975), 157-169, esp. 157f.; O. Eissfeldt, "Etymologische und archäologische Erklärung alttestamentlicher Wörter," *KlSchr,* IV (1968), 285-296; *idem,* "Kultvereine in Ugarit," *KlSchr,* V (1973), 118-129; *idem,* "Neue Belege für nabatäische Kultgenossenschaften," *KlSchr,* V (1973), 127-135; *idem,* "מַרְזֵחַ und מַרְזְחָא Kultmahlgenossenschaften im spätjüdischen Schrifttum," *KlSchr,* V (1973), 136-142; H.-J. Fabry, *Studien zur Ekklesiologie des AT und der Qumrangemeinde* (Habil., Bonn, 1979), 48-130; T. L. Fenton, "The Claremont 'MRZḤ' Tablet, Its Text and Meaning," *UF,* 9 (1977), 71-75; R. E. Friedman, "The *Mrzḥ* Tablet from Ugarit," *Maarav,* 2 (1979-80), 187-206; J. Greenfield, "The *Marzeaḥ* as a Social Institution," *Wirtschaft und Gesellschaft im alten Vorderasien,* ed. J. Harmatta and G. Komoróczy. *AAH,* 22/1-4 (1974), 451-55; O. Loretz, "Ugaritisch-biblisch *mrzḥ* 'Kultmahl, Kultverein' in Jer 16,5 und Am 6,7," *Künder des Wortes. Festschrift J. Schreiner* (1982), 87-93; P. D. Miller Jr., "The *MRZḤ* Text," *Claremont Ras Shamra Tablets,* ed. Fisher, 37-48; M. H. Pope, "A Divine Banquet at Ugarit," *The Use of the OT in the New. Festschrift W. F. Stinespring* (Durham, N.C., 1972), 170-203.

1. On the form see *NSS,* 240f.
2. *GesTh,* 1280.

together," positing a totally separate development of biblical *marzēaḥ* and Can. *mrzḥ*. There is, however, no evidence for such separate development. Rudolf Meyer therefore uses the theory of semantic opposition to account for *rzḥ:*[3] "be loud, make noise" led to the meaning "cultic association," "festivity," as well as "funeral repast." This etymology, however, is problematic.[4]

One must either look for a fundamental meaning lying behind all the occurrences, which Ugaritic usage suggests might have been something like "gather together," or stick to clearly attested evidence. Of the latter, however, there is only an Arab. *razaḥa,* "collapse, sink to the ground,"[5] from exhaustion or sickness. In this case, *rāzaḥ* + *m-* (locative preformative[6]) denotes a place where people sink down, whether originally in orgiastic ecstasy[7] or in idolatrous *proskynesis.* In the course of semantic development, this purely locative sense was weakened and the term was applied to the participants in this cult and to the cult itself.

II. Extrabiblical Occurrences.

1. *Ugaritic.* The earliest occurrences of this word are probably from Ebla, where we find *mar-za-*u_9 with the meaning "observance of the *marzēaḥ.*"[8] Next come the Ugaritic texts. There are 15 occurrences, with varying orthography: besides the basic form *mrzḥ* (*KTU,* 1.1 IV, 4; 1.114, 15; 3.9, 1, vo. 3; 4.52, vo. 12 [text?]; 4.399, 8; 4.642, 2-6), we find *mrzʿy* (*KTU,* 1.21 II, 1, 5) and in syllabic Akkadian documents *marziḫu* (*RS,* 14.16, 3; 15.70, 4, 7, 10, 15; 15.88, 4, 6; 18.01, 7, 10). The different morphemes do not appear to mark any semantic distinctions.[9] An occurrence in EA, 120, 21 is highly dubious.[10] These morphemes denote a religio-cultic institution the purpose of which is to seek and achieve communion with a patron deity, whose name is sometimes associated with the observance. This communion is to be achieved through a (regular?) meal with the deity. The central ritual of the cultic fellowship was therefore a cultic meal. The communion of the *bny mrzḥ* with the deity also constitutes the bond linking the members of the fellowship. This religious fellowship developed into a social fellowship. In the *mrzḥ,* eating and drinking as acts of fellowship take on theological significance. The sacral foods, accompanied by wine, do not appear to have been specified. Wild game and oil play a certain role. The danger of orgiastic excess became apparent early on, as is made clear especially by the transfer of the *mrzḥ* ritual to the mythical sphere of a banquet with the deity El.[11] The *mrzḥ* institution would seem to

---

3. *Festschrift C. F. A. Schaeffer. UF,* 11 (1976), 603f.
4. Cf. Loretz.
5. Wehr, 336; Lane, 1075f.
6. *GK,* §85e.
7. See F. Stolz, "Rausch, Religion und Realität in Israel und seiner Umwelt," *VT,* 26 (1976), 170-186.
8. G. Pettinato, *Testi amministrativi della Biblioteca L. 2769* (Naples, 1980), 46, vo. 2.
9. Bryan, 151.
10. *AHw,* II, 617 notwithstanding.
11. See esp. *KTU,* 1.114, where El is described as being totally drunk. Cf. (among others)

be incompatible with the Baʿal cult in the narrow sense, since it appears only in association with El and ʿAnat. This restriction would make it much easier for the institution subsequently to enter the Israelite sphere.

The Ugaritic *mrzḥ* possessed property, assembly halls *(byt mrzḥ),* and generally vineyards. The frequent references to a *mrzḥ* in the Rephaim texts (*KTU,* 1.21 II, 1, 5) have given rise to the theory that the *mrzḥ* was associated with the cult of the dead.[12] This association must be rejected insofar as it is based on the Rephaim, since they cannot be tied to this cult.[13] The cultic association constituting the human community had its prototype in the myth of the *mrzḥ* of El's pantheon.[14] The treaty text *KTU,* 3.9 shows that a *rb* ("superior") functioned as leader in the *mrzḥ.*[15] "Probably only men of great wealth could assume leadership of a *mrzḥ* and administer the common treasury."[16] We see from *KTU,* 3.9 that there could be disputes within a *mrzḥ,* since its structure allowed for accusations.

2. *Aramaic.* The only occurrence of *mrzḥ* in Aramaic is on an ostracon from Elephantine.[17] The ostracon makes no reference to any religious (-ecclesial) functions of the *mrzḥʾ,* but merely requests payment of a member's account. The text does not make it possible to interpret the *mrzḥ* unambiguously as a "funerary association."[18]

3. *Phoenician.* The Phoenician evidence documents the spread of the *mrzḥ* institution through the western Mediterranean region. The regulations contained in the Marseilles sacrificial tariff speak of a *mrzḥ ʾlm* that did not have its own meeting place but brought its offerings to the temple of Baʿal Zaphon.[19] It is mentioned in conjunction with *mzrḥ* [*sic*] and *špḥ,* two terms denoting groups of people that are hard to differentiate. The emphasis is less on the institution itself than on the cultic ceremony it performed,[20] which took the form of a lengthy celebration. Thus the Phoenician evidence marks a turning point in the semasiology of the term.

S. Loewenstamm, "Eine lehrhafte ugaritische Trinkburleske," *UF,* 1 (1969), 71-77; B. Margalit, "The Ugaritic Feast of the Drunken Gods," *Maarav,* 2 (1979-80), 65-120. To interpret this text as a medical text assailing the consequences of excessive revelry seems misguided, contra H. M. Barstad, "Festmahl und Übersättigung," *AcOr,* 39 (1978), 23-30.

12. W. F. Albright in Miller, 47, n. 1; Pope, 192f.; Loretz; M. Dietrich, et al., "Die ugaritischen Totenregister *rpu(m)* und die biblischen Rephaim," *UF,* 8 (1976), 45-52.

13. → רפא *rāpāʾ.* See S. B. Parker, "The Feast of Rāpiʾu," *UF,* 2 (1970), 243-49; *idem,* "The Ugaritic Deity Rāpiʾu," *UF,* 4 (1972), 97-104; C. E. L'Heureux, "The Ugaritic and Biblical Rephaim," *HTR,* 67 (1974), 265-274; and esp. J. C. de Moor, "Rāpiʾūma — Rephaim," *ZAW,* 88 (1976), 323-345; A. Caquot, "La tablette RS 24.252 et la question des Rephaim ougaritiques," *Syr,* 53 (1976), 295-304.

14. → סוד *sôḏ.*

15. M. Dietrich and O. Loretz, *UF,* 10 (1978), 421f.

16. Dietrich and Loretz, *UF,* 14 (1982), 71-76.

17. *RES,* 1295, 3; cf. *LidzEph,* III, 119.

18. B. Porten, *Archives from Elephantine* (Berkeley, 1968), 179-186, esp. 184.

19. *KAI,* 69, 20.

20. Cf. *KAI,* 60, 1.

4. *Nabatean.* All the Nabatean occurrences date from the first century A.D.[21] The texts show that the *mrzḥ* was an association drawn from the wealthy upper class; it recognized a fellowship with a tutelary deity, but there are no further religious details. A leader *(rb mrzḥ')* exercised authority over the members (*bny mrzḥ'* or *ḥbryn*[22]).

5. *Palmyrene.* The *mrzḥ* in Palmyra was clearly very similar to the Nabatean *mrzḥ*. The abundant sources include inscriptions and inscribed terra-cotta tokens.[23] Several Palmyrene-Greek bilinguals treat *thíasos* as the equivalent of *mrzḥ;* the same word is applied occasionally to the early church.[24] The *mrzḥ* had a clear hierarchical structure: the president *(rb mrzḥ),* priest or layman, was elected for a term and could simultaneously hold major political offices. His functions included liturgical leadership, divination, and charity. It seems that these functions could also be delegated.[25] The members *(bny mrzḥ)* sometimes played important roles in the *mrzḥ* as scribes or assistants.[26] The *mrzḥ* was named after its patron deity or (in *st. determinatus*) Bêl, the head of the Palmyrene pantheon. Its central ritual was a banquet. Here the tesserae serve a variety of purposes: they depict the banquet participants, including deities; they depict the elements of the banquet, baked goods and wine; they admitted their bearers to the banquet and were also distributed to needy persons who were not members of the *mrzḥ*. The purpose of the *mrzḥ* was thus to secure the weal of its members through communion with the deity in the banquet. This benefit then found expression in the charitable work of the *bny mrzḥ*. There is no necessary connection with the cult of the dead or funerary rites.

III. OT. In the OT *marzēaḥ* occurs only in Am. 6:7 (misread by the LXX); Jer. 16:5 (LXX *thíasos*). Am. 6:7 is textually difficult. The versions — especially the LXX recensions — attest to a complex textual history. A series of misreadings (possibly deliberate) produced the MT, which reads literally: "The revelry of the loungers *(mirzaḥ sᵉrûḥîm)* shall pass away." The original text can be reconstructed as: *lāḵēn ʿattâ yiglû bᵉrōʾš gōlîm wᵉsār mirzaḥ śārîm min ʾeprāyim,* "They shall therefore now be the first to go into exile, and the *mrzḥ* of the princes of Ephraim shall depart."[27] This reconstruction renders superfluous the myriad conjectures concerning a usable meaning.[28] The woe oracle in Am. 6:1-7 is for the most part authentic and is directed against the

---

21. *LidzEph,* III, 278; A. Negev, *IEJ,* 111 (1961), 135; 13 (1963), 113-17; J. Naveh, *IEJ,* 17 (1967), 187ff.

22. → חבר *ḥāḇēr* (IV, 193-97).

23. For the former see J. T. Milik, *Dédicaces faites par des dieux et des thiases sémitiques à l'époque romaine* (Paris, 1972). For the latter see R. du Mesnil du Buisson, *Le tessères et les monnaies de Palmyre* (Paris, 1962).

24. Eusebius *HE* 1.3.12; 10.1.8.

25. J. Teixidor, *CRAI,* 1981, 301-314, esp. 310.

26. H.-J. Fabry, "Der altorientalische Hintergrund des urchristlichen Diakonats," *Der Diakon. Festschrift A. Frotz* (Freiburg, ²1981), 15-26.

27. For details see Fabry, *Studien,* 108-111.

28. See H. W. Wolff, *Joel and Amos. Herm* (Eng. trans. 1977), 273, 277f.

upper class of Samaria. The conduct excoriated by the prophet in vv. 4-6 is in fact typical of the basic practices of the pagan *mrzḥ* together with their excessive perversions.[29] This *marzēaḥ* of the Samaritan upper class Amos considers the root of all evil. The prophet does not indicate whether he is thinking in terms of religious polemic. His attack can also be interpreted within the existing system, in the sense that the *mrzḥ* is not doing justice to his own (social) mission.

Jer. 16:5 does not present such textual problems. The versions unanimously interpret *bêṯ marzēaḥ* as a "house of banqueting" or the like; the only exception is the Syr.: *byt mrqwdt',* "house of mourning." Literarily, the text exhibits several layers of composition. What was probably its original core (vv. 1,5a,8) describes the prophet's commission to perform a fourfold symbolic action: he is not to enter the *bêṯ marzēaḥ*, mourn for the dead, show sympathy, or enter the *bêṯ-mišteh.* This commission is in the form of a chiasm with double antithetical parallelism. In meaning, *bêṯ marzēaḥ* and *bêṯ-mišteh* are more closely related than entering the *bêṯ marzēaḥ* and mourning the dead. Furthermore, *bêṯ marzēaḥ* cannot be translated "house of mourning,"[30] since this meaning is conveyed in the OT by *bêṯ 'ēḇel* (cf. Eccl. 7:2,4 par. *bêṯ mišteh;* 4QQoh[a] reads *bêṯ śimḥâ*[31]). It appears that the prophet is here forbidden to carry out actions that are clearly part of normal everyday behavior in order to represent symbolically the abnormality of the situation of judgment.

According to the basic stratum of Jeremiah, therefore, entering a *marzēaḥ* was not unusual and clearly not forbidden. The institution had been adapted, since it derived from the El cult. Religious toleration of the *marzēaḥ* began to vanish, however, as this institution became increasingly dubious, whether through its antisocial conduct (Am. 6:7) or its growing association with the cult of the dead and funerary rites (as reflected in the secondary additions in Jer. 16:2,6,7). At the time of the Deuteronomic or Deuteronomistic recension of Jeremiah, the *marzēaḥ* was rejected as being an idolatrous institution (Deuteronomistic verses: Jer. 16:3,4,9,10-13).[32] The associations with "mourning" and "idolatry" are therefore secondary and were not originally connected with the *marzēaḥ*.[33] This conclusion still leaves open the question whether from the very beginning the *marzēaḥ* in its early form was compatible with Yahwism. It clearly constituted an "integrating element of social life."[34]

IV. Rabbinic Literature. For the rabbis the *marzēaḥ* was no longer a cultic institution.[35] It became synonymous with *śimḥâ,* "joy," and *mišteh,* "banquet," and was associated with the Maiumas festival. Occasional metaphorical references to mourning can be accounted for by their contexts. The Madeba map, from the vicinity of Baal-peor,

---

29. Cf. *KTU,* 1.114 above.
30. J. Schreiner, *Jeremia 1–25,* 14. NEB (1981), in loc.; NRSV.
31. J. Muilenburg, *BASOR,* 135 (1954), 27.
32. W. Thiel, *Die deuteronomistische Redaktion von Jeremia 1–25. WMANT,* 41 (1973), 196.
33. Contra Loretz, 89.
34. *Ibid.,* 91.
35. *WTM,* III, 247.

identifies the *BHTOMAPCEA* with the Maiumas festival, widely celebrated in the Levant, exhibiting a geographical locus for such a tradition.[36] The rabbinical commentaries on Nu. 25:1f. also refer to the pagan rites observed there as *marzēaḥ*.[37] The abstruse rites connected with this site[38] indicate that this *mrzḥ* tradition had long since diverged from the mainstream.

Fabry

---

36. H. Donner and H. Cüppers, *Die Mosaikkarte von Madeba,* I (Wiesbaden, 1977), figs. 17, 53-55, 105.
37. E.g., Sifre on Nu. 131.
38. Pope, 196f.

מרר *mrr;* מַר *mar;* מֹרָה *mōrâ;* מָרוֹר *mārôr;* מְרִירוּת *m^e^rîrûṯ;* מְרֵרָה *m^e^rērâ;* מְרוֹרָה *m^e^rôrâ;* מֶמֶר *memer;* מַמְרֹרִים *mamrōrîm;* תַּמְרוּרִים *tamrûrîm*

Contents: I. 1. Etymology; 2. Occurrences. II. Usage: 1. Taste; 2. Emotion; 3. Derivatives. III. 1. LXX; 2. Dead Sea Scrolls.

I. 1. *Etymology.* At least two homonymous roots *mrr* are found in the Semitic languages. One appears in Akk. *marāru* (only EA), Ugar. *mrr,* "go away,"[1] and Arab. *marra,* "pass by." The other, meaning "be bitter," appears in Akk. *marāru,* Arab. *marra,* Aram. (including Syr.) *mrr,* and Eth. *marara, marra.* The last is often associated with Ugar. *mrr,* "strengthen, bless,"[2] and Arab. *marīr,* "strong"; this association assumes semantic ambivalence *(jidd)* in the root. It has been suggested that the first of these roots is reflected in Heb. *mar,* "drop" (Isa. 40:5);[3] the other is common and appears in many derivatives.

2. *Occurrences.* The verb *mrr (mar)* appears 6 times in the qal, 3 times in the piel ("make bitter"), 4 times (+ conj. in Ps. 4:5 [Eng. v. 4]; 106:33) in the hiphil ("embitter, distress, lament bitterly"), and twice in the hithpael. The adj. *mar* appears 38 times.

---

mrr. M. Dahood, "Qoheleth and Recent Discoveries," *Bibl,* 39 (1958), 302-318, esp. 308ff.; D. Pardee, "*m^e^rôrăt-p^e^tanîm* 'Venom' in Job 20,14," *ZAW,* 91 (1979), 401-416; S. Rin and Sh. Rin, "Ugaritic–OT Affinities II," *BZ,* n.s. 11 (1967), 174-192, esp. 189.

1. *WUS,* no. 1658.
2. *WUS,* no. 1659.
3. D. Winton Thomas, " 'A Drop of a Bucket': Some Observations on the Hebrew Text of Isaiah 40_{15}," *In Memoriam Paul Kahle. BZAW,* 103 (1968), 219-221.

The distinction between the qal perfect and the adjective is not always clear. The following derivatives are also found: *mōrâ,* "bitterness" (2 times); *mārôr,* "bitter" (5 times); *m*ᵉ*rērâ* and *m*ᵉ*rôrâ,* "gall bladder" (once each; the last also occurs once in the sense of "poison"[4]), *m*ᵉ*rîrûṯ* and *memer,* "bitterness, distress" (once each); *mamrōrîm,* "bitterness" (once); and *tamrûrîm,* "bitterness" (3 times; to be distinguished from the homonym meaning "road markers," Jer. 31:21).

Ringgren

The textually problematic phrase *mê hammārîm,* "bitter water," occurs in Nu. 5:18; the context is an ordeal following the complaint of a jealous husband. Jack M. Sasson proposes to derive *mārîm* from Ugar. *mrr,* "strengthen, bless," citing also → מרה *mārâ,* "rebel."[5] One may also compare *tammēr* (Ex. 23:21) and the proposals to derive it from *mrr.*[6]

Fabry

II. Usage.

1. *Taste.* In the first instance, *mrr* denotes a bitter taste; as Isa. 5:20; Prov. 27:7 show, it is an antonym of *māṯôq,* "sweet." In Ex. 15:23, e.g., the water of Marah was "bitter" and therefore undrinkable. After the fall of the great city in the Isaiah apocalypse, the inhabitants of the earth no longer drink wine with singing, and strong drink tastes bitter (Isa. 24:9). In Ex. 12:8; Nu. 9:11, *mārôr* denotes the bitter herbs of the Passover meal. In Lam. 3:15, in parallel with → לענה *la*ʿ*ᵃnâ* (traditionally translated "wormwood"; cf. also Prov. 5:4), it likewise refers to bitter herbs, metaphorically describing Israel's emotional reaction to the taunts of the nations. Dt. 32:32 is also figurative: "Their grapes are grapes of poison *(rôš),* their clusters are bitter *(m*ᵉ*rōrōṯ),*" for their vines are like those of Sodom and Gomorrah. It is unclear from the context whether these words refer to devastated Israel or to the nations.[7] Since other passages use the vine to symbolize Israel (e.g., Isa. 5:1-7; Ps. 80:9-20[8-19]), that is probably the case here as well; the verse then means that Israel is as degenerate as Sodom and Gomorrah.

2. *Emotion.* A bitter taste evokes a negative emotional response. Therefore *mar* is frequently used figuratively for feelings and emotions.

a. In describing her distress to her daughters, Naomi uses the phrase *mar lî,* "it is bitter to me," or more freely "I am sorry on your account" (Ruth 1:13). In v. 20 she

---

4. P. Fronzaroli, "Studi sul lessico comune semitico, II: Anatomia e Fisiologia," *AANLR,* 19 (1964), 254, 267.

5. J. M. Sasson, "Nu 5 and the 'Waters of Judgement,' " *BZ,* n.s. 16 (1972), 249-251. See also above; and D. Pardee, "The Semitic Root mrr and the Etymology of Ugaritic *mr(r)* par. *brk,*" *UF,* 10 (1978), 249-288; G. R. Driver, "Two Problems in the OT, II: The 'Waters of Bitterness' (Numbers, v.11-28)," *Syr,* 33 (1956), esp. 73-77.

6. Sh. Rin and S. Rin, *Leš,* 32 (1967/68), 236f. (Heb.); E. Y. Kutscher, *Leš,* 32 (1967/68), 343-46 (Heb.).

7. See the comms.

asks to be called Mara instead of Naomi, because Shaddai has dealt bitterly (*mrr* hiphil) with her. Referring to his illness, Hezekiah says (Isa. 38:17): "Surely it was for my welfare that I had great bitterness" (*mar lî mār;* the second *mar* should probably be read as *m*ᵉ*'ōḏ*). Zion is described in Lam. 1:4: "Her young girls grieve (*nûgôṯ;* יגה *yāgâ*), and her lot is bitter."

b. We often find *mar* in association with *nep̱eš,* either attributively or in the construct phrase *mar-nep̱eš.* The particular nuance ("sad," "embittered") must be determined in each case from the context. Sorrow and distress may be involved: Hannah is "distressed" and weeps because she is childless (1 S. 1:10); the Shunammite woman who comes to Elijah is "distressed" because her son has died (2 K. 4:27); Ezekiel describes a bitter lament *(mispēḏ mar)* over Tyre, depicted as a sunken ship, with bitter crying and lamentation (*z'q;* Ezk. 27:30f.). Job speaks in general terms of the bitterness of his soul (Job 7:11, par. *ṣar rûḥî;* 10:1; cf. also 21:25, "dying in bitterness of soul" in contrast to "tasting of good [*ṭôḇ*]"; 27:2); Hezekiah does likewise (Isa. 38:15; the rest of the verse is obscure). According to the teaching of King Lemuel (Prov. 31:6f.), wine should be given to those in bitter distress, that they may forget their trouble (*'āmāl).* Prov. 14:10 is equally general: the heart knows its own bitterness. In this last passage, the antonym is joy *(śimḥâ).*

Elsewhere we find concrete situations: the people are bitter and seek to stone David (1 S. 30:6); the "hot-tempered" Danites threaten to slay Micah and his family (Jgs. 18:25); David collects men who are discontented, in debt, or "desperate" (1 S. 22:2); David and his men are "enraged" like a bear robbed of her cubs (2 S. 17:8).

c. We find many of these same nuances in conjunction with *rûaḥ.* Esau's concubines made life bitter *(mōrâ)* for his parents (Gen. 26:35). Ezekiel is borne away by the Spirit, "bitter in the heat of [his] spirit" (Ezk. 3:14; *mar* is absent from the LXX, and may be an addition to explain or mitigate the daring expression "in the heat of my spirit"[8]). When Sir. 7:11 says, "Do not despise a person who is embittered in spirit," the reference is probably to those who are in desperate straits, from the context probably those who are desperately poor. The text of Sir. 4:1 must be corrupt; this verse, too, probably refers to those who are desperately poor.

d. Ezk. 27:30 connects *mar* with *z'q,* "cry out, lament."[9] It appears similarly as an attribute of *ṣ*ᵉ*'āqâ/z*ᵉ*'āqâ* in Gen. 27:34; Est. 4:1.

e. We read in 2 K. 14:26 that when he saw the bitter distress *('*ᵒ*nî)* of Israel during the reign of Jeroboam II, Yahweh helped them with the aid of Jeroboam. The words recall Ex. 1:14, which tells how the Egyptians made life bitter (*mrr* piel) for the Israelites; *'*ᵒ*nî* is also used for the suffering of the Israelites in Egypt (e.g., Ex. 3:7). Ps. 64:4(3) speaks of the "bitter" words of the enemy, which strike the psalmist like arrows. In Isa. 33:7 we read how, during the eschatological attack of the enemy, the warriors[10] cry out *(ṣā'aq)* and the envoys of peace weep bitterly: the enemy refuses peace

---

8. See W. Zimmerli, *Ezekiel 1. Herm* (Eng. trans. 1979), 94.
9. See above.
10. For the textual problem see *BHS.*

negotiations, demanding unconditional surrender.[11] In 1 S. 15:32 Agag says upon meeting Saul that his "bitterness of death" is past *(sār).* It is unclear whether he is hoping for mercy or speaking ironically in fear of death. Sir. 41:1 also speaks of the bitterness of death (cf. Prov. 5:4 below and 2 S. 2:26: "the bitter end").

Describing eschatological catastrophe ("on that day"), Am. 8:9f. (authenticity questionable) mentions all kinds of mourning customs: lamentation, sackcloth, baldness, mourning as for an only son;[12] it will be "a bitter day." In a similar vein, Zeph. 1:14 says that on the day of Yahweh warriors will cry out *mar.* Zec. 12:10 likewise speaks of bitter mourning for a firstborn or only son, although here the hiphil of the verb is used; cf. *tamrûrîm* in a similar context in Jer. 6:26.

Jer. 2:19 states that the wickedness *(rāʿâ)* and apostasy *(m^e^šûḇâ)* of the people are the cause of their punishment, and that it is bitter *(mar)* and evil *(raʿ)* to forsake God. The conjunction of *raʿ* and *mar* recurs in Jer. 4:18: "Your ways and your doings have brought this upon you. This is your doom; how bitter it is!" Here the text is difficult; we should possibly read "your wickedness and your recalcitrance *(meryēḵ).*"[13]

Eccl. 7:26 states that the woman who is a trap is "more bitter than death"; "one who pleases God escapes her, but one who displeases God is taken by her."[14] Prov. 5:4 speaks of the bitter end that results from consorting with the "strange woman" ("bitter as wormwood").

In a unique passage in the Blessing of Jacob (Gen. 49:23), we read that archers "fiercely attacked" him (*mrr* piel par. *śāṭam,* "press hard").

Dnl. 8:7; 11:11 use the hithpael to describe violent attacks: the goat against the ram, and the king of the south against the king of the north.

3. *Derivatives.* The remaining derivatives have nothing new to offer. In Ezk. 21:11(6) *m^e^rîrûṯ* is used for the bitter moaning of the prophet. In Dt. 32:24 *m^e^rîrî* describes a dreadful pestilence. The noun *mamrōrîm* appears in Job 9:18: "he fills me with bitterness"; cf. 13:26 ("you write bitter things [*m^e^rōrôṯ*] against me"); Lam. 3:15 ("he has filled me with bitter food [*m^e^rôrîm*]").[15] In Prov. 17:25 *memer,* "bitterness, grief," parallels *kaʿas,* "anger." Hos. 12:15(14) uses *tamrûrîm* similarly in conjunction with the hiphil of *kʿs:* "Ephraim has given bitter offense." In Jer. 31:15 the same word describes Rachel's bitter weeping in Ramah.

Ringgren

The nouns *m^e^rērâ/m^e^rôrâ,* "gall, gall bladder," also the "venom" that was associated with the gall of a serpent,[16] appear only in the book of Job (16:13; 20:14,25).

11. O. Kaiser, *Isaiah 13–39. OTL* (Eng. trans. 1974), 344f.
12. → יחד *yāḥaḏ* (VI, 40).
13. *BHS; HAL,* II, 629.
14. Cf. Rin and Rin, *BZ,* 11 (1967), 174-192; Dahood, 308f.
15. M. Dahood, "Hebrew-Ugaritic Lexicography V," *Bibl,* 48 (1967), 427.
16. A. van den Born, *BL*², 510.

Suggesting the most terrible poison imaginable,[17] they serve as a metaphor for evil and its consequences, as well as denoting one of the innermost organs of the human body, an injury to which spells swift and certain death.[18] Despite their Greek equivalent *cholḗ*, *m^e^rērâ/m^e^rōrâ* are not associated with any feeling or emotion in the OT. Gall was used medicinally; the book of Tobit mentions such use of fish gall.[19]

Fabry

III. 1. *LXX.* The usual LXX translation is *pikrós,* along with such derivatives as *pikría* and *pikraínein.* We also find *odýnē* and its derivatives, *elegmós,* and a wide range of translations occurring only once.

Ringgren

2. *Dead Sea Scrolls.* The verb *mrr* occurs only twice in the Dead Sea Scrolls (11QTemple 64:2,5); both instances are scribal errors for → מרד *māraḏ.* But the adj. *mārôr* occurs 10 times, almost exclusively with an anthropological sense in laments of a Qumran Essene. Not only the presence of sinners round about him but also insight into his own sinfulness occasion "bitterness" of soul (1QH 5:12, par. *ṣāraṯ nep̱eš;* 5:32, par. *ḥāsaḵ, mašḥôr;* 8:28, par. *k^e^'ēḇ 'ānûš,* "unceasing pain"; 11:19). The eschatological situation of imminent expectation involves on the one hand bitterness over the wicked enemies of the community (1QpHab 9:11; 1QS 4:13; 4Q179 [4QapocrLamA] 2:7 [cf. Lam. 1]) and on the other personal bitterness within the worshiper (1QH 5:34; 11:22), a hopeful endurance that awaits the "end of wickedness," coming close to the Pauline *stenázein* (Rom. 8).

Fabry

---

17. G. Fohrer, *Das Buch Hiob. KAT,* XVI (1963), 330; cf. Pardee.

18. H. W. Wolff, *Anthropology of the OT* (Eng. trans., Philadelphia, 1974), 64f.; E. Dhorme, *L'emploi métaphorique des noms de parties du corps en hébreu et en akkadien* (1923, repr. Paris, 1963), 130.

19. W. von Soden, *AfO,* 21 (1966), 81f.; W. Bunte, "Galle," *BHHW,* I (1962), 512; → דג *dāgh* (III, 139).

מַשָּׂא *maśśāʾ*; **מַשֹּׂא** *maśśōʾ*; **מַשָּׂאָה** *maśśāʾâ*; **מַשְׂאוֹת** *maśʾōṯ*; **מַשְׂאֵת** *maśʾēṯ*; *__מִשֵּׂאת__ *miśśēʾṯ*; **שְׂאֵת** *śᵉʾēṯ*; ***שִׂיא** *śîʾ*

Contents: I. Etymology and Forms. II. *maśśāʾ* I, "Burden": 1. Literal Usage; 2. Figurative Usage; 3. Metonymy. III. *maśśāʾ* II, "Utterance": 1. General Usage; 2. Prophetic Oracles. IV. Special Cases. V. 1. Versions; 2. Dead Sea Scrolls.

I. Etymology and Forms. The noun *maśśāʾ* can mean either (1) "burden" or (2) "utterance." There is no doubt that in both senses it derives from *nśʾ*, "bear, lift."

In either case it is a verbal noun of the *maqṭal* form, which denotes an object affected by the action of a transitive verb, which is used to name the object. Thus *maśśāʾ* means "that which one bears," i.e., "burden," as well as "that for which one raises (one's voice)," i.e., "utterance." Analogous formations include *maʾᵃḵāl,* "food," *maḥmāḏ,* "treasure," *mattān,* "gift," and *marʾeh,* "appearance."[1] Most likely the corresponding feminine forms *(maqṭalat) maśśāʾâ* and *maśʾēṯ* were originally *nomina vicis* denoting a single instance of the action (cf. Arab. *faʿlat*^{un}[2]).

In the late period (under Aramaic influence?), *maqṭal* > *miqṭal* is used regularly as a qal infinitive, as in the phrases *lāhem lᵉʾên maśśāʾ*, "until they could carry no more" (2 Ch. 20:25), and *ʾên-lāḵem maśśāʾ bakkāṯēp,* "you need no longer carry it on your shoulders" (2 Ch. 35:3) (cf. Middle Heb. *maśśāʾ ûmattān,* "taking and giving" > "commerce"). We find variant formations in the phrases *maśśōʾ pānîm,* "partiality" (2 Ch. 19:7), and *lᵉmaśʾôṯ ʾôṯāh miššᵒrāšêhā,* "to pull it from its roots" (Ezk. 17:9). Cf. *maśʾôṯ,* "portions" (Gen. 43:34), "utterances" (Lam. 2:14). We also find *miqṭal* + *-t* in *ûmiśśʾēṯô lōʾ ʾûḵāl,* "and I could not face (his majesty)" (Job 31:23b).[3]

The nominalized inf. *śᵉʾēṯ* I, "exaltation, majesty," and the hapax legomenon *śîʾ*, "height" (Job 20:6), are used like the infinitive of *maśśāʾ* I.

P. A. H. de Boer questions whether *maśśāʾ* II, "utterance," is in fact a meaning distinct from *maśśāʾ* I, "burden": he argues that the passages claimed for *maśśāʾ* II

---

maśśāʾ. P. A. H. de Boer, "An Inquiry into the Meaning of the Term משא," *OTS,* 5 (1948), 197-214; H. S. Gehman, "The 'Burden' of the Prophets," *JQR,* N.S. 31 (1940), 107-121; G. Lambert, "Mon joug est aisé et mon fardeau léger," *NRT,* 77 (1955), 963-69; W. McKane, "משא in Jeremiah 23, 33-40," *Prophecy. Festschrift G. Fohrer. BZAW,* 150 (1980), 35-54; J. A. Naudé, "*maśśāʾ* in the OT with Special Reference to the Prophets," *OTWSA,* 12 (1969), 91-100; G. Rinaldi, "Alcuni termini ebraici relativi alla letteratura," *Bibl,* 40 (1959), 267-289, esp. 278f.; V. Sasson, "An Unrecognized 'Smoke-Signal' in Isaiah XXX 27," *VT,* 33 (1983), 90-95; F. Stolz, "נשׂא *nśʾ* 'to lift, bear,' " *TLOT,* II (1997), 769-74, esp. 769f.,773f.

1. *BLe,* §61x$^{\varepsilon}$-p$^{\zeta}$; Meyer, II, §40, 4a.

2. W. Fischer, *Grammatik des klassischen Arabisch* (Wiesbaden, 1972), §232.

3. On the inf. **miśśēʾṯ* see W. von Soden, "Zum hebräischen Wörterbuch," *UF,* 13 (1981), 159.

refer specifically to "a heavy burden, a judgment of God."[4] In support of this view he cites Hugo Grotius, the thesaurus of Eliezer Ben Yehudah, and Henry S. Gehman. Those who agree include Gustave Lambert, Walter A. Maier, and Fritz Stolz.[5] Since Karl Heinrich Graf,[6] however, most scholars prefer to derive *maśśā'* II from *nś' qôl,* "raise one's voice,"[7] or from an elliptical use of *nś'* in the sense of "speak," as in Isa. 3:7; 42:2 (with the obj. *qôl* in the parallel strophe), 11; Job 21:12. There may also be a connection with *nāśî',* "speaker" > "chief."[8] We find *nś'* with "oracle" as its object in the phrase *wayyiśśā' mᵉšālô* (Nu. 23:7,18; 24:3,15,23). The verb *nś'* with *maśśā',* "utterance," as paronomastic object appears in 2 K. 9:25, followed in v. 26 by an oracle of Yahweh. In Jer. 17:21,27, however, *nś' maśśā'* clearly means "bear a burden" (Dt. 1:12; Sir. 51:26).

Several arguments favor a distinct *maśśā'* II, "utterance," derived from *nś' qôl.* (1) Prov. 30:1; 31:1; Sir. 9:18 use *maśśā'* in the general sense of "saying" without specific reference to a prophetic oracle of disaster. (2) Even in prophetic contexts, *maśśā'* is not limited to the meaning "burden of disaster" > "oracle of disaster"; in Zec. 9:1; 12:1; Mal. 1:1; 1Q27 fr. 1 1:8 it means simply "(prophetic) oracle." (3) The use of *maśśā'* in the metonymic sense of "leading music" in 1 Ch. 15:22,27[9] cannot involve *maśśā'* I, "burden"; it can be explained only by reference to *nś' qôl* or *nś' zimrâ,* "lead singing" (Ps. 81:3[Eng. v. 2]; cf. Am. 5:1; Isa. 37:4; cf. also *nś' 'bᵉṯōp' wᵉḵinnôr* in Job 21:12). For Northwest Semitic, the verb *nś'* is closely associated with the obj. "voice"; cf. the Ugaritic phrase *nš' g,* "raise one's voice"; contrast Akk. *rigma(m) šakānu(m)* with the same meaning.[10]

II. *maśśā'* I, "Burden."

1. *Literal Usage.* The noun *maśśā'* I, "burden," is used primarily in a concrete, literal sense: the "burden" under which a donkey lies (Ex. 23:5) or which must not be "borne" on the Sabbath (Jer. 17:21,27), i.e., neither "carried out" of Jerusalem (v. 22) nor "brought in" (v. 24); cf. Neh. 13:15,19. Modified by a genitive denoting a beast of burden, *maśśā'* I can be used as a unit of quantity, denoting the load that can be carried by that animal, e.g., *maśśā' ṣemeḏ-pᵉrāḏîm,* "two mule loads" (2 K. 5:17), or *maśśā' 'arbāʿîm gāmāl,* "forty camel loads" (2 K. 8:9).

2. *Figurative Usage.* In Isa. 46:1f. *maśśā'* I provides material for a simile. The (corrupt) text speaks of the "burden" that the images of the gods Bel and Nebo are for

---

4. P. 214.

5. Maier, *The Book of Nahum* (St. Louis, 1959), 146; Stolz, 773f.; on p. 769, however, Stolz contradicts his own etymology.

6. K. H. Graf, *Der Prophet Jeremia* (Leipzig, 1862), 315.

7. *HAL,* II, 725, s.v. *nś'* qal 8.

8. On Akk. *našû[m],* "utter," in the Alalakh texts see M. Tsevat, "Alalakhiana," *HUCA,* 29 (1958), 119; on Eth. *'awše'a,* "speak," see *HAL,* II, 725, s.v. *nś'* qal 8.

9. M. Gertner, "The Masorah and the Levites," *VT,* 10 (1960), 252.

10. For the Ugaritic see *WUS,* no. 1859; for the Akkadian, *AHw,* III, 982, s.v. *rigmu(m)* 2.

the weary (animals?), who must bear them away for their disappointed worshipers (cf. the "bearing" of idols in Am. 5:26). Isa. 22:25 is similar: the *maśśā'*, "load," of Eliakim's ancestral house will perish together with the "peg" supporting it, i.e., Eliakim the upstart ruler (vv. 20-23). For the fool, wisdom is *'bn mś'*, a "burdensome stone" that he would happily cast aside (Sir. 6:21); 51:26 enjoins the reader to bear "(wisdom's) burden" (cf. 6:25; Mt. 11:29f.). In Ps. 38:5(4) *maśśā'* is the object of comparison, linked by *k^e*, "like," with the subject: the psalmist's iniquities are "like a heavy burden," i.e., "they are too heavy for me."

Zeph. 3:18 uses *maś'ēṯ* metaphorically: *maś'ēṯ 'āleyhā ḥerpâ* means "the reproach burdening (Jerusalem)"; cf. *nś'* with *ḥerpâ* as object in Ps. 15:3. Also metaphorical is the phrase *hāyâ l^emaśśā' 'al,* "become a burden to" (2 S. 15:33; 19:36 [reading *'al*]). In Job 7:20 Job asks why he has become a "burden" to Yahweh (reading *'ālēyḵā*). In Nu. 11:11,17; Dt. 1:12, the genitive following *maśśā'* refers to the Israelites, who have become a "burden" to Moses. The "burden" that Israel has become to Yahweh is the point of the phrase *'attem hammaśśā'*, "you are the burden," in Jer. 23:33 (conj.).[11] These words pun on the preceding question, *mah-maśśā' YHWH,* "What is the utterance of Yahweh?" itself parallel to "What has Yahweh answered (you)?" and "What has Yahweh spoken?" in vv. 35,37. Vv. 34,36,38 build on this wordplay, using *maśśā' YHWH* frequently with the connotation of the burden of disaster Yahweh has laid upon his people.

3. *Metonymy.* At a relatively late date, the figurative use of *maśśā'* I gives rise to metonymic meanings. In Nu. 4:15 it refers to the cultic "service" of the Kohathites at the tent of meeting; cf. vv. 19,24,27,31f.,47,49, where *maśśā'* is used in conjunction with *'bd,* "serve (cultically)." In Ezk. 20:40 *maś'ôṯ* refers to "offerings," and in 2 Ch. 17:11 *maśśā'* means "tribute," as does *maśēṯ.*[12]

The use of *maśśā'* for "cultic service" might be related to → מַס *mas,* "compulsory service, forced labor," if the latter likewise derives from *nś'*,[13] although the elision of the third radical ' is hard to account for. Akk. *massu,* "corvée worker," in the Alalakh and Amarna texts appears to be borrowed from *mas.* In Punic, *nš'* I, "offer, sacrifice," and *nš'* II, "sacrificial offering," are relatively common;[14] the latter competes with *mš'*, "sacrificial offering."[15]

III. *maśśā'* II, "Utterance."

1. *General Usage.* In Prov. 31:1 the Masoretic accentuation suggests *maśśā'* II, in parallel with the preceding phrase *diḇrê l^emû'ēl meleḵ,* "the words of King Lemuel." The relative clause *'^ašer-yiss^erattû 'immô,* "that his mother taught him," follows; it must refer to *maśśā'* rather than the distant *diḇrê,* which already has a genitive

11. P. Wernberg-Møller, *VT,* 6 (1956), 415.
12. *HAL,* II, 640, s.v. 2.
13. *HAL,* II, 603f., s.v. *mas.*
14. *DISO,* 186f.
15. *CIS,* I, 408, 2; *DISO,* 169: *mš'* II.

qualifier.[16] This analysis makes it most likely that in Prov. 30:1 *hammaśśā'* means "utterance," in parallel with the preceding and following nouns *dibrê* . . . , "words of . . . ," and *n^e'um* . . . , "declaration of. . . ." In Prov. 30:1; 31:1, therefore, *(ham)maśśā'* denotes the essence of a wisdom "utterance": the term refers to a solemn and ceremonious style of speech for which "the voice is raised," as also in the effective pronouncement of a curse (cf. *nś' 'ālâ,* "pronounce a curse," 1 K. 8:31; 2 Ch. 6:22[17]). There is no necessary reference, however, to a specific content such as the "burden" of announced disaster. Sir. 9:18 has *mś' 'l pyhw,* "utterance from (?) his mouth," i.e., the mouth of the eloquent. Here, too, the word conveys a negative sense: it parallels *byṭh,* "idle talk" (cf. *bṭ'/h,* "rash words," in Prov. 12:18; Sir. 5:13), and the predicate *yśwn'* states that it is "hated."[18] Again the meaning "burden" is most unlikely.

2. *Prophetic Oracles.* When *maśśā'* II refers to a prophetic oracle, it usually means a proclamation of disaster (J. A. Naudé: "verdict, sentence"), directed against foreign nations (Isa. 13:1; 14:28; 15:1; 17:1; 19:1; 21:1,11,13; 23:1; 30:6; Nah. 1:1;[19] Hab. 1:1 [?]), Judah (Jer. 23:33; Ezk. 12:10; Hab. 1:1 [?]), or individual Israelites (2 K. 9:25; Isa. 22:1; 2 Ch. 24:27). In Lam. 2:14, however, *maś'ôṯ šāw' ûmaddûḥîm,* "false oracles and enticements (?)," refers to the false oracles of salvation spoken by preexilic prophets.

The overwhelming preponderance of disaster oracles may be due to overtones of the meaning "burden," as in Jer. 23:33-38. It would be inappropriate, however, to argue on these grounds against the denotation "utterance" in all cases, precisely because such an argument would destroy the contrast between *maśśā'* II, "utterance," in 23:33 versus *maśśā'* I, "burden," in vv. 34,36,38, depriving 23:33-38 of its linguistic and literary appeal.

It is probably also inappropriate to explain the use of *maśśā'* II followed by a parallel *d^ebar YHWH,* "word of Yahweh," in the headings of late collections of optimistic prophecies such as Zec. 9:1; 12:1; Mal. 1:1 as an inversion of the meaning of *maśśā'* I, "burden." In 1Q27 fr. 1 1:8, *mś'* also appears in parallel with the quite general expression *hdbr lbw',* "the word concerning the future," which again does not suggest specifically a burden of disaster. Finally, such terms as *maśśā',* like *d^ebar YHWH,* can be used as the subject of *hāyâ* in the sense of "come" (Isa. 14:28) and as the object of *ḥāzâ,* "see" (Isa. 13:1; Hab. 1:1; Lam. 2:14). In 4Q160 fr. 1 4, *mś',* "utterance," stands for MT *mar'eh,* "vision," in 1 S. 3:15.[20] These uses at the very least do not contradict a general meaning "utterance" for *maśśā'* II in prophetic contexts.

---

16. Contra B. Gemser, *Sprüche Salomos. HAT,* XVI (^{2}1963), 108.
17. On the reading *w^enāśā'* instead of MT *w^enāšā',* see M. Noth, *Könige 1–16. BK,* IX/1 (^{2}1983), 173.
18. G. Sauer, *Jesus Sirach. JSHRZ,* III/5 (1981), 528.
19. K. J. Cathcart, *Nahum in the Light of Northwest Semitic. BietOr,* 26 (1973), 36f.
20. *HAL,* II, 640, s.v. *maśśā'* II.

IV. Special Cases. In certain passages, other objects than *qôl,* "voice," must be understood with *maśśā'* from *nś'*. For example, the sons and daughters of whom the Jerusalemites are bereft in Ezk. 24:25 are called *maśśā' napšām,* "the affection of their soul [NRSV 'heart']." The idiom in the background is *nś' nepeš,* "set one's soul/heart upon."[21] In Dt. 24:15; Hos. 4:8, this phrase means "be eager for"; in Ps. 25:1f.; 143:8, it means "trust"; in Ps. 24:4; 86:4; Prov. 19:18, it means more generally "think about."[22] The use of *maś'ēṯ* with genitives like *kappay,* "the lifting up of my hands (in prayer)," *yd 'l yśr'l 'l,* "the lifting up of the hand of the God of Israel against" (1QM 18:3; cf. 18:1), or *he'āšān,* "the sending up of the fire signal" (Jgs. 20:38,40; Lachish ostracon 4[23]), reflects the use of *nś'* with the object in question.

In Gen. 43:34 *maś'ôṯ* and its const. sg. *maś'aṯ* are used elliptically in the sense of "portion(s) of food." Similar are the elliptical use of *maśśā'â,* "exaltation," in Isa. 30:27[24] and Middle Heb. *maśśā' ûmattān,* "taking and giving" > "commerce." In none of these cases is the object of *nś'* specified.

V. 1. *Versions.* The LXX uses a surprising variety of equivalents for *maśśā'*.[25] Most common are the verb *aírein* (Nu. 4:15,24,31f.,47,49; 2 Ch. 35:3 [*epaírein* LXX^{A}]), its related nouns *ársis* (2 K. 8:9; used for *maś'ēṯ* in 2 S. 11:8), *éparsis* (Ezk. 24:25; for *maś'ēṯ* in Ps. 141[LXX 140]:2), and *árta* (Nu. 4:27 [MSS]), and their homonyms such as *anaphorá* (Nu. 4:19), *bástagma* (2 S. 15:33; Jer. 17:21f.,24,27; Neh. 13:15,19), *gómos* (Ex. 23:5; 2 K. 5:17), *lḗmma* (2 K. 9:25; Jer. 23:33f.,36,38; Nah. 1:1; Zec. 9:1; 12:1; Job 31:23), and *phortíon* (2 S. 19:36; Isa. 46:1; Ps. 38[LXX 37]:5; Job 7:20); but the frequencies of these forms do not yield a clear picture. That the LXX must have been aware of a distinct *maśśā'* II, "utterance," is shown by the translations *rhḗma* (2 K. 9:25; Isa. 14:28; 17:1; 23:1; Jer. 23:33 [LXX^{S1}]), *chrēmatismós* ("document" [?], Prov. 31:1), and derivatives of *ádein,* "sing" (1 Ch. 15:22,27).[26]

2. *Dead Sea Scrolls.* In the Dead Sea Scrolls *maśśā'* (etc.) appears 8 times. The semantic range corresponds to that of the OT. In 1QSa 1:19f. the notion of "burden"[27] is extended through "service" to serve as a term for "office" in the community *('ēḏâ).*

Müller

21. *HAL,* II, 725, s.v. *nś'* qal 11.
22. See Stolz, 772.
23. *KAI,* 194, 10.
24. Contra Sasson; for the meaning "exaltation," cf. *ś^{e}'ēṯ,* "ascension, loftiness," and *śî',* "loftiness" (Job 20:6).
25. De Boer, 200-204.
26. On the Targ., Peshitta, and Vulg., see de Boer, 204-9.
27. See II.3 above.

מִשְׁבָּרִים *mišbārîm*

Contents: I. Linguistic Evidence: 1. Etymology and Basic Meaning; 2. Contextual Sense; 3. Versions, Commentaries, Dead Sea Scrolls. II. OT: 1. Mythological Usage; 2. Figurative Usage; 3. Theological Usage.

I. Linguistic Evidence.

1. *Etymology and Basic Meaning.* The word *mišbārîm* occurs 5 times in the OT, always in the plural and always in the construct or with a suffix; it also occurs in Postbiblical Hebrew. The root *šbr,* "break," has the same meaning in other Semitic languages (Akk. *šebēru,* Ugar. *t̠br,* Aram. *tbr,* etc.); but in none of these do we find a noun form corresponding to our word. The *miqṭal*[1] derivative of this root, with the basic meaning "breaking," can have either active or passive force: the surf, i.e., the "breaking" of the waters that the sea throws up and appears to shatter[2] or the waves that are broken.[3] A noun with the identical consonants, *mašbēr* (const. *mišbar,* Hos. 13:13), refers to the "breaking forth" of a newborn child. Later linguistic use established a connection between the homonyms.[4]

2. *Contextual Sense.* The word is used as an emphatic synonym of *gal,* "wave" (Ps. 42:8[Eng. v. 7] and the derivative Jon. 2:4[3][5]); it also appears in the construct with the genitive *yām,* "sea" (Ps. 93:4). The context establishes the meaning "waves." It is not so easy to establish the meaning of the two other occurrences. In Ps. 88:8(7) our word directly parallels *ḥēmâ,* "wrath (of Yahweh)," referring to the punishments Yahweh imposes; the larger context (v. 7[6]), however, speaks of the "depths of the Pit" and the "deep." In 2 S. 22:5 *mišbᵉrê-māweṯ,* "the *mišbārîm* of death," parallels "torrents of perdition"; but the context (v. 6) also mentions "cords of Sheol" and "snares of death." In these last two passages, it is possible that the word should be

---

mišbārîm. C. Barth, *Die Errettung vom Tode in den individuellen Klage- und Dankliedern des ATs* (Zurich, 1947); O. Eissfeldt, "Gott und das Meer in der Bibel," *Studia orientalia Ioanni Pedersen septuagentario* (Copenhagen, 1953), 76-84 = *KlSchr,* III (1966), 256-264; T. H. Gaster, *The Dead Sea Scriptures* (New York, 1956), 135-37, 210; G. Jobes, *Dictionary of Mythology, Folklore, and Symbols* (New York, 1962), II, 1669 ("Waves of the Sea"); O. Kaiser, *Die mythische Bedeutung des Meeres in Ägypten, Ugarit und Israel. BZAW,* 78 ([2]1962); H. G. May, "Some Cosmic Connotations of *Mayim Rabbîm,* 'Many Waters,' " *JBL,* 74 (1955), 9-21; P. Reymond, *L'eau, sa vie, et sa signification dans l'AT. SVT,* 6 (1958); S. Thompson, *Motif-Index of Folk-Literature* (Bloomington, [2]1966), index, s.v. "Waves" (vol. VI, 853); A. Wünsche, *Die Bildersprache des ATs* (1906), 171-76.

1. *VG,* I, 375-78; *BLe,* §§488-492.
2. Rashi on Jon. 2:4.
3. Rashi on Ps. 42:8 (Eng. v. 7); Kimchi on 2 S. 22:5; et al.
4. See below.
5. A. Weiser, *Der Buch der zwölf kleinen Propheten, I. ATD,* 24 ([7]1979), 222.

understood not in its specialized sense but rather according to its etymology as "breaking, destruction" in general. In fact, the parallel text (Ps. 18:5[4]) reads *ḥeḇlê-māweṯ* instead of *mišbᵉrê-māweṯ; ḥeḇlê* is usually understood as "snares,"[6] but the ancient versions (LXX, Latin Psalters, Targ.) and commentators (Ibn Ezra) interpret it as "pangs."[7] This reading accords with the explanation of our word as meaning "disaster."

3. *Versions, Commentaries, Dead Sea Scrolls.* In the Psalms and Jonah, the LXX translates *mišbārîm* with *meteōrismoí,* a neologism probably meant to refer to "towering (waves)." The Roman and Gallican Psalters echo this translation in the *excelsa* (Ps. 42) and *elationes* (Pss. 93 and 88 [where, however, the Gallican Psalter has *fluctus*]). The Psalterium iuxta Hebraeos revises the translations to *fluctus* (Pss. 88, 93) and *gurgites* (Ps. 42), i.e., "waves" and "eddies."[8] Only once (Jonah) does the Targ. provide a translation that clearly refers to "waves"; elsewhere it prefers to etymologize (root *tbr*) or interpret: "disasters (that shatter someone)" (Ps. 88:8[7]). The earlier Hebrew exegetes interpret the word in these passages as "waves of the sea."

The situation differs in 2 S. 22:5, where most interpretations are etymological: LXX, *syntrimmoí* (from *syntríbein,* "smash to pieces"); Vulg., *contritiones;*[9] Targ. (paraphrasing), the pains a woman undergoes on the *maṯbᵉrā',* "birth stool" (cf. Middle Heb. *mašbēr* with the same meaning, which goes back, however, to the OT *mašbēr,* "[place of] breaking forth [of a newborn child]"[10]). Kimchi says that *mišbᵉrê-māweṯ* means "great pangs" — *mišbᵉrê* because they "break" *(šbr)* the human heart. He does, however, cite "waves" as a possible meaning. Another exegete (Metzudat David) translates the phrase as "pangs of death."

The Dead Sea Scrolls bear important witness to the ambiguity of the word in antiquity. There are 12 occurrences of *mišbārîm* in the *Hodayoth;* the contexts suggest both "waves" (1QH 6:23) and "pangs" (1QH 9:4-7). This ambiguity is used deliberately in 1QH 3:6-19, which combines the image of birth pangs with that of a stormy sea. In 3:6 *mišbᵉrê māweṯ* refers to pain and means "pangs of death"; in 3:16 *mišbᵉrê mayim* means "towering waves"; in 3:12 the *mišbārîm* of *šaḥaṯ,* the "Pit," remain ambiguous.

II. OT.

1. *Mythological Usage.* In all occurrences of our word, the context clearly reveals its originally mythological background. In Ps. 93, a hymn, we hear echoes of the motif of the rebellious floods of chaos, familiar primarily from Babylonian and Ugaritic mythology.[11] In Ps. 42, a lament, v. 8(7) refers not to a realistic natural

6. → חבל *ḥbl* I (IV, 176).
7. → חבל *ḥbl* IV (IV, 191f.).
8. Luther: *Wogen* and *Fluten.*
9. Cf. Luther: *Schmerzen.*
10. Cf. I.1 above.
11. → ים *yām* (VI, 87-98).

phenomenon[12] but to the primordial depths *(tᵉhôm-ʾel-tᵉhôm).* 2 S. 22 speaks of death *(māweṯ),* Sheol, and the "torrents of perdition" *(naḥᵃlê ḇᵉlîyaʿal);*[13] in addition to *šᵉʾôl* and *tᵉhôm,* Jon. 2 mentions → מצולה *mᵉṣûlâ,* "the deep," *lᵉḇaḇ yammîm,* "the heart of the sea," and *nāhār,* "the flood"; Ps. 88 speaks of the pit and the grave, darkness and the depths of *mᵉṣōlôṯ,* identifying the realm of the dead with the waters of chaos. Since *mišbārîm* appears only in such contexts, we may assume that it denotes elements of the primeval ocean, which can be viewed in a sense as its agents.[14]

2. *Figurative Usage.* The figurative language of the OT turns these mythological notions into metaphors. The *mišbārîm,* the "breakers" that "pass over" (*ʿbr:* Jon. 2:4[3]; Ps. 42:8[7]) or "encompass" (*ʾpp:* 2 S. 22:5) the speaker of the lament, threatening to drown him, symbolize terrible tribulation.

Similar images occur in other literatures. In Akkadian laments, we read: "You became enraged at your servant . . . he was cast into the raging flood,"[15] or "Your servant . . . who lies in swampy waters."[16] A Sumerian hymn praises the god who "destroys like a flood."[17] In Homer the "swelling waves of the sea" symbolize the nations gathered before the gates of Troy.[18]

3. *Theological Usage.* In the Psalms where the verses in question are found, the psalmist agonizes over the separation from God that has befallen him — surely not just physical separation from the temple and its cult but also the consequent spiritual torment — and the mockery of his enemies to which he is exposed. But suffering and tribulation, the faithful psalmist knows, are sent — like everything — by Yahweh: *mišbāreyḵā,* "your waves," he calls them in his prayer. Thus the rebellious powers of the mythological underworld are reduced to instruments in the hand of Yahweh. To be delivered from them, the psalmist cries in lamentation for help from the same God who unleashed them.

Kedar-Kopfstein

12. E.g., W. Staerk, *Lyrik. SAT* III/1 (²1920), 220.
13. → בליעל *bᵉliyyaʿal* (II, 131-36).
14. Kaiser, 66.
15. *SAHG,* 263.
16. *Ibid.,* 228.
17. *Ibid.,* 146.
18. *Iliad* 2.144.

מֹשֶׁה *mōšeh*

Contents: I. The Era of Moses; II. The Pre-Prophetic Moses; III. Moses in the Prophets; IV. Moses in Deuteronomy and the Deuteronomistic Literature; V. Moses as Mediator in the Post-exilic Cult; VI. Moses in Postexilic Literature; VII. Moses in Intertestamental Literature; VIII. Later Developments.

---

mōšeh.

1. *General.* E. Auerbach, *Moses* (1965; Eng. trans., Detroit, 1975); H. Cazelles, "Moïse," *DBS,* V (1957), 1308-31; *idem,* et al., *Moise, l'homme de l'alliance* (Paris, 1955); O. Eissfeldt, "Mose," *OLZ,* 48 (1953), 490-505 = *KlSchr,* III (1966), 240-255; A. Gélin, "Moses im AT," *BiLe,* 3 (1962), 97-110; M. Greenberg, "Moses," *EncJud,* XII (1971), 371-411; A. H. J. Gunneweg, "Mose — Religionsstifter oder Symbol," *Der evangelische Erzieher,* 17 (1963), 41-48; S. Herrmann, "Mose," *EvT,* 28 (1968), 301-328; S. Horn, "What We Don't Know about Moses and the Exodus," *BAR,* 3/2 (1977), 22-31; C. A. Keller, "Vom Stand und Aufgabe der Moseforschung," *TZ,* 13 (1957), 430-441; A. Neher, *Moses* (Eng. trans., New York, 1959); H. M. Orlinsky, "Moses," *Essays in Biblical Culture* (New York, 1974), 15-37; E. Osswald, *Das Bild des Mose in der kritischen alttestamentlichen Wissenschaft seit J. Wellhausen. AzT,* 18 (1963) (cf. *TLZ,* 82 [1957], 391f.); H. Schmid, "Der Stand der Moseforschung," *Jud,* 21 (1965), 194-221; W. H. Schmidt, *Exodus, Sinai und Mose. EdF,* 191 (1983); F. Stier and E. Beck, *Moses in Schrift und Überlieferung* (1963); R. Smend, *Das Mosebild von Heinrich Ewald bis Martin Noth* (Tübingen, 1959); R. J. Thompson, *Moses and the Law in a Century of Criticism since Graf. SVT,* 19 (1970); G. Widengren, "What Do We Know About Moses?" *Proclamation and Presence. Festschrift G. H. Davies* (London, 1970), 21-47; F. E. Wilms, "Die Frage nach dem historischen Mose," *TTQ,* 153 (1973), 353-363; F. Wüst, P. de Caprona, and M. Faessler, *La figure de Moïse* (Geneva, 1978).

2. *History of Religions.* S. Abramsky, "On the Kenite-Midianite Background of Moses' Leadership," *Nelson Glueck Memorial Volume. ErIsr,* 12 (1975), 35-39; W. F. Albright, "From the Patriarchs to Moses," *BA,* 36 (1973), 5-33, 48-76; *idem,* "Moses in Historical and Theological Perspective," *Magnalia Dei. Festschrift G. E. Wright* (New York, 1976), 120-131; M. Astour, "Les étrangers à Ugarit et le statut juridique des Ḫabiru," *RA,* 53 (1959), 70-76; R. Borger, "Das Problem der ʿapīru ('Ḫabiru')," *ZDPV,* 74 (1958), 121-132; J. Bottéro, *Le problème des Ḫabiru. Cahiers de la Société asiatique,* 12 (Paris, 1954); P. Buis, "Qadesh, un lieu maudit?" *VT,* 24 (1974), 268-285; E. F. Campbell, "Moses and the Foundations of Israel," *Int,* 29 (1975), 141-154; H. Cazelles, *À la recherche de Moïse* (Paris, 1979); B. Childs, "The Birth of Moses," *JBL,* 84 (1965), 109-122; D. Daiches, *The Quest for the Historical Moses* (London, 1974); J. Ebach, "Moses," *LexÄg,* IV (1982), 210f.; C. H. J. de Geus, *The Tribes of Israel. SSN,* 18 (1976), esp. 182-87; R. Giveon, *Les bédouins Shosou des documents égyptiens. DMOA,* 18 (1971); H. Gressmann, *Mose und seine Zeit. FRLANT,* N.S. 1 [18] (1913); J. G. Griffiths, "The Egyptian Derivation of the Name Moses," *JNES,* 12 (1953), 225-231; A. H. J. Gunneweg, "Mose in Midian," *ZTK,* 61 (1964), 1-9 = *Sola Scriptura* (Göttingen, 1983), 36-44; S. Herrmann, *Israel in Egypt. SBT,* 2/27 (Eng. trans. 1973); J. P. Hyatt, *The Origin of Mosaic Yahwism* (Waco, 1964), 85-93; A. Jirku, *Die Wanderungen der Hebräer im 3. und 2. vorchristlichen Jahrtausend. AO,* 24/2 (1924); A. Lods, *Israel from Its Beginnings to the Middle of the Eighth Century* (Eng. trans., London, 1932); E. Meyer, *Die Israeliten und ihre Nachbarstämme* (1906, repr. Darmstadt, 1967), 41-100; H. H. Schmid, *Mose: Überlieferung und Geschichte. BZAW,* 110 (1968); W. H. Schmidt, "Jahwe in Ägypten," *Sefer Rendṭorff. Festschrift R. Rendtorff. BDBAT,* 1 (1975),

In view of the extensive bibliography cited, it should come as no surprise that scholars have widely differing views concerning Moses. There is Martin Noth's Moses, of whom nothing is known except the site of his burial outside Israel. There is Julius Wellhausen's Moses, the liberator who led the Israelites to the oasis of Kadesh. There are Moses the priest of Eduard Meyer, Moses the prophet of André Neher and Martin

---

94-112 = *Kairos,* N.S. 18 (1976), 43-59; K. Schubert, "Das Problem des historischen Moses," *BiLi,* 38 (1964), 451-460; E. Sellin, *Moses in seiner Bedeutung für die israelitisch-jüdische Religionsgeschichte* (Leipzig, 1922); T. L. Thompson and D. Irwin, "The Joseph and Moses Narratives," *Israelite and Judaean History,* ed. J. H. Hayes and J. M. Miller. OTL (1977), 149-212 (cf. J. B. Geyer, review, *JSOT,* 15 [1980], 51-56; Thompson, response, 57-61); J. R. Towers, "The Name Moses," *JTS,* 36 (1935), 407-9; R. de Vaux, "Sur l'origine kénite ou madianite du Yahvisme," *Festschrift W. F. Albright. ErIsr,* 9 (1969), 28-32; P. Volz, *Mose und sein Werk* (Tübingen, 1932); M. Weippert, "Semitische Nomaden des zweiten Jahrtausends," *Bibl,* 55 (1974), 265-280.

3. *History and Theology.* F. Baumgärtel, "Der Tod des Religionsstifters," *KuD,* 9 (1963), 223-233; D. N. Freedman, "The Poetic Structure of the Framework of Deuteronomy 33," *The Bible World. Festschrift C. H. Gordon* (New York, 1980), 25-46; H. Gese, "Bemerkungen zur Sinaitradition," *ZAW,* 79 (1967), 137-154; J. Gray, "The Desert Sojourn of the Hebrews and the Sinai-Horeb Tradition," *VT,* 4 (1954), 148-154; A. H. J. Gunneweg, *Leviten und Priester. FRLANT,* 89 (1965); K. Koch, "Der Tod des Religionsstifters," *KuD,* 8 (1962), 100-123; R. Michaud, *Moïse* (Paris, 1979); E. W. Nicholson, *Exodus and Sinai in History and Tradition* (Richmond, 1973); G. von Rad, "The Origin of Mosaic Monotheism," *God at Work in Israel* (Eng. trans., Nashville, 1980), 128-138; R. Rendtorff, "Mose als Religionsstifter?" *GSAT. ThB,* 57 (1975), 152-171; H. Ringgren, *Israelite Religion* (Eng. trans., Philadelphia, 1966), 28-40; H. H. Rowley, "Moses and Monotheism," *From Moses to Qumran* (New York, 1963), 35-63.

4. *Exegetical History.* G. W. Ahlström, "Another Moses Tradition," *JNES,* 39 (1980), 65-69; W. F. Albright, "Jethro, Hobab and Reuel in Early Hebrew Tradition," *CBQ,* 25 (1963), 1-11; W. Beyerlin, *Origins and History of the Oldest Sinaitic Traditions* (Eng. trans., Oxford, 1966); B. Boschi, "Il suocero di Mose," *RivBibl,* 23 (1975), 329-335; P. Buis, "Les conflits entre Moïse et Israël dans Exode et Nombres," *VT,* 28 (1978), 257-270; A. Caquot, "Les énigmes d'un hémistiche biblique," *Dieu et l'être,* ed. P. Vignaux (Paris, 1978), 17-26; H. Cazelles, "Pour une exégèse de Ex 3,14," *Dieu et l'être,* ed. Vignaux, 27-44; *idem,* "Rédactions et traditions dans l'Exode," *Studien zum Pentateuch. Festschrift W. Kornfeld* (Vienna, 1977), 37-58; G. W. Coats, "Despoiling the Egyptians," *VT,* 18 (1968), 450-57; *idem,* "An Exposition for the Wilderness Traditions," *VT,* 22 (1972), 288-295; *idem,* "History and Theology in the Sea Tradition," *ST,* 29 (1975), 53-62; *idem,* "The Sea Tradition in the Wilderness Theme," JSOT, 12 (1979), 2-8; *idem,* "The King's Loyal Opposition," *Canon and Authority,* ed. G. W. Coats and B. O. Long (Philadelphia, 1977), 91-109; *idem,* "Moses in Midian," *JBL,* 92 (1973), 3-10; *idem,* "Moses versus Amalek," *Congress Volume, Edinburgh 1974. SVT,* 28 (1975), 29-41; *idem, Rebellion in the Wilderness* (Nashville, 1968); *idem,* "A Structural Transition in Exodus," *VT* 22 (1972), 129-142; *idem,* "The Traditio-historical Character of the Reed Sea Motif," *VT,* 17 (1967), 253-265; F. M. Cross and D. N. Freedman, "The Blessing of Moses," *JBL,* 67 (1948), 191-210; D. Daiches, *Moses, Man in the Wilderness* (London, 1973); H. Dreyer, "Tradition und heilige Stätte" (diss., Kiel, 1952); J. Dus, "Moses oder Josua," *ArOr,* 39/1 (1971), 16-45; H. Eising, "Die ägyptischen Plagen," *Lex tua veritas. Festschrift H. Junker* (Trier, 1961), 75-87; J. Finegan, *Let My People Go* (New York, 1963); G. Fohrer, *Überlieferung und Geschichte des Exodus. BZAW,* 91 (1964); V. Fritz, *Israel in der Wüste. MarTS,* 7 (1970); W. Fuss, *Die deuteronomistische Pentateuchredaktion in Exodus 3–17. BZAW,* 126 (1972); O. Garcia de la Fuente, "La figura de Mose in Ex 18,5 y 33,7," *EstBíb,* 29 (1970), 351-370; H. Gross, "Der Glaube an Mose nach Exodus (4. 14. 19)," *Wort — Gebot — Glaube. Festschrift W. Eichrodt. ATANT,* 59 (1970), 57-65;

Buber, Moses the Egyptian of Sigmund Freud and A. Slosman, Moses the lawgiver of Jewish tradition, Moses the theologian of the Koran, Moses the mystic of Gregory of Nyssa, and many more. Since the extrabiblical texts of Moses' era do not mention him, all these aspects of his personality derive from the biblical tradition and document its fullness. Biblical criticism permits us to assign these various theological aspects of the

---

J. Jeremias, *Theophanie. WMANT,* 10 (^{2}1977), 90-111; R. Knierim, "Exodus 18 und die Neuordnung der mosaischen Gerichtsbarkeit," *ZAW,* 73 (1961), 146-171; J. C. H. Laughlin, "A Study of the Motif of Holy Fire in the OT" (diss., Southern Baptist Theological Seminary, 1975), 9-18, 22-29; I. Lissner, "The Tomb of Moses Is Still Uncovered," *BA,* 26 (1963), 106-8; S. L. Loewenstamm, "The Presence of Mount Sinai," *Immanuel,* 5 (1975), 20-27; D. J. McCarthy, "Moses' Dealings with Pharaoh: Ex 7,8–10,27," *CBQ,* 27 (1965), 336-347; S. Mittmann, "Ri 1,16f. und das Siedlungsgebiet, der kenitischen Sippe Hobab," *ZDPV,* 93 (1977), 213-235; M. Mulhall, "Aaron and Moses" (diss., Catholic University of America, 1973); E. W. Nicholson, "The Covenant Ritual in Exodus xxiv 3-8," *VT,* 32 (1982), 74-86; G. von Rad, "Beobachtungen an der Moseerzählung, Exodus 1–14," *EvT,* 31 (1971), 579-588; A. N. Radjawane, "Israel zwischen Wüste und Land (Deut 1–3)" (diss., Mainz, 1972); J. M. Schmidt, "Aaron und Mose" (diss., Hamburg, 1963); F. Schnutenhaus, "Die Entstehung der Mosetradition" (diss., Heidelberg, 1958); S. M. Schwertner, "Erwägungen zu Moses Tod und Grab in Dtn 34,5.6," *ZAW,* 84 (1972), 25-46; H. Seebass, *Der Erzvater Israel und die Einführung der Jahweverehrung in Kanaan. BZAW,* 98 (1966); *idem, Mose und Aaron, Sinai und Gottesberg. Abhandlungen zur evangelischen Theologie,* 2 (1962); P. W. Skehan, "The Structure of the Song of Moses in Deuteronomy (Dt 32,1-43)," *CBQ,* 13 (1951), 153-163 = *Studies in Israelite Poetry and Wisdom. CBQMS,* 1 (1971), 67-77; E. Starobinski-Safran, "Le rôle de signes dans l'episode du buisson ardent (Ex 3,2)," *Jud,* 35 (1979), 63-67; J. H. Tigay, " 'Heavy of Mouth' and 'Heavy of Tongue': On Moses' Speech Difficulty," *BASOR,* 231 (1978), 57-67; *idem,* "Moses' Speech Difficulty," *Gratz College Jewish Studies,* 3 (1974), 29-42; H. Valentin, *Aaron. OBO,* 18 (1978); K.-H. Walkenhorst, *Der Sinai im liturgischen Verständnis der deuteronomistischen und priesterlichen Tradition. BBB,* 33 (1969); N. Walker, *The Name of "Moses"* (West Ewell, 1948); P. Weimar, *Die Berufung des Mose. OBO,* 32 (1980); *idem* and E. Zenger, *Exodus: Geschichten und Geschichte der Befreiung Israels. SBS,* 75 (^{2}1979); W. Weinberg, "Language Consciousness in the OT," *ZAW,* 92 (1980), 195f.; F. V. Winnett, *The Mosaic Tradition* (Toronto, 1949); N. Wyatt, "The Development of the Tradition in Exodus 3," *ZAW,* 91 (1979), 437-442; E. Zenger, *Israel am Sinai* (Altenberge, 1982); *idem, Die Sinaitheophanie. FzB,* 3 (1971).

5. *Various Aspects of Moses.* C. Barth, "Mose, Knecht Gottes," *Parrhesia. Festschrift K. Barth* (Zurich, 1966), 68-81; D. M. Beegle, *Moses, the Servant of Yahweh* (Grand Rapids, 1972); W. Feilchenfeldt, "Die Entpersönlichung Moses in der Bibel und ihre Bedeutung," *ZAW,* 64 (1952), 156-178; W. Holladay, "Jeremiah and Moses: Further Observations," *JBL,* 85 (1966), 17-27; J. Jensen, "What Happened to Moses?" *CBQ,* 32 (1970), 404-417; T. W. Mann, "Theological Reflections on the Denial of Moses," *JBL,* 98 (1979), 481-494; G. S. Ogden, "Moses and Cyrus," *VT,* 28 (1978), 195-203; G. von Rad, *Moses* (London, 1960); J. Schildenberger, "Moses als Idealgestalt eines Armen Jahwes," *À la rencontre de Dieu. Mémorial A. Gelin* (Le Puy, 1961), 71-84; E. Sellin, "Hosea und das Martyrium des Mose," *ZAW,* 46 (1928), 26-33; A. Slosman, *Moïse l'égyptien* (Paris, 1981).

a. *Royal Figure.* J. R. Porter, *Moses and Monarchy* (Oxford, 1963); D. J. Silver, " 'Moses Our Teacher Was a King,' " *JLA,* 1 (1978), 123-132.

b. *Prophet.* K. Gouders, "Die prophetische Berufungsberichte Moses, Isaias, Jeremias und Ezechiels" (diss., Bonn, 1971), 15-61, 190-99; A. Penna, "Mosè profeta e più che profeta," *BiOr,* 12 (1970), 145-152; L. Perlitt, "Mose als Prophet," *EvT,* 31 (1971), 588-608; W. Richter, *Die sogenannten vorprophetischen Berufungsberichte. FRLANT,* 101 (1970); D. J. Silver, " 'By a Prophet the Lord Brought up Israel,' " *Essays on the Occasion of the 70th Anniversary of Dropsie*

figure of Moses to various redactions through a series of historical periods. It is this theology of Moses that is the subject of this article rather than the life of the historical Moses. We shall first discuss (1) the religious problems of the Mosaic (premonarchic) era, then sketch (2) the figure of Moses presented by pre-prophetic texts, followed by (3) Moses in the prophets, (4) Moses in Deuteronomy and the Deuteronomistic litera-

---

University (Philadelphia, 1979), 423-440; D. L. Tiede, "The Charismatic Figure as Miracle-Worker" (diss., Harvard, 1971); P. Volz, *Prophetengestalten des ATs* (Stuttgart, 1938), 42-76.

c. *Mediator.* C. Hauret, "Moïse était-il prêtre?" *Bibl,* 40 (1959), 509-521; A. M. Vater, "The Communication of Messages and Oracles as a Narration Medium in the OT" (diss., Yale, 1976), 78-80, 189-193.

d. *Lawgiver.* T. C. Butler, "An Anti-Moses Tradition," *JSOT,* 12 (1979), 9-15; *idem,* "Anti-Moses Tradition," *Lexington Theological Quarterly,* 14 (1979), 33-39; H. Cazelles, *Études sur le code de l'Alliance* (Paris, 1946); *idem,* "Die Thora des Moses und der Erlöser Christus," *Concilium,* 1 (1965), 819-830; M. Chigier, "Codification of Jewish Law," *JLA,* 2 (1979), 3-33; E. Nielsen, "Moses and the Law," *VT,* 32 (1982), 87-98; H. H. Rowley, "Moses and the Decalogue," *BJRL,* 34 (1951/52), 81-118 = *Men of God* (London, 1963), 1-36; H. Schmidt, "Mose und der Dekalog," Εὐχαριστήριον. *Festschrift H. Gunkel,* 2 vols., *FRLANT,* N.S. 19 (1923), I, 78-119; L. Szondi, *Moses Antwort auf Kain* (Bern, 1973); D. Timpe, "Moses als Gesetzgeber," *Saeculum,* 31 (1980), 66-77; E. Zingg, "Ehe und Familie nach den Gesetzen Moses," *Jud,* 20 (1964), 121-28; *idem,* "Das Strafrecht nach den Gesetzen Moses," *Jud,* 17 (1961), 106-119; additional bibliog. in works on Israel's law by such scholars as D. Daube, Z. Falk, S. Paul, and R. Yaron.

e. *Teacher.* N. Lohfink, "Glauben lernen in Israel," *Katechetische Blätter,* 108 (1983), 84-99, esp. 96; E. Schawe, "Gott als Lehrer im AT" (diss., Fribourg, 1979).

6. *Intertestamental Literature.* J. Gager, *Moses in Greco-Roman Paganism. SBLMS,* 16 (1972); R. Goulet, "Porphyre et la datation de Moïse," *RHR,* 192 (1977), 136-164; S. Isser, "Dositheus, Jesus, and a Moses Aretalogy," *Christianity, Judaism, and Other Greco-Roman Cults,* IV. *Festschrift M. Smith. SJLA,* 12 (1975), 167-189; W. A. Meeks, "Moses as God and King," *Religions in Antiquity. Festschrift E. R. Goodenough. SNumen,* 14 (1968), 354-371; G. W. Nickelsburg, *Studies on the Testament of Moses. SBLSCS,* 4 (1973); D. J. Silver, "Moses and the Hungry Birds," *JQR,* N.S. 64 (1973/74), 123-153.

7. *Jewish Tradition.* A. Amar, *Moïse ou le peuple séparé* (Paris, 1977); M. Buber, *Moses* (1946, repr. New York, 1958) = *Werke,* II (1964), 9-218; K. Haacker and P. Schäfer, "Nachbiblische Traditionen vom Tod des Mose," *Josephus-Studien. Festschrift O. Michel* (1974), 147-173; M. Ish-Shalom, "The Cave of Machpela and the Sepulchre of Moses: The Development of an Aggadic Tradition," *Tarbiz,* 41 (1971/72), 203-210; L. Landman, "Some Aspects of Traditions Received from Moses at Sinai," *JQR,* N.S. 65 (1974/75), 111-128; H. W. Obbink, "On the Legends of Moses in the Haggadah," *Studia Biblica et Semitica. Festschrift T. C. Vriezen* (Wageningen, 1966), 252-264; N. Pavoncello, "Il 7 de Adar, nascita e morte del propheta Mosè," *RivBibl,* 19 (1971), 233-240; K. Schubert and U. Schubert, "Die Errettung des Mose aus den Wassern des Nil in der Kunst des spätantiken Judentums und das Weiterwirken dieses Motivs in der frühchristlichen und jüdisch-mittelalterlichen Kunst," *Studien zum Pentateuch. Festschrift W. Kornfeld* (Vienna, 1977), 59-68; A. Shinan, "Moses and the Ethiopian Woman," *ScrHier,* 27 (1978), 66-78; C. Sirat, "Un midraš juif en habit musulman: La vision de Moïse sur le mont Sinai," *RHR,* 168 (1965), 15-28; A. Sur Min, "Mosesmotive in den Fresken der Katakombe der Via Latina im Lichte der rabbinischen Tradition," *Kairos,* N.S. 17 (1975), 57-80.

8. *Other Traditions.* T. Rajak, "Moses in Ethiopia," *JSS,* 29 (1978), 111-122; E. Ullendorff, "The 'Death of Moses' in the Literature of the Falashas," *BSOAS,* 24 (1961), 419-443; M. Wurmbrand, "Remarks on the Text of the Falashas," *BSOAS,* 25 (1962), 431-37.

9. *Christian Tradition.* M. R. DiAngelo, *Moses in the Letter to the Hebrews. SBLDS,* 42

ture, (5) Moses the mediator in the postexilic cult, (6) Moses in the postexilic period, and (7) Moses in the Dead Sea Scrolls and apocalyptic literature.

I. The Era of Moses. The Mosaic era is roughly the thirteenth century, before the Egyptian armies in Canaan came upon Israel (the Merneptah stela, ca. 1220). Until the time of Rameses II, the Egyptians know only the *ʿapiru* (cuneiform *ḫabiru,* Ugar. *ʿprm*), the Hebrews of the Bible, a group to which Moses belonged (Ex. 2:6).[1] In the polytheism of their environment, the Israelite tribes confronted a variety of religious options:

1. Egyptian religion was both erudite and popular, with a systematic theology (Heliopolis, Hermopolis, Memphis). Its focus was the cult of the pharaoh, at whose court the unity of the divine was recognized behind the multiplicity of divine manifestations. Under Amenhotep IV, the "god of the sages," often unnamed and represented by the sun-disk, was recognized as the "only god." This nature monotheism, however, did not last long.

2. The Semitic religions were cosmological rather than political. El, the supreme god, was a beneficent deity dwelling at the distant source of all rivers. The most active deity was the storm-god Baʿal (equivalent to Egyptian Seth), who brought fertility through rain. His virility, like that of El, was represented by the bull. One of the Amarna letters says that he causes the earth to tremble and makes his voice thunder.[2]

3. Some deities affected the human body. They could be beneficent; the verb → רפא *rp'* means "heal" or even "endow with new vitality." But there were also deities that brought sickness; magic was often used to combat them.

4. Human beings had tutelary deities, "personal gods," who accompanied their devotees everywhere. These gods could become enraged when people under their protection refused to believe their promises of offspring, prosperity, or possession of the land. The God of Abraham was such a personal god. Since the protection of this god extended to the offspring of the devotee, he became the "God of the father" (Gen. 28:13; 31:53; Ex. 3:6) and finally the God of the dynasty and the nation.

All these features appear in the biblical Moses tradition. His figure occupies a religious intersection between Semites and Egyptians, city-states and nomadic tribes. Moses was a leader, endowed with the religious prerogatives of the leaders of his era; like Noah and Abraham, he could build simple altars. Shortly before, the tribal leaders in Moab had similar functions. But this feature does not seem to be important in most of the biblical traditions. Moses leaves to Jethro (Ex. 18:12), to young people (24:5), or above all to Aaron the responsibility of offering sacrifice. We must note, however, that this borderland between Egypt and Canaan plays a different role in the biblical traditions.

(1979); P. von der Osten-Sacken, "Geist im Buchstaben," *EvT,* 41 (1981), 230-35; C. Perrot, "Les récits d'enfance dans la Haggada," *RSR,* 55 (1967), 481-518; T. Saito, *Die Mosevorstellungen im NT. EH,* 23/100 (1977).

1. See W. H. Schmidt, *EdF,* 191, 109, 24-31.
2. EA, 147, 15.

The name *mōšeh* has no satisfactory Hebrew derivation, despite the popular etymology that connects it with *mšh,* "draw out" (v. 10), for which a pass. ptcp. *māšûy* would have been required.[3] The name most likely derives from Egyp. *mśy,* "give birth to," with a theophoric element (cf. Thut-moses): "The deity N has given birth to."[4] "A wide range of conclusions has been drawn from the fact that Moses bears an Egyptian name. . . . The name Moses has nothing definite to say about its bearer, but the tradition that a man with an Egyptian name dwelt in the land of the Nile is very probably correct."[5] With Noth, we should probably locate this man in the setting of the deliverance from Egypt.

If we are to wrest the theological personality of Moses from the biblical traditions, we must use traditio-historical methods to analyze the text. A pre-prophetic Yahwistic (Judahite) story focuses on family (i.e., dynastic) questions. A prophetic redaction (Gen. 20:6; Nu. 11f.) is less well preserved; it corresponds to the Elohistic material, often doublets of the Yahwistic texts. Finally, there is a JE redaction (frequently with Deuteronomistic features); this redaction is not itself a literary work but an attempt to combine two divergent texts. Each by itself enjoyed such accepted authority that they could not be integrated into a single literary unit.

II. The Pre-Prophetic Moses. There is no unanimity concerning the boundary between J and E in the Exodus texts about Moses. The traditions are quite complex, and scholars have felt compelled to postulate a pre-Yahwistic source (J^1, N, S, etc.). A distinction between prophetic and pre-prophetic traditions can yield fairly clear results (e.g., in Nu. 11f.; more subtly in Ex. 32f.):[6] Yahweh accompanies Israel (J, Sinai); Yahweh's angel, not Yahweh, accompanies Israel (E); finally, Yahweh can mitigate the punishment (JE). In any case, it would be a methodological error to isolate the major traditions (exodus, Sinai, desert, occupation of Canaan) as though they had developed independently. Analysis shows that the Sinai texts in Ex. 19–24 are repeated at Horeb (Ex. 33); the manna traditions in Ex. 16 have parallels in Nu. 11. Moses' intercession (Ex. 33) has its parallels in Nu. 14. The tradition did not develop historically through literary units but rather in horizontal strata, as "documents."

For example, Ex. 19–24 contains some "Sinaitic" elements, while other verses mention only the "mountain of God." The latter should be analyzed separately.[7] Neither would it be appropriate to treat the Horeb traditions in 3:1; 17:6; 33:6 as misplaced additions. The only method that allows us to determine how the theological syntheses J (J^1) and E, combined in JE, were put together is to begin with the concrete data: geographical (Goshen, A. H. J. Gunneweg's Midian, Amalek, Baal-zaphon . . .), tribal (Levites, Reuben . . .), domestic (the different names of Moses' father-in-law: Reuel, Jethro, Hobab, or unnamed; the varying number of Moses' sons . . .), sociological (Pharaoh or the king of Egypt, the scribes of Pharaoh or scribes of the Israelites, sacrifice

3. On the literary structure of Ex. 2, see W. H. Schmidt, *Exodus 1–6. BK,* II/1 (1988), in loc.
4. *Ibid.,* 73f., with bibliog.
5. W. H. Schmidt, *EdF,* 191, 34ff.
6. Cf. Cazelles, *Festschrift Kornfeld;* Weimar; Childs.
7. Fritz.

or *ḥag,* elders, camp . . .), and historical (the exodus as flight or expulsion). This material is clearly incoherent; but it seems that one can recover a coherent picture if one keeps in mind the divergences in the life and history of the tribes that preserved these traditions. As a function of the theological and political problems of the period, the pre-prophetic Yahwist attempted to sketch a history of a united Israel (cf. the similar program of the Sumerian King List).

Several observations help define the theological figure of Moses according to J. (1) The accounts in the books of Samuel of how the Judahite monarchy was established never mention Moses. (2) The Mosaic traditions are rooted much more firmly in the north than in the south: Hos. 12:14 (Eng. v. 13];[8] the Ephraimite Joshua as Moses' servant (Ex. 24:13; 33:11; Nu. 11:28); the Danite priesthood, which derives from Moses (Jgs. 18:30); Moses as leader of Israel alongside Aaron and Miriam (Mic. 6:4); Moses interceding like Samuel (Jer. 15:1); no mention in Isaiah or Amos. (3) Strong links bound the Jerusalem court to Egypt: the marriage of Solomon[9] and the training of its scribes. In fact, the Israelite tradition does not allow Moses to enter Judah; the redaction of Jgs. 1 has Judah conquer the Negeb in league with the Kenites (v. 16) and capture Hormah with the aid of Simeon (v. 17). J knows Moses through the traditions of Northern Israel (Ephraim, Dan, and Reuben) and through southern traditions (the Kenites of the Negeb as neighbors of the Amalekites; the Calebites of Kadesh, who advanced as far as Hebron; the Levites, related to Aaron). Furthermore, it is likely that the Egyptian scribes at the court of Solomon added the tradition of the exodus as expulsion[10] to the version that depicted it as flight. Here the exodus that avoided the land of the Philistines (Ex. 13:17) was assimilated to the exodus describing the driving out of the Hyksos. This assimilation is supported especially by the mention of Baal-zaphon, i.e., Mt. Casios on the Mediterranean coast: the camp opposite Baal-zaphon presupposes a route along the Philistine road.

Finally, the special character of Ex. 34, with its ritual and liturgical overtones, in comparison to 20:24–23:19 should lead one to assign the more ritual and liturgical elements (3:5; cf. v. 12b) to the pre-prophetic Moses. But cultic elements appear to be found in other traditions as well.

The essential function of J's Moses is to break the forced bond with Pharaoh and establish the covenant at Sinai with Yahweh, the God of the fathers. The piel impv. *šallaḥ* (e.g., Ex. 5:1), which J uses as a refrain following the seven plagues of Egypt, does not mean "let go" but "send away." The verb is a weakening of *grš,* the term used for driving out (the Hyksos). The people are to be sent back in order to be joined with *YHWH qannā'* (34:14), whom they must "serve" by offering sacrifice on the mountain of Yahweh (Nu. 10:33), identified with Sinai.

The people prepare themselves ritually for the sacrifice (Ex. 19:10-13), but must

---

8. E. Zenger, " 'Durch Menschen zog ich sie . . .' (Hos 11,4)," *Künder des Wortes. Festschrift J. Schreiner* (Würzburg, 1982), 183-201.

9. M. Görg, "Die 'Sünde' Salomos," *BN,* 16 (1981), 42-59, recalling the role of Pharaoh's daughter in Ex. 2:10; 1 K. 3:1 (cf. 11:1).

10. De Vaux.

keep their distance from the holy site (19:12; 34:2f.), which only Moses may approach. It is with him that Yahweh makes the covenant (cf. 34:10 [stated more precisely in the LXX], 27 [except for the last two words, which are syntactically secondary]).

The pre-prophetic Moses of J is thus the rival of the king of Egypt, who wanted to "deal shrewdly" *(niṯhakkᵉmâ)* with the people to destroy them (Ex. 1:9f.). Not himself a king, Moses has features that are royal[11] and above all patriarchal. He is adopted by Pharaoh's daughter (2:10) and marries under circumstances that recall Jacob. His father-in-law is Hobab, a Kenite (Jgs. 1:16; 4:11; Nu. 10:29) chased from his "nest" by Edom (Nu. 24:21) and living as a nomad in the southern desert of Judah. There, "beyond the wilderness," the theophany of Yahweh's angel in the burning bush takes place (Ex. 3:2). This is a holy place, where the "God of his father" commissions Moses to "bring the people up" into the land of the Canaanites and Jebusites, out of the sphere of influence of their oppressors. Yahweh has "come down" (3:7-9) and will be "with" Moses (3:12). The people are dwelling in the land of Goshen, where J says they had been settled by Pharaoh in the time of Joseph (Gen. 45:10; Ex. 8:18[22]; 9:26). This Goshen is located in the southern region of Judah, in the territory of Simeon (Josh. 10:41; 11:16; 15:51[12]), not far from Edom. It is far from Egypt and the Egyptians, but under Egypt's political control.[13] Meyer already noted that the people driven from Egypt were led there by a route along the Mediterranean Sea.[14] Fear of the Hebrews and their God made the Egyptians let them go to Sinai to offer sacrifice (Ex. 8:24[28]). It is Moses who holds in "his" hand the staff that is the symbol of power.[15] Thanks to this staff in Moses' hand, the military Joshua of J (17:9; cf. 32:17) — in contrast to the Joshua of E, who guards the sacred tent (33:11; cf. Nu. 11:28) — gains victory over the Amalekites, who dwell in the Negeb of Judah (1 S. 15:6, as neighbors of the Kenites; 30:1).

Together with the Levite Aaron (who died at the border of Edom), Moses takes part in battles with the armies of the Egyptian king (Ex. 15:3f.). With Aaron's "sister" Miriam, he sings of the victory over the sea (Ex. 15); he heals her at Kadesh (Nu. 12:11-16), just as he makes the waters of Marah drinkable (Ex. 15:25) and heals the Israelites who had been bitten by serpents (Nu. 21:8f.). From Kadesh, south of Beersheba, he sends Caleb to explore the land as far as Hebron, where the Calebites will settle and where David will be made king. There is no mention of Moses in connection with the capture of Hormah (Nu. 21:1-3), a Simeonite city (Jgs. 1:17; but cf. Josh. 19:2-8); this capture was a first stage. Neither does Moses play any role in the prophecies of Balaam (Nu. 24), which refer to all Judah's southern and eastern neighbors. Thus J brings together some material concerning these southern neighbors (Kenites,

---

11. Porter.

12. Cazelles, *Festschrift Kornfeld.*

13. Other scholars propose a different location: *GTTOT,* §285ff.; M. Noth, *Das Buch Josua. HAT,* VII (^{3}1971), 97.

14. E. Meyer, "Die Mosessagen und die Leviten," SPAW, Phil.-hist. Kl., 31 (1905), 640-652 = *KlSchr,* I (1910), 315-332.

15. → מטה *maṭṭeh* (VIII, 241-49).

Calebites, Goshen, the Sinai of Jgs. 5:5 [cf. v. 4]; Dt. 33:2 [cf. v. 16]) as well as distant memories of wars with the Egyptian king.

Thus the pre-prophetic Moses (J) is attested as a controversial leader in the traditions of the northern tribes such as Joseph. In monarchic Israel his role as covenant mediator constitutes a counterpoise to the selection of a more or less pharaonic dynasty. To him is traced the aniconic cult with its cycle of agrarian festivals (Ex. 34:17): the Feast of Unleavened Bread, which coincided with Passover (34:25), the sacrifice after a journey of three days (5:3; 10:24-27).

III. Moses in the Prophets. The prophetic Moses is the prophet who "brought Israel up from Egypt" (Hos. 12:14[13]) and through whom Israel was "guarded *(nišmar)* (in the covenant)."[16] According to Jer. 15:1, Moses, like Samuel, has access to God's presence and can intercede for the people. Since the north is more complex than the south, the Elohistic Pentateuch texts concerning Moses are also more complex. Here we find Midianite traditions from Transjordan transmitted through Reuben and Gad; Ephraimite traditions linked with the Ephraimite Joshua, a follower of Moses; Levite traditions preserved at the sanctuaries of Dan (Jgs. 18:30) and Bethel (Aaronide: 1 K. 12:28; cf. Ex. 32:4). The society presupposed by the prophetic Moses is not based on a religious monarchy; it is a society with elders (sometimes an archaizing seventy) or an Israel encamped in tents. Judicial functions are performed by Moses' subordinates, who also perform military functions (Ex. 18:25). In Midianite tradition (east of the Gulf of Akaba), Jethro is Moses' father-in-law; the Aaronide tradition calls him Reuel, an Edomite name (Gen. 36:4,10,13,17).

The prophetic Moses, son of a Levite (Ex. 2:1), is a judge who is forced to flee when he seeks to mediate a quarrel (v. 14). He flees to Midian, where he marries the Cushite Zipporah; Cush is a Midianite tribe (execration texts cited by Georges Posener; Hab. 3:7). In the vicinity of Midian, at Horeb, God reveals his name to Moses in a burning thornbush: "I am" (*'ehyeh;* Ex. 3:14, explaining the name Yahweh) and sends him to the elders (vv. 14,16) in the name of the God of the fathers.[17] He meets Aaron at the "mountain of God" (4:27). With the aid of "signs" (*'ōṯōṯ:* vv. 28,30; cf. vv. 8,17; J speaks of "wonders" [*niplā'ôṯ*]), they persuade the people and demand permission from Pharaoh not so much to go three days' journey into the desert to offer sacrifice to Yahweh as to celebrate a festival *(ḥag).* After the plagues (v. 9: transformation of water into blood; treated differently in the account of J and P in 7:14-25), Moses instructs the elders in the Passover rite with the application of blood to the lintels and doorposts (12:21-23).

Now begins the fugitive exodus through the southern isthmus, avoiding the route via Philistia (Ex. 13:17). At Moses' intercession, the angel of God protects the escape,

16. But contra H. W. Wolff (*Hosea. Herm* [Eng. trans. 1974], 216), see F. I. Andersen and D. N. Freedman (*Hosea. AB,* XXIV [1980], 621f.), who suggest another prophet, Elijah or Samuel.

17. On the relationship between the God of the fathers and Yahwism, see W. H. Schmidt, *EdF,* 191, 45-48; *idem, BK,* II, 147-153.

appearing in the pillar of cloud and coming between the Egyptians and Israel. Immediately afterward, Moses gives the people the law (*ḥōq* and *mišpāṭ:* 15:25). The people are put to the test (17:7b): "Is Yahweh among us or not?"[18] It is less the authority of Moses that is at stake at Horeb (17:6a) than faith in the God of the exodus (v. 7b). Aaron (a Levite) and Hur (a Midianite) (Nu. 31:8) hold up Moses' weary "hands" (Ex. 17:12; not "hand") in the battle against Amalek. At the "mountain of God" (18:5), Moses meets Jethro, who has come from Midian; there Aaron also comes to meet him (with the elders of the Israel, v. 12b). At Jethro's suggestion Moses appoints "able men" *('anšê-ḥayil)* as judges (18:25), while reserving to himself the legislative function (v. 20).

In the cloud on the mountain, God once more puts the people to the test (Ex. 20:18-21) and reveals his "words" to Moses alone (20:1-17, Deuteronomistic and P additions). Aaron and Hur remain behind at the foot of the mountain (24:12-14) to judge the people. In Moses' absence, the people force Aaron to permit a festival in honor of the golden calf (32:1-5).[19] Then, in the Midianite tradition of Horeb, the people repent (33:6). Only the angel[20] of God will go with the people during the conquest of Canaan (23:20f.; 33:2). At the intercession of Moses, God has vouchsafed forgiveness; but God will no longer dwell personally in the midst of the people. The tent where God meets with Moses in the cloud stands outside the camp, guarded by Joshua, the servant of Moses (33:7-11).

The prophetic Moses is already the Moses of the four-stage historical sequence illustrated by the judges: apostasy, calling on God, repentance, and deliverance. The spirit no longer comes upon the king, understood as a charismatic figure; instead, the spirit rests "on Moses." God takes some of the spirit of Moses and puts it on the seventy elders (Nu. 11:16f.) to make them prophets (vv. 24f.). But they do not remain prophets. The spirit also makes prophets out of some who had not come to the tent (Eldad and Medad, vv. 26-30), and Moses does not object. Aaron and Miriam also count as prophets (12:2), but they transgress by speaking against Moses; for God speaks to Moses (unlike the other prophets) "mouth to mouth," and Moses "sees God's form (*t^emûnâ*)" (12:8). He sees this form "from behind" (Ex. 33:18-23); for according to E "no one can see God and live" (v. 20), while according to J Yahweh and the people see each other "face to face" (Nu. 14:14).

Hormah is no longer the site of a victory: Nu. 14:40-45 recounts a defeat in battle against the Amalekites and Canaanites. Moses does not play a military role — in the conflict with Reuben (Dathan and Abiram, Nu. 16), in the conquest of Amorite Transjordan (Nu. 21), or in relations with Moab (Balaam, Nu. 22 and part of 23). In all likelihood, Moses made the covenant of Ex. 24:3-6,8 in Moab between Baal-peor and Gilgal. This covenant still involves a blood ritual like the Passover of Ex. 12:22, but with an altar at the foot of the mountain and with twelve pillars, which appear to

---

18. On the question as a primary theme of R^P, see Zenger, *Israel am Sinai,* 50ff., 56ff., 67.

19. J. Davenport, "A Study of the Golden Calf Tradition in Ex 32" (diss., Princeton, 1973); J. Hahn, *Das goldene Kalb. EH,* 23/154 (1981).

20. → מלאך *mal'āḵ* (VIII, 308-325).

correspond to the twelve stones of Josh. 4:1-9. Moses wrote down the ten "words" (Ex. 24:3b; cf. 34:27) as the basis of the covenant. This covenant ritual is preceded by the "Covenant Code," which begins with the altar law (20:24) and includes "ordinances" (*mišpāṭîm:* 21:1; cf. 24:3) in addition to the "words" *(d^e^ḇārîm).* The prophetic Moses of the Elohistic texts is thus not just a mediator of the covenant, as in J, but also a judge, the ideal prophet, a scribe, and a lawgiver. He no longer has any royal or patriarchal features. Like Abraham (Gen. 12:7f.; cf. 22:8ff.), Moses builds an altar; but the sacrifices are offered by twelve young men representing the twelve tribes (Ex. 24:5).

IV. Moses in Deuteronomy and the Deuteronomistic Literature. The prophetic Moses owes his complexity to the traditions of the northern tribes, which combine a Midianite tradition (Horeb; Zipporah; Gershom [one son], whom Moses brings with him on his return from Midian [Ex. 2:22; 4:24-26; cf. Jgs. 18:30]) and an Aaronide tradition (mountain of God; Cushite wife; Gershom and Eliezer [two sons; cf. 1 Ch. 23:15], whom Jethro brings to Moses at the mountain of God). There is also an independent Ephraimite tradition that preserved the memory of a fugitive exodus by an unspecified southern route. This tradition culminates in the Blessing of Moses (Dt. 33): Reuben is the firstborn, but is on the point of vanishing from history; Joseph is the "prince *(nāzîr)* among his brothers" (v. 16); and the Levites see that God's will is carried out. Judah is a marginal tribe who must return to his brothers (v. 7).

By contrast, the Deuteronomistic Moses is a homogeneous figure, even though we must note the presence of several Deuteronomistic redactions. He resembles the prophetic Moses insofar as he is the prophet par excellence (Dt. 18:15), upon whom the other prophets are to pattern themselves. He is also the sole mediator of the covenant, made at Horeb and in Moab (28:69[29:1]). Only exceptionally does he function as judge (1:17), but he organizes the judicial system; judges have precedence over kings in the Deuteronomistic code. These judges are no longer "able men" (as in Ex. 18:25) and military figures but "wise and reputable" individuals (Dt. 1:15; cf. 16:19). Scribes *(šōṭ^e^rîm)* are also mentioned; they record decisions and maintain census lists. Except for the song mentioned in Dt. 31:22, these scribes rather than Moses do the writing; for it is Yahweh, their God, who himself wrote the Ten Commandments (5:22; 10:4).

Above all, the Deuteronomistic Moses is understood as a speaker, who gives instruction like the wisdom teachers of the scribal schools. Even Israel's neighbors acknowledge the law he expounds to be the highest form of wisdom; it was given to Israel in the form of statutes and ordinances more "just" than any others (Dt. 4:6-8). The Deuteronomistic Moses, speaker and wisdom teacher, teaches above all the worship of a single God.[21] The people must love Yahweh alone, as vassals love their lord; they must listen to Yahweh alone; they must not forget Yahweh or forsake Yahweh to run after other gods. This Deuteronomistic Moses formulates the basic monotheistic principle: "Yahweh is the only God, there is no other" (4:35).

---

21. N. Lohfink, "Gott im Buch Deuteronomium," in J. Coppens, et al., *La notion biblique de Dieu. BETL,* 41 (1976), 101-126, esp. 104.

This wisdom teacher Moses becomes a historian, recalling how on the day of the *qāhāl* the God of Horeb chose a people. Thus "all Israel" became a "church" (→ קהל *qāhāl,* Gk. *ekklēsía*) to be Yahweh's "treasured possession" (→ סגלה *s^egullâ*), a "people holy to Yahweh" (Dt. 7:6). Just as Yahweh chose only one from among all the peoples, so too Yahweh chose only one cultic site. The Deuteronomistic Moses totally disregards the patriarchs, retaining only the promises and the oath God swore to them. The sanctuaries reverenced for their association with them, in both north and south, are condemned as hotbeds of immorality. Moses eliminates them, just as he would have preferred to eliminate the vanquished nations: the Deuteronomistic Moses is highly exclusive. This sage sees his people forced to decide between life and death (30:15); he would like to eliminate all the sources of death that spring from the nations and their gods.

Above all, besides being a prophet and sage, the Deuteronomistic Moses is a lawgiver. All the texts authoritative for Israel — statutes, ordinances, precepts, dicta, etc. — constitute the one "law" (*tôrâ;* Dt. 1:5; 4:44; 31:12), which is entrusted to the Levitical priests (18:1-5). Moses was unsuccessful in controlling the people so as to prevent their defeat at Hormah (1:44), but he organized the land and established the places of asylum (4:41). He communicated the Torah orally; it is the Torah of Moses. He himself did nothing wrong, but suffered God's wrath on account of the Israelites (1:37; 3:26; 4:21); according to 9:18-20, God was angry only with Aaron.

Moses is mentioned 36 times in Deuteronomy and 53 times in Joshua; in the rest of the Deuteronomistic corpus, however, he plays a very minor role (1 S. 12:6,8): 2 K. 18:4 recalls that he made the bronze serpent (→ נחשתן *n^eḥuštān;* cf. Nu. 21:9) that Hezekiah broke in pieces. He is described as "God's servant" in 15 Deuteronomistic texts, e.g., Josh. 1:7 ("all the torah that my servant Moses commanded you"), 15; 8:31,33 (*sēp̱er tôraṯ mōšeh,* 2 K. 14:6; cf. Dt. 28:61; 29:20[21]); 2 K. 18:12. He is also called "man of God" (*'îš 'elōhîm,* Josh. 14:6), like Samuel in 1 S. 9:6 and like many other prophets in the Deuteronomistic history (Shemaiah, 1 K. 12:22; Elijah, 1 K. 17:18; Elisha, 2 K. 4:7).

V. Moses as Mediator in the Postexilic Cult. A priestly redaction also appears in the book of Joshua. Expressions in texts like Josh. 14:2; 21:8 that speak of Moses' power ("hand") may with some caution be ascribed to the language of P (cf. Nu. 36:13), which mentions Moses most frequently.

According to P, Abraham, not Moses, is the mediator of the covenant.[22] But at Sinai Moses renews the covenant of Abraham (Ex. 16:2ff.) and maintains it (Lev. 26:9,15,42,45) against the danger of being broken, as Deuteronomy foresaw (Dt. 31:16,20).[23] Ezekiel is the first to speak of the covenant of peace, the perpetual covenant that cannot be broken (Ezk. 16:60; cf. 34:25; 37:26; Jer. 32:40). This

22. W. Zimmerli, "Sinaibund und Abrahambund," *TZ,* 16 (1960), 268-280.

23. H. Cazelles, "Alliance du Sinaï, alliance de l'Horeb et renouvellement de l'alliance," *Beiträge zur alttestamentlichen Theologie. Festschrift W. Zimmerli* (Göttingen, 1977), 69-79.

language is based on P's idea of the covenant as found in the covenants with Noah (Gen. 9:16) and with Abraham (Gen. 17:7; Ex. 6:4; 31:16). In words spoken by Moses to Aaron, the support of the priesthood through sacred offerings is called a "covenant of salt[24] forever" (Nu. 18:19; cf. Lev. 2:13). After the incident of the Baʿal of Peor, Yahweh gives his eternal covenant of peace to Phinehas, the grandson of Aaron; it is to be a "covenant of perpetual priesthood (*kᵉhunnaṯ*)" (Nu. 25:12f.). Mal. 2:8 mentions this "covenant of Levi": through the revealed liturgy, God and God's people can live together by virtue of the forgiveness of sins. The renewal at Sinai of the covenant with Abraham (Ex. 6:4-8; 19:5) makes the people "a priestly kingdom and a holy nation" (19:6). Aaron and his sons officiate in this liturgy of atonement, in which the glory of God is manifested. Aaron is also associated closely with Moses. In the P texts concerning the plagues of Egypt, it is he rather than Moses who bears the staff of divine power. It is this staff that puts forth buds and blossoms, and bears fruit (Nu. 17:23ff.[8ff.]). Aaron is even described as Moses' elder brother (Ex. 6:20; 7:7).

It is Moses, however, who is the author of this perpetual Levitical covenant. Aaron is only the prophet of Moses, to repeat to Pharaoh whatever Moses says to him (Ex. 7:2). Yahweh makes Moses like "God" before Pharaoh (7:1). He does in fact have access to the sphere of the divine; he enters into the cloud on the mountain where Yahweh is present in his *kāḇôḏ,* which the Israelites can only view from afar. There he receives from God the plan for the sanctuary where the most holy God resides, whom only the holy priests can approach.[25] Moses does not write; he speaks, he conveys directives from God, he is a lawgiver and inaugurates rites through which the people are called to holiness. Above all, Moses speaks to Aaron to give him the commandments (*miṣwôṯ,* Lev. 27:34; Nu. 36:13) and ordinances that, taken together, constitute the legislation of Sinai. It is the function of the Aaronic priesthood to interpret and apply them, but not to change them.

As the sole lawgiver, Moses also has authority to consecrate. After the sanctuary is built, Moses first consecrates this dwelling place of God and its furnishings, then Aaron and his vestments; for Aaron is to have charge of liturgical worship. The Deuteronomistic Moses was the supreme prophet; the Priestly Moses is a high priest. Moses continues to function as leader after the consecration of Aaron and outside the limits of the Levitical covenant. When Aaron dies, he invests Eleazar with the priestly vestments. Shortly before his death, Moses separates the functions of the priest from those of the political leader (cf. the theology of Ezekiel), who "makes the Israelites go out and come in." As political leader he appoints Joshua, who, like Moses, is full of the Spirit (E; Nu. 27:18; Dt. 34:9). In the presence of Eleazar, whom he had already appointed priest, Moses lays his hands on Joshua.

Despite his greatness, the Moses of P also (like Aaron) has his faults. Nu. 20:12 makes no palliative attempt to ascribe God's anger to the sins of the people. Moses'

---

24. → מלח *melaḥ* (VIII, 331-33).
25. M. Haran, *Temples and Temple-Service in Ancient Israel* (Oxford, 1978), e.g., 149ff.

lack of trust had prevented God from manifesting his glory. The immediate context does not specify Moses' failing; it might have been in action (cf. Dt. 1:37: halting a campaign against Canaan) or in words, as Ps. 106:32f. might suggest. Since P often develops the traditions of J, it may preserve here a reminiscence of J without insisting on all the details.

Cazelles

When compared with Ex. 17:1-7, Nu. 20:1-13 provides an insight into the changing picture of Moses in the corpus of Priestly traditions: J still viewed Moses essentially as the mediator of Yahweh's words; JE depicted Moses as a prophetic miracle worker. P^G now sees in Moses and Aaron representatives of the spiritual office, which is subjected to massive criticism in Nu. 20 (v. 12). "This criticism of the office, which as a text inspired by P represents impressively bitter self-criticism, was probably . . . too one-sided for P^S and the redactor of the Pentateuch and appeared prejudicial to the reputation of Moses."[26] By making the people share in the transgression (20:4), P^S exonerates Moses. In the postexilic period, R^P undertook a thorough revision of the figure of Moses, characteristically emphasizing the divinizing of Moses (20:5aβ,6aα; esp. Ex. 4:16; 34:29-35). For R^P, Moses essentially ceases to be an individual and becomes a stylized medium of divine revelation.[27]

Fabry

VI. Moses in Postexilic Literature. The postexilic Moses retains these features. The Psalms mention him only 8 times. The superscription of Ps. 90 describes him as "the man of God." Ps. 77:21(20) looks on him as a leader of the people, together with Aaron. The final redaction of 99:6[28] sees in him a priest like Aaron, who intercedes for the people. The historical Pss. 103, 105, and 106 mention him most frequently, describing him as "chosen."[29] In a historical retrospect concerning the Holy Spirit and the lack of trust shown by the people in the wilderness, Isa. 63:11f. makes the only mention of Moses in the postexilic prophets.

In contrast, Moses appears 31 times in the Chronicler's history. There he is a "man of God" (1 Ch. 23:14; Ezr. 3:2) and "servant of God" (2 Ch. 24:9; Neh. 9:14; 10:30[29]). God entrusted the Torah to him (1 Ch. 22:13; Neh. 1:7) and enabled it to guide the people through the "hand" of Moses (2 Ch. 35:6; Neh. 8:14). But we are also told of taxes that Moses "levied" on the people (2 Ch. 24:6). The Chronicler refers to the torah of Moses (Ezr. 3:2; 7:6; Neh. 8:1). Eight texts mention a writing *(ktb)* or book of Moses without specifying who wrote it. These numbers do not suggest particularly high esteem for Moses: David is mentioned much more frequently. Even when the Chronicler speaks of the sanctuary, it is not the sanctuary created by Moses

---

26. Zenger, *Israel am Sinai,* 65.
27. See F. L. Hossfeld, *Der Dekalog. OBO,* 45 (1982), 185ff., etc.
28. See E. Lipiński, *La royauté de Yahwé dans la poésie et le culte de l'ancien Israël. VVAW.L,* 27/55 (1965), 296.
29. → בחר *bāchar* (II, 73-87).

but the temple whose construction David began (1 Ch. 22:19; 2 Ch. 29:21; Neh. 10:40[39]).

Wisdom Literature from Proverbs through Ecclesiastes says nothing of Moses, not even when the book of Job clearly alludes to the Torah. The situation changes in the book of Sirach and the book of Wisdom ascribed to Solomon. Following the lead of the historical psalms, Sirach calls to remembrance the great men of the past. The memory of Moses is blessed; his glory is like that of the saints (Sir. 45:1f.).[30] He is the chosen one, permitted to enter into the cloud to receive "the law of life and understanding" as well as the precepts he was called on to teach Jacob and Israel (vv. 4-6). These 6 verses concerning Moses (45:1-6) are few compared to the 16 verses devoted to Aaron. Joshua, "Moses' successor in the prophetic office," likewise receives 6 verses. But Wisdom, which proceeds from the mouth of the Most High and is established in Israel, is identified with "the book of the covenant of the Most High God, the law that Moses enjoined upon us" (24:3,8,23). In its meditations on the exodus, the book of Wisdom does not mention Moses; neither does it speak of the patriarchs or Adam. But Wis. 10:16 probably does allude to Moses: "[Wisdom] entered into the soul of the Lord's servant."

VII. Moses in Intertestamental Literature. References to Moses become more numerous in the era of the apocalypses. The book of Wisdom, redacted in this period, also begins with a description of the last judgment (Wis. 1–4). This era begins with the book of Daniel and the desecration of the temple; it ends after the destruction of the temple. Dnl. 9 reaches back into history, twice mentioning the "law of Moses," God's servant (vv. 11,13), before describing the tribulations of the last weeks of years and the end.

The Dead Sea Scrolls contain more than 20 texts referring to Moses: his law (CD 15:2), his book (4QFlor 2:3), and his intercession (1QM 10:7; 1QH 17:12). A frequent theme, which never appears in the OT, is "return to the law of Moses" (CD 15:9,12; 16:1,4; 1QS 5:8, etc.); the context associates this theme with reception of novices into the community. The expression implies strict interpretation of and obedience to the Torah of Moses as well as the numerous additional revelations and regulations (1QS 5:8; 4QpPs^a [4Q171] 3:9f.).[31] The Words of Moses (1QDM [1Q22]) are less a midrash than a "new Deuteronomy."[32] Finally, it is interesting that the Temple Scroll does not mention Moses, although its legislation reflects the Torah.

In the contemporary literature Moses plays a significant role, not only as lawgiver but also as mediator of revelation. The Ascension and Testament and other pseudepigrapha of Moses consider him the prophet of the end time.[33]

---

30. V. Hamp (*Sirach. EB,* XIII/2 [1951], in loc.) translates: "like a god."

31. H.-J. Fabry, *Die Wurzel Šûḇ in der Qumran-Literatur. BBB,* 46 (1975), 28-32; → שׁוב *šûḇ*.

32. J. Carmignac; see D. Barthélemy and J. T. Milik, *Qumran Cave I. DJD,* I (1955), 91-96.

33. See A. Denis, *Intro. aux pseudépigraphes grecs de l'AT* (Leiden, 1970), 128-141.

VIII. Later Developments. The Moses of the Pharisaic Rabbis is the great lawgiver not merely because of his written law but also by virtue of his oral tradition, which goes back to Sinai. The Moses of the NT is discussed elsewhere.[34]

Cazelles

---

34. J. Jeremias, "Μωϋσῆς," *TDNT,* IV, 848-873; *TWNT,* X/2, 1184f.; also G. Fitzer, "Μωϋσῆς," *EDNT,* II (1991), 450-52.

מָשַׁח *māšaḥ* I; מָשִׁיחַ *māšîaḥ*

Contents: I. 1. Etymology; 2. Occurrences. II. Meaning and Usage of *māšaḥ* I: 1. General; 2. Kings; 3. P. III. *māšîaḥ:* 1. Usage; 2. Distribution; 3. David; 4. Psalms; 5. Prophets; 6. Late Texts. IV. Later Development: 1. LXX; 2. Sirach; 3. Dead Sea Scrolls.

---

māšaḥ. S. Amsler, *David, Roi et Messie. CahTh,* 49 (1963); K. Baltzer, "Das Ende des Staates Juda und die Messias-Frage," *Studien zur Theologie der alttestamentlichen Überlieferungen. Festschrift G. von Rad* (Neukirchen, 1961), 33-43; P. A. H. de Boer, *De Zoon van God in het OT. Leidse Voordrachten,* 29 (1958); H. Cazelles, *Le Messie de la Bible. Collection "Jésus et Jésus-Christ,"* 7 (Paris, 1978); J. Coppens, *Le messianisme royal. LD,* 54 (1968); E. Cothenet, "Onction," *DBS,* VI, 701-732; H. L. Ellison, *The Centrality of the Messianic Idea for the OT* (London, 1954); J. A. Emerton, review of E. Kutsch, *Salbung als Rechtsakt im AT und im Alten Orient, JSS,* 12 (1967), 122-28; H. Gressmann, *Der Messias. FRLANT,* 43 (1929); F. Hahn, *The Titles of Jesus in Christology* (Eng. trans., London, 1969); F. Hesse, "χρίω B: משח und מָשִׁיחַ in the OT," *TDNT,* IX, 496-509; A. R. Johnson, *Sacral Kingship in Ancient Israel* (Cardiff, [2]1967); M. de Jonge, "χρίω C.III: Apocrypha and Pseudepigrapha," *TDNT,* IX, 511-17; U. Kellermann, "Die politische Messias-Hoffnung zwischen den Testamenten," *Pastoral Theologie,* 56 (1967), 362-377, 436-447; J. Klausner, *The Messianic Idea in Israel* (Eng. trans., New York, 1955); R. Knierim, "Die Messianologie des ersten Buches Samuel," *EvT,* 30 (1970), 113-133; E. Kutsch, *Salbung als Rechtsakt im AT und im Alten Orient. BZAW,* 87 (1963); E. Lipiński, "Le poème royal du Psaume LXXXIX 1-5.20-38," *CahRB,* 6 (1967), 45-52; D. Lys, "De l'onction à l'intronisation royale," *ETR,* 29 (1954), 1-54; T. N. D. Mettinger, *King and Messiah. CB,* 8 (1976), esp. 185-232; H. S. Moon, "The Origins of Messianism in the OT," *NEAJT,* 11 (1973), 1-15; S. Mowinckel, *He That Cometh* (Eng. trans., Nashville, [2]1959); C. A. North, "The Religious Aspects of Hebrew Kingship," *ZAW,* 50 (1932), 8-38; M. Noth, "Office and Vocation in the OT," *The Laws in the Pentateuch and Other Studies* (Eng. trans., Edinburgh, 1966), 229-249; G. von Rad, "The Royal Ritual in Judah," *The Problem of the Hexateuch and Other Essays* (Eng. trans., New York, 1966), 222-231; H. Ringgren, "König und Messias," *ZAW,* 64 (1952), 120-147; *idem, The Messiah in the OT. SBT,* 1/18 (1956); L. Schmidt, "König und Charisma im AT," *KuD,* 28 (1982), 73-87; *idem, Menschlicher Erfolg und Jahwes Initiative. WMANT,* 38 (1970), esp. 172-188; W. H. Schmidt, "Die Ohnmacht des Messias," *KuD,* 15 (1969), 18-34; K. Seybold, *Das davidische Königtum im Zeugnis der Propheten. FRLANT,* 107 (1972); J. A. Soggin, "מֶלֶךְ *melek* 'king,'" *TLOT,* II, 672-680, esp. 676f.; R. de Vaux, "The King of Israel, Vassal of Yahweh," *The Bible and the Ancient Near East* (Eng. trans., Garden City, N.Y., 1971), 152-166; K. R. Veenhof, review of E. Kutsch, *Salbung als Rechtsakt im AT und im*

I. 1. *Etymology.* Heb. *māšaḥ* I derives from the root *m-s/š-ḥ/ḫ,* which (esp. in West Semitic) has the basic meaning "rub, anoint." We may posit a homonymous (?) root *māšaḥ* II that denotes the semantic domain of "measuring."[1] In Akkadian we find Middle and Late Bab. *mašāḫu(m)* I and its derivatives, "measure, measure out," and Neo-Bab. *mašāḫu(m)* II, "flare up." Closer to West Sem. *mšḥ* I may be Akk. *namšāḫu(m),* "a leather container for unguents?"[2] But the Akkadian verb *pašāšu(m),* "anoint, rub in," largely covers the semantic range of West Sem. *mšḥ* I: *paššum,* "anointed"; *piššatu,* "anointing oil"; *pašīšu(m),* "anointed one (= priest)."[3] The Amorite PNs *Ma-si-ḫa-an* and *Ma-su-ḫu-un* can be derived from a *qāṭīl* form of the verb *mšḫ* I.[4] In Ugaritic, too, the verb *mšḥ* is attested, albeit rarely, with the meaning "anoint,"[5] as is the subst. *mšḥt,* "anointing" ([*šm*]*n mšḥt kṯpm,* "anointing oil of the enchanters"[6]). Other texts with *mšḥ* in the sense of "shatter, strike down,"[7] or the like remain unexplained.

The Aramaic branch is highly developed. The root *mšḥ* I and its derivatives are attested from Old Aramaic on,[8] especially in the later dialects; there are fewer occurrences of *mšḥ* II, "measure." Nominal forms include *mᵉšaḥ, mišḥā',* "anointing oil," and, with increasing frequency, the technical term *mᵉšiḥā'.*[9]

The Arabic verb *masaḥa* clearly encompasses the full range of meanings: "rub, wipe"; "measure out"; "rob of, deprive of"[10] — possibly within the more inclusive sense "move one's hand over something." This usage suggests an original meaning "rub," developing such senses as "anoint," "measure," "take," "extinguish," etc., as well as derivation from an onomatopoeic biliteral *m/pš* or *šḥ/ḫ* echoing the sound of rubbing; but this theory remains speculative.[11]

2. *Occurrences.* The following derivatives of *mšḥ* I occur in the OT:

a. the verb *māšaḥ* (68 occurrences, not counting 2 S. 1:21 MT or the 2 occurrences of the fem. inf. *mošḥâ*[12]), found primarily in the qal and niphal;

Alten Orient, BiOr, 23 (1966), 308-313; H. Weinel, "משח und seine Derivate," *ZAW,* 18 (1898), 1-82; A. S. van der Woude, *Die messianischen Vorstellungen der Gemeinde von Qumran* (Assen, 1957); *idem,* "χρίω C.I-II, IV," *TDNT,* IX, 509f., 517-520; → מלך *meleḵ* (VIII, 346-375).

1. G. R. Driver, *JTS,* 41 (1940), 169f. For the possibility of a verbal root *mšḥ* III, see *HAL,* II, 644; A. Guillaume, *JBL,* 76 (1957), 41f.; also J. Barr, *Comparative Philology and the Text of the OT* (London, 1968), 284f.

2. *AHw,* III, 1574, with a possible derivation from *mašāḫu(m)* III.

3. *AHw,* II, 845; cf. J. Renger, *ZA,* 59 (1960), 143ff.

4. *APNM,* 145, 232.

5. *UT,* no. 1561: two texts, one uncertain.

6. *Ugaritica,* V (1968), 574ff., 601.

7. *WUS,* no. 1689.

8. Sefire A, 21; *KAI,* 222.

9. *HAL,* V, 1741; *DISO,* 170; *MdD,* 280; M. Baillet, et al., *Les "Petites Grottes" de Qumrân. DJD,* III (1962), s.v.; see III below.

10. Wehr, 907.

11. Weinel, 9ff.

12. See (2) following.

b. the inf. form *mošḥâ*[13] (2 occurrences);

c. the subst. *mišḥâ,* a feminine segholate[14] (21 occurrences, not counting 2 K. 23:13 conj., *har-hammišḥâ,* "Mount of Olives," for MT *har-hammašḥîṯ,* "Mount of Destruction" [cf. Targ.]), found only in P texts (H, Lev. 21:10,12) and always in the genitive with *šemen,* "anointing oil";

d. the subst. *māšîaḥ*[15] (39 occurrences, including 2 S. 1:21 MT conj., *māšûaḥ*), always linked syntagmatically with YHWH except in 2 S. 1:21; Dnl. 9:25,26;

e. the Aram. noun *mᵉšaḥ,* "oil" (2 occurrences).

II. Meaning and Usage of *māšaḥ* I.

1. *General.* The verb *māšaḥ* I denotes the act and process of wetting, rubbing, smearing, or anointing something, exclusively and usually implicitly with oil (→ שמן *šemen;* Am. 6:6: "with the finest oils") or paint, probably oil-based (*šāšar,* "minium," for painting a house [Jer. 22:14; cf. Ezk. 23:14]). In this usage it corresponds to *sûḵ* (Akk. *sâku,* "pour out"), a by-form of *nāsaḵ* (cf. Isa. 30:1; Ps. 2:6), which usually appears in conjunction with *rāḥaṣ,* "wash," and is limited to cosmetic anointing in the context of bodily hygiene. Also secular in usage is the verb *māraq* I and its derivatives (rare in the OT), "rub, polish, scour, cleanse" (cf. Est. 2:3,9; Prov. 20:30).

The verb may have as its accusative object either things (wooden shields covered with leather [Isa. 21:5; cf. 2 S. 1:21], house walls [Jer. 22:14], loaves of bread [e.g., Ex. 29:2; Lev. 2:4], pillars [Gen. 31:13], altars [Lev. 8:11], cultic paraphernalia [Exodus, Numbers (P)]) or persons (Am. 6:6), especially kings, priests, and prophets (the last: 1 K. 19:16; Isa. 61:1). The majority of texts refer to the anointing of kings, so that in the OT we may say that the verb has become a technical term with this specialized sense. It also appears in various idioms and formulas.

2. *Kings.* The frequent construction of the verb with *lᵉ* (*lᵉḵōhēn, lᵉnāḇî, lᵉnāḡîḏ,* with implicit or explicit reference to a person) shows that the process means a change of status,[16] especially with the specification *lᵉmeleḵ* (16 occurrences), which reveals the relationship of the act to the enthronement of the king. The OT describes the following kings as being "anointed" (beside the bramble of the fable in Jgs. 9:15): Saul (1 S. 9:16; 10:1; 15:1,17 [LXX 11,15]), David (1 S. 16:3,12f.; 2 S. 2:4,7; 3:39; 5:3,17; 12:7; 1 Ch. 11:3; 14:8; Ps. 89:21[Eng. v. 20]), Absalom (2 S. 19:11[10]), Solomon (1 K. 1:34,39,45; 5:15[1]; 1 Ch. 29:22), Jehu (1 K. 19:16; 2 K. 9:3,6,12; 2 Ch. 22:7), Joash (2 K. 11:12; 2 Ch. 23:11), Jehoahaz (2 K. 23:30), possibly an unnamed king of the northern kingdom (Ps. 45:8[7]?), and Hazael of Damascus (1 K. 19:15). This evidence shows that the absolute use of *māšaḥ* is elliptical (e.g., 2 S. 19:11[10]; 1 K. 1:39).

---

13. *BLe,* §316d.
14. *BLe,* §601b.
15. *BLe,* §470n; Meyer, §37.4.
16. Mettinger, 191.

The subject doing the anointing may be YHWH (1 S. 10:1; 15:17; 2 S. 12:7; 2 K. 9:3,6,12; 2 Ch. 22:7; Ps. 89:21[20]; cf. Ps. 45:8[7]; Isa. 61:1), Samuel (1 S. 9:16; 10:1; cf. 11:15 LXX; 1 S. 16:3,12,13; 11QPs^a 28:8,11 [Ps. 151A:5,7]), a prophet (1 K. 1:34,45; 19:15,16; cf. 2 K. 9:3,12,13), a priest (1 K. 1:34,39,45; 2 Ch. 23:11; cf. 2 K. 11:12), or a variety of agents (Jgs. 9:8,15; 2 S. 2:4,7; 5:3 par. 1 Ch. 11:3; 2 S. 5:17; 19:11[10]; 1 K. 5:15[1]; 2 K. 11:12; 1 Ch. 29:22; cf. 2 K. 23:30).

a. *Plural Agency.* We may assume that formulations expressing plural agency refer to the earliest form of royal anointing used in Israel.[17] According to 2 S. 2:4a, "the men of Judah came [to Hebron], and there they anointed David king over the house of Judah." The evidence of 1 S. 30:26 suggests that the "men" were probably the elders of Judah.[18] It is clear that the text describes a juridical act of choosing and installing a king (omitted by the Chronicler in favor of an anointing over "all Israel"). Because the action is not described in detail, we may assume that the significance of the rite was familiar to the participants and listeners (2 S. 2:7). From 2 S. 5:3 we learn more about the juridical significance of anointing. Here it is "all the elders of Israel" who come "to the king at Hebron." "King David made a covenant *(b^{e}rîṯ)* with them at Hebron before Yahweh, and they anointed David king over Israel." Here the anointing is the second part of a legal covenant ceremony; it is the contribution of the elders, expressing the obligation they undertake after the Judahite king has come to an agreement (not further specified) with them. Once again, the language indicates only that the initiative was on the side of those representing the people, who were choosing themselves a king.

The notion that anointing substantiates the choice of a king clearly lies behind the other texts with plural subjects; the fable of Jotham may serve as a model: "The trees once went out to anoint a king over themselves" (Jgs. 9:8; cf. v. 15). The same basic idea, adapted to individual circumstances, appears in the other cases: a passage from the story of Absalom's rebellion (2 S. 19:11[10] with the abbreviated formulaic expression "whom we have anointed over us"); the account of the installation of Joash, the legitimate heir to the throne, by the partisans of the priest Jehoiada (2 K. 11:12: "He brought out the king's son, put the crown on him, and gave him the testimony [? *hā'ēḏûṯ*]; they [MT; LXX sg., 2 Ch. 23:11 pl.] proclaimed him king, and anointed him; they clapped their hands and shouted, 'Long live the king!' "); and the description of how the *'am hā'āreṣ,* the free population of the countryside, intervened in the royal succession (2 K. 23:30: "The people of the land took Jehoahaz son of Josiah, anointed him, and made him king in place of his father").

Only in a limited sense can one assign 1 K. 5:15(1) to this category. The text of 1:45 ("the priest Zadok and the prophet Nathan") can explain the plural verb (cf. 1:34,39), but there is no representative body that chooses the king. It is better to follow the LXX of 5:15(1) and the parallel in Hos. 12:2(1),[19] interpreting the text as referring

17. Kutsch, Mettinger.
18. Contra Hesse, 487f.
19. Also *KBo,* I, 14; EA, 34; cf. Mettinger, 225ff.

to a gift of oil and "diplomatic anointing," a gesture of homage or an acknowledgment of treaty obligations.[20]

This seems to have been the case especially at the beginning but even at the end of the period of the monarchy. There is little agreement as to its origin and spread (Franz Hesse: Canaanite; Ernst Kutsch: Hittite; Roland de Vaux: Egyptian).

b. *1 K. 1.* The account of the Davidic succession in 1 K. 1 also provides a historically precise use of *māšaḥ*.[21] As requested by David, the priest Zadok and the prophet Nathan performed the anointing of Solomon (vv. 34,45). Zadok, however, was the actual agent: he took the horn of oil (*qeren;* 1 S. 10:1; 2 K. 9:1,3 use *pak̲,* probably "vial") from the tent (sanctuary) and "anointed Solomon" (1 K. 1:39). (In 1 Ch. 29:22 the assembly [*qāhāl*] anoints Solomon as king and Zadok as priest.) The whole ceremony took place at Gihon in the presence of Benaiah and the "servants of the king," the Cherethite and Pelethite mercenaries. Then a trumpet was blown, and "all the people" cried, "Long live King Solomon!" Then all returned to the royal residence. Here *māšaḥ* denotes the crucial action; its sacral effectiveness and legal force are strongly emphasized (1 K. 1:45ff.). The plural formulation indicates that 1 K. 1 is seeking to justify the integration of the ceremony into the system of dynastic succession, which effectively rules out any free initiative and choice on the part of the representative. Thus Solomon became king over "Israel" (MT; the LXX adds "and over Judah"; 1:34).

c. *1 S. 16.* In 1 S. 16:1-13 we have what is probably the earliest theological explanation of the divine anointing of the king, i.e., the texts where Yahweh is the subject of *māšaḥ*. The traditional account of David's anointing by Samuel is rightly considered the *hieros logos* of the sacral anointing of the king, which clearly formed part of the accession ritual since the time of Solomon. Now the theological formulation of the sacral action is *ûmāšaḥtā lî,* "and you shall anoint for me [Yahweh]" (v. 3; cf. vv. 12f.).

Three factors define the significance of this sacral action. (1) It is no longer preceded by a public selection of the king in a council of the elders but by divine election (*rā'â* or *bāḥar* instead of *mā'as*): "Yahweh descries his anointed." Anointing is a visible sign of divine election. (2) A representative of Yahweh — Samuel, Elijah, a *nabi* — is sent *(šālaḥ)* to give ritual expression to Yahweh's election. The consent of those performing the ceremony and an acclamation by the participants are not needed: anointing is a symbolic cultic act that conveys the king's divine mission and authority (cf. 11QPs[a] 28:8; LXX Ps. 151A:5,7). (3) As an immediate consequence, the Spirit of Yahweh enters into *(ṣālaḥ)* the king, who is endowed with a special charisma (1 S. 16:13). Anointing signifies the manifestation of the gift of the Spirit. The verb *māšaḥ* becomes a theologoumenon; it takes on the weight and burden of a theological concept with more or less fixed implications. This process is clearly already beginning in the period of Solomon.

d. *The Saul and David Cycle.* In the cycle of traditions surrounding Saul and in the

---

20. Cf. *šmn šlm,* "oil of peace," *KTU,* 1.101, 14.

21. See II.2.a above for 2 S. 19:11(10) and II.1 above and II.3 below for 19:22(21); 2 S. 12:7 is probably a Deuteronomistic formulation (see III.1, 3 below).

context of the court history of David, we find uses of *māšaḥ* that obviously have been influenced by the theological tendency just described. This influence appears in the theological use of the title *nāgîḏ* for Yahweh's designated king (1 S. 9:16; 10:1 MT and LXX [it appears in conjunction with *māšîaḥ* in 1 S. 24:7,11; 26:9,11,16,23; 2 S. 1:14,16[22]]) and the theological statement that the king rules *ʿal-ʿammî yiśrāʾēl* or the like (1 S. 15:1,17). It is therefore doubtful that Saul was actually anointed.[23] The remaining texts exhibit the polished style that betrays Deuteronomistic origin (2 S. 3:39 conj.; 12:7; cf. 1 S. 12:3,5).

Ps. 45:8(7) ("therefore Yahweh your God has anointed you with the oil of gladness beyond your companions") is probably addressed to a king of the northern kingdom. It is not clear whether the words refer to his anointing as king or to some other festal cultic act. The former is suggested by the theologoumenon, the latter by the expression "oil of gladness" and the context (vv. 9f.[8f.]).

e. *Prophetic Tradition.* In the Elijah and Elisha traditions, we can recognize a reawakening of early ideas about anointing, albeit with fresh nuances. For the act itself, the tradition uses the phrase "pour the vial of oil upon the head of so-and-so." The verb *māšaḥ* is sometimes used performatively with Yahweh as 1st person subject: "I hereby anoint you king over Israel" (the so-called coincidence case, 2 K. 9:3,6,12) or in the jussive: "You shall anoint . . ." (1 K. 19:15ff.). Thus the theological heritage of the term is reactualized in prophetic word and deed. At the same time, we can see that the notion of choosing a king without dynastic constraints, even from outside the borders of Israel (Hazael: 1 K. 19:15), is still alive, being reclaimed and practiced by prophetic circles.

3. *P.* The P literature uses *māšaḥ* almost exclusively in the context of consecrations, usually in conjunction with the piel of *qdš* (consecration of the high priest: Ex. 29; Lev. 8; consecration of the tent sanctuary and the cultic paraphernalia: Ex. 40). Three observations are noteworthy. (a) Expressions like "pour oil" (*yāṣaq šemen;* frequently *šemen hammišḥâ,* "anointing oil), "anoint," "sanctify" (*qdš* piel), and occasionally "function as a priest" (*khn* piel) refer to one and the same ceremony, clearly conveying the technical, explicative, and functional aspect of the action (see, e.g., Ex. 29:36; Lev. 8:11 [with l^e + inf.]; Ex. 30:29; 40:9ff.; Lev. 8:10 [with w^e + perf.][24]). It is possible that *māšaḥ* denotes the verbal side of the process as in the coincidence of 2 K. 9 (cf. Ps. 2:7ff.; 110:1ff.). In any case, by alluding to the history of the term, it effects a theological definition and categorization of what is taking place. That the traditional implications of *māšaḥ* in the royal anointing continued to echo in the consecration of the high priest in the postexilic period (1 Ch. 29:22; Zec. 4:14) is a safe assumption.[25] (b) The immediate context includes detailed directives and cultic instructions (e.g., the

22. See below.
23. Mettinger, 194ff.
24. Hesse, 486.
25. Kutsch and Hesse.

preparation of anointing oil: Ex. 30:22ff.). (c) Except in Lev. 16:32; Nu. 35:25 (pass.), the agent performing the action is exclusively the Moses of P, representing the highest authority of the priestly office.

III. *māšîaḥ*.

1. *Usage.* The noun *māšîaḥ* is a *qāṭîl* formation with passive meaning. In contrast to the form *māšûaḥ,* with punctiliar meaning, *māšîaḥ* probably conveys customary meaning, "permanently endowed with a status."[26] It has become a fixed theologoumenon; in the OT it appears almost exclusively in syntagmatic association with Yahweh. Only in the late text Dnl. 9:25f. do we find it used anarthrously as a technical term for the high priest. By way of comparison, the early text 2 S. 1:21 (MT) uses *māšîaḥ* as a passive participle modifying the shield of Saul, to be "anointed with oil no more" after his death; if the text is not corrupt (21 MSS. read *māšûaḥ*), this usage suggests that the noun was still as flexible as the verb (cf. Isa. 21:5) and had not undergone the specialization noted above. Conversely, the difficult passage 2 S. 3:39 (MT) uses the passive participle to modify *meleḵ* — clearly a textual error. To date, no ancient Near Eastern parallel has been found to *mᵉšîaḥ YHWH* as a title of theological provenience. Transferences of what was originally a royal honorific attest its theological consistency, as does its appearance as a loanword, primarily after the OT period, in the Judeo-Christian vocabulary.[27]

2. *Distribution.* The word exhibits a distinctive distribution, both literarily and traditio-historically. A large number of occurrences are found in the sources of Deuteronomistic historiography: the story of David's rise (1 S. 16:6; 24:7[6][twice],11[10]; 26:9,11, 16,23; 2 S. 1:14,16,[21]), the story of the Davidic succession (2 S. 19:22[21]), and other Davidic traditions (2 S. 23:1), as well as Deuteronomistic texts (1 S. 2:35; 12:3,5; 2 S. 12:7). An almost equally large number appear in the psalmodic tradition (Ps. 2:2; 18:51[50] par. 2 S. 22:51; Ps. 20:7[6]; 28:8; 84:10[9]; 89:39,52[38,51], 105:15 par. 1 Ch. 16:22; Ps. 132:10 par. 2 Ch. 6:42; Ps. 132:17; 1 S. 2:10; Lam. 4:20; Hab. 3:13), where it is always a royal title, as also in the only occurrence in prophetic literature (Isa. 45:1; cf. Hab. 3:13). The remaining occurrences are in P texts referring to the (high) priest (Lev. 4:3,5,16; 6:15[22]) and in Dnl. 9:25f. Chronologically, the occurrences cover the period of the monarchy down to the exile (Lam. 4:20), always as a royal title (including Isa. 45:1 [Cyrus]). In the postexilic period, it became an honorific title of the (high) priest. The focus of its usage is Jerusalem (Davidic tradition and royal psalms). Except for Saul, none of the northern kings is so characterized. The description of the patriarchs as "anointed" represents a transference (Ps. 105:15 par. 1 Ch. 16:22).

3. *David.* Comparison with the notion of a divinely initiated anointing associated with the verb *māšaḥ*[28] shows that the exclusively theological expression *mᵉšîaḥ YHWH*

---

26. Weinel, 13f.; cf. *GK,* §84ᵃl.
27. *HAL,* II, 645.
28. See II.2.c above.

originated and found general use in conjunction with that conception.[29] This would mean that the title came into being during the time of Solomon under the influence of a developing official Jerusalemite royal theology and ideology.[30] This conclusion is confirmed by the anointing etiology in 1 S. 16:6: "Surely Yahweh's anointed now [stands] before him." This fits with the observation that the earlier succession narrative contains only a single occurrence (2 S. 19:22[21], referring to David).[31] During the period of David, the word still had primarily a verbal meaning (2 S. 1:21, if this text dates from this period). A substantial group of occurrences does not appear until the traditions of David's rise (dating from the post-Solomonic period).

In this case, the conclusion is inescapable that the Saul texts[32] should be interpreted more theologically than historically. In fact, the two parallel traditions in 1 S. 24 and 26 together with 2 S. 1 treat a fundamental theme of royal ideology: the question of immunity and the indelible character bestowed as a charisma by anointing. The insistent repetition of the justification formulas with *m^e^šîaḥ YHWH* suggest that they may well be the product of theological stylization.[33] The Deuteronomistic occurrences in 1 S. 2:10; 2 S. 12:7 carry no independent weight, for they take the title from or adapt it to the context. We may therefore assume that the title arose in connection with the development of the royal ideology and the institution of the Judahite royal ritual, probably under marked Egyptian influence, and soon found wide acceptance in Jerusalemite circles.[34] As a theologoumenon it was able to combine the following elements:

a. It designated an exclusive relationship with Yahweh that finds expression in the restricted use of the term — probably a reflection of the traditional belief in the exclusivity of the relationship between "Israel" and Yahweh. The further evolution of this element in Jerusalem during the monarchy produced the notion of the "Davidic covenant" (cf. 2 S. 23:1 and 23:5; Ps. 89:39,52[38,51] and 89:4,29,35,40[3,28,34, 39]),[35] intended to summarize the special relationship between the Davidic ruler and Yahweh.

b. It defined the status of the king and legitimated sacral kingship in Israel with the aid of ancient Israelite notions of election (1 S. 16). In agreement with the spirit of the age, it also drew on traditions of royal ideology that were probably Egyptian in origin (anointing of high officials and vassals),[36] so that the Davidic king could be proclaimed "Yahweh's vassal" with the full range of ideas implied by this claim (cf. the prophetic criticism of the Judahite kings).

c. It integrated the institution of the monarchy into the nascent conception of the

---

29. Mettinger, 198ff.

30. → מלך *meleḵ* (VIII, 346-375).

31. T. Veijola (*Die ewige Dynastie. AnAcScFen,* 193 [1975], 33f.) claims that this text is Deuteronomistic. On 1 K. 1 see II.2.b above.

32. See II.2.d above.

33. H.-J. Stoebe, *Das erste Buch Samuelis. KAT,* VIII/1 (1973), in loc.

34. → מלך *meleḵ* (VIII, 346-375, esp. 362f.).

35. Mettinger, 224ff., 275ff.

36. Kutsch, de Vaux, Cothenet.

(universal) kingdom of God, in which the anointed one is given a singular and outstanding role (cf. the Royal Psalms), so that the title could independently designate this function and become the embodiment of eschatological expectations.

d. It introduced the conception of a single individual chosen by God, which went on to become the paradigm of a privileged relationship with God and the representative personification of all humanity, eventually leading to the notion of the image of God.

4. *Psalms.* The psalmodic literature constitutes a second domain where the term occurs with some frequency. It is not always clear what elements of the *m*ᵉ*sîaḥ YHWH* concept are present if the context does not emphasize them. The texts include several passages from the so-called Royal Psalms (Pss. 2,18,20,89,132), which deal centrally and explicitly with the Judahite monarchy. Others mention the anointed only in passing, as either a petition or an expression of trust in prayers of an individual (Pss. 28,84; 1 S. 2; Hab. 3; cf. Ps. 20). Lam. 4; Pss. 151A,105 are unique cases. Except in the case of Ps. 105, all the texts refer to regents and kings of the Davidic dynasty, although only 2 S. 23:1; Pss. 132,151 mention the name of the anointed (David). As one might expect, the actual psalm texts cease with the exile (Lam. 4:20). Even if one assumes the postexilic composition of psalms like 89 and 132, the reference is still to the Davidic kings, albeit now belonging to the past.

In Ps. 2 the term appears in a clearly secondary addition (v. 2b), which nevertheless matches the meaning of the psalm precisely: the rebellion of the nations is directed "against Yahweh and his anointed." The mere juxtaposition of the two recalls the traditional kingship formula,[37] which is the focus of the psalm and is quoted by the royal psalmist (vv. 6,7-9). It is noteworthy that this formula is presented as being spoken by Yahweh, in part as a divine proclamation (v. 6), in part as the recitable substance of a divine decree (*ḥōq,* vv. 7ff.). In addition, the meaning of ritual anointing, also clearly central to Ps. 2, begins with the theological metaphor "I have *poured (nāsaḵtî)* my king on Zion, the hill of my sanctuary" (v. 6), an allusion to the effectual and juridical nature of the act of anointing. Finally, the threatened king has recourse to the universal position and function he has been promised, expressed in the categories of divine sonship, direct access to God, victory, and sovereignty over the nations. In this way, Ps. 2 offers a comprehensive realization of the *māšîaḥ* concept.

The same holds true to some extent for Pss. 18 and 89. Here, however, the theological concept associated specifically with the anointing of the king plays a smaller role, as evidenced by the fact that the term appears with its special accent only in 89:39f.(38f.). In his lament, the psalmist blames God for the fate of the king, which runs counter to all trusting hopes and expectations: "You have spurned and rejected him; you are full of wrath against your anointed. You have renounced the covenant with your servant; you have defiled his crown in the dust." These verses allude to the privileges promised to the anointed (election, covenant, royal insignia). Yahweh's actions appear inconsistent with the "steadfast love of old, which by your faithfulness you swore to David"

---

37. See III.2 above.

(89:50[49]). Like Ps. 18:51(50); 132:17; 1 S. 2:10 (cf. Ps. 28:8), Ps. 89 concludes with a petition that Yahweh will remember his anointed once more.

In a few passages, a prayer for the king combines the title with an expression of help and deliverance (*yšʿ:* Ps. 18:51[50], par. *ḥeseḏ;* 20:7[6],[10(9)]); 28:8; Hab. 3:13; 1 S. 2:10), clearly recalling the special intensity of the relationship: "Yahweh is the strength of his people and the saving refuge of his anointed" (Ps. 28:8).

The anointed brings life and salvation to his people. Ps. 84:10(9) uses the metaphor of a shield[38] ("behold our shield"; cf. 89:19[18]), while Lam. 4:20 says: "Yahweh's anointed, the breath of our life, was taken in their pits — the one of whom we said, 'Under his shadow we shall live among the nations.' "

Twice a horn symbolizes the enduring favor Yahweh shows his anointed: 1 S. 2:10, "exalt the horn"; Ps. 132:17, "cause a horn to sprout." The latter verse uses → נר *nēr,* "lamp," as a parallel ("I have prepared a lamp [upon Zion] for my anointed one").

In later ages, the memory of David appears to have played an important role. He was the prototype — and the "Davidic covenant" made with him the basis — of the relationship between Yahweh and his anointed: "For your servant David's sake do not reject your anointed one" (Ps. 132:10). Ps. 151A (11QPs^a 28) is also framed as a paraphrase of 1 S. 16: "He sent his prophet Samuel to anoint me" (vv. 8f.); "he took me away from the flock and anointed me with holy oil [or 'oil of the sanctuary']" (vv. 10f.).

In the so-called Last Words of David (2 S. 23:1-5; difficult to date, possibly to be included with the David traditions), the title appears in the unique phrase "the anointed of the God of Jacob." Two theologoumena, a divine predicate from the patriarchal era and an honorific from the early monarchy, appear to have been combined here to parallel the relationship with God that each represents — like the term *b^{e}rîṯ* in v. 5.

Ps. 105:15 is exceptional: it is the only text in the Psalms that uses the title for someone other than a king. In extending its usage to the plural and applying it to the patriarchs, this passage uses what had probably become a fossilized designation of a type to emphasize the special character of the patriarchs, calling them both "my anointed" and "my prophets." The former recalls 1 S. 24 and 26 and alludes to the immunity of the anointed. We may possibly see here the influence of the shift in meaning that marks the postexilic development of the term.[39]

5. *Prophets.* The prophetic literature is familiar with the Jerusalemite royal theology and the Judahite royal ritual, as well as the theological implications of anointing (Isa. 11:1ff.; Zec. 4:1ff.). But the term "the anointed of Yahweh" (cf. *māšaḥ* in 1 K. 19:16; Isa. 61:1) appears in only a single passage in Deutero-Isaiah (Isa. 45:1): "Thus says Yahweh to his anointed, to Cyrus, whose right hand I have grasped." Deutero-Isaiah employs the ancient honorific with great freedom and audacity. (a) Contrary to the entire weight of tradition as well as contemporary prophecy (Ezekiel, Haggai, Zechariah), the title is taken from the Davidic dynasty, Davidic kings past or future — as is

38. → מגן *māḡēn* (VIII, 74-87).
39. See III.5 below.

the privilege of the covenant relationship and its associate benefits (55:3ff.). (b) With prophetic authority, it is bestowed on a non-Israelite ruler, who appears to have made no such claim himself even though he entered juridically into the Davidide succession. (c) Cyrus is thus accorded the role the anointed is to play in the program of universal kingship (cf., e.g., 45:1ff.). (d) The prophet consciously accepts that Cyrus neither knew nor wanted to know anything about these privileges; his primary concern was clearly that the function of the anointed simply be recognized. This advance by Deutero-Isaiah was probably unique. Postexilic prophecy returned to the traditional promise to David, though not without new emphases (cf. the two "sons of oil" — *b^e^nê-hayyiṣhār* in Zec. 4:1-14 — elsewhere always → שמן *šemen* in this context).

6. *Late Texts.* Finally, *māšîaḥ* occurs sporadically in P and in Apocalyptic Literature, but only with reference to the high priest. Lev. 4:3,5,16; 6:15(22), which belong to late strata of P,[40] clearly use the word once more as an attributive participle in the phrase *hakkōhēn hammāšîaḥ* (cf. 2 S. 1:21; then the normal form in 2 S. 3:39; P: Ex. 29:2; Lev. 2:4; 7:12; Nu. 3:3; 6:15), with no observable reference to the preexilic royal title. The phrase seems already to have become a technical term. The word *māšîaḥ* simply stands for *gāḏôl.* "The rivalry of the Davidides (Zec. 4) no longer needs to be taken into account"[41] or is deliberately ignored by this language.[42] In contrast to other and probably later P strata, which require all priests to be anointed (e.g., Ex. 40:15; Nu. 3:3),[43] the claim to anointing and the title are here reserved for the high priest.

The late midrash in Dnl. 9:1-3,21-27, dating from the years 167-164 B.C., uses the anarthrous term "anointed one" for the high priest, probably Joshua, calling him *māšîaḥ nāgîḏ* ("an anointed one [and] prince" [v. 25]; on this usage of *nāgîḏ,* cf. 1 Ch. 9:11; 2 Ch. 31:13; Neh. 11:11; Dnl. 11:22). The age of the Aaronide "princes" begins 70 weeks of years after Jeremiah and extends for 62 weeks of years until an anointed one is cut off (*yikkārēṯ māšîaḥ:* Dnl. 9:26), probably Onias III.[44] After a further week of years of extreme oppression and tribulation (v. 27), the apocalypticist expects his conception of the "messianic" age, in which "a most holy place will be anointed," i.e., the eschatological sanctuary will be consecrated (v. 24).

IV. Later Development.

1. *LXX.* The LXX usually translates the forms of *māšaḥ* precisely and consistently with forms of *chríein (christós, chrísma),* whose meanings correspond.[45] It takes another course only for the anointing of a stone (Gen. 31:13: *aleíphein*) and of priests (Ex. 40:15; Nu. 3:3), the rubbing of a shield (Isa. 21:5: *hetoimázein*), and spreading of cakes (Lev.

40. K. Elliger, *Leviticus. HAT,* IV (1966), 57ff.
41. *Ibid.,* 68.
42. Hesse, 495.
43. Cothenet, 722ff.
44. A. Bentzen, *Daniel. HAT,* XIX (1952), 73ff. Cf. 2 Mc. 1:10: Aristobulus "from the line of the anointed priests" *(apó toú tṓn christṓn hieréōn génous).*
45. Grundmann, *TDNT,* IX, 485f.

2:4; 7:2,12: *diachríein*), and correctly paraphrases 2 S. 3:39 with *kathistánai* (treated differently by Aquila and Symmachus). Both *chrísis* and *chrísma* translate *mišḥâ;* in Ex. 40:15 *chrísma* also represents *mošḥâ,* in Dnl. 9:26 (LXX, Theodotion) it represents *māšîaḥ.* Elsewhere *māšîaḥ* is always translated with *chrístos,* with the exception of Lev. 4:3, where the participial function of the Hebrew term is emphasized: *archiereús ho kechrisménos* (cf. 2 S. 1:21: *thyreós Saoul ouk echrísthē*). The translation follows the diction of the Hebrew: *ho hiereús ho christós* is the high priest (cf. Lev. 4:5,16; 6:15[22] and 4:3). There is no clear instance of *ho christós* used absolutely in the LXX.[46] The passages where the LXX introduces *chríein* on its own do not change the picture: Am. 4:13 (probably misread); 2 S. 3:39;[47] 2 Ch. 36:1 for *mlk* hiphil; Isa. 25:6; Hos. 8:10; Ezk. 43:3 (probably also misreadings); cf. Symmachus on 1 S. 15:11; Ps. 2:6.

2. *Sirach.* The use of *mšḥ* in Sirach corresponds in the paraphrases to the convention of its model: Sir. 45:15, "Moses anointed [Aaron] with holy oil"; 46:13, "Samuel anointed princes *(ngydym, árchontes)* over the people of God"; 48:8, Elijah "anointed *(mwšḥ, chríōn* [ptcp.]) kings and prophets"; 46:19 clearly reflects 1 S. 12:5 *(mšyḥw, christoú autoú).*[48]

3. *Dead Sea Scrolls.* The Dead Sea Scrolls clearly continue the OT usage of *mšḥ* and its derivatives.[49] Especially important is the use of forms of the noun *mšyḥ.* In the plural it occasionally denotes the OT prophets (CD 2:12; 6:1; 1QM 11:7 [disputed]). In the singular it refers once to the prophetic messenger of joy who ushers in the *eschaton* (*mšyḥ hrwḥ,* "the one anointed with the Spirit"). In the majority of passages, however, it denotes the priestly and/or royal anointed one expected "at the end of days." The expectation of two messianic figures, usually termed "the anointed of Aaron" and "the anointed of Israel," probably derives from the idea based on Zec. 4:14 that the functions of the anointed one would be divided into a royal and a (high) priestly office.[50] The earliest evidence for the use of the absolute form *hmšyḥ* for the anointed one(s) of the *eschaton* may be 1QSa 2:12 (cf. 4QPBless 3).[51]

The later development of the Hebrew term as a loanword in its Hellenistic transcription *Messías* (Jn. 1:41; 4:25 [anarthrous]) or its Ethiopic form *Ma(s)siḥ* (1[Eth.] En. 48:10) is beyond the scope of this article.[52]

Seybold

---

46. See the discussion of the questionable passages by van der Woude, *TDNT,* IX, 510, n. 74.
47. See above.
48. De Jonge, 511.
49. Van der Woude, *TDNT,* IX, 517ff.
50. Van der Woude, *Vorstellungen,* passim; *idem, TDNT,* IX, 517ff.
51. For further discussion of this complex of problems, see van der Woude, *TDNT,* IX, 517ff.; K. Weiss, "Messianismus in Qumran und im NT," *Qumran-Probleme,* ed. H. Bardtke (Berlin, 1963), 353-368; R. B. Laurin, "The Problem of Two Messiahs in the Qumran Scrolls," *RevQ,* 4 (1963), 39-52.
52. See *HAL,* II, 645; A. S. van der Woude, "Messias," *BHHW,* II, 1197ff.

מָשַׁךְ *māšak̲*

Contents: I. Etymology; II. General Usage; III. Special Instances of the Qal; IV. Niphal and Pual; V. LXX.

I. Etymology. Heb. *māšak̲* corresponds to Arab. *masaka,* "grasp,"[1] OSA *msk,* "take, seize,"[2] Eth. *masaka,* "draw (a bow)," and Jewish Aram. *m*ᵉ*šak̲,* "draw, pull." Ugar. *mṯk,* "extend (a hand)," might correspond to Heb. *māšak̲,* but the *ṯ* rules out the other words (equivalent forms, e.g., would be Arab. **maṯaka,* Aram. **m*ᵉ*ṯak̲*). If Heb. *mešek̲,* "leather bag," belongs to this root ("something pulled off" [from *māšak̲,* "pull off"], i.e., "skin"),[3] there are parallels in several Aramaic dialects with *ma/eškā',* "skin,"[4] as well as Arab. *mask,* "pulled-off skin," and Akk. *mašku,* with the same meaning. Ugar. *ṯ* still remains a problem. It is more likely, however, that *mešek̲* should be considered a primary noun.

II. General Usage. Heb. *māšak̲* appears 36 times as a verb: 30 times in the qal and 3 each in the niphal and pual. It is an everyday word with the basic meaning "draw" and a wide range of connotations, e.g., lift out of a pit (Joseph: Gen. 37:28; Jeremiah: Jer. 38:13), pull out (a crocodile) with a fishhook (Job 40:25[Eng. 41:1]), draw a bow (1 K. 22:34 par. 2 Ch. 18:33; Isa. 66:19), blow the *yôb̲ēl* trumpet (Ex. 19:13; Josh. 6:5), go (Jgs. 4:6; 20:37; cf. also Ex. 12:21: *mišk̲û ûq*ᵉ*ḥû,* "go and take (a lamb)." These and some additional texts are scarcely relevant theologically.

III. Special Instances of the Qal. The following passages, where *māšak̲* occurs in theologically interesting contexts, merit special attention:

1. With *ḥesed̲* or *'ap̲, māšak̲* means "extend in time," i.e., "prolong." In Ps. 36:11(10) the psalmist prays that God will continue his steadfast love for those who know him and his "righteousness" to the upright of heart. This text assumes a mutuality in human relationships with God, such that knowledge of God and uprightness have as their consequence God's enduring faithfulness and favor. Ps. 85, a communal lament, records the impatient question, "Will you be angry *('ānap̲)* forever and prolong your anger *('ap̲)* to all generations?" (v. 6[5]). The duration of God's anger is here emphasized by the expressions *l*ᵉ*'ôlām* and *l*ᵉ*d̲ôr wād̲ôr.* The curse in Ps. 109:12 says of the usurer: "May there be no one to extend him *ḥesed̲.*" Here the emphasis is not on how long the *ḥesed̲* is not extended, but it is clear that *māšak̲ ḥesed̲* represents a fixed idiom.

1. A. Guillaume, *Abr-Nahrain,* 2 (1960/61), 23f.
2. ContiRossini, 179.
3. P. Fronzaroli, *AANLR,* 19 (1964), 252, 266.
4. *DISO,* 170; *LexSyr,* 407.

Therefore Jer. 31:3 probably also belongs here: "I have loved you with an everlasting love; therefore I have continued my faithfulness to you." The KJV translates: "Therefore with lovingkindness have I drawn thee" (Martin Luther: ". . . to me"), taking *ḥesed̲* (with LXX and Syr.) as an adverbial accusative; but *'ahᵃḇaṯ 'ôlām* supports the meaning "prolong." Luther's "to me" is not in the text, and the suffix in *meᵉšaḵtîḵā* can very well function as a dative.[5] The fundamental basis for the restoration of Israel (Jer. 31:4f.) is thus the constant love and faithfulness of Yahweh.

In Neh. 9:30 we find a briefer idiom: *māšaḵ 'al* means "have patience"; the length of time is emphasized by "many years." The context is a penitential prayer that emphasizes, among other things, that God long had patience with his people but finally had to hand them over to their enemies; he will, however, have mercy on them once more.

2. Hos. 11:4 is especially difficult: *bᵉḥaḇlê 'āḏām 'emšᵉḵēm ba'ᵃḇōṯôṯ 'ahᵃḇâ,* "with cords of human beings (= human cords?) I drew them [the Israelites], with bands of love." Although the language here resembles that of Jer. 31:3 *(māšaḵ, 'ahᵃḇâ),* the mention of cords and bands points in a different direction. If MT *'ōl* ("yoke") is retained in the following line, the image appears to refer to the taming of a draft animal. The rest of the passage, however, speaks of the son Yahweh has brought up. If *'ōl* is emended to *'ûl* ("suckling"), the reference to cords and bands becomes difficult. Since *māšaḵ* is not connected with *'ahᵃḇâ,* an interpretation based on Jer. 31:3 is uncertain. In any case, the passage speaks of Yahweh's loving guidance of Israel.[6]

3. The verb *māšaḵ* is also associated with *ḥeḇel* in Isa. 5:18, where the MT reads: "Woe to those who drag iniquity along with cords of falsehood *(šāw')* and sin with cart ropes." This seems to say that sinners by their conduct recklessly and inescapably bring about their own punishment or even, as the following verse suggests, hasten it. The text may also be corrupt. Scholars usually emend *šāw'* to *šôr,* to give the meaning "with cords of oxen." Mitchell Dahood interprets *šw'* as equivalent to Ugar. *ṯ't,* "mother sheep," and *'ᵃgālâ* as *'ēgel,* "calf."[7] Otto Kaiser therefore translated: "Woe to those who draw guilt with <sheep cords> and sin with <calf ropes>."[8]

4. In Ps. 28:3 the psalmist prays: "Do not drag me away with the wicked." He seeks refuge from his enemies, is convinced that they will receive their just punishment, and now prays that he will not have to be dragged away with them. According to Ps. 10:9, enemies seize the poor and drag them off in their nets (or draw their nets around them). Job 40:25(41:1) asks: "Can you draw out Leviathan [the crocodile] with a fishhook?" Of course the answer is no. In Cant. 1:4 the bride says to her beloved: "Draw me after you," i.e., "Take me to your chambers."

---

5. *GK,* §117x.
6. → IV, 177.
7. *CBQ,* 22 (1960), 75.
8. *Isaiah 1–12. OTL* (Eng. trans. 1972), 64. In the 2nd ed. of his comm. (Eng. trans. 1983), however, he returned to the MT.

5. Hos. 7:5 states: *māšak yāḏô 'eṯ-lōṣᵉṣîm,* "He [the king?] stretched out his hand with mockers [?]." The context is obscure. Scholars since Julius Wellhausen have seen 7:1-7 as alluding to a conspiracy against the king: he was made drunk and then murdered. In good faith he had consorted (exchanged handshakes) with the conspirators — conduct here represented as blameworthy. This is all quite uncertain; it is clear only that "he" is accused of having performed some kind of act with wicked people that somehow symbolized fellowship. H. S. Nyberg finds here an allusion to a cultic festival ("day of our Melek") that involved drinking wine and making a compact with the god Melek.[9] Opinions differ about *lōṣᵉṣîm.* It is usually derived from *lyṣ* and translated "mockers" (Nyberg: "the abandoned").[10] Other suggestions include "babblers" or "drunkards," "spies" (cf. Arab. *laḏlaḏa,* "spy out"), and "deviates" (cf. Arab. *lwṣ,* "turn aside").[11]

6. In the Song of Deborah, Jgs. 5:14b reads: "From Machir come commanders *(ḥōqᵉqîm),* and from Zebulun *mōšᵉkîm bᵉšēḇeṭ sōpēr.*" The *mōšᵉkîm bᵉšēḇeṭ* are clearly scepter bearers, i.e., princes; the meaning of *sōpēr* is obscure. If it is related to Akk. *šapāru,* "send, write; rule," the phrase would refer to a ruler's scepter. Others connect the work with Akk. *siparru,* "bronze."

7. Am. 9:13 includes the following description of the coming time of salvation: "The one who plows shall overtake *(māšak)* the one who reaps, and the treader of grapes the one who sows the seed." In other words, because of the rich harvest the vintage will last until it is time to plow; sowing will hardly be completed when the harvest begins again.

IV. Niphal and Pual. The niphal and pual agree with the qal sense of "prolong." At the end of the prophecy against Babylon in Isa. 13, v. 22 states that the day of catastrophe is "close at hand" and will not be delayed *(yāmêyhā lō' yimmāšēkû).* In a similar vein, Ezk. 12:25,28 promise that what Yahweh has spoken will be accomplished without delay. A similar notion is found in the Habakkuk commentary from Qumran: the men of truth will not slacken in serving the truth if the last age is prolonged, for God's ages come in their order as God has ordained (1QpHab 7:12).

This nuance is present in the 3 occurrences of the pual. Prov. 13:12 speaks of hope deferred *(mᵉmuššāk)* that makes the heart sick, whereas a desire fulfilled is "a tree of life," a psychological observation that is immediately understandable. Isa. 18:2,7 speak of a people tall *(mᵉmuššāk)* and smooth ([mᵉ]*mōrāṭ,* probably = "bald"), most likely the Egyptians.

---

9. *Studien zum Hoseabuche. UUÅ,* 6 (1935), 50f.
10. → VII, 548f.
11. See, respectively, H. N. Richardson, *VT,* 5 (1955), 166f.; P. Ruben, *AJSL,* 52 (1935/36), 36; T. H. Gaster, *VT,* 4 (1954), 79.

V. LXX. Most of the translations used by the LXX are forms of *helkýein* with various prefixes. For the niphal it uses *mēkýnein* and *chronízein*.

Ringgren

מִשְׁכָּן *miškān*

Contents: I. 1. Etymology; 2. Occurrences. II. 1. Secular Usage; 2. P; 3. The Dwelling of Yahweh outside P. III. 1. Dead Sea Scrolls; 2. LXX.

I. 1. *Etymology.* The noun *miškān* is an *m*-prefix formation from the root *škn,* "dwell"; it denotes the place where the action expressed by the root *škn* takes place, i.e., "dwelling (place)" or "habitation." Analogous formations appear in several Semitic languages. Akk. *maškanu* denotes a threshing floor, a storage place, or a house.[1] It also appears in Sumerian as the loanword *maš-gána* with the meaning "storage place."[2] One passage in the Mari texts refers to a *maškanu* guarded by an *āpilum,* so that Abraham Malamat proposes the meaning "tent sanctuary" for Heb. *miškān.*[3]

Akk. *maškanu* or *maškattu/maškantu*[4] probably appears as a loanword in Hebrew in *miskᵉnôṯ,* found only in the plural (Ex. 1:11; 1 K. 9:19; 2 Ch. 8:4,6; 16:4; 17:12; 32:28). Ex. 1:11 describes the cities Pithom and Rameses as *ʿārê miskᵉnôṯ*. Heinrich K. Brugsch therefore compares *miskᵉnôṯ* to Egyp. *meskenet* (clearly meaning *msḫn.t,* "resting place, temple").[5] It would not be wise to follow this suggestion, because the phonetic correspondence is too vague. 1 K. 9:19 (par. 2 Ch. 8:4,6), an account of Solomon's fortresses, refers to the *ʿārê miskᵉnôṯ* that Solomon had; LXX[A] here confuses

---

miškān. F. M. Cross Jr., "The Tabernacle," *BA,* 10 (1947), 45-68 = *BA Reader,* I (1961, repr. 1975), 201-228; V. Fritz, *Tempel und Zelt. WMANT,* 47 (1977); M. Görg, *Das Zelt der Begegnung. BBB,* 27 (1967); M. Haran, *Temples and Temple-Service in Ancient Israel* (Oxford, 1978); D. R. Hillers, "Mškn', 'Temple' in Inscriptions from Hatra," *BASOR,* 207 (1972), 54-56; W. Michaelis, "σκηνή," *TDNT,* VII, 368-394; L. Rost, "Die Wohnstätte des Zeugnisses," *Festschrift Friedrich Baumgärtel. ErF,* A10 (1959), 158-165; W. H. Schmidt, "מִשְׁכָּן als Ausdruck Jerusalemer Kultsprache," *ZAW,* 75 (1963), 91f.; R. Schmitt, *Zelt und Lade als Thema alttestamentlicher Wissenschaft* (Gütersloh, 1972).

1. *AHw,* II, 626b; *CAD,* X/1, 369-373.
2. See A. Falkenstein, *HO,* I, 2, sections 1-2, fascicle 1 (1959), 15. A. Goetze takes a different approach, pointing out that the meaning "threshing floor" can hardly derive from Akk. *šakānu,* so that the Akkadian word most likely borrowed this meaning from Sumerian ("The Meaning of Sumerian kislaḫ and Its Akkadian Equivalents," *AJSL,* 52 [1936], 154-56).
3. Malamat, "History and Prophetic Vision in a Mari Letter," *ErIsr,* 5 (1958), 67-73. For the Mari passage see A. Finet, *L'accadien des lettre de Mari. Compte-rendu des séances de la commission d'histoire,* ser. 2, 50/1 (1956), 58.
4. *AHw,* II, 627; *CAD,* X/1, 375f.
5. *Geschichte Ägyptens unter den Pharaonen* (Leipzig, 1877), 549.

misk^{e}nôṯ and *mišk^{e}nôṯ*. In a description of Jehoshaphat's wealth, 2 Ch. 17:12 mentions the *ʿārê misk^{e}nôṯ* built in Judah along with fortresses. We find *misk^{e}nôṯ* without *ʿārê* in 16:4; 32:28. In 16:4 some scholars, citing 1 K. 15:20, suggest that *misk^{e}nôṯ* came from *kinn^{e}rôṯ* > *kikk^{e}rôṯ*, replaced by *s^{e}ḇîḇôṯ* (cf. LXX *perichōrous*).[6] If instead *misk^{e}nôṯ* means "storehouses" (cf. Akkadian), then 2 Ch. 16:4 means that the commanders of Ben-hadad conquered not only Ijon, Dan, and Abel-maim, but also all the storehouses of the cities of Naphtali. In 32:28, finally, *misk^{e}nôṯ* for the yield of grain, wine, and oil are mentioned alongside stalls for cattle and treasuries (v. 27). This refers to storehouses serving as depots.[7] Heb. *misk^{e}nôṯ* thus borrowed and retained a specialized meaning of Akk. *maškanu*.

In two important passages in the Ugaritic texts, *mšknt* refers to the heavenly dwelling of the gods; both passages use *'hl,* "tent," in parallel.[8] In the Aramaic dialects, Jewish Aramaic and Christian Palestinian Aramaic examples are found as well as Syr. *mašk^{e}nā'*.[9] In the Ḥaṭra inscriptions *mškn'* appears in 281.3 with the meaning "tent";[10] it is probably a toponym for Maškēna = Maskin = Dujail in 50.3; 79.10.[11]

The word *maškna* plays a special role among the Mandeans. For example, Theodore ben Konai calls the Mandeans *mašk^{e}naiê,* "Maškeneans," i.e., "Templers," obviously because the earlier texts call their cultic sites *maškna*.[12] These "templets" (or, better, "cultic huts"), gabled rectangular structures made of reeds and clay, resemble ordinary huts in form. The term *maškna* merely borrows the OT technical term for the desert sanctuary without continuing a tent or dwelling-place tradition.

Finally, Arab. *maskan/maskin,* means "dwelling, house, residence."

2. *Occurrences.* The noun *miškān* appears 139 times in the Hebrew OT; 103 of its occurrences are in P (58 in Ex. 25–40; 30 in Nu. 1–10). The phrase *miškan hāʿēḏûṯ* appears 6 times (Ex. 38:21; Nu. 1:50,53[twice]; 10:11; 16:9) alongside *'ōhel hāʿēḏûṯ* (cf. Nu. 9:15; 17:23[Eng. v. 8]; 18:2). Apart from 8 occurrences in 1–2 Chronicles and Josh. 22:19,29; 2 S. 7:6, occurrences are in Isaiah (3), Jeremiah (3), Ezekiel (2), Habakkuk (1), Psalms (11), Job (3), and Song of Songs (1). The word appears once in an Aramaic context (Ezr. 7:15). A feminine plural form in *-ôṯ* appears 18 times (Nu. 24:5; Job 18:21; 21:28; 39:6; Ps. 43:3; 49:12[11]; 78:28; 84:2[1]; 87:2; 132:5,7; Cant. 1:8; Isa. 32:18; 54:2; Jer. 9:18[19]; 30:18; 51:30; Hab. 1:6), while a masculine plural form in *-îm* appears only twice (Ezk. 25:4; Ps. 46:5[4]). In Ps. 43:3; 84:2(1); 132:5,7, *miškānôṯ* denotes the temple as the dwelling place of Yahweh in Jerusalem; the plural

---

6. E.g., W. Rudolph, *Chronikbücher. HAT,* XXI (1955), 246.

7. Cf. P. Welten, *Die Königs-Stempel. ADPV* (1969), 124f.

8. *KTU,* 1.15, III, 18f.; 1.17, V, 32f. See Schmidt; cf. also M. Dahood, *RSP,* II, 15.

9. *LexSyr,* 776b.

10. R. Degen, *Neue Ephemeris für semitische Epigraphik,* 3 (Wiesbaden, 1978), 68f.; F. Vattioni, *Le iscrizioni di Ḥatra. AIONSup,* 28 (1981), 90.

11. Contra D. R. Hillers, who here and as a conj. in 29:9 reads *mškn',* for which he assumes the meaning "temple."

12. K. Rudolph, *Die Mandäer,* I (Göttingen, 1960), 31ff., 257f.

form is used as a kind of plural of majesty, not because the temple comprises a whole complex of structures.[13] Elsewhere *miškānôṯ* can be understood as a plural consisting of individual segments. By contrast, the masculine plural can be interpreted as a collective plural. In Ezk. 25:4 the phrase *nāṯan miškānîm* is presumably a periphrastic expansion of *šāḵan* analogous to Eng. "take up lodging" from "lodge." "In Ps. 46:5(4) the collective plural in *-îm* is highly meaningful as a superlative construction."[14]

II. 1. *Secular Usage.* The noun *miškān* is used only rarely to denote a human dwelling. It would be wrong to ascribe too much weight to Nu. 16:24,27, which speak of the *miškān* of Korah or of Korah, Dathan, and Abiram; in both cases we are dealing with the secondary redactional fusion of two narrative variants. The original text probably spoke of the *miškān* of Yahweh.

In Nu. 24:5; Job 21:28; Isa. 54:2; Jer. 30:18, *miškān* parallels → אהל *'ōhel.* In Nu. 24:5 Balaam in his third blessing praises the magnificence of Israel, which he perceives when he sees them encamped at his feet: "How fair are your tents, O Jacob, your dwellings, O Israel." Here *'ōhālîm* and *miškānôṯ* used in parallel clearly denote the lodgings of nomadic tribes. In the summation of Bildad's speech about the end of the ungodly in Job 18, v. 21 states: "Surely such are the dwellings of the ungodly, such is the place of one who does not know God." Here *māqôm* and *miškānôṯ* are parallel. It is questionable whether *miškānôṯ* can simply be translated as a singular.[15] It is better to follow Eduard König in taking *'awwāl* as a categorical term,[16] so that the text refers to the dwellings of the wicked — unless the plural reflects v. 14b and suggests the various sites of a tent within an area *(nāweh).*

In v. 28 of Job's sixth speech (Job 21:1-34), which describes the apparently wonderful life of the godless, Job addresses the question of his friends: "Where is the tent, the dwellings of the wicked?" The implication of the question is that the houses and dwellings of the wicked suddenly vanish away. The nouns *'ōhel* and *miškānôṯ* are apparently doublets. With MS. Kennicott 111 and the Vulg., one may delete *'ōhel,*[17] if the text does not allude once again to the various sites of a tent (cf. 18:21 and 18:14f.), so that *miškānôṯ* is added to *'ōhel.*

According to Ps. 78:28, the camp of the Israelites consisted of *miškānôṯ,* meaning tents, as several recent translations, including the EÜ, recognize. In Ezk. 25:1-5, an oracle against the Ammonites, v. 4 threatens that peoples of the east, unidentified desert tribes, will set up their encampments *(ṭîrôṯ)* in the territory of Ammon, thus taking up lodging *(nāṯan miškānîm)* there.

In Cant. 1:8 the Shulammite's beloved summons her to follow the tracks of the flock to come to the *miškānôṯ* of the shepherds, so that she can pasture her kids there; thus her beloved will find her. The noun *miškānôṯ* can hardly refer to fixed refuges; it means

---

13. As claimed, e.g., by H. Gunkel, *Die Psalmen. HAT,* II/2 (^{5}1968), 370.
14. D. Michel, *Grundlegungen einer hebräischen Syntax,* I (Neukirchen-Vluyn, 1977), 47.
15. As proposed, e.g., by G. Fohrer, *Das Buch Hiob. KAT,* XVI (1963), 297.
16. *Das Buch Hiob* (Gütersloh, 1929), 184.
17. As Fohrer does, for example.

the stopping places where the shepherds set up their camps for protection during the night.

Deutero-Isaiah's call to Jerusalem (Isa. 54:2) to extend without limit the curtains *(yᵉrîʿôṯ)* of her dwellings for the expected multitude of future inhabitants also uses the poetic metaphor of a tent camp. Hab. 1:6 states that at Yahweh's behest the Chaldeans will seize dwellings not their own. In a similar vein, in Jer. 9:18(19) the prophet hears the sound of wailing from Zion, which includes the destruction of Zion's dwellings. Neither passage refers explicitly to solid buildings in contrast to tents; the texts are speaking of dwellings without further qualification. Jer. 51:30, which threatens the dwellings of Babylon with fiery destruction, is to be understood in the same way. This more general sense of *miškān* is also found in 30:18: Yahweh will have compassion on the tents and dwellings of Jacob. Job 39:6 speaks in even more general terms of the dwelling places *(miškᵉnôṯāyw)* of the wild ass in the salt land *(mᵉlēḥâ)*.

By contrast, in Isa. 32:18 the promise of secure habitation envisions towns and villages. Isa. 22:16 calls the splendid tomb of the steward Shebna a *miškān,* thinking of a tomb formed like a small house, a houselike block cut from rock, containing a small chamber. Ps. 49:12(11) (where *qirbām* should probably be emended to *qᵉḇārîm*) refers similarly to graves as homes and dwelling places.

When Ps. 87:2 says that Yahweh loves the gates of Zion more than all the dwellings of Jacob, the reference is clearly to the election of the Jerusalem temple. In the light of Nu. 24:5; Jer. 30:18, however, it is unlikely that *miškᵉnôṯ yaʿᵃqōḇ* refers to cultic sites outside Jerusalem, i.e., all the other temples in Israel.[18] The dwellings of Jacob are a metaphor for the commonwealth and its members.

We have seen that *miškān* in the sense of human habitation is frequently used with *'ōhel;* in a few places, however, it can also refer to fixed settlements and villages. Manfred Görg may be correct in thinking that *miškān* can describe a habitation where one dwells without right of ownership — not a permanent residence but a temporary domicile.[19]

2. *P.* In the present complex text of P, two notions are interwoven: one envisions a tent, the other a wooden structure. It is an open question whether the two notions can be assigned to two distinct literary strata or tradition-historical considerations instead account for the material discrepancies in descriptions of the "dwelling."[20] It is also possible that directions for constructing a wooden building modeled on the Jerusalem temple were incorporated by P into earlier rituals associated with making the tent.[21] Apart from this question, it must be noted that the current text presents a construction that cannot function in reality: the wooden structure, e.g., does not fit into the tent.[22]

---

18. As proposed by H.-J. Kraus, *Psalms 60–150* (Eng. trans., Minneapolis, 1989), 186.

19. Pp. 106ff.

20. For the former see K. Galling, *Exodus. HAT,* III (1939), 132ff.; for the latter see M. Noth, *Exodus. OTL* (Eng. trans. 1962), 211ff.

21. K. Koch, *Die Priesterschrift von Exodus 25 bis Leviticus 16. FRLANT,* 71 (1959), 8f., 13ff.

22. Galling, 135.

Ex. 26:1,6 describe the *miškān* as being made up of curtains (*y*ᵉ*rî*ʿ*ōṯ*); 26:15-30 orders the *miškān* to be made as a wooden structure that originally has nothing to do with the tent in 26:1-14. The wooden framework is roofless and open in front because the structure is to be lodged inside the tent: its roof is replaced by the roof of the tent and its front or east side is replaced by the curtain provided at the entrance to the tent. It is not always clear how the wood is assembled. Since each frame is to be a cubit and a half wide, the north and south sides, consisting of twenty frames (26:18,20), are both 30 cubits long. It is more difficult to determine the width of the structure. Six frames are to be made for the west side, so that commentators usually speak of 10 cubits in round numbers. The obscure and probably revised text in 26:23f. mentions two corner frames; it is unclear whether these are two additional frames (as v. 25 assumes) or two of the six frames making up the rear wall that are specially fabricated. Yohanan Aharoni has observed that the ratio of 20 to 6 frames corresponds to the dimensions of the Arad temple: 20 by 6 cubits.[23] If we reject the attempt to make the dimensions of the *miškān* half those of the Jerusalem temple (60 cubits long, 20 wide [1 K. 6:2]), this observation could show that the original figures in 26:15ff. preserve a construction tradition that is not identical with that of Jerusalem but reflects an "ancient Israel temple construction tradition,"[24] associated secondarily with the dimensions of the Jerusalem temple.

In the secondary sections of P, most of the occurrences of *miškān* (e.g., Ex. 35:15,18; 36:14,20,22; but also Nu. 3:23,25,26,29,35,36,38; etc.) have come to denote the complex tent sanctuary; the noun is thus another name, with different nuances, for the *'ōhel mô*ʿ*ēḏ*. When Ex. 38:21; Nu. 1:50,53(twice); 10:11; 16:9 speak of the *miškān hā*ʿ*ēḏûṯ* (alongside *'ōhel hā*ʿ*ēḏûṯ:* Nu. 9:15; 17:23[8]; 18:2), they are thinking of the *miškān* as the repository for the ark with the testimony (*'ᵃrôn hā*ʿ*ēḏûṯ:* Ex. 25:22; 26:33f.; etc.). When these passages call the tent of meeting the "dwelling of the testimony," there is a tendency to turn the tent into a "reliquary." "Now there dwells in the midst of the people only the document in which Yahweh proffers himself to his people as God; the immediacy of 'I am with you' threatens to vanish."[25]

3. *The Dwelling of Yahweh outside P.* The language and conceptual world of Josh. 22:9-34 are dependent on P; in the midst of reproaches against the eastern tribes, v. 19 points out that the dwelling of Yahweh already dwells (*šāḵan*) in Yahweh's own land, so that it would be wrong to build more altars (cf. the exculpatory response in v. 29). Here it is probably the sanctuary at Shiloh that is called *miškān YHWH*. In the Psalms, too, one text (78:60) mentions the *miškān* of Shiloh. The other texts (26:8; 43:3; 46:5[4]; 74:7; 84:2[1]; 132:5,7) always refer to the Jerusalem sanctuary: it is the goal of

23. "The Solomonic Temple, the Tabernacle and the Arad Sanctuary," *Orient and Occident. Festschrift C. H. Gordon. AOAT,* 22 (1973), 1-8.

24. Fritz, 164.

25. Rost, 165.

pilgrimage (132:7; cf. also 43:3); it is lovely (84:2[1]) and especially loved by the psalmist (26:8) because the glory of Yahweh dwells there. In a similar vein, Yahweh proclaims in Ezk. 37:27 that his dwelling place will be in the midst of his people for all time; thus the nations shall know that Yahweh sanctifies Israel. The term *miškān* here refers to the Jerusalem temple.

Chronicles employs the language of P. When 1 Ch. 23:26 records that the Levites used to carry the dwelling, *miškān* means the tent sanctuary of the desert period. In 1 Ch. 6:23; 2 Ch. 29:6, however, the reference is to the Jerusalem temple as successor to the desert sanctuary. The pleonastic phrase *miškan 'ōhel mô'ēḏ* in 1 Ch. 6:17 appears already in Ex. 39:32; 40:2,6,29. The expression *miškan YHWH* in 1 Ch. 16:39; 21:29 also has its prototype in P (Lev. 17:4; Nu. 16:9; 19:13). Only the phrase *miškan bêṯ hā'elōhîm* in 1 Ch. 6:33 is not dependent on formulations found in the Pentateuch. This independent creation of the Chronicler links the temple of Solomon, the "house of God," with the term "dwelling," the sanctuary of the desert period, thus making an identification also undertaken in Ps. 74:7; 84:2(1); 132:5; Ezk. 37:27; 2 Ch. 29:6.[26]

The language of 2 S. 7:6 presents a special problem. Yahweh rejects David's plan to build a temple, saying that he has never dwelt in a house since he brought the Israelites out of Egypt; he has instead been moving about *be'ōhel ûḇemiškān.* It is hardly allowable to understand the phrase as a hendiadys for "tent dwelling" or to interpret the *waw* as a *waw explicativum* in the sense of "with a tent for a dwelling."[27] In the parallel text, 1 Ch. 17:5, the MT reads *mē'ōhel 'el-'ōhel ûmimmiškān.* Many exegetes add *'el-miškān,* following the Targ., so that the meaning is that Yahweh has moved about from tent to tent and from dwelling place to dwelling place. Some scholars consider this the original text and emend 2 S. 7:6 accordingly; Wilhelm Rudolph, e.g., identifies the original text as reading "I moved about in a tent from dwelling place to dwelling place"; he cites the Targ., which explicitly mentions Nob, Shiloh, and Gibeon as stopping places of the tent sheltering the ark.[28] This approach is hardly appropriate, for it puts too much faith in the text of Chronicles.

The formulation *be'ōhel ûḇemiškān* in 2 S. 7:6 (perhaps originally with the article) is probably based on the notion of the tent and framework desert sanctuary of Ex. 26. If Priestly traditions and notions find expression in the language of 2 S. 7:6, the purpose might be "to emphasize the continued existence of the desert sanctuary until the building of the temple (1 K. 8:4)."[29] The sanctuary at Shiloh was not taken into consideration, possibly because it was considered cursed since its destruction.

III. 1. *Dead Sea Scrolls.* The word *miškān* does not play any role in the Dead Sea Scrolls — not even in the Temple Scroll. Only in two fragmentary liturgical texts do we find one occurrence each of *mškn.* The *miškān* is mentioned in conjunction with Jerusalem

---

26. Ibid., 161.

27. For the former see, e.g., R. Kittel, *Das zweite Buch Samuel. HSAT,* I (^{4}1922), in loc. For the latter see, e.g., F. Stolz, *Die erste und zweite Buch Samuel. ZBK,* 9 (1981), 298.

28. W. Rudolph, *HAT,* XXI, 130ff.

29. Schmitt, 302.

in 4QDibHam[a] (4Q504) fr. 1-2 4:2, while a liturgy for the Sabbath burnt offering (4QshirShabb[f] [4Q405] fr. 20-22 7[30]) uses *miškān* to refer to the heavenly temple.

2. *LXX.* The LXX's rendering of *miškān* as *skēnḗ* (93 times; once *kataskḗnōsis,* 17 times *skḗnōma*) is striking. Since *skēnḗ* also translates *'ōhel,* the LXX ignores P's distinction between *'ōhel* and *miškān,* apparent even at the level of literary analysis. The use of *skēnḗ* has been cited as evidence that *miškān* originally meant "tent."[31] The LXX translators, however, probably chose *skēnḗ* to translate *miškān* because both words contain three similar consonants in the same order *(s-k-n).*[32]

D. Kellermann†

---

30. J. Strugnell, "The Angelic Liturgy at Qumran — 4Q Serek Šîrôt ʿŌlat Haššābāt," *Congress Volume, Oxford 1959. SVT,* 7 (1960), 318-345, esp. 335ff.
31. Cross, *BA Reader,* I, 227.
32. *TDNT,* VII, 371f.

מָשַׁל *māšal* I; מָשָׁל *māšāl*

Contents: I. 1. OT; 2. Other Semitic Languages; 3. Etymology. II. *mšl* I and *māšāl:* 1. *māšal* I; 2. *māšāl;* 3. Origin of the Term.

I. 1. *OT.* The verbal root *mšl* occurs in the OT with two different semantic domains, which etymologically represent two distinct roots. (a) The denominative verb *māšal* I (qal and piel), "formulate an expression," derives from *māšāl,* "saying, proverb."[1]

---

māšal I. A. Alt, "Die Weisheit Salomos," *KlSchr,* II (1953), 90-99; O. Eissfeldt, *Der Maschal im AT. BZAW,* 24 (1913); P. Fiebig, *Altjüdische Gleichnisse und die Gleichnisse Jesu* (Tübingen, 1904); idem, *Die Gleichnisreden Jesu im Lichte der rabbinischen Gleichnisse des neutestamentlichen Zeitalters* (Tübingen, 1912); H. Fuchs, "Sprichwörter," *Jüdisches Lexikon,* V (1930), 580f.; A. H. Godbey, "The Hebrew *Mašal,*" *AJSL,* 39 (1922/23), 89-108; F. Hauck, "παραβολή. B. OT, Septuagint, Later Judaism," *TDNT,* V, 747-751; P. Haupt, "Moses' Song of Triumph," *AJSL,* 20 (1903/4), 149-172; J. Hempel, *Die althebräische Literatur und ihr hellenistisch-jüdisches Nachleben* (1934; Berlin, [2]1967); A. S. Herbert, "The 'Parable' *(māšāl)* in the OT," *SJT,* 7 (1954), 180-196; H.-J. Hermisson, *Studien zur israelitischen Spruchweisheit. WMANT,* 28 (1968); A. R. Johnson, "מָשָׁל," *Wisdom in Israel and in the Ancient Near East. Festschrift H. H. Rowley. SVT,* 3 (1955), 162-69; J. Krengel, "Maschal," *Jüdisches Lexikon,* III (1929), 1411-15; G. M. Landes, "Jonah: A *Mašal,*" *Israelite Wisdom. Festschrift S. Terrien* (Missoula, 1978), 137-158; T. Polk, "Paradigms, Parables, and *mešālîm,*" *CBQ,* 45 (1983), 564-583; G. Rinaldi, "Alcuni termini ebraici relativi alla letteratura," *Bibl,* 40 (1959), 279-281; D. W. Suter, "*Māšāl* in the Similitudes of Enoch," *JBL,* 100 (1981), 193-212.

1. *HAL,* II, 647f.

One should note also a niphal meaning "be like," a hithpael "become like," and a hiphil "compare," which clearly derive from Proto-Sem. **mṯl* with a basic meaning "be like" no longer found in the OT. (b) *mšl* II, "rule," derives from Proto-Sem. **mšl*.[2]

2. *Other Semitic Languages.* In Akkadian the verbal root *mšl* I appears as *mašālu(m)* with a basic meaning "be(come) equal," which extends to the concept of equal portions (*mišlu,* "half"; *mišlānu,* "half share").[3] While the root *mšl* I (< *mṯl*) is not yet attested in the Ugaritic lexicon, it appears in the Northwest Semitic languages in Jewish Aram. and Syr. *mᵉṯal,* "compare," as well as in Arab. *maṯala,* "resemble" (cf. *miṯl,* "similarity"), OSA *mṯl,* "similar; likeness," and Eth. *masala,* "resemble."

3. *Etymology.* Although the root *mšl* II, "rule," and its derivatives are used more frequently than *mšl* I (98 and 58 occurrences, respectively), scholarly discussion has focused primarily on the literary genre associated with the term *māšāl.* Only rarely has the relationship between the two different meanings been discussed. As mentioned above, two distinct roots are involved. Attempts to derive them from a common basic meaning[4] depend for the most part on intellectual abstraction and run counter to the lexicographic evidence just cited.

For the verbal root *mšl* of Biblical Hebrew, it is likely that the basic meaning of the qal as evidenced by the meanings of the hithpael, niphal, and hiphil as well as by the parallels in related Semitic languages has been displaced by the denominative meaning "formulate an expression, show a parable; recite derisive verses,"[5] related to the noun *māšāl,* which clearly denotes a literary concept. The original meaning appears to be preserved only in the derivative *mōšel,* "equal," in Job 41:25(Eng. v. 33): "On earth it [Leviathan] has no equal." What relationship (if any) there is between the noun *māšal,* which denotes a kind of saying, and the verb *māšal* I, with the basic meaning "be like," will be examined later.[6]

II. *mšl* I and *māšāl*.

1. *māšal I.* The original meaning of the verb *mšl* I, "be like,"[7] has been preserved only in the derived stems (hithpael, niphal, hiphil), as well as in the derivative *mōšel* mentioned above. The majority of texts express the futility of life, describing a human being who becomes like the dead in the underworld (Isa. 14:10: the king of Babylon; Job 30:19; Ps. 28:1; 49:13,21[12,20]; 143:7: the speaker). Only in Isa. 46:5 does Yahweh speak of his own incomparability (*mšl* par. *dmh* piel par. *šwh* hiphil).

---

2. Ibid., 647.

3. *AHw,* II, 623f., 661.

4. *WTM,* III, 280; Hempel, 44; B. Gemser, *Sprüche Salomos. HAT,* XVI (^{2}1963), 8; cf. Eissfeldt, 1-6.

5. *HAL,* II, 647.

6. See II.3 below.

7. Eissfeldt, 6.

2. *māšāl.* Whether the noun *māšāl* is a literary term is disputed. The book of Proverbs bears the superscription *mišlê šᵉlōmōh* (Prov. 1:1), and this designation recurs at the beginning of the smaller collections that the book comprises (10:1; 25:1). By clearly listing several synonyms, 1:6 illustrates the range of meanings covered by *māšāl* in the book of Proverbs. Eccl. 12:9 uses *māšāl* in the same sense. The nature and purpose of such sayings are indicated in Prov. 1:2-6 (cf. also 26:7,9). The claim of Solomonic authorship for the biblical books of Proverbs and Ecclesiastes is based on 1 K. 5:12(4:32), although we must note that this passage probably refers also to kinds of sayings and proverbs other than those in these particular books.[8] The expansion of individual didactic sayings into discursive instruction is likewise called *māšāl* (cf. Ps. 49:5[4]), as is retrospective reflection on the history of the nation, because it gives instruction (78:2). Job's general discourses are also called *māšāl* (Job 27:1; 29:1). There are, however, situations where such instruction couched in wise sayings is of dubious value (13:12: "Your maxims are proverbs of ashes").

Didactic sayings and discourses like those found in OT Wisdom Literature are not, however, the only literary genres called *māšāl.* The word also has its place in prophetic proclamation, where it refers to an oracle spoken as the result of a vision or inspiration (cf. the Balaam oracles in Nu. 23:7,18; 24:3,15,20f.,23). It is also applied to a veiled statement concerning the future, more like a riddle[9] or allegory; Ezekiel frequently uses such statements (Ezk. 17:2; 24:3; cf. the complaint of his hearers over this form of prophetic proclamation cited in 21:5[20:49]).

To find the basic meaning of the noun *māšāl,* we must draw on the utterances called *māšāl* that are quoted verbatim; these are found in 1 S. 10:12; 24:14(13); Ezk. 12:22; 18:2.[10] Since they are quoted frequently and in varied form (1 S. 10:12 par. 19:24 [cf. Jer. 23:28b]; Ezk. 18:2 par. Jer. 31:29; 1 S. 24:14[13] resembles Ezk. 16:44; Ezk. 12:22 is turned on its head by v. 23), they can be called "proverbs" or "maxims."

By reversal of the notion found in Gen. 12:3; 48:20, the expression "become a proverb" (Dt. 28:37) comes to signify Yahweh's punishment of his people (1 K. 9:7 par. 2 Ch. 7:20; Ps. 44:15[14]; Jer. 24:9; Ezk. 16:44; Mic. 2:4) as well as mockery of the misfortunes of others (Isa. 14:4: the king of Babylon in the underworld; Ezk. 14:8: the idolaters among the people of Israel; Hab. 2:6: the oppressors of Israel; Ps. 69:12[11]: the devout psalmist; Job 17:6: Job himself). People who are experts at taunt songs are therefore called *mōšᵉlîm* (Nu. 21:17 [here a war or victory song]; Isa. 28:14; Ezk. 16:44 clearly uses a proverb in a mocking sense).

3. *Origin of the Term.* This survey raises the questions of how so many different literary forms have come to bear this collective designation *māšāl,* with which of these concepts the word was originally associated, and how they are related among them-

---

8. Alt (p. 91) thinks in terms of "scholarly lists" based on Egyptian models and more like natural science.

9. → חידה *ḥîḏâ* (IV, 320-23).

10. Eissfeldt, 7f.

selves. Despite the methodological objections of H. J. Hermisson, Otto Eissfeldt is probably correct in seeing a development from simple, prosaic popular proverbs to taunt songs on the one hand and to poetically framed wisdom sayings on the other.[11] He also brings together parable, oracle, and allegory. The term *māšāl* was applied to the two literary genres of "proverb" and "parable" until well into the rabbinic period.[12]

The use of the word *māšāl,* from the verbal root *mšl* I, "be like," is easy to explain for parables; note the introductory formula *'emšōl lᵉḵā māšāl: lᵉmâ haddāḇār dômeh.*[13] This is not true for proverbs, since they do not always comprise two equal halves[14] nor do they always contain an extended simile, like many of the sayings in Prov. 25f. (25:13; 26:1f.,8,11).

Closer examination of the proverbs cited by Eissfeldt[15] shows, however, that they all deal with two entities that are compared on the basis of some relationship: Saul and the prophets (1 S. 10:12; 19:24), the wicked and their deeds (1 S. 24:14[13]), straw and wheat (Jer. 23:28b), the prophetic oracle and its realization (Ezk. 12:22f.), mother and daughter (16:44), the actions of the fathers and the effects they have on the sons (18:2 par. Jer. 31:29). Thus these sayings are rightly called *māšāl* (possibly: "similitude" or "simile") in the sense of a simple popular saying figuratively representing a relationship of likeness or unlikeness. These may then be considered the primary form of the *māšāl,* which Eissfeldt thinks was "no longer extant."[16]

This kind of proverb continued to be common well into the NT period. Jesus quotes such a proverb in Lk. 4:23 ("Doctor, cure yourself");[17] like the OT proverbs, it deals with a relationship between the doctors and the medical arts they practice. They can help others, but they cannot help themselves.

We conclude, then, that the term *māšāl* originally denoted only a simple popular proverb that figuratively described a comparative relationship, capable of generalization, between two entities, which were judged accordingly to be "like" or "unlike." The proverb form led to artfully structured poetic sayings, while the similes at the heart of such sayings developed into parables. The word *māšāl* in its original sense goes back directly to the basic meaning of the verbal root *māšal* I, "be like." The denominated meaning now found in the OT is a later development.

Beyse

11. Eissfeldt, 42f.; cf. Hermisson, 38-49.
12. Hauck, 750f.; Fiebig, *Gleichnisreden,* 6.
13. Fiebig, *Gleichnisreden,* 17.
14. As claimed by Haupt, 150.
15. See above.
16. P. 42.
17. Hauck, 750.

מָשַׁל *māšal* II; מֹשֶׁל *mōšel;* מִמְשָׁל *mimšāl;* מֶמְשָׁלָה *memšālâ*

Contents: I. The Root *mšl,* "Rule": 1. Statistics; 2. LXX. II. OT Usage: 1. General; 2. Political; 3. "Self-Control"; 4. Yahweh; 5. Nouns; 6. Theological Significance. III. Dead Sea Scrolls.

I. The Root *mšl,* "Rule." Heb. *mšl* represents the coalescence of two different roots: *mšl* I = Proto-Sem. **mṯl,* "be like, resemble, speak a parable, sing a taunt song"; *mšl* II = Proto-Sem. **mšl,* "rule, govern." In Northwest Semitic (Phoenician, Punic, Old Aramaic), the meaning "rule" is attested in only a few texts.[1]

1. *Statistics.* The root *mšl* occurs 79 times in the OT: 76 times in the qal (including 24 occurrences of the ptcp.) and 3 times in the hiphil. It is especially frequent in the Pentateuch, the Deuteronomistic history, Psalms, Proverbs, and Isaiah. Occurrences of the verb are distributed as follows: Pentateuch, 10; Deuteronomistic history, 13; Chronicles, 5; Nehemiah, 1; Psalms, 10; Job, 1; Proverbs, 11; Ecclesiastes, 2; Lamentations, 1; Isaiah, 9; Jeremiah, 5; Ezekiel, 2; Daniel, 5; Joel, 1; Micah, 1; Habakkuk, 1; Zechariah, 1. Three nouns derive from *mšl: mōšel* (Dnl. 11:4; Zec. 9:10), *mimšāl* (1 Ch. 26:6; Dnl. 11:3,5), and the comparatively frequent *memšālâ,* which appears 17 times (Genesis, 2; Kings, 2; 2 Chronicles, 2; Psalms, 5; Isaiah, 2; Jeremiah, 2; Daniel, 1; Micah, 1). The root is used 20 times in the Hebrew text of Sirach; 15 of these occurrences are forms of the participle.[2]

2. *LXX.* The LXX usually uses *árchein* or *kyrieúein* to translate *mšl,* without apparent distinction. The translator of Proverbs prefers *krateín,* while the translator of Psalms uses *despózein* for the dominion of God. On rare occasions, *dynasteúein* is used. The translator of Sirach adds *krítēs, hēgoúmenos,* and *exousía.*

II. OT Usage.

1. *General.* Throughout the entire OT, *mšl* appears in texts that substantiate the all-embracing order of the whole created world and assign the activity of ruling to both God and human beings. Thus the divine plan determines the course of the world and human life. Ps. 8:7(Eng. v. 6) may be considered paradigmatic: all human dominion derives from God, who alone empowers mortals to exercise dominion. In this group

---

māšal II. W. H. Brownlee, *The Midrash Pesher of Habakkuk. SBLMS,* 24 (1979), 143f.; N. Lohfink, "*melek, šallîṭ* und *môšēl* bei Kohelet und die Abfassungszeit des Buches," *Bibl,* 62 (1981), 535-543; J. A. Soggin, *Das Königtum in Israel. BZAW,* 104 (1967); *idem,* "משל *mšl* 'to rule,' " *TLOT,* II, 689-691; → מלך *melek̠* (VIII, 346-375).

1. *DISO,* 171.

2. F. Vattioni, *Ecclesiastico, testo ebraico* (Naples, 1968); D. Barthélemy and O. Rickenbacher, *Konkordanz zum hebräischen Sirach* (Göttingen, 1973), 243f.

of texts, *mšl* is usually constructed with b^e. God gives human beings dominion over other people (Gen. 3:16 [male over female]; Ex. 21:8; Dt. 15:6; cf. Prov. 22:7; 1QS 9:22; CD 13:12; 1QH 12:23; for the dominion of human beings over creation, Gen. 1:28 uses → רדה *rādâ,* found elsewhere only in 1QS 3:17f. with *memšālâ*). Such dominion can be treated as a curse (Gen. 3:16) or lead to disaster (37:8).[3] God can also punish people by depriving them of a ruler (Hab. 1:14). To have evil rulers is a sign of God's judgment and punishment (Ps. 106:41; Prov. 12:24; 17:2; Lam. 5:8). The sons of Jacob take offense when Joseph claims dominion over them (Gen. 37:8: *mālak̠, māšal*). The wide range of meanings associated with *mšl* is also illustrated by its use in Gen. 24:1; Ps. 105:21 for the administration of property.

2. *Political.* In the majority of texts, this general meaning of *mšl* moves in the more specialized direction of political dominion. Its meaning thus comes close to that of → מלך *mlk.* In comparison with *mlk,* however, *mšl* focuses less on the person of the ruler and more on the rule or dominion itself. In Gen. 45:8,26, *mšl* denotes Joseph's rule over Egypt under Pharaoh. Josh. 12:2,5 similarly describe the rule of various Transjordanian kings, and Jgs. 14:4; 15:11 speak of the Philistines' dominion of the land of Canaan. In Jgs. 8:22f. Gideon refuses to rule over Israel, since to do so would impugn the kingship of Yahweh. In 1 K. 5:1(4:21); 2 Ch. 9:26, *mšl* describes Solomon's rule over the Israelite empire (cf. 2 Ch. 7:18; 4QpGen^a [4Q252] 5:1).

According to Isa. 3:4,12; 14:5; 19:4, incompetence or tyrannical cruelty characterizes the rule of the sovereigns Yahweh sends as punishment for both his own people and Egypt (cf. Jer. 51:46; Prov. 29:12; Eccl. 9:17[4]). The ptcp. *mōšēl* is used neutrally in Prov. 23:1; 29:26; Eccl. 10:4, which give advice on how to behave in the presence of rulers. In Jer. 30:21; Zec. 6:13, the verb is used positively for the restoration of the people under a new ruler of their own.[5] The apocalyptic interpretation of history in Dnl. 11:3-5,39,43 uses *mšl* and its derivatives for the enormous power and authority wielded by future kings as world rulers.

3. *"Self-Control."* In a different kind of specialization, *mšl* is used for self-control. In Gen. 4:7 Yahweh tells Cain to resist "sin," his enemy, and master it. The psalmist prays in Ps. 19:14(13) that Yahweh will protect him from the dominion of the insolent. According to Prov. 16:32, one who exercises self-control is better than the mighty and victorious conqueror of cities (cf. 17:2; 22:7; 29:2).

4. *Yahweh.* All these texts ultimately reflect the fundamental biblical notion that in the strict sense Yahweh is the ruler pure and simple, as Job 25:2 states absolutely. Here the participle is used abstractly.

This fundamental principle applies in a special way to Israel, which in the earliest

---

3. For the former → ארר *'arr* (I, 405-418); for the latter see below.
4. See Lohfink, 541ff.
5. See below for a discussion of Mic. 5:1(2).

premonarchic period considered itself a theocracy and recognized Yahweh as its true king even in the sphere of earthly politics, as Jgs. 8:23 illustrates. Hand in hand with this understanding goes the conviction that Yahweh is the ruler of the universe by virtue of his act of creation. In the prayers of David (1 Ch. 29:12) and Jehoshaphat (2 Ch. 20:6), *mšl* therefore refers to God's universal kingship. Knowing that Yahweh rules the whole world, Isa. 40:10 promises the special intervention of this royal God to accomplish the second exodus, from Babylon. In a similar vein, in 63:19 the people pray that God will appear to exercise judgment on the nations.

The steadfast faith that Yahweh is ruler of the whole universe by virtue of creation and absolute sovereignty in history finds particular expression (with *mšl*) in the Psalms. In their various ways, Ps. 22:29(28); 59:14(13); 66:7; 103:19[6] affirm Yahweh as lord of the nations and ruler of the universe. In 89:10(9) Yahweh's incomparable power is demonstrated in a natural phenomenon; the text celebrates the God for whom it is child's play to subdue even water, the most violent element.

Mic. 5:1(2) uses the qal active participle in promising the future messianic ruler for Israel. The choice of *mšl* instead of *mlk* may indicate that the rule of the Messiah is not a continuation of the Jewish kingship but signifies a new beginning, in which a qualitatively different dominion is realized. On the intimate involvement of the Davidides in this notion, cf. Mic. 4:8; Jer. 33:26; Zec. 9:9f.; negatively Jer. 22:30. In a similar fashion, the unique dominion of the Messiah is distinguished from the theocracy of Yahweh. Use of *mlk* could have suggested a kind of "competition" with the kingship of Yahweh (Pss. 47,93,96–99; but cf. 22:29[28]; 103:19; 145:13, where both *mlk* and *mšl* are used with reference to God). For the early period of Israel, the same eschewing of *mlk* and the concomitant emphasis on the unique kingship of God are attested by Jgs. 8:22f.; 9:2, in which the verb *mšl* is chosen deliberately for both God and the earthly ruler. Contrariwise, *mšl* is not used for the priestly supremacy expected in the future (cf. Zec. 6:13).

5. *Nouns.* In Dnl. 11:3,5, the rare noun *mimšāl* envisions the extraordinary power of the future rulers; in 1 Ch. 26:6 it denotes the authority exercised by the heads of families. As a rule, however, it suggests a claim to dominion over extensive territory. It is used in 1 K. 9:19; 2 Ch. 8:6, e.g., to emphasize the vast empire of Israel under King Solomon. Similarly 2 K. 20:13 par. Isa. 39:2 describes the extensive territory ruled by Hezekiah; Jer. 34:1; 51:28 depict the broad extent of the Babylonian Empire. Mic. 4:8 states that Israel will be restored to its former dominion by Yahweh, its God, that former dominion having been made by the deliverance from Egypt (Ps. 114:1f.; cf. the parallel: Judah becomes the sanctuary [*qōdeš*] of Yahweh).

God's dominion endures everlastingly from generation to generation (Ps. 145:13). The same noun is used in 2 Ch. 32:9 to describe the great "forces" of Sennacherib (par. 2 K. 18:17, *ḥayil kāḇēḏ*). But Isa. 22:21 uses the same term for the "authority" of Shebna, the governor of Palestine, again illustrating the wide semantic range of *mšl.*

---

6. See M. Dahood, *Bibl,* 48 (1967), 434.

6. *Theological Significance.* According to Ps. 8:7(6), all dominion originates in the fundamental divine order governing the universe, especially the human realm. It is meant to serve this superior purpose (cf. Gen. 1:26,28, where *rāḏâ* is used instead). This notion helps explain the striking use of *mšl* in Gen. 1:16-18 to describe the function of the heavenly bodies: they serve as God's world clock, a necessary preparation for the biosphere, without which there could be no vegetation and no life on earth. Ps. 136:8f. takes up this idea and relates it back to Yahweh in a hymn of praise. This singular usage also demonstrates that *mšl* includes an element of service, an aspect that is demonstrably present in most texts (in contrast to the usage of *mlk*). Seldom, however, does this element stand so much in the foreground as in these passages about the task of the sun, moon, and stars.

According to Gen. 3:16; Dt. 15:6; Ps. 106:41, dominion is connected directly or indirectly with judgment on sin. Thus dominion can become a punishment for a now sinful humanity and a sinful people. Jgs. 2:23; Job 25:2; Ps. 8:7(6) trace all manifestations and varieties of *mšl* back to the absolute dominion of God and derive it from God. God is the beginning and end of all "dominion" in the universe and among human beings.

III. Dead Sea Scrolls. The Dead Sea Scrolls largely continue OT usage. The root is comparatively frequent in 1QS, 1QH, 1QM, and 1QpHab. The last (1QpHab 8:9) uses *māšal,* "rule," to interpret *māšāl,* "taunt song," in Hab. 2:6.[7] Nouns are twice as common as the verb. In Ps. 151:4,11 (11QPs[a]), the qal active participle appears twice. It is noteworthy, however, that the word appears more frequently in negative contexts, e.g., to describe domination by an evil spirit (1QH 13:15; CD 12:2; cf. 1QS 1:18,23f.; 1QM 1:5; etc.). Messianic dominion is nevertheless still associated with the Davidic dynasty (1QSb 5:20; 4QpIs[a] 4:4).

On the basis of Ps. 114:2, the Qumran community considers itself the *memšālâ* of God (1QS 9:24). This *memšālâ* will ultimately gain victory over Belial (cf. 1QM 18:1,11). When the scrolls speak of the dominion *(memšālâ)* of the heavenly bodies (developing the idea of Gen. 1:16ff.: 1QS 10:1; 1QH 12:6,9; 1Q34 fr. 3 2:3), the notion of "management" appears alongside that of dominion. Of special interest is 1QH 1:17, according to which everything in the world has its place and its temporally limited *memšālâ*.

H. Gross

---

7. See Brownlee, 143.

מִשְׁמֶרֶת *mišmereṯ*

Contents: I. Akk. *maṣṣartu.* II. Heb. *mišmereṯ/šōmēr mišmereṯ:* 1. P; 2. Ezekiel; 3. Postexilic Literature. III. Other Forms: 1. *hāyâ leмišmereṯ;* 2. *mišmereṯ YHWH.* IV. Postbiblical Usage.

I. Akk. *maṣṣartu.* Heb. *mišmereṯ* has a parallel in Akk. *maṣṣartu,* whose basic meaning in combination with the related verb *naṣāru (naṣāru maṣṣarta = šāmar mišmereṯ)* is "watch, attend to, observe." This idiomatic phrase appears frequently in the general sense of being diligent or attentive in one's occupation or profession.[1] A further nuance is discernible when the object being watched is vulnerable or threatened, which is usually the case in military contexts, e.g., "they should protect the town and work their fields" *(maṣṣarti ālam liṣṣurū u eqelšunu līpušū).*[2]

The ambiguity of many contexts conceals the inherent nuances of the term. In general we must rely on contextual evidence such as military terminology to determine the specific differentia of "watching." Significant for *mišmereṯ* is the use of *maṣṣartu* with reference to the temple, sometimes with the meaning "guard": "in order to increase the security of Esagila I had Babylon surrounded with a wall" *(aššum maṣṣarti Esagila dunnuni . . . dūra danna . . . Bābilam ušaḫir);*[3] and: "I rebuilt the enclosure wall and made that temple into a secure place" *(bīta šuāti ana maṣṣartim dannatim aškunšu).*[4]

In numerous other examples *maṣṣartu* is used with reference to the temple, but we cannot with certainty define the meaning as "guard" or more generally "watch over" in the sense of conscientious stewardship. One text uses *dullu,* the Akkadian equivalent of Heb. *ʿaḇōḏâ,* in parallel with *maṣṣartu:* "I shall do corvée work on my fief, I shall perform my duty on my fief" *(dulli šá bīt bēlēia eppaš maṣṣartu ša bīt bēlēia anaṣṣar).*[5] Sometimes the aspect of stewardship stands clearly in the foreground: "Be not careless in the service of Eanna (specifically) with regard to the land of the farmworkers and whatever else I have entrusted to you" *(ina muḫḫi EN.NUN maṣṣarti ša Eanna zēri ša ikkārāti u mimma mala apqidakku la taselli).*[6]

---

mišmereṯ. A. Cody, *A History of OT Priesthood. AnBibl,* 35 (1969); M. Haran, "The Priestly Image of the Tabernacle," *HUCA,* 36 (1965), 191-226; J. Liver, *Chapters in the History of the Priests and Levites* (Jerusalem, 1968); J. Milgrom, "Israel's Sanctuary, the Priestly 'Picture of Dorian Gray,'" *RB,* 83 (1976), 390-99; *idem, Studies in Levitical Terminology* (Los Angeles, 1970).

1. A. Tremayne, *Records from Erech: Time of Cyrus and Cambyses. YOSBT,* VII (1925), 156, 14; *ABL,* 337, rto. 8.
2. *ARM,* IV, 10, rto. 11; quoted from *CAD,* X/1, 335b.
3. *VAB,* IV, 118, ii, 57; quoted from *CAD,* X/1, 337.
4. A. T. Clay, *Miscellaneous Inscriptions in the Yale Babylonian Collection. YOSBT,* I (1915), 45, ii, 17; quoted from *CAD,* X/1, 337b.
5. *ABL,* 778, 15-17; quoted from *CAD,* III, 173b.
6. *BIN,* I, 26, 6; quoted from *CAD,* X/1, 340a.

An interesting passage in which the verb *naṣāru* is used with *maškanum* (probably the equivalent of Heb. → מִשְׁכָּן *miškān,* "sanctuary") is: "The prophet of Adad, lord of Kallassu, guards the threshing floor of Alaḫtu for Neḫlatu" *(āpilum ša Adad bēl Kallassu maškanam ša Alaḫtim ana Neḫlatim inaṣṣar).*[7]

The phrase *mišmereṯ YHWH*[8] has an equivalent in Akk. *maṣṣartu ša šarri,* "observance of the precepts, regulations, or laws of the king." On the one hand, it can be used quite particularly with reference to specific precepts: "He who does not bring bowmen to the police post *(bît kādu)* and does not perform the king's service *(maṣṣartum ša šarri la inaṣṣaru)* commits a sin against the king."[9] On the other hand, it can refer in a very general sense to faithfulness in observing the ordinances of the king: "Many people in Babylon are (still faithfully) serving the king" *(maṣṣarti ša šarri inaṣṣaru).*[10] Heb. *mišmereṯ YHWH* is used also with reference to a specific command from God (Nu. 9:23) as well as in the more general sense of "faithfulness" in God's service (2 Ch. 13:10f.).

II. Heb. *mišmereṯ/šōmēr mišmereṯ*.

1. *P.* In P *mišmereṯ* and *šōmēr mišmereṯ* in the context of the tent sanctuary refer to the function of the Levites: "But the Levites shall camp around the tabernacle of the covenant, that there may be no wrath on the congregation of the Israelites; and the Levites shall perform the guard duty *(mišmereṯ)* of the tabernacle of the covenant" (Nu. 1:53). This guard duty is the lifelong responsibility of the Levites, in contrast to physical labor *(ʿᵃḇōḏâ),*[11] which consists in taking down the sanctuary, transporting it, and reconstructing it — a duty from which those over the age of fifty are exempt: "From twenty-five years old and upward they shall begin to do duty in the service of the tent of meeting; and from the age of fifty years they shall retire from the duty of the service and serve no more. They may assist their brothers in the tent of meeting in carrying out their duties *(mišmereṯ),* but they shall perform no service *(ʿᵃḇōḏâ)*" (Nu. 8:24-26).

This distinction between physical labor and guard duty also explains the double census of the Levites in Nu. 3 and 4: the former deals with guard duty *(mišmereṯ),* the latter with physical labor *(ʿᵃḇōḏâ).* The enrollment of the Levites to determine how many workers are available includes only those between the ages of thirty and fifty: "All those who were enrolled of the Levites, whom Moses and Aaron and the leaders of Israel enrolled, by their clans and their ancestral houses, from thirty years old up to fifty years old, everyone who qualified to do the work of service and the work of bearing burdens relating to the tent of meeting, their enrollment was eight thousand five hundred eighty" (Nu. 4:46-48).

By contrast, Levitical service could employ not only the older Levites (Nu. 8:25f.)

---

7. A. Malamat, "History and Prophetic Vision in a Mari Letter," *ErIsr,* 5 (1958) 67-73.

8. See III.2 below.

9. R. P. Dougherty, *Records from Erech: Time of Nabonidus. YOSBT,* VI (1920), 151, 16; quoted from *CAD,* X/1, 339b.

10. *CAD,* X/1, 339a.

11. Milgrom, *Studies,* 60f.

but theoretically also the very young — those over the age of one month. Clearly, from P's perspective all but very young children should perform guard duty or be trained for it. Therefore the number of those eligible for guard duty is substantially greater than the number of physical laborers: "The total enrollment of the Levites whom Moses and Aaron enrolled at the commandment of Yahweh, by their clans, all the males from a month old and upward, was twenty-two thousand" (Nu. 3:39).

Nu. 3:5-10 says that the Levites performing this function are to represent the Israelites and to assist the priests: "They [the Levites] shall perform duties for him [Aaron] and for the whole congregation in front of the tent of meeting, doing service at the tabernacle; they shall be in charge of all the furnishings of the tent of meeting, and attend to the duties for the Israelites as they do service at the *miškān*" (Nu. 3:7f.). Both verses are necessary for defining the service of the Levites as a whole: when encamped (v. 7) and during transport (v. 8). Mention of the sacred furnishings makes the reference to transport clear: while the Israelites were traveling, the Kohathites carried and watched over these furnishings (3:31; 4:15). In camp the furnishings were guarded by the priests (18:5), and the Kohathites were even forbidden to look directly on them (4:17-20).

When the Israelites were encamped, the Levites performed their service at the sanctuary (Nu. 1:53). Nu. 3:23,29,35 contain more details about the guard assignments of the Gershonites, Kohathites, and Merarites in relationship to the camp. It is probable that those encamped to the north, west, or south performed guard duty on that side of the sanctuary. The priests camped on the east side at the entrance to the sanctuary (3:38) and were responsible for guard duty there and within the sacred precincts (3:38; 18:2b). When traveling, each group watched over the portion of the sanctuary entrusted to it: the curtains of the tent were assigned to the Gershonites (3:25f.), the sacred furnishings to the Kohathites (v. 31), and the framework of the *miškān* to the Merarites (vv. 36f.).

In ancient Near Eastern religions, there was a common perception that the dwelling place of the deity had to be protected against invasion by demonic powers, which could evict the deity from his or her residence. Outside Israel, we find apotropaic rites and images of tutelary figures set up at the entrance to a temple. In Israel, however, these demonic forces were no longer an object of belief. They are replaced by human beings:[12] only the action of a human individual can evict God from his sanctuary. Since responsibility for sin rests entirely in human hands, the protective circle of priests and Levites is designed to guard God against human intrusion. The texts discussing the appointment of the priests and Levites as guards therefore stipulate that improper intrusion must be punished by death (Nu. 1:51; 3:10,38; 18:7).

After the revolt of Korah (Nu. 16f.), 18:1-7 redefines the *mišmereṯ* of the Levites: *mišmereṯ* in the sanctuary is reserved to the Aaronides. Only they may enter the tent of the covenant *('ōhel hā'ēḏûṯ)*. Under them come the Levites, who are to perform the *mišmereṯ* at the tent of meeting *('ōhel mô'ēḏ)*, all the service of the tent *(leḵol 'aḇōḏaṯ*

12. Milgrom, *RB,* 83 (1976), 390-99.

hā'ōhel) (vv. 3f.). Only the Aaronides are permitted *mišmeret̲* at the altar and with the sacred furnishings. All others are forbidden to intrude under pain of death (vv. 3,7).

J. Milgrom — L. Harper

The discussion in Nu. 18:1-7 is so confused "that one can scarcely expect any consistency of thought."[13] Literary criticism, however, can help resolve the problems of this passage by distinguishing an Aaronide stratum and a Levite stratum. A. H. J. Gunneweg has discussed the postulates behind such redactions.[14] It has also been suggested that the *mišmeret̲* of the Levites refers to military service.[15]

Fabry

In the present context, following the plague that had broken out on account of Korah's revolt (Nu. 17:11-15[16:46-50]), these directives are associated with the fear of the people that they will perish if they approach the sanctuary (17:28[13]). The directives not only constitute a revision of the directives governing service at the sanctuary already laid down in 1:53; 3:1-51, but contain a new element: priests and Levites alone must bear the punishment for any future offenses on the part of the laity and clerics (18:1,3,23). The Levites are now made responsible for guard duty round about the sanctuary and are to assist the priests in their service at the entrance to the holy place. Thus a fundamental hierarchy of responsibilities is established: the priests protect the most sacred furnishings within the sacred precincts against unauthorized approach by Levites or unqualified priests (3:10; 18:1b,7a), the Kohathites shield them from the laity during transport (18:1a; 4:15-20), and the Levites are in charge of setting up the whole complex (18:22f.).

The distinction between priestly service within and nonpriestly service without has parallels in the ancient Near East. The Hittite "Instructions for Temple Duties"[16] have a series of regulations for temple service that assign priests to guard duty in the temple and nonpriests to duties outside the temple. In addition, the entrance of the Hittite temple — like that of the tent sanctuary — was overseen by priests (Nu. 3:38; 18:2b). Like the Levites, the nonpriestly Hittite guardians are under priestly supervision; the Merarites and Gershonites are under the supervision of Ithamar (4:28,33), while the Kohathites are under the command of Eleazar (v. 16). Only at the command of the priests may the nonpriestly Hittite guardians perform services within the sacred precincts. The Levites, too, may leave their posts to accompany the laity inside the sacred precincts and help them prepare their offerings (16:9), but also to assist the priests in guarding the sacred furnishings against unauthorized approach, especially during transport (3:6b,7a; 18:2-4). Like the Levite guardians, the nonpriestly Hittite guardians are threatened with death if they approach without authorization. The Hittite guardians, however, are slain by human beings, whereas

13. M. Noth, *Numbers. OTL* (Eng. trans. 1968), 135.

14. *Leviten und Priester. FRLANT,* 89 (1965).

15. G. Schmitt, "Der Ursprung des Levitentums," *ZAW,* 94 (1982), 575-599, esp. 587 (→ VII, 498f.).

16. *ANET,* 207-210; cf. Milgrom, *Studies,* 50ff.

the Levites expect their punishment from God. In the view of P, the punishment for an offense is distributed equally among all the Levites.

As guardian of the sanctuary at Shiloh, Samuel performed nonpriestly sanctuary service; to do so he slept within the sacred precincts (1 S. 3:3,9). It is recorded that Joshua similarly "would not leave the tent," while Moses returned to the camp (Ex. 33:11). Both examples recall the *sâdin* of Arab nomads,[17] who guarded the sanctuary and of necessity also slept there. With the development of an extensive organization at sanctuaries such as Shiloh, the inclusion of nonpriestly guardians who also functioned as gatekeepers was no longer something unusual.

Responsibility for guarding the sanctuary required the Levites to be armed. In the view of P, they had the right to kill unauthorized intruders.[18] Thus they had not only a police function but also a military function. For P this was important, since any forbidden contact with the sacred furnishings provoked God's wrath, bringing plagues that could endanger the existence of the entire community. Intruders had to be stopped at all costs to spare the community the deadly consequences. Therefore the institution of the protective circle of Levites is often coupled with the reason for its existence: "that there may be no wrath upon the Israelites" (Nu. 1:53; 8:19; 18:5).

The innovation following Korah's revolt is the limitation of guilt for unauthorized intrusion to the intruder and the Levites who failed to prevent the intrusion. Because their duty is dangerous, the Levites receive the tithe as their reward (Nu. 18:22-24). Finally, it is also the *mišmereṯ* that entitles the Levites to a portion of the Midianite booty (31:30,47).

2. *Ezekiel.* Ezekiel keeps the meaning "guard duty" for *mišmereṯ/šōmēr mišmereṯ,* as well as the function of sanctuary guards for the priests and Levites. Ezekiel describes the Levites as guards at the temple gates and as temple servants, who slaughter the burnt offering and sacrifice for the people and attend them (Ezk. 44:11). The assignment of the duty of slaughtering to the Levites is new in Ezekiel and contradicts P's understanding of the sanctuary, in which the laity alone are responsible for offering their own sacrifices (Lev. 1:5,11; 3:2,8,13; 4:24,29,33). Ezekiel finds it necessary to disallow the people their rights in this matter because he blames the laity — and to a lesser degree the Levites — for allowing foreigners into the sanctuary (Ezk. 44:6-8). That foreigners served as guards of the first temple is clear from 2 K. 11:4. By reassigning ritual slaughtering to the Levites (Ezk. 44:11), Ezekiel punishes the people, who are now kept away from the inner gates where the slaughtering takes place (40:39-42).

Ezekiel also differs from P in reserving altar service to the Zadokite priests alone (Ezk. 40:45f.; 44:15f.). We may assume that for P the priestly service was performed in turn. The areas associated with priestly service are the same for Ezekiel as for P: the altar and the sanctuary (Nu. 18:5a, where *qōḏeš* refers to the sanctuary[19]).

---

17. Cody, 78f.
18. Milgrom, *Studies,* 21f.
19. *Ibid.,* 39, n. 149.

3. *Postexilic Literature.* In Chronicles the phrase *šōmēr mišmereṯ* keeps the meaning "guard." This can be seen from 1 Ch. 12:30(29), which speaks of the Benjaminites who "do guard duty" in the court of Saul. The Chronicler is aware that the Levites served as temple guards (9:27). This is also shown by the story of Jehoiada's revolt, in which the Chronicler replaces the soldiers guarding the child Joash (2 K. 11:5-9) with Levites (2 Ch. 23:4-8). The reason for this change is evident: laypeople were not permitted to enter the temple, as the Chronicler explains in an addition (23:6). Armed Levites surround the king to kill any intruder (vv. 6f.). Since the Chronicler does not give any reason for his variant, this can only mean that he knew the former function of the Levites as temple guards; therefore no explanation was needed. This story also reveals his knowledge that the Levites were originally armed, as we also find in P.

In the preexilic sources, *mišmereṯ* is used only as a noun with the meaning "guard duty" or "supervision" (e.g., 1 S. 22:23; "guardhouse" or "prison," 2 S. 20:3; "guard post," Isa. 21:8; Hab. 2:1). In this usage *mišmereṯ* is clearly a feminine abstract noun from the masc. *mišmar.*

In the postexilic sources, the usage of *mišmereṯ* varies. Sometimes the usual meaning "guard duty" is adopted, as in 1 Ch. 9:27; 25:8. In other texts it has a more general meaning such as "service" or "duty" (Neh. 12:45; 1 Ch. 23:32; 2 Ch. 13:11; 23:6). Nowhere do we find the postbiblical meaning "division" or "watch" (as a unit of time).

The pl. *mišmārôṯ* first appears in postexilic literature, usually with the meaning "guard units." In Chronicles, however, this term is the plural of *mišmereṯ,* "duty" (2 Ch. 7:6; 31:16; 35:2; and esp. 8:14), and should simply be translated "duties." In at least one passage, it refers to divisions (1 Ch. 9:23; probably also 26:12); but in this case it refers to units of the guard and is thus the plural of *mišmār* rather than *mišmereṯ.* The same is true for the occurrences in Ezra-Nehemiah (Neh. 4:3,16[9,22]; 7:3). In 12:9; 13:30, the context does not permit any certain conclusions about the word's semantic valence. It may refer to "divisions," in the first case perhaps the division of temple singers. In Neh. 11f., confusion reigns (esp. in the use of *mišmār* in 12:25), and it appears that singers and gatekeepers have been interchanged. If so, *mišmārôṯ* could be taken as the plural of *mišmār,* which would agree with usage elsewhere in the book of Nehemiah. In any case, it is dubious whether "divisions" are meant, since this meaning is not found elsewhere in the biblical text. More likely the plural is used abstractly for "duty."

III. Other Forms.

1. *hāyâ lᵉmišmereṯ.* The phrase *hāyâ lᵉmišmereṯ* retains the sense of guarding and should be translated "kept under supervision or protection." The lamb for the Passover sacrifice must be "watched over" during the four days from its selection to its slaughter in order to guarantee that it may remain unblemished and to prevent any incident that might render it unfit for use (Ex. 12:6).[20] For similar reasons, it is necessary to keep

20. *Ibid.,* 16, n. 51.

watch over the ashes of the red heifer (Nu. 19:9).[21] In putting aside manna[22] for the Sabbath (Ex. 16:23), the need to guard it is associated with its uniqueness, since food for the Sabbath is involved. A portion of manna must be preserved for future generations as evidence of the desert experience (16:32-34). Aaron's rod is also preserved (Nu. 17:25), presumably for the same reason.

2. *mišmereṯ YHWH.* When God is the object of *mišmereṯ,* the context always contains divine commandments and prohibitions, so that the meaning "observe" remains but in a figurative sense: the individual must be kept from transgressing the commandments laid down by God. The offenses range from cultic infractions (Lev. 8:35; 22:9; Nu. 18:8; Neh. 12:45; Ezk. 44:16; 48:11) to transgressions of contractual or legal restrictions (Gen. 26:5; Lev. 18:30; Nu. 9:19,23; Dt. 11:1; Josh. 22:3; 1 K. 2:3; 2 Ch. 13:11; 23:6; Zec. 3:7; Mal. 3:14). In one case the transgression concerns the charge that God alone is to determine the course of the desert wandering (Nu. 9:19,23; cf. "according to the command of the Lord," repeated 7 times in vv. 18,20,23).

IV. Postbiblical Usage. In the Qumran literature, as in later rabbinic literature, the pl. *mišmārôṯ* clearly has the meaning "cultic services" or duties: "The twenty-six leaders of the cultic services shall perform the cultic services" (1QM 2:2).

Although the word *mišmereṯ* is not used, the function of the Levites and priests as guardians of the sacred precincts continues in the rabbinic vision of the second temple (Sifre *Zuṭa* on Nu. 18:2; Sifra *Ṣaw* pereq 2:12; 3:5; Mishnah *Tam.* 1.1f.). There were twenty-four guard posts at the entrance to the sanctuary; three were occupied by the priests, the others by the Levites. The Levites are always presented as outside guards.

Finally, Philo provides a Greek translation of Nu. 8:24-26 in a treatise on the function of the Levites as workers and guardians of the sanctuary. He appears to follow the text of the LXX until v. 26, where he omits part of the verse and substitutes his own translation in order to juxtapose the two jobs of the Levites and thus emphasize the difference between them: "From (the age of) fifty years shall he cease from the ministry, and shall work no more, but his brother shall minister. He shall keep watch, but shall not work."[23]

J. Milgrom — L. Harper

21. *Ibid.,* 12, n. 43.

22. → מן *mān* (VIII, 389-395).

23. Philo, *That the Worse Is Wont to Attack the Better. LCL,* II, 245f., §63. For further citations see E. E. Urbach, "*Mišmārôṯ* and *Maʿᵃmāḏôṯ,*" *Tarbiz,* 42 (1973), 304-327 (Heb.); G. Moscati-Steindler, "Le *mišmārōt* in una iscrizione di Beit Hadir," *AION,* n.s. 34 (1974), 277-282.

מִשְׁפָּחָה mišpāḥâ

Contents: I. 1. Etymology; 2. Occurrences; 3. Meaning; 4. LXX. II. Secular Usage: 1. Definition of the Clan; 2. Clans of Nations and Lands; 3. Clans of Cities; 4. Figurative Usage. III. Religious Usage: 1. Legal Significance of the Clan; 2. The Clan as a Cultic Association; 3. Theological Contexts. IV. Dead Sea Scrolls.

I. 1. *Etymology.* It is most unlikely that the *m*-prefix noun *mišpāḥâ* derives from a root *špḥ,* "pour out" (cf. Arab. *safaḥa,* etc., with reference to semen).[1] OSA *sfḥ,* "call together," is closer to the mark.[2] The best parallels are Ugar. *špḥ* and the Punic noun *špḥ,* both of which mean "clan."[3]

2. *Occurrences.* The OT has 303 occurrences of *mišpāḥâ;* 159 and 47 of these are in Numbers and Joshua, respectively, primarily in P texts. Then come 1 Chronicles (19), Genesis (12), Zechariah (11), Jeremiah (9), Judges (8), Exodus and 1 Samuel (7 each), Leviticus (6), Psalms (3), 2 Samuel, Amos, Job, Ruth, and Esther (twice each), and Deuteronomy, Ezekiel, Micah, Nahum, and Nehemiah (once each). There are 17 occurrences in the Qumran literature, 10 of *špḥ* in Ugaritic, and 2 of *špḥ* in Punic.[4]

---

mišpāḥâ. A. Causse, *Du groupe ethnique à la communauté religieuse* (Paris, 1937), 17ff.; C. H. J. de Geus, *The Tribes of Israel. SSN,* 18 (1976), esp. 133-150; M. Haran, *"Zeḇaḥ hayyāmîm," VT,* 19 (1969), 11-22; W. Johnstone, "OT Technical Expressions in Property Holding," *Ugaritica,* VI (1969), 308-317, esp. 313f.; G. van der Leeuw, *Religion in Essence and Manifestation,* 2 vols. (Eng. trans., New York, 1963), §33; A. Malamat, "Aspects of Tribal Societies in Mari and Israel," *Les Congrès et Colloques de l'Université de Liège,* 42 (1967), 129-138; I. Mendelsohn, "Guilds in Ancient Palestine," *BASOR,* 80 (1940), 17-21; J. M. Milgrom, "Priestly Terminology and the Political and Social Structure of Pre-Monarchic Israel," *JQR,* 69 (1978/79), 65-81 = *Studies in Cultic Theology and Terminology. SJLA,* 36 (1983), 1-17; F. A. Munch, "Verwandtschaft und Lokalität in der Gruppenbildung der altisraelitischen Hebräer," *Kölner Zeitschrift für Soziologie und Sozialpsychologie,* 12 (1960), 438-458; R. Patai, *Sitte und Sippe in Bibel und Orient* (Frankfurt, 1962); J. Pedersen, *ILC,* I-II, 46-60; J. van der Ploeg, "Les 'nobles' israélites," *OTS,* 9 (1951), 49-64; L. Rost, "Die Bezeichnungen für Land und Volk im AT," *Festschrift Otto Procksch* (Leipzig, 1934), 125-148 = *Das kleine Credo* (Heidelberg, 1965), 76-101; G. Sauer, "Sippe," *BHHW,* III (1966), 1808f.; Å. Sjöberg, "Zu einigen Verwandtschaftsbezeichnungen im Sumerischen," *Heidelberger Studien zum Alten Orient* (Wiesbaden, 1967), 201-231; E. A. Speiser, " 'People' and 'Nation' of Israel," *JBL,* 79 (1960), 157-163 = *Oriental and Biblical Studies* (Philadelphia, 1967), 160-170; R. de Vaux, *AncIsr,* 7-8.

1. *GesB,* 467.
2. Beeston, 124.
3. → II, 110. On the Ugaritic term see *WUS,* no. 2664; for the Punic term see *DISO,* 316.
4. *CIS,* I, 165.16; *LidzEph,* I, 169.7.

3. *Meaning.* In Ugaritic, *špḥ* parallels *yrṯ*, "heir," *ǵlm*, "youth," and *bnm*, "sons."[5] It accordingly means "scion, offspring."[6] In Punic the meaning "family, clan" is likely.[7] The meaning of Heb. *mišpāḥâ* is clear from Josh. 7:14-18. In order to determine the guilt of Achan by lot, the selection process first finds the guilty tribe *(šēḇeṭ)*, then the guilty *mišpāḥâ*, then the correct household. Finally, members of this household are examined one by one. A similar process is described in the selection of the first king (1 S. 10:19-21): tribe by tribe, *mišpāḥâ* by *mišpāḥâ*, finally one man at a time. We can also see from 1 S. 9:21 that *mišpāḥâ* refers to an entity that stands between tribe and family or household. This suggests the translation "extended family" or "clan."

4. *LXX.* The LXX, especially when translating P texts, prefers *dḗmos* (189 times). We also find *phylḗ* (41 times, primarily in P), *patriá* (26 times), *syngéneia* (18 times), *génesis* (6 times), *geneá* (3 times), *génos* (twice), and *genetḗ* and *eídos* (once each). In 16 passages the LXX does not provide an equivalent.

II. Secular Usage.

1. *Definition of the Clan.* The word *mišpāḥâ* does not denote a regional or political entity but rather an ethnic or restricted human community. Est. 9:28 divides provinces into cities; in similar fashion it divides generations *(dôr)* into clans. In the Table of Nations (Gen. 10:5,20,31,32), P proceeds similarly, introducing the sons of Japheth, Ham, and Shem divided into clans, languages, lands, and nations.[8] The clan of Rahab includes her father, mother, brothers, and "all who belonged to her" (Josh. 6:23; cf. 2:13,18). And Abimelech addresses the "sons of his mother" and "the whole clan of the house of his mother's father" (Jgs. 9:1). A *mišpāḥâ* is therefore defined by kinship structures and includes more than just the nuclear or extended family of the man or woman. It is hard to be more precise; although different terms are used for communities of different size, no system of clear distinctions among them is convincing.

The clearest organization is found in P. In Nu. 1:1-43 each of the twelve tribes of Israel is subdivided into clans, and each clan is subdivided into "fathers' houses" *(bêṯ 'āḇôṯ)*. In 26:5-58 "these 'families' [are] explained as being the posterity of the descendants of Jacob"[9] (similarly 36:12; differently 36:1; cf. also P in Ex. 6:14ff.). P follows a similar approach in the census of the Levites (Nu. 3:14–4:49). Here, too, the clans are understood as the kinship groups descended from Levi's grandsons, subdivided into "fathers' houses." In the lists detailing the distribution of the land (Josh. 13–21), the tribes *(maṭṭeh)* of Reuben, Gad, and half Manasseh are mentioned first

---

5. For parallels with *yrṯ* see *KTU*, 1.14, I, 24; with *ǵlm*, 1.14, III, 49f.; VI, 33f.; with *bnm*, 1.16, I, 10, 21; II, 48.

6. *WUS*, no. 2664: "lineage, offspring, scion"; cf. *TDOT*, II, 110: "family, dynasty, ruler's house."

7. *'dr špḥ*, "leader of the clan" (?): *LidzEph*, I, 169, 7; other meanings are suggested on the previous page.

8. Cf. Speiser, 159: *mišpāḥâ* is "basically an administrative rubric."

9. M. Noth, *Numbers. OTL* (Eng. trans. 1968), 17.

(13:15-31), followed by Judah (15:1-20), Ephraim (16:5-8), and half Manasseh (17:1ff.), then Benjamin (18:11ff.), Simeon (19:1ff.), Zebulun (19:10ff.), Issachar (19:17ff.), Asher (19:24ff.), Naphtali (19:32ff.), and Dan (19:40ff.), each with its clans.

The list in Josh. 21:4-40 is organized similarly. The failure of some texts to mention fathers' houses must not lead to the conclusion that P does not presuppose such a subdivision in all the texts. It did not seem necessary to mention this structure explicitly. The situation is probably analogous with regard to whether the "fathers' houses" are to be understood as identical with "families" or as comprising several "families." Job 32:2 at least presupposes the latter: Elihu belongs to the family of his father Barachel, the family to the extended family of Buz, and the extended family to the clan of Ram (cf. Ruth 2:1,3).

Convincing as this organization into families, extended families ("fathers' houses"), clans, tribes, and nations is, at least in this developmental perfection it appears to reflect late theory.[10] That every Israelite belonged to a tribe *(šēḇeṭ)* and a clan is also stated by Jgs. 21:24 (cf. Dt. 29:17[18]). What is noteworthy, however, is that in some texts it is hard to distinguish between clans and fathers' houses (cf. also Ex. 12:21; 1 S. 9:21). Shimei son of Gera, e.g., is identified as coming from "the clan of the house of Saul" (2 S. 16:5). In the story of the wooing of Rebekah, the expressions "my father's house" (Gen. 24:38,40) and "my clan" (vv. 38,40,41) appear to be parallels from the E and J versions.[11] This would mean that in the early period the organizational structure of Israel consisted of families and clans, the latter comprising several families.[12]

In other texts, the ambiguity moves in the direction of identifying clans and tribes. We are told that Manoah was of the clan of the Danites (Jgs. 13:2). Hans Wilhelm Hertzberg suggests that this verse may reflect the historical reality that the tribe of Dan had been dissolved as a group and only remnants of it were still living in the south.[13] The fact that other texts exhibit the same ambiguity argues against this theory. According to Jgs. 18:2, spies are sent from the clan of the Danites; 18:11 states that 600 armed men from the clan of the Danites set forth and asked the priest Micah whether he preferred to be a priest "to the house of one man" or "to a tribe *(šēḇeṭ)* and clan in Israel" (v. 19). Jgs. 17:7 speaks of a Levite of "the clan of Judah"; if the text is correct, here, too, there is no clear distinction between clans and tribes.[14] Although the word *mišpāḥâ* is not used in 5:14,17, the same ambiguity is probably present, because Machir and Gilead are numbered among the tribes (for Machir, cf. 2 S. 9:4: *bêṯ māḵîr*). This situation may best be explained by Martin Noth's observation that the terms "nation" and "tribe" "are part of human history, rather than of human reproduction,"[15] so that

---

10. As argued correctly by Pedersen, *ILC,* I-II, 46. Cf. M. Noth, *OT World* (Eng. trans., Philadelphia, 1966), 63-66.

11. O. Eissfeldt, *Hexateuch-Synopse* (Berlin, 1922), 40*; for a different interpretation, see M. Noth, *A History of Pentateuchal Traditions* (Eng. trans., Englewood Cliffs, N.J., 1972), 29, n. 90.

12. *AncIsr,* 8; → II, 114.

13. W. Hertzberg, *Richter. ATD,* IX (1954), 225.

14. *ILC,* I-II, 47.

15. *OT World,* 64.

we are dealing with different aspects when one and the same human community is now called a "clan," not a "tribe."

The head of a clan may have been called *nāśî'* (Gen. 17:20; 25:16; Nu. 7:2);[16] Roland de Vaux thinks instead of *zāqēn.*[17] De Vaux's theory is at odds with the observation that "elders" belong more to the tribal organization[18] and function as tribal elders. Noth associates the elders with the extended families, so that the governing body of a clan was an "assembly of elders."[19] This conclusion is in total accord with Julius Wellhausen's statement that the polity of early Israel was that of a "commonwealth without a ruling body." Citing Gen. 36:40-43, Georg Sauer also includes the *'allûp̱* here; but de Vaux (probably correctly) associates this term with the military leader, usually called *śar,* because in theory a division comprised a thousand *('elep̱)* men.

2. *Clans of Nations and Lands.* The use of the term "clan" clearly developed further under the influence of preexilic prophecy. The people of Israel are called "the whole clan" that Yahweh brought up out of Egypt (Am. 3:1 [according to Hans Walter Wolff,[20] a Deuteronomistic addition]). The threat that follows begins with the words: "You only have I known of all the clans of the earth" (v. 2). In Jer. 2:4 "house of Jacob" and "all the clans of the house of Israel" stand in *parallelismus membrorum.* Referring to the northern and southern kingdoms, Jer. 33:24 speaks of "the two clans"; 25:9 speaks of "all the clans of the north" as instruments of God's judgment. Finally, prophets can speak almost contemptuously of "this evil clan" (8:3) or "this clan" (Mic. 2:3),[21] meaning Judah.

In consequence of this rhetorical figure, *mišpāḥâ* can parallel *gôy* (Jer. 10:25; Ezk. 20:32; Nah. 3:4; cf. Gen. 10:5,20,31f.; Zec. 14:18). The text can also speak of the clans of the Canaanites (Gen. 10:18) and the clan of Egypt (Zec. 14:18). In the language of the Psalms we find the expression "clans of the peoples *('ammîm)*" (Ps. 96:7 par. 1 Ch. 16:28); for Ps. 22:28(Eng. v. 27), "all the ends of the earth" are identical with "all the clans of the nations *(gôyim).*"

Last but not least we come to J's expression "all the clans of the earth," who are to bless themselves with Abraham/Jacob (Gen. 12:3; 28:14). This closes the circle with Am. 3:2.

In all these texts, the clan is the preferred designation for nations or portions of nations. This usage once more calls attention to the "feeling of solidarity" or "sense of unity" that comes from shared ancestry and represents something like a "psychic community."[22] As Leonhard Rost puts it, "The nation is . . . like a large extended

16. Sauer, 1808, with a question mark.
17. *AncIsr,* 8.
18. → IV, 127.
19. *OT World,* 64.
20. *Joel and Amos. Herm* (Eng. trans. 1977), 175.
21. W. Rudolph, *Micha. KAT,* XIII/3 (1975), 51.
22. See, respectively, Sauer, 1808; Van der Leeuw, §33.2; *ILC,* I-II, 50.

family."[23] It is important to note that these texts use a word with ethnic rather than historical or political overtones.

3. *Clans of Cities.* This notion probably also accounts for the usage, first attested in Chronicles but long an open possibility,[24] that speaks of the clans of a city or town (1 Ch. 2:53; 4:2; cf. also 9:3-9; Neh. 11:4-8) or organizes the names of Esau's chiefs by clans, localities, and names (Gen. 36:40 [P]). This resembles the allocation of free cities to Levitical clans (1 Ch. 6:40-66[55-81]).

4. *Figurative Usage.* The sense of solidarity established by shared ancestry also enables the term *mišpāḥâ* to be used figuratively. In 1 Ch. 2:55 we read of the "clans of the scribes" and in 4:21 of the "clans of the linen workers." Both passages presuppose something like a guild system, so that *mišpāḥâ* acquires the sense of a community based on a common profession.[25] Classification by species suggests speaking of animals "according to their clans" with reference to wild animals, cattle, birds, and vermin (Gen. 8:19). Jer. 15:3 names the four "clans" of God's punishment: the sword, dogs, birds, and wild animals.

III. Religious Usage.

1. *Legal Significance of the Clan.* When we turn to religious usage in the broader sense, we must first address the legal significance of clans. It is chiefly the clan, not the family or tribe, that appears as an independent autonomous entity. Lev. 25:10,41, and similar passages decree that in the Jubilee Year tenants are to return to their clans. In the law of inheritance, too, the clan is the accepted framework within which matters are settled (Nu. 27:11); for if the deceased left neither a son nor a brother, the nearest blood relative from the clan inherits. This legal concept probably also explains why the land apportioned by lot was given to the tribes "according to their clans" (Nu. 33:54; Josh. 13ff.). Finally, Nehemiah's stationing of the people by clans (Neh. 4:7[13]) illustrates the organizational form of the postexilic community, which appears to be modeled on the cultic and legal community of the premonarchic period.

That the clan represents a self-contained autonomous group is also clear from those cases where its members share communal culpability. If anyone gives his child to Molech, he and his clan must be punished (Lev. 20:5). The reverse is true when the whole clan profits from the good deed of a single individual, like that told of the prostitute Rahab (Josh. 6:23) and the man from Bethel (Jgs. 1:25); the same idea is expressed in Ex. 20:5f.; Dt. 5:9f. Finally, we must note the clan's responsibility for upholding the law, e.g., by putting to death a fratricide from among them (2 S. 14:7). Job 31:34 reflects a similar notion, in that the clan has to react to the sin of an individual by treating him with contempt and disdain.

---

23. *Credo,* 86.
24. See III.2 below.
25. See Mendelsohn, 18f.

2. *The Clan as a Cultic Association.* It is therefore natural that the clan should represent an independent entity in the cultic realm as well. It seems convincing to Saul that David should ask leave of Jonathan in order to participate in the annual sacrifice of his clan at Bethlehem (1 S. 20:6,29). The instructions concerning the Passover also require lambs to be selected according to clans (Ex. 12:21). When the festival of Purim is to be celebrated throughout every generation *(dôr wāḏôr)* clan by clan *(mišpāḥâ ûmišpāḥâ)* in every province and city (Est. 9:28), the regional entities of province and city are echoed by the ethnic structures of generation and clan. Finally, we hear that the people wept "throughout their clans, all at the entrances of their tents" because they were sick and tired of manna (Nu. 11:10); and the communal lament in Zec. 12:12-14 is organized by clans, within which the men and women are separated. These texts show that the clan was something like the smallest religious unit within the congregation of Israel. It is also the primary locus for the demonstration of grace and favor.[26]

In contrast to this notion of the clan as a cultic community, texts like 1 S. 1:21; 2:19 describe "sacrifice limited to a family"; Hans Joachim Stoebe rightly explains this as "the later form of the description."[27] Menaḥem Haran points out that the annual sacrificial festival of the clan of Jesse mentioned in 1 S. 20 might resemble the sacrifice with Samuel in 9:12 in the participation of the whole local populace.[28]

3. *Theological Contexts.* A variety of theological meanings are associated with the clan concept. The "humility motif"[29] found in David's words "Who am I and who is 'my clan'?" (1 S. 18:18) may have given rise to the notion of the election of the most humble. Saul, who comes from the humblest of all the clans of the tribe of Benjamin (9:21), is chosen king. Jgs. 6:15 expresses much the same thought but using *'elep̱* (cf. also Dt. 7:6-8).

It is therefore understandable that the clan concept should enter the semantic field of the exodus, election, and covenant and thus become a vehicle for theological ideas. Yahweh says of "the whole clan" that he brought up out of Egypt that he has known it alone "of all the clans of the earth" (Am. 3:1f.). This text alludes to the election of God's people; loss of this privilege can find expression in the despairing language of the people in exile, who have become "like the pagans, like the clans of the [pagan] countries" (Ezk. 20:32). Yahweh's favor toward the needy *('eḇyôn)* and the upright *(yāšār)* justifies the statement that he has multiplied their clans like flocks (Ps. 107:41f.). The people lament that Yahweh has now rejected "the two clans" that he had chosen (Jer. 33:24), referring to the northern and southern kingdoms as parts of the people of God. The promise in Jer. 31:1 is formulated in similar terms: at that time Yahweh will be the God of "all the clans of Israel," and they will be his people. The covenant idea concerns the covenant people of God, understood here as a collection of clans rather

26. → חסד *ḥeseḏ* (V, 44-64).
27. Stoebe, *Das erste Buch Samuelis. KAT,* VIII/1 (1973), 373f.
28. P. 17.
29. Stoebe, *KAT,* VIII/1, 351.

than tribes. The concept of kinship bonds based on clan solidarity shapes the idea of the people of God. When Israel wants to express its own uniqueness, it prefers the term *mišpāḥâ* (or *ʿam*[30]), because this word expresses a solidarity based on natural factors established, as it were, through creation. At the same time it has overtones of a future perspective based on God's blessing in creation.[31]

Since the people addressed by Jeremiah can be described as "this evil clan" (Jer. 8:3), our term can also appear in prophecies of disaster as "this clan" (Mic. 2:3).[32] Finally, in Jeremiah we even find the notion that Yahweh will summon "all the clans of the north" to execute his judgment (Jer. 25:9; cf. 1:15).

Following God's judgment, Jeremiah believes, Yahweh will not bring back the entire nation but only part of it. He clothes this belief in the statement that Yahweh will "take one from a city and two from a clan" and bring them to Zion (Jer. 3:14). Because Yahweh is enthroned on Zion and is the highest God, "all the clans of the *gôyim*" (Ps. 22:28[27]) or "the clans of the *ʿammîm*" (Ps. 96:7 = 1 Ch. 16:28) are called upon to worship him. Those among "the clans of the earth" who do not go up to Jerusalem will be punished (Zec. 14:17; cf. v. 18). These words echo the promise to Abraham that "all the clans of the earth" will bless themselves in him (Gen. 12:3 [J]). This statement about God's unique relationship with Israel and his relationship with the gentile world through Israel is repeated in 28:14 (J), which emphasizes that this promise is addressed to Jacob/Israel, who is also its mediator to the gentile world. That these texts of promise choose clan terminology for the entire world should probably be interpreted as reflecting the idea of God as creator. The population of the world, once a great human community divided solely into clans, will once more become this harmonious community through devotion to the mountain of God or participation in the blessing of God's people.

IV. Dead Sea Scrolls. In the Dead Sea Scrolls the clan is a subdivision of the people of God, as in the P material of the OT. This is clearest in 1QM 4:10: the standards bear the inscriptions "Congregation of God," "Camps of God," "Tribes of God," "Clans of God," and "Brigades of God." Thus each tribe is made up of clans, which in turn are divided into brigades (cf. also 1QM 3:6; 1QSa 1:9,15,21; CD 20:13). Even if it is not stated explicitly, this same idea seems to be reflected in 1QM 2:14 ("the sons of Ham, according to their clans, in their dwelling places") and CD 3:3 ("the sons of Noah and their clans"). According to 1QM 10:14, God "created the dwelling place of the clans." CD 14:10 assumes that each clan speaks its own dialect. 4QpNah 2:9 looks forward to the destruction of cities and clans. In 11QTemple 57:17ff. the law concerning the king of Dt. 17:14-29 is expanded by requiring that the king may take a wife only from the *mišpāḥâ* of his father. No specifically theological meaning can be seen in the usage of Qumran.

Zobel

---

30. → גוֹי *gôy* (II, 432f.).
31. C. Westermann, *Genesis 1–11* (Eng. trans., Minneapolis, 1984), 509.
32. See II.2 above.

מִשְׁפָּט mišpāṭ; שֶׁפֶט šep̱eṭ; שְׁפוֹט šᵉp̱ôṭ

Contents: I. Occurrences and Meaning. II. OT Usage: 1. Oracles and Casting Lots; 2. Jurisprudence; a. General; b. Legal Case; c. Verdict; d. Punishment and Deliverance; 3. Right; a. Legal Right; b. Righteousness; 4. Law; a. God's *mišpāṭîm;* b. Human *mišpāṭîm;* c. Commandment, Statute; 5. Custom; 6. Moderation. III. LXX. IV. Dead Sea Scrolls.

---

mišpāṭ. A. Alt, "The Origins of Israelite Law," *Essays on OT History and Religion* (Eng. trans., Oxford, 1966), 79-132; J. Becker, *Das Heil Gottes. SUNT,* 3 (1964); J. Begrich, "Die priesterliche Tora," *Werden und Wesen des ATs. BZAW,* 66 (1936), 63-88; E. Berkovits, "The Biblical Meaning of Justice," *Judaism,* 18 (1969), 188-209; O. Betz, "Rechtfertigung in Qumran," *Rechtfertigung. Festschrift E. Käsemann* (Tübingen and Göttingen, 1976), 17-36; H. J. Boecker, *Law and the Administration of Justice in the OT and Ancient East* (Eng. trans., Minneapolis, 1980); *idem, Redeformen des Rechtslebens im AT. WMANT,* 14 (²1970); O. Booth, "The Semantic Development of the Term מִשְׁפָּט in the OT," *JBL,* 61 (1942), 105-110; G. Braulik, "Die Ausdrücke für 'Gesetz' im Buch Deuteronomium," *Bibl,* 51 (1970), 39-66; D. Cox, "*ṣĕdāqâ* and *mišpaṭ,*" *SBFLA,* 27 (1977), 33-50; A. Deissler, *Ps 119(118) und seine Theologie. MTS,* I/11 (1955); M. Delcor, "Contribution à l'étude de la législation des sectaires de Damas et de Qumran," *RB,* 61 (1954), 533-553; 62 (1955), 60-75; H. Donner, "Die soziale Botschaft der Propheten im Lichte der Gesellschaftsordnung in Israel," *OrAnt,* 2 (1963), 229-249; K. H. Fahlgren, *ṣᵉdāqāh* (Uppsala, 1932), 120-138; Z. W. Falk, "Hebrew Legal Terms," *JSS,* 5 (1960), 350-354; *idem,* " 'Words of God' and 'Judgment,' " *Studi in onore di Edoardo Volterra,* 6 (1969), 155-59; H. Gese, *Lehre und Wirklichkeit in der alten Weisheit* (Tübingen, 1958); R. Hentschke, *Satzung und Setzender. BWANT,* 5/3 (1963); H. W. Hertzberg, "Die Entwicklung des Begriffes משפט im AT," *ZAW,* 40 (1922), 256-287; 41 (1923), 235-259; F. Horst, "Naturrecht im AT," *Gottes Recht,* ed. H. W. Wolff. *ThB,* 12 (1961), 235-259; *idem, Das Privilegrecht Jahwes. FRLANT,* 45[28] (1930) = *ThB,* 12 (1961), 17-154; K. Koch, "Die Entstehung der sozialen Kritik bei den Profeten," *Probleme biblischer Theologie. Festschrift G. von Rad* (Munich, 1971), 236-257; *idem,* "Wesen und Ursprung der 'Gemeinschaftstreue' im Israel der Königszeit," *ZEE,* 5 (1961), 72-90, esp. 83-87; L. Köhler, "Appendix: Justice in the Gate," *Hebrew Man* (Eng. trans., New York, 1956), 127-150; H.-J. Kraus, "Zum Gesetzesverständnis der nachprophetischen Zeit," *Kairos,* 11 (1969), 122-133; G. Liedke, *Gestalt und Bezeichnung alttestamentlicher Rechtsätze. WMANT,* 39 (1971); *idem,* "שׁפט *špṭ* 'to judge,' " *TLOT,* III, 1392-99; M. Limbeck, *Die Ordnung des Heils* (Düsseldorf, 1971); R. Martin-Achard, "Brèves remarques sur la signification théologique de la loi selon l'AT," *ETR,* 57 (1982), 343-359; A. Marzal, "The Provincial Governor at Mari," *JNES,* 30 (1971), 186-217; D. A. McKenzie, "Judicial Procedure at the Town Gate," *VT,* 14 (1964), 100-104; J. Miranda, *Marx and the Bible* (Eng. trans., Maryknoll, N.Y., 1974); G. Östborn, *Torah in the OT* (Lund, 1945); J. van der Ploeg, "*Šāpaṭ* et *Mišpāṭ,*" *OTS,* 2 (1943), 144-155; *idem,* "Studies in Hebrew Law," *CBQ,* 12 (1950), 248-259, 416-427; 13 (1951), 28-43, 164-171, 296-307; W. Richter, *Recht und Ethos. SANT,* 15 (1966); M. S. Rozenberg, "The *Šōp̱ᵉṭîm* in the Bible," *ErIsr,* 12 (1975), 77*-86*; *idem,* "The Stem *špṭ*" (diss., Univ. of Pennsylvania, 1963); N. H. Snaith, *The Distinctive Ideas of the OT* (London, 1944), 72-78; L. H. M. A. Temba, "A Study of the Hebrew Root *špṭ* with Reference to Yahweh" (diss., Harvard, 1978); H. C. Thomson, "*Shopheṭ* and *Mishpaṭ* in the Book of Judges," *GUOST,* 19 (1961/62), 74-85; R. de Vaux, *The Early History of Israel* (Eng. trans., Philadelphia, 1978), 766-773; K. Whitelam, *The Just King. JSOT Sup,* 12 (1979).

I. Occurrences and Meaning. The word *mišpāṭ* is a *ma*-noun derived from → שׁפט *šāpaṭ*. In addition to Biblical and Postbiblical Hebrew, it is found in Ugaritic and Phoenician with the meaning "government, authority."[1]

The word occurs 422 times in the OT, distributed among most of the books; only Ruth, Esther, Song of Songs, Joel, Obadiah, Jonah, and Nahum do not have it. In Hebrew, *ma*-nouns have a wide range of use. They can refer to the place where the activity denoted by the root takes place, the action as such, the result of the action, and the means by which the action is performed.[2] Within this range, *mišpāṭ* exhibits a variety of semantic variants. The question of its "basic meaning" cannot be separated from consideration of the verb (→ שׁפט *šāpaṭ*) with regard to the same question.[3] For *mišpāṭ* the focal point clearly lies in the realm of justice, judgment, and law. But in several texts the meaning "decision" is sufficient, without its being understood as correct and positive. Other passages tend in the direction of "claim, demand," emphasizing positive engagement on behalf of a particular position. This range confronts us with a variety of starting points for determining a basic meaning.

Since most occurrences appear in close association with justice and law, it has seemed reasonable to begin with a meaning in this area. For example, *GesB* (12th ed.) lists the following meanings: "(1) judgment; (2) a matter under judgment; (3) what is determined by judges and lawgivers, what is right, justice." Within the third meaning, "customary law" leads to "custom" and "manner."

As a new point of departure, Hans Wilhelm Hertzberg takes the volitional proclivity ascribed to David in 1 S. 27:11, defining *mišpāṭ* as a "constant certainty of action" and an "expression of a centrifugal confirmation of the will," an "expression of a volitional proclivity."[4] Following Klaus Koch and Hans Walter Wolff, Gerhard Liedke describes *mišpāṭ* as a domain and the act of *špṭ* as an act through which the damaged order of a community (bound by law) is restored.[5] Here modern liberation theology enters the field, finding in the *mišpāṭ* of the poor the starting point for biblical interpretation.[6] Others take "decision" as their starting point.[7] This decision can be defined more precisely in the sense of "legislation" or "verdict."[8] Other theories have been

---

1. For Ugaritic see *UT,* no. 2727; *WUS,* no. 2921; W. Richter, *ZAW,* 77 (1965), 60; W. H. Schmidt, *Königtum Gottes in Ugarit und Israel. BZAW,* 80 (1966), 28. For Phoenician see *DISO,* 171; Z. S. Harris, *A Grammar of the Phoenician Language. AOS,* 8 (1936), 153; T. Ishida, *RB,* 80 (1973), 518.

2. *BLe,* 488ff.; H. S. Nyberg, *Hebreisk grammatik* (Uppsala, 1952), 205ff.

3. See esp. H. W. Hertzberg, "Die Entwicklung des Begriffes *mšpṭ im AT,*" *ZAW,* 40 (1922), 256-287; 41 (1923), 16-76; Booth; Fahlgren; Liedke, *Gestalt,* 73-100; *idem, TLOT.*

4. For the first two quotations see *ZAW,* 40 (1922), 263; for the last, *ZAW,* 41 (1923), 73.

5. For the former see Liedke, *Gestalt,* 77; cf. Koch, "*ṣdq* im AT" (diss., Heidelberg, 1953), 35ff.; Wolff, *Amos the Prophet* (Eng. trans., Philadelphia, 1973), 59-67. For the latter, Liedke, *TLOT,* III, 1393.

6. Miranda, 109ff.

7. L. Köhler, *Deuterojesaja stilkritisch untersucht. BZAW,* 37 (1923), 110; *idem, Hebrew Man,* 133f.

8. For the former see O. Grether, "Die Bezeichnung 'Richter' für die charismatischen Helden

proposed.[9] Many scholars emphasize that *mišpāṭ* derives from the exercise of authority in general and should not be limited to the judicial process in the strict sense.[10] K. H. Fahlgren does not accept the basic meaning of "judgment," preferring to take the *mišpāṭ* of the individual as his starting point, although he rejects Hertzberg's view that every *mišpāṭ* should be based on a particular "volitional proclivity."[11] As the basic meaning, Fahlgren prefers "manner, characteristic." Similar meanings are proposed by Osborne Booth and Eliezer Berkovits.[12]

No semantic development of *mišpāṭ* can be detected when one compares its occurrences in earlier and later texts, although certain specialized meanings or specific constructions may be present in particular texts.[13]

II. OT Usage.

1. *Oracles and Casting Lots.* Reaching decisions is an important aspect of *mišpāṭ*. But caution is advisable in proposing this as the "basic meaning," even when the verb is also considered. Liedke comments: "*špṭ* seems to belong to the category of roots in which the search for a 'basic meaning' is not illuminating."[14] Despite this reservation, however, it must be said that this meaning provides a good starting point for access to the various usages of *mišpāṭ*.

This is clear, first, from the use of *mišpāṭ* in the context of casting lots, where it stands for the decision of a priest reached by lot. The priest is to inquire "by the *mišpāṭ* of Urim" (Nu. 27:21). In Ex. 28:15,29f., the breastpiece of the high priest, which contains the oracular lots Urim and Thummim, is called *ḥōšen (ham)mišpāṭ*.[15] In this way Aaron is to "bear the *mišpāṭ* of the Israelites on his heart continually" (28:30).

The result of casting lots is also called *mišpāṭ* (Prov. 16:33). Jgs. 4:5 is cited as an example of a text that associates *mišpāṭ* with oracles: Deborah spoke *mišpāṭ* under the "palm of Deborah."[16] Hertzberg goes a step further, theorizing that the judicial system as such emerged from consultation of oracles.[17] In these examples, however, it is better to understand *mišpāṭ* as meaning "decision, answer, opinion." Even if the answer was given within the framework of an oracle, the suggested translation

---

der vorstaatl. Zeit," *ZAW,* 57 (1939), 110-121. For the latter see J. Begrich, *Studien zu Deuterojesaia. BWANT,* 77 (1938), 161ff.

9. E.g., van der Ploeg, *OTS,* 2 (1943), 144-155; *idem, CBQ,* 12 (1950), 248-259; Thomson, 84; I. L. Seeligmann, "Zur Terminologie für Gerichtsverfahren im Wortschatz des biblischen Hebräisch," *Hebräische Wortforschung. Festschrift W. Baumgartner. SVT,* 16 (1967), 251-278, esp. 273, n. 1; L. Monsengwo Palsinya, *La notion de* nomos *dans le Pentateuque grec.* AnBibl, 52 (1973), 97ff.; de Vaux; and *HAL,* II, 651, which cites "ruling" as its point of departure.

10. E.g., Rozenberg.

11. P. 124.

12. Booth, 107; Berkovits, 188-209.

13. See below.

14. *TLOT,* III, 1393.

15. → חשן *ḥōšen* (V, 259-261).

16. Rozenberg, *ErIsr,* 12 (1975), 77f.*; Whitelam, 66, 84.

17. *ZAW,* 40 (1922), 269.

suffices. One might also add that God's *mišpāṭ* is autonomous and not limited by oracular technique.[18]

2. *Jurisprudence.* a. *General.* Like oracles, judicial dicta have the nature of decisions. When a judge has chosen between the available alternatives, he renders his decision, which is called *mišpāṭ.* This decision, however, also entails the substance and consequences of the decision. Therefore, *mišpāṭ* often stands for the entire judicial procedure, the forensic situation in its widest sense, as in Ps. 1:5.[19] Even in cases where *mišpāṭ* refers to a particular element of the forensic process, other semantic nuances are in the background.

In many texts *mišpāṭ* has the general meaning "justice." One comes before the king or judge *lammišpāṭ,* for a judicial decision (Jgs. 4:5; 2 S. 15:2,6); a slayer must stand before the congregation *lammišpāṭ* (Nu. 35:12; Josh. 20:6); parties draw together *lammišpāṭ* (Isa. 41:1; 54:17). The judge (divine or human) also comes *l^{e}mišpāṭ/lammišpāṭ* (Ps. 9:8[Eng. v. 7]; 76:10[9]; 122:5; Isa. 3:14; Ezk. 44:24; Mal. 3:5). In Job 9:19 *l^{e}mišpāṭ* means "if it is a matter of justice."

When *mišpāṭ* is used in the general sense of "justice," it often follows the prep. *b^{e}*. Injustice must not be done *bammišpāṭ,* in judgment, in court (Lev. 19:15; Dt. 1:17; Prov. 24:23); by *mišpāṭ* a king gives stability to the land (Prov. 29:4). Here the general sense of "administration of justice" suggests itself.[20] The prep. *'el* can also precede *mišpāṭ:* in Dt. 25:1 the parties come *'el-hammišpāṭ,* "to court." Here the meaning is almost locative, a sense expressed elsewhere by further qualifying the more general term *mišpāṭ: 'ulām hammišpāṭ,* "hall of justice" (1 K. 7:7); *m^{e}qôm hammišpāṭ,* "place of justice" (Eccl. 3:16). The construction with the prep. *'al* probably belongs here as well: "the one who sits in judgment *('al-hammišpāṭ)*" (Isa. 28:6). The toponym *'ên mišpāṭ* (Gen. 14:7) can also be explained in this way.[21]

b. *Legal Case.* In some passages the best translation appears to be "(legal) case." Moses brings the *mišpāṭ* of Zelophehad's daughters before Yahweh (Nu. 27:5). Job wants to bring his case before God (Job 13:18; 23:4). In 2 S. 15:4 this sense of *mišpāṭ* is defined more precisely by association with → ריב *rîḇ,* "lawsuit." Similar parallelism appears in Isa. 50:8, where "Who will contend *(yārîḇ)* with me?" parallels "Who is my adversary *(ba'al mišpāṭ)*?" The Levitical priests and the judge are to announce *d^{e}ḇar hammišpāṭ* (Dt. 17:9). Here the legal case issues in a decision. These meanings coalesce in the same way in 2 Ch. 19:6.

A legal case always includes a claim.[22] In this context, Liedke, following Hans-Jochen Boecker, proposes to give *mišpāṭ* the specific meaning "proposed verdict," "pleading."[23] This proposal, Liedke avers, was occasionally put forward both by the

18. Gese, 48.
19. See R. P. Merendino, *VT,* 29 (1979), 51.
20. See below.
21. G. von Rad, *OT Theology* (Eng. trans., 2 vols., New York, 1962-65), I, 12.
22. See II.3 below.
23. Liedke, *Gestalt,* 88-92; *idem, TLOT,* III, 1396-97; Boecker, *Redeformen,* 72.

parties involved and by the judge. Such a theory seems hardly necessary, since the meaning "case" or "claim" is sufficient in these passages.

c. *Verdict.* Among the texts using *mišpāṭ* in a general forensic context, one group has special reference to the decision reached, the verdict. Of course the whole judicial process cannot be divorced from the verdict, not even in those passages stating in general terms that God or the king administers justice (2 S. 8:15; 1 K. 3:28; Jer. 9:23[24], where the verb *ʿāśâ* is used). But this more general activity issues in a decision, a verdict, that summarizes the proceedings. Judgment is God's (Dt. 1:17); a case *(dāḇār)* can be too difficult to decide *(lammišpāṭ)* (Dt. 17:8); God leaves judgment to Oholibah's enemies (Ezk. 23:24).

The oral, audible nature of *mišpāṭ* sometimes finds expression: the Levites "announce" *mišpāṭ* (Dt. 17:11); it is on the lips of the king (Prov. 16:10) and is uttered by God (Ps. 105:5 = 1 Ch. 16:12). In Zeph. 3:8 Yahweh says: "For my *mišpāṭ* is to gather nations." Here *mišpāṭ* can be understood as "decision, determination"; its substance, however, is defined by the gathering of the nations.

That *mišpāṭ* sometimes has only the formal sense of "decision, verdict" is also clear from texts where it is qualified by other terms, positive or negative: *mišpaṭ-māweṯ,* "sentence of death" (Dt. 19:6; 21:22; Jer. 26:11,16); *mišpaṭ dāmîm,* "bloodguilt" (Ezk. 7:23); *mišpaṭ-ṣeḏeq,* "just decision" (Dt. 16:18); *mišpaṭ ʾᵉmeṯ,* "true decision" (Ezk. 18:8; Zec. 7:9); *mišpāṭ šālôm,* "decision making for peace" (Zec. 8:16). In 2 Ch. 19:8 *mišpāṭ YHWH,* "judgment of Yahweh," is conjoined with *rîḇ* to describe the judicial function of the Levites. The phrase might emphasize that the Levites are responsible before God when they utter judgments (cf. 2 Ch. 19:6); or it might refer to different types of cases, some being matters of God and others matters of the king (cf. v. 11).

d. *Punishment and Deliverance.* A verdict or judgment can also refer to the nature of the judgment: positive for those who are just and innocent, but negative for the wicked and sinful. With respect to the latter, several passages use *mišpāṭ* without further qualification to mean "sentence" or "punishment." When *mišpāṭ* has this meaning, it is synonymous with *šepeṭ* and *šᵉpôṭ,* both of which have only this negative sense. The noun *šepeṭ* is found only in the plural: Yahweh will intervene in Egypt with mighty acts of punishment (Ex. 6:6; 7:4); punishments await fools (Prov. 19:29); Yahweh will send four punishments (Ezk. 14:21). The usual construction is *ʿāśâ šᵉpāṭîm bᵉ,* "execute punishments upon (someone)" (Ex. 12:12; Nu. 33:4; 2 Ch. 24:24; and frequently in Ezekiel: 5:10,15; 11:9; 16:41; 25:11; 28:22,26; 30:14,19). Ezk. 23:10 uses the plural of *šᵉpôṭ* in the same construction; the singular appears in 2 Ch. 20:9, in a list of punishments.

When *mišpāṭ* is used in the sense of sentence or punishment, it is usually in the singular. The Babylonian foe passes *mišpāṭ* on the captive King Zedekiah (2 K. 25:6; the parallel text Jer. 39:5; 52:9 uses the pl. *mišpāṭîm*). The sword of Yahweh descends on Edom *lᵉmišpāṭ* (Isa. 34:5; cf. also Dt. 32:41). When the oracle of disaster against Moab in Jer. 48:47 ends with the words "thus far is Moab's *mišpāṭ,*" this refers not just to the verdict, the decision reached concerning Moab, but also to all the disasters listed, the entire fate of Moab. In Jer. 49:12, too, *mišpāṭ* means "fate, lot": "Those whose *mišpāṭ* was not to drink the cup."[24] The punishment of Yahweh strikes the wicked among the people of Israel (Ps. 1:5; Isa. 5:16; Ezk. 5:8; Hos. 5:1; 6:5), the enemy (Ps. 7:7[6]; 9:17[16]; Jer. 48:21; 51:9; Ezk. 39:21), the whole earth (Isa. 26:9 [pl.]). In executing sentence, Yahweh can make use of the enemy: he has established them *l^emišpāṭ,* for punishment (Hab. 1:12).

One can pray to God but not enter into judgment with God (Ps. 143:2). Here *bô' b^emišpāṭ (bammišpāṭ)* is used; cf. Job 9:32; 22:4; hiphil: Job 14:3; Eccl. 11:9; 12:14; *hālaḵ 'el-'ēl bammišpāṭ:* Job 34:23). In Zeph. 3:15 Jerusalem is told that Yahweh has taken away her *mišpāṭîm* and (in parallel) turned away her enemies. Finally, *mišpāṭ* as punishment can be presented and understood as chastisement with a positive goal, as illustrated by Job 36:17 in its context.

When God's punishment strikes the enemy, it means salvation and deliverance for the innocent and oppressed. Thus punitive *mišpāṭ* can also have positive content. The psalmist waits for God's *mišpāṭ* against the enemy (Ps. 119:84; 149:9). God's people execute the righteousness *(ṣiḏqaṯ)* of Yahweh and his sentences (*mišpāṭāyw:* Dt. 33:21). Therefore, they wait for God's *mišpāṭîm* and rejoice over them (Ps. 48:12[11]; 97:8; Isa. 26:8). Less clear is the reference to a forensic situation in 1 Ch. 16:14; Ps. 10:5; 105:7; here the meaning "law, ordinances" seems more apposite.[25]

Isa. 53:8 remains uncertain: "From *'ōṣer* and *mišpāṭ* he was taken (away)." Was the servant deprived of a saving verdict or judgment, or was he delivered from punishment? J. A. Soggin suggests understanding the text as meaning that the servant was led away after a sentence that was formally unimpeachable.[26]

3. *Right.* a. *Legal Right.* A positive verdict in favor of one party in a case vindicates that party's claim to be right, but the claim was valid even before the verdict was pronounced. Although a just verdict vindicates the right of the innocent, it is also true that it merely confirms an already existing right. Used in this sense, *mišpāṭ* stands for the rightful claim of the innocent party. Yahweh upholds the just cause of the oppressed or of his people (1 K. 8:45,49,59; 2 Ch. 6:35,39; Ps. 9:5[4]; 140:13[12]; 146:7; Mic. 7:9). Here the work of Yahweh is expressed by *'āśâ mišpāṭ.* With the same meaning, we also find *mišpāṭ* as the object of *šāpaṭ* (Jer. 5:28; Lam. 3:59) or *nāṯan* (Job 36:6). The psalmist prays that Yahweh will arise for his *mišpāṭ* (Ps. 35:23). A person's *mišpāṭ* can come from God (17:2) like the noonday (37:6); it is found with God (Prov. 29:26; Isa. 49:4) but can also be hidden (Isa. 40:27; Job 19:7). A female slave intended for the son of the house is to be dealt with *k^emišpaṭ habbānôṯ:* she can claim the rights of the daughters (Ex. 21:9). Jer. 30:18 says of the citadel that it shall be set on its rightful place *('al-mišpāṭô).*[27] This is its prescribed place, but also the place that it may claim.

It is also possible to deprive individuals of their right, the *mišpāṭ* that is properly

24. Cf. also the examples cited in II.5 below.
25. See II.4 below.
26. Soggin, *ZAW,* 87 (1975), 347. For further discussion see Liedke, *Gestalt,* 87.
27. See van der Ploeg, *OTS,* 2 (1943), 154.

theirs. Various constructions express this idea. God asks Job whether he wants to "break" God's *mišpāṭ,* put God in the wrong (*prr* hiphil: Job 40:8); Job insists that God has taken away his right (*sûr* hiphil: 27:2; 34:5f.). Other expressions for violating or infringing on someone's right include *gzl* (Isa. 10:2); *rṣṣ* (Hos. 5:11); *m's* (Job 31:13); and above all *nṭh* hiphil, "pervert someone's right" (Ex. 23:6; Dt. 16:19; 24:17; 27:19; 1 S. 8:3; Prov. 18:5; Lam. 3:35).

The noun *mišpāṭ* can also denote the right or authority that emanates from the power of a ruler. In Ezk. 21:32(27) the prophet speaks of the coming ruler to whom *mišpāṭ* belongs; Hab. 1:7 says of the Chaldeans that they cause *mišpāṭ* to proceed from themselves or seize *mišpāṭ* for themselves. Here we are close to the development from "legal right" to "law." Other passages use *mišpāṭ* in this sense with a further qualification to denote a particular right: *mišpaṭ habbᵉḵōrâ,* "right of the firstborn" (Dt. 21:17); *mišpaṭ haggᵉ'ullâ,* "right of redemption" (Jer. 32:7); *mišpaṭ hayᵉruššâ,* "right of possession" (Jer. 32:8; "right of first refusal" is also possible here).

To this category also belong *mišpaṭ hammeleḵ,* "right of the king" (1 S. 8:9,11), and *mišpāṭ hammᵉluḵâ,* "right of kingship" (1 S. 10:25). In this context *mišpāṭ* can be understood as the king's right or as the law governing the king and kingship. Dt. 18:3 employs a similar usage: *mišpaṭ hakkōhᵃnîm,* the right of the priests to a share of the sacrifice. In the Samuel passages, Berkovits argues for the possibility that *mišpāṭ* should be understood to mean "the manner of the king," the way kings behave.[28] Especially in the case of *mišpaṭ hammᵉluḵâ,* a royal compact or "constitution of the monarchy" is a real possibility.[29] Z. Ben-Barak sees in *mišpaṭ hammeleḵ* the Canaanite conception of kingship, and in *mišpaṭ hammᵉluḵâ* the specific form in which it developed in the Israelite monarchy.[30]

b. *Righteousness.* A just cause coincides with the substance of a right verdict. In this context *mišpāṭ* often has the meaning "what is right and proper, righteousness." Here *mišpāṭ* stands as an absolute entity, almost "world order," "the God-given norm to ensure a well-ordered society."[31] Proper conduct in all spheres is to be done in *mišpāṭ* or in conformity with *mišpāṭ.* The king is to reign *lᵉmišpāṭ* (Isa. 32:1); "in *mišpāṭ*" you shall swear (Jer. 4:2); Yahweh leads the humble in *mišpāṭ* (Ps. 25:9); Elihu asks whether Job's claim is real *lᵉmišpāṭ,* i.e., justified (Job 35:2). The devout psalmist expects help from God *kᵉmišpāṭ* (Ps. 119:132).

---

28. Pp. 199f.

29. H. J. Boecker, *Die Beurteilung der Anfänge des Königtums in den deuteronomistischen Abschnitten des 1. Samuelbuches. WMANT,* 31 (1969), 56; for further discussion, see Horst, *Gottes Recht,* 107ff.; A. Alt, "Der Anteil des Königtums an der sozialen Entwicklung in den Reichen Israel und Juda," *KlSchr,* III (1959), 367; H. Wildberger, "Samuel und die Entstehung des israelitischen Königtums," *TZ,* 13 (1957), 442-469, esp. 458; Liedke, *Gestalt,* 93; T. Mettinger, *King and Messiah. CB,* 8 (1976), 80-88.

30. Z. Ben-Barak, " 'The Manner of the King' and 'The Manner of the Kingdom' " (diss., Jerusalem, 1972). On the problem see also W. I. Wolverton, "The King's 'Justice' in Pre-Exilic Israel," *ATR,* 41 (1959), 276-286.

31. P. Uys, *NedGTT,* 9 (1968), 185.

In a series of passages *mišpāṭ* in this sense takes on overtones of deliverance, emphasized by the parallel use of the root → צדק *ṣdq* (Job 29:14; Ps. 72:2; 89:15[14]; 97:2; Isa. 1:27; 5:7; 9:6[7]; Hos. 2:21[19]) or *yš'* (Isa. 59:11). Ezk. 34:16 summarizes the actions of the good shepherd thus: "I will feed them *b^emišpāṭ,* 'as is right.' " Ps. 111:7 describes the works of Yahweh's hands as *mišpāṭ* and *'^emeṯ;* the thoughts of the righteous are *mišpāṭ* (Prov. 12:5); *mišpāṭ* (par. *g^eḇûrâ*) can fill the prophet (Mic. 3:8) or (together with *ṣdq*) Jerusalem/Zion (Isa. 1:21; 33:5). As the "right way," *mišpāṭ* can be conjoined with *dereḵ* (Dt. 32:4; Jer. 5:4,5), *nāṯîḇ* (Prov. 8:20), and *'ōraḥ* (Isa. 40:14; Prov. 2:8; 17:23). The *mišpāṭ* in a land may be snatched away (Eccl. 5:7[8]) and not be found (Isa. 59:8,15). Honest balances *(mō'z^enê mišpāṭ)* are from Yahweh (Prov. 16:11); cf. *mō'z^enê ṣeḏeq* with the same meaning. The people ask, "Where is the God of justice *('^elōhê hammišpāṭ)*?" (Mal. 2:17). God acts with a spirit of justice *(rûaḥ mišpāṭ,* Isa. 4:4; 28:6).

In the two last examples, the meaning tends in the direction of God's active intervention, to deliver or to punish. Even when *mišpāṭ* has the general sense of "right," predicate verbs and metaphors suggest activity. For example, Am. 5:24 looks for *mišpāṭ* (in parallel with *ṣ^eḏāqâ*) to roll down like waters.[32] Aberrant *mišpāṭ* springs up like poisonous weeds (Hos. 10:4). It is impossible for *mišpāṭ* to come forth, because it is perverted (Hab. 1:4); it will dwell in the wilderness (Isa. 32:16); it is far away and turned back (59:9,14). These last three passages in Isaiah use *ṣ^eḏāqâ* in parallel with *mišpāṭ*. Ps. 94:15 says that *mišpāṭ* will return to *ṣeḏeq*. Here *ṣeḏeq* is understood as the normative principle and *mišpāṭ* as the principle of conduct, which must conform to *ṣeḏeq* (cf. Ps. 119:160). M. Weber defines the relationship between *ṣeḏeq* and *mišpāṭ* with the aid of the conceptual pair "subjective/objective": *ṣeḏeq* is "the subjective sense of right, righteousness," and *mišpāṭ* is "objective right, the universally binding norm of justice."[33]

In the sense of right as a principle, *mišpāṭ* appears as the object of various verbs: Yahweh or the king loves *mišpāṭ* (Isa. 61:8; Ps. 33:5; 37:28; 99:4); *mišpāṭ* can be chosen (Job 34:4), sought (Isa. 1:17; 16:5), known (Mic. 3:1; Eccl. 8:5), heard (1 K. 3:11), learned (Prov. 1:3), sung of (Ps. 101:1). Right as a normative principle also appears as a decision reached in a concrete situation.[34] It can serve as a plumb line (Isa. 28:17; here again in parallel with *ṣ^eḏāqâ*). Negatively, *mišpāṭ* can be mocked (Prov. 19:28), abhorred (Mic. 3:9), hated (Job 34:17), perverted (Job 8:3; 34:12; 37:23), or turned to wormwood and poison (Am. 5:7; 6:12). The active nature of *mišpāṭ* often comes to the fore: *mišpāṭ* can be spoken (Isa. 32:7; Ps. 37:30; Jer. 12:1[35]), established (Am. 5:15; Isa. 42:4), brought forth (42:1,3).[36] It serves as a light (51:4; Zeph. 3:5; cf. Isa. 59:9;

---

32. On the position and development of *mišpāṭ* in this parallel, see H. W. Wolff, *Joel and Amos. Herm* (Eng. trans. 1977), 264.

33. M. Weber, *Jüdisches Lexikon,* IV/1 (Berlin, 1930), 1277.

34. See M. Noth, *Könige. BK,* IX/1 (1968), 51, on 1 K. 3:11.

35. S. Blank, *Jeremiah: Man and Prophet* (Cincinnati, 1961), 119, understands *mišpāṭ* here as "certain cases" that the prophet brings before God.

36. The broad meaning of *mišpāṭ* in Isa. 42 is underlined by W. A. M. Beuken, "Mišpāṭ: The First Servant Song and Its Context," *VT,* 22 (1972), 1-30; and J. Jeremias, "Mišpāṭ im ersten Gottesknechtslied," *VT,* 22 (1972), 31-42.

Mic. 7:9; Ps. 37:6). Here it is common for *mišpāṭ* to appear with a form of *ṣdq*. Above all, *mišpāṭ* as a principle is the object of *ʿāśâ,* "do" (Gen. 18:19,25; Dt. 10:18; 1 K. 10:9; Jer. 5:1; 7:5; 22:3,15; 23:5; 33:15; Mic. 6:8; Ps. 99:4; 103:6; 119:121; Prov. 21:3,7,15; 1 Ch. 18:14; 2 Ch. 9:8). Here too it is common to find *mišpāṭ* in parallel with a form of *ṣdq:* the righteous man does *mišpāṭ* and *ṣᵉḏāqâ* (Ezk. 18:5,19,21,27; 33:14,16,19; 45:9). Ps. 106:3 uses the parallelism "observe *mišpāṭ* and do *ṣᵉḏāqâ*"; here the meaning "law, commandment" suggests itself.[37]

4. *Law.* a. *God's mišpāṭîm.* The meaning "law, commandment" occupies an important place in the usage of *mišpāṭ*. When it denotes that which has been established, the law, *mišpāṭ* usually appears in the plural. God's *mišpāṭîm* are the individual commandments as well as the summary of the entire law. Moses or God in person commanded these laws (*ṣiwwâ:* Nu. 36:13; Dt. 6:1,20; Mal. 3:22[4:4]; 2 Ch. 33:8), gave them (*nāṯan:* Lev. 26:46; Ezk. 20:25; Ps. 72:1; Neh. 9:13), spoke them (*dibbēr:* Dt. 4:45; 5:31[28]; Jer. 1:16; 4:12), set them (*śîm:* Ex. 21:1), declared them (Ps. 147:19), and taught them (*limmaḏ:* Dt. 4:1,5,14; Ps. 119:108; *hôrâ:* Dt. 33:10; *hôḏîaʿ:* Ezk. 20:11). Moses tells *(sippēr)* the people all the *mišpāṭîm* of Yahweh (Ex. 24:3; the same verb is used in Ps. 119:13 for counting all the *mišpāṭîm* from God's mouth). Israel is to hear God's *mišpāṭîm* (*šāmaʿ:* Dt. 5:1; 7:12; with *ʾel,* Dt. 4:1), keep them (*šāmar:* Lev. 18:5,26; 19:37; 20:22; 25:18; Dt. 7:11; 11:1; 12:1; 26:17; 30:16; 1 K. 2:3; 8:58; 9:4; 2 K. 17:37; Ezk. 11:20; 18:9; 20:19; 36:27; 2 Ch. 7:17), and do them (*ʿāśâ:* Lev. 18:4; Dt. 11:32; 26:16; 1 K. 6:12; 11:33; Ezk. 18:17; Neh. 10:30; 1 Ch. 22:13; 28:7). Judgment shall conform to these *mišpāṭîm* (Nu. 35:24; Ezk. 44:24; 2 Ch. 19:10); in the happy future, people will walk in God's *mišpāṭîm* (Ezk. 37:24). The *mišpāṭîm* of Yahweh are found in Israel in contrast to the other nations (Dt. 4:8); they are plain to see (2 S. 22:23 = Ps. 18:23[22]). God's *mišpāṭîm* are described in more detail by association with other concepts: they are truth (*ʾᵉmeṯ:* Ps. 19:10[9]), like the great deep (36:7[6]), good (*ṭôḇîm:* 119:39), right (*yāšār:* 119:137), and righteous (*ṣeḏeq:* 119:75). The construct phrase *mišpᵉṭê-ṣeḏeq,* "laws of righteousness," appears in Isa. 58:2; Ps. 119:7,106.

Various expressions are used to denote contempt for and rejection of God's *mišpāṭîm* and disobedience toward them: *gāʿal* (Lev. 26:15), *māʾas (bᵉ)* (Lev. 26:43; Ezk. 5:6; 20:13,16), *mārâ* hiphil (Ezk. 5:6), *ḥāṭāʾ bᵉ* (Neh. 9:29), *sûr min* (Dnl. 9:5), *lōʾ hālaḵ bᵉ* (Ps. 89:31[30]), *bal yāḏaʿ* (Ps. 147:20), *lōʾ (lᵉḇiltî) šāmar* (Dt. 8:11; Ezk. 20:21; Neh. 1:7), *lōʾ ʿāśâ* (Ezk. 5:7; 11:12; 20:24).

Other words besides *mišpāṭîm* are used for God's commandments and ordinances, e.g., *tôrâ, ḥōq,* and *miṣwâ.* Albrecht Alt identified the *mišpāṭim* with casuistic law;[38] but further attempts to find apodictic law in *ḥōq,* e.g., must rely on the argument from silence.[39] As Sigmund Mowinckel notes, the *mišpāṭ* form and the apodictic form have

---

37. See below.
38. Alt, 92.
39. Liedke, *Gestalt,* 177ff. For further discussion → חקק *ḥāqaq* (V, 139-147).

influenced each other mutually.[40] We can say in general that the wide range of usage of *mišpāṭ* displays very little difference in meaning between *mišpāṭ* and the other words for "commandment"; *mišpāṭ* repeatedly transcends the boundaries of the various specialized meanings. The conjoining of synonyms serves to emphasize the multitude or totality of the commandments rather the specific meanings of the individual words. A good example is Ps. 119, where the various terms of *tôrâ* piety are woven into a pattern so artful that the possible differences between *mišpāṭ* and other terms for the law pale into insignificance.[41]

b. *Human mišpāṭîm.* Ezekiel also uses the pl. *mišpāṭîm* in the sense of human laws and ordinances. These *mišpāṭîm* stand in negative contrast to God's *mišpāṭîm:* "You have acted according to the *mišpāṭîm* of the pagan nations" (Ezk. 11:12); "Do not follow the *mišpāṭîm* of your fathers" (20:18). Relatively speaking, however, these human *mišpāṭîm* can constitute a good: "You have not followed my commandments and have not [even] acted according to the commandments of pagan nations" (5:7); "According to their own *mišpāṭîm* I will judge them" (7:27); "They will judge you according to their *mišpāṭîm*" (23:24). In some of these passages, the translation "custom, practice" is also possible; this leads to another section of our discussion.[42]

c. *Commandment, Statute.* In a series of texts, the sg. *mišpāṭ,* "right," appears in the specific sense of "law, commandment, statute." If an ox gores a boy or a girl, the owner shall be dealt with according to the same *mišpāṭ,* the same rule laid down in the preceding discussion (Ex. 21:31). One and the same *mišpāṭ* is to govern both the alien and the citizen (Lev. 24:22; Nu. 15:16). God's *mišpāṭ* is to be done (Zeph. 2:3), maintained (Isa. 56:1; Hos. 12:7[6]), known (Jer. 5:4,5; 8:7[43]), and not forsaken (Isa. 58:2). In this context, *mišpāṭ* may parallel *ḥōq* (Ex. 15:25; Josh. 24:25; Ps. 81:5[4]; Ezr. 7:10) or appear in the construct phrase *ḥuqqaṯ mišpāṭ* (Nu. 27:11; 35:29).

In cultic contexts an appended *kᵉmišpāṭ* or *kammišpāṭ* often indicates that a sacrifice or ceremony is to be carried out "according to regulation" (Lev. 5:10; 9:16; Nu. 9:3,14; 15:24; 29:6ff.; Ezr. 3:4; Neh. 8:18; 1 Ch. 6:17[32]; 15:13; 23:31; 24:19; 2 Ch. 30:16; 35:13). Discussing the celebration of Passover, Nu. 9:3 says that it is to be kept at the appointed time *kᵉḵol-mišpāṭāyw* (par. *kᵉḵol-ḥuqqōṯāyw*). The lampstands in 2 Ch. 4:7,20 are likewise made "as prescribed." In Ex. 26:30 *mišpāṭ* apparently stands for the plan or model of the tabernacle. The preceding text uses the word *taḇnîṯ* twice in this sense (25:9,40). This often leads to the assumption that *mišpāṭ* and *taḇnîṯ* here have the same meaning. We must note, however, that *mišpāṭ* is not used here simply as a full synonym of *taḇnîṯ;* it moves away from the concrete in the direction of a summary specification.

---

40. S. Mowinckel, *Israels opphav og eldste Historie* (Oslo, 1967), 215ff. On the subject see also Östborn, 45f.; E. Gerstenberger, *Wesen und Herkunft des sogenannten apodiktischen Rechts im AT. WMANT* 2 (1965); Hentschke, 112f.; Richter, 82, n. 119; Braulik, 61ff.; Boecker, *Law,* esp. 191-97.

41. S. Bergler, "Der längste Psalm — Anthologie oder Liturgie?" *VT,* 29 (1979), 257-288.

42. See II.5 below.

43. According to R. Albertz, *ZAW,* 94 (1982), 41f., *mišpāṭ* here refers to an early form of the Deuteronomic law.

The words are also translated differently by the LXX (*parádeigma, týpon* vs. *eídos*). Note also the translation of the two words as "model — ordinance" and "design — pattern,"[44] as well as the listing of the passage under "סדר ומנהג קבוע" by Ben-Yehuda.[45] The same usage appears in 1 K. 6:38 (cf. also Jer. 30:18; Ezk. 42:11).

Position in a series can also be defined by regulation. The priests were assigned to divisions according to the ordinance of David (2 Ch. 8:14), and barley and straw were delivered from time to time *k^e mišpāṭ* (1 K. 5:8).

5. *Custom.* In 2 K. 17:26f. we are told that the new settlers in Samaria brought there by the Assyrians did not know the *mišpāṭ* of the god of the land and were therefore attacked by lions. After receiving proper instruction, they worshiped Yahweh but continued also to worship the gods according to the *mišpāṭ* of the nations (v. 33). They continued to practice their former customs *(kammišpāṭîm hāri'šōnîm)* and did not follow the *mišpāṭ* of Israel (v. 34). In this account *mišpāṭ* clearly means not only "law" but also "procedure, custom, tradition, manner."

In the same way *mišpāṭ* is used in Ezk. 16:38 (pl.) and 23:45 (sg.) for "the law of women who commit adultery and murder." This *mišpāṭ* does not issue from legislators but from the situation; it denotes the proper procedure to be followed in this case. Here *mišpāṭ* also has overtones of "fate, lot." In Jgs. 13:12 Manoah asks the angel what should be the child's rule of life: "What should be the *mišpāṭ* of the boy and his conduct *(ma'^a śēhû)*?" The parallel here suggests the meaning "proper procedure." God has taught the farmer the proper procedure *(lammišpāṭ)* (Isa. 28:26). Every matter has its time and its *mišpāṭ,* "manner" (Eccl. 8:6).

Several texts suggest the translation "custom, usage, manner, practice" (cf. *dereḵ*): the people live securely, after the manner of the Sidonians (Jgs. 18:7); they cut themselves with swords and lances, as was their custom (1 K. 18:28); such was David's practice all the time (1 S. 27:11); David established this as a rule and practice (*l^e ḥōq ûl^e mišpāṭ:* 1 S. 30:25); the king stood by the pillar, according to custom (2 K. 11:14). In Gen. 40:13 the chief cupbearer is told that he will serve Pharaoh in "the previous manner" *(kammišpāṭ hāri'šôn).* Here the meaning is simply "as before." The Israelites marched around the city in the same manner *(kammišpāṭ hazzeh)* seven times (Josh. 6:15). In 2 K. 1:7 the question is asked: "What was the *mišpāṭ* of the man?" The answer is that he wore a hairy cloak and a leather belt around his waist. The man's *mišpāṭ* is thus understood as his characteristic appearance, his particular demeanor.

6. *Moderation.* In some passages *mišpāṭ* means "moderation." Jer. 10:24 speaks of chastisement *b^e mišpāṭ,* and 30:11; 46:28, *lammišpāṭ.* All three passages represent this chastisement as being less than total destruction: it is chastisement "in just measure, in equity." This meaning also appears in negations: "Like a bird sitting upon eggs that

---

44. For the former see K. Galling, *Exodus. HAT,* III (1939), 130, 132; for the latter, B. Childs, *The Book of Exodus. OTL* (1974), 513f., 523.

45. E. Ben-Yehuda, *Thesaurus totius hebraitatis,* 8 vols. (repr. New York, 1960), VII, 3410.

it did not lay [or: 'does not hatch'], so is one who amasses wealth, but not *bᵉmišpāṭ*" (17:11); "Woe to him who builds his house without *ṣeḏeq* and his upper rooms *bᵉlō' mišpāṭ*" (22:13). Here negated *mišpāṭ* refers to unrighteousness in general, but particularly to lack of moderation, the senseless accumulation of wealth. The negated form *bᵉlō' mišpāṭ* also appears in Ezk. 22:29: the people are oppressing aliens without justice (or "without measure"; the first part of the verse speaks of all kinds of violence). Similar examples are found in Prov. 13:23 ("The field of the poor may yield much food, but one can perish *bᵉlō' mišpāṭ*") and 16:8 ("Better is a little with righteousness [*biṣḏāqâ*] than large income *bᵉlō' mišpāṭ*"). Even though the general meaning "what is right and proper" makes good sense here, these passages refer to situations that suggest transgression of equitable limits.[46]

III. LXX. The LXX generally uses different Greek words to translate the various Hebrew words meaning "right, righteousness, law, statute." The standard translation of *mišpāṭ* is *kríma* or *krísis.* Consciously or unconsciously, the translators have thus singled out decision as an important element within the concept of *mišpāṭ.* In Ezk. 44:24 this element is underlined by the translation *diakrínein.* When the forensic activity associated with the root *krínein* does not quite fit, some twenty different translations are offered in particular passages, primarily *dikaíōma,* which is used some 40 times for *mišpāṭ* in the sense of "commandment, precept, specification." With the same meaning we also find *próstagma* (7 times) and *sýntaxis,* "regulation, specification" (3 times). The semantic nuances of *mišpāṭ* are reflected also in unique translations such as *katá tḗn archḗn,* "as before," in Gen. 40:13, and *eídos,* "form, image," in Ex. 26:30.[47]

IV. Dead Sea Scrolls. At first glance, the use of *mišpāṭ* in the Dead Sea Scrolls (about 260 occurrences) conforms to OT usage. In many passages it means "judgment," especially punitive judgment or the last judgment.[48] In these contexts we also find the noun *špṭ* as a synonym (1QM 11:16; 1QH 15:19). Also common is the meaning "commandment, statutes," both the commandments of God and the regulations of the community as an expression of God's will.[49] As in the OT, at Qumran *mišpāṭ* can also refer to a judicial process, a decision, a verdict (1QS 6:23; 7:25; 9:7,15,17; 1QSa 1:14,20; 1QH 1:6; CD 8:16; 13:5), right as a principle or entitlement (1QS 1:5; 1QH 4:25), and the "covenant of righteousness" (*bᵉrîṯ mišpāṭ:* 1QS 8:9). The meaning "manner" is suggested in CD 12:15: "This is the *mišpāṭ* of their [the locusts'] nature." The meaning "lot, destiny" also fits well. In negated form, *mišpāṭ* occurs with the meaning "without good reason" (1QS 7:4,8,18).

The meaning "(punitive) judgment" is underlined by parallelism with words from the roots *pqd* and *ng'.* When *mišpāṭ* appears with the meaning "law, statutes," parallels

---

46. See → חקק *ḥāqaq,* V, 142f.

47. See also F. Büchsel and V. Herntrich, *TDNT,* III, 920-25.

48. For further discussion, see A. Dietzel, "Beten im Geist," *TZ,* 13 (1957), 12-32, esp. 20; and Becker, 162f., 188f., noting development toward a negative meaning of *mišpāṭ.*

49. Delcor, *RB,* 61, 541; Becker, 143; Limbeck, 122.

include such words as *tôrâ* and *ḥōq*. In connection with the latter, one should note that in the Dead Sea Scrolls the root *ḥqq* is associated closely with divine predestination.[50] The idea of predestination has also colored the concept of *mišpāṭ* in the Qumran texts. In 1QS 11:12,14, Otto Betz translates *mišpāṭî* as "the (predestinizing) judgment of God concerning me"; Jürgen Becker translates similarly.[51] Cf. also 1QH 5:8f.: *l^emišpāṭ yissaḏtanî*, "you have destined me for justice."

B. Johnson

---

50. → חקק *ḥāqaq*, V, 147.
51. Betz, 31; Becker, 122.

מת *mt*

Contents: I. Etymology. II. OT Usage: 1. Secular Usage; 2. Theological Usage. 3. Personal Names.

I. Etymology. In the OT the word *mt* occurs only in the plural; the lexicons therefore list the singular without vocalization. It derives from East Semitic, although there appear to be clear connections with Egyptian and Ethiopic (*mĕt*, "husband").[1] For the Akkadian, Wolfram von Soden cites "husband" as well as the rarer meaning "warrior."[2] W. Eilers suggests that *mutum*, "man, human being," "from the biliteral root *mt*, originally meant 'mortal,' as in Indo-European."[3] In Akkadian texts the primary meaning of *mutu* is "husband."[4] The word has this same sexually determined sense in an Ugaritic text where two female deities engaged in the act of procreation with the god El cry out "Oh, man, oh, man," repeatedly and ecstatically.[5]

---

mt. W. F. Albright, "The Babylonian Matter in the Predeuteronomic Primeval History (JE) in Gen 1–11," *JBL*, 58 (1939), 91-103; J. Barth, *NSS;* H. Bauer, "Die Gottheiten von Ras Schamra," *ZAW*, 51 (1933), 81-101; 53 (1935), 54-59; *idem*, review of *IPN*, *OLZ*, 33 (1930), 588-596; H. B. Huffmon, *APNM;* T. Nöldeke, *NBSS;* M. Tsevat, "The Canaanite God Šälaḥ," *VT*, 4 (1954), 41-49.

1. *NSS*, 5; *VG*, I, 332f.; *AHw*, II, 690f.; contra *NBSS*, 146, n. 1. Egyp. *mt* is attested only as the phonetic value of the determinative of *ṯ3y*, "man."
2. *AHw*, II, 691f.
3. W. Eilers, *WO*, III/1 (1964), 120, n. 3. Cf. also J. J. Glück, "*Mat — 'nš* = Mortal," *Papers of the VI World Congress of Jewish Studies*, I (Jerusalem, 1977), 121-26.
4. *ARM*, III, 16, 7; V, 8, 13; in the latter text *mutu* is associated with "women" as an antonym.
5. *KTU*, 1.23, 40, 46.

The meaning of *mt* in the Aramaic Zinjirli inscriptions is disputed.[6] G. A. Cooke begins by listing a variety of meanings the word might have in its various occurrences, but then concludes: "It seems more reasonable to give *mt* the same meaning throughout."[7] Citing Mark Lidzbarski, he translates *mt* as "surely, indeed." Herbert Donner and Wolfgang Röllig call *mt* an "emphatic particle of unknown etymology," whose meaning ("an indefinite pronoun") and origin remain obscure "for lack of clear textual settings."[8] In the disputed Phoenician text from Parahyba, *mt* appears to mean "mighty man."[9]

II. OT Usage.

1. *Secular Usage.* In East Semitic and Ugaritic, *mt* appears with the meaning "man, husband." This usage is found in the OT where the text emphasizes the sex of the referent (Isa. 3:25, par. *g^e^ḇûrîm*). This is clear in the book of Job, where Job speaks of his "contemporaries" (*m^e^ṯê ʾoh^o^lî:* 31:31), who are also his partners in the dialogue (11:3; 19:19). The scene has to recall Gen. 18:1ff., where Abraham talks with his guests while his wife is off in the tent preparing the meal.

The phrase *ʿîr m^e^ṯîm* in Dt. 2:34 and 3:6 is unusual; it may also occur in Jgs. 20:48. Using the hiphil of → חרם *ḥrm* and → נכה *nkh,* the text describes the destruction of an enemy city and its inhabitants. The article is never used. This phrase, similar to a proper name, clearly represents an idiom that may refer to a city together with its population fit for military service. This usage could be related to the secondary meaning found in Akkadian.[10]

Similarly, *m^e^ṯîm* could be understood in the collective sense ("people") in the following passages, whose interpretation is disputed. In Isa. 5:13 *m^e^zēh rāʿāḇ,* "dying of hunger," should be read instead of *m^e^ṯê,* in parallel with *ṣiḥēh ṣāmāʾ,* "parched with thirst"; the only other occurrence of *māzeh* is in Dt. 32:24. In Ps. 17:14 most commentators emend the two occurrences of *mim^e^ṯîm* to forms of the verb *mwt* or its derivatives, while Artur Weiser translates: "before people."[11] In Job 24:12, too, the MT *m^e^ṯîm* is uncertain. Although the phrase *ʿîr m^e^ṯîm* recalls Dt. 2:34; 3:6, the following line (*nepeš ḥ^a^lālîm t^e^šawwēaʿ,* "the souls of the wounded cry out for help") suggests emending *m^e^ṯîm* to *mēṯîm* (*mēʿîr mēṯîm yinʾāqû,* "from the city of the dead they groan").

2. *Theological Usage.* The phrase *m^e^ṯîm mispār,* "men/people of [small] number," is used in secular contexts in Gen. 34:30 and Dt. 33:6; but it also appears in texts of

---

6. *DISO,* 172; *KAI,* 214, 12-14, 28; 215, 4, 10, 16.

7. G. A. Cooke, *A Text-Book of North-Semitic Inscriptions* (Oxford, 1903), 167.

8. *KAI,* II, 219.

9. See C. H. Gordon, *Or,* 37 (1968), 76.

10. See I above. Cf. also *GesTh,* II, 830; N. Lohfink (→ V, 187): *ʿîr mēṯîm* probably refers to a segment of the enemy population.

11. A. Weiser, *Die Psalmen. ATD,* 14 (^4^1955), 120 [not in the Eng. trans.]. For emendations to forms of the verb see Gunkel, *Die Psalmen. HKAT,* II/2 (^4^1926), 59; and to derivatives, H.-J. Kraus, *Psalms 1–59* (Eng. trans., Minneapolis, 1988), 244-45, 249.

theological import. Either the "small number of people" is the result of and punishment for apostasy from Yahweh (Dt. 4:27; 28:62), or the passage extols the rise and increase of the people under Yahweh's leadership, giving thanks in the form of a confession of faith (Ps. 105:12; 1 Ch. 16:19; cf. Dt. 26:5: *m^e^tê m^e^ʿaṯ*). This brings comfort to the "small number of people," called a "remnant" (*š^e^ʾērîṯ*) (Jer. 44:28). Deutero-Isaiah even calls the *m^e^ṯê yiśrāʾēl* "you worm Jacob" (*tôlaʿaṯ yaʿ^a^qōḇ*, Isa. 41:14).

Beyse

This interpretation, defended by Karl Elliger, was first proposed by Heinrich Ewald.[12] It requires emending the text, reading *rimmaṯ yiśrāʾēl* instead of *m^e^ṯê yiśrāʾēl* in order to yield a parallel to *tôlaʿaṯ yaʿ^a^qōḇ*. But the interpretation of the ancient versions cannot simply be rejected as an ad hoc solution and the 1QIs[a] reading *wmyty* called "not a solution to the problem"; they support the MT. A derivation from → מות *mwt* makes no sense in this passage, however; neither does recourse to the semantically pallid *mt* help. Therefore emendation has been proposed. Now the construct phrase *tôlaʿaṯ mtym* occurs in 1QH 6:34; 11:12 (the latter in the context of a soteriological confession). While Karl Georg Kuhn is undecided, Eduard Lohse commits himself to the translation "worm of the dead," without supporting his interpretation.[13] The anthropological overtones of the occurrences in the Dead Sea Scrolls (cf. Ps. 22:7[6]; Job 25:6) clearly suggest the semantic component "mortal" for *mt*, so that these passages should be cited in explaining Isa. 41:14.

Fabry

In contrast to the quantitative concept of *m^e^ṯê mispār*, *mt* is associated with a qualitative concept in the lamentation of a psalmist (Ps. 26:4) and in the theological disputes of Job with his friends (Job 11:11; 22:15). In Ps. 26:4 *m^e^ṯê šāwʾ*, "worthless people," parallels *naʿ^a^lāmîm*, "hypocrites." In Job 11:11 it parallels *ʾāwen*, "iniquity," while Job 22:15 speaks of *m^e^ṯê ʾāwen*, "wicked people," who have lived in Job's day and cannot be considered exemplary.

3. *Personal Names*. It has long been recognized that the PNs Methushael (Gen. 4:18) and Methuselah (5:21) must derive from *mt*.[14] Hans Bauer interprets them as "kinship names," in which the kinship term in the construct is followed by the name of a deity; thus *m^e^ṯu-* means "man/worshiper of the god N."[15] Elsewhere he proposes associating the *mt* element with the Ugaritic deity Mot.[16] The first interpretation is supported by the PN *mt-bʿl*, found several times in the Ugaritic texts.[17] According to

12. Ewald, *Commentary on the Prophets of the OT*, 5 vols. (Eng. trans., London, 1875-81), IV, 266; Elliger, *Deuterojesaja. BK*, XI/1 (1978), 146.

13. Kuhn, 118, 138; Lohse, *Die Texte aus Qumran* (Munich, 1971), in loc.

14. *NSS*, 5; *NBSS*, 146; H. Holzinger, *Genesis. HSAT* (1922), 53.

15. "Personennamen," 593f.

16. *ZAW*, 51, 94ff.; 53, 54ff.

17. *KTU*, 4.75 V, 21; 4.130, 10; 4.310, 4. See *WUS*, no. 1706; for other occurrences in Semitic,

Claus Westermann, the interpretation of the name *mᵉṯûšā'ēl* as "man of God" is disputed.[18]

Beyse

see Albright, 97; and Tsevat, 41. Tsevat attempts to prove the existence of a Canaanite deity *Šelaḥ* (→ לח *laḥ* [VII, 514]).

18. C. Westermann, *Genesis 1–11* (Eng. trans., Minneapolis, 1984), 328f.

מָתַי *māṯay*

Contents: I. Etymology; II. Akkadian; III. OT; IV. *ʿaḏ-'ānâ*.

I. Etymology. Heb. *māṯay,* "when?" has reflexes in most Semitic languages: Can. (Amarna) *matima,* Phoen. *mtm,* Syr. *'emmaṯ(y),* Arab. *matā,* OSA *mt, mtm,* Amhar. *matu,* Akk. *mati,* all with the same meaning.[1]

II. Akkadian. Akk. *mati* is in the first instance an ordinary interrogative: "When did I do such and such?" "When shall we hire reapers?" "When can I repay you the favor you have done me?"[2] Special interest attaches to the phrase *adi mati,* "until when, how long," which occurs frequently in impatient questions, e.g., "How long do I have to keep sending tablets [letters]?" "How long do I have to stay here?" "How long do we have to be at odds?"[3] It appears as a formula in laments and penitential prayers, where it can be considered a stylistic element comparable to the language of the Hebrew psalms. Among the passages cited, one occurs in a late Sumerian prayer (possibly under Akkadian influence), the rest in Akkadian texts: "How long, my God, until your angry heart is soothed?"[4] "How long, O my Lady, are my enemies to look darkly upon me, are they to plan evil things against me with lies and deception, are my persecutors and those who envy me to rejoice over me? How long, O my Lady, are the cripples and the fools to pass by me (in contempt)?"[5] "How long will you be

māṯay. H. Gunkel and J. Begrich, *Einleitung in die Psalmen. HKAT,* Erg. (^{2}1966), 230; E. Jenni, "מָתַי *māṯay* 'when?' " *TLOT,* II, 691-92; C. Westermann, "The Structure and History of the Lament in the OT," *Praise and Lament in the Psalms* (Eng. trans., Atlanta, 1981), 165-213, esp. 177f.

1. On Phoenician see *DISO,* 155; on Old South Arabic, ContiRossini, 181; not in Biella.
2. For these and other examples see *CAD,* X/1, 407.
3. For these and other examples see *CAD,* I/1, 119.
4. *SAHG,* 227.
5. *NERT,* 110f.

angry, my Lady, and is your face turned away? How long, my Lady, will you be wrathful and your heart enraged?"[6] "How long, O Lady, have you inflicted on me an unceasing sickness?"[7] "How long, O God, will you do this to me?"[8]

III. OT. In Hebrew both *māṯay* and the phrase *'aḏ-māṯay* appear in impatient questions, e.g., Ex. 10:3, "How long will you refuse? . . . Let my people go"; 10:7, "How long shall this fellow be a snare to us?"; 2 S. 2:26, "How long will it be before you order your people to turn from the pursuit of their kinsmen?" (cf. also Nu. 14:27; 1 S. 1:14). These impatient questions, which are often rhetorical, are concentrated in psalmodic literature, frequently serving as introductory formulas:

Ps. 42:3(2): When shall I come and behold the face of God?
Ps. 101:2: When will you come to me?
Ps. 6:4(3): My soul is struck with terror, while you, O LORD — how long?
Ps. 74:10: How long, O God, is the foe to scoff? Is the enemy to revile your name forever?
Ps. 80:5(4): How long will you be angry with your people's prayers?
Ps. 90:13: Turn *(šûḇâ)* to us, Yahweh — how long?
Ps. 94:3: How long shall the wicked . . . rejoice?
Jer. 12:4: How long shall the land wither?
Zec. 1:12: How long will you withhold mercy from Jerusalem?

The primary purpose of these questions is to be heard as petitions: act, intervene! Therefore Ernst Jenni rightly sees them as a topos rooted in the communal and individual lament.[9]

We also find the question "How long?" in prophetic discourse, possibly modeled on the language of the psalms:

Hos. 8:5: How long will they be incapable of innocence?
Jer. 4:14: How long shall your evil schemes lodge within you?
Jer. 31:22: How long will you waver, O faithless daughter?
Jer. 47:5: How long will you gash yourselves?

Such impatient, reproachful questions are also exhortations to repent, issuing from anguish over the delayed *kairos,* but also from anger at the people's hardness of heart.

From the language of prophecy, the formula entered the later language of wisdom: "How long, O simple ones, will you love being simple?" (Prov. 1:22); also the ironic question in Prov. 6:9: "How long will you lie there, O lazybones?"

IV. *'āḏ-'ānâ.* We find *'āḏ-'ānâ* (or *'ad-'ān,* Job 8:2) used similarly to *'aḏ-māṯay,* in laments:

---

6. *SAHG,* 333.
7. *SAHG,* 267.
8. *SAHG,* 270.
9. P. 692.

Ps. 13:2f.(1f.): How long, O LORD? Will you forget me forever? How long will you hide your face from me? How long must I bear pain . . . , how long shall my enemy be exalted over me?

Hab. 1:2: How long, O Yahweh, shall I cry for help, and you will not listen?

and in reproachful questions: Ex. 16:28; Nu. 14:11; Josh. 18:2; Job 8:2; 19:2. In Jer. 47:7 the impatient question is addressed to Yahweh's sword: "How long can you be quiet?"

Ringgren

מָתַק *māṯaq;* מָתוֹק *māṯôq;* מֹתֶק *mōṯeq;* מֶתֶק *meṯeq;* מַמְתַקִּים *mamᵉṯaqqîm*

Contents: I. 1. Etymology, Meaning; 2. Occurrences; 3. Semantic Parallels. II. 1. Literal Usage; 2. Figurative Usage; 3. Theological Usage.

I. 1. *Etymology, Meaning.* The root *mtq,* found in the various Semitic languages, may be onomatopoeic in origin, imitating the sound of licking or smacking one's lips (cf. *mṣṣ, mwṣ,* etc.). If so, its original meaning would be something like "eat with pleasure." This basic meaning easily accounts for the following semantic ramifications: Akk. *matqu,* "sweet"; *matāqu,* "be(come) sweet"; *muttāqu* and *mutqû,* "sweet cake";[1] Ugar. *mtq,* "sweet";[2] Syr. *mᵉṯaq,* "suck happily"; Jewish Aram. *mᵉṯaq,* "taste, lick"; Middle Heb. *māṯaq,* "be sweet, tasty," piel "suckle, soothe," etc.;[3] Arab. *mtq* (*t* before *q* assimilated to *ṭ*[4]), stem V "taste with pleasure, smack one's lips"; *mtk* (*k* assimilated to *t*), "(sucking) proboscis of a worm";[5] Tigr. *maṭṭaqa,* "sweet."[6] It is undeniable, however, that the connection between the stative verb *mtq,* "be sweet," and the active verb "suck" remains obscure.

2. *Occurrences.* The root appears 25 times in the OT: 6 times as a verb, twice in a toponym, and elsewhere as a noun or adjective. The verb in the qal means "become

---

māṯaq. A. Jirku, *Materialien zur Volksreligion Israels* (Leipzig, 1914), 34-40; B. Kedar, *Biblische Semantik* (Stuttgart, 1981), 154f., 174f.; W. Michaelis, "μέλι," *TDNT,* IV, 552-54; B. Olsson, "Die verschlungene Buchrolle," *ZNW,* 32 (1933), 90ff.; J. Streitberg, "Der Mensch in der Bildersprache des ATs" (diss., Bonn, 1935), 42-44; E. Struck, *Bedeutungslehre* (²1954), 113-18, 131; G. Widengren, *Literary and Psychological Aspects of the Hebrew Prophets. UUÅ,* 10 (1948), 100ff.; A. Wünsche, *Die Bildersprache des ATs* (1906), 96; J. Ziegler, *Dulcedo Dei. ATA,* XIII/2 (1937).

1. *CAD,* X/1, 405, 413f.; *AHw,* II, 632f.
2. *UT,* no. 1576.
3. Jastrow, 864; *WTM,* III, 301f.
4. *VG,* I, 161.
5. E. Ben-Yehuda, *Thesaurus totius hebraitatis,* 8 vols. (repr. New York, 1960), VII, 3453ff.
6. *HAL,* II, 655.

sweet" (Ex. 15:25) and "be sweet," i.e., be perceived as sweet, taste sweet (Prov. 9:17). The hiphil has a similar meaning where, as a reflexive-transitive modification of the basic meaning "sweet," it indicates that this taste arises in the subject (Job 20:12; Sir. 49:1). Elsewhere, however, the causative sense "sweeten, make sweet" is clear (Sir. 38:5; Ps. 55:15[Eng. v. 14]).

The toponym *miṯqâ* (LXX *mad/tekka,* Sam. *mtykh*) is the name of one of the camps on Israel's journey through the wilderness (Nu. 33:28f.); the name probably reflects the presence of a sweet-water spring (cf. Targ. Yerushalmi; Jerome, *De nominibus heb.: "mathca, dulcedo vel saturatis* [*mathca,* sweetness or richness]").

The suffixed form *moṯqî* in Jgs. 9:11 implies an abstract noun *mōṯeq,* "sweetness." The construct *meṯeq* in Prov. 16:21 has a similar meaning, suggesting either an identical absolute form or an adjectival form **māṯēq* (cf. const. *keḇeḏ* < *kāḇēḏ*); an erroneous vocalization of *māṯōq* has also been proposed.[7] The theory of an adjective form is supported by the parallel word in the second hemistich (const. *ḥᵃḵam*). The noun *meṯeq* in Prov. 27:9, a difficult text, is discussed below.

The preformative form *mamᵉṯaqqîm* (instead of *mamtaqqîm* or *mamtāqîm*[8]) occurs twice. In Neh. 8:10 it is a plural denoting a product ("sweet wine," par. *mašmannîm,* "fat food)"; in Cant. 5:16 (par. *maḥᵃmaddîm*), it is a plural of amplification intensifying the abstract concept "sweetness."[9] The adj. *māṯôq* also has the feminine form *mᵉṯûqâ* and pl. *mᵉṯûqîm;* the variant vowel is explained most simply as a reduction of *o* to *u* in an unaccented syllable.[10] We may therefore classify *māṯôq* as an original *qaṭāl* form.[11]

The meaning — with the exception of Job 24:20, to be discussed below — is always "sweet" in the literal or figurative sense. The LXX consistently uses *glykýs* (and derivatives) in translating the root; the Vulg. generally uses *dulcis* (and derivatives). Greek and Latin also use these words metaphorically.[12] Only for *mamᵉṯaqqîm* does the Vulg. prefer some different translations: *suavissimus* in Song of Songs and *mulsum,* "honied wine," in Nehemiah. Lat. *dulcis* also represents other Hebrew words when the text is describing jubilation (Isa. 24:8), a lovely voice (Cant. 2:14; 4:3; Ezk. 33:32), or a pleasant sleep (Jer. 31:26). Like the Greek word, it can also be used for *ʿāsîs,* "must, grape juice" (Am. 9:13). Finally, it describes the "gentle *(nimlᵉṣû)*" words of God (Ps. 119:103: Gk. *glykéa,* Lat. *dulcia* [Gallican Psalter]). This translation and the association with Ps. 34:9(8) later gave rise to the notion of the sweetness of God, epitomizes God's goodness and love: "What is sweeter than the LORD *(quid dulcius domino)?*"[13]

---

7. Torczyner, *ZDMG,* 64 (1910), 273.
8. *GK,* §85g, n. 1; §93ee; *NSS,* 174c.
9. For the former see *GK,* §124l-m; for the latter, §124e.
10. *VG,* I, 143.
11. Contra *NSS,* 23b; P. Lagarde, *Übersicht über die im Aramäischen, Arabischen und Hebräischen übliche Bildung der Nomina* (Göttingen, 1889), 60.
12. Struck.
13. Jerome, *Ep.* 78, 25, on the Psalm verses in question. See Ziegler.

The Targ. avoids the word *m^eṯîq,* using instead the two words *hālê* and *bāsîm* without distinction, so that their divergent basic meanings (sweet taste and pleasant odor, respectively) become totally blurred.

3. *Semantic Parallels.* There are clearly profound physiological reasons why we find a sweet taste pleasant: sugar in its various forms is needed by the body and is indispensable for the functioning of all the body's organs. The individual sensory realms influence each other, and we perceive an association between the impressions evoked by the various senses. It is therefore possible to apply the terminology of "tasting sweet" to other sensory spheres and finally to mental impressions.

Of the countless examples we could cite from a wide range of languages, we shall list a few that exhibit particular similarities to OT usage. An Akkadian text extols the goddess who "makes girls sweet *(mumattiqat).*"[14] Ugaritic verses speak of El's kissing his wives and describe their "lips as sweet as pomegranates" *(hn špthm mtqtm mtqtm klrmnm).*[15] Egyp. *bnr* means a "sweet" taste as well as "pleasant, gentle" speech, a "beloved" person, and the like; its synonym *nḏm* means not only "sweet" but also "fragrant," "refreshing," and finally "pretty" and "happy" *(nḏm ἰb).*[16] Homer celebrates the "tongue from which flows speech sweeter *(glykíōn)* than honey"; Euripides praises the "sweet light" *(hēdý gár tó phṓs).*[17] The rhetorician Seneca speaks of a "sweet color" *(color dulcis),* and Goethe of the "sweet light of sounds."[18] But sweetness can also represent a false, seductive charm concealing mischief and evil: "te veneni calicem circumlinere melle voluisse, ut simulata dulcedo, virus pessimum tegeret."[19]

II. 1. *Literal Usage.* It is the nature of the OT writings to be concerned less with depicting concrete situations than with interpreting them. Therefore determination of the literal meaning associated with *mtq* has to rely on just a few occurrences and limit itself to the most immediate context. A statement like "The drippings of the honeycomb are *māṯôq* to your taste" (Prov. 24:13) clearly indicates that "sweet tasting" is the concrete meaning of the Hebrew word; but even here, as the following verse shows, we are ultimately dealing with a metaphorical facade.

Above all, *māṯôq* describes honey (Jgs. 14:18; Prov. 24:13), which served as sugar in days gone by.[20] Our word thus stands in close relationship with the words for honey and nectar (Ps. 19:11[10]; Prov. 16:24; etc.): *nōpeṯ* ("honey from the comb") and *māṯôq* appear as corresponding elements in poetic parallelism (Prov. 27:7), and similes often declare that something is as sweet as or even sweeter than honey.[21] Fruit is *māṯôq*

---

14. *CAD,* X/1, 405.
15. *KTU,* 1.23, 50.
16. *WbÄS,* I, 462f.; II, 379f.
17. Homer *Iliad* 1.249; Euripides *Iphigeneia at Aulis* 1.1218.
18. Seneca *Controversiae* 1.4.7; Goethe, *Des Epimenides Erwachen,* 1, 17.
19. *Contra Rufinum* 1.7.
20. → דבשׁ *d^ebhash* (III, 128-131).
21. See II.2 below.

(Cant. 2:3), e.g., figs (Jgs. 9:11). Something sweet is good (*ṭôḇ:* Prov. 24:13); as food, it is pleasant (*yinʿām:* 9:17) and healthful (*marpēʾ:* 16:24). Sweet wine *(mamᵉṯaqqîm)* is drunk at festivities (Neh. 8:10).

The quality frequently named as the opposite of *māṯôq* is *mar,* which means "bitter" and "pernicious."[22] The water at Marah, the first oasis on the journey through the desert, was bitter until Moses threw a piece of wood into it and it became sweet (i.e., potable; *wayyimtᵉqû;* Ex. 15:23-25). The relativity of our tastes did not escape the notice of the sages: one who is full spurns even sweet food, but to someone who is hungry anything bitter is *māṯôq* (Prov. 27:7). Food acquired unlawfully tastes seductively good, and stolen water seems sweet (*yimtāqû:* 9:17).

The original meaning of the root *mtq,* "suck with pleasure," appears to be preserved in Job 24:20: *mᵉṯāqô rimmâ,* "worms have sucked him" (NRSV: "the worm finds [him] sweet"), but we may be dealing with an Aramaism. The text is difficult; in any case the verse describes the fate of the dead. The Vulg. *dulcedo illius vermes* reflects the reading *moṯqô rimmâ.* The feminine subject is preceded by a masculine verb because the subject is an animal.[23] The Midrash, however, takes God as the subject: "who causes the worm to suck them *(šemmittēq).*"[24]

2. *Figurative Usage.* Figurative usage resembles that found in other languages. A synesthetic extension of meaning enables light to be described as *māṯôq* (Eccl. 11:7). Here the physiological foundation has already vanished. The synesthesia is emotional: in this context the sunlight is an image of life, which is perceived as *māṯôq* in contrast to the darkness of death.

The refreshing sleep of the laborer is sweet (*mᵉṯûqâ:* Eccl. 5:11[10]). The Targ. finds here a reference to eternal rest, clearly a mistaken interpretation; but Job 21:33 does in fact speak of the sweet repose of the dead: "The clods of the valley are sweet *(māṯᵉqû)* to them."

Above all, the ecstasy of love is perceived as *māṯôq.* What now appears to be a veiled answer to Samson's riddle in fact has love as its subject: "What is sweeter *(māṯôq)* than honey? What is stronger than a lion?" (Jgs. 14:18). This was probably originally an independent riddle, to which the answer was: "Love."[25] The theory that the riddle in 14:14 refers to sexual intercourse appears dubious, as does the conjecture that it deals with adultery.[26] It might, however, be an ancient hunters' proverb expressing satisfaction that a ravening beast can yield a tasty meal *(maʾᵃḵal . . . māṯôq).*

In one of the descriptive lyrics of the Song of Songs, the beloved lists among the merits of her lover his mouth, which is sweetness (*mamᵉṯaqqîm:* 5:16). The text probably allludes to kisses rather than sweet words. More explicit eroticism appears in

---

22. → מרר *mrr.*
23. *GK,* §145o.
24. *Gen. Rab.* 33.32.
25. Gunkel, *Reden und Aufsätze* (Göttingen, 1913), 53.
26. For the former see Eissfeldt, "Die Rätsel in Jdc 14," *ZAW,* 30 (1910), 132-35. For the latter see Gressmann, *Die Anfänge Israels. SAT,* I/2 (²1922), 250f.

2:3, where the lover is compared to an apple tree in whose shadow his beloved longs to sit and whose fruit is *māṯôq* to her taste. This refers not to "the security and joys of marriage" but to sexual intercourse.[27]

Sweetness can also represent enticement to foolishness and misconduct, which are followed by bitter punishment. "The rascal enjoys the sweet taste *(tmtyq)* of what he has begged" (Sir. 40:30), but afterward it burns like fire within him. Sinners hide wickedness under their tongues, for "wickedness tastes sweet *(tamtîq)* in their mouth" (Job 20:12); ultimately, however, it kills them like the poison of asps. Folly is seductive: "Stolen water is sweet *(yimtāqû)*" (Prov. 9:17); but those who follow its counsel are condemned to Sheol. This text expresses a general observation about the attractiveness of what is forbidden, but it probably thinks particularly of sexual debauchery and adultery.

For the most part, however, the concept of "sweetness" serves to represent positive values. "Sweetness of the lips" *(meṯeq śᵉp̄āṯayim)* (Prov. 16:21), i.e., pleasant speech, is recommended for the sage; for pleasant words are "sweet *(māṯôq)* to the soul and healthful to the body" (16:24).

This is probably also the meaning of *ûmeṯeq rēʿēhû,* literally, "sweetness of a friend," in Prov. 27:9 — in other words, "a pleasant word from a friend," as interpreted by the rabbinic commentaries. The text, however, is uncertain; the LXX reads a single word, *ûmiṯkārēaʿ* ("is torn"?).

The bonds of friendship are perceived as sweet: "you . . . with whom I kept sweet [i.e., pleasant] company" (Ps. 55:15[14]), the psalmist addresses a perfidious friend. In the prophet's woes against perversion of justice (Isa. 5:20), injustice is described as bitter, whereas righteousness is good, bright, and *māṯôq.* Knowledge and wisdom, which result in moral conduct, are to the soul what honey from the comb is to the lips (Prov. 24:13f.).

3. *Theological Usage.* As the embodiment of what is good and true, useful and healthful, the term *māṯôq* can be applied to the words of Yahweh. The prophet Ezekiel ingests the scroll with the divine message like food; in his mouth, it is "like honey in its sweetness *(lᵉmāṯôq)*" (Ezk. 3:3; cf. Rev. 10:9). The second section of Ps. 19 (vv. 8-12[7-11]) glorifies the law of Yahweh, whose ordinances are true and righteous, more desirable than gold, and "sweeter *(mᵉṯûqîm)* than honey and drippings from the comb" (v. 11[10]). To those who keep them they bring health and refreshment.

Kedar-Kopfstein

---

27. Quotation from Budde, *Das Hohelied erklärt. KHC,* XVII (1898), 7. See P. Haupt, *Biblische Liebeslieder* (Leipzig, 1907), XI; on the apple tree as a symbol of love see H. Ringgren, *Das Hohelied. ATD,* XVI/2 (^{3}1981), 263.

נאה n'h; נָאוֶה nā'weh

Contents: I. Occurrences and Etymology: 1. OT Occurrences; 2. Etymology. II. Meaning: 1. Secular Usage; 2. Ethical and Theological Usage.

I. Occurrences and Etymology.

1. *OT Occurrences.* Three OT passages have verbal forms traditionally derived from the root *n'h:* Isa. 52:7; Cant. 1:10 *(nā'wû);* Ps. 93:5 *(na'ᵃwâ).* More common are the masculine (*nā'weh:* Prov. 19:10; 26:1; Cant. 2:14; 4:3) and feminine (*nā'wâ:* Ps. 33:1; 147:1; Prov. 17:7; Cant. 1:5; 6:4) forms used adjectivally. Both the verbal and the adjectival forms possess a broad spectrum of meanings, comprising aesthetic, ethical, and theological domains.[1] Sirach uses the root (with a different orthography) only in the ethical sense characteristic of proverbial literature. The root is not attested in other West Semitic dialects or in Akkadian.

2. *Etymology.* In Hebrew philology the etymology of the verbal and adjectival forms assigned here to the triliteral root *n'h* is disputed. The majority of scholars are inclined to derive this root from → אוה *'wh;* they analyze the attested forms as niphal perfect tense and participle. The passive notion "(be) desired" would yield the meaning "(be) beautiful" in the aesthetic sense, as found in the Song of Songs; the meaning "(be) proper, correct" as an ethical and theological term would then represent a secondary abstraction. Wilhelm Gesenius instead sees in the verbal forms a pilel of *n'h,* similar to the hithpael form of *šḥw* = *šḥh,* with the meanings "be beautiful," "be seemly."[2] While in his *Wörterbuch* Gesenius called *n'h* a by-form of *nwh* (deriving from it the form *'anwēhû,* "I will glorify him," in Ex. 15:2), in his *Thesaurus* he sought to combine the meanings of *n'h* and *nwh* and derive from *na'ᵃwâ lᵉ,* "suit, become someone," the concept of "seemly" on the one hand and "beautiful" on the other. In this case, the basic meaning would be found in the concept "seemly, becoming," which reflects the usage of the word in proverbial wisdom; the aesthetic categories of beauty and attractiveness as well as the word's theological use (as found in the Psalms)[3] would then derive from this meaning. The OT texts where *nā'weh* appears as an adjective (Jer. 6:2; Ps. 68:13[Eng. v. 12]) are textually uncertain and cannot be used for etymological purposes.

---

n'h. J. Barth, review of *NBSS, DLZ,* 39 (1911), 717-732, esp. 731; J. Blau, "*Nāwā ṯhillā* (Ps. cxlvii 1): Lobpreisen," *VT,* 4 (1954), 410f.; C. Brockelmann, "Zur hebräischen Lautlehre," *ZDMG,* 58 (1904), 518-524; T. Nöldeke, review of M. Hartmann, "Die Pluriliteralbildungen in den semitischen Sprachen" (diss., Halle, 1875), *ZDMG,* 30 (1876), 184-88, esp. 185; *idem, NBSS.*

1. See, respectively, II.1, II.2.a, and II.2.b below.

2. *GesB,* 477. *HAL* (I, 295f.), however, analyzes forms like *hištaḥᵃwâ* as the eshtaphel of *ḥwh;* see already Nöldeke's discussion in *ZDMG,* 30 (1876), 186; → חוה *ḥwh* (IV, 248-256).

3. See II.2.b below.

II. Meaning.

1. *Secular Usage.* The Song of Songs is a collection of secular love songs.[4] In this book, as one would expect, the verbal and adjectival forms of *n'h* are used aesthetically to describe the outward appearance of the young woman. She calls herself beautiful despite her sun-darkened skin (1:5); the young man describes her face, whose cheeks are surrounded with chains and strings hanging down from her hair or headdress,[5] as attractive (1:10); and he extols her lovely voice (4:3; cf. 2:14).

2. *Ethical and Theological Usage.* a. *Ethical Usage.* The usage of the adj. *nā'weh* in proverbial wisdom leads into the realm of ethical conduct. The negations *lō' nā'weh* and *lō' nā'wâ* criticize the conduct of the fool *(nāḇāl, k^esîl)* as inappropriate, unseemly: "Like snow in summer or rain in harvest, so honor is not fitting for a fool" (Prov. 26:1).[6]

b. *Theological Usage.* In Ps. 33:1; 147:1, the statement that it is fitting for the upright to sing Yahweh's praises is formulated as a religious obligation.[7] This usage leads into the theological and cultic realm. Ps. 93:5 likewise belongs to the cultic sphere; here, however, *na'^{a}wâ* expresses the essential bond between the house of God and its sacred character: "to your house holiness is due."[8]

The words of Isa. 52:7 effect a kind of integration of the secular and theological aspects: the news conveyed by the "beautiful feet" of the messenger is comforting and joyous; it promises the stricken nation peace, good fortune, and deliverance; it is an "evangel"[9] that makes the world beautiful and whole.

Beyse

4. O. Eissfeldt, *The OT: An Intro.* (Eng. trans., New York, 1965), 486f.
5. W. Rudolph, *Das Hohelied. KAT,* XVII (1962), 127.
6. Cf. B. Gemser, *Sprüche Salomos. HAT,* XVI (1963), 92.
7. But cf. Blau, who takes *nā'wâ* in parallel with *zamm^{e}râ* as a "feminine infinitive"; the same approach is taken by H.-J. Kraus, *Psalms 60–150* (Eng. trans., Minneapolis, 198), 555.
8. Cf. Kraus, *ibid.,* 232.
9. → בשׂר *bśr* (II, 313-16).

נְאֻם *n^e'um*

Contents: I. Occurrences and Etymology. II. Semantic Development. III. Usage. IV. Theological Meaning. V. Dead Sea Scrolls, LXX.

n^e'um. F. Baumgärtel, "Die Formel *n^e'um jahwe,*" *ZAW,* 73 (1961), 277-290; R. Rendtorff, "Zum Gebrauch der Formel *n^e'um jahwe* im Jeremiabuch," *ZAW,* 66 (1954), 27-37 = *GSAT. ThB,* 57 (1975), 256-266; G. Rinaldi, "Alcuni termini ebraici relativi alla letteratura," *Bibl,* 40

I. Occurrences and Etymology. The word *n^e'um* occurs 376 times in the OT; 365 times it is used as a formula for an utterance of Yahweh, 11 times for a human utterance. It is common in Jeremiah (176), Ezekiel (85), and Isaiah (25). In proportion to the length of the books, the number of occurrences in Amos (21), Haggai (12), and Zechariah (20) is noteworthy. There are 5 occurrences in Zephaniah, 4 in Hosea, 2 each in Obadiah, Micah, and Nahum, and 1 each in Joel and Malachi. Outside the prophetic books, *n^e'um* occurs 4 times in 2 Kings, twice each in 1 Samuel, 2 Samuel, and Psalms, and once each in Genesis, Proverbs, and 2 Chronicles. Numbers has 6 occurrences in the Balaam oracles plus 1 additional occurrence.

A verb *n'm* appears only in Jer. 23:31. It has been compared to Arab. *na'ama,* "roar, growl, sigh," probably a variant of *nhm.*[1] Despite the archaic feel of the verb, the suggestion that it means "murmur" is probably wrong; mostly likely it is denominative and means simply "speak." We often find *n^e'um* in parallel or variation with → דבר *dābhār* (e.g., Jer. 23:31; Ezk. 37:14; Zec. 12:1; Prov. 30:1). In Jer. 23:28 God denies that the false prophets who "utter utterances" (*wayyin'^{a}mû n^e'um,* v. 31) speak his *dāḇār.*

Giovanni Rinaldi nevertheless claims to detect a difference in meaning: in his opinion, *n^e'um* means the active revelation of God, whereas *dāḇār* means the inspired utterance of the prophet.[2] Therefore *dāḇār* introduces the latter, while *n^e'um* stands at the end of the utterance to emphasize its divine origin and guarantee.

II. Semantic Development. From the early Balaam oracles in Nu. 24, where *n^e'um* in the mouth of a seer serves as a self-presentation formula, Claus Westermann and Dieter Vetter see a development leading to a divine utterance, through which the prophets bear witness that their message originates in divine revelation and that they have been sent by God.[3] Both 2 S. 23:1 and Prov. 30:1 are probably late emulations of "seer oracles."

III. Usage. The normal, most common use of the Yahweh utterance formula is to conclude a rhetorical unit beginning with a *dāḇār* such as "thus says Yahweh" or "the word of Yahweh came." Such a unit may consist of a single verse (e.g., Jer. 31:36; 34:17; Ezk. 26:5; 30:6). On a somewhat larger scale, a condition may lead to a promise

---

(1959), 271-73; T. Seidl, "Die Wortereignisformel in Jeremia," *BZ,* 23 (1979), 20-47; D. Vetter, *Seherspruch und Segensschilderung. CThM,* ser. A, 4 (1974); *idem,* "נאם *n^e'um* 'utterance,' " *TLOT,* II, 692-94; C. Westermann, *Basic Forms of Prophetic Speech* (Eng. trans., Philadelphia, 1967); H. Wildberger, "Jahwewort und prophetische Rede bei Jeremia" (diss., Zurich, 1942); H. W. Wolff, "Die Begründungen der prophetischen Heils- und Unheilssprüche," *ZAW,* 52 (1934), 1-22.

1. *HAL,* II, 657, 676.
2. Pp. 271-73.
3. Westermann, 188f.; Vetter, *TLOT,* II, 693. See also Wolff, *Joel and Amos. Herm* (Eng. trans. 1977), 143, who, citing Am. 3:15; 9:7, sees this development beginning with Amos. On Nu. 24 see W. Rudolph, *Der "Elohist" von Exodus bis Josua. BZAW,* 68 (1938), 120.

(e.g., Jer. 15:19,20; 28:2,4). In longer units, *dāḇār* and *n*^e^*'um* may frame an oracle concerning Babylon (Jer. 51:36,39) or Gog (Ezk. 39:1,5). Sometimes the alternation of the two forms results in an artful stylistic structure (Ezk. 14:12-20; Hag. 2:4-9; Zec. 1:3-4). It is rare for the Yahweh utterance formula by itself to characterize words as coming from God. In Zeph. 1:2 a redactional introduction is followed by a threat, attested to be the "word of Yahweh" (cf. also Isa. 14:22; 30:1; Ps. 110:1). The formula serves as an introduction in six texts in Amos; Hans Walter Wolff rightly asks whether this usage is not a sign of later redaction.[4]

Especially in Ezekiel, the Yahweh utterance formula often concludes extensive rhetorical units (e.g., Ezk. 22:23,31). It also appears frequently at the boundary between prose and poetry (e.g., Jer. 8:3[Eng. 9:1]; 21:10; Ezk. 14:23; 21:12; Isa. 66:17), where it might serve to conclude a unit, but might also be associated with the compilation of the prophetic utterances. The same is true when the formula marks a change of theme (Jer. 27:22; 31:14). But we must also reckon with the possibility that within a lengthy discourse the prophet found it appropriate to emphasize that it was ultimately not he who was speaking but God.

The Yahweh utterance formula can also coincide with a logical transition: it may signal a conclusion (e.g., Isa. 1:24; Jer. 23:1f.; Ezk. 18:30) or introduce a particularization (Jer. 2:19f.; Ezk. 11:8; Zeph. 1:2f.) or an antithesis (Jer. 22:16; 29:19f.). In short, it can be associated with a wide range of rhetorical transitions; we should not assume automatically that its presence is redactional.

In some passages the formula must be original because it is indispensable to the context: without it the speaker would not be identified. Here and there it even seems to be a characteristic of prophetic discourse to begin with an uncertain subject in order to arouse interest by raising a question; then the Yahweh utterance formula makes the situation clear. For example, Isa. 49:14 begins by asking whether Yahweh has forsaken Zion; then the unwavering love of a mother for her child is cited as a counterexample. Not until v. 18 does the formula make clear that God is asking the question. In Jer. 23:9,10a, an unidentified subject speaks in the 1st person, while Yahweh is mentioned in the 3rd person. Then the formula explains that Yahweh is in fact the speaker (cf. also Zec. 10:11f.). Such alternation between speaking about Yahweh and the Yahweh utterance formula can lead to extraordinarily dramatic discourse, as in Am. 4:4-11. Often the prophet appears to be speaking; the formula, however, traces the words back to God, thus making clear (as in messenger speech) how the God who speaks to and through his prophets is conceived and represented as being one with them in their proclamation.[5]

It is also a mark of lively rhetorical style that the Yahweh utterance formula can even stand parenthetically within a clause, as in Jer. 2:9: "Therefore once more I accuse you — utterance of Yahweh — and I accuse your children's children" (there are 12 instances in Jeremiah [e.g., 7:30], 8 in Ezekiel [e.g., 16:8], and 7 elsewhere in the OT). The verb *'āmar* is used in the same way (Gen. 3:3a; Isa. 45:24a; etc.).

---

4. Wolff, *Joel and Amos,* 143.
5. See Wolff, *ZAW,* 52, 6.

IV. Theological Meaning. After noting the occurrences and usage of the Yahweh utterance formula, we must turn our attention to what is being said when it is used. It is comparable to the phrase "I am Yahweh" that motivates cultic and social ordinances in Lev. 19.[6] Our formula emphasizes that the message of the prophets comes from God, through whom their words are true and effectual. That the formula refers above all to God's truthfulness is shown by the addition in Ezk. 37:14 (cf. 35:8): "I have spoken and will act." The same point is made by the 21 passages where our formula underlines an oath spoken by God (cf. Jer. 22:5; 49:13). This occurs 14 times in Ezekiel (e.g., 34:8; 35:11).

The distinction expressed by the formula is important when God's word conveys a threat: 8 times in Isaiah (e.g., 17:3), 29 in Jeremiah (e.g., 13:25), 27 in Ezekiel (e.g., 23:34), and 8 elsewhere in the OT. Even more often the formula is associated with promises: 6 times in Isaiah (e.g., 37:35), 47 in Jeremiah (e.g., 32:44), 12 in Ezekiel (e.g., 18:9), and 3 elsewhere. The texts where God's word is directed against Israel's enemies may also be counted among the promises. It is true, however, that many of the promises appear to be the product of later redaction, especially when they are appended with the formula to long threat discourses (e.g., Jer. 46:26; 48:47; 49:39).

Not uncommonly the Yahweh utterance formula appears in conjunction with the phrase "the days will come" or "on that day." The point is to indicate that Yahweh knows the future, that he governs the course of world history and controls future destiny. Such statements are frequent in Jeremiah (26 times; e.g., 3:16; 30:8) and occur 19 times elsewhere in the OT. They concern weal and woe in the realm of history; once, at most, in the victory over Gog (Ezk. 38f.), they rise to the level of eschatology.

Sometimes the Yahweh utterance formula does not stand independently but is expanded by an important addition. In Ezk. 16:62f.; 20:44; 34:31; 37:14; 43:27, it is linked with "you shall know that I am Yahweh" (the "recognition formula").[7] We may recall Ex. 3, where the name of God bears witness that Moses has been sent by God, and God seeks to show that he stands by his people and fulfills the promises to their ancestors. Jer. 31:32 and Ezk. 16:62 speak of the covenant in conjunction with the formula. The same notion is present in Ezk. 34:15,31: Israel is God's flock and God is the shepherd of his people. Isa. 17:6 similarly adds "God of Israel" and 1:24 *'^{a}ḇîr yiśrā'ēl*. Finally, our formula is constructed 25 times with *YHWH ṣ^{e}ḇā'ôṯ* (e.g., Isa. 22:25; Jer. 25:29; Hag. 1:9; 2:4,8,9,23), which expresses God's "royal sovereign power."[8]

In three passages (Jer. 46:18; 48:15; 51:57) our formula reads "utterance of the King." The important role played by the divine name is demonstrated, however, by the addition of "whose name is *YHWH ṣ^{e}ḇā'ôṯ*" in each instance. The same meaning is

6. → III, 348-350.
7. → III, 350-52; V, 471-76.
8. A. S. van der Woude, *TLOT,* II, 1045.

expressed by the addition of *'ªḏōnāy* to "Yahweh" (83 times in Ezekiel; only 4 exceptions); it is intended to characterize God as "ruler."[9] This understanding of the name takes concrete form in Isa. 66:2: all things belong to Yahweh, because he created them. It is Yahweh who set a boundary to the sea (Jer. 5:22). God fills heaven and earth (Jer. 23:24), so that the false prophets cannot hide from this "God near by." Zec. 8:17 uses the Yahweh utterance formula to say that God hates evil and false oaths; in Isa. 1:24 he threatens to avenge himself on his foes.

But the formula can also be used to express salvific situations. God calls the faithless children to return (Jer. 3:14); acts with steadfast love, justice, and righteousness (9:23[24]); looks on the oppressed (Isa. 66:2); and will gather once more the outcasts of Israel (56:8). If, following Hans Wildberger, we interpret 31:9 as an assurance of deliverance,[10] then "utterance of Yahweh" serves also to signal Yahweh's intimate association with Zion. Thus *nᵉ'um YHWH,* with its many associated statements, is a confession of the self-revealing God of Israel.

V. Dead Sea Scrolls, LXX. The only occurrence in the Essene documents from Qumran (CD 19:8) replaces the *nᵉ'um YHWH ṣᵉḇā'ôṯ* of Zec. 13:7 with the sg. *nᵉ'um 'ēl.*

The LXX almost always uses *légein* to translate *nᵉ'um.*

Eising(†)

---

9. → I, 62.

10. *Jesaja 28–39. BK,* X/3 (1982), 1246; contra O. Kaiser, *Isaiah 13–39. OTL* (Eng. trans. 1974), 318f.

נָאַף *nā'ap̱*

Contents: I. Survey. II. Adaptation of the Decalog by the Prophets. III. Metaphorical Use: 1. General; 2. Child Sacrifice. IV. LXX.

---

nā'ap̱. G. Delling, "Ehebruch," *RAC,* IV (1959), 666-677; A. Eberhardter, *Das Ehe- und Familienrecht der Hebräer. ATA,* 5 (1914); F.-L. Hossfeld, *Der Dekalog. OBO,* 45 (1982); W. Kornfeld, "L'adultère dan l'Orient antique," *RB,* 57 (1950), 92-109; *idem, Studien zum Heiligkeitsgesetz* (Vienna, 1952), 69-89; B. Lang, " 'Du sollst nicht nach der Frau eines anderen verlangen,' " *ZAW,* 93 (1981), 216-224; H. McKeating, "Sanctions against Adultery in Ancient Israelite Society," *JSOT,* 11 (1979), 57-72; A. Phillips, *Ancient Israel's Criminal Law* (Oxford, 1970); *idem,* "Another Look at Adultery," *JSOT,* 20 (1981), 3-25; H.-F. Richter, *Geschlechtlichkeit, Ehe und Familie im AT und seiner Umwelt. BBET,* 10 (1978); L. Rosso Ubigli, "Alcuni

I. Survey. While the verb *nā'ap* is also attested in Jewish Aramaic and Palestinian Aramaic, its derivatives *na'ᵃpûp* and *ni'ûp* appear only in the Hebrew Bible. The 34 occurrences in the OT are concentrated in the prophetic literature (24), especially Jeremiah (9), Ezekiel (7), and Hosea (6). It appears 6 times in the Pentateuch (once each in the Decalogs and 4 times in Lev. 20:10) and 4 times in the Wisdom Literature. Analysis of its distribution shows clearly that the term was shaped by the Priestly tradition to denote an offense against marital law. The prophets borrowed this terminology to describe offenses against the covenant between Yahweh as husband and Israel his wife.

Since the Decalog itself does not go into further detail to explain its sixth (seventh) commandment, *lō' tin'āp,* the meaning must be determined from other texts. In Lev. 20:10-21, a list of casuistic laws dealing with sexual transgressions, v. 10 states: "If a man commits adultery *(yin'ap)* with the wife of his neighbor, both the adulterer *(nō'ēp)* and the adulteress *(nō'epet)* shall be put to death" (the repetition of *'îš . . . 'et-'ēšet* is dittography).

Since nothing is said about whether the adulterer is married, this question clearly does not matter in the situation. The woman's status, however, is defined, and therefore represents a critical factor. The man commits adultery against the woman's husband, not against the woman herself or against his own wife, should he be married. The woman offends against her husband and their mutual relationship. The practice of polygamy by the patriarchs, rare instances of bigamy in later times, royal harems, regulations governing plural marriages, and the terminology of marital status in cases of adultery show that we are never dealing with an offense against the wife of the adulterer (if he is married). (Although most Israelite marriages were monogamous, monogamy was the product of social status and property considerations, not morality.)[1]

The offense, however, is more than just a violation of property rights. If a man (married or unmarried) had sexual intercourse with an unmarried woman, he did not have to fear the death penalty; he had instead to pay the bride-price (Ex. 22:16f.). The woman's father could give her to the man to be his wife or refuse to do so; in either case, the bride-price had to be paid, since the financial value of the woman to her father or guardian had been reduced through loss of her virginity. But both Decalogs and Lev. 20:10 treat adultery as a capital offense. The adulteress is not a piece of property whose decreased value must be compensated for but the wife of a man whose relationship with her has been profaned.

---

aspetti della concezione della 'porneia' nel tardogiudaismo," *Henoch,* 1 (1979), 201-245; J. Scharbert, "Ehe und Eheschliessung in der Rechtssprache des Pentateuch und beim Chronisten," *Studien zum Pentateuch. Festschrift W. Kornfeld* (Vienna, 1977), 213-225; H. J. Schoeps, "Ehebewertung und Sexualmoral der späteren Judenchristen," *ST,* 2 (1950/51), 88-102; S. Schreiner, "Mischehen — Ehebruch — Ehescheidung," *ZAW,* 91 (1979), 207-228; H. Schüngel-Straumann, *Der Dekalog — Gottes Gebote? SBS,* 67 (1973), 47-53; → זנה *zānāh* (IV, 99-104); → שׁכב *šākab.*

1. See T. Kronholm, "Polygami och Monogami i Gamla Testamentet," *SEÅ,* 47 (1982), 48-92.

Finally, adultery must be distinguished from fornication and prostitution. Ezk. 16:1-43a describes Israel's idolatry as prostitution *(zānâ)* and adultery. We read in vv. 31b-34:

> You were not like a whore *(zōnâ),* because you scorned pay. Adulterous wife *(hā'iššâ hammᵉnā'āpeṯ),* you receive strangers instead of your [MT: her] husband. Gifts are given to all whores; but you gave your gifts to all your lovers, bribing them to come to you from all around for your whorings *(taznûṯ).* So you were different from other women in your whorings *(bᵉṯaznûṯayiḵ):* no one solicited you to play the whore *(zûnnâ);* and you gave payment, while no payment was given you; you were different.

An adulteress is therefore a woman who has sexual intercourse with others instead of her own husband. A prostitute is paid for her sexual favors (vv. 31b-32). This terminological difference between *nā'ap̱* and *zānâ* is also evident in the father's warning to his son in Prov. 6:20-35. The father points out to his son that a prostitute *('iššâ zōnâ)* sells her favors for "a loaf of bread." The man pays, and the consequences, if any, are minimal. By contrast, the adulteress in her passion seeks to devour the man, with fatal consequences. The enraged neighbor seeks revenge and will be content only with the death of the adulterer (v. 34); compensation or bribes are fruitless (v. 35).

Prostitution *(zᵉnûnîm, zᵉnûṯ, taznûṯ)* is thus the offer of sexual intercourse for sale; adultery *(ni'ûp̱, na'ᵃp̱ûp̱)* is sexual intercourse with another's spouse, the violation of a marital relationship. The result of the latter is dishonor, disgrace, and death (cf. David and Bathsheba, 2 S. 11:1–12:23); the effect of the former is loss of the price of a loaf of bread (cf. Prov. 2:16-19; 5:1-14; 7:5-27; 9:13-18).

The terms, however, are not mutually exclusive: a prostitute can be married and thus be an adulteress, and an adulteress can accept payment for sexual favors (Jer. 5:7f.; Hos. 4:13f.). Hosea's wife Gomer is an example of terminological interaction, for she is both an adulteress and a prostitute (Hos. 2:4[2]; 3:1-3).

II. Adaptation of the Decalog by the Prophets. Hos. 4:2 and Jer. 7:9f. are examples of flexible adaptation of the Decalog on the part of the prophets, who charge Israel with violating the covenant. Comparison of the two lists with the Decalog shows that the prophets combined and rearranged the material in different ways.

1. Both prophets eliminate the four commandments least concerned with the direct relationship between offender and victim (prohibition of images, Sabbath, parents, coveting); the accusations actually cited concern transgressions of the covenant that directly affect the human rights of the victim.

2. Both prophets list Israel's transgressions in affirmative style (finite verbs + inf. abs.), not the traditional apodictic style ("You shall not . . ."). What Israel should not do, it has done.

3. Both lists comprise five elements, four of which are the same. The last element differs. Hosea and Jeremiah charge Israel with perjury, murder, adultery, and stealing (kidnaping). Hosea's fifth charge has to do with lying, i.e., false witness; Jeremiah's fifth charge has to do with worship of other gods, the only transgression not infringing on human rights. (Since *nā'ap̱* includes idolatry as well as violation of marital bonds, and since the rites of the Baʿal cult included sexual intercourse and thus necessarily resulted in violation of the marital relationship, Jeremiah's fifth charge is understandable.)

4. The prophets do not cite the Decalog of Ex. 20 verbatim. They use the same verbs for "kill" *(rṣḥ),* "commit adultery" *(nā'ap̱),* and "steal" *(gānaḇ),* but otherwise the terminology is different. Finally, they vary the sequence of the commandments in the two lists: Hos. 4:2 lists perjury, lying, murder, stealing (kidnaping), and adultery; Jer. 7:9f. lists stealing (kidnaping), murder, adultery, perjury, and offering incense to Ba'al and going after other gods.

These passages show that the prophets used the Decalog as a barometer to determine the social and religious climate of the community, but its text could be interpreted, shortened, and adapted to suit the purpose of the author in question.

In addition, *nā'ap̱* and its derivatives are used in other contexts to denote sexual infidelity by a married woman and her partner; in this context *nā'ap̱* generally appears in conjunction with the terminology of covenant violation: Jer. 9:1f.(Eng. vv. 2f.); 29:23; Hos. 7:1b,4; Mal. 3:5 (*nā'ap̱* par. *šqr*); Ps. 50:18 (*nā'ap̱* par. *gānaḇ*); Job 24:14f. (*nā'ap̱* par. *rāṣaḥ, gānaḇ*).

All these passages use *nā'ap̱* in conjunction with *šqr* (5 times) and *gānaḇ* (5 times). This might suggest that the two concepts are related, i.e., when adultery is committed, other violations of the covenant follow. The adulterer has wronged his neighbor by taking what rightfully belonged to his neighbor; in the final analysis, he has stolen and exploited a human being bound to another.[2] The adulteress has wronged her husband in respect to their relationship and has lied to him by breaking the marriage oath. In any case, the breakdown of the social integrity of the nation is a well-known charge against the covenant community; and adultery is one of the most frequent signs of social chaos and violation of the covenant, along with stealing (kidnaping), perjury, and murder.

III. Metaphorical Use.

1. *General.* Since the prophetic movement found it appropriate to describe the relationship between Yahweh and Israel in terms of the relationship between husband and wife, it likewise characterizes religious transgression as adultery. This is especially clear in Jer. 3:8-9 (*nā'ap̱* par. *zānâ*). Addressing the Judahites of the seventh/sixth century, he speaks of their sister nation Israel as an adulteress who has received her decree of divorce. This divorce, manifest in the destruction of the nation, was the direct result of Israel's infidelity "on every high hill and under every green tree" (v. 6). The prophet charges Judah with having learned nothing from the fate of her sister nation; she must therefore expect the same terrible reaction on the part of Yahweh.[3] The prophet beseeches Judah to turn from her adultery "with stone and tree" (v. 9) and from "scattering her favors among strangers under every green tree" (v. 13).

The prophetic condemnation of the adultery of Israel and Judah by no means refers only to the spiritual adultery of idolatry; it includes the actual adultery of the worshipers

2. → גנב *gānabh* (III, 39-45).

3. For further discussion see G. Hall, "The Marriage Imagery of Jeremiah 2 and 3" (diss., Union Theological Seminary of Virginia, 1980).

who surrender themselves to cultic prostitution in the Canaanite fertility cult. Although the situation remains obscure, Gomer's violation of her marriage with Hosea may have resulted from participation in cultic prostitution (Hos. 2:6-13[4-11]). In this case, we may be dealing with actual adultery, and we would have here an example of how the Israelites committed adultery when they took part in the worship of Baʿal.

This close relationship between sexual intercourse on the part of the devotees and the worship of Canaanite gods to the exclusion of Yahweh explains why the prophetic movement used *nā'ap* and its derivatives to describe Israel's infidelity. The use of this term was based on the fact that adultery against Yahweh represented adultery against one's own marital partner (cf. Jer. 5:7f.; 13:27; 23:9-14).

We can draw a further conclusion from the prophetic use of *nā'ap:* the term seems to have coalesced with *zānâ,* and both words became synonymous with Israel's immorality and infidelity toward Yahweh. The distinction between violation of a marriage contract and sexual intercourse for pay was lost, and both terms developed into an expression of flagrant disobedience toward the covenant between Israel and God.

2. *Child Sacrifice.* In the prophetic literature, three texts associate Israel's adultery toward Yahweh with child sacrifice, which appeared in Israel during the eighth century and was practiced until the exile. Trito-Isaiah speaks explicitly of the adulteress/whore who sacrifices her children (Isa. 57:1-6, esp. vv. 3-5, *meṉā'ēp* par. *zônâ,* MT: *wattizneh*).

First, the association of adultery with child sacrifice derives from the prophetic notion that violation of Israel's marriage with Yahweh is seen most clearly in cultic prostitution and child sacrifice. The gravity of Israel's adultery with other gods is revealed in the enthusiastic sacrifice of children. Second, the connection can also find expression in a cyclic round of cultic observances. Men and women enter the sanctuary and surrender themselves to sexual intercourse in fertility rites, thus committing adultery against their own spouses and against Yahweh. It is quite possible that the children sacrificed were the very children begotten in cultic intercourse.

In two passages (Ezk. 16:35-43; 23:43-49) Ezekiel also illustrates the connection between Judah's adultery/whoredom and child sacrifice. In 16:38 the prophet proclaims the criteria for God's judgment: "I will judge you as women who commit adultery *(nō'ᵃpôṯ)* and shed blood are judged, and bring blood upon you in wrath and jealousy." V. 36 makes clear whose blood Judah has shed: the blood of her children. The terms *nā'ap* and *šāpaḵ dām* occur together not only because they represent the two most common violations of the covenant but also because they were performed together within a cultic ritual. The ultimate fulfillment of the fertility ritual was probably the birth of children, who were then sacrificed to the god who had bestowed this fertility, or in order to appease him in a time of great distress. The combination of *nā'ap* and *šāpaḵ dām* shows that the prophet intends to assail this very cycle.

Ezekiel also damns these practices in his diatribe against Oholah and Oholibah (23:36-49). One of the charges is that "they have committed adultery, and blood is on their hands; with their idols they have committed adultery; and they have even offered up to them for food the children whom they had borne to me" (v. 37). A second time Ezekiel attacks the adultery and bloodshed of Israel and Judah (vv. 43ff.). The repulsive practice of slaying the children of adulterous relationships in the sanctuary as a sacrifice to the deity is the final, unforgivable violation of the marriage bond between God and his people.

Freedman — Willoughby

IV. LXX. The LXX generally uses *moicheúō* to translate *nā'ap,* distinguishing it systematically from the semantic realm of *zānâ (pornéō).* Adultery and prostitution are thus linguistically distinct phenomena.[4] The root has not yet been found in the Dead Sea Scrolls.

Fabry

4. See F. Hauck, *TDNT,* IV, 729-732; Hauck and S. Schulz, *TDNT,* VI, 584f.

נָאַץ *nā'aṣ;* נְאָצָה *n^{e}'āṣâ;* נֶאָצָה *ne'āṣâ*

Contents: I. 1. Root; 2. Statistics; 3. Semantic Field. II. 1. Meaning; 2. Theological Usage. III. 1. Sirach and Dead Sea Scrolls. 2. LXX.

I. 1. *Root.* The root *n'ṣ* and its derivatives are attested in West and East Semitic as well as in the Hebrew OT. In Middle Hebrew we find both the verb and the new noun *nî'ûṣ* (= Heb. *n^{e}'āṣâ*); the Aramaic of the Targs. uses only the corresponding noun *nî'ûṣā',* "abuse, slander."[1]

In Ugaritic there are 5 certain occurrences of the root *n'ṣ,* "despise."[2] The verb appears once in narrative in an ʿAnat text.[3] The active participle *(n'ṣ)* with a suffix occurs 4 times; 3 of these are in the Aqhat epic,[4] each time with reference to the potential enemies of Danel who denigrate his royal appearance. The active participle also occurs in a poorly preserved text in the Baʿal-ʿAnat cycle.[5]

nā'aṣ. H. Wildberger, "נאץ *n'ṣ* 'to disdain,' " *TLOT,* II, 694-96. On II: A. Geiger, *Urschrift und Übersetzung der Bibel* (1857, Frankfurt am Main, [2]1928); M. J. Mulder, "Un euphémisme dans 2 Sam xii 14?" *VT,* 18 (1968), 108-114. On III: N. Peters, *Liber Jesu Filii Sirach sive Ecclesiasticus hebraice* (Freiburg im Breisgau, 1905); H. Preisker and G. Bertram, "μυκτηρίζω, ἐκμυκτηρίζω," *TDNT,* IV, 796-99; H. Seesemann, "παροξύνω, παροξυσμός," *TDNT,* V, 857.

1. *WTM,* 323.
2. *WUS,* no. 1731; *UT,* no. 1589.
3. *KTU,* 1.1, IV, 23.
4. *KTU,* 1.17, I, 29; II, 3, 18; the reconstructed text of I, 47 might also be included.
5. *KTU,* 1.5, IV, 26.

In Akkadian we find *nâṣu(m)* or *na'āṣu,* "look upon with disdain."[6] Two uses of the root are of special interest. In the Babylonian Theodicy, the sufferer laments that he is "treated with contempt" (*i-na-a-ṣa-an-ni;* l. 253); but he must let his friend accuse him of himself "despising" (*ta-na-ṣu:* l. 79) the plans of (his) god.[7] The form *na'āṣu* is found in the Amarna letters:[8] Rib-Adi, the ruler of Byblos, complains that his is "despised" *(ti-na-i-ṣú-ni, ia-an-aṣ-ni)* on account of his military weakness.

Akk. *na'āṣu,* "bite or chew to pieces," is not related to our root (cf. Arab. *nhš,* "bite"), although there may be a connection with Arab. *nwṣ,* "avoid."[9]

2. *Statistics.* The verb *n'ṣ* occurs 24 times in the OT: 8 times in the qal, 15 in the piel, and once in the disputed participial form *minnō'āṣ* (Isa. 52:5).[10] Nominal forms are *n^{e}'āṣâ* (2 K. 19:3 par. Isa. 37:3) and *ne'āṣâ,* an aramaizing piel infinitive with 3 occurrences (Ezk. 35:12; Neh. 9:18,26).[11] The 8 occurrences of the verb in the qal are in Proverbs (3), Jeremiah (2), Deuteronomy, Psalms, and Lamentations (1 each); the 15 piel occurrences are in Psalms (4), Numbers and Isaiah (3 each), 2 Samuel (2), Deuteronomy, 1 Samuel, and Jeremiah (1 each). There are also 3 occurrences of piel participles with personal suffixes (1st person sg.: Nu. 14:23; Jer. 23:17; 2nd person sg.: Isa. 60:14), as well as an infinitive absolute (2 S. 12:14).

3. *Semantic Field.* The following parallels constitute the primary semantic field of *n'ṣ:* → חרף *ḥrp* II, "despise, reproach, scoff" (Ps. 74:10,18); → מאס *mā'as,* "reject" (Isa. 5:24; Jer. 33:24); → עזב *'āzab̲,* "forsake" (Isa. 1:4); → מרה *mārâ* hiphil, "be rebellious" (Ps. 107:11; Neh. 9:26); → מרד *mārad̲,* "rebel" (Neh. 9:26); → שׂנא *śānē',* "hate" (Prov. 1:30); → נבל *nbl* piel, "dishonor" (Jer. 14:21); → חמס *chāmās,* "do violence to" (Lam. 2:6); → שׁחת *šḥt* piel, "destroy" (Lam. 2:6).

Usage that is clearly theological is exhibited in the parallels → פרר *prr* + *b^{e}rîṯ,* "break the covenant" (Dt. 31:20; Jer. 14:21); → עבד *'āb̲ad̲* with *'^{e}lōhîm '^{a}ḥērîm* as its object, "serve other gods" (Dt. 31:20); *zwr* niphal + *'āḥôr,* "turn back" (Isa. 1:4); *hālak̲* + *bišrirûṯ lēb̲,* "walk in hardness of heart" (Jer. 23:17); and *šlk* + *'aḥ^{a}rê gaw,* "cast (the law of Yahweh) behind one's back, refuse to observe" (Neh. 9:26; cf. also 1 K. 14:9; Ezk. 23:35; with *gēw:* Isa. 38:17).

As antonyms we may note: → שׁמר *šāmar,* "heed" (Prov. 15:5); → אבה *'āb̲â,* "desire" (negated: Prov. 1:30); *hištaḥ^{a}wâ* (→ חוה *ḥwh*), "bow down" (Isa. 60:14); → אמן *'āman* hiphil, "trust, believe" (negated: Nu. 14:11); and finally *zāk̲ar b^{e}rîṯ,* "remember the covenant" (Jer. 14:21), and → בחר *bāchar,* "choose" (Jer. 33:24).

Verbs with similar meanings include: → קלל *qll* piel, "call contemptible," hiphil

6. *AHw,* II, 758a.
7. *BWL,* 86, 76; also translated in *AOT,* 285f., and *ANET*[3], 603f.
8. EA, 137, 14, 23.
9. Contra *KBL*[2], 585b. On Arab. *nhš* see Wehr, 1003; on Arab. *nwṣ* see Wehr, 1010; *HAL,* II, 658a; cf. also A. Guillaume, *Abr-Nahrain,* 4 (1963/64), 18.
10. See II below.
11. *BLe,* 479nγ.

"treat as contemptible"; *bwz/bāzâ* (→ בזה *bāzāh*), "despise"; → קלס *qls* piel, "scorn," hithpael "make fun of"; → גדף *gādhaph* piel, "revile"; *gā'al* and → תעב *t'b* piel, "abhor"; and *sālâ* qal, "dismiss," piel "reject."

II. 1. *Meaning.* It is hard to distinguish the qal from the piel with respect to the basic meaning of *n'ṣ*. According to Hans Wildberger, the qal should be understood as meaning "fail to perceive, misjudge the significance of something," the piel as meaning "treat with contempt."[12] But the 3 occurrences of the qal in which Yahweh is the subject (Dt. 32:19; Jer. 14:21; Lam. 2:6) contradict this distinction: they speak of something more than disrespect. The contexts suggest instead that the qal of *n'ṣ* is close to meaning "spurn" (Dt. 32:19f.), "reject" (Jer. 14:21), or "destroy" (Lam. 2:6). The meaning of the qal is thus not estimative but effectual.[13] It goes far beyond the meaning that Wildberger assigns to the piel. The basic meaning behind both the qal and piel of *n'ṣ* is "disparage, disrespect."

Only in two areas do we find traces of secular usage of the root and its derivatives.[14] In Jer. 33:24, in words addressed to Jeremiah (the passage is not authentic), Yahweh takes offense because there are people who "hold his people in such contempt" (*n'ṣ* qal) that they no longer regard them as a nation. Of course the theological context shows that these people, presuming to know that Yahweh has rejected *(m's)* the two families, have drawn the correct conclusion concerning the degradation of the people of God. Here we may also note the use of *n^{e}'āṣâ* in 2 K. 19:3 par. Isa. 37:3, which speaks of a "day of distress, of rebuke, and of 'disgrace.'" Finally, we come to Ezk. 35:12, with the suffixed plural of *ne'āṣâ (nā'ṣôteykā)* dependent on *'mr* ("utter"): here a divine oracle accuses Edom of having uttered "abusive speech" against the mountains of Israel.

Fundamentally, then, the qal of *n'ṣ,* used with respect to relationships between nations, means "reduce (in significance), make contemptible," or "treat with contempt." The passage in the Amarna letters cited above shows that in pre-Israelite Palestine Akk. *na'āṣy* was already used for disparagement of a king (cf. also the Ugaritic passages in Aqhat). Against this background, we may interpret the 3 occurrences of *n'ṣ* qal just mentioned and its derivatives as showing that the verb *nā'aṣ,* used in the first instance in a general sense, took on theological significance when used with Israel as its object, touching on or illuminating antithetically the nation's understanding of itself and its election by God.

The 3 occurrences of *n'ṣ* qal in Proverbs illustrate the other *Sitz im Leben* of the root: the educational system or wisdom instruction. The fool "despises" a parent's instruction *(mûsār)* (Prov. 1:15); those who "despise" the reproof *(tôkaḥaṯ)* of wisdom (1:30; 5:12) must bear the terrible consequences of their actions. No one can "despise" with impunity the ordering of life on the basis of experience (15:5) or wisdom (1:30;

12. P. 695.
13. *HP,* 225.
14. Wildberger, 695f.

15:5). While Babylonian wisdom in the Babylonian Theodicy (l. 79) cited above speaks of despising the plans of the deity, the texts in Proverbs have a remarkably secular ring. Even here, however, people are required to conform to the given order of the world, which may well (through wisdom) emanate from God, if they are not to suffer for their disregard. Furthermore, special weight attaches to Prov. 1:30, where personified Wisdom, created by God (cf. 8:22), warns explicitly against disregarding her own reproof *(tôḵaḥtî),* an opinion parallel to hating knowledge, rejecting the fear of God (1:29), and refusing her counsel (1:30). In 1:30 at the latest, therefore, the initially secular usage of *n'ṣ* qal in the context of wisdom merges into theological usage.

Thus only 4 occurrences of *n'ṣ* qal (Jer. 33:24; Prov. 5:12; 15:5;), two of *neʼāṣâ* (2 K. 19:3 par. Isa. 37:3), and one of *ne'āṣâ* (Ezk. 35:12) can be assigned at least initially to secular usage — although the context certainly lends even these occurrences "theological significance."[15]

2. *Theological Usage.* No less than 21 occurrences betray theological usage with Yahweh or God as subject or object. When we list the examples, we note that the qal is reserved almost exclusively for use with a divine subject, whereas the piel is used with a divine object (exceptions: Ps. 107:11 [qal]; Isa. 60:14 [piel]); this distribution can hardly be the result of chance. In fact the qal expresses a "real act and decision," whereas the piel denotes an "attitude . . . expressed in certain actions as an estimative or declarative outcome."[16] Avoidance of the qal with God as direct object means that it is impossible for human *n'ṣ* really to affect God; with the help of the piel, *n'ṣ* is "limited to the mental intent and attitude of the blasphemer."[17]

a. As the earliest (preexilic) text using the qal with a divine subject, Jer. 14:21 has special significance. The context is a communal lament that probably goes back to Jeremiah himself (14:9-22). The substance of the prayer is that, for the sake of his name, Yahweh will not "reject" *n'ṣ* or "dishonor" (*nbl* piel) his glorious throne (i.e., Jerusalem; cf. Jer. 3:17), but will "remember" *(zkr)* his *beríṯ* and not "break" (*prr* hiphil) it. Here *n'ṣ* has already become synonymous with *m's* (reject). The passage therefore presupposes belief in God's election *(bḥr),* at least of Zion.

Lam. 2:6 and probably also Dt. 32:19 look back on the rejection only feared in Jer. 14:21 as having already occurred: the rejection of king and priest, probably along with the institutions they represent, is a terrifying fact, the more so because their (sacral) foundation has been destroyed with the destruction of the temple: Yahweh has "broken down" (*nbl* piel) his booth *(sukkâ),* "destroyed" (*šḥt* piel) his tabernacle *(môʻēḏ),* and "abolished" (*škḥ* piel) festival and Sabbath. In Dt. 32:19, unfortunately, it is not entirely clear whether "his sons and daughters" *(bānāyw ûḇenôṯāyw)* are the object of *nā'aṣ* or are dependent on the adverbial qualifier "out of vexation" *(mikkaʻas).* If the former, we would be dealing with Yahweh's plan (subsequently changed, according to vv.

15. *Ibid.,* 696.
16. *HP,* 225.
17. *Ibid.*

26-36) to destroy Israel (cf. vv. 15-28); if the latter, we would be dealing only with Yahweh's scorn for Israel's infidelity and idolatry (cf. vv. 15-18). The latter reaction, however, would seem to be too mild. The verses that follow also demand the first interpretation. A later transposition of *wayyik̠ʿās wayyin'aṣ*[18] does not seem advisable, not least because of the semantic parallel in Lam. 2:6 (*wayyin'āṣ beza'am 'appô* + obj.). A later glossator, however, might well have found the message of rejection too harsh and hard to reconcile with vv. 26ff., and therefore mitigated it by deliberately changing the *b* to an *m* (*bek̠aʿas* > *mikkaʿas*).

Ps. 107:11 speaks of a group participating in a thanksgiving liturgy who once found themselves in prison for "rebelling" (*mrh* hiphil) against the words of God (*'imrê 'ēl*) and "spurning" (*n'ṣ* qal) the "counsel of the Most High" (*ʿaṣat̠ ʿelyôn*) (cf. vv. 10-14). The indirect rejection of God is manifested in contempt for God's will, probably as expressed in the (ethical?) commandments of the law.

b. Of the 15 occurrences of the piel, 14 have to do with despising or disdaining God or God's acts. The earliest texts are probably those in J. Yahweh asks Moses rhetorically how long "this people" (*hāʿām hazzeh*) will continue to despise him (Nu. 14:11a); he also threatens that "none of those who despised me [piel ptcp.] shall see it [the land]" (14:23b). These texts refer to the spies and those Israelites who, discouraged by the spies' report, decided to return to Egypt (cf. 13:31; 14:4). Their offense is primarily to treat Yahweh's trustworthiness and faithfulness contemptuously. Their conduct exhibits a lack of faith (*lō'-ya'amînû*), in the OT sense, as v. 11b (probably redactional) interprets their words. As a punishment, they are kept from entering the promised land, because they doubted God's promise (14:23b). One can also assign 16:30 to J: Moses declares that the ground will swallow up Dathan and Abiram as a sign "that these people have despised Yahweh." Their rebellion against Moses (16:12-25 [J]) is interpreted and requited as contempt for Yahweh himself.

In Dt. 31:20, in a Deuteronomistic speech addressed to Moses by God, *n'ṣ* piel signalizes Israel's total rejection of Yahweh. Here the piel of *n'ṣ* parallels turning (*pānâ*) to other gods, serving (*ʿāb̠ad̠*) them, and breaking God's covenant (*prr* hiphil + *berît̠*; cf. Jer. 14:21, with God as subj.). The context (Dt. 31:16-22) serves as an introduction to the Song of Moses in Dt. 32. Under the influence of that text, 31:20 may well be using Israel's rejection of Yahweh (*n'ṣ* piel) to motivate Yahweh's rejection of Israel (32:19: *n'ṣ* qal), experienced in the catastrophe of 586 B.C.

Like the Levites Dathan and Abiram in Nu. 16, Hophni and Phinehas, the priestly sons of Eli in the Deuteronomistic account of 1 S. 2, sinned through their contemptuous attitude toward Yahweh in carrying out their own priestly tasks: they "treated with contempt" the offerings (*minḥâ*) intended for Yahweh, a terrible offense in Yahweh's eyes (2:17; cf. 2:29: *bʿṭ*, "spurn"). Divine vengeance is announced to their father by a man of God (2:17-36); both are killed in a battle with the Philistines (4:17).

The Isaianic text Isa. 5:24b is a redactional conclusion summarizing the charges of the woes in Isa. 5: those addressed have "rejected" (*m's*) the (prophetic) *tôrâ* of Yahweh

---

18. *BHS,* in loc.

Sebaoth and "despised" (*n'ṣ* piel) the word *('imrâ)* of the Holy One of Israel. This verse probably refers to transgression of the divine law. Isaiah's rebuke in the woe of 1:4 goes even further, charging the "sinful nation" with doing evil, "forsaking" *('āzab)* Yahweh, and "despising" (*n'ṣ* piel) the Holy One of Israel. The continuation "and they have turned their backs" (*zwr* niphal + *'āḥôr*) may be a gloss. According to Wildberger, the parallel terms *'āzab* and *ni'ēṣ* do not actually mean apostasy and the worship of other gods, as in later (Deuteronomic and Deuteronomistic) texts, but "the overall breaking away from the daily relationship with Yahweh . . . the refusal to trust and be obedient."[19]

In Jer. 23:17, in a message from God, Jeremiah accuses the false prophets of proclaiming well-being and security to "those who despise the word of Yahweh" *(limna'aṣê debar YHWH)*[20] and everyone who "follows his own stubborn heart" *(hôlēk biširirûṯ libbô)*.

Ps. 74 is a communal hymn of prayer, probably dating from the end of the exile; it reflects the internal afflictions of the people of God.[21] The psalmist grapples with the problem of how the "enemy" *('ôyēb)* or "an impious people" *('am nābāl)* can "revile" (*n'ṣ* qal par. *ḥrp* piel) Yahweh's name with impunity (vv. 10,18). The "impious people" (→ נבל *nābāl*) are those "who challenge the activity of God."[22] God's name (i.e., honor) has been impugned and disparaged by their disbelief.[23]

In Ps. 9/10, a postexilic acrostic thanksgiving hymn, the psalmist likewise laments that the wicked (10:2) can boast of "wickedness," the greed of their throat, extol "profit," and "despise" Yahweh (10:3).[24] He agonizes over the problem of how the wicked can simply "revile" God (10:13). Their contempt for God is made clear when they say, "You will not call us to account" (10:13).

Even David is charged by Nathan with having "scorned" (*n'ṣ* piel, intensified by the inf. abs.) Yahweh through his adultery with Bathsheba and the murder of Uriah (2 S. 12:14). In the MT the object of the verb is *'ôyebê YHWH*. Either this is an ancient gloss based on religious aversion to charging the devout king with such a serious offense, or *'ôyebê YHWH* is to be understood as a euphemism, introduced relatively early out of similar considerations, like the "enemies of David" for "David" in 1 S. 25:22.[25] M. J. Mulder shows that *n'ṣ* piel cannot have causative meaning.[26] He also draws attention to the disjunctive *passeq* supplied by the Masoretes in Ps. 10:3,13, likewise to avoid blasphemy. It is easy to understand that already in the OT period pious circles would be offended at the notion that David, who had evolved into the

---

19. *Isaiah 1–12* (Eng. trans., Minneapolis, 1991), 23f.
20. Conj.; cf. *BHS*.
21. See H.-J. Kraus, *Psalms 60–150* (Eng. trans., Minneapolis, 1989), 96f.
22. Kraus, 100.
23. *Ibid.*, 101.
24. The readings "wickedness" and "profit" are conjs.; cf. *BHS*.
25. The former theory was first proposed by Geiger, 267; cf. *GesB*, 478a; *HAL*, II, 658b; and most comms. For the latter theory see Mulder.
26. P. 111, contra W. H. Hertzberg, *I and II Samuel. OTL* (Eng. trans. 1964), 314f.

ideal of the devout king, at one time actually behaved like a despiser of God. Because of this behavior, however, he was punished by the death of the child born of his adulterous union with Bathsheba (2 S. 12:14; cf. 12:15-23), despite his confession (12:13).

In an oracle of salvation on the rebuilding of Jerusalem and the temple (Isa. 60:10-16), Trito-Isaiah proclaims to the city of Jerusalem that the sons of her oppressors *(b^{e}nê m^{e}ʿannayiḵ)* will come to her, and all who have "despised" her *(kol-m^{e}na'^{a}ṣayiḵ)* will bow down at her feet (v. 14). The use of the piel here is significant. No more than Yahweh or his name can effectively be disdained, rejected, or despised (*n'ṣ* piel) can this be possible in the case of Jerusalem. Like Yahweh, she can only be "treated as despised" (*n'ṣ* piel) for a time, without impugning her respect in the eyes of Yahweh.

This theological usage of the piel of *n'ṣ* casts some light on the grammatically obscure participial form *minnō'āṣ* in Isa. 52:5, in the context of a "marginal prose gloss."[27] This might be a hithpoel participle with an assimilated *t* or a hybrid poel/hithpael.[28] But parallels in which Yahweh's name is likewise "treated as despised" (Ps. 74:10,18: *n'ṣ* piel) suggest following Franciscus Zorell in reading the ptcp. *minnō'āṣ* as a pual *(m^{e}nō'āṣ)*.[29] The MT appears to be a pis aller.

A similar theme appears in Ezk. 35:12 in a "proof-saying"[30] against Edom (35:10-13). The mountains of Israel are the object of Edom's blasphemous abuse: "They are laid desolate, they are given us to devour." This attempt to annex Yahweh's land cannot go unpunished: Edom shall know that Yahweh is Israel's God and that he has heard the abuse (v. 12), and shall itself be made desolate (vv. 14,15b; cf. vv. 3f.).

Twice in a penitential prayer (Neh. 9:6-37) we find one of the Chronicler's stock phrases: "They committed great blasphemies" (*wayya^{ʿa}śû nā'āṣôṯ g^{e}ḏôlôṯ:* vv. 18,26). The background here is the Deuteronomistic interpretation of history, which the Chronicler borrowed and developed into the notion of the violent fate of the prophets.[31]

III. 1. *Sirach and Dead Sea Scrolls.* Sirach contains only a single occurrence of *n'ṣ,* and that textually uncertain: after making a gift, one should not "despise" the recipient (?) (Sir. 41:22).[32] Norbert Peters points as a piel, whereas M. H. Segal reconstructs the text ("contempt").[33] The LXX translates: *mḗ oneídize.*

According to Karl Georg Kuhn's concordance, the verb *n'ṣ* appears 5 times in the Dead Sea Scrolls, the noun *nṣh/n'ṣ* twice; the verb also appears once in an apocryphal prophetic quotation (1Q25 4:6). Totally within the framework of OT usage, CD 1:2 speaks of "all the despisers of God," 1QS 5:19 of "all the despisers of his word" (*n'ṣ*

---

27. C. Westermann, *Isaiah 40–66. OTL* (Eng. trans. 1969), 248.
28. For the former see *BLe,* 198g; *HAL,* II, 658b; for the latter see Meyer, II, 126.
29. *LexHebAram,* 491a.
30. W. Zimmerli, *Ezekiel 2. Herm* (Eng. trans. 1983), 232.
31. O. H. Steck, *Israel und das gewaltsame Geschick der Propheten. WMANT,* 23 (1967), 60-64.
32. Cairo MS. B; cf. the Jerusalem ed., in loc.
33. Peters, in loc.; Segal, *Sēper ben Sîrâ haššālīm* (Jerusalem, 1958), in loc.

ptcp., probably piel). In CD 1:3 we find the parallel term "forsake" *('zb);* in 1QS 5:19, the parallel phrase "not know his covenant" *(lō' yāḏaʿ 'eṯ bᵉrîṯô).* These texts refer to the Jewish contemporaries of the Qumran community who did not recognize the community's distinctive way or, possibly, had forsaken it.

In three of the Thanksgiving Hymns *(Hodayoth),* probably attributable to the Teacher of Righteousness himself, the psalmist (i.e., the Teacher) is quite surprisingly the object of *n'ṣ:* 1QH 4:22 (par. *bzh* par. *l' ḥšb*), 1QH 7:22 (par. *'nšy mlḥmty,* "men of the battle [waged] against me" par. *bʿly ryby,* "lords of the conflict with me": 1QH 7:23). While the first passage looks forward confidently to victory, the second already looks back on the failure of the Teacher's enemies, brought about with God's help. The third passage is 1QH 6:2, "my heart with scorning[s]" *(lby bn'ṣ[wt]);* the context is damaged.

Quite singular is the statement of 1QH 4:12 that God *('dwny)* "despises" (*n'ṣ* piel) or "rejects" (qal) all the designs of Belial, where "Belial" is probably a code name for enemies who have deserted the Teacher. A quotation of Josh. 6:26 referring originally to Jericho is reinterpreted in 4QTestim (4Q175) 28 to apply to Jerusalem: "they" (probably the eschatological enemies of the Qumran community: the priests of Jerusalem [?]) will commit *(ʿśh)* wickedness *(ḥnwph)* in the land and a great outrage *(nṣh* [conj. *n'ṣh*] *gdwlh)* among the sons of Jacob (cf. Neh. 9:18,26).

2. *LXX.* The LXX offers a wide spectrum of translations. Surprisingly, it regularly renders the piel with divine object as *paroxýnein,* "provoke" (Nu. 14:11,23; 16:30; Dt. 31:20; 2 K. 12:14; Ps. 9:25,34[MT 10:3,13]; 73[74]:10,18; Isa. 5:24). In other words, it interprets scorn and contempt for God as a provocation of God (also the qal in Ps. 107:11). We also find *atheteín,* "look down on" (1 S. 2:17), *apōtheísthai,* "dismiss" (Jer. 23:17), and *parorgízein,* "provoke to anger" (Isa. 1:4, as well as variants in 2 S. 12:14; Ps. 9:34[10:13]).

The three texts that consider rejection of Israel or Jerusalem and its representatives possible or even assume it to have taken place are all mitigated: "The LORD was jealous *(ezḗlōsen)* and became provoked *(parōxýnthē)* by anger against his sons and daughters" (Dt. 32:19, with a double translation of MT *wayyin'āṣ mikkaʿas*); "through the fierceness of his anger he provoked *(parṓxynen)* king, priest, and prince" (Lam. 2:6); and finally the prayer in Jer. 14:21: "Show restraint *(kópason)* for the sake of your name."

Other Greek equivalents include *myktērízein,* "turn up one's nose" (Prov. 1:30), *oneidízein,* "disgrace" (Sir. 41:22), and *ekklínein,* "turn aside" (Prov. 5:12). In Isa. 52:5 the pual (or hithpoel?) is rendered with *blasphēmeísthai.* The noun *nᵉ'āṣâ* (Ezk. 35:12) is translated *blasphēmía,* "blasphemy"; *ne'āṣâ* is translated *oneidismós,* "disgrace," and *orgḗ,* "anger" (Isa. 37:3 par. 2 K. 19:3: *parorgismós*); the plural forms are translated *parorgismoí,* "deeds of wrath" (Neh. 9:18,26).

Ruppert

נבט *nbṭ*

Contents: I. Etymology; II. Occurrences, Semantic Field; III. With Human Subjects; IV. With God as Subject; V. 1. LXX; 2. Dead Sea Scrolls.

I. Etymology. The etymology of *nbṭ* has little to offer. Arab. *nabaṭa* means "pour forth," IV "bring to light."[1] The causative of OSA *nbṭ* means "dig a well until water is found," i.e., probably "cause (water) to spring forth"; in personal names, however, it means "look graciously upon." Akk. *nanāṭu* means "shine forth,"[2] Jewish Aram. *n^eḇat,* "spring up" (not found in Syriac). Ugar. *nbṭ* means "appear, come to light."[3] The causative meaning "look at" in Hebrew could derive from what seems to be the common basic meaning: "appear, become visible."

II. Occurrences, Semantic Field. The verb appears 67 times in the hiphil. In addition, the form *nibbaṭ,* which might be either piel or niphal, occurs in Isa. 5:30;[4] the similar passage 8:2 has the hiphil *hibbîṭ.* The verb means "look in a specific direction, watch, look at, etc." It appears with striking frequency in conjunction with *rāʾâ,* "see," e.g., 1 S. 17:42: *wayyabbēṭ wayyirʾeh,* roughly "when he [David] looked, he saw"; 1 K. 19:6 is similar. The same construction is used with the hiphil of *šqp,* e.g., 2 S. 24:20: *wayyašqēp̄ ʾ^arawnâ wayyarʾ ʾeṯ-hammeleḵ,* "When Araunah looked down, he saw the king" (the par. 1 Ch. 21:21 has *wayyabbēṭ*); cf. Lam. 3:50. Other texts using *rāʾâ* include Isa. 42:18; 63:15; Ps. 33:13; 80:15(Eng. v. 14); 142:5(4); Lam. 1:12; 5:1; cf. also Ps. 91:8. Elsewhere *rāʾâ* precedes (Hab. 1:5; Lam. 1:11; 2:20; Ps. 84:10[9]) or parallels *hibbîṭ* (Job 28:24; cf. also 2 K. 3:14; Isa. 22:8).

III. With Human Subjects. The subject of the verb may be either a human being or God. In the former case, the act of looking is a very ordinary occurrence, although it may occasionally stand in a momentous context. Abraham looks toward heaven and counts the stars; thus he learns how numerous his descendants will be (Gen. 15:5). Elijah's servant looks toward the sea; the seventh time, he sees a little cloud that signals rain (1 K. 18:43). The people watch Moses when he prepares to enter the tent of meeting (Ex. 33:8). The caravans look for the watercourses but find them empty (Job 6:19). Lot's wife looks back and is turned into a pillar of salt (Gen. 19:17,26). The victims bitten by serpents look at the bronze serpent and are healed (Nu. 21:9). When God speaks to Moses out of the burning bush, Moses hides his face, "for he was afraid to look at God" (Ex. 3:6; cf. 2Q21 5), for whoever sees God must die.[5] Notwithstanding,

---

1. A. Guillaume, *Abr-Nahrain,* 3 (1961/62), 4f.
2. *AHw,* II, 697.
3. *UT,* no. 456; cf. *WUS,* no. 607: *bṭ(w),* "chatter."
4. For the piel see *HAL,* II, 661a. For the niphal see *HP,* 257 and n. 292.
5. → VIII, 198.

Nu. 12:8 says that Yahweh speaks with Moses face to face (cf. Dt. 34:10) and that Moses sees his "form" *(t^e^mûnâ).* This statement is at odds with Ex. 33:18-23 and may be a secondary addition; it can be understood, however, as a "pertinent interpretation" of the intimate relationship between Moses and God.[6]

The direction in which the subject looks is often introduced by *'el.* In the Psalm of Jonah, the psalmist laments that he will never again look on the temple of Yahweh (with reverence? Jon. 2:5[4]). Those who look to Yahweh will be radiant (with joy, Ps. 34:6[5]). Zec. 12:10 is difficult: "They will look upon the one [MT: me] whom they have pierced." The context at least makes clear that there will be bitter mourning for the one who has died, but who that is remains obscure. Does the "looking" here imply appreciation?[7] Looking directly ahead without glancing to the side and without turning aside to evil is the point of Prov. 4:25 (cf. v. 27). The meaning of Isa. 8:22 is reasonably clear: if one looks at the earth, there is nothing but distress and darkness there; but the significance of the verse in the larger context is hard to determine.

Often *hibbîṭ* connotes paying close attention: Lam. 1:12: "Come, all of you who pass by, look and see if there is any sorrow like mine"; Hab. 1:5: "Look *(r^e'û)* among the nations and see *(habbîṭû),* for I am doing a work in your days"; Isa. 42:18: "Listen, you that are deaf; and you that are blind, look up and see," i.e., pay attention to what Yahweh intends to do; Ps. 91:8: "With your own eyes you will look and see the punishment of the wicked." Rather more neutral are Nu. 23:21: "There is no misfortune to behold in Jacob, no trouble to see in Israel"; Isa. 38:11: "I thought, I shall no longer see the land of the living, I shall no longer look upon a human being among the inhabitants of the world." Here *hibbîṭ* is almost a parallel to *rā'â.*

Other passages imply esteem for what is looked at, e.g., 1 S. 16:7, where Yahweh says to Samuel with reference to Eliab, David's brother: "Do not look on his appearance or on the height of his stature." This command is explained as follows: "For God does not see *(rā'â)* as mortals see; they look on the outward appearance *(la'ênayim),* but Yahweh looks on the heart." In 2 K. 3:14, in a critical situation, Elisha says to the king of Israel: "Were it not that I have regard for *(nāśā' pānîm)* King Jehoshaphat of Judah, I would give you neither a look (*nbṭ* hiphil) nor a glance *(rā'â),*" i.e., I would not bother with you. In a series of woes Isa. 5:12 castigates those who "do not regard (*nbṭ* hiphil) the deeds of Yahweh or see the work of his hands." Ps. 119 uses the hiphil for obedient observance of the Torah (vv. 6,15; cf. v. 18).

In Isa. 51:1f. Deutero-Isaiah admonishes his listeners to look to the rock from which they were hewn and the quarry from which they were dug, i.e., to heed their ancestors Abraham and Sarah and to learn from the blessing they experienced.[8]

In Ps. 92:12(11) *hibbîṭ b^e^* means exactly the same as *rā'â b^e^,* i.e., "see with delight": "My eyes look with delight on [the downfall of] my enemies."

Hab. 2:15 contains a woe against him (the Chaldean) "who makes [his] neighbors

---

6. See M. Noth, *Numbers. OTL* (Eng. trans. 1968), 96.
7. See below.
8. → מקבת *maqqeḇeṯ* (VIII, 531f.).

drink . . . until they are drunk, in order to gaze on their nakedness." The text may be understood quite literally: the overlord takes delight in seeing his guests in this disgraceful condition. The words are probably metaphorical, however, and refer to the Chaldeans' degrading treatment of their enemies. The passage is applied to the Teacher of Righteousness in 1QpHab 11:2ff.: he is persecuted by the Unrighteous Priest and disgraced "at the time of the festival, during the quiet of the Day of Atonement." This interpretation presupposes the reading *môʿadêhem,* "their festivals," instead of *meʿôrêhem,* "their nakedness."

IV. With God as Subject. With God as its subject, the hiphil of *nbṭ* is found in statements and petitions. It is stated that God looks to the ends of the earth and sees everything (Job 28:24), that in the course of history God looked down from heaven at the earth (*hišqîp* and *hibbîṭ*) to hear grievances and free prisoners (Ps. 102:20f.[19f.]; cf. 33:13), that God will quietly (*šqṭ;* or should we read *šqp*?) look down from his "height" and wait for the time to intervene (Isa. 18:4). A different aspect appears in Ps. 104:32: when God looks at the earth, it trembles. Different again is Hab. 1:13: Yahweh cannot look on wrongdoing; he cannot abide it (par. *rāʾâ*). According to Isa. 66:2, Yahweh looks with favor on one who is humble and contrite in spirit; according to Am. 5:22, he will not look upon the offerings of the people (par. *rāṣâ,* "take pleasure in").

Petitions are found primarily in the Psalms and Lamentations. For example, Ps. 13:4(3) reads: "Look upon me, answer me"; 80:15(14): "God of hosts, look down from heaven, and see, have regard for this vine [i.e., Israel]." By using the imperatives "look" and "see," the author of Lamentations seeks to attract the attention of Yahweh to the sufferings of his people (Lam. 1:11; 2:20; 3:63; in 5:1 also *zeḵôr*). Similar pleas are heard in Isa. 63:15: "Look down *(habbēṭ)* from heaven and see *(reʾēh)* from your holy and glorious habitation. . . . Do not hold back, for you are our father"; and 64:8(9): "Do not be exceedingly angry, Yahweh, and do not remember *(zkr)* iniquity forever. Look, we pray *(habbeṭ-nāʾ),* we are all your people" (cf. also 4QLam [501] 1:5).

V. 1. *LXX.* The usual LXX translations are *epiblépein, emblépein,* or *katanoeín;* we also find *anablépein, epistréphein,* etc.

2. *Dead Sea Scrolls.* In the Dead Sea Scrolls *nbṭ* appears 16 times, primarily in 1QS and 1QH. Here it denotes an intensive, existential attention to the works of God on the part of the faithful (1QS 11:19; 1QH 10:20). God personally opens the eyes of human beings that they may "see" (1QS 11:3; 1QH 18:19). In some texts, the looking clearly implies an element of confident expectation: the apostate "beholds" darkness (1QS 3:3), one who is pure "beholds" the light of life (3:7) or eternity (11:6).

Ringgren

נָבִיא nāḇîʾ; נבא nbʾ niphal and hithpael; נְבִיאָה n^eḇîʾâ; נְבוּאָה n^eḇûʾâ

Contents: I. Semitic Parallels: 1. The Verb *nby/ʾ;* 2. Nominal Derivatives; 3. The Denominative Verb *nbʾ;* 4. *n^eḇûʾâ* and Parallels; 5. *nbʿ.* II. "Prophecy" in the Ancient Near East: 1. Mari; 2. Canaan; 3. Neo-Assyrian Prophetic Oracles; 4. Among the Arabs. III. Usage: 1. Amos; 2. Prophetic Narratives before Amos; 3. From Hosea to the Exile; 4. Exilic Prophecy; 5. Postexilic Prophecy.

---

nāḇîʾ. G. André, "Ecstatic Prophecy in the OT," *Scripta Instituti Donneriani Aboensis,* 11 (1982), 187-200; D. E. Aune, "The Use of προφήτης in Josephus," *JBL,* 101 (1982), 419-421; K. Baltzer, *Die Biographie der Propheten* (Neukirchen-Vluyn, 1975); G. Brunet, "Y eut-t-il un manteau de prophète?" *RSO,* 43 (1968), 145-162; M. Burrows, "Prophecy and the Prophets at Qumrân," *Israel's Prophetic Heritage. Festschrift J. Muilenburg* (New York, 1962), 223-232; J. L. Crenshaw, *Prophetic Conflict. BZAW,* 124 (1971); R. Coggins, et al., eds., *Israel's Prophetic Tradition. Festschrift P. Ackroyd* (Cambridge, 1982); J. B. Curtis, "A Folk Etymology of *nāḇîʾ*," *VT,* 29 (1979), 491-93; M. Dietrich, "Prophetie in den Keilschrifttexten," *Jahrbuch für Anthropologie und Religionsgeschichte,* 1 (1973[1976]), 15-44; W. Dietrich, *Prophetie und Geschichte. FRLANT,* 108 (1972); B. Duhm, *Israels Propheten* (Tübingen, 1916, ^{2}1922); F. Ellermeier, *Prophetie in Mari und Israel* (Herzberg am Harz, 1968); E. Fascher, ΠΡΟΦΗΤΗΣ (Giessen, 1927); G. Fohrer, "Neuere Literatur zur alttestamentlichen Prophetie," *TRu,* 19 (1951), 277-346; 20 (1952), 193-271, 295-361; *idem,* "Neue Literatur zur alttestamentlichen Prophetie," *TRu,* 40 (1975), 337-377; 41 (1976), 1-12; 45 (1980), 1-39, 109-132, 193-225; 47 (1982), 105-135, 205-218; *idem, Studien zur alttestamentlichen Prophetie. BZAW,* 99 (1967); *idem,* "Zehn Jahre Literatur zur Prophetie," *TRu,* 28 (1962), 1-75, 235-297, 301-374; M. Görg, "Der *Nāḇîʾ,* 'Berufener' oder 'Seher,' " *BN,* 17 (1982), 23-25; *idem,* "Weiteres zur Etymologie von *nāḇîʾ*," *BN,* 22 (1983), 9-11; K. Goldammer, "Elemente des Schamanismus im AT," *Ex orbe religionum. Festschrift G. Widengren. SNumen,* 21-22 (1972), II, 266-285; H. Gunkel, *Die Propheten* (Göttingen, 1917); F. Haeussermann, *Wortempfang und Symbol in der alttestamentlichen Prophetie. BZAW,* 58 (1932), esp. 3-28; J. G. Heintz, "Langage prophétique et 'style de cour' selon ARM X et l'AT," *Sem,* 22 (1972), 5-12; S. Herrmann, *Ursprung und Funktion der Prophetie im alten Israel* (Opladen, 1976); A. Heschel, *The Prophets* (New York, 1962); G. Hölscher, *Die Profeten* (Leipzig, 1914); J. A. Holstein, "The Case of *'ʾîš hāʾ^{e}lōhîm'* Reconsidered," *HUCA,* 48 (1977), 69-81; F.-L. Hossfeld, "Wahre und falsche Propheten in Israel," *BiKi,* 38 (1983), 139-144; F.-L. Hossfeld and I. Meyer, *Prophet gegen Prophet* (Fribourg, 1973); A. Jepsen, *Nabi* (Munich, 1934); J. Jeremias, *Kultprophetie und Gerichtsverkündigung in der späten Königszeit Israels. WMANT,* 35 (1970); *idem,* "נביא *nāḇîʾ* 'prophet,' " *TLOT,* II, 697-710; A. R. Johnson, *The Cultic Prophet and Israel's Psalmody* (Cardiff, 1979); *idem, The Cultic Prophet in Ancient Israel* (Cardiff, ^{2}1962); O. Keel, "Rechttun oder Annahme des drohenden Gerichts?" *BZ,* N.S. 21 (1977), 200-218; K. Koch, "Die Briefe 'profetischen' Inhalts aus Mari," *UF,* 4 (1972), 53-77; *idem, The Prophets* (Eng. trans., 2 vols., Philadelphia, 1983-84); G. Lanczkowski, "Ägyptischer Prophetismus im Lichte des alttestamentlichen," *ZAW,* 70 (1958), 31-38; B. Lang, "Prophetie, prophetische Zeichenhandlung und Politik in Israel," *TTQ,* 161 (1981), 275-280 (with bibliog.); *idem, Wie wird man Prophet in Israel* (Düsseldorf, 1980); J. Lindblom, *Prophecy in Ancient Israel* (Philadelphia, 1962); *idem,* "Zur Frage des kanaanäischen Ursprungs des altistraelitischen Prophetismus," *Von Ugarit nach Qumran. Festschrift O. Eissfeldt. BZAW,* 77 (1958), 89-104; A. Malamat, "Prophetic Revelations in New Documents from Mari and the Bible," *Volume du Congrès, Genève 1965. SVT,* 15 (1966), 207-222 = *ErIsr,* 8 (1967), 231-240 (Heb.); R. Micheel, *Die Seher- und Prophetenüberlieferung in der Chronik. BBET,* 18 (1983); S. Mowinckel, *Proph-*

I. Semitic Parallels. The Hebrew verb *nb'*, found in the niphal and hithpael, derives from the noun *nāḇî'*;[1] the noun, however, derives from the West Semitic root *nb'*, a verb of speaking. Because the term is deeply rooted in a group of Semitic languages, an Egyptian etymology must be ruled out as long as a Semitic derivation appears possible.[2]

---

ecy and Tradition (Oslo, 1947); *idem, Psalmenstudien.* III: *Kultprophetie und prophetische Psalmen* (1923; repr. Amsterdam, 1961); B. D. Napier, "Prophet, Prophetism," *IDB*, III, 896-919; P. H. A. Neumann, ed., *Das Prophetenverständnis in der deutschsprachigen Forschung seit Heinrich Ewald. WdF,* 307 (1979); E. Noort, *Untersuchungen zum Gottesbescheid in Mari. AOAT,* 202 (1977) (with bibliog.); H. M. Orlinsky, "The Seer in Ancient Israel," *OrAnt,* 4 (1965), 153-174; S. B. Parker, "Possession and Trance and Prophecy in Pre-exilic Israel," *VT,* 28 (1978), 271-285; L. Perlitt, "Mose als Prophet," *EvT,* 31 (1971), 588-608; A. Philipps, "The Ecstatics' 'Father,' " *Words and Meanings. Festschrift D. Winton Thomas* (Cambridge, 1968), 183-194; O. Plöger, "Priester und Prophet," *ZAW,* 63 (1951), 157-192 = *Aus der Spätzeit des ATs* (Göttingen, 1971), 7-42; J. R. Porter, *"bᵉnê hannᵉḇî'îm," JTS,* N.S. 31 (1981), 423-29; G. Quell, *Wahre und Falsche Propheten. BFCT,* 46/1 (1952); G. von Rad, *OT Theology,* II (Eng. trans., New York, 1965); L. Ramlot, "Prophétisme," *DBS,* VIII, 811-1222; R. Rendtorff, "Erwägungen zur Frühgeschichte des Prophetismus in Israel," *ZTK,* 59 (1962), 145-167; *idem,* "נָבִיא in the OT," *TDNT,* VI, 796-812; G. Rinaldi, "Profetismo," *RivBiblIt,* 11 (1963), 396-99; H. Ringgren, ed., *Israels profeter* (Stockholm, 1974); J. F. Ross, "Prophecy in Hamath, Israel, and Mari," *HTR,* 63 (1970), 1-28; J. M. Schmidt, "Ausgangspunkt und Ziel prophetischer Verkündigung im 8. Jh.," *VF,* 22 (1977), 65-82; *idem,* "Probleme der Prophetenforschung," *VF,* 17 (1972), 39-81; *idem,* "Prophetie und Tradition," *ZTK,* 74 (1977), 255-272; W. H. Schmidt, "Prophetie," *Neukirchener Arbeitsbücher AT* (1983), 114-146; *idem, Zukunftsgewissheit und Gegenwartskritik* (Neukirchen-Vluyn, 1973); A. Schmitt, *Prophetischer Gottesbescheid in Mari und Israel. BWANT,* 114 (1982) (with bibliog.); J. Schreiner, " 'Prophet für die Völker' in der Sicht des Jeremia-Buches," *Ortskirche, Weltkirche. Festschrift J. Döpfner* (Würzburg, 1973), 15-31; I. L. Seeligmann, "Die Auffassung von der Prophetie in der dtr. und chr. Geschichtsschreibung (mit einem Exkurs über das Buch Jer)," *Congress Volume, Göttingen, 1977. SVT,* 29 (1978), 254-284; A. van Selms, "CTA 32: A Prophetic Liturgy," *UF,* 3 (1971), 235-248; P. Seidensticker, "Prophetensöhne, Rechabiter, Nasiräer," *SBFLA,* 10 (1959/60), 65-119; S. Shaviv, "*nāḇî'* and *nāḡîḏ* in 1 Samuel ix 1–x 16," *VT,* 34 (1984), 108-113; O. H. Steck, *Israel und das gewaltsame Geschick der Propheten. WMANT,* 23 (1967); *idem, Überlieferung und Zeitgeschichte in den Elia-Erzählungen. WMANT,* 26 (1968); W. Thiel, *Die deuteronomistische Redaktion von Jeremia. WMANT,* 41, 52 (1973-81); B. Uffenheimer, *Ancient Prophecy in Israel* [Heb.] (Jerusalem, 1984); *idem, "nāḇî', nᵉḇû'ā," EMiqr,* V (1968), 690-732; *idem, "nāḇî' šäqär," ibid.,* 739-744; P. Volz, *Prophetengestalten im AT* (²1949); N. Walker, "What Is a *nābhî?*" *ZAW,* 73 (1971), 99f.; M. Weinfeld, "Mesopo.tamian Prophecies," *ShnatMikr,* 3 (1978), 263-276; M. Weippert, " 'Heiliger Krieg' in Israel und Assyrien," *ZAW,* 84 (1972), 460-493; C. Westermann, *Basic Forms of Prophetic Speech* (Eng. trans., Philadelphia, 1967); *idem,* "Die Mari-Briefe und die Prophetie in Israel," *Forschung am AT,* [I]. *ThB,* 24 (1964), 171-188; C. F. Whitley, *The Prophetic Achievement* (Leiden, 1963); J. G. Williams, "The Prophetic 'Father,' " *JBL,* 95 (1966), 444-48; R. R. Wilson, "Prophecy and Ecstasy," *JBL,* 98 (1979), 321-337; H. W. Wolff, "Die eigentliche Botschaft der klassischen Propheten," *Beiträge zur alttestamentlichen Theologie. Festschrift W. Zimmerli* (Göttingen, 1977), 547-557; *idem,* "Hauptprobleme alttestamentlicher Prophetie," *EvT,* 15 (1955), 146-168 = his *GSAT. ThB,* 22 (²1973), 206-231; W. Zimmerli, "Der 'Prophet' im Pentateuch," *Studien zum Pentateuch. Festschrift W. Kornfeld* (Vienna, 1977), 197-211; *idem, Studien zur alttestamentlichen Theologie und Prophetie. ThB,* 51 (1974).

1. Rendtorff, *TDNT,* VI, 796; *HAL,* II, 661; Jeremias, *TLOT,* II, 697; et al.
2. See Walker, Görg; on Egyp. *nbꜣ* see 1 below.

1. *The Verb nby/ʾ.* The G and D stems of a verb *nby* (more precisely, *nbī*) meaning "name, call" are attested in North Semitic (Eblaite and Amorite) and East Semitic (Akkadian). Eblaite lexical texts equate Sum. *pà(d),* "name, call, swear," with Eb. *na-ba-um* or *na-<ba->ù-um.*[3] Finite G stem forms are found in personal names such as *i-bí* + divine name, "DN named," as well as forms with a singular pronominal suffix, e.g., *ib-bí-ni,* "named me," *i-bí-ka, i-bí-su/sù.*[4] A finite D stem form with a paronomastic D infinitive is attested in the contextual form *ù-na-ba-kà-ma na-bu-ù (ʾunabbaʾ-ka-ma nabbuʾu),* "and I shall certainly name you."[5]

In Akkadian texts *nabāʾum* > *nabû(m)* II is represented by the logogram SA$_4$, corresponding to Sum. *sa$_4$,* "name." In lexical lists from Babylonia, the identification with *pà(d),* attested at Ebla, is only one among many.[6] The G stem is used frequently in Akkadian; in some rare instances it can change the basic meaning "name" to "decree (a fate)" and "create."[7] Being named with a name becomes the quintessence of existence;[8] cf. the expression *mala/ša šuma nabû,* "whose name is always named," for "everything, everyone,"[9] and Heb. *qrʾ* niphal + *šēm* (Jer. 44:26; Ruth 4:14; Eccl. 6:10).

In personal names we find the syntagmemes *i-bí* + divine name, "DN named/called," and *na-bí* + divine name, "named/called by DN," as early as Old Akkadian.[10] Despite the arguments of J. J. Stamm,[11] I believe it is possible that in Akkadian as well as in Amorite and at Ebla the "naming" of a child by a deity could refer also to its creation. In royal names like Ibbisuen, in royal epithets, and in contextual forms like royal inscriptions with the king as object, the meaning is that the deity called the king to his royal office.[12] Also germane are the phrase *nibīt* + divine name, "the named one of DN,"[13] the use of *nabû(m),* "decree," with the obj. *šarrūtu(m),* "kingship," etc.,[14] the Sumerian royal name *mès-an-né-pà-da,* "youth whom An has called," and the royal epithets cited by M.-J. Seux.[15]

---

3. G. Pettinato, "Testi lessicali bilingui della biblioteca L. 2769," *Materiali epigrafici di Ebla,* IV (Naples, 1982), 281, no. 725.

4. H.-P. Müller, "Neue Erwängungen zum eblaitischen Verbalsystem," *Il Bilinguismo a Ebla,* ed. L. Cagni (Naples, 1984), 167-204.

5. TM, 75. G. 1444, XIII, 12f.; D. O. Edzard, *Studi Eblaiti,* 4 (1981), 43, 53; cf. M. Krebernik, *ZA,* 73 (1983), 28.

6. *CAD,* XI/1, 32f.

7. *Ibid.,* 37f. and 34, respectively; cf. also *AHw,* II, 699, s.v. G.I.

8. *AHw,* II, 699, s.v. G.I.1f.; 700, s.v. II.2.

9. *CAD,* XI/1, 35, s.v. 1.b.2′.c′.

10. I. J. Gelb, *MAD,* 3 (^{2}1973), 194f.; *AHw,* II, 700, s.v. G.II.1; *CAD,* XI/1, 31, s.v. *nabû* (adj.) b.

11. *AN,* 141.

12. For the royal epithets see Seux, 175-79. For the contextual forms see *AHw,* II, 699, s.v. G.I.1.a; 700, s.v. N.2; *CAD,* XI/1, 36f., s.v. 3.b; for the verbal adj. *na-bi-ù,* etc., see also *CAD,* XI/1, 31, s.v. *nabû* (adj.).

13. *AHw,* II, 785, s.v. *nibītu*[*m*] 2; *CAD,* XI/2, 202, s.v. 4; Seux, 205-7.

14. *AHw,* II, 700, s.v. G.II.4; *CAD,* XI/1, 38, s.v. 4b.

15. Seux, 433-36.

Less common than the G stem are the D and N stems. The former has the meaning "lament," for which *CAD* also lists two G stem citations (cf. *nubû,* "lamentation"; *menambû*[*m*], "lamentation priest").[16] The Š stem means "cause to be named," with only one clear instance.

To some extent, *nabû* is synonymous with *zakāru(m),* with which it is sometimes parallel.

In Amorite, *nby* appears in personal names.[17] I. J. Gelb also finds the noun *nabi'um,* "prophet";[18] but such forms as *na-bi* (+ DN) are better understood in the nontechnical sense "called (by DN)," to the extent that they are not in fact Akkadian forms.

A similar PN (obviously hypocoristic) *nb*[ʾ] *bn* [ʾ]*rš* also appears in a Punic inscription.[19] There is one uncertain Ugaritic occurrence.[20]

Manfred Görg notes an Egyptian root *nbꜣ,* "rave, be excited," found in medical texts.[21] But it may be a borrowing from Sem. *nby/ʾ.*

The North and East Semitic primary verb *nby* also appears in West Semitic, as *nb'*.[22] Arab. *naba'a* (I: "he uttered a loud voice or sound, cried, barked"; II and IV: "inform"; X: "inquire") is not a denominative from *nabīy/'^{un},* "prophet";[23] on the contrary, the Arabic primary verb *naba'a* has nominal derivatives in *naba'^{un},* "report, information," and *nab'at^{un},* "soft sound." OSA *tnbʾ,* "promise, vow (an offering to a deity)," is probably also a primary verb, especially if the absence to date of a noun from which it might derive is not accidental, if, as in Arabic, the fifth stem is often denominative (cf. Eth. *naba'a,* "murmur, speak").[24]

A primary verb *nby/nb'* is easy to analyze in the structural and semantic categories of Semitic verb formation: its biconsonantal base *by/b'* obviously represents onomatopoeically a particular kind of articulation or sound production. A root augment *n-* is common, especially in onomatopoeic verbs.[25]

2. *Nominal Derivatives.* A *qaṭil* > *qaṭīl* nominal derivative of *nby/'* is found in most Semitic languages. The lengthened *qaṭīl (parīs)* form represents nominalized adjectives of the form *qaṭil (paris).*[26] In Akkadian the verbal adj. *paris,* which is identical with the stative, already has passive (better: ergative) force: "called" > "one who has been called."

---

16. XI/I, 39, s.v. *nabû* B.
17. See *APNM,* 236.
18. I. J. Gelb, *Computer-Aided Analysis of Amorite. AS,* 21 (1980), esp. 26.
19. *CIS,* I, 451.4.
20. See 2 below.
21. "Weiteres," with additional bibliog.
22. Contra Görg, *"Nābî."*
23. Lane, 2752f.; cf. A. Wahrmund, *Praktisches Handbuch der neu-arabischen Sprache,* 3 vols. in 2 (Giessen, ^{3}1898), s.v.; contra *HAL,* II, 659.
24. On Old South Arabic see Beeston, 90; Biella, 289f.; on Ethiopic, W. Leslau, *Contributions,* 32.
25. *GaG,* §102b; S. Segert, *Altaramäische Grammatik* (Leipzig, 1975), §4.6.3.2.1.
26. *GaG,* §55i, 10.

This is the etymology of Akk. *nabīum* > *nabû(m)* I, "one who has been called."[27] The word generally designates the king; it never means a mediator called by a deity to speak, a "prophet." A fossilized epithet serving as a divine name appears in ^{d}*Na-bi-um,* ^{d}*Na-bu-um,* ^{d}*Na-bu-ú,* etc., designating the relatively late deity Nabu, the patron of scribes and wisdom (cf. Heb. *n^{e}ḇô* in Isa. 46:1). Although it is possible morphologically to interpret the G ptcp. *nābiu(m)* > *nābu(m)* as active,[28] the force of the verbal adjective with stative/passive (ergative) meaning is more likely here as well. A popular etymology of the term "one who has been called" applied to the vizier of Marduk is found in a Sumerian attribute of Nabu, ^{d}*Mu-du^{10}-ga-sa$_{4}$-a* and Emesal, ^{d}*Mu-zé-eb-ba-sa^{4}-a,* "who has been named with a good name."[29]

In Ugaritic the noun *nbʾ* may occur in the PN *(bn) nbʿm* (< **nbʾ ʿm,* "called one [?] of [the god] ʿAmm").[30] It is found in Punic in the PN *nbʾ* cited above.

In the other West Semitic languages, the passive (ergative) *qaṭīl* noun seems to be borrowed from Heb. *nāḇîʾ* (fem. *n^{e}ḇîʾâ*). In both Hebrew and these other languages, it denotes a mediator who has been called by God to speak on God's behalf. The Western European languages use the word "prophet," borrowed from Greek, for such a person. This word itself reflects biblical usage, so that — if we disregard colloquial and arbitrary extensions of meaning, such as "weather prophet" — no other word adequately translates the Hebrew word. For the syntagmatics of *nāḇîʾ,* see *HAL.*[31]

Although earlier scholars preferred to assume an active basic meaning "speaker, proclaimer" for Heb. *nāḇîʾ,*[32] this theory is less plausible. Agent nouns formed like the Aramaic peal act. ptcp. *qāṭil* do not occur in Hebrew; moreover, *qaṭil* and *qaṭīl* at least are not specific to agent nouns.[33] On the contrary, analysis of Akk. *nabīum,* etc., as "one who is called" suggests that Heb. *nāḇîʾ* should also be considered a passive (ergative) verbal adjective or a noun formed from such an adjective with the same meaning as in Akkadian; it is not necessary to postulate an Akkadian loanword.[34] Similar Hebrew *qaṭīl* forms include *ʾāsîr,* "prisoner"; *bāḥîr,* "chosen one (of God)"; *yāḏîḏ,* "beloved"; *māšîaḥ,* "anointed one (of God)"; *nāzîr,* "dedicated one (of God)"; *śāḵîr,* "hireling"; etc. Fritz Werner has theorized that in Biblical Hebrew the *qaṭīl* form was especially productive of nouns and nominalized adjectives, while in Modern Hebrew the pure *qaṭīl* adjective has overtaken the noun.[35] This analysis agrees with my findings.

Semantically, such an etymology of *nāḇîʾ* can be compared to the use of *qrʾ,* "call," with Yahweh as subject and the object either the servant of Yahweh (Isa. 42:6; 49:1;

27. *AHw,* II, 697b; *CAD,* XI/1, 31, s.v. *nabû* adj.
28. *AN,* 141, 218.
29. F. Pomponio, "Nabû," *StSem,* 51 (1978), 6-8.
30. *PNU,* 17, 39, 164.
31. *HAL,* II, 661f.
32. See the bibliog. in Rendtorff, *TDNT,* VI, 796, n. 105.
33. For examples see *VG,* I, §138b; cf. *BLe,* §61n$^{\alpha}$.
34. Contra Rinaldi, 398, see Jeremias; *HAL,* II, 661f.
35. F. Werner, *Die Wortbildung der hebräischen Adjektiva* (Wiesbaden, 1983), 131.

cf. 22:20), Abraham (41:9; 51:2), or Israel (Hos. 11:1; Isa. 54:6). Morphosemantically comparable is the construct plural in *q*ᵉ*rî'ê hā'ēḏâ,* "called to the congregation" (Nu. 1:16 [*K*]; 16:2; 26:9 [*Q*]; cf. *q*ᵉ*rû'ê hā'ēḏâ* 1:16 [*Q*]; 26:9 [*K*]).

The technical military language of the Lachish letters (3:20; 16:5) may exhibit a metonymic shift of meaning.[36]

From Hebrew (including Middle Hebrew), *nāḇî',* "prophet," entered the Aramaic languages, from which Arabic and Ethiopic obviously borrowed it. Although the primary verb *nb'* with its G stem meaning is attested in both Arabic and Ethiopic, the nouns *nabīy/'un* (Arabic) and *nabīy* (Ethiopic) and their derivatives do not appear to be autochthonous.[37]

3. *The Denominative Verb nb'.* In Hebrew the noun *nāḇî',* derived from a Northwest Semitic verb *nb',* itself gave rise to a denominative verb in the niphal and hithpael meaning "act as a *nāḇî',* prophesy." The hithpael in particular sometimes takes on the derogatory sense of "behave like a prophet" (1 K. 18:29; Jer. 14:14; 29:26f.; Ezk. 13:17; a different sense in Jer. 26:20; Ezk. 37:10). On the syntagmatics of *nb'* niphal and hithpael, see *HAL;* Jürgen Jeremias outlines the distribution of *nāḇî'* and *nb'*.[38]

The hithpael is also found in Biblical Aramaic (Ezr. 5:1), as well as in other Aramaic dialects.[39] Syriac has both an etpaal and a less common pael with the same meaning.[40]

Although Arabic has primary verbal forms of *nb'* in stems I-IV and X, the fifth stem exhibits denominative forms with the meaning "he arrogated to himself the gift of prophecy or office of a prophet."[41] The latter is plainly a borrowing modeled on Hebrew and Aramaic (unlike OSA *tnb'* discussed above). Forms of the seventh stem, corresponding to the Hebrew niphal, are not found, obviously because the borrowing was by way of Aramaic and Syriac, which do not have a niphal.[42]

4. *n*ᵉ*ḇû'â and Parallels.* From the noun *nāḇî',* the Chronicler's history derives the technical term *n*ᵉ*ḇû'â,* "oracle" (2 Ch. 15:8; Ezr. 6:14 [Aram.]; Neh. 6:12) or "story of a prophet" (2 Ch. 9:29). The term appears later in Sir. 44:3 (par. *tbwntm,* "their understanding"); 46:1,13,20 as an abstract noun meaning "prophecy." It is also found in the Dead Sea Scrolls, and it undergoes a rich semantic development in Middle Hebrew.[43] Its parallel in Jewish Aramaic is *n*ᵉ*ḇû'*ᵃ*ṯā',* "prophecy"; in Syriac, *nḇîwūṯā',*

36. See provisionally H.-P. Müller, "Notizen zu althebräischen Inschriften I," *UF,* 2 (1970), 240-42, with bibliog.

37. See Leslau, 32.

38. *HAL,* II, 659; Jeremias, *TLOT,* II, 697f.

39. *WTM,* III, 323f.; Jastrow, 868.

40. *LexSyr,* 411.

41. Lane.

42. On stems II and IV in Arabic see also F. Leemhuis, "About the Meaning of *nabba'a* and *'anba'a* in the Qur'ān," *Akten des VII. Kongresses für Arabistik und Islamwissenschaft,* ed. A. Dietrich. *Abhandlungen der Akademie der Wissenschaften in Göttingen,* Phil.-hist. Kl., ser. 3, no. 98 (1976), 244-49.

"prophecy"; and in Arabic, *nubūʼat^un^*, "prophecy, the gift of prophecy; office, function of a prophet."[44]

5. *nbʻ*. The root *nbʻ*, "gush," found in Akkadian (*namba'u*, "spring"), Hebrew (*nbʻ*), Arabic (*nbǵ*), and Ethiopic, is not related to *nbʼ*, since ʻ is distinct from ʼ and *ī*. The notion of "gushing" ecstatic speech therefore has nothing to do with the etymology of Heb. *nbʼ*.[45] The metaphorical use of *nbʻ* to describe speech (qal: Sir. 50:27; hiphil: Ps. 19:3[Eng. v. 2]; 78:2; 119:171; 145:7; cf. 71:16) is etymologically irrelevant.

II. "Prophecy" in the Ancient Near East. If we understand a "prophet" to be a mediator of divine words, we find prophetic phenomena more or less consistently (1) at Mari in the eighteenth century B.C., (2) in Canaan in the fifteenth, eleventh, and eighth centuries, (3) in the Neo-Assyrian Empire, and (4) among the Arabs.In these four areas of the ancient Near East, the terminology for prophetic figures contains equivalents to concepts related to *nāḇîʼ*; it is not yet possible to saying anything about Eb. *nabiʼūtum*.[46] A detailed study of the semantic field of "prophecy" in Semitic, particularly Hebrew, is still a desideratum.[47]

Claims that prophecy is found elsewhere in Mesopotamia, at Ugarit, and above all in Egypt deserve critical caution.[48] In advanced civilizations, the need for divination is met largely by technical means in the broadest sense, provided by sacral institutions. Historical schemata with a finalistic view of the present, which appear to anticipate apocalypticism,[49] for this very reason do not fall within the realm of prophecy.

1. *Mari.* The Mari letters use the word *maḫḫûm* > *muḫḫûm*, fem. *muḫḫūtum*, "ecstatic" (already found in Old Akkadian), for the mediator of a divine message.[50] The noun, a *parras* form designating a function, derives from *maḫû(m)*, "rave (ecstatically)." This etymology accords with the Mari evidence: the use of the N stem of *maḫû(m)* for the inspired state of the mediator dispels any doubt concerning the latter's ecstatic condition.[51] It must remain an open question, however, whether *kumrum*, like Heb. *kmr* niphal, "become excited" (cf. **kōmer*, "idol priest"), denotes an ecstatic.[52] In addition, we find *āpilu(m)*, "answerer," the G stem participle of *apālu(m)*, and its

43. On the former see *HAL*, II, 660; on the latter, *WTM*, III, 324f.
44. For Jewish Aramaic see *WTM*, III, 325; *ChW*, II, 85; Jastrow, 867. For Arabic see Lane.
45. Contra *GesTh*, II/2, 838a; Jastrow, 868; et al.
46. G. Pettinato, *BA*, 39 (1976), 49.
47. Brief surveys are given by Rendtorff, *TDNT*, VI, 809f.; Jeremias, 698f.; and many others.
48. For Mesopotamia see M. Dietrich; for Ugarit, van Selms; and for Egypt, Lanczkowski; cf. Rendtorff, *TDNT*, VI, 801.
49. W. W. Hallo, "Akkadian Apocalypses," *IEJ*, 16 (1966), 231-242.
50. *ARM*, III, 40:9, 19; 78:12, 20, 27; A 455; the fem. occurs in VI, 45:9; X, 50:22.
51. *ARM*, X, 7:7; 8:7; contra Noort, 24f.
52. *ARM*, VIII, 1:37-39, 44. See J. Renger, *ZA*, 59 (1969), 219, n. 1042.

feminine equivalent *āpiltum.*[53] Except at Mari, however, the use of *āpilu(m)* and *āpiltum* for "prophet" appears to be rare.[54]

The use of *apālu(m),* "answer," for a prophetic oracle is analogous to the use of Heb. → ענה *'ānâ* for the communication of a divine oracle in response to a lament, as in Ps. 22:22(21), *'anîṯānî,* "you have answered me," i.e., "you have granted my request," and the petition *'anēnî,* "answer me," in Ps. 13:4(3). We find a similar usage in prose, e.g., 1 S. 28:6. Abraham Malamat also compares the second element of the enigmatic phrase *'ēr we'ōneh* in Mal. 2:12 to Akk. *āpilu(m)* ("he who is aroused and he who responds").[55]

The ecstatic character of inspiration is not at odds with the mediator's self-perception as a messenger of the deity, an understanding expressed in the legitimation elements of the language associated with prophecy at Mari.[56] In the case of the Hebrew prophets, too, the ecstatic impulse can occasionally be translated into reflection and be articulated to those addressed as 1st-person discourse spoken by God. The "way" that leads from impulse to articulation is symbolized as the consequence of being sent (Akk. *šapāru[m];*[57] cf. Heb. → שׁלח *šālaḥ* used of prophets: Isa. 6:8; Jer. 1:7; 19:14; 25:15,17; 26:12,15; 42:5,21; 43:1f.; Ezk. 2:3f.; 3:6; Hag. 1:12; Zec. 2:12f.[8f.],15[11]; 4:9; 6:15; etc.).

2. *Canaan.* The Taanach Letter (15th century B.C.) speaks of an *ú!-ba?-/ma?-an dA-ši-rat,* "finger/(oracle-giving) pundit of Asherah" (ll. 20f.);[58] a "sign" (*it-ta-am,* l. 23) and "word" (*a-wa-tam,* l. 24) are anticipated. William F. Albright associated the *ummān Aširat* with the *"neḇî' 'Ašeráh"* of 1 K. 18:19.[59] Authenticating signs are associated with oracles in several texts, e.g., Ex. 3:12; 4:8f.,17,28,30; Isa. 7:11-14; also Dt. 13:2(1). Ps. 74:9 may allude to interpretation of signs as oracles by a cultic (?) prophet (cf. Jgs. 6:17; 1 S. 14:10; Ps. 86:17).

The story of Wen-Amun speaks in a nontechnical sense of a *'ḏd 'ȝ,* "old [?] man," a priest (?) associated with the prince of Byblos, who became possessed by a god while offering sacrifice and raved through the night. During that time (or afterward?) he conveyed a message from the god correcting the conduct of the prince.[60]

The stela of King Zakir of Hamath and L'š speaks of *ḥzyn,* "seers," and *'ddn,* "oracle

---

53. *ARM,* X, 9:6; 53:5; XIII, 23:6, 16; A 1121:24, 26, 30, 37, 41; the fem. occurs in X, 81:4; A 1121:30.

54. *AHw,* I, 58a; *CAD,* I/1, 170, s.v. *apilu* A.1.

55. Pp. 211-13. Other words were used occasionally for "prophet" at Mari; see, e.g., Koch, *UF,* 4:76. For a general discussion of Old Babylonian terms for prophets see Renger, 219ff. (for Mari, 222).

56. Westermann, *Forschung,* I, 178f.; Koch, *UF,* 4:62.

57. *ARM,* II, 90:19; III, 40:13; XIII, 114:11.

58. First published by F. Hrozný in E. Sellin, *Tell Ta'annek. AWW Denkschrift,* 50/IV (1904), 113f. On the reading *ú-ma-an* see W. F. Albright, *BASOR,* 94 (1944), 18 and n. 28; *ANET,* 490.

59. Albright, *BASOR,* 94 (1944), 18, n. 28.

60. Following the translation of E. Edel, based on A. Scharf, *ZÄS,* 74 (1938), 147, found in *TGI*³, 41-48, esp. 43; with bibliog.

interpreters (?)," who pronounce a formal oracle of disaster against the king's enemies as the "answer" of the god Bʿlšmyn to his prayer.[61] The term "seer" recalls Balaam (Nu. 24:4,16; cf. now also the phrase *'š ḥ[z]h 'lhn,* "the man who sees the gods," from the ink inscription of Deir ʿAllā), who among other things (?) pronounces an oracle against his own people.[62] The long-enigmatic *ʿdd* of the Afis stele[63] resembles Heb. *ʿôḏēḏ,* a name obviously invented ad hoc for a fictive prophet in 2 Ch. 28:9 (cf. 15:1,8 [text?]); the name may have derived from a half-forgotten term denoting a profession or function.

Ugaritic parallels to Aram. *ʿdd* have been cited by James F. Ross (*tʿdt,* "embassy"; cf. Heb. *ʿwd* hiphil, "warn"; *tʿdh,* Isa. 8:16,20; etc.) and by J. Sanmartín.[64] Aelred Cody has proposed a connection with Egyp. *ʿḏd.*[65]

3. *Neo-Assyrian Prophetic Oracles.* Neo-Assyrian prophetic oracles call those who pronounce them *rāgimu* (G ptcp. of *ragām,* "call"), fem. *rāgintu;* according to Wolfram von Soden, a *rāgamu/raggimu,* like an *āpilu(m),* is an oracle priest.[66] Neo-Assyrian "prophecy" is discussed by Manfred Weippert and by M. Dietrich. Weippert cites several " 'spontaneous' oracles, namely, dreams or divine utterances comparable to the words of the OT prophets," in connection with the "holy wars" of the Assyrians.[67] Dietrich points to the preservation of prophetic utterances both in royal letters and in compilations like the tablet IV R 68;[68] the latter resemble the smaller literary units (like Isa. [6:1–]7:1-8,18) on which the prophetic books are based.

4. *Among the Arabs.* The pre-Islamic *kāhin*^{un}, fem. *hāhinat*^{un}, are not actually priests but soothsayers (cf. *kahana,* "foretell"). Their mantic activity appears to have evolved from priestly extispicy and oracular practice at sanctuaries; they are also consulted for decisions in legal matters. The Koranic *nabīy/'*^{un} is discussed elsewhere.[69]

III. Usage.

1. *Amos.* Am. 7:12-16 is characteristic of the cautious use earlier preexilic written prophecy makes of *nāḇî'* and *nb'.* Amaziah addresses Amos as *ḥōzeh,* "seer" (v. 12),

---

61. *KAI,* 202A, 13-15.

62. See H.-P. Müller, "Die aramäische Inschrift von Deir ʿAllā und die älteren Bileamsprüche," *ZAW,* 94 (1982), 214-244, with bibliog.

63. *KAI,* 202A, 12.

64. *KTU,* 1.2, I, 22, 26, 28, 30, 40f., 44. See Ross, 5ff.; J. Sanmartín, "Zu den ʿd(d)-Denominderungen im Ugaritischen," *UF,* 12 (1980), 345-48.

65. A. Cody, "A Professional Oracular Medium," *JEA,* 65 (1979), 99-106; cf. J. Ebach and U. Rüterswörden, "Die byblitische Ekstatiker," *Göttinger Miszellen,* 20 (1977), 17-22; M. Görg, "Die Ekstatiker von Byblos," *ibid.,* 23 (1977), 31-33. See above.

66. *AHw,* II, 942.

67. Pp. 471ff.

68. Pp. 38ff. See *ANET*^{3}, 605. The text is from H. C. Rawlinson, *The Cuneiform Inscriptions of Western Asia* (London, 1861-84).

69. H. Speyer, *Die biblischen Erzählungen im Qoran* (Hildesheim, ^{2}1961), 416-423; Zimmerli, "Der Prophet im AT und im Islam," *Studien,* 284-310; also Leemhuis.

and forbids him (using the niphal of *nbʾ*) to continue to appear as a *nāḇîʾ* in Israel (vv. 12f.). In what follows, Amos does not return to this form of address, obviously because he does not perceive it as a challenge. On the contrary, he takes the use of *nbʾ* niphal to describe his activity as an occasion emphatically to reject his identification as a *nāḇîʾ*, "prophet," or *ben-nāḇîʾ*, "member of a band of prophets" (v. 14a). If this referred to a typical cult prophet, Amos would also be disputing the right of the priest (as in Jer. 29:26f.) to ban him from the "royal sanctuary" and "imperial temple." Amos, however, is concerned primarily to refute the imputation that he makes his living through prophecy (v. 12b) and is consequently greedy or venal (cf. Mic. 3:5; Ezk. 13:19). In v. 14b, therefore, he emphasizes that he earns his bread by agriculture. In v. 15b (as in 3:8), of course, he must himself use *nbʾ* niphal for his own prophetic ministry, exercised under divine constraint.

Some scholars attempt to reconcile *lōʾ nāḇîʾ ʾānôḵî* in v. 14a with the impv. *hinnāḇēʾ* in v. 15b by interpreting v. 14a as a preterit: "I was not a prophet — until Yahweh 'took' me." Apart from the banality of such a statement, neither in v. 14a nor in 14b can an atemporal noun clause be read as a statement about past time. The form *lōʾ hāyîṯî* with a predicate noun would have been available had the reference been to the past.[70]

The prophecy of disaster that follows (v. 17) is preceded by an accusation (v. 16) that places in Amaziah's mouth the use of *nbʾ* niphal in parallel with *nṭp* hiphil, "cause to drip" > "slaver (ecstatically)" (cf. Mic. 2:6,11; Ezk. 21:2,7[20:47; 21:2]). The priest is characterized once more in terms of his aristocratic disdain for the *neḇîʾîm,* among whom he includes Amos.

In Am. 2:11f.; 3:7, where *nbʾ* niphal and *nāḇîʾ* are used positively, we are dealing with "Deuteronomistic" redaction.[71] In 2:12 *neḇîʾîm* and Nazirites represent a conservative nomadic set of values that the preexilic Israelites wanted to silence (cf. the Deuteronomistic commendation of the Rechabites in Jer. 35:13-17). If the Deuteronomistic perspective accurately reflects the thinking of the prophets, they were mirroring (belatedly) the problems that beset the ancient Hebrew religion with the change to an agrarian and urban milieu and the encounter with the higher civilization of the Canaanites and their hierarchical social structure.

2. *Prophetic Narratives before Amos.* It is relatively easy to date these Amos texts. We shall now turn our attention to prophet narratives that are in part later compositions although set in the period before Amos.

a. The "judge" Deborah is called *ʾiššâ neḇîʾâ,* a "prophetic woman" (Jgs. 4:4; cf.

---

70. Contra H. H. Rowley, H. Graf Reventlow, et al.; see the bibliog. in H. W. Wolff, *Joel and Amos. Herm* (Eng. trans. 1977), 312, n. 30. A totally different approach is taken by Z. Zevit, "A Misunderstanding at Bethel: Amos VII 12-17," *VT,* 25 (1975), 783-790; *idem,* "Expressing Denial in Biblical Hebrew and Mishnaic Hebrew, and in Amos," *VT,* 29 (1979), 505-8; see the remarks of Y. Hoffmann, "Did Amos Regard Himself as a *Nābîʾ*?" *VT,* 27 (1977), 209-212.

71. W. H. Schmidt, "Die deuteronomistische Redaktion des Amosbuches," *ZAW,* 77 (1965), 168-193; cf. Wolff, *Joel and Amos,* 112f.

ʾîš nāḇîʾ in 6:8 [Deuteronomistic]); alongside the military charisma of Barak, the phrase suggests words that predict victory and inspire to battle (vv. 6f.,9,14). When Ex. 15:20 calls Miriam *nᵉḇîʾâ,* however, the title represents an attenuated concept of the *nāḇîʾ*, albeit expressive of high esteem.

This is also true in 1 S. 3:20, which says of Samuel that *neʾᵉmān . . . lᵉnāḇî lᵉYHWH,* "he was esteemed as a prophet for Yahweh" (cf. 2 Ch. 35:18; Sir. 46:13,(15),20. Nowhere else is Samuel called *nāḇîʾ;* only in 1 S. 19:22-24, in the context of a comparatively late narrative, is Samuel described as leader of a group of *nᵉḇîʾîm.* In the legendary narrative of Saul's search for the strayed donkeys, Samuel is called *ʾîš (hā)ʾᵉlōhîm,* "man of God" (9:6-8,10). In the following scene with the girls at the well, he is introduced at first anonymously as *rōʾeh,* "seer" (vv. 11f.); he himself claims this title when speaking with Saul (vv. 18f.; on Samuel as "seer," cf. 1 Ch. 9:22; 26:28; 29:29). Strangely, v. 9 relates the terms *nāḇîʾ* and *rōʾeh,* even though the context (vv. 1-9) uses *ʾîš (hā)ʾᵉlōhîm* and the following section (vv. 11-21) uses *rōʾeh.* John B. Curtis treats v. 7 as a popular etymology.

In 2 S. 24:11; 1 Ch. 21:9, Gad is called *ḥōzēh ḏāwiḏ,* "David's seer," clearly a more accurate term (cf. *ḥōzēh-hammeleḵ* in 2 Ch. 29:25). The appositive *hannāḇîʾ*, without a genitive, is added to his name in 1 S. 22:5; 2 S. 24:11. This is another example of attenuated usage, especially in the latter verse, a product of Deuteronomistic redaction, where it redundantly precedes *ḥōzēh ḏāwiḏ.* The (a?) Deuteronomistic redactor also uses *hannāḇîʾ* appositively with Nathan's name (2 S. 7:2; 12:25; 1 K. 1:8,10,22ff.,32, 34,38,44f.; cf. Ps. 51:2[superscription]), although Nathan plays a "prophetic" role at best in 7:2. The term also appears in apposition with the names of Ahijah (1 K. 11:29; 14:2,18) and Jehu (16:7,12).

In 1 K. 18:22 Elijah calls himself *nāḇîʾ lᵉYHWH;* he "alone remained" as such during the persecution, in contrast to the 450 prophets of Baʿal (cf. 19:10). Therefore the Deuteronomistic redactor (DtrP?) adds *hannāḇîʾ*, "the (true) prophet," attributively to Elijah's name in v. 36 (cf. *ho prophḗtēs* in the LXX [except the Lucianic recension] of 1 K. 17:1; on Elijah as an eschatological figure, see also Mal. 3:23). Connotatively similar are the expressions *nāḇîʾ bᵉyiśrāʾēl,* "prophet in Israel" (2 K. 5:8 [Deuteronomistic]; cf. 6:12), and *hannāḇîʾ ʾᵃšer bᵉšōmᵉrôn,* "the prophet in Samaria," used by a captive Israelite slave girl to describe Elisha (5:3); cf. Elisha's call *lᵉnāḇî* (1 K. 19:16; also 2 K. 3:11; 5:13; 9:1,4). More commonly, of course, Elisha is called *ʾîš (hā)ʾᵉlōhîm,* "man of God"; this title and the concomitant motifs associated with being a miracle worker were then applied to Elijah (1 K. 17:18,24; 2 K. 1:9-13).

An anonymous *nāḇîʾ* is described in 1 K. 20:13,22 as predicting a victory; when this prediction is fulfilled, he gives military advice (1 K. 20:13,22). Hostility between the *nāḇîʾ lᵉYHWH* Micaiah ben Imlah, who predicts disaster, and the four hundred optimistic court prophets of the "king of Israel" is presupposed in 1 K. 22:6,10,12f.[72]

Also anonymous is the old *nāḇîʾ* of Bethel in the legend of 1 K. 13; he leads an equally anonymous *ʾîš (hā)ʾᵉlōhîm* from Judah (identified with Amos by Julius Well-

---

72. On vv. 19-23 see 2.c below.

hausen, Otto Eissfeldt, et al.) into temptation, pretending to have received a *d^eḇar YHWH* from a *mal'āḵ* (v. 18).[73] Catching the miscreant red-handed, he predicts disaster, which naturally ensues, so that the legend can function as a burial site etiology (cf. 2 K. 23:16-18). Each title (*'îš* [*hā*]*'^elōhîm* and *nāḇî'*) is assigned consistently to one of the actors; only in the words of introduction, *gam-'^anî nāḇî' kāmôḵā,* "I also am a prophet as you are," addressed to the "man of God" (v. 18a) might we find a violation of this principle. Are we dealing here with repressed polemic against the institution of the "man of God," if indeed there was such a specific institution or function?[74] The text clearly acknowledges that "men of God" also come forward *biḏḇar YHWH,* "at the command of Yahweh" (v. 1), so that the conflict between the functionaries appears to be displaced onto the deity. It is also unclear whether the "son" (v. 11 [text?]) and the "sons" (vv. 12f.,27,31) of the *nāḇî',* whom v. 11 refers to as their "father," are his children or his disciples (on the *'āḇ* of a group of prophets, cf. 1 S. 10:12; 2 K. 2:12; 6:21).[75]

b. Moses is occasionally called a *nāḇî'*. The earliest stratum of his call narrative, Ex. 3:1-4a*,5,7f.*,16f.* (the association of which with the original Yahwist Martin Noth finds dubious), presupposes a prophetic role for Moses: he receives a typical oracle of salvation (vv. 7f.) and is commanded to proclaim it (vv. 16f.).[76] Since there are no convincing historical grounds for categorizing Moses as a prophet,[77] the question arises as to what historical ideology led the author of the text to this picture of him. A relatively early understanding of Moses as a *nāḇî'* is also found in Hos. 12:14(13), which, like Ex. 3:4b,6,9-14(15) (E), clearly envisions a politically involved prophet like Elisha.

Nu. 12:6-8a (linked to its secondary context by v. 8b) is difficult to categorize both traditio-historically and literarily. It counts Moses among the *n^eḇî'îm:* Yahweh speaks to him not only through visions and dreams (v. 6), and therefore "in riddles," but "mouth to mouth" (v. 8aα; cf. "face to face": Ex. 33:11; Dt. 34:10b). According to v. 8aβ (secondary?), he "beholds the form of Yahweh." Thus he is Yahweh's "servant" (vv. 7a,8b; cf. the Deuteronomistic [DtrN?] texts Dt. 3:24; 34:5; Josh. 1:1f.,7,13,15; 1 K. 8:53,56; 2 K. 21:8; also Ps. 105:26; Mal. 3:22). Moses is "entrusted *(ne'^emān)* with all [Yahweh's] house" (v. 7b; cf. Samuel in 1 S. 3:20b). But the terminology used is inappropriate: speaking "in riddles," i.e., in visions or dreams, is characteristic of those whose dreams come true (Gen. 37, 40f.; Jgs. 7:13f.; Dnl. 2, 4), not of *n^eḇî'îm.*

---

73. See Wellhausen, *Die Composition des Hexateuchs* (Berlin, ³1899), 277f.; Eissfeldt, "Amos und Jona in volkstümlicher Überlieferung," *KlSchr,* IV, 137-142. For analysis and dating see E. Würthwein, *1 Könige 1–16. ATD,* 11/1 (1977), 168ff.

74. Contra Holstein.

75. See Williams; Philipps. On 1 S. 10:12 see 2.c below.

76. M. Noth, *A History of Pentateuchal Traditions* (Eng. trans., Englewood Cliffs, N.J., 1972), 30, n. 103, etc.; but cf. the cautious discussion by L. Schmidt, "Überlegungen zum Jahwisten," *EvT,* 37 (1977), 233-36. On the form see C. Westermann, "The Way of the Promise through the OT," *The OT and Christian Faith,* ed. B. W. Anderson (Eng. trans., New York, 1969), 200-224, esp. 202ff.

77. See Perlitt.

Moses becomes the prototype of all prophets in Dt. 18:15,18 (Deuteronomistic [DtrN?][78]); in Dt. 34:10a, however, as in Nu. 12:6-8a, the prototype eclipses his successors. Nu. 11:14-17,24b-25,30, a late episode,[79] legitimizes "seventy elders" in an undefined leadership role (contrast their cultic function in Ex. 24:9-11 and their judicial role in Ex. 18:13-26; Dt. 1:9-18); they receive a share of the "spirit" that rests on Moses and fall into a frenzy (*nb'* hithpael: Nu. 11:25-27). The mention in vv. 26-29 of two outsiders who also share in the spirit because they were "registered" (v. 26aβ; a gloss?) is also secondary;[80] v. 29 calls the ecstatics *neḇî'îm.*

We are dealing with a late extension of terminology when Gen. 20:7 (E) calls Abraham a *nāḇî'*. Ex. 7:1 (P) even calls Aaron the *nāḇî'* of Moses (cf. 4:16). Ps. 105:15 calls the ancestors of Israel "anointed ones" and "prophets" of Yahweh. Finally, even David, whom the Deuteronomistic history already calls Yahweh's "servant,"[81] becomes *'îš hā'elōhîm* in Neh. 12:36 and the mediator of a *neḇû'â* recorded in Psalms (11QPs[a]).[82]

c. Two parallel narratives use the pl. *neḇî'îm* for groups of prophets Saul meets (*ḥeḇel neḇî'îm* in 1 S. 10:5,10; *lahaqaṯ* [?] *hanneḇî'îm* in 19:20), who infect him and his messengers with their frenzy (10:6,10; 19:20f.,23f.). The stories are told to explain a *māšāl* that includes Saul in a group of contemptible people (10:11f.; 19:24); 19:23f. tacks on some repugnant details. The *neḇî'îm* themselves would be especially contemptible if we had to think of the *bāmâ* at *giḇ'aṯ hā'elōhîm,* from which 10:5 says they came with all the paraphernalia for their frenzy, as a Canaanite sacrificial high place; the second story is set *benāwî/ôṯ* (?) in Ramah, where David is granted sacral asylum. But 10:5ff. makes the theory of Canaanite or canaanizing cultic prophecy unlikely: the etiology of the *māšāl* is used instead to represent Saul as a man endowed with the Spirit of Yahweh.[83] The question in 10:12a about the "father" (i.e., leader) of the group is unmotivated and intrusive: only in 19:19ff. is a leader mentioned.

Along with "dreams" and *'ûrîm,* 1 S. 28:6(15) speaks of *(han)neḇî'îm* as vehicles for an (oracular) answer from Yahweh; when (as here) such divination fails (cf. 1 S. 3:1b), it is a sign of God's withdrawal.

The Elijah legends include the *neḇî'ê YHWH* among those persecuted by Ahab and Jezebel (1 K. 18:4,13; cf. 19:1,10; also 2 K. 9:7, Deuteronomistic [P?]); the latter in particular plays the role of an antihero against the proponents of Yahweh's claim to exclusive worship.[84] The statement in 1 K. 18:22 that Elijah alone is left as a prophet of Yahweh is hard to reconcile with the hundred prophets saved by Obadiah (18:4,13);

---

78. See 4.a below.

79. For dating, see Wellhausen, *Composition,* 99f.; M. Noth, *Numbers. OTL* (Eng. trans. 1968), 83f.

80. Hossfeld and Meyer, 19-21.

81. See 4.b below.

82. *DJD,* IV, 92:11.

83. H. Wildberger, *TZ,* 13 (1957), 454 = his *Jahwe und sein Volk. GSAT,* ed. H. H. Schmid and O. H. Steck. *ThB,* 66 (1979), 40; see also J. Sturdy, "The Original Meaning of 'Is Saul also among the Prophets?' " *VT,* 20 (1970), 206-213.

84. Steck, *Überlieferung;* U. Winter, *Frau und Göttin* (Freiburg and Göttingen, 1983), 577-588.

Georg Hentschel therefore argues that vv. 3b,4,12b,13(14) are a secondary addition.[85] The opposing group to the prophet(s) of Yahweh are the 450 *nᵉḇî'ê habbaʿal* said to be maintained by Jezebel (vv. 19,22,25,40; cf. *hannᵉḇî'îm* in v. 20); the "400 prophets of Asherah" mentioned in isolation in v. 19 are most likely an outgrowth of the history of the text.[86]

The image of the *nᵉḇî'ê habbaʿal* in 1 K. 18:19ff. would suggest Canaanite cult prophets, were it not the product of the black-vs.-white imagery that belongs to the dynamics of the legend. In 2 K. 10:19 "all the prophets of Baal" are generalized by the addition of *kol-ʿōḇᵉḏāyw* ("all his worshipers" [text?]) and "all his priests"; this language robs the image of the prophets of Baʿal of its specificity, at least if the cycle of Elijah legends in 1 K. 17f.(19) presupposes Jehu's revolution,[87] and 1 K. 18:40 (albeit traditio-historically secondary[88]) is intended simply to legitimize the slaughter of all the followers of Baʿal in 2 K. 10:(14),18-24.

In 1 K. 22:19-22(23), a Judahite interpolation into what was probably already a reworked North Israelite narrative,[89] a *rûaḥ šeqer* ("lying spirit") from Yahweh's council fills the 400 optimistic court prophets of the "king of Israel," identified in v. 20 (Deuteronomistic [P?]) as Ahab. The "king of Israel" is deceived by them, just as the "man of God" in 1 K. 13 was deceived by a *nāḇî'* of Yahweh.

The scene of the council assembled around Yahweh's throne has a history that stretches back to the Sumerian royal chronicle.[90] This mythological concept serves to derive the conflict between true and false prophets of Yahweh from a providential decision on the part of Yahweh; the underlying motif of divine deception projects onto the deity a contradiction in the relationship of human beings to their religious and social world. The deceptive oracle is fulfilled, although the "king of Israel" attempts to escape his fate by disguising himself (vv. 30ff.). A similar theme appears in the *Iliad* (2.1ff.): Zeus, who can think of nothing better in the conflict among the gods, uses a "deluding dream" represented as a personal emissary to send Agamemnon into a hopeless battle.

d. The plural phrase *bᵉnê hannᵉḇî'îm,* "sons of the prophets, members of a company of prophets" (cf. *ben-nāḇî':* Am. 7:14), is used throughout 2 K. 2:3–9:7 for the circle around Elisha; they sit "before" their master and enjoy table fellowship with him (4:38). The contrast with the court prophets of the North Israelite kings is noted in 3:13. The members of this circle have wives (4:1ff.); it includes *nᵉʿārîm* (5:22), one of whom is

---

85. G. Hentschel, *Die Eliaerzählungen. ETS,* 33 (1977), 67-69.

86. Wellhausen, *Composition,* 279, n. 1, and many others.

87. R. Smend, *VT,* 25 (1975), 540.

88. E. Würthwein, *ZTK,* 59 (1962), 134.

89. E. Würthwein, "Zur Komposition von I Reg 22 1-38," *Das ferne und nahe Wort. Festschrift L. Rost. BZAW,* 105 (1967), 245-254, esp. 252; Hossfeld and Meyer, 32-34; for a different view, see H. Schweizer, "Literarkritischer Versuch zur Erzählung von Micha ben Jimla," *BZ,* 23 (1979), 1-19.

90. H.-P. Müller, "Die himmlische Ratsversammlung," *ZNW,* 54 (1963), 254-267; *idem,* "Glauben und Bleiben," *Studies on Prophecy. SVT,* 26 (1974), 25-54, esp. 29ff.; → סוד *sôḏ.* On the function of similar motifs in oral tradition, see A. B. Lord, *The Singer of Tales* (Cambridge, 1960), 146ff.

the *na'ar hannāḇî',* the "servant" of Elisha (9:4). While groups (1 S. 10, 19) and even masses (1 K. 18, 22) of prophets appear earlier, the appearance of a new collective designation shows that they now constitute closely linked companies.

In 1 K. 20:25, a late legend related to 1 K. 13, there appears *'îš 'eḥāḏ mibbᵉnê hannᵉḇî'îm* ("a certain man of the sons of the prophets"), a prophet of disaster who uses an exemplary story (cf. 2 S. 12:1ff.; 14:5ff.; Isa. 5:1-7) to force the king of Israel (once again Ahab, according to 1 K. 20:2,13f., Deuteronomistic [P?][91]) to pronounce his own doom. When he uncovers his eyes and forehead, which he had bandaged to give the impression of having come directly from the battlefield, the king recognizes him as *mēhannᵉḇî'îm* ("[one] of the prophets," v. 41) — possibly because he had shaved his temples (cf. Jer. 9:25[26]; 25:23; 49:32; also the prohibition in Lev. 19:27; 21:5) or more likely because he had a *tāw* tattooed (?) on his forehead (cf. Ezk. 9:4,6; also *zikkārôn bên 'êneyḵā:* Ex. 13:9 [Deuteronomistic]).[92]

e. The Deuteronomistic sections of 1 Samuel and 1 Kings use the niphal of *nb'* just 3 times. In 1 S. 10:11; 19:20, the participle denotes the existence of a state of ecstatic frenzy; the extension to Saul of the taunts in 1 S. 10:11f. and 19:24 lends the texts an ambivalent overtone. In 1 K. 22:12 the participle likewise denotes ecstatic speech that clearly went on for some time. On the frequent attribution of ecstatic frenzy to the *rûaḥ YHWH* or *rûaḥ 'ᵉlōhîm* ("divine Spirit"; cf. 1 S. 10:6,10), note already the identification of Sum. *ˡúan-ni-ba-tu,* "one who has been entered by a divine power," with Akk. *eššebû* as the designation of an ecstatic priest, identified in turn with *maḫḫû.*[93]

By contrast, the hithpael is relatively frequent in the early period. The scenes in 1 S. 10:5ff. and 19:20ff. use the participle (10:5) to describe the ongoing ecstatic frenzy of the group and the narrative tense (10:10) or consecutive perfect (10:6) ingressively for Saul's falling into a frenzy (10:6,10) or his messengers' doing the same (19:20f.). In 18:10 the hithpael of *nb'* similarly describes Saul's (depressive?) raving under *rûaḥ 'ᵉlōhîm rā'â,* "an evil divine spirit." Beginning with *wayyēleḵ hālôḵ,* "while he went there," 19:23 uses the narrative tense of the hithpael (cf. Targ.^f, Syr.: inf.) for falling into an ecstatic frenzy; contrast 10:13, where *wayᵉḵal mēhiṯnabbôṯ* refers to the ending of the frenzy. In 1 K. 18:29 the narrative tense followed by a temporal expression clearly has derogatory overtones: "behave (constantly) like a *nāḇî'.*" Like the niphal participle in 1 K. 22:12, the hithpael participle in v. 10 describes the extended ecstatic speech of the false prophets.[94] The verb form itself, however, does not express a derogatory judgment; for the same text uses the negated hithpael imperfect of the true prophet, who continually "prophesies to the king of Israel nothing favorable, but only disaster" (vv. 8,18). The hithpael is used positively in Nu. 11:25-27;[95] the narrative tense seems again to be used for the ingressive aspect (vv. 25f.), the participle for the durative or stative (v. 27).

---

91. W. Dietrich, 121.
92. See B. Stade, *ZAW,* 14 (1894), 301; Lindblom, *Prophecy,* 67f.
93. *CAD,* IV, 371; see II.1 above.
94. But see Schweizer, 11.
95. See 2.b above.

3. *From Hosea to the Exile.* a. Unlike Amos, Hosea sees a continuity between himself and earlier "prophets," whose words brought disaster. Through them, Yahweh hewed and killed his people (6:5), after he had spoken in vain to (?) prophets *('al*[!]-*hannᵉḇî'îm),* "multiplied visions *(ḥāzôn),*" and "depicted (the future) through them" (*'ᵃḏammeh* < *dmh* I) (12:11[10]). The sacred history of Israel began with the prophetic figure of Moses (12:14[13])[96] and has been continued ever since through prophecy of disaster and repentance. When the "sentinel of Ephraim" (rightly identified as a *nāḇî'* by the gloss in 9:8; cf. Jer. 6:17; Ezk. 3:17; 33:2,6f.) is threatened by snares, his protest represents the beginning of a prophetic self-understanding as one who suffers in fulfilling Yahweh's commission. Hosea is not prevented from using the term *nāḇî'* in a positive sense by his opponents' defamation of the *nāḇî'* (whom they also call *'îš hārûaḥ,* "man of the [ecstatic] spirit") as *'ᵉwîl,* "a fool," even *mᵉšuggā',* "mad" (Hos. 9:7; cf. 2 K. 9:11; Jer. 29:26). A society that had long lived secure without having to mobilize its reserves of vitality in a struggle for survival obviously no longer had any need or sympathy for ecstatic agencies of strength and power, so that ecstatic phenomena degenerated into pathology. Hosea knows how to neutralize the mockery of his enemies: the "iniquity" and "hostility" of his mockers rob the prophet of his sanity (v. 7b). That the (hostile) prophet, like the priest, should stumble under Yahweh's judgment may be a Judahite glossator's addition to 4:5.[97]

b. Despite calling his wife *nᵉḇî'â* (Isa. 8:3), Isaiah never calls himself *nāḇî'*. The proclamation of disaster in 3:1-3 encompasses *nāḇî'* and *qōsēm* ("diviner")[98] along with the other functionaries of Jerusalem and Judah (cf. the addition in 9:14[15]). Otto Kaiser, who maintains that the prophecy of Isaiah is a fifth-century fiction, ascribes the words *wᵉnāḇî' wᵉqōsēm* to a glossator.[99] During the sacrificial meal, "priest and prophet" become drunk; the latter are impeded in their "vision" (reading *bārō'â*), the former in giving priestly "judgment" (reading *biplîlîyâ*) (28:7). By contrast, Isaiah feels solidarity with *rō'îm* and *ḥōzîm,* "seers," who are forbidden to deliver an authentic message (30:10f.); here, too, Kaiser finds a fragment of later prophetic theology (cf. Am. 2:12b ["Deuteronomistic"]).[100] These appraisals of the prophets and seers recall Amos's rejection of the appellation *nāḇî'* while allowing himself to be addressed as *ḥōzeh* (Am. 7:12ff.). Isaiah seems to have been influenced by the "school" of Amos, especially in the early period of his ministry.[101] Like other prophetic narratives, the Isaiah legend uses *hannāḇî'* in apposition to the prophet's name (Isa. 37:2; 38:1; 39:3; cf. 2 K. 19:2; 20:1,11,14).

c. Micah is the first to proclaim an oracle of disaster against the *nᵉḇî'îm* as a group (Mic. 3:5-8; cf. 2:6-11). In 3:9-12 they are among the dignitaries threatened with

---

96. See 2.b above.

97. H. W. Wolff, *Hosea. Herm* (Eng. trans. 1974), xxxii, 70f., 77f.; cf. W. Rudolph, *Hosea. KAT,* XIII/1 (1966), 96f.; J. Jeremias, *Der Prophet Hosea. ATD,* 24/1 (1983), 63, 66.

98. See 3.c below.

99. *Isaiah 1–12. OTL* (Eng. trans. ²1983), 8, 66.

100. Already in *Isaiah 13–39. OTL* (Eng. trans. 1974), 292f.

101. R. Fey, *Amos und Jesaja. WMANT,* 12 (1963).

judgment: they are accused of venality (v. 5) and facile trust in Yahweh (v. 11; cf. Ezk. 13:19). V. 11 links them with the priests (cf. Zeph. 3:4). The use of the root → קסם *qsm* appears to associate the activity of the *n*ᵉ*ḇîʾîm* with oracles in the technical sense (*qsm* is associated with oracular divination, Ezk. 21:26f.[21f.]; *kōh*ᵃ*nîm* with *qōs*ᵉ*mîm,* 1 S. 6:2; *n*ᵉ*ḇîʾîm* with *qōs*ᵉ*mîm,* Isa. 3:2; Jer. 27:9; 29:8 ["Deuteronomistic"]; Ezk. 22:28). The announcement of disaster in Mic. 3:6 proclaims the end of all "vision" *(ḥāzôn)* and "revelation" *(q*ᵉ*sōm);* cf. *haḥōzîm* par. *haqqōs*ᵉ*mîm* in v. 7. Mic. 2:6 recalls the use of *nṭp* hiphil in Am. 7:16 for the despised and forbidden proclamation of oracles of disaster.

The verb *nb'* is not used in Hosea, Isaiah, or Micah.

d. The book of Jeremiah uses *nāḇîʾ* and *nb'* more frequently than all the other prophetic writings. Here for the first time conflict with hostile *n*ᵉ*ḇîʾîm* (esp. Jer. 14:13-16; 23:9-32[-40]) leads to the beginnings of real reflection on Jeremiah's function as *nāḇîʾ*, in the course of which earlier motifs of prophetic self-understanding are collected and developed.

The accusations leveled against *n*ᵉ*ḇîʾîm* in Jeremiah's oracles of disaster are in part those already mentioned: facilely making soothing predictions of well-being (4:10; 5:12f.; "Deuteronomistic": 14:13; 23:17; 27:9f.,14,16; 28:9; and probably 37:19), which do not demand the repentance required (23:22b "Deuteronomistic") and are therefore of no profit either to "this people" or to their authors (v. 32b "Deuteronomistic"); greediness, which (as in the case of the priests) leads to "deceit" (6:13; 8:10; *šeqer* in association with *nāḇîʾ* and its derivatives: 5:1; also the "Deuteronomistic" texts 14:14; 23:25f.,32; 27:10,14-16; 29:9,21,31b), immoral conduct (23:14f.; 29:33), etc.

New in comparison to 1 K. 22:19-23 is the blunt denial that the false prophets have been sent by Yahweh or even have a revelation at all (Jer. 23:21; "Deuteronomistic": 14:14f.; 23:32; 29:31 [contrast v. 15]); they did not "stand in the council of Yahweh" (23:22; "Deuteronomistic": v. 18), although v. 30 appears to accuse them of plagiarizing words of Yahweh from each other. Dreams are their source of revelation (23:15f.; "Deuteronomistic": vv. 27f.; 29:8f.). Their words are ascribed rationalistically to "deceit" (23:26; "Deuteronomistic": 14:14) or "the visions of their own hearts" (23:16; cf. Ezk. 13:2). "Prophesying" *babbaʿal* ("in the name of Baal"), however, seems to be a thing of the past (Jer. 2:8; 23:13).

Therefore, the *n*ᵉ*ḇîʾîm* must hear Yahweh's defiance (23:30ff.), just as they had previously been devoured by the sword (2:30). The message of doom is addressed to both priests and prophets (*minnāḇîʾ w*ᵉ*ʿaḏ kōhēn:* 6:13; 8:10; also 14:18; 23:11; and the gloss 2:26b [cf. Zeph. 3:4]). Other groups, specifically identified as dignitaries, can be included (Jer. 4:9; 13:13; 26:7; 29:1; "Deuteronomistic": 8:1; 32:32; also 23:33f.; cf. the quotation from unconcerned opponents in 18:18). Here, as in Isa. 28:7; Mic. 3:11, the frequent juxtaposition of "priests" and "prophets" probably points to cultic prophecy (cf. *nb'* niphal with priestly subj. in Jer. 20:6 ["Deuteronomistic"]; also 2 K. 23:2; Lam. 2:20; Neh. 9:32).

In Jer. 26:11,16, priests and *n*ᵉ*ḇîʾîm* appear as Jeremiah's enemies in his trial; cf. also their interference with his ministry in 11:21; 29:26f.; 32:3; 37:21. The use of *hannāḇî'* in apposition with Jeremiah's name is frequent in the so-called Baruch biography, beginning with 20:2, as though to indicate that Jeremiah's prophetic preaching was repeatedly both the cause and the scandal of his martyrdom (outside the Baruch biography: 29:29; 32:2; and 25:2; 29:1; 34:6). In ch. 28 both Jeremiah (vv. 5f.,10-12,15) and Hananiah (vv. 1,5,10,15[!],17) are so designated.

Jeremiah's unique designation of himself as *nāḇî' laggôyim* ("prophet to the nations," 1:5) reappears in v. 10 as *'al-haggôyim w^e'al-hammamlāḵôṯ* (similarly vv. 15f.). It is explained in 25:13 and 28:8 in terms of prophecies against various nations, so that Jeremiah's continuity with the earlier prophets is underlined ("the prophets who preceded you and me from ancient times": 28:8a). Continuity with the *n^eḇî'îm* sent by Yahweh (also called *'^aḇāḏay,* "my [Yahweh's] servants") ever since the exodus from Egypt is emphasized in 7:25f. ("Deuteronomistic") and elsewhere.

4. *Exilic Prophecy.* a. Dt. 18:9-22 records the law governing prophecy; in its present form, it has been shaped by one or more Deuteronomistic redactors. According to vv. 15,18 (DtrN?), a *nāḇî'* like Moses is the positive alternative to the mantics and magicians prohibited in vv. 10f. V. 20 declares that any "prophet" not legitimated by Yahweh's command (*ṣwh* piel [positive], v. 18) shall die (cf. Jer. 14:15 ["Deuteronomistic"]). According to Dt. 13:2,4,6(1,3,5), the same applies to a "prophet or dreamer" (cf. Jer. 23:25-28; "Deuteronomistic": 23:32; 27:9) who calls on the people to worship "other gods." Otherwise the criterion of true prophecy is whether what has been predicted takes place (*hāyâ, bô';* Dt. 18:22; cf. 1 S. 9:6a; prophecy of salvation: Jer. 5:13; 28:9; prophecy of disaster: Ezk. 33:33; Zec. 1:6), with the important exception recorded in Dt. 13:2(1)ff. False prophecy is attributed to presumption (*yāzîḏ,* 18:20; *zāḏôn,* v. 22); it can clearly include prophecy of disaster, as the gloss *lō' tāḡûr mimmennû* ("do not be frightened by it") in v. 22bβ shows.

b. The Deuteronomistic history and its prophetic or nomistic redactional strata (DtrP, DtrN)[102] follow Dt. 18:22 by emphasizing the precise correspondence between prophecy and fulfillment (e.g., 1 K. 14:18; 16:12; 2 K. 14:25, where *hannāḇî'* is used in apposition with the names of the prophets; also 2 K. 17:23). Both Moses[103] and David have already often been called Yahweh's servants; now the prophets, too, who constitute an uninterrupted succession, receive the attribute *'^aḇāḏay* or *'^aḇāḏāyw* (2 K. 9:7; 17:13,23; 21:10; 24:2; cf. *'aḇdô,* etc.: 1 K. 14:18; 15:29; 18:36; 2 K. 14:25). They were often persecuted (2 K. 9:7).[104]

In contrast to the preaching of Amos (4:6-12; 8:2; 9:1), prophecies of disaster are intended as calls to repentance, verbally anticipating the judgment of Yahweh so as to render its reality needless (e.g., 2 S. 12:13f.; 1 K. 21:17-29; 2 K. 22:15-20). As early as Jgs. 6:7-10, Yahweh sent an *'îš nāḇî'* (cf. the role of the angel in 2:1-5) — to no avail, as was always to be true. This failure is summarized retrospectively in 2 K.

---

102. See esp. W. Dietrich and R. Smend, *Die Entstehung des ATs* (Stuttgart, ^{3}1984), 122f.
103. See 2.b above.
104. See Steck, *Israel,* 110ff.

17:13-23; 24:2 by the formulaic use of the pl. *hannᵉḇîʾîm,* and so on. In the prophetic interpretation of Israel's disastrous history, the criterion of theodicy is the Deuteronomic torah; the two oracles of "the prophetess Huldah" are characteristic of its simultaneous threat and promise (2 K. 22:16f.,18-20; on the threat, cf. v. 13).[105]

The verb *nb'* is not used in the redactional sections of the Deuteronomistic history — in contrast to the "Deuteronomistic" Jeremiah texts and Am. 2:12 ("Deuteronomistic").

c. In the book of Ezekiel the conflict with hostile *nᵉḇîʾîm* manifests itself once again in an oracle of disaster addressed specifically to them, ch. 13. The paradox of prophet against prophet is already determined in the introductory command: "Son of man, prophesy against the prophets who prophesy 'out of their (own) hearts' " (v. 2, conj.); Ezekiel's prophetic opponents "follow [?] their own spirit and have seen nothing" (v. 3). Clearly the "daughters of (the) people" claim to act as prophetesses (*nb'* hithpael) out of their own imagination (v. 17). The normal function of prophets, to preach repentance so as to prevent judgment through their message, probably lies behind the accusation in v. 5: in view of the actual situation, the "falsehood" and "lies" of prophetic vision and speech (vv. 6-8), i.e., the false prophecy of peace (v. 16), are like whitewash on a cracked (?) wall, which increases the danger when the storm comes (vv. 10-15; cf. 22:28; Lam. 2:14). Ezk. 13:17-21 describes the magical ambitions and greed of prophetic work performed by women for individual clients.

At present, God does not speak to the prophets (Ezk. 22:28), so that it is as vain to seek "revelation" *(ḥāzôn)* from them as to seek instruction from the priests or counsel from the elders (7:26, the opposite of the claim cited in Jer. 18:18; cf. Lam. 2:9; Ps. 74:9). If a prophet nevertheless speaks a *dāḇār,* Yahweh has "deceived" that prophet (Ezk. 14:9): both the inquirer *(dōrēš)* and the prophet must bear their *ʿāwōn* (v. 10; on the guilt of prophets and priests, cf. Lam. 4:13); for Yahweh now gives answer only directly (Ezk. 14:4,9) — in judgment.

Ezekiel nevertheless claims to be a *nāḇîʾ* called by Yahweh; if he speaks now to deaf ears, when the prophesied judgment takes place the Israelites will "know that there has been a *nāḇîʾ* among them" (2:5; 33:33; cf. 1 K. 18:36; 2 K. 5:8, Deuteronomistic [P?]). Indeed, Ezekiel understands himself as a "sentinel" *(ṣōp̄eh)* warning the "house of Israel" (Ezk. 3:17; 33:2,6f.; cf. Jer. 6:17), as though through his watchfulness some individuals might still escape the unavoidable. In this vein, Ezk. 3:18-21 and 33:2-9 even develop a casuistry of punishment.

With striking frequency, the niphal impv. *hinnāḇēʾ* appears formulaically in the elaborate introductions to several rhetorical units (Ezk. 6:2 et passim; cf. the consecutive perfect in 4:7): the repetition is intended to counter a weaker and weaker legitimation of prophetic speech.

---

105. On the assignment of parts of these oracles to DtrP and DtrN by W. Dietrich (*Prophetie,* 55-59; *idem, VT,* 27 [1977], 25-29), see E. Würthwein, *ZTK,* 73 (1976), 404f.; M. Rose, *ZAW,* 89 (1977), 54-57; and, with exaggerated emphasis on the unity of the present text, H.-D. Hoffmann, *Reform und Redeformen. ATANT,* 66 (1980), 170-180.

Ezekiel's appeal to the *rûaḥ* ("Spirit") or *yaḏ* ("hand") of Yahweh (11:4f.; 37:1), as well as his trance (4:7f.) and rapture (37:1), have something of an archaic and shamanistic air that does not eschew the pathological. But the attitude of those he was addressing also included such elements of traditionalism if they needed such manifestations. In 21:19(14), Yahweh's command to prophesy is associated with instructions for magical clapping. On the association of magic with prophecy, cf. 11:13; 37:7ff.; also facing in the direction of those addressed while prophesying: 4:7 (esp.); 6:2; 13:17; 21:2,7; etc.

In continuity with earlier prophecies, the "extension" of the Gog prophecy in 38:17 describes this very prophecy in language with Deuteronomistic overtones. There is a hint of apocalypticism when prophecies speak *lᵉyāmîm rabbîm* and *lᵉʿittîm rᵉḥôqôṯ*, "to many years ahead and distant times."

Ezk. 40–48, Deutero-Isaiah, and "Trito"-Isaiah do not use *nāḇîʾ* and its derivatives.

5. *Postexilic Prophecy.* a. In Haggai and Zechariah, as is often the case in prophetic narratives, *hannāḇîʾ* is linked as a formulaic appositive with the name of the prophet (Hag. 1:3,12; 2:1,10; Zec. 1:7; cf. the superscriptions Hab. 1:1; 3:1; Hag. 1:1; Zec. 1:1 [Ps. 51:2(superscription)]). Only in Zechariah do we find other uses of the root. His interpretation of the futile mission of the preexilic prophets of disaster as preachers of repentance (1:4-6; 7:7,12) echoes the Deuteronomistic history. Only now, after judgment, do those affected respond with a doxology (1:6), consult priests and prophets for ritual instruction (7:3), and hear their message of comfort (8:9), which differs from the preaching of the "former prophets" (7:12).

b. Like the Deuteronomistic history, the Chronicler's history understands the preexilic prophets as preachers of repentance: if they are heeded, their prophecies of disaster may go unfulfilled, at least in part (2 Ch. 12:5ff.; 15:1ff.; 28:9ff.; cf. 33:10-13). Usually, however, there is no repentance (20:37; 21:12ff.; 24:20; 36:12), and the prophet comes to a violent end (24:21). The retrospective summaries in 2 Ch. 36:16 and Neh. 9:26ff. describe the law by which rejection of the prophets brings God's wrath, against which there is no remedy.

Already in the Deuteronomistic history, the prophets as preachers of repentance are exegetes of the Torah; in Ezr. 9:10f., where they are again called Yahweh's "servants," they are actually the givers of the "commandments" (similarly in 1QS 1:3; 8:15f.; and possibly CD 5:21; 6:1a). In 2 Ch. 20:20, in the light of an impending war, King Jehoshaphat calls for faith (*ʾmn* hiphil) in both Yahweh and the prophets (cf. *ʾmn* niphal with *nbyʾyk* as subj. in Sir. 36:16).

Ezr. 5:1f.; 6:14 (1 Esd. 6:1; 7:3 LXX) emphasize the leading role played by postexilic prophecy, beginning with Haggai and Zechariah, in the building of the second temple. By contrast, the use of *nbʾ* for the performance of music in the cult (1 Ch. 25:1-3) and the identification of Nathan as the founder of such music may reflect the decline of earlier cultic prophecy to the Levites' temple music.

According to Neh. 6:7, Nehemiah's enemies charge him with having hired "prophets" to proclaim him as (messianic?) pretender to the throne. In vv. 10ff. he himself speaks of a hired "oracle" *(nᵉḇûʾâ),* of "prophets" (including a woman) frightening him at the behest of these same enemies. Shemaiah, Nehemiah's chief enemy among the prophets, is described (v. 10) as *ʿāṣûr,* "(legally?) restrained" (cf. Jer. 36:5) or "in an ecstatic trance" (cf. LXX *synechómenos*), at any rate "in (a kind of) confinement" (cf. *neʿṣār* in 1 S. 21:8[7]).

The records of certain "prophets" mentioned by name (*diḇrê . . .:* 1 Ch. 29:29; 2 Ch. 9:29; 12:15; 26:22; 32:32; *neḇûʾaṯ ʾaḥîyâ . . . ḥazôṯ yeʿdî [K] haḥōzeh:* 2 Ch. 9:29; *miḏraš hannāḇîʾ ʿiddô*) are considered historical sources. On written prophecy see 2 Ch. 21:12.[106]

Using Jer. 25:11f.; 29:10 as texts (Dnl. 9:2), Dnl. 9 seeks to interpret the present as a sealing of *ḥāzôn wenāḇîʾ* (v. 24; similarly 1QpHab 7:8). The role of *ʿaḇāḏeyḵā hanneḇîʾîm* (Dnl. 9:6,10; cf. 1QpHab 2:9; 7:5) is the same as in the Chronicler's history. Outside ch. 9, the book of Daniel does not use *nāḇîʾ* or its derivatives.

Isolated prophetic utterances are also cited and interpreted with reference to a present viewed eschatologically in 4QFlor 1:15f.; cf. CD 4:13f.; 7:10ff.; 19:7, where the interpretation contributes probative texts for new eschatological prophecies, in part *ex eventu.*[107]

c. For an eschatological future in Jerusalem, Zec. 13:2-6 proclaims the end of a prophecy conscious of its special position; such prophecy will have fallen into total disrepute. Should such prophets appear, their parents will consign them to the death decreed in Dt. 13:6; 18:20 (Zec. 13:3). The former marks of a prophet, visions and an archaic hairy mantle (cf. 1 K. 19:13,19; 2 K. 1:8; 2:8,13f.),[108] will bring disgrace (Zec. 13:4). People will accept the onus of the most disgraceful excuses to explain the scars left by ecstatic frenzy (v. 6).

If Zec. 13:2-6 referred to *all* kinds of prophecy, the author of the present utterance, like Amos himself (cited with exaggeration in v. 5), would not have considered himself a prophet: it would finally have become clear that loss of functionality had reduced all forms of prophetic stimulation to arrogant presumption. V. 2, however, speaks of the *neḇîʾîm* in the immediate context of the "spirit of uncleanness" and in the broader context of idolatry (cf. 1QH 4:15f.; CD 6:1b); one might therefore think rather of a revived interest in canaanizing ecstatic practices (cf. the self-laceration in 1 K. 18:28f.). But when could pagan enthusiasm, actually claiming to speak in the name of Yahweh (Zec. 13:13), have made such inroads into the postexilic cultic community?

It is therefore better to begin by interpreting the "spirit of uncleanness" (v. 2) as

---

106. On the history of scholarship in this area see D. Mathias, "Die Geschichte der Chronikforschung im 19. Jh. unter besonderer Berücksichtigung der exegetischen Behandlung der Prophetennachrichten des christlichen Geschichtswerkes" (diss., Leipzig, 1977); *idem, TLZ,* 105 (1980), 474f.

107. See F. du T. Laubscher, "A Suggested Reading for 4QFloril I:15," *JNSL,* 6 (1978), 25-31. On the use of *prophḗtēs* in 1, 2, and 4 Maccabees, Sirach LXX, Tobit, and Wisdom, see Fascher, 144-48; on Philo, Josephus, and rabbinic literature, see *ibid.,* 152-164; on Josephus, see also Aune; W. C. van Unnik, *Flavius Josephus als historischer Schriftsteller* (Heidelberg, 1978), 41-54.

108. But see Brunet.

the antithesis to the "spirit of compassion and supplication" poured out on the house of David and the inhabitants of Jerusalem (12:10aα; cf. Ezk. 36:26f.; 39:29; 1QH 7:6f.).[109] In this reading, Zec. 13:2-6 is an antithesis to the pouring out of the Spirit "upon all flesh" prophesied in Joel 3:1f.(2:28f.): according to Joel, all Israel receives the gift of prophecy, so that there can no longer be a restricted circle of prophets, especially prophets exhibiting extravagant behavior. The eschatological egalitarian utopia may also include an element of nomistic rationalism that looks on self-aggrandizing enthusiasm as *šeqer* and *kaḥēṣ,* "lies" (Zec. 13:3f.; cf. the LXX translation of *nᵉḇîʾîm* in v. 2 as *pseudoprophḗtas,* although the book of Jeremiah also uses *pseudoprophḗtēs* for *nāḇîʾ*[110]).

Before the eschatological day of Yahweh, according to Mal. 3:23f.(4:5f.), the prophet Elijah will return in Israel to preach repentance and reorient the people to the Torah of Moses, thus resolving the problem of religious conflict between generations and averting the "curse" on the land. In other words, he will bring to pass what the preexilic prophets, in the view of the Deuteronomistic history and the Chronicler's history, failed to accomplish. The Qumran community looks for the coming of an eschatological *nāḇîʾ* before the appearance of the *mšyḥy ʾhrwn wyśrʾl* ("messiah of Aaron and Israel"), i.e., a priestly messiah and a royal messiah (1QS 9:11).

The word *nāḇîʾ* and its derivatives are not found in Wisdom Literature except for Sirach (*nbyʾ:* 36:16; 48:1,8; 49:7,10; *nbwʾh,* "prophecy": 44:3; 46:1,13,29; almost exclusively in praise of those of earlier days). There are only 3 occurrences in the Psalms: 51:2(superscription); 74:9; 105:15. Ps. 74:9 suggests cultic prophecy.

d. The LXX uses *prophḗtēs* to translate *nāḇîʾ*.[111] In Chronicles *prophḗtēs* also represents *ḥōzeh, rōʾeh,* and (in one text, 2 Ch. 36:15) *malʾāḵ;* it also translates *rōʾeh* in Isa. 30:10. For *nᵉḇîʾâ* we find *prophḗtis;* for *nbʾ*, *prophēteúein;* and for *nᵉḇûʾâ, prophēteía.*[112]

H.-P. Müller

---

109. W. Rudolph, *Sacharja 9–14. KAT,* XIII/4 (1976), 288; et al.
110. Rendtorff, *TDNT,* VI, 812.
111. On *pseudoprophḗtēs* see c above.
112. The details are discussed by Fascher, 102-152; and Rendtorff, *TDNT,* VI, 812.

נָבֵל *nāḇēl* I; נְבֵלָה *n^eḇēlâ;* נֹבֶלֶת *nōḇeleṯ*

Contents: I. 1. Etymology and Meaning; 2. Distribution; 3. Semantic Field; 4. Syntax; 5. LXX. II. The Verb: 1. Figurative Sense; 2. Literal Sense. III. Nouns: 1. Human *n^eḇēlâ;* 2. Dt. 21:22f.; 3. Isa. 26:19; 4. Regulations concerning the *n^eḇēlâ* of Animals. IV. Dead Sea Scrolls.

I. 1. *Etymology and Meaning.* Since our root is not attested with certainty outside Hebrew (Akkadian occurrences being related to Heb. → נפל *nāpal*[1]), the problem of its etymology is extraordinarily difficult. The many proposals fall into two basic groups:

a. Some scholars assume that a single root *nbl* became differentiated semantically into *nāḇēl* I, "wither," and *nāḇal* II, "be foolish."[2] An older lexicography claimed "wither" > "be foolish" as the inherent semantic value of the etymon; other suggestions are "break loose, tear out" (Akk. *nabālu*) or "fall" (→ נפל *nāpal*) or "not exist, go out of existence" (*bl* + augment *n*).[3]

b. Since a semantic connection between *nbl* I and *nbl* II can be established only by artificial arguments, the theory of two separate homonymous roots *nbl* I, "wither," and *nbl* II, "be foolish," is more likely.[4] Other etymological theories are occasionally suggested (e.g., *n^eḇēlâ* < Arab. *nabala,* "shoot arrows," stem VIII "be killed, die"[5]), but they have nothing to offer until new textual citations from the ancient Near East can be evaluated.

2. *Distribution.* The verb *nāḇēl* occurs 19 times in the OT. It is especially common in the book of Isaiah (11 occurrences); it appears 3 times in the Psalms, twice in the Pentateuch, and once each in the Deuteronomistic history, Jeremiah, and Ezekiel. Establishing the chronological sequence of the occurrences involves some uncertainties, but is generally possible. The earliest might go back to the early period of the monarchy (Ps. 18:46[Eng. v. 45] par. 2 S. 22:46) but are textually not incontestable. The two

---

nāḇēl. J. Blau, "Über homonyme und angeblich homonyme Wurzeln, II," *VT,* 7 (1957), 98-102, esp. 99; M. Dahood, "Congruity of Metaphors," *Hebräische Wortforschung. Festschrift W. Baumgartner. SVT,* 16 (1967), 40-49; E. Dhorme, *L'emploi métaphorique des noms de parties du corps en hébreu et en akkadien* (Paris, 1923, repr. 1963); G. Gerleman, "Der Nicht-Mensch," *VT,* 24 (1974), 147-158; A. Guillaume, "Hebrew and Arabic Lexicography," *Abr-Nahrain* 2 (1960/61), 5-35, esp. 24f.; P. Joüon, "Racine נבל au sens de *bas, vil, ignoble,*" *Bibl,* 5 (1924), 357-361; *idem,* "Verbe נָבֵל *defluere,*" *ibid.,* 356f.; G. Rinaldi, "*nebēlâ* Dt 28, 26," *BiOr,* 22 (1980), 30; W. M. W. Roth, "NBL," *VT,* 10 (1960), 394-409.

1. Contra Roth, 394-97.

2. Barth, *NSS;* König; Caspari; *LexHebAram,* 494; Caquot; Gerleman; with some hesitation: Joüon; Roth; *KBL*², 589; *HAL,* II, 663.

3. See, respectively, Roth, 394-97 (incorrect; cf. *AHw,* II, 733f.); A. Caquot, "Sur une désignation vétérotestamentaire de 'l'insensé,' " *RHR,* 155 (1959), 1-16; Gerleman.

4. M. Sæbø, *TLOT,* II, 710f.; → נבל *nāḇāl* II. Cf. *GesTh,* s.v.

5. Guillaume, 24f.; cf. Wehr, 940.

occurrences in Ex. 18:18 (E) are semantically unique. Only some of the many occurrences in the book of Isaiah are authentic. Isa. 1:30; 28:1,4 go back to Isaiah himself, while 40:7,8 are exilic, 34:4 (3 times) and 64:5 are postexilic, and 24:4 (2 times) is late postexilic. Jer. 8:13 was spoken during the reign of Jehoiakim (ca. 605; Ezk. 47:12 belongs to the first revision of the temple vision [ca. 571]).[6] The two texts in the Psalms (1:3; 37:2) are clearly postexilic; the date of the latter is already suggested by the late verb *'umlal.* The conjectural emendation of *npl* (→ נפל) to *nbl* in Job 14:18 and Prov. 11:28 also belong to this period.[7]

The distribution of *n^e^ḇēlâ* (48 occurrences) is quite different. It occurs 24 times in the Pentateuch, 11 in the Deuteronomistic history, 8 in Jeremiah, twice each in Isaiah and Ezekiel, and once in the Psalms. This word does not belong to the ancient vocabulary stock: it first appears shortly before the exile (Isa. 5:25; Jeremiah; Dt. 21:23 [pre-Deuteronomic]; Ezk. 4:14). Ps. 79:2; Ezk. 44:31, and the late additions Dt. 14:8,21; 28:26 are exilic. The exact chronology of the occurrences in the Deuteronomistic history is hard to determine. All the occurrences in the Pentateuch belong to the postexilic P^S traditions. The latest occurrence is in Isa. 26:19. The only occurrence of *nōḇeleṯ* is in Isa. 34:4 (clearly postexilic).

3. *Semantic Field.* In most of its occurrences, *nāḇēl* is used to denote the familiar biological process of withering. This usage is soon extended metaphorically to all conceivable statements expressing transitoriness, substantially expanding the word's semantic field. The core comprises the verbs → יבשׁ *yāḇēš,* → חרב *ḥārēḇ,* → אבל *'ābhal* II, *qāmal, 'umlal, mālal* I, *'āḇaš,* and *ṣāmaq,* all expressing the meaning "wither, dry up, shrivel." The noun *š^e^ḏēpâ/šiddāpôn* stands for the "scorching" of grain. The noun *n^e^ḇēlâ,* "corpse," is a logical extension of the notion of transitoriness. Here we approach the semantic field of → מות *mûṯ,* "death." Other Hebrew words for lifeless bodies are → גויה *g^e^viyyāh, gûpâ, mappeleṯ,* → פגר *peger,* → עצם *'eṣem,* and (only of animals) *t^e^rēpâ.*[8]

4. *Syntax.* The verb appears only in the qal; the prefix conjugation is much more common than the suffix conjugation or the participle. The intransitive verb in its finite inflections is used almost exclusively in the 3rd person singular or plural (exceptions: Ex. 18:18; Isa. 64:5). The commonest subjects are leaves (*'āleh),* flowers (*ṣîṣ),* grass, and herbs, but we also find human beings, foreigners, Moses (Ex. 18:18), and the stars of heaven. The noun *n^e^ḇēlâ* never appears in the plural and must therefore be treated semantically as a collective noun. In only a quarter of the texts is it used absolutely or as the *nomen regens* of a construct phrase; elsewhere it appears in the construct in a variety of linkages or with a suffix (only once with the 1st person singular: Isa. 26:19). With striking frequency, *n^e^ḇēlâ* is the subject of the verb → היה *hāyāh.*

---

6. H. Gese, *Der Verfassungsentwurf des Ezechiel (Kap. 40–48). BHT,* 25 (1957), 90-95; W. Zimmerli, *Ezekiel 2. Herm* (Eng. trans. 1983), 552.

7. Dahood.

8. See G. Harder, *TDNT,* IX, 96f.; F. Baumgärtel, *TDNT,* VII, 1044f.

5. *LXX.* The LXX translation of *n*ᵉ*ḇēlâ* is anything but uniform, although the LXX was dealing with a semantically stable word. It uses compounds of *píptein* (7 times; the same stem is used almost 400 times for *nāpal*), *phtheírein* (3 times; usually used for *šaḥat,* "be marred"), *bállein* (twice; otherwise used for *nāpal*), and *rheín* (twice; in Prov. 17:21 Aquila treats *nbl* the same way, although the LXX, Theodotion, and the MT point to *nbl* II). Twice the LXX uses the word *palaioún* (2 S. 22:46 par. Ps. 18:46[45]), which suggests that the original text had the Hebrew root *blh.* The LXX usually (31 times) translates *n*ᵉ*ḇēlâ* by *thēsmiaíos,* followed by *sōma* (9 times; also used to translate *g*ᵉ*wîyâ, gēw, peger, gûpâ,* and Aram. *g*ᵉ*šēm*), *nekrós* (4 times), and *nekrimaíos* (once).

II. The Verb.

1. *Figurative Sense.* In what are probably the earliest texts, the verb *nāḇēl* is used figuratively. Referring to the excessive burden of Moses' judicial activity, Jethro says, "You will surely wear yourselves out *(nāḇōl tibbōl),* both you and these people with you"; he then suggests decentralizing the administration of justice (Ex. 18:18). Scholars generally ascribe Ex. 18:13ff. to E; it was probably composed with immediate reference to the legal reform of Jehoshaphat or to legitimize a similar reform on the part of David.[9] Martin Noth suggests a judicial system before the development of the state parallel to the organization of the levy, but the text is not detailed enough to allow reconstruction of nomadic jurisprudence.[10] The appearance of *nāḇēl* in *figura etymologica* as well as its use in a figurative sense with human beings as subjects shows that in the eighth century *nāḇēl* was part of everyday vocabulary.

In 2 S. 22:46 par. Ps. 18:46(45),[11] *nāḇēl* is used in the same way: "Foreigners lose heart, they come trembling *(ḥārag)* out of their strongholds." The hapax legomenon *ḥārag* does not help define the meaning of *nāḇēl* more precisely, because it draws on the latter for much of its own meaning; therefore the parallel *kāḥaš* in v. 45b must be used to help interpret *nāḇēl.* This parallel permits interpreting *nāḇēl* in the biological sense as "languish, waste away,"[12] but this meaning does not fit the larger context. Vv. 38ff. display the vast military superiority of the royal psalmist over his enemies, who in order to survive have no choice but to "serve" (*ʿāḇaḏ,* v. 44) and "obey" (*šāmaʿ,* v. 45b) him, to "feign submission" (*kāḥaš,* v. 45a),[13] "collapse utterly" (i.e., display

---

9. For the former see R. Knierim, "Exode 18 und die Neuordnung der mosaischen Gerichtsbarkeit," *ZAW,* 73 (1961), 146-171; G. C. Macholz, *ZAW,* 84 (1972), 322f. For the latter see H. Reviv, "The Traditions concerning the Inception of the Legal System in Israel," *ZAW,* 94 (1982), 566-575.

10. See W. H. Schmidt, *Exodus, Sinai und Mose. EdF,* 191 (1983), 118; cf. Noth, *Exodus. OTL* (Eng. trans. 1962), 150.

11. Text-critical issues are discussed by G. Schuttermayr, "Studien zur Text du Psalmen 9/10 und 18" (diss., Munich, 1966), 197f.; F. M. Cross Jr. and D. N. Freedman, *Studies in Ancient Yahwistic Poetry* (1975, repr. Grand Rapids, 1997), 105, n. 103; and H.-J. Kraus, *Psalms 1–59* (Eng. trans., Minneapolis, 1988), 256. The psalm has been dated from David to DtrN.

12. Roth, 400; Blau, 99; EÜ.

13. → כחש *kāḥaš* (VII, 134).

total subjection; *nāḇēl,* v. 46a), and "come trembling out of their strongholds" *(ḥāraḡ,* v. 46b). The behavior of the psalmists' enemies moves graphically from defeat in battle to a climax of total capitulation.

2. *Literal Sense.* In texts that use *nāḇēl* in the literal sense of the "withering" of vegetation, it always functions in a metaphor that becomes a commonplace in prophecies that threaten transiency. Isaiah was the first to incorporate *nāḇēl* into prophetic threats: "For you [idolaters] shall be like an oak whose leaves wither, and like a garden without water" (Isa. 1:30). This image, borrowed directly from the visual realm, casts a revealing light on the preexilic understanding of the cult: it is understood to be the source of life, whereas idolatry effects the reverse.

Despite text-critical problems, the meaning of Isa. 28:1,4 is clear. While Samaria thinks of itself as a "proud garland," in the eyes of the prophet it is nothing but a "fading flower" (*ṣîṣ nōḇēl*[14]) that vanishes in a moment.

In a threat against apostates (Jer. 8:13-17), Jeremiah compares them to a vine without grapes and a fig tree without figs, whose leaves are withered (v. 13). Not only has Israel failed to live up to its call, but it has also been robbed of all vitality through its apostasy. The juxtaposition of this verse with v. 12 has created a notable cluster of catchwords: *nāp̱al,* "fall"; *kāšal,* "stumble"; *nāḇēl,* "wither."

During the exile, Ezk. 47:12 uses the image of withering leaves or grass to express the opposite idea: the rivers springing from the temple mountain have so much water that the vegetation along their banks will never wither, a metaphor depicting the blessing that will go forth from Zion.

In the postexilic period, the commonplace appears in laments (Isa. 40:7,8; 64:5; 34:4 [3 times]; 24:4 [twice; very late]). As we approach the age of apocalyptic literature, we note an increasing universalization of the commonplace. According to 34:4, the whole sky will roll up like a scroll and the stars will wither like leaves that have withered and fallen from a tree. The great Isaiah apocalypse develops this apocalyptic motif: "The earth mourns *('āḇal)* and withers *(nāḇēl),* the circle of the earth languishes *('umlal)* and withers *(nāḇēl)*" (24:4). This elaboration of the theme of the apocalypse (v. 1) sketches a progressive desolation of earth, an increasing contraction of the biosphere and its vitality.

Independently of this development, Israel's wisdom tradition expressed the awareness that the righteous are like a tree whose leaves do not wither (Ps. 1:3; cf. the Wisdom of Amenemope[15]). By contrast, the wicked fade *(mll)* like the grass and wither like the green herb (Ps. 37:2). Prov. 11:28 (textually problematic) also speaks within the framework of retributive justice. To draw on the commonplace of withering leaves as a formal criterion for reconstructing the text nevertheless appears dubious.[16]

---

14. On the difficult *ṣîṣaṯ nōḇēl* of v. 4, see Meyer, §97.6; and P. Wernberg-Møller, *ZAW,* 71 (1959), 63, n. 39.

15. *AOT,* 39.

16. See Dahood for references.

III. Nouns. The two nouns *n*ᵉ*ḇēlâ* and *nōḇeleṯ* are not found in the vocabulary of early Hebrew. The former makes its first preexilic appearance in Isaiah, is used copiously in the purity legislation of P, and finally parallels *mēṯîm* in the very late verse Isa. 26:19, an interesting and much-debated text in the Isaiah apocalypse.

1. *Human n*ᵉ*ḇēlâ.* In the preexilic period, *nāḇēl* almost without exception refers to human corpses; this term, too, occurs with surprising frequency in prophetic threats (Isa. 5:25; Jer. 7:33; 9:21[22]; 16:4; 19:7; 34:20; 36:30; 1 K. 13:22; 2 K. 9:37). These threats lend stereotyped expression to the fundamental human fear of going unburied:[17] the *n*ᵉ*ḇēlôṯ* lie in the streets like refuse, food for the birds of the air. This was felt to be the worst disgrace imaginable; it is therefore no wonder that such threats are also found in the formularies of ancient Near Eastern curses (cf. Dt. 28:26).[18] One would wish such a fate to befall one's worst enemy. To the exilic psalmist, this scene of horror describes the situation during and after the destruction of Jerusalem (Ps. 79:2; cf. 4QTanḥ [4Q176] fr. 1-2 1:3).

The Deuteronomistic history contains a series of passages showing that the language of the prophets reflects actual practice. We may even detect various gradations within the general situation: The body of a man of God is left lying in the road (1 K. 13:22), but is guarded by a lion (vv. 24-28) until a *nāḇî'* gives it honorable burial (vv. 29f.). The body of the hanged king of Ai was thrown down at the entrance of the city gate and covered with stones (Josh. 8:29); the body of Uriah was thrown into the burial place of the common people (Jer. 26:23); Jehoiakim's body will lie in the road exposed to heat and cold (Jer. 36:30). Finally, Jezebel's body will be like dung on the field (2 K. 9:37), torn to bits by dogs (v. 35), for she is a "cursed woman" (*'ᵃrûrâ,* v. 34).

2. *Dt. 21:22f.* Dt. 21:22f. requires the burial of a person who has been executed. The text clearly provides that after execution the corpse will be hung *(tālâ)* on a stake; it must not, however, remain there overnight, but must be buried before sunset. The parallel ordinance in 11QTemple 64:10f. provides that someone guilty of a capital offense "shall be hung on the tree so that he dies *(wayyāmōṯ).*" This passage has raised the question whether the Temple Scroll does not already envision crucifixion as a means of execution (as commonly among the Romans), while Deuteronomy is thinking instead of using the corpse as a deterrent demonstration. This is also the view of the Mishnah (*Sanh.* 6.4). Nevertheless, 4QpNah 1:6-8 appears to allude to Jewish use of crucifixion (Alexander Jannaeus?).[19]

---

17. *AncIsr,* 56-61; B. Lorenz, "Überlegungen zum Totenkult in AT," *MTS,* 33 (1982), 308-311; L. Wächter, *Der Tod im AT. AzT,* II/8 (1967), 171-180. The last speaks in this context of "aggravated forms of death."

18. D. R. Hillers, *Treaty-Curses and the OT Prophets. BietOr,* 16 (1964), 68f.; F. C. Fensham, "Common Trends in Curses of the Near Eastern Treaties and *kudurru*-Inscriptions Compared with Maledictions of Amos and Isaiah," *ZAW,* 75 (1963), 155-175, esp. 161ff. → פגר *peger.*

19. For a discussion of the issue, see Y. Yadin, *The Temple Scroll,* 3 vols. (Eng. trans., Jerusalem, 1983), I, 378f.; A. Dupont-Sommer, "Observations nouvelles sur l'expression 'sus-

3. *Isa. 26:19.* The words *yiḥyû mēṯeyḵā nᵉḇēlāṯî yᵉqûmûn* in Isa. 26:19 may be translated: "Your dead shall live, my corpses shall rise" (this translation is generally accepted because of the form of the verb, although *nᵉḇēlāṯî* is sg.). This passage is a challenge to the exegete.[20] The problems center on *nᵉḇēlāṯî*. The consensus of present-day scholarship is that v. 19 belongs contextually to the communal lament in vv. 7-18.[21] This justifies accepting MT *nᵉḇēlāṯî* instead of the Peshitta *niḇlōṯām* or the conjectural emendation *niḇlōṯeyḵā*.[22] The change of suffix, *mēṯeyḵā/nᵉḇēlāṯî,* is explained by assuming different speakers in v. 19aα and 19aβ:

a. Israel/Yahweh.[23] Yahweh accepts the "dead" of Israel as his own corpses and promises that they shall rise. Such resurrection means primarily national restoration.[24]

b. Yahweh/Israel.[25] Yahweh's promise "Your dead shall live" is accepted with confidence by the community. This might refer to a collective resurrection in the literal sense.

c. Yahweh/a secondary interpreter.[26] In this view v. 19aβ is a gloss made by a reader who wants to be certain that he was included explicitly in the hope of resurrection. This solution best does justice to the singular form *nᵉḇēlāṯî;* all other occurrences are also singular. This implies individual resurrection.

All three proposals understand *nᵉḇēlâ* as denoting something that has "withered away," a term compatible with the positive possibility of a promised resurrection (in contrast to *gᵉwîyâ* and *peger*).

4. *Regulations concerning the nᵉḇēlâ of Animals.* The OT regulations governing contact with animal *nᵉḇēlâ* are quite extensive. The purity regulations of P^S in particular

---

pendu vivant sur le bois,' " *CRAI,* 1972, 709-720; J. M. Baumgarten, "Does *tlh* in the Temple Scroll Refer to Crucifixion?" *JBL,* 91 (1972), 472-481; J. M. Ford, " 'Crucify Him, Crucify Him' in the Temple Scroll," *ExpT,* 87 (1976), 275-78.

20. For bibliog. see F. J. Helfmeyer, "Deine Toten — meine Leichen, Heilszusage und Annahme in Jes 26,19," *Bausteine biblischer Theologie. Festschrift G. J. Botterweck. BBB,* 50 (1977), 245-258.

21. H. D. Preuss, " 'Auferstehung' in Texten alttestamentlicher Apokalyptik," *Linguistische Theologie,* 3 (1972), 101-133; H. Wildberger, *Isaiah 13–27* (Eng. trans., Minneapolis, 1997), 556, 567f.

22. For the former see E. A. Leslie, *Isaiah* (New York, 1963); W. Elder, "A Theological-Historical Study of Isaiah 24–27" (diss., Baylor, 1974); et al. For the latter see W. R. Millar, *Isaiah 24–27. HSM,* 11 (1976); P. L. Redditt, "Isaiah 24–27" (diss., Vanderbilt, 1972); et al.

23. M. L. Henry, *Glaubenskrise und Glaubensbewährung in den Dichtungen der Jesajaapokalypse. BWANT,* 86 (1967), 106; Wildberger, 567; Preuss; J. Lindblom, *Prophecy in Ancient Israel* (1962, repr. Philadelphia, 1973), 414f.

24. But cf. G. Habets, "Die grosse Jesaja-Apokalypse" (diss., Bonn, 1974), 146f.: literal resurrection.

25. Helfmeyer.

26. Wildberger, 556.

make a basic distinction clear: on the one hand, n^e*ḇēlâ* means any dead animal not ritually slaughtered; on the other hand, *ṭ*^{e}*rēp̄â* denotes a dead animal that has been killed because of a blemish or disease, or that has been torn by another animal. Both are considered unclean, and Israelites are forbidden to eat their flesh. A technical distinction is made, however, between the n^e*ḇēlâ* of an unclean animal (Lev. 5:2; 11:8,11,24,28,35-38; Dt. 14:8) and that of a clean animal (Lev. 7:24; 11:39,40; 17:15). The former makes the person coming in contact with it unclean under all circumstances, whereas the latter can be used for certain purposes. Priests were required to abstain from all animal n^e*ḇēlâ* (Ezk. 4:14; 44:31 [Zadokite stratum]). A later addition in Dt. 14:21 states that all animal n^e*ḇēlâ* is incompatible with the holiness of the people of God. This summary rule later became fundamental (cf. 11QTemple 48:6).

IV. Dead Sea Scrolls. The verb appears only twice in the Dead Sea Scrolls. In the context of a hymn by the Teacher, the tree metaphor describing the righteous (Ps. 1:3) is applied to the community, which is in full bloom. If God withdraws his protecting hand, the leaves will "wither" (1QH 8:26). In 1QH 10:32 *nāḇēl* appears in the anthropological metaphor in the context of a lowliness doxology. The devout member of the community sees himself withering away like a flower.

The noun n^e*ḇēlâ* occurs in 4 passages, all of which directly cite OT texts: 4QTanḥ fr. 1-2 1:3 (Ps. 79:2-3); 11QTemple 48:6 (Dt. 14:21); 51:4 (Lev. 11:25); 64:11 (Dt. 21:22f.).

Fabry

נָבָל *nāḇāl;* נְבָלָה n^e*ḇālâ*

Contents: I. 1. Etymology; 2. Meaning. II. 1. OT Occurrences; 2. Verb; 3. Noun and Adjective; 4. n^e*ḇālâ;* 5. Summary; 6. LXX. III. Dead Sea Scrolls.

---

nāḇāl. O. Bächli, "Amphiktyonie im AT," *TZ,* Sond. 6 (1977), 130-142; J. Barr, "The Symbolism of Names in the OT," *BJRL,* 52 (1969), 21-28; J. Barth, *Wurzeluntersuchungen zum hebräischen und aramäischen Lexikon* (Leipzig, 1902), 28f.; G. Buccellati, *The Amorites of the Ur III Period* (Naples, 1966), 152f.; A. Caquot, "Sur une désignation vétérotestamentaire de 'l'insené,'" *RHR,* 155 (1959), 1-16; W. Caspari, "Über den biblischen Begriff der Torheit," *NKZ,* 39 (1928), 668-695; A. J. Desečar, *La sabiduría y la necedad en Sirach 21–22* (Rome, 1970); Y. Devir, "Nabal — The Carmelite," *Leš,* 20 (1956), 97-104 (Heb.); T. Donald, "The Semantic Field of 'Folly' in Proverbs, Psalms, and Ecclesiastes," *VT,* 13 (1963), 285-292; K. H. J. Fahlgren, *ṣ*^{e}*dāqāh, nahestehende und entgegengesetzte Begriffe im AT* (Uppsala, 1932), 28-32 = K. Koch, *Um das Prinzip der Vergeltung in Religion und Recht des ATs. WdF,* 125 (1972), 115-120; G. Gerleman, "Der Nicht-Mensch," *VT,* 24 (1974), 147-158; W. H. Gispen, "De stam NBL," *GTT,* 55 (1955), 161-170; P. Joüon, "Racine נבל au sens de *bas, vil, ignoble,*" *Bibl,* 5 (1924), 357-361; *idem,* "Verbe נָבֵל *defluere,*" *ibid.,* 356f.; H. W. Jüngling, *Richter 19 — ein Plädoyer für das Königtum. AnBibl,* 84 (1981); J. D. Levenson, "1 Samuel 25 as Literature and

I. The etymology of the root *nbl* is problematic and has not been accounted for satisfactorily. Its basic meaning is disputed and translations have varied, beginning with the LXX and Vulgate. Modern translations, probably building on this tradition, generally assign *nbl* to the semantic field "fool, folly, be foolish."

1. *Etymology.* There is no clear evidence of the root *nbl* and its derivatives *nāḇāl* and *n^eḇālâ* in the Semitic languages apart from Hebrew, with the possible exception of the Syr. pael *nabbel.*[1] Some lexicons still cite Arab. *nabal,* "wretched stuff."[2] More recently, Johann Jakob Stamm has returned to Theodor Nöldeke's citation of the Arabic root *nbl* with its contrary meanings (*nabal,* "wretched stuff"; *nābil,* "noble, eminent") to explain the relationship between the name Nabal and the root *nābal* II.[3] This theory sees the name Nabal in 1 S. 25 as a relic of the root's positive sense, while elsewhere the pejorative dominates.

To date, the Ugaritic evidence includes only *nbl* = Heb. *nēḇel* I, "jar, leather bottle," and *nblt,* "flame(s)."[4] An Ugaritic occurrence of a verb *nbl,* "wither," parallel to Heb. *nāḇal,* "fall, wither" (leaves, flowers, fruit), and Akk. *abālu* has been proposed by Meindert Dijkstra and Johannes C. de Moor on the basis of the reconstruction *yb*[*l*], parallel to [*t*]*hmṣ,* "become sour."[5] There is an occurrence of *nēḇel* in Punic, and possibly of *nēḇel* II (a stringed instrument).[6] In a Punic inscription of the third to first century B.C. from El Hofra (Constantine, Algeria), *ḥmlkt* son of *bʿšrt* son of *nbl* pledges a child sacrifice to Baal Hammon and Tinnit.[7]

Martin Noth associates *nbl* with the name Nabal in 1 S. 25:25, as does Frank L. Benz.[8] There is no basis for seeing a relationship to the semantic field of *nāḇāl.*[9] The same is true for two cuneiform names cited by H. Schult,[10] *ià-an-bu-li* and *sa-amsu-*^d*na-ba-la;* Schult claims that these names raise the suspicion that the OT explanation

History," *CBQ,* 40 (1978), 11-28; M. Noth, *Das System der zwölf Stämme Israels. BWANT,* 4/1 (1930), 104-6; A. Phillips, "NEBALAH, A Term for Serious Disorderly and Unruly Conduct," *VT,* 25 (1975), 237-242; W. Richter, *Recht und Ethos. SANT,* 15 (1966), 50f.; W. M. W. Roth, "NBL," *VT,* 10 (1960), 394-409; M. Sæbø, "נָבָל *nābāl* 'fool,'" *TLOT,* II, 710-14; H. Schult, "Vergleichende Studien zur alttestamentlichen Namenkunde" (diss., Bonn, 1967), 93f.; U. Skladny, *Die ältesten Spruchsammlungen in Israel* (Göttingen, 1962); J. J. Stamm, "Der Name Nabal," *Beiträge zur hebräischen und altorientalischen Namenkunde. Festschrift J. J. Stamm. OBO,* 30 (1980), 205-213.

1. *LexSyr,* 411: *increpavit, obiurgavit.*
2. *GesB,* 480; cf. *HAL,* II, 663: "miserable witness."
3. Stamm, 210ff.; Nöldeke, *NBSS,* 94f.
4. On *nbl* see *UT,* no. 1598; Whitaker, 441; M. Dahood, *RSP,* I, 272f.; J. Khanjian, *RSP,* II, 375. On *nblt* see *UT,* no. 1599; *WUS,* no. 1739; A. Schoors, *RSP,* I, 25f.: I, 19.
5. *KTU,* 1.19, I, 18; M. Dijkstra and J. C. de Moor, *UF,* 7 (1975), 200; *KTU,* however, reads *yḥ.*
6. *RES,* 942, 5; cited by *DISO,* 173.
7. *KAI,* 105.
8. Noth, *IPN,* 228f.; Benz, 358; see also the citations on pp. 33, 146.
9. As Benz (358) appears to do.
10. Pp. 93f.

of the name should not be accepted uncritically. Giorgio Buccellati thinks these names may be related to Nabal in 1 S. 25:25, but he interprets *ià-an-bu-li* as "(God) fights for me" on the basis of Arab. *nabala*, "shoot arrows."[11]

In the search for an extrabiblical etymon, Wolfgang Roth, following an initial negative judgment by Jacob Barth and a reference by André Caquot, has reintroduced Akk. *nabālu/napālu* into the discussion.[12] Assuming a basic meaning "break forth, destroy," he considers likely a direct connection with the two Hebrew word groups *nāḇēl/nᵉḇēlâ*, "separate from life/corpse," and *nāḇāl/nᵉḇālâ*, "separate from the community." As cognates to *napālu(m)* I, "cause to fall, break down (buildings), destroy," D~G stem "ransack, blind," N stem "sag," however, Wolfram von Soden cites Ugar., Heb., and Aram. *npl*, "fall."[13] But the context of the Akkadian citations differs totally from that of the biblical semantic field. At the present time, therefore, a basic Akkadian meaning appears far from clear enough to support such extensive etymological associations.

Appealing to the principle of verb formation (defined by von Soden) that uses *n* as a root augment added to a biconsonantal base, Gillis Gerleman explains *nbl* (*n + bl;* cf. *bᵉlî* as a negation element) as nonbeing, nonbecoming, "a nonentity in the broadest sense."[14] Apart from the philological hypothesis, this theory needs to be tested against the actual biblical texts.

The hapax legomenon *naḇluṯâ* (with 3rd person fem. sg. suf.) in Hos. 2:12(Eng. v. 10) represents a special problem. The usual translation is "(female) pudenda."[15] Since P. Steininger, most scholars have derived it from Akk. *baltu* < *baštu,* "shame"; but *baltu* is now translated "dignity."[16] Paul Joüon derives it from "low."[17]

2. *Meaning.* The preceding discussion indicates that *nbl* is a typical Hebrew root. This conclusion raises the question, however, whether within Hebrew itself *nbl* II is a single root or has a basic meaning that can explain both *nāḇēl/nᵉḇēlâ* and *nāḇāl/nᵉḇālâ*.

The theory of a single basic root is supported by Eduard König ("wither — feeble — be foolish"); by Wilhelm Caspari, who associates *nᵉḇēlâ,* "something withered" (Isa. 28:1,4; 40:7), with *nāḇāl/nᵉḇālâ,* "bringer of destruction, destructive"; and by Caquot, who considers "fall" to be the common element of the root, which might be related to *npl.*[18] In Joüon's cautious words, *nāḇāl* in the sense of "low, mean, ignoble" might be associated with *nāḇēl,* "fall *(defluere).*"[19] Following this lead, Franciscus

---

11. Pp. 152f. For discussion of this name, see Barr, Stamm, and *HAL,* II, 663f.
12. Roth, 394-97, 409; Barth, 28f.; Caquot, 13f.
13. *AHw,* II, 773f., contra Roth, 397.
14. Gerleman, 153-56, quotation, 156. On the principle of verb formation see *GaG,* §102, 1.2.
15. *HAL,* II, 664.
16. *CAD,* II, 142-44. Cf. Steininger, *ZAW,* 24 (1904), 141f.; W. Rudolph, *Hosea. KAT,* XIII (1966), 64; Meyer, II, 35, §36.5.
17. *Bibl,* 5 (1924), 360; cf. also Rudolph, *KAT,* XIII, 64, 70; *HAL,* 664.
18. König, *Handwörterbuch zum AT* (1910), 261; Caspari, 668-671; Caquot, 13f.
19. P. 360.

Zorell suggests as the basic meaning of the verb "marcescit . . . delabitur, defluit," metaphorically "in miserum statum delabitur," hence "humilis, vilis," with reference to both status and attitude.[20] Such a development is clearly both consistent and possible, albeit not always simple from the perspective of the texts.[21]

Others support the theory of two semantically different roots, *nbl* I, "wither, fall," and *nbl* II, "act disgracefully" or "be worthless, foolish."[22] Since the meaning of a word is revealed less by a debatable etymology than by careful observation of its actual usage, we shall determine the meaning of *nbl* II from its various contexts without presupposing an association with *nbl* I.

II. 1. *OT Occurrences.* Statistical analysis of the word group *nbl* II, usually (but not aptly) translated "(be) foolish, folly," reveals the following picture: verbal forms of *nbl* II occur 5 times and related nouns or adjectives 18 times in the proto-canonical writings and 4 times in the Hebrew fragments of Sirach; the abstract noun *n*ᵉ*ḇālâ* occurs 13 times. In short, the root occurs a total of 36 times (40 counting Sirach). This count does not include the name Nabal in 1 S. 25 or *naḇlûṯ* in Hos. 2:12(10).

Considered in more detail, the various forms are distributed as follows: the verb appears once in Deuteronomy, Jeremiah, Micah, Nahum, and Proverbs; the noun/adj. *nāḇāl* appears 5 times in Psalms, 3 in Proverbs, twice each in Deuteronomy, 2 Samuel, Isaiah, and Job, once each in Jeremiah and Ezekiel, and 4 times in Sirach (Hebrew). The abstract noun *n*ᵉ*ḇālâ* appears 4 times in Judges, twice in Isaiah, and once each in Genesis, Deuteronomy, Joshua, 1-2 Samuel, Jeremiah, and Job. All in all, these data reveal a rather broad and uniform distribution throughout the OT (Pentateuch 5, Deuteronomistic history 9, Psalms 5, Wisdom Literature 7 [11 with Sirach], Prophets 10), suggesting no conclusions with respect to special emphasis or association with a particular literary genre or time period.

Comparison with the semantic field of "folly" in Proverbs, Job, Ecclesiastes, and Psalms confirms that *nbl* II is not specific to Wisdom Literature: *k*ᵉ*sîl,* 49 of 70 occurrences in Proverbs, 18 in Ecclesiastes; *'*ᵉ*wîl,* 42 of 51 occurrences in Proverbs; *pth,* 14 of 18 occurrences in Proverbs; *lēṣ,* 14 of 16 occurrences in Proverbs.[23] Furthermore, of these characteristic wisdom terms, only *k*ᵉ*sîl* appears in parallel with *nāḇāl* (once only, Prov. 17:21). The only positive wisdom antonym is *maśkîl* (Ps. 14:2; cf. also Dt. 32:6: *lō' ḥāḵām*). The specific meaning of the root, for which it is probably impossible to find a single consistent translation, will be revealed by analysis of its various forms in their contexts.

2. *Verb.* As the totally different terms chosen by the LXX show,[24] the five verbal forms are very difficult to translate. The perfect form in Prov. 30:32 is the only

20. *LexHebAram,* 494.
21. *TLOT,* II, 710.
22. *GesB,* 503; *BDB,* 614f.; *HAL,* II, 663.
23. Donald.
24. See II.6 below.

occurrence of the qal stem: *'im nāḇaltā bᵉhiṯnaśśē' wᵉ'im zammôṯā yāḏ lᵉpeh.* The parallelism of *nāḇalatā* with *zammôṯā* admits a variety of translations: "act like a *nāḇāl*" par. "ponder wisely" (antithetical) or "devise evil" (syn.; cf. Jgs. 20:6). So does the syntax: a main clause ("Watch out") completing the two conditional clauses understood synonymously ("act like a *nāḇāl*" par. "devise evil")[25] or decomposition into two separate antitheses: "If you are a fool, (this will reveal itself in your) exalting yourself; but if you reflect, (then you will place your) hand over your mouth."[26] But one could also understand *'im — 'im* as a double question, supply *hiṯnaśśē'* in the second hemistich, and take *yāḏ lᵉpeh* (impv.) as an apodosis.[27] As regards the meaning of *nāḇaltā,*[28] the preceding numerical saying in Prov. 30:29-31 concerning the proud demeanor of rooster, he-goat, and king calls special attention to *hiṯnaśśē'* (hithpael), which always denotes arrogant, presumptuous, or rebellious self-exaltation (Nu. 16:3; 23:24; 24:7; 1 K. 1:5; 1 Ch. 29:11; Ezk. 17:14; 29:15; Dnl. 11:14). Both the antonym *zmm* and the motivation stated in Prov. 30:33 emphasize the aspect of an act that stirs up strife without considering the consequences for the community (Buber: "foolhardy"). Both translations — "If you act rashly (defiantly, recklessly), (it will be revealed) in (emphatic) superiority; but if you reflect, (then you will place your) hand over your mouth," or "If you have acted rashly (recklessly) by displaying an air of superiority, or if you have thought of doing so, (then place) your hand over your mouth" — counsel as the opposite of *nbl* a modest, discreet, circumspect demeanor that avoids *rîḇ* (v. 33). The verb *hiṯnaśśē'* makes the suggested aspect of wrath unlikely.[29]

The piel occurs 4 times; Nah. 3:6 is the only instance of the suffix conjugation. In the context of a woe cry and lament over Nineveh's debaucheries and sorceries among the nations (vv. 1-4), Yahweh announces his judgment: the city will be exposed naked among the nations (v. 5). Yahweh himself will throw filth at her (v. 6a); as a synonym of this forceful statement, *wᵉnibbaltîḵ* with Yahweh as subject (cf. Jer. 14:21) probably means something more than "treat as worthless."[30] Ernst Jenni translates the verb as "treat with contempt."[31] But the context, speaking of disgrace among the nations (v. 5) that flee the sight of Nineveh (v. 7), suggests something more concrete: exclusion from society, brought about by Yahweh (Roth: "treat as a pariah").

Jer. 14:21 and Dt. 32:15 use the verb in the prefix conjugation, the former in the setting of a communal lament over a drought, following God's negative response to a first petition and the prophet's intercession (vv. 7-9,10-18). A question concerning God's

---

25. R. B. Y. Scott, *Proverbs. AB,* 18 (1965), 180; W. McKane, *Proverbs. OTL* (1970), 260, 664f.

26. G. Sauer, *Die Sprüche Agurs. BWANT,* 5 (1963), 111.

27. M. Buber, *Der Buch der Gleichsprüche. Der Schriftswerke* (1962), 271; W. Bühlmann, *Vom rechten Reden und Schweigen. OBO,* 12 (1976), 221-28.

28. *GesB,* 503: "act disgracefully"; *HAL,* II, 663: "be futile, foolish"; *LexHebAram,* 494: "lapsus es in defectum (non praevidens)."

29. Bühlmann, 223f.

30. Gerleman; *HAL,* II, 663.

31. *HP,* 40f., 286.

rejection of Judah and loathing for Zion (v. 19) and a confession of sin (v. 21) are followed by an even more urgent petition, underscored by the threefold repetition of *'al.* Recalling the promise in Jer. 3:16f., the people have already appealed to the throne of Yahweh's glory and his name in Jerusalem (v. 9); their question in v. 19 recalls once more Yahweh's ties with Judah and Zion. The climax in v. 21 summarizes their prayer that this solidarity with Yahweh will endure: *'al-tᵉnabbēl* parallels (and intensifies?) the prayer that Yahweh will not dishonor *(n'ṣ)* the throne of his glory (cf. 3:16) and — further emphasized by *zᵉḵōr* — will not break his *bᵉrîṯ* with the worshipers. In this context the verb denotes an act on the part of God that surrenders Jerusalem to disgrace as a sign of the breach between Yahweh and his people. It impugns sacred ordinances and signs of solidarity established by Yahweh himself (cf. Josh. 7:15: *'āḇar bᵉrîṯ* and *nᵉḇālâ* describing the sin of Achan).

In the Song of Moses (probably exilic),[32] Dt. 32:15 uses the verb in a series of statements concerning the ingratitude of Jacob/Jeshurun[33] despite his election (vv. 8f.), Yahweh's guardianship, and the wealth of the land (vv. 9-14). Jacob has become sated, fat, and refractory (v. 15a); v. 15b heightens this insensibility: *wayyiṭṭōš 'ᵉlôah 'āśâû wayᵉnabbēl ṣûr yᵉšu'āṯô.* The phrase "*nbl* the rock of his salvation" parallels "abandon *(nṭš)* his creator," i.e., *nbl* means something more than "consider foolish or worthless"; at the very least it means "treat contemptuously."[34] Abandonment and making Yahweh jealous with strange gods (v. 16) might even suggest "break off relationships contemptuously, repudiate" (cf. vv. 6,21).

The participle in Mic. 7:6a clearly emphasizes breaking off relations with someone in one's intimate circle:[35] among a people who bear no fruit and must look for God's visitation, not only does public morality degenerate (vv. 2-4a), but so do relations between neighbors, friends, and family: one must be on guard against neighbors, friends, even one's own wife (v. 5); within a household, daughter-in-law rises up against mother-in-law (v. 6b). According to v. 6a, *bēn mᵉnabbēl 'āḇ baṯ qāmâ ḇᵉ'immāh,* i.e., the son as *mᵉnabbēl 'āḇ* parallels the rising up *(qwm)* of daughter (daughter-in-law) against *(bᵉ)* mother (mother-in-law). "Son treats father with contempt" describes the corruption as a breach of the fundamental ties binding a family together.[36] The conclusion of v. 6 describes the situation brutally: "A man's enemies — his own household."

This destruction of communal bonds observable in the context of these forms of the verb (Yahweh/Israel: Dt. 32:15; Jer. 14:21; Yahweh/Nineveh/nations: Nah. 3:6; father/son: Mic. 7:6) goes beyond the estimative and declaratory meaning of the piel,

32. A. S. Carrillo, "Género literario del Cántico de Moisés," *EstBíb,* 26 (1967), 69-75, 143-185, 227-248, 327-351; G. Braulik, *Testament des Mose. Stuttgarter kleiner Kommentar. AT,* 4 (1976), 78f.

33. → ישורון *yᵉšurûn* (VI, 472-77).

34. For the former see EÜ and Gerleman. For the latter, G. von Rad, *Deuteronomium. ATD,* 8 (1964), 137 (not in Eng. trans.); F. Horst, *Hiob. BK,* XVI/1 (1968), 29.

35. Fahlgren, 28f.

36. *HP,* 84; Roth, 407.

"consider contemptible, treat with contempt."[37] It also seems hard to reconcile with a derivation from *nāḇēl* with the basic meaning "pass away, come to nothing," or "fall, fade."[38]

3. *Noun and Adjective.* With 18 occurrences (plus 4 in Sirach), the substantival-adjectival use of *nāḇāl* is most frequent. This observation probably accounts for the proposal to derive the intensive stem from the substantive/adjective.[39] Once again, the translation "fool(ish)" does little justice to the various contexts; specifically, it seems to be too weak. More apposite is "futile, worthless (socially), godless."[40] A primary text, both chronologically and materially, is 2 S. 3:33a, in David's lament for Abner, victim of Joab's blood vengeance in a treacherous attack (v. 27). The lament exhibits strict parallelism and is set in a formal framework; it compares Abner's sudden death to the death of a *nāḇāl* (v. 33a), described in vv. 33b-34a: "Your hands were not bound, your feet were not fettered." V. 34b goes on: "As one falls before the wicked *(bᵉnê ʿawlâ).*" Abner did not die the (honorable) death of a warrior or prisoner but the dishonorable death due a *nāḇāl* (cf. Jer. 17:11). K. H. J. Fahlgren speaks of "death like a criminal pariah"; Roth finds here the earliest instance of *nbl* as "outcast."[41] At the very least, it means "good-for-nothing";[42] the context seems to demand "malefactor, commoner," or the like. Gerleman's suggestion that Abner is called a "real coward" because he did not fight seems forced.[43]

In 2 S. 13:13 *nāḇāl* must be understood in the context of Amnon's *nᵉḇālâ* against Tamar.[44] Tamar pleads with Amnon not to commit a *nᵉḇālâ* in Israel (v. 12), then adds (v. 13): "As for me, where could I carry my shame?" These words are echoed precisely by her threat to Amnon: "You would be as one of the *nᵉḇālîm* in Israel." This expression, which reappears in Job 2:10 without the reference to Israel, describes the *nāḇāl* of v. 13 from the perspective of v. 12: he is someone who has seriously damaged the community of Israel through a sexual transgression.

The few texts from proverbial wisdom include the *nāḇāl* among those who are low and common, both in social class and in character. Prov. 30:21-23, from the numerical sayings of Agur, speaks of three/four kinds of people under whom the earth trembles and cannot bear up; these include the *nāḇāl* (v. 22). To a slave who becomes king (v. 22a), v. 23 adds an unloved woman *(śᵉnûʾâ)* when she gets a husband, and a maid *(šip̱ḥâ)* when she supplants (inherits from?) her mistress. Vv. 22f. add a *nāḇāl* who is glutted with food as a further example of such insufferable or dangerous people: most likely a low and common individual who oversteps his limits when things are going well.

---

37. *HP,* 84.
38. For the former see Gerleman; for the latter see Joüon; *LexHebAram.*
39. Barth, 29; *LexHebAram,* 494a; Roth, 407.
40. *HAL,* II, 663.
41. P. 402.
42. *HAL,* II, 663.
43. P. 152.
44. See below.

By contrasting the *nāḇāl* with a noble person *(nāḏîḇ),* Prov. 17:7 probably emphasizes a societal aspect of the *nāḇāl,* a lowly status without respect. By introducing the element of speech, it also describes personal conduct: false speech *(śᵉpaṯ šeqer)* unbecoming to a ruler (v. 7b) is parallel to *nāḇāl śᵉpaṯ yeṯer* in v. 7a. Walter Bühlmann renders this difficult phrase as "grandiose speech" (in the sense of generosity), since he understands *nāḇāl* as a covetous person; *HAL* takes the same tack.[45] The broader antithesis "aristocratic[46]/common, low" also seems more appropriate to *nāḏîḇ/nāḇāl* in Isa. 32:5 (cf. also the syns. *nāḏîḇ/ṣaddîq* in Prov. 17:26), as does "presumptuous speech" for *śᵉpaṯ yeṯer.*

Prov. 17:21 is not all that enlightening: "The one who begets a *kᵉsîl* gets trouble; the father of a *nāḇāl* has no joy." This is the only instance of *nāḇāl* in parallel with the primary term for folly; it does not justify translating *nāḇāl* uniformly as "fool."

Among the other *nāḇāl* texts in Wisdom Literature, Job 30:8 (in Job's lament over those who mock him) uses *bᵉnê bᵉlî-šēm,* "people without name," i.e., without power or respect, who have been whipped out of the land, in parallel with *bᵉnê-nāḇāl.* Like Prov. 17:7; 30:22; Isa. 32:5, this passage suggests "low" (in status and conduct); it can hardly refer to demonic creatures of the underworld, after the analogy of the mockery of the Babylonian king in Isa. 14:16.[47] The language with which Job rebukes his wife in 2:10, "You speak as one of the *nᵉḇālôṯ* would speak," recalls 2 S. 13:13. There is no direct reference to Israel, as in 2 S. 13:13, but the transgression is just as great: Job's wife is one of the *nᵉḇālôṯ* because she has urged Job to blaspheme God instead of maintaining his integrity before God in his afflictions (v. 9). Here, as in Isa. 9:16(17); 32:5; Ps. 14:1; 74:18,22, the term refers to violation of the religious dimension: "irreverent, impious," even "godless."[48]

Apart from Isa. 9:16(17) *(nᵉḇālâ),* the earliest occurrence of *nāḇāl* in the prophets is Jer. 17:11. This verse illustrates the word of Yahweh in v. 10 concerning recompense for human ways and actions. V. 11b says of one who unjustly amasses wealth: "In the middle of his days it shall leave him, and at his end he will prove to be *(yihyeh)* a *nāḇāl.*"

Recollection of the ultimate end of human actions *('aḥᵃrîṯ)* is a wisdom commonplace (Prov. 5:4,11; 29:21; Ps. 73:17); not to remember this end is the mark of a fool. According to 2 S. 3:33; 13:13, the end of the *nāḇāl* is associated with shame and disgrace. With the strong emphasis on trust in Yahweh in Jer. 17:5,6f.,13, the end of the *nāḇāl* reveals not merely a person who is unjust, covetous, or foolish, but also a godless person, one who has forsaken Yahweh by building on false sources of security (17:13). In the woe cry of Ezk. 13:3, the *nᵉḇî'îm hannᵉḇālîm*[49] ("high-handed," "pre-

45. Pp. 142-45; *HAL,* II, 663.

46. O. Plöger, *Sprüche Salomos. BK,* XVIII (1989), 198, 202: "responsible, noble."

47. Caquot, 7ff.

48. Fohrer, *Das Buch Hiob. KAT,* XVI (1963), 103; *HAL,* II, 663; N. H. Tur-Sinai, *The Book of Job* (Eng. trans., Jerusalem, ²1967), 26f.: "one of the wicked."

49. W. Zimmerli (*Ezekiel 1. Herm* [Eng. trans. 1979], 285, 292) argues that the MT is a secondary interpretative miswriting of *nᵉḇî'îm millibbām.*

sumptuous and contemptuous of Yahweh") follow their own spirit *(rûḥām)* without having seen anything (cf. Ezk. 13:5-9; Jer. 29:23).

The *nāḇāl* is described in detail in Isa. 32:1-8, a postexilic promise of the king of salvation.[50] Among the human endowments that will flourish once more is speech. V. 5 describes one of the consequences: "A *nāḇāl* will no longer be called *nāḏîḇ,* nor a villain said to be honorable." V. 5b identifies *nāḇāl* with the not entirely clear *kîlay,* "scoundrel, schemer"; less ambiguous are the antonyms *nāḏîḇ* and *šôaʿ,* both of which denote someone aristocratic or noble (cf. Prov. 8:16; Job 34:18f.). As in Prov. 17:7; 30:22; Job 30:8, therefore, *nāḇāl* here refers to someone of low social class,[51] who also thinks and acts in a low and common manner.

Isa. 32:6-8 develop the catchwords *nāḇāl, kîlay,* and *nāḏîḇ.* V. 6ab describes the speech of a *nāḇāl* chiastically: it is *nᵉḇālâ* and consists in perversity against Yahweh. The plotting of iniquity *(ʾāwen)* and the practice of ungodliness *(ʿāśâ ḥōnep̱)* confirm transgression against reverence for God. V. 6c adds harsh treatment of the hungry and thirsty (cf. the lies and oppression of the poor characteristic of the *kîlay*). The *nāḇāl* of Isa. 32:6, the antithesis to the *nāḏîḇ* of v. 8, who is noble in status, deportment, and public actions, is very close to the *nāḇāl* of Ps. 14.

The adjective is used quite specifically in Dt. 32:6,21 (cf. also vv. 15f.[52]). V. 6 asks, "Do you thus repay the LORD?" The question concerns the contrast between God's faithfulness and Israel's apostasy (vv. 4f.). Israel is addressed as *ʿam nāḇāl wᵉlōʾ ḥāḵām,* words that go beyond the realm of foolish vs. wise, touching the plane of Israel's special relationship with God: *nāḇāl* means oblivious to the fundamental relationship of the people of Israel to their father and creator (v. 6b; cf. also vv. 9,18f.,43).[53] Yahweh's reaction in v. 21, whose hemistichs are symmetrical with the motifs of vv. 6 and 16, confirms this conclusion. Just as Yahweh's sons and daughters (v. 19), a perverse generation and faithless *(lōʾ-ʾēmun)* sons (v. 20b), have aroused his jealousy with what is no god *(lōʾ-ʾēl)* and provoked him with vaporous beings *(hᵃḇālîm),* so Yahweh will arouse Israel's jealousy with what is no people *(lōʾ-ʿām)* and challenge them with a *gôy nāḇāl.* Both terms denote a theological reality: the challenge to Jacob/Israel as Yahweh's people and heritage (v. 8; cf. vv. 6,9,36,43) among the nations (vv. 8,21,43) through a "non-people" who are also allotted to a "non-god" (cf. v. 12). Therefore *gôy nāḇāl* is a godless nation, which serves other gods (from the perspective of the Song, possibly Babylon[54]) and thus challenges *ʿam nāḇāl* Israel, a godforsaken nation that contemns and shatters its relationship with its father, creator, and savior (cf. also Ps. 74:18; Sir. 50:26).

Recalling both aspects in Dt. 32 (godforsaken, ungrateful Israel/godless nations), *nāḇāl* appears twice in Ps. 74 (a communal lament) describing the enemies of Yahweh,

---

50. H. Wildberger, *Jesaja 28–39. BK,* X/3 (1982), 1252f.

51. *Ibid.,* 1258f., with Sæbø, 713; and Gerleman.

52. Discussed in II.2 above.

53. See also N. Lohfink, "Beobachtungen zur Geschichte des Ausdrucks עם יהוה," *Probleme biblischer Theologie. Festschrift G. von Rad* (Munich, 1971), 275-305.

54. Carrillo, 243.

both times motivating God's intervention. V. 18, "Remember this, how the enemy mocks Yahweh, an *ʿam nāḇāl* reviles your name," goes beyond v. 10, describing the enemies who revile (*ḥrp, nʾṣ* niphal) Yahweh or Yahweh's name as *ʿam nāḇāl.* V. 22 beseeches: "Rise up, O God, plead your cause; remember how the *nāḇāl* scoffs at you all day long," against associating the *nāḇāl* with mockery *(ḥerpâ)* of God. The verbs and nouns (*ʾôyēḇ:* vv. 10,18) here lend active, aggressive overtones to the meaning "irreverent, godless" (cf. Isa. 32:6).

Ps. 39:9(8) prays: "Deliver me from all my transgressions; let me not be *ḥerpaṯ nāḇāl.*" V. 9b(8b) can mean "do not let me become a jest of the fool,"[55] with a broad interpretation of *nāḇāl.* But it is also conceivable that it is a prayer that God will not treat the psalmist as an ignominious *nāḇāl* ("godless, impious person") on account of his sins;[56] cf. also v. 12(11), which speaks of chastising *ʿāwōn.* Hans-Joachim Kraus and *BHS* emend MT *pᵉšāʿay* to *pōšᵉʿay,* "those who rise up against me";[57] in this interpretation, too, the *nāḇāl* of v. 9b(8b) is an enemy or transgressor.

In Ps. 14:1 (par. 53:2[1]), *nāḇāl* once again has more prophetic than wisdom overtones. In vv. 1-4 the *nāḇāl* is characterized as denying God's effective existence (vv. 1,2f.,4b). The clause "The *nāḇāl* says in his heart, 'There is no God' " (v. 1), means denial of God's efficacy; this is the voice of the wicked *(rāšāʿ)* in 10:4(3) and of the inhabitants of Jerusalem in Zeph. 1:12: "Yahweh will not do good, nor will he do harm." The *nāḇāl* disparages God's reality in word and deed; Yahweh's inspection of humanity contrasts such persons with the wise *(maśkîl),* who seek after God (Ps. 14:2: *dāraš ʾeṯ-ʾᵉlōhîm*) and those who have knowledge (v. 4a; cf. Jer. 10:21; 29:12-14). Ps. 14:4 reinforces the description by adding rejection of the prayer relationship: "They do not call upon Yahweh." But the *nāḇāl* is not simply "godless"; he abrogates and destroys the bonds of human society. V. 1b ("they are corrupt, they do abominable deeds, there is no one who does good") recalls the protests of the prophets concerning the total corruption of Israel/Jerusalem even in the social realm: "The faithful have disappeared from the land, and there is no one left who is upright" (Mic. 7:2; cf. Jer. 5:1; 8:6; Isa. 59:4,15). In Ps. 14:4 the psalmist speaks unmistakably of the evildoers *(pōʿᵃlê ʾāwen)* who eat up the people (like bread?) (cf. Mic. 3:3). Like Isa. 32:5f., Ps. 14 (53) draws a comprehensive picture of the *nāḇāl,* who is degenerate in his relationship with God and with other human beings. Of the terms used by Wisdom Literature, "fool" might best express the malicious breach of these relationships. Udo Skladny locates the *nāḇāl* more in the realm of the *rāšāʿ;* for Fahlgren, he is "someone who has contemptuously broken the ties binding him to others and to God."[58]

The 4 occurrences in the Hebrew fragments of Sirach are obviously late. The first occurrence of the noun, "Do not subject yourself to a *nāḇāl*" (4:27a), clearly contrasts the *nāḇāl,* who is low in social status or deportment, with the "rulers" *(môšᵉlîm)* in v. 27b,

55. H.-J. Kraus, *Psalms 1–59* (Eng. trans., Minneapolis, 1988), 415.
56. Gerleman, 152.
57. Kraus, *Psalms 1–59,* 416.
58. Skladny, 33; Fahlgren, 28.

whether the verse is read "Do not resist the rulers" with the Hebrew or emended to "Show no partiality to the ruler" following the Greek, which is more appropriate to the context of vv. 26,28. Sir. 33(36):5, "The heart of a *nāḇāl* is like a cart wheel, and his thoughts like a turning axle," describes the *nāḇāl* as unstable and unreliable (cf. also 33:2b,3b,6). Two texts use *nāḇāl* adjectivally in the phrase *gôy nāḇāl.* Sir. 49:5 summarizes the history of the kings of Judah (except for David, Hezekiah, and Josiah): "They [Greek; Heb. 'he'] gave their power to others and their glory to a godless foreign nation." As in Dt. 32:21, *gôy nāḇāl* undoubtedly means Israel's godless foreign neighbors, ultimately the Babylonians sent to punish Israel for its own godlessness. The numerical saying in Sir. 50:26 apostrophizes the inhabitants of Shechem as a "nonpeople" *('ênennû ʿam)* and *gôy nāḇāl,* probably suggesting the aspect "not elect; foreign and godless" (cf. Dt. 32:15f.,21).

4. *n^eḇālâ.* The relation of the abstract noun *n^eḇālâ* to *n^eḇēlâ,* "corpse," is discussed elsewhere.[59] It is striking to observe that 9 of its 13 occurrences are in a set formula; the 4 exceptions are 1 S. 25:25; Isa. 9:16(17); 32:5f.; Job 42:8. Many occurrences of the formula are undoubtedly earlier; some may even represent the earliest occurrences of the root *nbl*.

a. *Formulaic Use.* The formula *ʿāśâ n^eḇālâ b^eyiśrāʾēl* or *ʿāśâ n^eḇālâ hazzōʾṯ* occurs 9 times, with minor variations. In it *n^eḇālâ* is the result of human action. Four of these occurrences are in Judges, one each in Genesis, Deuteronomy, Joshua, 2 Samuel, and Jeremiah. In this formula *n^eḇālâ* is the object of human action. It is noteworthy that, except for Dt. 22:21, the formula does not occur in legal texts: it is found instead in narratives (Jgs. 19:23f.; 2 S. 13:12 in discourse). The form *ʿāśâ n^eḇālâ b^eyiśrāʾēl* occurs 6 times, in each of its settings as the motivation for punitive sanctions or in reaction to a serious transgression (Gen. 34:7; Dt. 22:21; Josh. 7:15; Jgs. 20:6,10; Jer. 29:23). The form *ʿāśâ n^eḇālâ hazzōʾṯ* occurs 3 times as a warning: twice as a vetitive with *ʾal* (Jgs. 19:23; 2 S. 13:12), once as a prohibitive with *lōʾ* (Jgs. 19:24). Twice it is followed by the apodictic statement "Such a thing ought not to be done" (Gen. 34:7) or "Such a thing is not done in Israel" (2 S. 13:12).

The transgressions incriminated by the formula involve extremely grave circumstances in various realms: Gen. 34:7; Dt. 22:21; Jgs. 19:23,24; 20:6,10; 2 S. 13:12; Jer. 29:23 concern sexual offenses; Jgs. 19:23,24; 20:6,10 are also (and primarily) concerned with the law of hospitality; Josh. 7:15 concerns Yahweh's prerogatives, as does Jer. 29:23. The common and clearly decisive element of disqualification in all these offenses consists not just in the transgression of fundamental social or religious principles but in the consequent violation *(n^eḇālâ)* of the Israelite community. Besides mentioning Israel explicitly, some passages emphasize this aspect by other means: Jgs. 20:6,10 by the consent or participation of "all Israel," Dt. 22:21 by the *biʿartā* formula,[60] and Josh. 7:12-15 similarly by the restoration of Israel's purity and holiness. The severity of the sanctions (capital punishment) also plays a role in Dt. 22:21; Josh. 7:15; Jgs. 20:6,10; Jer. 29:23.

---

59. See I.1 above.
60. → II, 203.

Any attempt to sketch the history of the formula must be hypothetical. The earliest text, with the most intensive use of *n^eḇālâ,* is probably Jgs. 19–20, the story of the outrage committed by the men of Gibeah against the concubine of a Levite. This narrative probably originated during the early monarchy, possibly at the court of David.[61] Noth even thinks it contains a premonarchic nucleus.[62] The formula appears naturally and with a certain flexibility in the repeated warnings of the host to the *'anšê bᵉnê bᵉlîya'al,* increasing in urgency from vetitive to prohibitive. Before the breach of the already established hospitality relationship, Jgs. 19:23 warns: "No, my brothers, do not sin *('al-tārēʿû nā')* against this man who has come into my house; do not commit this outrage *('al-taʿᵃśû 'eṯ-hannᵉḇālâ hazzō'ṯ).*" V. 24b uses the prohibitive formulation and refers (more restrictively) to the crime that would be committed against the guest by ravishing his concubine: *lō' taʿᵃśû dᵉḇar hannᵉḇālâ hazzō'ṯ.*[63] The absence of any direct reference to Israel (in contrast to 20:6,10) may indicate that this is the original use of the formula: it simply introduces fundamental limits or norms for life within a social community or the moral code of a group.[64] The formula "such a thing ought not to be done" (Gen. 34:7), too, need not be specific to Israel; the same holds true for violation of the code of hospitality, the real offense in Jgs. 19–20.

Jgs. 20:6,10 and all the other texts speak only of *nᵉḇālâ* in Israel. Since Noth, therefore, most scholars have considered *ʿāśâ nᵉḇālâ bᵉyiśrā'ēl* to denote an offense against the amphictyonic code ("unwritten customary law") and theorized that the amphictyony was the formula's *Sitz im Leben.*[65] But Jgs. 19:23 at least leaves open the possibility that at an early date the formula denoted an "outrage" without specific reference to Israel; there is also the question of the concrete form such an amphictyonic code might have taken.[66]

Tamar's plea to her half-brother Amnon in 2 S. 13:12 recalls Jgs. 19:23f. in its flexible use of the formula in dialogue as well as the alternation of vetitive and prohibitive: "No, my brother, do not *('al)* force me; for such a thing is not *(lō')* done in Israel. Do not commit this outrage *(nᵉḇālâ).*" In Jgs. 19f. and 2 S. 13:12 (cf. 2 S. 13:13[67]), the person who commits the *nᵉḇālâ* callously disregards not only the norms of the community but also human warnings and pleas. The sociological traditions behind Gen. 34 may even antedate those in Jgs. 19; the characterization of the rape of Dinah by Shechem, a non-Israelite, as *nᵉḇālâ* in Israel (v. 7) may point to the period of the formula's integration into Israelite traditions (or it may be a gloss).[68]

---

61. Jüngling, 294f.
62. Pp. 104f.
63. Jüngling, 214-17.
64. For the former see Bächli, 140f.; for the latter see Richter, 50f.
65. Noth, 100-106; Roth, 405; most recently A. H. J. Gunneweg, *Geschichte Israels. TW,* 2 (^{3}1979), 51: "the prerogatives of the God of Israel."
66. The debate is summarized by Bächli, 140f.
67. See II.3 above.
68. A. de Pury, *Promesse divine et légende cultuelle dans le cycle de Jacob. ÉBib,* 2 vols. (1975), II, 540. On the sociological traditions see de Pury, *RB,* 85 (1978), 617; C. Westermann, *Genesis 12–36* (Eng. trans., Minneapolis, 1985), 535-37.

Despite its grammatical similarity to Gen. 34:7 (formula + inf. const.), Dt. 22:21 is a special case: *n*ᵉ*ḇālâ* appears in a casuistic law dealing with premarital sexual intercourse on the part of an Israelite woman. The punishment of stoning is justified ("because she committed a *n*ᵉ*ḇālâ* in Israel") and reinforced ("so you shall purge the evil from your midst"). In Deuteronomy the *biʿartā* formula following the stipulation of a punishment in a series of laws (e.g., Dt. 22:13-21,22,23f.) emphasizes the need to preserve the purity of the tribe or nation.[69] The non-Deuteronomic character of the phrase *ʿāśâ n*ᵉ*ḇālâ* would not lead one to expect that the amphictyonic formula has been incorporated secondarily into v. 21aβ (cf. Jgs. 20:10-11,13).[70]

Josh. 7 recounts the story of Achan's sin against Yahweh by holding back some of the devoted things. Vv. 12ff. expressly require the Israelites to sanctify themselves by removing the devoted things and the transgressor from their midst. Over and above the impairment of Israel's sanctity, the parentheses of vv. 11a,15baα explicitly define the *n*ᵉ*ḇālâ* as transgression *(ʿāḇar)* of the *b*ᵉ*rîṯ YHWH,* i.e., a direct and personal breach with Yahweh. The question whether *ʿāśâ n*ᵉ*ḇālâ* belonged to the narrative from the very beginning[71] is hard to decide; literarily, the formula has the air of an addition to the Deuteronomistic theme of the *b*ᵉ*rîṯ* in vv. 11a,15baα.

Jer. 29:23 is probably the latest text. Here social and religious transgressions are already combined. The explanation of God's judgment against the prophets Ahab and Zedekiah states that "they have perpetrated *n*ᵉ*ḇālâ* in Israel" because "they have committed adultery with their neighbors' wives, and have spoken in my name lying words that I did not command them." Adultery, which damages the sociosexual order in Israel, and false prophecy, which deliberately scorns Yahweh, are described together as *n*ᵉ*ḇālâ* in Israel. This text prepares the way for Ezk. 13:3.[72]

The formula leaves no doubt that from the very beginning *n*ᵉ*ḇālâ* characterized an act as a derangement of the community in critical areas (hospitality, sexual order, Yahweh's royal prerogatives); very early on, such an act was understood to impugn the community of Israel as a religious and ethical entity. This early (premonarchic?) understanding of *n*ᵉ*ḇālâ* as a grievously culpable derangement of communal society may also bear on the question of the basic meaning of the root *nbl.*

b. *Other Texts.* Of the 4 texts where *n*ᵉ*ḇālâ* appears apart from the formula, the earliest is 1 S. 25:25. In this wisdom narrative the wealthy Nabal of Maon is not the focus of attention, but he probably represents a vivid contrast to the figures of Abigail and David.[73] V. 25 takes the name "Nabal," which can hardly have originated as a purely pejorative appellation,[74] and clearly tries by means of poetic wordplay to associate it with *n*ᵉ*ḇālâ* or to find *n*ᵉ*ḇālâ* in the name and nature of Nabal (cf. Isa. 32:6). Abigail asks David not to take Nabal seriously: "For as his name is, so is he; Nabal

69. → II, 203f.
70. Contra R. P. Merendino, *Das deuteronomische Gesetz. BBB,* 31 (1969), 258ff.
71. As maintained by Roth, 405.
72. See II.3 above.
73. P. Kyle McCarter, *I Samuel. AB,* 8 (1980), 389-402.
74. See the discussion in I.1 above; also Barr and Stamm.

is his name, and n^e*ḇālâ* is with him." The precise meaning of the abstract noun must be determined from the narrative as a whole. 1 S. 25:3 already describes Nabal as "surly and mean"; vv. 10f. develop this description as arrogant and callous treatment of David's servants, vv. 10,14 as rudeness. According to vv. 17,25, Nabal is *ben-/'îš* b^e*lîyaʿal.* The term b^e*liyaʿal* appears primarily in contexts dealing with derangement of the social order, as the description of the men of Gibeah in Jgs. 19:22 illustrates.[75] It is impossible to speak to Nabal (vv. 17,19,36). He has displayed ingratitude toward David (vv. 4-8,15f.,21f.). Vv. 3,21,39 explicitly depict Nabal as malicious. Despite the contrasting figure of the beautiful and sagacious Abigail, n^e*ḇālâ* is not simply folly; neither is it breach of a personal relationship; it is something worse and more general than lack of generosity.[76] Nabal's n^e*ḇālâ* as malicious treatment of David, David's servants, and his own household (vv. 17,19,36) is fully on a plane with the meaning of the formulaic construction.

Isa. 9:16(17) is in the second (vv. 12-17[13-18]) of three oracles of judgment against the northern kingdom (vv. 7-20[8-21]). It justifies God's judgment against all classes of the people: "For everyone is godless and wicked and every mouth speaks n^e*ḇālâ.*" As in Isa. 32:6,[77] the parallel terms *ḥānēp,* "godless," and *mēraʿ,* "wicked," suggest that n^e*ḇālâ* means "malicious, destructive, mean" toward God and other human beings.

The must unusual use of the abstract noun is in Job 42:8. Enraged at Eliphaz and his friends, Yahweh orders them to go to Job, offer up a burnt offering, and ask Job to pray for them, "for only to him will I listen so as not to do you n^e*ḇālâ;* for you have not spoken of me what is right, as my servant Job has done."

Twice Yahweh is the subject of the verb *nbl:* not only does he treat Nineveh with contempt (Nah. 3:6), but according to Jer. 14:21 he gives the throne of his glory in Jerusalem over to contempt. In Job 42:8 Yahweh is the subject of *ʿāśâ* n^e*ḇālâ ʿim.* The need for burnt offering and the intercession of Job, to whom alone Yahweh will listen, indicates that the threatened n^e*ḇālâ* is a serious matter; the translations "abomination" and "outrage" are on the mark.[78] The analogy of the expression to *ʿāśâ ḥeseḏ ʿim*[79] does not necessarily point to a mitigating, generalizing idiom. Something of how n^e*ḇālâ* imperils the social community can also be suggested when, in order to punish, God brings someone not *ḥeseḏ* but n^e*ḇālâ.*[80] "I will show you consideration and not treat you as your heedlessness deserves" is an accurate translation.[81]

5. *Summary.* A semantic history of the root, formerly associated with the fringes of Wisdom Literature,[82] can hardly be constructed; many of the texts are difficult to date.

---

75. → II, 134f.; Jüngling.
76. On the last two see, respectively, Roth, 406; Gerleman, 150.
77. See II.3 above.
78. See, respectively, Buber; and Fohrer, *Das Buch Hiob. KAT,* XVI, 538, 540.
79. Fohrer, *KAT,* XVI, 540; Tur-Sinai, *Job,* 590.
80. Roth, 408.
81. L. Alonso Schökel and J. L. Sicre Díaz, *Job* (Madrid, 1983), 601.
82. See II.1 above.

It seems safe to conclude that the broadest meaning is found primarily in late texts (cf. Isa. 32:5f.; Ps. 14 par. 53), in association with markedly religious statements,[83] as Dt. 32:6,15,21; Job 2:10; Ps. 14; 74:18,22 illustrate. Otherwise *nbl* cannot be located on the secular/religious continuum. This holds true especially for its broad spectrum of meanings and translations. In wisdom terminology the force of the expression most closely approximates "fool."[84] More justice is usually done the texts by expressions that somehow signal graphically a breach or derangement of the bonds that unite human beings with each other or with God, whether expressed in status, attitude, word, or deed. The question may remain open as to the extent to which the wisdom notion of an ordered world lies in the background.[85]

6. *LXX*. The translators of the LXX already found it difficult to translate *nāḇāl;* the wide range of equivalents they used exhibits no uniformity.[86] For the verb, we find *atimázein* (Prov. 30:32; Mic. 7:6), *aphistánai* (Dt. 32:15), *apollýnai* (Jer. 14:21), *tithénai eis parádeigma* (Nah. 3:6). For the noun and adjective, we find primarily *áphrōn* (2 S. 13:13; Jer. 17:11; Ps. 14:1 [par. 53:2(1)]; 39:9[8]; 74:18,22; Job 2:10; 30:8; Prov. 17:7; 30:22), but also *mōrós* (Dt. 32:6; Isa. 32:5,6; Sir. 4:27; 33[36]:5; 50:26) and *asýnetos* (Dt. 32:21). For *n*ᵉ*ḇālâ,* we find *aphrosýnē* (Dt. 22:21; Jgs. 19:23,24; 20:6,10; 1 S. 25:25), *áschēmon* (Gen. 34:7), *anómēma* (Josh. 7:15), *anomía* (Jer. 29:23), *ádika* (Isa. 9:16[17]), *mōrá* (Isa. 32:6), and *apollýnai* (Job 42:8). Only *áphrōn/aphrosýnē* are used with some consistency, and possibly *mōrós*. This shift to a wisdom interpretation is thus clearly complete.

III. Dead Sea Scrolls. According to Karl Georg Kuhn,[87] *nāḇāl* appears in 1QS 7:9: *dbr nbl* is among the culpable offenses against the community. In a similar vein, CD 10:18 forbids speaking a *dāḇar nāḇāl w*ᵉ*rēq* on the Sabbath. 1QS 10:21f., "Belial I will not keep in my heart and *nblwt* shall not be heard in my mouth," associates *n*ᵉ*ḇālâ* with Belial, thus emphasizing the (negatively) religious character of the root. Kuhn reconstructs *nblwt* in 1QH 5:21.

Marböck

---

83. Roth, 407.

84. *BDB,* 614: "foolish, senseless. . . . (impious and presumptuous) fool"; Caquot: "insensé").

85. Sæbø, 713f.; with G. von Rad, *Wisdom in Israel* (Eng. trans., Nashville, 1972), 64f.

86. G. Bertram, "μωρός," *TDNT,* IV, 833-36; *idem,* "φρήν," *TDNT,* IX, 225.

87. Kuhn, 139.

נֵבֶל nēḇel

Contents: I. Etymology and Distribution. II. Meaning. III. Usage.

I. Etymology and Distribution. Heb. *nēḇel/neḇel* is probably a monosyllabic, onomatopoeic primary noun with the basic vowel *a,* distinct from נבל *nbl* with the basic vowel *i* (**ni/ēbl* in contrast to **na/ebl,* LXX[B] *nabal,* LXX[A, R] *nabla*).[1] Several pieces of evidence support this conclusion: (1) Ugar. *nbl,* "jar," in contrast to *nbl',* "harp";[2] (2) the Greek transliteration in the LXX: *nébel* (1 S. 1:24; Hos. 3:2; etc. [? *nebl* Sixt.]) in contrast to *nábla/ē, náblas, naúlon, nábal,* and the like (Lat. *nablium*); (3) the pointing of the MT: *nēḇel, niḇlê,* etc., in contrast to *neḇel, nāḇel* (MS. Ec 18 on Ps. 144:9, e.g., *bᵉnaḇal*); (4) Syr. *nbl* in contrast to *nablā* (?), Eth. *nēbāl/nēbēl,* "jar," in contrast to *nabal,* "flame"; (5) 1 S. 10:3,5, where both nouns appear without any recognizable distinction in the same rhetorical unit. The relationship to Akk. *nablu,* "flame," "flaming arrow, tongue of fire, flame," specifically "fire pan," is obscure.[3]

The noun *nēḇel* II occurs 28 times in the OT, including Am. 6:5 but omitting 2 occurrences in Sirach. It is thus somewhat less common than its counterpart *kinnôr* (40 occurrences). More than two-thirds of its occurrences are in the Chronicler's history (12) and Psalms (9). It therefore came into widespread use comparatively late; the oldest texts in which it appears are 1 S. 10:5; 2 S. 6:5; Am. 5:23; Isa. 5:12. It is used in parallel or in conjunction with *kinnôr* some 20 times. The most important occurrences without *kinnôr* are Am. 5:23; (6:5?); Isa. 14:11; Ps. 144:9. It appears in the Dead Sea Scrolls in 1QS 10:9; 1QM 4:5; 1QH 11:23; 11QPs[a] 28:4.

II. Meaning. If *nbl* II is to be kept distinct from *nbl* I, "jar (for wine or oil)," this holds true also for attempts to define more precisely the musical instrument it denotes. The following evidence emerges from the usage of the word. In contrast to *kinnôr,* "lyre," its origins are Semitic; this fact, together with its sonic form, may suggest an

---

nēḇel. → כנור *kinnôr* (VII, 197-204); P. Casetti, "Funktion der Musik in der Bibel," *Freiburger Zeitschrift für Philosophie und Theologie,* 24 (1977), 366-389; G. Delling, "ὕμνος," *TDNT,* VIII, 489-503; A. Draffkorn-Kilmer, "The Cult Song from Ancient Ugarit," *RA,* 68 (1974), 69-82; E. Gerson-Kiwi, "Musique," *DBS,* 5, 1411-1468, esp. 1422-26; P. Grelot, "L'orchestre de Daniel III 5,7,10,15," *VT,* 29 (1979), 23-38, esp. 33ff.; R. Hammerstein, "Instrumenta Hieronymi," *Archiv für Musikwissenschaft,* 16 (1959), 117-134, esp. 125ff.; O. Keel, *The Symbolism of the Biblical World* (Eng. trans., New York, 1978), 346-352, 408f.; H. P. Kümmel, "Zur Stimmung der babylonischen Harfe," *Or,* N.S. 39 (1970), 252-263; H. Seidel, *Der Beitrag des ATs zu einer Musikgeschichte Altisraels* (Leipzig, 1970); D. Wulstan, "Music from Ancient Ugarit," *RA,* 68 (1974), 125-28.

1. J. J. Stamm, *ZAW,* 90 (1978), 114. Listed in *HAL,* II, 664, as נֵבֶל II.

2. On Ugar. *nbl* see *Ugaritica,* V (1968), 558; *UT,* no. 1598; on *nbl'* see *UF,* 12 (1980), 339.

3. For the first definition see *CAD,* XI/1, 25-27; for the second, *AHw,* II, 698; for the third, W. C. Delsman, *UF,* 11 (1979), 188; W. Mayer, *ibid.,* 584.

indigenous plucking instrument. According to 1 S. 10:5, it is portable and belongs to an instrumental group that includes *tōp,* "tambourine," *ḥālîl,* "double flute (?)," and *kinnôr,* "lyre." Since it heads the list, it may have been conspicuous. A similar grouping appears in Isa. 5:12, and in somewhat different form in 2 S. 6:5, which mentions lyre, double flute, and tambourine along with castanets and cymbals. The Qumran texts also associate it with the *ḥālîl* flute. According to 1 K. 10:12, it could be made of *'almuggîm* wood, like all the woodwork of the palace (and the *kinnôr*).

When it is not associated with *kinnôr* (Ps. 144:9; Isa. 14:11; also Am. 5:23; [6:5?]), an association with the king or at least with the royal court is suggested.[4] The other occurrences in the Psalms associate the two instruments with vocal music (*šîr* and *zimmēr* appearing frequently), clearly to accompany the singing of a "thanksgiving hymn" (*hôḏâ,* Ps. 33:2; 57:9[8]; 71:22; 81:3[2]; 144:9; also probably 150:3). Note the description in 92:4(3): "to the music of *'āśôr* and *nāḇel,* to the melody of *kinnôr*" (cf. Am. 6:5).

This stringed instrument (so described in Sir. 39:15), of which there was a ten-stringed variant (Ps. 33:2; 144:9; 92:4[3]), appears to have been given a permanent role in the Levitical temple orchestra (Neh. 12:27; 1 Ch. 15:16ff.; etc.), especially to accompany singing (*baššîr:* 1 Ch. 25:6; 15:16; 2 Ch. 5:12ff.). The *kinnôr* and *nēḇel* were termed *kᵉlê ḏāwîḏ,* "instruments of David" (2 Ch. 29:25f.; cf. Neh. 12:36); Josephus speaks of the ten-stringed *kinýra* and the twelve-note *nábla* as instruments introduced by David.[5]

The LXX often simply transliterates (*hai náblai:* 1 S. 10:5; 2 S. 6:5; 1 K. 10:12; always in Chronicles; cf. also 1 Mc. 13:51). In the Psalms and Neh. 12:27, it uses *psaltḗrion* (Ps. 71:22: *psalmós*), and in Am. 5:23; 6:5, *órganon.*[6]

Identification of the actual instrument is not certain. If *nēḇel* always denotes the same instrument — uncertainty clearly begins with the LXX, which can equate *nēḇel* and *kinnôr* — the most likely candidate is the arched lyre or angled harp, both members of the harp family, with strings tuned to fixed pitches played by the fingers of both hands.[7] Such an instrument, however, is not yet attested archaeologically in Palestine. It is also conceivable that **nabl* was originally the indigenous word for portable stringed and plucked instruments in general and over time remained associated with a particular type when differentiation began (lyre, kithara, lute, harp, sambuca, etc.[8]). That the word is used somewhat less frequently than *kinnôr* may be due to the greater skill the *nēḇel* demanded of the player (cf. Ps. 81:3[2]: ". . . and also the *nāḇel*").

III. Usage. The procession of *nᵉḇî'îm* in 1 S. 10:5, the court celebration when the ark was brought to Jerusalem in 2 S. 6:5, and the employment of the *nēḇel* for

4. Keel, 349.
5. *Ant.* 7.12.3 §306.
6. On *psállō/psaltḗrion* see Delling, 490ff.; on *pᵉsanterîn,* Gk. *psaltḗrion,* see Grelot, 33ff.; on *psalterium* see Hammerstein, 125ff.
7. H. P. Rüger, *BRL*², 235.
8. See Grelot.

instrumental accompaniment or as part of the temple orchestra illustrate the religious significance of the *nēḇel* harp in the context of the music in which it played a part. Two aspects of the instrument itself are theologically significant. First is the function of accompanying the chant of individuals singing songs of praise and thanksgiving *(hôḏâ, hillēl, zimmēr)*. With harmonious chords (*prṭ ʿal-pî:* Am. 6:5 [?]) or a drone, music undergirds and sustains the performance of lay chant ("a new song") as liturgically appropriate, "elevated" speech in the presence of Yahweh and the congregation, playing a supporting role similar to that which it plays for the dance. Second, together with lyres, cymbals, etc., as governed by liturgical regulations, it belongs to the special institution of the Levitical temple orchestra, which serves (as Chronicles attests) to support hymnic chant ("after the manner of young girls" [?]: 1 Ch. 15:20) and thus in a special way to celebrate the epiphany and presence of God in the sanctuary.

Seybold

נגד *ngd*

Contents: I. 1. Etymology; 2. Meaning. II. 1. Verbal Communication; 2. Nonverbal Communication. III. 1. Occurrences; 2. Semantic Field. IV. Most Important Texts: 1. Prophetic Contexts; 2. Cultic Contexts; 3. Wisdom Contexts. V. 1. LXX; 2. Dead Sea Scrolls; 3. Jewish Literature.

I. 1. *Etymology.* The root *ngd* appears in Phoenician as a masculine personal name; in Arabic as a verb ("overcome, help," II "furnish, inform"), noun (*najdah,* "help, courage"), and adjective (*najīd,* "courageous"); in Aramaic (*n*ᵉ*gaḏ,* "pull"; Syriac also "lead"); and Ethiopic (*nagada,* "travel, engage in trade"). In Hebrew it is found as a verb (hiphil and hophal), in *negeḏ* (a noun used adverbially), and in the noun → *nāgîḏ,* "prince."

Attempts have been made to establish a connection between *ngd* and Akk. *naqādu,*

---

ngd. M. Dahood, "Denominative *riḥḥam,* 'To Conceive, Enwomb,' " *Bibl,* 44 (1963), 204-5; *idem,* "Qohelet and Northwest Semitic Philology," *Bibl,* 43 (1962), 349-365; O. Garcia de la Fuente, *La búsqueda de Dios en el AT* (Madrid, 1971); H. Haag, " 'Offenbaren' in der hebräischen Bibel," *TZ,* 16 (1960), 251-58; J. Harvey, *Le plaidoyer prophétique contre Israël après la rupture de l'Alliance* (Bruges, 1967); A. Lemaire, *Inscriptions hébraïques.* I: *Les ostraca* (Paris, 1977); I. L. Seeligmann, "Zur Terminologie für das Gerichtsverfahren im Wortschatz des biblischen Hebräisch," *Hebräische Wortforschung. Festschrift W. Baumgartner. SVT,* 16 (1967), 251-278; A. Schoors, "Les choses antérieures et les choses nouvelles dans les oracles Deutéro-Isaïens," *ETL,* 40 (1964), 19-47; M. Weinfeld, *Deuteronomy and the Deuteronomic School* (Oxford, 1972); Y. Yadin, *The Scroll of the War of the Sons of Light against the Sons of Darkness* (Eng. trans., London, 1962); W. Zimmerli, "Der 'Prophet' im Pentateuch," *Studien zum Pentateuch. Festschrift W. Kornfeld* (Vienna, 1977), 197-211.

"be in a critical situation," but these two roots are etymologically distinct.[1] There may, however, be some connection between Heb. *neged, nāgîd* and Tuareg *nkd,* "go before, go to meet," appearing in the Punic translation *(mynkd)* of Lat. *imperator.*[2] This theory should not be rejected out of hand.

The verb *ngd* probably derives from the subst. *neged,* which means literally something like "front, face," but is in fact used only as an adverb or preposition: "in front of, opposite." The only exception is Gen. 2:18,20, where *keneḡdô* means "as his counterpart," i.e., suitable for him.[3] This etymology is supported by the general tendency of Ugaritic and Hebrew to form denominative verbs from words denoting parts of the body.[4]

2. *Meaning.* From these observations, it is clear that the primary and most immediate meaning of *ngd* is "place opposite, place before, confront with." From this sense derives the most common meaning, "report, inform, show, explain, announce, reveal," with a wide range of nuances from the semantic field of communication. These nuances will be discussed in greater detail below.

II. 1. *Verbal Communication.* As a rule, *ngd* refers to verbal communication. This observation, which can be supported by numerous texts, is especially evident in those cases where *ngd* appears in conjunction with the expressions "open the lips" (Ps. 51:17[Eng. v. 15]) and "in the ears of" (Jer. 36:20; cf. Isa. 48:14).[5] In addition, Isa. 48:20 refers explicitly to the "voice" *(qôl)* as a means of communication; and in several texts "words" *(debārîm)* is the object of *ngd* (Gen. 44:24; 1 S. 18:26; 19:7; 25:12; 2 K. 6:12). Verbal communication is intended to convey a message. This operation implies a referent, a channel, and of course a sender and a receiver. In most cases, the sender (speaker) and receiver (hearer) are human beings; the referent (the subject matter of the message) likewise generally belongs to the human realm. This explains why *ngd* functions primarily in the secular sphere.

Human communication covers a very wide range; examples of the usage of *ngd* therefore are extremely varied: stating a truth (Gen. 3:11), answering a question (Gen. 32:30[29]; 43:7; Jer. 36:17; 38:14f.,27: *šā'al — higgîd*), conveying information (Gen. 14:13; 26:32; 46:31; 1 S. 4:13f.; Job 1:15-17,19), interpreting a dream (Gen. 41:24; Dnl. 2:2), concealing or revealing a secret (Gen. 31:20; Josh. 2:14,20; Jgs. 16:6,10,13, 15,17f.) or a name (Jgs. 13:6), solving a riddle (Jgs. 14:12-29; 1 K. 10:1-3), explaining a ritual or sign (Ex. 13:8; Dt. 32:7; Ezk. 24:19; 37:18), etc. In some cases a human being is the speaker and God is the hearer (Ex. 19:9; Ps. 142:3[2]); in others, God is

---

1. W. Richter, *BZ,* N.S. 9 (1965), 72, n. 7, contra J. J. Glück, "Nagid — Shepherd," *VT,* 13 (1963), 144-150; *AHw,* II, 743.

2. *KAI,* II, 126f.

3. W. J. Gerber, *Die hebräischen Verba denominativa* (1896), 189; C. Westermann, *TLOT,* II, 714.

4. Dahood, *Bibl,* 43, 364; 44, 204f.; *idem, Psalms. AB,* 16 (1965), 84, 237; 17A (1970), 385.

5. See III.2 below.

the sender and a human being the receiver (Gen. 41:25; 2 S. 7:11; Jer. 42:3; Mic. 6:8; Ps. 147:19). God is represented anthropomorphically, and one may therefore hope that he will "open his lips" (Job 11:5f.) and communicate "his word" *(dāḇār)* (Ex. 4:28; Dt. 5:5). Divine communication may be direct or indirect (Dt. 4:13; Jer. 9:11[12]); it may also use a mediator or messenger (1 S. 3:17f.; 9:8; Isa. 21:10; Jer. 16:10; 42:20f.; Ezk. 24:19ff.).

Syntactically and stylistically, the relationships sketched above are generally expressed by the hiphil of *ngd* + indirect object with l^e + (sometimes) direct object or other expression, e.g., 1 S. 19:7: *wayyaggēḏ lô yᵉhônāṯān 'eṯ-kol-haddᵉḇārîm hā'ēlleh.* On rare occasions the indirect object is introduced by *'el: wayyaggēḏ mōšeh 'eṯ-diḇrê hā'ām 'el-YHWH* (Ex. 19:9; cf. 1 S. 3:15). Instead of a direct object, we may find b^e + place (1 S. 4:13; 2 S. 1:20; Jer. 4:5; 5:20) or other adverbial expressions.

2. *Nonverbal Communication.* The verb *ngd* can also denote nonverbal communication. Without speech, without words, without audible voice, Ps. 19:2-4(1-3) declares, the heavens tell the glory of God and the firmament proclaims his handiwork (cf. also 50:6; 97:6; Job 12:7). We are dealing here with a special kind of "language": despite the absence of "words" *(dᵉḇārîm)* and "voice" *(qôl),* it is universal and extends throughout the entire world. The senders are the heavenly realms, the receivers the earthly. The message consists in the proclamation of God's glory, the revelation of the mighty God.

Thus *ngd* expresses not only communication among human beings but also God's communication through his word and through nature. As a rule, *ngd* means making someone else share in something previously unknown. It involves informing, making known, revealing in the broadest sense. When the subject is God, the verb can denote revelation in the strict sense; when God does this through a messenger, his word can be a prophetic message.

III. 1. *Occurrences.* The are 334 occurrences of the verb *ngd* in the hiphil: 48 in the Pentateuch (31 in Genesis — 14 in the story of Joseph), 138 in the Deuteronomistic history (27 in Judges — 23 in the story of Samson; 80 in 1-2 Samuel; 30 in 1-2 Kings), 70 in the prophetic books (29 in Isaiah — 21 in Deutero-Isaiah; 28 in Jeremiah), and 78 elsewhere (20 in Psalms, 17 in Job).

To these occurrences one may add the following conjectural emendations: Dt. 13:10, *haggēḏ taggîḏennû* for MT *hārōḡ tahargennû;*[6] 1 S. 12:7: inserting *wᵉ'aggîḏâ lāḵem* with the LXX;[7] Isa. 41:27: *higgaḏtî* for MT *hinnēh hinnām.*[8]

There are 35 occurrences of *ngd* in the hophal: 5 in Genesis, 8 in 1-2 Samuel, and 7 in 1-2 Kings.

---

6. Cf. LXX; *BHS;* Seeligmann, 261f.; Weinfeld, 94-97.

7. Cf. *BHS;* H. J. Stoebe, *Das erste Buch Samuelis. KAT,* VIII/1 (1973), 233; P. K. McCarter, *I Samuel. AB,* 8 (1980), 210.

8. Cf. *BHS;* C. F. Whitley, *JSS,* 2 (1957), 327f.; K. Elliger, *Deuterojesaja. BK,* XI/1 (1978), 174f.

The verb *ngd* also appears in extrabiblical Hebrew texts, e.g., Lachish ostracon 3.[9] The introductory formula "Your servant X has sent to tell (*ngd* hiphil) my lord N . . ." recalls formulas in the Amarna letters ("I have sent you this tablet to tell you . . .") and a few biblical passages such as Gen. 32:6: "I have sent to tell (*ngd* hiphil). . . ."[10]

2. *Semantic Field.* In Biblical Hebrew the semantic field of *ngd* includes above all → ידע *yāḏaʿ*, → שׁמע *šāmaʿ*, and → כחד *kiḥēḏ*.[11] If the basic meaning of *higgîḏ* is "cause to know," it is logical that the verb should have close associations with *yāḏaʿ*, as in Isa. 19:12; 41:22f.,26; Job 11:6; 38:4,18; Ruth 4:4; Eccl. 6:12. Ezk. 23:36 uses *higgîḏ* instead of *hôḏîaʿ* (cf. Ezk. 20:4; 22:2; also compare Ex. 13:8 to Josh. 4:22). Finally, we may note that, while the LXX uses *anangéllein* to translate *higgîḏ,* it occasionally uses the same verb for *hôḏîaʿ* (Ps. 104:1).

The relationship between *higgîḏ* and *šāmaʿ* is evident. We are dealing with the correlation between speaking and hearing, which in this case manifests itself in two ways: (a) parallelism of *higgîḏ* and *hišmîaʿ* (Isa. 41:22b,26b; 42:9; 43:9,12; 44:7a[*BHS*], 8; 45:21; 48:3,5,6,20; Jer. 4:5,15; 5:20; 46:14; 50:2); (b) use of the *higgîḏ-šāmaʿ* relationship (Gen. 21:26; Isa. 21:10; 48:6; Jer. 31:10; 36:13; 42:21; Ezk. 40:4; Prov. 29:24; see also Isa. 40:21 [*ngd* hophal]).

There is antithetical parallelism between *ngd* and *kḥd,* although the two verbs appear in synonymous parallelism when *higgîḏ* is used affirmatively and *kḥd* is negated (Josh. 7:19; 1 S. 3:18; Isa. 3:9; Jer. 38:25; 50:2; Job 15:18; cf. Jer. 38:14f.). We may observe analogous correlation between *ngd* and *ʿlm* (1 K. 10:3 par.; 2 Ch. 9:2; 2 K. 4:27; cf. Job 42:3) and between *ngd* and *ḥāšâ* (2 K. 7:9; Isa. 57:11f.).

IV. Most Important Texts. It is not always easy to categorize a text as belonging to a particular stream of tradition. In the following discussion, therefore, we use the term "context" in a broad sense. From the theological perspective, the verb *ngd* is used primarily in prophetic and cultic contexts, although some relevant examples also appear in Wisdom Literature. The theological meaning of a passage can exhibit a variety of semantic nuances and be embodied in a variety of literary forms. For example, *ngd* appears several times in texts of the *rîḇ* genre (Isa. 48:14; 57:12; 58:1; Mic. 6:8; Ps. 50:6).[12] Without losing its theological import, in these and other texts *ngd* acquires certain juridical overtones. Other nuances may depend on the direct object or parallel verbs and forms.

1. *Prophetic Contexts.* a. The earliest texts in which *ngd* appears in a prophetic context are probably in the Pentateuch. We are not always dealing with prophecy in the strict sense, but the association is clear.

---

9. *KAI,* 193, 2 (hiphil), 13 (hophal).

10. Lemaire, 101-4. On the Amarna texts see A. F. Rainey, *El Amarna Tablets 359-379. AOAT,* 8 ([2]1978), nos. 367, 2-4; 369, 2-4 (pp. 36ff.).

11. See IV.2.c below.

12. Harvey, 109, n. 2.

(1) In the Joseph story, Gen. 41:24f. is a theologically programmatic text[13] in which the verb *ngd* is repeated. In form and content, these verses recall 41:15f. and 40:8 (cf. 37:5ff.). Pharaoh tells Joseph that he has had a dream that his magicians have been unable to interpret (v. 24). In verbal communication, the message sent can convey information only when sender and receiver share a common code: the sender encodes and the receiver decodes the message. The magicians cannot decode the message because they do not know the code, as one would expect in this case, since it is not a human code. The usual word for dream interpretation in the Joseph story is *pāṯar* (40:8,16,22; 41:8,12,13,15). In 41:24 *higgîḏ* is used instead, with the same meaning and in a similar form of expression: *ûpôṯēr 'ên 'ōṯô* (40:8; 41:15)/*wᵉ'ên maggîḏ lî* (41:24).

Here we catch an echo of the general notion that dreams have prophetic significance.[14] Both dreams and their interpretation come from God (cf. 40:8; 41:25). Joseph is "not a trained dream interpreter," like the magicians of Pharaoh, but he "depends on God's inspiration"; he is a charismatic.[15] Future events belong to God and those to whom he wishes to reveal them. The essence of the revelation is not in the dream but in its divine interpretation. The dream of Pharaoh is a message from God: "What God is about to do, he has proclaimed *(higgîḏ)* to Pharaoh" (41:25) — even more, it is a message of favor (v. 16). This dream, together with its interpretation, is tantamount to a divine revelation of prophetic character, announcing God's favor.

The notion that dreams embody a revelation is an idea common to the Elohistic texts, to which Gen. 40–41 belong (cf. 20:3ff.; 28:12ff.). In the context of a dream, Abraham is given the title *nāḇî'* (20:7); and we are told that Joseph possesses "the spirit of Elohim" (41:38). Joseph is not only a sage or magician but a prophet, who receives the divine revelation through which he interprets dreams. "A prophet, not a magician, is the proper interpreter of dreams."[16] In 41:24f., therefore, *higgîḏ* far transcends simple explication: it belongs in the category of authentic prophetic interpretation, in the context of the revelation and proclamation of God.

Hos. 4:12 accords with these texts; like them, it originated in the northern kingdom. It is the only passage in Hosea to use *higgîḏ,* and it refers to the technique used to achieve contact with the Deity.[17]

Similar to these texts are Isa. 19:12; Jer. 9:11; and above all Dnl. 2:2 (+ 2:26ff.), which probably depends on Gen. 40–41. Common to all these passages is the contrast between the sages and soothsayers of other nations and the prophets of Israel.[18] Dreams and visions come from God and pass the comprehension of sages and court soothsayers: they give foolish counsel, because they are not guided by the true prophetic spirit.

---

13. G. von Rad, *Genesis. OTL* (Eng. trans. 1972), 375.
14. → חלם *ḥālam* (IV, 421-432).
15. Von Rad, *Genesis,* 375. Quotation from H. Gunkel, *Genesis* (Eng. trans., Macon, Ga., 1977), 412.
16. O. Procksch, *Genesis. KAT,* 1 (1913), 394; cf. Gunkel, *Genesis,* 412; H.-C. Schmitt, *Die nichtpriesterliche Josephsgeschichte. BZAW,* 154 (1980), 98f.
17. J. L. Mays, *Hosea. OTL* (1969), 73.
18. O. Kaiser, *Isaiah 13–39. OTL* (Eng. trans. 1974), 103.

(2) The understanding of Israelite prophecy as different from magical interpretation, latent in the Joseph story, appears openly in the Balaam cycle, most concretely in Nu. 23:3ff. (E). The author contrasts the magical apprehension of Balak's ritual sacrifice to the prophet's subjection to the word of God.[19] The primary source of prophecy is the word of God; the prophet repeats the words God tells him (23:5,7,12,16f.; 22:35,38) or the vision God shows him (23:3). Balaam does not dare express his own opinion; he does not speak prematurely, but awaits the word event in a meeting with God. J. de Vaulx compares Balaam to Moses, who climbs the mountain to meet Yahweh (Ex. 19:3: *higgîḏ*).[20] In Balaam's case the meeting takes the form of vision and audition (Nu. 23:3,5). Balaam conveys *(higgîḏ)* to Balak what God has shown him, what God reveals to him (23:3).

Moses' preeminence as mediator of God's word is illustrated by two texts from the northern tradition, Ex. 4:28[21] and Dt. 5:5. Both emphasize Moses' role as mediator; their almost identical formulation *(higgîḏ + l^e + 'eṯ . . . d^eḇar YHWH)* suggests not only a connection between the two texts but dependence of the latter on the former.[22] The relationship between the expression *d^eḇar YHWH* and prophetic revelation on the one hand and between Moses' role as mediator and the function of the prophets on the other appears to be undeniable.[23]

This relationship is accentuated even more if one acknowledges the connection between Mic. 6:8 and Dt. 5:5. Micah affirms that Yahweh has made known *(higgîḏ)* his will to Israel, i.e., has told Israel what is required. Artur Weiser connects the passage with the Decalog, and Hans Walter Wolff thinks that the terminology of Mic. 6:8 recalls that of Dt. 4:13 and 5:5 (*higgîḏ* in all three cases).[24] One should note, however, that Dt. 4:13 represents a tradition different from 5:5; the former emphasizes the directness of divine communication. The mediation of Moses expressed by *higgîḏ* also appears in Ex. 19:9, but in the opposite direction: from the people to God.

The Pentateuch texts here analyzed use the verb *ngd* in the context of primitive witnesses to the prophetic tradition. Although they do not belong to classical prophecy, these texts (esp. those of northern origin) represent in a sense the foundation pillars of Israelite prophecy. In them the verb *ngd* moves in the domain of prophetic interpretation, revelation, inspiration, and prediction. At the same time, it instantiates the mediating role of Moses and Balaam, an essential function in both communication theory and prophetic activity.

b. In the "Former Prophets" (Deuteronomistic history), we shall focus on three

---

19. M. Noth, *Numbers. OTL* (1968), 182.

20. *Nombres. SB* (1972), 275.

21. Assigned to E by G. Fohrer, *Überlieferung und Geschichte des Exodus. BZAW,* 91 (1964), 28ff., 124; J. P. Hyatt, *Exodus. NCB* (repr. 1981), 88; et al.

22. Contra G. Seitz, *Redaktionsgeschichtliche Studien zum Deuteronomium. BWANT,* 93 (1971), 49; A. D. H. Mayes, *Deuteronomy. NCB* (1979), 166.

23. G. Gerleman, *TLOT,* I, 331; Zimmerli, 202ff.

24. Weiser, *Das Buch der zwölf Kleinen Propheten. ATD,* 24 (1956), 281; Wolff, *Micah* (Eng. trans., Minneapolis, 1990), 179.

places where the verb *ngd* occurs in a context relevant to the theology of prophecy: the call of Samuel (1 S. 3), Samuel's appointment of Saul as *nāgîḏ* (1 S. 9:1–10:16), and an anecdotal story about Elisha (2 K. 4). All these texts belong to the northern stream of tradition, and in them we can observe some significant points of contact with the Pentateuch texts just discussed.

(1) Like Balaam, Samuel is a seer (1 S. 9:9) and receives his prophetic call in the setting of a vision (3:15). Like Elisha, Samuel is an *'îš 'ᵉlōhîm* (9:6; 2 K. 4:8ff.); both possess extraordinary powers through which they can come in contact with supernatural forces. In the account of Samuel's call, *higgîḏ* expresses the communication of the divine revelation to Eli: the concern is to tell the vision (*haggîḏ 'eṯ-hammar'eh:* 1 S. 3:15) and convey the words of Yahweh (*wayyaggēḏ šᵉmû'ēl 'eṯ-kol-haddᵉḇārîm:* v. 18). Vision and audition are the usual channels of prophetic revelation (cf. the discussion of Balaam above).

(2) When Samuel anoints Saul, he acts as God's agent. The verb *ngd,* which is especially frequent in this narrative (1 S. 9:6,8,18,19; 10:15f. [4 times]), exhibits various nuances. Saul hopes that the "man of God" will give him information *(higgîḏ)* about the stray donkeys (v. 6b). Indeed, he expects more than just information, knowing quite well that the man of God is endowed with special powers, so that "whatever he says always comes true" (v. 6a). But he certainly does not expect as much as the man of God will actually tell him, since he does not know that Yahweh has commanded Samuel to anoint him as *nāgîḏ* over Israel (9:15f.; 10:1). In this context, the meaning of *ngd* wavers between "inform" and "interpret prophetically" (9:6,19). Indeed, because of the etymological connection with *nāgîḏ, haggîḏâ-nā' lî* could even mean "designate me."[25]

In 1 S. 10:15f. *higgîḏ* takes on a new aspect. It refers simultaneously to both the revelation (v. 16a) and concealment (negated: v. 16b) of a matter. Saul's conduct toward his servants in concealing a portion of the truth recalls the behavior of Samson toward his parents: there too *higgîḏ* appears with the identical meaning (Jgs. 14:4,6,16).

(3) Not only Samson and Saul but also Yahweh is depicted as concealing or revealing *(higgîḏ)* something. The "man of God" Elisha says that Yahweh hid the distress of the Shunammite woman from him and did not tell him about it (*wᵉYHWH heʿᵉlîm mimmennî wᵉlō' higgîḏ lî:* 2 K. 4:27). Since *heʿᵉlîm* has a clear cognitive connotation, the parallel expression encompasses the same meaning: Yahweh did not inform Elisha concerning the event. God's word remains hidden within God as his "plan" (Dt. 29:28[29]; Am. 3:7).

(4) In the story of Samuel's call in 1 S. 3, vv. 11-14 are a Deuteronomistic addition.[26] In this section the object of *higgîḏ* is an oracle of judgment against the house of Eli. By contrast, in 2 S. 7:11 (also Deuteronomistic[27]) the object is an oracle of divine favor toward the house of David. These observations illustrate the semantic range of *ngd* in

---

25. McCarter, *AB,* 8, 179.
26. T. Veijola, *Die ewige Dynastie. AnAcScFen,* 193 (1975), 38f.
27. *Ibid.,* 79f., 132f.

the Deuteronomistic history. Its occurrences extend from the ancient stories revised by a prophetic redactor to its inclusion in the framework of the Deuteronomistic history.

c. In classical prophecy, *ngd* occurs primarily in late texts. There are, however, some noteworthy preexilic texts.

(1) Among the earliest texts (apart from Hos. 4:12 and Mic. 6:8, discussed above) are Isa. 3:9 and Mic. 3:8; in both, *higgîḏ* has *ḥaṭṭāʾṯ* as its object. In Mic. 3:8 the prophet represents himself as God's true messenger, sent to declare *(higgîḏ)* to Jacob his transgression *(pešaʿ)* and to Israel his sin *(ḥaṭṭāʾṯ)*. It is a thankless task, but essential to his prophetic activity. Here the verb expresses the prophetic charge against the false prophets (vv. 5-7). Using an almost identical formula, Isa. 58:1 says that the prophet has been charged with revealing the sin of the people (cf. Job 21:31).

In Isa. 3:9 *higgîḏ ḥaṭṭāʾṯ* has a different meaning: here the wicked themselves do not hide their sin but proclaim it openly. Thus *higgîḏ* becomes a public confession, proud and insolent in contrast to Ps. 51:5(3), where a similar formula gives voice to a recognition and humble confession of sin (*BHS* proposes *ʾaggîḏ* for *negdî*). Cf. also Am. 5:12; Isa. 59:12; Job 13:23; 36:9 *(ngd/ydʿ + ḥaṭṭāʾṯ/pešaʿ)*.

A second group of preexilic texts, later than these, is found in the book of Jeremiah (4:5,15; 20:10; 31:10; 46:14; 48:20). With the exception of 4:15, the impv. *haggîḏû* is followed by an indication of place introduced by *bᵉ* (cf. also 5:20; 50:2,28: exilic). This construction is characteristic of (but not unique to; cf. Ps. 9:12[11]) Jeremiah; on occasion it appears in solemn introduction to an oracle in order to announce a happy or tragic event. In 4:5, for example, disaster is announced for Judah and Jerusalem; in 31:10 a message of salvation is proclaimed. Jer. 46:14 and 48:20 contain oracles against Egypt and Moab.

(2) Among the late texts, those in Deutero-Isaiah stand out on account of their theological richness. One of Deutero-Isaiah's favorite expressions, especially in chs. 40–48, is *higgîḏ* (hophal in 40:21). Of the 21 occurrences of the hiphil, only 3 have a human subject (42:12; 45:21a; 48:20); in most of the rest, the subject is Yahweh or the gods. Syntactically and stylistically, the number of interrogative clauses introduced by *mî* is significant (41:26; 43:9; 44:7; 45:21; 48:14), as well as the many instances of combination with *šāmaʿ*.[28] In 40:21 the hophal of *ngd* parallels not only *šāmaʿ* but also *bîn* and *yāḏaʿ*. Strictly speaking, this series of relationships shows that not just speaking and hearing are involved but also understanding in the broadest sense, and that knowledge of God comes from hearing the proclamation.[29]

In Deutero-Isaiah *higgîḏ* usually means "predict." This meaning is emphasized by objects and modifiers: "what is to come" (*ʾôṯîyôṯ:* 41:23; 44:7), "what will take place" (cf. *ʾᵃšer lōʾ naʿᵃśû:* 46:10), "new things" *(ḥᵃḏāšôṯ)* par. "before they spring forth" (42:9), "from long ago" *(mēʾāz)* par. "before they came to pass" (48:5), "from ancient times" (*miqqeḏem:* 46:10).[30] In 41:22-27 much more is involved than mere prediction:

28. See III.2 above.
29. Elliger, *BK,* XI/1, 82f.
30. Schoors, 26.

higgîḏ refers to interpretation of both the present and the past.[31] Between the past and the future, the word constitutes a revelatory act in the present. In 43:12; 48:14f., the proclamation includes implicitly or explicitly the notion of salvation. In 48:20 all the Israelites are called on to proclaim (*haggîḏû;* cf. 42:12) the salvation accomplished by Yahweh. They are to be heralds of the good news before the nations. The passage is in the form of a herald's instructions, the central theme of which is proclamation of the salvific event that has taken place.[32]

Among the late texts, some exilic passages in First Isaiah, Jeremiah, and Ezekiel deserve mention. In Isa. 21:1-10 *ngd* appears at the beginning (v. 2 [hophal]), in the middle (v. 6), and at the end (v. 10). In v. 2 the object of *ngd* is *ḥāzûṯ,* which includes both vision and audition.[33] This explains the different formulas in vv. 6 and 10: *'ašer yir'eh yaggîḏ* and *'ašer šāmaʿtî.* While *ngd* in v. 2 refers to divine revelation, in vv. 6 and 10 it refers to the proclamation of this revelation: God reveals himself in visions and words, and the watchman reports what he sees and hears (cf. Ezk. 40:4).

In Jer. 16:10; 33:3; 42:4,20f., also, *higgîḏ* means "reveal." In Jer. 9:11(12); Ezk. 24:19; 37:18, the reference is probably to prophetic interpretation; here *ngd* appears in requests for an explanation or interpretation.

2. *Cultic Contexts.* In cultic contexts *ngd* appears primarily in relatively late texts. Some early occurrences, however, are associated with the institution of consulting God through a priest.

a. The OT contains only two more or less complete formularies for consulting Yahweh, one in David's inquiry in the midst of a war (1 S. 23:9-12), the other in connection with identification of a guilty party (14:41f.).[34] Both use *higgîḏ,* the former as part of the inquiry formula (23:11), the latter in close connection with it (14:43). In 23:11 *higgîḏ* expresses the answer to the inquiry through Abiathar. The request for an oracle appears as a formal prayer, part of a ritual rooted in the cult.[35] In 14:41 lots (Urim and Thummim) are cast to determine the guilty party. In this context we are dealing with a sacral ceremony, a divine determination in which God is called on repeatedly (14:38ff.). In this setting, *higgîḏ* is used once again. It would not suffice for the lot to fall on a person: that person must also acknowledge his or her guilt.

Josh. 7:14-19 describes a situation that has several points of contact with the scenes just described. The formula using *ngd* is almost identical with 1 S. 14:43 (*wᵉhaggēḏ-nā' lî meh ʿāśîṯā:* Josh. 7:19; *haggîḏâ lî meh ʿāśîṯâ:* 1 S. 14:43). The basic problem is also similar. In the setting of the Achan story, which is an etiological tale with marked liturgical elements,[36] there is mention of a sin that has been committed among the

31. Elliger, *BK,* XI/1, 192, 196.

32. F. Crüsemann, *Studien zur Formgeschichte von Hymnus und Danklied in Israel. WMANT,* 32 (1969), 50f.; R. P. Merendino, *Der Erste und der Letzte. SVT,* 31 (1981), 534.

33. H. Wildberger, *Isaiah 13–27* (Eng. trans., Minneapolis, 1997), 315.

34. See Garcia de la Fuente, 24.

35. *Ibid.,* 222f.

36. M. Noth, *Josua. HAT,* VII (²1953), 43ff.

Israelites (vv. 11f.). In a cultic ceremony beginning with ritual purification (v. 13), lots are cast to identify the guilty party (vv. 14-18). The ceremony culminates in a doxology and confession spoken by the guilty man (v. 19).[37] Just as the transgression has a double aspect — being an offense against both God and the community — so the confession must take place before God and the people. The formulas employed are in part complementary, in part parallel: *śîm-nā' kāḇôḏ lᵉYHWH . . . wᵉṯen-lô tôḏâ wᵉhaggeḏ-nā' lî meh ʿāśîṯā* (v. 19). This parallelism is accentuated when we compare Isa. 42:12: *yāśîmû lᵉYHWH kāḇôḏ ûṯᵉhillāṯô bā'îyîm yaggîḏû.* The formula *śîm-nā' kāḇôḏ lᵉYHWH* is characteristic of cultic worship (cf. Ps. 66:2).[38] Its close association with the *higgîḏ* formula gives this verb a special religio-cultic connotation. In Josh. 7:19 *higgîḏ* takes on the meaning "confess": a quasi-sacramental confession of Yahweh and Yahweh's representatives before the community.

The book of Jonah tells a story that coincides in part with the preceding. A storm arises at sea, awakening the crew's suspicion that someone guilty is on board (1:4ff.). Lots are cast, and the lot falls on Jonah, who is ordered to confess (*ngd* hiphil: v. 8). Here we are hardly dealing with a cultic ceremony, although it might be possible to speak of a cultic parody.[39]

The occurrence of *ngd* in these texts concerning the discovery of a transgression is certainly significant. The verb always appears in the second section, after identification of the guilty party, who must now confess what he has done. In such solemn contexts with a religio-cultic dimension, the scope of *ngd* transcends simple human declaration.

b. The law governing the offering of firstfruits (Dt. 26:1-11) contains two different rituals (vv. 3f. and 5ff.) whose central motif is a confession of faith by the Israelites. In vv. 3f. (a secondary addition by P[40]), the formula *higgaḏtî hayyôm lᵉYHWH 'ᵉlōheyḵā* occurs as a central element of the ritual. It is introduced by a ritual directive *(ûḇā'ṯā 'el-hakkōhēn)* with a few parallels in other texts where the verb *ngd* also occurs (Dt. 17:9; cf. Lev. 14:35). This introduction emphasizes the importance of the formula with *higgîḏ,* which refers to a solemn public proclamation. The liturgical "today" is an actualization of the historical "today" of the occupation. This "today" reappears in Dt. 30:18 in a curse formula, introduced by *higgaḏtî lāḵem hayyôm kî.* Here too *ngd* refers to a solemn proclamation, pronounced in the fictive setting of the covenant liturgy.[41]

c. In the Psalms, especially in the hymns, *ngd* is used repeatedly to express the proclamation of Yahweh's saving acts, the praise of the God who manifests himself to human beings. The hymnic formulas are not limited to the Psalms, but occur also in Isa. 42:12 and Am. 4:13.

(1) In Ps. 147:19f. *ngd* is synonymous with *ydʿ* and means "reveal, make known":

---

37. F. Horst, *Gottes Recht. ThB,* 12 (1961), 162.
38. Westermann, *TLOT,* II, 598.
39. R. G. Boling, *Joshua. AB,* 6 (1982), 354.
40. Seitz, *BWANT,* 93, 248.
41. P. Buis, *Deutéronome. SB* (1963), 187.

God reveals his word, makes known his statutes and ordinances. The word of God is creative (vv. 15-18) and revelatory (vv. 19f.). The doxology in Am. 4:13 represents Yahweh under this double aspect: creator and revealer. God reveals *(higgîḏ)* to mortals his plan for the world and his nature. One can say that Ps. 147:15-20 reflects a liturgy; the doxology in Amos is likewise a liturgical addition for the response of the congregation to the recitation of the prophetic text.[42] Ps. 111:6 states that Yahweh makes known the power of his works. This text uses the word *ma'ᵃśeh,* which also appears in conjunction with *higgîḏ* in Ps. 19:2(1): the firmament proclaims God's handiwork. According to Ps. 50:6; 97:6, the heavens declare the righteousness *(ṣeḏeq)* of God (cf. Ps. 22:32[31]; 71:18f., where *ngd* + *ṣdq* also appears). The whole creation is a language for the praise of God's revelation to humankind. In these texts, *ngd* means both praise of God, the proclamation of God's righteousness and works, and the revelation or manifestation of God. "The whole of Nature is in the service of a Supreme Being; its duty is to sing the praise of God and to be the vehicle of his revelation."[43]

(2) Yahweh opens the lips of the faithful and they proclaim his praise (*tᵉhillâ:* Ps. 51:17[15]). To declare God's praise is the same as to give God glory (Isa. 42:12), sing of God's wondrous deeds (Ps. 40:6[5]; 71:17), and proclaim God's greatness (71:19). The psalmist is to proclaim God's steadfast love and faithfulness (30:10[9]; 92:2f.[1f.]). Here *ngd* has as its objects *ḥeseḏ* and *'ᵉmeṯ,* two terms with clear liturgical overtones that are repeated frequently in the Psalms (25:10; 40:11f.[10f.]; 57:4[3]; 61:8[7]; 85:11[10]; 86:15; 115:1; 138:2) to describe an attribute or activity of God.[44] In 30:10(9) and 92:2f.(1f.), the parallelism is intensified by making both words dependent on the same verb *ngd,* but also by the relationship between *higgîḏ* and *hôḏâ.* To proclaim God's *ḥeseḏ* and *'ᵉmeṯ* is the same as to give God thanks (92:2f.[1f.]).

(3) The praise of God is to go on from mouth to mouth, "from generation to generation" (Ps. 145:4; cf. 22:31f.[30f.]; 71:18), "from day to day" (19:3[2]). These two expressions used in conjunction with *higgîḏ* point to a living tradition that constantly tells and proclaims the praise and acts of God. Ps. 145:4-7 specifies some of these acts of God, which we have already noted in conjunction with *higgîḏ: ma'ᵃśeykā* (v. 4a), *gᵉḇûrōṯeykā* (v. 4b), *kᵉḇôḏ hôḏekā* (v. 5a), *niplᵉ'ōṯeykā* (v. 5b), *gᵉḏōlōṯeykā* (v. 6b), *ṭûḇᵉkā* (v. 7), and *ṣiḏqāṯᵉkā* (v. 7b). Here we find most of the terms used in the Psalms as objects of *higgîḏ* to describe the proclamation of the acts and greatness of God, God's honor and majesty. In Ps. 145 these terms are introduced by a variety of verbs, all of them sometimes synonymous with *ngd: šibbaḥ,* "laud" (v. 4a, par. *higgîḏ*), *dibber* (v. 5; syn. with *ngd* in 40:6[5]), *'āmar* (145:6a, frequently interchangeable with *ngd*), and *sipper,* "tell" (v. 6b, par. *ngd* in 19:2[1]). Thus Ps. 145 furnishes a synthesis of the usage, meaning, and parallels of *higgîḏ,* without exhausting the richness of the verb in cultic contexts. From generation to generation, from day to day, the whole

---

42. See Weiser, *Psalms. OTL* (Eng. trans. 1962), 836; W. Brueggemann, "Amos IV 4-13 and Israel's Covenant Worship," *VT,* 15 (1965), 1-15.

43. Weiser, *OTL,* 198; cf. 633.

44. J. Scharbert, "Formgeschichte und Exegese von Ex 34,6f und seiner Parallelen," *Bibl,* 38 (1957), 130ff.

world (*kol-'āḏām:* 64:10[9]) is to proclaim the works of God. It is the eternal actuality of God's activity and its constant actualization in prayer and worship.

3. *Wisdom Contexts.* Finally, some texts from Wisdom Literature deserve mention.

a. Prov. 29:24 speaks of those who do not disclose a crime in court, even though failure to do so makes them vulnerable to the curse. The situation is the same as in Lev. 5:1 (cf. Jgs. 17:2), and the formulas employed are practically identical: *šāma' 'ālâ* and *lō' yaggîḏ.* The context is that of juridical wisdom with a religious background, since the curse presupposes an appeal to God against the one who refuses to testify.

Dt. 17:8-13 combines two legal systems, that of the priests, which finds expression in a *tôrâ,* and that of the judges, formulated in a *mišpāṭ.* The close linkage of the two pairs *tôrâ/mišpāṭ* and *hôrâ/higgîḏ* lends *ngd* a juridical and sapiential flavor.[45]

b. In wisdom the principle of tradition is fundamental. This principle is set down in various texts that use *ngd.* The traditions of the elders are the object of instruction of sons by their fathers (Ex. 13:8), the new generation by older generations (Dt. 32:7; Job 15:18; Eccl. 6:12). In this context *higgîḏ* takes on the sense of handing on or teaching everything that constitutes the religious and cultural heritage of the people, the wisdom of the elders.[46]

c. In Job 11:6 *higgîḏ* means "reveal" and has as its object "the secrets of wisdom." In this text, which formally resembles Ps. 51:7(5), Zophar expresses the wish that God would "open his lips" to instruct Job in the secrets of wisdom (v. 6). Divine wisdom surpasses human wisdom; Job discovers his ignorance through God's questions that he cannot answer (*higgîḏ:* 38:4). In the end Job acknowledges that he has spoken of wonders that transcend his comprehension: *higgaḏtî w^elō' 'āḇîn . . . w^elō' 'ēḏa'* (42:3).

V. 1. *LXX.* The LXX usually translates the hiphil of *ngd* with *anangéllō* or *apangéllō.* The former predominates in the prophetic books (47 out of 70 times), the latter in the Deuteronomistic history (95 out of 138). Other translations are relatively common in late documents: *deíknymi* (Gen. 41:25; Ezk. 40:4; 43:10), *hypodeíknymi* (Est. 2:10a,20; 3:4; 4:7a; 8:1; Dnl. 9:23; 10:21; 11:2; 2 Ch. 2:2[3]), *légō* (2 K. 22:10; Isa. 41:22b; Ruth 3:16; Est. 4:8), *prolégō* (Isa. 41:26b), *apokalýptō* (Josh. 2:20). In the last two verbs, we see the translator's intent to accentuate the sense of prediction or revelation.

2. *Dead Sea Scrolls.* The verb *ngd* does not appear often in the Dead Sea Scrolls; *neged* is more frequent, especially in 1QH, analogously to the OT. Of the occurrences of *higgîḏ,* 3 are especially interesting: 1QM 10:1 has Moses as subject and refers to theological "instructions."[47] The 2 other texts are also in the War Scroll and refer to earlier revelations. In 1QM 11:5 we find the formula *ka'^ašer higgaḏtâ lānû mē'āz lē'mōr,*

---

45. Weinfeld, 235f.

46. See IV.2.c above.

47. M. Burrows, "The Meaning of *'šr 'mr* in DSH," *VT,* 2 (1952), 255-260; I. Rabinowitz, *JBL,* 69 (1950), 45; Yadin, 314.

an allusion to Nu. 24:17-19; and 1QM 11:8 speaks of those who have seen the oracles *(ḥôzê tᵉʿûd̠ôt̠)* "through which God has predicted for us *(higgad̠tâ lānû)* the times of the wars of his hands."

3. *Jewish Literature.* The hiphil and hophal of *ngd* appear in the Targums, the Talmud, and midrashic literature with a meaning similar to that in the Bible. In this literature the most important term is *haggādâ,* which in later rabbinic literature denotes the nonlegal portions of biblical interpretation.[48]

Garcia-López

48. E. L. Dietrich, "Haggada," *RGG*³, III, 23f.

נָגַהּ *nāg̠ah;* נֹגַהּ *nōg̠ah;* נְגֹהוֹת *nᵉg̠ōhôt̠*

Contents: I. Occurrences. II. Meaning. III. Dead Sea Scrolls and LXX.

I. Occurrences. The root *ngh* occurs 6 times as a verb and 19 times as the noun *nōg̠ah.* In addition, *nᵉg̠ōhôt̠* is found in Isa. 59:9 and Aram. *nᵉg̠ōah* in Dnl. 6:20(Eng. v. 19). Cognates include Akk. *na/egû,* "be happy"; Ugar. *ngh,* "glow, shine"; Syr. *ngh,* "gleam," as a noun *nôghā',* "morning star."

Occurrences in combination with *'ôr* (Am. 5:20; Isa. 59:9; 60:19; etc.) as well as with *'ēš* (Isa. 4:5) and *lappîd̠* (Isa. 62:1), together with Prov. 4:18 and Dnl. 6:20(19), show that the use of *ngh* in the context of religious salvation and theophanies is based on the natural experience of pleasurable brightness.

II. Meaning. The usage of the verb, Prov. 4:18 (*nōg̠ah* as *nomen rectum*), and Ezk. 1:4,13,27f. together show that the root denotes not so much a source of light as the brightness emanating from it. It is used thus in theophanies, where fire and glowing coals emit *nōg̠ah* (Ezk. 1:13,27; Ps. 18:13[12] par. 2 S. 22:13f.). In Ezk. 1:28 "brightness" is likened to a rainbow. In 10:4 it emanates from the "glory of Yahweh"; cf. Isa. 4:5, where the → כבוד *kāḇôd̠* spreads over the pillar of clouds and fire, the latter characterized by *nōg̠ah.* In Hab. 3:4 God's glory is hidden in brightness like the sun.

The brightness associated with a theophany also means salvation for humankind. From gloom without brightness (*minnōg̠ah:* Isa. 8:22, emended on the basis of the LXX), a great light shines forth for the people (Isa. 9:1[2]). Kings shall come to its

nāg̠ah. F. Schnutenhaus, "Das Kommen und Erscheinen Gottes im AT," *ZAW,* 76 (1964), 1-22.

radiance (Isa. 60:3). God lightens the king's darkness (2 S. 22:29). Righteousness will shine out like the dawn (Isa. 62:1), and light shines on the way of the righteous (Job 22:28; Prov. 4:18). Eschatological hopes reach the point that neither the light of the sun nor the brightness of the moon will be needed, but God himself will be light and "glory" *(tip̱'ārâ)* (Isa. 60:19).

This meaning is underlined by antithetical statements concerning disaster, when the brightness of God's salvation fails. The day of Yahweh is darkness, not light (Am. 5:20). Then the stars will withdraw their shining (Jo. 2:10; 4[3]:15). The bright fire of the wicked is put out (Job 18:5). When God appears for judgment, *nōg̱ah* can also be used for the gleam of his flashing spear (Hab. 3:11). In the judgment against Babylon, sun, moon, and stars do not give their light (Isa. 13:10). Even in this context, however, an allusion to salvation is not absent: "The one who walks in darkness and has no light, let him trust in the name of Yahweh" (50:10; cf. 59:9).

Eising(†)

III. Dead Sea Scrolls and LXX. Despite the highly developed light/darkness dualism of the Essene documents from Qumran, *ngh* appears in this context only once, in 4Q184 8, where *nôgah* denotes the "shining brightness" that cloaks the righteous. In 4Q401 (ShirShab) B 6, the "brightness" of the *kāḇôḏ* of the Lord is mentioned (cf. Ezk. 1:27).

The LXX clearly did not have an exact notion of what the verb means, since it uses 5 different translations for 5 occurrences (e.g., *lámpein, phōtízein*). The noun *nōgah* created similar problems, even though here the translations *phéngos* (12 times) and *phō̂s* (4 times) predominate.

Fabry

נָגִיד *nāgîḏ*

Contents: I. Ancient Near East: 1. Aramaic; 2. Phoenician; 3. Ammonite; 4. Arabic; 5. Ethiopic; 6. Mandaic; 7. Samaritan. II. 1. Etymology; 2. Statistics; 3. Distribution; 4. Related Terms; 5. LXX; 6. Basic Meaning. III. Contexts: 1. Monarchy; 2. Temple; 3. Elsewhere. IV. Dead Sea Scrolls and Sirach.

---

nāgîḏ. A. Alt, "The Formation of the Israelite State in Palestine," *Essays on OT History and Religion* (Eng. trans., Oxford, 1966), 171-237; M. Buber, "Die Erzählung von Sauls Königswahl," *VT,* 6 (1956), 113-173; G. Buccellati, "Da Saul a David," *BibOr,* 1 (1959), 99-128; R. A. Carlson, *David, the Chosen King* (Stockholm, 1964); F. M. Cross, *Canaanite Myth and Hebrew Epic* (Cambridge, Mass., 1973); J. W. Flanagan, "Chiefs in Israel," *JSOT,* 20 (1981), 47-73; J. de Fraine, "Teocrazia e monarchia in Israele," *BibOr,* 1 (1959), 4-11; V. Fritz, "Die Deutungen des Königtums Sauls in den Überlieferungen von seiner Entstehung I Sam 9–11," *ZAW,* 88 (1976), 346-362, esp. 351-53; H. Gese, "Der Davidsbund und die Zionsbewegung," *ZTK,* 61

I. Ancient Near East.

1. *Aramaic.* In Old Aramaic the word *ngdy* appears in Sefire III, 10, with the meaning "my high ones," "my officers," or "my generals."[1] The context speaks of avenging the political murder of one of the partners in the treaty between King Bar-Ga'yah of Ktk and King Mati'-Il of Arpad (mid-8th century B.C.): "And if any of my brothers or any of my father's house or any of my sons or any of my high ones *(ngdy)* or any of my officers or any of the people who are subject to me . . . seeks my head to kill me — if they actually do kill me — you must come and avenge my blood."[2] The use of *ngdy* in the sequence "brothers — father's house — sons — high ones *(ngdy)* — officers ([*p*]*qd*)"[3] is informative with respect to the meaning of *nāgîḏ.* It shows that *ngdy* is a general term for "high" or "exalted" individuals, who either belong to the royal house by virtue of having been elevated to it or, if subordinate to it, are still superior to the military or civilian administrators, i.e., the "officers." Cautiously, therefore, we may conclude that "my high/exalted ones" *(ngdy)* refers to aristocrats or nobles who can hardly be understood simply as "generals" or military "commanders."

The word *ngdy* in Sefire III, 10 has also been read as *ngry,* "officer, prefect," and its meaning explained on the basis of Akk. *nāgiru(m),* "steward, military commandant, prefect," but *ngdy* appears to be the better reading.[4] We may also note, on the evidence

---

(1964), 10-26 = *Vom Sinai zum Zion. BEvT,* 64 (1974), 113-129; J. J. Glück, "Nagid-Shepherd," *VT,* 13 (1963), 144-150; S. D. Goitein, "The Title and Office of NAGID," *JQR,* 53 (1962), 93-119; B. Halpern, *The Constitution of the Monarchy in Israel. HSM,* 25 (1981), 1-11; T. Ishida, "נגיד, a Term for the Legitimation of Kingship," *AJBI,* 3 (1977), 35-51; P. Joüon, "Notes de lexicographie hébraïque, X: נָגִיד 'préposé,' d'où 'chef,' " *Bibl,* 17 (1936), 229-233; F. Langlamet, "Les récits de l'institution de la royauté (1 Sam., VII-XII)," *RB,* 77 (1970), 161-200; E. Lipiński, "Nāgīd, der Kronprinz," *VT,* 24 (1974), 497-99; G. C. Macholz, "NAGID, der Statthalter, 'praefectus,' " *Sefer Rendtorff. Festschrift R. Rendtorff. BDBAT,* 1 (1975), 59-72; T. N. D. Mettinger, *King and Messiah. CB,* 8 (1976); J. van der Ploeg, "Les chefs du peuple d'Israel et leurs titres," *RB,* 57 (1950), 40-61, esp. 45-47; W. Richter, "Die *nāgīd*-Formel," *BZ,* 9 (1965), 71-84; E. I. J. Rosenthal, "Some Aspects of the Hebrew Monarchy," *JSS,* 9 (1958), 1-18; L. Schmidt, *Menschlicher Erfolg und Jahwes Initiative. WMANT,* 38 (1970), esp. 141-170; S. Shaviv, "*nābî'* and *nāgîd* in 1 Samuel IX.1–X.16," *VT,* 34 (1984), 108-113; J. A. Soggin, "Charisma und Institution im Königtum Sauls," *ZAW,* 75 (1963), 53-65; *idem, Das Königtum in Israel. BZAW,* 104 (1967); T. Veijola, *Die ewige Dynastie. AnAcScFen,* 193 (1975); Y. Yeivin, "The Administration in Ancient Israel," *The Kingdom of Israel and Judah,* ed. A. Malamat (Jerusalem, 1961), 47-65 (Heb. with Eng. summary).

1. *KAI,* no. 224. For the first meaning see O. Rössler, *TUAT,* I/2 (1983), 187. For the second, J. A. Fitzmyer, *The Aramaic Inscriptions of Sefîre. BietOr,* 19 (1967), 112; *idem, CBQ,* 20 (1958), 459; cf. Cross, 220, n. 5; similarly E. Lipiński, *NERT,* 264: "commanders." For the third, Lipiński, *Studies in Aramaic Inscriptions and Onomastics,* I (Louvain, 1975), 56.

2. Sefire III, 9-11.

3. See R. Degen, *Altaramäische Grammatik der Inschriften des 10.-8. Jh.s v. Ch.* (Wiesbaden, [2]1978), 119; *TSSI,* II, 49; et al. On "officers," *pqd* (Sefire III, 4, 10, 13), see *DISO,* 234; Degen, 58; cf. Akk. *paqdu(m),* "agent, steward," *AHw,* II, 827; W. Eilers, *AfO,* 9 (1933/34), 333, with n. 4.

4. For *ngry* see A. Dupont-Sommer, *BMB,* 13 (1956), 32; *idem, Sem,* 1 (1948), 52; followed by M. Noth, *ZDPV,* 77 (1961), 150, with n. 88; *KAI,* I, 44; Degen, 21; S. Segert, *Altaramäische Grammatik* (Leipzig, 1975), 494; etc. For *ngdy* see Fitzmyer, 112f.; *DISO,* 174; followed by many others.

of many texts, that for much of its history and over a wide territory Akk. *nāgiru(m)* meant "herald"; only in one or two texts from the Elamite Empire does it have the meaning "high official," authorized, among other things, to command troops.[5] Thus the theory, based on the comparative evidence of Akk. *nāgiru(m),* that the Aramaic reading *ngry* means "officer, prefect" proves untenable.

In the Saqqara Papyrus (7th/6th century B.C.), the so-called Letter of Adon, the words *wngd' znh* [. . .] in l. 8 (fragmentary) have been translated "and this commandant [. . .]."[6] An alternative reading *ngr',* "officer, commander, official," from Akk. *nāgiru(m),* "steward, military commandant, prefect," has also been proposed.[7] As noted above, Akk. *nāgiru(m),* "herald," supports neither the alternative reading nor its proposed meaning. The reading *ngw',* "island, coastland, territory," instead of *ngd'* likewise has little to recommend it.[8] We may therefore understand the noun *ngd'* as a title meaning "high, exalted," denoting someone who has the authority to appoint a *pḫh,* "governor,"[9] and thus turns out to be superior to the latter. Whether the *ngd'* played any military role remains unproved. An Aramaic PN *ngd* appears in the seventh/sixth century B.C.[10]

The reading *ngydh* in a fragmentary context in one of the Elephantine papyri is to be understood either as the city name *Negîdâ,* a passive participle meaning "it is designated," or, less likely, a noun meaning "keel (of a ship)."[11] A fragmentary Aramaic text from Memphis (5th century) includes the word *ngyd,* which may mean "leader."[12]

Middle Hebrew and Jewish Aramaic use, respectively, *nāgîḏ* II and *neg̱îḏā',* "leader, prince," and *nāg̱ôḏ* and *nāg̱ôḏā',* "leader, director," in various contexts.[13]

2. *Phoenician.* The Old Phoenician Nora inscription (mid-9th century B.C.) uses the word *ngd.*[14] This might be the name of the colony *NGD.*[15] More likely it should be

---

5. For "herald" see *AHw,* II, 711; *CAD,* XI/1, 115-18. For "high official" see *CAD,* XI/1, 117f.

6. Dupont-Sommer, *Sem,* 1 (1948), 52; J. A. Fitzmyer, *Bibl,* 46 (1965), 45. See *KAI,* no. 266; see S. H. Horn, "When and Where Was the Aramaic Saqqara Papyrus Written?" *AUSS,* 6 (1968), 29-45.

7. Dupont-Sommer, *Sem,* 1 (1948), 52; but *KAI,* II, 314, remains undecided between *ngd'* and *ngr'.*

8. Fitzmyer, *Bibl,* 46 (1965), 55; contra H. L. Ginsberg, *BASOR,* 111 (1948), 25, n. 4c; followed by W. D. McHardy, *Documents from OT Times,* ed. D. Winton Thomas (New York, repr. 1961), 254; *TSSI,* II, 113, 115; et al.

9. *KAI,* II, 313; cf. II, 227f.

10. *CIS,* II, 112; cf. S. A. Cook, *A Glossary of the Aramaic Inscriptions* (Hildesheim, ^{2}1974), 80.

11. *AP,* 26, 8. For the first meaning see E. Sachau, *Aramäische Papyrus und Ostraka aus einer jüdischen Militär-Kolonie zu Elephantine,* 2 vols. (Leipzig, 1911), 46; for the second, *AP,* pp. 92, 94; for the third, R. A. Bowman, *AJSL,* 58 (1941), 309; cf. the Aram. root *ngd* I in *DISO,* 174.

12. N. Aimé-Giron, *Textes araméens d'Egypte* (Cairo, 1931), 13f.; for a different interpretation see Bowman, 310.

13. For Middle Hebrew see *ANH,* 262; *ChW,* I, 89; cf. Jastrow, 871f. For Jewish Aramaic see *WTM,* 332; cf. *ANH,* 262.

14. *KAI,* 46.

15. Z. S. Harris, *A Grammar of the Phoenician Language. AOS* (1936), 123; *KAI,* II, 63, reads *NGR.*

vocalized as *nagīd* and translated either as military "commandant" or "overseer" of the temple.[16] Although the meaning of the Nora inscription as a whole is not clear, it is reasonably certain that *ngd* in its immediate context has the meaning of *nagīd,* denoting the function and title of a "high" or "exalted" individual associated with the military or the temple.

3. *Ammonite.* In Ammonite the reading *ngd,* probably to be vocalized **nāgid,* appears for the first time in the recently discovered (and to date unpublished) Heshbon Ostracon XIII (6th century B.C.). Although the fragmentary nature of this difficult text does not permit a clear decision whether it is a PN *Nāgid,* a title in the sense of a military "commander,"[17] or a more general honorific "high, exalted," this inscription may be counted among the important occurrences of the word *nāgîḏ* outside Israel.

4. *Arabic.* In the Sabean dialect of Old South Arabic the noun *ngd* occurs in the sense of "upland, plateau."[18] The verbal forms of Classical Arab. *najada* I, "be high, rise up, arise, become manifest," and IV, "be exalted," as well as the modern Arabic noun *najd,* "upland, plateau,"[19] point to the long usage of various forms of the root *njd* with the basic meaning "be high, exalted."

5. *Ethiopic.* From the Ethiopic root *ngd,* "travel," derive in the Harari dialect the verb *nigdî,* "engage in trade (with or by means of caravans)," and the noun forms *näggade,* "wares," and *nugda,* "guest."[20] The Ethiopic root *ngd* is associated variously with Aram. *ndg,* "pull, flow," or Jewish Aram. *ngd',* "leader."[21]

6. *Mandaic.* Mandaic has the verb *ngd,* "pull, draw forward, pull out, spread; extend, expand, extract, lengthen," and the derived noun *ngada,* "extension, punishment, torture, pain."[22] It is unclear whether the root *ngd* in Mandaic is related directly to occurrences in Aramaic, Phoenician, Ammonite, etc., discussed above.

7. *Samaritan.* In Samaritan the qal stem of *ngd,* "lead, guide," is represented by the nominal ptcp. *ngwd* (vocalized *nāgūde*), "leader, guide."[23]

---

16. For the vocalization see Cross, 220, n. 5. The translation "commandant" was first proposed by F. Pili, *Frontiera,* III/7 (1970), 270; followed by B. Peckham, *Or,* 41 (1972), 465; et al. For "overseer" see A. Dupont-Sommer, *CRAI,* 1948, 15-24; *TSSI,* III, 27.
17. Oral communication from F. M. Cross, Harvard, December 1983.
18. Biella, 291.
19. Lane, I/8, 2752f.
20. W. Leslau, *Etymological Dictionary of Harari* (Berkeley, 1963), 118.
21. *HAL,* II, 665.
22. *MdD,* 288.
23. F. Rosenthal, ed., *An Aramaic Handbook. PLO,* 10 (1967), II/2, 7.

II. 1. *Etymology.* The subst. ptcp. *nāgîḏ* is a nominal *qaṭîl* formation.[24] It is not easy to determine whether it derives from the act. ptcp. (**qaṭil* >) *qaṭîl* or the pass. ptcp. *qaṭîl,* because in Hebrew the two forms coalesced phonologically, so that a *qaṭîl* form can derive from either the active or the passive participle.[25] In the latter case, however, the qal form is normally a *qaṭūl* formation.[26] For this reason, *nāgîḏ* probably derives from the qal active participle of the Hebrew verbal root *ngd.*[27]

Albrecht Alt has attempted to explain *nāgîḏ* as a passive participle of the hiphil form *higgîḏ,* denoting someone "proclaimed" by Yahweh.[28] But it can hardly be correct to base an etymology on the hiphil meaning of the Hebrew root.[29] The theory that derives *nāgîḏ* as a qal passive participle from the root *ngd,* with an original meaning "heir-apparent designated by the reigning king,"[30] must be considered improbable, because the qal passive participle normally results in a nominal *qaṭūl* formation,[31] so that the form would have to be *nāgûḏ*.

Other etymological theories derive *nāgîḏ* from the Hebrew prep. *negeḏ,* "in front of, before," in the sense of "one who is before others."[32] As an extension of this etymology, the meaning "principal, leader, prefect" has been proposed for *nāgîḏ*.[33] It remains to be shown, however, how the *qaṭîl* form *nāgîḏ* could have developed out of the prep. *negeḏ* or the original subst. *negeḏ,* "that which is facing, correspondence," since to date no such development has been found in Hebrew.[34]

J. J. Glück has attempted to connect the title *nāgîḏ* etymologically with the term *nōqēḏ,* "shepherd," deriving both words from a Semitic root *ngd/nqd,* so that *nāgîḏ* also means "shepherd."[35] This attempt might have been inspired by Henri Cazelles,[36] but was proposed independently by Glück. Against Glück's theory, it has been shown that the alternation of *g* and *q* is "methodologically inaccurate" with respect to his

---

24. E. König, *Historisch-kritisches Lehrgebäude der Hebräischen Sprache,* 2 vols. in 3 (Leipzig, 1881-97), II/2, 141; cf. Meyer, II, §37.4.

25. E. A. Speiser, *CBQ,* 25 (1963), 114, n. 10; Liver, 753; Richter, 72, n. 6. For the act. ptcp. see *NSS,* 184e, in the sense of "sayer"; cf. *GK,* §84[a]l; *BLe,* 470, §61nα; cf. → נביא *nāḇî'.* For the pass. ptcp., albeit with active meaning, see E. I. J. Rosenthal, *JJS,* 9 (1958), 7, n. 17 = *Studia Semitica,* 2 vols. (Cambridge, 1971), 9, n. 17.

26. Meyer, II, §37.5.

27. *HAL,* II, 667; *KBL*[2], 592; *GesB,* 483.

28. Alt, 195, n. 54.

29. Gese, 12, n. 7 = *BEvT,* 64 (1974), 115, n. 7.

30. Mettinger, 71f.; similarly T. C. G. Thornton, *JTS,* 14 (1963), 8.

31. Meyer, II, §37.5; cf. Richter, 72, n. 6.

32. Joüon, 229f.: "celui qui est devant les autres"; cf. *BDB,* 617; *LexHebAram,* 495; K. Seybold, *Das davidische Königtum im Zeugnis der Propheten. FRLANT,* 107 (1972), 30, n. 35.

33. Joüon, 229, 231; cf. Macholz, 65.

34. Meyer, II, §34; cf. E. Brønno, *Studien über Hebräische Morphologie und Vokalismus* (Leipzig, 1943), 242f.; W. J. Gerber, *Die hebräischen Verba denominativa* (1896), 139. On the derivation see *HAL,* II, 666; Meyer, II, §87.3f.

35. Pp. 144-150.

36. H. Cazelles, review of R. de Vaux, *AncIsr, VT,* 8 (1958), 321-26; cf. C. Schedl, *History of the OT,* 5 vols. (Eng. trans., Staten Island, 1972), III, 57-59.

Semitic examples and remains totally unproved in Semitic.[37] The evidence of comparative Semitic linguistics does not support Glück's theory, and therefore his approach has gained no following.[38] Furthermore, the meaning "shepherd" does not agree with the usage of the *nāgîḏ* concept in the context of the Israelite monarchy or in other OT usage.

On the basic of comparative Semitics,[39] we may hypothesize a qal form *ngd,* of West Semitic origin; this form is not attested in the OT, which uses only the hiphil. The various West Semitic usages of the verbal and nominal forms point to the meaning "be high, be exalted" for the Hebrew qal.[40] The meaning of the qal *ngd* is suggestive for the meaning of the subst. *nāgîḏ,*[41] which derives from the qal active participle, a *qaṭîl* formation.

2. *Statistics.* The word *nāgîḏ* occurs 44 times in the OT.

To explain the difficulty of the MT in 1 Ch. 27:4, some scholars delete as corrupt the words *ûmaḥ^a^luqtô ûmiqlôṯ hannāgîḏ,* which are not represented in LXX^B^ and other LXX MSS.; others claim that the words are a marginal gloss to v. 4a that has intruded into the text of 27:4 on account of the name in 11:12.[42] It is quite possible, however, that the *lectio difficilior* is the original reading. In 2 Ch. 6:6 the word *nāgîḏ* is inserted into the statement "and I have chosen David to be [*nāgîḏ*] over my people Israel" on the evidence of the Peshitta, the Targ., and a few Hebrew MSS.[43] Scholars resort to other conjectural emendations in 1 S. 16:6, changing the literal translation "his anointed stands before Yahweh" to "the *nāgîḏ* [MT: *negeḏ*] of Yahweh, his anointed, stands."[44] The fact that *nāgîḏ* always stands in relationship to the people by itself rules out this emendation. In 2 Ch. 6:6 *nāgîḏ* would not be out of place, but the context and meaning of the passage do not require it. In Prov. 8:6 some scholars have repointed *n^e^gîḏîm,* "exalted things, noble things," as *n^e^gāḏîm,* "upright things, right things" (from *negeḏ*); others have emended it to *n^e^ḵōḥîm,* "upright things, just things."[45] Here, too, however,

---

37. Richter, 72, n. 7; on other grounds: Gese, 12, n. 7 = *BEvT,* 64, 115, n. 7; Carlson, 53, n. 1.

38. Macholz, 71, n. 38; Ishida, 49, n. 8; Halpern, 257, n. 2; etc.

39. See I.1-4 above.

40. See I above; *GesTh,* 485f.; *GesB,* 482; Fritz, 351; similarly J. de Fraine, *L'aspect religieux de la royauté israélite. AnBibl,* 3 (1954), 98, who assigns the Hebrew qal stem the meaning "s'élever [rise]" on the basis of limited comparative evidence.

41. See II.6 below.

42. For the former see *BHK*[3]; *BHS; HAL,* II, 668. For the latter see W. Rudolph, *Chronikbücher. HAT,* XXI (1955), 178; cf. J. M. Myers, *I Chronicles. AB,* 12 (1965), 179, n. a; Mettinger, 152.

43. *BHK*[3]; *BHS;* J. M. Myers, *II Chronicles. AB,* 13 (1965), 31.

44. F. Perles, *Analekten zur Textkritik des ATs,* I (1895), 64; Glück, 149, with n. 6; etc.; *BHK*[3]; *KBL*[2], 592; *HAL,* II, 668 (with "?").

45. For the former see L. H. Grollenberg, *RB,* 59 (1952), 40f.; followed by W. McKane, *Proverbs. OTL* (1970), 345; *BHK;* mentioned by *HAL,* II, 666 (with "?"). For the latter see, e.g., R. B. Y. Scott, *Proverbs. AB,* 18 (1965), 66, with n. b.

it is possible to retain the MT and read n^e*gîḏîm* as an abstract plural: "I speak exalted things."[46] It seems best to let matters rest with the 44 occurrences of the MT.[47]

3. *Distribution.* The noun *nāḡîḏ* occurs in 14 OT books. These occurrences are concentrated especially in the historical books, with 33 occurrences (1-2 Chronicles: 21; 1-2 Samuel: 7; 1-2 Kings: 4; Neh. 11:11). There are 4 occurrences in Wisdom Literature (Job 29:10; 31:37; Prov. 8:6; 28:16), 3 in the Major Prophets (Isa. 55:4; Jer. 20:1; Ezk. 28:2), and 3 in Apocalyptic Literature (Dnl. 9:25,26; 11:22). There is a single occurrence in the Psalms (Ps. 76:13[Eng. v. 12]). It is particularly noteworthy that in the historical books the earliest occurrences refer to Saul (1 S. 9:16; 10:1); no *nāḡîḏ* is mentioned before him in the period prior to the Israelite state.[48] Most occurrences of the term refer to persons who were or were to become kings: Saul (2), David (7), Solomon (2), Jeroboam, Abijah, Baasha, and Hezekiah (1 each). A special concentration (11 occurrences) refers to the three kings who reigned over all Israel. The second greatest concentration (8 occurrences) refers to officials with responsibilities in or over the temple (1 Ch. 9:11,20; 26:24; 2 Ch. 28:7; 31:12,13; 35:8; Neh. 11:11). The remaining occurrences refer to various persons both within and without Israel.[49]

4. *Related Terms.* In Ps. 76:13(12) the plural of → מלך *meleḵ* appears in parallelism with n^e*gîḏîm,* "exalted ones, high ones" (traditionally: "princes"). The title of rank, however, is by no means identical with the "kings of the earth"; it is also used when the "exalted ones" and the "kings of the earth" belong to the powers hostile to Zion/Jerusalem, the city of God (46:7[6]; 48:5[4]). In the early period of the monarchy, *nāḡîḏ* is by no means identical with *meleḵ.*[50] The theory that *nāḡîḏ* is the Deuteronomistic alternative to *meleḵ* has also been rejected, correctly.[51] The term *nāḡîḏ* can refer to persons who are to become king but are not equated with the king before their acclamation.[52] In the title "king," primary emphasis is on the political element, while in the *nāḡîḏ* title the religious and sacral element stands in the foreground. A special notion of majesty and honor is peculiar to the *nāḡîḏ* title, so that *nāḡîḏ* and *meleḵ* may not simply be employed indiscriminately.[53] Both titles may be associated with a single person, but each retains its distinctive elements (cf. 2 S. 5:2f.).

It is important to examine the relationship between *nāḡîḏ* and → קָצִין *qāṣîn,* because

---

46. H. Ringgren, *Sprüche. ATD,* 16/1 (^{3}1981), 38; B. Gemser, *Sprüche Salomos. HAT,* XVI (^{3}1963), 44; O. Plöger, *Sprüche Salomos. BK,* XVII (1983), 85f.

47. Mettinger, 152, et al.

48. See II.4 below.

49. See III.3 below.

50. Contra Rosenthal, 8, et al.

51. Contra esp. Carlson, 52-55; see W. Richter, *Traditionsgeschichtliche Untersuchungen zum Richterbuch. BBB,* 18 (1963), 149ff., 215f.; *idem, BZ,* 9, 74, n. 9; W. Dietrich, *Prophetie und Geschichte. FRLANT,* 108 (1972), 15ff., 51-55, 112ff.; Mettinger, 166f.; et al.

52. J. A. Soggin, *TLOT,* II, 676.

53. W. Eichrodt, *Theology of the OT. OTL,* 2 vols. (Eng. trans. 1961-67), I, 444; contra Rosenthal; Carlson; I. Lewy, *VT,* 7 (1957), 325.

Martin Noth's suggestion that in the premonarchic period *nāgîḏ* "meant the man called by God to undertake a military action"[54] has been accepted in various quarters. The *nāgîḏ* is looked on as the "leader of the militia" in the period of the judges, a military commander, a "person endowed with judicial and military charisma," or an individual "placed at the head of the amphictyony, exalted."[55] This is not the place to pursue the problem of the existence of an Israelite amphictyony.[56] Another theory assigns the *nāgîḏ* title quite generally to the leader of the (holy) wars of Yahweh in the premonarchic period;[57] this theory, too, is problematic.

Insuperable problems stand in the way of these various hypotheses connected with the military history of the premonarchic period: (1) Many scholars have pointed out that the term *nāgîḏ* does not appear in any of the passages or historical texts of the premonarchic period.[58] (2) The title *qāṣîn* is used in the sense of "leader of the militia" in Josh. 10:24; Jgs. 11:6,11; Isa. 22:3; and finally Dnl. 11:18.[59] The premonarchic period is thus familiar with the title "leader of the militia," but this title is *qāṣîn,* not *nāgîḏ*. (3) The title *śar* frequently denotes the "commander-in-chief," "supreme commander," or "field commander," especially in the construct phrase *śar ṣāḇā'* (Gen. 21:22,32; 26:26; Josh. 5:14; Jgs. 4:7; 1 S. 12:9; 14:50; 17:55; etc.), but never in conjunction with the formulaic phrase "*nāgîḏ* over my/his people" (1 S. 9:16; 13:14; 25:30; 2 S. 6:21; 7:8; 1 K. 14:7; 16:2; etc.); here too there is no support for associating *nāgîḏ* with military leadership. (4) Some have proposed that the word → עם *ʿam* in the phrase "*nāgîḏ* over my/his people" denotes the "free male property owners capable of bearing arms" dwelling in the hereditary territory assigned to the amphictyonic league and thus supports "leader of the militia" or the like as the premonarchic meaning of the title *nāgîḏ*.[60] This theory has been disproved by the demonstration that in the passages in question the term *ʿam* means "relatives" or "clan."[61] These problems make hypotheses concerning the *nāgîḏ* title as denoting a premonarchic military leader appear unlikely and in need of demonstration.

We must examine briefly the relationship between *nāgîḏ* and → שׂר *śar,* "commander, chief," because three passages use both terms in semasiological proximity

---

54. M. Noth, *History of Israel* (Eng. trans., New York, ^{2}1960), 169, n. 1.

55. For the first see Schmidt, *WMANT,* 38, 91, 123, 144, 152ff. For the second see Cross, 120; W. F. Albright, *Samuel and the Beginnings of the Prophetic Movement* (Cincinnati, 1961), 15f.; Veijola, 129, n. 16. For the third see Soggin, *ZAW,* 75 (1963), 61. For the last see Gese, 12 = *BEvT,* 64, 115.

56. See R. de Vaux, *The Early History of Israel* (Eng. trans., Philadelphia, 1978), 695-716.

57. Richter, *BZ,* 9, 82; R. Smend, *Die Bundesformel. ThS,* 68 (1963), 19.

58. Ishida, 41f.; et al.

59. On Josh. 10:24 see de Vaux, *Early History,* 761; on Isa. 22:3 see H. Wildberger, *Isaiah 13–27* (Eng. trans., Minneapolis, 1997), 362; on Dnl. 11:18 see L. F. Hartman and A. A. Di Lella, *Daniel. AB,* 23 (1978), 268.

60. Richter, 77; similarly Smend, *Bundesformel,* 11ff.

61. N. Lohfink, "Beobachtungen zur Geschichte des Ausdrucks עם יהוה," *Probleme biblischer Theologie. Festschrift G. von Rad* (Munich, 1971), 283-86; cf. A. R. Hulst, *TLOT,* II, 905f.

(1 Ch. 13:1; 2 Ch. 32:21; Job 29:9f.). The usage of the term *śar* in the time of Saul (1 S. 14:50; 17:18,55; 18:13; 22:2; 26:5) shows clearly that the bearer of this title exercised military leadership as a "commander" or "officer."[62] This observation makes it difficult to understand Saul bearing the title *nāḡîḏ* as a military commander or commandant. The term *śar* conveys this meaning, but not *nāḡîḏ*. In the army as organized under David (2 S. 18:1-5; 24:1-9), *śar* became a technical term for any kind of military commander. According to 1 Ch. 13:1, David consulted "with the commanders *(śārîm)* of the thousands and the hundreds and with all the exalted ones [*n*ᵉ*ḡîḏîm:* traditionally 'princes']." Here we can see a distinction between the "commanders" of the army and the "exalted ones," the aristocracy or nobility of the "assembly" (→ קהל *qāhāl*) of Israel (v. 2), which included the elders and the heads of tribes and families. In Job 29:9f. *śar* parallels *nāḡîḏ:* "the chiefs *(śārîm)* refrained from talking, . . . the voice of the exalted *(n*ᵉ*ḡîḏîm)* was hushed." The two terms are related in meaning but not synonymous. A tripartite division of the Assyrian camp is attested in 2 Ch. 32:21: "all the mighty warriors [*kol-gibbôr,* collective sg.] and superiors [*nāḡîḏ,* collective sg.] and commanders *(śārîm)*" were cut off by the angel of Yahweh. Like the warriors and commanders, the "superiors" belonged to the leadership of the Assyrian army.

Another term associated with *nāḡîḏ* and its semantic field is → רֹאשׁ *rō'š,* used figuratively from early times for the "head" of a social group,[63] in the sense of "chiefs of the people" (*rā'šê hā'ām:* Nu. 25:4), "head of a clan" (*rō'š 'ummôṯ:* Nu. 25:15), "heads" of your tribes (Dt. 1:15; 5:23), "heads of the tribes" (Nu. 30:2; 1 K. 8:1). The use of the term *rō'š* for the "head" or chief of the people, family, or clan in the premonarchic and monarchic period is significant, because it also addresses the question whether the *nāḡîḏ* played the sociological role of a leader or "chief."[64] The proposal to understand *nāḡîḏ* as the "chief" of a social group appears to find little support in OT usage or in the ancient Near East.

Another sociopolitical theory understands *nāḡîḏ* as "governor" or "prefect," exercising political authority over a specific territory.[65] This hypothesis, too, is unsatisfactory. It is based on 1 K. 1:35 and disregards earlier texts as secondary.[66] We must also not overlook that the term for "governor" or "prefect" was *śar hā'îr* (1 K. 22:26; 2 K. 23:8; 2 Ch. 34:8; Jer. 51:59).[67]

This survey of OT titles or terms from the sociological, political, and military spheres has shown that *nāḡîḏ* is not used synonymously with any other term. Each has its own semantic domain.

---

62. C. Schäfer-Lichtenberger, *Stadt und Eidgenossenschaft im AT. BZAW,* 156 (1983), 250f.

63. J. R. Bartlett, "The Use of the Word ראשׁ as a Title in the OT," *VT,* 19 (1969), 1-10; H.-P. Müller, *TLOT,* III, 1184-94.

64. Yeivin, 47ff.; *idem,* "Administration," *The Age of the Monarchies: Culture and Society,* IV/2, ed. A. Malamat (Jerusalem, 1979), 171; Flanagan, 67f.

65. Macholz, 64.

66. See the criticism by Ishida, 40f.

67. Yeivin, *Age of the Monarchies,* IV/2, 167.

5. *LXX.* The LXX uses five different nouns to translate *nāḡîḏ*. The most frequent is *hēgoúmenos* (28 times).[68] There are 8 occurrences of *árchōn,*[69] besides one additional occurrence in an expansion of the text of 1 S. 10:1 not found in the MT. In the various translations it is impossible to detect a principle that would explain why the title *nāḡîḏ* is rendered differently even when the same person is involved. The term *basileús* is used in 1 Ch. 28:4; 29:22; Prov. 28:16.[70] Here the notion of kingship stands in the foreground. The other terms emphasize the notion of leadership or official authority. In Neh. 11:11 the prep. *apénanti* replaces the noun *nāḡîḏ,* and in three poetic texts (Job 29:10; 31:37; Prov. 8:6) the translation is so periphrastic that no Greek noun represents the word *nāḡîḏ*.

6. *Basic Meaning.* The qal of the Hebrew root *ngd* means "be high, exalted."[71] The *qaṭîl* form *nāḡîḏ* derived from this stem thus has the original basic meaning "high, exalted."[72] In the first instance, *nāḡîḏ* appears to have denoted a function;[73] the diversity of OT usage indicates that it became an honorific and specifically a title of nobility for people appointed to various positions. This broad definition of the word's basic meaning does justice to the wide range of OT usage.[74]

III. Contexts.

1. *Monarchy.* The term *nāḡîḏ* first appears in 1 S. 9:16; 10:1 with reference to Saul in the account of how the monarchy began (9:1–10:16), which account is probably contemporary with Saul.[75] Samuel is informed that he is to anoint a man from the land of Benjamin "to be *nāḡîḏ* over my people Israel" (9:16). The traditional translation of *nāḡîḏ* is "prince," but this translation fits neither the context nor the philological evidence;[76] here it is better translated "Highness" as a title of majesty. Saul is chosen by Yahweh in a charismatic call like that of a prophet and is anointed to this high position (10:1). God's choice of Saul as *nāḡîḏ* is a response to Israel's outcry (→ זעק *zāʿaq*), to save (→ ישׁע *yšʿ*) Israel from the hand of the Philistines (9:16). This had formerly been the function of the judges (Jgs. 3:31; 6:14f.,31,36f.; 10:1; 13:5) and was later the function of the king (1 S. 10:27; Hos. 13:10; Jer. 23:6).[77] In a private ceremony Samuel anoints Saul to be the exalted ruler *(nāḡîḏ)* over Yahweh's heritage (→ נחלה

68. See F. Büchsel, "ἡγέομαι," *TDNT,* II, 907f.
69. G. Delling, *TDNT,* I, 488f.
70. G. von Rad, *TDNT,* I, 565-571.
71. See II.1 above.
72. Similarly Gese, 12 = *BEvT,* 64, 115: "one raised up."
73. Van der Ploeg, 47: "eminent person," citing Arab. *najada*.
74. See III below. Cf. W. Zimmerli, *Ezekiel 2. Herm* (Eng. trans. 1983), 76f.; Halpern, 266, n. 78.
75. T. Ishida, *The Royal Dynasties in Ancient Israel. BZAW,* 142 (1977), 43; Richter, 72f.; etc. Various attempts at source analysis are noted in B. C. Birch, *The Rise of the Israelite Monarchy. SBLDS,* 27 (1976), 29-42; Ishida, *BZAW,* 142, 26-54; Halpern, 152f.; etc.
76. Cf. *HAL,* II, 668: "leader." See II.1 and II.6 above.
77. H. J. Boecker, *Redeformen des Rechtslebens im AT. WMANT,* 14 (1964), 61-66.

naḥ^a^lâ) (1 S. 10:1). Saul's anointing as *nāgîḏ* by the seer Samuel is not identical with his acclamation as king by the people (10:17-27) or his later anointing as king (15:1,17).[78] The divine call to be *nāgîḏ* and the prophetic anointing as *nāgîḏ* empower the one on whom the title "Highness" is bestowed to perform the function of saving the people from the hand of the enemy and to exercise broadly defined rulership over the heritage of Yahweh (10:1).[79] (The LXX has a longer text: "Has the Lord not anointed you as leader over his people, over Israel? And you are to rule among the people of the Lord, and you are to save them from the hand of their enemies. And this shall be the sign to you, that the Lord has anointed you as leader over his own.")[80]

The *nāgîḏ* title is applied most frequently to David (1 S. 13:14; 25:30; 2 S. 5:2 par. 1 Ch. 11:2; 2 S. 6:21; 7:8 par. 1 Ch. 17:7). In the context of Saul's failure, Samuel announces that Yahweh has sought a man after his own heart and "appointed him to be *nāgîḏ* over his people" (1 S. 13:14).[81] In the story of David's rise (1 S. 16:14–2 S. 5), Abigail uses equally formulaic language to announce that Yahweh "has appointed [David] *nāgîḏ* over Israel" (1 S. 25:30; the perf. *w^e^ṣiww^e^ḵā* is to be understood syntactically as a past tense[82]). David speaks to Michal about his appointment as *nāgîḏ* in place of Saul and Saul's household (2 S. 6:21). These statements emphasize Yahweh's appointment of David as *nāgîḏ*. Nonetheless, at Hebron he is anointed as king by the elders of the Israelite tribes, following a covenant ceremony (2 S. 5:3 par. 1 Ch. 11:3). However, Samuel had already privately anointed David as king (1 S. 16:13), so that we are left with the impression that charismatic, sacral, and political ceremonies are closely conjoined. It is clear that being chosen as *nāgîḏ* by God is a legitimation of leadership over Israel (cf. 2 Ch. 6:5); the anointing as king that follows is a ceremony that provides popular recognition in the presence of the elders of the people.

The prophecy of Nathan (2 S. 7) cites the words of Yahweh of hosts: "I took you from the pasture, from following the sheep, to be *nāgîḏ* over my people Israel" (v. 8; cf. 1 Ch. 17:7). David's exaltation from tending sheep (cf. 1 S. 16:11f.; 17:15-19,34f.; Ps. 78:70f.) to being *nāgîḏ* over the people of Yahweh is an act of divine election (→ לקח *lāqaḥ:* Ps. 78:70) to leadership over God's own people.[83]

In the context of the Davidic succession (1 K. 1:1–2:46) and the threat to it in the person of Adonijah (1:15-27), David determines his successor by decree: "There [by the Gihon] let the priest Zadok and the prophet Nathan anoint him [Solomon] as king over Israel. . . . It is he [Solomon] that shall be king in my place; for I have appointed him to be *nāgîḏ* over Israel and Judah" (1:34f.). Here we see that being *nāgîḏ* and becoming king are closely conjoined but are nevertheless not identical: being *nāgîḏ* is expressed by the perfect, and becoming king, a future event, is expressed by the imperfect. (Richter interprets the tenses as all referring to the future, but others reject

---

78. See II.4 above; cf. Alt, 189ff.
79. See II.4 above.
80. H. J. Stoebe, *Das erste Buch Samuelis. KAT,* VIII/1 (1973), 197.
81. *Ibid.,* 251f.
82. Halpern, 5; contra Richter, 75.
83. Seybold, *FRLANT,* 107 (1972), 30.

this interpretation with weighty arguments.)[84] Here designation as *nāg̱îḏ* is neither selection as "crown prince" nor appointment as "governor."[85] It is to be understood as a title of majesty, whereby David hands on to his successor the status of *nāg̱îḏ* to which he had been elevated by Yahweh, thus legitimizing and safeguarding the succession by an appeal to Yahweh (contra Trygvve Mettinger, who uses a questionable dating of 1 K. 1:35 to argue for an original and "normal" [i.e., secular] usage of *nāg̱îḏ,* from which the theological meaning was later derived and applied redactionally to Saul and David[86]). The subsequent anointing of Solomon as king by the priest Zadok makes Solomon David's coregent (1 K. 1:39; 1 Ch. 29:28). 1 Ch. 29:22 tells of the appointment and anointing of Solomon as the *nāg̱îḏ* of Yahweh.[87] We must not overlook that the appointment of Solomon as *nāg̱îḏ* "over Israel and Judah" (1 K. 1:35) serves both to safeguard the royal succession and to maintain the political unity of all Israel.[88] We must remember that the words "over Israel" in the appointment of Saul (1 S. 9:16) and David (1 S. 25:30; 2 S. 5:2; 6:21; 7:8) as *nāg̱îḏ* can hardly be used as an argument for a premonarchic or North Israelite origin of the title *nāg̱îḏ;*[89] neither can they be limited to the North Israelite tribes alone and their territory during the later period of the divided kingdoms. Each of the three rulers of all Israel — Saul, David, and Solomon — bears personally the twin titles *nāg̱îḏ* and "king." The transfer of the *nāg̱îḏ* title from David to Solomon points to a function as ruler that the *nāg̱îḏ* can pass on to his successor. Here we see an additional aspect of the *nāg̱îḏ* title, which had been used previously only by Samuel (1 S. 9:16) and Nathan (2 S. 7:8), as a term denoting a charismatic call and exaltation. In the context of royal succession, the status of *nāg̱îḏ,* established by Yahweh, can be transferred to secure the succession. I conclude, therefore, that *nāg̱îḏ* does not have simply the profane sense of "king designate," "designated heir," or "crown prince"; for the Israelite expression for these terms is "king's son" (2 K. 15:5), corresponding to Akk. *mār šarri.*[90]

Rehoboam, too, the son of Solomon, appointed his son Abijah, the son of Maacah (2 Ch. 11:18-20), "as chief [→ ראשׁ *rō'š*], as *nāg̱îḏ* among his brothers, for he intended to make him king" (11:22). The brothers were made local governors (v. 23), and Abijah was to be over them as "chief" and "Highness." This reference shows that the *nāg̱îḏ* was not a "governor,"[91] but was superior to governors. It also illustrates the decided difference between *nāg̱îḏ* and king *(meleḵ):* Abijah is not yet king; he is *nāg̱îḏ* and will eventually become king. But becoming king does not depend absolutely on being *nāg̱îḏ.*

---

84. Contra Richter, 75, see Mettinger, 162; Halpern, 6f.

85. For the latter see Macholz, 64. For the former see Thornton, *JTS,* 14, 8: "heir to the throne"; Lipiński, *VT,* 24, 498: "crown prince"; cf. Ishida, *AJBI,* 3, 39, against this interpretation.

86. Pp. 162-67.

87. W. Rudolph, *HAT,* XXI, 192f.; cf. Halpern, 7, with suggested emendations.

88. Richter, *BBB,* 18 (^{2}1966), 291.

89. Halpern, 6-8; Macholz, 65f.; et al.

90. *AHw,* II, 615b. For the translations see, respectively, Ishida, 39f.; Mettinger, 160; Lipiński, 499.

91. Contra Macholz, 59ff.

Of the forty-three kings of Israel, only seven were *nāgîḏ* (Saul, David, Solomon, Abijah, Jeroboam, Baasha, and Hezekiah). Every one of these seven *n*[e]*gîḏîm* was or became king, but not every Israelite king was *nāgîḏ*.

The prophet Abijah instructs the wife of King Jeroboam to convey to her husband the word of Yahweh: "Because I exalted you from among the people, made you *nāgîḏ* over my people Israel . . . yet you have not been like my servant David, who kept my commandments, . . . therefore behold, I will bring evil upon the house of Jeroboam" (1 K. 14:7-10). Here we are not told when and how Jeroboam became *nāgîḏ,* but only *that* he was exalted (→ רום *rûm*) and thus became Yahweh's *nāgîḏ* over his people.

The prophet Jehu proclaims a threat from Yahweh against Baasha: "Since I exalted you out of the dust and made you *nāgîḏ* over my people Israel, but you have walked in the way of Jeroboam, . . . behold, I will consume Baasha and his house" (1 K. 16:2f.). "Exalting out of the dust" appears to be related to Akk. *mār lā mammānim,* "son of a nobody,"[92] i.e., someone of lowly origin; the expression emphasizes Yahweh's raising *(rûm)* of Baasha, which is connected with his exaltation to the status of *nāgîḏ*.

A word concerning Hezekiah comes to Isaiah, in which the king is called "*nāgîḏ* of my people" (2 K. 20:5). In this context the concern is preservation of the Davidic dynasty and the city of Jerusalem (v. 6) in the face of Assyrian assault. Yahweh speaks as "God of your father David," and Hezekiah bears the title of majesty "*nāgîḏ* of my people," in which we hear his dynastic position as David's successor.

In summary, the title *nāgîḏ* was first used in ancient Israel at the beginning of Saul's reign; with the exception of Hezekiah, it was used of Israelite rulers only in the period from Saul to Baasha. The meaning "exalted, Highness" for *nāgîḏ,* embodying election, appointment, exaltation, and anointing, is based on philological and contextual evidence. From the beginning, its theological usage reflected Yahweh's initiative; this usage was preserved even when the one who had personally been chosen and "exalted" by Yahweh handed on the status and authority of *nāgîḏ* to his successor (David to Solomon and Rehoboam to Abijah) when the dynastic succession was in danger or in question. Every *nāgîḏ* in Israel was or became king, but not every king was or became *nāgîḏ*. The titles *nāgîḏ* and "king" were not synonymous or interchangeable. The authority and dignity of the *nāgîḏ* derived directly from God, even when they were handed on by a father to his son or by a king to his successor. The one "exalted" by God exercised rule and leadership only over the people of Yahweh, in every case "his/my people." Never are they described as the people of the earthly *nāgîḏ*. Being *nāgîḏ* was therefore always a divine gift, which had its full meaning and fundamental significance in the proper relationship of God's covenant (cf. 2 S. 7). When this covenant was violated, the status of *nāgîḏ* could be withdrawn (1 K. 14:7f.; 16:1-7) and given to another.

The Chronicler's history contains several texts that apply the title *nāgîḏ* to the king (1 Ch. 5:2; 22:1 par. 2 S. 5:2; 17:7 par. 2 S. 7:8; 28:4; 29:22; 2 Ch. 6:5; 11:22). In 1 Ch. 5:2 a Judahite who can only be David is called *nāgîḏ*. In an address concerning

92. *AHw,* II, 601.

his successor (1 Ch. 28:1-10), David refers to his own divine election as king and Judah's election as *nāgîḏ* (v. 4). In this text, unique in the OT, election by Yahweh and Judah's exaltation to *nāgîḏ* are linked in such a way as to legitimize David and his successor Solomon.

2. *Temple.* The term *nāgîḏ* appears frequently in the Chronicler's history as a title of individuals who exercise primary authority in or over the "house of God," i.e., the temple. In 1 Ch. 9:11 (par. Neh. 11:11), we find the titular phrase *n^egîḏ-bêṯ-hā'^elōhîm,* "exalted one of the house of God" (traditionally, "prince in the house of God"; NRSV: "chief officer of the house of God"), probably referring to the high priest in Jerusalem.[93] The title *nāgîḏ* is to be distinguished from the term *pāqîḏ,* "overseer" (→ פקד *pqd*), of priests (Neh. 11:14; cf. 11:22; 12:42), for the *pāqîḏ* can be an agent of the high priest (2 Ch. 24:11).[94] In Jer. 20:1 there is a unique occurrence of the expression *pāqîḏ nāgîḏ,* referring to the priest Pashhur, who combines in his own person the administrative duties of the *pāqîḏ,* the "overseer" of the temple, and the *nāgîḏ* or high priest. The title *nāgîḏ* is also applied to the high priest in 2 Ch. 31:13. The title "exalted one of the house of God" may be abbreviated to *n^egîḏ-habbayiṯ,* "exalted one of the house," in 28:7. Even in this abbreviated form, it refers to the high priest, or possibly to the "overseer of the [king's] house."[95] The pl. *n^egîḏîm* in 35:8 refers to a number of "exalted ones of the house of God," cultic functionaries in the temple. They include the "chief officer *(nāgîḏ)* over the contributions" (31:12), assisted by other cultic officials as "overseers" (*p^eqîḏîm:* v. 13). The chief treasurer of the house of God is also entitled *nāgîḏ* (1 Ch. 26:24). The gatekeepers of the temple, too, had their *nāgîḏ,* who served as their chief (1 Ch. 9:20). The honored position of the temple *n^egîḏîm* appears to reflect, even in late texts of the OT, the divine appointment and charismatic origin of the title *nāgîḏ*.

3. *Elsewhere.* 2 Ch. 19:11 has a totally secular usage of the term *nāgîḏ;* the context is the definition of responsibilities in the reorganized judicial system. Zebadiah, the "*nāgîḏ* of the house of Judah," is the "senior elder" or, more accurately, "chief" of the tribe;[96] he is placed in charge of the high court for civil cases in Jerusalem. In a list of the leaders of the tribes of Israel (1 Ch. 27:16-22) the title *nāgîḏ* designates the "chief officer of the tribe" (v. 16).[97]

The *nāgîḏ* can also be a military commander. The Aaronite high priest Jehoiada is both "*nāgîḏ* over the house of Aaron" (1 Ch. 12:28[27]) and a commander of the standing army (27:5). Mikloth is "*nāgîḏ* of his division" of twenty-four thousand

---

93. Yeivin, *Age of the Monarchies,* IV/2, 171.

94. W. Schottroff, *TLOT,* II, 1020.

95. For the former see Yeivin, *Age of the Monarchies,* IV/2, 171; for the latter see de Vaux, *AncIsr,* 210.

96. For the former see Rudolph, *HAT,* XXI, 257. *HAL,* II, 667, erroneously translates as "court official."

97. See II.2 above.

(27:4)[98] and thus their commander. Rehoboam appoints *n^eḡîḏîm* over the fortress cities of Jerusalem (2 Ch. 11:11); they function as commandants.

The term *nāḡîḏ* appears 4 times in Wisdom Literature (Job 29:10; 31:37; Prov. 8:6; 28:16). The two occurrences in Job speak of the *nāḡîḏ* as an exalted "aristocrat," referring to a person who enjoys high social status.[99] In Prov. 28:16 the *nāḡîḏ* is someone with an "exalted" role in society who multiplies oppression through lack of understanding.[100] The abstract pl. *n^eḡîḏîm* appears once (Prov. 8:6) with the meaning "noble things."[101]

A single passage in the book of Isaiah, which also reflects the prophecy of Nathan (2 S. 7),[102] uses the title *nāḡîḏ* theologically in the following sequence: "a witness to the people, *nāḡîḏ* and commander for the peoples" (Isa. 55:4). The reference is to David (not to the people, as some exegetes attempt to read by emending *nttyw* to *nttyk*[103]), who receives promises that include messianic elements,[104] spoken for the benefit of (cf. *lāḵem* in v. 3) the people of God.

OT Apocalyptic Literature contains three much-discussed texts in which the title *nāḡîḏ* appears (Dnl. 9:25,26; 11:22). The unique phrase *ʿaḏ-māšîaḥ nāḡîḏ* in 9:25 combines both terms as titles, and should be translated "until [the coming of] an anointed one, an exalted one [traditionally: prince]." The translation "an anointed prince/leader" is inappropriate: the absence of any conjunctions means that *māšîaḥ nāḡîḏ* cannot be understood as a hendiadys.[105] The primary emphasis is on the *nāḡîḏ,* a figure "exalted" by God, in whom the exaltation inherent in the term finds expression in leadership and rule. This exalted figure has been identified variously with historical figures (Cyrus, Zerubbabel, Joshua ben Jozadak, Onias III) and messianically with Christ.[106] The historical identification of the *nāḡîḏ* in 9:26 is likewise disputed (Onias III, Titus, Antichrist, Christ).[107] In 11:22 we find the unusual phrase *n^eḡîḏ b^erîṯ,* traditionally "a prince of the covenant" or, more precisely, "an exalted one of a covenant" or "covenant chief."[108] This figure has also been identified variously.[109]

---

98. Inappropriately translated "head of a family" by *HAL,* II, 667.

99. See II.4.

100. C. H. Toy, *Proverbs. ICC* (1899), in loc.; Gemser, *HAT,* XVI, 99; Scott, *AB,* 18, 165, delete *nāḡîḏ* as a gloss; *BHS* deletes it *metri causa;* following the majority of exegetes, however, one may accept the MT.

101. See II.2 above for a discussion of proposed emendations.

102. See III.1 above.

103. E.g., J. L. McKenzie, *Second Isaiah. AB,* 20 (1968), 141; for arguments against the emendation, see J. M. Vincent, *Studien zur literarischen Eigenart und zur geistigen Heimat von Jesaja, Kap. 40–55. BBET,* 5 (1977), 84.

104. On the promises see J. H. Eaton, *ASTI,* 7 (1968/69), 37. On the messianic elements see J. Coppens, *NRT,* 90 (1968), 626.

105. So R. J. Williams, *Hebrew Syntax* (Toronto, 1967), 17f., contra O. Plöger, *KAT,* XVIII, 134; L. F. Hartman and A. Di Lella, *AB,* 23, 240, 244.

106. For the former see the comms. in loc. For the latter see Keil, Liefoth, Young, Walvoord, Baldwin, et al.

107. See the comms. in loc.

108. Plöger, *KAT,* XVIII, 153.

109. See the comms.

Three passages use *nāgîḏ* in a secular sense with reference to the "princes" of non-Israelite peoples. Ps. 76:13(12) seems to have in mind the *n^{e}gîḏîm,* "exalted ones" or "princes," of the nations, but hostile princes from Judah are conceivably possible. This is the only occurrence of the term in the Psalter.

In Ps. 54:5c(3c) Mitchell Dahood proposes the emendation *lin^{e}gîḏî-m* with enclitic *mem* for MT *l^{e}negdām,* translating "but it was not known to them that God is my leader."[110] He makes the same emendation in 86:14, translating "they do not view you as my leader."[111] In 16:8, too, he finds the divine epithet by emending MT *l^{e}negdî* to *lin^{e}gîḏî:* "I have chosen Yahweh as my leader forever."[112] In 138:1 he also emends *negeḏ* to *nāgîḏ* and addresses Yahweh as "leader of the gods."[113] Later, however, he rejected this emendation as "unlikely."[114] The emendations in 54:5(3); 86:14; 16:8 are also unlikely, because no OT text refers to Yahweh or Elohim as *nāgîḏ,* no manuscript supports the reading (not even 11QPs), and the Hebrew expressions do not agree with OT usage.

In Ezk. 28:2 the king of Tyre is called the "exalted one of Tyre" on account of his overbearing arrogance;[115] judgment is proclaimed against him. The judgment of God also befell Assyria and its "exalted ones" or "officers" (2 Ch. 32:21).[116]

IV. Dead Sea Scrolls and Sirach. One would expect to find *nāgîḏ* as a term for military commanders in the War Scroll (1QM) or for cultic officials in the Temple Scroll (11QTemple). To date, however, it has been found only in 4Q504 (4QDibHam^a) 4:7, a text dating from ca. 150 B.C.[117] This text, messianic in content, uses the phrase *ngyd ʿl ʿmkh,* "exalted one over my people," with reference to David, whom God chose from the tribe of Judah and with whom God established a covenant relationship. The text alludes to the prophecy of Nathan (2 S. 7:6-8), pregnantly associating the ideas of election and covenant with messianic elements.

One may also note Sir. 46:13, which speaks of the "prophet Samuel," who established the monarchy and "anointed *n^{e}gîḏîm* over the people." The reference is to the anointing of Saul (1 S. 10:1) and David (1 S. 16:13).

Hasel†

---

110. *Psalms II. AB,* 17 (^{2}1973), 23f.
111. *Ibid.,* 292.
112. *Ibid.,* 24, changing his earlier reading in *Psalms I. AB,* 16 (1965), 86.
113. *AB,* 17, 25.
114. *Psalms III. AB,* 17A (1970), 276.
115. Zimmerli, *Ezekiel 2. Herm,* 77.
116. See II.4 above.
117. M. Baillet, *Qumrân Grotte 4. DJD,* VII (1982), no. 504.

נָגַע nāga'; נֶגַע nega'

Contents: I. Etymology. II. Occurrences and Usage. III. "Touch": 1. General; 2. Sacral Law; 3. Theophanies. IV. Figurative Usage: 1. Law; 2. "Strike with Affliction or Disease." V. Spatiotemporal Usage: 1. "Extend to"; 2. "Reach, Attain." VI. *nega'*: 1. Affliction, Disease; 2. Leprosy; 3. Bodily Harm. VII. Dead Sea Scrolls and LXX.

I. Etymology. The root *ng'* does not belong to the common Semitic root stock.[1] With the meaning "touch," the verb is found in the Egyptian Aramaic of Ahikar and in Jewish Aramaic.[2] It occurs in Mandaic with the meaning "strike, injure."[3]

II. Occurrences and Usage. The verb *ng'* occurs 150 times in the OT: 107 times in the qal (27 in Leviticus, 10 in Numbers, 7 in Job, 6 each in Genesis and Daniel, 5 each in Exodus [Ex. 4:25 hiphil, not qal],[4] 1 Kings, and Jeremiah), 38 times in the hiphil (8 in Esther, 6 in Isaiah, 4 in 2 Chronicles, 3 each in Psalms and Ecclesiastes), 3 times in the piel, and once each in the pual (Ps. 73:5) and niphal (Josh. 8:15).

The derived noun *nega'* occurs 78 times in the OT; 61 of these are in Lev. 13–14, and there are 4 occurrences each in Deuteronomy and Psalms. In the Hebrew text of Sirach, the verb *ng'* in the qal and hiphil and the noun *nega'* appear frequently.[5] With the qal, in most cases (80 times) the object is introduced by the prep. *bᵉ;* 8 times it is introduced by *'el* ("touch lightly[?],"[6] "reach"), and 4 times by *'al* ("be close upon," with disaster as subject: Jgs. 20:34,41; "touch," with lips as object: Isa. 6:7; Dnl. 10:16). In 3 cases we find a direct object (Gen. 26:29; Ruth 2:9; Isa. 52:11), 2 of which are suffixed.[7] The verb is used without an object 5 times, twice as a passive participle (Isa. 53:4; Ps. 73:14: "struck [by God]").[8] In Hag. 2:12 the object touched is introduced by

---

nāga'. G. Brunet, "Les aveugles et boiteux Jébusites," *Studies in the Historical Books of the OT. SVT,* 30 (1979), 65-72; *idem,* "David et le *ṣinnôr,*" *ibid.,* 73-86; M. Delcor, "נגע *ng'* 'to touch,' " *TLOT* II, 718-19; P. Hugger, *Jahwe, meine Zuflucht. Münsterschwarzacher Studien,* 13 (1971), esp. 224ff.; J. Jeremias, *Theophanie. WMANT,* 10 (²1977); E. König, *Stilistik, Rhetorik, Poetik in Bezug auf die biblische Literatur komparativisch dargestellt* (1900); H. Schulz, *Das Todesrecht im AT. BZAW,* 114 (1969); T. Seidl, *Tora für den "Aussatz"-Fall. ATS,* 18 (1982); K. Seybold, *Das Gebet des Kranken im AT. BWANT,* 99 (1973); H. J. Stoebe, "Die Einnahme Jerusalems und der Ṣinnôr," *ZDPV,* 73 (1957), 73-99.

1. For Ethiopic see Leslau, *Contributions,* 33.
2. Ahikar 165f.; *AP,* 218; *DISO,* 174. For Jewish Aramaic see *ANH,* 263a.
3. *MdD,* 25a.
4. Listed as qal by Lisowsky, 899b; see *TLOT,* II, 718.
5. D. Barthélemy and O. Rickenbacher, *Konkordanz zum hebräischen Sirach* (Göttingen, 1973), 252f.
6. Cf. JM, §125b.
7. *Ibid.*
8. *HP,* 208.

the prep. *'el,* and the means of touching ("corner of a garment," distinct from the subj.) by the prep. *bᵉ*.

The hiphil is the causative of the qal (Isa. 5:8; 6:7); it also functions as an internal causative with the same or similar meaning. The object is introduced by a preposition, usually *lᵉ* (10 times) or *'el* (8 times). The piel, which has factitive meaning ("make struck down [with afflictions]"),[9] is always used transitively (Gen. 12:17; 2 K. 15:5; 2 Ch. 26:20).

III. "Touch."

1. *General.* With the meaning "touch," *nāgaʿ* can denote the state of ongoing contact between inanimate objects (1 K. 6:27 with the preps. *bᵉ* and *'el* par. 2 Ch. 3:11f. hiphil with the prep. *lᵉ*; v. 12b: *dbq*). It can also denote the action of simple contact with an inanimate object (2 K. 13:21: a dead body; Isa. 6:7 [*ʿal*]: a glowing coal; Ezk. 17:10: the east wind) or with an animal (Dnl. 8:5, negated), a person (2 S. 23:7; Job 6:7; Est. 5:2), God's messenger (Jgs. 6:21; 1 K. 19:5,7), or a human figure (Dnl. 8:18; 10:10 [subj.: a hand],16 [*ʿal*],18) as subject. It can even denote the action of being "touched" violently by a "great wind" (Job 1:19).[10] Used literally, however, *nāgaʿ* never denotes being struck by a violent blow (→ נכה *nkh* [hiphil]).[11] Even in Gen. 32:26,33(Eng. vv. 25,32]), *nāgaʿ* should be translated "touch." The text does not mean a violent blow on the hip joint but a "magic touch."[12]

As a rule *nāgaʿ* denotes the action of outward contact, in contrast to → דבק *dābhaq,* which refers more to the condition of inward adherence (Sir. 13:1: "Pitch clings to *(dbq)* the hand of whoever touches *(ngʿ)* it"[13]). In the normal causative use of the hiphil ("cause to touch"), the subject may be a person (Isa. 5:8 [acc. + *bᵉ*] par. → קרב *qrb* hiphil; Ex. 4:25; 12:12 [partitive *min* + *'el*]), a seraph (Isa. 6:7 [*ʿal*]), or Yahweh (Jer. 1:9 [*ʿal*], preceded by "put out his hand").

With "ground" or "dust" as prepositional object, the hiphil of *nāgaʿ* occurs 4 times with the meaning "throw someone or something to the ground." In parallel we find → נפל *npl* hiphil (Isa. 25:12; 26:5; Ezk. 13:14), → שחח *šḥḥ* hiphil (Isa. 25:12), → הרס *hāras* (Ezk. 13:14; Lam. 2:2), and →חלל *ḥll* piel (Lam. 2:2). The subject in all these passages is Yahweh; the direct object may be fortifications (Isa. 25:12), a wall (Ezk. 13:14), a high city (Isa. 26:5), or, figuratively, kingdoms and rulers (Lam. 2:2).

In 1 S. 10:26 there is the unique expression "touch someone on the heart," with God as subject. "Heart" also appears as genitive object in 1 K. 8:38 and as prepositional object in Jer. 4:18.[14]

---

9. *Ibid.*

10. F. Horst, *Hiob. BK,* XVI/1 (1968), 2: "struck."

11. Contra Delcor, *TLOT,* II, 718.

12. C. Westermann, *Genesis 12–36* (Eng. trans., Minneapolis, 1985), 513, 517; cf. III.2 below; on 2 S. 5:8 see V.2 below.

13. R. Smend, *Sirach* (Berlin, 1900), 15, 21.

14. See below, VI.1; V.2, respectively.

2. *Sacral Law.* Almost half the occurrences of the qal are found in the P regulations governing sacrifice, food, and purity, and in the allied tradition. In most cases the subject of *nāga'* is an unspecified person ("whoever," "everyone who"). In Lev. 15:11f. the subject is "someone with a discharge"; in Nu. 19:22, "an unclean person"; and in Lev. 7:19, "(sacrificial) flesh." As object we find: an unclean person (Lev. 15:7,19), human uncleanness (5:3; 7:21; 22:5), a dead body (Nu. 19:11,13,16,18; 31:19; 2 K. 13:21), an unclean animal (Lev. 7:21; 11:26; 22:5), the carcass of an unclean animal (5:2; 11:8,24,27,31,36; Dt. 14:8) or of a clean animal (Lev. 11:39), an unclean object or an object rendered unclean (15:5,10,12,21-23,27; Nu. 19:16,18,21), something unclean in general (Lev. 7:19). The object may also be something holy (12:4; Nu. 4:15 [with *'el*]), an offering by fire (Lev. 6:11[18]), holy food (6:20[28]), the holy altar (Ex. 29:37), or cultic objects (Ex. 30:29). In these passages *nāga'* refers to direct contact (in Hag. 2:12f., contact mediated by clothing) between two mutually exclusive realms: life and death, clean and unclean, sacred and profane.[15] Contact must not occur between these two realms. If it does, the result is calamitous (Gen. 3:3; Ex. 19:12b,13 [an expansion of R^P?[16]]; Nu. 4:15). The purpose of the regulations is to limit the consequences of such taboo violations brought about by physical contact. Such calamitous contact can involve a touch so gentle that the person in question does not even notice it immediately (Lev. 5:2f.). In these passages *nāga'* is distinguished from carrying (*nś'*: 11:25,28,40; 15:10), which has more power to make a person — as well as that person's clothing (11:25,28,40) — unclean than does simple contact (15:10).

3. *Theophanies.* With God as subject, *nāga'* in the sense of "touch" occurs 3 times in theophany accounts:[17] in Ps. 104:32, the 3rd person imperfect is part of a hymn praising God's creative power; in the concluding doxology of the book of Amos (9:5f.), the participle is used attributively to characterize "Yahweh of hosts" in the style typical of hymnic predication; and in Ps. 144:5, the imperative is addressed to God in a royal prayer for a theophany. The prep. *b^e* introduces the objects: "the mountains" in Ps. 104:32; 144:5, "the earth" in Am. 9:5. Yahweh's touch brings violent upheavals to the natural order: the mountains smoke (Ps. 104:32; 144:5) and the earth melts (Am. 9:5). Even here, *nāga'* does not denote violent contact.[18] The point is the contrast: even Yahweh's slightest touch (Ps. 104:32 par. "look upon") causes tumult in the natural realm.[19]

IV. Figurative Usage.

1. *Law.* In legal contexts *nāga'* denotes infringement of the rights enjoyed by a person or group, in some cases even guaranteed by treaty (Gen. 26:28f.; Josh. 9:19).[20]

15. See III.3 below.
16. E. Zenger, *Israel am Sinai* (Altenberge, 1982), 131.
17. Jeremias, *Theophanie,* 160-62.
18. As argued by *GesB,* 484; *HAL,* II, 668.
19. See III.2 above.
20. Schulz, 103f.

In this usage, it always has negative connotations and is best translated "harm (someone or something)" or "afflict (someone)." The object, introduced by *b^e* or appended directly to the verb as a pronominal suffix (Gen. 26:29; Ruth 2:9), may be particularly vulnerable or defenseless people, such as strangers (Gen. 25:11,29; Josh. 9:19; Ruth 2:9f.; Ps. 105:12-15 par. 1 Ch. 16:19-22, where it parallels *r''* hiphil, "do harm") and widows (2 S. 14:10; Ruth 2:9), but also a heritage coveted by "evil neighbors" (Jer. 12:14; cf. Zec. 2:12[8]). In Josh. 9:18f. *nāga'* follows → נכה *nkh* hiphil ("slay") and contrasts with *ḥyh* hiphil ("let live"), which follows in v. 20.

In 2 S. 14:10 *nāga'* follows "say something against." In Gen. 26:29 negated *nāga'* is explicated by "do nothing but good" and "send away in peace."

The verb *nāga'* can also refer to the prohibited sexual approach of a man to a woman, which God intervenes to prevent (Gen. 20:6), or which is vigorously warned against (Prov. 6:29). The OT does not, however, use *nāga'* as a euphemism for sexual intercourse itself, like the expressions *yāḏa'* (e.g., Gen. 4:1), *bô' 'el-'iššâ* (e.g., 38:2f.) *qārab 'el-'iššâ* (e.g., Isa. 8:3), and *šākab* (Gen. 30:15f.);[21] the verb refers rather to the treatment of a married woman by a man who intends a sexual relationship prohibited by law (Prov. 6:29: adultery). In Ruth 2:9 *nāga'* probably does not have any sexual connotations, the opinion of many exegetes notwithstanding; as in 2 S. 14:10, it refers to infringement of the rights of a defenseless widow.[22]

2. *"Strike with Affliction or Disease."* Besides its meaning in legal contexts, *nāga'* has a second figurative meaning: "strike, punish, inflict pain." In this usage, the subject is always God or Yahweh (qal: Job 1:11; 2:5, preceded by "stretch out your hand"; piel: Gen. 12:17; 2 K. 15:5; 2 Ch. 26:20) or God's hand (1 S. 6:9; Job 19:21); otherwise the verb appears in the qal passive (Isa. 53:4 [God as the logical subj.[23]]; Ps. 73:14), the pual (Ps. 73:5), or the niphal (Josh. 8:15, for military defeat). Here it comes very near the figurative usage of → נכה *nkh* hiphil and → נגף *nāgap*. With the exception of Job 1:11 ("possessions") and 2:5 ("bones"), the objects are always persons: in 1 S. 6:9 a group, elsewhere an individual. Except for Josh. 8:15 and Job 1:11, all the passages probably refer to a disease:[24] 2 K. 15:5 and 2 Ch. 26:20 mention disease explicitly (pual ptcp. of *ṣr'*[25]); it is suggested by the context in Gen. 12:17 (*figura etymologica* with *n^egā'îm*); 1 S. 6:9 (v. 4: *maggēpâ;* 1 S. 5:6,9,12; 6:5: *'ōpel*); Isa. 53:4; Ps. 73:5,14 (par. *ykḥ*[26]); and Job 19:21 (cf. v. 20). In 1 S. 6:9 "his hand has punished *(ng')* us" parallels "he has done us great harm." Synonymous expressions appear in the extended context: the hand of Yahweh (God) was heavy (*kbd:* 5:6,11; *qš:* 5:7) upon the Philistines;

21. See König, *Stilistik,* 38f.

22. See above, contra W. Rudolph, *Das Buch Ruth. KAT,* XVII/1-3 (²1962), 48; E. Würthwein, *Ruth. HAT,* XVIII (²1969), 14.

23. JM, §121p.

24. Seybold, 25.

25. See VI.2 below.

26. Text following *BHS* and H.-J. Kraus, *Psalms 60–150* (Eng. trans., Minneapolis, 1989), 84.

Yahweh's hand struck (*nkh* hiphil) the Philistines with tumors (5:6; cf. v. 9). In Isa. 53:4 the passive participle of *nāga'* is used to describe the Servant of God, parallel to *nkh* (hophal ptcp.: "struck") and *'nh* (pual ptcp.: "humbled").

V. Spatiotemporal Usage.

1. *"Extend to."* In several passages the qal or hiphil of *nāga'* is used to express not the act of touching as such but spatial extension (topographically: Zec. 14:5 [hiphil]) or proximity, especially in a figurative sense: Isa. 16:8c (par. *t'h;* v. 8d: *nṭš* par. *'br*); Jer. 48:32 ("your branches extended [*'br*] to the sea, reached [*ng'*] as far as Jazer"); Mic. 1:9 (par. *bô' 'aḏ*); Jer. 4:10 ("the sword reached as far as [*'aḏ*] the throat"); Isa. 8:8 (hiphil); Gen. 28:12 (hiphil with locative acc.); Jer. 51:9b ("her judgment has reached up to [*'el*] heaven and has been lifted up [*nś'* niphal] even to [*'aḏ*] the skies"); Job 20:6 (hiphil); 2 Ch. 28:9 (hiphil); Hos. 4:2 ("bloodshed follows bloodshed"; cf. Isa. 5:8 [hiphil]); Ps. 88:4(3); 107:18. In a figurative sense, this meaning of *nāga'* hiphil is also found in Lev. 5:7, in the unique expression "if his hand does not extend to the price of a sheep."

2. *"Reach, Attain."* Especially in late texts, we find *nāga'* (15 times in the hiphil, 8 in the qal) used in the sense of "reach, arrive at (someone or something)." The subject may be a person (1 S. 14:9; 2 S. 5:8; Isa. 30:4; Dnl. 9:21 [qal]; 12:12; Est. 4:14; 6:14), an animal (Dnl. 8:7), news (Jon. 3:6 [qal]), "the king's command and decree" (Est. 4:3; 8:17; 9:1), "disaster" (qal: Jgs. 20:34,41; Job 5:19 [negated]); "rush of mighty waters" (Ps. 32:6), and "turn" in the phrase *haggîa' tōr* + acc., "be someone's turn" (Est. 2:12,15). In Eccl. 8:14 (hiphil ptcp. with *'el:* ". . . who are treated as . . ."), Est. 9:26, Job 4:5 (qal: "it has come to [*'aḏ*] you" par. *bô' 'el*]), and Jer. 4:18 (qal: "it has reached to [*'aḏ*] your very heart"), the verb is used impersonally.

The object may be introduced by the prep. *'el* (1 S. 14:9; Ps. 32:6; Jon. 3:6; Eccl. 8:14; Est. 9:26; Dnl. 9:21), *'al* (Jgs. 20:34,41: "disaster befell them"), b^e (2 S. 5:8; Job 5:19), *'aḏ* (Jer. 4:18; Job 4:5), l^e (Est. 4:14; Dnl. 12:12), *'ēṣel* (only Dnl. 8:7), or appended directly as an accusative (Isa. 30:4; Est. 2:12,15; 4:3; 8:17; 9:1). In Est. 6:14 *nāga'* is used absolutely. The difficult phrase *w^{e}yigga' baṣṣinnôr* in 2 S. 5:8 makes most sense with the meaning "meet at the *ṣinnôr,* reach the *ṣinnôr.*"[27] Here there may be overtones of the notion of magical contact.[28]

Only in the latest texts do we find *nāga'* with a temporal expression as subject (qal: Ezr. 3:1 par. Neh. 7:72; hiphil: Cant. 2:12; Eccl. 12:1 [par. *bô'*]; Ezk. 7:12 ["the time has come *(bô'),* the day has drawn near *(ng')*"]).

VI. *nega'*. The noun *nega'* is found with three different meanings: (1) a general term for an affliction or a disease sent by God; (2) a technical term in the realm of sacral medicine, denoting a particular kind of "leprosy" found on skin, fabric, or the

---

27. See Stoebe, 93f.; Brunet, 75-78; R. Wenning and E. Zenger, *UF,* 14 (1982), 280.

28. On Gen. 32:26,33, see III.1 above; on the role of the "blind and lame," see Brunet, 65-72.

walls of houses (Lev. 13–14; Dt. 24:8); (3) a technical term in the legal realm denoting bodily harm.[29]

1. *Affliction, Disease.* As a general term for an affliction or a disease sent by God, the noun *nega'* occupies the same semantic space as the verb *nāga'* in the piel, pual, and qal passive.[30] This is particularly clear in Gen. 12:17, where *n^e^gāḏîm g^e^ḏōlîm* is used as an adverbial accusative with the piel of *nāga'*, with Yahweh as subject. In 1 K. 8:37 (Deuteronomistic; par. 2 Ch. 6:28), we find a list of afflictions: famine *(rā'āḇ),* plague *(deḇer),* blight *(šiddāpôn),* mildew *(yērāqôn),* locust *('arbeh),* caterpillar *(ḥāsîl),* and enemy (i.e., war: *'ōyēḇ*). These are summarized by means of the two terms "whatever affliction *(nega'),* whatever sickness *(maḥ^a^lâ),*" and interpreted in a secondary addition (1 K. 8:38bα)[31] as "the affliction of his heart" *(nega' l^e^ḇāḇô).* Ex. 11:1, too, retrospectively calls the plagues of Egypt *nega'* (cf. Ex. 9:14: *maggēpâ*). The "onslaught of disease"[32] with which God afflicts people and from which the sufferer prays for deliverance (Ps. 38:12[11]; 39:11[10]; Isa. 53:8) is called *nega'*. In Ps. 91:10 *nega'* and *rā'â* together summarize all the perils that threaten human life (vv. 3,5-7), from which God protects the faithful. In Prov. 6:33 *nega'* (par. *qālôn,* "dishonor") does not clearly suggest disease.

Deuteronomistic texts use *nega'* in parallel with → שׁבט *šeḇeṭ,* "rod," for the means (obj. of the prep. *b^e^*) of punishment with which God threatens conduct contrary to the commandments (Ps. 89:33[32]: *pqd;* 2 S. 7:14: *ykḥ* hiphil; cf. the similar usage [Deuteronomistic] with *maḥ^a^lâ:* Ex. 15:26; 23:25; 1 K. 8:37).

2. *Leprosy.* The noun *nega'* occurs 61 times in Lev. 13–14;[33] in 13 of these occurrences it is a *nomen regens* with → צרעת *ṣāra'aṯ* (elsewhere only in Dt. 24:8[34]). In Lev. 13:1-46 *nega' ṣāra'aṯ* is a technical term for various skin diseases ("leprosy").[35] There is a suspicion of *nega' ṣāra'aṯ* when human skin exhibits any of the following symptoms: swelling *(ś^e^'ēṯ),* eruption *(sappaḥaṯ),* or spot *(bahereṯ).* The proof of *nega' ṣāra'aṯ* is normally the observation that the hair of the affected area has become white and that the disease appears to be deeper than the rest of the skin (13:1-3,20,25). A priest makes the diagnosis. If *nega' ṣāra'aṯ* is present, the sick individual must be declared unclean and excluded from society (13:3,45f.). What skin disease(s) the passage actually refers to is not clear.[36]

Since at least some of these diseases were curable (13:15-17), we should think of psoriasis, impetigo, or leucoderma[37] rather than true leprosy (Gk. *elephantíasis*). Instead

29. Seybold, 25f.
30. See IV.2 above.
31. M. Noth, *Könige. BK,* IX/1 (1968), 188.
32. Seybold, 25f.
33. See Seidel for a discussion of the difficult literary problems presented by this complex.
34. K. Elliger, *Leviticus. HAT,* IV (1966), 180, nn. 2, 3.
35. *Ibid.,* 159ff., 180.
36. For a summary of the various theories see Seidl, 85-88, nn. 56, 58.
37. W. Kornfeld, *Levitikus. NEB* (1983), 50.

of the full expression *nega' ṣāra'at,* we also find just *ṣāra'at* ("leprosy": 13:8,11-15,30,42f.) or *nega'* (13:22; LXX, Syr.: *nega' ṣāra'at*[38]). In other passages that use *nega'* absolutely, it refers to an infection that has not yet been diagnosed ("diseased area": 13:3,5f.,17a,29,42; etc.) or — probably as an abbreviation for *'îš hannega'* — the individual afflicted with the suspicious symptoms (13:4 [but not 5],13,17b).[39] The notion of such an "attack of leprosy" on which this Priestly tradition is based does not appear to reflect primarily observation of bodily injuries resulting from a blow, but rather the idea of a mysterious contact with the realm of impurity and death (cf. Lev. 14:34: Yahweh sends *nega' ṣāra'at*).[40] This notion appears also to lie behind the regulations governing *nega' ṣāra'at* affecting cloth and leather (13:47-59) and the walls of houses (14:33-53).

3. *Bodily Harm.* In Dt. 17:8 *nega'* appears as a legal term in a list with → דם *dām* ("bloodshed") and → דין *dîn* ("legal claim"); it is subordinate to the terms *dābār lammišpāṭ* ("judicial decision") and *dibrê rîbôt* ("matters of dispute"). In Dt. 21:5 (probably a secondary addition in the context of regulations governing murder by persons unknown), "every *rîb* and every *nega'*" is to be decided by the Levitical priests. Here *nega'* is probably used as a legal term for bodily harm, as distinct from murder and other matters of dispute.

VII. Dead Sea Scrolls and LXX. The Dead Sea Scrolls use the verb *nāga'*, "touch," in sacral legislation (1QS 5:13; 7:19; 8:17; CD 10:13; 12:17); it also occurs with the figurative sense of "strike" (1QpHab 9:1; 1QSa 2:3-6,10: "be struck by uncleanness") and "approach, reach" (1QM 17:11; 1QH 8:29; CD 15:5). The noun appears primarily in the *Hodayoth* (1QH) with the meaning "affliction, disease" (21 times). In CD 13:5 *nega'* has the meaning "leprosy."[41] In 4QDibHam[a] (4Q504) fr. 1-2 5:18; 6:7, it means "stroke of fate" (par. *nswyym*). Finally, 4Q512, a purification liturgy, speaks of *mng' hndh,* "stroke of uncleanness" (5:17).

The LXX usually translates *nāga'* with *háptesthai* and *nega'* with *haphḗ* (twice with *mástix*).

Schwienhorst

38. Elliger, *HAT,* IV, 163.

39. *HAL,* II, 669.

40. See III.2 above; cf. Gen. 32:26,33 (III.1 above). See also Elliger, *HAT,* IV, 180; Seybold, 32f., 43f. Cf. Seybold, 32f., n. 10; cf. also Hugger, 225: "The similarity between an open wound resulting from a blow with a stick and the sores associated with skin diseases probably led to the use of נָגַע to describe the latter phenomenon."

41. See VI.2 above.

נָגַף nāg̱ap; נֶגֶף neg̱ep; מַגֵּפָה maggēp̱â

Contents: I. Root, Occurrences, Semantic Field, LXX. II. Usage: 1. Earthly Subjects; 2. Yahweh as Subject; 3. Derivatives.

I. Root, Occurrences, Semantic Field, LXX. The root *ngp* is also found in other Semitic languages: Middle Hebrew, Samaritan, Jewish Aramaic, as well as Ethiopic, Arabic, and Akkadian.[1] To date, the root has not been identified in Canaanite, Punic, or Ugaritic.[2]

The verb *nāg̱ap* occurs 49 times in the OT. Of these occurrences, 26 are in the qal, with the meanings "strike, smite, plague": Ex. 7:27(Eng. 8:2); 12:23 (twice),27; 21:22,35; 32:35; Josh. 24:5; Jgs. 20:35; 1 S. 4:3; 25:38; 26:10; 2 S. 12:15; Isa. 19:22 (twice); Zec. 14:12,18; Ps. 89:24(23); 91:12; Prov. 3:23 (twice); 2 Ch. 13:15,20; 14:11; 21:14,18. The niphal is used 22 times ("be struck"): Lev. 26:17; Nu. 14:42; Dt. 1:42; 28:7,25; Jgs. 20:32,36,39; 1 S. 4:2,10; 7:10; 2 S. 2:17; 10:15,19; 18:7; 1 K. 8:33; 2 K. 14:12; 1 Ch. 19:16,19; 2 Ch. 6:24; 20:22; 25:22. The hithpael appears once, in Jer. 13:16, in the context of a warning oracle (vv. 15-17): "Give glory to Yahweh your God . . . before your feet 'stumble' on the dark mountains." The verb does not occur in the Hebrew text of Sirach.

The derivative *neg̱ep* occurs 7 times. Once (Isa. 8:14) it means "stumbling (block), offense"; cf. the quotations in 1Q38 1f. and Sir. 35:20 (B + E). Elsewhere it means "plague" or "(divine) punishment": Ex. 12:13; 30:12; Nu. 8:19; 17:11,12; Josh. 22:17. Another derivative, *maggēp̱â,* occurs 26 times: Ex. 9:14; Nu. 14:37; 17:13,14,15 (16:48,49,50); 25:8,9,18,19; 31:16; 1 S. 4:17; 6:4; 2 S. 17:9; 18:7; 24:21,25; Ezk. 24:16; Zec. 14:12,15 [twice],18; Ps. 106:29,30; 1 Ch. 21:17,22; 2 Ch. 21:14; cf. Sir. 48:21 (B). These nouns often appear in the same context as the verb and can therefore be discussed with the verb.

The Dead Sea Scrolls use *neg̱ep* only in 1Q38 1f., quoting Isa. 8:14; *maggēp̱â* occurs only in 1QM 18:1,12 ("stroke" in the sense of "defeat"). The verb, both qal (1QM 1:13; 3:9) and niphal (1QM 3:2; 9:2,3; 17:15), belongs to the military terminology of 1QM. God appears as the subject only in 1QM 3:9, in a trumpet inscription.

The semantic field includes above all the verbs → נכה *nkh* and → נגע *nāg̱aʿ* (often as the opposite of → רפא *rp'*) and the nouns → דבר *debher, ḥºlî, maḥªleh* (→ חלה *chālāh*), *makkâ, neg̱aʿ,* and *peg̱aʿ* (→ פגע *pgʿ*).

---

nāg̱ap. J. Hempel, *Heilung als Symbol und Wirklichkeit im biblischen Schrifttum* (Göttingen, ²1965) (see index); K. Seybold, *Das Gebet des Kranken im AT. BWANT,* 99 (1973), 26; P. Welten, *Geschichte und Geschichtsdarstellung in den Chronikbüchern. WMANT,* 42 (1973), 121, 133 (verb).

1. *HAL,* II, 669; *AHw,* II, 718a: *nakāpu(m).*
2. See also → נקף *nāq̱ap* I.

The LXX makes substantially more semantic distinctions in its various translations of both the verb (primarily *patássein,* but also *ptaíein, thraúein,* and *propoún,* as well as six other verbs, sometimes used only once) and the nouns (usually *plēgḗ* for *maggēp̱â,* but also *thraúsis, pteúsis, ptaíoma,* and other nouns).

II. Usage.

1. *Early Subjects.* In the Covenant Code, Ex. 21:35 stipulates the damages when a goring ox (→ שׁוֹר *šôr*) kills another ox;[3] 21:22 deals with the case of men "injuring" a pregnant woman while they are fighting, causing her to miscarry.

People kill each other in battle (→ מלחמה *milḥāmâ*) or are killed in battle (niphal: 2 S. 2:17; 10:15,19; 18:7; 2 K. 14:12; cf. 1 Ch. 19:16,19; 2 Ch. 25:22; with noun: 2 S. 17:9; 18:7).

2. *Yahweh as Subject.* Yahweh is usually the subject of the verb in the qal. "Smiting" is principally part of a punitive act. If it affects Israel's enemies, an indirect element of salvation for Yahweh's people is implicit.

Thus Yahweh "smites" or "plagues" the Egyptians but not the Israelites (Ex. 7:27[8:2]; 12:23 [twice], 27 [probably J]; cf. Ex. 12:23 verb [P]; also the retrospective summary in Josh. 24:5). By contrast, the verb also appears in a (secondary) oracle of salvation for Egypt in Isa. 19:22.[4] The Philistines are also smitten by Yahweh (1 S. 7:10; divine panic as an element of Yahweh war plays a role here[5]).

Yahweh also smote Nabal so that he died (1 S. 25:38; cf. 2 Ch. 13:15), and David says that Yahweh will smite Saul (1 S. 26:10). Yahweh smote David's child, so that he became deathly ill (2 S. 12:15).

Yahweh smote the Benjaminites by (!) Israel (Jgs. 20:35), and the Benjaminites smote each other (at the same time and as a result, v. 39 [niphal]; note the repetition of the verb in vv. 29ff.). But Yahweh also smote Israel before or by the Philistines (1 S. 4:3; cf. niphal in vv. 2,10). It is Yahweh the warrior who uses human beings to smite others.

If Yahweh is not in the midst of his people, they will be struck down (Nu. 14:42 [J], spoken by Moses; cf. the noun in v. 37). Dt. 1:42 depends on Nu. 14:42, deliberately reinterpreting the text and adding emphasis (Moses quotes words spoken by Yahweh). Martin Rose has the relationship between these texts backward.[6]

Chronicles shows a special interest in Yahweh's "smiting," mentioning it frequently in texts that have no equivalent in the books of Kings (2 Ch. 13:15; 14:11; 20:22; 21:14,18).[7]

The psalmist who trusts in Yahweh is promised guidance and protection, so that he

---

3. Cf. the Laws of Eshnunna, §§53-54 A. IV: *TUAT,* I/1, 38.
4. H. Wildberger, *Isaiah 13-27* (Eng. trans., Minneapolis, 1997), 277f.
5. G. von Rad, *Holy War in Ancient Israel* (Eng. trans., Grand Rapids, 1991), 48.
6. M. Rose, *Deuteronomist und Jahwist. ATANT,* 67 (1981), 264ff.
7. See the discussion by Welten.

will not strike his foot against a stone (Ps. 91:12; cf. Isa. 8:14 as a contrast). Wisdom can make the same promise to those who listen to her (Prov. 3:23).

It is also promised that Yahweh will smite those who hate his king (Ps. 89:24[23], in the exilic section of the psalm, which contains promises) and that Yahweh will smite the nations (Zec. 14:12,18 [verb and noun]; cf. also Sir. 48:21[B], the Assyrians).

According to Lev. 26:17 (spoken by Yahweh; cf. Dt. 28:25, spoken by Moses), Yahweh will smite Israel by means of their enemies. Here too theological reflection is dealing with the reality of the exile. In Dt. 28:7 it is the enemies who will be smitten (cf. 1 K. 8:33 [Deuteronomistic]; 2 Ch. 6:24). All these texts use the niphal.

3. *Derivatives.* The usage of the nouns also makes clear that Yahweh is usually looked upon as the subject of the "smiting" expressed by *ngp* and its derivatives. Only in 1 S. 4:17 and 2 S. 17:9 does *maggēp̄â* denote military defeat inflicted by human beings on others.

According to Isa. 8:14, Yahweh himself will become a "stone of stumbling" *(negep̄)*[8] for Israel and Judah (cf. Sir. 35:20 [B + E]; also 1Q38 1f. and Jer. 13:16 with the verb in the hithpael; for the opposite statement, see Ps. 91:12 (verb[9]) and Isa. 28:16.

A punishment in the form of a "plague" *(maggēp̄â),* a sudden punitive blow or sudden death, is sent by Yahweh to punish the people for turning from him to Baal-peor or for rebelling against their leaders (Nu. 14:37 [spies]; 17:13-15[48-50]; 25:8,9,18,19; 31:16; cf. Ps. 106:29; cf. also the use of *negep̄* with reference to Nu. 25 in Josh. 22:17, an example of "P" language). These texts are primarily assignable to P or exhibit P influence. The use of *maggēp̄â* (and *negep̄*) in association with Yahweh is common in P, an observation showing that these derivatives of *ngp* occur primarily in later texts of the OT. This category also includes 2 Ch. 21:14, in one of the "letters" typical of the Chronicler; there is no equivalent in Kings.[10]

P also speaks of a plague as Yahweh's punishment for the Egyptians in Ex. 9:14 *(maggēp̄â)* and 12:13 (*negep̄;* cf. the verb in v. 23 [J]). In an oracle of judgment, Zec. 14:12,15 (probably secondary;[11] cf. the verb in vv. 12,18) speak of Yahweh's plagues on the nations and their animals that attack Jerusalem or refuse to come to Jerusalem as pilgrims. V. 18 sounds the note of the pilgrimage of the nations to Zion,[12] but here with overtones of judgment.

Sudden death by and after disease is envisioned in Ezk. 24:16, where *maggēp̄â* denotes the sudden death of Ezekiel's wife. According to 1 S. 6:4, the ark of Yahweh brings a plague on the Philistines.[13] According to 2 S. 24:21,25 (cf. 1 Ch. 21:17,22), by building an altar David averted a plague *(maggēp̄â)* sent as punishment for a census. If this is to be considered an act of atonement, we have here a precursor of the thought

---

8. → I, 51.
9. See II.2 above.
10. See II.2 above.
11. K. Elliger, *Das Buch der zwölf kleinen Propheten, II. ATD,* 25 (^{2}1951), in loc.; et al.
12. → צִיּוֹן *ṣîyôn.*
13. → ארון *'ᵃrôn* (I, 363-374).

later found in P. Ex. 30:12 speaks of a similar act of atonement to avert a plague *(negep)* in conjunction with a census.[14] Similarly but with a more explicit theological concern, Nu. 8:19 (P) speaks of averting such a plague *(negep)* through an act of atonement when approaching the sanctuary (cf. Ex. 30:12 [P]; Josh. 22:17 ["P"?]). The texts in Nu. 17 (vv. 11ff.: *negep;* vv. 13,15: *maggēpâ*) likewise establish a connection with atonement.[15] Yahweh's "smiting" with a plague and the possibility of averting it become elements of priestly theological reflection.

Preuss(†)

---

14. On atonement see → כפר *kipper* (VII, 288-303).
15. On the strata and historical backgrounds of Nu. 16–17 see F. Ahuis, *Autorität im Umbruch. CThM* (1983).

נָגַשׂ *nāgaś*

Contents: I. Etymology, Occurrences; II. Participle; III. Verbal Forms; IV. Semantic Development; V. LXX.

I. Etymology, Occurrences. Outside Hebrew, the root *ngś* occurs in Ugaritic (*ngṯ,* "seek");[1] otherwise it is found only in South Semitic.[2] It is unclear whether Eth. *nagša,* "be king *(nĕgūš),*" belongs here; the verb is intransitive. The Hebrew verb occurs 4 times in the qal and 3 times in the niphal. The ptcp. *nōgēś* occurs 15 times.

II. Participle. The participle, used as a noun, is semantically quite similar to Eth. *nĕgūš* (Isa. 3:12; 9:3[Eng. v. 4]; 14:2,4; 60:17; Zec. 9:8; 10:4; Job 3:18; 39:7; Dnl. 11:20). In Ex. 3:7; 5:6,10,13,14, however, it denotes the Egyptian taskmasters, so that we may conclude that the term is semantically considerably broader than "king." Significantly, Targ. Onqelos translates it as *maplaḥ* (Ex. 3:7) or *šilṭôn* (5:6,10,13,14), while 11QTgJob translates it as *šallîṭ,* "ruler" (Job 39:7). Targ. Ps.-J. on the Prophets translates *nōgēś* as *šallîṭ* (Isa. 3:12), *šilṭôn* (Isa. 9:3[4];[3] 60:17; Zec. 9:8), *meša'bēd,* "oppressor" (Isa. 14:2), or *parnās,* "overseer" (Zec. 10:4). The term frequently has a pejorative nuance that is based on concrete experience but is also suggested by its etymology.

---

nāgaś. J. Pons, *L'oppression dans l'AT* (Paris, 1981).

1. *UT,* no. 1612; cf. B. Margulis, *UF,* 2 (1970), 136.
2. *HAL,* II, 670.
3. B. Kedar-Kopfstein, *ZAW,* 93 (1981), 274.

III. Verbal Forms. The verb *nāgaś* means "seize, take possession of," especially in the legal sense. We see from 2 K. 23:35 that the king of Judah can "seize" or exact silver and gold from his subjects to pay the tribute demanded by Pharaoh Necho. According to the regulations of Dt. 15:2f., which presuppose a practice similar to the Mesopotamian *mazzazānūtu(m), ngś* denotes a legal proceeding initiated by a creditor against an insolvent debtor on the basis of personal liability. During the Sabbatical Year creditors cannot enforce claims against debtors who are fellow Israelites; they may, however, enforce claims against foreigners.

The postexilic oracle in Isa. 58:3 attacks creditors who distrain their insolvent debtors in person without regard for the fast day. This text uses the hapax legomenon *ʿaṣṣēḇ* for the debtors, which corresponds to Arab. *ǵāṣib,* "usurper"; the Vulg. correctly translates *debitores.* The noun *ʿaṣṣēḇ* refers to persons who have not paid their debts on time, i.e., "insolvent debtors."

The same meaning appears in the niphal. Isa. 53:7 says that the Servant of Yahweh was "seized" for the guilt of the people, a notion confirmed by v. 8. According to Isa. 3:5, the anarchy in Jerusalem is manifested particularly in the Israelites' "seizure" of their fellow Israelites, reducing them to servitude for nonpayment of debts. The expression *niggaś hāʿām* (Isa. 3:5) is also found in 1 S. 13:6; here, however, the exact meaning is hard to determine (perhaps it is a variant reading for *kî ṣar lô*).

IV. Semantic Development. The verb *ngś* appears to reflect ancient legal terminology. It denotes the assertion of a right to seize property; the sovereign had this right within his state (2 K. 23:35), and creditors had it by virtue of the personal liability of debtors (Dt. 15:2f.; Isa. 58:3). The paucity of texts makes it impossible to be more precise or to determine the circumstances under which this right was invoked.

The ptcp. *nōḡēś* probably originally denoted someone who exacted property by virtue of a right, i.e., a "collection agent." Usage in Biblical Hebrew illustrates a semantic development that can be traced easily in the socioeconomic context of the ancient Near East. The tax collector or overseer of the corvée was also the ruler or dictator. Cf. Dnl. 11:20: "Then shall arise in his place one who shall send a *nōḡēś* in the finery of the kingdom" (reading *maʿᵃmîḏ*[4]). This passage is generally assumed to refer to Heliodorus, who was commissioned by Seleucus IV Philopator (187-175) to requisition the temple treasure. Therefore many translate *nōḡēś* here as "tax collector." In this late period, however, it is unlikely that *nōḡēś* had this etymological meaning. In fact, half a century later the author of 11QTgJob substituted *šallîṭ,* "ruler," for *nōḡēś* in Job 39:7. This very meaning appears already in Isa. 14:4, where *nōḡēś* denotes a Mesopotamian ruler.

The term expanded semantically until it referred to a "ruler" in general, since the ruler was usually perceived as the one who imposed taxes and forced labor and exercised his authority.

---

4. See *BHS; HAL,* II, 841f.

V. LXX. The LXX clearly had problems translating the root, since no predominant equivalent emerges. Besides *apaiteín* and *ergodiṓktēs* (4 times each), we find *(ex-) elaínein, phorológos,* and still other words. To date, the root has not been found in the Dead Sea Scrolls.

Lipiński

נָגַשׁ *nāgaš*

Contents: I. Etymology. II. 1. Occurrences; 2. LXX. III. Usage: 1. Qal and Niphal; 2. Hiphil. IV. Dead Sea Scrolls.

I. Etymology. Heb. *nāgaš,* "approach," has cognates in Ugar. *ngṯ* with the by-form *ngš* and Akk. *nagāšu,* "go."[1] A Can. *nagāšu (ngṯ)* is attested in a letter from Tell Taʿanak.[2]

II. 1. *Occurrences.* The basic form of the verb occurs in the qal and niphal; the perfect and the participle are represented by the niphal, the other forms by the qal. The hiphil (37 times), hophal (twice), and hithpael (once) also occur. Of the 84 occurrences of the qal and niphal, 19 are in Genesis, 20 in the other narrative and legal sections of the Pentateuch, 24 in the Deuteronomistic history, 5 in the Chronicler's history, 13 in the prophetic books, and one each in Psalms, Job, and Ruth.

2. *LXX.* In most cases the LXX translates the qal and niphal with *engízein* (or *prosengízein*) or *prosérchesthai,* the hiphil with *proságein, prosengízein,* or *prosphérein.* A few other translations are also found.

III. Usage.

1. *Qal and Niphal.* a. The qal and niphal forms mean "approach, come near" in a quite general sense. The goal or destination, introduced by *ʾel,* is usually a person. Jacob approaches Isaac (Gen. 27:22), Judah approaches Joseph (44:18), Joseph approaches his brothers (45:4). The children of Gad and Reuben approach Moses (Nu. 32:16), the children of Judah approach Joshua (Josh. 14:6), the family heads of the Levites approach Eleazar and Joshua (24:1). David approaches the Philistine Goliath (1 S. 17:40). At Mt. Carmel, Elijah steps before the people (1 K. 18:21) and says, "How

---

nāgaš. R. Rendtorff, *Studien zur Geschichte des Opfers im Alten Israel. WMANT,* 24 (1967); J. Milgrom, "The Cultic Use of נָגַשׁ," *Proceedings of the World Congress of Jewish Studies,* 5 (1969), 75-84, 164; E. Ullendorff, "Ugaritic Marginalia, II," *JSS,* 7 (1962), 340.

1. See *WUS,* no. 1749f.; *AHw,* II, 710.
2. W. F. Albright, *BASOR,* 94 (1944), 22, n. 63.

long will you go limping with two different opinions?" Then he says to the people, "Approach," and all the people come closer to him (18:30). A prophet approaches Ahab (20:13,22), the disciples of the prophets approach Elisha (2 K. 2:5), etc.

In most cases there is a reason for approaching someone, usually clear from the context and often expressed by *l*ᵉ + infinitive (examples below) or an immediately following verb, e.g., *g*ᵉ*šû w*ᵉ*šimʿû* (Josh. 3:9), *g*ᵉ*šû ûd*ᵉ*ʿû* (1 S. 14:38), *gaš p*ᵉ*ga*ʿ (2 S. 1:15). Note also the idiom *nāg̱aš lammilḥāmâ,* discussed below.

With an impersonal complement, *nāg̱aš* can be used with reference to the altar, which the priests approach "to minister in the holy place *(l*ᵉ*šāreṯ baqqōḏeš)*" (Ex. 28:43) or "to minister, to make an offering by fire to Yahweh *(l*ᵉ*šārēṯ l*ᵉ*haqṭîr 'iššeh l*ᵉ*YHWH)*" (30:20). The first passage deals with garments to protect the priests from the holiness of the altar; the second requires the priests to wash with water "so that they may not die." Lev. 21:16-23 contains a series of prohibitions forbidding priests with a physical defect to approach the altar; the purpose of approaching is *l*ᵉ*haqrîḇ 'eṯ-'iššê YHWH* (v. 21) or *l*ᵉ*haqrîḇ leḥem 'ᵉlōhāyw* (vv. 17,21). The approaching is expressed in vv. 17ff. by *qāraḇ* (cf. Ex. 32:19; 40:32; Lev. 9:7f.; Nu. 18:3), in vv. 21,23 by *ngš.*[3] Priestly ministry is also the subject of 2 Ch. 29:31: "Come near, bring *(hāḇî'û)* sacrifices and thank offerings to the temple"; thereupon the assembly (!) brings (*bô'* hiphil) the sacrifices.

Nu. 4:19 deals with the sacred vessels in the tent sanctuary (v. 15 speaks of *haqqōḏeš* and *kol-k*ᵉ*lê haqqōḏeš,* v. 19 of *qōḏeš haqq*ᵒ*ḏāšîm*), which the Kohathites who carry them must not look upon. Nu. 8:19 says that the Israelites must not approach *haqqōḏeš.* What *qōḏeš* means here is obscure; the verse is difficult, since the Levites otherwise have nothing to do with making atonement. Even when Ex. 34:30 says that the people were afraid to come near Moses when he came down from the mountain with his face shining,[4] we are dealing with fear of the holy (cf. v. 32, which says that the people nevertheless came near). The text of Isa. 65:5 is problematic; the idolaters say: "Do not come near me, lest I make you holy" (if we may read *qiddaštîḵā* for *q*ᵉ*ḏaštîḵā,* "I am holy to you" [?]). In any case, the text is a warning against contact with holiness.

"Come near to God" has several meanings. It can refer simply to priestly ministry, as in Ezk. 44:13: the Levites who have worshiped idols must bear their guilt, "they shall not come near to me *(lô'-yigg*ᵉ*šû 'ēlay)* to serve me as priest *(l*ᵉ*ḵahēn lî),* nor come near any of my sacred offerings, the things that are most sacred *(lāgešeṯ ʿal-kol-qoḏāšay 'el-qoḏšê haqq*ᵉ*ḏāšîm)*"; the expression is totally analogous to the passages just discussed, which refer to the altar. The same is probably true of Ex. 19:22: "Even the priests who [normally] are allowed to approach Yahweh must consecrate themselves." Cultic terminology is used to described the encounter with God at Sinai, and the sentence in fact means only that the priests normally perform cultic duties. The only surprising thing is that the passage already presupposes the existence of priests. In Ex. 20:21, however, Moses approaches "the thick darkness (→ ערפל *ʿᵃrāpel)* where

---

3. For literary analysis see K. Elliger, *Leviticus. HAT,* IV (1966), 283f.

4. → קרן *qeren.*

God is," i.e., he approaches God, who appears in the darkness of clouds, to serve as mediator between God and the people. Cf. 24:2: Moses alone, not the people, may come near Yahweh, i.e., climb up the mountain.

According to Jer. 30:21, the ruler *(mōšēl)* of the coming age of salvation may approach God (Yahweh will bring him near [*hiqrîḇ*]) without endangering his life; he enjoys the privilege of a priest and functions as a sacral king — or as a mediator like Moses? In any case, he represents his people before God and has direct access to God. In Isa. 29:13, however, the word is used in a general expression: "These people draw near with their mouths and honor me with their lips, while their hearts are far from me." Although there is a stylistic antithesis between "draw near" and "be far," and although the people rather than the priests are the subject, *ngš* suggests that the verse refers to cultic worship: it is mere lip service and does not involve the heart.

b. In conjunction with *milḥāmâ, ngš* means "go into battle." In Jgs. 20:23, e.g., the Israelites seek an oracular answer to the question: "Shall we again draw near to battle against our kinsfolk the Benjaminites?" The answer is: "Go up *(ʿᵃlû)* against them." In 1 S. 7:10 the Philistines advance to attack Israel; in 2 S. 10:13 (par. 1 Ch. 19:14), Joab advances against the Arameans. The threat against Egypt in Jer. 46 begins with a call to prepare weapons and advance to battle (v. 3). This is probably also the meaning of Jo. 4:9(Eng. 3:9): "Proclaim a holy war, stir up the warriors. Forward, up *(yiggᵉšû yaʿᵃlû)* [LXX reads impvs.], all the men of war"; the continuation contains a call to beat plowshares into swords. We also find *ngš* in a military context in 2 S. 11:20f.: advance against the city or its wall.

c. Another meaning of *nāgaš* is "go to court." Ex. 24:14 stipulates that in Moses' absence, whoever has a dispute *(baʿal dᵉḇārîm)* may turn to *(nāgaš ʾel)* Aaron and Hur. They are thus appointed as arbiters, and "come before them" means to accept their judgment. We find *nāgaš* used similarly in the fundamental precept of Dt. 25:1: "If two men have a dispute *(rîḇ)* and enter into litigation *(wᵉniggᵉšû ʾel-hammišpāṭ)* and the judges decide between them *(ûšᵉpāṭûm),* the one in the right is to be vindicated *(wᵉhiṣdîqû ʾeṯ-haṣṣaddîq)* and the one in the wrong is to be condemned *(wᵉhiršîʿû hārāšāʿ)*." Although this text has been interpolated into a law regulating flogging, it is a general description of correct legal procedure (cf. also Dt. 25:9, which deals with a particular case).

This usage is reflected in Deutero-Isaiah, who makes use of the lawsuit form. In Isa. 41:1 he summons the "isles" and the peoples to come before Yahweh: "Let them approach *(ngš),* then let them speak (*dbr* piel), let us together draw near for judgment *(qrb lammišpāṭ)*." Interestingly, *qrb* is used here as a synonym of *ngš*. In a similar vein Isa. 50:8, in the third Servant Song, says: "He who vindicates me *(maṣdîqî)* is near *(qārôḇ)* [cf. Dt. 25:1], who will contend *(rîḇ)* with me? Let us stand up *(ʿāmaḏ)* together. Who is my adversary *(baʿal mišpāṭî)*? Let him confront me *(yiggaš ʾēlay)*." The whole passage bears the stamp of legal terminology.

d. There is also a more general meaning of *ngš*. Am. 9:13 contains a promise of a time of salvation, when "the one who plows shall overtake *(ngš)* the one who reaps, and the treader of grapes the one who sows the seed." In other words, the land will be so fertile that sowing and harvest will follow hard on each other. Ps. 91:7 says that disaster will not come near someone under the protection of the Most High, though thousands and ten thousands fall (die of pestilence?) round about. Cf. Am. 9:10 (hiphil).

2. *Hiphil.* a. The basic meaning of the hiphil is simply "bring," e.g., 1 S. 15:32: "Then Samuel said, 'Bring Agag to me' "; 23:9: "Bring the ephod here" (similarly 30:7, with a statement that the order was carried out; probably also 14:18 LXX, where the MT has *'arôn 'elōhîm*); 2 K. 4:5f.: vessels are brought (to be filled).

The story of Jacob's ruse to obtain his father's blessing (Gen. 27) depends in part on a pun involving *ngš*. After Isaac's request to bring (*bô'* hiphil) savory food is fulfilled (vv. 4f.,7,10), Isaac asks Jacob to come near (*ngš* qal) so that Isaac can touch him (v. 21, carried out in v. 22). Then follows another request to bring food (*ngš* hiphil, v. 25a; carried out in v. 25b; *bô'* hiphil is used for the wine). The qal of *ngš* is used twice for coming near to be kissed (vv. 26f.). Then, when Esau brings the food he has prepared, only *bô'* hiphil is used; the food is not actually served up *(higgîš)*.

In Gen. 48:9f. *ngš* hiphil is used synonymously with *lāqaḥ*. Jacob (Israel) says to Joseph: "Please bring them *(qāḥem-nā')* to me, that I may bless them." Then we are told that "Joseph brought them near him (*ngš* hiphil) and he kissed them and embraced them." In v. 13 he brings them once more to Jacob, who pronounces his blessing on them.

Several times it is food that is brought. In 1 S. 14:34 Saul says: "Let all bring their oxen and their sheep here to me, and slaughter them here, and eat. . . . Then all the people brought what they had and slaughtered it." In 28:25 a woman who has slaughtered a calf and baked bread puts them before Saul and his servants. In 2 S. 13:10f. Amon says to Tamar: "Bring *(hāḇî'î)* the food into the chamber." She takes the cakes and brings them in (*bô'* hiphil) and offers them *(wattaggēš)* to him. In 17:29 all kinds of food are brought to David and his troops. Jgs. 6:19 also belongs in this context.

b. According to 1 K. 5:1(4:21), the whole world brings tribute (→ מנחה *minḥâ*) to Solomon. Elsewhere, however, it is clear that *minḥâ* refers to a sacrificial offering. The general term for offering a sacrifice is *hiqrîḇ*.[5] Lev. 2:8, however, uses three verbs: "You shall bring (*bô'* hiphil) the *minḥâ* . . . and he shall present (*qrb* hiphil) it to the priest, that he may take (*ngš* hiphil) it to the altar." Here we can distinguish three stages of the offering. The unusual terminology may point to "the special status of Lev. 2."[6] In Ex. 32:6 (in the episode of the golden calf), *'ālâ* hiphil is used for the burnt offering, *ngš* hiphil for the *šelāmîm* offering; Lev. 8:14 uses *ngš* hiphil for the sin offering. In 1 S. 13:9 *higgîš* is used for the bringing in of the sacrificial animals, *he'elâ* for the sacrifice of the burnt offering. In 2 Ch. 29:23 we read that the male goats for the sin offering were brought to the king and the assembly; *ḥiṭṭē'* is used for the sprinkling of blood on the altar. Am. 5:25 asks: "Did you bring (*ngš* hiphil) to me sacrifices *(zeḇāḥîm)* and offerings *(minḥâ)* in the desert?"[7] In Malachi *higgîš* has almost become the normal

---

5. Elliger, *HAT,* IV, 129, n. 7; Rendtorff, 90-92.
6. Rendtorff, 184.
7. See the comms. for the meaning of the verse.

expression for the offering of sacrifice. He castigates the sacrifice of defective animals (1:7f. [3 times]) and speaks of sacrifice being offered to Yahweh throughout the whole world (1:11; *ngš* hophal) and of right offerings (3:3; cf. also 2:12: an offering to Yahweh).

c. In legal usage the hiphil of *ngš* denotes the presentation of a case. For example, Isa. 41:21f. reads: "Set forth your case *(qrb rîḇ),* says Yahweh, bring (*ngš* hiphil) your proofs *(ʿ^{a}ṣumôṯ)* concerning what is to happen." And Isa. 45:20f.: "Assemble yourselves (*qbṣ* niphal) and come together, draw near (*ngš* hithpael, 'come before the court'), you survivors of the nations. . . . Declare *(haggîḏû)* and present your case (*haggîšû).*" The nations are to bear witness that Yahweh announced everything long before.

d. Am. 9:10 is a special case. Here *taggîš* parallels and is almost synonymous with *taqdîm:* the arrogant think that evil will not overtake or meet them (cf. the qal in Ps. 91:7; perhaps the qal should be read here too).

IV. Dead Sea Scrolls. In their use of *ngš,* the Dead Sea Scrolls stand for the most part within the tradition of the OT. In 1QM we find 2 instances of *nāgaš lammilḥāmâ* (4:7,11) and 2 of the coming of the high priest to address the warriors (16:13; 19:11, dependent on Dt. 20:2; similarly 11QTemple[a] 61:15). CD 4:2 speaks of priests who offer the fat and the blood. In 1QSa 1:13 we read that a member who is thirty years old may come forward to decide *(rîḇ)* legal cases *(rîḇ ûmišpāṭ).* The use of *higgîš* together with *qrb* for induction into the community represents a special development (1QS 9:16). This same meaning appears also in a few poetic passages, although sometimes there are echoes of the more general meaning of spiritual community (1QS 11:13; 1QH 12:23; 14:13; 18:19; probably also 16:12). Priestly ministry is the subject of 11QTemple[a] 63:3.

Ringgren

נדב *ndb;* נְדָבָה *n^{e}ḏāḇâ;* נָדִיב *nāḏîḇ;* נְדִיבָה *n^{e}ḏîḇâ*

Contents: I. 1. Occurrences; 2. Basic Meaning; 3. LXX. II. *ndb* and *n^{e}ḏāḇâ:* 1. Freewill Offering; 2. Freewill Contribution; 3. Freewill Decision; 4. Free Divine Favor. III. *nāḏîḇ* and *n^{e}ḏîḇâ.* IV. Dead Sea Scrolls.

---

ndb. R. Albertz, *Persönliche Frömmigkeit und offizielle Religion. CThM,* A/9 (1978); J. Conrad, *Die junge Generation im AT. AzT,* I/42 (1970); A. Fitzgerald, "*MTNDBYM* in 1QS," *CBQ,* 36 (1974), 495-502; J. A. Fitzmyer and D. J. Harrington, *A Manual of Palestinian Aramaic Texts. BietOr,* 34 (1978); S. Légasse, "Les pauvres en esprit et Les 'volontaires' de Qumran," *NTS,* 8 (1961), 336-345; J. Licht, "The Concept of *Nedabah* in the DSS," *Studies in the Dead Sea Scrolls. Festschrift E. L. Sukenik* (Jerusalem, 1957), 77-84; S. Nyström, *Beduinentum und Jahwismus* (Lund, 1946); J. van der Ploeg, "Les chefs du peuple d'Israël et leurs titres," *RB,* 57 (1950), 40-61; R. Rendtorff, *Studien zur Geschichte des Opfers im Alten Israel. WMANT,* 24 (1967); U. Skladny, *Die ältesten Spruchsammlungen in Israel* (Göttingen, 1962).

I. 1. *Occurrences.* The verb *ndb* occurs 17 times in the Hebrew text of the OT (3 times in the qal, otherwise in the hithpael) and 3 times in Biblical Aramaic (hithpaal). Only in the Hebrew text are the following derivatives found: *n^e^d̲āḇâ* (25 occurrences besides Ps. 110:3aα, where *ʿimm^e^ḵā n^e^d̲îḇôṯ* should be read, following the LXX[1]), *nāḏîḇ* (26 occurrences, although the text of Cant. 6:12 is totally uncertain[2]), and *n^e^ḏîḇâ* (3 occurrences, plus a conjectural occurrence in Ps. 110:3[3]). The verb *ndb* (qal perf.) is also contained in the PNs *nāḏāḇ, y^e^hônāḏāḇ/yônāḏāḇ, n^e^ḏaḇyâ, ʾ^a^ḇînāḏāḇ, ʾ^a^ḥînāḏāḇ,* and *ʿammînāḏāḇ* (a total of 60 occurrences). These are phrase names with a theophoric element.[4] *nāḏāḇ* is an abbreviated form from which the theophoric element has been dropped.[5] The kinship terms *ʾāḇ, ʾāḥ,* and *ʿam* are ancient divine appellatives.[6]

This group of words is also found in Postbiblical Hebrew and the Jewish Aramaic dialects.[7] There is also an occurrence in early Aramaic (Ya'udic: noun *ndb* + suf.).[8] In Northwest Semitic and Old South Arabic the verb *ndb* is also found in phrase names formed analogously to the Hebrew names mentioned above.[9] In the other Semitic languages (with the exception of North Arabic[10]), only uncertain instances of the root are found. In these cases too we are probably dealing primarily with names.[11]

2. *Basic Meaning.* For all occurrences of the word group in the OT, as well as in Postbiblical Hebrew and Jewish Aramaic, the element of free will is determinative. The act of giving, the gift, and the decision are all free and voluntary. The basic meaning of the root *ndb* can therefore be defined as "prove oneself freely willing." This meaning corresponds to the meaning of the verb *naduba* in North Arabic ("be willing, noble, generous").[12] The same meaning may be postulated for the qal of *ndb* in the phrase names cited ("the deity has proven to be willing, generous" [in the birth of the child[13]]). In the OT, however, the independent forms of the qal have transitive meaning, with either *lēḇ* (Ex. 25:2; 35:39) or *rûaḥ* (Ex. 35:21) as subject. In this case the North Arabic verb *nadaba* ("call, incite") can be cited for comparison.[14] This usage may actually

---

1. H.-J. Kraus, *Psalms 60–150* (Eng. trans., Minneapolis, 1989), 344; cf. *BHK, BHS.*
2. See the comms.
3. See above.
4. See *IPN,* 20f.
5. *IPN,* 22.
6. *IPN,* 66-82.
7. For Sirach see II.3 below; for the Dead Sea Scrolls see IV below; for later texts see *WTM,* III, 339f. For Jewish Aramaic see *WTM,* III, 339f.; Fitzmyer and Harrington, 256 (= A11, 4).
8. *KAI,* 214, 33.
9. *IPN,* 193, n. 1, and the parallels to the Hebrew names cited in *KBL*^{2}; *HAL.*
10. See I.2 below.
11. For Akkadian see *AHw,* II, 700b; but cf. *CAD,* XI/1, 41. For Ugaritic see *WUS,* no. 1752-54; *UT,* no. 1613; cf. also J. C. de Moor, *UF,* 2 (1970), 216f.; M. Dietrich, et al., *UF,* 7 (1975), 545. For Punic see *DISO,* 174 (*ndb* I).
12. Lane, I/8, 2779.
13. See II.4 below.
14. Lane, I/8, 2778f.; according to *KAI,* II, 222, this meaning is also found in the noun *ndb* in no. 214, 33 (see I.1 above); *DISO,* 174, assigns this occurrence to *ndb* II.

reflect the original meaning of the root *ndb* in all cases: cf. Arab. *nadaba* VIII, "follow a call to service, follow willingly."[15] Chaim Rabin also proposes this meaning for the hithpael of *ndb* in Jgs. 5:2.[16] The meaning of *nāḏîḇ,* "noble," represents a special development.[17]

3. *LXX.* The LXX uses a wide range of equivalents for this group of words and often translates very freely. For the qal of *ndb* we find *dokeín* (Ex. 25:2; 35:21) and *phérein* (35:29); for the hithpael we always find *ekousiázein* or *prothymeísthai.* The most common equivalent for *n^eḏāḇâ* in the sense of "freewill offering" is *tó hekoúsion;* for *nāḏîḇ* in the sense of "noble," it is *árchōn* (the noun is interpreted as a name in Cant. 6:12; 7:2). Noteworthy is the use of *elpís* for *n^eḏîḇâ* in Job 30:15.

II. *ndb* and *n^eḏāḇâ*.

1. *Freewill Offering.* The verb *ndb* and the noun *n^eḏāḇâ* refer primarily to the cultic realm; they therefore appear with by far the greatest frequency in P and the Chronicler's history. The noun *n^eḏāḇâ* denotes a cultic ceremony in the strict sense of the word. In the majority of its occurrences, it means "freewill offering" and refers to the offerings of private individuals outside the regular sacrificial system. It is always assumed that this takes place at major sanctuaries with a highly developed cult. The earliest text (pre-Deuteronomic) is Am. 4:5, which speaks of the sanctuaries of Bethel and Gilgal. All the other occurrences of the term presuppose Jerusalem or the central sanctuary (Deuteronomy, P) as the locus of the cult. The offering may be an → עלה *ʿōlâ* (Lev. 22:18; Nu. 15:3; Ezk. 46:12; Ezr. 3:5 [here together with *ndb* hithpael and *n^eḏāḇâ*][18]) or a *zeḇaḥ, zeḇaḥ š^elāmîm,* or *š^elāmîm* (Lev. 7:16 [cf. v. 11]; 22:21; Nu. 15:3; Ezk. 46:12 [→ זבח *zābhach*]). Nu. 29:39 clearly speaks of *ʿōlâ,* → מנחה *minḥâ, neseḵ* (→ נסך *nāsaḵ*), and *š^elāmîm.* Such offerings could certainly be made at any time, but the preferred occasions were definitely the major festivals, where they were proclaimed in public and appreciated as "good works" (Am. 4:4f.).

Nothing is said about the concrete reasons for such offerings; it is clear, however, that they were intended primarily to express thanksgiving to Yahweh. In Am. 4:5 *n^eḏāḇâ* is associated closely with the thank offering *(tôḏâ;* → ידה *ydh).* This association fits with the intimate relationship between *n^eḏāḇâ* and vow *(neḏer).* Most texts juxtapose the two terms, and P undoubtedly treats them on occasion as a fixed pair (Lev. 7:16; 22:18,21; Nu. 15:3; 29:39; cf. also Lev. 23:38; Dt. 12:6,17). It is clearly impossible to draw a strict distinction between the two (cf. also Dt. 23:24[Eng. v. 23], which speaks of "freely vowing" [*n^eḏāḇâ* used adverbially], and Ps. 54:8[6][19]).

In the case of vows, we are dealing primarily with fulfillment of an obligation to give thanks for divine help prayed for in affliction and then experienced (→ נדר *nāḏar;*

15. Lane, I/8, 2779.
16. C. Rabin, "Judges V,2 and the 'Ideology' of Deborah's War," *JSS,* 6 (1955), 125-134.
17. See III below.
18. W. Rudolph, *Esra und Nehemia. HAT,* XX (1949), in loc.
19. See below.

thus there is also a close relationship between *neḏer* and *tôḏâ* [→ ידה *ydh*][20]). Very often, therefore, the purpose of a *n*ᵉ*ḏāḇâ* was to thank Yahweh for demonstrations of favor and acknowledge Yahweh as helper and deliverer (cf. Ps. 54:8[6], where the afflicted psalmist looks forward to sacrificing a freewill offering [*binḏāḇâ*] after receiving help). A vow implies the notion of offering something to Yahweh in return; the offering is understood to be bountiful and generous. The same is probably true of a *n*ᵉ*ḏāḇâ.* For this reason, a major festival was the preferred occasion for offering it: it could then be witnessed and acknowledged by a great multitude. Quite logically, this very point is the occasion for prophetic criticism (Am. 4:5).

Despite all the similarities and points of contact, *n*ᵉ*ḏāḇâ* cannot simply be equated with *neḏer* or *tôḏâ.* Lev. 22:23 makes a clear distinction. The special mark of a *n*ᵉ*ḏāḇâ,* as the meaning of the root would lead one to expect, is that it was offered totally voluntarily and spontaneously; it was therefore less controllable and calculable than a vow offering. In this sense, it occupied a unique place within the framework of the otherwise strictly regulated cult (cf. the special provisions in Ezk. 46:12; also 2 Ch. 31:14[21]). This is probably also the reason why Lev. 22:23 ascribes to it a lesser degree of holiness than to other sacrifices.[22] Nonetheless, this very difference made it an especially appropriate vehicle for expressing praise, joy, and thanksgiving to Yahweh freely and unconditionally.

This interpretation is particularly suggested by Dt. 16:10, which provides only a freewill offering for the Festival of Weeks. Other witnesses, however, attest that this festival included the offering of firstfruits, in other words, regular sacrificial offerings (Ex. 23:16; 34:22; Lev. 23:17). When Deuteronomy does not require the sacrifice of firstfruits or other regular offerings, it can only mean that the celebration of this festival is meant to be not an obligation but an act of joyous thanksgiving for Yahweh's blessings (cf. vv. 10b,11), an act that can find appropriate expression only in a freewill offering. (It is also conceivable that *n*ᵉ*ḏāḇâ* serves here as a comprehensive term including regular offerings, chosen to make clear that this festival is to be nothing other than a festival of joy and thanksgiving.)

In Ps. 119:108 the offering has been spiritualized and turned into prayer.

2. *Freewill Contribution.* In P and the Chronicler's history the noun *n*ᵉ*ḏāḇâ* serves not only as a sacrificial term but more generally as the designation of any freewill contribution to the central sanctuary. Similarly, in these texts the verb *ndb,* sometimes appearing in the same context as *n*ᵉ*ḏāḇâ,* denotes the act of making a voluntary donation to this sanctuary. The occasions when such contributions are reported are always of great importance: the erection of the tabernacle (*ndb* qal: Ex. 25:2; 35:21,29; *n*ᵉ*ḏāḇâ:* 35:29; 36:3) and the Jerusalem temple (*ndb* hithpael: Ezr. 1:6; 2:68; *n*ᵉ*ḏāḇâ:* 1:4; 8:28), as well as the reorganization of its cult under Josiah (*n*ᵉ*ḏāḇâ:* 2 Ch. 35:8) and Ezra (*ndb* hithpaal [Aramaic]: Ezr. 7:15f.; *n*ᵉ*ḏāḇâ:* 8:28). The contributions mentioned include large quantities of precious metal, costly materials for furnishing the sanctuary,

---

20. See III.1.c below.
21. See II.2 below.
22. L. Köhler, *OT Theology* (Eng. trans., Philadelphia, 1957), 191.

and substantial numbers of sacrificial animals (for regular sacrifices). The primary emphasis, therefore, is less on the voluntary nature of the contribution than on its abundance and opulence. The generosity of the contribution is what matters.

This could be the special mark of a freewill contribution as distinct from a freewill offering. We must remember, however, that the texts cited — at least those in P and Chronicles — reflect a highly idealized presentation and can hardly be claimed as authentic historical evidence. They permit no firm conclusions concerning the circumstances under which freewill contributions were actually given or about their nature. The purpose of these texts is rather to express the special significance of the central sanctuary and the necessary readiness of the whole cultic community to furnish it elaborately (by way of contrast, cf. Hag. 1:2-4). In reality, there was probably no fundamental difference with respect to nature and purpose between freewill offering and freewill contribution. We may therefore ask whether all the texts cited in II.1 above refer in fact to offerings or only to freewill contributions.[23]

3. *Free Decision.* In some cases, the hithpael or hithpaal (Aramaic) of the verb *ndb* suggests a free decision or choice of a particular action. Examples include the willingness to go into battle expressed in the Song of Deborah (Jgs. 5:2,9; the same is probably true in 2 Ch. 17:16), to return from exile under the leadership of Ezra (Ezr. 7:13 [Aramaic]), and to resettle Jerusalem under the leadership of Nehemiah (Neh. 11:2). In this context we may also mention Sir. 45:23, which (citing Nu. 25) extols a ready zeal to contend against idolatry (*ndb* qal). All these actions are of great import and entail substantial risk, so that the decision to proceed demands total commitment and suppression of reservations. It is clear, furthermore, that the choice directly or indirectly involves a decision in favor of Yahweh, who initiated these actions and in whose name they are carried out.

4. *Free Divine Favor.* Yahweh appears as the subject of *ndb* qal in the phrase names *yᵉhônāḏāḇ (yônāḏāḇ)* and *nᵉḏaḇyâ* (as well as the short form *nāḏāḇ*[24]). These names all refer to the birth of the person bearing the name, whose parents attest that Yahweh has proved to be generous. In other words, the (male) child born to them is a wonderful free gift from Yahweh.[25] In view of the role played by the family in biblical society, this gift has a very concrete meaning. Only through a son could the father's name and possessions be preserved, hence guaranteeing the continuance of the family as the fundamental social and economic unit.[26] The name thus gives voice to Yahweh's favor toward the family as a whole, securing its future through the gift of the child. The names with a kinship term as the theophoric element also show that we are dealing here with a very ancient notion, found also outside Israel.[27]

---

23. See W. Rudolph, *Chronikbücher. HAT,* XXI (1955), in loc.
24. See I.1 above.
25. Noth discusses gratitude names in *IPN,* 192f.
26. Conrad, 13-18.
27. See I.1 above; according to Albertz, 49-77, such names express a widespread form of personal devotion.

Two texts associate *n^eḏāḇâ* with Yahweh. According to Ps. 68:10(9), Yahweh showers abundant rain, thus demonstrating his favor toward his people and his intent to secure them a comfortable life. In the context of the psalm, the setting is the entry into the promised land; but the words make a fundamental statement that holds true also for the present day of the psalmist (*n^eḏāḇôṯ* is to be understood as an abstract pl.). Hos. 14:5(4) states that Yahweh loves Israel of his own free will and promises renewed favor to the extent that Israel is prepared to repent. The noun *n^eḏāḇâ* is used adverbially, modifying *'hb.*[28] It is clearly intended to express Yahweh's unconditional and unrestricted love for his people, whose repentance, necessary as it is (vv. 2-4[1-3]), must not be misunderstood as a precondition making this love possible.[29]

III. *nāḏîḇ* and *n^eḏîḇâ.* In a small number of texts, the noun *nāḏîḇ,* like the verb *ndb,* describes the act of making a voluntary contribution for cultic purposes (materials for furnishing the tabernacle: Ex. 35:5,22;[30] the offering of *'ôlôṯ:* 2 Ch. 29:31 [probably a reference to voluntary contributions,[31] although the other sacrifices and offerings mentioned in vv. 31ff. are clearly voluntary, so that v. 31bβ must refer to additional offerings above and beyond those listed]) or a constant ready devotion to Yahweh (Ps. 51:14[12]). In 1 Ch. 28:21bα the text clearly refers to all those who volunteer their craftsmanship *(ḥoḵmâ)* for the construction of the temple.[32]

In all other cases (none in P or the Chronicler's history), *nāḏîḇ* is a social category. It denotes a noble, a leader among the people. Other terms denoting members of this class therefore appear frequently in parallel, sometimes in groups (esp. → שׂר *śar:* Nu. 21:18; Job 34:18f.; Prov. 8:16; other parallel terms in Ps. 83:12[11]; Job 12:17-21; 34:18f.; Prov. 8:15f.; 25:6f.). The *nāḏîḇ* therefore enjoys special respect (Prov. 25:7; cf. 17:26; Cant. 7:2[1]); also Nu. 21:18, which describes a well as being especially valuable,[33] and Isa. 13:2b, which refers to especially magnificent or important gates, the capital, or important cities as a whole[34]). In addition, the *n^eḏîḇîm* as a group embody the highest human power in tribe and state (Ps. 118:9; 146:3; with reference to foreign nations: 47:10[9], accepting the emendation proposed by *BHK* and *BHS* in v. 10aβ; 83:12[11]). Therefore *meleḵ* appears as a parallel term in Job 34:18; Prov. 8:15f.; 25:6f.; in Ps. 47:10(9) *māginnê-'ereṣ* probably also refers to kings, namely, those of the nations.[35] The noun *n^eḏîḇâ* likewise reflects this meaning, referring to the dignity or majesty ascribed to those who are noble and powerful (Job 30:15; referring to the king: Ps. 110:3 [emended[36]]).

The respect enjoyed by a *nāḏîḇ* is based in the first instance on his wealth, which

---

28. → אהב *'āhabh* IV.1 (I, 113f.).
29. Contra W. Rudolph, *Hosea. KAT,* XIII/1 (1966), 251.
30. See II.2 above.
31. See II.1 above.
32. Emended text; see *BHK, BHS.* → חכם *chākham,* IV.5 (IV, 378).
33. H. Gressmann, *Die Anfänge Israels. SAT,* I/2 (^{2}1922), 107.
34. O. Kaiser, *Isaiah 13–39. OTL* (Eng. trans., 1974), 13.
35. H.-J. Kraus, *Psalms 1–59* (Eng. trans., Minneapolis, 1988), 465, 470.
36. See I.1 above.

makes him widely influential (Prov. 19:6). There is accordingly a fundamental contrast with → דל *dal* and → אביון *'eḇyôn* (1 S. 2:8; Ps. 107:40f.; 113:8; Sir. 11:1). Wisdom texts, however, suggest that it was primarily his blameless conduct that set him apart from others. Like the righteous *(ṣaddîq),* he is innocent (Prov. 17:26); he acts with divine wisdom, like an upright judge (8:16). False speech[37] is foreign to his nature (17:7b). He therefore stands in sharpest contrast to the "fool" (→ נבל *nāḇāl*), who is immersed in lies (17:7 [emended[38]]), spreads iniquity and ungodliness, and oppresses the poor without restraint (Isa. 32:6-8). The *nāḇāl* may be equated with the "wicked" *(rāšā'),* who is the antitype to the *ṣaddîq* throughout Proverbs.[39] Thus the *nāḏîḇ* embodies the wisdom idea of the righteous sage and represents human perfection.[40] This is also the sense of *n^eḏîḇâ* in Isa. 32:8.

Of course, this ideal of the perfect aristocrat does not correspond to reality. It is not by chance that the book of Job vividly expresses the contrast. In one of Job's discourses, *nāḏîḇ* and *rāšā'* are parallel terms (Job 21:28). This incongruity must be accepted, however, because there is no divine retribution for the wicked (cf. vv. 29-31). Another of Job's discourses says that Yahweh can pour contempt[41] even on the *n^eḏîḇîm* (12:21). This is not, however, an act of retribution but a demonstration of Yahweh's incalculable wisdom and power (vv. 13f.). The words of Elihu, too, assume that the *nāḏîḇ* can become one of the wicked *(rāšā')* (34:18). Elihu, however, expresses his conviction that Yahweh does not approve of this and therefore intervenes (vv. 19-22).

According to Isa. 32:5, the incongruity that a "fool" *(nāḇāl)* can be called *nāḏîḇ* is resolved only in a future age of salvation. Hymnic texts, however, bear witness to Yahweh's incalculable freedom, praising him for placing the "poor" *(dal, 'eḇyôn)* on a par with the *nāḏîḇ* (1 S. 2:8 [cf. vv. 6f.]; Ps. 113:8) or for pouring contempt on the latter and exalting the former (Ps. 107:40f.; v. 40a is identical with Job 12:21a, discussed above). Here, however, the psalmist sees this as a salvific act of God. There is an element of genuine wisdom in the statement of Sir. 11:1 that wisdom can place one of the "poor" *(dal)* among the circle of the *n^eḏîḇîm.*

A general qualification is stated in Ps. 118:9; 146:3: even the *n^eḏîḇîm* are only human and therefore do not deserve full confidence. Concerning the *n^eḏîḇîm* of other nations, we are told only that they too are subject to Yahweh's sovereignty (47:10[9]) and will be destroyed if they are among Israel's enemies (83:12[11]).

We may also assume the aspect of free will as a fundamental element in the meaning of the noun *nāḏîḇ* as a social category. As a rule, scholars cite modern Bedouin society, where the wealthy, especially the tribal leader *(šēḫ),* use their wealth not for themselves but for the benefit of the tribal community and its guests, distinguishing themselves by their generosity.[42] The use of *nāḏîḇ* to designate a noble is thus associated with nomadic

---

37. → שקר *šqr.*
38. See *BHK, BHS.*
39. → רשע *rš';* see Skladny, 33, on this identification.
40. → צדק *ṣdq;* → חכם *chākham* (IV, 364-385).
41. → בזה *bāzāh* (II, 60-65).
42. Nyström, 132-34.

concepts. But a different line of development is also possible. In all its occurrences (except Nu. 21:18), *nādîḇ* refers not to a nomadic figure but to a member of the upper class in a socially stratified society, such as developed in Israel during the course of the monarchy. Such individuals enjoyed far greater wealth and influence than did members of the poorer classes, who increasingly became economically dependent. This social and economic superiority generally made it possible for the nobility to be lavishly generous and thus to embody a particular ideal of nobility[43] — a dubious ideal, insofar as it presupposed a corresponding impoverishment of the lower classes. According to this theory, the use of *nādîḇ* to designate a noble originated during the monarchy. This theory is also buttressed by the fact that its primary support is texts influenced by wisdom, which made its first appearance in Israel during the monarchy.

IV. Dead Sea Scrolls. The word group based on *ndb* is also found in the Dead Sea Scrolls. Semantically, there is a large area of agreement with the corresponding OT occurrences. For example, the noun *n^e^ḏāḇâ* means a freewill offering (CD 16:13 [to fulfill a vow]; 4Q509 fr. 131-32 2:6, in connection with the Festival of Weeks;[44] spiritualized in 1QS 9:5 [qualified by → מנחה *minḥâ*]),[45] a free decision (to engage in battle in the eschatological war: 1QM 7:5; cf. *nādîḇ* in 1QM 10:5),[46] or free devotion to God (1QH 14:26; 15:10 [qualifying *'āhaḇ* as in Hos. 14:5(4), but here referring to a human person];[47] cf. 1QS 9:24). In 1QSb 3:27f.; 4QM^a^ (4Q491) fr. 11 1:12,[48] the *n^e^ḏîḇîm* are the representatives of foreign nations, who are made subject to God or excluded from salvation;[49] cf. also the quotation from Ps. 107:40 and Job 12:21 in 1Q25 1:7.

Other texts, however, exhibit a special accent. According to CD 6:2-10, for example, the *n^e^ḏîḇîm* (and *śārîm*) of Nu. 21:18 are the converted of Israel, who have left the land of Judah and live strictly according to the law, in other words, all those who have freely joined this new community. Above all, this special meaning lies behind the participial forms of the verb *ndb* (hithpael: 1QS 5:1,6,8,10,21f.; 6:13; 1QpMic [1Q14] 10:7; 1Q31 1:1; niphal: 1QS 1:7,11; pual[?]: 4Q501 3;[50] these are the only attested forms of the verb *ndb*). These forms are virtually technical terms for the members of the community, identified by their rigorous separation from all who are ruled by evil and by their free submission to the ordinances of the community as the new Israel.[51]

Conrad

---

43. Van der Ploeg, 56f.
44. M. Baillet, *Qumrân Grotte 4 III. DJD,* VII (1982), 203.
45. See II.1 above.
46. See II.3 above.
47. See II.4 above.
48. *DJD,* VII, 27.
49. See III above.
50. *DJD,* VII, 79.
51. See Fitzgerald.

נָדַד nāḏaḏ

Contents: I. Etymology. II. LXX. III. Forms. IV. Syntax and Meaning. V. Usage with Animate Subjects: 1. Secular Contexts; 2. Secular Meaning in Theological Contexts; 3. Theological Meaning.

I. Etymology. Besides *ndd,* the biliteral base *nd* gives rise in Hebrew to the semantically related roots *nd',* *ndh,* and *nwd.* Associated with *ndd* is the abstract *qaṭûl* form *n^eḏuḏîm* (always pl.), "restlessness." The verb *ndd,* "flee," appears in the Aramaic dialects (e.g., Biblical Aramaic, Jewish Aramaic, Mandaic) and in Arabic. In Syriac it has the meaning "shrink in terror from, loathe." In Akkadian the G stem *nadādu* appears only as an Aramaic loanword in Late Babylonian.[1] Since we can only guess at its meaning,[2] any etymological and semasiological connection with the Old and Middle Assyrian D stem *nuddudu* and its suggested meanings "sweep up, bring together, seek, comb" must remain an open question. For Ugaritic the meaning of *ndd* is defined as "go or come hastily, wander about, go away" or "go back and forth."[3]

II. LXX. The LXX uses many words to translate *ndd,* attempting to reproduce the appropriate contextual nuance in each case. Most common is *pheúgō* (4 times) together with *diapheúgō* and *phyadeúō* (once each), followed by *exístēmi/amai* (4 times), *aphístēmi/amai* (3 times, always with "sleep" as the subj.), and *apopēdáō* (twice). There is one occurrence each of *aníptamai, apoxenóomai, aphállomai, exōthéomai, katapetánnymai, katatáttomai, pétomai, eínai planḗtai,* and *ptoéomai.*

---

nāḏaḏ. M. H. Gottstein, "Bemerkungen zu Eissfeldt's Variae Lectiones der Jesaia-Rolle," *Bibl,* 34 (1953), 212-221; B. Grossfeld, "The Relationship Between Biblical Hebrew ברח and נוס and Their Corresponding Aramaic Equivalents in the Targum — ערק, אפך, אזל," *ZAW,* 91 (1979), 107-123; C. Hardmeier, *Texttheorie und biblische Exegese. BEvT,* 79 (1978); E. Jenni, " 'Fliehen' im akkadischen und im hebräischen Sprachgebrauch," *Or,* 47 (1978), 351-59; E. Y. Kutscher, *The Language and Linguistic Background of the Isaiah Scroll (1QIsa^a). STDJ,* 6 (1974); B. Landsberger, "Einige unerkannt gebliebene oder verkannte Nomina des Akkadischen," *WO,* 3 (1964), 48-79, 246-268; E. Lipiński, "Banquet en l'honneur de Baal: CTA 3 (V AB), A, 4-22," *UF,* 2 (1970), 75-88; H. N. Richardson, "The Last Words of David," *JBL,* 90 (1971), 257-266; A. Salonen, *Vögel und Vogelfang im Alten Mesopotamien. AnAcScFen,* 180 (1973); M. S. Segal, ספר בן סירא השלם (Jerusalem, 1953); W. von Soden, "Aramäische Wörter in neuassyrischen und neu- und spätbabylonischen Texten. Ein Vorbericht. II (n-z und Nachträge)" *Or,* 37 (1968), 261-271.

1. Von Soden, 261, no. 98.
2. *CAD,* XI/1, 41: uncertain; *AHw,* II, 700f.: "retreat?" Using a text note cited in *CAD* or *AHw,* Landsberger (263, n. 57, with an erroneous semantic citation of Heb. *ndd*) and Salonen (359) arrive at the meaning "scare away (a bird)."
3. For the former see *WUS, UT.* For the latter see Lipiński, 77f.

III. Forms. There are 25 certain occurrences of *ndd* in Hebrew and 1 in Aramaic (Dnl. 6:19[Eng. v. 18]; Lisowsky omits Prov. 27:8). Two additional occurrences are probable: 2 S. 23:6 (if the verb form does not derive from *nûḏ*[4]) and Jer. 9:9(10); the same expression recurs in Jer. 50:3, but with *nûḏ* (by confusion?[5]). Four conjectures include *ndd:* Isa. 17:11; 38:15 (with 1QIs^a);[6] Ezk. 31:12; Dnl. 2:1. The only probable conjecture is Ezk. 31:12. There is one occurrence in the Hebrew text of Sirach: 34:20c (*wndd yšynh,* LXX *agrypnías* [disregarding the *waw*], "sleeplessness"[7]).

The verb appears 24 times in the qal; most of these texts use the suffix conjugation or the participle. There are 4 instances of the prefix conjugation (Gen. 31:40; Nah. 3:7; Ps. 68:12[11] [twice]), one of the infinitive construct (Ps. 55:8[7]), and one of the polal using the suffix conjugation: Nah. 3:7 (the Masoretic pointing of the text is dubious if only by virtue of the number; since, however, there is no recognizable passive meaning, it is reasonable to follow *HAL* in treating the form as an active polel.[8] We also find one instance of the hiphil (prefix conjugation: Job 18:18) and two of the hophal (one prefix [Job 20:8], one ptcp. [2 S. 23:6]).

The conjugation of *ndd* follows a variety of paradigms: (1) פ״ן or ע״ע: the participle, suffix conjugation, and infinitive construct *(n^eḏōḏ)* of the qal; (2) פ״ן or, if ע״ע, "aramaizing": the prefix conjugation qal *wattiddaḏ* (Gen. 31:40) and *yiddōḏûn* (Ps. 68:13[12]), and the prefix conjugation hophal *w^eyuddaḏ* (Job 20:8); (3) פ״ן, ע״ע unlikely on account of the *plene* orthography: the prefix conjugation qal *yiddôḏ* (Nah. 3:7);[9] (4) ע״וי or ע״ע (helped by semantic overlap), but not פ״ן: the suffix conjugation polal (passive?) *w^enôḏaḏ* (Nah. 3:17) and hophal ptcp. *munāḏ* (2 S. 23:6); (5) only ע״ע, clearly not פ״ן: the prefix conjugation hiphil *y^eniddubû* (Job 18:18). The pairs *w^eyuddaḏ/munāḏ* and *wattiddaḏ/yiddōḏûn* stand in opposition within the same partial paradigm; do they reflect dialectal differences or merely problems of Masoretic orthography? The verb *ndd* is described correctly as doubly weak.[10] Bauer-Leander's thesis that verbs with identical second and third radicals are never doubly weak and that in the case of *ndd* only the first consonant is weak, while the other two (!) are strong, is disproved by the forms that cannot be explained as פ״ן forms.[11]

IV. Syntax and Meaning. Most occurrences of *ndd* are exilic or postexilic. Apart from the figurative expression that sleep flees from the eyes, all are in poetic contexts exhibiting elevated language. In statements using the verbs *bāraḥ* and *nûs,* which in

---

4. Richardson, 265.

5. G. Bergsträsser, *Hebräische Grammatik,* 2 vols. (Leipzig, 1918-29), II, 140, §27q, note.

6. Gottstein, 218; Kutscher, 263f., 301, 330.

7. Segal, 193; D. Barthélemy and O. Rickenbacher, *Konkordanz zum hebräischen Sirach* (Göttingen, 1973), 254.

8. *HAL,* II, 672.

9. Bergsträsser, II, 132, §27a. *BLe,* §58q′, argues instead that the form represents "late *plene* orthography." The latter became standard in the Dead Sea Scrolls: *'dwdh* (1QIs^a 38:15), *ydwdw* (4QpNah 3:5).

10. *GK,* §76.

11. *BLe,* §58q′.

Hebrew dominate the semantic realm of flight, "we are told with roughly equal frequency what the subject is fleeing from and where the subject is fleeing to."[12] The verb *ndd* differs characteristically. With four exceptions (Isa. 10:14; Hos. 9:17; Job 15:23; Dnl. 6:19 [18]), statements with *ndd* either do not include any syntagmeme making the meaning more precise (the most common pattern) or add only a prepositional compound with *min* (9 examples). This verb, therefore, in its usage and probably also in its meaning is interested at most in where the flight begins, not in its goal.

The prepositional compounds with *min* speak of: (1) in unpolitical terms, the region from which the subject flees (the world: Job 18:18; home: Prov. 27:8b; a nest: Prov. 27:8a); (2) dangers (swords: Isa. 21:15; the sound of tumult: Isa. 33:3) or persons (a sick person, unjustly persecuted: Ps. 31:12[11]; Nineveh, represented as a woman: Nah. 3:7; Yahweh: Hos. 7:13); (3) eyes, in the figurative statement that sleep flees from human eyes (Gen. 31:40); in Biblical Aramaic the idiom is formulated with *ʿal* (Dnl. 6:19[18]).

We observe the same phenomenon in expressions used in parallel with or in the context of *ndd:* the act of fleeing denoted by *ndd* is viewed from the perspective of the point of departure. In the perfect the verb expresses the result that the individual or group in question has vanished, not that it has arrived somewhere or been saved. Examples include: *ndḥ* niphal, "be scattered" (Isa. 16:3; Jer. 49:5); *brḥ,* "flee" (Isa. 22:3); *npṣ,* "disperse" (Isa. 33:3); *ʾên,* "cease to exist" (Jer. 4:25); *hlk,* "go away" (Jer. 9:9[10]); "no one knows where they have gone" (Nah. 3:17); "be forgotten" (Ps. 31:13[12]); *ʿwp,* "fly away" (Nah. 3:16,17; Ps. 55:7,8[6,7]; Job 20:8[13]); *rḥq* hiphil, "go far away" (Ps. 55:8[7]); *ʾbd,* "perish" + *hdp,* "drive away" (Job 18:17,18), "not be found, not be seen" (Job 20:8,9). There is only one contextual counterexample (Isa. 10:31: *ʿwz,* "flee for safety") and one prepositional counterexample (Job 15:23, where *l*ᵉ introduces the goal: "he wanders about for bread"). Many commentators, however, like Georg Fohrer and Marvin Pope, follow the LXX and translate the expression as "he wanders about as food for vultures." In this case there is not a single instance of *ndd* with a statement of the goal.

Therefore *ndd* is particularly appropriate for restless, aimless, panicky wandering; the participle denotes someone still in hazardous flight (Isa. 16:3; 21:14; Jer. 49:5). In Hos. 9:17 the prepositional compound with *b*ᵉ refers not to the realm where the fleeing Israelites find rest but to the nations among whom they ceaselessly wander without rest (LXX: *planḗtai*). In contrast to their use of *nûs* and *nûḏ,* the prophets do not use *ndd* when calling on people to flee.

Except for the figure that speaks of sleep fleeing (Gen. 31:40; Dnl. 6:19[18]; Est. 6:1; cf. the simile in Job 20:8: "like a dream"; also Sir. 34:20c) and the passive construction in 2 S. 23:6 (where the subj. is thorns or possibly wick trimmings), the subjects of *ndd* are always animate — for the most part humans (individual, nations, the inhabitants of a town, etc.) but sometimes animals, almost exclusively birds (Isa.

12. Jenni, 355; cf. Grossfeld, 108, n. 3, with earlier bibliography.
13. See M. Dahood, *RSP,* III, 112, no. 211.

10:14; 16:2; Jer. 4:25; Prov. 27:8; cf. Jer. 9:9[10]: from birds to cattle; only in passive construction, Nah. 3:17: locusts, i.e., flying insects; birds also appear in the immediate context in Hos. 7:11-13 and Ps. 55:7,8[6,7]). Here belongs the unique construction of *ndd* in Isa. 10:14, where the participle without a preposition governs an undetermined noun, which, however, specifies the action instrumentally: flapping with wings. The irregular flight of birds — up, down, back and forth — is described especially well by *ndd*.

The reasons for flight are panic fear or terror evoked by a fearsome sight, and in one instance (Hos. 7:13) anger with Yahweh. Like *nûs,* therefore, *ndd* can describe the act of running away from a catastrophe (but without a place of refuge); like *brḥ,* it can describe escape from the structures of society.[14] As its own particular nuance, it adds the connotation of haste, panic, and aimlessness.

V. Usage with Animate Subjects.

1. *Secular Contexts.* The verb *ndd* appears primarily in secular contexts and with secular meaning.

a. *Wisdom Literature.* In Wisdom Literature the subject is the typical fate of the individual. The verb describes the situation of the godless or persecuted. They must flee from their social support system, from the very context of their lives, without hope of finding refuge. They are even banished from the memory of their associates, or their misfortune may provoke these same associates to take flight. To the inner torment of the wicked there is added outward suffering: they wander aimlessly and unceasingly, terrified like an animal trying to escape a bird of prey (Job 15:23).

The memory of the wicked is totally lost, as though they had been banished from the light of day and from the face of the earth (Job 18:18). Like a dream, they vanish without a trace in an instant (20:8). Evildoers are there like scattered thorns (2 S. 23:6).

Innocent victims of persecution or those who are seriously ill are considered such dangerous signs of divine displeasure that even their familiar friends flee their presence (Ps. 31:12[11]). The victim of persecution would flee into the desert, far from his enemies in the city (55:[7]). Prov. 27:8 describes the situation of someone forced to leave home.

b. *Prophetic Texts.* The prophetic texts that use *ndd* in secular contexts reflect a wide variety of genres and dates. Most of them refer to the horrors of war: (1) a group fleeing from the enemy, or (2) the situation of the fugitives.

(1) During Sennacherib's siege of Jerusalem in 701, the cowardly officers and nobles of Jerusalem tried unsuccessfully to flee (Isa. 22:3). The inhabitants of Madmenah fled from a surprise attack by the Assyrians (10:31). The king of Assyria likens himself as conqueror to one who gathers eggs, while the birds from whom they are taken cannot even flap their wings (10:14). Threatened by an unnamed enemy, the fleeing Moabite women resemble fluttering birds (16:2).

(2) A Moabite delegation in Jerusalem pleads in vain(?) for total protection for their

---

14. See Jenni, 355f.

fugitives (Isa. 16:3). The caravans of Dedan, an Arabian oasis, have fled into the desert to escape a mighty enemy. There the inhabitants of the oasis town of Tema are asked to feed the fugitives (21:14f.). Nah. 3:17 resembles more the use of *ndd* in wisdom contexts: at the news of the fall of Nineveh, throughout the whole Assyrian Empire the Assyrian guards and officials have vanished in an instant without a trace, like locusts warmed by the first rays of the rising sun. Here *ndd* describes how the locusts suddenly fly away in a totally unknown direction, finally vanishing from view.

2. *Secular Meaning in Theological Contexts.* Without losing its secular meaning, *ndd* appears also in theological contexts where Yahweh fights against (a) Israel's enemies or (b) his own people.

a. Yahweh will so devastate Nineveh that all will shrink and flee from the sight of it (Nah. 3:7). Yahweh punishes the Ammonites for dispossessing Israel, devastating their land so completely that no one can gather the scattering fugitives (Jer. 49:5). A postexilic "apocalypse" describes how the nations flee at the sound of the tumult when Yahweh arises in response to his people's cry for help, attacking the nations of the "destroyer" and leaving them to be despoiled (Isa. 33:3). Ps. 68:13(12) also belongs here: the tidings of victory tell how the kings of the Canaanite armies fled when Yahweh intervened during the wars of Israel's settlement.

b. By means of the foe from the north, Yahweh has so devastated Judah that not just the people but even the birds have vanished (Jer. 4:25). Jer. 9:9(10) goes even further: because of the people's depravity, Yahweh attacks Jerusalem and the towns of Judah. The enemy has already so devastated the towns that all living creatures, from birds to cattle, have fled. The earliest occurrence of *ndd* in such a context is Hos. 9:17: after interceding in vain, the prophet accepts Yahweh's judgment and prays or declares that Yahweh will reject Israel for its disobedience. This rejection means that Israel must permanently wander aimlessly as a fugitive among the nations.

3. *Theological Meaning.* In Hosea we also find the only occurrence of *ndd* with theological meaning: 7:13, probably to be interpreted in conjunction with 9:17 in the sense of retributive justice. The text is a woe cry against Israel, threatening or proclaiming physical suffering.[15] Instead of seeking help from Yahweh, Israel has entered into coalitions, now with Egypt, now with Assyria, thus rebelling against Yahweh and fleeing from him. (Elsewhere *brḥ* denotes flight from God, but, in contrast to *ndd,* usually with a statement of the goal: Jon. 1:3,10; 4:2; Ps. 139:7). In contrast to all other instances of *ndd,* this flight was not occasioned by fear or horror, but by disobedience toward the one who could have delivered Israel but now punishes Israel by making it a fugitive among the nations.

W. Gross

---

15. Hardmeier, 195, n. 82.

נִדָּה *niddâ*

Contents: I. 1. Etymology and Basic Meaning; 2. LXX and Targum. II. Meanings: 1. In Connection with Menstruation; 2. In General; 3. Purification. III. Lam. 1:8. IV. Dead Sea Scrolls.

I. 1. *Etymology and Basic Meaning.* The etymology of *niddâ* is unclear. Some derive it from the root *ndd,*[1] which in the qal means "leave, flee, wander" (Isa. 21:15; Hos. 9:17), in the hiphil "put to flight, chase away" (Job 18:18); cf. Ugar. *ndd,* "wander, go," Akk. *nadādu,* "retreat(?)."[2] Others derive it from *ndh,*[3] found only in the piel with the meaning "chase away, move aside" (Isa. 66:5; Am. 6:3); cf. Ugar. *ndy*(?), "drive away," Akk. *nadû,* "throw, throw down." Morphologically, the word represents a nominal form of an ע״ע root, like *bizzâ, middâ,* etc.[4] When considering its etymology, however, one must remember that ל״ה and ע״ע verbs with corresponding radicals often have similar or synonymous meanings (e.g., *šgg/šgh, qṣṣ/qṣh*). Since *ndd* and *ndh* are almost synonymous, further semantic differentiation is superfluous for the derivation of *niddâ*.

Both *ndd* and *ndh* share the meaning "chase away, drive away." If *niddâ* can be assigned the putative basic meaning "expulsion, exclusion," the opposite meanings of the word are comprehensible. In the case of a menstruating woman, the word originally denoted the discharge or elimination of the menstrual blood; it then came to denote the impurity of a menstruating woman in particular or impurity in general. In the phrase *mê niddâ,* too, the word conveys the meaning "expulsion": "water of expulsion (of impurity)," or simply "water of purification." The word *ḥaṭṭā'ṯ* in Zec. 13:1 suggests this interpretation of *mê niddâ.* The noun *ḥaṭṭā'ṯ* (derived from a privative piel), "purification," corresponds to the piel *ḥiṭṭē',* "purify."[5] In other words, in Zec. 13:1 *ḥaṭṭā'ṯ* and *niddâ* are synonymous, and the phrase is to be translated "for cleansing and for purification." This meaning of *niddâ* appears also in the designation of the water used for purification of the Levites, *mê ḥaṭṭā'ṯ,* "water

---

niddâ. J. Döller, *Die Reinheits- und Speisegesetze des ATs* (Münster, 1917); M. Greenberg, "The Etymology of נִדָּה, '(Menstrual) Impurity,' " *Solving Riddles and Untying Knots,* J. Greenfield Festschrift, ed. Ziony Zevit, et al. (Winona Lake, 1995), 69-77; H. J. Hermisson, *Sprache und Ritus im altisraelitischen Kult. WMANT,* 19 (1965), 84ff.; J. Milgrom, "The Paradox of the Red Cow," *VT,* 31 (1981), 62-72; W. Paschen, *Rein und Unrein. SANT,* 24 (1970); S. Wefing, "Beobachtungen zum Ritual mit der roten Kuh (Num 19,1-10a)," *ZAW,* 93 (1981), 341-364; I. Zatelli, "Il campo lessicale degli aggettivi di purità in ebraico biblico," *Quaderni di semitistica,* 7 (1978), 37-42, 89-100.

1. *BDB,* 622; Rashi; et al.
2. → נדד *nāḏaḏ.*
3. *KBL*², 596; but not *HAL,* II, 673.
4. JM, §88Bh.
5. J. Milgrom, "Sin-Offering or Purification-Offering?" *VT,* 21 (1971), 237-39.

of purification" (Nu. 8:7). Thus both *mê niddâ* and *mê ḥaṭṭā't* refer to a kind of water used in purification.

2. *LXX and Targum.* The LXX uses a variety of substantives to translate *niddâ: áphedros* (11 times), *rhantismós* (5 times), *akatharsía* (4 times), *chōrismós* (3 times), and *agnismós* (once). The translations *metakineín* and *metakínēsis* appear to have read a form of *ndh* I. In Nu. 19 the LXX and Targ. translate *niddâ* as though derived from Arab. *ndy,* "sprinkle."[6] Thus the LXX reads *hýdōr rhantismoú,* Targ. Onqelos and Targ. Jonathan have *mê 'addāyûṯā',* "water of sprinkling" (cf. Targ. Onqelos in Nu. 31:23), and the Vulg. has *aqua aspersionis.*

II. Meanings. The noun *niddâ* occurs 29 times in the OT (the form *nîḏâ* in Lam. 1:8 probably does not belong here). It is found in three semantic domains: (1) impurity in connection with menstruation; (2) impurity in general, abomination; and (3) purification.

1. *In Connection with Menstruation.* We find *niddâ* most often as a technical term for the impurity of a menstruating woman (Lev. 15:19,20,33). Intercourse with a menstruant brings the same impurity on the man (v. 24; cf. 18:19; 20:18). A woman afflicted with a discharge of blood outside the normal menstrual cycle is also considered unclean (vv. 25-30). According to Lev. 12:2,5, immediately after childbirth a woman is in a condition "as at the time of her menstruation."

Ezekiel shows clearly that he stands firmly in the priestly tradition in his usage of *niddâ* (Ezk. 18:6: the phrase *'iššâ niddâ* comprises two nouns in apposition, the second functioning as an attribute of the first; cf. 22:10; 36:17).

2. *In General.* We also find *niddâ* used quite generally for "impurity, uncleanness." 2 Ch. 29:5 offers an instructive example: the Levites are told to remove the *niddâ* from the sanctuary. But v. 16, which describes how these instructions were carried out, uses the word *ṭum'â,* which suggests that *niddâ* is used in a general sense (cf. also Ezk. 7:19f.; Lam. 1:17; Ezr. 9:11).

Once *niddâ* occurs with the meaning "abomination, atrocity": If a man takes his brother's wife, he is guilty of *niddâ* (Lev. 20:21). Other sins are categorized similarly with expressions like *zimmâ,* "depravity" (18:17; 20:14), *tô'ēḇâ,* "abomination" (18:23; 20:12), and *ḥeseḏ,* "disgrace" (20:17).

3. *Purification.* In the final group of texts, *niddâ* develops a meaning antithetical to the sense just discussed, namely, "purification." Someone who touches a corpse must be sprinkled with *mê niddâ* (water mixed with the ashes of a red heifer: Nu. 19:9,13,20,21; 31:23). A similar meaning of *niddâ* occurs in Zec. 13:1: "A fountain shall be opened . . . for *ḥaṭṭā't* and for *niddâ.*" Most scholars interpret *mê niddâ* as

6. → נזה *nāzâ.*

"water (for the removal) of impurity," but the context here suggests the meaning "purification" for *niddâ*.[7]

III. Lam. 1:8. In Lam. 1:8 *nîḏâ* is often understood as a form of *niddâ*.[8] It is better, however, to associate this word with the root *nwd* and the idiom *hēnîḏ bᵉrōš* (Jer. 18:1; Ps. 44:15[Eng. v. 14]), with the meaning "(object of) scorn, mockery."[9]

Milgrom — Wright

IV. Dead Sea Scrolls. The Dead Sea Scrolls make frequent use of *niddâ* (40 occurrences); the highest concentrations are in 1QS (9), 4Q512 ("Ritual of Purification"; 8), and 11QTemple (5). Surprisingly, *niddâ* appears in 1QS only in the latest literary stratum (100-75 B.C.); in other words, it plays no role in the primary formulations of the fundamental regulations governing the Qumran Essenes, while the word group → טהר *ṭhr* already appears twice in the first revision (1QS 8:17,24), the "penal code," and more frequently in the second revision, the Community Rule itself. Only long after consolidation of the community did religious difficulties arise concerning "pure/impure," requiring codification. There came into being a manual for novices (1QS 3f.), the *maśkîl* law (1QS 4), and the purity catechesis (5:13-20), which defined purity more sharply through extensive contrastive examples. Purity/impurity was established in both the anthropological realm (cf. also 1QH 1:22; 11:11; 12:25; 17:19; CD 3:17) and above all in the moral and ethical realm (1QS 4:10; 5:19; 10:24; CD 12:2). Membership in the community is an essential criterion of human purity (1QS 3:4,9; CD 2:1). One can escape *niddâ* by obedience to the Torah (1QS 5:19). Only then the purification rituals with *mê niddâ* (3:4) and *mê ḏôḵî* (v. 9) achieve their true meaning. For the Qumran Essenes, it is a fundamental article of faith that human *niddâ* is ultimately removed by God in person through sprinkling (→ נזה *nāzâ*) with the "holy spirit" *(rûaḥ qōḏeš)* and the "spirit of truth" *(rûaḥ ʾᵉmeṯ)* (4:21f.). The hymnic conclusion of the Manual of Discipline formulates this belief in dogmatic terms: "By his righteousness he purifies me from human impurity *(minniddaṯ ʾᵉnôš)* and from the sin of humankind" (11:14f.).

In the Thanksgiving Hymns *niddâ* appears several times as one of many terms for human sinfulness: "source of impurity" (1QH 1:22; 12:25), "abomination of impurity and sin of unfaithfulness" (11:11),[10] "I have wallowed in impurity" (17:19); cf. also fr. 3 16.

The occurrences in 4Q have nothing further to add. Some in 4Q512 occur in combinations that are very interesting linguistically (e.g., *negaʿ hanniddâ,* "blow of impurity" [5:17]; *niddôṯ ṭumʾâ,* "impurities of impurity" [12:9]); but they remain essentially within the domain of Nu. 19 (cf. also 11QTemple 49:18).

---

7. See I.1 above.
8. *BDB,* 622; *KBL*², 596; but cf. *HAL,* II, 696.
9. D. Hillers, *Lamentations. AB,* 7A (1972), 9f.; et al.
10. For the first two meanings → VIII, 548.

The occurrences in the Temple Scroll refer as a rule to impurity occasioned by sexual phenomena (pollution: 45:10; menstruation: 48:16f.). 11QTemple 66:13 reflects Lev. 20:21, describing intercourse between people related by marriage as *niddâ*. Here *niddâ* moves into the semantic domain of taboo terminology.[11]

Fabry

11. See also G. W. Buchanan, "The Role of Purity in the Structure of the Essene Sect," *RevQ*, 4 (1963), 397-406; *idem, The Consequences of the Covenant. NovTSup*, 2 (1970); S. B. Hoenig, "Qumran Rules of Impurities," *RevQ*, 6 (1969), 559-567; B. E. Thiering, "Inner and Outer Cleaning at Qumran as a Background to NT Baptism," *NTS*, 26 (1979/80), 266-277; H. Thyen, *EDNT*, II, 218-220; L. Goppelt, *TDNT*, VIII, 317-322.

נָדַח nāḏaḥ; מַדּוּחִים maddûḥîm

Contents: I. Etymology. II. Usage: 1. Survey; 2. Qal; 3. Niphal; 4. Pual; 5. Hiphil; 6. Hophal; 7. *maddûḥîm*. III. Dead Sea Scrolls. IV. LXX.

I. Etymology. Almost all earlier scholars thought that there was only a single root *ndḥ* in the OT.[1] This root, which in most OT texts has the basic meaning "impel, drive out, scatter," or the like, is also found in Middle Hebrew.[2] It appears as well in Ethiopic (*nadḥa* I, "wield, strike, impel"), Tigré, and Arabic (*nadaḥa*, I: "widen, enlarge," V: "become dispersed"; it is also found in stem VII).[3]

Citing Arab. *nadaḫ*, G. R. Driver proposes the existence of a verb *ndḥ* II in the OT. He argues that the LXX recognized such a root in Prov. 7:21, where it translates (incorrectly, according to Driver) the Hebrew with *exokéllein*, and claims to find the hypothetical root in 3 OT passages: Dt. 20:19 (qal): *lindōaḥ ʿālāyw garzen*, "to drive/impel an axe against it"; Dt. 19:5 (niphal): *wᵉniddᵉḥâ* [Sam.: *wndḥ*] *yāḏô ḇaggarzen*, "his hand is laid/applied to the axe"; 2 S. 15:14 (hiphil): *wᵉhiddîaḥ ʿālênû ʾeṯ-hārārʿâ*, "he impelled, i.e., set in motion, the evil against us." He concludes: "Thus the first verb describes turning cattle out into the open fields or driving people either into a strange country or into license to do what they ought not, while the latter describes driving a tool home; they describe the same action though carried out in opposite

nāḏaḥ. G. R. Driver, "Hebrew Roots and Words," *WO*, 1 (1950), 406-415; H. D. Preuss, *Deuteronomium. EdF*, 164 (1982).

1. E.g., *GesTh*, 854.
2. Jastrow, 878.
3. See, respectively, *LexLingAeth*, 679f.; *WbTigr*, 338b; Lane, 1780. On stem VII see J. G. Hava, *Arabic-English Lexicon* (Beirut, 1951), s.v.; *HAL*, II, 673, incorrectly cites VIII.

directions and ought therefore to be similarly kept apart in the dictionaries, even though they may be ultimately derived from a common root."[4] On these weak grounds, some lexicons now list a separate verb *ndḥ* II.[5]

The root *ndḥ* appears to be related to *dḥh/dḥy,* and probably also to *dwḥ* and *dḥḥ;* cf. also *dḥp* (qal: "push away") and *dḥq* (qal: "oppress," "thrust, urge," etc.).[6]

II. Usage.

1. *Survey.* The Hebrew verb *ndḥ* occurs 58 times in the OT (3 times *ndḥ* II[7]); there are 2 occurrences of the qal (2 S. 14:14 [not cited in *HAL*!]; Dt. 20:19), 25 of the niphal (including 4 of *niḏḥê yiśrā'ēl* [Isa. 11:12; 56:8; Ps. 147:2; Sir. 51:12; sometimes interpreted incorrectly as the niphal of *dḥh*[8]] and Dt. 19:5, which *HAL* assigns to *ndḥ* II[9]), 1 of the pual (Isa. 8:22 [possibly to be read *minnōgâ*]), 29 of the hiphil (including 2 S. 15:14, which *HAL* assigns to *ndḥ* II;[10] 2 K. 17:21 [*Q*]; Sir. 8:19; and a conjectural emendation in Jer. 51:34 [*wᵉhiddîḥānî*]), and one of the hophal (Isa. 13:14).

The 58 occurrences of *ndḥ* cluster primarily in Jeremiah (19, including 51:34 conj.) and Deuteronomy (10). The others are distributed as follows: Isa. 1–39, 6; 2 Samuel, 4; Ezekiel and Psalms, 3 each; 2 Chronicles and Sirach, 2 each; Micah, 2 Kings, Deutero-Isaiah, Zephaniah, Joshua, Proverbs, Nehemiah, Job, and Daniel, 1 each.

Among the roots that function in some way as synonyms of *ndḥ* are *ndd* (e.g., Isa. 16:1-4; Jer. 49:5); *pwḥ* hiphil (e.g., Dt. 30:3f.; Jer. 23:2f.); *rdp* (e.g., 29:18). The primary antonym of *ndḥ* is the piel of *qbṣ* (e.g., Dt. 30:3f.; Jer. 29:14; 32:37; 49:5; Mic. 4:6; Zeph. 3:39; Neh. 1:9), but others are *šwb* qal (e.g., Dt. 30:3f.; Jer. 29:14; 43:5) and hiphil (e.g., Dt. 22:1; Jer. 16:15; 32:37; Ezk. 34:4,16), *bw'* hiphil (e.g., Dt. 30:4f.; Jer. 23:8; Neh. 1:9), and *lqḥ* (e.g., Dt. 30:4). The combination of *ndh* niphal with *hištaḥᵃwâ* and *'bd* in Dt. 4:19 and 30:17 is unique.

The only derivative of *ndḥ* in the OT is the hapax legomenon *maddûḥîm* (Lam. 2:14).

2. *Qal.* The 2 OT occurrences of *ndḥ* in the qal can be understood quite naturally on the basis of a common meaning "push (away)." The early pre-Deuteronomic formulation of one of the laws governing war in Deuteronomy reads: "If you besiege a town for a long time, making war against it in order to take it, you must not destroy its trees by wielding an ax against them" (. . . *lō'-taškîṯ 'eṯ-'ēṣâ lindōaḥ 'ālāyw garzen:* 20:19).[11] In the artfully framed conversation between David and the wise woman of

---

4. P. 409.
5. *CHAL,* 229; *HAL,* II, 673 (with a question mark).
6. *HAL,* I, 219. The relation to *dḥh/dḥy* was already noted by *GesTh,* 854. For the relation to *dwḥ* and *dḥḥ* see Driver, 409, n. 22.
7. Driver, *HAL,* et al.
8. E.g., Mandelkern, 293.
9. *HAL,* II, 673.
10. *Ibid.*
11. Preuss, 55, 139f.

Tekoa, who at Joab's request tries to intercede on behalf of Absalom, who has fled from Jerusalem to Geshur, the argument runs: "(God) will devise plans so as not to cast away (*yiddaḥ* qal) one who has been cast out (*niddāḥ* niphal)" (2 S. 14:14).[12] G. R. Driver's arguments notwithstanding,[13] this text does not use two different verbs that "describe the same action though carried out in opposite directions": in both cases, the action of "casting" proceeds from the subject (God and Israel, respectively).

3. *Niphal.* All 25 occurrences of the niphal can be interpreted as reflexive or passive equivalents of the qal. This is true also in Dt. 19:5:[14] the Deuteronomic laws governing the cities of refuge address the case of someone who accidentally kills his neighbor when they have gone into a forest to cut wood: "and his hand is stretched out with the ax to cut down a tree" *(wᵉniddᵉḥâ* [Sam.: *wndḥ*] *yāḏô ḇaggarzen liḵrōṯ hāʿēṣ).*[15]

Many instances of the niphal make clear that *ndḥ* belongs to the language of animal husbandry. An early (pre-Deuteronomic?[16]) law in Deuteronomy requires that one take back a neighbor's oxen or sheep that have strayed (*niddāḥîm:* 22:1). This concrete language could naturally be used metaphorically: Israel, Yahweh's flock, repeatedly "strayed" and became "scattered." This usage is especially transparent in Ezekiel's invective and threat against the false shepherds of Israel during the exile: "You did not gather the strayed" (*wᵉʾeṯ-hanniddaḥaṯ lōʾ hᵃšēḇōṯem:* 34:4); therefore, says Yahweh, "I will bring back the strayed" (*wᵉhanniddāḥâ ʾāšîḇ:* v. 16). The parallel oracle of Yahweh in Mic. 4:6 concerning the new Jerusalem may be based on Ezk. 34: "I will gather those who have been driven away" *(wᵉhanniddāḥâ ʾᵃqabbēṣ).*[17]

The same metaphorical shepherd language, albeit not always so clear, lies behind the occurrences in the book of Jeremiah. An exception is 30:17, which calls the northern kingdom in the period ca. 622-612 an "outcast (woman)" *(niddāḥâ).*[18] Elsewhere the image of the scattered herd (Judah, Ammon, Elam) dominates the scene. The account of Gedaliah's governorship and murder (40:7–41:18; once independent) reports that the diaspora Judeans came to Gedaliah in the land of Judah "from all the places to which they had been scattered" (40:12). Baruch's account of the migration to Egypt (42:1–43:7) says that Johanan son of Koreah and all the commanders took all the remnant of Judah that had returned "from all the nations to which they had been driven" (43:5) and led them to Egypt. In the collection of oracles against the nations (chs. 46–51), the oracle of Yahweh against Ammon (49:1-6) says: "You will be scattered, each headlong, with no one to gather the fugitives" (v. 5); and the oracle against Elam (49:34-39) says: "There shall be no nation to which the exiles from Elam will not come" (v. 36).

---

12. But see S. R. Driver, *Notes on the Hebrew Text and the Topography of the Books of Samuel* (Oxford, ²1913), 308.
13. P. 409.
14. *HAL: ndḥ* II.
15. E. König, *Das Deuteronomium. KAT,* III (1917), 145.
16. Preuss, 56.
17. H. W. Wolff, *Micah* (Eng. trans., Minneapolis, 1990), 123f.
18. On the text see W. Rudolph, *Jeremia. HAT,* XII (³1968), 188-193.

The same usage has penetrated the (late exilic?) Deuteronomistic strata of Deuteronomy, in the great farewell discourse of Moses (Dt. 29–30): "Even if you are exiles to the end of the heavens, from there Yahweh your God will gather you, and from there he will bring you back" (30:4).[19] This passage is adapted freely in the prayer of Nehemiah (Neh. 1:5-11a: v. 9).[20] Late exilic at the earliest is the related formulation in the concluding promise of the book of Zephaniah (3:16-20): "I will gather the outcast [Zion]" (v. 19).

The other instances of the usage are almost without exception postexilic. This is true of Job 6:13: *ha'im 'ên 'ezrāṯî ḇî wᵉṯušîyâ niddᵉḥâ mimmennî,* which may mean: "Is not the possibility of my helping myself as nothing, and has not all means of help been driven from me?"[21] It is clearly also true of the four passages in Isa. 1–39: 16:3,4, the "outcasts of Moab"; 27:13, "those [Israelites] who were driven out of the land of Egypt."[22] Only the common phrase "outcasts of Israel" (*niḏḥê yiśrā'ēl:* 11:12, where it is postexilic[23]) may be somewhat earlier (56:8), but it survives in later usage (Ps. 147:2[24]), e.g., in Sir. 51:12 as a term denoting the diaspora communities: "Give thanks to the one who gathers the outcasts of Israel."[25]

A unique tolerative meaning of the niphal of *ndḥ,* "allow oneself to be led astray," is found in two texts in Deuteronomy, both probably exhibiting Deuteronomistic language.[26] A vigorous warning is sounded against departing from the Deuteronomic and Deuteronomistic ideal of monolatry: "do not be led astray and bow down to them [sun, moon, stars, and host of heaven] and serve them" (*wᵉniddaḥtā wᵉhištaḥᵃwîṯā lāhem wa'ᵃḇaḏtām:* 4:19); "lest you be led astray to bow down to other gods and serve them" (*wᵉniddaḥtā wᵉhištaḥᵃwîṯā lē'lōhîm 'ᵃḥērîm wa'ᵃḇaḏtām:* 30:17).

4. *Pual.* The only pual form of *ndḥ* found in the MT is in Isa. 8:22, the so-called memorial of Isaiah, which deals with the prophet's ministry in the period of the Syro-Ephraimite war (6:1–9:6[Eng. v. 7]). Here the short passage 8:21-23aα(9:1aα) (probably genuine) speaks of the "oppressive darkness" *(wa'ᵃpēlâ mᵉnuddāḥ)* of a group of North Israelites.[27]

---

19. Preuss, 60, 160f.

20. F. Michaeli, *Les Livres des Chroniques, d'Esdras et de Néhémie. CAT,* XVI (1967), 309.

21. E. Dhorme, *Job* (Eng. trans., repr. Nashville, 1984), 83f.

22. On 16:3,4 see H. Wildberger, *Isaiah 13–27* (Eng. trans., Minneapolis, 1997), 141f.; W. Rudolph, "Jesaja xv-xvi," *Hebrew and Semitic Studies. Festschrift G. R. Driver* (Oxford, 1963), 136. On 27:13 see Wildberger, *Isaiah 13–27,* 598f.

23. Wildberger, *Isaiah 1–12* (Eng. trans., Minneapolis, 1991), 489f.

24. H.-J. Kraus, *Psalms 60–150* (Eng. trans., Minneapolis, 1989), 554-56.

25. G. Sauer, *Jesus Sirach. JSHRZ,* III/5 (1981), 489, 635.

26. Preuss, 47, 60.

27. Wildberger, *Isaiah 1–12,* 376-382. He rightly says of the interpretation offered by Guillaume and G. R. Driver: "In this case also, making use of the Arabic seems too risky" (377). The reading *minnōgah,* suggested by *BHS,* is also possible.

5. *Hiphil.* Like the niphal, the causative hiphil of *ndḥ* is used for the most part metaphorically. The shepherd language in the background is nevertheless clear in two Jeremiah passages, especially in the oracle against Babylon (50:1–51:58): "A stray sheep was Israel, chased by lions" (*śeh pᵉzûrâ yiśrā'ēl 'ᵃryôṯ hiddîḥû:* 50:17, reading *hiddîḥûḥû* or *hiddîḥûhā*[28]). An oracle of Yahweh against the kings of Judah (21:11–23:8) says: "You have scattered my sheep and driven them away *(wattaddiḥûm)*. . . . I myself will gather the remnant of my sheep out of all the lands where I have driven them" (23:2f.).

This metaphorical use of the hiphil, found already in Jer. 23:2f., becomes an effective tool for theological interpretation of the exile: the people of God were indeed scattered by hostile lions (Assyria, Babylon: Jer. 50:17; cf. also 51:34, if we may read *hiddîḥānî* instead of MT *Q hᵉḏîḥānî*[29]); but the real tragedy is this: behind all the scatterings of Israel Yahweh, the shepherd of Israel, stands sovereign. A series of exilic texts in Jeremiah, Ezekiel, and Deuteronomy used the hiphil of *ndḥ* to express the repulsing, scattering activity of Yahweh, either in the 1st person (Ezk. 4:13 [possibly secondary; cf. LXX]; Jer. 8:3; 23:3,8; 24:9 [possibly a secondary addition based on Dt. 28:37[30]]; 27:10,15; 29:14,18; 32:37; 46:28; cf. Joel 2:20) or in the 3rd person (Dt. 30:1 [*hiddîḥᵃḵā;* Sam.: *ydyḥk*]; Jer. 16:15). In the same context, however, the image of Yahweh as the faithful shepherd is underlined by a promise, as in Jeremiah's letter to the deportees of 598 (Jer. 29): "I will gather you from all the nations and from all the places where I have driven you" (v. 14; cf. also 23:3,8; 32:27; 46:28; Dt. 30:1-4). This language can still be heard in the penitential prayer of Daniel (Dnl. 9:4-20): *bᵉḵol-hā'ᵃrāṣôṯ 'ᵃšer hiddaḥtām šām* (v. 7).[31]

The same metaphorical language is sometimes used in other contexts. Ps. 5, a preexilic hymnic prayer,[32] calls on God to cast out *(haddîḥēmô)* the psalmist's enemies (v. 11[10]). In the words of King Abijah to the king and people of the northern kingdom (2 Ch. 13:4b-12; special material of the Chronicler), Abijah criticizes his listeners because they have driven out the Aaronite priests and the Levites (v. 9). The composite passage Jo. 2:18–3:5(2:18-32) says of "the northern one" *(haṣṣᵉpônî)* that Yahweh will drive him into a parched and desolate land (v. 20).[33] The only occurrence in a wisdom context is Sir. 8:19: "Reveal your heart to no one, lest you drive something good away."[34]

It is clear, however, that the hiphil of *ndḥ* also has roots in the language of love. In

---

28. *BHS.*

29. Rudolph, *HAT,* XII, 312.

30. *Ibid.,* 156.

31. On the language see L. F. Hartman and A. A. di Lella, *Book of Daniel. AB,* 23 (1978), 248f.

32. W. Beyerlin, *Die Rettung den Bedrängten in den Feindpsalmen der Einzelnen auf institutionelle zusammenhänge untersucht. FRLANT,* 99 (1970), 90.

33. A. Lauha, *Zaphon. AnAcScFen,* 49/2 (1943); H. W. Wolff, *Joel and Amos. Herm* (Eng. trans. 1977), 62.

34. Sauer, *Sirach,* 526.

the wisdom warning against the temptress (Prov. 7), we read: "With much seductive speech she persuades him [the foolish youth], with her smooth talk she compels him" (*beḥēleq śepāṯeyhā taddîḥennû:* v. 21).[35] This mode of expression can be used metaphorically of seductive ways of the enemy, for example, in the hymnic prayer of an individual: "They take pleasure in seduction" (*yāʿaṣû lehaddîaḥ:* Ps. 62:5[4]).[36]

The same usage may be reflected in a few texts that speak of religious seduction (in parallel with the niphal: Dt. 4:39; 30:17[?]). The language is probably Deuteronomistic. For example, Dt. 13:6(5) declares that the prophet or dreamer must be put to death because he "made you stray from the way" *(lehaddîḥaḵā min-hadderek);* a brother who tempts someone into apostasy must be stoned (13:11; both passages are Deuteronomistic[37]), as must those who "lead the inhabitants of the town astray" into idolatry (13:14[13]; Deuteronomic?[38]). In the Deuteronomistic history it is Jeroboam: he "drove Israel from following Yahweh" (2 K. 17:21); in the Chronicler's history it is Jehoram: he "made Judah go astray" (2 Ch. 21:11; special material of the Chronicler).

Another passage in the Deuteronomistic history, however, must be distinguished clearly from this usage. Speaking of Absalom, David says to his officials in Jerusalem: "Let us flee, lest he overtake us and bring disaster down upon us" (*wehiddîaḥ ʿālênû 'eṯ-hārāʿâ:* 2 S. 15:14). This is not a different verb,[39] but the hiphil of *ndḥ* with the normal meaning "cause to fall upon" (cf. Eth. *nadḥa,* "impel"[40]).

6. *Hophal.* The only occurrence of the hophal in the OT is used in a concrete sense. The post-Isaianic oracle concerning the fall of Babylon and Israel's return (dating from the end of the Neobabylonian Empire?) says that the Babylonians will flee "like a hunted gazelle *(kiṣbî muddāḥ),* or like sheep with no one to gather them" (Isa. 13:14).[41]

7. *maddûḥîm.* The only derivative of the verb *ndḥ* in the OT is *maddûḥîm.*[42] The eyewitness account of the catastrophe of 587 in Lam. 2 says of Zion/Jerusalem: "Your prophets have seen for you false and deceptive visions . . . , deception and exile" (*šāw' ûmaddûḥîm:* v. 14).[43] From the context, *maddûḥîm* here means neither "seduction" nor "false claims" (cf. Arab. *tanaddaḫa*), but "driving out, exile."[44]

---

35. O. Plöger, *Sprüche Salomos. BK,* XVII (1984), 73-81.
36. But A. Weiser (*Psalms. OTL* [Eng. trans. 1962], 445) and others translate: "They plan to bring/thrust him down"; cf. EÜ and NRSV.
37. Preuss, 52.
38. *Ibid.,* 53.
39. Contra Driver, *CHAL,* and *HAL.*
40. See I above.
41. Wildberger, *Isaiah 13–27,* 3-28.
42. *BLe,* §61gη; *GK,* §124f.
43. On the text and its context, see W. Rudolph, *Hosea. KAT,* XVII/1-3 (1966), 216-227.
44. Cf. LXX, Vulg.; for "seduction" see Syr., Targ., EÜ; for "false claims" see Driver, 409, n. 22.

III. Dead Sea Scrolls. The root *ndḥ* occurs a few times in the Dead Sea Scrolls. In 1QM 14:9f. the remnant of the people of God say of the malevolence of Belial: "And through all the mysteries of his malevolence, they have not led (us) astray (*ndḥ* hiphil) from your covenant" (cf. in the OT esp. Dt. 13:6[5], with *min*). In 1QH 4:8f. the root *ndḥ* occurs twice (hophal and niphal?). The worshiping community speaks as a collective "I" concerning the followers of Belial: "For I was cast out by them, and they paid me no regard, although you show yourself mighty on my behalf; for they drove me out of my land [*ky' ydyḥny m'rṣy;* cf. in the OT esp. Jer. 51:34 conj.; 2 Ch. 17:20 *Q;* also Sir. 8:19[45]] like a bird out of its nest. And all my friends and family have been turned away from me [*ndḥw mmny;* cf. in the OT esp. Dt. 4:19; 30:17] and think of me as a useless implement."

The root also occurs in the texts from Cave 4.[46] Two of the passages are damaged: in 4QM[a] (4Q491) 8-10 1:7, we have a parallel to 1QM 14:9f.; in a halakhic fragment (4QOrd[b] [4Q513] 18:2), we find the word [*y*]*dyḥn*[*w*], perhaps to be read as *lw' ydyḥnw* and interpreted as a reference to the release of slaves in the Sabbatical Year.[47] In the liturgical collection 4QDibHam[a] (4Q504) fr. 1-2 5:11-14, God is addressed: "You have shown your favor toward your people Israel in all the lands where you have driven them *(bkwl* [*h*]*'rṣwt 'šr hdḥtm šmh),* that they may decide to return to you and hearken to your voice, according to all that you have commanded through your servant Moses." Finally, there are two occurrences in 4QPrFêtes[c] (4Q509). A very fragmentary passage (fr. 12 i and 13) begins: "The exiles *(hmnwdḥym)* who stray without anyone to bring them back"; and in fr. 183 7, without any legible context, we find *hdḥtw b,* which might possibly be interpreted as "you have scattered them in. . . ."[48]

IV. LXX. The LXX uses a wide variety of words to translate *ndḥ.* The most common is *exōtheín* (qal once; niphal 4 times; hiphil 13 times); *maddûḥîm* (Lam. 2:4) is represented similarly by *exṓsmata* (elsewhere *exōtheín* is used for *dwḥ* hiphil, *dḥh* pual, *k'h* niphal, *lqḥ, nd'* hiphil, *ndd* hophal, *ndp* niphal, *nsḥ, rḥq* hiphil, *t'h* hiphil). Among the other translations of *ndḥ* in the LXX are: qal: *epibállein* (once); niphal: *diaspeírein* (twice), *diasporá* (3 times), *planán* (5 times), etc.; pual: *skótos hṓste mḗ blépein* (Isa. 8:22, probably reflecting a different text than MT *'ᵃpēlâ mᵉnuddāḥ,* possibly *'ᵃpēlâ mērᵉ'ôt*[49]); hiphil: *diaspeírein* (3 times), etc.; hophal: *pheúgein* (once). Finally, we may note that the occurrences assigned by *HAL* to *ndḥ* II are translated as follows: Dt. 20:19 (qal): *epibállein;* Dt. 19:5 (niphal): *ekkroúein;* 2 S. 15:14 (hiphil): *exōtheín;* these translations at least suggest that the LXX did not recognize a root *ndḥ* II.

Kronholm

---

45. See also S. Holm-Nielsen, *Hodayot* (Aarhus, 1960), 81.
46. M. Baillet, *Qumrân Grotte 4. DJD,* VII (1982), index.
47. *Ibid.,* 293.
48. *Ibid.,* 207.
49. Wildberger, *Isaiah 1–12,* 376f.

נָדַר *nāḏar;* נֶדֶר *neḏer*

Contents: I. 1. Etymology; 2. Forms and Usage in Other Languages; 3. Formulas. II. 1. Religious Usage in the OT; 2. Occurrences. III. Vows as Conditional Promises: 1. Psalms; 2. Vow Narratives. IV. Vows of Abstinence: 1. Nazirites; 2. Other Self-Imposed Obligations. V. LXX.

I. 1. *Etymology.* There are identical or equivalent verbs corresponding to Heb. *nāḏar,* "make a vow," in Ugaritic, Imperial Aramaic, Palmyrene, Punic, Jewish Aramaic, Samaritan, Syriac, and Mandaic.[1] The same is true of the noun *neḏer* (more rarely *nēḏer*), "vow, vow offering," in Ugaritic, Phoenician, Punic, Jewish Aramaic, Syriac, and Mandaic.[2] Old Aram. *nzr,* Arab. *naḏara,* "consecrate," *naḏr,* "vow, consecrated offering," *nāḏīr,* "consecrated one," as well as Sab. *nḏr* I, "make atonement," together with Heb. → נזר *nzr* niphal, "abstain," *nāzîr,* "consecrated one," and *nezer,* "consecration," raise a difficult problem of historical linguistics: the relationship of the roots *ndr, nzr,* and *nḏr.*[3] Akk. *nazāru,* "revile, curse," Arab. *naḏira* IV, "warn," and Sab. *nḏr* II, "warn, threaten," must also be taken into account.[4]

---

nāḏar. J. Gold, *Das Gelübde nach Bibel und Talmud* (1926); M. Joseph, "Vow (Jewish)," *ERE,* XII, 657-59; C. A. Keller, "נדר *ndr* 'to vow,' " *TLOT,* II, 719-22; B. Kötting (B. Kaiser), "Gelübde," *RAC,* IX, 1059-66; J. E. McFadyen, "Vows (Hebrew)," *ERE,* XII, 654-56; S. B. Parker, "The Vow in Ugaritic and Israelite Narrative Literature," *Festschrift C. F. A. Schaeffer. UF,* 11 (1979), 693-700; H. G. Perelmuter, "Gelübde," *TRE,* XII, 304f.; H. D. Preuss, "Gelübde," *TRE,* XII, 302-4; W. Richter, "Das Gelübde als theologische Rahmung der Jakobsüberlieferungen," *BZ,* N.S. 11 (1967), 21-52; A. Wendel, *Das freie Laiengebet im vorexilischen Israel. JEOL,* 5/6 (1931), 100-122; *idem, Das israelitisch-jüdische Gelübde* (Berlin, 1931).

Ancient world: (a) Ancient Near East and Egypt: J. Assmann, "Gelübde," *LexÄg,* II, 519-521; E. Ebeling, "Gelübde," *RLA,* III, 200f.; B. Kötting (B. Kaiser), "Gelübde," *RAC,* IX, 1057-59.

(b) Phoenicians in North Africa: G. Garbini, *I Fenici: Storia e religione* (Naples, 1980), 175ff.; S. Gsell, *Histoire ancienne de l'Afrique du Nord,* IV (1924), 404-425.

(c) Arabs: W. Gottschalk, *Das Gelübde nach älterer arabischer Auffassung* (Berlin, 1919); J. Pedersen, *Das Eid bei den Semiten* (Strassburg, 1914); cf. *idem, "nadhr," Handwörterbuch des Islam* (Leiden, 1941), 564f.

(d) Greeks and Romans: W. D. H. Rouse, *Greek Votive Offerings* (Cambridge, 1902); W. Eisenhut, *PW Sup,* XIV, 964-973; B. Kötting (B. Kaiser), *RAC,* IX, 1072-84.

1. See *WUS,* no. 1758; *DISO,* 174f.; R. S. Tomback, *A Comparative Semitic Lexicon of the Phoenician and Punic Languages. SBLDS,* 32 (1978), 210f.; *WTM,* III, 345f.; Z. Ben-Ḥayyim, *The Literary and Oral Traditions of Hebrew and Aramaic among the Samaritans,* 3 vols. (Jerusalem, 1957-61), II, 446; *LexSyr,* 416; *MdD,* 290a.

2. On *nēḏer* see *BLe,* 459f., 566f.; on Ugaritic, *WUS,* no. 1758; on Phoenician and Punic, Tomback, 211; on Jewish Aramaic, *WTM,* 346f.; on Syriac, *LexSyr,* 416; on Mandaic, *MdD,* 281b, 297a.

3. For Old Aramaic see the Barhadad inscription, *KAI,* 201, 4; *TSSI,* II, 1, 4; for Arabic, Lane, 2781f.; Wehr, 953; for Sabaic, Beeston, 91; Biella, 294f. For the relation see G. Garbini, *Il Semitico di Nord-Ovest* (1960), 195; cf. *VG,* I, 237; Keller, *TLOT,* II, 719.

4. See *AHw,* II, 772b; Lane, 2781f.; Wehr, 953; Beeston, 91; Biella, 290.

2. *Forms and Usage in Other Languages.* In Ugaritic, *ndr ṯ̱t* means "vow an offering" and *ndr dbḥ* means "vow a sacrifice."[5] The noun form *mḏr,* "vow," is dubious, however.[6] It is noteworthy that, despite the wealth of Palmyrene inscriptions in comparison to Punic, the noun is not found in them and the verb is attested only once.[7] The Ugaritic PNs *bn ndr* and *ndrg[d]* are problematic in the light of the readings in *KTU,* 1.79, 4; 1.18, 18.[8] For now, clear evidence of personal names formed by use of the root *ndr/nḏr* appears to be limited to Nab. *ndrw* and Saf. *nḏr'l,* together with the short forms *nḏr* and *mnḏr.*[9] These observations may be accounted for by the hypothesis that, as a rule, children born after a vow received a name expressing thanksgiving.[10]

3. *Formulas.* Formulas and formulaic expressions found in the OT include: (1) *nāḏar neḏer,* "vow a vow, make a vow" (Gen. 31:13; Nu. 6:2; 30:3,4[Eng. vv. 2,3] par. 11QTemple 53:11; 2 S. 15:8; Isa. 19:21; Jon. 1:16; cf. 11QTemple 53:14; Ep. Jer. 35; 2 Mc. 3:35); note also the usual formula introducing a vow narrative: *wayyiddōr neḏer,* "and he made vow" (Gen. 28:20; Nu. 21:2; Jgs. 11:30; 1 S. 1:11 [fem.]); (2) the retrospective or prospective statement *neḏer ʾ^a^šer nāḏar/yiddōr* (Nu. 6:21; Dt. 12:11,17; 2 S. 15:7); (3) several formulas belonging to the register of cultic language, including *šillēm neḏer,* "fulfill a vow" (2 S. 15:7; Ps. 22:26[25]; 50:14; 61:9[8]; 65:2[1]; 66:13; 116:14,18; Prov. 7:14; Job 22:27; cf. Isa. 19:21; Ps. 56:13[12]; 76:12[11]; Dt. 23:22 par. 11QTemple 53:11; Eccl. 5:3f.[4f.]); *ʿāśâ neḏer,* "perform a vow" (Jer. 44:25; Jgs. 11:39; cf. Nu. 30:2[1]; Dt. 23:24); *hēqîm neḏer,* "validate a vow" (Nu. 30:14,15[13,14] par. 11QTemple 54:3; Jer. 44:25); *hēp̄ēr neḏer,* "nullify a vow" (Nu. 30:9[8]; cf. vv. 13[12],16[15] [11QTemple 54:1-3]), along with the expressions *qûm neḏer,* "a vow remains binding" (Nu. 30:5,8[4,7] par. 11QTemple 53:19; 54:4), and *lōʾ yāqûm,* "ceases to be binding" (Nu. 30:6[5] par. 11QTemple 53:21). The formulas **pillēʾ neḏer* (Lev. 22:21; Nu. 15:3,8) and *hip̄lîʾ neḏer* (Lev. 27:2; Nu. 6:2) are associated with the Priestly language of the cult. It is debated whether they should be translated "make a special vow" or simply "fulfill a vow," or even be accepted only in the piel with the meaning "make a vow."[11] As is shown by the different translations of the LXX in Leviticus and Numbers and the translation of the Vulg., which represents the second interpretation, the controversy is of long standing. (4) In

5. For the former see Parker, 694f.; for the latter see III.f.(1) below.

6. *KTU,* 1.119, 30.

7. H. Ingholt and J. Starcky, "Receuil des inscriptions sémitiques," *La Palmyrène du Nord-Ouest,* ed. D. Schlumberger (Paris, 1951), no. 14, 5 (pp. 148f.).

8. For the former see *PRU,* II, 154, 4; cf. Prov. 31:3. For the latter see *PRU,* II, 4, 18; cf. *PNU,* 164, 402.

9. *RyNP,* I, 236 and 136.

10. See, e.g., *IPN,* 169ff.; R. Albertz, *Persönliche Frömmigkeit und offizielle Religion. CThM,* A, 9C (1978), 49ff., with the table on 61f., and the comments of Benz, 313f., 421; *PNU,* 135f.; *PNPI,* 89b; F. Vattioni, *Le iscrizioni di Ḥatra. AION.Sup,* 28 (1981), 114a.

11. For the first see *HAL,* III, 927; for the second, *GesB,* 641b; *LexHebAram,* 649a; for the third, D. Kellermann, *Die Priesterschrift in Numeri 1:1 bis 10:10. BZAW,* 120 (1970), 83.

Priestly language a vow of abstinence, *'issār,* means acceptance of a binding negative obligation. It is undertaken by means of an oath *(šᵉḇûʿâ),* and is to be distinguished from an ordinary vow (Nu. 30:3[2]; cf. Ps. 132:2ff.). It appears in ritualized form as *neḏer nāzîr* (Nu. 6:2). (5) The noun *nᵉḏāḇâ,* "freewill offering," denotes a subordinate (and therefore inferior) offering related to *neḏer* (Lev. 7:16; 22:18; 23:38; Nu. 29:39; Dt. 12:6,17; cf. 23:23).

II. 1. *Religious Usage in the OT.* An oath is a solemn promise to a deity to perform a certain act if the deity acts in a certain way. It is thus a prayer demanding emphatically that God act. A special form is the unconditional self-imposed obligation that binds the person making the vow to a particular way of life for a period of time or perpetually. Both forms are widespread in developed civilizations and thus appear also in the OT,[12] where the only legitimate recipient of a vow is Yahweh. In the OT, therefore, only Jer. 44:25 speaks of a vow made to another deity, *malkaṯ haššāmayim,* whose votaries are accordingly threatened with destruction by Yahweh.[13] The high esteem enjoyed by vows in Israel can be seen from the fact that their fulfillment in Judah (Nah. 2:1[1:15]) and even in Egypt (Isa. 19:22) is counted among the signs of the age of salvation.[14] Mal. 1:14; Lev. 22:20; CD 16:13ff. (cf. 6:15) indicate and attack the human weaknesses that appear in the fulfillment of vows, as does the wisdom warning against making rash vows (Prov. 20:25; Eccl. 5:3f.[4f.]). The casuistic addition to Dt. 23:19(18) in vv. 22-24(21-23) inculcates fulfillment of vows as an absolute obligation,[15] since otherwise Yahweh will intervene to punish the failure, but leaves quite free the decision to make a vow. This accords with the statement of Qoheleth that it is better not to make a vow than to fail to fulfill it (Eccl. 5:4[5]).

2. *Occurrences.* The root *ndr* occurs 91 times in the OT. Of these occurrences, 31 are of the verb in the qal and 60 are of the noun, 5 in the form *nēḏer.* Statistics of distribution alone show that the root is concentrated in (1) vow narratives (21 times: e.g., Gen. 28:20 with 31:13; Nu. 21:2; Jgs. 11:30,39; 1 S. 1:11,21 [cf. Prov. 31:3]; 2 S. 15:7f.; Jon. 1:16; Ps. 132:2), (2) cultic *tôrôṯ* (44 times: e.g., Lev. 7:16; 22:18,21,23 [cf. Mal. 1:14]; 23:38; 27:2,8; Nu. 6:2,5,21; 15:3,8; 29:39; 30:3-15[2-14] [cf. 11QTemple 53:16–54:7]; Dt. 12:6,11,17,26 [cf. 11QTemple 53:9f.]; 23:19[18] [cf. CD 18:17ff.];

12. See the bibliog.

13. On the secondary nature of the passage, see K.-F. Pohlmann, *Studien zum Jeremiabuch. FRLANT,* 118 (1978), 181f.; on the actual religious situation in the preexilic period, see G. W. Ahlström, "An Archaeological Picture of Iron Age Religions in Ancient Palestine," *StOr,* 55/3 (1984) 115-145.

14. On the exilic dating of Nah. 2:1(1:15) see J. Jeremias, *Kultprophetie und Gerichtsverkündigung in der späten Königszeit Israels. WMANT,* 35 (1970), 13f. On the late redactional character of Isa. 19:22 see O. Kaiser, *Isaiah 13–39. OTL* (Eng. trans. 1974), 105; R. E. Clements, *Isaiah 1–39. NCB* (1980), 170.

15. W. Richter, *Recht und Ethos. SANT,* 15 (1966), 133.

23:22-24[21-23] [cf. 11QTemple 53:12-14]; [Prov. 20:25; Eccl. 5:3f.[4f.]), and (3) cultic poetry (12 times: individual songs of thanksgiving: Ps. 22:26[25]; 56:13[12]; 116:14,18; Jon. 2:10; individual laments: Ps. 61:6,9[5,8]; hymns: 65:2[1];[16] 76:12[11]; cultic psalms: 50:14;[17] 132:2; cf. also Prov. 7:14; Job 22:27; Nah. 2:1[1:15]; Isa. 19:21). The 9 occurrences in wisdom contexts (Job 22:27; Prov. 7:14; 20:25; 31:2; Eccl. 5:3f. [5 times]) and the 10 occurrences in the Prophets (Isa. 19:21 [twice]; Jer. 44:25 [4 times]; Jon. 1:16; 2:10; Nah. 2:1[1:15]; Mal. 1:14) do not constitute independent groups; as the individual citations show, they belong to one or another of the groups already identified.

III. Vows as Conditional Promises.

1. *Psalms.* Except for Ps. 132,[18] the occurrences in the Psalms can be interpreted in the light of 50:14f.: in v. 15 Yahweh urges his *ḥ^{a}sîḏîm* to call on him in the day of trouble and promises to deliver them. That a vow is expected to accompany the invocation can be seen from the command in v. 14 to offer a sacrifice of *tôḏâ* to God and pay *(šillēm)* him his vows.

Theories to the contrary notwithstanding,[19] the phrase *z^{e}ḇaḥ tôḏâ* is not to be understood figuratively, as an expression divorced from its concrete cultic meaning and referring instead to a song of thanksgiving, since v. 5 alludes to the *b^{e}rîṯ* made with *zebaḥ.* In vv. 8-13, the introduction to vv. 14f., the point is not rejection of sacrifice per se but the absence of any need on God's part, since anything a mortal could sacrifice already belongs to him. In contrast to Ps. 51, where the offering of praise in vv. 18f.(16f.) is related by vv. 20f.(18f.), a later addition, to the normative sacrificial system, the polemic of Ps. 50 is directed not against sacrifice as such but against an attitude that would see sacrifice as establishing a claim on God.[20]

The individual songs of thanksgiving that speak of paying vows (Ps. 22:26[25]; 56:13[12]; 66:13; 116:14,18; Jon. 2:10[9]) refer also to prayers answered by God (Ps. 22:25[24]; 66:19f.; 116:14; Jon. 2:10[9]; also Ps. 65:3[2]), but the introductory laments in the first two psalms do not mention any corresponding vow (of sacrifice). This indicates either that the oath was dropped from the lament when or after it was joined to the song of thanksgiving or that the ritual recitation of the lament referred to a thank offering as a matter of course. Ps. 61, an individual lament, includes such a vow in v. 9(8), although here it is unclear whether we may be dealing with a promise of continual praise, possibly different from v. 6(5).[21]

---

16. F. Crüsemann, *Studien zur Formgeschichte von Hymnus und Danklied in Israel. WMANT,* 32 (1969), 199, 201.

17. O. Loretz, *Die Psalmen. AOAT,* 207/2 (1979), 291.

18. See IV.2 below.

19. E.g., A. Weiser, *Psalms. OTL* (Eng. trans. 1962), 397.

20. H.-J. Hermisson, *Sprache und Ritus im altisraelitischen Kult. WMANT,* 19 (1965), 35f.

21. Weiser, *OTL,* 445; A. R. Johnson, *The Cultic Prophet and Israel's Psalmody* (Cardiff, 1979), 358. On vows of praise in psalms of lamentation, see the tabulation in E. Gerstenberger, *Der bittende Mensch. WMANT,* 51 (1980), 133.

The fundamental association of prayers and vows is also illustrated in the OT by 1 S. 1:10,12 and outside the OT by the prayer vow of the Hittite queen Puduḫepa.[22] That vows were fulfilled by sacrifice is shown by Ps. 56:13(12); 116:17-19. Although offering a *zeḇaḥ (šᵉlāmîm)* was the norm (2 S. 15:8,11; Jon. 1:16; Lev. 7:16; 22:21), Lev. 22:18 shows that it was also possible to offer an *ʿōlâ,* a more significant sacrifice (cf. Ps. 66:13).[23] A different meaning may be intended in Ps. 76, an eschatological song of Zion, where v. 12(11) is addressed to the nations as well as to Israel,[24] commanding them to bring gifts to the awesome God (cf. Isa. 60:5ff.).

The site of the sacrifice was obviously the sanctuary, after the exile the outer court of the Jerusalem temple (Ps. 116:19), in the presence of God's people (116:14,18) or a large congregation (22:26[25]). It is noteworthy that the texts almost always speak of fulfilling vows in the plural (*nᵉḏāray:* 22:26[25]; 56:13[12]; 61:9[8], but cf. v. 6[5]; 66:13; 116:14,18; *neḏer* in 65:2[1] is to be understood collectively). If the plural does not refer to sacrificial offerings (66:15), a secondary collective interpretation of the Psalms is possible. It would not be surprising, however, for ritual texts to suggest extensive votive offerings.

Vows are clearly addressed to Yahweh, and it is Yahweh who receives the offerings (Ps. 76:12[11]; 116:14,18; 56:13[12]; 65:2[1]; 66:13; Jon. 2:10[9]) and hears *(šāmaʿ)* the crying (*šwʿ* piel: Ps. 22:25[24]), the vows (61:6[5]), and the spoken prayer (*qôl tᵉpillâ:* 66:19) of the worshiper.

The occasion of a vow can be seen as mortal danger, and the occasion of thanksgiving as divine deliverance from it (Ps. 56:14[13]; cf. 22:21f.[20f.]; 116:3,8). The danger seems to come from enemies (56:3[2]; 61:4[3]; 66:10ff.; 22:13ff.).[25] Jon. 2:3ff.(2ff.) was composed for its context, although it is a secondary interpolation into the book of Jonah.[26] The worshiper's statement that he is paying a vow when he announces his sacrifice (Ps. 22:26[25]; 56:13[12]; 66:13; 116:14,18; Jon. 2:10[9]) reflects the vow of thanksgiving in a lament (Ps. 61:9[8]) and is so much a matter of course that it can also be incorporated into a hymn as a statement (65:2[1]) or command (76:12[11]; cf. also 2 S. 15:7; Jon. 1:6).

2. *Vow Narratives.* Because the Psalms were intended for repeated use in a ritual context, the light they can throw on the actual practice of vows in the OT is limited to generalities. The situation changes when we turn to the vow narratives preserved in the OT: Gen. 28:20-22; Nu. 21:1-3; Jgs. 11:30-40; 1 S. 1; 2 S. 15:7-12. The first four,

---

22. For the OT see Wendel, "Laiengebet," 105f.; for the Hittite material see *ANET,* 394f.; E. Laroche, *RA,* 43 (1949), 55ff., esp. 62.

23. On the probably postexilic date of this psalm see A. Deissler, *Die Psalmen,* 3 vols. (Düsseldorf, ²1979), 254f.

24. Weiser, *OTL,* 528.

25. On the problem of identifying these enemies see H.-J. Kraus, *Theology of the Psalms* (Eng. trans., Minneapolis, 1986), 129ff.; Johnson, *Cultic Prophet,* 352ff.

26. O. Kaiser, *EvT,* 33 (1973), 97; H. W. Wolff, *Obadiah and Jonah* (Eng. trans., Minneapolis, 1986), 125ff.

admittedly, are clearly literary compositions; it is not impossible that the fifth is also.[27] We may nevertheless impute to them reliable knowledge of Israelite vow practice, so that they can help us reconstruct the vow formulary, picture concretely the occasions that brought forth vows, and extend our knowledge of the matter of vows.

a. *Form.* The structure of the vows recorded in these narratives is so constant "that we must be dealing with a fixed form."[28] In all 5 instances (Gen. 28:20-22; Nu. 21:2; Jgs. 11:30f.; 1 S. 1:11; 2 S. 15:8), the vow is preceded by the introductory formula *wayyiddōr (X) neder (leYHWH) (lē'mōr/wayyō'mar)* (cf. Gen. 28:20a; Nu. 21:2a; Jgs. 11:30a; 1 S. 11aα [3rd person sg. fem.]; 2 S. 15:8a [inversion with description of the situation]). If there is no explicit statement that the vow was made to Yahweh, this fact is clear from the wording of the vow itself (Gen. 28:20b,22a with the additions in vv. 21b,22b[29]). Jon. 1:16 precedes the clause *wayyiddérû neḏārîm* with *wayyizbeḥû zeḇaḥ leYHWH;* in theory this might suggest a sacrifice preceding the vow and serving to undergird it, like the sacrifice that some evidence suggests accompanied OT laments.[30] But v. 15b suggests rather that we are dealing here with a thank offering for deliverance from peril at sea and an oath for a successful conclusion of the journey.[31]

Surprisingly, only Hannah's vow in 1 S. 1:11 is introduced by an invocation of the Deity (Yahweh of hosts). Adolf Wendel claims that this feature and the odd discontinuity between the condition (Yahweh addressed in the 2nd person sg. masc.) and the promise (Yahweh addressed in the 3rd person sg. masc.) establish a similarity to the oath formula.[32] Although some evidence supports mutual influence between oaths and vows, the fundamental difference between the two must be emphasized: a vow is "undertaken solely by the person making it, but is addressed to God as witness and recipient of what is vowed; by contrast, an oath requires both a person to swear it and a person to receive it; God serves only as a witness, not as the beneficiary of the performance."[33]

As we see from the Hittite examples cited in III.1 and the vow of King Keret, with

---

27. On Gen. 28 (E) see E. Otto, "Jakob in Bethel," *ZAW,* 88 (1976), 165-190; P. Weimar, *Untersuchungen zur Redaktionsgeschichte des Pentateuch. BZAW,* 146 (1977), 166; H.-C. Schmitt, *Die nichtspriesterliche Josephsgeschichte. BZAW,* 154 (1980), 104ff.; also C. Westermann, *Genesis 12–36* (Eng. trans., Minneapolis, 1985), 453; R. Rendtorff, *ZAW,* 94 (1982), 511ff. On Nu. 21:1ff., usually assigned to J and described by M. Noth (*A History of Pentateuchal Traditions* [Eng. trans., Englewood Cliffs, N.J., 1972], 135f.; *Numbers. OTL* [Eng. trans. 1968], 154) as a supplement in J, see M. Rose, *Deuteronomist und Jahwist. ATANT,* 67 (1981), 295ff., 304, arguing for a late Deuteronomistic date. In the case of Jgs. 11:30f.,38f., W. Richter, *Bibl,* 47 (1966), 503ff., has observed affinities with E. Recently, 1 S. 1, along with chs. 2 and 3, has been called Deuteronomistic by J. van Seters, *In Search of History* (New Haven, 1983), 153; and R. K. Gnuse, *The Dream Theophany of Samuel* (Lanham, Md., 1984), 179f. In my opinion one must think at least in terms of post-Deuteronomistic redaction. Van Seters (277ff.) takes a unique position in dating the Succession Narrative in the 5th century.

28. Richter, *BZ,* N.S. 11, 22.

29. On the secondary nature of these additions see most recently Rendtorff, *ZAW,* 94, 516.

30. Gerstenberger, *Der bittende Mensch,* 51, 149f.

31. Wolff, *Obadiah and Jonah,* 121f.; also Ps. 107:23ff.

32. Wendel, "Laiengebet," 110f.

33. Gottschalk, 34f.; quotation, 36f.

its invocation of the goddess *'ṯrt ṣrm wɜlt ṣdynm,* the absence of an invocation is by no means a matter of course.[34] Whether its absence in Gen. 28:20b; Nu. 21:2b; Jgs. 11:30b (it would not be expected in 2 S. 15:8) is due to the form or to the narrators' concentration on the progress of their narratives is best left an open question, since the number of texts is so small. There would be a natural explanation for regular omission of the invocation if a vow was normally preceded by a prayer addressed to Yahweh, as we would expect apart from extreme situations.

An oath consists of a protasis or *paradosis* introduced by *'im,* "if," stating the condition under which the promise that follows will be carried out, and an apodosis stating the promise. The reverse sequence is found, for example, in an Egyptian vow.[35] The condition can be simple (Nu. 21:2bα; Jgs. 11:30b; 2 S. 15:8bα) or include multiple elements (Gen. 28:20b-21a; 1 S. 1:11aα). The condition in the Bethel narrative nevertheless reduces to a desire for divine help expressed in the clause *'im-yihyeh 'ᵉlōhîm ʿimmāḏî,* the situation (imminent departure) lending this desire concrete form: protection during the journey, food and clothing, and a safe return (cf. Gen. 28:15). The reduction is even clearer in 1 S. 1:11aα, where Yahweh's looking on Hannah's misery, remembering her and not forgetting her, is to be demonstrated in the gift of a son, described poetically as *zeraʿ 'ᵃnāšîm:* this is the actual condition. The introductory conditions are intended to demonstrate Hannah's humility.

In the condition, Yahweh is usually addressed directly. The exception in 2 S. 15:8bα is due to the incorporation of the vow into Absalom's account. The exception in Gen. 28:20b shows the extent to which the vow has become an element of the narrative, in which it functions to establish the arch that stretches from departure for a foreign land to return home (31:13) and the building of a massebah at Bethel (35:7,14). The patriarch experiences the divine aid requested in his vow, fulfills his promise, and thus becomes the founder of the sanctuary at Bethel.[36] In short, Gen. 28:20-22 does not record a vow as it was actually spoken: it is a literary construct.[37] This is also apparent in the absence of the infinitive absolute, normally used in the condition to emphasize the finite verb in the modal imperfect, strengthening the force of the obligation.[38]

Elsewhere the syntax of compound conditions is what we would expect: simple verbal clauses are linked with the so-called consecutive perfect (Gen. 28:20bα$_2$β,21a; 1 S. 1:11aα$_{3/1}$), negations are included by means of *wᵉlō'* and the imperfect, while a following positive verbal clause returns to the so-called consecutive perfect (1 S. 1:11a).[39] As we see in *KTU,* 1.14, IV, 40f., the condition can also speak of the success

34. *KTU,* 1.14, IV, 38f.; Parker, 693f. Cf. also the modern Arabic vow in P. Kahle, *PJ,* 8 (1913), 111; the problem is discussed by A. Caquot, et al., *Textes ougaritiques, I. LAPO,* 1 (1974), 530, n. w.

35. Stele Berlin 23077, 13ff.; A. Erman, *SPAW,* 49 (1911), 1095.

36. See also Rendtorff, *ZAW,* 94, 514.

37. Westermann, *Genesis 12–36,* 458.

38. Wendel, "Laiengebet," 107.

39. See the tables in Wendel, "Laiengebet," 112ff.; and Richter, *BZ,* N.S. 11, 22.

of the votary instead of the action of a deity (cf. also Gen. 28:21a). It is clearly presupposed, of course, that this success results from the action of the deity invoked.

The promise always follows the condition in the 1st person singular of the so-called consecutive perfect, "in the sense of an assured pledge for the future."[40] This element, too, may be simple (Nu. 21:2b; 2 S. 15:8b) or compound (1 S. 1:11b). Except in the secondary expansion in Gen. 28:22b, Yahweh or Elohim is always spoken of in the 3rd person as the recipient of the vow.

The syntactic structure of Jgs. 11:31 is complex: the double promise in v. 31b is preceded by an involved description of what is being vowed, so that v. 31a contains an expansion of the condition stated in v. 30b. This complexity may be viewed as a stylistic device used to represent Jephthah's inner uncertainty.[41] In Gen. 28:21b,22 we now have a triple promise; v. 21b is a late Yahwistic interpolation that transforms and inverts what had been a single promise in v. 22a. Finally, v. 22b was added, promising to give God a tithe; the use of the 2nd person singular to address God directly in itself shows that this promise is secondary.[42]

b. *Threat.* A threat may be viewed as a secondary form of a vow, promising negative consequences if the deity refuses to help. It is hardly accidental that examples are found in Egyptian pyramid, coffin, and magical texts.[43] A hybrid form comprising a negative vow and a positive vow also appears in a coffin text.[44]

c. *Place.* We learn directly from 1 S. 1:11,19 and indirectly from Gen. 28:20ff. that vows were made at sanctuaries. Since a temple as *bêṯ YHWH* was the place of Yahweh's presence in a very special way, it is not surprising that people visited temples — and later *the* Jerusalem temple — not only for prayer and sacrifice (1 S. 1:3; 1 K. 8:28ff.) but also to perform solemn vows.[45]

Thus the narrator has Hannah choose the yearly family pilgrimage to the temple of Yahweh at Shiloh, probably at the time of the autumn festival (1 S. 1:3,21),[46] as the occasion to express her heart's desire and make her vow. The narrator of Gen. 28:20ff. clearly has in mind an extension of the massebah sanctuary already consecrated by Jacob (v. 17); this extension takes place in 35:7, when Jacob builds an altar there and calls the place El-bethel. It is noteworthy, however, that 35:7 ascribes the building of the altar to a divine command (35:1) rather than to Jacob's vow.[47] We are to picture the vow in Nu. 21:2 as being spoken before the imagined assault of the Israelites on

---

40. Richter, *BZ,* N.S. 11, 23.

41. R. Bartelmus, *Münchener Universitätsschriften,* 17 (1982), 223.

42. Westermann, *Genesis 12–36,* 459f.

43. G. Roder, *Die ägyptische Religion in Text und Bild,* 4 (Zurich, 1961), 182ff., 223; Wendel, "Laiengebet," 122.

44. G. Roeder, *Urkunden zur Religion des alten Ägypten* (Jena, 1923), 210f.

45. R. E. Clements, *God and Temple* (Oxford, 1965); M. Metzger, "Himmlische und irdische Wohnstatt Jahwes," *UF,* 2 (1970), 139-158. See also *KTU,* 1.14, IV, 31ff.

46. H. J. Stoebe, *Das erste Buch Samuelis. KAT,* VIII/1 (1973), 95f.

47. E. Otto, *ZAW,* 88, 178ff.; *idem, Jakob in Sichem. BWANT,* 110 (1979), 72f.; for a different view, see Westermann, *Genesis 12–36,* 549-552. On El-bethel see M. Köckert, *Vätergott und Väterverheissung. FRLANT,* 142 (1988).

the Canaanite towns near Hormah, at the edge of the Negeb. Jephthah's vow in Jgs. 11:30f. is clearly made while the Israelites are advancing against the Ammonites. Absalom's vow, which he uses as a pretext for a conspiratorial meeting, is supposed to have been made at Geshur, in the territory of his grandfather Talmai, an Aramean king (2 S. 15:8; cf. 3:3; 13:37). It is clear, therefore, that a vow could be made to Yahweh not only in one's own land but also in a foreign land. The sailors in Jon. 1:16 make their vow while at sea. Although a sacred place had the advantage of God's presence,[48] anyone in distress could make a vow to God at any time and in any place, to gain God's help by promising something in return.

d. *Occasion.* The Psalms provide a general picture of the circumstances occasioning vows and the sacrifices offered. The extant vow narratives supplement this picture and give it concrete form. The Psalms suggest danger from enemies as the primary occasion of vows but do not describe the nature of these enemies. Nu. 21:1 and Jgs. 11:30f. speak of an advance to meet an attacking enemy of the people, suggesting a military context. During the period of the monarchy, it would hardly be off the mark to see the king[49] or the military commander on the scene as making such a vow, with the individual soldiers following suit progressively: victory (Nu. 21:2; Jgs. 11:30) and safe return (Jgs. 11:31aβ) are here the obvious concerns. The private realm is represented by the fugitive's prayer to return home safely (Gen. 28:20b). Also in the private realm is the vow made by a barren woman (1 S. 1:11). Such a vow is implicit in Prov. 31:2, where Lemuel's mother addresses her son as *bar-n^e^dāray.*[50]

In this context we may also recall the vow of King Keret, who promised Princess Ḥurray's weight in gold and silver on the condition that she be brought home.[51] According to another passage, he either personally made a vow for Ḥurray's fertility or accepted responsibility for the corresponding vow on her part.[52] To fill out the catalog, we may cite Ps. 107, adding wanderers, prisoners, the sick, and (with the supplement) those in peril at sea.[53] With regard to sickness and health, we may also cite the vow of Puduḫepa on behalf of the king and the vow of Neb-Re, the "painter of Amon in the city of the dead," for his son Nakht-Amon.[54] Deliverance from peril at sea recalls the vow of the sailors in Jon. 1:16 and Jonah's declaration of deliverance (2:10[9]).[55]

In the nature of the case, any such list must be incomplete. In general, however, we may say that in Israel vows were considered the means of obtaining God's help for the people or an individual in any time of need.

---

48. Wendel, *Gelübde,* 121.
49. Cf. Ps. 56; Johnson, *Cultic Prophet,* 331ff.
50. See I.2 above.
51. *KTU,* 1.14, IV, 40f.
52. *KTU,* 1.15, III, 25ff.; cf. ll. 20ff.; Caquot, et al., *LAPO,* 1, 541, n. r.; Nu. 30:11ff.(10ff.).
53. On the analysis of this psalm, see W. Beyerlin, *Werden und Wesen des 107 Psalms. BZAW,* 153 (1979), 102ff.
54. For the former see III.1 above; for the latter see Stele Berlin 23077, 13ff., and III.2.b above.
55. For other occasions of vows in Jewish practice see Wendel, *Gelübde,* 115ff.

e. *Offerings.* (1) *Votive Sacrifices.* As the discussion above indicates, the offerings associated with vows were primarily cultic sacrifices.[56] In 1 S. 1:21; 2 S. 15:12, such a sacrifice is called *zeḇaḥ;* in Ps. 116:17; 107:22, *zeḇaḥ tôḏâ.* Priestly language distinguishes *zeḇaḥ hattôḏâ* or *zeḇaḥ šᵉlāmîm*[57] from simple *zeḇaḥ* (Lev. 7:11f.; cf. Nu. 15:8, although the distinction is not entirely clear). Karl Elliger theorizes that the terminology refers to official and unofficial sacrifices; Rolf Rendtorff thinks in terms of the same occasion reflected in different stages of tradition.[58] In any case it is clear that the *zeḇaḥ šᵉlāmîm* as a thank offering included an offering of food (Lev. 7:11-14), which Nu. 15:1-11 shows was later transformed, supplemented by a drink offering, and differentiated according to the animal sacrificed. In addition, the flesh of the *zeḇaḥ šᵉlāmîm* had to be consumed on the day of the sacrifice, whereas the flesh of the *zeḇaḥ* on the occasion of a *neḏer* or *nᵉḏāḇâ,* a freewill offering, could still be consumed on the following day.

According to Ps. 66:13-15; Lev. 22:18,[59] an *ʿōlâ,* a whole burnt offering, could replace the *zebaḥ* sacrifice. Since this meant that the worshiper did not partake at all of the animal, the promise of an *ʿōlâ* was certainly considered superior to the promise of a *zeḇaḥ.* In the case of an *ʿōlâ,* only male cattle, sheep, and goats could be offered, whereas the sex did not matter in the case of a *zeḇaḥ šᵉlāmîm* (Lev. 22:17-22). Naturally the sacrificial animals had to be without blemish (v. 20). For a *nᵉḏāḇâ,* however, an animal with a limb that was too long or too short might be offered (22:23). This fact and the mention of *nᵉḏāḇâ* after *neḏer* show that the latter was considered superior (7:16; 22:18,21; 23:38; Nu. 15:3; 29:39; Dt. 12:6,17; 23:24).

In Priestly language the sacrifice was termed *qorbān,* "offering" (Lev. 7:16; 22:18; Nu. 15:4), because it was offered to Yahweh (*hiqrîḇ:* Lev. 22:18; Nu. 15:4). In the postexilic period, of course, Dt. 12:6,11 required the votive sacrifice to be brought to a place chosen by Yahweh (cf. also 12:26) to be slaughtered and eaten (vv. 17f.; cf. Ex. 29:42ff.).

An Ugaritic extispicy text mentions a *ndr dbḥ* among the monthly sacrifices.[60] One gets the impression from 1 S. 1:21 that the vow was paid once a year on the occasion of a pilgrimage to the temple (but cf. Ex. 34:18ff.; 23:15ff.; Dt. 16:16). The narrator may, however, have used this statement to emphasize the importance of Shiloh,[61] without necessarily contradicting Lev. 23:38 and Nu. 29:39, which state that votive sacrifices were performed as part of the three great pilgrimage festivals. It is hardly

---

56. See II.2 above.

57. B. Janowski, "Erwängungen zur Vorgeschichte des israelitischen *šᵉlamîm-Opfers,*" *UF,* 12 (1980), 231ff.

58. K. Elliger, *Leviticus. HAT,* IV (1966), 100; R. Rendtorff, *Studien zur Geschichte des Opfers im Alten Israel. WMANT,* 24 (1967), 137.

59. On Nu. 15:3 see *ibid.,* 85.

60. *KTU,* 1.127, 2; see J.-M. de Tarragon, *Le culte à Ugarit d'après les textes de la pratique en cunéiformes alphabetiques. CahRB,* 19 (1980), 66; but cf. also P. Xella, *I testi rituali di Ugarit, I. StSem,* 54 (1981), 181.

61. K. Budde, *Die Bücher Samuel. KHC,* VIII (1902), 3f.

proper to conclude on the basis of this evidence that the offering of votive sacrifices was possible only during these festivals.

(2) *Other Offerings.* Apart from votive sacrifices, a catalog of votive offerings must be no less selective than a catalog of occasions for vows, because the biblical narrative records only the most significant.

Without prejudice to the narrator's etiological and redactional purpose, when Jacob vows that the massebah he has set up will become a *bêṯ *ᵉ*lōhîm* (Gen. 28:22a), he is acting as the king acted in the historical era (1 K. 12:31).[62] A popular etymology in Nu. 21:2b,3 (cf. Dt. 20:16f.) derives the ban *(ḥērem)* imposed on towns of the enemy, i.e., the extermination of their entire population, from the name of the town Hormah.[63] In the historical era, a similar vow would once again be conceivable only in the mouth of a king, as the inscription of Mesha, the Moabite king, shows.[64] The problem becomes more difficult in the case of Jephthah's promise (Jgs. 11:31), which can refer only to a human sacrifice;[65] it propels him into tragedy, so that he must sacrifice his daughter as an *ʿōlâ,* an act that the narrator tactfully paraphrases in v. 39a.[66]

1 S. 1:11,24ff.; 2:1,11, concern a more everyday realm, even though the texts deal with Samuel. The firstborn son of a previously barren woman is dedicated to Yahweh, so that he serves in the temple. The transfer is expressed by the lifelong prohibition imposed on him, forbidding him to shave the hair on his head.[67]

In principle, Israelites — like Jews of a later era — could vow anything that was not excepted by religious tradition or law.[68] In the OT Dt. 23:19(18) forbids bringing the fee of a prostitute *('eṯnan zônâ;* cf. Prov. 19:13 LXX) or the wages of a male prostitute *(mᵉḥîr keleḇ,* lit. "wages of a dog")[69] into the sanctuary as a votive offering. If we follow Wilhelm Rudolph on the basis of Dt. 23:18(17), we must reckon with the possibility that in the OT the term was applied also to profane male prostitution (Lev.

---

62. G. W. Ahlström, *Royal Administration and National Religion in Ancient Palestine* (Leiden, 1982), 46.

63. → V, 189.

64. *KAI,* 181; *TSSI,* I, 16, 14-18.

65. H. Gressmann, *Die Anfänge Israels. SAT,* I/2 (^{2}1922), 227f.

66. See the discussion by W. Baumgartner, *ARW,* 18 (1915), 240ff.; also Richter, *Bibl,* 47, 511, n. 1. On child sacrifice among the Greeks, see W. Burkert, *Homo necans: The Anthropology of Ancient Greek Sacrificial Ritual and Myth* (Eng. trans., Berkeley, 1983), 84ff. On child sacrifice in Israel, see A. R. W. Green, *The Role of Human Sacrifice in the Ancient Near East. ASORDS,* 1 (1975), 149ff.; P. G. Mosca, "Child Sacrifice in Canaanite and Israelite Religion" (diss., Harvard, 1975), 117ff.; O. Kaiser, "Der Erstgeborenen deiner Söhne sollst du mir geben," *Dankender Glaube. Festschrift C. H. Ratschow* (Berlin, 1976), 24ff.

67. J. Henninger, *Arabica Sacra. OBO,* 40 (1981), 286ff.; Stoebe, *KAT,* VIII/1, 96f.; on the *nᵉṯînîm* see J. P. Weinberg, "*Nᵉtînîm* und 'Söhne der Sklaven Salomos' in 6.-4. Jh.v.u.Z.," *ZAW,* 87 (1975), 355-371.

68. Wendel, *Gelübde,* 121ff.; a rhyton is mentioned as a votive offering in *KTU,* 6.62 (Xella, 295f.).

69. Cultic: D. Winton Thomas, *VT,* 10 (1960), 423ff.; noncultic: W. Rudolph, *ZAW,* 75 (1963), 68. See also M. Delcor, *UF,* 11 (1979), 161f.; → VII, 155f. On cultic prostitution in general see B. Menzel, *Asyrische Tempel. StPohl,* ser. maior, 10/1 (1981), 28; 10/2, 27f.*, with n. 308.

18:22). CD 16:13ff. forbids vowing or dedicating to God something obtained by force *('nws),* one's own food *(m'kl pyhw),* or someone else's property (cf. also CD 6:15).

It is noteworthy that no Israelite votive steles and altars have been preserved, although they are well represented in the Semitic and Greco-Roman world.

(3) *Excursus: Punic Steles Recording Child Sacrifice.* Apart from two Ugaritic texts and the earliest Syrian example,[70] the thousands of Punic *tophet* inscriptions are striking. On the whole, their content is stereotyped. The basic Carthaginian formula runs: *lrbt ltnt pn bʿl sl'dn lbʿl ḥmn 'š ndr X.*[71] It can be expanded by adding the names of the father, grandfather, great-grandfather, and great-great-grandfather, and above all by including the reason for setting up the stele in the form of a *kšmʿ ql' brk'* in full or short form.[72] Women also appear as votaries.[73] Information concerning the occupation (up to chief magistrate) of the votaries or their ancestors provides some sociohistorical insights.[74] Today it is beyond doubt that all these inscriptions refer to child sacrifice (or a substitute).[75]

(4) *Redemption of Votive Offerings.* The law governing redemption of votive offerings or consecrated property (Lev. 27),[76] dating from the postexilic period, allows us to expand the catalog of what could be promised. In this context the distinction between a vow and simple conveyance to the deity ultimately plays no role.

Here we learn that even though children were no longer sacrificed, they could be vowed to Yahweh (vv. 2-8; *hip̱lî neḏer:* v. 2). Unlike the situation presupposed in 1 S. 1:11ff., there was no longer any need for additional temple personnel, so that the only interest in such a vow was the monetary value of the person vowed. The equivalent *(ʿēreḵ)* was determined not by how much work the person could do[77] but by his or her value as a slave, depending on age and sex. The inclusion of young children and infants (v. 6) shows that individuals could vow others as well as themselves. Sacrificial animals vowed to Yahweh could not be exchanged but could be redeemed for a surcharge of 20 percent (v. 13).[78] Unclean animals had to be assessed by a priest (vv. 9-13; cf. also vv. 26f.,30ff.). Under certain circumstances, the consecration *(hiqdîš)* of a house might represent an attempt to keep an urban dwelling out of the hands of creditors (vv. 14f.). The rules governing the consecration of fields (vv. 16-24) give rise to the same suspicion. If redemption was impossible, human beings, animals, and fields came under the ban *(ḥērem)* (v. 28; cf. also v. 29 with Ezr. 10:8).

---

70. On *KTU,* 6.13, 14 see Xella, 297ff. For the Syrian example see *KAI,* 201; *TSSI,* II, 1.

71. See, e.g., *CIS,* 3328, 3330, 3439.

72. See, e.g., *CIS,* 3388, 2; 3386, 3f.; 3407, 2f.; 3524, 3ff.; see also 3778, 7ff. (15 ancestors!). For the full form see, e.g., *CIS,* 33390, 3; 3770, 6ff.; 4283, 3f. (*ybrk':* 3522, 3; 3911: 5; *tbrk':* 3777, 2). For the short form see, e.g., *CIS,* 3263, 3; 3278, 4.

73. E.g., *CIS,* 3323, 3f.; 3334, 2f.; 3356, 3; 3829, 3f.; 3456, 2; 3459, 2f.; 3460, 3.

74. E.g., *CIS,* 3321, 3f.; 3432, 3; 3567, 6.

75. See → מלך *mōleḵ* (VIII, 375-388); also Mosca, 1-116; Garbini, *Fenici,* 175ff., 191ff.; O. Kaiser, "Salammbo, Moloch, und das Tophet," *Nordafrika: Antike und Christentum. Die Karawane,* 19 (1978), 2, 3ff., 130ff.

76. See Elliger, *HAT,* IV, 386ff.

77. Contra G. B. Gray, *Sacrifice in the OT* (Oxford, 1925), 36.

78. Elliger, *HAT,* IV, 387f.

f. *Remission of Vows.* The law in Nu. 30 concerning the obligation of vows *(neḏer)* and pledges *('issār)* also brings us into the area of postexilic casuistry; it was not developed completely and systematically, and therefore gave rise to supplementary interpretations in rabbinic discussion.[79] A man *('îš)* was forbidden to break *(hēḥēl deḇārô)* a vow or a pledge of abstinence. The spoken word made them binding (v. 3[2] [all citations of Nu. 30 in the following discussion are to the MT versification]; cf. 11QTemple 53:14f.). The situation was different in the case of vows made by an unmarried woman still living in her father's house (vv. 4-6; cf. 11QTemple 53:16-21) or a married woman whose vow antedated her marriage (vv. 7-9) or was made thereafter (vv. 11-16; 11QTemple 54:1-3 generalizes the question and thus avoids the casuistry of Nu. 30:6-9,11-16). In the first case the father, in the second and third the husband, upon learning of the vow, could nullify (*hēp̄ēr,* "break": vv. 9aα,13aαbβ,14b,16a) it by disapproval (*hēnî':* vv. 6aαbβ,9a,12), making it invalid (*lō' yāqûm:* v. 6a). By his silence, however, he could confirm (*hēqîm:* vv. 14b,15aαbα) it, so that it remained in force (*yāqûm:* vv. 5bαβ,8bα,12bαβ). If the vow was nullified, the woman was innocent (*weYHWH yislaḥ-lāh:* vv. 6bα,9b,13bβ); the man bore her guilt *('awônāh).* For a widow or a divorced woman, by contrast, the law was the same as for a man (v. 10; cf. 11QTemple 54:5). When Nu. 30 was composed, vows uttered thoughtlessly (*miḇṭā' ṣep̄āṯeyhā:* vv. 7bα,9aβ) seem to have presented a special problem. 11QTemple ignores this problem, but closes this section in 54:5f. with a general exhortation to fulfill vows diligently.

Dt. 23:22-24(21-23) takes the position that every vow must be fulfilled straightaway to avoid incurring guilt and being called to account by Yahweh; it emphasizes that what has been spoken must be performed, while refraining from making a vow incurs no guilt (*ḥēṭ';* cf. Eccl. 5:3-4[4-5]; Prov. 20:25). 11QTemple 53:11-13 reproduces Dt. 23:22-24(21-23) with minor variations and stylized as spoken by God at the beginning of its law governing vows.[80] CD 16:6f. incorporates Dt. 23:24(23), while limiting it to a binding oath *(šeḇû'aṯ 'issār)* to carry out a specific commandment of the Torah; this obligation cannot be evaded even at the cost of death *(bmḥyr mwt).*

The modern reader should not look on these regulations and the Jewish craving for specificity as curiosa, but as expressing the seriousness with which both God's word and one's own word are taken (cf. Eccl. 5:4[5]; Matt. 5:37).

IV. Vows of Abstinence.

1. *Nazirites.* In the OT the primary form of a vow of abstinence was the *neḏer nāzîr* taken by a man or a woman, through which one dedicated oneself to Yahweh for a specific period of time (Nu. 6:2). For the duration of the vow (*kol-neḏer nizrô:* v. 5), the consecrated individual was forbidden to enjoy any products of the grapevine (vv. 3f.), to shave the hair of the head (v. 5), or to have any contact with the dead or dying

79. For rabbinic discussion and practice, see tractate *Nedarim* of the Talmud, esp. 10f.; also Wendel, *Gelübde,* 134ff.; for additional bibliog. see Perelmuter, *TRE,* XII, 305.

80. Y. Yadin, *The Temple Scroll,* 3 vols. (Eng. trans., Jerusalem, 1983), II, 168f., 258f.

(vv. 6ff.). V. 9 shows that consecration of the hair was the essential element. Accidental contact with the dying made reconsecration necessary: the head was shaved and two pigeons were offered, one for a *ḥaṭṭā'ṯ* and one for an *'ōlâ*. At the end of the period of consecration, a male lamb was sacrificed as an *'ōlâ,* a female lamb as a *ḥaṭṭā'ṯ,* and a ram with a *minḥâ* as a *šᵉlāmîm;* the head was finally shaved and the hair burned in the fire (vv. 13ff.). V. 21 shows that additional votive offerings were expected.[81] In the OT, Samson was set apart by the angel of Yahweh as a lifelong *nᵉzîr YHWH* even before his birth (Jgs. 13:4f.); by Hannah's vow Samuel was likewise forbidden to shave the hair of his head throughout his lifetime (1 S. 1:11).

2. *Other Self-Imposed Obligations.* Ps. 132 (late exilic or early postexilic[82]) speaks of David's vow in the form of an oath (v. 2) with the triple obligation (vv. 3-4a) to grant himself no rest until he should find a dwelling place for Yahweh, thus lending a legendary background to the theme of the bringing of the ark to Jerusalem (2 S. 6). This text is significant, because it illustrates the otherwise unattested realm of self-imposed obligations outside the cult in Israel.

V. LXX. The LXX translates *nāḏar* with *eúchesthai* (28 times), *euchḗ* (twice), and *homologeín* (once); *neḏer* with *euchḗ* (52 times), *homología* (3 times), and *dṓron* and *eúchesthai* (once each).

Kaiser

81. For a literary analysis of the *tôraṯ hannāzîr* (Nu. 6) see Kellermann, *BZAW,* 120, 83ff.; on the offering of hair see Henninger, *Arabica Sacra,* 286ff.

82. T. Veijola, *Verheissung in der Krise. AnAcScFen,* 220 (1982), 161f.

נָהַג *nāhag*

Contents: I. *nhg* I, "Drive": 1. Etymology; 2. LXX; 3. Forms, Phrases, and Meanings; 4. Theological Usage. II. *nhg* II, "Moan."

nāhag. G. Braulik, *Die Mittel deuteronomischer Rhetorik erhoben aus Deuteronomium 4,1-10. AnBibl,* 68 (1978); E. Jenni, *HP;* W. Leslau, "Observations on Semitic Cognates in Ugaritic," *Or,* 37 (1968), 347-366; *idem,* "Southeast Semitic Cognates to the Akkadian Vocabulary," *JAOS,* 89 (1969), 18-22; N. Lohfink, *Kohelet. NEB* (1980); W. W. Müller, "Altsüdarabische Beiträge zum hebräischen Lexikon," *ZAW,* 75 (1963), 304-316; N. Peters, *Der jüngst wiederaufgefundene hebräische Text des Buches Ecclesiasticus* (1902); O. Rickenbacher, *Weisheitsperikopen bei Ben Sira. OBO,* 1 (1973); O. Rössler, "Der semitischen Charakter der libyschen Sprache," *ZA,* 50 (1952), 121-150; S. A. Ryder II, *The D-Stem in Western Semitic. Janua Linguarum,* Ser. Practica

I. *nhg* I, "Drive."

1. *Etymology.* In Hebrew the *nomen actionis minhāg,* "manner of driving a chariot," derives from *nhg* I, although it is not entered as a derivative under *nhg* in *HAL.*[1] Outside Hebrew, *nhg* I is found with certainty only in Jewish Aramaic ("lead, practice, be accustomed to") and Arabic (*nahj/nāhij/manhag/minhāj,* "open, clear, easy path"; *nahaja,* "make a path, proceed, behave").

The only Old South Arabic occurrences, *mnhg,* "path," may be a misreading of *mnhl.*[2] Since August Dillmann, Eth. *'anhaga,* "drive cattle," has been associated etymologically with *nhg* I. This would be the only occurrence of the root in Ethiopic, and Wolf Leslau therefore questions this explanation.[3] Derivation from Amhar. *mänga,* "herd," favored since Praetorius, should probably be given up in favor of a Cushite etymology.[4] Otto Rössler postulates for Kabylic *inig,* "travel," a middle radical *h* that has vanished in Libyan and associates it with the Semitic root *nhg.*[5]

2. *LXX.* The LXX usually uses *ágō* and its compounds to translate both the qal and piel of *nhg:* qal: *ágō/omai, apágō/omai;* also *aichmalōteúō* (once), *hodēgéō* (twice), and *paralambánō* (3 times); piel: *ágō, anágō, eiságō, epágō;* also *parakaléō* (once) and *poimaínō* (once). Three additional translations occur in Sirach: *apóllymai, diágō,* and *elaúnō* (once each).

3. *Forms, Phrases, and Meanings.* The verb *nhg* occurs 20 times in the qal and 10 times in the piel. It is also conjectured in Lam. 1:4, on insufficient grounds,[6] and appears 4 times in the Hebrew fragments of Sirach (3:16b; 38:25c,27b; 40:23a).

a. *Qal.* The text refers occasionally simply to the pure action denoted by the verb: Sir. 38:27b; 2 K. 9:20. In the latter passage an object may have been omitted, to be understood from the context (v. 16: *rkb*): a chariot or the horses pulling it. Elsewhere the qal of *nhg* is almost always realized as a bivalent (subj. + direct obj. or prepositional obj.) or trivalent (subj. + direct obj. + directive)[7] verb. The subject is always animate, usually human (once, in a figurative expression, the human heart: Eccl. 2:3); twice it is Yahweh (Ps. 80:2[Eng. v. 1]; Lam. 3:2). The object is usually animate: a human being or an animal. In 2 S. 6:3; 1 Ch. 13:7, the object is inanimate: a cart; the text is probably thinking of the animals doing the pulling. In those passages that omit the

131 (1974); W. von Soden, "*n* als Wurzelaugment im Semitischen," *Studia Orientalia in memoriam Caroli Brockelmann* (Halle, 1968), 175-184; H. Stadelmann, *Ben Sira als Schriftgelehrter. WUNT,* II/6 (1980).

1. *HAL,* II, 675.
2. Cf. Müller, 312; Biella, 295.
3. *Contributions,* 33.
4. Leslau, *Etymological Dictionary of Gurage,* 3 vols. (Wiesbaden, 1981), 408f.
5. P. 132, no. 38.
6. Cf. G. Bergsträsser, *Hebräische Grammatik,* 2 vols. (Leipzig, 1918-29), II, 128, §26g, with note: niphal ptcp. of *ygh.* On the conjectural pual of *nhg* I, see II below.
7. The third syntagmeme of W. Richter, *Grundlagen der althebräischen Grammatik. ATS,* 13 (1980), 40ff.

object, it is always named just before and understood from the context: 1 S. 30:1f., the women; 1 S. 30:22, wives and children; 2 K. 4:25, a donkey. The form in Isa. 60:11 should probably be repointed as an active participle: the kings are driving their nations, or beasts of burden, laden with treasure. In 2 S. 6:3 the qal has a direct object; the parallel in 1 Ch. 13:7 uses a prepositional object instead. The latter construction appears to be restricted to late texts (cf. Isa. 11:6; Sir. 38:25), and may be characteristic of a later state of the language. This observation supports Norbert Lohfink's interpretation of the construction and meaning of Eccl. 2:3 ("while my mind led my knowledge to pasture"): the prepositional linkage with b^e is not a free circumstantial qualifier of manner or instrument, but a prepositional object as required by the valency of the verb.[8] As a trivalent verb, *nhg* requires an indication of direction, as in Ex. 3:1. Other occurrences may express the direction by means of a second verb in the following clause (Gen. 31:18; Cant. 8:2; Lam. 3:2; 2 Ch. 25:11); alternatively, the directive or separative qualifier is implicit in the context of *nhg* qal ("lead away, drive away") or the following verb of motion (cf. 1 S. 23:5; 30:2,22; 2 K. 4:24; Isa. 20:4; Job 24:3).

The basic meaning of *nhg* appears in the occurrences with human subject and animal object: "drive animals or flocks." This meaning is also illustrated by Ps. 80:2(1), with a different structure. The verb does not, however, specify the nature of the driving, which is defined by the context: lead one's flock as a shepherd to new pastures far distant (Ex. 3:1); tend in peace (Isa. 11:6; also probably the figurative usage in Eccl. 2:3); drive away livestock secretly or illegally (Gen. 31:18; Job 24:3 [par. in v. 2: *gāzal,* "steal"]); take away by force as the spoils of battle (1 S. 23:5; 30:20); urge on a mount (2 K. 4:24); and (probably as a further development of this last meaning) drive a cart or chariot (2 S. 6:3; 2 K. 9:20; 1 Ch. 13:7). The qal can have these same nuances when the object is human: lead an army into battle (1 Ch. 20:1; 2 Ch. 25:11); deport prisoners of war (Isa. 20:4); carry people off as booty (1 S. 30:2); leave with members of one's family (1 S. 30:22). Thus in 1 S. 30 *nhg* describes both the violent abduction of women by the enemy (v. 2) and the men's recovery of the rescued women and children (v. 30). It is clear from this observation that the nuance of violence versus peaceful, tender care is not determined by the verb *nhg*. The two occurrences with divine subject fit easily into this framework; here too it is the context that determines the peaceful or hostile nuance of the action: Yahweh has led Israel attentively, like a shepherd (Ps. 80:2[1]), and he has driven the lamenting speaker malevolently into darkness (Lam. 3:2). In Sir. 38:25c *nhg* probably does not mean "drive cattle to pasture." It is used in chiastic asyndeton with the poel of *šûḇ:* "the one who leads the steer, the one who turns the ox"; both verbs together probably refer to plowing.[9] In Sirach *nhg* also appears to mean "occupy oneself (with something)" (Sir. 3:26b?;[10] 38:27b).

b. *Piel.* The piel offers a totally different picture. Except in Gen. 31:26, the subject is always Yahweh, and the object is never an animal. Apart from the figure of speech that describes Yahweh as causing a storm to break loose (Ex. 10:13 [plague of locusts]; Ps.

8. P. 26.
9. See Stadelmann, 285; Rickenbacher, 180.
10. Peters, 7.

78:26 [quails in the desert]) and the statement that he caused the wheels of the Egyptian chariots or the Egyptians to advance with great difficulty (Ex. 14:25), only humans are the objects of *nhg* piel. Furthermore, only in Gen. 31:26, the sole occurrence with a human subject, are individuals the objects; elsewhere the object is always a collective: Israel, the people of Yahweh, the exiles. Yahweh's treatment of Israel denoted by *nhg* piel is hostile only in Deuteronomy (Dt. 4:27; 28:37: deportation into exile); elsewhere it is a mark of loving care (Isa. 49:10; 63:14; Ps. 48:15[14]; 78:52). Since these same nuances, with the same subjects and human objects, are also attested for the qal (cf. esp. 80:2[1] [qal] and 48:15[14]; 78:52 [piel]), it is difficult to suggest a specific semantic function for the piel with a human object. Accepting Gotthelf Bergsträsser's statement that there is "sometimes a secondary semantic difference" between the qal and the piel, "with one of the two forms being used more in the literal sense, the other in the figurative sense," Ernst Jenni claims that the occurrences of the piel have "a more figurative meaning," especially insofar as they have Yahweh as subject.[11] This theory is hardly convincing; it is even less persuasive when Jenni applies it to the only occurrence with a human subject: "In Gen. 31:26, 'Laban said to Jacob, What have you done, deceiving me and taking my daughters away like prisoners of war?' we could replace *taking away* with *'carrying off,'* in quotation marks to indicate the figurative use of the verb." As we have just seen, the qal of *nhg* can likewise be used for the carrying off of prisoners of war, so that the object makes no difference. Furthermore, just a few verses before, v. 18 uses the qal of *nhg* to say: "He [Jacob] drove away all his livestock." Jenni's reference to an "accusatory resultative" may possibly help explain the use of the piel in v. 26.

4. *Theological Usage.* In theological contexts *nhg* can be used in either a negative or a positive sense. In a negative sense it serves the theological interpretation of the end of Jerusalem and the exile. Just as the emperor of Assyria will lead away the Egyptians as captives and the Cushites as exiles, like captured livestock (Isa. 20:4), so Yahweh will treat Israel. Because his people have broken the covenant, specifically by disobeying the prohibition of images, Yahweh will inflict on them the curses of the covenant; Yahweh will personally remove them from the land and drive them out among the peoples (Dt. 28:37; 4:27). His action will be the opposite of that of a shepherd: he will scatter them among the peoples so that they perish (4:27; note the three rhetorical constituents of this verse and the use of *nhg* piel and *pwṣ* hiphil for the scattering of Israel[12]); the remnant will become an object of horror, a proverb, and a byword (28:37). In Lam. 3:1,2, an individual laments that Yahweh in wrath has driven him like an animal with his rod and brought him into the deathly realm of darkness.

In texts that are equally late or later, *nhg* describes Yahweh's beneficent protection of Israel. Yahweh's relationship to Israel is depicted figuratively as that of a shepherd to his flock. The verb can denote Yahweh's specific acts in the past as well as his general present and future mode of conduct. When *nhg* refers to the past, Yahweh's deliverance of Israel at

---

11. *HP,* 201, no. 198, citing Bergsträsser, II, 93, §17a, on p. 135.
12. Braulik, 55, 130.

the Reed Sea and his guidance through the desert are meant; but *nhg* never came to be used in formulaic language. A community lament describes God's saving acts of the past in singular language: Yahweh led Israel through the sea as safely and securely as a herd of cattle going down into the valley at evening to drink (Isa. 63:14; cf. v. 11: "his flock"). Ps. 78:52 ("like sheep, like a flock") uses *nhg* to describe Yahweh's safe and careful guidance through the desert (v. 53 uses *nāḥâ,* "lead," in parallel). Even more wonderfully, according to Deutero-Isaiah, at the second exodus Yahweh will lead the exiles (Isa. 49:10) like a flock to rich pasture (v. 9: *rāʿâ,* "pasture"; v. 10: *nāhal,* "guide," in parallel). Ps. 48:15(14) associates *nhg* with the Zion tradition: the glory of Zion inspires confidence that Yahweh will continue to lead his people like a guardian shepherd. Ps. 80:2(1), however, combines lament with petition: in their distress, Israel reminds Yahweh of his past acts of mercy, appealing to him as the one who led Joseph as a shepherd leads *(rōʿeh)* his flock.

II. *nhg* II, "Moan." The etymology of Heb. *nhg* II, "moan, sigh," must be considered in conjunction with the related roots *n'q,* "groan," and *nhq,* "bray." In many פ״ן verbs, the *n* is an augment of a biliteral root that may, among other things, "onomatopoeically describe sounds that are characteristic of an action."[13] These include Heb. *nhq,* "cry haq haq" = "bray." Like Hebrew, other Semitic languages possess this root as well as one or more phonetically related roots describing the crying and groaning of human beings. As one would expect in onomatopoeic verbs, the third and occasionally the second radical are subject to variation in different languages. For the braying of an ass (Heb. *nhq*), one may compare the Ugar. noun *nqht,* "braying of an ass," Jewish Aram. *nᵉhaq,* Arab. *nahaqa/nahiqa;* but Tigr. *näḥaqa,* Akk. *nagāgu.*[14] The variant with *g:* Heb. *nhg* denotes human sighing or moaning; cf. Syr. *nᵉhag,* "groan, roar" (also of animals), Arab. *nahija,* "be out of breath, gasp," modern South Arab. (Soq.) *nhg,* "cry";[15] variant: Eth. *nĕhĕka,* "sigh" (not *nĕhĕqa*[16]). For Akk. *nâqu* I, "cry," *AHw* gives no Semitic equivalent; Leslau, however, associates it with Heb. *n'q, nhq,* and *nhg,* as well as Eth. *naqawa,* "call out."[17] With respect to Heb. *nā'aq,* "groan," compare the verb *'ānaq* (with metathesis), with the same meaning.

There is only one occurrence of *nhg* II, the piel participle in Nah. 2:8(7).[18] It describes sounds of mourning and despair at the fall of Nineveh: "Its slave women moan like doves." According to Jenni, *nhg* II is in the piel here because "a continued sound" is being described.[19]

W. Gross

---

13. Von Soden, 176.

14. For Ugaritic see *WUS,* no. 1761, *UT,* no. 1622. For Tigré see Leslau, *Etymological Dictionary,* 458.

15. Leslau, *Lexique Soqoṭri* (Paris, 1938), 259f.

16. Leslau, *Or,* 37 (1968), 359, no. 1622.

17. *AHw,* II, 744; Leslau, *JAOS,* 89 (1969), 21; *idem, Etymological Dictionary,* 458.

18. With the LXX, Vulg., and Targ., W. Rudolph (*Nahum. KAT,* XIII/3 [1975], 168) repoints the text as the pual of *nhg* I, "are taken away"; but this reading postulates a textual lacuna.

19. P. 247. This theory is treated with skepticism by Ryder, II, 130ff., esp. 135.

נָהַל nāhal

Contents: I. Etymology; II. Occurrences; III. LXX, Dead Sea Scrolls.

I. Etymology. Heb. *nhl* may be related to Akk. *nâlu, na'alu,* "lie down, rest."[1] There is a possible but not certain relationship with Arab. *manhal,* "watering place, resting place." Heb. *nah^{a}lōlîm* appears in Isa. 7:19 with the meaning "watering places." The verb *nhl* is found only in the piel (9 times) and hithpael (once).

II. Occurrences. The Song of the Sea uses *nhl* in parallel with *nāḥâ,* "guide," to describe how God in his steadfast love led his people to his holy abode to give them rest there (Ex. 15:13). Gen. 47:17 proves that the verb has nothing to do with the commonly assumed meaning "lead,"[2] saying of Joseph: *way^{e}nah^{a}lēm balleḥem,* "he gave them rest with bread." Deutero-Isaiah uses the verb several times. In a promise of salvation to the people coming out of captivity, Isa. 49:10 says: "He who has pity on them will lead them, and by springs of water will given them rest" *(w^{e}ʿal-nabbûʿê mayim y^{e}nah^{a}lēm).* Isa. 51:18, a passage about Jerusalem, says similarly that "there is none to give her rest among all the sons that she has borne, none to take her by the hand among all the sons she has brought up." Isa. 40:11 describes Yahweh as the shepherd of the people of Jerusalem: he will gather the lambs in his arms and carry them in his bosom and "give the mother sheep rest."

The use of the verb in Ps. 23:2 is familiar: "By still waters he gives me rest" *(ʿal-mê m^{e}nuḥôṯ y^{e}nah^{a}lēnî);* cf. Ps. 31:4(Eng. v. 3): "You are indeed my rock and my fortress; for your name's sake you lead me and bring me to rest." In 2 Ch. 28:15 we read: "They let the feeble rest *(nhl)* on donkeys and brought them to Jericho, the city of palm trees." The usage is even clearer in 32:22: "So Yahweh saved Hezekiah and the inhabitants of Jerusalem from the hand of King Sennacherib of Assyria and from the hand of all the enemies, and gave them rest on every side" *(way^{e}nah^{a}lēm missāḇîḇ).*

The hithpael puts more emphasis on the element of activity. The only occurrence is Gen. 33:14: "Let my lord pass on ahead of his servant, and I will continue on in peace" *('eṯnāh^{a}lâ l^e'iṭṭî).*

The meaning "give rest, bring to rest" is clear if we let the texts speak for themselves.

---

nāhal. F. Delitzsch, *Prolegomena eines neuen Hebräisch-aramäischen Wörterbuchs zum AT* (Leipzig, 1886), 17ff.; W. J. Gerber, *Die hebräischen Verba denominativa* (1896), 28f.; P. Haupt, "The Hebrew Stem *nahal,* to Rest," *AJSL,* 22 (1905), 195-206; T. Nöldeke, review of Delitzsch, *Prolegomena, ZDMG,* 40 (1886), 728; A. Schultens, *Origenes Hebrææ* (1724).

1. *AHw,* II, 725.
2. As already pointed out by Haupt: "Fr. Delitzsch's view that *nhl* means throughout *to rest* is correct" (p. 195); "There is no verb *nhl to lead* in Hebrew, only a stem *nhl to rest*" (p. 202).

III. LXX, Dead Sea Scrolls. The translation of the LXX is totally heterogeneous; only 3 times is a compound of *tréphein* used. The only certain occurrence in the Dead Sea Scrolls, 1QH 18:7, is textually corrupt.

Kapelrud(†)

נָהָר *nāhār*; נְהַר *nahar*

Contents: I. Ancient Near East: 1. Egypt; 2. Mesopotamia; 3. Ugarit. II. Etymology. III. Occurrences and Meaning. IV. Rivers as Natural Phenomena: 1. Boundaries; 2. Beyond the River; 3. Dry Rivers. V. River of Living Water: 1. Blessings of Water; 2. Rivers of Paradise and the Temple; 3. Rivers Arise and Dry Up. VI. Rivers as Sacred Places. VII. Destructive Rivers. VIII. LXX, Dead Sea Scrolls.

I. Ancient Near East.

1. *Egypt.* Egyp. *ỉtrw,* "river," refers primarily to the Nile, whereas *ḥʿpy,* the usual term for the Nile, actually refers to the inundation.[1] Hapi can be identified with the waters of Nun, and is thus linked with the primal sea.

2. *Mesopotamia.* Akk. *nāru* means both "river" and "watercourse, canal." The Euphrates is the river par excellence; *eber nāri,* "beyond the river," is Syria (cf. Aram. *ʿa̱bar nahărā*ʾ).[2]

The Assyro-Babylonian pantheon includes a "god River"; the name is written with the ideogram *ID* and was probably pronounced "id," since *nāru* is feminine. This deity is invoked as "creator of all," and is called giver of all good things and judge of humankind.[3] As the abode of Ea, Id is associated with Apsu.

---

nāhār. Y. Aharoni and M. Avi-Yonah, *The Macmillan Bible Atlas* (New York, 1968, ³1983); R. T. O'Callaghan, *Aram Naharaim. AnOr,* 26 (1948); J. A. Emerton, " 'Spring and Torrent' in Psalm 74:15," *Volume du Congrès, Genève 1965. SVT,* 15 (1966), 122-133; N. Glueck, *Rivers in the Desert* (New York, 1959); O. Keel, *The Symbolism of the Biblical World* (Eng. trans., New York, 1978); O. Kaiser, *Die mythische Bedeutung des Meeres in Ägypten, Ugarit und Israel. BZAW,* 79 (²1962); H. G. May, "Some Cosmic Connotations of *Mayim Rabbîm,* 'Many Waters,' " *JBL,* 74 (1955), 9-21; K. H. Rengstorf, "ποταμός," *TDNT,* VI, 595-607; A. Schwarzenbach, *Die geographische Terminologie im Hebräischen des ATs* (Leiden, 1954); J. J. Timmers, *Symboliek en iconographie der christelijke kunst* (1947); W. A. Ward, "Notes on Some Semitic Loanwords and Personal Names in Late Egyptian," *Or,* 32 (1963), 413-436, esp. 420ff.; A. J. Wensinck, *The Ocean in the Literature of the Western Semites. Verhandelingen van de Koninklijke Academie der Wetenschappen,* 19/2 (1968).

1. → יְאֹר *yᵉʾōr* (V, 359-363); see also "Nil, Nilgott," *LexÄg,* IV, 480-83, 485-89.
2. *AHw,* I, 181.
3. *AOT,* 130.

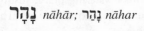

In the underworld is the river *Ḫubur.* To cross *(ebēru)* this river means "to die."[4] This river is identified with Tiamat ("Mother Ḫubur, who creates everything"; cf. the river as creator above).[5]

The river plays a special role in trial by water.[6] The Code of Hammurabi decrees that someone accused of sorcery or adultery must go to the (divine) river, i.e., undergo trial by water.[7] The procedure is not described; other texts suggest that a guilty person sinks, whereas an innocent person does not.[8] In a later period an oracular site by a river was called *ḫursānu* (Sum. *ḫursag*), a word scholars often associate with the homonymous word for "mountain," finding in it certain associations with the underworld.[9] But the two words can hardly be identical.

A world map calls the waters surrounding the flat earth *nāru marratu,* "bitter river" (cf. *marratu,* "salt sea").[10] It is also interesting that Gilgamesh may dwell *ina pī nārāti,* "at the mouth of the rivers," probably the land of Dilmun at the edge of the world.

3. *Ugarit.* In Ugaritic texts *ṯpṭ nhr,* "Judge (or perhaps better: Lord) River (or Stream)" appears as a parallel designation of *zbl ym,* "Prince Sea," overcome by Baʿal.[11]

Ringgren

II. Etymology. Heb. *nāhār,* "river," corresponds to Ugar. *nhr,* Akk. *nāru,* Aram. and Syr. *n^ehar, nahrā',* and Arab. *nahr,* all with the same meaning.[12] OSA *nhr* means "canal."[13] The word is not found in Ethiopic. It is probably a primary noun.

Two verbs *nāhar* are distinguished by *HAL.*[14] The first (*nhr* I) is taken as a denominative from *nāhār* and translated "flow, stream" (Isa. 2:2 par. Mic. 4:1; Jer. 51:44). The second (*nhr* II), meaning "be radiant (with joy)," occurs in Isa. 60:5; Jer. 31:12; Ps. 34:6(Eng. v. 5); it is related to Syr. *n^ehar,* "be radiant," and Arab. *nahār,* "bright daylight."

Closer examination of the texts in question, however, makes it dubious that a verb *nāhar* meaning "stream" ever existed (*nāhar,* "to stream," is also unknown to the

---

4. *AHw,* I, 352.
5. EnEl, I, 133.
6. A. Falkenstein, *AfO,* 14 (1942), 333ff.
7. CH, §§2, 132, respectively.
8. A Mari text in J. Bottéro, "L'ordalie en Mésopotamie ancienne," *Annali della Scuola Normale, Superiore di Pisa,* III/11 (1981), 1005-1067; J. M. Sasson, *BA,* 47 (1984), 117f.; a text in E. Ebeling, *Tod und Leben* (Berlin, 1931), 99; a Nabonidus text, published most recently by W. von Soden, *Archäologische Mitteilungen aus Iran,* Erg. 10 (1983), 65.
9. Cf. *AHw,* I, 359f.; Ebeling, *RLA,* III, 98; *CAD,* XI/1, 374f.; see also P. Kyle McCarter, "The River Ordeal in Israelite Literature," *HTR,* 66 (1973), 403-412, who points to possible similarities in the OT.
10. *BuA,* II, 378.
11. → יָם *yām,* VI, 90.
12. See *WUS,* no. 1762; *AHw,* II, 749.
13. Biella, 296.
14. P. 676.

Mishnah, Talmud, and Targums). In contrast to Isa. 2:2, Mic. 4:1 uses the prep. *ʿal*, "over, above," which fits poorly with a verb of motion. Whereas Isa. 2:2 uses *ʾel*, "to," 1QIs^a has *ʿal*. If we accept the latter reading, Jer. 31:12 is the only occurrence remaining. Here too we find *nāhar ʾel*, but both Syr. and Targ. read "shine, be radiant." Bertil Wiklander translates "rejoice."[15] Isa. 2:2 and Mic. 4:1 would then mean: "and nations shall rejoice over it, and many peoples shall come."[16] Hans Wildberger, however, sees in *nāhar*, "stream," an allusion to *nāhār* in the Zion hymn Ps. 46:5(4).[17]

A derivative of *nāhar*, "be radiant," is *n^{e}hārâ*, "light" (Job 3:4; Sir. 43:1), usually described as an Aramaic loanword. The hapax legomenon *minhārâ* in Jgs. 6:2 is problematic. It is translated by *HAL* as "caves cut out of the rock-face as subterranean hideaways)."[18] J. A. Soggin translates it as "hiding places," with good contextual support but without etymological basis.[19]

There could be a connection between *nāhar*, "be radiant," and *nāhār*, "river," if one were to think of the glittering surface of a great river. It must be noted, however, that *nāhar* II is related closely to the root *nwr* (Akk. *naw/māru*, "be radiant, shine"; *nûru*, "light"; Arab. *nûr*, "light").

III. Occurrences and Meaning. The word *nāhār* occurs 110 times in the OT. In Isa. 43:19 1QIs^a supports the reading *n^{e}ṯîḇôṯ* for *n^{e}hārôṯ*. In Job 20:17 *nah^{a}rê* is sometimes deleted as a marginal gloss. A. B. Ehrlich may be correct, however, in understanding *biplaggôṯ* as an abstract plural ("division") and connecting it with *nah^{a}rê*: "He takes no pleasure in the division of his rivers into streams of honey and curds." The wicked busy themselves with dividing the spoil into various kinds of booty, but they do not get to enjoy it.[20] On the metaphor, cf. Job 29:6.

The noun *nāhār* is masculine. In ancient Semitic and Greek mythology, river deities are usually gods, not goddesses. The normal plural suffix, however, is *-ôṯ* (31 times); *n^{e}hārîm* occurs 6 times. Hab. 3:8f. uses *n^{e}hārîm* twice and *n^{e}hārôṯ* once. It is an open question whether this variation is due to linguistic carelessness or whether the text is making a distinction, so that *n^{e}hārîm* is to be understood as a plural of amplification,[21] "much water, a sea," and *n^{e}hārôṯ* (v. 9) as referring to the streams issuing from the subterranean sea. Others see in *n^{e}hārôṯ* a plural of *n^{e}hārâ*, "light," i.e., "lightning flashes."[22] Otherwise only the rivers of Nubia are called *n^{e}hārîm* (Isa. 18:1f.,7; Zeph. 3:10). This usage, too, must be a plural of amplification; this is suggested also by the word *yām*, which in Isa. 18 (as occasionally elsewhere; cf. 19:5) refers to the Nile. The

---

15. B. Wiklander, "The Context and Meaning of *nhr ʾl* in Jer 51:44," *SEÅ*, 43 (1978), 40-64.
16. The same interpretation is proposed by H. Cazelles, *VT*, 30 (1980), 418.
17. *VT*, 7 (1957), 62ff.
18. *HAL*, II, 600.
19. J. A. Soggin, *Judges. OTL* (Eng. trans. 1981), 110.
20. *Randglossen zur hebräischen Bibel*, 7 vols. (Leipzig, 1908-14), VI, 261.
21. *GK*, §124d-f.
22. E.g., W. Rudolph, *Habakuk. KAT*, XIII/3 (1975), in loc.

verb *bāzā'* occurs only in Isa. 18:2,7. The meanings "wash away" and "cut through" remain conjectural.[23]

A *nāhār* is a perennial river. For a *nāhār* to run dry is unusual (Nah. 1:4; Ps. 74:15; cf. Ps. 66:6; Job 14:11), in contrast to a → נחל *naḥal,* which flows only during the rainy season.

Several rivers are mentioned by name in the OT: the Abana and Pharpar, the rivers of Damascus (2 K. 5:12); the Ahava (Ezr. 8:15); the Chebar (Ezk. 1:1), the Tigris and the Euphrates (*ḥiddeqel, pᵉrāṯ:* e.g., Gen. 2:14). The latter is often referred to simply as "*the* river" (Gen. 31:21; Ex. 23:31; Nu. 22:5; Josh. 24:2; etc.) or "the great river" (Gen. 15:18; Dt. 1:7; 11:24; Josh. 1:4). The OT always calls the Nile → יאר *yᵉ'ōr* (except in Gen. 15:18, where it is called "the river of Egypt"), a word that the LXX interpreted generically, as the translation *potamós* shows. This is also the case in the MT of Dnl. 12:5, where *yᵉ'ōr* refers to the Tigris.

It is noteworthy that no river in Israel is called *nāhār.* The text speaks only of *nᵉḥālîm:* Jabbok, Arnon, Kishon (Dt. 2:36; Gen. 32:24[23]; Jgs. 4:7), etc. Even the most famous river of Israel is called simply → ירדן *yardēn.* Here too we are probably dealing with a generic term, since Job 40:23 uses *yardēn* in parallel with *nāhār* (like *yᵉ'ōr* in Am. 8:8; 9:5) and Dt. 3:27; 4:21f.; 31:2; Josh. 1:2,11 speak of *hayyardēn hazzeh.*

In some texts *nᵉhārôṯ* must be interpreted as a plural of amplification or extension: it refers to the great river, the sea (Isa. 44:27; 50:2; Ps. 78:16; 137:1), or the deep (24:2; 74:15; Hab. 3:8). This usage is comparable to the use of *yᵉ'ōrîm,* "the great river," in Nah. 3:8; Isa. 7:18, and *tᵉhômôṯ* for the Sea of Reeds in Isa. 63:13.

It is more surprising that the sg. *nāhār* is sometimes equated with *yām,* "sea": Isa. 19:5 (the sea is the Nile); Ps. 66:6 (the river is the Sea of Reeds); 114:3,5 (the sea is the Jordan; cf. Isa. 48:18). The usage of Ugar. *nhr* is comparable.[24]

The phrase *'ᵃram nahᵃrayim* (Gen. 24:10; Dt. 23:5[4]; Jgs. 3:8; Ps. 60:2[superscription]) is not a dual but a locative.[25] It denoted initially "the area surrounded by the great bend of the Euphrates from Aleppo to the river חָבוּר, later incorporated into Greater Syria,"[26] the middle stretch of the Euphrates, inhabited by the Arameans and called in Akkadian *mātu ina birit* ^nār^*diqlat u* ^nār^*puratti,* "the land between the rivers Tigris and Euphrates," or simply *birit nārim.*

IV. Rivers as Natural Phenomena.

1. *Boundaries.* Streams often represent barriers to caravans and armies (Josh. 24:11; Isa. 47:2; 43:2) and therefore function (like wadis or mountains) as boundaries. In Numbers and Joshua the *nᵉḥālîm* Arnon and Jabbok as well as the Jordan are mentioned as tribal and national boundaries (Nu. 34:12; Josh. 13:23; 19:22; Dt. 3:16; cf. Jgs. 11:13;

---

23. For the former see *HAL,* I, 117; for the latter see H. Wildberger, *Isaiah 13–27* (Eng. trans., Minneapolis, 1997), 206, 208.

24. M. Dahood, *Bibl,* 48 (1967), 437: "ocean current." See I above.

25. O'Callaghan, 131.

26. *HAL,* II, 677.

Josh. 12:2; etc.). The *naḥal* of Egypt (Wadi el-Arish) was considered the southern boundary of Canaan or Israel (Nu. 34:5; 1 K. 8:65). In the promise to Abraham, however, the boundary line is the *nāhār* of Egypt (Gen. 15:18), i.e., the Nile (probably the easternmost distributary of the Delta). 1QGenApoc calls this river Gihon, meaning the Nile.[27]

Kings David and Solomon ruled "from the Euphrates to the *naḥal* of Egypt" (1 K. 5:1,4[4:21,24]; cf. Dt. 11:4; Josh. 1:4; 2 S. 8:3; Isa. 27:12; also Ps. 80:12[11]). The Euphrates appears also as the boundary of the territory controlled by Egypt under Necho (2 K. 23:29; 24:7; Jer. 46:2). The worldwide rule of the ideal king is described in these terms: "May he have dominion from sea to sea, and from the River [Euphrates] to the ends of the earth" (Ps. 72:8); or: "His dominion shall be from sea to sea and from the River to the ends of the earth" (Zec. 9:10). These texts not only define western and eastern boundaries, the Mediterranean and the Euphrates, but use *nāhār* synonymously with *yām* to refer to the ocean surrounding the world.[28] The phrase *'apsê hā'āreṣ* suggests Akk. *apsū,* the primal sea where the land ends.[29] The royal dominion thus comprises the whole inhabited world.[30]

2. *Beyond the River.* The notion of the river as boundary echoes also in the phrase *'ēḇer hannāhār,* "beyond the river," which refers to a foreign land with different laws (Ezr. 8:36; Neh. 2:7,9; 3:7). Beyond the river lies a distant, sinister, hostile world (Isa. 7:20; cf. Jer. 2:8). Joshua recalls that Israel's ancestors dwelt beyond the Euphrates, where they served other gods (Josh. 24:2). Beyond the river is also the cruel place of exile (1 K. 14:15). The people beyond the rivers of Cush are horrifying (Isa. 18:1).

The OT knows nothing of a *nāhār* of death.[31]

3. *Dry Rivers.* Rivers and seas act as obstacles for human beings and animals. Several texts refer to Yahweh's help in such situations. He stands by the returning exiles when they are blocked by water (or fire): "When you pass through waters, I will be with you; and through the rivers, they will not overwhelm you" (Isa. 43:2). Here "water and fire stand for dangers from any element."[32] This help can manifest itself in a desert storm so hot ("the heat of his breath") that the river almost dries up — only small channels remain ("seven *n^eḥālîm* [wadis]"), which can be easily crossed (11:15: possibly an allusion to rendering harmless the seven-headed serpent of 27:1). The mention of Egypt at the beginning of the verse recalls the exodus. When this scorching wind blows ("the panting of Yahweh": 42:14), the streams dry up: "I will turn the rivers into dry land (*'îyîm,* 'islands') and dry up the pools" (42:15). Thus a path is made for the returnees (v. 16). Isa. 44:27, too, stands in the context of the captives' return

27. J. A. Fitzmyer, *The Genesis Apocryphon. BietOr,* 18A ([2]1971), 131f.
28. See I above.
29. Wensinck, 21f.
30. → VIII, 351.
31. → VIII, 205.
32. C. Westermann, *Isaiah 40–66. OTL* (Eng. trans. 1969), 118.

from Babylon: "Who says to the deep *(ṣûlâ),* 'Be dry, I will dry up your rivers *(n^ehārôṯ).*' "[33] The rivers of Babylon, or better the great river of Babylon (pl. of amplification), is a river that emerges from the subterranean ocean: it will be dried up to help the returnees.

In Job 14:11 the drying up of a river serves as a metaphor for the fading of human life. The usual translation of 28:11 suggests redirection of rivers through human intervention: "The underground watercourses he [the miner] blocks up" (i.e., he dams them so that no water leaks through). Marvin Pope is probably correct in reading *ḥippēṣ,* "probe," instead of *ḥibbēš:* "The sources of the rivers he probes, brings hidden things to light."[34]

Yahweh overcomes the river by a word of power (Isa. 44:27), just as his word caused the waters to come together into a single sea so that dry land appeared (Gen. 1:9). Isa. 50:2 and Ps. 106:9 speak of Yahweh's rebuke (→ גער *gā'ar*), which dries up the sea (cf. Nah. 1:4; Ps. 18:16[15]; 104:7). Here the sea and rivers take on cosmic, mythological dimensions.

V. River of Living Water.

1. *Blessings of Water.* Gardens with produce and fruit trees grow beside the river (Nu. 24:6). The stream flows with honey and curds (*d^eḇaš w^eḥem'â:* Job 20:17; probably a variation on the expression *'ereṣ zāḇaṯ ḥālāḇ ûd^eḇaš* [→ דבש *d^ebhash*]). Therefore an increase in prosperity *(šālôm)* can be likened to a river or stream (Isa. 66:12; cf. 48:18); here is also an echo of the life-giving power of water. Streams from the deep caused the cedars of Lebanon to flourish (Ezk. 31:4). Although Exodus does not speak explicitly of the benefits of the Nile's inundation, the account of the first plague in Egypt alludes to them: the water is changed into blood, the river stinks, and the fish die (Ex. 7:19ff.; cf. 8:5[9]).

2. *Rivers of Paradise and the Temple.* The rivers of paradise and the temple bring life and blessings to the world. "A river flowed out of Eden to water the garden, and from there it divided and became four branches (*rā'šîm,* 'major rivers')" (Gen. 2:10). The garden[35] is a huge oasis watered by a mighty spring, which gives rise to four rivers flowing through the whole world. Although *ḥiddeqel* and *p^erāṯ* are familiar names (Tigris and Euphrates), it would be foolish to try to locate the rivers of paradise on our maps. The world of the ancient narrator was totally different from ours. Furthermore, the rivers Gihon and Pishon are otherwise unknown.[36] The number four is significant, reflecting the four corners of the earth (Isa. 11:12; Ezk. 37:9; 1 Ch. 9:24). To be more precise, the Euphrates runs through the north (Jer. 46:6,10), the Tigris is the river of the east (Gen. 2:14), the Pishon is the river of the south (Havilah, the sands of Arabia;

---

33. On the notion of the subterranean ocean from which springs and rivers issue, see → מצולה *m^eṣûlâ* (VIII, 514-19).
34. M. Pope, *Job. AB,* 15 (³1973), 181.
35. → גן *gan* (III, 34-39); → עדן *'ēḏen.*
36. Westermann, *Genesis 1–11* (Eng. trans., Minneapolis, 1984), 217.

cf. Gen. 10:7,29; 25:18; 1 S. 15:7), and the Gihon is located in the west (Egypt/ Nubia).[37] The waters from paradise bring growth and fertility to the whole world.[38]

From the temple of Jerusalem, the dwelling place of God, there also runs a river that transforms the land into a luxuriant garden. In Ps. 46:5(4) this river is a *nāhār* feeding *p^elāgîm,* "watercourses, canals." The psalm describes how Yahweh exorcises the waters of the sea, the tumult of the nations (vv. 7,11[6,10]) — the realm of chaos. In the city of God, a river divides and flows through the land in all directions, i.e., God saves and blesses the land (cf. Ps. 87, which speaks of springs). Scholars rightly assume that the bronze sea and the ten basins on wheels in the temple (1 K. 7:23,43) symbolize the river *(nāhār)* and its branches in the cult.[39] Ps. 36:9(8) speaks of a river *(naḥal)* of delight flowing from the temple, from which people drink; v. 10(9) describes the result as light and life.

Isa. 33:21 describes the Jerusalem of the age of salvation as a paradise flowing with water. Where God dwells, there is "a place of broad rivers *(n^ehārîm)* and streams *(y^e'ōrîm).*" The statement that no ships sail on the rivers means that they are not navigable for commerce or for enemy fleets: they bring blessings only to the land. Ezk. 47:6 uses *naḥal* for the river that gives life and blessings to the whole land. Zec. 14:8 speaks of living water flowing from Jerusalem; one half flows toward the eastern sea, the other half toward the western sea (cf. Jo. 4:18[3:18]).[40]

3. *Rivers Arise and Dry Up.* Both promises of salvation and oracles of judgment draw on the notion of rivers as bringers of life and prosperity. Yahweh punishes the nations by making the rivers cease to flow and the springs to run dry, thus depriving the people of the necessities of life.[41] When a river dries up, the result is catastrophic. In the absence of life-giving water, the garden becomes a desert. For example, Egypt, which depends on the annual inundation of the Nile, will be smitten with drought (Isa. 19:5ff.). The water of the "sea" (i.e., the surface of the Nile) will dry up,[42] the river will be parched,[43] the *n^ehārôṯ* (lateral canals) will become foul, the *y^e'ōrîm* (tributaries) will diminish, reeds and rushes will rot away. When Yahweh appears in judgment, he rebukes the "sea" and makes it dry and dries up all the rivers; then Bashan and Carmel wither, and the bloom of Lebanon fades (Nah. 1:4). Lebanon is clothed in gloom (Ezk. 31:15). Ps. 107 describes God's power to avail: "He turned rivers into a desert, springs of water into thirsty ground, a fruitful land into a salty waste, because of the wickedness of its inhabitants" (vv. 33f.; v. 35 describes the

---

37. A. Dillmann, *Genesis,* 2 vols. (Eng. trans., Edinburgh, 1897), I, 123ff.; for Babylonian illustrations depicting four rivers, see Keel, 118, ill. 153a; 140, ill. 185.

38. A. van Selms, *Genesis. POT,* 2 vols. (1967), I, 54; cf. H. Gunkel, *Genesis* (Eng. trans., Macon, Ga., 1997), 8.

39. Keel, 142, ill. 188; cf. May, 20.

40. → II, 468.

41. See IV.3 above.

42. → חרב *ḥāraḇ* (V, 150-54).

43. → יבשׁ *yāḇēš* (V, 373-79).

opposite). The sea is dried up, the rivers become a desert — so Deutero-Isaiah depicts God's power (Isa. 50:2).

By contrast, Yahweh also provides the water in the rivers. The salvation that the prophets proclaim they often liken to water, rivers, and streams. This imagery recalls the miracles during Israel's desert wandering (Ex. 17:6; Nu. 20:8). Yahweh gives water in the wilderness, rivers in the desert, to give drink to his people (Isa. 43:20; cf. Ps. 78:6; 105:41). He opens rivers on the bare heights and springs in the midst of the valleys, he makes the desert a pool and the parched land a garden full of trees (Isa. 41:18). It is well known that flat portions of the desert turn into lakes following tropical rainstorms. They vanish quickly but support vegetation for some time (cf. Isa. 35:6f.).[44]

Ps. 74:15 appears to speak of a similar wonder in the desert: "You cut openings for springs and torrents." If so, the second part of the verse is problematic: "You dried up ever-flowing streams," which says just the opposite. In my opinion, J. A. Emerton has suggested a good solution to this problem, pointing out that v. 15 describes God's work of creation. Mythological language tells of God's victory over the powers of primordial chaos (vv. 13f.). Then, as a transition to the creation of day and night and establishing the bounds of the earth, God liberated the earth from the dark masses of water: "He made holes in the ground," through which the water could drain away, and "tore wadis in the land," through which the water could run off into the distant sea. V. 15b then is most appropriate: "You dried up the eternal sea (*n^{e}hārô*ṯ: not 'streams' but the ocean itself, *mayim rabbîm*)."

VI. Rivers as Sacred Places. The OT mentions the river Chebar several times. On the bank of this river in the land of the Chaldeans, Ezekiel had a heavenly vision (Ezk. 1:1,3), to which he refers with the words "what I saw by the river Chebar" (3:23; 10:15; 43:3). The Chebar is identical with the *nāru kabru,* i.e., the *šatt el-nīl,* which leaves the Euphrates near Babylon and rejoins it at Uruk.[45] The prophet is dwelling by the river "among the exiles" when he receives his vision. Daniel too has visions on the bank of a river (Ulai: 8:2; Tigris: 10:4). This location may be meant in a purely topographic sense. Walther Zimmerli, however, has rightly pointed out that "the Jewish diaspora of the New Testament period established its places for prayer preferably beside water."[46] According to Josephus, praying by the sea was "a custom inherited from the fathers."[47] Ps. 137:1 also speaks of assembling for worship by the river Euphrates (*ʿal nah^{a}rôṯ bāḇel*).

It is noteworthy, furthermore, that Ezekiel has other visions in a *biqʿâ* (Ezk. 3:23; 37:1ff.). This word means "valley," but are there valleys between mountains in the broad alluvial plain of Babylonia? Now the verb *bāqaʿ* means "split (the earth)," often so that water pours forth (Gen. 7:11; Dt. 8:7; Isa. 35:6; Hab. 3:9; Ps. 78:15; Prov. 3:20).

---

44. A. Parrot, *The Flood and Noah's Ark* (Eng. trans., London, 1958), 52; Glueck, 84f.
45. *BHHW,* III, 22.
46. *Ezekiel 1. Herm* (Eng. trans. 1979), 115.
47. *Ant.* 14.10.23 §258.

In Ezekiel, therefore, we are probably dealing with a topographical depression containing a spring, where grass grows and the flocks (not to mention the people) love to gather (Isa. 41:18; 63:14). Samuel Krauss notes a rabbinic text:[48] "Thus he spoke with them (outside the land of Israel), but only in a pure place with water, as it is written . . . (Dnl. 8:2; 10:4; Ezk. 1:3)." Water was needed for the prescribed ablutions.[49] Others find this explanation of prayers on the bank of a river unsatisfactory and think instead of archaic water deities. Otto Kaiser recalls appearances of angels at desert wells (Gen. 16:7ff.).[50] It is hard to say, however, what role this ancient popular response to nature played in the customs of the diaspora community.

VII. Destructive Rivers. Rivers can also bring destruction. The secure foundation of the wicked is washed away by a river (Job 22:16). The Psalm of Jonah speaks of a river that surrounds him. This river is *tᵉhôm,* the primordial deep; it is *šᵉ'ōl,* the realm of the dead. Jonah has sunk to the depths of the sea *(mᵉṣûlâ bilḇaḇ yammîm),* to the roots of the mountains that stand in this sea (Jon. 2:3,5f.). It is natural to describe enemies as "mighty waters" (Ps. 18:4,17[3,26] par. 2 S. 22:4,17) or "deep waters" (Ps. 69:15[14]). The advance of a devastating army is likened to "the mighty flood waters of the River," overflowing its banks and flooding the land of Judah (Isa. 8:7ff.). Egypt, too, rises like the Nile, whose waters advance like floods (*yiṯgā'ᵃšû;* not "rage"). It says: "I will rise, I will cover the earth, I will destroy the cities and their inhabitants" (Jer. 4:8). Other texts use the image of a hurricane (Isa. 4:6; Ezk. 13:13). God's judgment of wrath is like a river (Isa. 59:19).

The passages cited make clear that "sea" and "river" are parallel concepts, and also that the sea/river is viewed as a dangerous monster. Egypt is a dragon in the seas, thrashing about in the streams, troubling the water with its feet and fouling it (Ezk. 32:2; cf. Isa. 51:10; Ezk. 29:3). The sea is the chaos monster that Yahweh tames and overcomes (Ps. 77:17[16]; 78:13; 93:2ff.). As at Ugarit and in Mesopotamia, the motif of battle with the sea appears in the OT. Yahweh does battle with the power of chaos, the primordial deep. This battle is a contest fought in the context of the creation of heaven and earth. This is the sense, for example, of Ps. 24:2, which states that Yahweh founded the earth on seas *(yammîm)* and the ocean *(nᵉhārôṯ).*[51] Ps. 104:9 makes a similar statement about the waters of the Flood.

But this battle takes place also within history. The dividing of the Sea of Reeds is interpreted as a victory over the waters of chaos (*tᵉhômôṯ:* Ex. 15:8; Ps. 77:17-20[16-19]; cf. 114:3-7). Hab. 3:8f. recalls this glorious battle: "Is your wrath against the rivers [= the sea[52]] or your anger against the sea, that you drive your horses, your chariots to victory?" In a mighty storm, God reveals himself as victor over the sea; he conquers the enemy to save his people (v. 13). The earth splits, and the devastating rivers flood

---

48. Midr. *Mekilta* on Ex. 12:1.
49. S. Krauss, *Synagogale Altertümer* (Berlin, 1922), 281, 285.
50. Pp. 92-101.
51. See III above.
52. See above.

the land (v. 9). Torrential rains fall, the deep *(t^e^hôm)* surges up. God takes the field in a battle with the nations, destroying the enemies of Israel and delivering his people. The whole scene is described in mythological language that recalls the Ugaritic myth of Baʿal and Hadad. God fights by drying up the sea and the rivers, but also by destroying the enemy with a rushing flood (Nah. 1:4,8). Nineveh is flooded when "the gates of the river [i.e., the subterranean sea] are opened" (Nah. 2:7[6]). Thus God masters the enemies who threaten his creation. His throne rises above their throne, his sovereignty is unassailable. "The floods lift up, O Yahweh, the floods lift up their voice, the floods lift up their roaring; mightier than the thunders of many waters, mightier than the waves of the sea is Yahweh on high" (Ps. 93:3f.). And to Yahweh's servant David it is granted to lay his hand upon "the rivers" (= the sea). David conquers nations that represent chaos (89:26[25]; cf. v. 11[10]).

Timo Veijola expresses reservations concerning this "battle with chaos" mythology, preferring to return to a concrete geographical interpretation in which *n^e^hārôṯ* refers to the Euphrates and its tributaries (cf. Ps. 137:1).[53] In the framework of Ps. 89, which is conceived after the analogy of ancient Near Eastern treaties, v. 26(25) serves to define a geographical boundary.

Love, too, which is as strong as death, conquers the waters of chaos: "Many waters *(mayim rabbîm)* cannot quench love, neither can rivers *(n^e^hārôṯ)* drown it" (Cant. 8:7). The forces of evil in the world cannot destroy the love of Yahweh for his people.[54]

Snijders

VIII. LXX, Dead Sea Scrolls. The LXX had no problem with translating *nhr.* The few occurrences of the verb are represented by *hḗkein* (twice), *synágein,* and *phōtízein* (once each).[55] The noun *nāhār* finds its equivalent in *potamós* (131 times), *nah^a^rayim* in *Mesopotamía.*

In the major Dead Sea Scrolls, *nāhār* is quite rare and appears to have no special semantic overtones. Only once does *n^e^hārôṯ* appear in connection with regulations governing purification (1QS 3:5). The application of "garden of Eden" symbolism to the community is interesting. The community is thought of as a great tree, and all the *n^e^hārôṯ* of Eden water its branches (1QH 6:16). In 1QapGen *nāhār* occurs 11 times, almost always defined by a proper name, e.g., *tînâ, karmônâ, gîḥōn,* and *p^e^rāṯ.* The "river" with seven "heads" is mentioned in 19:12; the associated geographical clues suggest that this refers to the Nile with its Delta tributaries. Finally, according to 1QM 2:10, the decisive battle of the *eschaton* begins in Aram Naharaim.

Fabry

---

53. T. Veijola, "Davidverheissung und Staatsvertrag," *ZAW,* 95 (1983), 9-31, esp. 22-29; following M. Sæbø, *VT,* 28 (1978), 85f.

54. May, 18; on the cosmic overtones of this text, see H. Ringgren, *Das Hohe Lied. ATD,* 16/2 (³1981), 287.

55. See II above.

נוד nûḏ

Contents: I. Etymology; II. Meaning, Usage; III. LXX.

I. Etymology. The root *nwd* appears in Jewish Aramaic with the meaning "be mobile," in Syriac and Mandaic with the meaning "sway," and in Arabic with the meaning "sway," "shake (one's head)." It is clearly related to → נדד *nāḏaḏ*, "flee," etc. The two roots are sometimes confused in the OT, e.g., Jer. 50:3 *nwd,* and 9:9(Eng. v. 10) *ndd,* in otherwise identical contexts; Prov. 26:2 *nwd,* used of flitting birds, and 27:8 *ndd,* in a similar context. In the OT the word appears 19 times in the qal, 3 times in the hiphil, and 4 times in the hithpael.

II. Meaning, Usage.

1. The concrete meaning of the word is clear from 1 K. 14:15: Israel will be smitten so that it will " 'shake' like a reed in the water"; cf. also the hithpael in Isa. 24:20: "The earth staggers *(nûaʿ)* like a drunkard, it 'sways' like a hut." This meaning appears also (with the same combination of *nûaʿ* and *nûḏ*) in the judgment on Cain in Gen. 4:12: *nāʿ wānāḏ tihyeh bāʾāreṣ,* "you will be a fugitive and a wanderer on the earth" (cf. v. 14). The verse characterizes the unsettled wandering of a nomad as divine punishment; it also alludes to the land of Nod, where Cain settles.

A similar meaning may be present in Ps. 56:9(8): "You have kept count of my *nōḏ;* put my tears in your bottle *(nōʾḏ).*" Here *nōḏ* may mean something like "unsettled life" = "misery."[1] Other suggestions include "lamentation," shaking the head in penitential rites, and *n^eḏûḏîm,* "restlessness" = "sleepless nights."[2] In any case, the verse says that God cares for the psalmist and knows his suffering well. If the text is correct, there is wordplay involving *nōḏ* and *nōʾḏ;* the LXX, however, reads *negdeḵā,* "in your presence," instead of "your bottle."

The hiphil in 2 K. 21:8 also belongs in this group: this text cites Yahweh's promise to David (2 S. 7:10?) that he will never "cause Israel to seek refuge" from his land if the people keep his commandments — obviously a Deuteronomistic commentary on Manasseh's idolatry.

Elsewhere the word is often associated with flight. In Jer. 49:30, for example, the inhabitants of Hazor are exhorted: "Flee *(nusû),* get away quickly *(nuḏû)*" — the two verbs are more or less synonymous — to save themselves from Nebuchadnezzar. Jer. 50:8 is similar: "Flee *(nuḏû)* from Babylon . . . go out (*ṣēʾû* [*Q*] vs. *yṣʾw* [*K*])." Characteristically, the imperatives are written defectively in both cases (influenced by

---

1. H. Gunkel, *Die Psalmen. HAT,* II (1926), 245.

2. For the first see F. Perles, *Analekten zur Textkritik des ATs,* 2 vols. (1895), in loc.; D. Winton Thomas, *The Text of the Revised Psalter* (London, 1963), in loc. For the second, J. Eaton, *The Psalms. Torch Comm.* (1967), 149. For the third, *HAL,* II, 672, following B. Duhm, *Die Psalmen erklärt. KHC,* 14 (1899), 154.

ndd?). Jer. 50:3 describes how a nation from the north advances against Babylon and lays waste the land so that no one can live in it and human beings and animals "flee *(nûḏ)* and depart *(hālaḵ)*." In a similar context, Jer. 9:9(10) says that all of Judah is laid waste, and the birds and cattle have fled and departed *(hālaḵ);* this text, however, uses *ndd*.

By contrast, Jer. 4:1 is a promise to Israel: "If you return . . . you will not need to 'flee' from me" — not away from God, but back to God.

Prov. 26:2 likens an undeserved curse to a sparrow flitting away *(nûḏ)* and a swallow flying away *(ʿûp):* it will not achieve its purpose. (Prov. 27:8, however, uses *ndd* to describe a bird "that strays from its nest.") One may also note the striking summons in Ps. 11:1: "Flee like a bird to the mountains." The psalmist's enemies call on him to flee, but he knows that he can take refuge in God.

2. In another group of texts *nûḏ* means "show pity," obviously related to the gesture of shaking one's head (cf. the hiphil in Jer. 18:16: *kōl ʿōḇēr . . . yānîḏ rōʾšô,* "everyone who passes by . . . shakes his head"; and the hithpael in Jer. 48:27, Ps. 64:9[8]). The parallel expressions clearly indicate this meaning. In Isa. 51:19 Jerusalem, having drunk the cup of Yahweh's wrath, is asked: "Who will lament *(yānûḏ)* for you?" Her condition is so appalling that there is no one left to care for her. The same parallel appears in Job 2:11, 42:11 (Job's friends come to sympathize [*nûḏ*] and comfort), and Ps. 69:21(20): "I waited in vain for 'pity,' for a comforter, and found none." Jer. 15:5 again addresses Jerusalem as it lies in ruins: "Who will have pity on you *(ḥāmal),* who will 'bemoan' you?" And Nahum declares that Nineveh is devastated, and no one exhibits sympathy (Nah. 3:7b). In Jer. 48, an oracle against Moab, v. 17 says: " 'Mourn' over him, all you his neighbors."

In an oracle against Shallum, Jer. 22:10 says: "Do not weep for him who is dead, nor 'bemoan' him." And Jeremiah, lamenting his loneliness and isolation, says that God commanded him not to enter the house of mourning, not to participate in mourning for the dead, and to "show sympathy" (→ מרזח *marzēaḥ*).

III. LXX. The LXX does not translate the verb uniformly. It uses the following twice each: *kineín, metanasteúein, syllypeísthai, trémein,* and (for the hiphil) *saleúein;* other translations (e.g., *planán, seíein*) appear only once.

Ringgren

נָוֶה *nāweh*

Contents: I. 1. Etymology; 2. Occurrences. II. 1. Akk. *nawû;* 2. Usage. III. LXX.

I. 1. *Etymology.* Akk. *nawûm/namû* means "pasture, steppe"; OSA *nwy* means "watering place" or the like. In Arab. *nawā,* "destination," the primary emphasis is clearly on the notion of a goal (cf. *niya,* "intention," and Heb. **nāwâ,* "achieve one's aim" [Hab. 2:5]). Both Akk. *nawû* and Heb. *nāweh* would therefore be the goal of a nomadic tribe, a place where there is pasturage; this would lead to the meaning "stopping place, dwelling place." But *nawûm/nāweh* may also be a primary noun.

2. *Occurrences.* The noun *nāweh* occurs 45 times in the OT, almost exclusively in poetic texts (the exception being 2 S. 7:8). The form **nā'ōṯ,* found only in the const. *n^e'ôṯ,* serves as the plural of *nāweh.*

II. 1. *Akk. nawûm.* Akk. *nawûm* occurs frequently, especially in the Mari texts. Here, as D. O. Edzard has shown, it denotes "the flocks together with their shepherds." In later Babylonian texts it means "the pasturelands belonging to a city." We also find expressions like *nawûm ša karkamiš,* "the pasturelands of Carchemish," and *sippar u nawêšu,* "Sippar and its pasturelands."[1]

2. *Usage.* a. *Pasture.* In a number of OT texts, the connection with pasture and flocks is clear. We may note, for example, the phrase *n^{e}wēh rō'îm* (Jer. 33:12; Am. 1:2; Zeph. 2:6); the context often includes forms or derivatives of *rā'â,* "graze" (Isa. 27:10; Jer. 50:19; *mar'îṯ:* Jer. 25:36; *mir'eh:* Ezk. 34:14), forms or derivatives of *rāḇaṣ,* "lie down" (Isa. 27:10; Jer. 33:12; Ezk. 34:14; cf. Prov. 24:15), or *ṣō'n,* "sheep" (2 S. 7:8; Isa. 65:10; Jer. 23:3; 49:20; 50:45; Ezk. 25:5; Zeph. 2:6). The phrase *n^e'ôṯ midbār* also belongs here (Jer. 9:9[Eng. v. 10]; 23:10; Jo. 1:18f.; 2:22; Ps. 65:13[12]).

The pasture motif can be used in various ways. In 2 S. 7:8 (par. 1 Ch. 17:7; the prophecy of Nathan) it is quite neutral: Yahweh has taken David away from the pasture and the sheep *(ṣō'n)* to make him king.

Several passages speak of the transformation of settled areas into pasture: "I will make Rabbah a pasture for camels and Ammon a fold for flocks *(mirbaṣ ṣō'n)*" (Ezk. 25:5; cf. also Isa. 34:13, "the haunt of jackals, an abode for ostriches," and Isa. 35:7, where the probably corrupt text speaks of "the place where jackals dwelt"). There is

---

nāweh. M. Delcor, "Quelques cas de survivances du vocabulaire nomade en hébreu biblique," *VT,* 25 (1975), 307-322; D. O. Edzard, "Altbabylonisch *nawûm,*" *ZA,* 53 (1959), 168-173; A. Malamat, "Aspects of Tribal Societies in Mari and Israel," *XVe Rencontre assyriologique international* (1967), 129-138; R. Zadok, "Babylonian Notes," *BiOr,* 38 (1981), 547-551.

1. Malamat, 136.

also Zeph. 2:6: "I will make you [land of the Philistines] 'meadows' for shepherds and folds for flocks."[2] The Isaiah apocalypse bewails the devastated city: "It is a pasture, depopulated, forsaken like the desert; calves graze *(rāʿâ)* there, there they lie down *(rāḇaṣ)*" (Isa. 27:10).

In other passages, the pastures themselves are devastated. For example, the introductory words of the book of Amos say that the pastures of the shepherds wither when Yahweh roars from Zion (Am. 1:2; there may be an echo of this text in Jer. 25:30: Yahweh will roar from on high "against his pastures"). In the explanation of Jeremiah's vision of the cup of wrath (Jer. 25), where a universal judgment of the nations is announced, we read: "Yahweh is despoiling *(šdd)* their pasture *(marʿîṯ),* and the peaceful folds [*nᵉʾôṯ haššālôm;* cf. Isa. 32:18] are devastated (*dmm* niphal) before the blazing anger of Yahweh" (vv. 36c,37a). Two quite similar oracles concerning Edom and Babylon, Jer. 49:20 and 50:45, prophesy that the smallest of the sheep *(ṣᵉʿîrê haṣṣōʾn)* will be dragged away and their pasture (NRSV: fold) will be appalled. The same context (49:19; 50:44) has the phrase *nᵉwēh ʾêṯān,* "enduring pasture," probably to be understood as "oasis."[3]

Other statements are positive. In Jer. 23:3 Yahweh promises to "gather (*qbṣ* piel) the remnant of his flock [i.e., the people of Israel] and bring them back to their pasture"; 50:19, in the oracle against Babylon, says: "But I will restore Israel to its pasture, and it shall feed *(rāʿâ)* on Carmel and in Bashan." Ezekiel uses the same image: "I will guide them to good pasturage *(mirʿeh),* in the mountain heights of Israel shall be their 'pastures'; there they shall lie down *(rāḇaṣ)* in good 'grazing land,' and they shall feed on rich pasture *(mirʿeh)* on the mountains of Israel" (Ezk. 34:14). The people are the flock, and Yahweh will be their shepherd (v. 15). In Jer. 33:12 the pastures are literal: "In this place . . . there shall again be pasture for shepherds resting their flocks *(marbîṣê ṣōʾn)*." The same is true in Isa. 65:10: "For my people who have sought me, Sharon shall become a pasture for flocks *(nᵉwēh ṣōʾn),* and the Valley of Achor a place for herds to lie down *(rēḇeṣ bāqār)*." Isa. 32:18 occupies a middle ground: "My people will abide in a peaceful pasture *(nᵉwēh šālôm),* in secure dwellings *(miškᵉnôṯ miḇṭaḥîm),* and in quiet resting places *(mᵉnûḥōṯ šaʾᵃnannôṯ)*." The context also includes the terms *miḏbār* and *karmel,* as well as *ṣᵉḏāqâ* and *mišpāṭ.*

Also figurative but with more general import is Ps. 23:2. Here the *nᵉʾôṯ dešeʾ,* "green pastures," and *mê mᵉnuḥôṯ,* "waters of the resting places" (cf. Isa. 32:18), illustrate the function of the divine shepherd. We may also note the expression "he makes me lie down" (*rbṣ* hiphil [see above]).

To the same category belongs the phrase *nᵉʾôṯ miḏbār,* "pastures of the steppe." In Jer. 9:9ff.(10ff.) a lamentation *(qînâ)* is heard there and on the mountains, because they are scorched (*yṣt* hiphil) and their herds *(miqneh)* are gone; Jer. 23:10 laments the drying up *(yāḇēš)* of the pastures. The pastures of the steppe appear also in Jo. 1:15-20,

---

2. The text presents problems; cited here as reconstructed by W. Rudolph, *Zephanja. KAT,* XIII/3 (1975), in loc.

3. Rudolph, *Jeremia. HAT,* XII ([3]1968), 248; → נחל *naḥal.*

a communal lament, where v. 19 says that they have been devoured by fire; in 2:22ff. God's response is: "The pastures of the steppe are green" (*dāšᵉʾû;* cf. *dešeʾ* in Ps. 23:2). Here we may also recall Ps. 65:13, where the pastures "overflow" (? *rʿp;* in parallel with *gîl,* however, the reading *yārîʿû,* "rejoice," is attractive) as one expression of God's bounty.

b. *Dwelling Place.* In some texts *nāweh* parallels *ʾōhel,* "tent," or *bayiṯ,* "house." In these cases it appears to have the broader sense of "stopping place" or "dwelling place." The clearest example is Job 5:24: "You shall know that your tent is safe, you shall inspect your *nāweh* and miss nothing."[4] More difficult is 18:15, speaking of the wicked, where Friedrich Horst translates: "Nothing more of him *(mibbᵉlî lô;* possibly 'nothing alien to him') still dwells in his tent, on his abode *(nāweh)* sulfur is scattered."[5] Prov. 3:33 speaks of the blessing on the "abode" of the righteous (par. *bayiṯ*). The abode of the righteous appears again in 24:15, here in parallel with *rēḇeṣ,* "resting place." Prov. 21:20 speaks in general terms of the "abode of the wise," calling it a precious treasure; Job 5:3 speaks of the "dwelling of a fool," which must suddenly curse *(qbb)* him (after his downfall).

Ps. 79:7 (cited in Jer. 10:25) is problematic; it says that the nations have devoured *(ʾāḵal)* Jacob and laid waste (*šmm* hiphil) his *nāʾôṯ,* referring either to fields (pasture) or to dwelling places. The same is true of Lam. 2:2: "Yahweh has destroyed [*blʿ,* 'devoured'] the *nāʾôṯ* of Jacob and broken down the strongholds *(miḇṣār)* of Judah." Here the parallelism probably requires the meaning "dwelling places."

Equally unclear is the expression *nᵉʾôṯ ʾᵉlōhîm* in Ps. 83:13(12): the hostile kings seek to take possession of *(yāraš)* the *nāʾôṯ* of God. Does this mean "pasture" in the sense of "land?" Or does it refer to the "holy place" (see 2.c below; cf. also LXX *thysiastḗrion*)? The Targ. reads "beauty" (= *nāʾweh?*); cf. also Jer. 25:30 above. The meaning of *nāweh* in Ps. 74:20 is likewise quite obscure: the land is full of "dwelling places of violence" *(nᵉʾôṯ ḥāmās);* the LXX reads *oíkōn anomiṓn.*

A *nāwōṯ* or *nāyôṯ* (*Q; K* probably *nāwᵉyaṯ*) also appears in 1 S. 20:1 and 19:18f. as a place of refuge for David "in Ramah." The LXX interprets the word as a toponym; but it clearly refers to the abode of the prophets gathered around Samuel, although it cannot be a cloister in the strict sense of the word. P. Kyle McCarter translates it as "camps," assuming that the prophets dwelt in camps like those of shepherds.[6]

The text of Hos. 9:13 is almost certainly corrupt. Ephraim is apparently being compared to "Tyre, planted on the meadow," but this makes no sense in the context. Following the LXX, Hans Walter Wolff reads *lᵉṣayiḏ šāṯ lōh bānāyw,* "Ephraim exposed his sons to the wild animals";[7] but the presence of *bānāyw* in the following line makes

4. F. Horst, *Hiob. BK,* XVI/1 (1968), 88: "the security of one's dwelling place, here described in nomadic terminology as a 'tent' and 'stopping place' (lit.: pasture)."

5. *Ibid.,* 265.

6. *I Samuel. AB,* 8 (1980), 328; see also A. Haldar, *Associations of Cult Prophets among the Ancient Semites* (Uppsala, 1945), 142, n. 1.

7. *Hosea. Herm* (Eng. trans. 1974), 160f.

this unlikely. Francis I. Andersen and David Noel Freedman retain the MT and interpret *šᵉṯûlâ ḇᵉnāweh,* "planted on a meadow," as referring to the fig tree in v. 10.[8]

c. *Dwelling Place of Yahweh.* In a few instances *nāweh* clearly or possibly refers to Yahweh's dwelling place on Zion. At the very least, 2 S. 15:25 is clear. Fleeing from Jerusalem, David says to Zadok that he hopes Yahweh will "bring me back and let me see again *'ōṯô wᵉ'eṯ-nāwēhû.*" The question is whether *'ōṯô* refers to Yahweh or to the ark; in either case, *nāweh* denotes the tent sanctuary where the ark and Yahweh are present.[9]

McCarter refers here to Ex. 15, the so-called Song of the Sea, where v. 13 reads: "In your steadfast love you led *(nāḥâ)* the people, you guided *(nhl)* them by your strength to your holy abode *(nᵉwēh qoḏšeḵā).*"[10] Both *nhl* and (to some extent) *nāḥâ* are pastoral terms (cf. Ps. 23:2f; 77:21[20]). The abode could be the temple on Zion, but if so, the poem would date from the period of the monarchy at the earliest, a dating supported by the expressions "mountain of your possession," "place where you are enthroned," and *miqdāš* in Ex. 15:17. In "mountain of your possession" and "holy dwelling place," however, Martin Noth sees terms referring to the promised land as a whole.[11] Stig Norin finds Ugaritic parallels to *har naḥᵃlāṯᵉḵā, māḵôn lᵉšiḇtᵉḵā,* and *miqdāš,* all referring to the abode of the gods on Zaphon; there is no parallel to *nᵉwēh qōḏeš.*[12] According to Norin, the reference to Zion would be possible in a Deuteronomistic context.

The situation is clear, however, in Isa. 33:20, where images from pastoral life, including the expressions *nāweh ša'ᵃnan,* "quiet habitation," and "immovable tent"[13] express the security of the future Jerusalem. Jer. 31:23 is not entirely clear. It prophesies that once more people in Judah will say, "May Yahweh bless you, O abode of righteousness, O holy hill." Wilhelm Rudolph considers it possible that "holy hill" (as in Isa. 11:9) means the entire land, and correctly interprets *ṣeḏeq* as "salvation."[14] But the use of the words "in the land of Judah and in its towns" does not prove conclusively that the prophecy is addressed to the whole land; indeed, it makes Jerusalem alone more likely. The expression is then borrowed and reinterpreted in Jer. 50:7 (secondary): now Yahweh, against whom the people have sinned, is "the place of righteousness and the hope of the ancestors."

The *nᵉwaṯ bayiṯ* that divides the spoil in Ps. 68:13(12) probably does not belong here; it may mean "entrance hall" or "the beautiful woman of the house."[15] The expression *nᵉwaṯ ṣiḏqeḵā* (Job 8:6), "your rightful place," i.e., the restored abode of the penitent, argues otherwise.

---

8. *Hosea. AB,* 24 (1980), 544.
9. K. Rupprecht, *Der Tempel von Jerusalem. BZAW,* 144 (1977), 94.
10. *II Samuel. AB,* 9 (1984), 371.
11. *Exodus. OTL* (Eng. trans. 1962), 125f.
12. S. I. L. Norin, *Er spaltete das Meer. CB,* 9 (1977), 85ff.
13. → נסע *nāsa'.*
14. *HAT,* XII, 199.
15. See *HAL,* II, 679.

III. LXX. The translations of the LXX reflect the semantic breadth of the Hebrew words: *nomḗ,* "pasturage" (7 times), or *nomós,* "pasture" (Jer. 10:25); *tópos,* "place" (4 times); *épaulis,* "dwelling place" (3 times + Isa. 35:7?); *katályma* (twice) and *katálysis* (once), "refuge"; *mándra,* "fold" (2 S. 7:5 and par.; Ezk. 34:14); *díaita,* "abode" (Job 5:3; 8:6); and *euprépeia,* "beauty," or *euprepḗs* (2 S. 15:25; Job 5:24; Jer. 49:20).

Ringgren

נוּחַ *nûaḥ;* מְנוּחָה *m^e^nûḥâ*

Contents: I. General. II. Verb: 1. Qal; 2. Hiphil A; 3. Hiphil B. III. Noun: 1. For Humans; 2. For God. IV. Apocrypha and Dead Sea Scrolls.

I. General. The root *nûaḥ/nḥ/nḫ* is widely attested in both early (Old South Arabic, Canaanite, Old Sinaitic, Ethiopic, and Akkadian) and later Semitic languages (Middle Hebrew, Jewish Aramaic, Christian Palestinian Aramaic, Syriac, Mandaic), as well as Ugaritic.[1]

According to Mitchell Dahood, several translations have confused *nûaḥ* with *nḥh*

nûaḥ. G. R. Berry, "The Hebrew Word נוּחַ," *JBL,* 50 (1931), 207-210; G. Braulik, "Menuchah, die Ruhe Gottes und des Volkes im Lande," *BiKi,* 23 (1968), 75-78; W. Brueggemann, "Weariness, Exile and Chaos," *CBQ,* 34 (1972), 19-38; J. Ebach, "Zum Thema: Arbeit und Ruhe im AT," *ZEE,* 24 (1980), 7-21; O. Eissfeldt, "nûaḥ 'sich vertragen,'" *KlSchr,* III (1966), 124-28; J. Frankowski, "Requies, Bonum Promissum Populi Dei in VT et in Judaismo," *VD,* 43 (1965), 124-149, 225-240; O. Hofius, *Katapausis. WUNT,* 11 (1970), esp. 22-50; A. R. Hulst, "De betekenis van het woord מְנוּחָה," *Schrift en uitleg. Festschrift W. H. Gispen* (Kampen, 1970), 62-78; W. C. Kaiser Jr., "The Promise Theme and the Theology of Rest," *BS,* 130/518 (1973), 135-150; *idem, Toward an OT Theology* (Grand Rapids, 1981), 127-130 (see also index); M. Metzger, "Himmlische und irdische Wohnstatt Jahwehs," *UF,* 2 (1970), 139-158; G. von Rad, "There Remains Still a Rest for the People of God," *The Problem of the Hexateuch and Other Essays* (Eng. trans., New York, 1966), 94-102; *idem, OT Theology,* 2 vols. (Eng. trans., New York, 1962-65), II, 373f.; G. Robinson, "The Idea of Rest in the OT and the Search for the Basic Character of the Sabbath," *ZAW,* 92 (1980), 32-42; W. Roth, "The Deuteronomic Rest Theology," *BR,* 21 (1976), 5-14; F. Stolz, "נוח *nû^a^ḥ* 'to rest,'" *TLOT,* II, 722-24; cf. also 790; P. Welten, *Geschichte und Geschichtsdarstellung in den Chronikbüchern. WMANT,* 42 (1973), 17f., 49, 97, 201; H. W. Wolff, *Anthropology of the OT* (Eng. trans., Philadelphia, 1974), 134-142; *idem,* "The Day of Rest in the OT," *CTM,* 43 (1972), 498-502.

1. For Canaanite see EA, 147, 56; for Ethiopic, W. Müller, *ZAW,* 75 (1973), 312; for Akkadian, *AHw,* II, 716; for the later Semitic languages, *HAL,* II, 679; *DISO,* 146; *KAI,* 58; also K. Beyer, *Die aramäischen Texte vom Toten Meer* (Göttingen, 1984), 634; for Ugaritic, *WUS,* no. 1772; *UT,* no. 1625 (*n* and *nt*), also M. Dahood, *RSP,* I, 221f. On Eccl. 10:4; Est. 9:17f., cf. Dahood, *RSP,* I, 276, with an analogous double occurrence; on Ex. 23:12, cf. Dahood, *RSP,* II, 23; on Isa. 57:2 (cf. Isa. 32:18; 1 Ch. 22:9), cf. Dahood, *RSP,* II, 32; III, 161 (in combination with *šālôm*).

in a few passages (e.g., Isa. 63:14).[2] On Akkadian equivalents see also EA, 74, 27, 37.[3] Whether Est. 9:17f. and 2 Ch. 6:41 attest the existence of a subst. *nôaḥ* is disputed. There are also textual problems with Isa. 57:18 and 30:32.[4] On the name Noah in Gen. 5:29 (cf. Sir. 44:17), see Claus Westermann's commentary.[5]

The LXX equivalents for the verb are primarily *anapaúein* and *epanapaúesthai;* for the nouns, *anápausis* and *katápausis.* For the qal of the verb *aphíein/aphiénai* is less frequently used. For the hiphil the LXX has more than twenty different translations, including *kathízō* and *títhēmi.*

There are 30 occurrences of the qal of *nûaḥ,* meaning "settle down (to rest), become quiet and (consequently) rest." The hiphil A *hēnîaḥ,* often with *l*[e], occurs 33 times, with the meaning "cause to settle down, give rest, bring to rest." The opposite is not just motion, e.g., wandering, but (psychic) restlessness, so that sometimes (albeit rarely) the best translation is "satisfy, bring joy, calm" (Ex. 33:14; Prov. 29:17). The hiphil B *hinnîaḥ* (72 occurrences) means "lay, deposit, leave over, leave alone."[6] There are 4 occurrences of the equivalent hophal B (Ezk. 41:9; 41:11 [2 occurrences of *munnāḥ,* "free space"]; Zec. 5:11 [the basket is to be "set down"]), while the hophal A is found only in Lam. 5:5 *(Q):* "We are given no rest" — a sign of divine judgment.

The most important derivatives are *m*[e]*nûḥâ* (21 occurrences), with meanings that range from "resting place" through "rest (in the land)," "place of (God's) rest" to (psychic) "calm"; and *mānôaḥ* (7 occurrences), "resting place" (cf. Arab. *munāḥ,* "resting place," esp. for camels). In Gen. 49:15 Dahood would read *mānôaḥ* (with acc. ending) instead of *m*[e]*nûḥâ.*[7]

We may also note 2 Ch. 6:41, which incorporates Ps. 132:8 but changes the *m*[e]*nûḥâ* of the latter to *nôaḥ* (niphal inf.?). We also find *naḥaṯ* in Isa. 30:15 (contrasting with preparation for war); cf. Prov. 29:9; Eccl. 4:6; Job 17:16 ("rest").[8]

That the theme of "rest" addresses a matter of some substance for the OT is shown by the number and importance of its occurrences,[9] as well as by its relatively broad semantic field, which includes the following: → שׁקט *šqṭ* (and its derivatives), *šalwâ* (→ שׁלו *šlw*), *šûḇâ* (→ שׁוב *šûḇ*), → שׁכב *šāḵaḇ,* → ישׁן *yāšēn,* esp. → רגע *rāgaʿ* with its derivatives, and finally → שׁלום *šālôm* and → שׁבת *šāḇaṯ,* although the last appears in combination with *nûaḥ* only in Ex. 20:11; 23:12 (and there probably in secondary interpretations). Antonyms include → יעף *yʿp,* → נשׂא *nāśā',* → רגז *rāgaz,* and → רום *rûm* (with the hiphil).

---

2. *Bibl,* 48 (1967), 357f.; cf. *idem, RSP,* I, 191f.

3. See also Eissfeldt.

4. On the former text see J. S. Kselman, *CBQ,* 43 (1981), 539-542; on the latter see H. Wildberger, *Jesaja 28–39. BK,* X/3 (1982), 1209; also Stolz, *TLOT,* II, 722.

5. C. Westermann, *Genesis 1–11* (Eng. trans., Minneapolis, 1984), 359f., with bibliog.

6. See II.1-3 below for further discussion.

7. M. Dahood, *Bibl,* 48 (1967), 427f.

8. Cf. Ugaritic and Karatepe I, 17f.; *KAI,* no. 26. On → ניחוח *nîḥôaḥ* see *HAL,* II, 696.

9. See II-IV below.

II. Verb.

1. *Qal.* Only a few occurrences of the qal represent strictly secular usage. David's followers waited (rested) (1 S. 25:9); Rizpah did not allow the birds of the air to alight on the sackcloth she had spread out (2 S. 21:10).

When Noah's ark (Gen. 8:4 [P]) or the ark of the covenant (Nu. 10:36) comes to rest, the meaning is positive (cf. also Josh. 3:13). It is negative, however, when locusts settle on the land of Egypt (Ex. 10:14 [J?]) or the fly of Assyria and the bee of Egypt settle on Israel (Isa. 7:19) (representing judgment; cf. also Isa. 23:12; Hab. 3:16; Lam. 5:5 [hophal]).

The qal is often associated with the gift of the Spirit,[10] as in Nu. 11:25f. with reference to the seventy elders and other men; in 2 K. 2:15 with reference to Elisha, on whom the spirit of Elijah rests (according to the company of prophets); and in Isa. 11:2, which states that the Spirit of Yahweh will rest on the shoot from the stump of Jesse.

The qal of *nûaḥ* is also used frequently to express the wisdom principle of retributive justice (Prov. 14:33; 21:16; cf. Eccl. 7:9), so that the concept also plays a role in Job's critical dispute with this ideology. In light of life's troubles, Job longs for death: then he would have rest, but not in this life (Job 3:13,17,26) — a wish rarely expressed in the OT. Dnl. 12:13 is the only other text that speaks of death as rest, albeit with a prospect of resurrection not ventured elsewhere. An expression of hope strongly influenced by wisdom also occurs in Ps. 125:3.

That the OT views rest as a God-given gift is clear from various promises (Isa. 25:10; 57:2 [text unclear]; also 14:7). Rest (= relief) from enemies[11] is an aspiration of the Jews (Est. 9:16,22; cf. vv. 17f.); the historical retrospect in Neh. 9 uses the word in v. 28 (thus clearly displaying Deuteronomistic influence[12]) for the rest achieved in the period of the judges — which rest, however, tempted the people to apostasy.

Already in the Covenant Code (Ex. 23:12), the Israelite is called on to rest *(šbt)* on the seventh day, "so that your ox and your donkey may rest *(yānûaḥ)*." Dt. 5:14 extends this rest to male and female slaves, in the spirit of both Deuteronomic and Deuteronomistic thought.[13] In this context, finally, Ex. 20:11 even says that on the seventh day Yahweh "rested" (*wayyānaḥ;* then in Gen. 2:2 [probably with more emphasis on the Sabbath] *wayyišbōṯ*[14]); in any case, this is the only text that uses the verb *nûaḥ* for the semantic opposite of working (cf. Gen. 49:15). That this resting of Yahweh (as in Isa. 25:10 [Yahweh's *yāḏ*]; 2 Ch. 6:41) alludes to Zion is unlikely.[15] Rest is not to be a privilege of the gods (i.e., God) or of specific human social classes.

---

10. → רוח *rûaḥ.*

11. → I, 215.

12. See III below.

13. But cf. H. Rücker, *Die Begründungen der Weisungen Jahwes im Pentateuch. ETS,* 30 (1973), 108, who considers this text pre-Deuteronomic.

14. F.-L. Hossfeld, *Der Dekalog. OBO,* 45 (1982), 47ff., 247ff.; L. Ruppert, "Die Ruhe Gottes," *ZDMG Sup,* 5 (1983), 121-131.

15. Contra Robinson.

2. *Hiphil A.* Like the qal, the hiphil A *(hēnîaḥ)* of *nûaḥ* is used primarily in theological contexts. It is Yahweh who gives his people or their king rest from their enemies: Dt. 12:10; 25:19; Josh. 21:44; 23:1; cf. also 1 Macc. 14:4; 16:2; etc.; also 2 S. 7:1; analogously in 2 S. 7:11, but as a renewed promise; 1 K. 5:18(Eng. v. 4) (v. 17[3] contradicts 2 S. 7:1,11!); 1 Ch. 22:9,18; 23:25; 2 Ch. 14:5f.(6f.); 15:15; 20:30.

Even a brief survey of these texts makes three things clear: (a) for the most part, they are associated with Deuteronomistic thought and its influence; (b) they mean rest as relief from enemies and war (sometimes "on all sides" instead of "from the enemy"); (c) this relief from enemies is often expanded to peace and prosperity in the land (cf. *šālôm* explicitly in 2 Ch. 20:30). Deuteronomistic influence is clear in Dt. 3:20; 12:10; 25:19; Josh. 1:13,15; 21:44; 22:4; 23:1; 2 S. 7:1,11 (both verses belonging to the Deuteronomistic recension of the chapter); 1 K. 5:18. Here rest is living at peace in the land — a Deuteronomistic benefit of hope and the fruit of (Deuteronomistic) obedience, as well as the substance of God's promise.[16] The clustering of several of these texts around the figure of Solomon (1 K. 5:4,18; 1 Ch. 22:9; cf. also Sir. 47:13) represents this king as the king of peace, but also exhibits an intentional association with Yahweh's "resting" in the temple.[17] This notion of rest was popular in certain circles of the Deuteronomistic school, but was not shared by all Deuteronomistic groups and movements, as may be seen from its absence in the Deuteronomistic redactional sections of the book of Jeremiah. Deuteronomistic influence is probably present also in Ezk. 33:14.

Timo Veijola's study of the Deuteronomistic history quite logically includes the "rest formula," which admittedly does not exhibit the same wording in all Deuteronomistic passages.[18] Going into more detail, Wolfgang Roth theorizes that the stratum DtrN took a special interest in the promise of rest (e.g., Dt. 25:19; Josh. 23:1; 2 S. 7:1,11; 1 K. 5:18), while its association with such themes as the oath sworn to the patriarchs (Josh. 21:44) and Yahweh's promise (22:4) points to earlier Deuteronomistic strata.[19]

"Rest" correlates with the notion of journeying; it is associated with guidance (on the way to Canaan) and hence with the theology of the land. It is also related to the theological appraisal of the Jerusalem temple (Dt. 12:9; 1 K. 8:56). Georg Braulik has attempted a more detailed analysis of the Deuteronomistic texts and their mutual "reference systems," with the aim of assigning them to various Deuteronomistic strata;[20] his proposed four phases of the Deuteronomistic conception of rest should, however, be related more clearly to the exilic situation of the audience addressed. It is this exilic Israel that is "not yet" (again) at rest in the land. Yahweh's renewed promise and the call to renewed obedience are intended to bring this about.

---

16. Contra von Rad, "There Remains," who considers this concept Deuteronomic.
17. See III below.
18. T. Veijola, *Die ewige Dynastie. AnAcScFen,* 193 (1975), 72f.
19. See also H. D. Preuss, *Deuteronomium. EdF,* 164 (1982), 194.
20. G. Braulik, "Some Remarks on the Deuteronomistic Conception of Freedom and Peace," *The Theology of Deuteronomy* (Eng. trans., North Richland Hills, Tex., 1994), 87-98.

The books of Chronicles also fall within the domain of the Deuteronomistic history, reflecting the history of its influence and interpretation. In contrast to 2 S. 7:1,11, 2 Ch. 17:1,10 deliberately omit the lexeme, because the Chronicler attaches more importance (in view of the "wars of David") to Solomon and his temple, with which the notion of rest is here more strongly linked (cf. 1 Ch. 22:9,18; 23:25; 2 Ch. 14:5f.[6f.]; 15:15; 20:30 with verb and substantive — all without parallels in the books of Samuel and Kings).[21] The contrast between David the man of war and Solomon the king of peace is stated explicitly in connection with the "gift of rest" in 1 Ch. 22:9.[22] T.-S. Im sees here a piece of historical revisionism rather than an interpretation of the figures of David and Solomon.[23] The statement about "peace on every side" is transferred to 1 Ch. 22:18, since now it is only under David that the enemies surrounding Israel were conquered (1 Ch. 18–20).

The books of Chronicles link the rest brought to the people by Yahweh, who is "with" his people (1 Ch. 22:18), with the theology of Zion and the temple. Yahweh vouchsafes rest by being himself at rest in Jerusalem[24] and dwelling *(škn)* in Jerusalem forever (1 Ch. 23:25). That this rest is the opposite of war and is therefore associated with *šālôm* is likewise stated explicitly by such texts as 2 Ch. 14:5f.(6f.); 26:30. The predilection of the Chronicler's history for this gift of rest is found both in the core of the history and in the redactional additions. The continued influence of these ideas can still be observed not only in 1 Maccabees but also in Sirach.[25]

Like the qal, the hiphil A appears in conjunction with *rûaḥ* (Isa. 63:14; Zec. 6:8; cf. also Ezk. 37:1, where the form may be a hiphil B). According to Isa. 63:14, it was the Spirit of Yahweh that gave rest (Yahweh led his people). What the Spirit of Yahweh does in Ezk. 37:1 is done by the hand of Yahweh in 40:2. Whether these texts describe actual changes of location or visionary experiences on the part of the prophet cannot be determined simply from the use of the hiphil A of *nûaḥ*. With its reference to the land of the north, the promise in Zec. 6:8 probably refers to the Babylonian Diaspora (cf. 2:10).

The extent to which this rest is a divine blessing can be seen directly from its appearance in several promises of salvation (Isa. 14:3 [probably also exilic; cf. the Deuteronomistic history]; 28:12;[26] also Ezk. 44:30). This association of rest with salvation is confirmed indirectly by the prophecies of judgment that argue the contrary or speak of the "fury" that Yahweh will "bring down" (Ezk. 5:13; 16:42; 21:22[17]; 24:13).[27]

Isolated usages are found in Ex. 17:11 (when Moses "lowers" his hand, Amalek

---

21. See T. Willi, *Die Chronik als Auslegung. FRLANT,* 106 (1972), 143.

22. On 1 Ch. 22:18 see also K. Koch, "Gestaltet die Erde, doch heget das Leben!" *"Wenn nicht jetzt, wann denn?" Festschrift H.-J. Kraus* (Neukirchen-Vluyn, 1983), 29.

23. T.-S. Im, *Der Davidsbild in den Chronikbüchern. EH,* 23/263 (1986), 142ff.

24. See III below.

25. For 1 Maccabees see II.1 above; for Sirach, IV below.

26. → VI, 154.

27. On this combination → IV, 464f.; cf. also Isa. 30:32.

prevails rather than Israel) and Prov. 29:17 ("Discipline your son, and he will 'bring you joy' ").

Finally, Yahweh's words to Moses in Ex. 33:14 (not to be read as a question) promise that Yahweh's countenance[28] will go before Moses, "and I will give you rest." The formulation is deliberately ambiguous: the promise clearly refers to rest in the land; but at the same time Moses is "calmed" by the promise.

3. *Hiphil B.* The hiphil B is not used as frequently in theologically significant contexts. It means "lay, set down, leave": Gen. 2:15; 19:16; 39:16; Josh. 4:3,8; 1 S. 6:18; 10:25; 1 K. 7:47; 8:9; 13:29,31; 2 K. 23:18; 2 Ch. 1:14; 9:25; cf. also Josh. 6:23 ("lodge"). Someone or something is "left behind": Gen. 42:33; 2 S. 16:21; 20:3; 1 K. 19:3. In Ps. 17:14; Eccl. 2:18, the meaning is "leave something to one's descendants."

Cultic texts frequently speak of "leaving over" something (e.g., a portion of a sacrifice) or "setting down" clothing, the tithe, a basket, or the like: Lev. 7:15; 16:23; Nu. 17:19,22(4,7); 19:9; Dt. 14:28; 26:4,10; Jgs. 6:18,20; Ezk. 40:42; 42:13f.; 44:19; 2 Ch. 4:8. P texts of this nature often stress the correspondence between directive and performance (Ex. 16:23f.,33f.).

Several times we find a request like "let me alone" or "let me do such and such": Ex. 32:10 (in vv. 9-14, probably a Deuteronomistic addition); Jgs. 16:26; 2 S. 16:11. Hos. 4:17 should probably be interpreted in the light of these texts: the verb can hardly mean "tolerate him [Ephraim, in his idolatry]" (cf. 2 S. 16:11); a more likely translation would be "let him go" (cf. 2 K. 23:18; Ex. 32:10; and above all the immediate context, which clearly speaks of judgment [Hos. 4:15]).

Similar words of judgment appear in Isa. 28:2; 65:15; Ezk. 16:39; 22:20 (textually problematic[29]). The verb is also used in a punitive sense ("put in custody") in Lev. 24:12 and Nu. 15:34 with reference to an individual, and in Nu. 32:15 with reference to the people (abandoned in the wilderness as a punishment).

In Jgs. 2:23; 3:1, the meaning is "leave": Yahweh left certain nations instead of driving them out (Deuteronomistic theology); cf. also Jer. 43:6. In Est. 3:8 the verb means "tolerate."

Salvific elements, often associated with dwelling in the land, are found in Isa. 14:1 (where it is possible that the text should be emended[30]); Jer. 27:11; Ezk. 37:14 (both similar to Isa. 14:1, albeit with a different emphasis; textual emendation is also possible). The people can therefore pray to Yahweh, "Do not forsake us" (Jer. 14:9 in a prayer of lamentation, vv. 7-9; cf. Ps. 119:121). What Ps. 105:14 (par. 1 Ch. 16:21) states positively (Yahweh allowed no one to oppress Israel during its wanderings), Ps. 119:121 expresses in the form of a petition.

The "setting up" of idols is criticized in 2 K. 17:29 and mocked in Isa. 46:7.

Finally, Ecclesiastes uses the verb in wisdom aphorisms (5:11[12]; 7:18; 10:4b) and

---

28. → פנים *pānîm.*

29. W. Zimmerli, *Ezekiel 1. Herm* (Eng. trans. 1979), 462.

30. H. Wildberger, *Isaiah 13–27* (Eng. trans., Minneapolis, 1997), 35.

admonitions (10:4a [text? "do not leave your place = your position"? the context [v. 4b] suggests instead "maintain tranquility"; then also 11:6); this usage occurs with some frequency elsewhere in wisdom texts.

Am. 5:7 is unique: a woe cry speaks of bringing righteousness down to the ground (cf. Jer. 28:2).[31]

III. Noun. The noun *m*^e^*nûḥâ* (written defectively in Gen. 49:15; 2 S. 14:37; Isa. 11:15; pl. in Ps. 23:2) is found also (usually as *nḥt*) in Aramaic and Canaanite,[32] as well as in Middle Hebrew and Samaritan. In one Hebrew inscription the grave is a place of rest.[33] The term also occurs elsewhere outside the Bible.[34]

In Jgs. 20:43; 1 Ch. 2:52; 8:2, *m*^e^*nûḥâ* may be a toponym.

1. *For Humans.* The noun *m*^e^*nûḥâ* occurs 21 times in the OT text. In the majority of passages it means rest for an individual or a group, often the Israelites. Jgs. 20:43 says that the Benjaminites had no rest in battle. A woman finds and may be wished rest in the house of her husband (Ruth 1:9). Nu. 10:33 speaks of rest during a journey, and Jer. 51:59 mentions a *śar m*^e^*nûḥâ* (royal courier? quartermaster?).

The early text Gen. 49:15 (in Jacob's saying about Issachar) already links rest with dwelling in the land (here freedom to settle);[35] this is an important element of the gift of rest for human beings in the OT. Isa. 32:18 promises that the people will abide in secure resting places. The postexilic context (vv. 15-18,[20]) describes in detail what this means. Ps. 95:11 also understands rest as dwelling in the land; because the context (vv. 7b-11) is a prophetic admonition, the verse probably does not refer to Yahweh's resting. The use of words spoken by Yahweh in the 1st person to conclude the psalm (with → בוא *bô'*, as in Dt. 12:9) underlines the significance of the statement, which He. 3:7–4:13 (4:9!) developed in a manner that was to be extremely influential.[36] In a quotation within a prophetic oracle (probably reflecting later revision[37]), the rich who are denounced say to those who are driving them out, "This is no place of rest" (Mic. 2:10).

Like the verb, the noun clearly illustrates the special interest of Deuteronomistic texts and Chronicles in the notion of rest, conceived as rest in the land and rest from enemies (with clear overtones of "freedom"), as well as rest near the sanctuary, Yahweh's resting place.[38] Both reflect a major theological concern, especially of the exilic and postexilic periods.

---

31. See also C. Story, *VT,* 30 (1980), 72.

32. *KAI,* 223 B 4: Sefire: rest through obedience; *KTU,* 1.4, I, 33; 2.11, 14; cf. *UT,* no. 1640; also *KAI,* 1, 2: rest = peace.

33. N. Avigad, *IEJ,* 7, 239, cited by *DISO,* 159. Cf. *KAI,* 34, 5; 35, 2; also Dnl. 12:13 (verb); Job 3:13.

34. *KAI,* 26, I A 18; II 8, 13; Dahood, *RSP,* I, 221f.; on the word pairs in these texts, cf. Isa. 30:15; Prov. 19:9; Eccl. 4:6; 6:5; 9:17; Job 17:16; 36:16.

35. See Dahood, *Bibl,* 48 (1967), 427f.

36. See E. Lohse, *TDNT,* VII, 34f.; and Hofius.

37. H. W. Wolff, *Micah* (Eng. trans., Minneapolis, 1990), 75f.

38. See III.2 below.

The Deuteronomistic texts include Dt. 12:9 (cf. the verb in 12:10; 25:19; also Josh. 21:44; 23:1), where "you have not yet come to rest" is given a further theological qualification by the addition of *naḥ*^{a}*lâ*.[39] The reference is to the land west of the Jordan as the substance of a new Deuteronomistic (not Deuteronomic) promise. The contrast with Dt. 28:65 (likewise Deuteronomistic) is instructive (cf. also Lam. 1:3; 5:2-6). Solomon's prayer at the dedication of the temple (1 K. 8:56; Deuteronomistic) extols Yahweh for giving rest to his people in fulfillment of his promise (on the association of this idea with that of "being with" in v. 57, cf. 2 S. 14:17[40]). The Deuteronomistic history does not speak of such rest at any time after Solomon. It was the gift of the land that brought rest — and the entrance of the exilic community into the promised land will bring this rest once more. It was the age of Joshua that brought rest from enemies throughout the land; the period of the judges also provided this rest, but it was interrupted by military threats (Josh. 1:13,15; 21:43-45; 22:4; 23:1; Jgs. 3:30; 8:28). Then it was the age of David and above all that of Solomon that was able to grant complete rest (2 S. 7:1,11; cf. 1 S. 26:19; then 1 K. 5:18[4]; 8:56). These texts frequently use both verb and noun together; both are fundamental to the expression of the Deuteronomistic notion of rest, shared by the Chronicler.

To the Chronicler, Solomon is the "man of rest" (1 Ch. 22:9; cf. v. 8), for Yahweh will give him rest (verb) from his enemies. Therefore it was not David but Solomon who was able to complete the "house of rest" for Yahweh (1 Ch. 28:2).[41] Once again, the similarity to the notion of *šālôm* is evident.[42]

Zion as the site that vouchsafes rest is probably also the subject of Isa. 11:10, an addition to vv. 1-9 that speaks of the root of Jesse that will glorify his resting place. The explanatory addition in Isa. 28:12 (which also uses both noun and verb) likewise refers to Jerusalem.

Zec. 9:1 (cf. 1 K. 8:56f.) states that the word of Yahweh "is coming to rest," i.e., is affecting the course of historical events; the reference is to the present, not to future punishment.[43]

The extent to which the OT notion of rest is associated not only with the land, the promise, and the temple but also with the guidance of Yahweh is clear from Ps. 23:2: Yahweh leads the psalmist to "waters of rest" (a pasture with water).

In the OT, therefore, it is impossible to distinguish rest as a resting place from rest as a divine gift. The place and the gift go together.[44] As a result, "rest" (as we have already seen in the case of the verb) can be psychic as well as local. The word of the king sets one's mind at rest (2 S. 14:17); contrariwise, Baruch laments that he finds no rest (Jer. 45:3).

The noun *mānôaḥ* also generally denotes a resting place (Isa. 34:14; Ruth 3:1; 1 Ch.

39. → נחל *nḥl*.
40. See also II.2 above.
41. See III.2 below.
42. See also G. von Rad, *TDNT*, II, 404; *DISO*, 177, s.v. *nḥt* II.
43. K. Elliger, *Das Buch der zwölf kleinen Propheten, II. ATD*, 25 (^{2}1951), in loc.
44. Ebach.

6:16[31]: here for the ark in the house of Yahweh; in Gen. 8:9, for the dove sent out by Noah). But in this noun, too, we find inward and outward rest (or their absence) interwoven (Dt. 28:65 [together with *mᵉnûḥâ*]; Lam. 1:3), while Ps. 116:7 refers only to rest for the psalmist's soul.

2. *For God.* That the Jerusalem temple was considered Yahweh's resting place has already been noted in the examination of the hiphil A of the verb.[45] The noun is used for this theologoumenon in 1 Ch. 28:2 (cf. Isa. 11:10); we may also include here statements that otherwise refer to the ark (Nu. 10:33; 1 K. 8:56). Of course, the context of Dt. 12:9 suggests the temple (cf. the verb in v. 11). This notion is developed more fully in Ps. 132:8,14 (see the context; cf. also 94:11 LXX and its incorporation in Jos.As. 8:10),[46] and appears again in 1 Ch. 6:16(31) and 2 Ch. 6:41f., and in substance in 1 Ch. 23:25.[47] On the use of the noun in combination with → ישׁב *yāšaḇ* in Ps. 132:14, cf. Lam. 1:3.[48]

Despite the importance of "rest" in Israelite spirituality, it is interesting to note that it never appears as an aspect of eschatological hope in the OT.

Isa. 66:1 (in 1st person words spoken by Yahweh) even casts doubt on the notion that the temple is Yahweh's resting place. This text clearly presupposes 1 K. 8:56 and should probably be understood as a protest against the postexilic rebuilding of the temple, after people during the exile had learned to experience and believe in Yahweh's presence apart from the temple.

IV. Apocrypha and Dead Sea Scrolls. The significance of the notion of rest in Sirach has already been noted[49] (cf. also 1 Mc. 14:4; 16:2; etc.; also the qal of the verb in Sir. 5:6; 32:21; 34:3f.,21; 40:5; 44:23; 46:19; and the hiphil in 5:6; 6:3; 12:3; 38:7; 39:28,32; 44:9; 47:13). Unfortunately the text of 33:4 E is difficult, so that it is unclear whether and how *mānôaḥ* (or the hiphil of the verb) is used there. In 6:28 (cf. 4:15; 14:24-27; 51:26), however, it is no longer the land that provides rest but rather wisdom — who also seeks rest herself (cf. 24:7). In 30:17 (cf. Job 3:13; Dnl. 12:13) the noun *nûḥâ* refers to death as eternal rest.

Jos.As. 22:13 (thinking of rest as a divine gift) cites Isa. 66:2, while 8:10 cites Ps. 132 (cf. Ps. 94:11 LXX).[50]

In the Dead Sea Scrolls, 4QFlor 1:7 cites the promise in 2 S. 7:11, reinterpreted with reference to the writer's own age as rest from the followers of Belial. According to 1QpHab 11:6, the Day of Atonement is the festival of rest; 11:8 associates rest with

45. See II.2 above, and esp. Metzger.

46. On Ps. 132:14 see also H. Kruse, *VT,* 33 (1983), 287.

47. On the Chronicler's history, see also J. P. Weinberg, *VT,* 33 (1983), 310; also Willi, *Chronik.*

48. Cf. also Dahood, *RSP,* I, 222; III, 195.

49. See II.2 above.

50. On the use of the term in the apocryphal books, see esp. Frankowski, 225ff., where he also discusses rabbinic literature.

the Sabbath. This combination appears also in 1QM 2:9. Other texts include 1Q56 2; 4QDibHam[a] (4Q504) fr. 1-2 4:2;[51] and 4QOrd[a] (4Q159) 2:5.[52] The hiphil of the verb can also be used for cessation of the tumult of war (1QM 17:14; cf. 8:7,14: the "quiet" sound of the war trumpets). Of course fighting is forbidden on the Sabbath as a day of rest (2:9), and when the war is over the soldiers return to their camp of rest (12:9). We see from 1QH 8:30 (important for Jgs. 20:43?) and 9:5 that at Qumran, too, the gift of rest could be understood as inward rest.

In the Temple Scroll we find only the hiphil B of the verb (11QTemple 32:10; 58:15; probably also 33:4; 43:4) in the sense "set down, leave"; the contexts are not theologically significant.

Preuss

---

51. Text: M. Baillet, "Un recueil liturgique de Qumrân, Grotte 4: Les paroles des luminaires," *RB,* 68 (1961), 195-250.

52. Text: J. M. Allegro, "An Unpublished Fragment of Essene Halakah (4Q Ordinances)," *JSS,* 6 (1961), 71-73.

נוס *nûs;* מָנוֹס *mānôs;* מְנוּסָה *m[e]nûsâ*

Contents: I. Distribution: 1. Extrabiblical Evidence; 2. OT; 3. LXX and Targum. II. Meaning: 1. Qal Stem; 2. Derived Stems; 3. Nouns; 4. Related Verbs. III. Theological Usage: 1. Narrative Texts; 2. Wars of Yahweh; 3. Israel's Flight; 4. Mythology. IV. Dead Sea Scrolls.

I. Distribution.

1. *Extrabiblical Evidence.* The base *ns* does not occur in all Semitic languages: there are no occurrences in East Semitic. Apart from Hebrew, it is clearly attested in Old Aramaic, Syriac, and Arabic; its appearance in Ugaritic is questionable. It has acquired the sense of "flee" only in Hebrew. For Ugaritic the glossary of *CML*[2] cites 2 occurrences. The first is a fragmentary *'l yns,* translated "let him not escape"; but the isolated nature of the text makes the meaning highly uncertain.[1] Cyrus Gordon derives the form from *nsy.*[2] The second is the form *ʒts* (identified by Gordon as the Gt stem of *ns,* without

---

nûs. B. Grossfeld, "The Relationship Between Biblical Hebrew ברח and נוס and Their Corresponding Aramaic Equivalents in the Targum," *ZAW,* 91 (1979), 107-123; E. Jenni, " 'Fliehen' im akkadischen und im hebräischen Sprachgebrauch," *Or,* 47 (1978), 351-59; S. Schwertner, "נוס *nûs* 'to flee,' " *TLOT,* II, 725-27.

1. *KTU,* 1.4, III, 5.

2. *UT,* 444, no. 1661.

further evidence).[3] This occurrence is thus also uncertain. Close in meaning to Heb. *nûs* is the form *hns* used by several Old Aramaic inscriptions for removing a stele;[4] cf. the meaning of the hiphil of *nûs* in Jgs. 6:11. The meanings "shudder," "be in a state of motion, swing," cited by *HAL* on the basis of Syriac and Arabic, show only that the base represents a verb of motion in all the Semitic languages that use it.[5]

2. *OT.* In Hebrew the base *ns* appears as the qal stem *nûs,* the hiphil *hēnîs,* and the polel *nôsēs;* there are also two derived nouns, *mānôs* and *m^enûsâ.* There are 153 occurrences of the qal, plus the hiphils in Jgs. 7:21 and Jer. 48:44, which the Masoretic pointing requires reading as qal forms. In Jer. 48:44 this reading is supported by the parallel in Isa. 24:18. In Jgs. 7:21, too, the Masoretic reading is probably preferable; the hiphil reading may be based on a misunderstanding of the subject.[6] The hiphil occurs only 3 other times. The form *l^ehiṯnôsēs* in Ps. 60:6(Eng. v. 4) is probably an ad hoc creation for the sake of the play on *nēs;* even if the writer was thinking of *nûs,* we cannot draw any conclusions about the meaning of the form.

3. *LXX and Targum.* The LXX uses *pheúgein* and its compounds with *dia-, kata-,* and *ek-* quite consistently to translate *nûs.* The inf. *lānûs* is sometimes represented by a noun formed from the same stem. Variant translations *(anachōreín, apodidráskein, diṓkein)* are explicable either as fixed idioms or as due to a desire for variety. The translations *kineín* in Cant. 2:17; 4:6 and *phtheírein* in Dt. 34:7 attempt to avoid unfamiliar images or metaphors in Greek. In Zec. 14:5 the LXX *emphrássein* suggests that the translator read the niphal of *stm.* The homogeneous translation used by the LXX already indicates that *nûs* has a limited range of meanings. Bernard Grossfeld discusses the translation of the Targum.

II. Meaning. All occurrences of *nûs* and its derivatives exhibit the basic meaning "flee"; we must not, however, ignore the semantic nuances despite their narrow range. I shall defer discussing the necessary question of how *nûs* differs from the semantically similar verbs → ברח *bāraḥ,* → נדד *nāḏaḏ,* and *'ûz* hiphil until we have studied its own semantic nuances more closely.

1. *Qal Stem.* a. The qal stem of *nûs* appears frequently in the context of war and battle; it denotes the flight of an individual or an entire army from a superior or victorious foe. Defeated by the Judahites, Adoni-bezek flees but is pursued and captured (Jgs. 1:6). This example illustrates the terms often associated with *nûs* in this context, as in the flight of Sisera (Jgs. 4:15) or the Midianites (7:21f.). To flee from the enemy in battle is considered disgraceful: warriors who have fled from the battlefield must

3. *KTU,* 1.2, IV, 4; *UT,* 368, no. 416.
4. *KAI,* 202B, 20; 225, 6; 226, 8f.
5. *HAL,* II, 681.
6. W. Nowack, *Richter. HKAT,* I/4 (1902), 73.

steal secretly into the city (as do David's followers when their king is mourning Absalom's death [2 S. 19:4]). A collective as well as an individual can be the subject of *nûs.* If the entire army or the troops arrayed for battle take flight, it can signal the end of hostilities: "they fled, everyone to his tent" (1 S. 4:10; 2 S. 18:17; 19:9; 2 K. 8:21 — here the present text glosses over what actually happened, but the idiom refers, as always, to Israel's flight).

Of course, it is possible to feign flight in order to entice the foe into an ambush (Josh. 8:5ff.; Jgs. 20:32); *nûs* is also used for such a tactical retreat. If the purpose is to deceive the enemy into pursuit, we see here a further nuance that the verb *nûs* can take on: it can describe not only departure from battle but also flight from a pursuer at one's heels, so that it could be translated "be engaged in flight." In 2 S. 24:13 David finds himself forced to choose famine, flight *(nûsᵉḵā lip̱nê-ṣāreyḵā),* or pestilence; in a similar vein, Prov. 28:17 says: "Someone who is burdened with the blood of another must be a fugitive until death *(ʿaḏ-bôr yānûs)*" (the emendation proposed by *BHS* is unnecessary). The ptcp. *nās,* therefore, can denote a fugitive, regardless of what circumstances have driven him to flee (Jer. 48:19,45; 50:28).

b. The nuance of *nûs* just identified shows that *nûs* is not confined to military situations alone. The verb can appear whenever an individual or a group has to escape as quickly as possible from a concrete danger or a threatening situation. The danger can be in the form of an animal: Moses flees from the snake into which his staff has been transformed (Ex. 4:3); on the day of Yahweh, a man will flee as from a lion (Am. 5:19). The precarious situation into which Potiphar's wife has brought Joseph causes him to flee outside (*nûs haḥûṣâ:* Gen. 39:12). Jotham makes off after telling his fable to the inhabitants of Shechem (Jgs. 9:21). The citizens of the towns across the Jordan flee at the news of Saul's death, leaving their towns to the Philistines (1 S. 31:7).

Here *nûs* can express a meaning recognizably different from that of *bāraḥ.* Jotham runs away *(wayyānos)* from the top of Mt. Gerizim, where he has delivered his speech, betaking himself in exile to Beer, "fleeing *(wayyiḇraḥ)* from Abimelech" (Jgs. 9:21). We are told similarly that David fled *(nās)* from Saul's malicious attack — in other words, as the following narrative shows, he sought safety in his own dwelling. When Saul pursues him even there, he flees *(wayyiḇraḥ)* to Samuel (1 S. 19:10,12). Here *nûs* means instant escape from immediate danger, while *bāraḥ* expresses flight from the pursuer's sphere of influence. It would be wrong, however, to generalize this distinction between *nûs* and *bāraḥ.* Gen. 16:6,8 use the latter for Hagar's flight to escape harsh treatment at the hands of her mistress — i.e., the slave girl runs away from Sarah. But *nûs* can also be used for escape to a place of asylum,[7] beyond the power of the avenger of blood. It is noteworthy that both passages use other verbs to qualify *bāraḥ: wayyēleḵ . . . wayyēšeḇ šām* (Jgs. 9:21); *wayyēleḵ wayyimmālēṭ* (1 S. 19:12); *wayyimmālēṭ wayyāḇō' 'el-šᵉmû'ēl hārāmāṯâ* (19:18).

c. Up to this point, the reason for flight has been some kind of actual danger. We may note, however, that *nûs* can also denote flight occasioned by panic. In Nu. 16:34

7. See below.

it is possible still to assume that the Israelites fled at the destruction of the "Korah gang" because they were afraid that they might also be pulled down into the abyss. But what causes the Arameans besieging Samaria to flee (2 K. 7:7) is a sound produced by Yahweh: "the sound of chariots and of horses, the sound of a great army." This sound so fills them with terror that they desert their camp in panic and run for their lives *(wayyānusû 'el-napšām)*. Such panicky flight is always brought about by Yahweh. It is Yahweh who sows such confusion in the Egyptian camp that the army rushes headlong toward the sea (*nāsîm liqrā'tô:* Ex. 14:27); in the Midianite camp, Yahweh turns the warriors' swords against each other until the whole army flees in panic (Jgs. 7:21f.; the toponyms here do not define the goal of the Midianites' flight but rather illustrate vividly how far their panic scattered them). It is true that Ahithophel claims to be able to throw David and his camp into such terror that all the people will flee (2 S. 17:2); as everyone knows, however, his plan fails. Thus it remains true that flight in panic is always flight occasioned by God; it therefore belongs to the vocabulary of prophecies of disaster (Lev. 26:17; Isa. 30:16f.; Jer. 49:24).[8]

d. Especially when *nûs* is used with a statement of the goal (locative *hē, 'el, lᵉ,* or *'aḏ*), it also includes the aspect of "find safety," so that it can be translated "escape, take refuge." This aspect appears, e.g., in Gen. 14:10: the kings of Sodom and Gomorrah, having joined battle (v. 8), take flight *(wayyānusû);* when they are captured, the rest flee to the hill country (*nāsû:* v. 10). When Lot is commanded to take refuge *(himmālēṭ),* he suggests: "Look, that city is near enough to flee to *(lānûs šāmmâ)* . . . let me escape there" (Gen. 19:20). Cf. also Jgs. 9:51: all the men and women of Shechem take refuge in a strong tower. This nuance probably gave rise to the expression *nûs lᵉ'ezrâ* (Isa. 10:3; 20:6): one turns to someone for help like a supplicant fugitive. In this context the verb no longer expresses literal travel to a place of refuge; *nûs lᵉ'ezrâ* means simply "approach someone for help." Isa. 20:6 does not mean that the inhabitants of the coastal towns literally went to Egypt or Cush; the reading of 1QIsᵃ probably arose from such a misunderstanding.[9]

e. The use of *nûs* in legal contexts is closely allied to the specialized meaning discussed in §d above. The cities of refuge are set apart *lānûs šāmmâ hārôṣēaḥ* (Nu. 35:6ff.; Dt. 4:42; 19:3,10ff.; Josh. 20:3ff.; cf. also Ex. 21:13). Their purpose is to protect the slayer (here *rôṣēaḥ*[10] is a technical legal term; Nu. 35:15-21 distinguishes the offense from murder, and the following verses define it in greater detail) from the avenger of blood until a regular trial finds him guilty or innocent. In the latter case he may remain in the city of refuge until he can return home (v. 28). Here *nûs* includes not just escape from the avenger of blood but also the intention of remaining in the city of refuge for some time, a notion expressed elsewhere by → ברח *bāraḥ*.[11] The regulations in question presuppose the distinction between murder and manslaughter. Ex. 21:13f. is a secondary

---

8. See III.3 below.
9. Cf. H. Wildberger, *Isaiah 13–27* (Eng. trans., Minneapolis, 1997), 284, 286.
10. → רצח *rāṣaḥ*.
11. Schwertner, 725f.

addition, and the earlier version of Dt. 19:1-10 does not mention an extended stay in the city of refuge; the usage under discussion may therefore represent a later semantic development.

f. Almost always, *nûs* is used literally; only occasionally is it used figuratively. In Nah. 2:9(8) it describes water running out of a pool; in Ps. 104:7 it describes the waters retreating before the creator God; in Ps. 114:3,5, it describes the retreat of the sea at the exodus (par. to *yissōḇ 'āḥôr*). In Dt. 34:7 it represents the diminution of vigor *(lēaḥ)*. Isa. 35:10 (par. 51:11) foresees that when the exiles return to Zion, "sorrow and sighing shall flee away." The poetic expression "the shadows flee" (Cant. 2:17; 4:6) does not signify (as in English) the dawning of the day but rather the fading light of evening, when shadows vanish (not "lengthen";[12] *nûs* can hardly have the meaning "grow, increase"). Isa. 30:16 is a special case; for the sake of consonance, *nûs* is used to describe riding on proud steeds: "But you refused and said, 'No, we will ride [NRSV: flee] upon horses *('al-sûs nānûs)'*; therefore you shall flee *('al-kēn t^e^nûsûn)*."

2. *Derived Stems.* The meaning of the qal stem can also account for the rare instances of the other stems.

a. There are three clear hiphil forms.[13] In Dt. 32:30 *yānîsû* clearly has causative meaning: "How could one have routed a thousand, and two put a myriad to flight?" This reflects the meaning of the qal stem discussed under 1.a above. Ex. 9:20 should also be understood causatively ("put to flight"): the officials of Pharaoh who hearkened to Yahweh made their slaves and livestock "flee to their homes" *(hēnîs . . . 'el-habbāṯîm)*. With rare unanimity the ancient versions "render the Hebrew הניס . . . by some word meaning 'to gather in' ";[14] they were not interpreting a different text but merely trying to represent the meaning. In Jgs. 6:11 the hiphil serves as a causative of the meaning discussed under 1.d above, "bring to a safe place."

b. In the figurative language of Isa. 59:19, the polel of *nûs (nōs^e^sâ)* takes its meaning from the chosen simile: the storm drives on the waters of the stream as the pursuer drives the fugitives. Here, too, the sense is the causative equivalent to the basic meaning.

c. The form *hiṯnôsēs* in Ps. 60:6(4) has been discussed under I.2 above.

3. *Nouns.* The two nouns derived from the base *ns* have different meanings.

a. The noun *m^e^nûsâ* denotes the act of fleeing, "flight." In Isa. 52:12 it parallels *ḥippāzôn.*[15] Alluding to the exodus tradition in Ex. 12–13, the text emphasizes that the new exodus is superior to the old: it will not be like hasty flight. In Lev. 26:36 *m^e^nusaṯ-ḥereḇ* clearly associates the verb *nûs* in the same clause with its meaning in military contexts.

b. In Ps. 59:17(16); 2 S. 22:3 (lacking in the par. Ps. 18:3[2]); Jer. 16:19, the context

---

12. W. Rudolph, *Das Hohe Lied. KAT,* XVII/2 (1962), 135; G. Gerleman, *Das Hohelied. BK,* XVIII (1965), 128.

13. On Jgs. 7:21; Jer. 48:44, see I.1 above.

14. Grossfeld, 113.

15. → חפז *ḥāpaz* (V, 90f.).

indicates that *mānôs* means "(place of) refuge." In an expression of confidence, God is described as the one who grants the worshiper safety and security *(menûsî)*. The noun has the same meaning in Ps. 142:5(4): finding no one who will take notice, the psalmist seeks refuge with Yahweh. Here, as in the preceding texts, *mānôs* denotes a refuge in the metaphorical sense; unlike *mā'ôz* and *maḥseh,* it never refers to an actual place. Ps. 142:5(4) clearly uses it as part of a fixed idiom (cf. Job 11:20; Jer. 25:35; Am. 2:14). The phrase *'āḇaḏ mānôs min* describes a hopeless situation: every "refuge" has vanished, i.e., all prospects of deliverance have been taken away (cf. Job 11:20 LXX: *sōtēría . . . apoleípsei;* Jer. 25:35: par. *pelēṭâ*). But *mānôs* can also be used in the sense of *menûsâ,* simply meaning "flight." For example, Am. 2:14 does not mean that the "swift" do not know where to turn for refuge, but that even they will be unable to flee. This meaning is also present in the paronomastic phrase *nûs mānôs* in Isa. 46:5.

4. *Related Verbs.* There remains the question of differentiating *nûs* from other semantically related verbs.

a. The choice between *bāraḥ* and *nûs* can easily be influenced by objective criteria, since only *nûs* is used in the context of battle or specifically named dangers. We must also note, however, that this very usage lends *nûs* overtones of opprobrium (2 S. 19:4). These overtones may help explain the preference of the patriarchal narratives for *bāraḥ* (*nûs* being used only for Joseph's flight from Potiphar's wife) and the avoidance of *nûs* for David's flight from Saul (except in 1 S. 19:10). By contrast, *bāraḥ* seems to be preferred when the reasons for flight have to do with familial disputes.[16] Otherwise the distinctions between the two verbs are not all that clear. The difference between secret and open flight is not the decisive criterion; it is also not true that *nûs* is limited to running away from a danger and *bāraḥ* to escaping from an inherited situation.[17] Indeed, the two verbs converge and overlap semantically.

b. The verb *nāḏaḏ,* "flee, take flight," is never used in narrative texts; it is restricted to poetic and figurative language, as may be seen from its frequent use in metaphors (Gen. 31:40: sleep flees from the eyes; Isa. 10:14: wings flutter; 2 S. 23:6: thorns are thrown away [hophal]; etc.). The semantic nuance appears to consist in vigorous movement. A goal is never mentioned.

c. The meaning of *'ûz* (qal and hiphil) is much narrower than that of *nûs* (and *bāraḥ*) and is restricted to the notion of refuge: compare *hā'ēz* in Ex. 9:19 with *hēnîs* in v. 20. It can always be rendered as "bring to/be in a secure place."[18]

III. Theological Usage. Our word belongs to everyday language; even usage in theological or cultic texts did not transform it into a theological term. It is worth noting,

---

16. → II, 250f.

17. See, respectively, J. Kennedy, *Studies in Hebrew Synonyms* (1898), 1-7; Schwertner, 725f.

18. P. Hugger, *Jahwe, meine Zuflucht. Münsterschweizacher Studien,* 13 (1971), 91; Y. Avishur, "Biblical Words and Phrases in Light of Their Akkadian Parallels," *ShnatMikr,* 2 (1977), 11-19 (Heb.).

however, that the appearance of *nûs* in specific genres can make it a vehicle for certain specific theological statements.

1. *Narrative Texts.* Almost two-thirds of the forms in which *nûs* appears are 3rd person perfect or narrative; in other words, it is used predominantly in narrative texts. When the context is military, the appearance of this verb signals victory over the enemy or defeat. In the narratives shaped by the deliverance schema, *nûs* is thus one of the semantic signals indicating the deliverance wrought by Yahweh or the elimination of the danger facing Israel; examples include Jgs. 4:15ff. (Sisera), 9:12 (Zebah and Zalmunna), and 1 S. 14:22 (Saul's first victory over the Philistines). But the verb may also describe Israel's flight; when the narrative context deals with Israel's failure to carry out the ban or transgression of the express will of Yahweh, the use of *nûs* (often in conjunction with other verbs associated with military terminology) documents Yahweh's punitive response (e.g., Josh. 7:4; Jgs. 20:45ff.).

2. *Wars of Yahweh.* The enemy's fleeing in panic is a characteristic motif of the Yahweh war pattern.[19] In the narratives reflecting this pattern, the headlong flight of the enemy (Ex. 14:27; Jgs. 9:21f.; 1 S. 14:22 [cf. v. 15]) manifests Yahweh's incomparable power, which overwhelms all resistance. The ancient ark saying in Nu. 10:35, going back to the tradition of the Yahweh war, contains a formula stating that those who hate Yahweh flee before him (*w^{e}yānusû m^{e}śan'eyḵā mippāneyḵā;* cf. the echo in Ps. 68:2[1]). The prophetic oracles against the nations, which probably go back to the same source, use *nûs* in the same way to proclaim to Israel's enemies the failure of their plans and their own destruction (Isa. 17:3; 31:8; Jer. 46:5,21; 49:8,24,30; 50:16). In this context, a special stylistic device is the summons to flight (Jer. 48:6; 49:8,30; 51:6).[20] The victory hymn of the Yahweh war, which attests explicitly to Yahweh's participation in the battle and celebrates the victory he has vouchsafed, is the setting of the theophany description. It, too, uses the motif of the enemy's flight denoted by the catchword *nûs* (together with *nāḏaḏ:* Ps. 68:13[12]), e.g., Isa. 13:14, where it has been combined with the notion of the day of Yahweh.[21]

3. *Israel's Flight.* The catchword *nûs,* however, is not restricted to Yahweh's intervention against his or Israel's enemies. As in narrative texts, a proclamation of flight can be directed against Israel itself. Am. 5:19 uses the motif of flight in a metaphorical description of the day of Yahweh as a "day of darkness, not light," for Israel. In Lev. 26:17 and Dt. 28:15, flight before the enemy threatens to reverse the blessing promised in Lev. 26:7 and Dt. 28:7 (Yahweh war terminology) if Israel does not keep the covenant. Prophetic threats can use *nûs* in prophecies of disaster against Israel as well

---

19. R. Smend, *Yahweh War and Tribal Confederation* (Eng. trans., Nashville, 1970).
20. R. Bach, *Die Aufforderung zur Flucht und zum Kampf im alttestamentlichen Prophetenspruch. WMANT,* 9 (1962).
21. → יום *yôm* (VI, 7-32).

as against the nations (Isa. 10:29, where a threat directed originally against Jerusalem has been transformed into an oracle against Assyria). The proclamation of eschatological judgment leads to a generalized conception of flight on the eschatological day of judgment (Isa. 24:18, using words originally directed against a foreign nation; Jer. 48:44). Finally, proverbial literature applies the threat originally spoken against unfaithful Israel to "the wicked" in general (Prov. 28:1).

4. *Mythology.* Only in Ps. 104:7; 114:3,5 do we find the motif of the fleeing of the waters (of chaos) or the sea at the exodus. This may be a distant echo of the mythological figure of "fleeing Leviathan" (Isa. 27:1),[22] if it is not simply borrowed from the description of the flight of the enemy.

IV. Dead Sea Scrolls. In the Dead Sea Scrolls the verb is attested only in 1QM 3:5 (flight of the enemy; cf. *mānôs* in 4QMª [4Q491] 9) and 6Q9 33:3 (reminiscence of David's flight from Saul). The noun *mānôs* raises the total of occurrences to 6: 1QH 5:29; 6:33; 9:28 are anthropological, describing the worshiper as being in tribulation "without refuge." The only "refuge" (parallels: *miśgāḇ,* "fortress"; *selaʿ,* "rock"; *ʿôz,* "strength"; *mᵉṣûḏâ,* "stronghold") is God. In 3Q15 1:13 *mnws* may be a toponym.

Reindl

22. → II, 252.

נוּעַ *nûaʿ*

Contents: I. Etymology, Occurrences; II. Usage; III. LXX, Qumran.

I. Etymology, Occurrences. Besides Hebrew, the root *nwʿ* is attested in Jewish Aramaic with the meaning "move about" and in Arab. *nāʿa,* "sway" (of branches). A reduplicated form *nʿnʿ* is found in Modern Hebrew and Jewish Aramaic, as well as in Arabic (*naʿnaʿa,* "swing") and Ethiopic.[1] The Ugaritic occurrence cited by *HAL* is dubious.[2]

The verb occurs 20 times in the qal, twice in the niphal, and 14 times in the hiphil.

1. Leslau, *Contributions,* 33.
2. *HAL,* II, 681, citing *KTU,* 1.6, VI, 16: *ytʿn.*

II. Usage.

1. *Qal.* In the first instance, *nûaʿ* means "move back and forth," then either "sway, stagger" or "be unsettled, wander." It describes the swaying of trees in the wind (Isa. 7:2), the staggering of a drunkard (Isa. 24:20; 29:9; Ps. 107:27), the moving of lips in prayer (1 S. 1:13), and the shaking of the thresholds in Isaiah's temple vision (Isa. 6:4). It usually appears in figurative expressions and similes. The people "tremble" with fear during the theophany at Sinai (Ex. 20:18); the gods of Egypt "tremble" with fear when Yahweh appears upon the cloud (Isa. 19:1, par. *mss,* "lose heart"); the heart of Ahaz trembles "like trees in the wind" when he hears of the enemy's attack (7:2). In the great catastrophe depicted in the Isaiah apocalypse, the earth is broken *(rʿʿ)* and torn asunder *(prr),* it is shaken *(mûṭ),* it staggers *(nûaʿ)* like a drunkard and sways (*nûḏ* hiphil) — a concentration of words describing the disintegration of the ordered world (24:19f.). In 29:9, by contrast, "staggering" (par. *škr,* "be drunk" — but not with wine or beer) describes the helplessness of the blind inhabitants of Jerusalem, while Ps. 107:27 speaks of the desperation of the endangered sailors (with *ḥgg,* "jump about"). In Job 28:4 *nûaʿ,* together with *dll,* describes how the miners hang by ropes in their shafts, swaying back and forth.

The 3 occurrences in the parable of Jotham (Jgs. 9:9,10,13) are not entirely clear. The trees that are offered the kingship refuse it, saying, "Shall I give up my true nature to *nûaʿ* over the trees?" This can hardly mean something like "reign." More likely, the word means that when the other trees wave in the wind, the king is to tower high above them. The use of *nûaʿ* may also imply a concealed criticism of the monarchy.

Am. 4:8 describes how the inhabitants of the drought-stricken town wander about searching for water; in 8:12 the object of the search is a word from Yahweh (although everyone knows that God is silent and no such word will be found). Lam. 4:14 describes how the inhabitants of Zion wandered blindly through the streets on account of their sins, their clothes defiled with blood so that they were treated as unclean. "Then they fled [*nûṣ?* read *nûḏ?*], then they staggered *(nûaʿ)*" (v. 15). Jer. 14:10 describes the inconstant people as wavering back and forth.[3] Prov. 5:6 is not entirely clear. Describing the "alien woman" who is the adversary of Wisdom, it says: "That you may fail to recognize the path of life, her ways *(maʿgālôṯ)* 'wander,' and you do not know it." This seems to mean that she moves about to lead the disciple of Wisdom astray.

Gen. 4:12,14 use *nûaʿ* together with *nûḏ* to describe the nomadic wandering that is to be Cain's fate.[4] A similar meaning appears in Ps. 109:10, in the context of a curse upon the psalmist's enemy: "May his children wander about and beg, driven out of the ruins of their house."

2. *Niphal.* The two occurrences of the niphal speak of shaking. Am. 9:9 says: "I will shake (*nûaʿ* hiphil) the house of Israel [gloss: among all the nations] as one shakes [niphal] (grain) in a sieve, and no pebble shall fall to the ground." The image is not

---

3. B. Duhm, *Das Buch Jeremia. KHC,* XI (1901), 129: "Now they adhere to their Baals, now they go to Yahweh, they run tirelessly from one to the other."

4. → נוד *nûḏ.*

entirely clear; the text probably means that the grain falls through while pebbles and clumps of dirt remain in the sieve; cf. Sir. 27:4: "When a sieve is shaken, the refuse appears; so do a person's faults when one considers." Nah. 3:12 addresses Nineveh: "All your fortresses are like figs . . . if (the tree is) shaken, they fall into the mouth." In other words, they will fall to the enemy like ripe fruit.

3. *Hiphil.* Among the texts using the hiphil, a special group has the obj. *rō'š,* "head." Shaking the head is a gesture of scorn. Thus the psalmist laments in Ps. 22:8(Eng. v. 7): "All who see me mock (*lʿg* hiphil) me, they make mouths at me and shake their heads." Ps. 109:25 is even clearer: "I have become an object of scorn *(ḥerpâ)* to them; when they see me they shake their heads." To the Assyrian king Sennacherib, Isaiah says: "She despises *(bāzâ)* you, she scorns *(lāʿag)* you, the virgin, daughter Zion; daughter Jerusalem shakes her head over you" (Isa. 37:22 par. 2 K. 19:21). Job says to his friends (16:4): "I could join words together against you and shake my head at you." In Lam. 2:15 we read: "All who pass along the way clap *(sāpaq)* their hands at you; they hiss *(šāraq)* and shake their heads at daughter Jerusalem." Cf. also Sir. 13:7: the rich man is your friend so long as it benefits him, but then he will shake his head and pass you by. In Sir. 12:18 ("he shakes [*nûaʿ* hiphil] his head and waves [*nwp* hiphil] his hand"), it is not clear whether the gestures express open derision or feigned sympathy.

The other occurrences exhibit the usual alternation between "cause to wander" and "shake." Nu. 32:13 says that Yahweh made the people wander in the wilderness for forty years. Ps. 59:12(11) expresses the wish that God will not kill the psalmist's enemies but cause them to wander, that they may not be forgotten; in v. 15(14), however, the qal should be read (following *K*): they prowl around looking for something edible. In 2 S. 15:20 David, fleeing from Jerusalem, says to Ittai of Gath: "Shall I make you wander about with us, since I must go now here, now there?"

Zeph. 2:15 speaks of shaking the hand ("hissing [*šāraq*] and shaking the hand") as an apotropaic ritual; the object is the "exultant city" of the enemy. The gesture is both apotropaic and scornful.[5]

The usage in 2 K. 23:18 represents a special case: Josiah protects the tomb of a "man of God" and commands that his bones not be "disturbed."[6]

Finally, Dnl. 10:10 probably means simply that a hand helped Daniel move after his vision, so that he could get up on his hands and knees.

III. LXX, Qumran. In the LXX, *saleúein, kineín,* and *sténein* predominate, but other translations such as *seíein* also occur.

At Qumran there was a fund for the support of orphans, those in distress, the poor, prisoners, and the *'îš 'ᵃšer yānûaʿ*, the homeless wanderer (CD 14:15).

Ringgren

---

5. W. Rudolph, *Zephanja. KAT,* XIII/3 (1975), 283f.

6. The reference to G. Widengren, *Iranische Geisterwelt* (Baden-Baden, 1961), 217, in *HAL,* II, 682, is hardly relevant, for Bundahišn, ch. 34, speaks of bones being shaken at the resurrection.

נוף *nwp*; תְּנוּפָה *tᵉnûp̱â*

Contents: I. 1. Etymology and Meaning; 2. Occurrences. II. Usage: 1. Verb; 2. The *tᵉnûp̱â* Offering. III. LXX. IV. Qumran.

I. 1. *Etymology and Meaning.* There are two homonymous roots *nwp.* The first, usually translated "swing," appears in Hebrew, Jewish Aramaic ("move to and fro"; aphel: "swing") and Syriac ("bow"; aphel: "swing"). Akk. *nāpu,* "move," is dubious and should probably be disregarded.[1] There may also be a connection with Soq. *nwf,* "wave one's hand."[2]

The other root is represented by Arab. *nāfa(u),* "be high, exalted," "surpass" (cf. *nauf,* "top of a camel's hump," "surplus"), Jewish Aram. *nôp̱ā',* "treetop," and Akk. *nūptu,* "surplus." Ugar. *np šmm,* interpreted by some as "zenith," is disputed; a different *np* means "surplus."[3] This root is clearly represented by Heb. *nôp̱* (Ps. 48:3[Eng. v. 2]), which describes Mt. Zion as *yᵉp̱ēh nôp̱,* "beautiful in exaltation, lofty."

Godfrey Rolles Driver and Jacob Milgrom derive Heb. *hēnîp̱* — at least when it refers to the *tᵉnûp̱â* offering — from the second root. Driver translates it as "set apart as an additional offering," Milgrom as "lift up."[4] Milgrom points out that in Isa. 10:15 *hēnîp̱* stands in conjunction with *hērîm* and in 13:2 with *hērîm* and *nāśā'.* But this translation is not appropriate in contexts that clearly suggest back-and-forth movement (like that of the saw in 10:15).

2. *Occurrences.* The verb occurs 32 times in the OT in the hiphil and once each in the hophal (Ex. 29:27) and polel (Isa. 10:32 [1QIs[a] hiphil]). Its derivatives are *tᵉnûp̱â,* "wave offering" (30 occurrences), and *nāp̱â,* "winnowing fan" (Isa. 30:28: "to winnow the nations with the winnowing fan of destruction").

---

nwp. G. R. Driver, "Three Technical Terms in the Pentateuch," *JSS,* 1 (1956), 97-105; J. Milgrom, "The Alleged Wave-Offering in Israel and in the Ancient Near East," *IEJ,* 22 (1972), 33-38 = *Studies in Cultic Theology and Terminology. SJLA,* 36 (1983), 133-38; R. Rendtorff, *Studien zur Geschichte des Opfers im Alten Israel. WMANT,* 24 (1967); N. H. Snaith, "The Wave Offering," *ExpT,* 74 (1962/63), 127; L.-H. Vincent, "Les rites du balancement (tenoûphâh) et du prélèvement (teroûmâh) dans le sacrifice de communion de l'AT," *Mélanges syriens offerts à R. Dussaud,* 2 vols. (Paris, 1939), I, 267-272.

1. Letter from W. von Soden; see *AHw,* II, 742.
2. Leslau, *Contributions,* 33.
3. For the former, *WUS,* no. 1826, reads *npš mm,* "whirlpool." For the latter see *WUS,* no. 1813.
4. See II.2 below.

II. Usage.

1. *Verb.* The basic meaning of the hiphil is to wave one's hand or set an implement in motion (saw, staff: Isa. 10:15; sickle: Dt. 23:26[25]; chisel: Ex. 20:25; Dt. 27:5; Josh. 8:31; spear: Sir. 46:2).

Hands can be waved for various purposes. Naaman expected Elisha to "wave his hand over the (afflicted) spot [*māqôm;* cf. Lev. 13:19]" (2 K. 5:11). This is usually interpreted as a healing gesture, possibly of magical origin.[5] Milgrom cites Hittite and Akkadian rituals of purification and exorcism that involved moving a sacrificial offering back and forth.[6] Albert Šanda understands *māqôm* to mean the place where Naaman was standing, and Rudolf Kittel interprets it as the holy place: Elisha was expected to call on Yahweh and stretch out his hand in the direction of the sanctuary in a gesture of prayer.[7]

Otherwise the gesture is usually threatening in character. Assyria waves his hand (NRSV: "shakes his fist") against Mt. Zion, i.e., gives the signal to attack (Isa. 10:32[8]). The enemy gives a hand signal to show that it is time to enter the gates of mighty Babylon (13:2). Yahweh raises his hand in anger against the Euphrates *(nāhār)* to split it into seven channels (11:15); the parallel "tongue of the sea of Egypt" alludes to the exodus: Israel will be delivered once more through divine intervention. The Egyptians will tremble in fear when Yahweh raises his hand against them (19:16; *nwp* hiphil with *t^enûp̱â* as cognate acc.). According to Zec. 2:13(9), Yahweh will raise his hand against the nations; since the verse goes on to speak of plunder, this gesture is surely not just a threat but an attack. Sir. 36:3 (LXX 33:3) is similar: "Lift your hand against the foreign nation, that it may see your mighty deeds." When Job says that he has not raised his hand against the orphan (Job 31:21), the gesture may be either a threat or an act of violence.

As for moving an implement, I note first the prohibition against making an altar of hewn stones (Ex. 20:25). This prohibition is probably very ancient; the stated reason is that swinging a chisel *(ḥereḇ)* over the altar would profane (*ḥll* piel) it. According to Diethelm Conrad, *mizbaḥ 'ᵃḏāmâ* in v. 24 refers to an altar of sun-dried bricks; but the archaeological evidence he cites is not entirely comparable.[9] A simple altar of stones and earth is more likely.[10] Conrad may be correct, however, in arguing that the prohibition is directed against the Canaanite custom of building altars of hewn stones.[11] The precept reappears in somewhat altered form in Dt. 27:5, which speaks of an altar of

---

5. J. Fitzmyer, *CBQ,* 22 (1960), 284, n. 27; A. Dupont-Sommer, "Exorcismes et guérisons dans les récits de Qoumrân," *Congress Volume, Oxford 1959. SVT,* 7 (1960), 251.

6. Pp. 37f.

7. A. Šanda, *Die Bücher der Könige. EHAT,* 9/I-II (1911/12), in loc.; R. Kittel, *Die Bücher der Könige. HKAT,* I/5 (1900), in loc.

8. See I.2 above on the text.

9. D. Conrad, "Studien zum Altargesetz: Ex 20:24-26" (diss., Marburg, 1968), 21ff. Cf. → VIII, 218.

10. E. Robertson, "The Altar of Earth," *JJS,* 1 (1948), 12-21; B. S. Childs, *The Book of Exodus. OTL* (1974), 466.

11. Conrad, "Studien," 43ff.

unhewn stones and replaces *ḥereḇ* with the more general term *barzel*, "(implement of) iron." Josh. 8:31 is an account of how this command was carried out. Both texts are postexilic.

Isa. 10:15 castigates the arrogance of Assyria and its king: he imagines that he is exercising the initiative, but this is like a tool's wanting to exchange roles with the person using it. Here *hēnîp̱* is associated with both *maśśôr*, "saw," and *maṭṭeh*, "rod"; it therefore refers to different kinds of motion. Isa. 45:9f. expresses a similar thought using different words.

2. *The tᵉnûp̱â Offering.* The majority of hiphil occurrences refer to the so-called wave offering (*tᵉnûp̱â;* NRSV: "elevation offering"). In the case of the *šᵉlāmîm* offering (Lev. 7:1-21), the major portion of the sacrificial animal is consumed in a sacrificial meal (v. 15). The fat is burned on the altar (v. 31), while the breast is assigned to the priests, after they have set it apart as *tᵉnûp̱â* (v. 30). "The 'waving' should be pictured as a swinging of the sacrificial portions back and forth in the direction of the altar, as though to cast the offerings into the fire."[12] This ordinance is followed by another, according to which the right thigh is also assigned to the priests as *tᵉrûmâ*, "heave offering" (vv. 32f.). In Lev. 9:21; 10:15, the right thigh is also a "wave offering."

According to Elliger, the regulation that makes the right thigh a wave offering is literarily secondary. Driver has difficulties defining the relationship between *tᵉnûp̱â* and *tᵉrûmâ;* if the latter means "contribution" and the former "additional contribution," the sequence should be reversed.[13] Milgrom sees in the *tᵉnûp̱â* an elevation of the sacrificial offering, presenting it to God. As an analogy he cites Egyptian depictions of sacrificial offerings on a platter "being elevated before the face of the god" (cf. Heb. *hēnîp̱ lip̱nê*). The parallel, however, is not exact. In the Egyptian sacrificial ritual, the offerings are first "placed on the ground" *(wꜣḥ r tꜣ)* then "elevated before the god" *(fꜣy ḫft ḥr)*, i.e., presented to the god, and then set down again.[14] All one can say with assurance is that *hēnîp̱ tᵉnûp̱â* represents a symbolic offering of the sacrificial gifts.[15]

There would appear to be no connection with the waving back and forth *(šubû'u)* of incense and torches found in Akkadian purification rituals.[16] Ugar. *šnpt*, interpreted by Delbert Hillers as a wave offering, in fact means "two-thirds."[17]

The instructions for the ordination of priests in Ex. 29 (called by Martin Noth a "supplement to P"[18]) require certain choice portions of the ram of ordination (v. 22) and three pieces of bread (v. 23) to be offered before Yahweh by "waving" (v. 24). They are then burned on top of the already completed burnt offering (v. 25). Finally,

---

12. K. Elliger, *Leviticus. HAT,* IV (1966), 102.
13. P. 104.
14. Bonnet, *RÄR,* 555.
15. Cf. M. Noth, *Exodus. OTL* (Eng. trans. 1962), 232: "indicates the distributing of the food."
16. See *AHw,* I, 117; Milgrom, 37f.
17. See J. C. de Moor, *UF,* 2 (1970), 324; D. R. Hillers, *BASOR,* 198 (1970), 142.
18. Noth, *Exodus,* OTL, 229.

the ram's breast is "waved" and given to the priests (v. 26). Lev. 8:22-29 describes how these requirements were carried out (waving in vv. 27,29). "Waving" is also prescribed for the guilt offering at the cleansing of a leper (Lev. 14:12,24) as well as for the shoulder of a ram and two pieces of bread offered at the end of a Nazirite's term (Nu. 6:19f.).

The festival regulations of the Holiness Code (Lev. 23) require that at the beginning of the harvest[19] the first sheaf of barley be set apart by waving (v. 11); only then are the people free to enjoy the new harvest (v. 14). In addition to the wave offering, v. 20 mentions two lambs as a *šᵉlāmîm* offering; the dating in v. 15 indicates the Feast of Weeks.[20]

Finally, "waving" became a general term for offering and consecration. At the consecration of the Levites, Aaron can even "wave the Levites before Yahweh" (Nu. 8:11,13,15,21), thus setting them apart *(hiḇdîl)* from the rest of the Israelites so that they belong to Yahweh *(wᵉhāyû lî)* (v. 14). Offerings of gold and copper for the building of the tabernacle are also called *tᵉnûpâ* (Ex. 35:22; 38:24,29).

One finds *tᵉnûpâ* used figuratively in Isa. 30:32, a difficult text; the point is clearly to "consecrate the enemy like a sacrifice for slaughter."[21]

III. LXX. For the verb the LXX uses *aphorízein* (6 times), *epitithénai* (5 times), *anaphérein, apodidónai, aphaireín, phérein, epaireín,* etc. For *tᵉnûpâ,* it uses *epíthema, aphórisma, aphaírema, apódoma,* and four other words once each. This variety shows that the two words were not yet considered technical terms. The rendering of the Vulg. is equally diverse.[22] By contrast, the Syr. generally uses *pᵉraš,* the Targ. *'ᵃrîm* or *'ᵃrāmûṯā'*.

IV. Qumran. In the Dead Sea Scrolls the verb appears 4 times in conjunction with "hand": in 1QM 17:9 as a general term for God's saving work, in 1QH 8:22 to express preparation for an action ("when I set my hand to dig canals for the plantation"), and in 1QH 8:33, "I could not move any hand," in a series of expressions describing the speaker's desperate situation. 11QTemple uses both verb and noun as sacrificial terms: both together in 15:11f. and 20:16, the verb in 11:10 and 18:10 (with a sheaf as obj.), *tᵉnûpâ* alone in 22:9 (with *hērîm!*) and 60:2. The text is damaged in 18:12 and 19:4.

Another verb with the meaning "sprinkle" (cf. Prov. 7:17; Ps. 68:10[9]; Sir. 47:17) is found in connection with the Holy Spirit (1QH 7:7; 17:26; 1QH 23 fr. 2 9,13).

Ringgren

19. On the date see Elliger, *HAT,* IV, 314f.
20. *Ibid.,* 314.
21. O. Kaiser, *Isaiah 13–39. OTL* (Eng. trans. 1974), 309.
22. Driver, 101.

נָזָה nāzâ

Contents: I. Root and Related Words. II. Meaning: 1. Qal; 2. Hiphil; 3. Isa. 52:15; 4. Personal Name *yzyh.* III. 1. LXX; 2. Dead Sea Scrolls.

I. Root and Related Words. The root *nzh (*nḏy)* is attested in other Semitic languages: Akk. *nezû,* "excrete urine or feces";[1] Aram. *ndy/nd',* "sprinkle"; Syr. *n^edā',* "dilute, sprinkle, throw." It has been pointed out that the instance of *nzh* in Isa. 52:15 might be related to Arab. *nazā,* "jump, hop" *(nzw).*[2] If this is the case, then Heb. *nzh* reflects two originally distinct roots, *nḏy* and *nzw.*

II. Meaning. The verb *nāzâ* occurs 24 times in the OT: 4 times in the qal, otherwise in the hiphil. There is also a personal name that uses *nāzâ* as one of its elements. The verb is always associated with liquids, which spatter (qal) or are made to spatter, i.e., used to sprinkle something (hiphil). Isa. 52:15 is an exception.[3]

1. *Qal.* The qal is intransitive and means "spatter." The spattering liquid is always the subject. Since no other active subject is found, one may conclude that the verb denotes unintentional, accidental spattering. The qal is used to depict graphically how Jezebel's blood spatters on the wall and on the horses when she is thrown down to Jehu (2 K. 9:33), or to describe the spattering of the sacrificial blood of the purgation offering: "and when any of its blood spatters on a garment, you shall wash the bespattered part in a holy place" (Lev. 6:20 [Eng. v. 27]). It likewise describes the spattering of *nēṣaḥ* ([grape] juice?) on Yahweh's garments (Isa. 63:3). Here *w^eyēz* should be vocalized as a consecutive imperfect *(wayyēz);* the MT pointing appears to be an attempt to give the verb future meaning.[4]

2. *Hiphil.* The hiphil *hizzâ* is the causative of *nzh* and means "bespatter, sprinkle." Except in Isa. 52:15,[5] the hiphil always refers to intentional sprinkling of a liquid in a ritual context. The texts can be categorized as follows:

a. *Consecration of a Liquid.* The oil used on the eighth day to purify a leper is

---

nāzâ. H. Balz, "ῥαντίζω," *EDNT,* III, 207f.; C. H. Hunzinger, "ῥαντίζω," *TDNT,* VI, 976-984; R. Rendtorff, *Studien zur Geschichte des Opfers im Alten Israel. WMANT,* 24 (1967), 218-220; N. Snaith, "The Sprinkling of Blood," *ExpT,* 82 (1970/71), 23f.; T. C. Vriezen, "The Term *Hizza:* Lustration and Consecration," *OTS,* 7 (1950), 201-235.

1. *CAD,* XI/2, 200; *AHw,* II, 784.
2. See II.3 below.
3. See II.3 below.
4. *GK,* §107b, n. 2; §53p, n. 1; *BHS.* On the form see *GK,* §76c.
5. See II.3 below.

consecrated by means of two ritual acts: a *t^enûpâ*[6] (Lev. 14:12,24) and a sevenfold sprinkling of the oil before the Lord (vv. 16,27). This oil is secular by nature and belongs to the person who brings it (unlike, e.g., the "anointing oil" [*šemen hammišḥâ*], which is sacred from the outset and hence does not require a consecration ritual [cf. Ex. 30:22-34; Lev. 8:10-12]); therefore the *t^enûpâ* and sevenfold sprinkling must be performed to consecrate it for its ritual purpose. This double consecration does not mean, however, that something unnecessary is being done. The *t^enûpâ* effects a general consecration of the entire supply of oil, while the sprinkling serves to consecrate once more — particularly and exclusively — the oil in the priest's hand (cf. the repetition of *'^ašer 'al-kappô* in vv. 16-18), so that just this portion is made effectual for the purification of the leper.

In the ritual of the "red heifer," the sevenfold sprinkling of the blood toward the tent of meeting consecrates both the blood and the animal, to achieve a purifying effect against contamination caused by a dead body (Nu. 19:4).[7]

b. *Consecration of Objects or Persons.* One also finds sprinkling associated with consecration of an object or person. The clearest instance is the consecration of the altar on the day when the cult was inaugurated. The specially prepared anointing oil (Ex. 30:22ff.) is sprinkled seven times on the altar, which is then anointed (→ משׁח *māšaḥ*) along with its utensils, basin, and its base "to consecrate (→ קדשׁ *qāḏaš*) them" (Lev. 8:11; cf. Ex. 30:22-30; 40:9-14).

Again, Moses takes some of the blood on the altar together with anointing oil and sprinkles them on Aaron's garments (or on Aaron and his garments) as well as on his sons and their garments, to consecrate them and their garments (Lev. 8:30; Ex. 29:21).

c. *Consecration and Purification of Sanctuaries.* Two ritual sprinklings with the blood of the purgation offering take place on the Day of Atonement (implicit in Lev. 16:16b). One is performed at the exterior altar (vv. 18f.). Aaron is to take some of the blood of the bull and of the goat and put it on the horns of the altar; then he is to sprinkle the altar seven times with some of the blood. The reason for this double ritual is stated in v. 19bα: "Thus he shall cleanse and hallow it." It appears that smearing the blood on the horns effects purification, while sprinkling with blood effects consecration *(qdš)*.[8]

The other ritual of the Day of Atonement is more difficult to understand. After Aaron's bull has been slain, he is to take some of its blood behind the veil and sprinkle it once with his finger on the east side of the *kappōreṯ* (the cover of the ark);[9] then he is to sprinkle the blood seven times in front of it (v. 14). In the first case, therefore, the blood comes in contact with the *kappōreṯ*. In the following sevenfold sprinkling, the blood is simply sprinkled into the air in the holy of holies, where it falls to the

---

6. → נוף *nwp;* see J. Milgrom, *"Hattenûpâ," Studies in Cultic Theology and Terminology. SJLA,* 36 (1983), 139-158; *idem,* "Wave Offering," *IDB Sup,* 944-46.

7. J. Milgrom, "The Paradox of the Red Cow (Num. xix)," *VT,* 31 (1981), 66 = *Cultic Theology,* 89.

8. For purification → טהר *ṭāhar* (V, 287-296); for consecration → V, 293.

9. → כפר *kipper* (VII, 288-303).

ground. The same double ritual is performed with the blood of the *ḥaṭṭā'ṯ* goat of the people (v. 15). The purpose of all these blood rituals is purification (v. 16), as the entire ritual of the Day of Atonement suggests: atonement is made for the holy of holies, the tent of meeting, and the altar of burnt offerings (vv. 16,20,33).[10]

Another example of this category is the sevenfold sprinkling of blood in the tent of meeting during the *ḥaṭṭā'ṯ* offering of an anointed priest or the whole congregation (Lev. 4:6,17). There follows an application of blood to the horns of the incense altar. Both rituals serve for purification, as can be seen from the similarity of the procedure to Lev. 16:14-16a, where blood comes in contact with a holy object and is sprinkled into the air (although the sequence is different). Further evidence may be found in the likelihood that the blood ritual of Lev. 4:6f.,17f. was performed in the tent of meeting on the Day of Atonement (16:16b).

The final instance of sprinkling the *ḥaṭṭā'ṯ* blood is when pigeons are sacrificed as a substitute[11] (Lev. 5:7-10). The priest sprinkles some of the blood on the side of the altar and drains the rest at the base of the altar. This procedure is distinct from the *'ōlâ* of birds, in which the bird's blood is drained out against the side of the altar (1:15). The double ritual with the blood of the *ḥaṭṭā'ṯ* bird in contrast to the simple ritual of the *'ōlâ* bird has its parallels in the blood rituals involving larger animals, in which the blood of the *ḥaṭṭā'ṯ* is smeared on the horns of the altar and then poured out at the base of the altar (4:7,18,25,30,34), while the blood of the *'ōlâ* is sprinkled only toward the altar (vv. 1,5,11). The sprinkled blood of the *ḥaṭṭā'ṯ* bird is thus equivalent to the *ḥaṭṭā'ṯ* blood smeared on the horns of the altar and therefore effects purification.

d. *Purification of Persons or Objects.* Water or watery liquids can be sprinkled to purify persons or objects. As part of the ritual consecrating the Levites for service in the tent of meeting, Moses is to sprinkle them with "water of purgation" *(mê ḥaṭṭā'ṯ)* in order to purify them (Nu. 8:7).

Persons or objects that have been contaminated by contact with a dead body are sprinkled on the third and seventh days with "water of purification" *(mê niddâ)*[12] (Nu. 19:18,19,21). This passage displays several interesting pieces of philological information about *nāzâ*. The verb *zāraq*,[13] "throw," is used twice in the negated passive *(zōraq):* "the water of purification had not been dashed on them" (vv. 13,20). Some scholars have suggested that the use of *zāraq* instead of *nāzâ* is a sign that different authors have been at work here. But a different explanation is possible: the OT does not have a passive of the root *nāzâ* corresponding to the hiphil *hizzâ;* therefore *zōraq* functions as the passive of *hizzâ.*

Finally, a healed leper or a "leprous" house can be purified by sprinkling (Lev. 14:7,51).[14] A bird is slaughtered over fresh water in an earthen vessel. A living bird is

10. J. Milgrom, "The Function of the *ḥaṭṭā'ṯ* Sacrifice," *Tarbiz,* 40 (1970/71), 1-8 (Heb.); *idem,* "Sacrifices and Offerings," *IDB Sup,* 766-68.

11. → אשׁם *'āshām* (I, 429-437).

12. → נדה *niddâ.*

13. → זרק *zāraq* (IV, 162-65).

14. → IV, 163.

dipped into this mixture, together with cedarwood, crimson yarn, and hyssop. The individual or the house is then sprinkled seven times. The bird is then released.

3. *Isa. 52:15.* The meaning of *yazzeh* in Isa. 52:15 is unclear. The form appears to represent a 3rd person masc. sg. hiphil impf. of the root *nzh.* The syntax of the clause, however, with *gôyim rabbîm* as the direct object of the verb, precludes the translation "he will sprinkle many nations," since this meaning would require the prep. *'al.* Some scholars have proposed keeping the derivation from *nzh* and interpreting *yazzeh* with a direct object as "scatter, overcome." Others emend the text or connect the form with Arab. *nazā,* "jump, hop," and translate "cause to jump, startle."[15] None of these explanations is convincing. The last is the most satisfying, since it preserves the text and fits the context best.[16]

4. *Personal Name yzyh.* The root *nzh* is an element of the PN *yizzîyâ* (Ezr. 10:25), a theophorous name that possibly means "May God purify, sprinkle." The verbal element of the name is in fact a qal, but the Greek *(Iazia*[*s*], *Az*[*e*]*ia, Adeia)* can be read as a hiphil.[17]

Milgrom — Wright

III. 1. *LXX.* The LXX generally uses the verbs *raínein* and *rantízein* and their compounds to translate *nāzâ.* Isa. 52:15 has *thaumázein,* which helps improve the MT markedly;[18] the use of *katágein* in 63:3 shows that all of v. 3c is a free interpretation on the part of the LXX.

2. *Dead Sea Scrolls.* The verb occurs 9 times in the Dead Sea Scrolls; 6 of these are in the Temple Scroll. The 2 occurrences in 1QS (3:9; 4:21) belong to the final phase of redaction, which added an extensive induction ritual for novices preceding the Community Rule. The novice is sprinkled with "water of purification" (3:9); it is actually the Holy Spirit that is sprinkled over the novice like water of purification (4:21). The occurrences in the Temple Scroll are concentrated in the section dealing with removal of the impurity resulting from contact with a dead body (49:18,20; 50:3,14,15). In the "Ritual of Purification" (4Q512), *nāzâ* appears in 12:7, echoing its use in the regulations governing purification after contact with a dead body (Nu. 19). According to the rule of the Qumran Essenes, the impure individual must undertake a far from simple series of ablutions and sprinklings, in which an important role is played by "water of purification" *(my dwky),* "water of ablution" *(my rḥṣ),* and "water of sprinkling" *(my hzyh lṭhrw)* (*hzyh* has been added above the line, either correcting an omission [?] or providing a Late Hebrew interpretation). The phrase *my hzyh* stands

15. See *BHS* and comms.; *BDB,* 633.
16. But see now *HAL,* II, 683.
17. *IPN,* 245f. Cf. *BDB,* 633; *HAL,* II, 404.
18. *BHS.*

for the *mê hanniddâ* used in the text of Numbers. The nominal form *hazzāyâ* derived from *nzh* is Late Hebrew; it appears frequently in the Mishnah.[19] The ritual of the "red heifer" at Qumran is discussed elsewhere.[20]

Fabry

19. *WTM,* I, 461.
20. J. Bowman, "Did the Qumran Sect Burn the Red Heifer?" *RevQ,* 1 (1958), 73-84.

נָזַל *nāzal*

Contents: I. Usage in the Semitic Languages. II. OT Usage. III. Qal. IV. Participle. V. Hiphil.

I. Usage in the Semitic Languages. The verb *nzl* is a verb of motion, originally describing a downward movement. It has its widest range of usage in Arabic, where the lexicons cite the following meanings for *nazala* I: "descend (a ladder), disembark, fall (rain, water level), come down from heaven (= be revealed, esp. the Koran), descend (blows), drop (value, price), alight, take up one's abode, encamp, fall upon someone (attack, fight), befall (disaster, punishment)." Less frequent is Syr. *n^{e}zal,* "bend down, bend back"; *nazzēl,* "let down, hand down (hair)." Even rarer is Akk. *nazālu,* "pour out (water, molten metal)." The form *nzl* occurs also in Ugaritic; *WUS* translates "on hand for guests," citing Arab. *nuzl, nuzul, nazal,* "food reserved for one's guest," reflecting the verb's specialized meaning "take up one's abode, stop as a guest."[1] The root is not found in West Semitic inscriptions,[2] Ethiopic, or Old South Arabic. Aram. *'^{a}zal,* "go away," is related, whereas the *n^{e}zal* of the Targs. may be a Hebraism, as the few occurrences cited by Levy suggest.[3]

II. OT Usage. The root *nzl* occurs 15 times in the OT, 14 in the qal: 7 in the prefix conjugation (Nu. 24:7; Dt. 32:2; Isa. 45:8; Jer. 9:17[Eng. v. 18]; Ps. 147:18; Job 36:28; Cant. 4:16), another 7 in the form of the act. masc. pl. ptcp. *nōz^{e}lîm* (Ex. 15:8; Isa. 44:3; Ps. 78:44; Prov. 5:15; Cant. 4:15; written *plene* in Jer. 18:14; Ps. 78:16). The suffix conjugation of the hiphil occurs once (Isa. 48:21). It is strange that, in contrast to the other Semitic languages, Hebrew uses the root exclusively in association with water (twice figuratively) in the broadest sense of "flow (down, out)" (so that the Vulg.

1. *KTU,* 1.14, II, 16; III, 58; see *WUS,* no. 1765.
2. Cf. *DISO.*
3. *ChW,* II, 99.

translates 13 times with a form derived from *fluere*). It is used only in poetic texts, often metaphorically.

III. Qal. In Nu. 24:7, in one of the oracles of Balaam, the characteristic OT meaning "flow" describes the water flowing from a bucket (cf. the totally different, possibly interpretative [messianic] translation of the LXX, as well as Targ. and Syr.[4]), serving as an image of fertility and plentiful water. In Jer. 9:17(18), in a lament over Judah, the verb similarly provides a graphic image of the tears of the mourners, from whose eyelids the "water" streams (*nāzal* par. *yārad̲*).

The basic meaning of the root comes through most clearly in the pouring down of rain from the heavens. In the book of Job, Elihu's fourth discourse incorporates a hymn extolling the power of God in nature, beginning with a description of the miraculous origin of rain. In 36:28 the clouds (like the eyelids in Jer. 9:17[18]) are syntactically the subject of *nāzal* (and the par. *rāʿap̱,* "drop down"); logically, however, they are the source in both cases. The same construction occurs in the short hymn of Deutero-Isaiah, Isa. 45:8, which bids the clouds, as a metaphor for the divine realm, to shower righteousness (cf. Ps. 85:12[11]).

The OT thinks of the dew, like the rain, as falling from heaven (cf. Dt. 33:28; Zec. 8:12; Prov. 3:20). In the opening summons of the wisdom discourse referred to as the Song of Moses, Dt. 32:2 uses similarly figurative language to describe the speaker's teaching as dropping like the rain and his speech as "trickling down" like the dew (cf. Isa. 55:10f.). In Ps. 147, a hymn of praise based on observation of nature, v. 18 uses *nāzal* for the trickling away of the water when Yahweh sends forth his mighty word, thawing the ice with a warm wind. The notion of flowing water is probably also associated with the verb in Cant. 4:16, in the context of a love poem: the winds are to blow on a garden planted with exotic, aromatic herbs, that their fragrance may "flow."

IV. Participle. The nominalized qal active participle is used only in the plural: "flowing (waters)," a poetic term for a spring or stream. Jer. 18:14 uses this epithet for cold, flowing springs. Cant. 4:15 similarly calls the mountain streams "flowing down" from Lebanon *nōzᵉlîm.* Here the beloved is likened to a garden spring, whose "living" water in its freshness, purity, and abundance is equated with the wonderful waters of Lebanon. A similar metaphor appears in Prov. 5:15, which calls on the married man to remain faithful by slaking his thirst for love only on the water that flows from his own well.

In the other poetic texts, *nōzᵉlîm* appears in conjunction with the mighty acts of Yahweh. In Ex. 15:8 the Song of Moses uses this word (which elsewhere refers to "springs" or "streams") together with *tᵉhōmôt̲* for the waters of the sea, obviously as an antonym to *niṣṣᵉḇû,* in order to emphasize the startling contrast between the fluid motion of the sea and its sudden congealing (cf. Targ. Onqelos: *qāmû . . . 'āzᵉlayyā',*

4. More probable than the conj. proposed by *BHK, BHS.*

" 'the moving ones' . . . stood still"); *nēḏ,* "dam" (NRSV: "heap"), suggests poetic exaggeration describing the rise and sudden foaming collapse of high waves.

In the context of an oracle of salvation, Isa. 44:3 likens the revitalizing outpouring of God's Spirit on the despairing people to streams flowing over (LXX: *toís poreuoménois*) parched and thirsty land. Ps. 78:44 uses the word with "rivers" (clearly to include every channel through which water might flow) for the watercourses of Egypt, transformed into blood and undrinkable (cf. Ex. 7:19). In Ps. 78:16, by contrast, it denotes the stream of water that Yahweh caused to issue from the rock in the desert for his thirsty people.

In 1QH 8:4 *nōzᵉlîm* and several synonyms symbolize the community.

V. Hiphil. Isa. 48:21, a hymn of praise, alludes to the miraculous water in the desert. This, the only instance of *nāzal* in the hiphil, has a causative sense: Yahweh made water flow from the rock for them.

Maiberger(†)

נזר *nzr;* נֵזֶר *nēzer;* נָזִיר *nāzîr*

Contents: I. 1. Occurrences; 2. LXX. II. Usage: 1. The Charismatic *nāzîr;* 2. Naziriteship as an Act of Devotion; 3. Diadem; 4. Other Usage. III. Dead Sea Scrolls.

---

nzr. K.-H. Bernhardt, "Krönung," *BHHW,* II (1964), 1015f.; J. Blenkinsopp, "Structure and Style in Judges 13–16," *JBL,* 82 (1963), 65-76; M. Boertien, *Nazir (Nasiräer)* (Berlin and New York, 1971); K. Budde, "Das alttestamentliche Nasiräat," *Die Christliche Welt,* 24 (1930), 675-680; S. M. Cooke, "Nazirites," *ERE,* 9 (1917), 258-260; A. G. van Daalen, *Simson* (Assen, 1966); G. Delling, "Nasiräer," *BHHW,* II, 1288f.; W. Eichrodt, *Theology of the OT. OTL,* 2 vols. (Eng. trans. 1961-67), I, 303-6; G. Fohrer, *History of Israelite Religion* (Eng. trans., Nashville, 1972); K. Galling, "Priesterkleidung," *BRL*², 256f.; M. Görg, "Die Kopfbedeckung des Hohenpriesters," *BN,* 3 (1977), 24-26; *idem,* "Weiteres zu *nzr* ('Diadem')," *BN,* 4 (1977), 7f.; H. Gunkel, "Simson," *Internationale Monatszeitschrift für Wissenschaft, Kunst und Technik,* 7 (1913), 875-894; M. Haran, "נזיר," *EMiqr,* V (1968), 795-799 (Heb.); J. Henninger, "Zur Frage des Haaropfers bei den Semiten," *Die Wiener Schule der Völkerkunde* (Vienna, 1956), 349-368; S. Herrmann, *A History of Israel in OT Times* (Eng. trans., Philadelphia, ²1981), 224f.; M. Jastrow, "The 'Nazir' Legislation," *JBL,* 33 (1914), 266-285; E. Jenni, "Nasiräer," *RGG*³, IV, 1308f.; D. Kellermann, *Die Priesterschrift von Numeri 1,1 bis 10,10 literarkritisch und traditionsgeschichtlich untersucht. BZAW,* 120 (1970); J. Kühlewein, "נָזִיר *nāzîr* 'consecrated person,' " *TLOT,* II, 727-29; G. van der Leeuw, *Religion in Essence and Manifestation* (Eng. trans., New York, 1963); J. S. Licht, "כֶּתֶר וַעֲטָרָה, *EMiqr,* IV (1962), 399-408 (Heb.); C. Meister, "Kranz, Krone," *BHHW,* II (1962), 999f.; J. Milgrom, "Nazirite," *EncJud,* XII (1971), 907-910; J. Pedersen, *ILC,* III-IV, 77f., 264-66; G. von Rad, "The Royal Ritual in Judah," *The Problem of the Hexateuch and Other Essays* (Eng. trans., New York, 1966), 222-231; *idem, OT Theology,* 2 vols. (Eng. trans., New York, 1962-65), I, 62-64, 333f.; H. F. Richter, *Geschlechtlichkeit, Ehe und Familie im AT und seiner Umwelt. BBET,* 10 (1978); W. Richter, *Traditionsgeschichtliche*

I. 1. *Occurrences.* The root *nzr/nḏr* is found in all branches of Semitic (whether Akk. *nazāru,* "vilify," is related to it is questionable). The basic meaning is "withdraw from ordinary use, set apart."[1] In Biblical Hebrew the verb *nzr* appears 4 times in the niphal, with the meaning "refrain, consecrate oneself," and 6 times in the hiphil, with the meaning "consecrate oneself." The noun *nēzer,* which means both "consecration" and "diadem," occurs 24 times; *nāzîr,* "consecrated one, nazirite," occurs 16 times. Ezk. 14:5,7 show that *zwr* (Isa. 1:4; Ezk. 14:5) is related semantically to *nzr;* it is common for פ״ן verbs to become hollow verbs.[2] The text of Lev. 15:31 is disputed: emendation to *wᵉhizhartem* has been suggested on the basis of the Sam., LXX, Syr., and Vulg.[3] In Lam. 4:7 the conjectural emendation *nᵉʿāreyhā* has found support.[4]

2. *LXX.* The translation of the LXX is relatively constant. Some texts merely transliterate (*nazir:* Jgs. 13:5 [B]; *naziraíos:* Jgs. 13:5,7 [both A]; 16:17 [A]; Lam. 4:7; *nezer:* 2 K. 11:12) or attempt simply to convey the meaning (*hṓn hēgḗsato adelphṓn:* Gen. 49:26; *doxastheís en adelphoís:* Dt. 33:16; *eulabeís poiéō:* Lev. 15:31; *proséchō apó:* Lev. 22:2; *basíleion:* 2 S. 1:10; 2 Ch. 23:11; *keírō tḗn kephalḗn:* Jer. 7:29 [but cf. Symmachus: *tḗn kómēn tḗs nazraiótētós sou*]; *apallotrióomai:* Ezk. 14:7; Hos. 9:10; *ischýs:* Prov. 27:24). As a rule, however, we find a derivative of *hagi-* (*hagiázō:* Nu. 6:12; *hēgiasménos:* Am. 2:12; *hēgiasménon:* Lev. 25:11; *hagíasma:* Ex. 29:6; Lev. 25:5; Zec. 7:3; Ps. 89:40[Eng. v. 39]; 132:18; *hagiasmós:* Am. 2:11; *hágios:* Lev. 21:12; Jgs. 13:7 [B]; 16:17 [B]; Zec. 9:16; *hágion:* Lev. 8:9) or *hagn-* in the Priestly law of the nazirite (Nu. 6:1-21) (*hagneía:* v. 21; *aphagnízomai hagneían:* v. 2; *hagnízō:* v. 3; *hagnismós:* v. 5). Peculiar to Nu. 6 is the use of *euch-* (*eúchomai:* v. 5; *euxámenos:* vv. 13,21; *ēugménos:* vv. 18-20; *euchḗ:* vv. 4,6-9,12,13,18,19,21).

II. Usage.

1. *The Charismatic nāzîr.* In the eighth century *nāzîr* refers to a charismatic figure, called by Yahweh like a prophet (Am. 2:11).[5] In v. 12 a later hand accuses Israel of

---

Untersuchungen zum Richterbuch. BBB, 18 (1963); H. Salmanowitsch, *Das Naziräat nach Bibel und Talmud* (1931); C. Serfass, "Naziréat, Naziréen," *Dictionnaire encyclopédique de la Bible,* II (1932), 209f.; R. de Vaux, *AncIsr,* 102-7, 465-67; *idem, The Early History of Israel* (Eng. trans., Philadelphia, 1978), 644; *idem,* "The King of Israel, Vassal of Yahweh," *The Bible and the Ancient Near East* (Eng. trans., Garden City, N.Y., 1971), 152-166; H. Weippert, "Schmuck," *BRL²*, 282-89, esp. 287f. with fig. 75; Z. Weisman, "The Biblical Nazirite, Its Types and Roots," *Tarbiz,* 36 (1967), 207-220 (Heb.); J. A. Wharton, "The Secret of Yahweh," *Int,* 27 (1973), 48-66; H.-J. Zobel, *Stammesspruch und Geschichte. BZAW,* 95 (1965); E. Zuckschwerdt, "Zur literarischen Vorgeschichte des priesterlichen Nazir-Gesetzes (Num 6,1-8)," *ZAW,* 88 (1976), 191-205.

1. Kühlwein, 50; *HAL,* II, 684.
2. *GK,* §77c; G. Bergsträsser, *Hebräische Grammatik,* 2 vols. (²⁹1918-29, repr. Hildesheim, 1962), II, §31c.
3. K. Elliger, *Leviticus. HAT,* IV (1966), 192; *BHS.*
4. H.-J. Kraus, *Klagelieder. BK,* XX (1956), 72; *BHS.*
5. With W. Rudolph, *Amos. KAT,* XIII/2 (1971), 146f.; contra W. H. Schmidt, *ZAW,* 77 (1965), 174-183, who ascribes the verse to Deuteronomistic redaction.

having made the nazirites drink wine and forbidden the prophets to speak, conduct that provokes Yahweh's intervention. The relationship between the nazirite and God is so intimate that an attack on the integrity of the former impugns the latter.

Samson is called *nᵉzîr ʾᵉlōhîm,* "consecrated one of God" (Jgs. 13:5,7; 16:17); therefore no razor may touch his head. The prohibition against wine found in Am. 2:12 is repeated and even extended to all products of the vine and to beer *(šēḵār).* Since he is to be consecrated from his mother's womb until his death, the same prohibition is imposed on his mother before his conception, as well as refraining from unclean food (Jgs. 13:4,7,14); thus the holiness of the child, whose birth is predicted by an angel, is enhanced. The birth narrative in Jgs. 13 breathes a spirit very different from that of the narrative cycle in Jgs. 14–16. At the same time, apart from 16:17, ch. 13 alone bears the entire burden of depicting Samson as a nazirite. It is reasonable, therefore, to view ch. 13 as an interpretative addition to chs. 14–16.[6]

Consideration of the textual development of the Samuel narratives in 1 S. 1–16 supports this theory. In ch. 1 the story of Samuel's boyhood incorporates motifs that also characterize Samson's naziriteship: lifelong consecration and unlimited growth of hair (1:11,28). While vv. 13-15 of the MT merely allude to the required abstention from wine and beer, the LXX has added this element to Hannah's vow (v. 11 LXX). Later 4QSam[a] 1:22 and Sir. 46:13 (Heb.) explicitly give Samuel the title *nāzîr.*[7] They clearly find this term an appropriate expression of the status and close relationship with God (cf. Jer. 15:1; Ps. 99:6) enjoyed by Samuel, whom tradition sometimes calls a priest, sometimes a judge, and sometimes a prophet. The term *nāzîr* thus lent itself to characterizing heroic figures, since its definition reflected their holiness rather than their function. This usage appears also in Gen. 49:26 and Dt. 33:16, where the word characterizes Joseph's special relationship to God that sets him apart from his brothers; there is no need to invent the meaning "prince."

Some scholars find the origin of the *nāzîr* in the holy war, others more generally in a reaction against canaanizing tendencies. The former base their arguments on the narratives associated with Samson and Samuel, as well as the sayings concerning Joseph in Gen. 49 and Dt. 33. The latter cite abstention from alcohol and unlimited growth of hair. The first approach is ruled out by the redactional analysis outlined above, which justifies at best a reference to the birth stories of Samson and Samuel. The second approach also faces severe obstacles. Priestly abstinence from wine (Lev. 10:9; Ezk. 44:21) is generally interpreted as an echo of anti-Canaanite attitudes, but it cannot have been directed against wine in general as a product of civilization that has no place in the cult of Yahweh. It is well known that libations were associated with various offerings (Ex. 29:40; Nu. 15:5; 28:14; 1 Ch. 9:29), and the sacrificial meal included wine (Dt. 14:26). Amos and Isaiah criticize only the use of wine acquired through injustice (Am. 2:8) or intemperance (Isa. 28:7). The abstinence from wine required of priests during

---

6. E.g., Gunkel, 889f.; von Rad, *OT Theology,* I, 333f.; W. Richter, 142.

7. See F. M. Cross, "A New Qumran Biblical Fragment Related to the Original Hebrew Underlying the Septuagint," *BASOR,* 132 (1953), 15-26. Cf. also Mishnah *Naz.* 9.5.

their period of service suggests more the avoidance of artificially induced ecstasy. Just as the classical prophets received their calls and messages from God in a state of heightened consciousness rather than ecstasy, so too the *n^e^zîrîm,* called to special service by Yahweh, must be sober. Their hair must not be cut, because it embodies their consecration, symbolically and realistically.[8] A luxuriant growth of hair is evidence of their holiness. The only constant element in naziriteship is the special relationship to Yahweh; it is easy to envision a wide range of functions.

2. *Naziriteship as an Act of Devotion.* In Nu. 6:1-21 P deals at length with the regulations governing a temporary vow of naziriteship. The first section (vv. 3-7), framed by vv. 2,8, incorporates the familiar requirements of abstinence from alcohol and cutting one's hair and adds a prohibition against defilement by a corpse (vv. 6f.), in almost the same words Lev. 21:11f. uses for the high priest. Both the high priest and the *nāzîr* must avoid contracting impurity even from the closest members of their family: father or mother, and, in the case of the *nāzîr,* brother or sister. The version of the prohibition framed for ordinary priests makes explicit exception for these cases (Lev. 21:1-4; Ezk. 44:25). The explanation is also the same for both: their consecration (*nēzer:* Lev. 21:12; Nu. 6:7), which comes to the high priest through his anointing. Both sets of regulations probably derive from the same priestly circles. The addition of *kōl y^e^mê nizrô* at the end of the first prohibition (Nu. 6:4), *kol-y^e^mê neḏer nizrô* as an introduction to the second (v. 5), and *kol-y^e^mê hazzîrô l^e^ YHWH* before the third (v. 6) limit the duration of the triple abstinence.

Like the preceding section (v. 2b), the section comprising vv. 9-12 begins with the conjunction *kî.* It regulates what is to be done in case, despite all precautions, a nazirite has become unclean. The days of consecration already spent do not count. As required by 19:11,14,16, seven days must pass before the individual is clean once more; then the hair is shaved and the vow renewed. On this occasion two turtledoves or ordinary pigeons are brought to the priest to be offered as a sin offering and a burnt offering; a lamb one year old is also offered as a guilt offering. In the regulations governing the offerings, Diether Kellermann sees the text beginning with *bayyôm hašš^e^ḇî'î* in v. 9 as an addition by a later author, drawing on the special regulations applying to poor women after childbirth (Lev. 12:8), healed lepers (14:22,30), and men or women freed of a bodily discharge (15:14,19).[9]

To the same author he assigns the section Nu. 6:13-21, which governs the ceremonies at the end of the period of consecration.[10] Referred to as *tôrâ* in both superscription (v. 13) and colophon (v. 21), this section begins with a sacrificial gift (*qorbān:* v. 14): a male lamb as a burnt offering, a female lamb as a sin offering, and a ram as an offering of well-being, together with a basket of loaves and flat bread. The burnt offering includes a food offering comprising one-tenth of an ephah of fine flour mixed with one-fourth of a hin of oil, together with a libation of one-third of a hin of wine; the offering of well-being requires

8. Henninger, 365.
9. Pp. 88f., with table on p. 90.
10. *Ibid.,* 90-93.

as a food offering two-tenths of an ephah of flour and one-third of a hin of oil, with one-third of a hin of wine as a libation (quantities from Lev. 15:1-16). These offerings are followed by deconsecrating: the hair is shaved and burned (Nu. 6:18). The *nāzîr* is not allowed to drink wine, however, until the priest has performed the wave offering *(t^{e}nûpâ)*, which, as part of the offering of well-being, includes not only the usual thigh and breast (Lev. 7:32-34) but also a boiled shoulder. It is easy to see that, just as the figure of *nāzîr* was assimilated increasingly to that of the priest, so the institution became incorporated increasingly into the priestly system. If one assumes that the sacrificial regulations drawn upon here go back to the early postexilic period,[11] the *tôrâ* under discussion probably reflects the circumstances of the first half of the fifth century.

This situation did not remain unchanged, however. Later evidence, especially from the last years of the Second Temple, reveals that the vow of naziriteship became the most popular way to express thanksgiving for divine favors like deliverance from sickness or affliction, a safe return from war, or the fulfillment of a wish for a son.[12] If a different period was not named, the naziriteship lasted 30 days, probably a parallel to the 30 days of mourning during which male members of the deceased's family were forbidden to cut their hair.[13] To pay for the offerings of someone else was considered an act of piety.[14] Tradition preserves the names of a few women who made the nazirite vow: Berenice, the sister of Herod Agrippa II; Helena, the queen of Adiabene, a proselyte; and a certain Miriam of Palmyra.[15]

3. *Diadem.* The word *nēzer,* "diadem," denotes a metal band with holes for laces, ornamented with decorations such as rosettes, imitation floral wreaths,[16] or even precious stones (Zec. 9:16). As an emblem of royalty (2 S. 1:10), the priest gave it to the king along with the royal protocol at his enthronement (2 K. 11:12; 2 Ch. 23:11).[17] Its symbolic importance is illustrated by the use of the word in the lament over the decline of the kingdom (Ps. 89:40[39]) as well as in the promise to David (132:18). The diadem also played a role in the investiture of the high priest (Lev. 8:9; Ex. 29:6; 39:30). Wisdom speaks of the impermanence of diadems (Prov. 27:24).

Manfred Görg calls attention to the difference between the word's etymology ("consecration") and its semantics ("diadem") and postulates for *nēzer,* "diadem," a derivation from Egyp. *nṯr.t,* a term for the serpent goddess.[18] If this is true, the king's diadem would be functionally comparable to the apotropaic uraeus of the pharaohs.

---

11. E.g., Elliger, *HAT,* IV, 158, 176, with 67.
12. Josephus *BJ* 2.15.1 §313; Mishnah *Naz.* 2.7; 3.6.
13. For the former see Josephus *BJ* 2.15.1 §§313f.; Mishnah *Naz.* 1.3; 6.3; cf. also 1 Mc. 3:49. For the latter see Mishnah *Mo'ed Qaṭ.* 3.5; Talmud Bab. *Mo'ed Qaṭ.* 14b, 27b; cf. Nu. 20:29; Lev. 19:27; Dt. 14:1.
14. Josephus *Ant.* 19.6.1 §294; Acts 21:23f.; Mishnah *Naz.* 2.5; Talmud Jer. *Naz.* 54b, 5f.
15. On Berenice see Josephus *BJ* 2.15.1 §§313f.; on Helena, Mishnah *Naz.* 3.6; on Miriam, *ibid.,* 6.11.
16. Weippert, 287f.
17. Von Rad, "Royal Ritual"; cf. S. Yeivin, "'Eduth," *IEJ,* 24 (1974), 17-20.
18. "Headgear," following M. Noth, *Exodus. OTL* (Eng. trans. 1962), 225f.

4. *Other Usage.* Usage elsewhere in the OT does not diverge from the observations made above.

a. *Prophets.* Prophetic polemic against the various forms of idolatry uses the niphal of *nzr* (or of *zwr*[19]) for turning to other gods (Hos. 9:10) as well as for turning away from Yahweh (Isa. 1:4;[20] Ezk. 14:5,7). Also, when Jeremiah uses *nēzer* to refer concretely to long hair, he does so in the same context (Jer. 7:29). In Zec. 7:3 the verb refers to the modalities of mourning; the context suggests fasting.

b. *Holiness Code.* There are many occurrences in H, obviously in passages associated with Nu. 6.[21] The noun *nēzer* stands for the holiness of the high priest (Lev. 21:12); the vine that is not pruned during the Sabbatical or Jubilee Year is called *nāzîr* (25:5,11); the admonition to abstain from holy foods uses the niphal of *nzr* (22:2).

III. Dead Sea Scrolls. The noun *nēzer* occurs in the Dead Sea Scrolls with both abstract and concrete meaning. According to 1QSb 4:28, the priest should be a consecration for the holy of holies (not a "diadem": cf. Lev. 21:12). The eschatological king wears a diadem (4QpIs[a] fr. 8-10 19[22]). The niphal and hiphil of *nzr* describe life lived according to the covenant. A member of the community must abstain from godless possessions (CD 6:15). His consecrated way of life must eschew the company of prostitutes (7:1). By contrast, apostates are characterized by their refusal to separate themselves from the people (8:8; 19:20). The use of *nāzîr* is discussed in II.1 above.

G. Mayer

---

19. See I above.
20. W. L. Holladay, "A New Suggestion for the Crux in Isaiah I 4b," *VT,* 33 (1983), 235-37.
21. See II.2 above.
22. J. Allegro, *Qumrân Cave 4. DJD,* V (1968), 14.

נָחָה *nāḥâ*

Contents: I. Root: 1. Etymology; 2. Meaning; 3. Versions; 4. Lexical Field. II. Statistics: 1. Occurrences; 2. Distribution; 3. Syntactic Relationships. III. Theological Usage: 1. Ancient Near East; 2. God as Leader; 3. Variations in Meaning.

---

nāḥâ. L. Delekat, "Ein Septuagintatargum," *VT,* 8 (1958), 225ff., esp. 237-240; J. A. Emerton, "Notes on Jeremiah 12, 9 and Some Suggestions of J. D. Michaelis About the Hebrew Words *naḥā, ʿæbrā,* and *yadăʿ,*" *ZAW,* 81 (1969), 182-191; E. Jenni, "נחה *nḥh* 'to lead,'" *TLOT,* II, 729f.; W. Michaelis, "ὁδήγος, ὁδηγέω," *TDNT,* V, 97-102; G. Sauer, "דֶּרֶךְ *derek* 'way,'" *TLOT,* I, 343-46; *idem,* "הלך *hlk* 'to go,'" *TLOT,* 365-370; J. F. A. Sawyer, *Semantics in Biblical Research. SBT,* 2/24 (1972), 39.

I. Root.

1. *Etymology.* The Hebrew (and Modern Hebrew) root *nḥh* is usually associated with Arab. *naḥā,* "look or go sideways," and OSA *mnḥy,* "channel (for water)."[1] A semantic connection is possible: both Heb. *nāḥâ* and Arab. *naḥā* appear to embody the idea of "motion in a particular direction." The Arabic root, however, refers to the subjective act of turning or setting out in a direction,[2] a notion that is at best present incidentally in the usage of Heb. *nāḥâ* ("lead" [transitive]). Caution is therefore advisable in accepting the two roots as identical. John Sawyer's theory that *nāḥâ* is a by-form of *nûaḥ* is no longer accepted.[3] The hypothesis of a separate root *nḥh* II is discussed later.[4]

2. *Meaning.* In Biblical and Postbiblical Hebrew (1QS 9:18, the only occurrence in the Dead Sea Scrolls), the root appears only in the form of the verb *nāḥâ* (qal and hiphil). No other derivatives or personal names use the root. In both stems the verb generally means "lead." Depending on usage and context, one can distinguish three semantic variants.[5] If the emphasis is on the "initiative" of the leader, the verb can be interpreted as meaning "lead someone in the right way," "show someone the right way." If the context refers primarily to the action of the leader during a journey, the word can mean roughly "accompany someone for protection." In some cases the goal of the journey stands so clearly in the foreground that one can interpret *nāḥâ* as "lead someone safely to the goal."

3. *Versions.* Among the ancient versions, the LXX uses translations that reflect these variations in meaning, but not consistently. The commonest translation of *nāḥâ* is *hodēgeín* (20 times); we also find *euodoún* (Gen. 24:27,48; Gen. 24 uses the same word 5 additional times to represent → צלח *ṣlḥ* hiphil and → קרה *qrh* hiphil), *ágein* (Dt. 32:12; Job 38:32), *epágein* (Prov. 6:22), *deiknýein* (Ex. 13:21), *metapémpesthai* (Nu. 23:7), *kathizánein* (Prov. 18:16), and *parakaleín,* "comfort" (1 S. 22:4; Isa. 57:18). The verbs *hodēgeín, ágein,* and *parakaleín* are also used to translate the parallel words → נהל *nāhal* and נהג *nāhag; hodēgeín* represents → דרך *drk* hiphil 3 times (Ps. 25:5,9; 119:35). Generally (about 60 out of 80 occurrences), *parakaleín* translates → נחם *nḥm.*

The Vulg. generally uses *ducere* for *nāḥâ,* but sometimes *dirigere, perducere,* or *adducere; deducere* is quite frequent. Neither the LXX nor the Vulg. appears to distinguish clearly among our root, *nāhal,* and *nāhag.*

4. *Lexical Field.* The lexical field of *nāḥâ* includes primarily the piels of *nāhal* (Ex. 15:13; Ps. 23:2f.; 31:4[Eng. v. 3]) and *nāhag* (Ps. 77:21[20]; 78:52f.; Isa. 63:14), often used in poetic parallelism; in practice all three verbs are synonyms. For *nāhal* the

1. *GesB,* 495; *HAL,* II, 685. For OSA see Biella, 301.
2. Cf. J. B. Belot, *Vocabulaire arabe-français à l'usage des étudiants* (Beirut, 1883), 811f.
3. Jenni, 729.
4. See II.1.c below.
5. See III.3 below.

derived noun *nahᵃlōl,* "watering place" (Arab. *manhal*), suggests that this verb is favored to describe the way a shepherd leads a flock. In contrast with *nāhal* ("to escort, with care"[6]), *nāhag* appears to express a more energetic act, possibly involving force: "drive." It, too, is often used for the action of a shepherd. We accordingly find *nāḥâ* used as a synonym of the more general term → רעה *rāʿâ,* "pasture" (Ps. 78:72). The context frequently mentions the flock (→ צאן *ṣōʾn*).[7]

The act of leading includes the notion of a way *(dereḵ)* to be traveled by the one led and often by the one doing the leading as well (Gen. 24:27,49; Ex. 13:17,21; Ps. 5:9[8]; 23:3; 27:11; 77:20f.[19f.]; 139:24; 143:10; Prov. 6:22; Neh. 9:12,19). Therefore "lead" can be glossed by the hiphil of *yārâ* ("show [the way]": Ps. 27:11; cf. 25:8f.,12; 86:11).[8] Besides *yārâ* hiphil, we also find as parallels *yāṣāʾ* hiphil, "cause to go forth" (143:10f.; Job 38:32), *bôʾ* hiphil, "cause to enter" (Ps. 43:3; 78:53f.), *yāḇal* hiphil, "bring in" (60:11[9]; 108:11[10]), or simply *hālaḵ* hiphil, "cause to go" (Isa. 63:12-14; cf. Prov. 6:22) — naturally "on a level path" (*bᵉmîšôr:* Ps. 27:11; 143:10; cf. 5:9[8]) and "in safety" (*lāḇeṭaḥ:* 78:53).

The hand as an instrument of guidance is a further characteristic element in the lexical field of *nāḥâ.* The texts often speak of "grasping," "seizing," or "holding" (*ʾḥz, lqḥ, tmk*) the right hand or with the right hand (Ps. 63:9[8]; 73:23f.; 77:21[20]; 78:72; 139:10; cf. Isa. 51:18) — once with reference to a staff in the shepherd's hand (Ps. 23:4 conj.). The difficult phrase *ṣōʾn yāḏô* in Ps. 95:7 may refer to leading the flock "with one's hand."[9]

II. Statistics.

1. *Occurrences.* The verb *nāḥâ* occurs 39 times in the OT. Of these occurrences, 11 are in the qal (Gen. 24:17; Ex. 13:17; 15:13; 32:34; Isa. 58:11; Ps. 5:9[8]; 27:11; 60:11[9]; 77:21[20]; 108:11[10]; 139:24) and 28 in the hiphil (Gen. 24:48; Ex. 13:21;[10] Nu. 23:7; Dt. 32:12; 1 S. 22:4; 1 K. 10:26; 2 K. 18:11; Isa. 57:18; Job 12:23; 31:18; 38:32; Ps. 23:3; 31:4[3]; 43:3; 61:3[2]; 67:5[4]; 73:24; 78:14,53,72; 107:30; 139:10; 143:10; Prov. 6:22; 11:3; 18:16; Neh. 9:12,19[11]). Most of the qals are perfects, most of the hiphils imperfects or infinitives.[12] But this list requires correction.

a. In many cases the similarity between forms of *nāḥâ* and *nûaḥ* in the hiphil imperfect with suffixes has led to confusion in the MT.[13] In 1 S. 22:4 *wayyanḥēm,* "and he led them," is better read *wayyannihēm,* "and he left them," following the Vulg. *(reliquit).* The form *wayyanḥēm* in 1 K. 10:26 should be emended to *wayyannihēm,* "and he stationed them," following the LXX and 2 Ch. 9:25; the same

---

6. *HAL,* II, 675.
7. But see II.3.b below.
8. → ירה *yārâ* III (VI, 339-347).
9. → יד *yāḏ,* V, 420.
10. Lisowsky: qal.
11. Lisowsky: qal.
12. *GK,* §78c.
13. M. Dahood, *Bibl,* 49 (1968), 357f.

change should be made in 2 K. 18:11 ("and he settled them"), following the LXX, Vulg., and Syr. The form *we'anḥēhû* in Isa. 57:18 is semantically difficult in its context. Following Karl Marti, *BHS* rightly suggests reading *wa'aniḥēhû.*[14] In Job 12:23, too, the MT reading *wayyanḥēm* can hardly be correct. It agrees with the LXX, Syr., and Targ., but the parallelism with *ye'abbedēm* would lead one to expect a verb denoting judgment or destruction. The suggestion to read *wayyanniḥēm,* "and brings them to rest," following the Vulg. *(in integrum restituet),* does not meet this expectation.[15] Friedrich Horst suggests a venturesome but plausible solution: *wayyimḥēm,* "and wipes them out."[16] In Ps. 139:10 several modern translations assume an original *tiqqāḥēnî* instead of the less appropriate *tanḥēnî.* In Prov. 11:3a *tanḥēm,* "it [integrity] guides them," does not establish a real contrast with v. 3b, "it (crookedness) destroys them"; *BHS* therefore proposes reading *tanniḥēm,* "it gives them rest." In Prov. 18:16 the analogy of 1 S. 22:4[17] suggests reading *yannihennû,* "it causes him to abide," instead of *yanḥennû,* "it leads him." Finally, in Isa. 63:14 the reading *tanḥennû* (Vulg.) or *tanḥēm* (LXX, Syr., Targ.) appears superior to MT *tenîhennû.*

b. In unpointed texts the forms of *nāḥâ* in the hiphil imperfect with the 3rd person masc. pl. suffix can be confused with piel forms of → נחם *nāḥam,* "comfort." The difficult *tanḥēnî* in Ps. 61:3(2), for which the reading *tanniḥēnî* (hiphil of *nûaḥ; BHS*) has been proposed, was taken by the Syr. in the sense of *wattenaḥamûnî;* the Syr. offers the same variant in 73:24. In 43:3, too, the Syr. (possibly influenced by the similar construction in 23:4) appears to have read *yenaḥamûnî* instead of MT *yanḥûnî,* with a few Hebrew manuscripts. In Isa. 57:18 the LXX *(kaí parekálesa autón)*[18] may have had *wa'anaḥamēhû* as its text instead of MT *me'anḥēhû.* Conversely, Hermann Gunkel would replace the *yenaḥamûnî* of Ps. 23:4 with *yanḥûnî:* "your rod and your staff, they lead me" does make better sense than the traditional MT ". . . they comfort me."[19]

c. One apparent and two real qal perfect forms of *nāḥâ* require explanation. Lisowsky assigns *nāḥâ* in Isa. 7:2 to the root *nḥh;* it is actually a form of *nûaḥ.*[20] Among the versions only the Vulg. *(requievit)* has recognized this. The Vulg. also read *wenāḥakā* in Isa. 58:11 as a form of *nûaḥ* (*et requiem tibi dabit,* for *weyanniḥakā*?). But as a form of *nḥh* with the meaning "lead (to pasture)" the word provides sensible parallelism to v. 11b *(hiśbîa' napšekā),* so that the MT should be retained. In Ps. 60:11(9) par. 108:11(10), for MT *nāḥanî,* "he has led me," we should follow the versions in reading *yanḥēnî,* "he will lead me" (haplography?).

Thus after we eliminate Ps. 60:11(9) par. 108:11(10), only 9 of the 11 occurrences

---

14. See J. S. Kselman, "A Note on *w'nḥhw* in Isa. 57:18," *CBQ,* 43 (1981), 539-542.

15. See comms. by Hitzig, Delitzsch, in loc.

16. F. Horst, *Hiob 1–19. BK,* XVI/1 (1968), 180.

17. See above.

18. See I.3 above.

19. Cf. *BHS.*

20. On the hypothesis of a root *nḥh* II, "stick to" (*HAL,* II, 675), see Delekat; on the interpretation of *nûaḥ* as "alight upon, fall upon," see H. Wildberger, *Isaiah 1–12* (Eng. trans., Minneapolis, 1991), 283.

of the qal remain. Further, on the one hand, the 28 hiphil occurrences are reduced by the 9 texts where it is better to read a hiphil form of *nûaḥ* (1 S. 22:4; 1 K. 10:26; 2 K. 18:11; Isa. 57:18; Prov. 11:3; 18:16; Ps. 61:3[2]) or a form of some other verb (Job 12:23; Ps. 139:10). On the other hand, in four cases graphically similar forms of other verbs (Isa. 63:14: *nûaḥ;* Ps. 23:4: *nāḥam*) or what the MT presents as qal forms of *nāḥâ* (Ps. 60:11[9] par. 108:11[10]) should be reconstructed as hiphils of *nāḥâ.* There remain 23 certain occurrences of *nāḥâ* in the hiphil and only 32 occurrences in all.

2. *Distribution.* With the doubtful occurrences eliminated, the improved statistics of the usage of *nāḥâ* allow several conclusions with respect to its literary distribution in the OT.

a. An initial group of 8 occurrences is found in the Pentateuch, for the most part (with the exception of Nu. 23:7) in its later strata. The theme of "leading" is developed as a novella in Gen. 24 (vv. 27,48); the LXX emphasizes this theme even more.[21] In the summary account of Israel's journey through the wilderness, *nāḥâ* is a frequent catchword (Ex. 13:17,21; 32:34; Neh. 9:12,19; cf. Ps. 77:21[20]; 78:14,53).

b. By far the largest group of occurrences (19) is in the realm of sacral poetry. The genre of the individual prayer is represented frequently (Ps. 5:9[8]; 23:3,4 conj.; 27:11; 31:4[3]; 43:3; 73:24; 139:24; 143:10); but other genres, too, display an accentuated use of *nāḥâ* (Ex. 15:13; Dt. 32:12; Ps. 60:11[9] par. 108:11[10]; 67:5[4]; 77:21[20]; 78:14,53,72; 107:30).

c. In the corpus of prophetic literature, only Trito-Isaiah is represented (Isa. 58:11; 63:14 conj.; according to the MT, also 57:18).

d. The final group comprises 3 occurrences in later Wisdom Literature: Prov. 6:22; Job 31:18; 38:32. In the remaining occurrences (Prov. 11:3; 18:16; Job 12:23), the MT can hardly be correct.

3. *Syntactic Relationships.* To these statistics concerning usage, a survey of syntactic relationships should be joined, with special attention to the subjects and objects involved in the act of leading.

a. *Subjects.* Only rarely are humans named as the subject of the action. Balak "brought" Balaam from the distant east (Nu. 23:7). David "guided" his people with a skillful hand (Ps. 78:72; here, as in 67:5[4], *nāḥâ* approaches the sense of "govern"). In Job 31:18 textual problems make it difficult to determine the subject who does the leading; in the context of an "oath of purgation," Job is most likely. Again, Job is asked the ironic question whether he can lead forth the constellations in their season (38:32). Finally, Moses is entrusted with the task of leading Israel to Canaan (Ex. 32:34; cf. Ps. 77:21[20]). This example is listed last, because this function can be understood only as indirect, reflecting Yahweh's leadership.

In some texts the subject appears to be an abstraction: "your light and your truth" (Ps. 43:3[2]), "your good spirit" (143:10), "a mother's teaching" (Prov. 6:22 [cf.

21. See I.3 above.

v. 20]). Behind such abstractions, however, stands the divine leader. In the majority of texts (20 out of 32[22]), Yahweh is the explicit subject. As one would expect, sacral poetry heads the list (Ps. 5:9[8]; 23:3; 23:4 conj.; 27:11; 31:4[3]; 67:5[4]; 73:24; 77:21[20]; 78:14,53; 107:30; 139:24; Ex. 15:13; Dt. 32:12); there follow Pentateuchal narrative or its recapitulation (Gen. 24:27,48; Ex. 13:17,21; Neh. 9:12,19) and finally prophetic literature (Isa. 58:11; 63:14 conj.).

b. *Objects.* The object is almost always human: Abraham's servant (Gen. 24), Balaam (Nu. 23), the people of Israel (Ex. 13:17,21; 15:13; 32:34; Dt. 32:12; Isa. 58:11; 63:14 conj.; Ps. 77:21[20]; 78:14,53,72; Neh. 9:12,19), upright individuals (Ps. 5:9[8]; 23:3; 23:4 conj.; 27:11; 31:4[3]; 43:3[2]; 73:24; 107:30; 139:24; 143:10), widows and orphans (Job 31:18?), the nations of the earth (Ps. 67:6[5]; Job 12:23 MT). Only Job 38:32 speaks of the stars (constellations?), a nonhuman object (cf. *yṣ'* hiphil in Isa. 40:26).[23]

In contrast to *nāhag,* "drive," *nāḥâ* never has a flock as its direct object. Israel, however, is often likened to a flock led by God (*kaṣṣō'n:* Ps. 77:21[20]; 78:52; cf. 74:1; 79:13; 80:2[1]; 95:7; 100:3; also the use of *rā'â,* "pasture," in parallel: Ps. 78:71f.; Isa. 40:11).

III. Theological Usage.

1. *Ancient Near East.* The large number of references to Yahweh's leadership raise the question whether similar statements were common elsewhere in the ancient Near East. Some quotations will suggest the evidence for both Egypt and Mesopotamia.

"Amun, shepherd, early in the morning you care for your flock. . . . The shepherd drives the cattle to the grass; Amun, you drive me, the hungry one, to food" (hymnic prayer to Amon from an ostracon of the Ramesside period).[24] "Hail to him who sits on the hand of Amun, who directs the timid, who rescues the poor . . . the perfect guide for everyman" (hymnic prayer to Amon from an inscription on a wooden figure, ca. 13th century).[25] "It is God who leads men on the path of life" (scarab inscription, 14th-12th century).[26] "The beginning of the teaching of life, the instruction for salvation, . . . to direct a man rightly on the ways of life, to make him prosper on earth, to let his heart go down into his shrine, by steering him from evil" (Teaching of Amenemope, Introduction, 1, 1-10; 12th-11th century).[27] "Restrain your heart and strengthen your heart, do not make yourself the steersman of your tongue; man's tongue is (indeed) the rudder of the ship, (but) the all-lord is its pilot" (Amenemope, 18, 20, 3-6).[28] "I guide you . . . on the way of life, I will tell you your (right) way of life which leads to the city of rejuvenation; keep to my words" (inscription in the tomb of Petosiris,

22. See II.1 above.
23. → כוכב *kôkāḇ* (VII, 75-85).
24. *NERT,* 40.
25. *NERT,* 41.
26. *NERT,* 43.
27. *NERT,* 49f.; cf. *ANET*^{3}, 423f.
28. *NERT,* 59; cf. *ANET*^{3}, 423f.

end of the 4th century).[29] "Above, you direct the affairs of all men, shepherd, of those below, guardian of the world above" (Akkadian hymn to Shamash, after 1400).[30] "Loose my fetters, secure my deliverance, guide my path aright, so that I can (again) go (my) way among men" (Akkadian invocation to Ishtar, ca. 1500).[31] In an account of military operations, Shalmaneser III speaks of "Nergal, my leader."[32]

These texts express the shepherd and leader function of the deity often and clearly enough. Both quotations from Amenemope reflect the wisdom notion that the deity's leadership is mediated, being experienced through the leading function of teaching, instruction (cf. Prov. 6:20,22), or the "heart."

2. *God as Leader.* The OT texts that speak of Yahweh or God as a leader can be divided into two groups: the first describes a completed action in the past, the second a present or future action. We shall examine only the use of *nāḥâ*.

a. *Past.* The statement that Yahweh "led" or "guided" his people is a characteristic motif in Israelite hymns; it is also one of the fundamental "themes" of the Pentateuchal narrative.[33] The miraculous guidance of Israel through the wilderness is frequently extolled as a saving act of God in history (Ex. 15:13; Dt. 32:12; Ps. 77:21[20]; 78:53; cf. 136:16; Isa. 63:14 conj.) or described in narrative (Ex. 13:17,21). It is especially vivid in God's going before the people in the pillar of cloud and fire (Ex. 13:21; Ps. 78:14; Neh. 9:12,19).

The use of *nāḥâ* is a fixed element of the wilderness tradition; the same, however, cannot be said of the patriarchal tradition. That *nāḥâ* appears only marginally in Gen. 24 is all the more surprising because both the Jacob cycle and the Joseph novella may be considered true "guidance stories" (for examples of this genre, see the books of Ruth and Tobit).

Only a single text (Ps. 107:30) speaks of God's leadership in the immediate past (rather than in the distant past of sacral history). In the course of a festal thanksgiving liturgy, the final group of those who have been saved is a bunch of sailors who have escaped a storm; they are called on to thank Yahweh for delivering them and "bringing them to their desired haven." This is the only extant hymn of thanksgiving for divine leadership on the way.

b. *Present and Future.* In the Psalms most of the texts pray to God for leadership or express trust in God's leadership. The pure "prayer for leadership" is rare (5:9[8]; 27:11; 139:24), but the confession of trust (23:3; 23:4 conj.; 31:4[3]; 43:3[2]; 67:5[4]; 73:24; 143:10) often has the inherent character of a prayer or petition (esp. 31:4[3]; 43:2[2]; cf. 79:9; 143:10). Such prayers for God's leadership in the future often invoke the divine name (*lᵉmaʿan šᵉmô/šimḵā:* 23:3; 31:4[3]]; cf. 79:9; 143:10f.); the mention of enemies as the motivation (*lᵉmaʿan šôrᵉray:* 5:9[8]; 27:11; cf. 69:19[18]) may be understood to mean that the very people who despise God's name (74:10,18) are to

29. *NERT,* 62f.
30. *NERT,* 102.
31. *NERT,* 111; cf. *ANET*³, 385.
32. *ANET*³, 277, 279.
33. *A History of Pentateuchal Traditions* (Eng. trans., Englewood Cliffs, N.J., 1972), 58f.

learn to respect it (83:17[16]). The enemies will discover that Yahweh upholds the cause of those who lament.[34]

c. *Relationship.* The question whether there is a conscious relationship between the statements concerning God's leadership in the past and those concerning his leadership in the present and future can hardly be answered with certainty. On the one hand, we must recall that the initial acts of God were recited and celebrated from time immemorial as being exemplary for all time. On the other hand, the frequent appeals to God's "name," "righteousness," "faithfulness," etc., show that petitions and expressions of trust are based on what God is known to have done: Pss. 77 and 79 are clear examples. The prophetic promise — unique in its way — in Isa. 58:11 ("the LORD will guide you continually"), too, is to be interpreted as a triumphal renewal of God's miraculous intervention in history, as the reference to Dt. 32:13 in v. 14 shows.

3. *Variations in Meaning.* What does it actually mean to say "God leads" in the individual texts? Depending on the context, *nāḥâ* may mean "lead to (or: on) the right way," "accompany and protect on the way," or "lead to the goal of the way." Allowing for occasional overlapping, I venture the following analysis.

The first, "guiding" meaning of the word appears in texts like Gen. 24:48 *(b^e^ḏereḵ ʾ^e^meṯ),* Ex. 13:17 *(dereḵ hammiḏbār),* Ex. 13:21 *(hadderek),* Ps. 78:14 (*bammiḏbār,* v. 15), and Ps. 139:24 *(b^e^ḏereḵ ʿôlām).* In the wilderness tradition Yahweh leads by going before his people veiled and thus visible; to the individual (Gen. 24:48; Ps. 139:24), he shows the way in mysterious fashion.

Leadership in the "protective accompaniment" sense appears in Dt. 32:12 (vv. 10-11,13!) as well as the Psalms (5:9[8]; 23:3; 27:11; 31:4[3]; 73:24; 77:21[20]; 78:53; 143:10); in 67:5(4) (cf. 78:2) *nāḥâ* is used more in the sense of "govern." This side of leadership includes God's constant presence (23:4; 73:23; opposite *ʿzb,* "forsake": Neh. 9:19) with the wanderer, who is exposed to deadly danger.

The "goal-oriented" use of *nāḥâ* is marked by a following *ʾel* or *ʿaḏ.* It appears in everyday language in Nu. 23:7; Ps. 60:11(9) = 108:11(10) and with God doing the leading in Gen. 24:27 and Ps. 107:30. God's leading to the sacred precincts or land is exemplary for both Israel (Ex. 15:13; cf. 32:34) and the devout individual (Ps. 43:3).

A few passages express the sense that Yahweh, the holy and incomparable God of Israel, not just any god, is truly Israel's leader (Dt. 32:12). In the context of Ex. 15:13 we find the hymnic *mî ḵāmōḵā* (v. 11); the words *YHWH š^e^mô* (v. 3) likewise claim leadership for Yahweh alone, denying it to other gods.[35] The statement of Ps. 77:21(20) can be understood correctly only against the background of the confession *ʾattâ hāʾēl* in v. 15. Prophetic admonition therefore has its necessary place alongside the comforting promise of God's leadership (cf. Ex. 33:3b-6 following 32:4; Ps. 78, a penitential liturgy; the admonitory Isa. 58).

Barth†

---

34. H.-J. Kraus, *Psalms 1–59* (Eng. trans., Minneapolis, 1988), 296.

35. F. Crüsemann, *Studien zur Formgeschichte von Hymnus und Danklied in Israel. WMANT,* 32 (1969), 95.

נָחַל *nāḥal;* נַחֲלָה *naḥ^a lâ*

I. Semantics: 1. Literal Meaning; 2. *nḥl* and *yrš;* 3. *naḥ^a lâ* and *'^a ḥuzzâ.* II. Inheritance: 1. Terminology; 2. Primogeniture; 3. Daughters; 4. Distribution; 5. Collateral Lines; 6. Widows; 7. Division of Property; 8. Inalienability and Rights of the *gō'ēl.* III. Inheritance of the Tribes and Israel: 1. Division of the Promised Land; 2. Levites; 3. Israel/Jacob; 4. The New Age. IV. The King. V. Yahweh: 1. Mythology; 2. Double Meaning; 3. Yahweh's Land, Holy Land; 4. "Mountain of God's Inheritance." VI. Metaphorical Usage: 1. *ḥlq* Parallel to *nḥlh;* 2. Essene Theology of Predestination; 3. Synonym of "Give."

---

nāḥal. Z. Ben-Barak, "Inheritance by Daughters in the Ancient Near East," *JSS,* 25 (1980), 22-33; R. Bohlen, "Der Fall Naboth," *TTS,* 35 (1978), 320-350; G. Boyer, *ARM VIII: Textes juridiques* (1958), 190-97; E. W. Davies, "Inheritance Rights and the Hebrew Levirate Marriage," *VT,* 31 (1981), 138-144, 257-268; P. Diepold, *Israels Land. BWANT,* 95 (1972); H. Donner, "Die soziale Botschaft der Propheten im Lichte der Gesellschaftsordnung in Israel," *OrAnt,* 2 (1963), 229-245; F. Dreyfus, "Le thème de l'héritage dans l'AT," *RSPT,* 42 (1958), 3-49; *idem* and P. Grelot, "Inheritance," *Dictionary of Biblical Theology,* ed. X. Léon-Dufour (Eng. trans., New York, ^{2}1973), 255-57; J. Ebach, "Sozialethische Erwägungen zum alttestamentlichen Bodenrecht," *BN,* 1 (1976), 31-46; D. O. Edzard, "Mari und Aramäer?" *ZA,* 56 (1964), 142-49, esp. 146, §16; Z. W. Falk, *Intro. to Jewish Law of the Second Commonwealth,* part 2 (1978), 332-349; W. Foerster and J. Herrmann, "κληρονόμος," *TDNT,* III, 768-781; H. O. Forshey, "The Construct Chain *naḥ^a lat YHWH/'^e lōhîm,*" *BASOR,* 220 (1975), 51-53; *idem,* "The Hebrew Root *NḤL* and Its Semitic Cognates (Summary)," *HTR,* 66 (1973), 505f.; G. Gerleman, "Nutzrecht und Wohnrecht," *ZAW,* 89 (1977), 313-325; I. Gottlieb, "Succession in Elephantine and Jewish Law," *JSS,* 26 (1981), 193-203; J. Guillet, *Themes of the Bible* (Eng. trans., Notre Dame, 1960), 191-210; J. Halbe, *Das Privilegrecht Jahwes Ex 34,10-26. FRLANT,* 114 (1975), esp. 283f.; J. Henninger, "Zum Erstgeborenenrecht bei den Semiten," *Festschrift Werner Caskel* (Leiden, 1968), 162-183; F. Horst, "Zwei Begriffe für Eigentum (Besitz)," *Verbannung und Heimkehr. Festschrift W. Rudolph* (1961), 135-156; J. Huehnergard, "Five Tablets from the Vicinity of Emar," *RA,* 77 (1983), 11-43; A. Jaussen, *Coutumes des Arabes au pays de Moab* (1908), 19-24, 236-240; J. Klima, "Donationes mortis causa nach den akkadischen Rechtsurkunden aus Susa," *Festschrift J. Friedrich* (Heidelberg, 1959), 229-259; *idem,* "Quelques remarques sur le droit successoral d'après les prescriptions néo-babyloniennes," *ArOr,* 27 (1959), 401-406; *idem,* "Die Stellung der ugaritischen Frau," *ArOr,* 25 (1957), 313-333, esp. 325f.; *idem, Untersuchungen zum altbabylonischen Erbrecht* (Prague, 1940); *idem,* "Untersuchungen zum elamischen Erbrecht (auf Grund der akkadischen Urkunden aus Susa)," *ArOr,* 27 (1959), 401-6; *idem,* "Untersuchungen zum ugaritischen Erbrecht," *ArOr,* 25 (1956), 356-374; H. Langkammer, "Die Verheissung vom Erbe," *BiLe,* 8 (1967), 157-165; E. Lipiński, "La Terre promise, héritage de Dieu," *Essais sur la révélation et la Bible. LD,* 60 (1970), 115-132; S. E. Loewenstamm, *"B^e nôṯ Ṣ^e lŏpḥād," EMiqr,* II, 170f., 948; *idem, "Y^e ruššâ," ibid.,* III, 788-791; *idem, "Naḥ^a lâ," ibid.,* V, 815f.; A. Malamat, "Mari and the Bible," *JAOS,* 82 (1962), 143-150, esp. 148-150 = *Festschrift M. H. Segal* (Jerusalem, 1964), 19-32; E. Neufeld, *Ancient Hebrew Marriage Laws* (London, 1944), 259-265; M. Noth, "Das Krongut der israelitischen Könige und seine Verwaltung," *ZDPV,* 50 (1927), 211-244 = *Aufsätze zur biblischen Landes- und Altertumskunde,* ed. H. W. Wolff, 2 vols. (Neukirchen-Vluyn, 1971), I, 159-182; *idem,* "Die Ursprünge des alten Israel im Lichte neuer Quellen," *Veröffentlichungen der Arbeitsgemeinschaft für Forschung des Landes Nordrheim-Westfalen,* 94 (1961), 9-40, esp. 18-20 = *Aufsätze,* II, 244-272, esp. 254f.;

I. Semantics.

1. *Literal Meaning.* The verb *nāḥal* appears 59 times in the OT, the noun *naḥ^{a}lâ* 220 times. Both are found in a variety of Semitic languages and are attested as Amorite loanwords as early as the Old Babylonian documents from Mari. They reflect the legal language of the Northwest Semites: the verb means that a joint heir has received his portion by succession, while the noun denotes the portion received. In other words, the action denoted by the verb consists in transforming the right to a total estate into an exclusive right to a portion, called in Hebrew *naḥ^{a}lâ,* in Ugaritic *nḥlt,* and in Amorite *neḫlatu.* The meaning of *naḥ^{a}lâ* is thus narrower than that of "inheritance," because, strictly speaking, it cannot be applied to an undivided estate, as Dt. 25:5 and Ps. 133:1 implicitly illustrate. It is also more precise than the meaning of *ḥēleq,* "share," because *naḥ^{a}lâ* properly refers only to a portion of the patriarchal estate. The two terms appear in synonymous parallelism (Gen. 31:14; Nu. 18:20; Dt. 10:9; 12:12; 14:27,29; 18:1; 32:9), but there is a tendency to use *naḥ^{a}lâ* in a metaphorical or figurative sense (2 S. 20:1; 1 K. 12:16; 2 Ch. 10:16; Job 20:29; 27:13; 31:2).

2. *nḥl and yrš.* From the sixth century on, under the influence of Aramaic, which uses *yrṯ* > *yrt* in the same sense as Heb. *nḥl,* we find the noun *y^{e}ruššâ* used in the sense of "(inherited) portion" (Dt. 2:5,9,12,19; 3:20; Josh. 1:15; 12:6f.; Ps. 61:6[Eng. v. 5]; 2 Ch. 20:11; 1QS 4:24). The verb *yrš* also seems to have been used as a synonym of *nḥl* (e.g., Isa. 57:13; Ps. 69:36f.[35f.]), but it is difficult to determine this with assurance for the biblical period. Normally, only a direct male descendant could inherit. In reality, however, *yrš* expresses the opposite of regular succession from father to son: it describes the situation when someone comes into possession of alien property, whereas *nāḥal* refers to division of the entire patriarchal estate. It follows that *yrš* is used less in the sense of "become someone's heir, inherit from," than "acquire, take possession of, acquire illegally, dispossess, supplant, take someone's place."[1]

For example, Abraham laments that he has no offspring and therefore fears that "a slave will take my place" (*yôrēš 'ōṯî,* Gen. 15:3). Sarah demands that Hagar and Ishmael

---

J. Pedersen, *ILC,* I-II, 89-96; G. von Rad, "The Promised Land and Yahweh's Land in the Hexateuch," *The Problem of the Hexateuch and Other Essays* (Eng. trans., Philadelphia, 1966), 79-93; N. H. Snaith, "The Daughters of Zelophehad," *VT,* 16 (1966), 124-27; É. Szlechter, "Les lois néo-babyloniennes (II)," *Revue internationale des droits de l'antiquité,* 3rd ser., 19 (1972), 43-127, esp. 79-110; R. Taubenschlag, *The Law of Greco-Roman Egypt in the Light of the Papyri* (1955, repr. Milan, 1972), 137-166; W. Thiel, "Die Anfänge von Landwirtschaft und Bodenrecht in der Frühzeit Alt-Israels," *Altorientalische Forschungen,* 7 (1980), 127-141; E. E. Urbach, "Inheritance Laws and Afterlife," *Proceedings of the Fourth World Congress of Jewish Studies,* I (1967), 133-141, 263 (Heb.); A. van Selms, *Marriage and Family Life in Ugaritic Literature. POS,* 1 (1954), 137-143; R. de Vaux, *AncIsr,* 53-55, 164-69; G. Wanke, "נַחֲלָה *naḥ^{a}lâ* 'possession,'" *TLOT,* II, 731-34; J. Weingreen, "The Case of the Daughters of Zelophehad," *VT,* 16 (1966), 518-522; H. Wildberger, "Israel und sein Land," *EvT,* 16 (1956), 404-422; R. Yaron, *Gifts in Contemplation of Death in Jewish and Roman Law* (Oxford, 1960); *idem, Intro. to the Law of the Aramaic Papyri* (Oxford, 1961), 65-78; S. Zeitlin, "Testamentary Succession," *The 75th Anniversary Volume of JQR,* ed. A. A. Neuman and S. Zeitlin (Philadelphia, 1967), 574-581.

1. → ירשׁ *yāraš* (VI, 368-396).

be cast out "lest the son of this slave woman become an heir" *(lō' yîraš)* along with her son Isaac (21:10). It is unbearable "that a maid should succeed her mistress" (*tîraš;* Prov. 30:23). The fratricide who would succeed to the entire inheritance is called *yôrēš* in 2 S. 14:7, better translated "usurper" than "heir." The rare occasions when the verb *yāraš* does refer to a legitimate heir (Gen. 15:5; Jer. 49:1) involve a play on words; the context contrasts a legitimate heir and a usurper. The notion of "making someone an heir" or "taking someone's place" can be used in various ways. We may recall that *yāraš* can be used in poetic parallelism with → ישׁב *yāšaḇ,* "settle" (Jer. 49:1; Ps. 69:36[35]).

3. *naḥ^alâ and 'ᵃḥuzzâ.* The noun *naḥᵃlâ* is often associated with *'ᵃḥuzzâ,* "possession." The phrase *'ᵃḥuzzaṯ naḥᵃlâ* therefore means "possession of an allotted portion" of an estate (Nu. 27:7; 32:32), while *naḥᵃlaṯ 'ᵃḥuzzâ* is an "allotted portion that one possesses" (Nu. 35:2). *'ᵃḥuzzâ* usually refers to land, but it can also refer to slaves owned in perpetuity (Lev. 25:45f.). Legally, however, it cannot refer to real estate of which one has temporary usufruct but no right of ownership. Cf. Lev. 27:22-24, which speaks of a field that has been acquired for a specific period of time but without full title *('ᵃḥuzzâ).* This legal meaning of *'ᵃḥuzzâ* also occurs in 2 Ch. 11:14, where the pastureland *(migrāš)* of the Levites is distinguished from their *'ᵃḥuzzâ.* In fact, the former is generally considered to be communal property, while houses and the cultivated land are private property. For the same reason, Josh. 14:4 contrasts the arable parcels *(ḥēleq)* with the pastureland *(migrāš),* and Josh. 21:11f. makes a clear distinction between pastureland *(migrāš)* and cultivated land *(śāḏeh).*

Strictly speaking, *nḥl* refers only to an allotted portion to which one has a claim by right of inheritance, while *'ḥz* refers to all the property that one has actually acquired, whether by purchase or by some other bilateral transaction, gift, inheritance, prescription, usucapion, or the like. For this reason, the tribe of Levi has an *'ᵃḥuzzâ* (but cf. Ezk. 44:28), although it received no *naḥᵃlâ* in the strict sense. This distinction is already quite clear at Mari, where the verb *naḫālu* refers to the allotment of a hereditary portion from a parent's estate, while a causative form of *aḫāzu* refers to concession of landed property by the king.[2]

The strictly legal usage of the root *nḥl* is relatively rare in the OT, but it lies behind every instance of the theological or metaphorical sense, which appears in a significant number of texts. It is therefore important first to analyze the basic meaning, which represents the true semantic value of *nḥl.*

II. Inheritance.

1. *Terminology.* Although not a single written will survives from ancient Israel, it is certain that a father before his death "set his house in order" (2 S. 17:23; 2 K. 20:1 par. Isa. 38:1), i.e., he determined the division of the property he was leaving behind (Dt. 21:16; Sir. 14:13; 33:24). Furthermore, before his death he could make advances

2. *ARM,* X, 90, 29-31, 33-36, respectively.

from the estate. This is clear not only from a few relatively late texts (Tob. 8:21; Sir. 33:20-24; cf. Lk. 15:12), but also from the law governing crown property (Ezk. 46:16-18). This text distinguishes clearly between a gift to a son, who thus becomes legal owner of part of the inheritance, and a gift to a servant, who merely has right of usufruct until *šᵉnaṯ haddᵉrôr,* i.e., until the year of release for debts and encumbrances (but cf. Prov. 17:2). This may be the case with the portion of the inheritance entreated by the son in Lk. 15:12; there may be an allusion to this practice in Prov. 20:21: "An estate coveted in the beginning [cf. Arab. *mabḫala,* 'object of desire'] will not be blessed in the end." Sir. 45:25 (read *nḥlt 'š lb!ny kbwdw;* cf. Mal. 1:6) appears to imply the possibility of disinheriting an unworthy son.

The actual term for distribution of the estate was the hiphil of *nḥl* (Dt. 21:16; Ezk. 46:18; Prov. 13:22), with a double accusative specifying the recipients of the inheritance and the property distributed. In addition, the qal of *nḥl* with a singular object (Nu. 34:17f.; Josh. 19:49) and the piel with a plural object (Nu. 34:29; Josh. 13:32; 14:1; 19:51) are used in the same sense, while the hithpael serves as the reflexive of the piel without any additional nuance of its own (Lev. 25:46; Nu. 32:18; 33:54; 34:13; Isa. 14:2; Ezk. 47:13). This same meaning must be assigned to the form *inḫil* from Mari, which might, however, be a causative form **yanḫīl* > Akk. *inḫil,* because the verb *naḫālu* is used in the basic stem with the meaning "come into possession (of a *niḫlatu*)."[3] Since, however, Arab. *naḥala* I means "give, grant," *yinḥal* (qal) and the basic stem *inḫil* may be correct with the meaning "grant, bestow." The portion allotted to the rightful heir constitutes his *naḥᵃlâ* and legally becomes his *'ᵃḥuzzâ,* "property."

The qal of *nḥl* means "come into possession of a *naḥᵃlâ*" (Jgs. 11:2); the associated accusative refers to the allotted property: *'ereṣ* (Ex. 23:30; Josh. 19:49; Isa. 57:13; Ezk. 47:14) or *naḥᵃlâ* (Nu. 18:23f.; 35:8; Josh. 17:6). Note that the formula *naḥᵃlâ nāḥal* is already attested at Mari: *niḫlatam inaḫḫil,*[4] "he will inherit an inheritance" (probably from Sūmu-Epu, who has just died[5]), and possibly in the Phoenician inscription on the bronze spatula of ʿAzrubaʿal (end of the 11th century B.C.: *nḥl tnḥl*).[6]

Distribution of the estate should be governed by common and statutory law. Only three legal texts (Dt. 21:15-17; Nu. 27:1-11, supplemented by 36:6-9; Ezk. 46:16-18) deal with inheritance, and they discuss only special cases. It is therefore absolutely necessary to supplement these limited sources of information with the pieces of legal information scattered throughout the OT that are sometimes not easy to interpret.

2. *Primogeniture.* In principle only sons have a right to inherit. Among them, the firstborn has a special status: he receives not just a double portion but two-thirds of his father's estate, as *pî-šᵉnayim* states explicitly in Dt. 21:17 (cf. Mishnah *Bek.* 8.9).

This expression is used metaphorically outside the context of inheritance by a

3. *ARM,* I, 91, vo. 6.
4. *Ibid.*
5. *Ibid.,* 5.
6. *KAI,* 3, 3f.

firstborn son in 2 K. 2:9 and also in Zec. 13:8, where it clearly means "two-thirds." This accords with West Semitic practices attested at Amorite Mari as early as the eighteenth century B.C.

According to an adoption contract,[7] an adopted son enjoyed the right of primogeniture, including its material benefits with respect to the distribution of the estate: of the patrimony, he could withdraw a specific portion, *šittān,* "two-thirds." The same provision is found in a Neo-Babylonian law that reflects Aramean or Chaldean traditions but can apply collectively to the children born of two successive marriages by a common father, who has remarried after the death of his first wife.[8] The sons of the first marriage collectively receive two-thirds of the patrimony, the sons of the second marriage only one-third. This regulation gives the children of the first marriage the privilege otherwise associated with primogeniture.

The law in Dt. 21:15-17 protects the right of the firstborn: the father is forbidden to favor the son of a favorite wife to the detriment of the firstborn son of a less favored wife. In the case of twins, the first to emerge from the womb is the firstborn (Gen. 25:24-26; 38:27-30). Despite the legal privileges of the firstborn, the OT furnishes numerous examples of how younger children supplant the firstborn — besides the case of Esau, who sold his right of primogeniture to Jacob (25:29-34). These examples serve well to illustrate the gratuitous nature of divine election. They do not, however, show that the ancient Israelites had a customary law protecting the last-born, like that found among some peoples. This motif of gratuitous divine election is already attested at Ugarit, where the god El foretells that Keret's wife will bear him seven sons and seven daughters, declaring: "The youngest of them I will make the firstborn."[9]

The firstborn could, however, lose his right of primogeniture in consequence of a serious transgression. This might account for the division of the promised land among the sons of Jacob, in which Reuben, the firstborn, does not receive two-thirds. His incest (Gen. 35:22) lost him the right of primogeniture (49:3f.). According to a late tradition (1 Ch. 5:1f.), the right of primogeniture passed to Joseph's two sons, Ephraim and Manasseh, who shared equally the privilege of a complete inheritance from Israel/Jacob. This interpretation of 1 Ch. 5:1f. implies a development in the law of inheritance, awarding the firstborn merely a double portion of the patrimony. Later, the disposition described in the LXX and Targ. of Dt. 21:17 is explained in the same way. According to the earlier account (Gen. 48:5f.), each of Joseph's two sons received a full portion, because through adoption their grandfather had given them the same status as his own sons (cf. Prov. 13:22). Finally, Josh. 17:14-18 justifies the allotment of a double portion to the sons of Joseph on the grounds of their number.

3. *Daughters.* Daughters inherit only when there is no male heir. This legal principle was established with respect to the daughters of Zelophehad in Nu. 27:1-8 (cf. Josh.

---

7. *ARM,* VIII, 1.
8. §15.
9. *KTU,* 1.15, III, 16.

17:3-6), but subject to the condition that they must marry within their father's tribe, in order to prevent the family estate from falling into the hands of a different clan (Nu. 36:1-9). This restrictive condition, however, is cited only in late additions (Nu. 36:5-9), and seems to enshrine a modification of ancient legal custom. A similar practice is found, for example, in an Old Babylonian law from Nippur: "If a man dies and has no son, his unmarried daughters are to be his heirs";[10] there is no restriction on their right to marry. But the case of Eleazar's daughters, who married their cousins (1 Ch. 23:22), fits with the restriction ascribed to Moses in Nu. 36:5-9; this is probably the "decree of Moses" alluded to in Tob. 7:10-13.

There are, however, two noteworthy exceptions. In Gen. 31:14 Rachel and Leah lament that they cannot count on a *naḥᵃlâ* in the house of their father, who has spent everything. Job's three daughters receive a *naḥᵃlâ* along with their seven brothers (Job 42:13-15). These two exceptions are not expressions of later legal practice but reminiscences of a vanished era when a wealthy father could assign a portion of his estate to all his children. New material relating to this practice has been provided by the Emar tablets, dating from the thirteenth century B.C.[11] The practice is confirmed by a legal document from stratum VII at Alalakh (17th century B.C.), which deals with a lawsuit over the distribution of an estate within the royal family. Citing the deposition of a certain Abi-Haddu, King Niqmepa of Yamḫad determines that the lady Bitt-Haddi is to receive a portion of the inheritance after her brother Abba'el has chosen his portion from among the parcels defined by court officials.[12]

4. *Distribution.* Abba'el is accordingly the principal heir and may select the first portion, whatever he chooses. This right is normally assigned to the firstborn, who does not, however, himself undertake the division of the estate. This is done by referees, court officials as at Alalakh, or the youngest son, if the father has not done so during his own lifetime. From the texts describing the distribution of the promised land among the descendants of Israel/Jacob, we may conclude that a similar practice prevailed in ancient Israel.

Moses assigns their *naḥᵃlâ* to the tribes of Reuben, Gad, and the half-tribe of Manasseh (Josh. 13:15-32; cf. Nu. 32; 34:14f.). Note that although Reuben has presumably lost his right of primogeniture, he takes the first portion (Nu. 32:1-5). The distribution of a *naḥᵃlâ* to the tribes west of the Jordan is regulated by a group of referees: Eleazar, Joshua, and a leader from each tribe (Nu. 34:16-29; Josh. 14:1). Although economic considerations led to division of the land on the basis of the number of people in each tribe (Nu. 26:53-56; 33:54), it was ultimately done by lot,[13] which determined the *naḥᵃlâ* of each individual tribe (Nu. 26:55f.; 33:54; 34:13; 36:2f.; Josh. 13:6; 14:2; 15:1; 16:1; 18:6–19:49; Jgs. 1:3). This contradiction is probably due to the

---

10. M. Civil, *Studies in Honor of Benno Landsberger. AS,* 16 (1965), 4-6.
11. See Huehnergard.
12. Alalakh Tablets, *7.
13. → גורל *gôrāl* (II, 450-56).

influence of the laws governing distribution of an estate among brothers on the narratives describing the distribution of the promised land. The Middle Assyrian laws likewise envision a lottery that assigns each brother his portion after the firstborn has selected one of the two portions that are his by right according to Assyrian law.[14]

5. *Collateral Lines.* If a man dies without issue, his *naḥ^{a}lâ* passes to his male relatives on his father's side in the sequence: brothers, brothers of his father, nearest relatives within the clan (Nu. 27:9-11). The *naḥ^{a}lâ* could not pass from one clan to another (Nu. 36). The rule is implicit in the ordinance governing the estate of the crown (Ezk. 46:16ff.), which reflects an ancient tradition, as well as in the story of Naboth (1 K. 21:1-19). Some have argued on the basis of 1 K. 21:15f. that the *naḥ^{a}lâ* of someone condemned to death fell to the king; the narrative makes clear, however, that Ahab committed an arbitrary act of confiscation, provoking the vengeance of heaven. Mic. 2:2 likewise condemns those who take possession of fields and houses and confiscate "people and their *naḥ^{a}lâ*" in payment of debts (cf. Isa. 5:8). For the duration of her widowhood, Naomi ceded the usufruct of the parcel that had belonged to her deceased husband (Ruth 4:3-6); but this case merely confirms the principle that an estate is inalienable. Naomi does not sell the *naḥ^{a}lâ* itself: it remains the property of her husband's descendants, whom Ruth is to bear in accordance with levirate law (Ruth 4:9f.).[15]

6. *Widows.* In principle a widow has no right to the *naḥ^{a}lâ* of her husband, which constituted his estate in the strict sense. A different principle is found in an Akkadian will from Ugarit, in which a certain Yarimānu leaves all his property to his wife Bidawe and empowers her to disinherit any of his sons who should dispute her right of succession, while leaving the property to the son who shows her respect.[16] In Jewish circles we find such a provision only in contracts from Elephantine dating from the fifth century B.C., where a widow without children may enjoy the estate of her deceased husband. It is possible, however, that her right is restricted to usufruct. In the story of Judith, which dates from the Hellenistic period, Judith is left enormous wealth by her husband, including household goods and land (Jgs. 8:7). Before her death, she distributes it to her husband's next of kin and to her own (16:24). Tradition, however, provided that a childless widow should return to the house of her father (Gen. 38:11; Lev. 22:13; Ruth 1:8) with her dowry and personal property, unless a levirate marriage kept her with her husband's family.[17] This provision accords with the Babylonian laws and the customary law of Nuzi, which state explicitly that a widow keeps her dowry. It also explains how the mother of Micah (Jgs. 17:1-4) can possess personal property apart from the *naḥ^{a}lâ* of her husband.

---

14. Tablet B, §1.
15. → מכר *mkr* (VIII, 291-96).
16. RS, 8.145; *ANET*^{3}, 546b.
17. → יבם *ybm* (V, 367-373).

If the widow had adult children, they provided for her support. If the children were still young, however, she administered their *naḥ^{a}lâ* as guardian (cf. Prov. 15:25; 23:10). This explains the story of the Shunammite woman in 2 K. 8:3-6 and the case of Naomi, who took care of the *naḥ^{a}lâ* of her deceased husband (Ruth 4).

7. *Division of Property.* It is important to know what family property constituted the *naḥ^{a}lâ* of the father that was divided among their heirs, so that each of them then came into possession of a *naḥ^{a}lâ*. Some have assumed that chattels were divided among the male offspring, while to preserve the family assets the real property was allotted to the firstborn son or kept as an undivided estate. The texts, however, suggest otherwise. A legal transaction from Mari, characterized by the use of the verb *naḫālum,* refers to a parcel of land *(eqlum)* taken from the lands of the clan of Avin and allotted to Yarim-Addu by his thirteen "brothers."[18] In another text the object of the verb *naḫālum* is "a field and a garden" *(eqlam u kirām).*[19] One document speaks of *eqlat*^{meš} *na-ḫa-li,* the hereditary land of a certain Allanšerdanu.[20] Finally, Jephthah was driven away by his brothers (Jgs. 11:2) so that he would not inherit any of their father's property *(lōʾ-tinḥal b^{e}ḇêṯ-ʾāḇînû);* the term *bayiṯ* shows that the reference is primarily to real property. In Dt. 21:17 the law requires the father to give to his firstborn son "two-thirds of *all* that he has," not just chattels. Finally, all of the texts referring to the division of the promised land presuppose that landed property could be divided, each tribe or clan receiving its *naḥ^{a}lâ*. Individual cases show that this was true not only with respect to clans but also with respect to individuals. The daughters of Zelophehad receive a *naḥ^{a}lâ* among their father's brothers (Nu. 27:4-7; Josh. 17:4,6), who even fear that the portions of the daughters will be lost to the clan if they marry someone belonging to a different tribe (Nu. 36:2-4). Joshua receives his own *naḥ^{a}lâ* in the hill country of Ephraim (Josh. 19:49f.; 24:30; Jgs. 2:9), while Caleb receives Hebron (Josh. 14:9,13f.).

Others theorize that a *naḥ^{a}lâ* in the strict sense was a piece of real property: a "parcel of land" (*ḥelqaṯ haśśāḏeh:* Ruth 4:3), a "vineyard" (*kerem:* 1 K. 21:1-19), "a field and a vineyard" (*śāḏeh wāḵārem:* Nu. 16:14[21]), or more generally "landed property" or a "house" (*bayiṯ:* Jgs. 11:2; Mic. 2:2; Lam. 5:2; Prov. 19:14). But a *naḥ^{a}lâ* can also consist of a "flock" (*ṣōʾn:* Mic. 7:14), "slaves" (*ʿeḇeḏ w^{e}ʾāmâ:* Lev. 25:44-46; *ʿ^{a}ḇāḏîm ûš^{e}p̱āḥōṯ:* Isa. 14:2), "money" (*kesep̱:* Eccl. 7:11-12a), or "chattels" (*hôn:* Prov. 19:14). A document from Elephantine regulates the distribution of slaves at the time of inheritance.[22] The *naḥ^{a}lâ* thus appears to comprise both real and movable property. The former constitutes the bulk of an estate, and the expression "return to one's *naḥ^{a}lâ*" means "go home" (Josh. 24:28; Jgs. 2:6; 21:23f.; Jer. 12:15; cf. Neh. 11:20). It is also clear that keeping a patrimonial estate intact was a major concern.

---

18. *ARM,* VIII, 11.
19. *ARM,* X, 90, 30f.
20. RS, 16.251, 7 (*PRU,* III, 109).
21. Cf. *ARM,* X, 90.
22. *AP,* 28.

Such estates were delimited by heaps of stones serving as boundary markers *(gᵉḇûlôṯ),* which it was forbidden to move (Dt. 19:14; 27:17; CD 1:16; cf. Hos. 5:10; Job 24:2; Prov. 15:25; 22:28; 23:10). Both clan solidarity and common law insisted that this property must not be alienated or at least that it remain within the family. It was bequeathed to descendants "forever" (*lᵉʿôlām:* Ex. 32:13; Lev. 25:46; Ps. 37:18; 119:111; 1 Ch. 28:8), i.e., the act denoted by the verb *nḥl* indicated a permanent transfer of the object in question. Finally, as the example of Naboth shows (1 K. 21), a smallholder would never relinquish the *naḥᵃlaṯ ʾāḇôṯ,* the parcel inherited from his ancestors (Nu. 36:3,8; 1 K. 21:3f.; Prov. 19:14; cf. Nu. 27:7; Isa. 58:14), if only because it often contained the family tomb (Josh. 24:30,32f.; Jgs. 2:9; 1 S. 25:1; 1 K. 2:34; cf. Gen. 23).

8. *Inalienability and Rights of the gōʾēl.* When circumstances required someone to relinquish (→ *māḵar*) usufruct of an estate, one of his immediate relatives, the *gōʾēl,*[23] exercised his prerogative in order to prevent the alienation of family property. The pertinent law is codified in Lev. 25:25-28. Jeremiah acquires the field of his cousin Hanamel as *gōʾēl* (Jer. 32:6-15). The text speaks of his "right of *yᵉruššâ*" (v. 8). Here *yᵉruššâ* is not yet synonymous with *naḥᵃlâ:* it does, however, mean that the *gōʾēl* has taken possession of the property of his nearest relative (cf. Nu. 27:11). The same practice informs the story of Ruth: the right of levirate is invoked in order to nullify the rights of the *gōʾēl* over time (Ruth 4).

These concrete examples, unique in the OT, illustrate the normal result: in return for compensation, the *gōʾēl* took possession of the *naḥᵃlâ,* which was not returned to the impoverished blood relatives. The law in Lev. 25:25-28, however, reflects an earlier practice based on the principle that real estate was inalienable for compensation: it could only be transferred gratis to the "nearest *gōʾēl.*" The latter claimed his right by "coming to his brother," i.e., actually exercising his proprietary right to the clan or family property. This right was the basis of the institution of the *gōʾēl.* Here we can see the survival of a socioeconomic situation in which real property was held collectively. Therefore Lev. 25:25-28 does not use the term *naḥᵃlâ,* which denotes an allotted inheritance, but *ʾᵃḥuzzâ,* which can also mean the "collective property" (Gen. 17:8; 36:43; 48:4; Lev. 14:34; etc.) belonging to a clan or *mišpāḥâ* (Lev. 25:10,21).

When conditions changed, it became customary for the *gōʾēl* who took ownership of a parcel of land belonging to the clan to pay compensation. Possession became ownership, and exercise of the *gōʾēl* right was transformed into a contract of purchase. Even though Jer. 32:6-15 tries to avoid the vocabulary of purchase by using different terminology, the true nature of the act is immediately clear. A similar purchase contract is already found at Mari;[24] the verb *naḫālum* is used for the assignment of the real estate and its price. The procedure may be compared to adoption contracts at Nuzi, where the seller goes through the fiction of adopting the buyer so as to receive a gift, thus circumventing the prohibition against selling.

---

23. → גאל *gāʾal* (II, 350-55).
24. *ARM,* VIII, 13.

III. Inheritance of the Tribes and Israel.

1. *Division of the Promised Land.* Division of an estate among heirs served the authors of the Deuteronomistic history and P as a leitmotif for the division of the promised land among the descendants of Israel/Jacob. The distribution took place *b^{e}gōrāl,* "by lot" (Nu. 26:55f.; 33:54; 34:13; 36:2f.; Josh. 14–21; Jgs. 1:3), at the central sanctuary of Shiloh "before Yahweh" (Josh. 18:1-10; 19:51; cf. 13:6b). This account was revised by a redactor in Nu. 34:29; now it is Yahweh who gives the command "to apportion the inheritance for the Israelites in the land of Canaan" (cf. v. 2). The number of *n^{e}ḥālôṯ,* "inheritances" (Josh. 19:51; cf. Isa. 49:8), agrees with the number of the sons of Israel/Jacob (Nu. 32:32; 34:14f.; Dt. 29:7[8]; Josh. 13:8,23,28; 14:2f.; 15:20; 16:5,8f.; 18:2,4,7,20,28; 19:1-48; Jgs. 18:1), with the exception that Manasseh and Ephraim, the sons of Joseph, both receive a full portion, while Levi does not receive any portion at all (Nu. 18:20,23f.; 26:62; Dt. 10:9; 12:12; 14:27,29; 18:1f.; Josh. 13:14,33; 14:3; 18:7; Ezk. 44:28; Sir. 45:22; but cf. Ezk. 48:13f.), and Caleb receives a special portion (Josh. 14:9,13f.).[25]

2. *Levites.* The special case of Levi is explained by the fact that the Levites did not actually have their own territory. The theological explanation was that "Yahweh is their *naḥ^{a}lâ*" (Nu. 18:20; Dt. 10:9; 18:2; Josh. 13:33; Ezk. 44:28; cf. Ps. 16:5f.); but the situation was also described as a punishment for the rebellion of Korah (Nu. 18:20; cf. 16:14). Instead of their *naḥ^{a}lâ,* the Levites receive the income of the "priesthood of Yahweh" (Josh. 18:7), i.e., the "tithes" (Nu. 18:21,24,26) and the "sacrificial portions belonging to Yahweh" (Dt. 18:1; Josh. 13:14; Sir. 45:20-22,25), together with the Levitical cities, which were excluded from the lands belonging to the individual tribes (Nu. 35:2-8; Josh. 21:3).

3. *Israel/Jacob.* The division of the promised land "among the sons of Israel" presupposes that this land was the portion of their father, the property of Israel/Jacob (*naḥ^{a}laṯ yiśrā'ēl:* Jgs. 20:6; *naḥ^{a}laṯ ya'^{a}qōḇ:* Isa. 58:14; *naḥ^{a}laṯ bêṯ-yiśrā'ēl:* Ezk. 35:15), as distinct, e.g., from the *naḥ^{a}lâ* of Esau (Mal. 1:3), i.e., Edom (cf. Ezk. 35:15; 36:12), or the *naḥ^{a}lâ* of the nations (Jer. 12:15; cf. Ps. 111:6). In his prayer at the dedication of the temple, Solomon addresses the following petition to Yahweh: "Then hear in heaven . . . and grant rain on *your* land, which you have given to *your people* as an *inheritance*" (1 K. 8:36 [Deuteronomistic history] par. 2 Ch. 6:27). Israel — the name refers to both the eponymous ancestor and his lineage — received this portion from Yahweh. Although the words "father" and "son" do not even appear in the Deuteronomist's prayer, the theologoumenon implies the notion that Yahweh is Israel's father, has begotten Israel (Dt. 32:6; cf. Ex. 4:22f.; Isa. 63:13; 64:7[8]; Jer. 3:4; 31:9; Hos. 11:1; Mal. 1:6; Sir. 51:10), treated Israel as a favorite son and given him a glorious inheritance (Ps. 47:5[4]), or else wanted to adopt Israel in order to give him a beautiful *naḥ^{a}lâ* (Jer. 3:19).

---

25. On Joseph's sons see above; on Levi → לֵוִי *lēwî* (VII, 483-503).

This theme is undoubtedly based on the notion of patriarchal inheritance, although the "historical" traditions of the promise and occupation of the land also play a role. Thus the gift of this *naḥ^{a}lâ* to Israel is represented as the fulfillment of the promise to the patriarchs (Ex. 32:13; Ps. 105:8-11; Ezk. 47:14; 1 Ch. 16:15-18); the extermination of the Canaanite population becomes the means whereby Yahweh has his people take possession of the *naḥ^{a}lâ* (Ex. 23:30; Dt. 4:38; 20:16; Ps. 47:4f.[5f.]; 78:55; 135:10-12; 136:17-22; cf. Ps. 111:6). Later, the allotment of Canaan to Israel becomes a Deuteronomistic leitmotif (Dt. 4:21,38; 12:9f.; 15:4; 19:3,10,14; 21:23; 24:4; 25:19; 26:1; cf. Jer. 3:18; 12:14; 17:4; 11QTemple 64:13); it is Joshua's task to bring Israel into possession of its *naḥ^{a}lâ* (Dt. 1:38; 3:28; 31:7; Josh. 1:6; 11:23; 13:6f.; Sir. 46:1). This concept refers to the land but can include the cities of the vanquished nations (Dt. 20:16; 11QTemple 62:13) or their inhabitants (Josh. 23:4).

4. *The New Age.* Toward the end of the exile, the secondary material in Ps. 69:36f. (35f.) restricts the *naḥ^{a}lâ* to Zion and the cities of Judah, as the heritage of those who are faithful to Yahweh. This realistic perspective contrasts with the hopes that find expression in the prophetic writings of this era. According to Zeph. 2:9, the remnant of Israel will take possession *(yinḥālû)* of Moab and Ammon; according to Isa. 14:2, the house of Israel will take possession *(w^{e}yiṯnaḥ^{a}lû)* of the nations as their heritage, so as to enslave them. In Isa. 49:8, by contrast, Yahweh simply promises to establish Israel once more in its desolate heritage.

According to Ezk. 45:1-7; 47:13–48:29, the land of Canaan will be reapportioned after the exile. It will be divided into equal parallel tracts without regard for historical and geographical realities. The "holy district" *(qōḏeš)* of Yahweh (45:1-6; 48:8-21), which is reserved for the priests (45:5; cf. 48:9-12), will occupy the whole central region, with the sanctuary at its center (45:2f.; 48:8). A region with the same area as that of the priests and parallel to it is allotted to the Levites (45:5; cf. 48:13), who thus receive their own territory. The holdings of the city of Jerusalem (45:6; cf. 48:15-20) and the prince (45:7; cf. 48:21f.) will also be in the center of the land. The twelve tribes receive territories to the north and south of the lands constituting the heritage of the priests, the Levites, the city, and the prince (47:13–48:7; 48:23-29). The aliens who have dwelt among the Israelites for more than a generation are also conceded the right to a *naḥ^{a}lâ* (47:22f.).

Although the term *gôrāl* is not used in this context, the apportionment of the land by lot is implied semantically by the hiphil of *npl* (Ezk. 45:1; 47:22; 48:29). Ezekiel does not say who is to carry out this new distribution of the promised land; by using the hithpael of *nḥl* (47:13), he merely indicates that the tribes are to divide the land among themselves. The hithpael of *nḥl* appears also in Nu. 32:18; 33:54; 34:13 in the context of division of the land (cf. Isa. 14:2) and in Lev. 25:46 in the context of inheritance of alien slaves. Here the hithpael serves as the reflexive of the piel, which has the same meaning as the hiphil.

IV. The King. The father-and-son relation is associated also with the *naḥ^{a}lâ* Yahweh allots to the ruler. According to 2 S. 7:14 (cf. 1 Ch. 17:13; 22:10; 28:6); Ps. 2:7f.;

89:27f.(26f.), Yahweh is father to the king and the king is a son, even the firstborn son (Ps. 89:28[27]), to Yahweh. Therefore Yahweh gives the king a *naḥ*ª*lâ,* ideally all the nations of the earth (2:8) or hegemony over all the kings of the earth (89:28[27]). This notion is an expression of the royal ideology of the ancient Near East, which is grounded in the existence of a special relationship between the king and the deity.

This theme appears as early as text A 1121 from Mari.[26] In an oracle for King Zimri-Lim, the god Adad of Kalassu reminds him that he elevated him to the throne of his father, but that he can likewise "take back the heritage from his hand" *(niḫlatam ina qātišu eleqqe).*[27] The continuation of the oracle shows that this "heritage" comprises the throne, the land, and its capital.[28] If the king does not give the deity all the cattle that the latter demands, the deity can take back his "heritage." If the king is obedient, however, Adad of Kallassu will give him "throne upon throne, city upon city, and the land of the east and of the west."[29] "In view of this heritage (*ana niḫlatim*[ki])," the cult prophet *(āpilu)* of Adad of Kallassu "guards the territory of Alatum,"[30] a statement whose precise meaning is unknown.

V. Yahweh.

1. *Mythology.* Although the land of Canaan is frequently called the "heritage of Israel," many other texts call the land or the Israelites dwelling in it the "heritage of Yahweh." This double motif is of mythological origin and goes back to the notion of the division of the nations or their lands among the sons of the gods. According to Dt. 32:8 (LXX and 4QDt[j]), *ʿelyôn,* the Most High, "apportioned the nations as a heritage among the divine sons *(b*ᵉ*nê ʾ*ᵉ*lōhîm).*" The apportionment took place according to the number of the divine sons, called "sons of Elyon" in Ps. 82:6(5). The Ugaritic pantheon includes seventy sons of Athirat,[31] corresponding to the seventy nations listed in Gen. 10. The same number appears later in apocryphal texts (T.Naph. 8f.; 1 En. 89:59ff.; 90:22,25) as well as in the Talmud and Midrash,[32] which fix the number of the nations and their "angels" or "princes" at seventy (or seventy-two, to achieve a multiple of twelve; cf. Sir. 17:17). The Midr. *Pirqe de Rabbi Eliezer* 24 explicitly mentions Dt. 32:8 in this connection. The War Scroll from Qumran ascribes to God "the confusion of tongues and the dispersal of the nations, the dwelling place of the clans and the heritage of the lands *(nḥlt ʾrṣwt)*" (1QM 10:14f.), but does not mention angels.

In Ugaritic mythology the father of the gods gave a land to each of his children as an inheritance. Thus the city *hmry* is the heritage *(ʾrṣ nḥlt)* of Môt, while *ḥkpt* is the

---

26. Published by G. Dossin, "Une tablette inédite de Mari," *Studies in OT Prophecy. Festschrift T. H. Robinson* (Edinburgh, 1950), 103-6.

27. L. 15.

28. Ll. 16f.

29. Ll. 19-23.

30. L. 27.

31. *KTU,* 1.4, VI, 46.

32. *ZDMG,* 57 (1903), 474; *ZAW,* 19 (1899), 1-14; 20 (1900), 38ff.; 24 (1904), 311; *RÉJ,* 54 (1907), 54.

heritage of the god Qadeš-Amrur.[33] The mythological motif of apportioning the earth and the nations among the divine sons survived for centuries; it reappears in Philo of Byblos: "When Kronos was journeying through the inhabited world, he gave his daughter Athena dominion over Attica." Then "he gave the city of Byblos to the goddess Baaltis, alias Dione, and to Poseidon he gave Beirut. . . . When Kronos came to the land of the south wind, he gave all of Egypt to the god Tauthos [Thoth] as his residence."[34]

This tradition in Philo, along with the use of *'rṣ nḥlt* at Ugarit and the hiphil of *nḥl* in Dt. 32:8, leaves no doubt that the myth projects into the world of the gods the way a wealthy father determines the distribution of his estate as he pleases. According to OT tradition, Jacob would be the portion allotted to Yahweh (Dt. 32:9 ["Israel" in Sam., LXX]), even though all the nations should be Yahweh's portion, as Ps. 82:8 seems to claim *(kî 'attâ tinḥal bᵉkol-haggôyim).* In the OT, however, the identification of Yahweh with the Most High, who undertakes the distribution of the nations (cf. Dt. 7:6; Sir. 17:17), confuses the picture.

2. *Double Meaning.* The OT documents call the people Yahweh's *naḥᵃlâ* (Dt. 4:20; 9:26,29; 1 S. 10:1; 2 S. 20:19; 21:3; 1 K. 8:51,53; 2 K. 21:14; Isa. 19:25; 47:6; 63:17; Jer. 10:16; 12:8f.; 51:19; Jo. 2:17; 4:2[3:2]; Mic. 7:14,18; Ps. 28:9; 33:12; 74:2; 78:62,71; 94:5,14; 106:5,40) more often than they call the land his *naḥᵃlâ* (1 S. 26:19; 2 S. 14:16; Jer. 2:7; 12:7; 16:18; 50:11; Ps. 68:10[9]). The land is still called *naḥᵃlâ* in 1QM 12:12; 19:4, but the *Hodayoth* once again see God's *naḥᵃlâ* in his people (1QH 6:8).

According to OT tradition, Yahweh chose the people of Israel to make them his *naḥᵃlâ* (1 K. 8:53; Ps. 33:12), as Moses requested (Ex. 34:9). Israel became the "tribe of his heritage" (Isa. 63:17; Jer. 10:16; 51:19; Ps. 74:2) and the "flock of his heritage" (Mic. 7:14). The use of this figurative expression does not emphasize the transfer or inheritance of property, but rather the constant, enduring nature of its possession. The notion of permanent possession is in fact intimately associated with the concept of *naḥᵃlâ,* which constitutes a family's ancient property, an indisputable possession that could not be transferred from one clan to another.

Jer. 12:7-9 combines the two formulations of this motif: the *naḥᵃlâ* of Yahweh comprises both his people (vv. 8f.) and his land (*bayiṯ:* v. 7; cf. Hos. 8:1; 9:15; Zec. 9:8). Here the term *bayiṯ* does not mean "house" but "real property" (cf. Jgs. 11:2), "the land that is Yahweh's possession" (*'ereṣ 'ᵃḥuzzaṯ YHWH:* Josh. 22:19). The same idea is expressed in Lev. 25:23 (redactional): "The land is mine; with me you are but aliens and tenants."

3. *Yahweh's Land, Holy Land.* The first element of this statement, "the land is mine," reflects the text of the covenant promise as recorded in Ex. 19:5. The expression "alien

33. On Môt see *KTU,* 1.4, VIII, 11-14; 1.5, II, 15f. On Qadeš-Amrur see *KTU,* 1.3, VI, 15f.
34. Cited by Eusebius *Praep. Evang.* 1.10.30-39.

and settler *(gēr wᵉtôšāḇ)* beside someone" is a stereotyped formula (Gen. 23:4; Lev. 25:35-47; Nu. 35:15; Ps. 39:13[12]; 1 Ch. 29:15) denoting an alien given permanent welcome in a neighboring territory, but without all the rights of a native citizen. As a consequence, Canaan is not the "inheritance of Israel." Israel is to think of itself as a guest lodged by Yahweh in a land that is Yahweh's own possession and therefore holy. Therefore Jeremiah twice describes Canaan as the "inheritance of Yahweh" when attacking the desecration of the land through idolatry (Jer. 2:7; 16:18). Jer. 16:18 describes the idols as "carcasses" that, if not buried, pollute the land. Dt. 21:22f., too, requires the burial of executed criminals on the grounds that otherwise the land as *naḥᵃlâ* would be defiled. Similarly, the series of laws prohibiting incest (Lev. 18) concludes with an admonition making clear that dissolute sexual behavior defiles the land; this is why it vomited out the nations that dwelt in it before Israel (vv. 24-28). This commentary by the redactor of the Holiness Code therefore assumes that the land of Canaan already belonged to Yahweh before the tribes of Israel conquered it.

The land of Canaan is described also as Yahweh's inheritance in texts that speak of other lands as being unclean (Am. 7:17). Those who are exiled from the holy land are removed thereby from the presence of Yahweh; they no longer share in the *naḥᵃlâ* and must worship other gods. In the early period Yahweh was thought of as being associated so intimately with "his land" (Hos. 9:3; 1 K. 8:36 par. 2 Ch. 6:27) that people believed it impossible to worship him in an alien land. Even David could not imagine a cult of Yahweh outside the promised land, and lamented being forced into exile so that he no longer had any share in the *naḥᵃlaṯ YHWH* (1 S. 26:19). Naaman took some Israelite soil with him so that he could offer sacrifice to Yahweh (2 K. 5:17).

It was not only outside Israel that people felt it was impossible to sense the presence of Yahweh. The dead, too, were "cut off from the *naḥᵃlâ* of God" (2 S. 14:16) and were no longer able to give him praise (Ps. 6:6[5]; 30:10[9]; 88:11f.[10f.]; 115:17; Isa. 38:18f.). Furthermore, the soil of Canaan could be so defiled that Yahweh had to forsake it. The notion of such a departure by a national god was by no means unique to the religious mentality of Israel. The Moabite Mesha Inscription (9th century) furnishes an excellent extrabiblical parallel: Mesha considers that Omri's conquest of Moab was caused ultimately by the national god, "for Chemosh was angry with his land."[35] This anger led him to forsake his land and let it fall into the hands of strangers. In the OT, Jeremiah draws on this ancient notion, incorporating it in his prophetic message. He combines the theme of the land as Yahweh's inheritance with that of the people as Yahweh's inheritance. According to Jeremiah, therefore, Yahweh forsakes his *naḥᵃlâ*, his land (Jer. 12:7), because he has grown to hate his people (v. 8).

The notion reappears in Ezekiel: the glory of Yahweh[36] departs from the Jerusalem temple (Ezk. 9:3; 10:18f.; 11:22f.), an unmistakable sign of the imminent destruction of the city and the sanctuary. Ezekiel does not use the term *naḥᵃlâ*, but Ps. 79, which probably refers to these same events, speaks of the temple as the *naḥᵃlâ* of Yahweh

---

35. *KAI*, 181; *TSSI*, I, 74, 76, quotation from l. 5.
36. → כבוד *kāḇôḏ* (VII, 22-38).

(v. 1). Toward the end of the exile, Zec. 2:16(12) proclaims that Yahweh will once more take possession of his *naḥ^{a}lâ* in the holy land; now, however, his portion is limited to the territory of Judah.

4. *"Mountain of God's Inheritance."* Ps. 48:3(2) identifies Mt. Zion with Mt. Zaphon, which appears in Ugaritic literature as the inheritance of Baʿal *(ǵr nḥlty).*[37] This identification raises the question whether Ps. 79:1 does not contain an echo of this ancient Canaanite tradition, transferred to the temple mount.

Even if the Ugaritic documents did not influence the Israelite authors directly, the religion of the inhabitants of Ugarit was similar to that of the Canaanite population from which Israel borrowed so much, including its religious vocabulary. It is therefore not at all surprising to find an exact equivalent to *ǵr nḥlty* in Ex. 15:17, where Yahweh's dwelling place is called *har naḥ^{a}lāṯ^{e}ḵā.* Quite generally, this section makes reference to the "establishment and possession of the sanctuary on Zion by Yahweh."[38] It is highly probable, however, that Ex. 15:17 refers instead to the hill country west of the Jordan, since the text says that Yahweh planted his people on "the mountain of his inheritance" and made them dwell there. Now the place where Yahweh settled his people is not Mt. Zion but the land of Canaan, which the context of v. 15 mentions explicitly. The sanctuary that Yahweh established is therefore not the Jerusalem temple but the holy land, in which Yahweh settles his people after it has been taken from its earlier inhabitants. Furthermore, other OT texts use such expressions as "holy mountain" of Yahweh (Isa. 57:13), "mountains" of Yahweh (Isa. 65:9), "territory [*g^{e}ḇûl*] of holiness," and "mountain that his right hand created" (Ps. 78:54) for the promised land. Isa. 57:13 and Ps. 78:54f. even combine this terminology with the *naḥ^{a}lâ* theme, because those who are faithful to Yahweh "shall inherit [his] holy mountain" (*yinḥal* par. *yîraš:* Isa. 57:13), where Yahweh has prepared a *naḥ^{a}lâ* for them (Ps. 78:54f.). Thus the "mountain of God's inheritance" in Ex. 15:17 would appear to be the hill country of Ephraim, which was first occupied by the Israelite tribes (cf. Josh. 17:15-18).

In the OT tradition, then, we can see various adaptations of the Canaanite motif of the "holy mountain" as *naḥ^{a}lâ* of a deity. This image was applied first to the hilly regions west of the Jordan, then more comprehensively to the entire holy land, and finally to the temple of Jerusalem (Ps. 79:1).

VI. Metaphorical Usage.

1. *ḥlq Parallel to nḥlh.* The metaphorical use of *naḥ^{a}lâ*[39] manifests itself already in Sheba's call to revolt, where *ḥlq* parallels *nḥlh* (2 S. 20:1; 1 K. 12:16; 2 Ch. 10:16). The expression *lō' naḥ^{a}lâ-lānû b^{e}ḇen-yišay* means that Israel can expect nothing from David. The same parallelism of *ḥlq* and *nḥlh* also appears in Job, where *naḥ^{a}lâ* means

37. *KTU,* 1.3, III, 29f.

38. J. Jeremias, "Lade und Zion," *Probleme biblischer Theologie. Festschrift G. von Rad* (Munich, 1971), 196.

39. See above.

"lot" or "fate" (20:29; 27:13; 31:2). The word is used in the same way in Isa. 54:17 and somewhat later in the rule of the Qumran Community (1QS 4:16,24), where the use of the subst. *nḥlh* corresponds to that of the verb *nḥl*.

2. *Essene Theology of Predestination.* According to 1QS 4:26, God has assigned humankind portions *(wayyanḥîl)* in the spirit of truth and in the spirit of wickedness by casting lots *(gôrālôṯ)* over each individual to determine his or her spirit for the day of judgment. Thus God has given those he has chosen a portion in the lot of the holy ones (*wayyanḥîlēm b^egôral q^eḏôšîm:* 1QS 11:7f.). From that time on, all enter into possession *(yinḥ^alû)* of their fate. It follows that those who have received a portion of truth and righteousness hate wickedness, while those who have a share *(y^eruššâ)* in the lot of wickedness despise the truth (1QS 4:24f.).

Here a theology of predestination uses the terminology of inheritance. The fate of each individual, denoted by *naḥ^alâ* or *y^eruššâ,* is determined by God, who casts the "lot of the holy ones" *(gôral q^eḏôšîm)* or the "lot of wickedness" *(gôral ʿāwel)* over all of life. This inheritance terminology is also found in 1QH, where *naḥ^alâ* appears to presuppose the predestination theology of the Community Rule. The psalmist's statement that he will love every faithful member of the sect "according to the fullness of his *naḥ^alâ*" (1QH 14:19) means that this love will be determined by the share in the spirit of truth that has been allotted to the individual. To the "son of man" (apparently the psalmist) God has given a particularly rich *naḥ^alâ* with respect to knowledge of God's truth (1QH 10:28f.). At the end of the ages, God will distribute the totality of human glory *(l^ehanḥîlām b^eḵol k^eḇôḏ 'āḏām)* among his elect (1QH 17:15), an expression that recalls Prov. 3:35.

Even though the Bible itself does not exhibit this systematic theology of the Essenes, it does anticipate the extension of inheritance terminology in this direction. Not only is the subst. *naḥ^alâ* used in the sense of "fate" (Isa. 54:17; Job 20:29; 27:13; 31:2), but the verb *nḥl* governs objects that denote positive or negative values of a spiritual or moral nature. The psalmist has "inherited [Yahweh's] decrees forever" (*nāḥaltî ʿeḏôṯeḵā l^eʿôlām:* Ps. 119:111), for "their [the righteous] heritage will abide forever" (Ps. 37:18). The blameless "inherit the good *(ṭôḇ)*" (Prov. 28:10), and the wise "inherit honor" (8:35). Wisdom "appoints as heirs" *(hanḥîl)* those who love her (8:21), and God causes the poor and the needy to inherit *(yanḥîl)* a seat of honor (1 S. 2:8). Conversely, those who trouble their households "inherit wind" (Prov. 11:29), and the simple "inherit folly" (Prov. 14:18). Job laments that he has "inherited months of emptiness" (Job 7:3), and the ancestors of the nations "have inherited nothing but lies" (Jer. 16:19).

3. *Synonym of "Give."* In Zec. 8:12; Ps. 127:3, *naḥ^alâ* has a special meaning. Zec. 8:12 describes the coming of the new age after the return from exile: to the remnant of his people, God will "give as a heritage" *(w^ehinḥaltî)* the fruit of the vine, the produce of the ground, and the dew of the skies. This text is associated with the gift of the land to the chosen people, but the verb *nḥl* refers only to the promised gifts *(kol-'ēlleh),* not to the land itself. In Ps. 127:3 it is sons who are described as a *naḥ^alâ*

of Yahweh. Here God is not the possessing subject of *naḥ^{a}lâ* as elsewhere, but the creator or originator of the *naḥ^{a}lâ*. In both texts the verb and substantive are used in such a general sense that they practically serve as synonyms of "give" and "gift."

Lipiński

נַחַל *naḥal;* אֵיתָן *'êṯān*

Contents: I. 1. Etymology, Occurrences; 2. Meaning; 3. LXX. II. *naḥal 'êṯān.* III. Wadi: 1. Uncultivated Land; 2. Boundaries; 3. Dump Sites; 4. Sacrificial Sites. IV. Cultivated Land. V. The *naḥal* from the Temple. VI. Dead Sea Scrolls.

I. 1. *Etymology, Occurrences.* Heb. *naḥal,* "watercourse, wadi," occurs 141 times in the OT. It corresponds to Aram. and Syr. *naḥlā',* Akk. *naḫlu, naḫallu,*[1] Ugar. *nḫl,* and is therefore probably a primary noun (Arab. *naḫl,* OSA *nḫl* mean "palm tree"). It has been suggested that *naḥal* derives from *ḥll,* "bore," with an *n-* prefix,[2] but such a formation would be unique.

2. *Meaning.* A *naḥal* is the valley cut by a stream, often quite deep. The water, which runs down the mountains with great force during the rainy season (cf. Dt. 9:21), carves a channel in the soil. In contrast to a → נהר *nāhār,* which never dries up, a *naḥal* is a stream that flows only after a rain, but then with great force and volume. Qoheleth's description of a *naḥal* does not suggest a constant, monotonous flow. He emphasizes the futility of the stream: despite the torrents of water that make their way to the sea in the winter through the normally dry wadi, the sea is not filled (Eccl. 1:7).[3]

Job 6:15-17 describes a *naḥal:*

My companions are treacherous like a torrent bed *(naḥal),*
like the channel of wadis *('^{a}pîq n^{e}ḥālîm)* that overflow,
that run dark in the winter
when the snow melts on their banks.
In the time of heat they disappear,
when it is hot, they vanish from their place.

---

naḥal. D. Baly, *The Geography of the Bible* (New York, ²1974); I. Eitan, "Studies in Hebrew Roots, 6: *jtn,*" *JQR,* N.S. 14 (1923/24), 42-44; L. Krinetzki, " 'Tal' und 'Ebene' im AT," *BZ,* N.S. 5 (1961), 204-220; P. Reymond, *L'eau, sa vie, et sa signification dans l'AT. SVT,* 6 (1958), esp. 66-71; C. Schedl, "Aus dem Bach am Wege," *ZAW,* 73 (1961), 290-97; A. Schwarzenbach, *Die geographische Terminologie im Hebräischen des ATs* (Leiden, 1954).

1. *AHw,* II, 712.
2. Schwarzenbach, 32.
3. J. van der Ploeg, *Spreuken. BOT,* 8 (1952), 21.

In the winter, violent cloudbursts can inundate an entire region, and often the "streams" cannot contain the water (cf. 2 K. 3:20).[4]

Elijah hid himself by the Wadi Cherith, because he could get water to drink there; when the wadi dried up, he had to find a new hiding place (1 K. 17:4-7). During the rainy season, the wadis fill up (2 K. 3:16; Isa. 35:6; Ezk. 47:6; Ps. 78:20). Then the *n*ᵉ*ḥālîm* can become so swollen that they cannot be crossed (Ezk. 47:5) and the water reaches up to one's neck (Isa. 30:28). They can sweep everything away, and it is therefore no wonder that one can speak of torrents of perdition (*naḥ*ᵃ*lê b*ᵉ*lîya'al:* Ps. 18:5[Eng. v. 4] par. 2 S. 22:5). Tears can flow like a torrent (Lam. 2:18). Here the word *naḥal* conveys the impression of a sudden rush of tears.

If the text needs to emphasize that it is speaking of a flowing stream rather than an empty wadi, it uses the phrase *naḥal mayim* (Dt. 8:7; 10:7; Jer. 15:18). Jeremiah alludes to the drying up of a wadi when he compares God to "a deceitful brook and waters that fail" (Jer. 15:18). The word *'akzāḇ* found here and in Mic. 1:14 is usually translated "deceitful brook"; even though the word does not embrace the semantic element "wadi, stream,"[5] it is hardly possible to conceive of "deceitful water" apart from a spring or wadi.

Other Hebrew words for "valley" are *'ēmeq,* "lowland plain"; *biq'â,* a broad geological trough with smooth walls (from *bāqa',* "split, divide"); and *gay',* e.g., *gê' ḥinnōm,* the Valley of Hinnom. The noun *'āpîq* denotes the stream channel of a valley; *peleg* (from *pālag,* "split") refers to an artificial watercourse, a canal.

3. *LXX.* The LXX translates *naḥal* with *cheimárrous,* "winter stream," or *pháranx,* "ravine." The former emphasizes the water flowing in the wadi, the latter, the (empty or flowing) channel. These two elements are also found in the Vulg.: *torrens,* a violent torrent, and *vallis,* a valley.

II. *naḥal 'êṯān.* A flowing winter stream is also called *naḥal 'êṯān.* The form *'êṯān* is associated with *naḥal* three times and once (Ps. 74:15) with *nāhār.* It is usually translated "constant" or "ever-flowing"; but this translation is a *contradictio in adiecto,* because it is characteristic of a *naḥal* to flow only sporadically. There are in fact some "wadis" that, although called *naḥal,* are permanent streams, at least in their lower reaches: the Kishon, described by the MT of Jgs. 5:21 (corrupt?) as *naḥal q*ᵉ*ḏûmîm,* "the ancient wadi";[6] the Jabbok (Dt. 2:37; 3:16; Josh. 12:2); the Jarkon, referred to in the OT only in Josh. 19:46 as *mê yarqôn;* and the Jarmuk, not mentioned in the OT.

The subst. *'êṯān* is associated with Arab. *watana,* "be constant, flow constantly."[7] In Hebrew the verb *ytn,* "flow continuously," is found only in Isa. 33:16 and (possibly) Prov. 12:12. The reference is to food that is "constant," i.e., assured, and a root that

---

4. *EncJud,* IX, 182; Baly, 50.

5. → VII, 116f.

6. For a different interpretation see G. W. Ahlström, "Judges 5:10f. and History," *JNES,* 36 (1977), 287f.: *q*ᵉ*ḏûmîm* means "front," "outstanding part," i.e., "flooding."

7. Eitan; *HAL,* I, 44.

is "enduring," i.e., firm. The substantive describes a dwelling place as "enduring" (Nu. 24:21), a nation as "ancient" (Jer. 5:15, par. *mēʿôlām*), pain as "continual" (Job 33:19). It is easy to hear overtones of "strong" or the like. The Kenites' nest in the rock is "strong and secure," the ancient nation is "mighty" (Syr.: *ʿammāʾ ʿaššînāʾ,* "a mighty nation"; Vulg.: *gens robustus*), and the continual pain can also be severe (cf. Targ.).

The *ʾêṯānîm* of Job 12:19 have been interpreted in diverse ways. Edouard Dhorme thinks it refers to those whose power is unvarying, i.e., the authorities (cf. LXX *dynástai,* Vulg. *optimates*).[8] Nahum Sarna connects it with Ugar. *ytnm,* a term for a group of temple ministers (cf. Heb. *n^eṯînîm*).[9] Georg Fohrer finds an association with wadis: "It is as though in the natural realm God were to cause a permanent stream to run dry."[10]

In Gen. 49:24 some translate: "his bow endures"; others, however, take *ʾêṯān* to mean "strength."[11] Many scholars follow Julius Wellhausen in emending the text of Mic. 6:2, for *hāʾêṯānîm* reading *haʾᵃzînû,* "give hear," in parallel with *šimʿû.*[12] Wilhelm Rudolph, however, keeps the MT and translates: "You primeval ones [par. 'mountains'], you foundations of the earth."[13] It is possible that the text is more concerned to emphasize the stability than the age of the mountains (Vulg.: *fortia fundamenta*). A. S. van der Woude claims that the reference is to the potent, conclusive judgments of God.[14]

Since a *naḥal* by definition cannot be *ʾêṯān* in the sense of "permanently flowing," the expression probably describes a devastating torrent, like *naḥal* alone in such texts as Jgs. 5:21; Ps. 124:4 (*naḥlâ* being originally a locative form); Prov. 18:4; and esp. Isa. 30:28; 66:12; Jer. 47:2, which describe the torrent as *šōṭēp,* "devastating." In Am. 5:24 the mighty progress of justice and righteousness is compared to rolling *(gll)*[15] waters and a *naḥal ʾêṯān.* Here the basic meaning "flowing strongly" proposed by *HAL* fits the context well[16] (cf. righteousness [or "success"] like the "waves of the sea" in Isa. 48:18). The text of Sir. 40:13 is corrupt. The phrase *naḥal ʾēṯān* does, however, parallel *ʾāpîq ʾaddîr,* "mighty stream"; the reference to a storm once again suggests the notion of a devastating torrent.

The *nahᵃrôṯ ʾêṯān* of Ps. 74:15 are the primeval waters; the same verse also calls them *naḥal.*[17] The mighty waters are sundered by the creator God. The same idea probably lies behind Ex. 14:27: after the dividing of the Sea of Reeds, the water returns *lᵉʾêṯānô,* i.e., not to its "normal level"[18] but to its previous force.

---

8. E. Dhorme, *Job* (Eng. trans., repr. Nashville, 1984), 177.
9. N. M. Sarna, "אֵיתָנִים, Job 12:19," *JBL,* 74 (1955), 272f.
10. G. Fohrer, *Das Buch Hiob. KAT,* XVI (1963), 246.
11. Cf. *BDB,* 450; H. Gunkel, *Genesis* (Eng. trans., Macon, Ga., 1977), 460.
12. Cf. H. W. Wolff, *Micah* (Eng. trans., Minneapolis, 1990), 164f., who claims that the MT is syntactically enigmatic.
13. W. Rudolph, *Micha. KAT,* XIII/3 (1975), in loc.
14. *Micha. POT* (1976), 206.
15. → III, 21.
16. See *HAL,* I, 44.
17. Cf. J. A. Emerton, "Torrent and Spring in Ps 74,15," *Volume du Congrès. Genève 1965. SVT,* 15 (1966), 122-133.
18. *HAL,* I, 44f.

Dt. 21:4 (11QTemple 63:2ff.) is especially difficult. The context is atonement for a murder by persons unknown. A heifer is taken down (in)to a *naḥal 'êṯān,* where it is slain. The qualification "where there is neither plowing nor sowing" is more suggestive of a valley than a stream; in this case *'êṯān* cannot mean either "strong" or "permanently flowing." August Dillmann considers the possibility that the text may refer to a watercourse that is inundated repeatedly during the rainy season and therefore cannot be cultivated, but he decides in favor of the tradition meaning "wadi with a perennial stream."[19] Alfred Bertholet points out that wadis with perennial streams were popular cultic sites. "The fact that there is no plowing or sowing there confirms that the site is a sanctuary, withdrawn from all secular use and reserved for the numen."[20] We may agree with Gerhard von Rad "that originally it was not a matter of sacrifice at all. It was, on the contrary, a magical procedure for getting rid of sin."[21] Peter Craigie cites Ugaritic parallels.[22] Perhaps it was assumed that the stream would carry off the blood or even the entire body of the animal. Two points argue strongly in favor of interpreting *'êṯān* as referring to a torrent sweeping everything away: it was impossible to find perennial streams everywhere throughout the land, and a deserted area where no one dwelt and where the blood or the whole body of the animal could be washed away was ideally suited for such a ritual. The LXX speaks here only of a rugged or rocky valley *(pháranga tracheían);* the Vulg. has *vallem asperam atque saxosam,* a translation defended by H. Bar-Deroma.[23]

Finally, *'êṯān* became a generic term for "wadi" (Prov. 13:15?). Jer. 49:19 and 50:44 speak of a lion coming up from the thickets of the Jordan to a *n^{e}wēh 'êṯān.*[24]

III. Wadi.

1. *Uncultivated Land.* The *naḥal* of Dt. 21:4 is not just a wasteland. Isa. 57:6 and 1 S. 17:10 also suggest that it has stony soil. Job 22:24 says that gold as well as stones can be found here. Job 30:6 describes such a locale as terrifying.

2. *Boundaries.* Watercourses, often cut deep into the land, are well-defined markers; not rarely they are difficult to cross. It is therefore not surprising that wadis like the Arnon, Zared, and Jabbok served as boundaries between nations or tribes (Dt. 2:24; 3:16; Josh. 16:8; etc.). The most famous boundary is the *naḥal miṣrayim,* the "Wadi of Egypt" (Nu. 34:5; Josh. 15:4; 1 K. 8:65; 2 K. 24:7; Isa. 27:12), Akk. *naḫal* $^{m\bar{a}t}$*muṣri,*[25] generally identified with the Wadi el-ʿArish. Wadi Kidron is clearly a boundary of Jerusalem (1 K. 2:37; cf. 2 S. 15:23).

---

19. A. Dillmann, *Die Bücher Numeri–Josua. KEHAT* (^{2}1886), 338.
20. A. Bertholet, *KHC,* 5 (1899), in loc.
21. *Deuteronomy. OTL* (Eng. trans. 1966), 136.
22. P. C. Craigie, *The Book of Deuteronomy. NICOT* (1976), 278, n. 1.
23. H. Bar-Deroma, *A Series of Studies on the Bible and the Land of the Bible,* V (Jerusalem, 1968) (Heb.); see G. R. Driver's comments in *OT Booklist* (1969), 12.
24. *HAL,* I, 44: "pastureland by a constantly flowing stream"; others: "a perennial pasture."
25. *GTTOT,* §70.

3. *Dump Sites.* A *naḥal* could serve as a dump site for refuse from a town or village. The water, which sometimes flows swiftly, could wash away the garbage. Thus idols were burned in Wadi Kidron (1 K. 15:13; 2 K. 23:6,12), and everything unclean that was found during a purification of the temple was brought to Wadi Kidron (2 Ch. 29:16; 30:14). The dust remaining when the golden calf was burned was thrown into a *naḥal* (Dt. 9:21). According to 2 S. 17:13, an entire city was even dragged into a wadi with ropes.

4. *Sacrificial Sites.* Dt. 21:4 speaks of a *naḥal 'êṯān* as the site of a cultic ritual.[26] The Valley of Hinnom is famous for the child sacrifice practiced there (2 K. 23:10; 2 Ch. 28:3; 33:6; cf. Isa. 57:5).[27] We do not know why this site was chosen for the Canaanite practice.[28]

IV. Cultivated Land. During the dry season the winter rivers also bring fertility to a region. Cultivated fields can adjoin such *nᵉḥālîm.* The association of wadis with agriculture and settlement is attested frequently in the OT (e.g., Jgs. 16:4). Isa. 15:7 mentions a Wadi of the Willows (or Poplars) in Moab; 2 S. 17:13 speaks of a city on the edge of a *naḥal.* The grapes in Wadi Eshcol are famous (Nu. 13:23). A land with springs and wadis is a good land (Dt. 8:7). Rivers and wadis flow with honey and curds (Job 20:17). Balaam sees a nation and its dwellings "like wadis that stretch far away, like gardens beside a river" (Nu. 24:6). Wells for shepherds and their flocks can be dug at the bottom of wadis (Gen. 26:18f.).

V. The *naḥal* from the Temple. Particularly important is the *naḥal* that flows from the temple in Ezk. 47. The prophet paints a glorious picture of life-giving water streaming down the hill into the Wadi Kidron and flowing on as an ever-deepening river into the Dead Sea. Along both its banks grow trees bearing wonderful fruit. The "living water" purifies the Dead Sea. It is noteworthy that the prophet speaks of a *naḥal,* not a *nāhār.* There is no suggestion, however, that this beneficent stream will dry up again like a wadi; instead, it flows into the *naḥal qiḏrôn,* and we may assume that this circumstance has influenced the terminology. Just as the Wadi Kidron is dry and empty before the rainy season, so the sanctuary has been desolate and dead. Now, however, a new age has begun. The glory of Yahweh has entered the sanctuary. Worship at the altar has begun once more. The people are offered salvation and blessing once more (Ezk. 43ff.).

Ps. 36:9(8), too, speaks of life-giving water. The thirsty drink and are revived: "They feast on the abundance of your house [by participating in the sacrificial feast], and you give them drink from the river of your delights." The spring in the temple fills the stony channel of barren human life with the fresh water of God's blessing. The symbolism of the temple spring is in the background.[29]

---

26. See above.
27. → מלך *mōleḵ* (VIII, 375-388).
28. → תפת *tōpeṯ.*
29. → גיחון *gîchôn* (II, 466-68).

Ps. 110:7 likewise speaks of drinking from such a stream: "He will drink from the stream by the path; therefore he will lift up his head." Here the psalmist alludes to a sacramental action belonging to the coronation ceremony. The *naḥal* is probably the spring of Gihon, considered by mythology to be the wellspring of life par excellence. Claus Schedl reads a hiphil participle here, finding a reference to God as the one who "establishes an inheritance." Even more fanciful is Gillis Gerleman's proposal: "The verse recounts in veiled language the narrative of Gen. 38:13ff."[30] Maurice Gilbert and Stephen Pisano connect the verse with Jgs. 15:18ff., seeing in the chosen Davidide the legendary judge reincarnate.[31]

Snijders

VI. Dead Sea Scrolls. The word *naḥal* appears 12 times in the Dead Sea Scrolls published to date; its occurrences in 1QH are all cosmological and eschatological. The devastating effects of evil in the world are compared to the "torrents of Belial" (3:29),[32] which like "torrents of pitch" (3:31) lay waste all the realms of the cosmos (3:32). The 2 occurrences in 11QTemple 63:2,5 echo those in Dt. 21:1-9. The Copper Scroll speaks of a *naḥal hakkippā'* on the road from Jericho to Sekakah (3Q15 5:12) and of a *naḥal gāḏôl* (10:3-4); neither has been located or explained.[33]

Fabry

30. G. Gerleman, *VT,* 31 (1981), 15.
31. M. Gilbert and S. Pisano, "Psalm 110(109),5-7," *Bibl,* 61 (1980), 343-356.
32. See I.2 above.
33. See most recently B. Pixner, *RevQ,* 11/43 (1984), 348, 353f.

נחם *nḥm*

Contents: I. 1. Etymology; 2. Occurrences. II. Meaning and Theological Usage: 1. Niphal; a. With Yahweh as Subject; b. *nḥm ʿal-hārāʿâ;* c. Diachronic Development; d. Specialized Meanings; e. With Human Subjects; 2. Hithpael; 3. Piel; a. With Yahweh as Subject; b. With Human Subjects; c. Participle; 4. Substantives. III. 1. LXX; 2. Dead Sea Scrolls.

nḥm. B. W. Anderson, "'The Lord Has Created Something New': A Stylistic Study of Jer 31:15-22," *CBQ,* 40 (1978), 463-478; D. L. Bartlett, "Jer 31:15-20," *Int,* 32 (1978), 73-78; P. Berthoud, "Le discours de Jérémie dans le parvis du Temple," *Études évangéliques,* 36 (1976), 112-125; D. J. A. Clines, "Noah's Flood, 1: The Theology of the Flood Narrative," *Faith and Thought,* 100/2 (1972/73), 128-145; A. Deissler, *Psalm 119 (118) und seine Theologie. MTS,* I/11 (1955); W. Fuss, "II Samuel 24," *ZAW,* 74 (1962), 145-164; O. Garcia de la Fuente, "Sobre la idea de contrición en el AT," *Sacra Pagina. BETL,* 12-13, ed. J. Coppens, et al. (1959), I,

I. 1. *Etymology.* The root *nḥm* is not found in Akkadian. The verb *na'āmu(m),* "proceed boldly,"[1] is not related to *nḥm.* The verb *nâḫu* (Sem. *nūḫ*) can mean "become calm, be content" in the G stem, "calm, pacify" in the D stem,[2] meanings close to Heb. *nḥm,* "comfort." Jacob Levy therefore postulates a common root for *nḥ* and *nḥm,* with the basic meaning "rest."[3] The different *h* phonemes, however, rule out this theory. The root *nḥm* is not found in Biblical Aramaic, but it probably does appear in Imperial Aramaic and Western Aramaic.[4]

Syr. *nḥm* pael is usually translated "to raise the dead, raise to life, resuscitate," and in some cases "was comforted" (cf. Sir. 48:27 [Peshitta Mosul]).[5]

Most experts no longer accept an original semantic identification of Heb. *nḥm* with Arab. *nḥm,* "breathe heavily," both because of critical objections to deriving the meaning of a word from its etymology and because the concrete semantic field associated with *nḥm* in the OT clearly differs from that associated with Arab. *nḥm.*[6]

For Ugaritic, *WUS* connects the root with two personal names; *UT* lists a variety of forms.[7]

559-579; R. Gordis, "A Note on Lamentations 2:13," *Journal of Tamil Studies,* 34 (1933), 162f. = *The Word and the Book* (New York, 1976), 358f.; W. L. Holladay, *The Root ŠÛBH in the OT* (Leiden, 1958); J. Jeremias, *Die Reue Gottes. SBS,* 65 (1975); L. J. Kuyper, "The Repentance of God," *VT,* 9 (1959), 91-94; *idem,* "The Suffering and Repentance of God," *SJT,* 22 (1969), 257-277; B. Lindars, " 'Rachel Weeping for Her Children,' Jer 31:15-22," *JSOT,* 12 (1979), 47-62; D. Lys, *L'Ecclésiaste, ou Que vaut la vie?* (1973, repr. Paris, 1977); R. Mine, "Le verbe 'consoler' dans le livre de Ruth," *Israel Wochenblatt,* 69, 21 (1969), 41-43; J. Naveh, "The Title *ŚHD/ʿD* [Witness] and *MNḤM* [= paráklētos] in Jewish Epigraphic Texts," *Studies in the Bible and the Ancient Near East. Festschrift S. Loewenstamm,* 2 vols. (Jerusalem, 1978), II, 303-7 (Heb.; Eng. summary, I, 204); H. Van Dyke Parunak, "A Semantic Survey of *NḤM,*" *Bibl,* 56 (1975), 512-532; P. H. Plamondon, "Sur le chemin du salut avec le IIᵉ Isaïe," *NRT,* 114 (1982), 241-266; H. D. Preuss, E. Kamlah, M. A. Signer, and G. Wingren, "Barmherzigkeit," *TRE,* V (1979), 215-238; R. Rendtorff, "Gen 8, 21 und die Urgeschichte des Jahwisten," *KuD,* 7 (1961), 69-78 = *GSAT. ThB,* 57 (1975), 188-197; H. Graf Reventlow, "Gattung und Überlieferung in der 'Tempelrede Jeremias,' Jer 7 und 26," *ZAW,* 81 (1969), 315-352; J. Scharbert, *Der Schmerz im AT. BBB,* 8 (1955); H. J. Stoebe, "נחם *nḥm* pi. 'to comfort,' " *TLOT,* II, 734-39; A. Tosato, "La colpa di Saul (1 Sam 15,22-23)," *Bibl,* 59 (1978), 251-59; *idem,* "*NIHAM,* Pentirsi" (diss., Rome, 1974); P. Trible, "The Gift of a Poem," *Andover Newton Quarterly,* 17 (1977), 271-280; A. Weiser, "1 Samuel 15," *ZAW,* 54 (1936), 1-28; G. Wanke, *Untersuchungen zur sogenannten Baruchschrift. BZAW,* 122 (1971).

1. *AHw,* II, 694.
2. *AHw,* II, 716.
3. J. Levy, *Neuhebräisches und chaldäisches Wörterbuch,* 4 vols. (Leipzig, 1876-89), III, 370. Cf. Van Dyke Parunak, 514.
4. For Imperial Aramaic see *DISO,* 176; for Western Aramaic, *WTM,* s.v.
5. For the former see *CSD,* 335; cf. *LexSyr,* 423b. For the latter see R. Payne Smith, *Thesaurus Syriacus,* 2 vols. (Oxford, 1869-1901), II, 2338.
6. Cf. D. Winton Thomas, *ExpT,* 44 (1932/33), 191f.; 51 (1939/40), 252; N. H. Snaith, *ExpT,* 57 (1945/46), 48; the identification is still apparently accepted by *HAL,* II, 688; and *LexHebAram,* 510. On the critical objections see J. Barr, *The Semantics of Biblical Language* (Oxford, 1961), 116f.
7. *WUS,* no. 1770; *UT,* no. 1634. On the presence of the root in Ugaritic PNs see *PNU,* 165.

2. *Occurrences.* The root *nḥm* occurs 119 times in the OT (not counting PNs). Of these occurrences, 108 are verbal forms (48 niphal, 51 piel, 2 pual, 7 hithpael); the remaining 11 are nominal forms. Personal names using the root are: *mᵉnaḥēm,* king of Israel (2 K. 15:14,16,19-23); *naḥam,* a leader in Judah (1 Ch. 4:19); *naḥûm* (Nah. 1:1); *nᵉḥûm* and *naḥᵃmānî,* among those returning from exile (Neh. 7:7); *nᵉḥemyâ,* son of Hacaliah, governor of Judah under Artaxerxes Longimanus (Neh. 1:1; 8:9; 10:2[Eng. v. 1]; 12:26,47); ruler of half the district of Beth-zur (Neh. 3:16); one of the twelve leaders who returned with Zerubbabel (Ezr. 2:2; Neh. 7:7); *tanḥûmeṯ,* related to Seraiah, a Hebrew officer after the fall of Jerusalem (Jer. 40:8 par. 2 K. 25:23).[8] Apart from the personal names, only in Isaiah does the root occur with great frequency (13 times in the piel, 8 in Deutero-Isaiah). The piel occurs 12 times in Jeremiah, 6 each in Psalms, Job, and Lamentations. In the other books, the various forms counted individually occur no more than 4 times. The root is not found in Leviticus, 1-2 Kings, 2 Chronicles, Obadiah, Micah, Habakkuk, Haggai, Proverbs, or the Song of Songs.

II. Meaning and Theological Usage. The lexicons and commentaries suggest a substantial number of translations for *nḥm.* For the niphal, for example, we find "become remorseful, repent of something, regret, be sorry, feel sorrow or sympathy, find comfort, be comforted"; for the piel, "feel sympathy for someone, comfort, console, pity, requite, strengthen, ameliorate (someone's pain)." We also find several ad hoc translations: "take vengeance," "observe a period of mourning." In modern language the two broadest semantic domains ("repent [of]" for the niphal, "comfort" for the piel) often and primarily involve the emotional realm (a change of feeling on the part of the one who repents or comforts), coupled with de facto futility: regret over something that has already been done or cannot be altered, consolation for someone whom one cannot effectively help. In the majority of OT texts these meanings are not present or are present only secondarily. The only element common to all meanings of *nḥm* appears to be the attempt to influence a situation: by changing the course of events, rejecting an obligation, or refraining from an action, when the focus is on the present; by influencing a decision, when the focus is on the future; and by accepting the consequences of an act or helping another accept them, or contrariwise dissociating oneself emotionally from them, when the focus is on the past. This affective dissociation has various gradations, from regret that something specific has happened, through remorse that what has happened was influenced by the decision or direct involvement of the subject or intentional and explicit distancing from what has taken place, to determination to bring about a new situation that actually alters what has gone before. This determination is tantamount to a decision regarding a future situation.

The twin factors of decision/effect and emotion/affect are thus the rule in *nḥm;* they are indissolubly interwoven, even when in individual cases there may be greater emphasis on one element or the other. Furthermore, the niphal and piel make it possible

8. For the Ugaritic, Phoenician, and Egyptian Aramaic PNs, see *PNU,* 165; *APNM,* 237-39; Benz, 359f.; Vattioni, *Bibl,* 50 (1969), 387.

to emphasize, respectively, the alteration of the subject with regard to a specific situation and the subject's determination to change someone else's attitude with regard to the situation.

1. *Niphal.* a. *With Yahweh as Subject.* In nine different texts the niphal of *nḥm* refers to Yahweh's regret or an alteration of Yahweh's decision. Three of these texts associate Yahweh's *nḥm* with an act other than punishment. Gen. 6:5-8, the J prologue to the story of the Flood (Claus Westermann assigns vv. 5a,7a to the ancient tradition edited by J[9]), interprets the account — in contrast to the Mesopotamian versions — as an expression of the mysterious relationship between humankind and God. Humankind, created by God, had so multiplied its wickedness on earth and so profoundly compromised itself ("every inclination of the thoughts of their hearts was only evil continually") that Yahweh was sorry that he had made them (impf. consecutive of *nḥm* + *kî:* v. 6; perf. + *kî:* v. 7b) — not without deep sadness (*'ṣb* hithpael + *'el-libbô;* cf. 3:16f.; 5:29). But only 6:5-8 + 8:21 provide the correct proportion for the whole meaning of the narrative. In a first statement, 8:21 (J) alludes clearly to 3:17; in a second, it draws on 6:5b. It is hard to decide whether 8:21 primarily refers back to ch. 3 or concludes the account of the Flood (which is actually more concerned with the punishment of humankind and the preservation of a single group than with the fate of the earth as a human habitation[10]). It is clear, however, that the concluding statement of 8:21, "I will never again destroy every living creature," refers directly to a punishment of all humankind that will never be repeated. Yahweh's regret in 6:6a,7b is in its beginning stages; it is not final, but it cannot be retracted. In spite of everything, Yahweh remains faithful to the human race he has created, as 6:8 already suggests. The strange reason given in 8:21a for never again punishing humankind ("for the inclination of the human heart is evil from youth") — an observation already made by Yahweh in 6:5 — reveals the profound meaning of *nḥm* for Yahweh. Yahweh has not changed his mind because humankind has become better in consequence of its punishment; he has instead fully accepted the incorrigible nature of humankind with patience and mercy. "In view of the enduring character of human nature, [Yahweh's] patience is the only conceivable way to guarantee the ongoing existence of humankind."[11] Yahweh's *nḥm* is an act of identification with human frailty.

A similar situation obtains in 1 S. 15:11,35: Yahweh regrets (perf. + *kî*) having made Saul king. Yahweh's reaction paves the way for his irrevocable promise of steadfast love toward the house of David, alluded to in 15:28; Ps. 89:4f.,36f.(3f.,35f.); 132:11; 2 S. 7:12,16 (often with the verb *šb'*). The explicit contrast stated in 2 S. 7:15, "I will not take my steadfast love from him, as I took it from Saul, whom I put away from before you," accounts for the words of 1 S. 15:29, which appear to contradict vv. 11,35 ("the Glory of Israel will not recant or change his mind; for he is not a mortal, that he

9. C. Westermann, *Genesis 1–11* (Eng. trans., Minneapolis, 1984), 406f.
10. *Ibid.,* 454.
11. Jeremias.

should change his mind"; *nḥm* used absolutely twice). V. 29 is therefore not a theological correction of vv. 11 and 35 but a confirmation of v. 28. The proposed interpretation receives its full weight from two texts in which negated *nḥm* appears with Yahweh as subject: Ps. 110:4 in contrast to *šbʿ;* Nu. 23:19 (*nḥm* hithpael) with a motivation similar to that in 1 S. 15:29.[12] Yahweh's regret in the face of Saul's unfaithfulness is justified by Saul's guilt, but does not change his plans radically and definitively. Yahweh's title in 1 S. 15:29 ("Everlasting One"[13]) is an appropriate expression of the irrevocability of Yahweh's plans. Note that while the affirmative use of *nḥm* is associated with a specific situation (regret at having created humankind or having made Saul king), its use in negation is absolute: ultimately, Yahweh does not change his mind.

In the other texts where Yahweh is the subject, it is a punishment that is regretted (or not). In Jer. 4:28 negated *nḥm* parallels *šwb* and contrasts with *zmm* ("I have purposed"). Jer. 4:23-28 alludes to the creation, which is returning to primordial chaos (v. 23), and probably also to the Flood and the disappearance of humankind from the face of the earth (vv. 24f.). The words *lōʾ niḥamtî* take Yahweh's punishment to its final extreme, which in the account of the Flood is offset by the promise in Gen. 8:21.

The opposition *zmm/nḥm* (negated) appears also in Zec. 8:14, heightened by an additional expression (*šaḇtî zāmamtî,* "change one's purpose"). The connection between the two clauses is unique: Yahweh now changes his purpose with the same power with which he had stood by it *(kaʾᵃšer/kēn).* V. 14 transforms the promise of v. 13 into a general principle and points to a profound consistency in Yahweh, who does not feel constrained by his own previous purpose and changes his decision in response to the reaction of the accused.

In Jer. 20:16 *nḥm* (negated and used absolutely) appears as an adverbial modifier of *pwk,* describing the manner in which Yahweh carries out his destruction: without changing his purpose, without "regret," to the bitter end.

Negated *nḥm* used absolutely serves a similar function in Ezk. 24:14, contrasted with "act" and in parallel with *prʿ,* "neglect, refrain," and *ḥws,* "pity." The latter verb appears in the technical idiom "your eye shall not show pity," with reference to ineluctable punishment (Dt. 7:16; 13:9[8]; 19:13,21; 25:12).

In Jer. 15:6 *nḥm* also expresses a contrast with a previous action: *nilʾêṯî hinnāḥēm* (*lʾh* niphal + inf., "be weary of something, be unable to continue"[14]). The verse states Yahweh's self-justification with respect to the punishment announced in vv. 2-5. Yahweh cannot "relent," cannot alter the course of his determined purpose.

In two parallel visions, Am. 7:3,6 repeat the statement *niḥam YHWH ʿal-zōʾṯ,* i.e., he relented concerning the two punishments with which the people were threatened. The text does not suggest any change in the conduct of the people or reconsideration on the part of Yahweh regarding a punishment deemed too harsh. Only the prophet's

---

12. A. Tosato (*Bibl,* 59 [1978], 258f.) considers 1 S. 15:29 a gloss dependent on Nu. 23:19.
13. P. Kyle McCarter Jr., *I Samuel. AB,* 8 (1980), 264.
14. → לאה *lāʾâ* (VII, 395f.).

intercession ("forgive, cease": vv. 2,5), appealing to the weakness of the people, who would not survive such a punishment, effects a change in Yahweh's purpose: "This shall not be." Am. 7:7-9 and 8:1-3 are two parallel visions contrasting with the preceding pair. Here Yahweh does not remain indifferent to the transgressions of his people. The prophet does not understand the meaning of these visions; Yahweh must explain them in words. The visions do not present instruments of imminent punishment but rather objects associated with such punishment conceptually (plumb line) or phonetically *(qayiṣ/qēṣ)*. Finally, in contrast to the previous visions, the prophet does not burst forth spontaneously in intercession but responds intelligently to Yahweh's didactic questions. The absence of the prophet's intercession marks a radical contrast between the two pairs of visions. In the first two, Amos's intervention brought, if not pardon, at least remission of the punishment; here the absence of Amos's intercession gives Yahweh a free hand to prove his case, ending with condemnation. Intercession appears to make Yahweh's *nḥm* possible. Without this intercession, there is nothing to prevent Yahweh from carrying out his judgment.

b. *nḥm ʿal-hārāʿâ*. The problematic phenomenon of Yahweh's regret finds expression 12 times in the syntagmeme *nḥm (YHWH) ʾel/ʿal hārāʿâ* (once: *haṭṭôḇâ*) *(ʾašer)*. The use of this syntagmeme often appears concentrated in a single textual unit: Ex. 32:12,14; Jer. 18:8,10; 26:3,13,19; Jon. 3:10; 4:2. It is used also in 2 S. 24:16 par. 1 Ch. 21:15; Jer. 42:10; Jo. 2:13. In Job 42:11 the syntagmeme proper does not appear.

Ex. 32:9-14 is an addition in Deuteronomistic style that inappropriately anticipates the question of Israel's punishment.[15] Moses implores Yahweh (using the syntagmeme in v. 12) not to inflict severe punishment on Israel. His argument cites the derision of the Egyptians that would ensue and the promises to the patriarchs. The plea is introduced by the words *wayᵉḥal mōšeh ʾeṯ-pᵉnê YHWH,* "but Moses appeased the countenance of Yahweh" (v. 11; this expression also appears with *nḥm* in Jer. 26:19; Mal. 1:9; Ps. 119:58). V. 14 describes the result of Moses' intercession. The *nḥm* of Yahweh is thus presented as a response to Moses' appeasement. Yahweh's repentance is a change of purpose incidental to the circumstances, not a modification of the circumstances.

In 2 S. 24:16 an angel stretches out his hand toward Jerusalem to destroy it; but *wayyinnāḥēm YHWH ʾel-hārāʿâ,* and he commands the angel to stay his hand. Various points in vv. 16f. suggest that this passage is secondary: the presence of the destroying angel does not accord with punishment by pestilence; Yahweh's decision to forestall the punishment (v. 16) precedes David's prayer (v. 17); the punishment has already achieved its goal in v. 15 ("until the appointed time"), so that it seems superfluous to speak of Yahweh's "repentance"; the presence of the destroying angel at the threshing floor of Araunah in v. 16 is superfluous, since the angel takes no part in the narrative of vv. 18ff. The parallel account in 1 Ch. 21 attempts in vv. 16,18 (without parallel in 2 S. 24) to justify the problematic mention of the angel's presence in the overall narrative by introducing the angel into the scene with Ornan (Araunah) the Jebusite. 2 Sam. 24:15 has all the earmarks of the end of a narrative, while v. 18 feels like a

15. M. Noth, *Exodus. OTL* (Eng. trans. 1962), 244.

beginning. Thus 2 S. 24:16f. constitute a theological interpretation emphasizing the personal stature of David, who takes all the blame on himself, while alluding to the mercy of Yahweh, who "repents" or withholds the punishment, contrary to what is described in v. 15.

Jer. 18:7-10 presents proclamation of judgment, change of conduct, and Yahweh's change of mind as a general paradigm. Vv. 8 and 10 contain the syntagmeme in two parallel casuistic formations, concluding with the statement: "I will change my mind about the evil/good that I intended to bring on/do to them." Vv. 11f. apply the general principle to Judah and Jerusalem.

The materials of which Jer. 26 is composed — in partial agreement with Jer. 7, which describes the prophet's ministry more accurately — are used to exhort and to awaken hope among the exiles, the narrator's contemporaries. The syntagmeme plays a structural role in vv. 1-19, appearing once in each of the three sections of the narrative (vv. 2-6,7-15,16-19). In the first, Yahweh expresses the hope that the people will "turn from their evil way," that he "may change [his] mind about the disaster that [he] intended to bring on them." In the second, Jeremiah defends himself before the officials and the people with an exhortation to amend their ways, that Yahweh may change his mind about the disaster that he has pronounced *(dbr)* against them. In the third, the elders argue an historical precedent in defense of Jeremiah: Micah of Moresheth, too, was not condemned to death despite his harsh message, because he "appeased the countenance of the LORD," causing him to change his mind about the disaster that he had pronounced against them. The syntagmeme of Yahweh's repentance thus gives expression to Yahweh's profound and fundamental determination to forgive, gives meaning to the prophet's mission as one of intercession, and justifies the defense presented by the elders. Theologically, the planned/promised/determined punishment is not final; it allows room for change of conduct and intercession. Yahweh's change of heart varies in intensity, from a mere possibility linked to a condition in the future through a future that depends on hearkening to Jeremiah's exhortation to a declaration in the words spoken by the elders. The three modes of expression make clear that the punishment was not carried out.

Jer. 42:10 actually prophesies that the punishment will be retracted. Yahweh's promise to restore his people rather than destroying them, on the condition that they continue to dwell in the land, is based on Yahweh's regret for the disaster *'ᵃšer ʿāśîṯî lāḵem.*

The theme of Yahweh's repentance pervades the whole penitential liturgy of Joel 2:12-17, structured as a threefold exhortation to return to Yahweh: Yahweh's exhortation to the people, the prophet's exhortation to the people, and the prophet's exhortation to Yahweh. The prophet's exhortation to the people cites the characteristic attributes of Yahweh as *ḥannûn wᵉraḥûm* and includes in v. 13b the complete syntagmeme of Yahweh's repentance. V. 14a (only the verbal form of *nḥm*) suggests the possibility of forgiveness in the phrase *mî yôḏēaʿ* ("who knows?"). The exhortation beseeching Yahweh to be merciful uses instead the impv. *ḥûsâ ʿal* (together with *nḥm,* as in Ezk. 24:14), citing (like Ex. 32:12) the argument of potential derision on the part of the nations.

Jon. 3:9f.; 4:2 share with Jo. 2:13f. an expression of hope ("who knows?") and the argument that Yahweh is "a gracious God and merciful, . . . ready to relent from punishing." The text does not stop, however, with exhorting Yahweh to be merciful but goes on to say: "God changed his mind about the calamity that he said he would bring upon them; and he did not do it" (v. 10). This knowledge of Yahweh's nature and mode of action leads Jonah to yearn to die, since he cannot follow his God on the path of understanding and mercy. The clause *w^e šāḇ mēḥ^a rôn 'appô* in Jon. 3:9 resembles *šûḇ mēḥ^a rôn 'appeḵā* in Ex. 32:12. While Exodus and Joel refer to Israel, Jonah views the gentile nations from the same perspective.

c. *Diachronic Development.* The theme of Yahweh's change of mind thus exhibits a clear course of development. In the earlier texts (Gen. 6:6f.; 1 S. 15), regret merely leads up to the final affirmation of Yahweh's plans. We need not consider 2 S. 24:16 an exception, if the text is a later theological commentary.[16] From the eighth century on, Yahweh's repentance has to do with punishment. In Amos and Hosea the decision not to punish is not linked to forgiveness but is grounded on the weakness of the people, who could not survive the punishment. Hos. 11:8 and Am. 7:3,6 hope for Yahweh's *nḥm* in the immediate future. Hos. 13:14; Jer. 4:28; 15:6 treat *nḥm* retrospectively and negatively: Yahweh does not go back on his word, because he has so determined and because the people have not changed their ways. Since the time of Jeremiah's disciples (Jer. 26:3,13,19; 42:10), Yahweh's *nḥm* is offered as a possibility, conditional upon the people's return. Among the Deuteronomistic theologians, it became a theme of exhortation and a structural motif of theological reflection on the situation of all Israel (Joel) and the nations (Jonah) in their relationship with God, as well as an essential element of penitential liturgy (Jo. 2:12-17). In Jer. 18:8,10, the relationship between *nḥm* and change of conduct has become an almost juridical formula (cf. Ezk. 14:12-20). With the appearance of the formula *nḥm 'el/ʿal hārāʿâ '^a šer* in the time of Jeremiah's disciples, the disquieting theme of Yahweh's *nḥm,* which in Gen. 6 attempts to express the mystery of the relationship between divine and human freedom, becomes a standard theological and pastoral category.

d. *Specialized Meanings.* In four texts the niphal of *nḥm* with Yahweh as subject has a peculiar semantic force that is hard to associate with the regular meaning previously established: dissociation from a particular attitude or action in the past or future.

In Ps. 90:13 it is impossible to determine whether *w^e hinnāḥēm ʿal-ʿ^a ḇāḏeyḵā* means "rescind a punishment"[17] in direct reference to the wrath of Yahweh (vv. 7,9,11) or "have pity, console" as a programmatic introduction to the urgent prayer that follows (to rejoice and be glad, to see the manifestation of Yahweh's work: vv. 14-17). The use of *nḥm* in parallel with the impv. *šûḇâ* (used absolutely as in Jo. 2:14; cf. Ex. 32:12; Jer. 4:28; Jon. 3:9, with prepositional obj.) does not help decide between these interpretations. The generic meaning of *šûḇ,* "turn back, change one's mind,"[18] suggests a wider, positive sense: "have mercy."

---

16. See II.1.a above.
17. Van Dyke Parunak, 528.
18. Holladay, 76f.

In Ps. 106:45, too, *nḥm* has a broad meaning: Yahweh's change of mind with respect to his people. This meaning is shown by the general tenor of the psalm, which presents the entire history of Israel as an example of judgment interspersed with and suspended by acts of mercy on the part of Yahweh,[19] moved by the intercession of Moses (v. 23) and Phinehas (v. 30), and above all by faithfulness to the covenant. The direct parallelism (regard the distress of his people, hear their cry) demands that the focus of attention be not the punishment from which Yahweh would dissociate himself but the unhappy lot of the people, to which Yahweh cannot close his eyes.

The historico-theological retrospect in Jgs. 2 records a similar view. The cycle of apostasy, Yahweh's wrath, and punishment (vv. 11-15) is interrupted only by the sending of judges to deliver the people (v. 16), a decision reached by Yahweh when he hears the cries of his oppressed people, so as to have mercy on them. (There is little justification for H. Van Dyke Parunak's emphasis on the similarity of Jgs. 2:18 to Dt. 32:36 so as to translate and interpret both texts homogeneously ["retract punishment"].)[20]

The use of *nḥm* niphal + *min* in Isa. 1:24 presents a special problem. The parallel with *nqm* ("avenge") suggests the translation "execute wrath," even though this usage is admittedly unique. Comparison to Dt. 32:35 is not sufficient, since there *nqm* refers to the enemy, while *nḥm* refers to Israel and has the opposite meaning, "have mercy." The only possibility of assigning one of the incontestable meanings of the verb to *nḥm* niphal in this verse is to treat it as a reflexive, "console oneself" (at the expense of the enemy). The verb does not actually refer to revenge but only to the satisfaction enjoyed by the subject of *nḥm,* achieved by the revenge signified by *nqm.*

A similar meaning must be assigned to the hithpael of *nḥm* in Gen. 27:42: "Your brother Esau *miṯnaḥēm lᵉḵā lᵉhorgeḵā*" are Rebecca's words to Jacob. The expression refers not so much to "plotting revenge" against his brother as consoling himself with the thought of killing him (v. 41), a consolation all the more necessary after the disconsolate tears of v. 38.

In Ezk. 5:13, too, *wᵉhinneḥāmtî* is a hithpael associated with the meaning "take vengeance." The form (already slightly suspect as the only instance of assimilation of the *t* in the hithpael) may, however, be nothing more than an orthographically corrupt doublet of *wahᵃniḥōṯî.*[21] The latter interpretation is supported by the well-attested presence of the syntagmeme *hēnîaḥ ḥēmâ bᵉ* + suffix (Ezk. 16:42; 21:22[17]; 24:13). Then the meaning "take vengeance" would lose all textual support.

e. *With Human Subjects.* The niphal of *nḥm* is used in a variety of ways with human subjects (individuals or the nation).

(1) Used absolutely, it denotes consolation, i.e., a cessation in the subject of the pain caused by the death of someone near and dear (Gen. 24:26: Isaac is consoled after the death of his mother; 38:12: Judah is consoled after the death of his wife). It is not

19. H.-J. Kraus, *Psalms 60–150* (Eng. trans., Minneapolis, 1989), 322.
20. Pp. 529f.
21. W. Zimmerli, *Ezekiel 1. Herm* (Eng. trans. 1979), 152.

necessary to interpret the two passages in different ways, with the first referring to the end of the period of mourning, usually expressed by the phrase *ʿāśâ ʾēḇel.* The difference between being in mourning *(wayyiṯʾabbēl)* and being consoled *(nḥm)* is obvious in 2 S. 13:37,39.[22] In addition, the contrast between *nḥm* and "cease to be angry" in v. 39 confirms for *nḥm* the meaning "be consoled" as a restoration of inward equilibrium. The meaning includes an emotional element: pain is followed by resignation and inward peace. This is the composure Ephraim looks forward to after Yahweh transforms the situation of dispersion and the infertility of the land (Jer. 31:19).

In Job 42:6 *nḥm* par. *m's* (both used absolutely) might also denote a change in inward attitude. Rebellion is followed by submission. The verb *m's* can be assigned to the root *m's* II = → מסס *mss* (there is uncertainty in assigning texts to this root[23]), which used absolutely refers to the shriveling of skin (Job 7:5), destruction (Job 7:16, par. "I do not want to live"), and despair (Ps. 58:8[7]). In his final confession of faith, Job accepts his situation in the eyes of God and thus finds peace *(niḥamtî).* In any event, the common rendering of *m's* as "recant, retract, reject" (with an implied obj. such as "my words") as a parallel to "repent" (with its overtones of disavowing wrong or sinful conduct, a meaning rare in the OT[24]) is by no means certain here.

Jer. 31:15,16-20 comprise a double lament: Rachel, the inconsolable mother (symbolizing the earth), bewails both the devastation of the land and of Ephraim and the affliction of the exiles. She receives a double answer from Yahweh: do not weep, Ephraim is a beloved son. The repetition of the weeping motif in vv. 15f. and the contrast between "refuse *lᵉhinnāḥēm*" in v. 15 and *niḥamtî* in v. 19 caution against isolating vv. 17-19 and interpreting them as a prophetic penitential liturgy. The genre is more that of an oracle of consolation, presupposing repentance and return to Yahweh. Rachel declares that there can be no consolation so long as the land remains desolated, i.e., consolation can come only from Yahweh. Yahweh's explicit promise in vv. 16f. is followed by a statement of the accomplished change. In this context v. 19aα should not be translated "after I had turned away, I repented," but should be treated as an affirmation of hope: "after my return I am consoled" (the niphal having stative force). This induces Yahweh to decide finally to have mercy *(raḥēm ʾᵃraḥᵃmennû)* on his people (v. 20). V. 19 indicates that being known (*ydʿ* niphal) is an element of conversion. The ability to console is conditional upon knowing the distress of the weak; being consoled is conditional upon recognizing the situation of contingency.

(2) The niphal of *nḥm* uses *ʿal* to introduce the object that has occasioned despair (Absalom dead: 2 S. 13:39; Rachel's children: Jer. 31:15 [hithpael]). In Ezk. 32:31 (part of the commentary on the basic text 31:16 and inspired by it[25]), *ʿal* gives the reason for Pharaoh's consolation. The idea can be the same as that expressed in 31:16,

---

22. → אבל *ʾāḇhal* (I, 45), where the verb *nḥm* is not listed as a synonym.
23. Cf. *HAL,* II, 541; *LexHebAram,* s.v.; Kuyper, 92.
24. See (2) below.
25. W. Zimmerli, *Ezekiel 2. Herm* (Eng. trans. 1983), 178f.

where the trees of the underworld are consoled by the fall of the cedar (Pharaoh) in their midst (*nḥm* niphal, used absolutely).

When the niphal of *nḥm* + *ʿal* has *hārāʿâ* as the object of the preposition, the meaning "be consoled" appears impossible. In Jer. 8:6 ("No one *nḥm ʿal-rāʿāṯô,* saying 'What have I done?' "), the meaning that the expression has with Yahweh as subject is transferred to a human person: dissociation from a particular action or decision. In the case of Yahweh, *rāʿâ* was objective evil ("disaster") used as punishment, while now it refers to the subjective evil of blameworthy conduct. Vv. 4-7 (possibly a fragment of a prophetic penitential liturgy) are built around six contrasts between rhetorical questions or assertions and their negations (6 occurrences of *lōʾ/wᵉlōʾ/ʾên* and the negative verb *mʾn*): "no one *nḥm*" is glossed by "no one rises up, no one returns, they refuse to return, they speak what is wrong, they do not know the ordinance of Yahweh."

The use of *nḥm* (niphal) *ʿal-hārāʿâ* in Ezk. 14:22b sets itself apart from the construction discussed above;[26] it is also not consonant with the meaning of Jer. 8:6 (repenting of moral evil). It resembles more closely the meaning of Ezk. 31:16; 32:31. Someone — here the exiles — takes consolation from a punishment that has been inflicted on others (Jerusalem?). Ezk. 14:22b,23a interrupt the clear flow of vv. 22a and 23b, suggesting a different level of text. In any case, the interpretation of v. 23a ("they will console you [*nḥm* piel] when you see them"), which attempts to elucidate the thought of v. 22b, is obscure.

(3) The niphal of *nḥm* + *ʾel* expresses a feeling on the part of the subject for another person who is in danger or distress. Jgs. 21:6,15 use *nḥm* + *ʾel/lᵉ* to express the attitude of the Israelites (or "the people") toward the Benjaminites, who had been condemned to perish as a tribe because the other tribes had sworn not to give them any wives. It does not appear appropriate to describe the sympathy expressed as "suffering emotional pain."[27] The passage instead emphasizes a dissociation from earlier feelings of vengeance. The "sympathy" expressed by *nḥm* is manifested as a desire to find a concrete solution.

(4) In Ex. 13:17 *pen-yinnāḥēm hāʿām bᵉ* + verb cannot be assigned to the category "suffer emotional pain." God is afraid that the people will change their minds, i.e., alter their decision with respect to the dangers of the journey through the wilderness, and will want to return to Egypt. Here the meaning of *nḥm* is the same as when Yahweh changes his mind concerning a punishment he has determined to inflict.

2. *Hithpael.* Apart from the special meanings in Nu. 23:19 and Gen. 27:42; Ezk. 5:13,[28] the hithpael of *nḥm* expresses the affective and effective relationship between two parties: between Yahweh and the people or a specific person, or between individuals; the stronger party supports the weaker, takes an interest in their fate, takes them in hand, and helps rectify their problems. In Ps. 119:52 the psalmist is comforted by

26. See II.1.b.

27. Van Dyke Parunak.

28. On Nu. 23:19 see II.1.a above; on Gen. 27:42; Ezk. 5:13 see II.1.d above.

his recollection of Yahweh's saving decrees in the past. This same relationship between the experience of comfort and Yahweh's salvific judicial activity is also found in Dt. 32:36 par. Ps. 135:14 (*dîn* par. *nḥm*), even though the meaning of Dt. 32:36b is obscure. Both texts view the relationship not from the perspective of the weaker party, who experiences the beneficent influence of the stronger, but from the perspective of the stronger, who "has compassion." Compassion and comfort thus turn out to be correlative aspects of the same act, starting from opposite poles. If one of the two parties is not stronger than the other, comfort is impossible. In Gen. 37:35 Jacob refuses to be comforted because, in fact, no one can comfort him.[29]

3. *Piel.* a. *With Yahweh as Subject.* The usage of the piel of *nḥm* is more uniform and less nuanced. It can usually be translated "comfort" or "strengthen." When Yahweh is the subject, in many cases the texts express a fervent plea (Isa. 12:1: "Cease from your anger and comfort me"); it is difficult to draw the line between a fervent plea as such and the absolute assurance that Yahweh will not forsake his own (v. 2). More common is the clear statement (verb in the perf.) that Yahweh has comforted his people (Isa. 49:13; 52:9) or Zion (Isa. 51:3 [twice]) or the certainty that Yahweh will comfort Zion (Zec. 1:17). Often Yahweh personally assures his people that he will comfort them (Isa. 51:12; cf. also Jer. 31:13); and the prophet's rhetorical question in Isa. 51:19 (probably to be read in the 3rd person rather than the 1st person), "Who would be able to comfort you?" confirms that comfort comes only from Yahweh.

In Isa. 40:1 the subject of "Comfort, O comfort my people" is still a matter of debate. Although the function of giving comfort is characteristic of Yahweh, it seems difficult to imagine that such an imperative can be addressed to him. Of the two possible solutions, the more likely is that the prophet himself, as the protagonist of the text, is addressing those who keep watch over Jerusalem; this hypothesis finds support in Isa. 52:7-10; 62:6f.[30]

Yahweh's giving of comfort, expressed by the piel of *nḥm,* includes concrete aspects that can be brought out by parallel verbs or by the immediate context. Isa. 49:12-13 speaks of gathering the scattered people, which leads to the statement that Yahweh has comforted his people; in 51:3 the object of the verb "comfort" is "ruins," so that the verb includes the meaning "rebuild." In 52:9 *nḥm* is used in parallel with "redeem" *(g'l);* in 12:1 the comfort is the cessation of Yahweh's anger; in Zec. 1:17 it is the overflowing prosperity of the cities;[31] in Jer. 31:13 it is the joyful dancing of old and young. Never are words of encouragement the source of comfort: it always springs from an act of Yahweh that truly transforms the sorrowful situation. The comforting of those who mourn in Isa. 61:2 appears to include the concrete terminology (liberation of the deportees, return of the prisoners) of v. 1.

In Isa. 40:1f. the use of *dbr ʿal-lēḇ* in parallel with *nḥm* (cf. Gen. 50:21; Ruth 2:13)

---

29. See 3.b below.
30. Cf. R. P. Merendino, *Die Erste und der Letzte. SVT,* 31 (1981), 18-20.
31. K. Elliger, *Die Buch der zwölf kleinen Propheten, II. ATD,* 25 (^{7}1975), 117.

— assuming that the idiom is associated specifically with "the language of love"[32] — favors an interpretation of *nḥm* with strong affective overtones. This idiom, however, always appears in situations of grief, fear, sin, or offense, from which those who suffer are delivered by one who "speaks to their heart" and "comforts them."[33]

In prophetic texts, the piel of *nḥm* expresses Yahweh's comforting of the people as a group. By contrast, the Psalms apply the verb to the individual worshiper. Here the meaning of the piel has been spiritualized and generalized. In Ps. 23:4 "comfort" is tantamount to "deliver from fear" and in 71:21 to "revive, restore." In 86:17 it is used in a context that requires the meaning "support, help" *(ʿzr)* and "empower." In 119:76 the comfort is redress of humiliation; in 119:82 the psalmist longs for both comfort and deliverance.

The pual (Isa. 54:11; 66:13) exhibits no meaning distinct from the piel apart from its inherent passive sense. Zion and the inhabitants of Jerusalem are (or are not) comforted.

b. *With Human Subjects.* With human subjects the piel often governs a personal direct object (Gen. 5:29; 50:21; 2 S. 12:24; Ruth 2:13); the infinitive frequently indicates the finality or completion of a movement and act ("break bread") or an inner disposition ("strive") (Gen. 37:35; 2 S. 10:2 par. 1 Ch. 19:2; 1 Ch. 7:22; Isa. 22:4; Jer. 16:7; Job 42:11). The commonest situation demanding human comfort is the death of someone near and dear: the supposed death of Joseph, the death of Nahash, king of the Ammonites, or quite generally the death of anyone. Boaz comforts Ruth, alleviating her misery and hard labor; Job's misfortunes bring his friends to come and comfort him (Job 2:11); the destruction of the nation is so terrible that the prophet thinks there can be no comfort (Isa. 22:4).

On some occasions human comfort appears to meet with approval on the part of the text: this happens when the comforter possesses the means to alter an unfortunate situation (Boaz) or when the person in question somehow enjoys the privilege of Yahweh's special love (Noah, Joseph). David's consolation of Bathsheba appears to be nothing more than erotic diversion (2 S. 12:24); the efforts of Jacob's sons are in vain, for Jacob refuses to be comforted (Gen. 37:35b; cf. Jer. 31:15; Ps. 77:3[2] [niphal]).

Refusal to be comforted is not a voluntary decision: it signifies a realization that comfort is not within the power of those who offer it. David's message of consolation to Hanun (2 S. 10:3) is suspect; the attempt of Job's friends to comfort him is irrelevant (Job 16:2), futile (21:34), and too late (42:11; cf. v. 10). Also futile is the comfort essayed by the soothsayers in Zec. 10:2. The futility of human comfort is expressed most vividly in Isa. 22:4: *'al-tā'îṣû lᵉnaḥᵃmēnî* ("do not try to comfort me"); the verb *'yṣ* suggests urgency, often with negative connotations. The prophet contrasts the attempt to seek comfort through diverting words with the only correct perspective: acceptance of Yahweh's will, expressed in the tragic fate of Jerusalem. Human comfort

32. → III, 98; VII, 417f.; see also H. W. Wolff, *Anthropology of the OT* (Eng. trans., Philadelphia, 1974), 52.

33. G. Fischer, *Bibl*, 65 (1984), 246-250.

is useless because it does not change anything. Only Yahweh's comfort gives assurance (Isa. 12:1).

This same line of thought is represented by Lam. 2:13, the focus and turning point of ch. 2. Vv. 1-10 emphasize that it is indeed the Lord who has punished Zion; Israel's enemies are only an instrument in God's hand. Vv. 11-12 give voice to the prophet's emotions. Vv. 15-19 describe the reaction of those who pass by and of the enemy; the poet exhorts Jerusalem to entreat Yahweh without ceasing, and Jerusalem obeys. Vv. 13-14, in the middle of this composition, are different: the poet resists the temptation to find rhetorical comparison that might persuade Jerusalem that her fate is not the worst imaginable. In contrast to his own conduct, he calls to account the prophets who did not expose the iniquity of Jerusalem but instead reassured the people with false and deceptive visions. Any comfort the poet might have to offer would be a new deception, like the deception that brought the disaster. Human comfort is irreconcilable with open exposure of the true connection between sin and the punishment that has been inflicted on the city. In this context *mâ 'ašweh-lāḵ* (v. 13) can be translated: "What sense would it make to frame a comparison that would comfort you!"

c. *Participle.* Lam. 2:13 states in its most extreme form the theme the poet repeats obsessively in 1:2,9,16,17,21: "there is no comforter [ptcp.] for them/me," "a comforter is far from me." Here, too, there is a coherent train of thought. V. 2 still leaves room for illusion, suggesting that the friends who might actually comfort Jerusalem are unfaithful to her, whereas v. 16 states that the only possible comforter is far away. What one expects of a comforter is presented in Nah. 3:7: when Yahweh punishes (v. 5), there is no possibility of finding a comforter. The suffering servant in Ps. 69 knows that only from Yahweh can he expect deliverance and protection from his enemies; apart from Yahweh, he will find neither pity nor *m^e^naḥēm* (v. 21[20]).

Although it is clear that comfort always involves more than kind words, there is no real evidence to suggest that *m^e^naḥēm* has a specifically juridical sense — not even Eccl. 4:1.[34] The injustice suffered by the oppressed is one more concrete expression of the general meaninglessness of life, which equates the lot of human beings with that of animals (3:18). The absence of a comforter is an expression of God's silence in the midst of human life. One cannot argue for a juridical aspect of *m^e^naḥēm* on the basis of the parallel of *nḥm* piel with *g'l* in Isa. 52:9. The verb most frequently used in parallel with the piel of *nḥm* is *nwd,* which denotes the gesture of concern made in the presence of misfortune (Job 2:11; 42:11; Isa. 51:19; Nah. 3:7; Ps. 69:21[20]). This usage suggests sympathy for the sufferer, even though it is clear that this sympathy is useless when it comes from human beings. The uniqueness of Yahweh as the only true *m^e^naḥēm* is emphasized in Isa. 51:12.

The only legitimate comfort in the human realm is the comfort expressed in the gestures of mourning described in Jer. 16:5-9, especially *prs leḥem* and *šqh tanḥumîm.*[35]

---

34. Lys translates "réhabilitateur"; G. Lohfink (*Kohelet. NEB* [1980], 36) keeps the traditional translation "and no one comforts them."

35. On the meaning and legitimacy of such gestures see W. Rudolph, *Jeremia. HAT,* XII (^{3}1968), 107.

That the prophet is forbidden to perform these gestures serves as a sign that Yahweh has withdrawn his friendship from his people.

A clearer juridical aspect of *m^e^naḥēm* appears in Ezk. 16:54, where *b^e^naḥ^a^mēḵ* plays the same semantic role as the piel of *ṣdq* in vv. 51,52 ("make appear righteous," or, in Walther Zimmerli's bolder translation, "justify, show to be righteous"[36]), as the repetition of *(û)ś^e^'î ḵ^e^limmāṯēḵ* shows. Jerusalem's acceptance of her own disgrace is the necessary condition for the restoration of her former status; Samaria and Sodom return to their former status on account of Jerusalem's iniquity. This is the consolation Jerusalem has to offer her sister cities. By contrast, the consolation that the (new) exiles bring to the exiled community is only the observation that Yahweh will punish once more those who deserve punishment (14:23).

4. *Substantives.* Five substantive forms appear in eleven texts. In Isa. 57:18 *niḥumîm* (the obj. of *šlm*) appears in the context of previous divine anger and punishment already inflicted, in contrast to God's will to heal (vv. 18f.), lead (v. 18), and give peace (v. 19); it can only mean the comfort vouchsafed by Yahweh to his people as recompense for the calamity of the past. The *d^e^ḇārîm niḥumîm* that Yahweh gives to the angel to be told to the prophet are likewise de facto words of comfort. In Hos. 11:8 *niḥumîm* is the subject of *kmr.* The close association with the niphal of *kmr* + *raḥ^a^mîm* (Gen. 43:30; 1 K. 3:26) suggests a translation reflecting intense inner feelings (Joseph's leniency toward his brothers, the terror of the child's mother at Solomon's judgment, Yahweh's pity at seeing the consequences of the punishment his people deserve). The reason for Yahweh's inner turmoil and his decision not to punish his people is: "I am God and no mortal." In Nu. 23:19; 1 S. 15:29, these same words explain why God will not recant or change his mind.[37] Yahweh's very divinity makes it possible for his heart to feel pity so that he is not constrained, not even by the inflexible relationship between guilt and punishment. Yahweh's capacity for pity is ultimately the force that determines how he acts, even though he does not hesitate to fix responsibility.

In Hos. 13:14 *naḥam* can mean both caution and self-control,[38] or simply "compassion." The verse is hard to understand. If v. 14a is interpreted as a statement, it contradicts v. 14bβ; if it is taken as a rhetorical question expecting a negative answer, it contradicts v. 14bα. The statement *nōḥam yissāṯēr mē'ênay* suggests inflexibility on the part of Yahweh.

In Job 15:11 *tanḥûmôṯ* denotes the consolations that Job's friends believe spring from Yahweh's word. In 21:2 Job uses the same word polemically: if his friends would be silent for a moment and listen to him, that would be true consolation. In 6:10 *neḥāmâ* is the consolation Job hopes to find only in his own death; in Ps. 119:50 the psalmist associates it with Yahweh's word and with life.

The noun *tanḥûmîm* appears in a construct phrase in Isa. 66:11; in an image drawn

---

36. Zimmerli, *Ezekiel 1,* 332.
37. See II.1.a above.
38. Jeremias.

from the realm of mothering, it refers to the source of divine comfort *(šōḏ).* It can also refer to a means of human comfort (*kôs tanḥumîm:* Jer. 16:7). In Ps. 94:19 it denotes the comfort that comes from Yahweh.

III. 1. *LXX.* For the most part (at least 58 times), the LXX uses *parakaleín* to translate the niphal, piel, pual, and hithpael of *nḥm.*[39] It uses *metanoeín* only for the niphal, frequently to denote Yahweh's "remorse" (11 times), sometimes Israel's. It uses *eleeín* 4 times for the piel and once for the niphal, and *paúein* 5 times for the niphal. It is interesting to note that, while neglecting the possible influence of *nḥm,* the NT interpretation of *metanoeín/metánoia* is influenced heavily by the meaning of *šûḇ,* even though the LXX never uses *metanoeín* to translate *šûḇ.*[40]

Simian-Yofre

2. *Dead Sea Scrolls.* In the Dead Sea Scrolls *nḥm* is remarkably rare, occurring only 11 times (7 in 1QH, 2 in 4QTanḥ [4Q176], and once each in 1QS and 4QPrFêtes[c] [4Q509]). OT usage is continued but with significant additions: divine "comfort" is paralleled by "forgiveness" (1QH 9:13; 11:32; 16:17) and is linked to human "repentance" (1QS 10:21; 1QH 6:7; 16:17).[41] God is the "comforter" of those who mourn (1QH fr. 21 3), stumble (4Q509 12:1 + 13:5), or suffer affliction (1QH 9:13). The Qumran Essenes even had their own book of comfort (4QTanḥ) arranged as a pesher on the "Book of Comfort for Israel" (Isa. 40–55): fr. 1-2 1:4 cites Isa. 40:1; and fr. 9-11, 13 cite 54:4-10 as *tanḥûmîm,* interpreting them with reference to their own present affliction.

Human *nḥm* is "remorse" for one's own sinfulness, which results from recognition of the truth (1QH 9:13).

Fabry

---

39. On *parakaleín* see J. Thomas, *EDNT,* III, 22-27; on *paraklētós* see F. Porsch, *ibid.,* 28f., both with bibliog.

40. E. F. Thompson, *Μετανοέω and Μεταμέλει in Greek Literature Until 100 A.D.* (Chicago, 1909), 348-377. Cf. C. Spicq, *Theological Lexicon of the NT,* 3 vols. (Eng. trans., Peabody, Mass., 1994), II, 471-77, with bibliog. On the NT interpretation of *metanoeín/metánoia* see J. Behm and E. Würthwein, *TDNT,* IV, 975-1006; H. Merklein, *EDNT,* II, 415-19.

41. → שׁוב *šûḇ.*

נָחָשׁ *nāḥāš;* נחשׁ *nḥš;* אֶפְעֶה *ʾep̱ʿeh;* זָחַל *zāḥal;* עַכְשׁוּב *ʿakšûḇ;* פֶּתֶן *peṯen;* צֶפַע *ṣepaʿ;* צִפְעוֹנִי *ṣip̱ʿônî;* קִפּוֹז *qippōz;* שְׁפִיפֹן *šᵉpîp̱ōn*

→ לִוְיָתָן *liwyāṯān;* → שָׂרָף *śārap̱;* → תַּנִּין *tannîn*

Contents: I. 1. Etymology; 2. Distribution and Syntax; 3. Lexical Field and Parallels; 4. LXX. II. Zoology: 1. General; 2. *ʾep̱ʿeh;* 3. *zāḥal;* 4. *ʿakšûḇ;* 5. *peṯen;* 6. *ṣep̱aʿ/ṣip̱ʿônî;* 7. *qippōz;* 8. *šᵉpîp̱ōn.* III. Religious and Symbolic Usage: 1. Mesopotamia; 2. Egypt; 3. Canaan. IV. OT: 1. Gen. 3; 2. The Miraculous Staff; 3. Nu. 21; 4. Gen. 49:17; 5. Cosmic Peace; 6. Mythological Texts; 7. Wisdom; 8. Prophetic Threats; 9. Oracles of Salvation. V. Dead Sea Scrolls.

I. 1. *Etymology.* In Hebrew the consonant group *nḥš* includes the verb *nḥš* piel, "prognosticate," and the nouns *naḥaš,* "spell"; *nāḥāš* I, "serpent"; *nāḥāš* II, *nᵉḥûšâ, nᵉḥōšeṯ* I, "bronze," together with the adj. *nāḥûš,* "made of bronze"; *nᵉḥōšeṯ* II,

---

nāḥāš. W. Baudissin, *Adonis und Esmun* (Leipzig, 1911), esp. 325-339; *idem,* "Eherne Schlange," *RE,* XVII (1906), 580-86; C. H. Bowman and R. B. Coote, "A Narrative Incantation for Snake Bite," *UF,* 12 (1980), 135-39; M. Dietrich and O. Loretz, "Die Bannung von Schlangengift (KTU 1.100 und KTU 1.107:7b-13a, 19b-20)," *UF,* 12 (1980), 153-170; H. Egli, *Das Schlangensymbol* (Freiburg, 1982); M. Görg, "Das Wort zur Schlange (Gen 3,14f.," *BN,* 19 (1982), 121-140; O. Grether and J. Fichtner, "The Serpent in the OT," *TDNT,* V, 571-76; J. Haspecker and N. Lohfink, "Gn 3,15: 'weil du ihm nach der Ferse schnappst,'" *Scholastik,* 36 (1961), 357-372; J. Hehn, "Zur Paradiesesschlange," *Festschrift S. Merkle* (Düsseldorf, 1922), 137-151; J. Hofbauer, "Die Paradiesesschlange (Gn 3)," *ZKT,* 69 (1947), 228-231; K. R. Joines, "The Bronze Serpent in the Israelite Cult," *JBL,* 87 (1968), 245-256; *idem,* "The Serpent in Gen 3," *ZAW,* 87 (1975), 1-11; *idem,* "The Serpent in the OT" (diss., Southern Baptist Theological Seminary, 1967); *idem, Serpent Symbolism in the OT* (Haddonfield, N.J., 1974); P. Kjeseth, "Nehushtan (Num 21,4-9, 2 Kgs 18,4) and Ernst Bloch," *Dialog,* 17 (1978), 280-86; H. Lesêtre, "Serpent," *DB,* V (1912), 1671-74; H. Maneschg, *Die Erzählung von der ehernen Schlange (Num 21,4-9) in der Auslegung der frühen jüdischen Literatur. EH,* XXIII/157 (1981); R. G. Murison, "The Serpent in the OT," *AJSL,* 21 (1904/5), 115-130; B. Piperov, "Die Symbolik der Schlange bei den biblischen Schriftstellern," *Jahrbuch der geistlichen Akademie* (Sofia), 32 (1957), 369-390; B. Renz, "Die kluge Schlange," *BZ,* 24 (1938/39), 236-241; H. H. Rowley, "Zadok and Nehushtan," *JBL,* 58 (1939), 113-141; O. Sauermann, *Untersuchungen zu der Wortgruppe* נחשׁ (Vienna, 1955); G. Schneemann and J. Heller, "Feuerschlangen in Num 21,4-9," *ComViat,* 20 (1977), 251-58; P. A. Seethaler, "Kleiner Diskussionsbeitrag zu Gen 3,1-5," *BZ,* N.S. 23 (1979), 85f.; F. Thureau-Dangin, "Le serpent d'airain," *Revue d'histoire et de littérature religieuses,* 1 (1896), 151-58; M. Vernes, "Le serpent d'airain fabriqué par Moïse et les serpents guérisseurs d'Esculape," *Revue Archéologique,* 6 (1918), 36-49; P. Welten, "Schlange," *BRL*², 280f.; C. Westermann, *Genesis 1–11* (Eng. trans., Minneapolis, 1984), 237-240; H. Wohlstein, "Zur Tier-Dämonologie der Bibel," *ZDMG,* 113 (1963), 483-492; S. Yeivin, "The Brazen Serpent," *EMiqr,* 72 (1977), 10f. (Heb.); D. W. Young, "With Snakes and Dates: A Sacred Marriage Drama at Ugarit," *UF,* 9 (1977), 291-314; W. Zimmerli, "Das Bilderverbot in der Geschichte des Alten Israel (Goldenes Kalb, Eherne Schlange, Mazzeben und Lade)," *Schalom. Festschrift A. Jepsen. AzT,* 1/46 (1971), 86-96 = *Studien zur alttestamentlichen Theologie und Prophetie. ThB,* 51 (1974), 247-260.

"menstruation(?)"; and *n*ᵉ*ḥuštān* as the term denoting the "bronze serpent."[1] The etymology must therefore examine and explain the history of five roots and their relationship to each other.

a. The Hebrew verb *niḥēš,* "seek or give omens, prognosticate,"[2] also occurs in Aramaic, Syriac, and Mandaic. It is often associated with Arab. *naḥisa,* in the fifth stem "investigate," with the derived noun *naḥaš,* "spell, omen." There is no discernible connection with *nāḥāš,* "serpent," since serpents have no mantic associations in Israel. O. Sauermann derives the verb from the biliteral root *ḥš,* "make soft sounds, whisper," a theory that might establish a semantic link. E. L. Dietrich, however, proposes interpreting *niḥēš* as a denominative verb from *nāḥāš* or deriving it from a common Semitic root *nḥš,* "practice magic."[3] There is no evidence, however, for such a root.

b. Outside Hebrew, *nāḥāš,* "serpent," appears only in Ugaritic.[4] It is connected with Arab. *ḥanaš,* "serpent, insect, bird," *lḥš,* "whisper," or *rḥš,* "be excited, agitated."[5] Sauermann cites Egyp. *nḥśy,* "be dark, black" (usually "Negro" or "Nubian"; cf. Heb. *pînᵉḥās* < *pꜣ nḥsy,* "the Nubian"),[6] but is then forced to accept the unlikely conclusion that the common Hebrew word for "serpent" is an Egyptian loanword. It is therefore probable that *nāḥāš* is a primary noun.

c. The nouns *n*ᵉ*ḥûšâ* and *n*ᵉ*ḥōšeṯ,* "copper, bronze," are associated with Arab. *nuḥās,* "copper."[7] Mitchell Dahood cites Arab. *ḥasana,* "be beautiful"; others cite *naḥasa,* "be hard, firm" (rare). Here too Sauermann sees a direct borrowing from Egyptian,[8] with primary emphasis on the characteristic color of the metal. In one of the Amarna tablets, a Canaanite gloss uses the word *nuḫuštum,* "copper."[9]

d. The noun *n*ᵉ*ḥuštān* as a term for the "bronze serpent" *(n*ᵉ*ḥaš n*ᵉ*ḥōšeṯ)* may be associated with this group of words only because it sounds like *nāḥāš.*[10] It does not appear to be a word native to Hebrew-speaking circles.[11] Dietrich cites other personal names containing the element *nḥš* and thinks an East Semitic origin likely. Alfred Jeremias sees a connection with the Mesopotamian healing deity Šaḫan (by metathesis; cf. above), but this is hardly likely.[12]

---

1. *HAL,* II, 686, 690f. On *nḥš,* "prognosticate," and *naḥaš,* "spell," → כשׁף *kāšap̱* (VII, 360-66).
2. → VII, 365.
3. E. L. Dietrich, *ZDMG,* 113 (1963), 202ff.
4. *UT,* no. 1634.
5. The first, by metathesis; see *VG,* I, 275; J. Barr, *Comparative Philology and the Text of the OT* (London, 1968), 97. For the second see *HAL,* II, 527; but cf. W. von Soden, *WZKM,* 53 (1957), 157-160. The third is an association already proposed by L. Herzfeld in 1883.
6. *WbÄS,* II, 303.
7. *HAL,* II, 686; Lane, I/8, 2775.
8. See b above.
9. EA, 69, 28. Cf. *CAD,* XI/2, 322. → נחשׁת *n*ᵉ*ḥōšeṯ.*
10. E. L. Dietrich, 202ff.
11. See already P. de Lagarde, *AKGW,* 35 (1888), 188.
12. A. Jeremias, *Handbuch der altorientalischen Geisteskultur* (Berlin, ²1929), 57.

2. *Distribution and Syntax.* The noun *nāḥāš* occurs 31 times in the OT; 15 of these occurrences are in the Pentateuch (5 in J [Gen. 3], 2 in JE [Ex. 4:3; 7:15], 3 in P [Ex. 7:9f.,12]). The occurrences in Nu. 21:5-9 (3 times) and Gen. 49:17 are hard to assign. Dt. 8:15 is Deuteronomistic. Other occurrences: 2 each in Amos, Jeremiah, Proverbs, Psalms, Ecclesiastes, and the late apocalypse of Isaiah; one each in Isaiah, Trito-Isaiah, Job, and the Deuteronomistic history.

One finds the following phrases: *n*ᵉ*ḥaš (han)n*ᵉ*ḥōšeṯ,* "bronze serpent" (Nu. 21:9; 2 K. 18:4); *nāḥāš śārāp̱,* "fiery serpent" (Dt. 8:15), pl. *hann*ᵉ*ḥāšîm haśś*ᵉ*rāp̱îm* (Nu. 21:6); *n*ᵉ*ḥāšîm ṣip̱ʿōnîm,* "poisonous serpents" (Jer. 8:17); *nāḥāš bārîaḥ,* "fleeing serpent" (Job 26:13; Isa. 27:1); *nāḥāš ʿ*ᵃ*qallāṯôn,* "twisting serpent" (Isa. 27:1); the last two describe Leviathan (cf. the similar description of the chaos dragon in the Ugaritic Baʿal myth[13]).

Ps. 58:5(Eng. v. 4) speaks of *ḥ*ᵃ*maṯ-nāḥāš,* "venom of a serpent" (cf. *ḥ*ᵃ*maṯ ʿak̲šûḇ* in Ps. 140:4[3]), Isa. 14:19 of *šōreš nāḥāš,* "root of a serpent."

3. *Lexical Field and Parallels.* The lexical field "serpent" has been the subject of several studies, with the following conclusions.[14] The noun *nāḥāš* is a generic term meaning "serpent" in general; all the other words are subordinate to it, denoting particular types or species. "Serpents" together with the lower animals (e.g., *ʿaqrāḇ,* "scorpion": Dt. 8:15) belong in turn to the class of "crawling things of the earth" (*zōḥ*ᵃ*lê ʾereṣ:* Mic. 7:17), more generally the "animals of the field" (*ḥayyaṯ haśśāḏeh:* Gen. 3:1,14) or even *b*ᵉ*hēmâ* (3:14).[15] *śārap,* "fiery serpent," seems also occasionally (e.g., in Nu. 21) to be a generic term. The species mentioned in the OT are *peṯen,* "asp"; *ṣip̱ʿônî* and *ṣepaʿ,* "asp"; *ʾep̱ʿeh,* "viper"; *ʿak̲šûḇ,* "adder" (Ps. 140:4[3]); *š*ᵉ*p̱îp̱ōn,* "viper" (Gen. 49:17); and *qippōz,* "sand snake."

The language takes on mythological overtones when hybrid creatures are superimposed on the zoological notion of a reptile. This is occasionally true of *śārap* (Isa. 6); it is always true of *liwyāṯān, tannîn* (Isa. 27:1), and *rāhaḇ* (Job 26:12), as in Babylon.

Like the wolf *(z*ᵉ*ʾēḇ)* and lion *(ʾaryēh),* the *nāḥāš* is counted among the wild animals (Isa. 65:25), in contrast to the lamb *(ṭāleh)* and the ox *(bāqār).* The nature of their movement, like the flight of the eagle *(nešer),* arouses wonder in the wise (Prov. 30:19). Eccl. 10:11 plays on the words *nāḥāš* and *laḥāš,* "spell," which may also have a semantic affinity.

4. *LXX.* The LXX almost always uses *óphis* to translate *nāḥāš* (also *śārāp̱* and *ʾep̱ʿeh*); only in Job 26:13 and Am. 9:3 (where the context demands a sea serpent) does it use *drákōn,* which elsewhere represents *tan, tannîn,* and *liwyāṯān,* and once each *peṯen, ʿattûḏ* (in error for *árchontes:* Jer. 50[LXX 27]:8), and *k*ᵉ*p̱îr.* The LXX uses *aspís* for the individual species or distinguishes them with such terms as *basilískos, drákōn,*

---

13. *KTU,* 1.5, I, 1ff.; P. Humbert, *AfO,* 11 (1936), 235-37.
14. Murison, Lesêtre, Joines, and Grether and Fichtner.
15. → II, 18.

kerástēs, and *echínos.*[16] The Targs. regularly use Aram. *ḥiwyā'/ḥewyā'.*[17] In translating *nāḥāš* the Vulg. alternates among the synonyms *serpens, coluber,* and *draco.*[18]

II. Zoology.

1. *General.* The zoological information concerning the serpent in the OT is based entirely on observation; there are no flights of fancy. It lives in the *miḏbār haggāḏôl* (Dt. 8:15), on a rock (*ṣûr:* Prov. 30:19), or at the bottom of the sea (Am. 9:3). Neither explicitly nor implicitly does the OT distinguish poisonous vipers and asps from harmless species. It appears that mention of *hannāḥāš* (e.g., Nu. 21:7,9) implicitly brings with it a basic register of associations: its unusual way of moving (Gen. 3:14; Prov. 30:19), its predilection for hiding (Am. 5:19) and striking suddenly (Gen. 49:17), its dangerous bite and deadly poison (Gen. 3:15; Am. 5:19; Ps. 58:5[4]; Job 20:14), its sharp, forked tongue (Ps. 140:4[3]), and its threatening hiss (Jer. 46:22; cf. Wis. 17:9). It builds a nest where it hatches its brood (Isa. 34:15). Its eggs conceal all the treacherous cunning of its kind (Isa. 59:5).[19] Serpents devour each other (Ex. 7:12). Even the erroneous notion that serpents lick or eat dust (Mic. 7:17; Isa. 65:25) is based on the observation "that many species of snakes put spittle around their victims and thus get dust on their mouths."[20]

All these observations led people to consider serpents ugly, repulsive, sinister, and dangerous. This view expresses the profound aversion of human beings, who walk upright, toward everything that creeps or crawls. Nowhere in ancient Israel do we find any possibility of developing a positive attitude toward serpents, as was the case in Egypt, Greece, and Italy.[21] There was certainly never any serpent cult, as in Mesopotamia and Egypt.[22] This — more than the inclusion of serpents in Ugaritic mythology — accounts for the fact that serpents were considered cultically unclean.

2. *'ep̱'eh.* The noun *'ep̱'eh,* "viper" (Isa. 30:6; 59:5; Job 20:16), well attested in South Semitic, may be an onomatopoetic formation echoing the reptile's puffing breathing *(p'h).*[23] Its zoological identification is disputed, but it is probably an *Echis* (*arenicola, arietans, carinata,* or *colorata*),[24] an extremely dangerous sand viper. According to Job 20:16b, the tongue of the *reša'* is the tongue of an *'ep̱'eh,* which kills its owner. The LXX translation *basilískos* leaves the zoological realm, recalling the Greco-Egyptian myth of the basilisk, the "king of the reptiles."[25]

---

16. See Joines, "Serpent in the OT," 1-8.
17. See M. Görg, *BN,* 16 (1981), 57.
18. On the other versions see Sauermann, 5-9.
19. See IV.8 below.
20. L. Rost, *TDNT,* V, 572, n. 81.
21. Murison, 115f.
22. → נחשתן *n^eḥuštān.*
23. *HAL,* I, 79.
24. See, respectively, Joines, *Serpent Symbolism,* 5 ("maybe"); Murison; F. S. Bodenheimer, *Animal Life in Palestine* (Jerusalem, 1935), 190; *HAL,* II, 79.
25. L. Rost, "Basilisk," *BHHW,* I, 204.

3. *zāḥal.* The form *zāḥal* (found in Hebrew, Aramaic, Syriac, Arabic, and Old South Arabic) is not a term for a specific kind of serpent but a verb meaning "creep" (Job 32:6).[26] Only in Dt. 32:24 and Mic. 7:17 does the ptcp. *zōḥēl* refer clearly to a reptile, not identified further. According to 1 K. 1:9, Adonijah offered sacrifice by the *'eḇen hazzōḥeleṯ,* near the spring Rogel, in order to be acclaimed king there. The expression could refer to an ancient Canaanite sanctuary (cf. *'ên hattannîn* in Neh. 2:13).[27] There is no suggestion, however, of a serpent as a dynastic idol of the Davidides.[28] The association "serpent stone"–spring–bronze serpent is insecure at best, since the theory that the stone has something to do with a "serpent" is uncertain.[29]

4. *'aḵšûḇ.* The word *'aḵšûḇ* (Ps. 140:4[3]), "viper," is etymologically obscure; it denotes the horned viper *(Cerastes cornutus).*[30] In Targumic Hebrew it means "spider." According to Herodotus, the horned viper was sacred to Jupiter and was worshiped cultically at Thebes.[31]

5. *peṯen.* The noun *peṯen,* "asp," is an Aramaic term for the cobra or uraeus serpent *(Naha haia, Cerastes candidus);* it may be related etymologically to Gk. *pýthōn.*[32] The appearance of the word in Ugaritic *(bṯn),* Arabic *(baṯan),* and Syriac *(paṯnā')* suggests that in this word we have the generic Semitic term for "serpent" (cf. also Akk. *bašmu*), which may have entered Hebrew through Aramaic.[33] According to Ps. 58:5f.(4f.), this dangerous serpent (91:13) was used by magicians and enchanters. Its terrible poison (Dt. 32:33) causes illness (Job 20:14) or even death (v. 16). Sir. 39:30 calls the *peṯen* an instrument of God's punishment. Isa. 11:8 mentions the *peṯen* in painting a paradisal picture of eschatological peace among human beings and animals.[34]

6. *ṣep̄a'/ṣip̄'ônî.* The nouns *ṣep̄a'* (Isa. 14:29) and *ṣip'ônî* do not appear to have any Semitic etymology; they probably refer to the largest and most dangerous serpent found in Palestine, the *Daboia/Vipera xanthina.*[35] Since this snake is viviparous, 59:5 may

---

26. *HAL,* I, 267.

27. Joines, "Serpent in the OT," 32f.; *idem, Serpent Symbolism,* 92f.; R. Kittel, *Studien zur hebräischen Archäologie und Religionsgeschichte* (1908), 159-188.

28. R. Smith, Murison.

29. Advocating the association are Baudissin; Joines, *Serpent Symbolism,* 92f., 96, n. 43. But see, e.g., G. R. Driver, "Hebrew Notes," *ZAW,* 52 (1934), 51f.; cf. III.2 below.

30. *HAL,* II, 824; Bodenheimer, *Animal Life,* 190.

31. Joines, *Serpent Symbolism,* 6.

32. Murison, 3. See Bodenheimer, *Animal Life,* 190f.; G. Garbini, "Considerazioni sulla parola ebraica *peten,*" *RivBibl,* 6 (1958), 263-65.

33. See W. Eilers, *Symbolae biblicae et Mesopotamicae. Festschrift F. M. T. de Liagre Böhl. SFS,* 4 (1973), 134. On Ugaritic see *UT,* no. 546; on Arabic, M. Wagner, *Die lexikalischen und grammatikalischen Aramaismen in alttestamentlichen Hebräisch. BZAW,* 96 (1966), 97; on Syriac, *LexSyr,* 618; on Akkadian, *AHw,* I, 112.

34. See below.

35. Bodenheimer, *Animal Life,* 187ff. On the etymology see *HAL,* III, 1050.

contradict this identification; but the prophet is probably thinking only of the deadliness of this species without trying to describe it in detail.[36] It appears also in 11:8; 14:29; Jer. 8:17; Prov. 23:32. There is a possible connection with "Typhon," the name of a dragon.[37]

7. *qippōz.* The *qippōz* (Arab. *qiffazat*) is mentioned only in Isa. 34:15; this noun may refer to the arrow snake *(Coluber jugularis),*[38] so named because of its lightning speed. It is the commonest serpent in Palestine.[39] Isa. 34:15 prophesies that when Edom is laid waste this snake will make its nest there, to hatch and brood.

8. *šᵉp̱îp̱ōn.* The *šᵉp̱îp̱ōn* viper is mentioned only in Gen. 49:17; this is the horned viper (*Cerastes hasselquestii*[40]), an extremely poisonous reptile the color of sand, which reaches a length of 50 cm. (20 in.). The description by H. B. Tristram matches precisely the characterization in Gen. 49:17.[41] The comparison of the tribe of Dan to this malevolent creature is meant less to characterize the Danites pejoratively than to flaunt the victory of this small tribe over the superior forces of its enemies.

III. Religious and Symbolic Usage.

1. *Mesopotamia.* The serpent plays a role in Mesopotamian mythology and therefore is depicted frequently in art, especially on seals.[42] In the Gilgamesh Epic, a serpent robs Gilgamesh of the plant of life.[43] In the myth of Adapa, Tammuz and the serpent-god Gizzida offer Adapa the food of life, although Ea thwarts the offer by trickery.[44] In the symbolism associated with the gods, we find the most fantastic combinations, from an early Elamite figure with a human head on the body of a serpent to a human body with a serpent's head at Susa.[45] Finally, Ningishzida is represented as a human figure with serpents growing from his shoulders. Gudea of Lagash called the serpent-god Ningishzida his protector. His temple was richly adorned with sculptured serpents kept in boxes.[46] More than his father Ninazu, Ningishzida was associated directly with the realms of water, life, the tree of life, and the plant of life; he thus acquired the title "lord of life," from which developed, as one would expect, the "god of healing."[47]

---

36. H. Wildberger, *Isaiah 13–27* (Eng. trans., Minneapolis, 1997), 96.
37. Murison, 120.
38. Joines (*Serpent Symbolism,* 6), *HAL* (III, 1118), and Wildberger (*Jesaja 28–39. BK,* X/3 [1982], 1328f.) do not try to identify the species.
39. Bodenheimer, *Animal Life,* 185.
40. Joines, *Serpent Symbolism,* 6f.
41. *The Natural History of the Bible* (New York, 1867), 274.
42. G. Contenau, *La Glyptique Syro-Hittite* (Paris, 1922), 87ff.; E. D. Van Buren, *The Fauna of Mesopotamia as Represented in Art. AnOr,* 18 (1939), 97-101; *idem, Symbols of the Gods in Mesopotamian Art. AnOr,* 23 (1945), 40ff.
43. Gilg. XI, 304f.; *AOT,* 182.
44. *AOT,* 145; *ANET,* 101ff.
45. Contenau.
46. Van Buren.
47. Hehn, 146f. Cf. the Greek Asclepius and the Palmyrene Shadrapa: *Syr,* 26 (1949), 46, fig. 2.

In Mesopotamia the serpent was one of the chthonic deities and therefore is depicted frequently on boundary stones *(kudurru)*. This use already suggests an association with fertility, an aspect that becomes totally dominant in the motif (found from Ur I on) of the twining serpent, which according to E. Douglas Van Buren represents copulation, thus symbolizing fertility and constituting a favorable omen for human beings, animals, and the fruit of the ground.[48] Finally, the chthonic deities are also the gods of the underworld.

The so-called fall of man cylinder depicts a male figure (with the determinative of a deity) and a female figure under a date palm. There is a serpent behind the woman.[49] There is no reason, however, to see any connection with Gen. 3.[50]

2. *Egypt.* The relationship of the Egyptians to serpents was likewise characterized by both fear and veneration. People sought in many ways to protect themselves from dangerous serpents in both this world and the next, especially by magic. In the Egyptian view serpents came into being by spontaneous generation from the earth and renewed themselves by sloughing their skins. This made them important for theological symbolism (regeneration, resurrection). Many gods, especially the primeval gods, were represented in serpent form. The earth-god Geb had a serpent's head; the "serpent who created the earth" was worshiped at Thebes. Serpent deities controlled human life and the passage of time. People sought to make use of the danger associated with serpents, keeping a tutelary serpent *(ʿḥʿ.y)* as a domestic animal, a manifestation of the deity to protect life and property. The upright uraeus serpent exercised a central apotropaic function; it represented symbolically the omnipotent eye of the sun-god and in writing became the determinative for "goddess."[51] The use of "serpent stones" is attested in Egypt early on: two steles with the image of an upright serpent *(ʿḥʿ)* stood before the central sanctuary of the kingdom.[52] Their origin is debated, but their tutelary function is clear; they probably served primarily as instruments invigorating and renewing the king through the powers of the earth.[53]

3. *Canaan.* In the Ras Shamra texts *nḥš* appears some 50 times; many of these occurrences, however, are concentrated in *KTU,* 1.100 and 1.107, which are the subject of much scholarly debate.[54] We find the constantly repeated refrain:

---

48. *Symbols.*
49. O. Weber, *Altorientalische Siegelbilder. AO,* 17-18 (1920), II, no. 429.
50. Hehn.
51. A. Erman, *Die Religion der Ägypter* (Berlin, 1934), 21f.; O. Keel, *Jawhe-Visionen und Siegelkunst. SBS,* 84/85 (1977), 83ff.
52. See II.3 above.
53. *RÄR,* 584f.; S. Morenz, *Egyptian Religion* (Eng. trans., Ithaca, N.Y., 1973), 26, 33, 61; L. Störk, "Schlange," *LexÄg,* V, 644-652; D. Wildung, "Schlangensteine," *ibid.,* 655f.
54. Dietrich and Loretz.

Charm against the bite of the serpent,
against the poison of the scaly serpent.
From it let the charmer destroy,
from it let him expel poison.
Behold, let him lift high the serpent,
let him feed the scaly serpent.

It is clear that these words refer to charming a serpent; the ritual, however, is embedded in the myth of a sacral marriage between Ḥoron, god of the underworld, and an unnamed goddess (Astarte?), both of whom have the serpent as their symbolic animal.[55] Dwight Young theorizes that *KTU,* 1.100 is based on a Sumerian myth, Theodor Gaster cites Egyptian spells, Dennis Pardee points out Indic parallels, and finally Matitiahu Tsevat conjectures traditions from Asia Minor.[56] Manfred Dietrich and Oswald Loretz see a possible Indo-European or Hurrian background to the ritual.[57] They explain the rare combination of snake charming and myth by theorizing that the myth served the charmer in the ritual and explained the origin and power of the charm; the whole finally constituted a fertility ritual combining snake charming and sacral marriage.

The normal word for "serpent" at Ugarit is *bṯn;* in mythology this is an epithet of the chaos monster Lotan in the expressions *bṯn brḥ,* "fleeing serpent," and *bṯn ʿqltn,* "twisting serpent."[58]

In art the serpent appears as one of the symbols of the fertility-goddess of the Qadšu type. A golden pendant from Ugarit depicts the goddess as "mistress of the animals."[59] The aspect of fertility is emphasized by the inclusion of serpent, lion, and lotus symbols;[60] the particular symbolic value of the serpent cannot be determined.

In the private realm, earthenware serpents were kept in houses for apotropaic purposes.[61] The serpent sculptures in Canaanite temples, however, need not have played the same role, e.g., in the symbolic decoration of the temple paraphernalia (cultic standard from Hazor, incense stands from Beth-shan).[62] Bronze serpents have been found among the votive offerings at Tell Mubarak and Timnaʿ (cf. the serpent head from Tepe Gawra with a tongue made of copper wire[63]).

---

55. See Young. On Ḥoron see A. Caquot, "Horon, revue critique et données nouvelles," *Annales archéologiques arabes, syriennes,* 29/30 (1979/80), 173-180. Loretz disputes that the myth is a sacral marriage.

56. Young, 308; T. H. Gaster, *JANES,* 7 (1975), 50; D. Pardee, "*mᵉrôrăt-pᵉtanîm* 'Venom' in Job 20:14," *ZAW,* 91 (1979), 401-416; M. Tsevat, *UF,* 11 (1979), 776f.

57. P. 168.

58. E.g., *KTU,* 1.5, I, 1f.; cf. Isa. 27:1; → לויתן *liwyāṯān* (VII, 504-9).

59. *Ugaritica,* II (1949), 36, fig. 10.

60. Cf. *ANET,* 470ff.

61. E.g., at Taanach; cf. Welten. See III.1 above.

62. For Hazor see *BRL*², 79; for Beth-shan, *ibid.,* 190.

63. Van Buren, *Fauna,* 99; Joines, *Serpent Symbolism,* 109f.

IV. OT.

In the OT, serpents appear in several important contexts.

1. *Gen. 3.* The serpent in the story of the Fall (Gen. 2f.) is always called *nāḥāš*. Although it is a peripheral figure (mentioned only in 3:1,2,4,13,14), its interpretation is important. The fairy-tale motif of the speaking serpent has attracted little attention; scholars have emphasized symbolic meanings of the serpent or historical allusions of the Yahwist.

a. The serpent as a symbol of rejuvenation or regeneration and eternal life recalls the ancient human longing reflected in the myths of Gilgamesh and Adapa.[64] In Egyptian mythology the serpent appears as guardian of eternal life.[65] Although this theme is addressed in Gen. 2f., it is not associated with the serpent.

The name "Eve" *(ḥawwâ)* is often associated with Aram. *ḥiwyâ* (Syr. *ḥēwyā'*), "serpent," and both derived from *ḥāwâ/ḥāyâ*, "live,"[66] in order to account for the explanatory gloss in Gen. 3:20, "mother of all living." This interpretation is etymologically possible, but is only one of several possible explanations.[67]

b. The theory that the serpent is a symbol of wisdom probably does more justice to the text of Gen. 3.[68] V. 1 describes it as *'ārûm,* "crafty, clever";[69] the many occurrences of this word in Proverbs show that it was definitely perceived as a positive term. Most of the evidence for the serpent as a symbol of wisdom is Egyptian, but one may also cite the Mesopotamian association of the serpent with divination.[70]

c. It is not clear that the serpent was already considered a symbol of evil in the period of the Yahwist; it was not identified with Satan until the rabbinic and Christian period, although late Israelite traditions had already laid the groundwork (Wis. 2:23f.; Rev. 20:2). The notion of God's enemy as a serpent has parallels in Egypt.[71]

d. The serpent as a symbol of chaos seeks to pervert the order of creation; Karen Joines cites similar Mesopotamian, Egyptian, and Hittite notions.[72] Johannes Hehn's theory that the serpent of Gen. 3 embodies a reminiscence of the Babylonian underworld deity should be understood similarly.[73]

Any interpretation of the serpent as a symbol must be measured against the statement in 3:1 that it is also a creature made by *YHWH 'ᵉlōhîm.* Recent scholarship, therefore,

---

64. Joines, *Serpent Symbolism,* 17; for additional bibliog. see Westermann, 236f.

65. Joines, *Serpent Symbolism,* 19f.

66. First by Wellhausen, then W. Eilers, *Die vergleichende semasiologische Methode in der Orientalistik* (Wiesbaden, 1974), 53f.

67. See *DISO,* 84; *HAL,* I, 296; for other explanations see Westermann, 268f.; → IV, 257-260.

68. T. C. Vriezen, *Onderzoek naar de Paradijsvoorstelling* (Wageningen, 1937); Joines, *Serpent Symbolism,* 21-26.

69. Renz, Hofbauer; cf. Mt. 10:16.

70. G. Contenau, *La divination chez les Assyriens et les Babyloniens* (Paris, 1940), 222.

71. Murison, 127.

72. Joines, *Serpent Symbolism,* 26-30.

73. P. 149.

has largely distanced itself from the theory of a symbolic meaning, since this theory makes it all too easy to misinterpret the serpent as a contrary divine principle alongside *YHWH *ᵉlōhîm*. Scholars today look instead for an historical allusion on the part of the Yahwist.

e. One theory finds a criticism of Solomon's marital policies, since he formed a marriage alliance by taking one of Pharaoh's daughters into his harem (1 K. 3:1; cf. also 9:16f.; 11:1). The emphasis on the roles of the serpent and the woman (both with the definite article) displays J's aversion to this Egyptian woman and the cult of Renutet she imported to Jerusalem. "The serpent becomes a symbolic animal presenting wisdom without Yahweh."[74] On the identification of Egypt with a serpent, see also Jer. 46:22.

f. Joines reads the story of the Fall as an expression of Yahwistic monotheism.[75] A cosmic order in which mortals can become gods like Yahweh through their wisdom is a perversion.

g. William F. Albright, Kurt Galling, and others treat the serpent as a fertility symbol, believing that the material used by the Yahwist originally contained a positive allusion to a Canaanite fertility cult rampant in Israel.[76] Only the Yahwist's redaction lent the story its negative force.[77]

h. To explain Gen. 3:14f., a difficult passage, Manfred Görg theorizes that the curse reflects Hezekiah's two-faced policy.[78] On the one hand, as a distant descendant of "the woman," he destroyed the bronze serpent as a sign of the imported Egyptian cult (2 K. 18:4);[79] on the other hand, through his political toadying to Egypt he imperiled Judah's existence and thus drew Isaiah's criticism (e.g., Isa. 14:29). It would appear difficult, however, to read these verses as documenting the hereditary enmity between Egypt and Israel.

Furthermore, it is hardly possible to sustain exegetically the reading of Gen. 3:14f. as a *protoevangelium,* common since Irenaeus,[80] containing a messianic prophecy referring to Jesus and Mary. More likely it should be read as a promise in the context of the Yahwist's perspective on the future.[81]

The description and appraisal of the serpent in Gen. 3 are much more in the foreground, though no less thoughtful. In vv. 1-4 the serpent, a "wisdom" creature made by *YHWH *ᵉlōhîm,* leads the human couple astray. The Yahwist thus demonstrates that any further investigation into the origin of evil in this world has little hope for

---

74. M. Görg, "Die 'Sünde' Salomos," *BN,* 16 (1981), 42-59, esp. 53; cf. also W. von Soden, "Verschlüsselte Kritik an Salomo in der Urgeschichte des Jahwisten," *WO,* 7 (1973/74), 228-240.

75. Joines, *Serpent Symbolism,* 31.

76. O. Loretz, *Schöpfung und Mythos. SBS,* 32 (1968), 117; E. MacLaurin, "The Canaanite Background of the Doctrine of the Virgin Mary," *Religious Tradition,* 3 (1980), 1-11.

77. L. Ruppert, "Die Sündenfallererzählung (Gn 3) in vorjahwistischer Tradition und Interpretation," *BZ,* N.S. 15 (1971), 185-202; P.-A. Seethaler, "Kleiner Diskussionsbeitrag zu Gen 3,1-5," *BZ,* N.S. 23 (1979), 85f.

78. M. Görg, "Das Wort zur Schlange (Gen 3,14f)," *BN,* 19 (1983), 121-140.

79. Cf. already Murison; see e above.

80. See T. Gallus.

81. See esp. Ruppert, 199-202; J. Scharbert, *Genesis 1–11,* NEB (^{2}1985), 58.

success if it is based on "wisdom."[82] Instead, evil must have its abode in the power of free human beings to make decisions. Only a slight external impetus is needed to turn evil into actual sin. That the Yahwist is attacking a Canaanite serpent cult[83] as such an "impetus" does not emerge necessarily from the text, in which the serpent is a rather peripheral figure.

Vv. 14f. contain etiologies highly appropriate to the subsequent influence of a central text like the account of the Fall. The two verses can hardly come from the same hand. V. 14 uses the archaic form of the curse[84] to explain the peculiar form and habits of the serpent. Then v. 15 is appended to explain the enduring negative relationship between human beings and serpents as a consequence of the curse: "The enmity will work itself out by humans and the serpent continually . . . trying to kill each other."[85] The future, however, holds promise for human beings. Here we hear the voice of the Yahwist and his epigoni, who certainly wanted to be considered participants in the wisdom erudition of the royal court. Textually, this attempt to explain why human life bears the stamp of sin and death is not a collection of etiologies; by attracting such etiologies, however, it has become a compendium of ethically oriented attempts to explain the nature of the world.

2. *The Miraculous Staff.* The two accounts of the miraculous staff (the first, Ex. 4:3; 7:15; the second, 7:9-12) exhibit such close parallels that they cannot be independent. At the same time, however, the differences are so great that they must be deliberate. Scholars disagree as to what source strata are involved: Ex. 4:3; 7:15 are J, the *Vorlage* of JE, or JE;[86] 7:9f.,12 are P.

The earlier recension speaks of Yahweh's giving Moses a sign in the context of his call. Then his staff is transformed into a serpent *(nāḥāš)* as a sign of Yahweh's mighty aid. Moses flees in terror. At Yahweh's command, however, the serpent turns back into a staff. The flight motif in particular suggests that this recension has preserved the original form of the story. In Ex. 7:15 Yahweh commands Moses to go to Pharaoh with the staff "that was turned into a *nāḥāš,*" to poison the waters of the Nile. This description of the staff should be taken as an encouraging recollection of the authenticating sign. It is noteworthy that this recension associates Moses very closely with both the staff and the serpent (cf. also Nu. 21:5-9; 2 K. 18:4);[87] we may well ask whether it does not enshrine ancient memories.

P presents this tradition in a form so different that we must suspect both the incorporation of heterogeneous material and deliberate modification: Moses *and* Aaron go to Pharaoh and legitimate themselves by turning the staff into a *tannîn,* the word

82. Westermann, 238f.
83. See g above.
84. W. Schottroff, *Die altisraelitische Fluchspruch. WMANT,* 30 (1969).
85. Westermann, 259.
86. For J see Simian-Yofre, → VIII, 243f.; for the *Vorlage* of JE, P. Weimar, *Die Berufung des Mose. OBO,* 32 (1980), 237; for JE, W. H. Schmidt, *Exodus 1–6. BK,* II (1988), 193.
87. Schmidt, *BK,* II, in loc.

used for a sea monster in Gen. 1:21. When Egyptian magicians perform the same feat, Aaron's staff swallows up their serpents or staffs. Thus the legitimation is expanded to become a demonstration of power.

3. *Nu. 21.* Nu. 21:4-9 is actually a murmuring episode in which the people are attacked by serpents (*hannᵉḥāšîm haśśᵉrāp̱îm,* v. 6; *nᵉḥāšîm,* v. 7; *śārāp̱,* v. 8; *hannāḥāš,* v. 9). Yahweh commands Moses to make a *śārāp̱* and set it on a pole (→ נס *nēs*) (v. 8). Moses then makes the *nᵉḥaš nᵉḥōšeṯ* (v. 9a; with the definite article in v. 9b). Both 2 K. 18:4 and Wis. 16:5-11 allude to this story; the former identifies the *nᵉḥaš hannᵉḥōšeṯ* with → נחשתן *nᵉḥuštān.* Dt. 8:15 (Deuteronomistic or later[88]) likewise recalls this perilous situation in the wilderness, and even Jer. 8:17 (cf. Isa. 30:6f.) may reflect this danger faced by the Israelites.[89] One striking element in Nu. 21:4-9 is the obvious variation in the terminology used for the serpents. Since the content of the narrative does not require this constant variation and it cannot be explained by literary analysis, we should consider this text a literary product of the late period (R^P), which can easily contain earlier material (JE).[90]

Less noteworthy than the apotropaic function of the serpent on a pole (an Egyptian motif) is the association of the serpent image with sickness (more specifically snakebite) and healing. It is therefore reasonable to suppose that in the original recension the *nᵉḥaš (hann)nᵉḥōšeṯ* was the symbol of a healing deity. "Clearly, then, Yahweh is a secondary importation into what was originally a transparent symbol of a healing deity. That he never was seen unambiguously in this context can probably be explained by the removal of the cultic image during the reform under Hezekiah."[91] Nu. 21:4-9 is, however, no longer concerned with legitimizing the *nᵉḥuštān:* the text does not undertake any identification, and furthermore the cultic object mentioned in 2 K. 18:4 had long been forgotten. The healing effect is ascribed only to obedience to Yahweh (paradigmatically expressed by looking up [at the *śārāp̱:* vv. 9c,9b]). At the same time, we see in this passage a pragmatic interpretation of the prohibition against images, which was becoming increasingly important in the late period.

4. *Gen. 49:17.* The Blessing of Jacob characterizes the tribe of Dan as follows: "Dan shall judge his people, as one of the tribes of Israel. Dan shall be a snake *(nāḥāš)* by the roadside, a viper *(šᵉp̱îp̱ōn)* along the path, that bites the horse's heels so that its rider falls backward" (Gen. 49:16f.). The two sayings do not harmonize particularly well, hence we may assume separate origins. Although neither can be assigned to a particular source stratum, we can discern a series of twelve units belonging to JE and a framework surrounding Gen. 49 from the hand of R^P. It is impossible to date the

88. N. Lohfink, *"Ich will euer Gott werden": Beispiele biblischen Redens von Gott. SBS,* 100 (1981), 60, n. 133.
89. See the further discussion below.
90. Maneschg, 97f.
91. Lohfink, 42, n. 90.

comparison of Dan to a snake and a viper.[92] In any case, the saying must antedate Jer. 8:16f., where the prophet uses the familiar associations with "poison" (Dan in v. 16). The comparison to a snake is not necessarily intended to be negative; more likely the point of comparison is the wily and determined survival instinct of this small tribe (Jgs. 18), so that a dating of the saying as early as the period of the judges might be considered.[93] According to Stanley Gevirtz, the word *bāšān* in the parallel Dan saying in Dt. 33:22 also conceals the name of a serpent *(peṯen).*[94]

5. *Cosmic Peace.* The motif of eschatological peace among animals and between animals and human beings (Isa. 11:6-8) includes serpents: nursing children will be able to play safely over asps' hiding places. This passage should not be interpreted as an allegorical description of universal peace among all nations;[95] it is intended to show paradigmatically that nothing evil or dangerous will have any place in the world of the age of salvation (concentrated on the *har qoḏšî*).

Isa. 65:25 describes this situation in strikingly similar terms. It is noteworthy that in both passages the prophetic authors see the natural food chain interrupted at the *eschaton* (lions eat grass, serpents eat dust). The same idea appears in Mesopotamian mythology.[96]

In Isa. 34:9-15, by contrast, a late Israelite apocalyptic author paints a terrifying picture of Edom laid waste: owls, ravens, jackals, hyenas, poisonous snakes *(qippōz),* and vultures inhabit the ruins.

6. *Mythological Texts.* Texts colored or influenced by mythology mostly use *tannîn* as the word for "serpent." In these cases the motif of the battle with chaos is always in the background (Ps. 74:13; 148:7; Job 7:12; also Isa. 51:9; Jer. 51:34). Only Am. 9:3; Job 26:13; Isa. 27:1 use *nāḥāš.* All these passages are almost certainly late postexilic texts. Surprisingly, Isa. 27:1 contains echoes of Ugaritic mythology. Am. 9:3, which designates the serpent as an instrument of divine punishment, is atypical.

7. *Wisdom.* The serpent appears frequently as a metaphor in the *māšāl* of Wisdom Literature: the serpent's venom is the outstanding example of everything pernicious. The food of the wicked is transformed into venom within them (Job 20:14), and they ultimately perish as though poisoned (v. 18). The wicked speak with a double tongue; their lips conceal the venom of vipers (Ps. 140:4[3]). Ps. 58:5(4) (cf. Ps. 82) centers these proverbial dangers on corrupt judges. Dt. 32:33 uses the same language to describe

---

92. Westermann, *Genesis 37–50* (Eng. trans., Minneapolis, 1986), 220: "horned viper"; H. Gunkel, *Genesis* (Eng. trans., Macon, Ga., 1997), 459: "a small, very dangerous species of snake."

93. L. Ruppert, *Das Buch Genesis,* II (Düsseldorf, 1984), 411f.

94. S. Gevirtz, "Adumbrations of Dan in Jacob's Blessing on Judah," *ZAW,* 93 (1981), 21-37, esp. 30ff. See already W. F. Albright, cited by F. M. Cross and D. N. Freedman, *Studies in Ancient Yahwistic Poetry* (1975, repr. Grand Rapids, 1997), 80, n. 74.

95. Buber.

96. For citations see H. Wildberger, *Isaiah 1–12* (Eng. trans., Minneapolis, 1991), 479f.

the enemies of Israel. Prov. 23:32 departs from this metaphorical usage, comparing the effects of wine to the venom of serpents. Eccl. 10:8, "Whoever digs a pit can fall into it; whoever breaks through a wall can be bitten by a snake," warns against rashly trying to change the status quo. It is all too easy to burn one's fingers.

8. *Prophetic Threats.* Imagery derived from observation of the natural world finds a parallel in the threat pronounced in Am. 5:19: "It is as if someone fled from a lion, and was met by a bear; or went into the house and rested a hand against the wall, and was bitten by a serpent." In this vivid causal sequence, in which the serpent is the final instrument of God's punishment, Amos attempts to show that the confidence of the people who look forward to the "day of Yahweh"[97] is misplaced. A similar causal sequence appears in Isa. 14:29, an oracle against the Philistines. They are looking forward to the death of an oppressor (Tiglath-pileser?), but "from the root of the snake *(nāḥāš)* will come forth an adder *(ṣepaʿ),* and its fruit will be a flying fiery serpent *(śārāp̱ meʿōp̱ēp̱).*" "Whereas the Philistines regard the danger as past, they and . . . the whole world of the nations are in fact faced with an intensification of the threat from which there is no escape."[98] According to Mic. 7:17, God's judgment brings a proverbial humiliation upon the nations: they shall eat dust like a snake (cf. Gen. 3:14; Ps. 72:9; Isa. 49:23).[99]

In a threat against Egypt, Jer. 46:22 compares the land to a snake gliding away, which is nevertheless struck down as though by the blow of a woodsman's ax.

Finally, Isa. 59:5 compares the intrigues of the wicked to the hatching of adders' eggs and the weaving of webs. "Whoever eats their eggs dies, and the crushed egg hatches out a viper" expresses metaphorically the difference between the outward appearance and the true nature of the plotters.

9. *Oracles of Salvation.* Only once (and without the use of *nāḥāš*) are serpents mentioned in an oracle of salvation: "The one who lives in the shelter of the Most High" is borne up by angels so that he can tread on the lion (?) and the adder *(peṯen)* and trample the young lion and dragon *(tannîn)* underfoot (Ps. 91:13). Yahweh protects his own, even and especially against proverbial dangers.

V. Dead Sea Scrolls. Apart from the Damascus Document, serpents are not a theme in the Dead Sea Scrolls. Only in 11QTemple 60:18 does the piel of *nḥš* occur with the meaning "practice divination," an activity prohibited at Qumran (cf. Dt. 18:11). There are 3 occurrences of *zāḥal* and 5 of *peṯen; ṣep̱aʿ* occurs once.

In 1QH 5:27 the intrigues of the community's enemies are compared to the venom of serpents, for which there is no antidote. CD 5:14 cites Isa. 59:5 to describe those who violate the Torah; CD 8:19f.; 19:22f. cite Dt. 32:33 in proscribing apostates.

Fabry

---

97. → יוֹם *yôm* (VI, 7-32).
98. O. Kaiser, *Isaiah 13–39. OTL* (Eng. trans. 1974), 54.
99. → עָפָר *ʿāp̱ār.*

נְחֹשֶׁת *n*[e]*ḥōšeṯ*; נְחוּשָׁה *n*[e]*ḥûšâ*; נְחֻשְׁתָּן *n*[e]*ḥuštān*

Contents: I. 1. Etymology and Meaning; 2. Distribution; 3. Lexical Field; 4. Phrases; 5. LXX. II. 1. *nḥšt* in the Ancient Near East; 2. Copper/Bronze in the Ancient Near East. III. Bronze/Copper in the OT: 1. Everyday Life; 2. Military Technology; 3. Cultic Objects. IV. Metaphorical Usage: 1. Oracular Threats; 2. Oracles of Salvation; 3. Visions. V. The "Bronze Serpent." VI. Dead Sea Scrolls.

I. 1. *Etymology and Meaning*. The etymology of *n*[e]*ḥōšeṯ* appears to lie within West Semitic, since the Canaanite gloss *nuḫuštum* in EA, 69, 28 (glossing *erû*) already provides evidence of the word. Association with a verbal root *nḥš* II gains nothing, since such a root is not attested.

O. Sauermann associates the word with Egyp. *nḥś*, "black, dark,"[1] seeing the term for the metal as an outgrowth of its color. Karl H. Singer reverses the argument, deriving *n*[e]*ḥōšeṯ* from *nāḥāš*, "serpent," with the basic meaning "serpentlike": "this probably refers to the reddish-yellowish (copper pyrites) color of copper, which is reminiscent of the color of snakes."[2] These derivations are not particularly convincing, since all words for metals exhibit the same etymological problems. They have no adjective forms, and it is as easy to consider the verbs denominative as it is to consider the nouns deverbal.

The noun *n*[e]*ḥōšeṯ* II, "menstruation" (Ezk. 16:36), is associated with Akk. *naḫšatu*;[3] it probably has nothing to do with our etymon.

Besides EA, 69, 28, this etymon is found in Aramaic, Mandaic, Arabic, Ethiopic, and the Tigré dialects,[4] always with the meaning "copper" or "bronze." "Since it . . . is not always possible to decide whether copper or bronze is meant, we may establish the following rule: for all objects characterized by strength and hardness, we may

---

n[e]*ḥōšeṯ*. A. Alt, "Hic murus aheneus esto," *ZDMG*, 86 (1933), 33-48; J. Bottéro, "Métallurgie," *Dictionnaire archéologique des techniques*, II (1964), 649-657; T. A. Busink, *Der Tempel von Jerusalem von Salomo bis Herodes I. SFS*, 3 (1970), 232-35, and esp. 287f.; H. G. Conrad and B. Rothenberg, *Antikes Kupfer im Timna-Tal. Der Anschnitt*, Beihefte 1 (Bochum, 1980) (cf. G. Mansfeld, *ZDPV*, 99 [1983], 219-224); R. J. Forbes, *Studies in Ancient Technology*, VIII (Leiden, [2]1971); IX (Leiden, [2]1972); M. Gsell, "Eisen, Kupfer und Bronze bei den alten Ägyptern" (diss., Karlsruhe, 1910); M. Heltzer, *Goods, Prices, and the Organization of Trade in Ugarit* (Wiesbaden, 1978); K. D. Hill and I. Mundle, "Erz," *RAC*, VI, 443-502; J. L. Kelso, "Ezekiel's Parable of the Corroded Copper Caldron," *JBL*, 64 (1945), 391-93; J. D. Muhly, "Kupfer," *RLA*, VI, 345-364; K. H. Singer, *Die Metalle Gold, Silber, Bronze, Kupfer und Eisen im AT und ihre Symbolik. FzB*, 43 (1980); M. Weippert, "Metall und Metallbearbeitung," *BRL*[2], 219-224.

1. → נחשׁ *nāḥāš*, I.1.
2. P. 47.
3. *AHw*, II, 715b.
4. On Mandaic see *MdD*, 290; on Tigré, *WbTigr*, 324; here we also find the clearly denominative verb "apply verdigris."

assume that the material is bronze. If, however, we are dealing with *nᵉḥōšeṯ* as a raw material, an alloy in smelting, or a material constantly exposed to great heat, we may . . . assume copper."[5]

2. *Distribution.* The noun *nᵉḥōšeṯ* is a feminine form of *nuḥušt,* not an abstract noun formed from *naḥaš* + *t.*[6] It occurs 139 times in the OT, including 7 occurrences of the dual *nᵉḥuštayim* (only in texts exhibiting Deuteronomistic influence). It appears with significant frequency in Priestly literature (P^G, P^S, and R^P; 44 times), Ezekiel (7 times), Deuteronomistic literature (the Deuteronomistic history and Deuteronomistic passages in Deuteronomy, 41 times), Jeremiah (14 times), and Chronistic literature (26 times). The word is significantly rare in J (once), JE (? Nu. 21; twice), Trito-Isaiah (twice), Psalms, Lamentations, Zechariah, and Daniel (once each). This uneven distribution reflects the use of the material for cultic utensils (P, etc.), weapons, and temple furnishings (Deuteronomistic history, Chronicler's history); it is out of place in wisdom and poetry. The last uses *nᵉḥûšâ* instead (10 times: 4 times in Job, twice in Deutero-Isaiah, once each in Psalms [cf. also 2 S. 22:35], Micah, and H [Lev. 26:19]). The adj. *nāḥûš* occurs only once (Job 6:12); Singer considers this occurrence a misreading of the noun.[7]

The noun *nᵉḥuštān* appears only in 2 K. 18:4. *HAL* analyzes it as a hybrid form combining *nāḥāš,* "serpent," and *nᵉḥōšeṯ,* "copper, bronze"; according to Wolfram von Soden, the afformative serves to emphasize certain representatives (often unique) of the class denoted by the basic word (cf. *liwyāṯān*).[8] It is possibly only consonance that connects it with *nᵉḥaš nᵉḥōšeṯ.*[9] It is worth noting that all Hebrew nouns ending in *-ān* have something to do with serpents.[10]

3. *Lexical Field.* The OT does not possess any term denoting metal in general; it uses instead words for particular metals: → זהב *zāhābh,* "gold"; → כסף *kesep̱,* "silver"; *barzel,* "iron"; *bᵉḏîl,* "tin"; *ʿôpereṯ,* "lead." Whether *ʾᵃnāḵ* (Am. 7:7f., in the vision of the "plumb line") really means "tin" is highly dubious, since this interpretation makes the vision obscure.[11] The noun *sîg,* "galina, silver dross,"[12] probably does not mean pure metal but dross with a high metal content. Gold was of the highest importance in Israel, both as a metal and symbolically. Since there were probably various forms of gold for commercial purposes, Hebrew also has the more or less close synonyms *keṯem, paz, ḥārûṣ, beṣer,* and *sᵉg̱ôr.*[13]

The language also includes words for the two alloys known since the end of the

5. Singer, 46.
6. *BLe,* 609. Cf. *GK,* 86k.
7. P. 46, n. 3.
8. *HAL,* II, 692; *GaG,* §56r.
9. E. L. Dietrich, *ZDMG,* 113 (1963), 202ff.
10. *BLe,* 500r; → נחשׁ *nāḥāš,* I.1.
11. For further discussion see below.
12. *HAL,* II, 750.
13. → IV, 33-35.

third millennium: electrum (*ḥašmal,* a natural alloy of gold and silver) and bronze (*n*[e]*ḥōšeṯ,* an artificial alloy of copper and tin). The primary constituent of the latter, copper, is also called *n*[e]*ḥōšeṯ*. Brass, an alloy of copper and zinc, did not become common until the Roman period and plays no role in the OT.

That these words belong to the same lexical field is shown by their use in series and in parallelisms: gold, silver, bronze, iron, tin, and lead (Nu. 31:22); gold, silver, and bronze (Ex. 31:4; 35:2; 2 Ch. 2:6,13); silver, gold, and bronze (Josh. 22:8); bronze and gold (Isa. 60:17); bronze and silver (Ex. 35:24; 2 S. 8:10; Ezk. 22:20; 1 Ch. 18:10; 29:2); bronze and iron (Gen. 4:22; Nu. 31:22; Dt. 28:23; 33:25; Josh. 6:19,24; Jer. 1:18; 6:28; Ezk. 22:18; 1 Ch. 22:14,16; 2 Ch. 24:12); iron and bronze (Jer. 15:12).

4. *Phrases.* On the one hand, in construct phrases *n*[e]*ḥûšâ* appears only as a *nomen rectum:* *'*[a]*pîqê n*[e]*ḥûšâ,* "tubes of bronze" (Job 40:18); *dalṯôṯ n*[e]*ḥûšâ,* "doors of bronze" (Isa. 45:2); *mēṣaḥ n*[e]*ḥûšâ,* "forehead of bronze" (Isa. 48:4); *qešeṯ n*[e]*ḥûšâ,* "bow of bronze" (2 S. 22:35; Ps. 18:35[Eng. v. 34]). On the other hand, *n*[e]*ḥōšeṯ* does appear in the construct, but only in the phrase *n*[e]*ḥōšeṯ hatt*[e]*nûpâ,* "copper of contribution" (Ex. 38:29). As a *nomen rectum, n*[e]*ḥōšeṯ* appears in a great many phrases: *'aḏnê n*[e]*ḥûšâ,* "bases of bronze" (Ex. 26:37); *'ôpannê n*[e]*ḥûšâ,* "wheels of bronze" (1 K. 7:30); *b*[e]*rîaḥ n*[e]*ḥûšâ,* "bars of bronze" (1 K. 4:13); *dalṯôṯ n*[e]*ḥûšâ,* "doors of bronze" (Ps. 107:16; see also above); *hārê n*[e]*ḥûšâ,* "mountains of bronze" (Zec. 6:1); *ḥômaṯ n*[e]*ḥûšâ,* "wall of bronze" (Jer. 1:18; 15:20); *ḥôrēš n*[e]*ḥûšâ,* "forger of bronze" (Gen. 4:22; 1 K. 7:14; pl. 2 Ch. 24:12); *ṭabb*[e]*'ôṯ n*[e]*ḥûšâ,* "network of copper" (Ex. 27:4); *yām hann*[e]*ḥōšeṯ,* "sea of bronze" (2 K. 25:13, etc.); *kîḏôn n*[e]*ḥûšâ,* "javelin of bronze" (1 S. 17:6); *kîyôr n*[e]*ḥûšâ,* "basin of bronze" (Ex. 30:18, etc.); *k*[e]*lî n*[e]*ḥûšâ,* "vessel of bronze" (Lev. 6:21[28], etc.); *māginnê n*[e]*ḥûšâ,* "shields of bronze" (1 K. 14:27); *mûṣaq n*[e]*ḥûšâ,* "casting of bronze" (1 K. 7:16); *maḥtôṯ hann*[e]*ḥōšeṯ,* "censers of copper" (Nu. 17:4[16:39]); *mizbaḥ hann*[e]*ḥōšeṯ,* "altar of bronze" (Ex. 38:30, etc.); *mikbar n*[e]*ḥûšâ,* "grating of copper" (Ex. 35:16, etc.); *miṣḥaṯ n*[e]*ḥûšâ,* "greaves of bronze" (1 S. 17:6); *m*[e]*ṣiltayim n*[e]*ḥûšâ,* "cymbals of bronze" (1 Ch. 15:19); *mar'ēh n*[e]*ḥûšâ,* "appearance of bronze" (Ezk. 40:3); *mišqal hann*[e]*ḥōšeṯ,* "weight of bronze" (1 K. 7:47, etc.); *n*[e]*ḥaš (han)n*[e]*ḥōšeṯ,* "serpent of bronze" (Nu. 21:9; 2 K. 18:4); *sarnê n*[e]*ḥûšâ,* "axles of bronze" (1 K. 7:30); *'ammûḏê n*[e]*ḥûšâ,* "pillars of bronze" (2 K. 25:13); *qôḇa' n*[e]*ḥûšâ,* "helmet of bronze" (1 S. 17:38); *qarsê n*[e]*ḥûšâ,* "clasps of copper" (Ex. 26:11, etc.); *rešeṯ n*[e]*ḥûšâ,* "net of copper" (Ex. 27:4); *š*[e]*qālîm n*[e]*ḥûšâ,* "shekels of bronze" (1 S. 17:5); *t*[e]*rûmaṯ n*[e]*ḥûšâ,* "offering of bronze" (Ex. 35:24).

Finally, *n*[e]*ḥōšeṯ* is modified by the following adjectives: *m*[e]*mōrāṭ,* "burnished" (1 K. 7:45); *muṣhāḇ,* "polished" (Ezr. 8:27); *mārûq,* "burnished" (2 Ch. 4:16); *qālāl,* "smooth" (Ezk. 1:7, etc.); *rabbâ,* "much" (1 Ch. 18:8). As subject, *n*[e]*ḥōšeṯ* appears with *ḥāmam,* "become hot," and *ḥārâ,* "glow" (Ezk. 24:11); in the context of refining, it is the subject of *bô' bā'ēš,* "go through the fire" (Nu. 31:22). It appears as the object of *ḥāšaḇ,* "hew out, mine" (Dt. 8:9); *ṭāhēr,* "purify," *'āḇar* (hiphil) *bā'ēš,* "pass through the fire" (Nu. 31:23); *ḥāraš,* "forge" (Gen. 4:22); *yāra',* "break" (Jer. 15:12); and *šāqal,* "weigh" (1 Ch. 22:3). One can make *('āśâ)* objects of bronze (genitive of material) or overlay (*ṣāpâ:* Ex. 38:2,6) them with copper.

5. *LXX.* The LXX always uses *chalkós/chalkoús/chálkaios* to translate n^{e}*ḥûšâ/* n^{e}*ḥōšeṯ.*

II. 1. *nḥšt in the Ancient Near East.* In the ancient Near East the term *nḥšt* appears above all in Aramaic texts.[14]

a. In Imperial Aramaic, as the nature of the documents would lead one to expect, copper and bronze appear as precious metals in a wide variety of contracts and transfers of property. A list of materials guaranteeing a loan includes silver, gold, bronze, iron, slaves, barley, spelt, and other foodstuffs.[15] Copper and bronze were used frequently to make household furnishings, as their frequent mention in marriage contracts (bride price, etc.) shows — e.g., bronze mirrors *(mḥzy zy nḥšt),* bowls *(tmḥy? tms'?),* vases *(zlwʿ),* pots *(kp),* possibly even a bronze plow.[16] One invoice lists, together with many other utensils, such a bronze plow (?, *ḥrš' zy nḥš*) and bands of copper *(nḥšy').*[17] The meaning of the fragmentary text is obscure, but the last may have been used in the cultivation of palm trees. One text includes bronze vases *(mny zy nḥš)* among the gifts given to the king at his accession.[18] According to another text, bronze nails *(msmry nḥš)* and bronze plates *(ṭsn)* were used in shipbuilding.[19] Finally, we know from the petition to the governor of Judea that the temple of Yahweh in Elephantine has bronze doors *(dššyn)* with bronze hinges (? *ṣyryn,* "hole for door pivot").[20]

b. Phoenician inscriptions use *nḥšt* only in connection with dedications: Yehawmilk dedicates a bronze altar *(hmzbḥ nḥšt)* to the "Lady of Byblos,"[21] recalling Ex. 38:30 as well as the bronze altar from Beth-shan and the one from Ugarit.[22] Votive offerings included an image *(smlt),* a relief *(mš + pn),* and an inscribed bronze tablet *(dlt hnḥšt).*[23] The difficult phrase *r'št nḥšt* may denote copper of particularly high quality.[24]

c. In Punic inscriptions votive offerings include a bronze altar weighing some 33 kgs. (73 lbs.), a bronze statue on a base *(m's hnḥšt ʿl m'kn'),* and bronze doors *(dlht šnḥšt).*[25] There are similar texts from Palmyra.[26] Whether Nab. *nḥš* means "coppersmith" is questionable.[27]

---

14. *DISO,* 177; K. Beyer, *Die aramäischen Texte vom Toten Meer* (Göttingen, 1984), 635f.
15. *AP,* 10, 10f.; cf. the similar list in the context of a division of property in a divorce: *AP,* 14, 4.
16. See, respectively, *AP,* 15, 11,12,13; 36, 4; *BMAP,* 7, 13ff.
17. See, respectively, *AP,* 81, 37, 111.
18. *BMAP,* 13, 5.
19. *AP,* 26, 12,15,16.
20. *AP,* 30, 1; cf. *TGI*², 84ff. On *ṣyryn* see *HAL,* III, 1024.
21. *KAI,* 10, 4; *TSSI,* III, 25, 4 (pp. 93-99, esp. 96f.).
22. *Syr,* 10 (1929), pl. 60.
23. On the image see *KAI,* 33, 2; on the relief, 43, 7; *TSSI,* III, 36, 7 (pp. 134-141); on the tablet, *KAI,* 43, 12; *TSSI,* III, 36, 12.
24. *KAI,* 31, 1: "choiceness of copper." Cf. *TSSI,* III, 17, 1 (pp. 66-68).
25. On the altar see *KAI,* 66, 1; on the statue, 119, 4; on the doors, 122, 2.
26. *DISO,* 177.
27. *CIS,* II, 158, 1.

2. *Bronze/Copper in the Ancient Near East.* Copper was known throughout the entire Near East as early as the fifth millennium; the production of bronze began toward the end of the third millennium, possibly thanks to the fortuitous juxtaposition of supplies of copper ore and tin ore near Byblos.[28] Because they were relatively easily worked and were substantially less expensive than gold or silver, copper and bronze were the metals in commonest use. The earliest finds (end of the 4th millennium) come from Teleilat Ghassul and Tell Abu Maṭar; what is probably the most famous find, from Naḥal Mishmar, attests to the cultic use of this metal at an early date.[29] Large-scale imports during the Mari period, especially in the Late Bronze Age, illustrate the importance of these metals for the manufacture of weapons, household furnishings, and jewelry in Palestine before the first millennium. Sheets of copper and bronze castings served above all for the production of large sculptures of cultic significance.[30] The production of large bronze artifacts is attested in Egypt since the 18th Dynasty at the latest (the doors of the temple of Amon at Thebes), in Palestine since the time of Solomon (Jachin and Boaz, the bronze sea), and in Mesopotamia since Sennacherib at the latest (the pillars of the palace at Nineveh).

Copper *(ḥmty)* was produced in Egypt itself (Timna, Araba, Serabit al-Khadim), while bronze *(ḥzmn)* was imported from Syria. Bronze vessels sometimes even served as currency.

In Mesopotamia copper (Akk. *erû;* Sum. *urud*) and bronze (*siparru;* Sum. *zabar*) were common, but had to be imported from Tilmun, Oman, and Cyprus. Their value in relationship to silver varied greatly, between 1:80 and 1:140 (1:200 at Ugarit), and could be affected significantly by historical events and rising prices.[31] In addition to the common uses of these metals, copper was used as an additive in the manufacture of glass (to give the color of lapis) and for the medical treatment of eye diseases.[32]

The difficult word *'ᵃnāḵ* in Am. 7:7f. (Akk. *anāku*), often translated "tin," could refer to an alloy of copper and arsenic, characterized by unusual hardness.[33] If this theory is correct,[34] it would make possible a new interpretation of Amos's plumb line vision.

Finally, Mesopotamian mantics used copper figurines in the practice of sympathetic magic, while bronze, especially music played on bronze instruments, was thought to counteract spells.[35]

---

28. C. F. A. Schaeffer, "La contribution de la Syrie anciénne à l'invention du bronze," *JEA,* 31 (1945), 92-95.

29. P. Bar-Adon, *The Cave of the Treasure* (Jerusalem, 1971, 1980); see also W. G. Dever and M. Tadmor, *IEJ,* 26 (1976), 163-69.

30. For technological information, see Forbes; Weippert, *BRL*², 221ff.

31. W. Röllig, *RLA,* VI, 345-48.

32. R. C. Thompson, *Assyrian Medical Texts* (Oxford, 1923), 9, 1, 34, 39; see also *RAC,* VI, 490f.

33. E. R. Eaton and H. McKerrell, *World Archaeology,* 8 (1976), 169-191.

34. See the cautious discussion by J. D. Muhly, *RLA,* VI, 360.

35. On copper and magic see G. Meier, *BAfO,* 21 (1966), pl. II/91. On bronze and spells see *RAC,* VI, 481.

III. Bronze/Copper in the OT.

1. *Everyday Life.* These two metals are characterized by the ease with which they can be worked. Their hardness and durability (bronze) and flexibility (copper) are useful qualities, and their appearance is aesthetically pleasing. Since the natural resources of Israel were meager (despite the idealized picture of the land in Dt. 8:9), copper and bronze had to be imported or collected as tribute from subject peoples. The OT hardly mentions their everyday use. Gen. 4:22 calls Tubal-cain the father of all smiths (a reference to the Kenites); 1 K. 7:14 mentions the smith Hiram who was hired for the bronzework of Solomon's temple project; and Ezk. 27:13 speaks of the bronze trade of Tyre. Ex. 38:8 knows that women used copper mirrors. The temple musicians, finally, used copper or bronze instruments (1 Ch. 15:19).[36] We may assume that such agricultural tools as plowshares, axes, and sickles (1 S. 13:20) were made out of bronze.

2. *Military Technology.* The hardness and durability of bronze made it particularly suitable for the manufacture of weapons (1 S. 17:5f.,38; 2 S. 21:16; 22:35; 1 Mc. 6:35,39), chains (Jgs. 16:21; 2 S. 3:34; 2 K. 25:7; 2 Ch. 33:11; 36:6; Jer. 39:7; 52:11; Dnl. 4:12,20[15,23]; Lam. 3:7), and gate bars (Dt. 33:25; 1 K. 4:13). Goliath is paradigmatic of a warrior with bronze armor: 1 S. 17 describes him as wearing a helmet *(kôḇaʿ)*, coat of mail *(širyôn)*, and greaves *(miṣḥâ)* of bronze. On his back he carried a bronze javelin *(kîḏôn)* (cf. the exaggerated description in 2 S. 21:16,19f.). A "bronze bow" *(qešeṯ nᵉḥōšeṯ)* is mentioned as a weapon in 2 S. 22:35 and Job 20:24; in the latter passage it is probably an elliptical expression meaning "bronze arrow."[37] 1 K. 4:13 mentions sixty cities across the Jordan fortified with walls and gates having bronze bars *(bārîaḥ)*. Shields of bronze served as both a means of defense and a reserve for the city treasury. Solomon made such shields out of gold, which he stored in the House of the Forest of Lebanon (1 K. 10:16f.). When Pharaoh Shishak plundered them, Rehoboam replaced them with shields of bronze (1 K. 14:27). For defense of the city, they were set up in special wooden frames to protect the tower walls from missiles.[38]

According to the *ḥērem* law of the holy war, silver, gold, bronze, and iron had to be devoted to Yahweh (Nu. 31:22; Josh. 6:19,24).[39] This law was not always enforced to the letter, however: Josh. 22:8 mentions the division of silver, gold, bronze, iron, and clothing. Bronze is also mentioned in 2 S. 8:8; 1 Ch. 18:8 as booty and in 2 S. 8:10; 1 Ch. 18:10 as tribute. In order permanently to disarm Bronze Age Israel, the Philistines imposed a ban on metalworking (1 S. 13:19-22). The same tactic was pursued by the Babylonians, who exiled all the smiths of Judah (2 K. 24:14).

3. *Cultic Objects.* The hardness and durability of bronze together with its aesthetically attractive appearance and high value made it a prized raw material for the

---

36. On the use of such instruments to counter spells see *RAC,* VI, 482.
37. B. Couroyer, "NḤT: 'Encorder un arc'?" *RB,* 88 (1981), 13-18.
38. → מגן *māgēn* (VIII, 74-87).
39. → חרם *ḥāram* (V, 180-199).

manufacture of cultic objects, despite the fact that it was also used to make weapons. Only two situations are mentioned that disqualify this metal and objects made from it for cultic use: metal taken in battle that had been made unclean by the uncleanness of the military camp itself had to be purified by fire (Nu. 31:22f.; cf. 17:4 and the oracular threat in Ezk. 24:11), and any cultic vessel contaminated by a sin offering (which was considered extremely holy) had to be boiled thoroughly and scoured (an example of late priestly scrupulosity; Lev. 6:21[28]).

Copper and bronze were used extensively in Solomon's temple: according to 1 Ch. 22:3,14,16; 29:2,7, David had already begun procuring these precious metals "in quantities beyond weighing" for the building of the temple. Solomon established a copper industry in the southern region in order to realize the construction of his temple and palace (1 K. 7:47; 2 Ch. 4:18).[40] In Hiram he employed an expert and artistically talented smith (1 K. 7:14; 2 Ch. 2:13). Copper or bronze was used to make the following: the two pillars Jachin and Boaz (1 K. 7:15) together with their bronze capitals (v. 16; the Chronicler's parallel in 2 Ch. 3:15ff. does not indicate the material); ten stands *(m^eḵônôṯ)* holding basins for water (1 K. 7:27-39; 2 Ch. 4:6 [again without indication of the material]); the "brazen sea" (1 K. 7:23-26 par. 2 Ch. 4:2-5, but disagreeing over its capacity); pots, shovels, and basins (1 K. 7:45 par. 2 Ch. 4:16). Clearly secondary is the reference to the "bronze altar" in 1 K. 8:64, described in more detail in the Chronicler's parallel (2 Ch. 4:1). Nu. 17:1-5 provides an etiology for the bronze covering of this altar: it is an admonitory reminder that any utensil that has come in contact with something sacred must not be used for profane purposes. This altar must be distinguished from the bronze altar in front of the tabernacle (2 Ch. 1:5f.; cf. Ex. 31:1ff.), which consisted of a wooden core with copper gratings and copper-covered horns. According to 2 Ch. 6:13, Solomon also made a bronze platform on which he stood to pray before the assembly. Thus the Chronicler avoids describing Solomon in priestly terms (cf. 1 K. 8:22, where Solomon prays before the altar itself). Also secondary is the Chronicler's statement about the doors overlaid with bronze in the court of the priests (2 Ch. 4:9). These passages make clear that copper and bronze were used primarily outside the temple structure proper. The furnishings of the *bayiṯ* were gold (1 K. 7:48ff.). May this fact not account for the prohibition against using iron in the construction of the temple? Do these texts not preserve a building ritual that antedates the Iron Age?

The renovation of the temple under King Ahaz is reported in 2 K. 16:14ff.: the bronze altar was replaced with a new altar, i.e., it was discarded (v. 15). The theriomorphic base supporting the bronze sea was also removed.[41] Behind these actions we see Ahaz's attempt to requisition all but the most important objects made of precious metal for the payment of tribute to the Assyrians. We must note, however, that all these bronze cult objects, including the base of the bronze sea, are mentioned once more

40. B. Rothenberg, "Ancient Copper Industries in the Western Arabah," *PEQ*, 94 (1962), 5-71, esp. 40.
41. But cf. Busink, 330f.

(2 K. 25:13f.,16f.; cf. Jer. 52:17f.,20,22) when the Babylonians despoil the temple. Only the bronze altar is missing! It is mentioned again in Ezk. 9:2.

In P these texts are drawn upon and combined with P's own traditions to form an ideal model (Ex. 25:1–31:18) describing the construction and furnishings of the tabernacle.[42] As the Priestly understanding of obedience to the Torah would lead one to expect, this description is matched (in Ex. 35:1–40:38), with only minor adjustments, by a detailed account (secondary?) of how the work was carried out. In comparison with the copper and bronze furnishings of Solomon's temple, the following differences are significant: because the tabernacle is portable, a complex set of fittings for pitching the tent is described, including rings, pins, hooks, pegs, and footings of bronze (Ex. 26:11,37; 27:10-19; 36:18,38; 38:10-20); the bronze altar is fitted with rings for carrying (27:4; 35:16; 38:5), and the carrying poles are overlaid with copper (27:6; 38:6); in addition, it is to be pictured as an altar with horns (7:2; 38:2). Instead of the bronze sea and the ten basins on wheels, we now find a single copper basin (30:18; 38:8), which better reflects the meager furnishings of the postexilic temple. Ezr. 8:27 indicates that in the postexilic period the value of bronze had increased significantly, equaling that of gold.

IV. Metaphorical Usage. The symbolic value of copper and bronze is not especially expansive. The substantially lower value of these metals in normal times in comparison to gold and silver lets copper serve as a metaphor for anything base — ethically, evildoers. Bronze, however, symbolizes hardness and impregnability, so that its metaphorical use can be quite ambiguous. When metals characterize a list of eras, bronze can easily suggest a degenerate age; when political entities are compared, it can stand for an inferior empire.

1. *Oracular Threats.* In oracular threats the prophets often draw on the process of smelting and refining to lend color to their descriptions of judgment: "As one gathers silver, copper, iron, lead, and tin into a smelter, to blow the fire upon them in order to melt them, so I will gather you in my anger and in my wrath, and I will put you in and melt you" (Ezk. 22:18-20). It will then be impressively clear that Israel is nothing but dross. In Jer. 6:28 a glossator (thinking of Jeremiah's call; cf. 1:18) has inserted a similar image into the text: the people are so totally corrupt that even smelting cannot separate the elements, and everything must be discarded.[43] Copper is susceptible to verdigris *(ḥel'â),* which symbolizes sin and stubbornness; it can be removed only by intense heat (Ezk. 24:6,11f.). Since bronze symbolizes hardness, the destruction of Solomon's monumental bronzes in 587 must have been perceived as an especially harsh judgment (2 K. 25:13; Jer. 52:17; Dnl. 2:34). The obscure threat in Jer. 15:12 (a secondary addition to a confession) may refer to this event. Finally,

---

42. → אהל *'ōhel* (I, 118-130).

43. For a discussion of the passage see J. A. Soggin, "Jeremias VI 27-30," *VT,* 9 (1959), 95-98.

a post-Deuteronomic threat in Dt. 28:23 (cf. Lev. 26:19) curses disobedience to the law with this punishment: "The sky over your head shall be bronze, and the earth under you iron." The cosmos turns hostile to life. Texts from Egypt, Iran, and Greece also speak of a sky of bronze.[44]

2. *Oracles of Salvation.* A bronze chain symbolized captivity without prospect of escape (Lam. 3:7), from which in the end only God can deliver, by shattering bronze doors and breaking iron bars (Ps. 107:16). In the Blessing of Moses (possibly pre-Deuteronomic in the form of individual sayings), Asher receives the following promise: "May your bars be iron and bronze; have peace as long as you live" (Dt. 33:25), symbolic of unconquerable strength (cf. Isa. 45:2). It casts a bright light on the actual experience of the prophet's call when either he himself or one of his disciples incorporates into the account of his call a promise of salvation like "I have made you a bronze wall against the whole land" (Jer. 1:18; cf. 15:20; there is copious material of this nature in the prophetic tradition, based on real experience;[45] cf. also Ezk. 3:8f.). The prophetic individual needs superhuman hardness and ruggedness to carry out the office (cf. Isa. 50:7: "I have set my face like flint"). Using an ascending series of metals, the oracle of salvation in Isa. 60:17 predicts better times for Jerusalem: "Instead of copper I will bring gold, instead of iron I will bring silver."

3. *Visions.* Four prophetic visions mention copper/bronze. Burnished bronze has a supernatural glow that makes it useful for the description of heavenly beings (Ezk. 1:7; 40:3; Dnl. 10:6). The reference to the temple and tabernacle may also cast some light on the symbolic value of the metals. Just as gold is used only inside, i.e., in the immediate presence of God, so copper/bronze is used outside, i.e., in the immediate vicinity of God. Gold, the most precious metal, points to God; copper/bronze points to the messengers who surround him. The omission of silver from this symbolism has not been explained.

The two mountains of copper (with the definite article) in the eighth vision of the prophet Zechariah (Zec. 6:1) are difficult to interpret. Scholars suggest that they represent the two jambs of the gate of heaven, the twin (?) peaks of the world mountain, or even the temple pillars Jachin and Boaz;[46] but these theories are not persuasive. They clearly stand for something in the supernatural realm; further speculations are only unverifiable fantasy.

V. The "Bronze Serpent." Scholars have proposed many explanations of the origin and function of the bronze serpent.[47]

---

44. *RAC,* VI, 476.
45. *RAC,* VI, 492.
46. For the first see Rudolph, Singer; for instances of this notion in Egypt and Greece see *RAC,* VI, 477. For the second see M. Bič, *Die Nachgesichte des Sacharja* (Neukirchen, 1964). For the third see J. W. Rothstein, *Die Nachgesichte des Sacharja. BWA(N)T,* 8 (1910).
47. Maneschg, 84ff.

1. *Mosaic origin:*
   - a serpent image made at the same time as the ark and stored in it;[48]
   - a Syro-Phoenician emblem of Eshmun from Obot, a site in the desert;[49]
   - the staff of Moses with a sympathetic effect as a fetish.[50]
2. *Davidic origin:*
   - a totem of the house of David (cf. the many names containing the element *nḥš* in the genealogy of David);[51]
   - a military emblem of the Calebites, captured by David.[52]
3. *Egyptian origin:*
   - an Egyptian serpent staff (cf. Ex. 4:1-5; 7:8-14);[53]
   - an Egyptian symbol of sacral royal sovereignty;[54]
   - a symbol of the cult of Renutet, the influence of which in Jerusalem during the reign of Solomon was under attack.[55]
4. *Babylonian origin:*
   - an apotropaic talisman;[56]
   - a representation of serpentine tutelary genii in Babylonian temples;[57]
   - an association with *šarrāpu* (Nergal).[58]
5. *Canaanite origin:*
   - a relic of Canaanite serpent worship and the fertility cult;[59]
   - a non-Yahwistic cultic image in the Jebusite sanctuary of Jerusalem.[60]
6. *Phoenician origin:*
   - a serpent staff of the Phoenician god Eshmun (cf. Greek Asclepius).[61]

H. Maneschg holds that *n^eḥuštān* was a cultic image of the Canaanites borrowed by the Israelites.[62] After it had been incorporated into the cult of Yahweh, its origin

---

48. R. H. Kennett, *ERE,* I, 792f.
49. A. Vernes, *Revue Archéologique,* 6 (1918), 36-49.
50. H. Gressmann, *Die Anfänge Israels. SAT,* I/2 (^{2}1920), 106; cf. W. Eichrodt, *Theology of the OT. OTL,* 2 vols. (Eng. trans. 1961-67), I, 112f.
51. W. Robertson Smith, *Journal of Philology,* 9 (1880), 99f.
52. H. Cazelles, *Les Nombres. Sainte Bible* (1952), 101.
53. H. Wohlstein, *ZDMG,* 113 (1963), 486.
54. K. R. Joines, "Winged Serpents in Isaiah's Inaugural Vision," *JBL,* 86 (1967), 409-415; *idem,* "The Bronze Serpent in the Israelite Cult," *JBL,* 87 (1968), 245-256.
55. M. Görg, *BN,* 19 (1983), 133f.
56. F. Thureau-Dangin, *RHPR,* 1 (1896), 151-58.
57. T. C. Cheyne, *EncBib,* III (1902), 3387.
58. J. de Vaulx, *Les Nombres. SB* (1972).
59. See, respectively, F. Hvidberg, *VT,* 10 (1960), 288; K. R. Joines, *JBL,* 87.
60. H. H. Rowley, "Zadok and Nehushtan," *JBL,* 58 (1939), 113-141, esp. 132-141; *idem,* "Hezekiah's Reform and Rebellion," *BJRL,* 44 (1962), 395-431, esp. 425-27; possibly also W. Zimmerli, *Studien zur alttestamentlichen Theologie und Prophetie. ThB,* 51 (1974), 254ff., suggesting a chthonic deity invoked for healing.
61. M. H. Farbridge, *Studies in Biblical and Semitic Symbolism* (repr. New York, 1970), 75f., and many others.
62. P. 93.

was retrojected into the period of the desert. It was easy to find points of contact with a desert tradition. As a form, the familiar genre of the "murmuring" narrative was chosen. The image was disarmed: it no longer represented the Deity but symbolized the salvific intervention of Yahweh. Later, when it threatened to take on independent value as an image conveying grace, it was destroyed in the cultic reform of Hezekiah (2 K. 18:4).

If, however, Nu. 21:4-9 is dated in the period of R^P, the perspective shifts: with the help of the statement in 2 K. 18:4 but without identifying the bronze serpent with *n^eḥuštān,* Nu. 21:4-9 becomes an exemplary narrative inculcating salvific obedience to Yahweh, composed in the late postexilic period with a purpose that is clearly parenetic. The avoidance of the word *n^eḥuštān* suggests a superstitious origin, a further indication that Nu. 21:4-9 and 2 K. 18:4 ultimately have to do with two different objects.

By analyzing the itinerary and the archaeological evidence (esp. that of Benno Rothenberg), Maneschg concludes that the site of the plague of serpents reflected in Nu. 21 could well be located between Kadesh and the Gulf of Aqaba;[63] he is probably thinking primarily of Timna. Against this theory are the late date of Nu. 21:4-9, the late composition of the itinerary, the uncertain location of the *yam sûp,*[64] and the unresolved question of a connection with the Midianite sanctuary at Timna in the twelfth century B.C.

VI. Dead Sea Scrolls. In the Dead Sea Scrolls *n^eḥûšâ* appears only in 1QSb 5:26 (in a blessing formula that is already almost an apocalyptic apostrophe, the prince of the community is accorded horns of iron and hoofs of bronze), whereas *n^eḥōšeṯ* appears 9 times. Bronze shields ornamented with gold, silver, and copper are mentioned in 1QM 5:4,5,8. The lance is fashioned similarly. It is safe to assume that 11QTemple 3:7,15-17 refer directly to the account of Solomon's temple in 1 K. 6–8; and 11QTemple 49:15 speaks of purifying copper tableware after a death in the house.

The mention of a copper tablet in 11QTemple 34:1 is interesting even though it offers little textually. The Qumran community itself (?) used such copper tablets (3Q15) to list the property of their various annexes.[65] Since archaeological explorations have not yielded any positive results, a topographic interpretation remains dubious.[66] All we know for sure is that the use of this unusual and costly writing material must have something to do with the subject matter, for copper tablets were fashioned only for extraordinarily important purposes (cf. 1 Mc. 8:22; 14:18,26,48).

Fabry

63. A theory already proposed by R. de Vaux, "L'itinéraire des Israélites," *Hommages à A. Dupont-Sommer* (Paris, 1971), 331.

64. → סוּף *swp.*

65. H. Bardtke, "Qumrān und seine Probleme," *TRu,* 33 (1968), 185-204: "The scroll thus contained an inventory of the property belonging to the individual divisions" (189).

66. Contra, e.g., B. Pixner, "Unravelling the Copper Scroll Code," *RevQ,* 11/43 (1983), 323-361.

נָטָה nāṭâ

Contents: I. 1. Etymology; 2. Occurrences. II. Usage: 1. Qal; 2. Hiphil. III. Dead Sea Scrolls. IV. LXX.

I. 1. *Etymology.* Biblical Heb. *nāṭâ,* "stretch out," has cognates with the same meaning in Jewish Aram. *n*ᵉ*ṭā'* and Arab. *naṭā*ʷ. It is uncertain whether Eth. *naṭaya,* "tire," and Akk. *naṭû,* "strike,"[1] also belong here.

2. *Occurrences.* The qal of *nāṭâ* occurs 135 times, the niphal 3 times, and the hiphil 75 times. *HAL* lists 2 occurrences of the hophal: Isa. 8:8, where others interpret *muṭṭôṯ* as the plural of a subst. *muṭṭâ,* "span"; and Ezk. 9:9, where it is better to interpret *muṭṭeh* as "perversion (of the law)" (cf. Ezk. 7:10, where the MT reads *maṭṭeh,* "staff").[2] The distribution of the occurrences is hardly significant. We are dealing with a general word having many nuances; it can be used in a wide variety of situations.

The nouns *miṭṭâ,* "couch, bed,"[3] and probably → מטה *maṭṭeh,* "staff," derive from *nāṭâ.*

II. Usage.

1. *Qal.* a. *"Stretch Out One's Hand."* To "stretch out one's hand" means that one is ready to perform an action, usually hostile. Yahweh stretches out his hand against the Egyptians, and they know that he is Yahweh (Ex. 7:5). He stretches out his hand in anger against his people and strikes (*nkh* hiphil) them so that the mountains quake (Isa. 5:25). This image probably comes from the idea of Yahweh as a warrior. Yahweh has framed a plan to break Assyria (14:24-27): "This is the plan, . . . this is the hand that is stretched out against all the nations" (v. 26); no one can annul this plan: "his hand is stretched out, and who will turn it back?" (v. 27). In the oracle against Tyre in Isa. 23, v. 11 states that Yahweh has stretched out his hand against the sea and has shaken the kingdoms; he will destroy the fortresses of Canaan. Behind this image may lie the mythological notions of Baʿal's battle with the sea, especially meaningful in an oracle concerning the naval power Tyre. Ex. 15:12 describes Yahweh's actions at the Sea of Reeds in similar terms, but with *yāmîn* instead of *yāḏ.*

The expression is especially frequent in Ezekiel: against the people, to make the

---

nāṭâ. M. Dahood, "Hebrew-Ugaritic Lexicography, VI," *Bibl,* 49 (1968), 355-369; *idem,* " 'A Sea of Troubles': Notes on Psalms 55:3-4 and 140:10-11," *CBQ,* 41 (1979), 604-7; H. Gese, "Kleine Beiträge zum Verständnis des Amosbuches," *VT,* 12 (1962), 417-438; N. C. Habel, " 'He Who Stretches out the Heavens,' " *CBQ,* 34 (1972), 417-430; P. Humbert, " 'Etendre la main' (Note de lexicographie hébraïque)," *VT,* 12 (1962), 383-395; L. Kopf, "Arabische Etymologien und Parallelen zum Bibelwörterbuch," *VT,* 9 (1959), 247-287.

1. *AHw,* II, 768.
2. *HAL,* II, 693.

land desolate and waste (6:14); against a prophet who is deceived, to destroy him (14:9); against the land, to send famine upon it (14:13); against the whoring people, to "reduce their portion" (16:27); against Ammon, to cause the land to be despoiled (25:7); against Edom, to cut off from it humans and animals (25:13); against the Philistines, to exterminate the people (25:16); against Edom, to make it a desolation and waste (35:3). Zephaniah, too, uses the expression: Yahweh will stretch out his hand against Judah, to destroy those who worship Baal (1:4); against Assyria and Nineveh, to lay them waste (2:13). It is especially wicked to stretch out one's hand against God and defy him (Job 15:25 [Eliphaz, referring to Job]).

Only occasionally does the stretching out of a hand have positive significance, as in Prov. 1:24, where the expression describes the invitation of Wisdom. Isa. 65:2 uses *pāraś* in a similar context.

In the refrain contained in Isa. 5:25; 9:11,16,20(Eng. vv. 12,17,21); 10:4b, the outstretched hand of Yahweh symbolizes his repeated and enduring wrath (cf. 14:27 above).

In Deuteronomistic language the phrase *b^{e}yāḏ ḥ^{a}zāqâ ûḇizrōaʿ n^{e}ṭûyâ* describes the mighty acts of God during the deliverance of Israel from Egypt (Ex. 6:6; Dt. 4:34; 5:15; 7:19; 9:29; 11:2; 26:8; 2 K. 17:36; Jer. 32:21; more generally: 1 K. 8:42; 2 Ch. 6:32; cf. also in reverse sequence Jer. 21:5). In Jer. 27:5; 32:17, the phrase is applied to the creation of the world, and in Ezk. 20:33f. to God's sovereignty in general. In the account of the plagues in Ex. 7:8–10:29 the stretching out of the hand or staff of Moses or Aaron serves repeatedly as a symbolic action almost magical in its effect (7:19; 8:1f.,12f.[5f.,16f.]; 9:22f.; 10:12f.,21f.); it functions similarly in the passage through the sea (14:16,21,26f.).

A sword can also be stretched out: Joshua stretches out his sickle sword against Ai (Josh. 8:18f.,26) as a signal to attack (or possibly as a symbol of power[4]); the king of Babylon will stretch out his sword against Egypt (Ezk. 30:25); after David's census the angel of Yahweh stretches out his sword against Jerusalem, to destroy it (the parallel in 2 S. 24:16 says "hand").

b. *Spread, Extend.* "Spread a tent" refers in the first instance quite concretely to pitching camp (Gen. 12:8; 26:25; 33:19; 35:21; Jgs. 4:11) and to pitching a tent for the ark (2 S. 6:17; 1 Ch. 15:1; 16:1; 2 Ch. 1:4). Used elliptically without *'ōhel, nāṭâ* appears in Jer. 14:8 in the lament that God is like a traveler who spends only a night with his people (although here *nāṭâ lālûn* could also mean "turn aside from the way to spend the night"). Cf. also Jer. 43:10, with *šaprîr,* "pavilion," as object.

Then the spreading of a tent can be used figuratively for God's spreading out the heavens, especially in Deutero-Isaiah. God's creative power is underscored by the statement that he "stretches out the heavens like a curtain, and spreads *(nāṭâ)* them like a tent to live in" (Isa. 40:22; also 42:5; 44:24; 45:12; 51:13). The same idea also appears elsewhere: Jer. 10:12; 51:15; Zec. 12:1; Ps. 104:2; Job 9:8. Job 26:7 says that

---

3. → ערש *'ereś.*

4. R. G. Boling and G. E. Wright, *Joshua. AB,* 6 (1982), 240f.

God stretched out "the north" over the void *(tōhû)*. The question is whether *ṣāpôn* refers to the northern sky or to Mt. Zaphon as the dwelling place of God.[5] But does one spread out a mountain? Sir. 43:12 says that God spreads out the rainbow (not the "vault of heaven" [*ḥûg*][6]).

A few texts speak of extending a measuring line *(qaw)*, literally in Isa. 44:13 to measure the wood used to make an idol. Elsewhere the expression is used figuratively. In 34:11 the line of confusion *(tōhû)* and the plummet of chaos *(bōhû)* are extended over Edom; the consequence is total devastation. The same image appears in a prophetic oracle in 2 K. 21:13: Yahweh extends over Jerusalem the same line and the same plummet as over Samaria. Zec. 1:16 uses the niphal similarly to symbolize destruction. In Job 38:5, by contrast, the question "Who extended the line upon the earth?" points to the power of the Creator.

Used intransitively, *nāṭâ* sometimes has the meaning "extend, lengthen," especially with reference to the shadows that lengthen at evening (2 K. 20:10, in the context of Hezekiah's miraculous cure); Ps. 102:12[11]; 109:23, referring figuratively to human life; cf. the niphal in Jer. 6:4). It can also describe wadis that extend into the distance (Nu. 24:6).[7]

c. *Bow.* The Blessing of Jacob uses *nāṭâ* literally with the meaning "bow": Issachar bows his shoulder to the burden and becomes a slave at forced labor (Gen. 49:15; cf. the hiphil with a water jar as its obj. in 24:14). It is used figuratively of God appearing in a theophany: "he bowed the heavens and came down" (Ps. 18:10[9]), and in the petition "bow your heavens and come down" (Ps. 144:5, hiphil). In both cases the object is *šāmayim* and the result is expressed by *yāraḏ*. Klaus Koch thinks that Job 9:8, discussed above, may also belong here.[8]

Used intransitively, then, *nāṭâ* can denote God's "inclination" toward an individual. Thus the psalmist confesses in Ps. 40:2(1): "I waited patiently for Yahweh; he inclined to me and heard my cry." It is also possible that this usage represents an ellipsis for "he inclined his ear"; in this case, however, we would expect a hiphil.[9]

Whether Ps. 17:11 belongs here is unclear. The psalmist's enemies set their eyes *linṭôṯ bā'āreṣ,* "to cast [him] to the ground" (NRSV) — but the construction with *bᵉ* is difficult.

d. *Change Direction.* Often *nāṭâ* implies a change of direction in the literal or figurative sense, either toward or away from something. According to Nu. 20:17, the Israelites want to go straight through Edom, "not turning aside to the right hand or to the left" (cf. the similar statement about the land of Sihon in Nu. 21:22 and with *lāleḵeṯ* in 2 S. 2:19). Balaam's donkey turns off the road when it sees the angel of Yahweh (Nu. 22:23, twice).

---

5. For the former see E. Dhorme, *Job* (Eng. trans., repr. Nashville, 1984), 371f. For the latter see M. Pope, *Job. AB,* 15 (^{3}1973), 183.

6. *HAL,* I, 295.

7. For other interpretations, see *HAL,* II, 693.

8. *ZAW,* 86 (1974), 521.

9. See 2.a below.

The figurative usage is clear in Prov. 4:26f.: "May all your ways be sure *(yikkōnû);* do not swerve to the right or to the left; turn your foot away from evil." Cf. 4:5, "Do not turn away from the words of my mouth," and Ps. 119:51, "I do not turn away from your law" (v. 157: "your decrees"). In Ps. 44:19(18) the speakers avow that their hearts have not turned back *(swg)* from God, nor have their steps departed from God's way *('ōraḥ).* Job 31:7, too, speaks of steps that turn aside (here with *dereḵ*); in parallel we find "follow my eyes." Ps. 73:2 is not really comparable: here *regel* is the subject of *nāṭâ,* and *'aššûr* is the subject of *špk* pual ("be poured out," probably meaning "lose stability"). The text clearly refers to involuntary turning aside or stumbling: the psalmist experienced a crisis of faith when he thought about the prosperity of the wicked.

The change of direction can also be *toward* something. Judah turns aside from the road to Tamar (*wayyēṭ 'ēleyhā 'el-hadderek̲:* Gen. 38:16); he joins a man from Adullam (38:1; here with *'ad̲* instead of *'el*). Joab joined Adonijah rather than Absalom (*nāṭâ* twice with *'aḥarê;* 1 K. 2:28). According to Jgs. 9:3, the hearts of the citizens of Shechem inclined to follow Abimelech *(wayyēṭ libbām 'aḥarê).* The same idea is expressed in 2 S. 19:15(14) with the hiphil: David swayed the hearts of all Judah as one. The combination with *lēḇāḇ* can also have negative import: Solomon's heart turned away from Yahweh (1 K. 11:9). In Ps. 119:112 *lēḇ* is the object: "I have inclined my heart to perform *('āśâ)* your statutes." Here we may compare Ex. 23:2: "In a lawsuit, you shall not side with *(nāṭâ 'aḥarê)* the majority so as to pervert (justice) [*nāṭâ* hiphil; see below]"; also 1 S. 8:3: Samuel's sons turned aside after gain *(beṣa')* and perverted justice.

e. *With Abstract Objects.* Finally, I note some passages where *nāṭâ* is used with an abstract object and means roughly "extend" or "offer." In Isa. 66:12 Yahweh promises Zion that he will extend prosperity *(šālôm)* to her like a river; in Ps. 21:12(11) the psalmist's enemies want to inflict evil *(rā'â)* on him; and in Gen. 39:21 Yahweh gives Joseph the *ḥesed̲* of the chief jailer (par. *nāt̲an ḥēn*); cf. the hiphil with *ḥesed̲* in Ezr. 7:28; 9:9. A similar meaning is apparently present in 1 Ch. 21:10: "I offer you three (choices)"; here, however, the parallel in 2 S. 24:12 has *nṭl,* "impose."

2. *Hiphil.* a. *Stretch out, Extend.* The hiphil is often used in combinations similar to those that use the qal. One may stretch out a hand: Isa. 31:3 (Yahweh stretches out his hand and the helper stumbles); Jer. 6:12 (Yahweh stretches out his hand against the inhabitants of the land); 15:6 ("I have stretched out my hand against you [Jerusalem] and destroyed you"); or one may pitch a tent (2 S. 16:22: on the roof, for Absalom) or stretch out its curtains (Isa. 54:2, reading *haṭṭî* for *yaṭṭû*), or spread sackcloth on a rock (2 S. 21:10). According to *HAL,* the hophal form in Isa. 8:8 is used figuratively of outstretched wings.[10]

The hiphil is also used to say that God bows the heavens and comes down (Ps. 144:5).[11] Especially interesting is the expression "incline one's ear," i.e., pay special

10. *HAL,* II, 693. But cf. I.2 above.
11. See II.1.c above.

attention. Thus God bids the exiles to hear and heed his message of salvation (Isa. 55:3); the sage admonishes his listeners to heed his instruction (Prov. 4:20; 5:1; 22:17; cf. Ps. 78:1 and the admonition to the king's bride in 45:11[10]). In Jeremiah the complaint that the people have not inclined their ear to God and listened to him has become a virtual commonplace (Jer. 7:24,26; 11:8; 17:23; 25:4; 34:14; 35:15; 44:5). In Ps. 49:5(4) the psalmist says that he will incline his ear to a *māšāl.* The expression is also used in prayers to attract God's attention to the worshiper, e.g., "Incline your ear and hear, open your eyes and see" (2 K. 19:16 par. Isa. 37:17), "Incline your ear to me, hear my words" (Ps. 17:6; also 31:3[2]; 71:2; 86:1; 88:3[2]; 102:3[2]; Dnl. 9:18; as a statement: Ps. 116:2). Like the qal, the hiphil can mean "extend something to someone": Ezr. 7:28; 9:9; in both cases the object is *ḥesed.*

b. *Turn.* The hiphil can mean "turn in a specific direction." Balaam turns the donkey back onto the road (Nu. 22:23); Joab takes Abner aside in the gateway (2 S. 3:27); David takes the ark into the house of Obed-edom (2 S. 6:10).

c. *Turn Someone's Heart.* The hiphil appears with some frequency in the expression "turn someone's heart in a particular direction": "turn my heart to your decrees *('el-ʿēḏᵉwōṯeyḵā)*" (Ps. 119:36); "do not turn my heart to *(lᵉ)* evil" (Ps. 141:4); "[if you] incline your heart to *(lᵉ)* understanding" (Prov. 2:2); "put away the foreign gods that are among you and incline your hearts to *('el)* Yahweh" (Josh. 24:23); "[may Yahweh] incline our hearts to *('el)* him" (1 K. 8:58); "they [the foreign women] might incline your heart to follow *('aḥᵃrê)* their gods" (1 K. 11:2; this did indeed happen to Solomon, as vv. 3f. tell us).[12]

But the heart can lead someone astray from the right way. The idolater "feeds on ashes," says Deutero-Isaiah; his heart is deluded *(hûṯal)* and leads him astray *(hiṭṭāhû)* (Isa. 44:20). The strange woman persuades the young man with her seductive speech (Prov. 7:21, par. *ndḥ* hiphil). Elihu warns Job not to let the greatness of the ransom *(kōp̱er)* turn him aside from justice (Job 36:18).

d. *Turn Aside from the Way.* The hiphil *hiṭṭâ* is used intransitively with the meaning "turn aside from the way." Job says, "I have kept *(šāmar)* his way and not turned aside" (Job 23:11). Ps. 125:5 speaks of those who "turn aside to their own crooked ways *('ᵃqalqallôṯ).*" Isa. 30:11 quotes ironically what the people say to the prophet: "Leave *(sûrû)* the [right] way *(dereḵ),* turn aside *(haṭṭû)* from the [right] path *('ōraḥ).*"

e. *Pervert.* It is also possible to speak of "bending" or "perverting" a way or path. Prov. 17:23 warns against accepting a bribe "to pervert the ways of justice," i.e., to violate the principles of justice. This usage leads in turn to the expression "pervert justice." It appears already in the Covenant Code in the general prohibition "You shall not pervert the justice due to your poor in their lawsuits" (Ex. 23:6). The following verses expand on this principle: do not declare the innocent guilty, do not take bribes (vv. 7f.). This prohibition is then adopted by Dt. 16:19: "You must not pervert justice; you must not show partiality; you must not accept bribes" (even the motivating clause "for a bribe blinds the eyes of the wise" recalls Ex. 23). The prohibition takes special

---

12. On 2 S. 19:15 see above.

note of the *gēr,* the orphan, and the widow in Dt. 24:17 and the series of curses in 27:15ff.: "Cursed be anyone who perverts the justice of aliens, the orphan, and the widow" (the MT reads "aliens who are orphans," but the terms are probably coordinate[13]). Then we are informed that the sons of Samuel forsook the principles of their father and turned aside after gain (*nāṭâ 'aḥ^{a}rê habbāṣa'*[14]), took bribes, and perverted justice (1 S. 8:3). Finally, Lam. 3:35 says that God will not fail to take vengeance "when human rights are perverted in the presence of the Most High"; the parallel in v. 36 speaks of subverting (*'awwēṯ*) another in a lawsuit.

f. *Turn Away.* The thrust of Am. 2:7 is rather different. Here the people of Israel are castigated because, among other things, they "twist the way of the afflicted (*'^{a}nāwîm*)." The entire verse deals with oppression of the poor, and the expression is related to Prov. 17:23.[15] Similar is the charge in Isa. 10:2 that the needy (*dallîm*) are turned aside (*nāṭâ* hiphil) from justice (*dîn*). Prov. 18:5 uses the same verb for turning away the innocent (*ṣaddîq,* "one in the right") from justice, as does Isa. 29:21: "They turn away the innocent (*ṣaddîq*) by *tōhû* [i.e., without grounds]." Am. 5:12 elaborates on 2:7: they afflict (*ṣrr*) the *ṣaddîq,* take a bribe (*kōp̱ēr*), and turn away the needy (*'eḇyôn*) in the gate (i.e., in court). Compare also Job 24:4 ("They thrust the needy off the road"); Mal. 3:5 ("who deprive the aliens [*maṭṭēh-gēr*] in the land of their rights"). Here, too, belongs the noun *muṭṭeh,* "perversion of justice" (NRSV: "perversity"), in Ezk. 9:9 and probably also 7:10, where the MT reads *maṭṭeh.*[16]

Outside legal contexts, then, *hiṭṭâ* refers to turning away someone seeking help. In Ps. 27:9 the psalmist prays: "Do not turn your servant away in anger."

g. *Special Cases.* In Sir. 32:17 *yaṭṭeh tôḵāḥôṯ* means "he refuses correction"; the subject is probably to be read as *'îš ḥāmās,* "the man of violence"; in parallel is "pervert (*mšk*) the *tôrâ.*" Jer. 5:25 says that the iniquities of the people have brought total chaos (*hiṭṭû-'ēlleh*).

The text of Hos. 11:4 is corrupt. If we retain MT *'ōl,* we can follow H. S. Nyberg,[17] supplying an object and translating: "I bent [the fruit of the tree] to him and fed him." If, following most modern scholars, we read *'ûl,* "suckling," it is preferable to read *wā'ēṭ* (qal): "I bent down to him and fed him." An association with *l^{e}'aṭ,* "gentle," is to be rejected.[18]

III. Dead Sea Scrolls. The few occurrences of *nāṭâ* in the Dead Sea Scrolls stay totally within the framework of OT usage. In the Temple Scroll *hiṭṭâ mišpāṭ,* "pervert justice," occurs 4 times in conjunction with *šōḥaḏ,* "bribery" (11QTemple 51:13,17; 57:19f.). The War Scroll speaks of stretching out a hand for weapons of war (1QM

13. JM, §177o.
14. See above.
15. See above.
16. See I.2 above.
17. H. S. Nyberg, *Studien zum Hoseabuche. UUÅ,* 6 (1935), 86.
18. Contra H. Ewald, *Commentary on the Prophets of the OT, I: Joel, Amos, Hosea and Zechariah* (Eng. trans., London, 1875), in loc.; W. H. Gispen, *Het Boek Hosea. COT* (1953), in loc.

8:8). The bowing down of the heavens is mentioned in 1QH 1:9, and 1QJub[a] (1Q17) 1:4 speaks of turning aside from the way.

IV. LXX. The rich variety of translations used by the LXX reflects the broad semantic range of *nāṭâ.* For the qal the LXX uses primarily *ekteínein* (44 times) and *ekklínein* (24 times), but also *pēgnýnai* (8 times). For *n*[e]*ṭuyâ* we find *hypsēlós* (20 times). Many other translations occur only once or twice. The hiphil is represented primarily by *klínein* (24 times), but also by *parabállein* (5 times), *pēgnýnai* (3 times), *epiklínein, euthýnein,* etc.

Ringgren

נָטָע *nāṭaʿ*; מַטָּע *maṭṭāʿ*; נֶטַע *neṭaʿ*; נְטִעִים *n*[e]*ṭiʿîm*; שָׁתַל *šāṯal*

Contents: I. Occurrences: 1. The Roots *nṭʿ* and *štl;* 2. Outside Hebrew; 3. OT; 4. Ancient Versions. II. Meaning: 1. Verb; 2. Nouns; 3. Distinction between *nāṭaʿ* and *šāṯal.* III. Theological Usage: 1. With God as Subject; 2. As a Human Activity. IV. Dead Sea Scrolls.

I. Occurrences.

1. *The Roots nṭʿ and štl.* The Hebrew verb *nāṭaʿ* denotes a natural and oft-repeated activity in the everyday world of the settled farmer; we should therefore expect many occurrences, distributed widely. Indeed, *nāṭaʿ* occurs 55 times in the qal (and once in the niphal), as well as 11 occurrences of nominal derivatives. Surprisingly, the same activity is denoted by a second lexeme, *šāṯal,* which is substantially less common (10 occurrences) and is used only in a very circumscribed group of texts. The noun *šāṯîl* derives from *šāṯal.* This study includes both roots and their derivatives.

2. *Outside Hebrew.* a. The root *nāṭaʿ,* common in Hebrew, is attested only rarely in other Semitic languages. Ugaritic has only the plural noun *mṭʿt,* "plantings,"[1] which corresponds to Heb. *maṭṭāʿ.* Cyrus Gordon erroneously associates the form *nṭʿn* with *nṭʿ;* the former in fact represents an N stem of *ṭʿn.*[2] As a verb, *nṭʿ* is attested outside Hebrew only in Old South Arabic.

b. By contrast, the root *štl* is distributed more widely. It is common in the Aramaic

---

nāṭaʿ. R. Bach, "Bauen und Pflanzen," *Studien zur Theologie der alttestamentlichen Überlieferungen.* Festschrift G. von Rad (Neukirchen, 1961), 7-32; M. Delcor, "Le problème des jardins d'Adonis dans Isaie 17:9-11," *Syr,* 55 (1978), 371-394; I. Engnell, " 'Planted by the Streams of the Water,' " *Studia Orientalia Ioanni Pedersen* (Hauniae, 1953), 85-96; H. Ringgren, "The Branch and the Plantation in the *Hodayot,*" *BR,* 6 (1961), 2-8.

1. *KTU,* 1.20, II, 7 (cf. 9); probably also to be supplied in the fragmentary text *KTU,* 1.22, II, 26.

2. *WUS,* no. 1123. Cf. *UT,* no. 1643. The term occurs in *KTU,* 1.10, II, 24.

dialects with the basic meaning "plant," but is often used figuratively (*štl* peal; *šeṯel* and *šᵉṯîlā'*, "shoot, slip"; *šattālā',* "gardener"). In *nṣb* Syriac has at its disposal a much commoner verb for "plant," but also uses the base *štl* and its derivatives (in addition to *šᵉṯal* and the ethpeal, Syriac has the nouns *šetlā',* "plantation," and *štelta',* "plant"[3]). It is reasonable to ask whether the presence of both *štl* and *nṭʿ* in Hebrew is due to Aramaic influence, especially since *šāṯal* appears only in late texts (in Hos. 9:13, the MT reading *šᵉṯûlâ* is dubious; most scholars follow the LXX, emending the text to read *lᵉṣayiḏ šāṯ lōh bānāyw;* in this division of the consonantal text *štl* does not appear[4]).

3. *OT.* a. Except for the niphal in Isa. 40:24, Biblical Hebrew uses the base *nṭʿ* only in the active qal stem; it serves to denote an action performed on an object (only in Isa. 65:22; Jer. 1:10; 18:9; 31:28; 45:4; Eccl. 3:2 is *nāṭaʿ* used absolutely). The object of *nāṭaʿ* may be an individual plant: a tamarisk (Gen. 21:33), the cedars of Lebanon (Ps. 104:16), a laurel (Isa. 44:14), a vine (Ps. 80:9[Eng. v. 8]), an *'ᵃšērâ* (Dt. 16:21). The *'ᵃhālîm* of Nu. 24:6 is questionable; elsewhere (Ps. 45:9[8]; Prov. 7:17; Cant. 4:14) it is named as an aromatic along with cassia and myrrh (aloe, *Aquilaria agalocha,* "a large tree in India with dark brown, hard wood"[5]). Primarily, however, the objects of the verb are tracts of cultivated plants: vineyards (Dt. 6:11; 28:39; Josh. 24:13; etc. [14 times in all]) or a vineyard (Gen. 9:20; Dt. 20:6; 28:30; Prov. 31:16); olive groves (always in conjunction with vineyards: Dt. 6:11; Josh. 24:13); gardens (Gen. 2:8; Jer. 29:5,28); plantations (*nᵉṭāʿîm:* Isa. 17:10; also Jer. 31:5 conj.); all kinds of trees (*kol-ʿēṣ:* Lev. 19:23; Eccl. 2:5 [here in conjunction with vineyards and parks, *pardēsîm*]). In the figurative sense the verb may denote the "planting" of the ear (Ps. 94:9), the fixing of nails (as sharp points in a goad: Eccl. 12:11), or the pitching of tents (Dnl. 11:45).

When God is the subject of the statement, the action denoted by *nāṭaʿ* almost always has to do with human beings: the whole people ("my people," "they," the Israelites: Ex. 15:17; 2 S. 7:10 par. 1 Ch. 17:9; Jer. 2:21; 11:17; Am. 9:15; Ps. 44:13[12]), the exiles (Jer. 24:6; 32:41), or those who remained in Judah after the catastrophe (42:10); even the wicked appear in one passage as the object of God's action (12:2). This last is also the only passage that addresses the fate of an individual (for the plural here does not refer to the wicked as a group). In both literal and figurative usage, the place where the object is planted can be stated (with *bᵉ*, e.g., Gen. 2:8; Jer. 31:5; 32:41).

Isa. 51:16 is the only passage that raises text-critical questions. On the one hand, the combination *nṭʿ šāmayim* is unique; on the other hand, not only is *nṭh šāmayim* common, it already appears in this context (v. 13), also in conjunction with *ysd 'ereṣ.* The LXX clearly read *nṭh,* for both here and in 40:22 it uses *histánein* to translate the verb.

b. The only passage that uses the niphal of *nāṭaʿ* in a clearly passive sense is Isa.

---

3. *LexSyr,* 812a.

4. For a different approach see W. Rudolph, *Hosea. KAT,* XIII/1 (1966), in loc.

5. J. Feliks, "Aloe," *BHHW,* I, 62; *KBL*², 17, suggests ice plant, *Mesembrianthemum nodiflorum.*

40:24. Both the LXX and Targ. Jonathan (to the extent that the heavily paraphrastic text can be relied on as evidence) appear to have read active forms of the verb (*nāṭᵉʿû* and *zārᵉʿû,* respectively); but the reading of the MT may be preferable, since it fits the context better syntactically (cf. the suffixes in v. 24b, which presuppose the comparison of *šôpᵉṭê ʾereṣ* to a tree).

c. Two nouns, *maṭṭāʿ* and *neṭaʿ*, derive from the base *nṭʿ*. The former, with its prefixed *m,* is a *maqṭāl* form, which can denote both the site and the result of the action referred to by the qal stem.[6] The latter is a segholate *(qaṭl)* denoting the result of planting. Both substantives appear to belong not to the realm of everyday language but to the elevated language of poetry and prophetic preaching.

In Ps. 144:12 the Masoretes used the pointing *nᵉṭiʿîm,* presupposing a noun *nāṭîaʿ*, not otherwise attested in Biblical Hebrew.[7] There is a subst. *nᵉṭîʿâ* (pl. *-îm*) in Middle Hebrew, but this does not guarantee the existence of such a form in Biblical Hebrew. The defective orthography of the consonantal text suggests rather the reading *nᵉṭāʿîm,* the plural of *neṭaʿ*. In any case, the ancient versions do not distinguish their translation of *nṭʿym* in Ps. 144:2 from their translation in other passages where they read *neṭaʿ* or its plural (LXX *neóphyton* in Isa. 5:7; Job 14:9; Syr. also has *nṣbtʾ,* which serves to translate *neṭaʿ* and *šāṯîl* [Ps. 128:3]). This evidence suggests that the versions, too, read the same noun *neṭaʿ*. The MT reading may have been influenced by the more common *nᵉṭîʿâ* of late Hebrew. If so, the identification of a lexeme *nāṭîaʿ*, assumed by *HAL,* is superfluous.[8]

4. *Ancient Versions.* In translating the verb *nāṭaʿ*, the ancient versions exhibit little tendency toward variation. The LXX consistently uses *phyteúein* or *kataphyteúein,* the latter especially (but not exclusively) when the meaning is "grow, cultivate." Only three passages deviate from this practice. In Nu. 24:6 the LXX renders *nāṭaʿ* with *épēxen,* possibly reflecting a reading *nāṭâ,* but dependent in either case on its translation of *ʾhlym* as *skēnaí* (for *ʾōhālîm*): "like tents that the LORD has pitched." In Dnl. 11:45, too, it translates *wᵉyiṭṭaʿ* (with the obj. "tents") with *stḗsei,* avoiding *(kata)phyteúein.* The combination of "plant" and "tents" apparently offended the translators' sense of language. In Isa. 51:16 *éstēsa* probably indicates that the LXX was translating a text that read *linṭôṯ šāmayim.*[9]

For the nouns *maṭṭāʿ* and *neṭaʿ*, too, the LXX uses derivatives of the root *phyt-* without exception: for *maṭṭāʿ*, *phytós* (Ezk. 34:29; 31:4) and *phyteía* (Mic. 1:6; Ezk. 17:7); for *neṭaʿ*, *neóphyton* (Isa. 5:7; Job 14:9) and *phýteuma* (Isa. 17:10). In Isa. 17:11 it uses a verbal form to translate *niṭʿēḵ.*

The Syr. exhibits a similar consistency, always using *nṣb* or a derivative. In the Targs., Onqelos always uses *nṣb,* while Jonathan, besides *nṣb,* uses the pael of *qwm* in Jeremiah, Ezk. 36:36, and Am. 9:15 (always when "planting" is meant figuratively).

---

6. JM, §88e.
7. *HAL,* II, 694.
8. *Ibid.*
9. See above.

The translators were not quite so consistent in their treatment of *šāṯal;* here too, however, the LXX prefers *phyteúein,* the Syr. *nṣb,* and the Targs. *nṣb* together with *štl.*

II. Meaning.

1. *Verb.* The almost monotonous translation of the ancient versions shows that *nāṭaʿ* is a verb with little variation in meaning. It nevertheless exhibits clearly recognizable semantic nuances. These are determined in the first instance by the possibility of using the verb "plant" either literally or figuratively.

a. The verb *nāṭaʿ* means "plant": the insertion of a slip (*neṭaʿ* or *šāṯîl*) into the soil; it thus belongs to the group of verbs that refer directly to the peasant who cultivates the land, such as → זרע *zāraʿ,* "sow," → חרשׁ *ḥāraš,* "plow," and *ʿdr* niphal, "hoe" (Isa. 5:6; 7:25). Nevertheless, consociation with terms belonging to this lexical field is remarkably rare (Dt. 28:39; Isa. 5:2; Jer. 35:7; Ps. 107:37). Direct antonyms are likewise rare in literal usage: the unique qal of *ʿāqar* in Eccl. 3:2, *nāṯaš* in Jer. 1:10, etc. (but always in a fig. sense), and *kāraṯ*. In light of its meaning in the Aramaic dialects, Syriac, and Mandaic, the meaning "tear out (by the roots)" should be kept for *ʿāqar.*[10] Only in Mic. 5:12(13) (tear out an *ʾᵃšērâ;* cf. Dt. 16:21) and Ezk. 19:12 (hophal, referring to a vine; cf. Ps. 80:9[8]) is *nāṯaš* used in a literal sense; when it appears as a direct antonym to *nāṭaʿ,* the meaning is always figurative.[11] Although it never stands in direct opposition to *nāṭaʿ, kāraṯ,* too, should be considered an antonym, since it can be done to the same objects that appear with *nāṭaʿ* (*ʾᵃšērâ:* Ex. 34:13; *ʿēṣ:* Dt. 19:5).

A semantic nuance results when the planting is viewed not as the result of an action performed while a farmer works the land but as the beginning of the growth of what has been planted, as in the extended imagery of Jer. 12:2 and Ps. 80:9ff.(8ff.). In this case the lexical field includes terms like "take root" *(šrš),* "grow," "spread out," "send out branches," and finally "bear fruit." The antithesis is seen when the planting is unsuccessful: the result is no fruit at all or not the expected fruit (cf. Isa. 5:2). Used in this sense *nāṭaʿ* is an affective term: an expectation or even a hope is bound up with the planting (*wayᵉqaw:* Isa. 5:2).

b. To this point the discussion has concerned the planting of an individual plant (or several plants); but *nāṭaʿ* can also refer to planting on a large scale, establishing an agricultural settlement, a garden (Gen. 2:8), a vineyard (Gen. 9:20; Prov. 31:16), or "all kinds of trees" (*kol-ʿēṣ:* Lev. 19:23). Gen. 9:20 treats the planting of a vineyard as a pioneering act of civilization, through which Noah proves himself *ʾîš hāʾᵃḏāmâ.* In Prov. 31:16 it is a sign of intelligent management on the part of a capable housewife; in Eccl. 2:4f. it is among the great works made possible by the possession of wealth. Here, too, we find the same nuances noted above. In particular, the planting of vineyards is considered so characteristic of sedentary agriculture that Rechab, devoted to nomadic ideals, commands his descendants: "You shall never build a house, or sow seed, or plant or own a vineyard" (Jer. 35:7). Dt. 6:11 numbers among the benefits of civilization

---

10. *HAL,* II, 874; contra M. Dahood, *Bibl,* 47 (1966), 270.
11. See below.

bestowed by Yahweh and awaiting Israel in Canaan, besides houses and cisterns, "vineyards and olive groves that you did not plant." Ps. 107:36f. describes the transformation of the desert into civilization (by Yahweh): "There he let the hungry live, and they established towns to live in; they sowed fields and planted vineyards."

Together with the building of houses and the sowing of fields, the planting of vineyards is a sign of normal civilized life. In this sense the promise vouchsafed to Hezekiah in 2 K. 19:29 (par. Isa. 37:30) signals the new beginning of normal life in the third year after the Assyrian disaster of 701. "It is apparently a considered estimate that the people of Jerusalem who are threatened by the Assyrians will be unable to gather in the harvest during the current year nor to plough the fields for sowing in the following year, so that the year after they will be dependent upon the second growth, and normal economic life will not return until the third year."[12] The verse immediately following, however, proposes to understand the promise of salvation, intended quite concretely, in a figurative sense, using "take root" and "bear fruit" as metaphors for the restoration of the house of Judah. For the Judahites in exile, at least, Jeremiah's call to "build houses and live in them, plant gardens and eat what they produce" (Jer. 29:5; cf. v. 28b) means that they should live their lives as normally as possible in their place of exile and stop waiting for a speedy return to their homeland. Conversely, in the promise of salvation appended to the oracle against Tyre in Ezk. 28:25ff., the building of houses and planting of vineyards is symptomatic of the stability that will be achieved after return from exile.

Anyone who plants a vineyard expects to enjoy its yield: the aspect of expectation associated with the nuance of large-scale planting is the same as that identified above in the discussion of the basic meaning "plant." The standard threat of future disaster accordingly includes a reference to the futility of investing such effort: "You build houses of hewn stones, but you shall not live in them; you plant pleasant vineyards, but you shall not drink their wine" (Am. 5:11; cf. Dt. 28:30,39; Isa. 17:10: Zeph. 1:13). Conversely, to enjoy the fruits of one's own labor is a sign that the time of judgment has ended and the age of salvation has begun: "They shall build houses and inhabit them; they shall plant vineyards and eat their fruit. They shall not plant and another eat; they shall not build and another inhabit" (Isa. 65:21f.; cf. Jer. 31:5; Am. 9:14).

c. Only rarely does *nāṭaʿ* have the meaning "cover with plants." This sense is expressed in Isa. 5:2 by means of a double accusative (suf. + acc.): "he planted it [the vineyard] with choice vines." In Ezk. 36:36 this meaning is established by the use of *n*ᵉ*šammâ* as an object: "I, Yahweh, will rebuild the ruined places and replant that which is desolate."

d. When *nāṭaʿ* is used figuratively, it is not difficult to recognize the basic literal meaning. Like a seedling planted in the soil (where it takes root), so is the ear, which God has "planted," i.e., set in its proper place (Ps. 94:9). In a similar manner, Eccl. 12:11 uses the verb of nails embedded in the point of an ox goad. Dnl. 11:45 is immediately clear: the tents with their pegs are, as it were, planted in the earth; it is

---

12. O. Kaiser, *Isaiah 13–39. OTL* (Eng. trans. 1974), 396.

therefore unnecessary to emend the text to *nṭh* here (Aram. *šᵉṯal* also frequently used for pitching tents). The metaphorical use of "plant" or its opposite "uproot" to describe the fate of an individual or a nation is readily explicable when the metaphor itself requires it. In Isa. 40:24 the familiar image of a withered plant describes how Yahweh brings down the powerful: "Scarcely are they planted, scarcely sown, scarcely has their stem taken root in the earth, when he blows upon them, and they wither, and the tempest carries them off like stubble." The imagery of Jer. 12:2 is rather different: the life of the wicked, successful and apparently secure, leads the prophet to suspect that Yahweh himself has planted them, so that they can take root and bear fruit. Here the planting represents the life of the wicked, apparently grounded on a firm foundation. Ps. 80:9ff.(8ff.) likewise employs the imagery suggested by the metaphor, using the familiar vine allegory to compare the settlement of Israel in Canaan to the planting of a vine. In Jer. 2:21, too, the metaphor of a choice vine (possibly borrowed from Isa. 5:2) is used with other images to represent the incomprehensibly wicked conduct of Israel; the metaphorical use of *nāṭa'* derives from the image employed, as it does also in Jer. 11:17 (the luxuriant olive tree).

This metaphorical usage explains how *nāṭa'* by itself, without further figurative elaboration, can stand for Israel's occupation of the land. In Ex. 15:17 the context emphasizes that Yahweh alone has done this. 2 S. 7:10 par. 1 Ch. 17:9 emphasizes more the element of security; Ps. 44:3(2) stresses the contrast between the driving out of the previous occupants of the land and the stable planting of Israel.

No trace of the vine, vineyard, or olive tree metaphor, however, appears in the characteristically Jeremianic sequence "build (and tear down), plant (and uproot)." Robert Bach has demonstrated that this usage goes back to Jeremiah himself. His derivation of the sequence "build — plant" from a felicitation formula, however, is less convincing. The supposed sequence exhibits too much variability and focuses its interest on too great a range of aspects to derive from a single root. The Jeremianic sequence characteristically gives no additional detail qualifying the building and planting. "This loss of concreteness lends the terms almost the character of ciphers. . . . They denote the salvation and disaster wrought by God as comprehensively and generally as possible: the concrete form of the salvation and disaster never comes into view."[13] Bach finds the origin of the sequence in Jeremiah's proclamation of disaster (Jer. 45:4); its use in the context of hope for salvation is therefore secondary (24:6; 31:28; 42:10). Its absolute use to characterize the ambivalence of the prophet's message stands accordingly at the end of its conceptual development (1:10; 18:9).

2. *Nouns.* The noun *neṭa'* can denote an individual plant or sapling, as in Ps. 144:12[14] and Job 14:9; both texts associate it with the idea of vigorous growth. In Isa. 5:7 *neṭa'* parallels *kerem* and therefore should be translated "planting, plantation"; it has the same meaning in Isa. 17:10, where the phrase *niṭ'ê naᵃmānîm* probably refers to the

---

13. Bach, 26f.
14. On the derivation of *neṭa'* see above.

so-called gardens of Adonis.[15] Otherwise the place where planting takes place is always referred to as *maṭṭā'*, literally in the sense of a place where plants are planted (Ezk. 17:7; 31:4; Mic. 1:6) or figuratively in the sense of "Yahweh's planting" (Isa. 60:21 [*Q*]; 61:3). In Ezk. 34:29 we should probably follow *BHS* in reading *maṭṭa' šālôm* (or *šālēm*[16]), "planting of salvation." The only passage with a different meaning is Isa. 17:11, where MT *niṭ'ēḵ* would have to mean "planting" in the sense of "being planted." The LXX translates it with a verbal form, interpreting it, probably correctly, as an infinitive construct.[17]

3. *Distinction between nāṭa' and šāṯal.* The verb *šāṯal* differs from *nāṭa'* in both usage and meaning. It appears exclusively in poetic language and has a very restricted distribution (Ezk. 17; 19 [6 times]; Jer. 17:8; Ps. 1:3 [in the metaphor of a tree by the water]; otherwise only Ps. 92:14[13], where it is used figuratively).[18] Eight of the ten occurrences are forms of the passive participle. In each case it refers to a single plant (in Ps. 92:14[13], an individual). The interest is always in the site (preferred, well-watered) — an aspect of no weight in the case of *nāṭa'*. The noun *šāṯîl* appears only in Ps. 128:3; it has the same meaning as *n^eṭi'îm*.

III. Theological Usage. In itself, "plant" is not a theological term; only its use in specific contexts and formulas lends the verb a theological quality.

1. *With God as Subject.* The theological sense is most striking when God is the subject.

a. In the literal sense the verb *nāṭa'* is predicated of God only in mythological language; Gen. 2:8 uses it to emphasize God's special care for his creation. When Nu. 24:6; Ps. 104:16 use the verb to describe enormous trees not planted by human hands, we are dealing with the figurative language of poetry.

b. In historical retrospect Ps. 80:9(8) describes Israel's entrance into Canaan as Yahweh's planting of a vine. This metaphorical language emphasizes that the gift of the land is Yahweh's own personal act; it can also be used to express Yahweh's special care and love (Isa. 5:2; Jer. 2:21) or to underpin Israel's claim over against that of the nations (Ps. 44:3[2]). Israel is Yahweh's planting (*maṭṭā':* Isa. 60:21; *neṭa':* 5:7). The Qumran community considered itself *maṭṭa'aṯ 'ôlām,* an "eternal planting" (1QS 8:5; 11:8; CD 1:7).[19]

c. This figurative language, used in the first instance to characterize past history, can then be applied to Yahweh's future actions: as a prediction of disaster or salvation,

15. See Delcor; on the questionable identification of the deity called *na'^amān,* see H. Wildberger, *Isaiah 13–27* (Eng. trans., Minneapolis, 1997), 182f.
16. W. Zimmerli, *Ezekiel 2. Herm* (Eng. trans. 1983), 211.
17. *BLe,* 343b; *HAL,* II, 694.
18. On Hos. 9:13 see I.2.b above.
19. See Ringgren; A. S. van der Woude, "Das Hiobtargum aus Qumran Höhle XI," *Congress Volume, Bonn 1962. SVT,* 9 (1963), 330.

the formula of "(tearing down and building), uprooting and planting," is used to proclaim Yahweh's sovereignty over history. It is ambivalent only when it describes the prophetic message (Jer. 1:10; 18:9); as a prediction of God's acts, it is always unambiguously negative (45:4) or positive (24:6; 42:10; 31:28; 32:41; Am. 9:15).

2. *As a Human Activity.* a. In itself the human activity of planting is theologically neutral. It can, however, become the object of an enjoinder: planting an *ʾašērâ* as a symbol of an alien cult is forbidden (Dt. 16:21); Lev. 19:23 associates an ancient taboo regulation with the establishment of an agricultural settlement; the exiles are commanded to build houses and plant vineyards (Jer. 29:5,28). Gen. 21:33 mentions Abraham's planting of a tamarisk as a praiseworthy cultic act.

b. Farmers by their labor lay the groundwork, but they cannot guarantee the outcome. Their experience constitutes the background for threats that promise the frustration of all human effort as a sanction for disobeying God's commandments (Dt. 28:30,39; Am. 5:11; etc.). Negation of such a threat (Isa. 65:22) or its conversion into a positive promise (v. 21) can be an oracle of salvation announcing the end of the time of judgment (Jer. 31:5; Ezk. 28:26; Am. 9:14). In Dt. 6:11; Josh. 24:13, a modification of this threat becomes a parenetic reminder that God freely gave the land to Israel.

Reindl

IV. Dead Sea Scrolls. In the Dead Sea Scrolls the verb *nāṭaʿ* occurs only in the Temple Scroll (11QTemple 51:20; 52:1), with reference to the "planting" of an *ʾašērâ* (Dt. 16:21f.). The nouns *maṭṭāʿ* and *maṭṭaʿaṯ* occur frequently as metaphors for the community: it is "an everlasting plantation, the holy house [temple] of Israel" (1QS 8:5; cf. 11:8) or "the root of a planting" that has sprouted from Israel and Aaron (CD 1:7). This notion is developed extensively in 1QH 8:5ff.[20] As in Isa. 41:19, God causes a planting of all kinds of trees to grow up, "trees of life in the secret source," nourished by living water. "They must make a shoot grow in the everlasting plantation" (similarly 1QH 6:15). Other trees (unbelievers), with access only to ordinary water, will grow tall in their plantation (cf. Isa. 17:11) and rise up against the eternal plantation. But the "true plantation" *(maṭṭaʿaṯ ʾemeṯ),* although hidden and unnoticed, will endure and its fruit will be preserved. The other trees will be destroyed, but the "plantation of fruit" will be an Eden, which the poet (probably the Teacher of Righteousness) will water by his teaching, and whose trees he will align with his level. The paradisal symbolism recalls T.Lev. 18:10f., which speaks of the priestly messiah opening the gates of paradise and giving the saints food from the tree of life. The notion of planting appears also in 1(Eth.) En. 10:16; 84:6.[21]

Ringgren

---

20. See Ringgren.
21. M. Delcor, *RB,* 58 (1951), 537f.

נָטַף nāṭap; נָטָף nāṭāp̱; נֶטֶף neṭep̱; נְטִ(י)פוֹת n^eṭîp̱ôṯ; נְטֹפָה n^eṭōp̱â; נְטֹפָתִי n^eṭōp̱āṯî

Contents: I. Etymology and Distribution: 1. Etymology; 2. The Verb in the OT; 3. Derivatives; 4. Phonetically Similar Words; 5. LXX. II. Human Subjects: 1. Hands; 2. Lips; 3. Speech; 4. Prophetic Speech. III. The Heavens, Clouds, and Mountains: 1. The Heavens; 2. Job 36:27; 3. Am. 9:13; Jo. 4:18(Eng. 3:18).

I. Etymology and Distribution.

1. *Etymology.* Outside Biblical Hebrew, the root *nṭp* in the sense of "drip, drop, melt" occurs in Samaritan, Syriac, Mandaic, Arabic, Ethiopic, and Tigré.[1] It occurs also in 4QEn^c (4Q204) fr. 1 1:6 in the sense of "resin" (cf. *nāṭāp̱*).[2] The Deir ʿAlla text (2:35f.) probably also uses the root with reference to *ṭal,* "dew," and *šr,* "rain," with the fields or mountains as subject, to symbolize a happy future.[3] According to William A. Ward, the root is an *n*-expansion of an element *ṭp,* related to Egyp. **df* (in a variety of specific forms: *dfy,* "large jug"; *dfdf.t,* "drop"; *dfdf,* "drip"; etc.).[4] Other expansions of the same element appear, for example, in Middle Heb. *ṭipṭēp̱,* "drip"; Arab. *ṭāfa,* Middle Heb. *ṭûp,* "overflow"; and Arab. *ṭafā,* "flow, swim." A connection with Akk. *naṭāpu,* "uproot," is semantically impossible.[5]

2. *The Verb in the OT.* The verb occurs 9 times in the qal: with the subj. *šāmayim/ʿāḇîm* (Jgs. 5:4; Ps. 68:9[8]) and the obj. *mayim* (Jgs. 5:); with the subj. *hārîm* and the obj. *ʿāsîs* (Jo. 4:18[3:18]); with the subj. *yāḏ/ʾeṣbāʿôṯ* and the obj. *môr (ʿōḇēr)* (Cant. 5:5); with the subj. *śip̱tê/śip̱tôṯ* and the obj. *nōp̱eṯ* (Prov. 5:3; Cant. 4:11); with the subj. *śip̱tôṯ* and the obj. *môr ʿōḇēr* (Cant. 5:13); and with the subj. *millâ* (Job 29:22). Most of the occurrences are in poetic texts. The verb also occurs 9 times in the hiphil; in 8 of these occurrences (Ezk. 21:2,7[20:46; 21:2]; Am. 7:16; Mic. 2:6 [3 times], 11 [twice]) it has no object and means "speak as a prophet." It also occurs in Am. 9:13 — like the qal in Jo. 4:18(3:18) — with *hārîm* as subject and *ʿāsîs* as object.

---

nāṭap. M. Dahood, "Honey That Drips," *Bibl,* 54 (1973), 65f.; K. Kob, "Noch einmal Netopha," *ZDPV,* 94 (1978), 119-134; E. Lipiński, "Juges 5,4-5 et Psaume 68,8-11," *Bibl,* 48 (1967), 185-206; E. Vogt, "'Die Himmel troffen' (Ps 68,9)?" *Bibl,* 46 (1965), 207-9; *idem,* "'Regen in Fülle' (Psalm 68,10-11)," *Bibl,* 46 (1965), 359-361; W. A. Ward, "Notes on Some Egypto-Semitic Roots," *ZÄS,* 95 (1969), 70-72.

1. *HAL,* II, 694.
2. J. A. Fitzmyer and D. J. Harrington, *A Manual of Palestinian Aramaic Texts. BietOr,* 34 (1978), 10:6 (pp. 64f.).
3. J. Hoftijzer and G. van der Kooij, *Aramaic Texts from Deir ʿAlla. DMOA,* 19 (1976), 251f.
4. Pp. 70f.
5. *AHw,* II, 767f.

3. *Derivatives.* Among the derived nouns, *nāṭāp̱* (Ex. 30:34) is a resinous exudate that was mixed with equal parts of *šᵉḥēleṯ* (onycha) and *ḥelbᵉnâ* (galbanum) and then combined with the same amount of frankincense[6] to make an aromatic mixture to be burned as a daily offering and in the holy of holies on the Day of Atonement. The basic material of this resin is a matter of debate: suggestions include the mastic terebinth, *Styrax officinalis,* myrrh, and balsam.[7]

On *neṭep̱/nᵉṭāp̱îm* as a drop of water in Job 36:27, see III.2 below.

Then there are the *nᵉṭîp̱ôṯ* mentioned in Jgs. 8:26; Isa. 3:19, probably ear pendants but possibly neck ornaments, worn by the defeated kings of Midian and by the flashy women of Jerusalem. Both texts speak of them in conjunction with *śahᵃrōnîm,* "little moons"; they may therefore have served not only as ornaments (Isa. 3:19) but as charms to protect fertility.[8]

The toponym Netophah appears in Ezr. 2:22 and Neh. 7:26 together with Bethlehem in the list of exiles who returned under Zerubbabel. Men from Netophah were among David's warriors (2 S. 23:28f.; 1 Ch. 11:30) as well as among the Levites and temple singers (1 Ch. 9:16; Neh. 12:28). They were also among those responsible for supplying the king (1 Ch. 27:13). "The Netophathite" is the brother of Bethlehem (1 Ch. 2:54). Most of the references to what was probably a tiny village date from the postexilic period; there is hardly any connection between the local tradition and the other *nṭp* texts (Ps. 68:9[8]; Jo. 4:18[3:18]?). Identification of the site does not appear to be certain;[9] the name at the edge of the desert of Judah is probably meaningful.

4. *Phonetically Similar Words.* Phonetically similar to *nṭp* is *dālap̱/delep̱* for a leaking roof, an image describing an indolent person (Eccl. 10:18) and a quarrelsome wife (Prov. 19:13; 27:15[10]), as well as a crying eye (Job 16:20; Ps. 119:28). Then there is *ʿārap̱* (Dt. 32:2; 33:28; Sir. 43:22); it is always used with *ṭal* to represent healing *(rāpāʾ, hôšîaʿ)* fertility for the parched land. Finally, there is *rāʿap* (Ps. 65:12[11]; Job 36:28; Prov. 3:20; hiphil in Isa. 45:8), a sign of the constantly recurring created order established by Yahweh; it is predicated of *šāmayim/šᵉḥāqîm,* the *maʿgᵉlê YHWH,* and the *nᵉʾôṯ miḏbār.* In the texts listed, "drip" or "drop" is usually a satisfactory translation. By contrast, the common verb *šāṭap,* phonetically similar but semantically different, refers to a substantial flow or an inundation.[11]

---

6. So U. Cassuto, *Exodus* (Eng. trans., Jerusalem, 1967), 400.

7. For the mastic terebinth see *AuS,* I, 541; *HAL,* II, 695. For *Styrax officinalis,* Cassuto, *Exodus,* 399f.; rejected by J. Feliks, *EncJud,* XV, 415f. For myrrh, A. Dillmann, *Die Bücher Exodus und Leviticus. KEHAT,* 12 (^{3}1897), 361. For balsam, Feliks, *EncJud,* IV, 142f.

8. See esp. H. Weippert, "Schmuck," *BRL*^{2}, 285f.; H. Wildberger, *Isaiah 1–12* (Eng. trans., Minneapolis, 1991), 151-56.

9. Kob, 119-134; O. Keel and M. Küchler, *Orte und Landschaften der Bibel,* 2 vols. (1982), II, 662: *ḫirbet bedd fālūḥ; rāmat rāḥel; ḫirbet umm ṭūba.*

10. *AuS,* I, 188f.

11. → מטר *māṭār,* VIII, 252f.

5. *LXX.* In the LXX most of the occurrences use the root *stag- (stázein, apostázein; stalázein, apostalázein; stagṓn, staktḗ),* which probably exhibits an onomatopoeic similarity.[12] It always means "drip" or "drop"; *staktḗ* is used for the resin in Ex. 30:34. The prep. *apó* is a special case, used onomatopoeically with the obj. *glykasmós,* "honey," in Prov. 5:3; Cant. 4:11; Am. 9:13; Jo. 4:18(3:18). Although the verb does not appear there, Job 29:22 belongs in the same semantic field, as does Mic. 2:6 with *klaíein* and *dakrýein.* There is an element of the tumultuous and the extraordinary in *existán,* used in Jgs. 5:4 (A; subj. *ouranós*), and *ochlagōgeín,* used in Am. 7:16 for the prophecy of Amos.[13] In Ezk. 21:2,7(20:46; 21:2) *epiblépein* plus a statement of direction parallels *prophēteúein.* Jgs. 8:26 and Isa. 3:19 use different roots: *hormískos — strangalís; káthema.* The word group *stázein,* etc., is also used to translate Hebrew words other than *nṭp.* Gk. *nétōpon,* "oil of bitter almonds," derives from the root *nṭp,* but does not appear in the LXX.[14]

II. Human Subjects.

1. *Hands.* In Cant. 5:5f. the hands of the beloved ("my hands dripped with myrrh") represent the opening (*pāṯaḥ,* twice) of a locked garden (cf. 4:12; 5:5f.). Here the image shifts from the house of vv. 2f. to the garden. It is probably also the garden of her body, her totality, including her inmost feelings (*mēʿay-yāḏay/ʾeṣbeʿōṯay;* cf. Jer. 31:20; Ps. 144:1; etc.[15]); myrrh is the embodiment of this garden and its riches (Cant. 4:6; 5:1). When the door is opened (5:5), the text speaks for the first time of overflowing (the probable meaning, not simply fluidity). All kinds of fragrances (4:14) are gathered in the hand as a symbol of anointing. The practice of smearing door bolts with unguents is widely attested.[16] The form of the poem may also echo the weeping at a lover's door,[17] but the image of the garden must not be overlooked.

2. *Lips.* The lips of the beloved dripping with myrrh, says Cant. 5:13, are lilies (*šûšannîm*). This metaphor may refer to their brilliant color, possibly their exquisite form; perhaps, however, the image of lilies[18] represents life and fertility; note the antonyms and synonyms: brambles (2:2); breasts, twins (4:5); belly, heap of wheat (7:3[2]); pasturing (2:16; 6:2,3). It probably means also that the beloved's lips are all of these when they speak of the bride, since elsewhere the imagery of lilies always refers to her. All the images in 5:12f. are in fact garden images, and the feminine forms are striking.[19] His locks, his eyes,

---

12. H. Frisk, *Griechisches etymologisches Wörterbuch,* 2 vols. (Heidelberg, 1960-70), II, 776.
13. "Court the mob": LSJ, 1281.
14. Frisk, II, 308; LSJ, 1170.
15. Dahood, *RSP,* I, 213.
16. Lucretius: W. Rudolph, *Das Hohe Lied. KAT,* XVII/2 (1962), 156; Mesopotamia: M. H. Pope, *Song of Songs. AB,* 7C (1977), 522.
17. Pope, 522f.; G. Krinetzki, *Kommentar zum Hohenlied. BBET,* 16 (1981), 159ff.; cf. also Prov. 7:17.
18. Lotus for "sister": see A. Hermann, *Ägyptische Liebesdichtung* (Wiesbaden, 1959), 125f.
19. F. Landy, *Paradoxes of Paradise* (Sheffield, 1983), 80.

his cheeks and lips, like those of the bride, are the garden; in him, in his lips, this profusion, this fecundity find their ultimate meaning and expression. His overflowing abundance *(ʿōḇēr),* his desirability (*mamṯaqqîm:* v. 16) are his brilliant, life-giving perfection.[20]

Cant. 4:11 speaks of the lips of the bride; up to this point, the emphasis has been on her beauty (4:1-10a: *yāpâ*). The image of dripping honey from the comb, found only here, is employed (note the 12 words beginning with *m-* in vv. 8-10). This image probably refers not only to the refreshing taste, the beautiful appearance of the bride (a crimson thread: v. 3), but also to her sweet and sparkling speech (*miḏbārêḵ nāʾweh:* v. 3; cf. Ps. 19:11[10]). The next image, honey and milk under the tongue, points in the same direction (cf. Ps. 66:17 [positive]; Job 20:12 [negative]). In ancient Mesopotamian literature honey frequently symbolizes love, especially to the beloved.[21]

Prov. 5:3-5, describing the lips of the strange woman *(zārâ, noḵrîyâ),* contrasts with Cant. 4:10f. Again the text speaks of lips dripping with honey, an image that elsewhere suggests the soothing, health-giving effect of words and even wisdom itself (Prov. 16:24; 24:13).[22] But the very next words take a different turn: instead of soothing, invigorating milk we find oil in the mouth, a plethora of words, smooth lips, speech, and kisses that seduce the youth (7:13-22, esp. 13,21) and finally lead him like an ox to the slaughter (v. 22). In the case of the strange woman, there can be no talk of love: instead of soothing milk and honey he finds bitter wormwood,[23] her tongue becomes a sword, and her legs lead onward to death on the path to Sheol. The image of the strange woman should not be construed as one-dimensional; she is primarily an antitype to the man's own wife or bride (*ʾiššâ:* Prov. 5:18; *kallâ:* Cant. 4:11).[24]

3. *Speech.* Job 29 speaks of happiness, respect, abundance, and vigor of days gone by (vv. 3-5,6-7,18-20). Young and old, nobles and princes (vv. 8-10), and especially the poor (vv. 11-16) attend to this abundance of vigor. Job is their eye, foot, hand, father, and light (vv. 13-16,24). They listen to his counsel, they wait for it in silence as one waits in silence for Yahweh (Ps. 37:7; Lam. 3:26).[25] They are like the parched earth; Job's word drops on them like rain (Job 29:22: *ʿālêmô tiṭṭōp millāṯî*), which otherwise is sent by God (28:26; 37:6; 38:28), like the latter rain *(malqôš)*[26] for which they open their mouths as for Yahweh's word (Ps. 119:131; cf. the wordplay in Job 29:22f.: *millāṯî — māṭār — malqôš; pîhem pāʿᵃrû*). It is also Job who puts on Yahweh's

---

20. A. Brenner, "Aromatics and Perfumes in the Song of Songs," *JSOT,* 25 (1983), 78f.; G. W. van Beek, "Frankincense and Myrrh," *BA,* 23 (1960), 70-95.

21. *ANET,* 645 ("man of honey"); H. Ringgren, "Hohes Lied und hieros gamos," *ZAW,* 65 (1953), 300-302; *idem, Das Hohe Lied. ATD,* 16/2 (³1981), 274, n. 9.

22. Dahood (65f.) particularly emphasized 5:2f.

23. → לענה *laʿᵃnâ* (VIII, 14-16).

24. For a balanced treatment, with bibliog., see U. Winter, *Frau und Göttin. OBO,* 53 (1983), 613-625.

25. → דמה *dāmāh* II (III, 264); → יחל *yāḥal,* VI, 51, 53f.

26. → מטר *māṭār,* VIII, 252, 255; *AuS,* I/2, 302-4.

ṣeḏeq and *mišpāṭ* like a garment (v. 14). This profusion of images may be relatively late.[27] In any case it probably presupposes texts such as Ps. 1; Jer. 17:8.[28]

4. *Prophetic Speech.* Job 29:22 may help us understand the difficult passages Am. 7:16; Ezk. 21:2,7(20:46; 21:2); Mic. 2:6,11, which deal with prophetic speech. These passages (all in the hiphil) never state explicitly the actual meaning of *nṭp.* The earliest is probably Am. 7:16 (secondary). Amos's *hiṭṭîp̱ ʿal-bêṯ yiśḥāq* parallels "prophesying" *(hinnāḇēʾ ʿal-yiśrāʾēl).* The same is true in vv. 12f., where prophesying is understood as a remunerative activity *(ʾᵉḵol-šām leḥem).* The LXX interprets v. 16 in a negative sense: *ochlagōgeín,* "be a demagogue" (cf. Symmachus: "reproach"); this meaning probably does not come out of the blue[29] but reflects v. 10: *qāšar ʿal,* "conspire against." In any case, the prophet's message is clearly one of disaster and is more than suspect to his audience.

This element is likewise not entirely absent from Ezk. 21:2,7(20:46; 21:2). Here *nṭp* is certainly part of the total act of prophetic speech *(śîm pāneyḵā dereḵ — haṭṭēp̱ ʾel — hinnāḇēʾ ʾel — ʾāmartā lᵉ),*[30] directed toward all points of the compass, and is therefore parallel to *hinnāḇēʾ.* As a message of ineluctable disaster *(lōʾ-ṯiḵbeh — lōʾ tāšûḇ),* it embraces all (*kol-pānîm — kol-bāśār:* vv. 3f.,10[20:47f.; 21:5] *ṣaddîq wᵉrāšāʿ:* v. 8[3]). The effect of this speech on the audience (*hᵃlōʾ mᵉmaššēl mᵉšālîm hûʾ:* v. 5[20:49]) is clearly negative.[31] The hiphil of *nṭp* is not simply synonymous with *hinnāḇēʾ;* rather, the basis of the comparison is probably the absence (also *mšl*) of rain and storm, and ultimately also of the blessing of the prophet's message. Nothing in these texts suggests anything like ecstatic "slavering"; furthermore, the verb never appears in passages that describe typically ecstatic speech.[32]

Mic. 2:6-11 is an oracle in the form of a discussion with the leaders of the house of Jacob.[33] The hearers object to this prophesying (*hiṭṭîp̱:* v. 6), which is obscure (*māšāl:* v. 4) and predicts only calamities (*kᵉlimmôṯ:* v. 6). The leaders want to remonstrate with Yahweh, to utter prophecies against him (v. 7), to listen to a prophet of empty falsehoods (v. 11), not one who devotes himself to "the favorite theme of the officers and soldiers,"[34] but in contrast to the proclaimer of disaster one who prophesies the salvation of an ideal future (cf. Am. 9:13; Jo. 4:18[3:18]).

The image of the lying prophet, who pours out the water of falsehood over Israel, appears later at Qumran in the Damascus Document as one who weighs wind (CD

---

27. F. Stier, *Das Buch Ijob* (Munich, 1954), 318f.

28. G. Fohrer, *Das Buch Hiob. KAT,* XVI (²1963), 410.

29. As argued by W. Rudolph, *Amos. KAT,* XIII/2 (1971), 251, among others.

30. F. Hossfeld, *Untersuchungen zu Komposition und Theologie des Ezechielbuches. FzB,* 20 (1977), 381f., 433; W. Zimmerli, *Ezekiel 1. Herm* (Eng. trans. 1979), 422f.

31. Contra Zimmerli; cf. H. W. Wolff, *Joel and Amos. Herm* (Eng. trans. 1977), 315.

32. F. Ellermeier, *Prophetie in Mari und Israel* (Herzberg a. Harz, 1968), 180f.; on slavering see A. Jepsen, *Nabi* (Munich, 1934), 11.

33. E. A. Neiderhiser, "Micah 2:6-11," *BTB,* 11 (1981), 104-7.

34. Wolff, *Micah* (Eng. trans., Minneapolis, 1990), 84.

8:13; 19:25) and leads the people astray into the desert (1:14f.); in 1QpHab 10:9 as one who builds a phantom city of blood and establishes a community based on falsehood; and in the pesher on Mic. 1:5-7 (1Q14 8-10).[35] This figure may pave the way for the prophet of lies in Rev. 16:13; 19:20; 20:10.[36]

III. The Heavens, Clouds, and Mountains.

1. *The Heavens.* Jgs. 5 is composed in the form of a hymn; vv. 2-9 are framed by praise of Yahweh *(bārᵉḵû YHWH),*[37] while vv. 4f. extol Yahweh as the God of Israel. In an awesome theophany Yahweh advances from Seir and Edom (probably parallel and equivalent[38]), which, like Sinai, Paran, and Teman in Dt. 33:2 and Hab. 3:3, may represent Yahweh's original home.[39] This is an advance into battle (*lāḥem:* Jgs. 5:8), to perform victorious deeds (*ṣiḏqōṯ:* v. 11); it is also a descent from Tabor, probably accompanying the warriors of Israel (vv. 11,13f.), with Yahweh their only shield and spear. The text envisions a concrete battle with the kings of Canaan (*nilḥam:* v. 19). When Yahweh advances, the earth trembles and tumult fills the cosmos (cf. esp. Ps. 77:18f.[17f.]; 18:8[7]; Isa. 24:18).[40] The heavens and the clouds drip — water! There is no good reason to abridge the text or to translate it differently (image of tottering); this repetitive style is typical of the Song of Deborah.[41] Cosmologically, water dripping from the heavens and the clouds bespeaks an overflowing abundance, as in the Flood (Gen. 7:11f.; 8:2).[42] Above all, Jgs. 5:21f. help interpret the image. Water from heaven[43] and from the abyss (*qᵉḏûmîm — qîšôn;* cf. the alliterating *ns* and *qs* in vv. 4f.,20f.) brings about the defeat of the Canaanite coalition. Similarly, the hills can be described as "flowing" *(nāzal),* parallel to the "dripping" *(nṭp)* of the mountains (Am. 9:13; Jo. 4:18[3:18]). It is likely that Yahweh was worshiped early on as "the one of Sinai," and then worshiped as a mountain god on Tabor.

Ps. 68 resembles a processional hymn, with its imperatives to praise God (vv. 5,33,35) and its repeated blessing formulas (*brk:* vv. 20,27,36).[44] In v. 8, unlike Jgs. 5:4, Yahweh does not come from a particular place; he is in his exalted sanctuary (Ps. 68:6,18f.,25,36) and in Jerusalem (v. 29); Sinai (vv. 9,18) is a name rather than a place

---

35. D. Barthélemy and J. T. Milik, *Qumran Cave I. DJD,* 1 (1955), 78.

36. M. A. Klopfenstein, *TLOT,* II, 610.

37. J. Blenkinsopp, "Ballad Style and Psalm Style in the Song of Deborah," *Bibl,* 42 (1961), 61-76.

38. M. Weippert, "Edom und Israel," *TRE,* IX (1982), 291.

39. M. Weippert, "Jahwe," *RLA,* V (1976/80), 250f., 252; → יצא *yāṣā',* VI, 232f.

40. → ארץ *'erets* (I, 388-405).

41. A. J. Hauser, "Judges 5: Parataxis in Hebrew Poetry," *JBL,* 99 (1980), 23-41; M. O'Connor, *Hebrew Verse Structure* (Winona Lake, Ind., 1980), 220, 362f., etc. On abridging the text see J. Jeremias, *Theophanie. WMANT,* 10 (²1977), 11, etc. For the image of tottering see Lipiński, 199; Vogt, "Himmel," 207-9.

42. E. F. Sutcliffe, "The Clouds as Water-Carriers in Hebrew Thought," *VT,* 3 (1953), 99-103; P. Reymond, *L'eau, sa vie, et sa signification dans l'AT. SVT,* 6 (1958), 202-7.

43. On the stars as bringers of rain, see Blenkinsopp, 73; R. G. Boling, *Judges. AB,* 6A (1975), 113.

44. This paragraph cites only the verse numbers of Ps. 68 in the Hebrew text; the English numbering is one fewer.

of origin.[45] Thence he arises and thither he returns from Bashan, from his enemies, from the "gables of the gods" (vv. 16f.,23; cf. the verbs *qûm, yāšaḇ, šāḵan, ʿālâ lᵉ* in vv. 2,17,19).[46] Yahweh goes before his people in the desert wilderness (*yᵉšîmôn* [anarthrous]: Dt. 32:10; Isa. 43:19f., etc.). Unlike Jgs. 5:4f., Ps. 68:9 begins again after a *selâ.* As in Jgs. 5:4f., the whole cosmos is in tumult; heaven and earth are shaken. The enemy will be struck — they will perish before God (*mippᵉnê:* 3 times in vv. 2f.,9), they will be scattered, be driven away, melt away, flee. But the combination of vv. 9,10 also gives *ntp* a positive aspect: Yahweh brings rain *(gešem)* to his parched, languishing heritage, he restores it (v. 10) — he, the "rider of the clouds" (vv. 15,18,34).[47]

2. *Job 36:27.* In Job 36:27 God himself *('ēl)* separates the water drops from the great reservoir above the firmament, drops that ultimately "distill" rain from the heavenly ocean *('ēḏ).*[48] Then the clouds can pour down *(nāzal)* rain, dripping upon the mass of humankind.[49] As in Jgs. 5:4f.; Prov. 3:20, the heavenly ocean and the clouds are involved; as in Ps. 68:9f.(8f.), this rain is both judgment (*bām yāḏîn ʿammîm:* Job 36:31) and salvation, i.e., food in abundance (v. 31b).[50] What God does in the firmament will not pass away (*mispar šānāyw wᵉlō'-ḥēqer:* v. 26b). It brings judgment and salvation to all (*'āḏām rāḇ:* v. 28b).

3. *Am. 9:13.* Am. 9:13-15 is probably a single unit;[51] a later addition, framed as an oracle from God, it highlights what Yahweh will do for Israel. He will lead his people home from captivity (v. 14a), giving them back their land to plant *(nāṯan/nāṭaʿ).* Fields (v. 13), cities, and gardens (v. 14) will be restored by God's act; his "replanting" of his people is reflected in human activity (*nāṭaʿ/ʿāśâ:* v. 13a). The earth will be restored in its fullness, the regular cycle of activity will replace destruction: building and dwelling, planting vineyards and making gardens and enjoying their produce (v. 14); the more restricted cycle of the year: cultivating and harvesting (v. 13a). Stability and fruition *(yāšaḇ — šāṯâ — 'āḵal)* are predicted, not so much the regular monthly cycle of fertility.[52] Thus the mountains' dripping sweet wine (v. 13; hiphil) is the soil's reaction to Yahweh's act, resembling the reaction of the human population. It is probably also a sign of unimagined, almost paradisal abundance, which eases the labor of human civilization. Just as the mountains will drip sweet wine, the hills will flow with it — the imagery recalls the description of Yahweh's judgment in 9:5. Now, however, the

45. Contra M. Dahood, *Psalms I. AB,* 17 ([2]1973), 143; H.-J. Kraus (*Psalms 60–150* [Eng. trans., Minneapolis, 1989], 54, etc.) is probably wrong in suggesting Tabor.

46. P. A. H. de Boer, *VT,* 1 (1951), 53f.

47. See L. Stadelmann, *The Hebrew Conception of the World. AnBibl,* 39 (1970), 115. → לאה *lā'â* (VII, 395f.); cf. *yᵉšîmôn.* Vogt ("Regen," 359-361) destroys the continuity by transposing vv. 9 and 10.

48. See N. Peters, *Das Buch Hiob. EHAT,* 21 (1928), 415; M. Pope, *Job. AB,* 15 ([3]1973), 273.

49. Not *rᵉḇîḇîm* with E. F. Sutcliffe, *Bibl,* 30 (1949), 82; and Pope, *Job,* 236.

50. Sutcliffe, 85.

51. Contra P. Weimar, "Der Schluss des Amos-Buches," *BN,* 16 (1981), 60-100, esp. 89-94.

52. Wolff, *Joel and Amos,* 354.

result is not mourning but drunkenness (the best translation of *mûg* in this context), tottering (cf. the parentheses in vv. 13aβ,14b,14aγ) from strong drink (*ʿāsîs*).[53]

4. *Joel 4:18(3:18).* Like Am. 9:13-15, Joel 4:18(3:18) is embedded in an oracle of Yahweh; it is also associated with the restoration of the nation. Yahweh's habitation is Zion (vv. 17,21[3:17,21]); the land round about resembles a new paradisal garden (cf. Isa. 51:3; Ezk. 36:35). The mountains, formerly the site of judgment (Joel 2:2,5), scorched by fire, now bear witness to the land's fertility (cf. the resurrection of Baʿal: "The heavens rain oil, the valleys flow with honey"[54]). The hills flow with milk where previously the animals groaned and the cattle wandered about (1:18). The drunkards and wine drinkers wailed over the sweet wine, cut off from their mouths (1:5); now it drips from the mountains for all. Joel 4:18(3:18) harks back to the image of abundant fertility in 2:18-27; the vivid, concrete imagery loses some of its vibrancy, but compensates for the loss by extension to all ages. The streambeds of Judah will always flow (*hālak̠);* the paradisal fertility is permanent. From Zion, from the house of Yahweh, which had been without offering (1:9,13f.,16) because the land was without food, goes forth a stream, like the stream issuing from the garden of Eden in Gen. 2:10, linking beginning and end (cf. Ezk. 47:1-12), watering the whole earth (cf. Zec. 14:8; Ps. 36:5ff.[4ff.]; 46:5[4]; 65:10[9][55]). The mention of Wadi Shittim may bring Judah back to the entrance to the new land (cf. Josh. 2:1; 3:1; possibly the wilderness [*yᵉšîmôn*] of Ps. 68:8[7]; Wadi Shittim and *nᵉṭāpôt̠* are related traditions), where it will dwell forever in full view of the desolate habitations of the enemy (Joel 4:19f.[3:19f.). Nothing is said of any human response, unless 3:1-3(2:28-30), the outpouring of the Spirit of God, can be associated with 4:18(3:18).

Madl

---

53. Not " 'rippling' of wine": *ibid.,* 354; softening the soil → מוג *mûg,* VIII, 150; see K. Koch, et al., *Amos. AOAT,* 30 (1976), 240f.; LXX *sýmphytoi ésontai;* "fully cultivated," LSJ, 1689.

54. *KTU,* 1.6, III, 6f., 12f.

55. → הר *har,* III, 446.

נָטַר *nāṭar;* מַטָּרָה *maṭṭārâ*

Contents: I. Etymology and Distribution: 1. Etymology; 2. The Verb and Its Synonyms in the OT; 3. Derivatives; 4. LXX; 5. Dead Sea Scrolls. II. Guard, Keep: 1. Guarding a Vineyard; 2. Keeping Words. III. Lev. 19:18. IV. Yahweh's Anger: 1. With His People; 2. With His Enemies.

---

nāṭar. G. R. Driver, "Studies in the Vocabulary of the OT, III," *JTS,* 32 (1931), 361-66; M. Held, "Studies in Biblical Homonyms in the Light of Accadian," *JANES,* 3 (1971), 46-55; W. J. Odendaal, "A Comparative Study of the Proto-Semitic Root *nṭr*" (diss., Stellenbosch, 1966); G. Sauer, "נצר *nṣr* 'to guard,' " *TLOT,* II, 762f.

I. Etymology and Distribution.

1. *Etymology.* It is possible that *nṭr* represents two homonymous roots. The first is related to Akk. *nadāru,* "be wild, rabid" (although there are phonological problems), and parallel to *šamāru* I, "rage."[1] This etymology has been proposed for Jer. 3:5; Am. 1:11 conj., as well as Lev. 19:18; Jer. 3:12; Ps. 103:9; Nah. 1:2.[2] The second homonym is related to Proto-Sem. *nṭr,* Akk. *naṣāru,* Ugar. *nǵr,* Egyp. Aram. *nṭr,* and early Heb. *nṣr;* it occurs in the later form *nṭr* in Cant. 1:6; 8:11f. (plus Dnl. 7:28 [Aramaic]) with the meaning "guard, keep." Aram. *nṭr* is first attested at Elephantine;[3] it is not clear whether Heb. *nṭr* developed under Aramaic influence or analogously to Aramaic.[4] Other scholars assume that all occurrences of *nṭr* represent the same root; in such passages as Jer. 3:5,12, they speak of "keeping anger," "being angry continually."[5]

Derivation from a single root seems to be supported by the various ways the continuation of anger is expressed: (1) the modifier *leʿôlām* (Jer. 3:5,12; Ps. 103:9; cf. Am. 1:11); (2) addition of such verbs as *šāmar* (Jer. 3:5; Am. 1:11), *rîḇ lāneṣaḥ* (Ps. 103:9), and *śānē'— 'āhaḇ* (Lev. 19:17) and the phrase *ḥāsîḏ 'anî* (Jer. 3:12), expressing a condition; (3) the verbal form of the active participle (Nah. 1:2).

2. *The Verb and Its Synonyms in the OT.* All occurrences of the verb are in the qal. Cant. 1:6; 8:11f.; Dnl. 7:28; Lev. 19:18 differ formally from the other texts by including an accusative object: *kerāmîm, karmî* (Cant. 1:6); *piryô* (Cant. 8:12 [cf. *kerem,* v. 11]); *milleṯā'* (Dnl. 7:28); *'eṯ-benê ʿammeḵā* (Lev. 19:18). As a prepositional object, *leṣārāyw* occurs in Nah. 1:2. Otherwise only the adverbial modifier *leʿôlām* occurs (Jer. 3:5,12; Ps. 103:9). As synonyms of the meaning "be angry," we find *nāqam* (Lev. 19:18; Nah. 1:2), *šāmar* (Jer. 3:5; Am. 1:11), *rîḇ* (Ps. 103:9), and *hippîl pānay bāḵem* (Jer. 3:12).

3. *Derivatives.* The noun *maṭṭārâ* derives from this root (*maṭṭārā'* [Aramaic orthography] in Lam. 3:12[6]). It means "target" in 1 S. 20:20; Job 16:12; Lam. 3:12; "guard" in Jer. 32:2,8,12; 33:1; 37:21 (twice); 38:6,13,28; 39:14,15; Neh. 3:25; and "guard gate" in Neh. 2:39. In 1 S. 20:20 the word refers concretely to the "target" for Jonathan's arrows.[7] In Job 16:12 and Lam. 3:12 it refers figuratively to the body or kidneys, respectively, of one who has been wounded by God's arrow.[8] Jeremiah is

---

1. See, respectively, *AHw,* II, 703; III, 1154.

2. First Driver, 361-63; then *KBL*², 613 (also *HAL,* II, 695); O. Rössler, *ZAW,* 74 (1962), 126; Held; K. J. Cathcart, *Nahum in the Light of Northwest Semitic. BietOr,* 26 (1973), 42-44; and Odendaal.

3. J. A. Fitzmyer, *JAOS,* 81 (1961), 202; *idem, Bibl,* 46 (1965), 54.

4. Odendaal, 158; for Aramaic, Nabatean, and Palmyrene see *DISO,* 178.

5. E.g., *GesTh,* 879; *GesB,* 502; *LexHebAram,* 514; *HAL,* II, 695. → נצר *nāṣar.*

6. *BLe,* §62x; M. Wagner, *Die lexikalischen und grammatikalischen Aramaismen in alttestamentlichen Hebräisch. BZAW,* 96 (1966), 83f.: fem.; cf. Aram. *manṭerā',* "guard," etc.; *DISO,* 159.

7. H. J. Stoebe, *Das erste Buch Samuelis. KAT,* VIII/1 (1973), 387; *AuS,* VI, 330-32; *BRL*², 49, 89.

8. On kidneys → כליות *kelāyôt,* VII, 179f.; on God's arrow, → חץ *ḥēṣ* (V, 118-124).

confined (*kālû'*: Jer. 32:2; *'āṣûr:* 33:1; 39:15; *yāšab̲:* 37:21; 38:13,21; 39:14) in the "court of the guard." He appears to enjoy a certain freedom of movement: he can make contracts (32:12), travel to certain destinations (37:11ff.; not to the temple: 36:5), speak freely (38:1), and receive sufficient rations (37:21); but he also faces the possibility of closer confinement (prison: 37:11-16; a cistern: 38:6ff.), which can lead almost to death.[9] In Neh. 3:25; 12:39, we are probably dealing with purely architectural terms.

4. *LXX.* The LXX uses several words to translate *nṭr: phylássō* (Cant. 1:6e); *phylákissa* (1:6d); *tēréō* (8:11,12); *syntēréō* (Dnl. 7:28). In the texts where the meaning is "be angry," we find *mēníō,* "rage, bear a grudge" (Lev. 19:18; Jer. 3:12; Ps. 103:9), *exaírō* (Nah. 1:2), and *diaménō/diaphylássō* (for *nāṭar/šāmar:* Jer. 3:5). This variety in itself reflects the difficulties the LXX had in translating the root. For "court of the guard" the LXX always uses *aulḗ tḗs phylakḗs;* Neh. 12:39 has *probatikḗ,* "sheep gate." 1 S. 20:20 has the otherwise unknown *amáttaris;* Job 16:12 and Lam. 3:12 use *skopós* — reflecting a broader meaning than *maṭṭārâ.*

5. *Dead Sea Scrolls.* In the Dead Sea Scrolls the verb is used primarily in the exegesis of Lev. 19:18 (1QS 7:8; CD 7:2; 8:5; 9:2,3; 13:18; 19:18); sometimes it refers to the members of the community (CD 7:2; 9:2,4; 13:18; 1QS 7:8: a concrete form of punishment), sometimes to apostates (CD 8:5; 19:18). CD 9:5 relates Nah. 1:2 to Lev. 19:18; 1QS 10:20 uses similar words to expound Jer. 3:12. With the meaning "be angry," *nṭr* occurs also in 4QFlor (4Q174) 4:2; with the meaning "guard, keep," it is found in 6Q31 fr. 1.

II. Guard, Keep.

1. *Guarding a Vineyard.* Cant. 1:6b is connected stylistically with 1:5-8;[10] the daughters of Jerusalem are possibly also the speakers of v. 8 (cf. 5:9; 6:1).[11] In any case, the beauty (*nā'wâ:* 1:5a) and fairness (*yāp̄â:* v. 8a) of the woman appear to bracket the passage.[12] "My mother's sons" parallels "the daughters of Jerusalem" — both with somewhat negative overtones. They made the woman keeper of their ("the") vineyards. She thus resembles the keeper of the garden mentioned in Papyrus Anastasi I, who surrenders herself in love to the visitor (with respect to the vineyard keeper, cf. Ugar. *nǵr krm*).[13] The vineyards are linked associatively with the love the bride shares with her "royal" beloved (2:15; 7:13[Eng. v. 12]). Her vineyard *(karmî)* is her body;[14] in their love (1:7), she cannot guard it.

---

9. *AncIsr,* I, 160.

10. Contra E. Würthwein, *Das Hohelied. HAT,* XVIII (^{2}1969), 40f.; G. Gerleman, *Das Hohelied. BK,* XVIII (^{2}1981), 99-104.

11. For recent discussions of the passage see N. Lohfink, *TP,* 58 (1983), 239-241; M. Görg, " 'Travestie' im Hohen Lied," *BN,* 21 (1983), 101-115; F. Landy, *Paradoxes of Paradise* (Sheffield, 1983), 142-152.

12. For a similar conclusion see G. Krinetzki, *Kommentar zum Hohenlied. BBET,* 16 (1981), 72.

13. For Papyrus Anastasi I see Görg, 109-111; for Ugaritic see *KTU,* 4.609, 12; 1.92, 23.

14. → VII, 324: *kerem* representing a woman's body.

Speaking of Solomon's vineyard, Cant. 8:11f. is more circumstantial. The rhetorical arc joins with 1:2,4; 2:4: his vineyard is also hers *(karmî šellî l^epānay).*[15] The vineyard is in fact the one in *baʿal hāmôn* — the one belonging to Abraham (?) (*'aḇ h^amôn:* Gen. 17:4f.), possibly the one belonging to Yahweh *(kerem hāyâ lîḏîḏî);* its fruit (Isa. 7:23) is the fruit of Israel (?). The keepers guard its fruit, but ultimately Yahweh himself is the guardian of the vineyard (*'^anî YHWH nōṣ^erâ:* Isa. 27:3). Raymond Tournay interprets the number one thousand as an allusion to 1 K. 11:3, Ernst Würthwein and Wilhelm Rudolph to Isa. 7:23.[16]

2. *Keeping Words.* Dnl. 7:28 concludes the vision in ch. 7 and is thus comparable to 8:24; 2 Esd. 10:50; 12:35; Rev. 13:9,18. Jacob kept the word (*šāmar 'eṯ-haddāḇār;* NRSV: "kept the matter in mind") concerning Joseph (Gen. 37:11); the wisdom teacher urges the hearer to keep *(nāṣar)* his commandments in his heart (Prov. 3:1). The idiom is related to the expression "not let a word fall to the ground" (1 S. 3:19; Est. 6:10). It means holding on to the words because one day they will come to pass (cf. Josh. 21:45; 23:14; 1 K. 8:56; 2 K. 10:10). One should keep all the words of God and ponder them in one's heart until they are fulfilled (cf. Lk. 2:19).

III. Lev. 19:18. In its present form (the positive statement is secondary[17]), Lev. 19:17f. are a unit framed by the contrasting terms *śānē',* "hate," and *'āhaḇ,* "love," in parallel. The admonition addresses intimate personal relations rather than the forensic realm (cf. the contrast *bammišpāṭ/bil^eḇāḇeḵā* in vv. 15a/17a). The verb "hate" is made concrete in specific repeated acts by the parallel use of *lō'-tiqqōm,* "not take vengeance," and *lō' tiṭṭōr,* "not bear a grudge" (v. 18). One must not confront a brother, sister, or neighbor with hatred smoldering in one's breast, but with clear, firm reproof. Hatred incurs guilt to the point of death; therefore a rejoinder must always be made in love, which must also be rooted in the heart.[18]

IV. Yahweh's Anger.

1. *With His People.* The earliest texts using *nāṭar,* "be angry," are probably Jer. 3:5,12. Jer. 3:5 is a double question asked by the people. The first, "Will he be angry forever?" is unambiguous; the second, *'im-yišmōr lāneṣaḥ,* can be understood either as a parallel or as an antithesis. The former depends on supplying *'aḇ* (cf. Am. 1:11;

---

15. R. Tournay, *Quand Dieu parle aux hommes le langage de l'amour. CahRB,* 21 (1982), 27.

16. *Ibid.;* Würthwein, *HAT,* XVIII, 70f.; Rudolph, *Das Hohe Lied. KAT,* XVII (1962), 184. On the image see *AuS,* IV, 316ff., 332ff.

17. H. Reventlow, *Das Heiligkeitsgesetz formgeschichtlich untersucht. WMANT,* 6 (1961), 62; E. Gerstenberger, *Wesen und Herkunft des "apodiktischen Rechts." WMANT,* 20 (1965), 81; → לב *lēḇ,* VII, 418.

18. The theme is discussed by F. Maass, "Die Selbstliebe nach Lev 19,18," *Festschrift F. Baumgärtel* (Erlangen, 1959), 109-113; J. L'Hour, "Pour une enquête morale dans le Pentateuque et dans l'historire du Deutéronomiste," *Morale et AT* (Louvain-la-Neuve, 1976), 57f.

the LXX takes a similar approach): what is kept is anger (parallel to most *hᵃ/'im* clauses in Jeremiah, except 2:14; *neṣaḥ* has negative overtones in 15:18; 50:39).[19] The latter interprets the question to mean "Or will he keep forever?" (with *šāmar* used positively, as in 5:24; 31:10). It is possible that 3:6-12a are secondary;[20] in any case, they conclude — in response to Israel's question in 3:5 — with Yahweh's forceful declaration of forgiveness: he is *ḥāsîḏ* and does not bear a grudge. He will not cause his face to fall before his people (NRSV: "I will not look on you in anger").[21]

In the middle of Ps. 103 (v. 8) stands the confession: "Yahweh is merciful and gracious, slow to anger and abounding in steadfast love." The same statement appears in Ex. 34:6; Ps. 86:15, transposed in Jo. 2:13; Jon. 4:2, and abbreviated in Nu. 14:18; Nah. 1:3.[22] The negative formulations in Ps. 103:9f. ("He will not always accuse [*rîḇ*], he will not be angry [*nṭr*] forever") are, as it were, an exegesis of the *raḇ-ḥeseḏ,* an expression of Yahweh's faithfulness (*'ᵉmeṯ:* Ex. 34:6). Indeed, Ps. 103:10 goes beyond the requital of evil in Ex. 34:7b. God's anger is opposed by his mercy as a father, his wrath is countered by his steadfast love from everlasting to everlasting (Ps. 103:17; *lāneṣaḥ — lᵉʿôlām:* v. 9).

2. *With His Enemies.* It is likely that the theophany in Nah. 1:3b-6 with its acrostic structure contains secondary elements.[23] According to v. 2, the wrathful God *(nōṭēr)* is the jealous God *(qannô'),* as the parallels to *nōqēm* indicate; before his indignation (v. 6) none can stand. His patience (v. 3) contrasts with the heat of his anger against the enemy (v. 6), which rages like fire and can break rocks. Yahweh is patient with those who take refuge in him (v. 7); his jealousy and anger are reserved for his enemies (*'ōyᵉḇāyw:* v. 2b) — possibly not so much the enemies of the people as those from his own ranks (*'ēl qn':* vv. 9-11,14).

Madl

---

19. This is the interpretation of most comms.; see B. O. Long, "The Stylistic Components of Jeremiah 3:1-5," *ZAW,* 88 (1976), 386-390; D. Jobling, "Jeremiah's Poem in III 1–IV 2," *VT,* 28 (1978), 45-55.

20. Argued persuasively by W. McKane, "Relations between Poetry and Prose in the Book of Jeremiah," *Congress Volume, Vienna 1980. SVT,* 32 (1981), 220-237; contra J. A. Thompson, *Jeremiah. NICOT* (1980), 193; J. Schreiner, *Jeremia 1–25,14. NEB* (1981), 25f.

21. See J. Reindl, *Das Angesicht Gottes im Sprachgebrauch des ATs. ETS* (1970), 125f.; → פנים *pānîm.*

22. J. Scharbert, "Formgeschichte und Exegese von Ex 34,6f und seiner Parallelen," *Bibl,* 38 (1957), 130-150.

23. The unity of vv. 2-8 is argued by S. J. de Vries, "The Acrostic of Nahum in the Jerusalem Liturgy," *VT,* 16 (1966), 476-481; C. A. Keller, *Nahoum. CAT,* XIb (1971), 109-114; D. L. Christensen, "The Acrostic of Nahum Reconsidered," *ZAW,* 87 (1975), 17-30.

נָטַשׁ *nāṭaš;* נְטִישָׁה *n^eṭîšâ*

Contents: I. Meaning, Occurrences. II. Concrete Usage. III. Theological Usage: 1. Yahweh and Israel: The Covenant Relationship; 2. Yahweh and the Nations: Creation and Chaos; 3. Wisdom Literature.

I. Meaning, Occurrences. The various meanings of the verb *nāṭaš* derive from a fundamental notion of separation. In Biblical and Postbiblical Hebrew, *nāṭaš* means "to lay out, stretch out, give up."[1] A connection with Arab. *naṭisa,* "be demanding, precise, shrewd," also "move away from something unclean,"[2] is uncertain. The root is unknown in Ugaritic. The LXX translates *nāṭaš* variously. In passages where Yahweh abandons (or does not abandon) Israel, especially in the Deuteronomistic history and Psalms, the normal translation is *apōthéō*.

a. The qal of *nāṭaš* occurs 33 times in the OT (+ Sir. 8:8). It usually means "abandon, discard," occasionally "spread out." In both poetry and prose *nāṭaš* is commonly associated with *ʿāzaḇ* (1 K. 8:57; Jer. 12:7; Ps. 27:9). To judge from the context, *nāṭaš* can mean "abandon" in a concrete and, as it were, negligent sense. In Jer. 7:29; Sir. 8:8f., *nāṭaš* and *mā'as* are parallel.

The verb can also refer to a more neutral "leaving" (like *ʿāzaḇ*). In 1 S. 17:20,22, David does not abandon his sheep and the provisions he needs for battle: he leaves them behind under guard. His brother Eliab nevertheless chastises him for having deserted the sheep: "With whom have you left those few sheep in the wilderness?" (v. 28).

In the laws governing the Sabbatical Year, *nāṭaš* takes on a positive sense. In Ex. 23:11 *n^eṭaštāh* means "you shall leave it [the land] to itself," i.e., let it lie fallow. In Neh. 10:32(Eng. v. 31) *niṭṭōš* means "we will forego" the crops and now also the exaction of debts. In Ex. 23:11 *nāṭaš* follows *šāmaṭ,* "let loose, let drop," defining it more precisely.

In Prov. 17:14 *n^eṭôš* means "stop"; the semantic connection with *ḥāḏal* is discussed below. In 1:8 and 6:20 *'al-tiṭṭōš* means "do not reject" or "do not despise."

Abandoning something (or not doing so) can therefore imply a moral imperative. Since abandoning generally involves a deliberate, intentional act (as is always true in the case of Yahweh), the one who abandons something bears responsibility for the act. When Israel abandons Yahweh, it is negligent and therefore sinful (Dt. 32:15ff.). When Yahweh abandons Israel, Israel's transgressions justify his action (e.g., 2 K. 21:14f.). To abandon Israel means deliberately letting Israel fall into the hands of its enemies (Jer. 12:7).

---

1. *HAL,* II, 695; *ANW,* 269.
2. G. W. Freytag, *Lexicon Arabico-Latinum,* 4 vols. (Halis Saxon, 1830-37), IV, 295; Lane, 2810.

Something that has been abandoned is left to its fate (Ezk. 29:5; 31:12; 32:4; cf. *nṭš* niphal in Am. 5:2). The verb thus covers a range from thought to energetic action. Kish, Saul's father, no longer worries about "the matter of the donkeys," i.e., he has given up searching for them (1 S. 10:2). Here *nāṭaš* comes close in meaning to *ḥāḏal,* "desist from something" (cf. the par. *pen-yeḥdal 'āḇî min hā'ᵃṯōnôṯ* in 9:5). In most texts, however, *nāṭaš* involves an action. "Abandon" can then mean simply "leave" or "let fall" or "discard." In Nu. 11:31 a wind sent by Yahweh brings quails and lets them fall into the desert camp *(wayyiṭṭōš ʿal-hammaḥᵃneh).* In Hos. 12:15(14) Ephraim's crimes are not simply "left" on his shoulders: they are "brought down" on him (the corresponding term in v. 15c[14c] is *yāšîb*).

In prophetic discourse *nāṭaš* often means "discard"; here "abandon" represents a violent action. The LXX recognizes this fact, translating *nṭš* with *rássō* (Jer. 23:33,39) or *katabállō* (Ezk. 29:5; 31:12).[3] Only in two texts does the qal of *nāṭaš* mean "disperse" (cf. the niphal) in the negative sense of "scatter, confuse." A scene of confusion is described in 1 S. 30:16: the Amalekites are "scattered"[4] while they eat, drink, and dance. In 4:2 *wattiṭṭōš hammilḥāmâ* means "and the battle spread" (or "surged back and forth"). A root *yṭš* meaning "collide," proposed by G. R. Driver on the basis of Arab. *waṭasa,* is not attested.[5] Mitchell Dahood finds here a second root *nṭš* as a by-form of *lāṭaš,* "sharpen": "the battle grew fiercer."[6] This hypothesis, however, is unnecessary.

In Gen. 31:28 *nāṭaš* functions as an auxiliary verb with the meaning "let": "let me kiss my sons and say farewell to my daughters." In Isa. 21:15 the phrase *ḥereḇ nᵉṭûšâ* means "drawn sword."[7]

b. The niphal of *nṭš* occurs 6 times in the OT. In Am. 5:2 *niṭṭᵉšâ* means "forsaken" or "stretched out." Jgs. 15:9 and 2 S. 5:18,22 use *yinnāṭᵉšû* in the sense of "they deployed themselves (for battle)." Isa. 16:8 says that "shoots spread abroad"; 33:23 says that a ship's rigging "hangs loose."

c. The pual appears only in Isa. 32:14 (par. *ʿāzaḇ*), with the meaning "be forsaken."

d. The noun *nᵉṭîšôṯ* (only pl.) occurs 3 times (Isa. 18:5; Jer. 5:10; 48:32); it means "branches" or "tendrils" (of a vine).

II. Concrete Usage. The concrete usage of *nāṭaš* in Judges and Samuel takes advantage of the nuances of the Hebrew word and raises questions that will take on even great weight in theological passages. In 1 S. 17 we are dealing with a situation that is normally associated with leaving and abandoning, and especially with the tension

---

3. In these last two passages G. R. Driver (*Bibl,* 35 [1954], 299, 301) prefers "throw down"; cf. also W. Zimmerli, *Ezekiel 2. Herm* (Eng. trans. 1983), 107, 144; and *HAL,* II, 695, which includes Ezk. 32:4 *(nᵉṭaštîḵā* par. *'ᵃṭîleḵā),* where the LXX translates *ektenō se.*

4. *HAL,* II, 695: "disbanded."

5. G. R. Driver, *JTS,* 34 (1933), 379. Cf. also H. J. Stoebe, *Das erste Buch Samuelis. KAT,* VIII/1 (1973), 129.

6. M. Dahood, *Bibl,* 49 (1968), 361f.

7. Contra Dahood.

between care and risk. When David leaves his sheep and provisions behind on the way to battle, he is separating from things that have been entrusted to him. In both cases, he evidences concern: he entrusts the sheep to a keeper (v. 20) and leaves the provisions in the care of the keeper of the baggage (v. 22). In v. 28, nevertheless, Eliab censures his carelessness. If the keeper of the sheep should prove incompetent and let something happen to the sheep, David would be held negligent; he could be accused of having abandoned them. Such abandonment exhibits two aspects: (1) a relationship is influenced negatively in some way, and (2) what has been abandoned is considered essentially lost. The strained relationship here is that of David to his elder brother, who represents the interests of the family. No matter how he assesses the abilities of the person to whom he has entrusted the sheep, however, David has good reasons for his conduct. The Philistines and Goliath have brought Israel into serious danger. For David, concern for the people takes precedence over concern for his family's sheep. In 10:2, again, abandonment is justified by a concern of overriding importance.

In passages describing scenes of actual battle, *nāṭaš* expresses dispersion and confusion. The Philistines "spread out for battle [with Israel]" (Jgs. 15:9; 2 S. 5:18,22). Prior to an attack, this can mean dispersion and confusion; but it may also mean a more orderly deployment of forces. Jgs. 15:9 has been interpreted variously. The Philistines advance but do not yet attack; perhaps the meaning is: "they deployed near Lehi."[8] In 1 S. 30:16 the Amalekites are "spread out all over the ground" after their raid on Philistia and Israel. Thus *nāṭaš* can describe preparations for battle as well as reckless disorderly conduct after battle, leaving the company vulnerable to attack. This is just what happens to the Amalekites, as the text that follows shows.

III. Theological Usage.

1. *Yahweh and Israel: The Covenant Relationship.* Although *nāṭaš* never occurs in conjunction with *b^{e}rîṯ,* the occurrences that are most important theologically presuppose the covenant relationship or bear directly on the root of that relationship. This usage alternates between mercy and judgment, affirmation and rejection of the covenant, Israel's abandonment of Yahweh and Israel's abandonment by Yahweh.

In the desert Yahweh provides his people with a great supply of quails from the sea. He "throws" them down on the camp in response to the people's plea for meat (Nu. 11:31). Although Yahweh acts fundamentally out of merciful compassion, he also treats Israel a bit negligently, because he is angry at their entreaty: the amount of quail is enough to make them sick (v. 33; cf. vv. 18-20). Later, Yahweh blankets the northern kingdom with his judgment: "Ephraim has given bitter offense, so his LORD will hurl his crimes down on him *(w^{e}ḏāmāyw ʿālāyw yiṭṭôš)*" (Hos. 12:15[14]). Human provocation is the reason for divine abandonment; cf. the association of *kāʿas* with *nāṭaš* in Dt. 32:15f.,19,21; 2 K. 21:14f.; Ps. 78:58ff.).

The regulations governing the Sabbatical Year require Israel to forego the harvest and remit all debts. The Covenant Code prescribes that the land be left to itself every

8. On 1 S. 4:2 see above.

seventh year (Ex. 23:11). No seed may be sown, vineyards and orchards may not be cultivated, fruit may be neither harvested nor sold. What grows of its own accord, however, may be eaten (cf. Lev. 25:1-7). This law was reaffirmed in the postexilic period by Nehemiah. At the same time, the people accepted the obligation to forego collection of all debts (Neh. 10:32[31]; cf. Dt. 15:1-6).

In the covenant context, abandonment is a very serious matter. In the covenant Yahweh as the God of Israel and Israel as the people of Yahweh have bound themselves to each other. If either breaks the covenant, serious consequences can be expected. Israel's early life under the Mosaic covenant is summarized in Dt. 32, the Song of Moses — a key passage, which influences all the subsequent preaching of the prophets and also provides a theological perspective for the Deuteronomistic history.[9] The poem dates at the latest from the beginning of the prophetic movement, i.e., the time of Samuel; it may, however, be earlier. Its theme is Yahweh's grace and favor. Israel responds to Yahweh's beneficence with ingratitude, abandoning Yahweh. This leads to Israel's punishment. But Yahweh sets Israel free for the sake of his holy name, after which he punishes the enemy. V. 15 uses *nāṭaš* to say that Jeshurun (= Israel) abandoned God who made him. This is the provocation *(kāʿas)* referred to in vv. 16,19,21.

Lundbom

George Mendenhall previously proposed the hypothesis that dates the Song of Moses in the time of Samuel.[10] It has found little support. Dt. 32 is usually dated in the exilic or postexilic period and interpreted not as anticipating prophetic preaching but as depending on it. "It closely resembles Deuteronomistic language and thought, and the wide range of influences — linguistic, stylistic, and theological (including wisdom) — make an earlier dating impossible."[11]

Fabry

Deuteronomic theology is expressed in the book of Judges by the concepts of sin, abandonment to the hand of the enemy, cry for help, and deliverance. Gideon fails to see this connection and asks the divine messenger: "Did not Yahweh bring us up from Egypt? But now Yahweh has cast us off *(neṭāšānû)* and given us into the hand of Midian" (Jgs. 6:13). According to Ps. 78:60, Yahweh abandoned his first sanctuary at Shiloh; the Deuteronomistic history found this memory too painful and did not mention the fact (but cf. Jer. 7:12-14). The psalmist explains the abandonment of Shiloh on the grounds that Israel had provoked (*kāʿas:* v. 58) Yahweh through idolatry. Deuteronomistic theology is speaking when Samuel addresses the people and accedes to their offensive request for a king (1 S. 12). Nevertheless, for the sake of his great name, Yahweh will not cast away his people (v. 22). Solomon, too, in his prayer at the

---

9. J. Lundbom, "The Lawbook of the Josianic Reform," *CBQ,* 38 (1976), 293-302.

10. "Samuel's 'Broken *Rîb*': Deuteronomy 32," *No Famine in the Land. Festschrift J. L. McKenzie* (Missoula, 1975), 63-74.

11. H. D. Preuss, *Deuteronomium. EdF,* 164 (1982), 167.

dedication of the temple, expresses the hope that Yahweh will not leave *(ʿāzaḇ)* or abandon *(nāṭaš)* Israel (1 K. 8:57). Ps. 27:9 contains a heartfelt prayer — in this case by an individual — not to be abandoned: *ʾal-tiṭṭᵉšēnî wᵉʾal-taʿazḇēnî ʾᵉlōhê yišʿî,* "Do not cast me off, do not forsake me, O God of my salvation!"

The message that Yahweh must abandon Israel appears primarily in the prophets. More than any others, they feel that the relationship has been broken and that Israel will fall into the hand of the enemy. Amos laments that Israel lies like a fallen maiden, "forsaken on her land, with no one to raise her up" (5:2). The *ésphalen* of the LXX reinforces the image of someone thrown violently to the ground. Here abandonment means that no one will pay any attention to Israel: the "corpse" lies helpless and alone, abandoned by God.[12] In an early oracle Isaiah proclaims the condemnation of Jerusalem, since Yahweh has forsaken his people on account of their idolatry (Isa. 2:6).[13] The populous city of Jerusalem will likewise be deserted *(ʿuzzāḇ)* and the palace forsaken *(nuṭṭāš),* until a new age when Yahweh's Spirit will be poured out (Isa. 32:14f.).

The vision of Jerusalem's abandonment becomes reality in the time of Jeremiah. Jeremiah's message exhibits affinities with Dt. 32:[14] Israel has once again rejected Yahweh (Jer. 15:6). Therefore Yahweh will deliver the whole nation into the hands of the Babylonians (7:29; 12:7). The people foolishly ask: "What is the burden of the LORD?" Jeremiah must reply: "You are the burden [LXX], and I will cast you off" (23:33). An entire people and an entire city will be cast away violently from Yahweh's presence (v. 39). In both passages the LXX translates *nāṭaš* with *rássō,* "lay low." In 5:10 the people are compared to alien vine branches *(nᵉṭîšôṯ)* that no longer belong to Yahweh (cf. 2:21); therefore they must be destroyed.

Alongside the prophetic prediction of certain abandonment, the OT contains the certain assurance that Yahweh will not forsake his people (cf. Ps. 94:14; 1 S. 12:22). If Israel breaks the Mosaic covenant, Yahweh must, according to its terms, likewise withdraw from the covenant. But there is an important difference. Israel's abandonment of God is the result of negligence, whereas Yahweh abandons Israel only with good reason. Nevertheless, the continuity of the relationship is maintained in two ways: (1) the unconditional covenant with Abraham undergirds the covenant relationship; and (2) the broken Mosaic covenant is replaced by a new covenant, easier to fulfill and more comprehensive in effect (Jer. 31:31-34).

2. *Yahweh and the Nations: Creation and Chaos.* Yahweh also sees to the abandonment and destruction of Israel's enemies. Isaiah bewails the destruction of the famed vineyards of Moab, which were like a giant vine with roots in Heshbon and Sibmah

---

12. H. W. Wolff, *Joel and Amos. Herm* (Eng. trans. 1977), 236.

13. For a different interpretation, see H. Cazelles, *VT,* 30 (1980), 412; B. Wiklander, *Prophecy as Literature. CB,* 22 (1984), 71f.; also H. Wildberger, *Isaiah 1–12* (Eng. trans., Minneapolis, 1991), 105f.

14. W. L. Holladay, "Jeremiah and Moses," *JBL,* 85 (1966), 18-21.

and whose clusters extended to Jazer in the north and to the desert in the east, whose "shoots spread abroad" *(šᵉluḥôṯeyhā niṭṭᵉšû)* to the Dead Sea in the southwest (Isa. 16:8). Jer. 48:32 is possibly a different version of the same oracle.

The spreading branches in Isa. 18:5 are the advancing shoots of Assyria, which Yahweh will cut off before they totally destroy Ethiopia. The text here is obscure. If it is intended to mean that Yahweh waits to intervene until the moment when one nation is on the point of destroying another (vv. 3f.), then it is a parallel to Dt. 32:26ff.: there Yahweh exercises restraint lest Israel be destroyed totally by the enemies sent to punish it. In both texts Yahweh ultimately intervenes to destroy the foe.

In Isa. 33:23 the unseaworthy ship with its rigging hanging loose *(niṭṭᵉšû)* could be a foreign power to which Yahweh wishes to deny access to the new Jerusalem (v. 21); but here, too, the text is obscure. The prophet or compiler possibly wanted to express the notion that chaos has no place in the new creation (cf. Rev. 21:27).

In three texts Ezekiel proclaims Yahweh's abandonment of Egypt — as well as his abandonment of Egypt's destroyers. In 29:5 Yahweh plans to throw (LXX: *katabalō*) Egypt and all the fish of the Nile into the desert. He had earlier done the same thing with quails, but now the emphasis lies on removal of his care for a haughty nation. Egypt and its fish will be fodder for the wild beasts and the birds (cf. also Ezk. 32:4). Egypt was once like a cedar of Lebanon, but now its enemies will cut it down and leave it: the nation that offered Egypt protection he will likewise abandon (Ezk. 31:12 [twice]). This abandonment is an act of violence. In v. 12a the LXX reads: *kaí katébalon autón epí tṓn oréōn,* "and cast them down on the mountains."[15]

3. *Wisdom Literature.* Prov. 1:8; 6:20 caution against rejecting parental instruction (cf. Sir. 8:8: *'l ṭṭš šyḥṭ ḥkmym,* "do not reject the speech of the wise"). The reason is that one can learn so much from parents or teachers that success will follow. In Prov. 17:14 the sage warns: "The beginning of strife is like letting out water; so stop *(nᵉṭôš)* before the quarrel breaks out."

15. Zimmerli, *Ezekiel 2,* 144.

Lundbom

נִיחֹחַ *nîḥôaḥ*

Contents: I. Formulaic Usage. II. Differing Interpretations. III. Deluge; Cult. IV. Late Usage.

nîḥôaḥ. P. A. H. de Boer, "God's Fragrance," *Studies in the Religion of Ancient Israel. SVT,* 23 (1972), 37-47; K. Elliger, *Leviticus. HAT,* IV (1966), 35f.; J. Hoftijzer, "Das sogenannte Feueropfer," *Hebräische Wortforschung. Festschrift W. Baumgartner. SVT,* 16 (1967), 114-134; L. Köhler, *OT Theology* (Eng. trans., Philadelphia, 1957), 186f.

I. Formulaic Usage. In the Hebrew OT *nîḥôaḥ* (a fossilized polel[1]) appears 43 times, always as a *nomen rectum* dependent on *rêaḥ,* and always referring to an offering. Except for Gen. 8:21 (usually ascribed to J) and four occurrences in Ezekiel (6:13; 16:19; 20:28,41), the texts belong to P or H. The word appears twice in Biblical Aramaic (Ezr. 6:10; Dnl. 2:46), both times in the plural and without reference to *rêaḥ.*

Besides being linked with *rêaḥ,* the 38 occurrences in P and H are incorporated into formulas: (1) *'iššeh* stands in apposition, either preceding (21 times) or following (6 times); (2) association with the divine realms is indicated by *leYHWH* (33 times) or *lip̄nê YHWH* (once); (3) the clause in question usually begins with the hiphil of *qṭr,* with a priestly subject, and the altar is the locus of the action. As an introductory verb we also find the more general *'āśâ* (12 times) or the hiphil of *qrb* (4 times). The texts clearly reflect an ancient sacrificial formula, probably: *wehiqṭîr hakkōhēn 'eṯ . . . ham-mizbēḥâ 'iššeh rêaḥ nîḥôaḥ leYHWH.* Since the noun clause frequently appears in the present text as a formula concluding sacrificial instructions (Lev. 1:9,13; Nu. 15:7,10; etc.), it probably played this role in the preexilic cultic rituals on which P is based.[2]

Two occurrences in which a suffix is added are exceptions to this fixed usage. In them we may observe the ambivalence of the formula, for the offering can be qualified as "your *nîḥôaḥ*" (Lev. 26:31; cf. Ezk. 20:28) as well as "my [God's] *nîḥôaḥ*" (Nu. 28:2).

The usage in Ezekiel is more varied, but still points to the realm of standardized cultic language, with the recipients of the offering (in this case idols) being introduced by *le* or *lip̄nê* (6:13; 16:19). The verbs *nāṯan* (6:13; 16:19) and *śîm* (20:28) are used to denote the action.

II. Differing Interpretations. The translation of *rêaḥ nîḥôaḥ* is disputed. Targ. Onqelos paraphrases: "be accepted with favor" (*[hiṯ]qabbēl bera'awā':* Gen. 8:21; Lev. 1:9; etc.). The LXX uses *osmḗ euōdiás,* "scent of perfume," like the Vulg. *odor suavitatis.* NRSV translates "pleasing odor." *GesB* gives the meaning as "pleasure, favor."[3]

By contrast, Ludwig Köhler views these translations as "foolish twists" and insists on "soothing" as the only possible meaning. With Ezekiel, the fundamental understanding of sacrifice is that it "appeases God's wrath"; this purpose is reflected in its description as an appeasing aroma.[4] As evidence, Köhler cites Ezk. 5:13: *wahaniḥôṯî ḥamāṯî bām,* "I soothe my fury toward them." But this text uses the verb *nûaḥ,* the many connotations of which cannot simply be extended to the noun; it is related etymologically but appears in totally different syntagmemes.

P. A. H. de Boer suggests a totally different approach. Noting that in ancient Near Eastern religions a pleasant aroma accompanies theophanies,[5] he sees in *rêaḥ nîḥôaḥ*

1. *BLe,* 475t.
2. Contra K. Koch, *Die Priesterschrift. FRLANT,* 71 (1959), 48.
3. P. 503.
4. *OT Theology,* 186f.; cf. *KBL*², 614; *HAL,* II, 696; F. Stolz, *TLOT,* II, 724; H. Ringgren, *Israelite Religion* (Eng. trans., Philadelphia, 1966), 169; and many others.
5. E.g., "God's vapor," *ANET,* 230a.

a salvific divine effect on human worshipers. In the earliest text, Gen. 8:21, Noah's offering has nothing to do with propitiation or gratitude. The causative verb should be translated: "and Yahweh spread a smell of peace, reassurance, security."[6] In the P formula that describes an offering as *rêaḥ nîḥôaḥ l^eYHWH,* the prep. *l^e* does not mean "for," but substitutes for the genitive. After God has accepted the sacrifice as his own act, the pleasant aroma that emanates from it is a sign of God's salvific presence.

III. Deluge; Cult. The Akkadian accounts of the deluge describe the reaction of the gods to the first sacrifice after the flood with the well-known words: "The gods smelled the aroma. The gods smelled the sweet aroma. The gods assembled like flies over the one offering sacrifice."[7] Here the pleasant aroma emanates from savory food. It has nothing to do with appeasement, since the hero of the Akkadian deluge story has not committed any sin; it reflects the conviction that feeding the gods is one of the primary purposes of human existence.[8] The Akkadian parallel demonstrates that Gen. 8:21, the only Hebrew occurrence of *nîḥôaḥ* outside Ezekiel and P, in fact represents an ancient tradition; at least in this passage, the OT is not thinking of appeasing divine wrath, which would be inappropriate with respect to Noah, who is offering the sacrifice.[9] Instead, the pleasant aroma of the burnt offering, which Yahweh inhales, makes it easier for him to express a change of heart: "I will never again curse the ground."

It is true that some Akkadian incantations employ the expression *linūḫ libbaka,* "May your heart be soothed (toward me)," which uses the same root *nḫ/ḥ* as the Hebrew lexeme and is sometimes associated with a confession of sin.[10] But we should not be too hasty in applying this association to OT usage. In P the *nîḥôaḥ* odor is expected primarily from a burnt offering (12 times), then also from a grain offering (6 times), a *zeḇaḥ* (Lev. 3:5,16; Ezk. 20:28), a consecration offering (Ex. 29:25; Lev. 8:28), or a festival offering in general (Nu. 29:6,8,13, etc.; Ezk. 20:41). It is noteworthy, however, that the expression does not occur in the context of rites whose primary purpose is removal of sin and guilt, namely, the *ḥaṭṭā'ṯ* and *'āšām* rituals. The only exception is Lev. 4:31, where such an odor is expected from the fat offered in the sin offering of a private individual (not of the community or the high priest). The odor here is probably meant "in a secondary and figurative sense."[11] For P and Ezekiel, then, *rêaḥ nîḥôaḥ* denotes the "comforting aroma" that arises during a festal sacrifice, which creates the proper climate for God's beneficent intercourse with the cultic

---

6. De Boer, 47.

7. Atraḫasis III, V, 34f. (W. G. Lambert and A. R. Millard, *Atra-ḫasīs: The Babylonian Story of the Flood* [Oxford, 1969], 98f.); Gilg. XI, 159-161 (*AOT,* 179; *ANET,* 95; *NERT,* 97).

8. A. L. Oppenheim, *Ancient Mesopotamia* (Chicago, 1964), 183ff.

9. Contra A. Heidel, *The Gilgamesh Epic and OT Parallels* (Chicago, ²1949, repr. 1970), 255f.

10. W. Mayer, *Untersuchungen zur Formensprache der babylonischen "Gebetsbeschwörungen." StPohl,* ser. maior, 5 (1976), 240f.; cf. *AHw,* II, 716.

11. J. Herrmann, *TDNT,* III, 305, with n. 22; B. Janowski, *Sühne als Heilsgeschehen. WMANT,* 55 (1982), 217, n. 176.

community. Therefore Ezk. 20:41 expects "pleasure" *(rāṣâ)* from it (cf. 1QS 3:11; 9:5; 1QM 2:5; 11QPs[a] 154).

IV. Late Usage. Only in the late period of Israel's history did the increasing emphasis of the temple cult on atonement[12] lead to the coupling of atonement *(kpr)* with an aroma pleasing to God. This association occurs first in Sir. 45:16, then in 1QS 3:11 *(kippûrê nîḥôaḥ);* 9:5; 1QM 2:5. It goes hand in hand with a spiritualization of the notion of sacrifice.[13] Whoever praises the Most High will be viewed by God with as much favor as one who sacrifices animals, as a *q[e]ṭōreṯ nîḥôaḥ* (11QPs[a] 154;[14] cf. 1QS 3:11; 8:9; 9:5). This development is continued in the NT (Eph. 5:2; Phil. 4:18).[15]

In Biblical Aramaic, *nîḥôaḥ* lost its connection with "odor" and became a general term for sacrificial offerings; therefore Ezr. 6:10 and Dnl. 2:46 use the plural.

Koch

12. K. Koch, "Sühne und Vergebung," *EvT,* 26 (1966), 217-239.
13. G. Klinzing, *Die Umdeutung des Kultes in der Qumrangemeinde und im NT. SUNT,* 7 (1971), 62, 64ff., 93-106.
14. J. A. Sanders, *The Psalms Scroll of Qumrân Cave 11. DJD,* IV (1965), 64f.
15. Cf. A. Stumpff, "εὐωδία," *TDNT,* II, 808-810.

נכה *nkh;* מַכָּה *makkâ;* נָכֶה *nāḵeh;* נכא *nk'*

Contents: I. 1. Occurrences; 2. LXX. II. Human Acts: 1. Violence; 2. Killing; 3. Military Defeat; 4. Symbolic Acts. III. Acts of Yahweh. IV. Other Subjects. V. *makkâ.* VI. *nāḵeh;* Derivatives of *nk'*.

I. 1. *Occurrences.* The root *nkh* is represented in the OT primarily by the hiphil of the verb (480 occurrences, plus 16 hophals) and the noun *makkâ* (47 occurrences; text corrupt in 2 Ch. 2:9[1]). Since both are used most often as terms for homicide or defeat in battle, respectively, they are found primarily in corresponding narrative texts in the Pentateuch, the Deuteronomistic history, and the Chronicler's history; they are also

nkh. P. C. Craigie, *The Problem of War in the OT* (Grand Rapids, 1978); D. Daube, *Studies in Biblical Law* (New York, 1947, ²1969); H. Schüngel-Straumann, "Tod und Leben in der Gesetzesliteratur des Pentateuch" (diss., Bonn, 1968); K. Seybold, *Das Gebet des Kranken im AT. BZAW,* 99 (1979), 26; F. Stolz, *Jahwes und Israels Kriege. ATANT,* 60 (1972); H. W. Wolff, *Anthropology of the OT* (Eng. trans., Philadelphia, 1974).

1. W. Rudolph, *Chronikbücher. HAT,* XXI (1955), ad loc.

comparatively frequent in prophetic oracles of disaster. In the case of the hiphil as a term for injuring or killing an individual, some 25 of the occurrences are concentrated in the applicable laws in the Pentateuch. The other stems and derivatives of *nkh* appear only rarely or as hapax legomena: the niphal occurs once, the pual twice, **nāḵeh* 3 times (plus Ps. 109:16; the text of Ps. 35:15 [*nēḵîm*] is probably corrupt),[2] *nāḵôn* (possibly from *kûn*[3]) only in Job 12:5. There is also the rare by-form *nk'* and its derivatives: one occurrence of the niphal, one of **nāḵā'*, three of *nāḵē'*. There are no occurrences in Biblical Aramaic.

Outside the OT the roots *nkh* and *nk'* or their derivatives are represented in Old and Middle Hebrew, most of the Aramaic languages (but not Imperial Aramaic), and South Semitic, albeit sometimes very sparsely.[4] Only highly dubious occurrences are known in Akkadian and Egyptian.[5] The basic meaning of the root is "smite, strike," usually with the negative aspect of harming or injuring. The OT evidence reflects this meaning, but with a special twist, because *nkh* most often means to strike fatally.

Except in the Temple Scroll (6 occurrences), *nkh* and *makkâ* appear only rarely in the Dead Sea Scrolls (only in Hebrew texts); *nāḵeh* probably occurs in 1QSa 2:5 (like Ps. 109:16[6]); it is unclear whether *nk'ym* and *nk'y* in 1QS 10:21; 1QM 11:10 (1QH 18:15) derive from *nkh* or from *k'h*. The range of meanings is basically the same as in the OT, but the context is sometimes extremely fragmentary.

2. *LXX*. The LXX uses some forty different verbs to translate *nkh*. The most frequent is *patássein* (344 occurrences); relatively common (20 to 30 occurrences each) are other verbs meaning "strike" (*týptein, paíein, plḗssein* [used exclusively for the niphal and pual, 9 times for the hophal], and *kóptein* and its compounds); infrequent (less than 10 occurrences) are *mastigoún* and verbs that mean "kill," "destroy," or "fight," as well as those that render or alter the meaning of the Hebrew text (*epibouleín* in Prov. 17:26). The noun *makkâ* is represented by *plēgḗ* (plus *sýntripsis* [Josh. 10:10], *kopḗ* [Josh. 10:20], *mástix* [Jer. 6:7], and *plḗssein* [Isa. 27:7]). The adjs. *nāḵeh, nāḵē'*, and *nāḵā'* are represented by a variety of equivalents. In Job 30:8 (*nk'* niphal), the LXX translation differs markedly from the MT.

II. Humans Acts.

1. *Violence*. In its basic meaning, the hiphil of *nkh* (and the corresponding hophal) denotes the act of striking a manual blow by a human agent, with or without an instrument.

---

2. On both these Psalm texts see *BHS; HAL*, II, 698.

3. *HAL*, II, 698.

4. On Hebrew see *DISO*, 178; *WTM*, III, 392f.; on the Dead Sea Scrolls see below. On Aramaic see *DISO*, 178 (*KAI*, II, 269); *WTM*, III, 392f.; *LexSyr*², 428; *MdD*, 296. On South Semitic see *HAL*, II, 697; cf. A. Jamme, *Cahiers de Byrsa*, 8 (1958), 165f.

5. For Akkadian see *AHw*, II, 724, contra *CAD*, XI/1, 197. For Egyptian, A. Goetze, *BASOR*, 151, 31, no. 7.

6. See above.

The object of the verb, too, is generally human.[7] The primary point is the use of physical force against others, resulting in infringement on their personal existence. On the one hand, therefore, the verb can mean the unjustified endangerment or injury or humiliation of others, like fighting during a quarrel (Ex. 2:13; Dt. 25:11; Isa. 58:4; Prov. 23:35) that results in bodily harm (Ex. 21:18f.; Zec. 13:6 [hophal]) or an insulting slap on the cheek (1 K. 22:24; Mic. 4:14[Eng. 5:1]; Job 16:10; cf. Lam. 3:30).[8] On the other hand, a beating can be a legitimate means of punishing a transgression (Dt. 25:2f.; Neh. 13:25; cf. Cant. 5:7). More often, however, it is a means of humiliating subject or disagreeable individuals or breaking their resistance (Ex. 2:11; 5:14,16 [hophal]; Isa. 50:6; Jer. 20:2; 37:15; 2 Ch. 25:16; with an animal as obj.: Nu. 22:23ff.; abuse resulting in bodily harm: Ex. 21:26; representing a perversion of personal relationships: Ex. 21:15; Prov. 17:26[9]). In early proverbial wisdom, it has a purely positive meaning: it is an educational tool (Prov. 23:13f.;[10] cf. 17:10; 19:25). In the context of battle, *nkh* can denote the wounding of an enemy (indirectly, by means of a projectile: 2 K. 8:28f.; 9:15; cf. 3:25). Finally, in a struggle with a beast of prey, blows help rescue the victim (1 S. 17:35a).

According to CD 11:6, beating animals on the Sabbath is prohibited. The meaning of *nkh* in 1 K. 20:35,37 is obscure (possibly stigmatization on the forehead [cf. vv. 38,44] or an ecstatic act [cf. 1 K. 18:28; Zec. 13:5,6a]). The figurative use of *nkh* is discussed in I.3, III, and IV below.

2. *Killing.* a. *Murder, Homicide, Expiation.* Most often, *nkh* hiphil (like the corresponding niphal and hophal) denotes a deadly blow, an injury caused by a human agent that leads to the immediate or rapid death of the victim, usually also a human being. Especially when death is immediate, this meaning is frequently made clear by addition of the verb → מות *mûṯ*. As one would expect, killing is, first of all, a crime, an act that entails bloodguilt and must be expiated. As such it is a subject of legislation. There is no distinction in principle between intentional and unintentional homicide, i.e., between murder and manslaughter (Ex. 21:12 [vv. 13f. are a later addition]; Lev. 24:17,21; in Dt. 21:1; 2 S. 14:6f., too, it is not clear whether the text refers to an intentional or unintentional act; according to Lev. 24:18,21, it is also a punishable crime to kill an animal [belonging to someone else]).

The casuistic law of the Covenant Code does single out one specific kind of homicide for special treatment (Ex. 22:1[2] [hophal]; 21:20f. probably also distinguishes between murder and manslaughter[11]). In apodictic legislation, especially heinous instances of deliberate homicide are also singled out (Dt. 27:24f.). Narrative texts describe other instances of deliberate homicide: political murder (2 S. 4:7; 20:10; 2 K. 19:37), attempted political murder (1 S. 18:11; 19:10; 20:33),[12] murder for personal reasons (2 S.

7. Inanimate objects are discussed in I.4 below.
8. → לחי *lᵉḥî*, 3 (VII, 518f.).
9. On *nāḏîḇ*, see → נדב *ndb*, III.
10. → יסר *yāsar*, III.4 (VI, 132f.).
11. M. Noth, *Exodus. OTL* (Eng. trans. 1962), 181; contra Schüngel-Straumann, 61f.
12. Murder in the context of usurpation is discussed in II.2.b below.

12:9 [in an extended sense, cf. 11:14ff.]; cf. Gen. 37:21). Only late legal texts distinguish between murder and manslaughter (Dt. 19:4,11; Nu. 35:11,15-18,21,24,30; Josh. 20:3,5,9).

Second, *nkh* can denote a punishment or act of expiation, viz., blood vengeance or execution in consequence of a murder (2 S. 1:15; 3:27 [here understood also as a political murder]; 2 K. 14:5f.; averted in Gen. 4:15b and Dt. 19:6 [the latter in the context of manslaughter]), punishment for other transgressions (idolatry: Nu. 25:14f.,18 [hophal]; political enmity: 2 K. 25:21; Jer. 29:21 [judicial murder in Jer. 26:23; cf. 18:18]; fig.: Isa. 11:4b [emended[13]]), or even an act of personal vengeance (Ex. 2:12; 2 S. 13:28). Isa. 66:3 probably refers to human sacrifice.[14]

Used in this sense, *nkh* resembles other verbs of killing, especially → הרג *hāragh,* → מות *mûṯ* hiphil, and → רצח *rāṣâ,* which can therefore appear as synonyms in the same context.[15] In the case of *nkh,* however, the focus of the statement is not on the fact of killing as such, but on the act causing the violent death; therefore the ensuing death is often expressed separately by the appended verb *mûṯ.* As the basic meaning of *nkh* would lead one to expect, the emphasis is on the sudden blow, well aimed either by design or by accident, that causes death, inevitably if not immediately, depriving the person struck of all defense.[16] The death of the victim is bought about violently; his or her fate is suddenly sealed. In the case of murder as well as in other instances of killing, this also means that the victim is an adversary or rival, who is removed definitively by the quickest possible means.

b. *Battle.* In military hostilities the primary goal is to get rid of the enemy, intentionally and speedily. Therefore *nkh* refers primarily to killing in battle. The object can be an individual, who is attacked and struck down (2 S. 11:15 [niphal]; cf. v. 21) or is taken by surprise (1 S. 13:3f.) or falls in single combat (2 S. 2:22f.). In the last case the opponent is usually especially dangerous, so that his removal quickly and definitively averts a serious threat (2 S. 21:16-19,21; 23:20f.). The killing of a beast of prey is also mentioned in connection with single combat (1 S. 17:35b,36; 2 S. 23:20). If the mightiest warrior or leader of an enemy army is killed in single combat or in the course of a general assault, this act spells the defeat of the entire army (1 S. 17:9,25-27,49f.; 1 K. 22:34; cf. 2 K. 3:23). If such a person is killed at the end of a battle or after the battle has been lost, then this final "blow" means the annihilation of the entire enemy force (Josh. 10:26; 11:17; cf. 1 S. 31:2).

Much more frequently, however, *nkh* denotes the killing of several opponents in a single action or in a brief period of time. A small group or a multitude may be killed in open combat (Josh. 7:5; Jgs. 20:31; 1 S. 14:14; 18:27; by an individual without military equipment: Jgs. 3:31; 15:15f.; 15:8 probably refers to killing also), the major part of an army in a pitched battle (e.g., 2 S. 8:5; 10:18; cf. Jer. 18:21 [hophal]), or

13. See *BHS.*

14. → חזיר *chᵃzîr* (IV, 291-300).

15. For the laws of the Pentateuch see Schüngel-Straumann.

16. See Daube, 111, 249f., on the expression *hikkâ nep̱eš* in Gen. 37:21; Lev. 24:17f.; Dt. 19:6,11; Jer. 40:14f.

even an entire host (Jgs. 3:29; cf. Jer. 37:10). Central, however, are the numerous texts in which not just the enemy army but the entire enemy population, usually the inhabitants of a city, is totally exterminated (e.g., Nu. 21:35; Josh. 8:22,24; Jgs. 1:8,25; 18:27; 21:10; 2 S. 15:14; cf. 2 K. 15:16; Jer. 21:7; extermination including animals: Jgs. 20:48; 1 S. 22:19; extermination of the males only: Dt. 20:13). The phrase *lᵉpî ḥereḇ* is usually added.[17] Raids and retaliatory actions of a military nature should be included in this context (Gen. 32:9[8]; 34:30; 1 S. 27:9; Job 1:15,17; Est. 9:5); cf. also the proverbial expression in Gen. 32:12bγ(11bγ), which also refers to extermination in battle (Hos. 10:14).

Used in this sense, especially in Deuteronomistic texts, *nkh* is frequently associated with the hiphil of *ḥrm,* denoting execution of the ban (cf. Josh. 10:28,35,37,39f.; 11:11f.; Jgs. 21:10f. [v. 11 being a later amelioration of v. 10]; also Dt. 13:16). We may therefore assume that other, similar texts where only *nkh* appears likewise refer to execution of the ban. Dt. 20:10-18 makes an explicit distinction, albeit artificial and schematic.[18] If we examine all the texts that refer to the killing of several opponents, it is clear once again that this root deals with definitive annihilation at a single stroke, as suggested by the basic meaning of *nkh,* even if it takes place concretely in a number of individual actions (cf. 1 K. 20:20).

Instances of usurpation likewise involve military action, albeit in the sphere of domestic politics. The primary goal is the killing of a particular individual, the reigning king — in other words, a political murder. In such cases the power and authority exercised by a king (cf. 2 S. 14–19) can lead to military conflict, in which the killing of the king (17:1f.) or the usurper (18:11,15) represents a military victory (cf. Saul's persecution of David in 1 S. 26 [v. 8]). Elsewhere we find a unilateral military action carried out by the usurper, to which the king, his family, and his supporters unexpectedly fall victim (as in the case of Jehu: 2 K. 9f. [*nkh* in 9:7,24,27; 10:9,11,17,25]; cf. texts such as 1 K. 15:27,29; 16:9-11). Even when the text mentions only the killing of the king, as in 2 K. 15:10,14f.,25,30, extensive military action may be implied. This is shown by the common use of the catchword → קשר *qāšar* in accounts of usurpation. A counteraction is described in 2 K. 21:24. The killing of Gedaliah in Jer. 40:13–41:18 (*nkh:* 40:14f.; 41:2f.,9,16,18) is comparable to such usurpations.

3. *Military Defeat.* In military contexts the hiphil of *nkh* (like the Eng. verb "beat") can convey the more general sense of inflicting (or, with the hophal, suffering) a devastating defeat: the enemy host is not annihilated totally but decimated and battered, and thus defeated definitively. This meaning is clear when the text speaks of scattering, routing, pursuing, or putting to flight the enemy (Nu. 14:45; 22:6; Josh. 7:5; 10:10; 13:12; 1 S. 11:11; 19:8; 2 K. 3:24a), or when the subsequent killing or exterminating of the enemy is distinguished clearly from a preceding military defeat (e.g., the execution of the ban in 1 S. 15:7f.; cf. also Dt. 7:2; another instance is Jgs. 12:4-6). This

---

17. → חרב *ḥereḇ,* II.1.b (V, 157-162).
18. On the problem of the ban in general, see → חרם *ḥāram* (V, 180-199).

meaning may also be assumed in all the texts that do not speak explicitly of exterminating the enemy host (e.g., 1 S. 23:2,5; 2 S. 8:1-3,9f.; 1 K. 20:21; 2 K. 13:17,19,25; Jer. 46:2; as the act of an individual: 2 S. 23:12). The same is probably true of the familiar quotation cited in 1 S. 18:7: "Saul has killed his thousands, David his ten thousands."[19]

Finally, similar are the texts in which *nkh* refers to the destruction of an enemy city or the ravaging of an entire region. These texts occur primarily in the prophetic books. The subject of *nkh* is a great power (Jer. 43:11; 46:13; 47:1; 49:28; cf. the ptcp. in Isa. 27:7a;[20] also 1QpHab 3:1; in the metaphor of corporal punishment: Isa. 10:20,24; 14:6,29 [also in the secondary addition 30:31b, probably with Assyria as subj.]; hophal: Ezk. 33:21; 40:1; cf. Gen. 14:7).

4. *Symbolic Acts.* The object of *nkh* can also be inanimate. Almost always (1 S. 2:14; 2 K. 11:12 being the only exceptions), such usage describes an effectual symbolic act performed at Yahweh's command or in Yahweh's name. These acts in turn anticipate or bring about extraordinary or portentous events. In 2 K. 11:12, for example, the clapping of hands in rejoicing over the king becomes a sign of Yahweh's triumph over Israel, thus anticipating the disaster that Yahweh is about to inflict on his own people (cf. Ezk. 6:11; 21:19[21]). Other anticipatory symbolic acts are described in Ezk. 5:2; Am. 9:1aα (describing a marvelous event accompanying a vision; emendation is unnecessary[22]). Striking the ground, a rock, or the water of the Nile symbolically anticipates victory (2 K. 13:18f.) or performs wonders for the immediate benefit of Israel (Ex. 7:20; 8:12f.; 17:5f.; Nu. 20:11).[23] According to 2 K. 2:8,14, such an act demonstrates the transfer of divine authority from one prophet to another. Since Yahweh is the real agent in all these actions, he can also appear as the subject in the same context or with reference to the same event (Ezk. 21:22[17]; cf. 22:13; cf. Ps. 78:20 with Ex. 17:5f.; Nu. 20:11).

III. Acts of Yahweh. Just as Yahweh is the real agent in symbolic acts, accounts of military actions often state explicitly that it is Yahweh who accomplishes the destruction of the enemy army or population, or the devastation of their territory, so that he is the indirect subject of the event (e.g., Jgs. 3:28 before v. 29; 1 S. 17:45-47 before vv. 49f.; Jer. 43:10 before v. 11).[24] But *nkh,* used figuratively, can also have Yahweh as its grammatical subject, so that in accounts of military action only his activity is expressed (Nu. 32:4; 2 S. 5:24 [cf. vv. 20,25]; Ezk. 32:15; Ps. 78:66; 135:10; 136:17). These texts presuppose that human agents are involved, but other passages make clear that Yahweh can intervene supernaturally to injure or destroy foreign powers and nations without

---

19. On its original meaning, see the comms.
20. See III below.
21. W. Zimmerli, *Ezekiel 1. Herm* (Eng. trans. 1979), 191, 434.
22. K. Koch, et al., *Amos. AOAT,* 30/2 (1976), 57.
23. On 2 K. 13:18f. → חץ *ḥēṣ* (V, 123f.); on Moses' staff → נטה *nāṭâ.*
24. See II.2.b, 3 above.

resort to military means: he kills the firstborn of Egypt (Ex. 12:12f.,29; Ps. 78:51; 105:36; etc.) and "strikes" people with severe or mortal illness (Ex. 9:15; 1 S. 4:8; 5:6,9 [hophal in v. 12]; Ezk. 39:3, too, probably refers to a plague that destroys the army[25]), strikes a hostile army with blindness (2 K. 6:18; Zec. 12:4), and smites people with destruction through natural catastrophes (universal destruction: Gen. 8:21; indirectly affecting the human population: Ex. 7:25 [corresponding to v. 17[26]]; Ps. 105:33; cf. Isa. 11:15; a natural catastrophe is probably also suggested by Zec. 9:4, reflected in vv. 10f. [emended[27]]). In Ex. 3:20 the verb with Yahweh as subject summarizes the events of the exodus.[28]

In the prophetic books the primary object "struck" by Yahweh is Israel, for the most part in oracles predicting future disaster. Israel is likewise the object in the curses of Lev. 26 and Dt. 28. Ezk. 7:9 uses the verb in a general sense; elsewhere various tribulations are mentioned: military attack with its consequences (Mic. 6:13[14f.]; cf. Mal. 3:24), pestilence in various forms (Lev. 26:24[25f.]; Jer. 21:[4f.]6), a wide range of afflictions (Dt. 28:22,27f.,35), and pestilence alone (Nu. 14:12).[29] Am. 3:15; 6:11 probably refer to a natural catastrophe (earthquake) in which the houses of the upper class are destroyed together with their owners. Postexilic prophetic texts speak retrospectively of a passing catastrophe: Isa. 57:17; 60:10; cf. Jer. 33:5; a later disaster in Isa. 27:7, which also mentions the destruction of the great power that has "struck" *(makkēhû);* in Jer. 30:14 the catastrophe of the northern kingdom appears to be interpreted in the same way (cf. vv. 16f.).

Other texts refer to partial catastrophes of the past and present, intended to make Israel reflect and return to Yahweh: Isa. 9:12; a severe disaster in Isa. 5:25 (war? earthquake?); figuratively in the form of corporal punishment in Jer. 2:30; 5:3; cf. Isa. 1:5 (hophal, possibly referring to the military disaster of 701 or 587[30]); crop failure in Am. 4:9; Hag. 2:17; the figure of severe corporal punishment also in Jer. 14:19 (drought: cf. v. 22) and Hos. 6:1 (Syro-Ephraimite war). According to 1 S. 6:19 and 2 S. 6:7, the desecration of the ark results in a deadly intervention on the part of Yahweh.[31]

Only rarely are individuals "struck" by God: with sickness in Isa. 53:4 (hophal); Ps. 69:27(26); with death in 2 S. 6:7; Zec. 13:7 (emended).[32] By contrast, Ps. 3:8(7) has Yahweh striking the enemies of an individual (metaphorically: either a degrading slap on the cheek or a broken jawbone in combat). The subject of *nkh* can also be a divine being acting on Yahweh's authority: → מלאך *mal'āḵ* in 2 S. 24:17; 2 K. 19:35

---

25. On the image of disarming an opponent in single combat see W. Zimmerli, *Ezekiel 2. Herm* (Eng. trans. 1983), 308.

26. Noth, *Exodus,* 73f.

27. See *BHS.*

28. → פלא *pl'.*

29. On the range of afflictions see Schüngel-Straumann, 71-74; on pestilence, → דבר *debher* (III, 125-27).

30. O. Kaiser, *Isaiah 1–2. OTL* (Eng. trans. ²1983), 19.

31. → ארון *'ᵃrôn* (I, 363-374). On 1 S. 6:19 see H. J. Stoebe, *Das erste Buch Samuelis. KAT,* VIII/1 (1973), in loc.

32. On 2 S. 6:7 see above; on Zec. 13:7 see *BHS.*

(pestilence); "men" in Gen. 19:11 (blindness); Ezk. 9:5,7f. (killing); → שׂטן *śāṭān* Satan in Job 2:7 (sickness of an individual). In every instance where Yahweh is the direct or indirect subject of *nkh,* the text suggests immediate definitive annihilation or severe injury; this usage manifests clearly God's superior power and might.[33]

IV. Other Subjects. Only rarely are other entities the subject of *nkh;* in all these cases the verb is used figuratively. First come animals and forces of nature, which, at Yahweh's behest, kill humans (1 K. 20:36; Jer. 5:6; Ex. 9:25; also 4QpNah 5, where a lion represents a power hostile to God), place them in mortal danger (Jon. 4:8 [heat-stroke]; cf. Isa. 49:10 and Ps. 121:6,[34] where Yahweh averts the danger), or cause destruction that injures them (Jon. 4:7; Ex. 9:31f. [pual]; also 9:25). In addition, comparison to events in the realm of plants and animals can illustrate events in the human realm: the tribulation of an individual, likened to the destructive effect of heat on grass (Ps. 102:5[4] [hophal]); the apostasy of Israel (Hos. 9:16a [hophal]); Yahweh's future deliverance (Hos. 14:6[5];[35] cf. the similar idea in 1QH 8:23); and the military defeat of an enemy power brought about by Yahweh (Dnl. 8:7; with an inanimate object as subj.: Jgs. 7:13). Finally, the subject of *nkh* can be the conscience (*lēḇ;* NRSV: heart), which figuratively hurts or punishes a guilty person (1 S. 24:6[5]; 2 S. 24:10); this usage can hardly be ascribed to observation of the heartbeat as a physiological phenomenon.[36]

V. *makkâ.* The noun *makkâ* has fundamentally the same range of meanings as the verb *nkh.* In about half its occurrences, the verb also appears in the immediate context. In its basic meaning it denotes a manual blow struck by a human being. The primary emphasis is on the action itself, quite clearly in the case of corporal punishment (Dt. 25:3) and blows that serve an educational end (Prov. 20:30).[37] When *makkâ* is used as a cognate accusative to denote the slaying of many adversaries in a military engagement or the inflicting of an annihilating defeat, the emphasis is likewise on the action that brings about the killing or the defeat (*makkâ gᵉḏôlâ* [*mᵉ'ōḏ*]: Josh. 10:10,20; Jgs. 11:33; 15:8, etc.; *makkaṯ ḥereḇ:* Est. 9:5; cf. Isa. 14:6). But the emphasis can also be on the result (killing: 1 S. 14:14; defeat: 1 S. 4:10; 14:30). Therefore when a blow inflicts injury, *makkâ* can take on the meaning "wound" (as the result of battle: 1 K. 22:35; 2 K. 8:29; 9:15; as the [alleged] result of a brawl: Zec. 13:6 [in fact, self-inflicted in an ecstatic experience[38]]).

In the figurative sense Yahweh himself may also deliver a blow or a number of blows, suddenly causing death, disease, or general destruction.[39] Again, the emphasis

33. For further instances of Yahweh's indirect agency see IV below.
34. On the association of sun and moon see → ירח *yārēaḥ,* II.1 (VI, 357).
35. W. Rudolph, *Hosea. KAT,* XIII/1 (1966), in loc.
36. → לב *lēḇ,* IV.1 (VII, 411f.); Wolff, 51.
37. → בטן *beṭen,* II.5 (II, 96f.).
38. Rudolph, *Sacharja 9–14. KAT,* XIII/4 (1976), in loc.
39. See III above.

may be on either the action as such (esp. when *makkâ* is a cognate acc.: Nu. 11:33; 1 S. 4:8; 6:19; Isa. 27:7; Jer. 30:14 [all but 1 S. 4:8 referring to Israel]; cf. Lev. 26:21 [Israel]; Isa. 10:26 [Midian]) or the result of the action (referring to Israel: Dt. 28:59,61; 29:21[22]; Jer. 19:8; referring to foreign nations: Jer. 49:17; 50:13). In the sense of "wound," *makkâ* can also be used figuratively to denote social injustice (Jer. 6:7), but above all to describe devastating catastrophes befalling Israel as the result of military actions, brought about in turn by Yahweh (*makkâ naḥlâ,*[40] Jer. 10:19; 14:17; 30:12; in Nah. 3:19 a catastrophe for Assyria; cf. Isa. 1:6; Mic. 1:9 [emended[41]]; referring to the suffering of an individual: Jer. 15:18; destruction of the adversaries of an individual: Ps. 64:8[7]). But Yahweh can also heal such "wounds" (Isa. 30:26; Jer. 30:17; cf. 1QM 14:6f.).

VI. *nāḵeh;* Derivatives of *nk'*. For derivatives of *nk'* and the adj. *nāḵeh,* the aspect of punishment and injury is determinative (*nk'* niphal, "be whipped out": Job 30:8; *nāḵeh* used figuratively for being crippled: 2 S. 4:4; 9:3; 1QSa 2:5). An important usage is the metaphor of a "broken spirit"[42] in the sense of being "disheartened" (*nāḵē':* Prov. 15:13; 17:22; 18:14; *nāḵeh* with → לב *lēḇ:* Ps. 109:16; cf. *nāḵā'* in Isa. 16:7) or positively in the sense of being humbled and open to Yahweh (*nāḵeh:* Isa. 66:2; possibly also 1QM 11:10 and [as a qualifier] 1QS 10:21[43]). The form in Ps. 109:16; 1QSa 2:5 was discussed at the beginning of this article.

Conrad

40. → חלה *chālāh,* II.1 (IV, 403).
41. See *BHS.*
42. → רוח *rûaḥ.*
43. But see I.1 above.

נכר *nkr;* נֵכָר *nēḵār;* נָכְרִי *noḵrî*

Contents: I. Meaning, Etymology. II. *noḵrî:* 1. Semantics; 2. Ruth; 3. The "Strange Woman" in Proverbs; 4. Inanimate Objects. III. *ben nēḵār,* "Foreigner." IV. *'elōhê nēḵār,* "Foreign Gods." V. 1. LXX; 2. Dead Sea Scrolls. VI. *nkr* II hiphil.

nkr. G. W. Ahlström, *Joel and the Temple Cult of Jerusalem. SVT,* 21 (1971); A. Aymard, "Les étrangers dans les cités grecques aux temps classiques," *Recueils de la Société Jean Bodin,* 9 (1958), 119-139; G. Bergsträsser, *Intro. to the Semitic Languages* (Eng. trans., Winona Lake, Ind., 1983), 210; A. Bertholet, *Die Stellung der Israeliten und der Juden zu den Fremden*

I. Meaning, Etymology. While some lexicons distinguish two homonymous roots, *nkr* I, "be foreign," and *nkr* II, "recognize," others attempt to make do with a single root *nkr* exhibiting semantic differentiation.[1] The assumption of a single root is based on the theory, borrowed from Arabic grammar, that the same root can be used to represent both its normal meaning and the opposite.[2] The hypothesis of a single root, however, leads to a very irregular lemma *nkr,* whose cohesion must be established by artificial etymologizing. It is therefore better to distinguish *nkr* I and *nkr* II.

From the root *nkr* I derive the words *nēḵār,* "foreign land" (36 occurrences), and *noḵrî,* "foreign(er)" (45 times). *ben nēḵār,* pl. *bᵉnê nēḵār,* "foreigner(s)," occurs 19 times. Occurring once each are **nōḵer* (Ob. 12) and *nēḵer* (Job 31:3), both of which mean "misfortune." As a verb, *nkr* niphal (Prov. 26:24) and hithpael (Gen. 42:7; 1 K. 14:5f.) mean "dissemble, conceal one's identity"; the piel (Jer. 19:4; Sir. 11:12) means "alienate." The piel form in Dt. 32:27 means "deny, dispute," like Akk. *nakāru* G and

(Freiburg im Breisgau, 1896); G. Boström, *Proverbiastudien: Die Weisheit und das fremde Weib in Spr 1–9. LUÅ,* N.S., Avd. 1, 30/3 (1935); A. Caquot, "Brève explication du livre de Malachie, I," *Positions Luthériennes,* 17 (1969), 187-201; *idem,* "La fin du livre des Douze," *Annuaire du Collège de France,* 82 (1981/82), 529-541; M. Dahood, "Causal *Beth* and the Root NKR in Nahum 3, 4," *Bibl,* 52 (1971), 395f.; Z. Falk, "נכרי וגר תושב במשפט העברי," *Mahᵃlakim,* 2 (1969), 9-15; M. Fortes, "Strangers," *Studies in African Social Anthropology. Festschrift I. Schapera,* ed. M. Fortes and S. Patterson (1975), 229-253; R. Gordis, "Some Effects of Primitive Thought on Language," *AJSL,* 55 (1938), 270-284; M. Guttmann, "The Term 'Foreigner' (נכרי) Historically Considered," *HUCA,* 3 (1926), 1-20; V. Haas, "Die Dämonisierung des Fremden und des Feindes im Alten Orient," *Rocznik orientalistyczny,* 41 (1980), 37-44; E. Häusler, "Sklaven und Personen minderen Rechts im AT" (diss., Cologne, 1956); F. Horst, "Das Eigentum nach dem AT," *Gottes Recht. GSAT,* ed. H. W. Wolff, *ThB,* 12 (1961), 203-221; P. Humbert, "Les adjectives *zār* et *nokrî* et la 'Femme étrangère' des Proverbes bibliques," *Mélanges Syriens offerts à M. R. Dussaud,* 2 vols. (Paris, 1939), I, 259-266 = his *Opuscules d'un hébraïsant* (Neuchâtel, 1958), 111-18; F. F. Hvidberg, *Weeping and Laughter in the OT* (Leiden, 1962); A. M. Ibn Ganāḥ, *Sepher Haschoraschim,* ed. W. Bacher (1896), 304f.; O. Keel, "Das Vergraben der 'fremden Götter' in Genesis XXXV 4b," *VT,* 23 (1973), 305-336; F. Kramer, "Fremd und freundlich," *Kursbuch,* 62 (1980), 17-26; B. Lang, *Die weisheitliche Lehrrede. SBS,* 54 (1972), 87-96; R. Martin-Achard, "נֵכָר *nēkār* 'stranger,' " *TLOT,* II, 739-741; R. Meyer, *Gegensinn und Mehrdeutigkeit in der althebräischen Wort- und Begriffsbildung. SSAW,* 120/5 (1979); T. Nöldeke, *NBSS;* L. Sabottka, *Zephanja. BibOr,* 25 (Rome, 1972); R. B. Salters, "Notes on the Interpretation of Qoh 6,2," *ZAW,* 91 (1979), 282-89; C. Schedl, *Rufer des Heils in heilloser Zeit* (Paderborn, 1973); S. Schreiner, "Mischehen — Ehebruch — Ehescheidung," *ZAW,* 91 (1979), 207-228; L. A. Snijders, "The Meaning of *zār* in the OT," *OTS,* 10 (1954), 1-154, esp. 60ff.; J. A. Soggin, "Jezabel, oder die fremde Frau," *Mélanges bibliques et orientaux. Festschrift H. Cazelles. AOAT,* 212 (1981), 453-59; J. J. Stamm, "Fremde, Flüchtlinge und ihr Schutz im alten Israel und seiner Umwelt," *Der Flüchtling in der Weltgeschichte,* ed. A. Mercier (Bern, 1974), 31-66; F. Steiner, "Enslavement and the Early Hebrew Lineage System," *Man,* 54 (1954), 73-75; A. D. Tushingham, "A Reconsideration of Hosea, Chapters 1–3," *JNES,* 12 (1953), 150-59; F. Vattioni, "La 'staniera' nel libro dei Proverbi," *Aug,* 7 (1967), 352-57; M. Zer-Kavod, "הנכרי הגר במקרא," *Sepher D. Ben-Gurion* (Jerusalem, 1964).

1. For the former see *GesB, BDB, LexHebAram.* For the latter see Jastrow, *KBL*²; also *LexLingAeth,* 666-68.

2. For a general discussion see Meyer; on *nkr* as a bipolar root see *NBSS,* 96; Gordis, 278; Humbert, *Opuscules,* 117; Tushingham, 153f.; Snijders, 60f.; Stamm, 33.

Arab. *nakira* IV; the piel form in 1 S. 23:7 means "transport someone to a different place," like Akk. *nakāru* D.[3]

The root *nkr* is widespread in the Semitic languages: Akk. *nak(a)ru,* "foreign, enemy," and *nakāru,* "be different, foreign, hostile"; Ugar. *nkr,* "foreigner"; Aram. *nkry'* pl., "foreigners"; Eth. *nakîr,* "foreigner."[4] Gotthelf Bergsträsser accordingly includes it in the common Semitic word stock.[5]

II. *nokrî.*

1. *Semantics.* The word *nokrî* always refers to a relationship, so that analysis must always take the relation into account.

a. *"Other."* One meaning of *nokrî* is "another," someone distinct from the subject: "another" should praise the subject (Prov. 27:2), "another" enjoys the subject's possessions (Eccl. 6:2).[6] Similarly, *bêṯ nokrî* (Prov. 5:10) is "the house of another" (NEB: "another man's family"); cf. also *ḥēq nokrîyâ* (Prov. 5:20), "the bosom of another, different woman" (not the subject's own wife). This meaning is also attested in Ugaritic, e.g., in the Krt Epic: "Let the newly married man go forth (to battle), let him bring his wife to another, his beloved to someone else *(nkr).*"[7]

b. *"Outside the Family."* In other texts the focus is on the family or clan, so that *nokrî* means "unfamilial," i.e., standing outside the family. Someone outside a family has not only no emotional and social ties with that family but also no legal ties. When a person is excluded from a family, all such ties are lost.[8] In Gen. 31:15 Rachel and Leah regard themselves as having been "sold"[9] by their father Laban; they are therefore "strangers" *(nokrîyôṯ)* to him and owe him nothing. Ps. 69:9 (Eng. v. 8) and Job 19:15 presuppose that in certain cases sick individuals were excluded from their families; the relatives of such persons no longer recognize any responsibility to provide for them. Job is even looked upon as a "stranger" *(nokrî)* by his own (former) female slaves, and none of his relatives takes notice of him. To his family, he is morally dead. The Babylonian poem "I Will Praise the Lord of Wisdom" *(ludlul bēl nēmeqi)* contains a pertinent text: the speaker, a brother, has become a stranger, and his family no longer counts him among its members: "My friend (Akk. *aḫû*) has become my foe . . . my family treat me as an alien."[10] In a legally important context, we also find the phrase *'am nokrî,* "a different, alien family" (Ex. 21:8): a rejected slave concubine may not be sold to an "alien family," but must return to her own clan through redemption. As an ordinary slave, she would no longer have had any connection with her own family;

3. On the G stem see *AHw,* II, 719a, no. 5; on the D stem, 719b, no. 6.
4. On Akkadian see *AHw,* II, 718-720, 723; *CAD,* XI/1, 159-171, 189-195. On Ugaritic, *WUS,* no. 1786. On Aramaic, *DISO,* 179.
5. Pp. 210f.
6. On the exegetical history of this text see Salters, 286-89.
7. *KTU,* 1.14, II, 48, 50; cf. M. Dietrich and O. Loretz, *UF,* 12 (1980), 194.
8. See Steiner.
9. → מכר *mkr* (VIII, 291-96).
10. Tablet 1.84, 92 = *BWL,* 34f.

as her master's concubine, however, this connection is recognized. This same familial meaning is also attested for Akk. *nakaru: awīlum awīl bītiya ul nakar,* "the man is a man of my house, not a stranger."[11]

c. *"Foreigner."* For a third group of texts, the OT itself provides definitions: "a *nok̲rî,* [someone] who is not of your people Israel and comes from a distant land" (1 K. 8:41); and "someone *nok̲rî,* [someone] who is not your brother" (Dt. 17:15) — in other words, a "foreigner." In this sense Ittai the Gittite is a *nok̲rî* (2 S. 15:19), Ruth the Moabite is a *nok̲rîyâ* (Ruth 2:10), Solomon's Moabite, Ammonite, etc., wives are *nāšîm nok̲rîyōt̲* (1 K. 1:11), and the Babylonian soldiers are *nok̲rîm* (Ob. 11). If genuine, Isa. 2:6 appears to be an early witness to this critical attitude toward foreigners: the prophet cites alienation by foreign soothsayers (Philistines), speaking in the same context of *yald̲ê nok̲rîm,* "foreign children."[12] (Even if the exact meaning of Isa. 2:6 remains obscure, the interpretation of *yald̲ê nok̲rîm* as "prophetic children" on the basis of a different root *nkr,* "know," has little to recommend it.)[13]

Nevertheless, isolation from foreigners or xenophobia does not appear in Israel during the monarchy but is first documented in the period of early Judaism, when the people were living under foreign domination and were concerned for their identity. For Deuteronomy (cf. Dt. 14:21), foreigners appear to fall into two groups: *gērîm,*[14] who are receptive to the religion of Yahweh (29:10[11]; 31:12), and *nok̲rîm,* for whom this is clearly not the case. Therefore the *nok̲rîm* ("foreigners") are accorded inferior treatment: creditors may exact claims from them during the Sabbatical Year, and they may be charged interest (15:3; 23:21[20]).

According to Dt. 15:3, foreigners do not share the privilege of the year of release. This restriction agrees with common practice in the ancient Near East. According to the Edict of Ammiṣaduqa,[15] remission of debts is granted only to Akkadians and Amorites, i.e., the autochthonous citizenry. A further paragraph (§8) of the same edict decrees that remission cannot be granted if an Akkadian or Amorite has received a loan for commercial purposes. In this case a native businessperson is on a par with a foreigner. This regulation reflects the distinction between consumer and producer credit. Credit qualifying for remission was intended in case of need to make it possible for a member of one's own people to consume and thus to survive. Credit for the purpose of production met no such immediate need and therefore did not qualify for remission.

While an animal that has died of natural causes may be "given" to a *gēr* to eat (instead of being thrown to the dogs: Ex. 22:30[31]), it is "sold" to a *nok̲rî* (Dt. 14:21). Of all those with whom Jews came in social contact, the *nok̲rî* was treated worst. The *gēr* can be confident of divine and human help (10:18; 14:29); nothing similar is said of the *nok̲rî.* In Israel there is nothing similar to Ζεὺς Ξένιος, the tutelary deity not of

---

11. T. Fish, *Letters of the First Babylonian Dynasty* (1936), no. 1, 22, cited by *CAD,* N/1, 191a.
12. H. Wildberger, *Isaiah 1–12* (Eng. trans., Minneapolis, 1991), 98: "strange mob."
13. Cf. Schedl, 58f.; Dahood, 396.
14. → גור *gûr,* II, 443-48.
15. *ANET,* 527.

the resident aliens but of travelers and unassimilated foreigners (2 Mc. 6:2; cf. Homer *Od.* 6.20f.; 9.270f.). It would be wrong, however, to conclude from these observations that the *nokrî* was totally without protection and rights, for hospitality appears to have been granted foreigners (Gen. 19 being a possible instance).

According to Josephus, Jewish law distinguishes between foreigners who wish to accept the Jewish way of life and those who merely happen to be staying among Jews *(hoi ek parérgou prosióntes)*[16] — an expression that appears to paraphrase *nokrî*. Israel shares this dichotomy between semi-assimilated *(gēr)* and unassimilated foreigners *(nokrî)* with many peoples,[17] especially the Hittites and Greeks. Thus we read in the Hittite "Instructions for Cultic Officials and Temple Personnel" (13th century): "But if a befriended citizen wants to come to one (of you), [he may] enter the temple. For he may cross the threshold of the gods and the king. [He is to be conducted?] up, and he is to eat and drink. But if he is a [foreig]ner, if he is not a citizen of Hattusa, he may [not enter in to the gods(?). Anyone] who (nevertheless) introduces him incurs the death penalty."[18] The privileged resident alien corresponds to the Heb. *gēr*, the discriminated-against foreigner to the *nokrî*. Comparable to this distinction is that between *métoikos* and *xénos* in the Greek cities of the classical period:[19] as a traveling foreigner staying only briefly in the city, the *xénos* corresponds to the Heb. *nokrî;* the *métoikos,* a local resident without full rights (prohibited from entering into a mixed marriage or own property, excluded from holding public office, but allowed to participate in the official cult), is comparable to the *gēr*. Sir. 29:22-28 calls such a person *pároikos* and laments his way of life, filled as it is with unpleasant and demeaning duties toward a native patron. Acts 17:21 distinguishes *epidēmoúntes xénoi,* "foreigners living (in Athens)," probably students and travelers seeking an education, from Athenians.

The characteristic unity of religion and state in Deuteronomy explains why a *nokrî* ("foreigner") must not become king of Israel (Dt. 17:15). Since foreigners belonging to the royal court could attain respectable positions, possibly as personal clients of the king, the law may be intended to make any possible succession by a foreigner illegitimate.[20]

In the postexilic period, marriage with "foreign women" *(nāšîm nokrîyôt)* was condemned (Ezr. 10:2-44; Neh. 13:26f.; cf. Mal. 2:11).

2. *Ruth.* The book of Ruth is based on the basic attitude of Israelites toward foreigners, clearly expressed in 2:10: hostility. The novella plots an instance when this hostility is overcome and a foreign woman, Ruth, becomes the wife of an Israelite. Because Ruth is not a blood relative of Boaz, he is under no obligation to show her amity. He does so nevertheless, and Ruth responds to the favor granted her during the grain harvest with an erotic offer that likewise has a dimension of amity, because Ruth

---

16. *Contra Ap.* 2.28 §210.
17. Fortes.
18. *KUB,* XIII, 4/5; translation from *NERT,* 182.
19. Aymard.
20. Bertholet, 40.

accepts the role of a true family member made possible by Boaz. Each of them, Boaz and Ruth, takes a step to meet the other, overcoming the conventional irreconcilability of foreign *(nokrî)* and friendly (*nkr* hiphil).

Unlike the Moabite Mesha stela[21] and Dt. 23:4(3) but like 1 S. 22:3f., the Ruth novella presupposes friendly relations between Moabites and Israelites (more precisely, people living in Bethlehem) as well as intermarriage: the sons of Naomi had married Moabite women in Moab; after the death of her Israelite husband, one of these women, Ruth, again marries an Israelite. Earlier exegesis saw in the book of Ruth an open attitude toward foreign women, contrasting it in this respect to the books of Ezra and Nehemiah (Ezr. 10; Neh. 13:26f.), whose rigorous opposition to mixed marriages the author of Ruth rejects and opposes. Today this interpretation of Ruth as a political tract is generally rejected. It is noteworthy, however, that earlier novellas speak of marriage with foreign women (the Joseph novella [Gen. 41:45]; Ruth), while a later novella describes marriage within the Jewish community (Tob. 7–8). Perhaps the novellas reflect the circumstance that Jews living in the Diaspora shunned mixed marriages, whereas Palestinian Jews were not totally opposed to such marriages.

3. *The "Strange Woman" in Proverbs.* There has been much controversy over the interpretation of the "strange woman" *(nokrîyâ)* against whom several school wisdom texts warn (Prov. 2:16; 5:20; 6:24; 7:5). Is she the wife of "another" (Israelite) or a foreign woman?[22] Recent studies suggest that the question is misstated. According to Otto Plöger, the warning is kept deliberately ambiguous so as to apply to a neighbor's wife, a foreign woman, and a prostitute.[23] A woman who ostracized herself by committing adultery was perhaps treated like a foreign woman.[24] This interpretation echoes a widespread topos of practical wisdom in Egypt, Mesopotamia, and Greece.[25]

4. *Inanimate Objects.* Several texts use *nokrî* as an adjective describing inanimate objects: *'ereṣ nokrîyâ,* "foreign land" (Ex. 2:22; 18:3: Midian); *'îr nokrî,* "foreign (Jebusite) city" (Jgs. 19:12, but cf. *BHS*). In the MT of Prov. 6:24 the phrase *lāšôn nokrîyâ* suggests "foreign language"; but we should probably follow the Syr., reading *l^ešôn nokrîyâ,* "tongue of a strange woman." In Zeph. 1:8 the meaning of *malbûš nokrî,* "foreign attire," is not clear from the context. Are we to look for the partisans of foreign attire criticized by the prophet among the court or the wealthy upper class, whose attire is a symptom of polytheistic tendencies (cf. Sir. 19:30; 2 Mc. 4:12)? Does such attire transgress the law against clothing of different materials (Lev. 19:19; Dt. 22:11), which law is suspended only for clothing worn in a cultic context (Ex. 28)? Or should we

---

21. *KAI,* 181.
22. For the former see Ibn Ganāḥ and Humbert; for the latter see esp. Boström.
23. O. Plöger, *Sprüche Salomos. BK,* XVII (1984), 56.
24. Soggin, 458f.
25. Instruction of Ani 3, 13-17 (*ANET,* 420); Instruction of Ptahhotep, 277-288 (*ANET,* 413); Counsels of Wisdom, 72-79 (*ANET*³, 595); Hesiod *Works* 328f., 697-705. See also Lang, 88f.

think of priests whose pagan "vestments" (the meaning of *malbûš* in 2 K. 10:22) indicate that they are not orthodox?[26]

Two passages use *nok̲rî* figuratively: *nok̲rîyâ ʿab̲ōd̲āt̲ô,* "strange is his deed" (Isa. 28:21); *haggep̲en nokrîyâ,* "the sick [?; NRSV: wild] vine" (Jer. 2:21). The meaning "sick" is suggested by Akk. *nakāru,* which can also mean "look unhealthy, sick," albeit only of persons.[27]

III. *ben nēk̲ār,* "Foreigner." While Deuteronomic and Deuteronomistic circles use *nok̲rî* to distinguish Israel from strangers, i.e., foreigners,[28] priestly circles and Ezekiel use *bᵉnê nēk̲ār.* This phrase denotes uncircumcised Gentiles, who are not allowed to eat of the Passover (Ex. 12:43) and, in the second temple, may not perform any priestly functions (Ezk. 44:7,9). The passage in Ezekiel casts light on the complex history of the Jerusalem priesthood, which resists schematization; it must long have included foreign (pre-Israelite?) non-Semitic elements. The foreigners are prohibited from selling defective animals to Jews for sacrifice (Lev. 22:25). According to Gen. 17:12,27, slaves purchased from *bᵉnê nēk̲ār* who were themselves foreigners must be circumcised.

The Chronicler's history uses both *nok̲rî*[29] and *ben nēk̲ār,* although the Deuteronomic usage predominates. In Neh. 9:2 the statement that "the seed of Israel separated itself from all foreigners *(bᵉnê nēk̲ār)*" refers to the dissolution of mixed marriages with Gentile women (Ezr. 9f.), breaking the extensive familial ties of affinity established by marriage. In Neh. 13:30 the phrase *kol-nēk̲ār,* "everything foreign," refers to the same situation; it is a displaced gloss on Neh. 13:23-27.

The exclusion of foreigners from the cultic and familial systems, closely linked in Judaism, is extended in the expectation that "foreigners," probably thought of as performing forced labor, would one day rebuild the walls of Jerusalem and take on the hard work of plowing (Isa. 60:10; 61:5). The oracle in 56:6 moves in a different direction, being distinctly favorable to foreigners: it welcomes to the temple "the foreigner *(ben nēk̲ār)* who joins himself to Yahweh," i.e., the proselyte. Thanks to a Greek inscription and Josephus, we know that only an outer "court of the Gentiles" was accessible to foreigners; they were forbidden on pain of death to enter the inner precincts.[30] The inscription uses the word *allogenḗs,* a term the LXX often uses to translate *ben nēkār* (Ex. 12:43; Lev. 22:25; Ezk. 44:7,9; etc.), whereas Josephus uses *alloethnḗs.*[31] In similar fashion 4QFlor 1:4 says that no "Ammonite, Moabite, bastard, foreigner *(bn nkr),* or proselyte *(gr)*" may enter the temple. Cf. 1 K. 8:41 par. 2 Ch. 6:32, which speaks of a *nok̲rî* worshiping in the temple but not offering sacrifice.

---

26. Rashi; Sabottka, 38.
27. *CAD,* XI/1, 163.
28. See II.1.c above.
29. See II.1 above.
30. See *TGI*³, no. 55; Josephus *Ant.* 15.11.5 §417.
31. Cf. *TDNT,* I, 266f.

IV. *'elōhê nēḵār,* "Foreign Gods." The phrase *'elōhê nēḵār,* "foreign gods," was coined during the exilic period of the sixth century, when large groups of the people came into unpleasant contact with foreign lands. The expression reflects a strict "Yahweh alone" point of view and implies that only Yahweh can be the "true" God: gods other than Yahweh, elsewhere neutrally called *'elōhîm 'aḥērîm,* "other gods,"[32] are referred to, with strong negative implications, as "foreign gods." The earliest texts belong without exception to Deuteronomistic circles: Dt. 31:16; 32:12; Josh. 24(LXX 14):20,23; Jgs. 10:16; 1 S. 7:3). This holds true also for Jer. 5:19, a secondary passage, and Gen. 35:2,4, an earlier text that has undergone Deuteronomistic editing.

Othmar Keel has shown that Gen. 35:2b,5 and the phrase *'elōhê hannēḵār* in v. 4 are secondary.[33] The hiding of divine images (teraphim?) was clearly already puzzling to the ancient readers. A redactor associated with Deuteronomistic circles interpreted the text on the basis of Jgs. 10:16 and 1 S. 7:3 as a necessary condition for God's intervention to help Israel. The Deuteronomistic expression *hāsîrû 'eṯ-'elōhê hannēḵār 'ašer beṯōḵeḵem,* "remove the foreign gods that are in your midst" (and its variants), appears in Gen. 35:2,4; Josh. 24(LXX 14):23; Jgs. 10:16; 1 S. 7:3; 2 Ch. 33:15.

The other occurrences of the phrase (Mal. 2:11: "daughter of a foreign god," i.e., a foreign woman); Ps. 81:10[9]; Dnl. 11:39; 2 Ch. 33:15) are dependent on Deuteronomistic usage, as are the phrases *haḇlê nēḵār,* "foreign nothings," i.e., idols (Jer. 8:19 [secondary]) and *mizbeḥôṯ hannēḵār,* "foreign altars" (2 Ch. 14:2). We should possibly also include here the plain phrase *'aḏmaṯ nēḵār,* "foreign land" (Ps. 137:4), for which the context suggests the connotation "land of exile" = "land of foreign gods."

The unusual phrase *baṯ-'ēl nēḵār,* "daughter of a foreign god," in Mal. 2:11 is sometimes interpreted to mean "goddess."[34] The parallel in Nu. 21:29 (Moabite women called "daughters" of Chemosh), however, suggests that it is a poetic expression for "foreign woman."[35] Why marriage with a "daughter of a foreign god" profanes the temple is not immediately clear. The most likely explanation is that the text — obscure to us but not to the prophet's contemporaries — refers to a specific mixed marriage: an older high priest has divorced his childless Israelite wife to marry a foreign woman, possibly an Edomite, and thus continue his line (Mal. 2:13-16). The prophet raises his voice in protest.[36]

V. 1. *LXX.* The LXX does not have any serious problems with translation. The meaning of the niphal of *nkr* (Prov. 26:24) is rendered appropriately with *epineúein,* "nod to"; the piel is represented by *apallotrioún* (3 times), the hithpael by *apoxenoún* (twice) and by *allotrioún* and *diestramménōs* (once each). The words *nēḵār* and *noḵrî*

32. → אחר *'achēr,* I, 202f.
33. O. Keel, *VT,* 23 (1973), 327-331.
34. Hvidberg, 121; Ahlström, 49.
35. Schreiner, 215.
36. Caquot (1969), 200; *idem* (1981/82), 538.

are translated primarily by *allótrios,* the former also by *allogenḗs* (9 times) and the latter by *xénos* (5 times).

2. *Dead Sea Scrolls.* The root is rare in the Dead Sea Scrolls. In CD 14:15 someone who has been held prisoner by a "foreign nation" *(gôy nēḵār)* (and returns home?) is listed with orphans, the poor, the elderly, and the homeless as needing support. Other texts reveal a clear sense of separation from everything "pagan." As "pagans," foreigners must not be allowed to enter the temple (4QFlor 1:4).[37] The Temple Scroll states that a bodyguard must protect the king from attack by people belonging to a foreign nation (11QTemple 57:11); death on a stake (or hanging on a tree) is the punishment for traitors serving a "foreign (pagan) nation" (*gôy nēkār,* 64:7f.). These laws are primarily theoretical; quite practical, however, is the regulation in CD 11:2, which testifies to opposition against a common custom: members of the Qumran community must not let a Gentile (the meaning here of *ben nēkār!*) perform domestic labor for them on the Sabbath; in other words, especially on the Sabbath they must not be dependent on pagan "Gentiles."

Lang

VI. *nkr* II hiphil. The basic meaning of the hiphil of *nkr* II is "recognize (a person)": Isaac does not recognize Jacob in disguise (Gen. 27:23), Joseph's brothers do not recognize their brother (42:7f., antonym *yd'* hithpael in 45:1), Job is so disfigured that his friends do not recognize him (Job 2:12), people do not recognize each other in the dark (Ruth 3:14; cf. also 1 K. 18:7; 20:41). Eliphaz recounts how God appeared to him in a form whose appearance he could not recognize (Job 4:16). In the coming age of salvation, the descendants of Israel will be known *(nôḏa')* among all the nations, and people will recognize *(nkr)* that Yahweh has blessed them (Isa. 61:9). In a similar fashion a person's voice is recognized (Jgs. 18:3; 1 S. 26:17).

Like *nāśā' pānîm,*[38] *hikkîr pānîm* means "regard a person," "be partial"; partiality in the administration of justice is forbidden (Dt. 1:17; 16:19) and is judged to be *lō'-ṭôḇ* in Wisdom Literature (Prov. 24:23; 28:21).

With *l^eṭôḇâ, hikkîr* means "regard with favor": God will look favorably on those who have been carried off to Babylon, just as one looks at good figs (Jer. 24:5). Even by itself *hikkîr* has this meaning: Boaz looks with favor on Ruth and takes notice of her (Ruth 2:10,19); the psalmist laments that no one "takes notice of him" or "asks after his life" (*dōrēš l^enapšî:* Ps. 142:5[4]).

In Dt. 33, the Blessing of Moses, Levi is praised for having "set aside all obligations of loyalty to his own kindred":[39] he did not "see" his parents, he did not recognize *(nkr)* his brothers, and he did not "know" *(yāḏa')* his own children. In a similar vein, Isa. 63:16 states that Abraham does not know *(nkr)* his own people and does not

37. See III above.
38. → נשׂא *nāśā';* → פנים *pānîm.*
39. G. von Rad, *Deuteronomy. OTL* (Eng. trans. 1966), 206.

acknowledge *(yāḏaʿ)* Israel — in other words, it is no longer possible to appeal to natural ancestry: only Yahweh is the father of the people.

When the wind passes over a flower, it perishes, and the place where it was knows *(nkr)* nothing of it — so transitory are humans (Ps. 103:16). Without any imagery, Job 7:10 says the same concerning humans, who die.

According to Job 24:17, sinners are "familiar" with the terrors of deep darkness; they rebel *(mrd)* against the light and do not "know" its ways (24:13). God, however, "knows" their works (34:25).

In Neh. 13:24 *hikkîr* is used in the sense of "knowing" or "mastering" a language.

Ringgren

נָמֵר *nāmēr*

Contents: I. Etymology, Meaning, and Distribution. II. Ancient Near East. III. OT: 1. Occurrences; 2. Names; 3. Hebrew; 4. Dnl. 7:6. IV. Ancient Versions.

I. Etymology, Meaning, and Distribution. The word *nāmēr (nᵉmar, nimrāʾ)* is found not only in the OT but in many other Semitic languages.[1] Pelio Fronzaroli posits an ancient root *nimr* as the basis from which the word developed in the various Semitic languages: Akk. *nimru(m),* Arab. *namir,* Eth. *namr,* Mand. *nimria* (sg. *namar* = *nimar*), Syr. *nemrāʾ*.[2] According to Frank L. Benz, the word is attested in the Phoenician and

---

nāmēr. F.-M. Abel, *Géographie de la Palestine. ÉBib,* 2 vols. (³1967), II; J. Aharoni, "Über das Vorkommen und Aussterben palästinischer Tierarten," *ZDPV,* 49 (1926), 247-262; A. Billiq, "נמר," *EMiqr,* V, 870ff.; S. Bochartus, *Hierozoicon, sive Bipertitum opus de animalibus S. Scripturae* (ed. tertia ex rec. Johannes Leusden) (1692), 791-805; F. S. Bodenheimer, *Animal and Man in Bible Lands,* 2 vols. (Eng. trans., Leiden, 1960-72); F. Frank, "Tierleben in Palästina," *ZDPV,* 75 (1959), 83-88; V. Haas, "Leopard und Biene im Kulte 'hethitischer' Göttinnen," *UF,* 13 (1981), 101-116; F. Hommel, *Die Namen der Säugethiere bei den südsemitischen Völkern* (1879); B. Landsberger and I. Krumbiegel, *Die Fauna des alten Mesopotamien nach der 14. Tafel der Serie Ḫar-ra-Ḫubullu* (1934); J. A. Rimbach, "Bees or Bears? Sefire I A 31 and Daniel 7," *JBL,* 97 (1978), 565f.; A. Salonen, *Jagd und Jagdtiere im alten Mesopotamien. AnAcScFen,* 196 (1976).

III.4: A. Caquot, "Les quatre bêtes et le 'Fils d'Homme' (*Daniel* 7)," *Sem,* 17 (1967), 37-71; *idem,* "Sur les quatre bêtes de *Daniel* VII," *Sem,* 5 (1955), 5-13; A. J. Ferch, "Daniel 7 and Ugarit," *JBL,* 99 (1980), 75-86; J. C. H. Lebram, "Daniel/Danielbuch," *TRE,* VIII, 325-349; H. H. Rowley, *Darius the Mede and the Four World Empires in the Book of Daniel* (Cardiff, 1935).

1. See III below; for the variants see A. Sperber, *HUCA,* 12/13 (1937/38), 242: Jerome has *nēmēr.*

2. Fronzaroli, *AANLR,* 365 (1968), 281. On Akkadian see *CAD,* XI/2, 234f.; *AHw,* II, 790. On Arabic, Hommel, 294-99. On Ethiopic, Hommel, 379. On Mandaic, *MdD,* 298. On Syriac, *LexSyr,* 431.

Punic world as well.[3] We find *nmr* also in the Deir ʿAlla text and in the story of Ahikar *(nmrʾ)*.[4]

There are two occurrences of *nmrh* in the Sefire inscriptions from the mid-eighth century B.C., which Herbert Donner and Wolfgang Röllig as well as Joseph Fitzmyer translate "panther."[5] According to Donner and Röllig, the word is a substantive in the absolute form; Fitzmyer considers it feminine.[6] More recently James Rimbach has noted the uncertainty of the reading and consequently proposed another meaning: *nmlh,* "ant."[7]

Etymologically, *nāmēr* has often been associated with Arab. *namira,* "be spotted."[8] Other etymologies have also been proposed that posit a connection with Akk. *namāru,* "shine, gleam."[9] But *namāru* is just a by-form of *nawāru,* and *nāmēr* is clearly a primary noun (Akk. *nimru[m]*). Hitt. *parsana* (sumerogram PIRIG.TUR, UG.TUR, or PIRIG.KAL) is connected with Gk. *párdalis* (since Homer), *pórdalis, pánthēr* (since Herodotus), *párdos* (Roman period), and *leópardos.*[10] The etymology of these last words is unknown, but they may derive from a non–Indo-European language of Asia Minor.[11]

The translation of *nāmēr* varies in most dictionaries, translations, and commentaries: sometimes "leopard," sometimes "panther," often without distinction.[12] Jer. 13:23 says that the *nāmēr* cannot change its *ḥᵃḇarburôṯ*. This suggests "spots,"[13] a meaning associated with "leopard," to be distinguished in the Palestinian region from the "panther," from which it also differs in minor features of appearance and anatomy.[14]

The panther *(Felis panthera)* is found primarily in Southeast Asia; its appearance in Palestine, even in the early period, is scarcely attested.[15] By contrast, the leopard *(Felis pardus tullianus)* was (and to some small extent still is) found in Asia Minor,

---

3. Benz, 147, 361.

4. Deir ʿAlla I, 17; cf. J. Hoftijzer and G. van der Kooij, *Aramaic Texts from Deir ʿAlla. DMOA,* 21 (1976), 219f.; H.-P. Müller, "Die aramäische Inschrift von Deir ʿAllā und die älteren Bileamsprüche," *ZAW,* 94 (1982), 214ff.; Ahikar 118f.

5. *KAI,* 222A, 31; 223A, 9; Fitzmyer, *The Aramaic Inscriptions of Sefîre. BietOr,* 19 (1967), 15, 49, 81.

6. *KAI,* II, 249. Cf. *DISO,* 179.

7. Cf. already D. Winton Thomas, *JSS,* 5 (1960), 283.

8. Already Bochartus, 785ff., as well as the early lexicons and such modern dictionaries as *HAL,* II, 701; cf. P. Fronzaroli, *AANLR,* 365 (1968), 281, 301.

9. E.g., *BDB,* 649.

10. W. Richter, *KlPauly,* IV, 475. On the Hittite see Landsberger and Krumbiegel, 76, n. 4, 77; Salonen, 219f.; cf. K. Butz, *BiOr,* 34 (1977), 289.

11. Haas, 106; cf. F. Schwally, *Idioticon des christlich palästinischen Aramaeisch* (1893), 121.

12. But see T. Wittstruck, *JBL,* 97 (1978), 100, n. 5.

13. Already Bochartus, 786; cf. *HAL,* I, 288.

14. Hommel, 294, n. 2.

15. Lesêtre, *DB,* IV, 172-75; Feliks, *BHHW,* III, 1382; H. Wildberger, *Isaiah 1–12* (Eng. trans., Minneapolis, 1991), 461.

Syria, Palestine, and North Africa. The swift "leopard" in Hab. 1:8 refers possibly to the hunting leopard or cheetah *(Felis acinonyx jubatus),* also called *bard*ᵉ*lēs* (related to Gk. *párdalis*) in later Hebrew literature (Mishnah *Sanh.* 1.4; *B. Qam.* 1.4; etc.).[16] Even today, leopards and cheetahs are found occasionally near the Dead Sea.[17] In ancient times cheetahs were sometimes domesticated.[18] It is not always possible to decide with certainty whether the word *nāmēr* refers to a leopard, cheetah, serval, or even a lynx.[19] The leopard sometimes appears in ancient art, e.g., in Egypt and Mesopotamia.[20] It might be best to avoid the translation "panther" for *nāmēr.* The leopard lives in thickets and among rocks (cf. Cant. 4:8).

II. Ancient Near East. In the religions of the ancient Near East, the leopard is quite often among the animals associated with a deity — in Hittite religion, e.g., with the goddess Inar(a), in whose temple a cup of wine was offered for the leopard.[21] Inar(a) was originally a Ḫatti deity of more than regional significance. The leopard was also sacred to the Ḫatti sun-goddess: it protected her spring. It already played an important role in the religious thought of the Neolithic period, as finds at the terraced settlement of Çatal Hüyük (7th-6th millennium) show.[22] Later the leopard appears in conjunction with the great goddesses of central Anatolia, e.g., in Hittite festival rituals such as the leopard dance.[23] According to Volkert Haas,[24] the association of the leopard with the Anatolian goddesses Cybele, Artemis, and Aphrodite (Urania) goes back to Hittite traditions.

In Sumerian literature the goddess Inanna is associated with the leopard; in Assyria the animal is connected with Ishtar of Arbela.[25] In Northern Arabia the leopard is sacred to Dusares.[26] In later classical literature, too, the leopard has religious associations not only with Cybele, Aphrodite, and Circe, but also with Dionysus/Bacchus and his retinue.[27] Hunting leopards is often considered a "religious act," as in ancient South Arabia.[28]

---

16. See S. Krauss, *Griechische und lateinische Lehnwörter im Talmud, Midrasch und Targum,* 2 vols. (Berlin, 1898-99), II, 164; Levy, *WTM,* I, 261f. On Hab. 1:8 see W. S. McCullough, *IDB,* III, 111.

17. Aharoni, 251f.; Frank, 83f.; Billiq, 871.

18. Bodenheimer, 100.

19. Richter, *KlPauly,* IV, 475f.

20. For Egypt see Billiq, 871f.; *ANEP,* nos. 52, 297. For Mesopotamia see *ANEP,* no. 678.

21. Haas, 107.

22. Haas, 104ff.

23. Haas, 108f.

24. P. 111.

25. For Sumerian see W. Heimpel, *Tierbilder in der sumerischen Literatur. StPohl,* 2 (1968), 331ff.; for Assyria see R. Frankena, *Tākultu* (Leiden, 1954), 95, no. 97.

26. M. Höfner, *WbMyth,* I, 434, 522; cf. R. Dussaud, *La pénétration des Arabes en Syrie avant l'Islam* (Paris, 1955), 57f.

27. Richter, *KlPauly,* IV, 476.

28. A. F. L. Beeston, "The Ritual Hunt," *Mus,* 61 (1948), 183-196.

III. OT.

1. *Occurrences.* In the OT *nāmēr* occurs in Isa. 11:6; Jer. 5:6; 13:23; Hos. 13:7; Hab. 1:8 (pl.); Cant. 4:8 (pl.); and Dnl. 7:6 (Aram. *n*ᵉ*mar*).

2. *Names.* Evidence for leopards in ancient Palestine includes the toponyms *nimrâ* or *bêṯ nimrâ* (Nu. 32:3,36; Josh. 13:27) and *mê nimrîm* (Isa. 15:6; Jer. 48:34) in Moabite territory not far from the Jordan and the Dead Sea.[29]

3. *Hebrew.* In the OT the leopard is not found either in immediate conjunction with the Deity or as a "sacred" animal. For the most part it appears in images and metaphors (as in many Akkadian texts).[30] In Jer. 13:23 the leopard serves as a parable expressing skepticism over the possibility of the people's changing their ways: "Can a Cushite change his skin or a leopard its spots? Then also you can do good, who are accustomed to do evil." Here the animal is a metaphor from the natural realm expressing an *adynaton.*[31] In Hos. 13:7f. God compares himself to a number of animals in his judgment on Ephraim: "So I will become like a lion *(šaḥal)* to them, like a leopard I will lurk on the way 'to Assyria.' "[32] The text also mentions a she-bear *(dōḇ),* a lion *(lāḇîʾ),*[33] and "beasts of the field" (*ḥayyaṯ haśśāḏeh* (NRSV: "a wild animal"). A similar menagerie also appears in Sefire texts in a so-called covenant imprecation.[34] Jer. 5:6 threatens the sinful people with a leopard as well as a lion *('aryēh)* from the forest and a wolf from the desert *(z*ᵉ*'ēḇ ʿ*ᵃ*rāḇôṯ).* The wolf of the "desert" or "evening"[35] also appears in the company of the leopard in Hab. 1:8. This verse likens the swiftness of the Chaldeans on their horses to the speed of leopards (cf. 1QpHab 3:6ff.). Cant. 4:8 speaks of the descent of the bride from Lebanon.[36] The mountains are described as the "dens of lions" and "mountains of leopards."[37] The mention of lions and leopards suggests the sinister and dangerous situation in which the poet imagines the bride. It is not impossible, of course, that the geographic

---

29. For the former see *GTTOT,* §300; Abel, 278. For the latter see *GTTOT,* §§1256-58; Abel, 399; Billiq, 871; A. H. van Zyl, *The Moabites. POS,* III (1960), 55ff.; cf. also T. Nöldeke, *ZDMG,* 29 (1875), 437, n. 3: "the 'leopardlike' spotted or striped appearance of the ground"; *HAL,* II, 701; Arab. *namīr,* "having abundant water."

30. *CAD,* XI/2, 235; cf., among others, Butz, *BiOr,* 34 (1977), 289; also for Egyptian texts H. Grapow, *Die bildlichen Ausdrücke des Ägyptischen* (1924, repr. Darmstadt, 1983), 73.

31. G. van der Leeuw, *JEOL,* 8 (1942), 635; E. Würthwein, *TDNT,* IV, 987.

32. L. Wächter, *Der Tod im AT. AzT,* 2/8 (1967), 45. The reading "to Assyria" follows LXX, Vulg., Syr., and many comms.

33. But see H. W. Wolff, *Hosea. Herm* (Eng. trans. 1974), 220, 226f.; J. L. Mays, *Hosea. OTL* (1969), 173, 176; and the apparatus of *BHK* and *BHS,* in loc.: *k*ᵉ*lāḇîm,* "dogs."

34. See T. Wittstruck, "The Influence of Treaty Curse Imagery on the Beast Imagery of Daniel 7," *JBL,* 97 (1978), 100-102; *KAI,* 222A, 30f.; 223A, 9; see I above.

35. K. Elliger, "Das Ende der 'Abendwölfe' Zeph 3,3; Hab 1,8," *Festschrift A. Bertholet* (Tübingen, 1950), 158-175.

36. → לבנון *l*ᵉ*ḇānôn,* II.2, 4 (VII, 451f., 455).

37. W. Rudolph (*Das Hohe Lied. KAT,* XVII/2 [1962], 147f.) prefers to read " 'caves' of leopards."

references in this verse derive originally from association with a cultic deity who dwelt in Lebanon.[38]

Peaceful coexistence among animals as well as between animals and human beings is one of the themes of the poem in Isa. 11:1-9. The wolf shall "be the guest" of the lamb, and "the leopard shall lie down with the kid" (v. 6). When this comes to pass, the peaceful kingdom of the Messiah will have arrived. The text lists a whole series of dangerous animals: wolf, leopard, young lion, bear, lion, asp, adder. They all live together in peace, because peace among animals is "a characteristic of paradise."[39] Here prophecy draws on more ancient popular traditions, using them to describe the eschatological age of salvation. The presence of the leopard in this description is probably deliberate,[40] although it is surprisingly not included in 65:25.

4. *Dnl. 7:6.* The leopard in Dnl. 7:6 has the strongest association with ancient mythological and popular motifs. Strictly speaking, the text does not refer to a leopard but to a leopardlike creature with four wings on its back, four heads, and "great power." It is the third of four beasts, none of which belongs to the fauna of the known world.[41] It comes after a lion with eagles' wings and a bear with three ribs between its teeth; they all arise out of the sea. We are clearly dealing here with features that "indicate the originally mythological nature of the symbolic event."[42] Whether this mythologization derives from the ancient Near East or is a product of the Hellenistic and Roman period is difficult to determine. According to Jürgen C. H. Lebram, the use of animals to symbolize world empires reflects neither a battle with chaos nor a creation myth; it is a "pseudoprognostic representation of the dominion of the world empires as an irruption of the forces of chaos into history."[43] Like the metals of the statue in ch. 2, the description of the beasts in Dnl. 7 reveals an increasing depravity that leads from the partially human features of the first empire to the bestiality of the fourth.[44] The "powerful" leopard occupies the third place in this series. It is difficult to determine what empire the beast symbolizes: it might represent the Lydian, Medo-Persian, Persian, Greek, Macedonian, Roman, or even the Christian Empire.[45] Most scholars assume that the third beast represents the Persian Empire.[46] It is nevertheless possible to interpret the four beasts as being present simultaneously,[47] so that they symbolize empires existing in the time of the author. In this reading it is not impossible that the

38. M. Haller, *Das Hohelied. HAT,* XVIII (1940), 35.
39. H. Gressmann, *Der Messias* (Göttingen, 1929), 151.
40. S. N. Kramer, *History Begins at Sumer* (Garden City, N.Y., ^{2}1961), 210; *ANET,* 38.
41. M. Haller, *Das Judentum. SAT* (^{2}1925), 296.
42. Lebram, 332.
43. P. 334; cf. 333, and Ferch, 81.
44. Lebram, *VT,* 20 (1970), 517ff.
45. Rowley, 184f.
46. C. Colpe, *TDNT,* VIII, 421, n. 164; K. Koch, *Das Buch Daniel* (1980), 187ff.; already Rowley, 144ff.
47. B. D. Eerdmans, *The Religion of Israel* (Leiden, 1947), 224f.; M. A. Beek, *Das Danielbuch* (Leiden, 1935), 26f., 49.

leopard with four wings and heads represents Rome, which was expanding in the Maccabean period (cf. also Rev. 13:2, the only mention of a leopard in the NT).

IV. Ancient Versions. The LXX translates *nāmēr* with *párdalis* (also Sir. 28:23; cf. *pardáleios* in 4 Mc. 9:28; T.Abr. A 19). Josephus includes the leopard among the unclean animals.[48] In addition to *párdalis,* the LXX uses *pánthēr* in Hos. 5:14; 13:7 to translate *šaḥal* (also Ps. 91:13; Job 4:10; 10:16; 28:8; Prov. 26:13), usually translated "lion."[49] The Vulg. uses *pardus* to translate *nāmēr* and *leaena* to translate *šaḥal.* The Syr. always uses *nemrā'* for *nāmēr,* except in Hab. 1:8, where it uses *nešrā',* possibly because of confusion with Jer. 4:13. In 2 Ch. 31:1; 33:3; 34:3, the Syr. uses *nemrā'* for *'ašērâ.* It is unlikely that this translation shows that images of leopards were still known to the Syr. translators.[50]

Mulder

48. *Ant.* 12.3.4 §146.

49. But see S. Mowinckel, "שַׁחַל," *Hebrew and Semitic Studies. Festschrift G. R. Driver* (Oxford, 1963), 95-103.

50. A. E. Shipley and S. A. Cook, *EncBib,* III, 2763.

נֵס *nēs;* נסס *nss* II

Contents: I. 1. Etymology; 2. Distribution; 3. Lexical Field; 4. Syntax; 5. LXX. II. Secular Usage: 1. Military Contexts; 2. Nautical Contexts. III. Theological Usage: 1. Nu. 21:8f.; 2. Ex. 17:15; 3. Metaphorical Usage in the Prophets; 4. Sign. IV. Dead Sea Scrolls.

I. 1. *Etymology.* Since the root is found only in Hebrew, Jewish Aramaic, Christian Palestinian Aramaic, and Syriac (in other words, only in languages dependent on Hebrew), its etymology presents a difficult problem. The following theories have been proposed.

nēs. B. Couroyer, "Un Égyptianisme en Exode, XVII,15-16: *YHWH-NISSI,*" *RB,* 88 (1981), 333-39; J. Fichtner, "Die etymologische Ätiologie in den Namengebungen der geschichtlichen Bücher des ATs," *VT,* 6 (1956), 372-396, esp. 388; M. Görg, "Der Altar; theologische Dimensionen im AT," *Freude am Gottesdienst. Festschrift J. Plöger* (Stuttgart, 1983), 291-306, esp. 302ff.; *idem,* "*Nes* — ein Herrschaftsemblem?" *BN,* 14 (1981), 11-17; K. Goldammer, "Die heilige Fahne," *Tribus,* N.S. 4/5 (1954/55), 13-55, esp. 34; R. Gradwohl, "Zum Verständnis von Ex. XVII 15f.," *VT,* 12 (1962), 491-94; R. Krauss, "Feldzeichen," *LexÄg,* II/9 (1975), 155-57; A. R. Müller, "Ex 17,15f. in der Septuaginta," *BN,* 12 (1980), 10-23; H. Schäfer, "Assyrische und ägyptische Feldzeichen," *Klio,* 6 (1909), 393-99, esp. 396; E. Strömberg Krantz, *Des Schiffes Weg mitten im Meer. CB,* 19 (1982), 122-26; H. Weippert, "Feldzeichen," *BRL*^{2} (1977), 77-79.

a. The noun *nēs* derives from *nss* I, "go to and fro, run zigzag," hithpolel "glitter."[1] For the verb, Gesenius also proposes the meaning "raise up,"[2] but this theory is rejected today.

b. The verb *nss* I, "go to and fro," has no connection with *nēs; nss* II (only hithpolel) is a denominative from *nēs.*[3]

c. There is no demonstrable connection with *nsh,* "test, try."[4]

d. Paul Haupt proposes a non-Hebrew etymology, citing the Akkadian loanword *nîšu.*[5] But this noun with the meaning "elevation" derives from the verb *nāšû*[6] and is related to → נשׂא *nāśā',* as Jerome noted in the Vulg.

e. B. Couroyer and Manfred Görg have independently proposed Egyptian etymologies.[7] Couroyer points to Egyp. *nś.t,* "seat, throne," and interprets *YHWH nissî* (Ex. 17:15) as "the throne of Yahweh." When later Hebrews no longer knew of this meaning, the phrase was interpreted in parallel with *kēs yāh* (v. 16).[8]

According to Görg, *nēs* can be interpreted without complications as the Hebrew version of the Egyptian title *ny.śwt,* "he who belongs to the *śwt* plant [sedge]," which originally was the title of the king of Upper Egypt and later became the general royal title. More a royal standard than a military standard, it symbolized the leadership role of the king as God's appointed regent, whose primary function was to protect the people from enemies.[9] The proposed mixture of iconography and etymology, however, counsels caution.

Although determining the etymology of *nēs* is probably a hopeless task, its use in several unambiguous contexts makes its meaning clear: "standard, pole, banner, sail," figuratively "danger signal" (Nu. 26:10; Isa. 11:10). The figurative meaning leads to the meaning "wonder, miracle" in Late Hebrew and Aramaic.[10] In rabbinic literature and the Talmud, *nēs* generally replaces the term *môpēṯ.*[11]

2. *Distribution.* The noun *nēs* occurs 21 times in the OT, with particular frequency in the books of Isaiah (8 occurrences in Proto-Isaiah, once each in Deutero-Isaiah and Trito-Isaiah) and Jeremiah (5 occurrences). The 4 occurrences in the Pentateuch (Ex. 17:16; Nu. 21:8f.; 26:10) are difficult to assign to literary sources. Ps. 60:6(Eng. v. 4) and Ezk. 27:7 stand in isolation.

A verb *nss* II occurs only in the hithpolel (Ps. 60:6[4]; Zec. 9:16); according to *HAL,*[12] it is a denominative from *nēs* and means "to assemble under the banner." But

---

1. *KBL*², 619f.
2. *GesTh,* II, 891.
3. *GesB,* 508; *HAL,* II, 704.
4. G. Gerleman, *TLOT,* II, 741.
5. P. Haupt, *JBL,* 19 (1900), 68.
6. *AHw,* II, 762.
7. Couroyer, citing N. Reich, *Sphinx,* 14 (1910), 29; Görg, *BN,* 14, 11-17.
8. → כסא *kissē'* (VII, 232-259).
9. *BN,* 14, 16f.
10. K. Beyer, *Die aramäischen Texte vom Toten Meer* (Göttingen, 1984), 637.
11. K. H. Rengstorff, *TDNT,* VIII, 123f.
12. P. 704.

even the ancient versions generally interpreted these texts as using a form of *nûs,* "seek refuge." Only the Vulg. and Symmachus (in Zec. 9:16) attest to the notion of elevation: "raise as a sign."[13]

3. *Lexical Field.* Twice *nēs* parallels *tōren,* "flagstaff" (Isa. 30:17), "mast" (Isa. 33:23; cf. Ezk. 27:5). The word *deg̱el,* used almost exclusively in P, clearly means something like "military standard" (cf. Nu. 2, 10); it can also refer to a tactical military unit ("squad") as *signum pro toto.* The noun has a similar meaning at Elephantine and in the Dead Sea Scrolls.[14] In Cant. 2:4 *deg̱el* probably refers to the "sign" of a tavern, its original meaning. Closely related but not totally synonymous are *môṭ/môṭâ,* "pole," but primarily in the sense of "carrying pole" or "yoke," and *ḥibbēl,* "mast" (Prov. 23:34). Also in the domain of military signaling is *maśʾēṯ,* "raising" (in Jgs. 20:38,40 as in the Lachish Letters[15]) a "smoke signal." Used figuratively, *nēs* is related to → אוֹת *ʾôth* and → מוֹפֵת *môpēṯ.*

4. *Syntax. nēs* occurs only in the singular and almost always anarthrously; in Nu. 21:9; Isa. 30:17, it is determined by the definite article, in Ex. 17:15; Isa. 49:22 (closely related texts) by the 1st person singular suffix. It appears as the object of → נשׂא *nāśāʾ,* "raise, set up" (Isa. 5:26; 11:12; 13:2; 18:3; Jer. 4:6; 50:2; 51:12,27), *hērîm,* "raise" (Isa. 49:22; 62:10), *pāraś,* "spread out," also possibly "slacken" (Isa. 33:23), *rāʾâ,* "see" (Jer. 4:21; Ps. 60:6); its use as the object of *hišmîaʿ,* "cause to hear" (Jer. 50:2), is exceptional.

A person or object can become a *nēs* (*hāyâ lᵉnēs:* Nu. 26:10; Ezk. 27:7) or stand (*ʿāmaḏ:* Isa. 11:10) as *nēs ʿammîm.* One may take refuge (*nss* hithpolel: Ps. 60:6[4]) by a *nēs* or flee from it (*ḥtt minnēs:* Isa. 31:9). The sites where a *nēs* is raised are: *har,* "mountain" (Isa. 13:2; 18:3), *giḇʿâ,* "hill" (Isa. 30:17), *ʾereṣ,* "land" (Jer. 51:27), *ḥômaṯ bāḇēl,* "city wall of Babylon" (Jer. 51:12), and *ṣîyônâ,* "toward Zion."

5. *LXX.* The LXX always translates *nēs* correctly with *sēmeíon* (9 times), *sēmaía* and *sēmeíōsis* (once each), or *sýssēmon* (3 times; used throughout by Aquila[16]). The other translations, *árchein, dóxa,* and *histíon,* are singular. Ex. 17:15 uses *kataphygḗ.*[17] The LXX has also understood *nᵉsâ-ʿalênû* in Ps. 4:7(6) as a form of *nēs (sēmeioún),* while deriving *nss* in Ps. 60:6(4) from *nws (phygeín).*

II. Secular Usage. The strictly secular use of *nēs* as a technical term of military operations or shipbuilding must remain speculative, since all the texts appear in theological and metaphorical contexts.

---

13. But see W. Rudolph, *Sacharja 9–14. KAT,* XIII/4 (1976), in loc.: *nṣṣ,* "sparkle."
14. For the former see *AP,* 12; for the latter see 1QM 5:3.
15. *KAI,* 194, 10.
16. J. Ziegler, *NGWG,* N.S. 1/4 (1939), 90.
17. See Müller.

1. *Military Contexts.* As a military standard, a *nēs* serves primarily as a marker, indicating where the army is to assemble (Isa. 5:26; 11:12) or pointing in the direction of advance and attack (Jer. 51:12).[18] It is usually set up on a mountain or hill to provide orientation (Isa. 13:2; 18:3; 30:17); but it appears also to advertise the victor's claim to possession when it is set up on the city wall of defeated Babylon (Jer. 50:2). The setting up of this standard is accompanied by trumpets (Isa. 18:3), horns (Jer. 4:21; 51:27), and battle cries (*qôl:* Isa. 13:2). As a military standard, comparable to the ark, the *nēs* appears to have been a divine emblem endowed with leadership qualities.[19] In the ancient Near East, standards symbolize concretely the gods advancing into battle.[20]

We must remember, however, that a *nēs* is not mentioned in any of the OT descriptions of battle;[21] it first appears in prophetic emulations of this form. The same holds true for the use of *degel* in P. All we know of the function of military standards comes through the prophets' metaphorical exploitation of the ritual of the holy war.

2. *Nautical Contexts.* In Isa. 33:23; Ezk. 27:7, *nēs* appears to denote part of a ship's tackle. A sail of fine embroidered linen *(miprāś)* is to serve as a *nēs.* To interpret this as meaning "flag" (LXX) seems reasonable, but there is no evidence for flags before the Persian period.[22] The necessary late dating of Isa. 33:23 would admit such an interpretation, but the parallelism with *ḥᵃḇālîm,* "ropes," and *tōren,* "mast," suggests a sail. Even though "sail" is the preferred interpretation in both texts, a signal function is not excluded, since bright (red) sails are known to have indicated a wealthy and eminent owner or passenger.[23] This interpretation does most justice to the context of both occurrences.

III. Theological Usage.

1. *Nu. 21:8f.* Reference to the appearance of a *nēs* appears in the account of the "bronze serpent" (Nu. 21:8f.: JE).[24] In this account, reshaped later by R^P, Moses is commanded to set a *śārap* on a *nēs;* those who see it will be protected from the bite of poisonous serpents. According to v. 9, Moses then sets a bronze serpent on this *nēs.* It would be hard to picture the *nēs* otherwise than as a pole (cf. Isa. 30:17), although its function as a support is of primary importance.[25] Archaeologically, standards with a serpent motif have been found in Late Bronze Age strata at Hazor.[26]

---

18. G. Schumacher, *ZDPV,* 9 (1886), 232.
19. See Weippert, Görg; on the ark → אהל *'ōhel* (I, 118-130); → ארון *'ᵃrôn* (I, 363-374).
20. M. Weippert, *ZAW,* 84 (1972), 477f.
21. → מלחמה *milḥāmâ* (VIII, 334-345).
22. Weippert, *BRL,* 78.
23. Strömberg Krantz, 126; G. R. Driver, *JSS,* 13 (1968), 54.
24. → נחש *nāḥāš* IV.3; → נחשתן *nᵉḥuštān* I.2; V.
25. See II.1 above.
26. Y. Yadin, *BA,* 20 (1957), 43; cf. also *BuA,* II, fig. 26.

2. *Ex. 17:15.* It is very difficult to interpret the phrase *YHWH nissî* (which also presents textual problems[27]), applied to the altar Moses is to build after the battle with the Amalekites at Rephidim (Ex. 17:15f.).[28] Whether this designation is anchored traditio-historically among the southern tribes of the premonarchic period or is associated with the later state is a minor problem[29] compared to the problem of the connection between the name of the altar and its interpretation in v. 16: *kî-yāḏ ʿal-kēs yāh,* "a hand upon the throne of Yahweh."[30] This banner formula together with its etiology must be considered a later appendix to the basic narrative. The battle cry on which v. 16 is based was probably a text to protect the soldiers in battle (with the Amalekites). They gained this protection by placing their hands on a banner *(nēs)* or on an altar of Yahweh conceived of as a throne *(kēs).*[31] The reading *kēs yāh* in v. 16 is virtually certain, since it is attested by all the ancient versions. The misunderstanding of the LXX (reading a form of *ksh*) is an excellent example.[32] The oath gesture is also a matter of debate.[33] Citing good archaeological evidence, Roland Gradwohl suggests a votive hand on a standard as a symbol of the supporting hand of God. There is, however, no other trace of such a notion in Israel.

The solution to these problems should probably be sought along the following lines: Just as the box-shaped ark could go forward as a military standard and emblem of Yahweh, so could a similarly shaped altar, which could be set up on the battlefield like the throne of a Near Eastern potentate.[34] Therefore the designation of the Rephidim altar as both *nēs* and *kēs* is quite possible; the one may even help explain the other through assonance. Görg has shown that the post-Yahwistic author used this designation of the altar as a means of making explicit reference to Yahweh.[35]

3. *Metaphorical Usage in the Prophets.* Most of the occurrences of *nēs* are in prophetic metaphors in the books of Isaiah and Jeremiah. In the prophetic oracles the texts in question focus on (a) the impending end of Israel and (b) the wonderful restoration of Israel after the exile.

a. According to Isa. 5:26, Yahweh raises a *nēs* for the Assyrians or Babylonians,[36] about which they are to assemble for their campaign to destroy Israel. A *nēs* points the way to Jerusalem for the foe from the north (Jer. 4:6). The judgment will be so terrible that the remnant of the people will look like a *nēs,* emaciated as a signal pole.

---

27. See the extensive discussion in B. S. Childs, *The Book of Exodus.* OTL (1974), 311f.

28. On the derivation from → נוס *nûs,* "he gives me refuge," → V, 515.

29. For the former see Weippert, *ZAW,* 84 (1972), 489, n. 145; for the latter see Görg, *BN,* 14 (1981), 14.

30. → VIII, 216.

31. For the former see V. Fritz, *Israel in der Wüste. MarTS,* 7 (1970), 57; for the latter → כסא *kissēʾ,* VII, 254f.

32. Müller.

33. Couroyer.

34. → כסא *kissēʾ* (VII, 232-259).

35. *Festschrift Plöger,* 302f.

36. For the former see H. Wildberger, *Isaiah 1–12* (Eng. trans., Minneapolis, 1991) 239f.; for the latter see O. Kaiser, *Isaiah 1–12. OTL* (Eng. trans. [2]1983), 112.

b. In prophecies of salvation the *nēs* functions similarly as an orientation signal for the expected deliverance. Isa. 31:9 already describes the divine panic caused by Yahweh's attack on Assyria: its officers abscond, deserting their *nēs.* In later texts the prophecies of salvation focus on Babylon (Isa. 13:2). To set up a *nēs* against Babylon means a declaration of war (Jer. 50:2; 51:12). Yahweh himself calls on Israel to set up a *nēs* against Babylon and raise a war cry (Isa. 13:2; cf. Jer. 51:27).

In the deliverance of Israel accomplished by the return from exile, a real *nēs* may well have played a role. However that may be, this event is itself to be a *nēs* for the nations (Isa. 49:22; 62:10). According to Isa. 11:10, the awaited scion from the root of Jesse is to be a *nēs* for the peoples, the place of assembly and rest. "He will raise a *nēs* for the nations, and will assemble the outcasts of Israel, and gather the dispersed of Judah from the four corners of the earth" (v. 12).

4. *Sign.* This usage opens the way for the semantic development of *nēs* in the direction of "sign."[37] Overtones of this meaning can be heard in the last passages cited; it is fully present in Ps. 60:6(4): "To those who fear you, you give a sign, that they may flee from the bow." According to Nu. 26:10, the fate of Korah and his band is a "warning" (cf. Nu. 16; Isa. 11:10).

V. Dead Sea Scrolls. To date, only 3 occurrences of *nēs* have been found in the Dead Sea Scrolls. Surprisingly, only one of these is in 1QM, and there it does not mean "military standard," for which 1QM uses *'ôṯ.* One of these standards bears the inscription *nēs 'ēl* (3:15); it ranks third in the series of standards, following *'am 'ēl,* "people of God." The whole series of inscriptions (cf. 4:6-13) can be divided into a tactical military group (*'am, mišpāḥôṯ, qāhāl,* etc.) and a metaphorical group (*kāḇôḏ, rîḇ, gᵉmûl,* etc.). According to 1QH 2:13, the teacher of the community thinks of himself as *nēs* of the community (par. *mēlîṣ,* "interpreter of mysteries"). 1QH 6:34 may allude to the miraculous sign of the resurrection: "the worm of the dead raises a *nēs.*" There is also an association of *nēs* with resurrection in Did. 16:6.[38]

Fabry

37. → מופת *môpēṯ* (VIII, 174-181); → אות *'ôth* (I, 167-188).
38. See also A. Stuiber, *JAC,* 24 (1981), 42-44; → נשׂא *nāśā'.*

נִסָּה nissâ; מַסּוֹת massôṯ; מַסָּה massâ

Contents: I. Etymology, Related Verbs. II. Secular Usage: 1. Testing Others; 2. Testing Oneself; 3. Testing Objects; 4. Intransitive Use. 5. Lexical Field. III. Theological Usage: 1. Testing God; 2. Testing by God. IV. *massôṯ*. V. *massâ*. VI. Dead Sea Scrolls.

I. Etymology, Related Verbs. The meaning of Ugar. *nsy/ysy*[1] has not been explained. Adrianus van Selms associates *nsy* with Heb. *nissâ* and translates it "undergo an experience."[2]

It is most unlikely that there is any connection between *nissâ* and *nāśā'*, despite the Akkadian use of *našû* with *rēšu* ("head") as its object ("lift up the head") in the sense of "take notice of, test," "check on quality or quantity of fields, materials, staples, animals," and "inspect, test (a medicine), investigate (personnel, also objects)."[3]

A connection with → נס *nēs,* "sign, standard," is also possible, especially if *nissâ* can be understood as a military term.[4] A *nēs* serves to characterize and identify a tribe or a military unit; *nissâ* similarly pursues the goal of knowing a person or an object.

In one of the Lachish ostraca,[5] the writer assures his superior that no one has ever — successfully — "tried" to read to him a document not intended for his ears.

The most important semantically similar verbs are → בחן *bāchan,* → חקר *ḥāqar,* and → צרף *ṣārap.* The first has a strongly cognitive character; *ḥāqar* refers to intensive investigation, thorough examination, leading to understanding; *ṣārap* denotes originally

---

nissâ. A. M. Dubarle, "La tentation diabolique dans le Livre de la Sagesse (2, 24)," *Mélanges E. Tisserant,* 7 vols. (Vatican City, 1964), I, 187-195; G. Gerleman, "נסה *nsh pi.* to test,' " *TLOT,* II, 741-42; M. Greenberg, "נסה in Ex 20:20 and the Purpose of the Sinaitic Theophany," *JBL,* 73 (1960), 30-54; R. Kilian, *Isaaks Opferung. SBS,* 44 (1970); *idem, Die vorpriesterlichen Abrahamsüberlieferungen literarkritisch und traditionsgeschichtlich untersucht. BBB,* 24 (1966); J. H. Korn, *ΠΕΙΡΑΣΜΟΣ; Die Versuchung des Gläubigen in der griechischen Bibel. BWANT,* 72 (1937); S. Lehming, "Massa und Meriba," *ZAW,* 73 (1961), 71-77; J. Licht, *Testing in the Hebrew Scriptures and in Postbiblical Judaism* (Jerusalem, 1973) (Heb.); N. Lohfink, " 'Ich bin Jahwe, dein Arzt' (Ex 15,26)," *"Ich will euer Gott werden." SBS,* 100 (1981), 11-73; *idem,* "Die Ursünden in der priesterlichen Geschichtserzählung," *Die Zeit Jesu. Festschrift H. Schlier* (Freiburg im Breisgau, 1970), 38-57; S. Lyonnet, "Le sens de peirazein en Sap 2, 24 et la doctrine du péché originel," *Bibl,* 39 (1958), 27-36; I. V. Oikonomos, Πειρασμοὶ ν τῇ Παλαιᾷ Διαθήκη (Athens, 1965); L. Ruppert, "Das Motiv der Versuchung durch Gott in vordeuteronomischer Tradition," *VT,* 22 (1972), 55-63; A. Sommer, *Der Begriff der Versuchung im AT und im Judentum* (Breslau, 1935); H. Seesemann, *TDNT,* VI, 24-27; W. Popkes, *EDNT,* III, 64-67.

1. *UT,* no. 1661; *KTU,* 1.4, III, 5; 1.9, 14.

2. A. van Selms, *UF,* 2 (1970), 264; it occurs in *KTU,* 1.2, IV, 4.

3. See W. J. Gerber, *Die hebräischen Verba denominativa* (1896). For the Akkadian definitions see *AHw,* II, 762f.; *CAD,* XI/2, 107.

4. O. Eissfeldt, *KlSchr,* III, 356-58.

5. *KAI,* 193.

the process of smelting used to test the quality of precious metals. These verbs share a teleological aspect with *nissâ:* something hitherto hidden is to be revealed and known.

II. Secular Usage.

1. *Testing Others.* People test others by asking riddles (1 K. 10:1 par. 2 Ch. 9:1), by affliction (Wis. 2:17; 4 Mc. 9:7), by friendly, ingratiating words (Sir. 13:11), and by reflection (Sir. 25:5,7; cf. 6:7: *peirasmós*). Skepticism is the motive for testing (1 K. 10:7), knowledge its goal (10:6f.). With her questions, the queen of Sheba seeks to test and know Solomon's wisdom and perhaps also to find out whether he is her equal.[6] When the wicked put the righteous man to the test by torture and condemnation to a shameful death (Wis. 2:19f.), they want to learn about his forbearance. They also want to find out whether the righteous man is, as he claims (v. 17), really God's son and enjoys divine protection (vv. 17f.).

These texts and themes show that talk of people testing others is rooted in the wisdom tradition, with its riddles, its ruminations, and its interest in the righteous and the wicked. Here a characteristic feature of *nissâ,* notable above all in its theological usage, is already suggested: it serves both an "etiological" and a "teleological" function. The question why Solomon is considered wise is answered in 1 K. 10:1-7; the question why the righteous person suffers is answered in Wis. 2:17-21. The goal of testing is an understanding of what a person can do, what one really has in oneself, and who one is.

2. *Testing Oneself.* The object of the testing that the Preacher essays (Eccl. 2:1) and that Jesus Sirach recommends (Sir. 37:27) is the heart. After two failures (Eccl. 1:14,17), the Preacher undertakes a further test: he will test his heart[7] with pleasure, i.e., he will acquaint it with pleasure to find out whether that brings enduring happiness. The result: "This also is vanity" (2:1). This testing involves not reflection but experience. Similarly in Sir. 37:27: one should test one's heart not in one's thoughts but in one's way of life to find out what is bad for one (or for one's heart), what one should avoid. Here, too, we note the wisdom setting, more specifically practical wisdom. Testing brings understanding that is necessary for knowing how to live.

3. *Testing Objects.* When someone tests something, it is to make sure of it, to become thoroughly familiar with it, because it is important for one's life.

In the setting of a miracle story (Jgs. 6:36-40), which "sees God at work in miracles, not in the normal course of events,"[8] we are told of Gideon's desire to "make trial with the fleece" (v. 39) to see whether the miracle (vv. 36-38) will be repeated. Although *nissâ* is not a theological term here,[9] in the background there is a testing of God on the part of Gideon, motivated by skepticism.

---

6. E. Würthwein, *1. Könige 1–16. ATD,* 11/1 (1977), 120f.

7. W. Zimmerli, *Prediger. ATD,* 16 (^{3}1980), 152.

8. W. Richter, *Traditionsgeschichtliche Untersuchungen zum Richterbuch. BBB,* 18 (^{2}1966), 213.

9. *Ibid.,* 216.

Whoever wants to wear armor must have tested it and be comfortable in it. The young David cannot move in Saul's armor because he lacks the requisite experience (1 S. 17:39). Whether this text allows us to understand *nissâ* as a technical military term is dubious.[10]

The Preacher's attempts to find enduring happiness remained unsuccessful. He also tried wisdom, his quest being "an experiment with wisdom,"[11] but it remained far from him (Eccl. 7:23f.).

One who is wise "travels in foreign lands, testing what is good and evil in the human lot" (Sir. 39:4). "Discernment of spirits" serves not just the end of theoretical knowledge; its goal is to seek God (v. 5). Those who belong to the devil's company must "explore" death, must experience it, must become thoroughly acquainted with it (Wis. 2:24).

The purpose of such testing is to gain experience in order to foster "assurance of a new call"[12] (Jgs. 6:39), fighting ability (1 S. 17:39), the search for enduring happiness (Eccl. 7:23), and the search for God (Sir. 39:4f.). In these texts the teleological nature of *nissâ* is primarily visible; Wis. 2:4 exhibits more its etiological character.

4. *Intransitive Use.* In Dt. 28:56; Job 4:2, *nissâ* is used intransitively, as is *peirázein* in 2 Mc. 11:19; 3 Mc. 1:25; 2:32; 4 Mc. 12:3 (*peirasmós* in 4 Mc. 8:1). The meaning is "try or undertake something," as an expression of intent (2 Mc. 11:19), a warning (3 Mc. 1:25), or an enticement (4 Mc. 8:1; 12:3). In Dt. 28:56 transitive use is not out of the question: the spoiled woman has not tested her foot, i.e., she has not accustomed it to step on the bare earth. The same may also be true for Job 4:2, especially since the expected infinitive is absent; possibly *nissâ* is used here (uniquely) with *'el* (or conj. *'eṯ*): the word puts Job to the test, it challenges him.

5. *Lexical Field.* People test others in order to "see" (*rā'â:* for 1 K. 10:1, cf. vv. 4,7; cf. Wis. 2:17) or "find out" (*gignōskein:* for Wis. 2:17, cf. v. 19) whether what has been said about them by others or by themselves is "true" (for 1 K. 10:1, cf. v. 6: *'ᵉmeṯ;* Wis. 2:17: *alēthḗs*). At issue, therefore, is demonstration of a truth that can be "seen," in contrast to a truth that is "believed" (for 1 K. 10:1, cf. v. 7; Sir. 6:7). Synonyms like *dokimázein,* "inspect, examine" (Wis. 2:19; Sir. 27:5), and *exetázein,* "examine, explore" (Sir. 13:11),[13] and testing by *(dia)logismós,* "conversation, deliberation" (Sir. 27:5,7), characterize the testing of others as a process, motivated by skepticism and accompanied by a demand for clarity, which aims at tangible proof of a truth.

When the Preacher "tests" or acquaints his heart with pleasure, the purpose is to "see" whether that is good (*rā'â:* Eccl. 2:1). This verse draws on the previous un-

---

10. *TLOT,* II, 742; contra Eissfeldt, *KlSchr,* III, 356-58.
11. *ATD,* 16^3, 207.
12. H. W. Herztberg, *Richter. ATD,* 9 (^{4}1959), 194.
13. Korn, 10-13, n. 6.

successful experiments (1:13-15,17; v. 13: *tûr,* "search out"; *dāraš,* "seek"; v. 17: *yāḏaʿ,* "know") and the test that follows (2:3: *tûr*). Here, too, the goal is "visible" demonstration. The widely accepted trust in wisdom, pleasure, and enjoyment of life is "checked out," made subject to scrutiny.

One who is wise tests what is good and evil in the human lot (Sir. 39:4), "exploring" (*dianoeísthai:* 38:34; 39:7) and "seeking out" (*ekzēteín:* 39:1,3) the answer. One is not content with mere observation of the surrounding world; one is concerned with its basic foundations, that one may devote one's heart to the eager search after God (39:5).

III. Theological Usage.

1. *Testing God.* a. *Survey.* Texts: Ex. 17:2,7; Nu. 14:22; Dt. 6:16; Ps. 78:18,41,56; 95:9; 106:14; Isa. 7:12; Wis. 1:2; Sir. 18:23; Jth. 8:12. The distribution reveals a concentration in the Psalms: cautionary and hortatory reminiscences of Israel's history, almost exclusively (except for Ps. 78:56) involving the generation of the exodus. The Psalms interpret Israel's demand for food and water in the wilderness as defiance of God (Ps. 78:18; 95:9; 106:14). For the most part, these texts are based on the tradition preserved in Ex. 17:2,7 (J); this holds true also for Dt. 6:16. Ps. 78:18 and 106:14 recall Ex. 16 (manna) and Nu. 11 (quails), interpreting the demand for bread and meat as a testing of God on the part of the exodus generation. Ps. 78:56 looks at the continuation of this calamitous "testing" in the promised land (cf. also Dt. 6:16; Isa. 7:12; Wis. 1:2; Sir. 18:23).

The association of Israel's testing of God with the story of the spies (Nu. 14:22) is unique. In contrast to the texts just discussed, the relevant texts in Wisdom (1:2), Sirach (18:23), and Judith (8:12) do not exhibit any association with earlier traditions.

b. *The Exodus Generation.* It is J who first mentions the Israelites' putting Yahweh to the test. Thirst moves them to ask, "Is Yahweh among us or not?" (Ex. 17:7). The answer will depend on whether Yahweh provides water (cf. v. 2). The Israelites' dispute with Moses (vv. 2,7) becomes a test of Yahweh's power and care, which test presupposes a lack of trust in Yahweh. To put God to the test means "to call into question the reality of God's power. . . . Mortals venture in their thinking to treat God like one of themselves. . . . 'Tempting' God means nothing less than seeking to test and judge God by human standards."[14]

Here J is not interested primarily in the etiology of a toponym but in the people's lack of faith, which Yahweh overcomes. In the realization of God's salvific will despite human sin, we see a characteristic feature of J. Against the background of wisdom, J seeks to call for trust in Yahweh alone. A limit is set to the arrogant and impatient desire of the sages to know everything as precisely as possible (cf. v. 7). Going beyond the geographical etiology, J provides here a theological etiology and answers the question why Israel sinned and how Yahweh nevertheless does not abandon his salvific will ("on the one hand, a demonstration of God's power, on the other, a testimony to the people's lack of faith"[15]).

---

14. Korn, 34.
15. Korn, 76.

Nu. 14:22 (with its context; Deuteronomistic?) answers the question why Israel spent long years in the wilderness and why the Calebites in particular came into possession of the Hebron region.[16] This etiology is clearly theological and parenetic in nature, as, e.g., the condemnatory synonyms show (vv. 9,11,22,27,34f.). This testing of Yahweh as an expression of deficient trust in and disrespect for Yahweh forgets Yahweh's acts in Egypt and in the wilderness (v. 22; cf. v. 11).

Dt. 6:16 recalls Ex. 17. In a legal parenesis (vv. 10-18) in the form of a commentary on the beginning of the Decalog,[17] the Israelites dwelling in the land are admonished not to put Yahweh to the test, as at Massah (v. 16). This admonition is possibly intended to "particularize and deepen"[18] the call to obedience issued in general terms by the context. Since references to historical events are not exactly rare in Deuteronomy (here v. 12 also), the reference in v. 16 need not be a secondary addition.[19] The focus is not, however, on the historical reference, but on the admonition: to forget Yahweh in a time of prosperity (v. 12), to fail to fear and serve him (v. 13), to follow other gods (v. 14), and to disregard Yahweh's commandments (v. 17) and not do what is good in Yahweh's eyes (v. 18) are to put his forbearance to the test, to test whether Yahweh will actually react — e.g., in anger (cf. v. 15). In the last analysis, it is Yahweh's trustworthiness that is put to the test; this comes close to "defying God."[20]

In the setting of a "prophetic" admonitory discourse (vv. 7b-11), Ps. 95:9 also recalls the sin of Israel's ancestors at Meribah and Massah and warns against repeating the mistake. The enormity of this sin is particularly clear in light of God's work on Israel's behalf (v. 9c). Whoever puts Yahweh to the test expresses (groundless) mistrust, demonstrating ignorance of Yahweh's ways in law and history (v. 10). The root of this sin lies deep in the human heart, which is hardened toward God (v. 8) and leads people astray (v. 10). The consequence is stated in v. 11: Yahweh's anger denies the sinners entry into the land of Yahweh's rest.

Ps. 78:18 and 106:14 see the demand for food as a testing of God on the part of the exodus generation. Ps. 78 is more than a "recapitulation of history":[21] after the manner of wisdom and Deuteronomistic historiography, it seeks to expose "the mysteries (riddles) of ancient times" (v. 2). The intent is didactic and parenetic (vv. 7f.). The focus is on gaining insight into the complexities of history and demonstrating the conclusions to be drawn from history. This is the context in which we are to understand the references to the exodus generation, which put God to the test (vv. 18,41,56). Their demand for food (vv. 18ff.; summarily in v. 41) and refusal to obey his decrees in the land (v. 56) are the "facts"; elucidation of the "mysteries (riddles)" reveals their significance: Israel thus put their God to the test.

Ps. 78 is a key text for the OT understanding of how Israel put God to the test, since

16. M. Noth, *Numbers. OTL* (Eng. trans. 1968), 109.
17. G. Seitz, *Redaktionsgeschichtliche Studien zum Deuteronomium. BWANT,* 93 (1971), 73.
18. G. von Rad, *Deuteronomy. OTL* (Eng. trans. 1966), 64.
19. *Ibid.*
20. Von Rad, *Deuteronomy,* 64; S. R. Driver, *Deuteronomy. ICC* (^{3}1895), 95.
21. A. Weiser, *Psalms. OTL* (Eng. trans. 1962), 538.

it explores the root, the expression, and the consequences of this testing. Those who put God to the test are forgetful: they do not remember God's powerful, redeeming hand (v. 42; cf. vv. 12-16,55). Those who forget cease to trust (v. 22) and pray; instead they demand (v. 18) and doubt (vv. 19f.). They slight God's decrees (v. 56) by worshiping other gods (v. 58). The consequences: God's anger (vv. 21,49,50,59), followed nevertheless by his actions on behalf of Israel (vv. 23ff.,51ff.,65ff.). Here above all the "mysteries (riddles) of ancient times" (v. 2) are laid bare: Yahweh's beneficence is mightier than Israel's sin.

In Ps. 106:14, too, forgetting (v. 13a) leads the exodus generation to put God to the test: Israel behaves as though it had never experienced God's saving acts. Another root of this sin is human impatience, which does not trust the divine plan of salvation and refuses to wait for its realization (v. 13b). Israel's ancestors in the wilderness replace memory and patience with a demand for food (v. 14a), thus putting Yahweh to the test (v. 14b). In this way they abandon belief in God's word (cf. v. 12).

c. *In the Promised Land.* When Israel had settled in the promised land, they continued to test God. As in the time of the exodus generation, this testing involved slighting God and God's word (for Dt. 6:16, cf. vv. 17ff.), including the demand for exclusive worship: by worshiping other gods, Israel put their God to the test (for Dt. 6:16, cf. v. 14; for Ps. 78:56, cf. v. 58). To put God to the test is to distrust God (Wis. 1:2) and to challenge his power (for Wis. 1:2, cf. v. 3).

The elders of Bethulia likewise went astray when they were in distress and challenged God's power, his readiness to act, with their demand for judgment, thus putting God to the test (Jth. 8:12). Here putting God to the test means wanting to bind God (v. 11), to plumb the mysteries of the almighty Lord (v. 13), to search out and comprehend God (v. 14), and thus put oneself in place of God (v. 12). To do so betrays a deficient understanding of God's nature (v. 13) and purposes (v. 14).

Even a "pious act" like a vow can be a testing and challenging of God on the part of a human being (Sir. 18:23), especially when it loses the character of an intensified prayer and becomes instead the vehicle of a mercantile *do ut des.* Above all, a vow that is not performed is a testing and challenging of God (for v. 23, cf. v. 22). Since those who make such vows are not thinking of "the day of wrath and the end of days" and "the moment of vengeance" (v. 24), they challenge God and question God's effectiveness.

Probably echoing Ex. 17 (cf. Dt. 6:16), Ahaz refuses to ask for any sign and thus put Yahweh to the test (Isa. 7:12) — apart from the context, theologically correct conduct. Here, however, the point is not a demand for a sign but Ahaz's reaction to the offer of a sign. Vv. 13ff. make clear that Ahaz's response is a "sign of disbelief."

d. *Lexical Field.* When people put God to the test, they have forgotten God (on Dt. 6:16, cf. v. 12; on Ps. 106:14, cf. v. 13), they no longer remember God's acts of deliverance (on Ps. 78:18,41,56, cf. v. 42; on Ps. 106:14, cf. v. 7), they fail to draw on this memory for its present relevance. Those who put Yahweh to the test refuse to trust him (on Ps. 78:18,41,56, cf. vv. 22,32,37) and will not wait for his counsel (on Ps. 106:14, cf. v. 13); with their impatient demands (Ps. 78:18) and cravings (106:14) they seek to force Yahweh to act (on Jth. 8:12, cf. v. 16). But this conduct is sinful (on Ps.

78:18,41,56, cf. vv. 17,32; on Ps. 106:14, cf. v. 6; on Wis. 1:2, cf. v. 4) and an expression of rebelliousness (on Ps. 78:18,41,56, cf. vv. 17,40,56; on Ps. 106:14, cf. v. 7), "a fundamental, evil opposition to everything revealed by Yahweh."[22] Those who put Yahweh to the test harden their hearts (on Ps. 95:9, cf. v. 8); their hearts go astray (on Ps. 95:9, cf. v. 10), they pursue foolish and perverted thoughts (on Wis. 1:2, cf. vv. 3-5). Hubris and lack of trust lurk in the background when people put God to the test and thus set themselves up in the place of God (Jth. 8:12), when they try to force God's decisions, threaten and seek to influence God (on Jth. 8:12, cf. v. 16). Thus they provoke God's jealousy (Ps. 78:18,41,56, cf. v. 58) and anger (on Jth. 8:12, cf. v. 14).

2. *Testing by God.* a. *Survey.* Texts: Gen. 22:1; Ex. 15:25; 16:4; 20:20; Dt. 4:34; 8:2,16; 13:4(Eng. v. 3); 33:8; Jgs. 2:22; 3:1,4; 2 Ch. 32:21; Ps. 26:2; Jth. 8:25,26; 1 Mc. 2:52; Wis. 3:5; 11:9; Sir. 2:1; 4:17; 33:1; 44:20. A survey of the texts that speak of God's testing people reveals concentrations in Deuteronomy and the Deuteronomistic history, as well as deuterocanonical or apocryphal Wisdom Literature. Afflictions such as those besetting Israel in the wilderness (esp. Deuteronomy and the Deuteronomistic history, together with the earlier texts Ex. 15:25; 16:4; 20:20) and the righteous (Wisdom and Sirach) are examined to determine the reason for them; they are understood as tests imposed by God and presented as being meaningful in light of their purpose. Behind this interpretation stands the question of the cause and purpose of such afflictions — a question certainly rooted in contemporary history. Deuteronomy and the Deuteronomistic history as well as the wisdom tradition clearly feel compelled to provide meaningful answers in times of national distress and religious conflict: the Deuteronomists in light of the national catastrophes inflicted on the northern (722 B.C.) and southern kingdoms (587/586 B.C.), the wisdom tradition in confrontation with the question of why the righteous suffer.

The groundwork is laid for the answers by the earlier traditions discussed above and Gen. 22 (note v. 1), which describe, respectively, the testing of Israel in the wilderness and the testing of Abraham. Here it is already made clear that the afflictions of Abraham and Israel are not blind chance but have meaning and purpose, because they proceed from Yahweh. The story of the testing of (righteous: 15:6) Abraham (22:1ff.) prepares for wisdom's answer to the question of why the righteous suffer, and the theme of testing by the law (Ex. 15:25; 16:4) is sounded by Dt. 8:2,16; 13:4(3) and probably also by Sir. 4:17 (and their contexts). Later the notion of discipline associated with testing (on Dt. 8:2,16, cf. v. 5) is taken up by wisdom (Wis. 11:9f.), as is the interpretation of testing as God's "humbling" of human beings (Dt. 8:2,16; on Sir. 2:1, cf. vv. 4b,5).

b. *The Testing of Abraham.* One of the purposes of E is to present the patriarchs as models. This purpose is reflected in Gen. 22:1-14a,19,[23] where God puts Abraham's fear of God to the test. Here E pursues "a paradigmatic and at the same time didactic

22. *TLOT,* II, 688.
23. Kilian, *Isaaks Opferung,* 21ff.

goal. With the help of the exalted figure of Abraham, he seeks to show how someone who fears and obeys God should relate to God."[24] This takes place in a "theological amplification and reinterpretation" of the tradition drawn on by E, which explained the establishment of a pilgrimage and cult.[25] A possible source of E's temptation narrative may lie in the cultic realm, in a ritual of divine judgment. The cultic traditions drawn on by E may have included this ritual, so that E could borrow it to describe — in an episode of "narrative theology"[26] — Abraham's fear of God, proved in his acknowledgment that Isaac, the son of promise, did not ultimately belong to him. For E, of course, this hypothetical cultic tradition recedes into the background. The point now is to apply "the idea of temptation or testing to the paradoxes of God's historical leading."[27] These "paradoxes" include God's casting doubt on fulfilled promises.

We can trace a kind of history of the influence exerted by the story of the testing of Abraham in Sir. 44:20; 1 Mc. 2:52; Jth. 8:25-27. In Sir. 44:20 the testing of Abraham serves to demonstrate the patriarch's faithfulness. A not insignificant result is that his offspring were numerous and became a blessing for the nations (v. 21). In Jth. 8:25-27 the threat to Bethulia is understood as a divine test and likened to the testing of the patriarchs. What is new here is God's testing of Isaac and Jacob: perhaps the tradition in Gen. 22 is understood as a testing of Isaac also;[28] Gen. 29:18-30; 31:7ff. may be behind the testing of Jacob in the Laban episode. What the patriarchs experienced and what now afflicts the inhabitants of Bethulia is not an accident; it comes from God, who has a purpose: to test their hearts and to lead them to wisdom (v. 27). Divine testing is a purification as by fire; it reflects the nature of God, who chastens those who are his friends (v. 27). Remembrance of these models from past history is designed to encourage imitation, zeal for the law, and faithfulness to the covenant (1 Mc. 2:50-64). The testing of Abraham is "connected as closely as possible with the covenant of grace with which God has blessed the people of Israel," and thus appears as "the first element in a list of acts of grace through which the covenant has been constantly renewed."[29]

c. *The Testing of Israel in the Wilderness.* In the wilderness, Israel was tested by privation (Dt. 8:2,16, and context; on Ex. 15:25, cf. v. 23; Dt. 33:8), by terrifying signs (Ex. 20:20; cf. Dt. 4:34), and by God's law (Ex. 15:25; 16:4). The gift and occupation of the land also depend on observing the law (Dt. 8:1), which serves to recall the wilderness period (vv. 2-5,16). During this period, God led, humbled, tested (vv. 2,16), and disciplined (v. 5) Israel. Here the testing is depicted as a means of discipline. Yahweh puts his people to the test to find out whether Israel will obey or disobey (v. 2) and to bring Israel to knowledge of divine discipline (v. 5). The text is legal parenesis, but it also has etiological and teleological aims: the question of why Israel suffered

---

24. *Ibid.*, 51.
25. Kilian, *Abrahamsüberlieferungen,* 274.
26. C. Westermann, *The Promises to the Fathers* (Eng. trans., Philadelphia, 1980), 72.
27. G. von Rad, *Genesis. OTL* (Eng. trans. ^{2}1972), 239f.
28. Korn, 50f.
29. Sommer, 14, citing also Sir. 44:20.

privation in the wilderness is answered by reference to God's testing, the objective of which is divine and human knowledge. The alleviation of the people's privation by the gift of manna likewise serves to humble and test Israel (v. 16); it is meant to elucidate the question of whether Israel will trust in God and recognize human dependence on God, thereby preventing arrogance (see v. 14).

Levi is also tested by affliction (Dt. 33:8), whether the background is Ex. 17:1-7, Nu. 20:2-13, or Ex. 32:26-29. The localization of the testing at Massah recalls Ex. 17:1-7 (cf. Nu. 20:2-13), even though there Israel tested Yahweh (v. 7) and quarreled with Moses (Nu. 20:3). Dt. 33:9 suggests an association with Ex. 32:26-29: with the command in vv. 26f., Yahweh (implicitly) used Moses to put the Levites to a very severe test, and they demonstrated that they were priests "who had determined to renounce all ties and devote themselves entirely to God."[30]

Ex. 20:18-21 (E) answers the question why terrifying phenomena accompany God's appearance: "to test you" (v. 20) — in other words, an etiology that also names the purpose: "to put the fear of him upon you so that you do not sin" (v. 20). Ex. 20:20 shares with Dt. 4:10 "the purpose of the theophany — to give Israel a direct, palpable experience of God."[31] The people assembled at Sinai passed the test: they "have shown the right 'fear' of God and have not attempted to go too near the theophany."[32]

The text therefore also answers the question why "the voice of God himself was no longer heard by the cultic community at the cultic recapitulation of the Sinai-theophany and why the mediating word of a man issued forth instead."[33] To the etiology mentioned above there is added "the aetiology of the office of a cultic spokesman,"[34] who appears, e.g., on the great Day of Atonement. The clouds and the sound of the ram's horn accompanying the theophany point in this direction.[35] The "fear of him so that you do not sin" mentioned in Ex. 20:20 may also suggest a connection with the great Day of Atonement. Such a connection would support the localization of the notion of testing by God in the cult that Gerhard von Rad proposed.[36]

In Dt. 4:34 it is generally accepted that *nissâ* is used in the sense of "make an attempt," a meaning that is rare in the context of testing by God. One can hardly deny that the text is overburdened (cf. *lāḇô' lāqaḥaṯ lô*). If we bracket *lāḇô' lāqaḥaṯ lô gôy miqqereḇ, gôy* appears as the object of *nissâ* and the original text reads: *'ô hᵃnissâ 'ᵉlōhîm bᵉmassôṯ bᵉ'ōṯôṯ gôy.* The nation put to the test by God is Egypt. It is possible that *lāḇô' lāqaḥaṯ lô gôy* has been misplaced and originally concluded v. 34. God put the Egyptian people to the test — most likely a reference to the plagues. The obedience of the Egyptians is put to the test; the purpose of this testing is stated in Ex. 7:5 and

30. Lehming, 76.
31. M. Greenberg, *JBL,* 79 (1960), 275.
32. M. Noth, *Exodus. OTL* (Eng. trans. 1962), 168.
33. W. Beyerlin, *Origins and History of the Oldest Sinaitic Traditions* (Eng. trans., Oxford, 1965), 139.
34. *Ibid.*
35. *Ibid.,* 134-36.
36. See the discussion of Gen. 22 above.

elsewhere. This purpose conflicts to some extent with the intention stated in Dt. 4:35: *Israel* is to acknowledge the uniqueness of Yahweh. That Yahweh should want to bring another nation than Israel to such "knowledge" appears to have been an alien or even offensive notion to the redactor responsible for Dt. 4:34f., who therefore added or shifted the words *lāḇô' lāqaḥaṯ lô gôy*.

Israel is put to the test by the divine commandments (Ex. 15:25); the people's response to the law is decisive for their trust, obedience, and salvation (cf. v. 26). It is not impossible that the idea of being tested by God was originally connected with the "bitter waters" (Marah, v. 23). If so, a later hand (Deuteronomistic?[37]) borrowed the Marah tradition and gave it topicality by associating testing by God with the law.

The portion of Ex. 16 that can probably be assigned to J, in the first instance vv. 1-5,[38] describes the murmuring of the people in the wilderness of Sin (vv. 2f.) and God's promise of manna (v. 4a). By demanding that the people gather only enough for their daily needs (v. 4b), Yahweh tests the people to see "whether they will follow my instruction or not" (v. 4c), whether they will trust Yahweh. V. 5 leads to the association of the gift of manna with the Sabbath (vv. 23-26,27-30) and thus sets the testing of the people's faith (v. 4) in a larger context: compulsory rest on the Sabbath is a kind of test of faith.

d. *The Testing of Israel in the Promised Land.* Once the people are settled in the promised land, Yahweh tests them with false prophets (Dt. 13:4[3]), with the other nations remaining in the land (Jgs. 2:22; 3:1,4), probably by refusing a miraculous sign (2 Ch. 32:31) and by political and military threats (Jth. 8:25f.; 1 Mc. 2:52). Here, too, the notion of testing by God answers the question of the reason and purpose behind the multitudinous afflictions of Israel. The psalmist's prayer to be tested in Ps. 26:2 should probably also be localized in the promised land. In most cases the purpose of God's testing is the familiar one: demonstration and acknowledgment of Israel's faithfulness and love toward their God (Dt. 13:4[3]; Jgs. 2:22; 3:4; 2 Ch. 32:31; on Ps. 26:2, cf. vv. 1,3-5,11f.; on Jth. 8:25f., cf. v. 27).

Dt. 13:4b(3b) (with vv. 5,6b[4,5b], formulated in the pl., possibly an expansion of the unit in vv. 1-4a,6a,6c[12:32;13:1-3a,5a,5c], formulated in the sg.[39]) states the reason why false prophets and diviners can appear in Israel and, by means of wonders, incite the people to follow other gods. The explanation that God is "testing" Israel is an "etiology," and the purpose of this testing is stated: "to know whether you love Yahweh" (v. 4[3]).

There are varying explanations of the motive and purpose behind God's using the nations remaining in the land to test Israel. In the context of Jgs. 2:11ff. and congruently with the Deuteronomist's objective of describing Israel's apostasy from Yahweh in Judges, Jgs. 2:22 cites Yahweh's anger over Israel's faithlessness (v. 20). Jgs. 2:22 and 3:4 identify the purpose of this testing as Yahweh's determination of Israel's obedience or disobedience; 3:1 cites the "military training of the second generation."[40]

---

37. Noth, *Exodus,* 127-29.
38. W. H. Schmidt, *Exodus, Sinai und Mose. EdF,* 191 (1983), 97: vv. 4f.
39. H. D. Preuss, *Deuteronomium. EdF,* 164 (1982), 113f.
40. Hertzberg, *Richter. ATD,* 9, 161.

The nature of God's testing of Hezekiah in 2 Ch. 32:31 is comprehensible only against the background of 2 K. 20:1-11,12-19. Yahweh leaves Hezekiah (v. 31), possibly without a miraculous sign — in contrast to what he did previously (2 K. 20:8-11; 2 Ch. 32:24,31). In this situation Yahweh leaves the king to himself, for any testing or temptation is a situation "where God leaves an individual to himself, to decide freely for or against God."[41]

In an individual lament or psalm of innocence, the psalmist prays that God will test him to demonstrate his innocence (Ps. 26:2). This text may reflect a liturgical testing ritual at the sanctuary (cf. 1 K. 8:31ff.).[42]

e. *The Testing of the Righteous.* The sages give their answer to the question of the reason and purpose of the suffering of the righteous, not least because of the action-issue nexus. They find the reason in God himself: he tests the righteous through suffering. He also determines the purpose: demonstration that the righteous are deserving and devout (Wis. 3:5; 11:9f.; Sir. 2:1; 4:17; 33:1).

The book of Wisdom views God's testing of the righteous as a means of divine discipline (Wis. 3:5; 11:9). The testing is "in the form of a transitory affliction, which is trifling in comparison to the eternal blessedness of the souls when they are 'in the hand of God.' "[43] Suffering therefore has two aspects: it disciplines the righteous and punishes the wicked.[44]

Sir. 2:1-18 (esp. vv. 1-5) answers in the form of a wisdom exhortation the question why the righteous must suffer. The sufferings of a righteous person are a divine test (v. 1), a calamity sent by God (v. 2; cf. v. 4a), a humiliation (vv. 4b,5). The righteous person is tested like gold; only in suffering is devotion proved genuine (v. 5). The righteous person must suffer, but "can sense God's gracious hand in this suffering." Since it is not a punishment for sin, it is not "authentic suffering." The testing of the righteous is instead "transitory in nature" and includes "the assurance . . . that God is graciously inclined toward the sufferer."[45] Thus the testing becomes a mark of the faithful, not of unbelievers.[46]

Wisdom tests her "children" through her laws, brings fear and dread on them, and subjects them to her training and discipline until they know her in their hearts (Sir. 4:17). Only then does Wisdom turn to them and reveal her secrets (v. 18).

The righteous are not spared testing, but will be delivered from it (Sir. 33:1). In contrast, sinners shun reproof (32:17) and fear (32:18).

f. *Lexical Field.* When God puts people to the test, this takes place through "humiliation" (Dt. 8:2f.: *ʿānâ*) in affliction and has "knowledge" *(yāḏaʿ)* as its objective: Yahweh will know that Israel is obedient to his commandments (v. 2), and

---

41. W. Rudolph, *Die Chronikbücher. HAT,* XXI (1955), 315; on being forsaken by God as a component of temptation, see Korn, 67.

42. H.-J. Kraus, *Psalms 1–59* (Eng. trans., Minneapolis, 1988), 325f., 326f.

43. Sommer, 17.

44. Cf. Oikonomos, 88.

45. Sommer, 16f.

46. Oikonomos, 89.

Israel is to know that they are dependent on Yahweh's words (v. 3) and discipline (v. 5).

Wisdom and Sirach understand God's testing of human beings as a means of divine discipline (Wis. 3:5; 11:9; Sir. 4:17: *paideúein/paidía*).

IV. *massôṯ*. In the context of the deliverance from Egypt, *massôṯ* is associated primarily with "signs," "wonders," and Yahweh's "mighty hand" and "outstretched arm." The signs and wonders are "tests" insofar as they focus on the reaction of those affected. Such phenomena are simply "earnest money": the question remains whether the people involved will draw the proper conclusions, whether they will acknowledge the God who works the wonders. This association accords with the use of *massôṯ* in legal parenesis (on Dt. 4:34, cf. vv. 39f.; on 7:19, cf. vv. 17f.,25f.; on 29:2[3], cf. v. 8[9]). The purpose of the *massôṯ* finds its clearest expression in Dt. 29:3(4): from them, Israel should gain an understanding heart (NRSV: "mind"), seeing eyes, and hearing ears. The signs and wonders are also "tests" in that they test Israel's trust in Yahweh.

The deuterocanonical books (Apocrypha) use *peíra* and *peirasmós* for God's testing of human beings (Sir. 2:1; 44:20; 1 Mc. 2:52), the testing of human beings by others (Sir. 6:7; 25:5,7), and being tested (experienced) in battle (2 Mc. 8:9). Wis. 18:20,25 recall the testing of the exodus generation; death and God's wrath, which also touch the righteous, are "a trial of death" and "a trial of wrath."

V. *massâ*. The first mention of the place called Massah is in Ex. 17:7 (D[47]): the place where Moses struck the rock and produced water he named Massah and Meribah. The double name of the spring "is hardly original."[48] A later tradition in Nu. 13 (P) mentions only Meribah in this context, and appears to locate it at Kadesh (cf. v. 1; Ps. 106:32); the same location probably holds true for Massah as well.[49] For this reason, and because Ex. 17:2,7, and Nu. 20:13 focus on the quarrel *(rîḇ)* of the people with Moses and Yahweh, "Meribah" may be the original name of the spring.[50] The other texts mentioning Massah (Dt. 6:16; 9:22; Ps. 95:8) do not offer any clues as to its location. Neither do we receive any help from the position of Massah between Taberah and Kibroth-hattaavah (Dt. 9:22), which cannot support the theory that a Massah narrative at one time stood between Nu. 11:3 and 11:35.[51]

If *massâ* in Dt. 33:8 is not to be translated "temptation"[52] (that it should not is argued by the unusual phrase *nissâ bᵉmassâ*), then this text locates a testing of Levi by God at Massah. S. R. Driver suggests the possibility "that another version of the incidents of Massah and Meribah was current, in which the fidelity of the tribe was in

47. E. Zenger, *Israel am Sinai* (Altenberge, 1982), 62.
48. Noth, *Exodus,* 139.
49. G. Morawe, *BHHW,* II, 1159.
50. Noth, *Exodus,* 139; S. Lehming, "Massa und Meriba," *ZAW,* 73 (1961), 71.
51. Lehming, 73.
52. Contra *ibid.,* 76f.

some manner tested directly by Jehovah."[53] This "other version" most likely appears in Ex. 32:26-29 (see the discussion of Dt. 33:8 above), which has nothing to do with what happened "at the waters of Meribah." Massah preserves the memory of a testing of Levi by Yahweh (Dt. 33:8), while Meribah recalls a quarrel of Israel with Moses and Yahweh (Ex. 17:2,7; Nu. 20:13).

VI. Dead Sea Scrolls. The verb *nsh* appears 5 times in the Dead Sea Scrolls, 3 times as the qal ptcp. *nswy,* "tested one," used by the faithful to describe themselves (1QS 1:18; 4QDibHam[a] [4Q504] 5:18; 6:7). The Teacher of Righteousness is obligated to examine *(bḥn)* the "men of truth" and put them to the test (1QH 2:14; cf. also 11QTemple 54:12 = Dt. 13:4[3]). In 1QH 2:14, among other things, the question of the reason and purpose of the sufferings of the righteous is answered. It was God who made the psalmist a disgrace (v. 9), pursuing a particular objective: God made him a sign *(nēs)* for the righteous elect and an interpreter of knowledge in wonderful mysteries (v. 13). By means of this "sign," he will examine *(bāḥan)* the "men of truth" and test *(nissâ)* the friends of discipline (vv. 13f.), probably in order to bring them to understand that the sufferings of the righteous are imposed by God for disciplinary purposes. Or perhaps the preaching of the "interpreter of knowledge" is "a decisive test permitting the 'men of truth' to be recognized."[54]

Helfmeyer

53. *Deuteronomy. ICC,* 400.
54. A. Dupont-Sommer, *The Essene Writings from Qumran* (Eng. trans., repr. Gloucester, Mass., 1973), 205, n. 3.

נָסַךְ *nāsak̲;* נֶסֶךְ *nesek̲;* נָסִיךְ *nāsîk̲;* מַסֵּכָה *massēk̲â;* מַסֶּכֶת *massek̲et̲;* סוּךְ II *sûk̲;* אָסוּךְ *'āsûk̲*

Contents: I. Distribution in Semitic. II. OT: 1. Verbal and Nominal Derivatives; 2. LXX. III. Usage: 1. Metalworking; 2. Libation; 3. Anointing; 4. Other. IV. Dead Sea Scrolls.

nāsak̲. F. Blome, *Die Opfermaterie in Babylonien und Israel,* I (Rome, 1934); J. P. Brown, "The Sacrificial Cult and Its Critique in Greek and Hebrew, II," *JSS,* 25 (1980), 1-21; A. Citron, "Semantische Untersuchungen zu σπένδεσθαι, σπένδειν, εὔχεσθαι" (diss., Bern, 1965); C. Dohmen, "Ein kanaanäischer Schmiedeterminus *(nsk),*" *UF,* 15 (1983), 39-42; F. Graf, "Milch, Honig und Wein," *Perennitas. Festschrift A. Brelich* (Rome, 1980), 209-221; E. Kutsch, *Salbung als Rechtsakt im AT und im Alten Orient. BZAW,* 87 (1963); O. Michel, "σπένδομαι," *TDNT,* VII, 528-536; R. Rendtorff, *Studien zur Geschichte des Opfers im AT. WMANT,* 24 (1967).

I. Distribution in Semitic. The root *nsk* is found in both East and West Semitic. Semantically, however, the individual languages use it in very different ways. For example, Akk. *nasāku* and its derivatives represent the semantic field of "throwing" in its broadest sense;[1] but there is no West Semitic usage comparable to that in East Semitic. In West Semitic the root *nsk* possesses a double semantic range: it is used in religious contexts with the meaning "offer, sacrifice," and in secular contexts with such meanings as "pour" or "bring."[2] It is important to note that in Southwest Semitic the occurrences are concentrated primarily in the former area. Arab. *nasaka* and its derivatives denote a wide range of cultic and religious acts and attitudes (*nusuk:* "offering," "offer," "be devout"[3]). In Northwest Semitic, besides being used in the sense of "pour, give (esp. as a libation)," *nsk* is used in the context of metalworking.[4] This usage appears first in Canaanite, from which it entered later branches of Aramaic, e.g., Syriac.[5] In this context *nsk* has the meaning "forge" rather than "pour." This meaning appears clearly in the Ugaritic trade designations *nsk ksp,* "silversmith," *nsk ṯlṯ,* "rough smith," and *nsk ḥḏm,* "tool smith," as well as in the Numidian-Punic bilingual from Dougga, where Pun. *hnskm š brzl* matches Numidian *nbṭn nzl'*.[6] The root appears also in terms for the products of metalworking, such as Heb. → מסכה *massēḵâ* and Pun. *nskh.*[7]

Etymological dependencies between East and West Semitic (or among West Semitic) occurrences of the root *nsk* cannot be determined directly, not least because phonetic homonymy caused by spirantization of the stops makes it difficult to distinguish *nsk* from the semantically similar root *ntk.*[8] It is better to assume a very broad semantic spectrum for *nsk* (like that still found to some extent in Akkadian), which crystallized into distinct ranges of usage in the individual languages. From the perspective of comparative semantics, we may consider a possible relationship between Heb. *nsk* II, "weave," and *nsk,* "forge, hammer," since there is a parallel in Egyptian, where *nbḏ* means both "sheathe" and "interweave."[9]

---

1. *AHw,* II, 752f.; III, 1579; *CAD,* XI/2, 15-20.
2. M. Dietrich and O. Loretz, *UF,* 11 (1979), 195, n. 56.
3. J. Wellhausen, *Reste arabischen Heidentums* (Berlin, ^{2}1927), 114, 118, 142; according to T. Nöldeke, *ZDMG,* 41 (1887), 791, it meant originally "pour."
4. *WUS,* no. 1801; *DISO,* 180; K. Beyer, *Die aramäischen Texte vom Toten Meer* (Göttingen, 1984), 638; *WTM,* III, 406f.; *ANH,* 272; *HAL,* II, 703.
5. *CSD,* 342.
6. For Ugaritic see Dohmen, 41. For the Dougga text see *KAI,* 100, 7; Dohmen, 42.
7. *DISO,* 180.
8. K. Tsereteli, "Zur Frage der Spirantisation der Verschlusslaute in den semitischen Sprachen," *ZDMG,* 130 (1980), 207-216.
9. W. Eilers, *Die vergleichend-semasiologische Methode in der Orientalistik. AAWLM,* 10 (1973). On *nsk* II see *HAL,* II, 703; cf. Arab. *nasağa,* "weave" (Wehr, 961), and its derivatives. On *nsk,* "forge," see Dohmen, 42. On the Egyptian parallel see *WbÄS,* II, 246; I. Grumach-Shirun, *LexÄg,* II, 260f.; R. Drenkhahn, *LexÄg,* V, 664f.; J. J. Janssen, *Commodity Prices from the Ramesside Period* (Leiden, 1975), 136-39.

II. OT.

1. *Verbal and Nominal Derivatives.* In the OT we find several derivatives of *nsk.* As a verb, *nsk* I, "pour," occurs 25 times (7 qal, 1 niphal, 1 piel, 14 hiphil, 2 hophal); the by-form *sûḵ* II, "anoint oneself,"[10] occurs 10 times. The verb *nsk* II, "weave," with the by-form → סכך *sāḵaḵ,*[11] occurs twice. Among the nominal derivatives of *nsk* I are *neseḵ,* "libation," with 60 occurrences; in 4 additional texts, it is synonymous with *massēḵâ.*[12] As a term designating the product of working with precious metals, *massēḵâ* occurs 25 times (2 Ch. 28:2 and Isa. 30:1 are discussed elsewhere[13]). As a derivative of *nsk* II, with the meaning "covering," *massēḵâ* occurs twice.[14] The noun *masseḵeṯ,* "warp-threads," from *nsk* II, occurs twice.[15] The noun *'āsûḵ,* from *sûḵ* II, occurs in 2 K. 4:2.[16]

In the Aramaic sections of the OT, *nsk* appears as a verb in Dnl. 2:46 with the meaning "offer," and as a noun, "drink offering," in Ezr. 7:17.

2. *LXX.* As the semantic range of the Hebrew occurrences would lead us to expect, the LXX uses an extensive palette of equivalents to translate the root. The most common are derivatives of *spéndein, poieín, chōneúein,* and *aleíphein.*[17]

III. Usage.

1. *Metalworking.* Hebrew provides some material reflecting the Canaanite use of the root *nsk* in the context of metalworking,[18] above all the noun → מסכה *massēḵâ.* As its contexts show, it is clearly restricted to designating an article fashioned by a goldsmith. Four postexilic passages (Isa. 41:29; 48:5; Jer. 10:14 par. 51:17) use the noun *neseḵ* with the same meaning; elsewhere it means "libation."[19] As Isa. 30:1 suggests, these texts appear to aim at a characterization of sinfulness established in this context by the mention of libation,[20] so that worship of images and worship of other gods are made parallel. Hebrew has a series of terms describing the various stages involved in metalworking; it is therefore easy to understand why little importance attaches to the general, undifferentiated term *nsk,* "forge" (*yṣq* being reserved for the more specific process of "casting").[21] The expression *nsk pesel,* which occurs only twice (Isa. 40:19; 44:10), has often led scholars to suggest an even more general basic meaning for *nsk,* such as "fashion, form," since the etymologically inherent basic

---

10. *HAL,* II, 704.
11. *HAL,* II, 712.
12. → מסכה *massēḵâ,* I.2 (VIII, 432).
13. → VIII, 435.
14. *HAL,* II, 605.
15. *HAL,* II, 605.
16. *HAL,* I, 71.
17. Michel, 531-33; H. Schlier, "ἀλείφω," *TDNT,* I, 229-232.
18. See I above.
19. See III.2 below.
20. See III.2 below; on Isa. 30:1 → VIII, 435.
21. On *yṣq* → VI, 256; on the stages of metalworking see *BRL*², 221f.

meanings of the two words — "cast" and "carve" — do not seem to correspond.[22] OT usage, however, does not restrict *pesel* to carved images; the word can be used for any kind of cultic image.[23] The expression *nsk pesel* probably has the general meaning "fashion (forge) an image."[24]

2. *Libation.* Throughout the ancient world, libation played an important role in a wide range of sacrificial practices. There was great variety in both the nature of the act (complete or partial emptying of the vessel, with or after other offerings, etc.) and the material offered (primarily water, wine, milk, and honey). Differing concepts of the nature of the offering — alimentation of the gods, tribute, propitiation, etc. — account for much of this variety. It is noteworthy that libation almost never appears as an independent sacrificial act; to the extent that it is not part of a divine meal, it is usually an ancillary or preliminary offering with a specific symbolic function.[25]

Libation plays a special role in both the Egyptian[26] and the Assyro-Babylonian cult. Its importance in the latter is illustrated by the fact that *naqû/nīqu,* the most frequent sacrificial terms,[27] derive etymologically from libation. In the OT, from the lexical field of pouring, nominal and verbal forms of *nsk* are used to denote libation, especially in the *figura etymologica nsk* (hiphil/hophal) *nese̱k.*[28] Only in 1 Ch. 11:18 does the piel appear; the parallel text 2 S. 23:16 uses the hiphil.[29] Rainer Degen suggests that this variation may be due to linguistic change.[30] The qal of *nsk* is used twice to denote libation; Hos. 9:4 may represent a deliberate anomaly, since the parallel sacrificial expression *ʿrb zibḥêhem* is likewise unique. The situation is similar in Ex. 30:9, a late addition to P concerning the incense altar, since the functional relationship of the offerings mentioned remains obscure.[31]

In the OT, libations also appear as ancillary offerings. P usually uses *nese̱k* in combination with → מנחה *minḥâ* as a supplementary offering associated with an → עלה *ʿōlâ.* The textual basis of this collocation is nevertheless narrow: it is concentrated in Nu. 28f. and Lev. 23:13,18,37, which are dependent on Nu. 28f. (cf. Nu. 6:15,17; 15:22f.; Ex. 29:38ff.; Ezk. 45:17).[32] In addition, Deuteronomistic terminology uses *nsk* (hiphil) *neśāḵîm* to characterize syncretism, especially in the Deuteronomistic redaction of Jeremiah (Jer. 7:18; 19:13; 32:29; 44:17-19,25) and Ezk. 20:28.[33] Apart from this

---

22. K. Elliger, *Deuterojesaja. BK,* XI/1 (1978), 74f.
23. → פסל *pesel.*
24. On the use of *nāsîḵ* in Dnl. 11:8 → IV, 1111.
25. Graf, esp. 211, 218f.; on the divine meal see Blome, nos. 280ff.
26. J. F. Borghouts, "Libation," *LexÄg,* III, 1014f.
27. *AHw,* II, 744f., 793; *CAD,* XI/1, 336-341; XI/2, 252-59.
28. → יצק *yāṣaq,* → נתך *nāṯak,* → שׁפך *šāpak;* → VI, 254f.
29. *HP,* 199.
30. R. Degen, *WO,* 6 (1970), 54.
31. Rendtorff, 170. On the late addition to P see M. Noth, *Exodus. OTL* (Eng. trans. 1962), 234f.
32. *Ibid.* The derivation of *yussaḵ* in Ex. 25:29 from *nsk* or *skk* is discussed by M. Haran, *Temples and Temple-Service in Ancient Israel* (Oxford, 1978), 216.
33. For the former see W. Thiel, *Die deuteronomistische Redaktion von Jeremia. WMANT,*

literary complex, the expression appears only twice: in the singular(!) in Gen. 35:14, where the redactor probably added it to mark the beginning of sacrificial worship at the sanctuary; and in the unique instance of Ps. 16:4, which mentions libations of blood.[34] These "offerings of blood" have nothing to do with the Israelite blood ritual, although the latter is sometimes associated mistakenly with libation; the terminology of the blood ritual is entirely different.[35] Instead, the *n^esāk̲îm middām* should be interpreted in parallel with the *minḥâ dam-ḥ^azîr* of Isa. 66:3 as false, illicit offerings.

3. *Anointing.* In the ancient Near East, anointing in the widest variety of forms is attested by both material and literary evidence.[36] In Hebrew the verb *sûk̲* encompasses only the secular realm (e.g., Dt. 28:40; 2 S. 14:2; Mic. 6:15; Ruth 3:3; Dnl. 10:3; 2 Ch. 28:15), not the cultic; the latter makes use primarily of → משח *māšaḥ.*[37] Cosmetic anointing is deeply rooted in the everyday life of the ancient Near East,[38] as is clearly illustrated by classic texts like Gilgamesh Pennsylvania Tablet III, 23-25, where the civilizing of the wild man Enkidu after his encounter with a prostitute is completed by anointing: *pagaršu šamnam iptašašma awēliš īwe,* "he anointed his body with oil and [thus] became a human being," and the Egyptian Songs of the Harpers, which extol anointing of the body in the context of enjoying life because it is transitory.[39] In Egypt anointing was even incorporated among the standard metaphors of the language.[40]

4. *Other.* Certain late texts exhibit a somewhat obscure use of *nsk* that may reflect a semantic shift influenced by Aramaic. In Isa. 29:10, e.g., the obduracy of the Jerusalem leaders[41] is described by the image of pouring out *(nsk)* a *rûaḥ tardēmâ.* Or should the verb here be derived from *nsk* II, conveying the sense that Yahweh has covered them with a "spirit of deep sleep," since other verbs are used to describe the pouring out of a spirit?[42]

A similar notion lies behind the use of *nsk* in Isa. 25:7, which uses the image of a shroud that covers all the peoples: *w^ehammassēk̲â hann^esûk̲â ʿal-kol-haggôyim.* The

---

41, 52 (1973-81), in loc.; H.-D. Hoffmann, *Reform und Reformen. ATANT,* 66 (1980), 340; M. Weinfeld, *Deuteronomy and the Deuteronomic School* (Oxford, 1972), 322. For the latter see F.-L. Hossfeld, *Untersuchungen zu Komposition und Theologie des Ezechielbuches. FzB,* 20 (^{2}1984), 32.

34. On Gen. 35:14 see C. Westermann, *Genesis 12–36* (Eng. trans., Minneapolis, 1985), 553f. On Ps. 16:4 see Rendtorff, 171.

35. → VIII, 222f.; → זרק *zāraq* (IV, 141-43); → יצק *yāṣaq* (VI, 254-57); → שפך *šāpak̲.*

36. For the material evidence see *BRL*^{2}, 260-64. For the literary evidence see Kutsch.

37. J. A. Soggin, *TLOT,* II, 676f.

38. E. Cassin, "Kosmetik," *RLA,* VI, 214-18.

39. M. Lichtheim, "The Songs of the Harpers," *JNES,* 4 (1945), 178-212; *idem, Ancient Egyptian Literature,* 3 vols. (Berkeley, 1973-80), I, 193-97; H. Brunner, "Wiederum die ägyptischen 'Make Merry' Lieder," *JNES,* 25 (1966), 130f.

40. H. Grapow, *Die bildlichen Ausdrücke im Ägyptischen* (Darmstadt, 1924, ^{2}1983), 146f.

41. H. Wildberger, *Jesaja 28–39. BK,* X/3 (1982), 1114; on obduracy ("hardness of heart") → VII, 20f.

42. *TLOT,* II, 1218f.

text can hardly be referring to knowledge of God, as in 1 Cor. 3:12ff.; the shroud is a sign of mourning.[43]

Many emendations have been proposed for *nsk* in Ps. 2:6.[44] The debate focuses on its meaning in the expression *nāsak̲tî malkî.* Many scholars follow the LXX in reading a niphal, which, citing *nesek̲,* "libation," and *nāsîk̲,* "prince," they interpret as meaning "be consecrated as prince (with a drink offering)."[45] Hartmut Gese has cast doubt on this interpretation, citing Prov. 8:23; Ps. 110:3; 139:13, and proposing a derivation from *skk,* with the meaning "fashion artfully."[46] The implicit need for this revocalization as *nᵉsakkōt̲î* is questionable; this text possibly provides evidence for a broader semantic range of *nsk.*[47]

IV. Dead Sea Scrolls. Among the Dead Sea Scrolls, only the Temple Scroll uses *nsk* and *nesek̲.* 11QTemple 19:11–21:10 describes a unique vintage festival (cf. 43:7-9), which is especially noteworthy in light of the fact that wine offerings do not play an important role in the OT (but note the directions concerning consumption of the tithe of grain and wine and oil in Jub. 32:11f.).[48] The extensive development of the ritual for drinking the new wine (first the priests, then the Levites: 11QTemple 21:4f.) is striking and might reflect the practices followed at meals of the Qumran community. 11QTemple 21:12–23:9 goes on to describe a new oil festival, including drink offerings after the analogy of the vintage festival.[49] We must note, however, that drink offerings are not mentioned elsewhere in the writings of the community; their absence agrees with the overall development of sacrificial theory in early Judaism.[50] They are not mentioned even in the central texts concerned with spiritualizing the cultic directives.[51] The earliest in this series of "spiritualizing texts" originates in the early days of the community but already looks back to the texts dealing with the community's founding;[52] for the first time it reinterprets *expressis verbis* the requirements of the temple cult, but says merely: "For divine approval for the earth, without the flesh of burnt offerings and without the fat of sacrifices, the offering of the lips in compliance with the decree will be like the pleasant aroma of justice and the correctness of behavior will be acceptable like a freewill offering" (1QS 9:3-5). Against this background, the unique character of the Temple Scroll stands out clearly.

Dohmen

---

43. Wildberger, *Isaiah 13–27* (Eng. trans., Minneapolis, 1997), 532.
44. H.-J. Kraus, *Psalms 1–59* (Eng. trans., Minneapolis, 1988), 124.
45. *HAL,* II, 702f., 703.
46. Gese, *"Natus ex virgine," Probleme biblischer Theologie. Festschrift G. von Rad* (Munich, 1971), 81f.
47. See I above. In Prov. 8:23 O. Plöger (*Sprüche Salomos. BK,* XVII [1984], 87) keeps the niphal of *nsk,* translating it "be appointed."
48. See Y. Yadin, *The Temple Scroll,* 3 vols. (Eng. trans., Jerusalem, 1983), I, 108-111. On wine offerings in the OT → VI, 63.
49. Yadin, I, 111-14.
50. Michel, 533f.
51. G. Klinzing, *Die Umdeutung des Kultus in der Qumrangemeinde und im NT. SUNT,* 7 (1971), 50-93.
52. C. Dohmen, "Zur Gründung der Gemeinde von Qumran," *RevQ,* 11 (1982), 89-92.

נָסַע nāsaʿ; מַסַּע massaʿ; מַסָּע massāʿ

Contents: I. 1. Etymology; 2. Occurrences; 3. Meaning. II. Usage: 1. Qal; 2. Niphal; 3. Hiphil; 4. Derivatives. III. LXX and Dead Sea Scrolls.

I. 1. *Etymology.* Outside Hebrew, the root *nsʿ* is attested in Ugaritic ("tear out"), Phoenician (Karatepe: "tear out, tear down," with objs. "city" and "gate"), and Jewish Aramaic ("drag off, pull").[1] Arab. *nazaʿa,* "pull out," and *nasaʿa,* "tear," as well as Eth. *nazʿa,* "tear out," may also be related, but not Akk. *nešû,* "be distant." Heb. *nāsaḥ,* "tear down, tear out," is probably a by-form.

2. *Occurrences.* The verb appears 135 times in the qal, twice in the niphal, and 8 times in the hiphil. There are two nominal derivatives: *massaʿ,* "breaking camp, day's journey" (12 occurrences), and *massāʿ,* "breaking" (once); *massāʿ* II, the name of a weapon, occurs once and is probably unrelated. Both the verb and the nouns appear primarily in narrative texts (the patriarchal narratives, the exodus, the forty years in the wilderness). Occurrences are rare in the prophetic books (2 in Isa. 37 par. 2 K. 19, 2 in Jeremiah, 1 additional occurrence in Isaiah, and 1 in Zechariah) and Wisdom Literature (2 in Job, 1 in Ecclesiastes); there are no occurrences in early poetry.

3. *Meaning.* The basic meaning of the verb is "set out, break camp, journey"; it is therefore a verb of motion. All its semantic nuances can be explained by its context or syntactic construction.

Kaddari

"Pull out (tent pegs)" is usually taken to be the original meaning, from which the senses "set out" and "journey" derive.

Ringgren

II. Usage.

1. *Qal.* The qal means (a) "move" (intransitive), (b) "start to move" (inchoative), (c) "be carried or brought" (with an inanimate subj.), (d) "move, carry, bring" (transitive with an inanimate obj.).[2]

---

nāsaʿ. M. Delcor, "Quelques cas de survivances du vocabulaire nomade en hébreu biblique," *VT,* 25 (1975), 307-322; A. Guillaume, "Hebrew and Arabic Lexicography," *Abr-Nahrain,* 1 (1959/60), 3-35, esp. 28f.

1. For Ugaritic see *WUS,* no. 1803; for Phoenician, *KAI,* 26A, III, 15, 17.
2. The ergative use of verbs of motion is discussed by M. Z. Kaddari, *Studies in Biblical Hebrew Syntax* (Ramat-Gan, 1976), 87ff. (Heb.).

a. The verb is usually used intransitively with a group of living creatures as subject, e.g., "(the inhabitants of) the whole earth" (Gen. 11:2), "the children of Israel" (Nu. 2:34), the Egyptians (Ex. 14:10), Judah and all its towns (Jer. 31:24, if the text is correct; we should possibly read *nōsᵉʿê bāʿēḏer,* "those who wander with their flocks" [cf. NRSV]). In Zec. 10:2 (text?), in a simile, a flock is the subject: "The people had to wander [i.e., were driven out] like sheep." The subject can also be a proper name, especially the name of a leader, e.g., Abram (Gen. 12:9), Lot (13:11), Jacob (33:17, etc.), or Sennacherib (2 K. 19:36 par. Isa. 37:37). It is used for the movement of God's angel and the pillar of cloud when they come between the Israelites and the Egyptians (Ex. 14:19) and for the wind from Yahweh that brings quails (Nu. 11:31). Sometimes contextual parallelism brings out semantic nuances, e.g., as an antonym to *ḥānâ,* "encamp" (Nu. 2:17,34, etc.), *ʿāmaḏ,* "stand still" (Ex. 14:19), or *hāyâ,* "remain"; or as a synonym to *hālaḵ,* "go" (e.g., Gen. 12:9: *hālôḵ wᵉnāsôaʿ*). The verb is usually modified by an adverbial expression indicating the place from which the subject leaves (Nu. 12:16), the direction in which the subject sets out (10:29), or both the starting point and the terminus of the journey (11:35). It can also be qualified by a general locative expression (Ex. 14:19: *mippᵉnêhem*) or some other adverbial modifier (*lᵉḏiglêhem:* Nu. 2:31). It also appears without further qualification (Nu. 10:28). The context can indicate that a long journey is in store, probably using mounts or carts, as in the case of Lot (Gen. 13:11) or the Egyptians (Ex. 14:10).

b. The inchoative *nāsaʿ,* "set out, leave a place," is often used in combination with other verbs of motion such as *hālaḵ* (e.g., Dt. 1:19: "we set out from Horeb and went . . ."), *qûm* (e.g., Dt. 2:24: "rise up, set out"), *qûm* and *ʿālâ* (Gen. 35:3,5: "let us rise up and go to Bethel . . . and they set out"), *pānâ* (Nu. 14:25: "turn and set out for the wilderness"), and *ʿālâ* niphal for the movement of the pillar of cloud (Nu. 9:21). In Jer. 4:7 it parallels *ʿālâ:* "a lion has gone up from its thicket, a destroyer of nations has set out."

Kaddari

The verb is a key word in the patriarchal narratives. Abraham sets out and journeys to the Negeb (Gen. 12:9; cf. 20:1). Esau says to Jacob, "Let us set out and go on our way" (*nisʿâ wᵉnēlᵉḵâ:* 33:12). Jacob sets out for Succoth (33:17). Jacob's family sets out from Bethel (35:5,16). Jacob (Israel) sets out and pitches his tent beyond the tower of Eder (35:21), and finally sets out and goes to Egypt by way of Beer-sheba (46:1). The verb reflects the wanderings of the nomadic patriarchs.

With the exodus a new journey begins. The Israelites set out from Rameses to Succoth (Ex. 12:37) and from there to Etham (13:20), and from Elim to the wilderness of Sin (16:1), whence "they journeyed from one resting place to the next *(lᵉmasʿêhem),* as Yahweh commanded" (17:1; cf. also 19:2).

The many occurrences of the verb in Numbers reflect the wilderness wanderings of the Israelites. The text emphasizes that they made camp and broke camp just as Yahweh commanded Moses (Nu. 2:34) or according to the command of Yahweh (*ʿal-pî:* 9:20). Nu. 33, with 42 occurrences, lists the stages of the desert journey.

Ringgren

c. With inanimate subjects, the verb is used only with reference to things of religious or national significance; here it implies being carried. With the *miškān,* it is an antonym to *ḥānâ* (Nu. 1:51); with the ark, it is an antonym to *nûaḥ,* "rest" (10:35f.). The *'ōhel môʿēḏ* also appears as its subject.

d. Used transitively, *nāsaʿ* has the meaning "remove, tear out," with reference to part of a structure or an object: doors of a city gate (Jgs. 16:3), a weaving pin with its warp threads (Jgs. 16:14), or tent stakes (Isa. 33:20).

Kaddari

Isa. 33:20 describes the future Zion as "a quiet habitation, a tent that cannot be moved *(ṣāʿan),* whose stakes will never be pulled up *(nāsaʿ),* and none of whose ropes will be broken (*ntq* niphal)." It is quite possible that this passage contrasts the "eternal sanctuary with the portable sanctuary of the time in the wilderness," but it is equally possible that it merely uses an apposite metaphor from pastoral life.[3]

Ringgren

2. *Niphal.* The niphal occurs only as the passive of intransitive *nāsaʿ.* In Isa. 38:12 it is predicated of *dôrî,* "my dwelling,"[4] in parallel with *niglâ minnî,* "is removed from me." "The expected end of [Hezekiah's] life is described in v. 12 in two very original metaphors, that of the striking of a Bedouin or shepherd's tent and that of the cutting off of the completed piece of cloth by the weaver from the supporting threads known as the thrum."[5] Job 4:21 states: "[Mortals'] tent-cord *(yeṯer)* is torn loose, and they die devoid of wisdom." The image of the destruction of the tent of life is the same as in the psalm of Hezekiah (Isa. 38:12). The meaning of *bᵉlō' ḥoḵmâ* is obscure: "for lack of wisdom," "unawares," or "without wisdom, i.e., senselessly"?[6]

3. *Hiphil.* With animate objects, the hiphil means "set a group of people or animals in motion." For example, Ps. 78:52 says that at the exodus God led his people out (caused them to set out) like sheep and guided (*nhg* piel) them through the wilderness like a flock. With personification, v. 26 uses the same two words for God's sending of the east wind (*qāḏîm,* a reference to Nu. 11:31): "He caused the east wind to break loose in the heavens, and by his power he led out (*nhg* piel) the south wind." Ex. 15:22 uses the verb with adverbial expression of place: "Moses ordered Israel to set out from the Sea of Reeds."

With inanimate objects, *nsʿ* hiphil means "remove, take away": a jar (2 K. 4:4), a stone (1 K. 5:31[Eng. v. 17]). The king commanded that great, costly stones be quarried to lay the foundation of the temple; cf. Eccl. 10:9: "Whoever quarries stones will be

---

3. O. Kaiser, *Isaiah 13–39. OTL* (Eng. trans. 1974), 348.
4. Contra H. S. Nyberg, *Festschrift H. Kosmala. ASTI,* 9 (1974), 90f.: "my people."
5. Kaiser, *Isaiah 13–39,* 405.
6. See F. Horst, *Hiob 1–19. BK,* XVI/1 (1968), in loc.; E. Dhorme (*Job* [Eng. trans., repr. Nashville, 1984], 59f.) connects 4:21a with 5:5c; the LXX has a totally different text.

hurt by them" — one of four lurking dangers. God is the subject of such texts as Ps. 80:9(8), "You brought a vine out of Egypt," which refers metaphorically to God's leading Israel out of Egypt and anticipates the metaphor of the planting of the vine in Canaan. The verb may also have an abstract noun as its object: "He broke me down *(ntṣ)* . . . and uprooted my hopes *(tiqwâ)* like a tree" (Job 19:10).

4. *Derivatives.* In the first instance, *massaʿ* as a *nomen actionis* refers to setting out or journeying; it can also mean the stages of a journey, of Israel's wandering in the wilderness (Ex. 40:36,38; Nu. 10:12; 33:1f.; cf. also Gen. 13:3; Ex. 17:1). In Nu. 10:2 it functions as an infinitive and is the object of the prep. *'eṯ:* the silver trumpets are to be used *lᵉmiqrā' . . . ûlᵉmassaʿ,* "for summoning the congregation and for breaking camp." In Dt. 10:11 Moses is to go at the head of the people as they set out.

The meaning of *massāʿ* I is uncertain. In the context of the construction of Solomon's temple, 1 K. 6:7 reads: *'eḇen šᵉlēmâ massāʿ niḇnâ.* Ernst Würthwein translates: "[the house] was built of unhewn quarry stones."[7] This text may refer to the altar law in Ex. 20:25, which prohibits building an altar with hewn stones. The noun *massāʿ* II appears in a list of weapons in Job 41:18(26): *ḥᵃnîṯ massāʿ wᵉširyâ,* "spear, projectile, and javelin." According to Gustav Dalman, *massāʿ* is the throwing stick used in hunting birds.[8]

III. LXX and Dead Sea Scrolls. The LXX usually uses *apaírein* (81 times) or *exaírein* to translate *nāsaʿ;* we also find simple *aírein,* as well as such verbs as *anazeugnýnai, kineín,* and *stratopaideúein.* The niphal in Job 4:21 is translated with *exérchesthai,* while Isa. 38:12 has a very different text. Several compounds of *aírein* are used for the hiphil: *apaírein, exaírein, epaírein,* and *metaírein.*

In the Dead Sea Scrolls the verb occurs only once, in CD 1:16, where a hiphil is used for moving boundary markers (cf. Dt. 19:14, which uses *taśśîg*); the context suggests a metaphor for altering the law. *massāʿ* occurs twice: in 1QM 3:5, the "trumpets of departure"; and in 1QSa 2:15, which speaks of hierarchy "in their camps and on their marches."

Kaddari

7. E. Würthwein, *Das erste Buch der Könige, Kapitel 1–16. ATD,* 11/1 (1977), 60.
8. *AuS,* VI, 333.

נַעַל *na'al*

Contents: I. Etymology and Meaning; II. Footwear; III. Symbolism; IV. Verb; V. LXX.

I. Etymology and Meaning. In all probability *na'al* is a primary noun; it is found in most Semitic languages: Arab. *na'l,* Syr. *na'lā',* Mand. *nala.*[1] Ugar. *n'l* is not related, since the context requires a meaning like "couch."[2] Strictly speaking, it refers to a sandal, a simple sole of wood or leather bound to the foot with thongs (Gen. 14:23; Isa. 5:27). It possibly also denotes other simple footwear (shoes). It is distinct from *s^{e}'ôn* (Isa. 9:4[Eng. v. 5]), the laced boot worn by Assyrian soldiers (Akk. *šênu;* cf. Ugar. *sȝn,* Jewish Aram. *šênā',* Syr. *s^{e}'ûnā',* Eth. *šā'en*).[3]

II. Footwear. Belted loincloth, shoes, and staff are signs of readiness to set out (Ex. 12:11). Belt and sandals, described in 1 K. 2:5 as being stained with innocent blood, probably represent standard battle gear. Here LXX^{R} has the 1st person singular pronominal suffix; if this reading is correct, David bears the bloodguilt of Joab's deeds. In Isa. 5:27 belt and sandals likewise represent the readiness for battle of the advancing enemy: "The leather girdles round the waists of the warriors and the thongs of their sandals are rigid and taut, and spur the army on to take no rest."[4]

Nonetheless, clothes (*śalmâ,* in some MSS. *śimlâ*) and shoes (Dt. 29:4[5]) are worn every day; it is a sign of God's care that they did not wear out *(bālâ)* during the forty years of wandering in the wilderness. Dt. 8:4 expresses the same idea in different language: the Israelites' clothes *(śimlâ)* did not wear out and their feet did not swell.

The same association with *bālâ* appears also in Josh. 9:5,13,[5] in a totally different context: the Gibeonites come to Joshua wearing worn-out clothes and patched shoes so as to look like refugees who have come a long distance. Since sandals can hardly be "patched" *(ṭl'),* this text may well refer to some other kind of simple shoes.

---

na'al. C. M. Carmichael, "A Ceremonial Crux: Removing a Man's Sandal as a Female Gesture of Contempt," *JBL,* 96 (1977), 321-336; H. W. Hönig, *Die Bekleidung des Hebräers* (Zurich, 1957), 82-88; E. R. Lacheman, "Note on Ruth 4,7-8," *JBL,* 56 (1939), 53-56; L. Levy, "Die Schuhsymbolik im jüdischen Ritus," *MGWJ,* 1918, 178-185; G. Rühlmann, " 'Deine Feinde fallen unter deine Sohlen,' " *WZ Halle,* 20 (1971), 61-84; E. A. Speiser, "Of Shoes and Shekels," *BASOR,* 77 (1940), 15-20; T. Thompson and D. Thompson, "Some Legal Problems in the Book of Ruth," *VT,* 18 (1968), 79-99; G. M. Tucker, "Witnesses and 'Dates' in Israelite Contracts," *CBQ,* 28 (1966), 42-45.

1. *MdD,* 283.
2. M. Dietrich and O. Loretz, *UF,* 10 (1978), 61; *WUS,* no. 1805; *KTU,* I.4, I, 36.
3. For the Akkadian see *AHw,* III, 1213f. For the archaeological evidence see *BRL*², 186; G. Fohrer, *BHHW,* II, 671f.; E. Höhne, *BHHW,* III, 1739.
4. O. Kaiser, *Isaiah 1–12. OTL* (Eng. trans. 1972), 138.
5. On the pl. forms see D. Michel, *Grundlegungen einer hebräischen Syntax,* I (Neukirchen-Vluyn, 1977), 58.

The descriptive poem in Cant. 7:2ff.(1ff.) depicts the dancing bride, emphasizing the beauty of her feet (or steps: *pa'am*) in their shoes (v. 2a[1a]); the text here very likely refers to decorated dancing shoes.

III. Symbolism. According to Ezk. 24:23, taking off headgear and shoes is a sign of mourning: the exiles are not to do so at the fall of Jerusalem; neither are they to mourn or weep, as they would normally do.

In Isa. 20:2 Isaiah takes off his sackcloth and sandals and goes naked (→ **ערום** *'ārôm*) and barefoot to symbolize the expected ignominious treatment of the Egyptians by the Assyrians.[6]

Ex. 3:5 and Josh. 5:15 presuppose that one removes *(šll)* one's shoes in a holy place. This action probably reflects the notion that shoes come into contact with dust and dirt more than other articles of clothing.[7] It is noteworthy that the detailed descriptions of the priestly vestments in Ex. 29 and 39 say nothing of shoes.[8] In Job 12:19 the priests are led away barefoot, a sign of disgrace.

Am. 2:6; 8:6 use the dual *na'^{a}layim,* "a pair of sandals," to represent something of no value. People "sell the righteous *(ṣaddîq)* for silver and the needy for a pair of sandals" (2:6), i.e., the poor person who is unable to pay is forced into servitude on account of a minor debt. People say, "Let us buy *(qānâ)* the poor *(dallîm)* for silver and the needy for a pair of sandals" (8:6). On the one hand, since the context involves deceit in commerce, the reference to debt servitude is somewhat inappropriate and might be an interpolation from 2:6. On the other hand, we note that the text speaks of buying rather than selling; the primary emphasis is on the eagerness of the people in question to ply a trade, which is then specified. A similar idea appears in Sir. 46:19, which says that Samuel never took a bribe, not even a pair of sandals. The Hebrew text reads *kôper w^{e}na'^{a}l[ay]im,* close to the reading *kōp̱er w^{e}na'^{a}layim* (instead of *w^{e}'a'lîm)* in 1 S. 12:3 (cf. LXX).

In Ps. 60:10(8) "throwing down one's shoe" on something is a sign of taking possession (the same text reappears in 108:10). Yahweh claims Edom as his possession. L. Levy already noted that the image expresses "more than taking possession: the element of humiliation and subjugation is also present."[9] Mitchell Dahood proposes to interpret the verb *hišlîḵ* as "plant," finding here a reference to the custom of placing one's foot on the neck of the vanquished.[10]

---

6. On the problem of prophetic symbolic actions see G. Fohrer, "Die Gattung der Berichte über symbolische Handlungen des Propheten," *Studien zur alttestamentlichen Prophetie. BZAW,* 99 (1967), 92-112.

7. Contra L. Dürr, "Zur religiongeschichtlichen Begründung der Vorschrift des Schuhausziehens an heiliger Stätte," *OLZ* (1938), 410-12, who claims that leather from dead animals is considered unclean; but cf. already J. Pedersen, *Der Eid ben den Semiten* (Strasbourg, 1914), 97.

8. Hönig, 85f.

9. Levy, 180.

10. M. Dahood, *Psalms II. AB,* 17 (^{2}1973), 80f. Cf. also Rühlmann.

Ruth 4:7 states that "in former times" in Israel it was the custom when "redeeming" *(g^eʾullâ)* or exchanging to confirm the transaction by "taking off *(šālap̱)* a shoe and giving it to the other." It is unclear who took the shoe off and who received it. E. A. Speiser cites material from Nuzi to show that this represents a mock payment. Gillis Gerleman sees in the symbolic act a renunciation of possession in contrast to the taking possession in Ps. 60:10(8).[11] After a thorough discussion, Edward Campbell concludes that the first redeemer *(gōʾēl)* gave Boaz his shoe (v. 8) to symbolize the transfer of his right.[12] However that may be, the case discussed in Dt. 25:9f. is not comparable. This text prescribes that when a man refuses to enter into levirate marriage with a woman, she is to pull *(ḥālaṣ)* his shoe off his foot and spit in his face. Here we are dealing with a gesture of contempt, not a normal legal action.[13]

IV. Verb. The verb *nʿl* is a denominative from *naʿal;* it occurs twice in the OT. In Ezk. 16:10 Yahweh says that he gave the woman representing Jerusalem embroidered cloth and sandals of *taḥaš* leather; the context makes clear that this was clothing of great value. The hiphil occurs in 2 Ch. 28:15, which tells how the prisoners of war sent back to the southern kingdom were furnished with clothing, shoes, and everything they needed.

This denominative verb is probably distinct from *nāʿal,* "lock" (Jgs. 3:23f.; 2 S. 13:17f.; Cant. 4:12), with its derivatives *manʿûl* (Cant. 5:5; Neh. 3:3,6,13,15) and *minʿāl* (Dt. 33:25), both of which mean "bolt."

V. LXX. The LXX usually translates *naʿal* with *hypódēma; sandálion* is used twice.

Ringgren

11. Gerleman, *Ruth. BK,* XVIII (1965), 37.
12. E. F. Campbell, *Ruth. AB,* 7 (1975), 149f.
13. W. Rudolph, *Das Buch Ruth. KAT,* XVII/1 (1962), 68; cf. also Carmichael, who finds in the gesture sexual symbolism alluding to the Onan episode in Gen. 38:8-10.

נָעַם *nāʿam;* נָעִים *nāʿîm;* נֹעַם *nōʿam;* מַנְעַמִּים *manʿammîm;* נַעֲמָנִים *naʿ^amānîm*

Contents: I. Etymology. II. Usage: 1. Survey; 2. Verb; 3. *nāʿîm;* 4. *nōʿam;* 5. *manʿammîm;* 6. *naʿ^amānîm.* III. LXX.

nāʿam. J. Gabriel, "Die Kainitengenealogie Gn 4,17-24," *Bibl,* 40 (1959), 409-427, esp. 418f.; K. Galling, "Die Τερπωλη des Alexander Jannäus," *Von Ugarit nach Qumran. Festschrift O. Eissfeldt. BZAW,* 77 (1958), 49-62, esp. 59-61; A. Jirku, "Niṭʿē naʿamanim (Jes. xvii 10, c) = niṭʿē naʿaman-ma," *VT,* 7 (1957), 201f.; W. Rudolph, *Das Buch Ruth. KAT,* XVII/1 (²1962), 38;

I. Etymology. The root, listed as *n'm* I in lexicons of Biblical Hebrew (cf. also *n'm* and *nḫm/nḥm*), is also found in Middle Hebrew and other Semitic languages: Arabic (*na'ima,* "enjoy, rejoice"), Amorite (PN *nḫm*), Ugaritic (*n'm,* "lovely, good," "attractiveness, something attractive, a lovely place," "well-being, health"; *n'mt,* "loveliness"; *n'my,* "loveliness, delight"; *n'mn,* "lovely, good," also a PN), Phoenician and Punic (*n'm,* "good, friendly, lovely," "joy, goodness"; *n'mt,* "good, beneficial," "goodness," etc.), Postbiblical Aramaic (e.g., *ne'îmtā',* "loveliness"; also a PN), and Syriac (*ne'îmā',* "lovely, beloved"; also a PN).[1]

This root is distinct from *n'm* II, which appears not only in Middle Hebrew (hiphil: "sing, accompany"; *ne'îmâ,* "song, sound," etc.), but also, e.g., in Arabic (*naǵama,* "hum, sing"; *naǵma,* "sound, melody"), Aramaic (e.g., *ne'îmtā',* "melody"), and Syriac (e.g., *na'matānāyā',* "pertaining to the modulation of the voice").[2] In the OT this root is attested only in derivatives (esp. *ne'îmâ,* "song, music," Sir. 45:9; the PN *na'amâ* I may mean "[female] singer," but it may also derive from *n'm* I and mean "lovely" or "friendly"; cf. also the roots *n'm* and *nḫm*).[3]

II. Usage.

1. *Survey.* The root *n'm* I is quite common in the OT. The verb appears only in the qal (8 occurrences: 3 in Proverbs and one each in Song of Songs, Ezekiel, Psalms, 2 Samuel, and Genesis), but the root occurs in the adj. *nā'îm* (13 occurrences: 6 in Psalms, 3 in Proverbs, 2 in 2 Samuel, and one each in Song of Songs and Job), and the nouns *nō'am* (7 occurrences: 3 in Proverbs, 2 each in Psalms and Zechariah), *man'ammîm* (once only: Ps. 141:4), and *na'amānîm* (once only: Isa. 17:10).

The root appears also in proper names such as *na'am* (masc.: 1 Ch. 4:15, in the genealogy of Judah), *na'amâ* (possibly from *n'm* II;[4] the daughter of Lamech: Gen. 4:22;[5] an Ammonite woman, the mother of Rehoboam: 1 K. 14:21,31; 2 Ch. 12:13),

---

J. M. Sasson, *Ruth* (Baltimore, 1979), esp. 17f.; H. Schmökel, *Heilige Hochzeit und Hoheslied* (1956); J. J. Stamm, "Hebräische Frauennamen," *Hebräische Wortforschung. Festschrift W. Baumgartner. SVT,* 16 (1967), 301-339, esp. 323.

1. For Biblical Hebrew see, e.g., *BDB,* 653b; *HAL,* II, 705. For the variants see *IPN,* 166, 175, 222; Z. S. Harris, *A Grammar of the Phoenician Language. AOS,* 8 (1936), 124; *RyNP,* I, 237; A. Vincent, *La religion des Judéo-Araméens d'Eléphantine* (Paris, 1937), 406f. For Middle Hebrew, Jastrow, 919f. For Amorite, *APNM,* 237f. For Ugaritic, *WUS,* no. 1806f.; M. Dahood, *RSP,* I, 277, no. 385; *PNU,* 163; Whitaker, 451f.; see also II.1 below. For Phoenician and Punic, *DISO,* 180f.; *KAI,* III, 16f.; *ANET,* 653, 656; R. S. Tomback, *A Comparative Semitic Lexicon of the Phoenician and Punic Languages. SBLDS,* 32 (1978), 215-17. For Postbiblical Aramaic, Jastrow, 919f. For Syriac, R. Payne Smith, *Thesaurus Syriacus,* 2 vols. (Oxford, 1879-1901), II, 2405f.

2. For Middle Hebrew see Jastrow, 919f. For Aramaic, Jastrow, 920. For Syriac, Payne Smith, II, 2406.

3. On *ne'îmâ* see *HAL,* II, 705. On the meaning of the PN, for the former see Gabriel, 418f.; for the latter see Stamm, 323.

4. See I above.

5. M. Flashar, *ZAW,* 28 (1908), 307f.; S. Mowinckel, *The Two Sources of Predeuteronomic Primeval History (JE) in Gen. 1–11. ANVAO* (1937), 2, 82.

naʿ^amān (masc.: name of Adonis; a descendant of Benjamin: Gen. 46:21; Nu. 26:40a [LXX *Noeman*]; 1 Ch. 8:4,7 [LXX *Nooma*]; a general of the king of Damascus: 2 K. 5:1-27 [LXX *Naiman, Neeman*]),[6] *noʿ^omî* (fem.: mother-in-law of Ruth: Ruth 1:2–4:17[7] [the ending *-î* is not a pronominal suf., "my lovely one," but a hypocoristicon from *-aya;*[8] cf. Ugar. *nʿmy, nʿmyn;*[9] Palmyr. *nʿmy,*[10] also LXX *Nōem/e/in*]), the toponym *naʿ^amâ* (near Lachish: Josh. 15:41; in Arabia[?], only in the gentilic *naʿ^amāṯî:* Job 2:11 [LXX *ho Minaíos*]),[11] the gentilic *naʿmî,* from *naʿ^amān* (Nu. 26:40b), and some compound PNs such as *'^aḇînōʿam* (father of Barak: Jgs. 4:6,12; 5:1,12)[12] and *'^aḥînōʿam* (Saul's wife: 1 S. 14:50; David's wife: 1 S. 25:43; 27:3; 30:5; 2 S. 2:2; 3:2; 1 Ch. 3:1).[13] With respect to the use of *nʿm* I in OT personal names in general, we may cite many West Semitic appellatives constructed with the root *nʿm.*[14]

In the Ugaritic texts the goddess ʿAnat is described as being equipped with *nʿm,* and *nʿm* is used as an epithet for Canaanite heroes (Keret/Aqhat) and gods.[15]

Among the roots that can appear in parallel with *nʿm* I, we note especially → טוב *ṭôḇ* (Gen. 49:15; Ps. 133:1; 147:1; Job 36:11; Prov. 24:25[?]), as well as *brk* (Prov. 24:25[?]), *yph* (Cant. 1:16; 7:7), *yqr* (Prov. 24:4), and *mtq* (Prov. 9:17). The clearest antonym is → מרר *mrr* (Ruth 1:20).

2. *Verb.* The 8 OT occurrences of the verb *nʿm* I are all in the qal; most are in poetry or Wisdom Literature, where it is often impossible to determine the precise semantic nuance. It is clear in any case that the primary context of *nʿm* I is the language of love, either in descriptions of the beauty and attractiveness of the beloved or in expressions praising the delights of erotic love. Cant. 7:7-10a(Eng. vv. 6-9a) is a poetic accolade, extolling the maiden's loveliness as an aspect of her perfect beauty, detailed in the poem: "How fair you are and how lovely, O loved one, delectable maiden" (*ma-yāp̄îṯ ûma-nāʿamt '^ahuḇâ* [MT: *'ah^aḇâ;* cf. Vulg., LXX] *baṯ taʿ^anûḡîm* [MT: *battaʿ^anûḡîm,* a hapax legomenon; cf. Aquila and Symmachus]: v. 7[6]). While here the loveliness of the beloved parallels her beauty (*yph;* cf. also 1:16), in the context of late wisdom we find a statement of the physical sweetness of erotic love, more specifically forbidden love, as Dame Folly describes it: "Stolen water is sweet *(yimtāqû),* and bread eaten in

---

6. H. Bardtke, *BHHW,* II, 1279. On Adonis see *WbMyth,* I, 234f.

7. *IPN,* 166; Rudolph, 38; Stamm, 323; Sasson, 17f.; E. F. Campbell Jr., *Ruth. AB,* 7 (1975), 52f.

8. Cf. *PNU,* 50, 211.

9. On *nʿmy* see *KTU,* 4.75, V, 5; on *nʿmyn* see *KTU,* 4.611, 9; Benz, 241-43; Glanzman, 205f.

10. *PNPI,* 99f.

11. On Josh. 15:41 see F.-M. Abel, *Géographie de la Palestine. ÉBib,* 2 vols. (1933-38), II, 393; W. F. Albright, *BASOR,* 18 (1925), 10; *GTTOT,* §318, B/15. On Job 2:11 see E. Dhorme, *Job* (Eng. trans., repr. Nashville, 1984), xxvii, 21.

12. *HAL,* I, 5b.

13. *HAL,* I, 34.

14. Benz, 362.

15. For ʿAnat see *KTU,* 1.10, I, 16; III, 10; 1.14, III, 41. For the heroes see *UT,* no. 1665. For the gods see *KTU,* 1.23, 1ff.; 1.5, III, 15; Sasson, 17.

secret is delicious *(yinʿām)*" (Prov. 9:17; with reference to the par. *nʿm/mtq,* cf. the antonyms *nʿm/mr'* in Ruth 1:20).

This kind of language can also be used in the setting of intimate friendship, as in David's lamentation over the death of Saul and Jonathan (2 S. 1:17-27): "I am distressed for you, my brother Jonathan; greatly beloved were you to me *(nāʿamtā lî meʾōḏ)*" (v. 26).

Metaphorically, *nāʿam* can stand for the beauty or attractiveness of the land of Israel. For example, the Blessing of Jacob (Gen. 49) says of Issachar: "And he saw that a resting place was good *(ṭôḇ),* and that the land was pleasant *(nʿm)*" (v. 15). There are probably overtones here of the fertility of the land, the "beloved" of all Israelites.[16] In the book of Ezekiel, the prophecy against Pharaoh and Egypt (29:1–32:32) asks ironically of the pomp of Egypt, "Are you more beautiful than all the rest?" *(mimmî nāʿāmtā,* lit.: "Whom do you surpass in beauty?" 32:19).[17]

A love metaphor clearly stands behind a late wisdom statement concerning the loveliness of knowledge: "[If you accept the words of wisdom], . . . understanding will come into your heart, and knowledge will delight your soul" *(weḏaʿaṯ lenapšekā yinʿām:* Prov. 2:10; the MT is superior to the emendation proposed by *BHS*).[18]

We find an isolated impersonal construction in one of the two remaining texts using the verb, namely, in the second collection (Prov. 24:23-34) of the admonitions and instructions (22:17–24:34) of older wisdom. Here we read of the well-being of those who stand up for what is right: "Those who stand up for what is right will have delight *(yinʿām),* and a good blessing will come upon them" (24:25).[19] The final occurrence, Ps. 141:6, is in a poetic prayer of the individual. The context is very obscure, and the text may also be corrupt. The psalmist pictures the wicked falling into the hands of those who will condemn them: "then they shall hear how pleasant my words are *('amāray kî nāʿēmû)*."[20] In any case, the function of the verb is clearly comparable to that of the adj. *nāʿîm* in two wisdom admonitions (Prov. 22:18; 23:8).[21]

3. *nāʿîm.* Like the verb *nʿm* I, the adj. *nāʿîm* belongs to the language of love. It appears in the song of the orchard (Cant. 1:15-17), where — together with *yāp̄â,* "beautiful" — it denotes the physical loveliness and attraction of the beloved: "Ah, you are beautiful, my beloved, truly lovely" *(hinnekā yāp̄eh dôḏî 'ap nāʿîm,* v. 16). In the context of intimate friendship, David's lamentation (2 S. 1:17-27) says: "Saul and Jonathan, beloved and lovely *(hanne'ehāḇîm wehanneʿîmim)!* In life and in death they were not divided" (v. 23).[22]

16. Cf. LXX; E. Nestle, *ZAW,* 26 (1906), 159f.

17. W. Zimmerli, *Ezekiel 2. Herm* (Eng. trans. 1983), 163.

18. *HAL* (II, 705) incorrectly cites the text as Ps. 2:10. See also O. Plöger, *Sprüche Salomos. BK,* XVII (1984), 12.

19. Following Plöger, *BK,* XVII, 285-87.

20. H.-J. Kraus, *Psalms 60–150* (Eng. trans., Minneapolis, 1989), 525-29.

21. See below.

22. S. R. Driver, *Notes on the Hebrew Text and the Topography of the Books of Samuel* (Oxford, ²1913), 238; *HAL,* II, 705, erroneously citing v. 21.

The use of *nāʿîm* as an epithet is clearly connected with this usage.[23] David is described as *mešîaḥ ʾelōhê yaʿaqōḇ ûneʿîm zemirôṯ* (2 S. 23:1), which is normally understood as "the anointed of the God of Jacob, the darling of the songs of Israel."[24] The proposed interpretation "singer of the songs of Israel," based on *nʿm* II, is to be rejected as "precarious."[25] The interpretation proposed by H. N. Richardson, "the beloved of the Guardian [*zmrwt/zmrt;* cf. Ugar. *ḏmr* and Amor. *zmr*] of Israel," is likewise unconvincing.[26]

In a few instances, *nāʿîm* simply parallels *ṭôḇ,* "good, fitting," as in the didactic poem Ps. 133: "Behold, how good *(ṭôḇ)* and pleasant *(nāʿîm)* it is, when brothers live together in unity" (v. 1; cf. the combination *baṭṭôḇ . . . banneʿîmîm* in Job 36:11[27]). Ps. 135:3 says that Yahweh is "good" *(ṭôḇ)* and his name "gracious" *(nāʿîm);* it is "good" *(ṭôḇ)* to play to him, "pleasant" *(nāʿîm)* to sing his praises (147:1); cf. the "sweet lyre" *(kinnôr nāʿîm)* in 81:3(2). The adj. *nāʿîm* has roughly the same meaning in three texts of the first collection of admonitions and instructions in Prov. 22:17–24:22: it is "pleasant" *(nāʿîm)* to keep the words of the wisdom instructor within one (22:18); "pleasant words" *(deḇāreyḵā banneʿimîm)* spoken to one who is hostile are wasted (23:8);[28] riches can also be "precious and pleasant" (*yāqār wenāʿîm,* 24:4).

Of the 3 remaining occurrences, 2 are in Ps. 16, a (preexilic?) prayer; one occurrence is masculine plural, the other feminine plural. The first is probably associated with the "loveliness" of the land (cf. Gen. 49:15; Ezk. 32:19): "The measuring line has fallen on pleasant ground for me" (*ḥaḇālîm nāpelû-lî banneʿimîm,* Ps. 16:6[5]), which Hans-Joachim Kraus compares to 84:4f.(3f.): "Lovely (נעם) is this highest good fortune: to be privileged to live in proximity to Yahweh, to live in Yahweh himself."[29] The concluding verse of Ps. 16 also speaks of "the bliss of the nearness to God":[30] "You show me the path of life. The fullness of you is joy, in your right hand are pleasures forevermore *(neʿimôṯ bîmîneḵā neṣaḥ)*" (16:11[10]). The third and final passage, in the fourth discourse of Elihu (Job 36–37), is connected with Ps. 16 both formally and contextually. Describing the righteous, Job 36:11 says: "They complete their days in prosperity *(baṭṭôḇ),* and their years in pleasantness *(banneʿîmîm).*"

4. *nōʿām.* Of the 7 occurrences of the noun *nōʿām* in the OT, at least 3 are in wisdom contexts (cf. the verb *nʿm* I in Prov. 2:10; 24:25; also 9:17; Ps. 141:6; also the adj. *nāʿîm* in Prov. 22:18; 23:8; 24:4). Here the noun functions as *nomen rectum,* twice in the phrase *ʾimrê-nōʿam:* "gracious words" are pure to Yahweh (15:26); indeed, they

---

23. In Ugaritic cf. *KTU,* 1.17, VI, 45; 1.15, II, 20; 1.14, I, 40, II, 8; see also II.1 below.
24. *HAL,* II, 705.
25. Driver, *Notes,* 357.
26. H. N. Richardson, *JBL,* 90 (1971), 259-262.
27. See below.
28. On the text of 23:6-8, see Plöger, *BK,* XVII, 263.
29. H.-J. Kraus, *Psalms 1–59* (Eng. trans., Minneapolis, 1988), 238. On Ezk. 32:19 see II.2 above.
30. Ibid., 241.

are like a honeycomb, sweet to the gums and healthy to the bones (16:24); the LXX summarizes: "their sweetness is medicine to the soul."[31] The phrase *darḵê-nōʿam* occurs in 3:17: the ways of wisdom and understanding are "ways of pleasantness."

It is highly dubious that *nōʿam* refers in a wisdom sense to the "friendliness" or "kindness" of Yahweh.[32] In a (preexilic?) prayer of a persecuted and accused individual (Ps. 27), the psalmist says: "One thing I asked of Yahweh, that will I seek after: to live in the house of Yahweh all the days of my life, to behold the *nōʿam* of Yahweh" (v. 4); the verse probably refers to "God's loving way of turning to him for deliverance, to which he looks forward in vv. 1-6."[33] Ps. 90 is a late communal prayer; vv. 13-17, an even later expansion, include the petition "Let the lovingkindness of the LORD be upon us" (v. 17; it is preferable to follow 2 MSS. and the Targ. in deleting MT *'ᵉlōhênû*[34]). Here *nōʿam* appears to express Yahweh's miraculous intervention to reestablish the people's life work.

The most difficult problem is the meaning of the subst. *nōʿam* in the parabolic shepherd narrative Zec. 11:4-17. Central to this passage — which exhibits a "dense interpenetration of initial action and subsequent adaptation to narrative form"[35] — is the episode of the two staffs (*šᵉnê maqlôṯ* [v. 7], → מקל *maqqēl*), which is probably related to Ezk. 37:15-28 (but cf. *ʿēṣîm* in Ezk. 37). At Yahweh's command, the prophet — it is just possible that Zechariah himself is the "I" of the original account[36] — uses two staffs to guard the people's sheep doomed to slaughter: "one I named Favor *(nōʿam)*, the other I named Unity *(ḥōḇᵉlîm)*." The (later?) interpretation of the continued account, which tells how the prophet-shepherd refused to guard the sheep and therefore broke his staffs, states that the staff named Favor was broken "to annul my [Yahweh's or the prophet's?] covenant that I had made with all the peoples" (v. 10), while Unity was broken "to annul the family ties between Judah and Israel" (v. 14).[37] In any case, the staff Favor is to be understood as a "symbol of the happy condition of a people under an ideal ruler."[38]

5. *manʿammîm.* The derived noun *manʿammîm*[39] appears only in a (postexilic?) individual prayer (Ps. 141). The psalmist pleads to be protected from the power of the wicked and prays that a guard will be set over the door of his lips (v. 3). The next verse is usually understood in something like the sense proposed by Kraus and the NRSV: "Do not turn my heart to any evil, to busy myself with wicked deeds in company with those

---

31. Plöger, *BK,* XVII, 187f., 194f.
32. M. Sæbø, *Sacharja 9–14. WMANT,* 34 (1969), 241, n. 9.
33. Kraus, *Psalms 1–59,* 334; theophany or oracle of salvation?
34. Kraus, *Psalms 60–150,* 214.
35. Sæbø, *Sacharja 9–14,* 34, 249.
36. *Ibid.,* 252.
37. The various possible interpretations of 11:4-17 are discussed by Sæbø, *ibid.,* 71-88, 234-252, 276-78.
38. H. G. Mitchell, *Zechariah. ICC* (1912), 308.
39. On the gemination see *BLe,* 558f.

who work iniquity; do not let me eat of their delicacies *(ûḇal-ʾelḥam bᵉmanʿammêhem).*"[40] In this interpretation,[41] the psalmist speaks literally of the delectable food of the wicked. The context, however, suggests a figurative meaning (cf. esp. v. 6: *ʾᵃmāray kî nāʿēmû*[42]). It is also possible that the wisdom tradition used *manʿammîm* in the sense of "delightful, sweet words" (see, e.g., Prov. 22:18; 23:8).[43] If so, in Ps. 141 the psalmist is praying in fact for protection against taking the sweet (i.e., unctuous) words of the wicked in his own mouth. The interpretation of the LXX suggests a third possibility: "and let me not be joined to their elect *(metá tṓn eklektṓn autṓn)*"; in this interpretation the text refers to an elite group of the wicked (deriving *ʾelḥam* from *lḥm* I, not from *lḥm* II[44]).

6. *naʿᵃmānîm.* The derivative *naʿᵃmānîm* is also a hapax legomenon in the OT. The word is neither a plural *tantum* nor a double plural, but an incorrectly vocalized *naʿᵃmān-ma* (the DN *naʿᵃmān* + *-îm* = the affixed particle *-ma* found in Ugaritic; cf. Dt. 33:1; Ps. 68:17[16]; 77:18[17]; 125:1).[45] In the OT *naʿᵃmānîm* occurs in Isa. 17:1-11, a single kerygmatic unit comprising several originally separate strata, now bearing the superscription "an oracle concerning Damascus" *(maśśāʾ dammāśeq).* In vv. 10f. (probably Isaianic and dating from the period of the Syro-Ephraimite War), a fem. "you" (Jerusalem?) is addressed: "Truly you have forgotten the God of your salvation, and have not remembered the rock of your refuge; therefore, you plant gardens for the pleasant one *(ʿal-kēn tiṭṭᵉʿî niṭʿê naʿᵃmānîm)*and sow them with the vines of an alien (god). . . . The harvest will flee away in a day of weakness."[46] Here we apparently have a reference to Adonis gardens (Gk.: *hoi Adṓnidos kḗpoi*); *naʿᵃmān* is to be understood as designating the god Tammuz-Adonis.[47] "These little gardens of Adonis make use of bowls, boxes, or earthenware vessels, which would have the seeds of fast growing types of plants planted in them. The fast sprouting and the withering, which took place just as fast, were supposed to symbolize the appearance and disappearance (or coming to life again and death) of the vegetation god."[48] In Isa. 17:10 the Adonis gardens probably visualize the frail and fading nature of the (political and military?) power in which the prophet's audience trusted.[49]

III. LXX. The LXX uses a wide variety of translations for the root *nʿm* I. The most important is *kalós,* which represents *nāʿîm* 4 times, *nōʿam* 3 times, and the verb once.

---

40. Kraus, *Psalms 60–150,* 525.
41. Cf. *HAL,* II, 603; also Phoen. *mnʿm,* "delicacies," *DISO,* 159.
42. See II.3 above.
43. See II.3 above.
44. Cf. *HAL,* II, 526, etc.
45. J. O'Callaghan, *VT,* 4 (1954), 170f. On the double plural see *BLe,* 517v. On the Ugaritic material see Jirku, 201f.
46. On the text see Wildberger, *Isaiah 13–27,* 155f., 160f. On the date see *ibid.,* 180-82.
47. Schmökel, 29, n. 4; cf. also H. Ringgren, *UUÅ,* 1952:5, 67, 87.
48. Wildberger, *Isaiah 13–27,* 182.
49. See also esp. W. W. Baudissin, *Adonis und Esmun* (Leipzig, 1911); Galling, 59-61; W. Baumgartner, *Zum AT und seiner Umwelt* (Leiden, 1959), 247-281.

We also find *hēdýnein* (verb twice, *nāʿîm* twice, *nōʿam* twice), *euprepḗs* (*nāʿîm* twice, verb once), and *terpnós/terpnótēs* (*nāʿîm* 3 times, *nōʿam* once). In Isa. 17:10b *(naʿ^{a}mānîm)* the LXX is rather free: *diá toúto phyteúseis phýteuma ápiston kaí spérma ápiston,* avoiding actually translating *naʿ^{a}mānîm.* The LXX's interpretation of *manʿammîm* is discussed elsewhere.[50]

Finally, the root *nʿm* I is not attested in the Dead Sea Scrolls.

Kronholm

---

50. See II.5 above.

נַעַר *naʿar;* נַעֲרָה *naʿ^{a}râ;* נְעוּרִים *n^{e}ʿûrîm;* נְעֻרוֹת *n^{e}ʿurôṯ;* נֹעַר *nōʿar*

Contents: I. Etymology: 1. *nʿr* I; 2 *nʿr* II; *nʿr* III. II. Ancient Near East: 1. Egypt; 2. Ugarit; 3. Phoenician Inscriptions; 4. Akk. *ṣuḫār(t)u.* III. OT: 1. Occurrences; 2. Synonyms and Antonyms; 3. *naʿar;* 4. *naʿ^{a}râ;* 5. *nōʿar, n^{e}ʿûrîm, n^{e}ʿurôṯ.* IV. 1. Dead Sea Scrolls; 2. LXX.

---

naʿar. N. Avigad, "New Light on the *Naʿar* Seals," *Magnalia Dei. Festschrift G. E. Wright* (Garden City, N.Y., 1976), 294-300; B. J. Bamberger, "Qetanah, Naʿarah, Bogereth," *HUCA,* 32 (1961), 281-294; B. M. Barstad, *The Religious Polemics of Amos. SVT,* 34 (1984), esp. 11-36; F. Bron, "Notes de lexicographie ougaritique," *Sem,* 30 (1980), 13-15; R. L. Cohn, "Form and Perspective in 2 Kings V," *VT,* 33 (1983), 171-184, esp. 177-180; J. Conrad, *Die Junge Generation im AT. AzT,* I/42 (1970); B. Cutler and J. Macdonald, "Identification of the *naʿar* in the Ugaritic Texts," *UF,* 8 (1976), 27-35; A. H. Gardiner, *The Kadesh Inscriptions of Ramesses II* (^{2}1975); W. L. Holladay, "The Identification of the Two Scrolls of Jeremiah," *VT,* 30 (1980), 452-467, esp. 454f.; R. Kilian, *Die vorpriesterlichen Abrahamsüberlieferungen. BBB,* 24 (1966); L. Köhler, *Hebrew Man* (Eng. trans., New York, 1956); V. Maag, *Text, Wortschatz und Begriffswelt des Buches Amos* (Leiden, 1951); J. Macdonald, "The Role and Status of *ṣuḫārū* in the Mari Correspondence," *JAOS,* 96 (1976), 57-68; *idem,* "The Status and Role of the *Naʿar* in Israelite Society," *JNES,* 35 (1976), 147-170; *idem,* "The Supreme Warrior Caste in the Ancient Near East," *Oriental Studies. Festschrift B. S. J. Isserlin* (Leiden, 1980), 39-71; *idem,* "The Unique Ugaritic Personnel Text KTU 4.102," *UF,* 10 (1978), 161-173; E. W. Nicholson, "The Covenant Ritual in Exodus XXIV 3-8," *VT,* 32 (1982), 74-86, esp. 81f.; I. Riesener, *Der Stamm ʿbd im AT. BZAW,* 149 (1979); H.-C. Schmitt, *Elisa* (Gütersloh, 1972); A. R. Schulman, "The Nʿrn at Kadesh Once Again," *Schriften der Studiengemeinschaft der Evangelischen Akademien,* 11 (1981), 7-19; *idem,* "The Nʿrn at the Battle of Kadesh," *JARCE,* 1 (1962), 47-53; N. Šcupak, "Some Common Idioms in the Biblical and the Egyptian Wisdom Literatures," *ShnatMikr,* 2 (1977), 233-266 (Heb.); H. P. Stähli, *Knabe — Jüngling — Knecht. BBET,* 7 (1978); Z. Weisman, "The Nature and Background of *bāḥûr* in the OT," *VT,* 31 (1981), 441-450; H. W. Wolff, *Anthropology of the OT* (Eng. trans., Philadelphia, 1974); Y. Yadin, *The Art of Warfare in Biblical Lands in the Light of Archaeological Discovery,* 2 vols. (Eng. trans., New York, 1963).

I. Etymology. The etymology of the nominal lexeme *nʿr* (fem. *nʿrh*) is uncertain; scholars have proposed various derivations.

1. *nʿr I.* F. E. C. Dietrich derives the noun *naʿar* from a root *nʿr,* "snarl, roar," which reproduces "onomatopoeically the rasping sounds of snarling, snoring, or the like that issue from the throat."[1] A *nʿr* is "actually in transition to puberty, when the voice changes, someone who speaks with a rasp" (cf. the rabbinic interpretation of Ex. 2:6: "[Moses] was a child [*yld*], and his voice was that of a boy [*nʿr*]"[2]). This interpretation is accepted by F. Mühlau and W. Volck.[3] It is presently supported for Ugar. and Heb. *nʿr* by Adrianus van Selms, who cites Jer. 51:38, and by Lothar Kopf, who cites Jgs. 13:5,7.[4]

Heb. *nʿr* I is attested only in Jer. 51:38, a late text. It is related to Akk. *naʾāru(m)/nēʾiru,* which denote primarily the roaring of a lion, the braying of an ass, or the screeching of a bird, but never the cry of a human being; cf. Aram. *ḥmr nʿr,* "braying ass," as well as the snarling of a camel.[5] Only Arab. *naʿara,* which covers a broad range of meanings, refers to a human sound, especially a war or battle cry; cf. also *naʿʿara,* "scolding woman."[6]

Heb. *nʿr* I is clearly an aramaism.[7] The root is not found in the other Northwest Semitic dialects. In contrast to Hebrew, there are no nominal derivatives of *nʿr* meaning "boy" or "servant" in Aramaic, Arabic, or Akkadian. We conclude that there is no etymological connection between Heb. *naʿar* and *nʿr* I.

2. *nʿr II.* Johann Buxtorf connects *naʿar* with *nʿr* II, "shake (off)." A *naʿar* is a "little boy, an infant," in that he has been "forced out of his mother's womb."[8] Franz Delitzsch takes as his starting point the striking use of *nʿr* in the Pentateuch to refer to a female, concluding that "originally it denoted a new-born infant of either sex," since it "is an ancient derived noun with the meaning 'shaking off, bringing forth' (cf. Job 39:3), concretely: that which has been brought forth, offspring."[9]

---

1. *GesB* ([5]1857), 35.
2. R. Jehuda, *Shem. Rab.,* 1, 24.
3. *GesB* ([8-11]1878-90).
4. A. van Selms, *Marriage and Family Life in Ugaritic Literature. POS,* I (1954), 95; L. Kopf, *VT,* 8 (1958), 183; cf. *KBL*[2], 623a, incorrectly citing H. L. Fleischer, *Kleinere Schriften,* I-III (1885-88). This etymology has been dropped by *HAL,* II, 707.
5. For the Akkadian see *AHw,* II, 694a, 709a; *CAD,* XI/1, 7f. On the Aramaic, for the former see Ahikar 79 (*AP,* 214); Bab. *Ber.* 3a, 56a; for the latter see Bab. *Yeb.* 120b; Jastrow, 922a.
6. For the former see Lane, 2815; for the latter, *Lisān al-ʿArab of Ibn-Mukarram* (Cairo, 1890), V, 220b.
7. Already B. Duhm, *Das Buch Jeremia. KHC,* XI (1901), 372; not noted as such by M. Wagner, *Die lexikalischen und grammatikalischen Aramaismen im alttestamentlichen Hebräisch. BZAW,* 96 (1966).
8. J. Buxtorf, *Lexicon hebraicum et chaldaicum* (1607), 477.
9. F. Delitzsch, "Pentateuch-kritische Studien, VIII," *Zeitschrift für kirkliche Wissenschaft und kirkliches Leben,* 1 (1880), 393-99.

Heb. *n'r* II, "shake (off)," appears in various contexts with a variety of objects: leaves (Isa. 33:9), dust (52:2), hands (33:15), locusts (Ps. 109:23), the fold of a garment (Neh. 5:13), and, figuratively, enemies (Jgs. 16:20; Ex. 14:27; Ps. 136:15). The OT does not use *n'r* II in connection with birth; nor does such usage appear in extrabiblical texts. The association of this root with *na'ar* therefore appears dubious.

3. *n'r III.* Heb. *na'ar* is probably a primary noun from a distinct root *n'r* III, whose basic meaning is unknown.[10]

II. Ancient Near East.

1. *Egypt.* Egyptian texts of the Ramesside period frequently use the word *n'rn.* It is not an Egyptian word but a Canaanite loanword denoting a military unit.[11] The descriptive legend on a relief depicting the battle of Kadesh speaks of *n'rn* of Pharaoh from the land of Amurru; their intervention saved Rameses from defeat.[12] Scholars have interpreted this text as referring to a specialized Egyptian unit, an Egyptian reserve corps, or an elite unit made up of young people from aristocratic families brought up at Pharaoh's court.[13] More likely the word denotes a Canaanite military unit in Pharaoh's service.

The Karnak Inscription of Merneptah (1224-1204) includes *n'rn* in a (fragmentary) list of the military hierarchy and the associated (?) units. Here *n'rn* parallels *ỉȝyw,* which means something like "veterans." The text does not indicate whether the two terms refer to the same group of people or to different units.[14] In any case, the term denotes an experienced, battle-tested unit.

Papyrus Anastasi I, a satirical polemic, speaks of a punitive expedition of Amenemope to Djahi, an unidentified Canaanite town, to put down a revolt of *n'rn.*[15] Hori, the author of this document, derisively calls his opponent "leader of the *n'rn,* who stands at the head of the *ḏȝbw*";[16] one may ask whether Amenemope himself was once commander of a Canaanite *n'rn* unit and whether it is perhaps his old unit that is rebelling in Djahi. It appears possible, at any event, that the *n'rn* in Canaanite territory played an important role not only militarily but also politically.

In the Onomasticon of Amenope, written around 1100 (toward the end of the Twentieth Dynasty), the toponym *n'ryn* appears in the so-called Syro-Palestinian list.[17]

---

10. *GesTh,* 894a; E. Ben-Yehuda, *Thesaurus totius hebraitatis,* 8 vols. (repr. New York, 1960), V, 3712a; *BDB,* 654b; Stähli, 37.

11. *WbÄS,* II, 209; cf. W. F. Albright, *AfO,* 6 (1930/31), 221.

12. G. A. Lehmann, *UF,* 2 (1970), 68f.

13. See, respectively, Gardiner, 8; Schulman, 48; and S. Yeivin, in *Military History of the Land of Israel in Biblical Times,* ed. J. Liver (Tel Aviv, 1964), 13 (Heb.).

14. For the former see Gardiner, 37: "veterans *(ỉȝyw)* of the army who were Ne'ārīn." For the latter see Schulman, 52; idem, "Military Rank," *MÄS,* 6 (1964), 118: "all the veterans (lit. old ones of the army), (and) the ones who were n'rn-troops with captures."

15. *AOT,* 101-5; *ANET,* 475-79.

16. *ANET,* 478b.

17. No. 259 in Gardiner, *Ancient Egyptian Onomastica,* I (Oxford, 1947); the list is nos. 250-270; see pp. 24ff. for the whole onomasticon.

This word is probably not connected with *n'rn* as a military unit; more likely it is associated with the Hebrew place name *n'rn* = *n'rh,* deriving from *n'r* II.[18]

2. *Ugarit.* Ugaritic texts use *n'r* (fem. *n'rt*) in a wide range of meanings. Like Egyp. *n'rn,* in the social structure of Ugarit *n'rm* may denote a group of high military rank, whose functions we cannot determine in detail.[19]

In addition, *n'r/n'rt* denotes persons belonging to the household of a paterfamilias. It can refer to servants, usually holding responsible positions.[20] Depending on the social status of the paterfamilias, a *n'r(t)* can be of distinguished birth and can occupy an important office.[21] Age is irrelevant.

This seems to be the case in *KTU,* 4.360, 5, and 4.367, 7, where *n'r* parallels *bn,* with which it appears to exhibit a certain synonymy. The first text lists as belonging to the family of Yrḫm 2 *bnh b'lm,* 3 *n'rm,* and *bt 'ḥt.* It is probably to be understood as meaning that Yrḫm married two wives[22] and had three minor sons. The meaning of *KTU,* 4.367, a list of the royal personnel from the town of *tbq,* is obscure. One portion of the text reads: *ṯn bn ʒwrḫz (n)'rm yṣr.* H. P. Stähli translates: "two sons of Iwrḫz, (being) *n'rm,* who are potters"; B. Cutler and J. Macdonald translate differently: "two sons of I. (who are) *n'rm;* a potter. . . ."[23] In their interpretation, *n'rm* does not refer to a legal status within the family — minors under their father's authority[24] — but rather denotes a specific office held by the sons at the court of the king of Tbq.

By contrast, *KTU,* 2.33, 29 is a clear instance of *n'r* with the meaning "child, youth."[25] The weakness associated with youth is alluded to in *KTU,* 1.107, 37, where *n'r* parallels *ṣǵr,* "small": the son of the goddess Šapaš cries like a *n'r* and pours forth tears like a *ṣǵr* — in other words, he cries like a young child.

The evidence for *n'r* as an element of theophorous names is unclear. *UT,* 10:16 has *n'r(?) ʒl,* "Servant of Il";[26] but now *KTU,* 4.12, 16 reads *nz*rʒl.* Franke Gröndahl interprets *n'r* in *KTU,* 3.7, 16 as a hypocoristic theophorous name, while Stähli suggests the possibility of a secular name.[27] We should probably follow Cutler and Macdonald, who think in terms of an office.[28]

3. *Phoenician Inscriptions.* A Phoenician marble tablet of the fourth or third century B.C. discovered near Larnaka contains a list of the expenditures of a temple adminis-

---

18. Contra Stähli, 66; cf. *HAL,* II, 708.
19. *KTU,* 4.68, 60; 4.126, 12; cf. Cutler and Macdonald, 32ff.; Stähli, 44ff.
20. *KTU,* 4.102, 17; cf. 8; 4.339, 3; cf. *UT,* no. 1666; for a different view, see van Selms, *Marriage,* 95.
21. Cutler and Macdonald, 27.
22. *UT,* no. 493; for a different interpretation, see *PRU,* V, no. 80, 4f.; Cutler and Macdonald, 31.
23. Stähli, 49, following *UT,* 284; Cutler and Macdonald, 31.
24. Stähli, 49.
25. Cutler and Macdonald, 35.
26. Stähli, 55; cf. *PNU,* 80.
27. See *PNU,* 50; Stähli, 55, citing *IPN,* 221.
28. P. 28.

tration in Kition.[29] Several times it names *nʿrm* among those receiving payments, clearly members of the temple personnel.[30] Nothing is said about their position or function. Whether they belonged to the cult personnel and might be called "sacred ministers of high rank"[31] remains dubious.

In *KAI,* 24, 12 we have the only instance of an abstract plural derived from *nʿr: lmnʿry (la-min-naʿ-ūrayyu).* In this inscription, composed around 825 B.C., Kilamuwa extols the general prosperity that his rule has brought: among other things, "he who had seen no linen from his youth was clothed with byssus in my days." This text is important because (together with *KTU,* 1.107; 2.33; 4.360) it shows that Can. *nʿr* refers primarily to age, albeit with connotations of the naturally associated social position of a leading personality within the extended family or the household.

4. *Akk. ṣuḫār(t)u.* Neither *naʿar* nor its feminine derivative occurs in Akkadian. The noun *na'āru(m)* derives from *nʿr* I.[32] The semantic equivalent to *nʿr* is *ṣuḫāru* or *ṣuḫārtu.*[33] Both occur frequently in Assyro-Babylonian texts as well as in the Mari letters; they have a broad range of meanings almost identical with that of *nʿr(t).*

The noun *ṣuḫār(t)u* can denote a particular age: "child, youth."[34] According to the Code of Hammurabi, a son described as *ṣiḫru* (adj.) is not yet legally competent. He cannot inherit his patrimony, hold property in fee, or marry.[35] Middle Assyrian law defines the minimum age for marriage as ten.[36] Young persons of either sex can be requisitioned for service by order of the king.[37]

In the majority of cases, *ṣuḫāru* denotes a servile relationship in a variety of positions and functions. Dependence on the master is reflected in such expressions as "my *ṣuḫāru,*" which parents never use of their children. One list illustrates the connection between age and position.[38] It names a series of occupations and the rations assigned to them; in each case the *ṣuḫāru* are listed last and their rations are substantially scantier than those of the others. They are clearly still apprentices in training.[39] Age is not significant. A *ṣuḫāru* is a servant. As such, he is dependent on his master, who can employ him in a variety of tasks — as basket maker, field hand, fisher, scribe, messenger.[40] Depending on his master's position, a *ṣuḫāru* may be of high birth and be responsible for important jobs.[41]

29. *KAI,* 37.
30. A 8, 10(?), 12; B 11.
31. Stähli, 68.
32. *AHw,* II, 694; *CAD,* XI/1, 7f.
33. See, respectively, *CAD,* XVI, 231b-35a, 229b-231b.
34. *CAD,* XVI, 231b-232b; *ARM,* I, 108, 6f.; II, 32, 13; 99, 8; V, 38, 10-14; VI, 43, 8f.; etc.
35. See, respectively, CH, §§177, 28f., 166.
36. *ANET,* 184a.
37. *ARM,* III, 38, 5ff.
38. *ARM,* IX, 24, I, 47, 55; II, 46.
39. M. Birot, *ARM,* IX, 357.
40. *CAD,* XVI, 132ff.
41. For the former see *ARM,* II, 79, 24, 28; VI, 20, 7; VII, 110, 3; etc. For the latter see *ARM,* I, 45, 13; II, 21, 15; IV, 31, 13f.; V, 11, 7ff.

The case of the *ṣuḫārtu* is similar. The feminine usually means "marriageable girl, young woman."[42] Infrequently in Old Babylonian texts but more often in the Mari letters and the Nuzi texts, it refers to women in various servile positions. They may be domestic servants or weavers.[43] Some of them occupy high positions in the palace of Mari.[44] They occasionally perform cultic functions, always referred to by the appropriate technical terms.[45] For this very reason, it is unlikely that *ṣuḫārtu* (or *ṣuḫāru*) can mean "cultic functionary."[46]

III. OT.

1. *Occurrences.* In the OT *na'ar* occurs about 239 times.[47] Almost one-third of these occurrences (86) are in Samuel (1 Samuel: 60; 2 Samuel: 26); then follow Kings with 35 (1 Kings: 11; 2 Kings: 24), Genesis with 27 (none in P), Judges with 23, Isaiah with 11, and Nehemiah with 8. The word does not appear in Leviticus, Ezekiel, the Minor Prophets (except for one occurrence each in Hosea and Zechariah), Song of Songs, or Daniel. Fewer than a quarter of the occurrences (49) are distributed among the remaining books.

The fem. *na'ᵃrâ* occurs 38 times: Gen. 24:16; Ex. 2:5; Dt. 22:19; Jgs. 19 (6 times); 21:12; Ruth 2:6,8,22f.; 3:2; 4:12; 1 S. 9:11; 25:42; 1 K. 1:2-4; 2 K. 5:2,4; Est. 2 (8 times); 4:4,16; Job 40:29(Eng. 41:4);[48] Prov. 9:3; 27:27; 31:15; Am. 2:7. Other derivatives are *nᵉ'ûrîm* (46 occurrences), *nᵉ'urôṯ* (Jer. 32:30), and *nō'ar* (Ps. 88:16[15]; Job 33:25; 36:14; Prov. 29:11).

A special feature is the *qere perpetuum* נַעֲרָ *na'ᵃrā:* Gen. 24 (5 times); 34:3,12; Dt. 22:15-29 (14 times). Delitzsch considers this a "linguistically indisputable archaism," showing that originally *n'r* was used for either sex without distinction.[49] More likely we have here an "orthographical oddity," a "survival of a system of orthography in which a final vowel was written defectively."[50]

In one group of texts (some 100 out of 239 occurrences), *n'r* is used absolutely (with or without the definite article *h-;* rarely in the pl.). The semantic context points exclusively to the realm of the extended family. Here *na'ar* denotes a son[51] living within the circle of the family. Such expressions as "my *na'ar*" are never used to convey the parent-child relationship.

A second group of texts uses *na'ar* (sg. and pl.) as *nomen regens* in a construct

---

42. *CAD,* XVI, 231.
43. For the former see *ABBU,* I, 21, 14, 20; 26, 6, 7; II, 108, 13; III, 11, 34; *ARM,* III, 38, 5-7; etc. For the latter see *ARM,* X, 125, 11-14.
44. *ARM,* V, 7; X, 100.
45. *ARM,* X, 124, 4f.; 140, 16-19; cf. *ARM,* III, 8, 6.
46. Despite *ARM,* 8, 6f.; XIII, 112.
47. Stähli, 72; *HAL,* II, 707.
48. Uncertain; see D. Winton Thomas, *VT,* 14 (1964), 115f.
49. P. 399; see I.2 above.
50. For the first quotation see JM, §16f, 3; for the second, *GK,* §17c; cf. §2n.
51. → בֵּן *bēn* (II, 145-159).

phrase or with a suffix. Here the contextual evidence reveals a more nuanced relationship of dependency associated with the *naʿar*.

2. *Synonyms and Antonyms.* In the broader and narrower context of *naʿar,* we find terms referring to age or stage of life that serve as parallels or antonyms,[52] e.g., *naʿar/zāqēn* (Gen. 19:4; Dt. 28:50; Isa. 20:4); cf. *bāḥûr/zāqēn* (Jer. 31:13); *naʿar/bāḥûr/zāqēn* (Ps. 148:12; Lam. 2:21); cf. *naʿar/ʾîš/zāqēn* (Josh 6:21); *yônēq/bāḥûr/ ʾîš śêḇâ* (Dt. 32:25); cf. *yônēq/ʿôlēl/ʾîš* (Jer. 44:7); *ṭap/naʿar/ʾiššâ/zāqēn* (Est. 3:13); cf. *ṭap/bāḥûr/ʾiššâ/zāqēn* (Ezk. 9:6); *naʿar/bāḥûr/ʾîš/zāqēn* (Jer. 51:22); cf. *ʿôlēl/bāḥûr/ʾîš/zāqēn/mᵉlēʾ yāmîm* (Jer. 6:11). The texts present very diverse divisions of human life into stages. Although some terms refer to a specific age bracket or stage of development *(yônēq, ʿôlēl, yeleḏ, ʿelem, bāḥûr, zāqēn),* it is hardly possible to assign definite ages to them and associate them with other corresponding terms,[53] despite many passages that include ages (Gen. 17:25; Ex. 30:14; Nu. 1:3,18; 4:3,23; 8:24; 14:29; 26:2; 32:11; Lev. 27:1-8; 1 Ch. 23:3; 2 Ch. 25:5). It is true, however, that *naʿar* always stands in contrast to *zāqēn;* in many passages, it has become part of a stock phrase as an antonym to *zāqēn: minnaʿar . . . ʿaḏ-zāqēn* (Gen. 19:4; Josh. 6:21; Est. 3:13), *naʿar wᵉzāqēn* (Ex. 10:9; Isa. 20:4; Lam. 2:21) or *zāqēn wᵉnaʿar* (Jer. 51:22; Ps. 148:12). These phrases are typical examples of merism, a figure that expresses a totality by emphasizing its opposite extremes: "young and old" (with the natural connotations of associated social rank) = "one and all."

These observations show that *naʿar* clearly refers to youth. The upper boundary varies: 20 (Ex. 30:14; Nu. 1:3,18; 14:29; 26:2; 32:11; 2 Ch. 25:5; etc.), 25 (Nu. 8:24), 30 (Nu. 4:3,23; 1 Ch. 23:3). The rabbis reflect similar uncertainty: *Midr. Prov.* on 1:4 states that one is a *naʿar* until age 25 (R. Meir), 30 (R. Akiba), or 20 (R. Ishmael), because from the age of 20 one is held accountable for one's sins.[54] In any case, for the rabbis both *naʿar* and the abstract *nᵉʿurôṯ* are precise terms for youth, with the particular connotation of vigor and strength.[55]

The antonym *ʾāḏôn* (Jgs. 19:11,12; 1 S. 25:14,17; 2 K. 5:20,22,25; 6:15; cf. 1 S. 20:38; 30:13; 2 S. 9:9; 2 K. 5:3) indicates the dependent or servile status of a *naʿar,* similar to that of an → עבד *ʿeḇeḏ.* In contrast to the latter, however, who as a slave "in the power of another" is not free, the *naʿar* is a free person who enters by choice into a servile relationship and may even under some circumstances possess *ʿᵃḇāḏîm* and *šᵉp̄āḥôṯ* (e.g., 2 K. 5:20-27[6-13]).[56]

3. *naʿar.* a. *Child, Youth, Young Man.* The three-month-old baby Moses is called a *naʿar.* When Pharaoh's daughter found a basket among the reeds and opened it, "she saw the child *(yeleḏ),* and behold, it was a crying *naʿar*" (Ex. 2:6 [J]). Judah calls his

52. See Köhler, 39ff., 74ff.; Wolff, 120ff.; Stähli, 77ff., 132ff.
53. Conrad, 10; Stähli, 84.
54. A. Wünsche, *Der Midrasch Mischle. Bibliotheca Rabbinica,* IV (Leipzig, 1883-85, [2]1967), 4.
55. Bab. *Giṭ.* 70a; *Shab.* 11a; cf. *Ber. Rab.* 48:19,22 on Gen. 18:11,13.
56. Riesener, 75ff. The quotation is from *AncIsr,* 84.

young brother Benjamin a *na'ar* (Gen. 43:8; 44:22,30-34 [J]); according to 44:20, Benjamin is a *yeleḏ zᵉqunîm qāṭān*. He lives with his father, whose protection he enjoys (44:20,30; cf. 44:22). Gen. 25:27 (J) calls the growing brothers Esau and Jacob *nᵉ'ārîm*. Shechem, a growing youth who already enjoys respect and honor, is likewise called a *na'ar;* he asks for Dinah's hand and negotiates the marriage terms with her family (34:19 [J]).

The story of Hagar's expulsion (Gen. 21:8-21 [E]) sometimes calls Ishmael a *yeleḏ* (vv. 14-16), sometimes a *na'ar* (vv. 12,17 [twice], 18-20). This is not evidence of different sources:[57] the two nouns are synonymous here. As a small *na'ar,* Ishmael is totally dependent on the protection and help of his mother (21:16). The *nᵉ'ārîm* Ephraim and Manasseh whom Joseph blesses are also small children (48:15f. [E]). The *na'ar* Isaac is somewhat older (22:5,12 [E]); he walks next to his father and carries the wood of the burnt offering.

Jgs. 13:5,7,8,12 speak of Samson as the *na'ar* to be born. V. 34 calls the grown boy a *na'ar.* According to 8:14, Gideon catches a *na'ar* from Succoth, who is still young and inexperienced but knows the information Gideon wants and can write it down.

Samuel's mother calls her child a *na'ar* both as a suckling (1 S. 1:22) and as a growing boy (vv. 24,25,27). The sons of Jesse are *nᵉ'ārîm* (16:11); they still live with their father but are old enough to share a sacrificial meal (v. 5). The story of Goliath (17:1–18:5) frequently calls the adolescent David a *na'ar* (17:33,42,55,58; 17:56 par. *'elem* [cf. 20:22]). David's seriously ill young son is called both *yeleḏ* (2 S. 12:15, 18f.,21f.) and *na'ar* (v. 16). The sons of David who live as young princes at court are *nᵉ'ārîm* (13:32). With particular emphasis, David calls his rebellious son Absalom (who has his own property and servants [13:23ff.]) a *na'ar* (14:21; 18:5,29; cf. 18:12,32), in order to play down his rebellion and make it out to be a foolish escapade of youth.

Jeroboam's son is called a *na'ar* in 1 K. 14:3,17 and a *yeleḏ* in v. 12. In 2 K. 4:18ff. we read of a boy who is not yet old enough to work but is old enough to go by himself to his father out in the field. In parallel with *yeleḏ* (vv. 18,26,34) he is also called *na'ar* (vv. 29f.,31f.,35). Here, too, the alternation between the two terms should not be taken as evidence of different sources.[58] Finally, 2 K. 2:23 speaks of *nᵉ'ārîm qᵉṭannîm* ("small boys") who make fun of Elisha.

Several texts in Isaiah use *na'ar.* Isa. 8:4, "Before the *na'ar* knows how to call 'My father' or 'My mother,' " refers to a child one or two years old. Isa. 7:17 reads: "Before the *na'ar* knows how to refuse the evil and choose the good"; this expression refers not so much to "freedom of choice based on personal experience," suggesting an age of about twenty, as to the ability to distinguish what is harmful from what is beneficial, which comes around the age of three.[59] Isa. 40:30 uses *nᵉ'ārîm* in parallel with *baḥûrîm*

---

57. Contra Kilian, 228ff., 236-249.

58. Contra Schmitt, 93ff.

59. H. Wildberger, *Isaiah 1–12* (Eng. trans., Minneapolis, 1990), 315; R. Kilian, *Die Verheissung Immanuels. SBS,* 35 (1968), 42f. For the quotation see O. Kaiser, *Isaiah 1–12. OTL* (Eng. trans. ²1983), 161.

to suggest the vigor of youth.[60] The prophecy of the coming age of salvation in 65:16b-25 promises long life for all.[61] No infant will die young, and the *naʿar* will live to be one hundred (v. 20).

Besides the youthfulness of the *naʿar,* wisdom texts emphasize his immaturity and dependence (par. *peṯî* and *kᵉsîl*). He is without sense (Prov. 7:7), is easily led astray and deluded (7:22f.), and needs strict discipline (22:6,15) if he is to become prudent and wise (*ḥāḵām*) (1:4; 22:15; 29:15) and thus be spared from death (23:13f.). To have a *naʿar* as king means the total breakdown of civil order and the downfall of the community (Eccl. 10:15f.; cf. Isa. 3:4f.).

Solomon's description of himself as a *naʿar qāṭōn* (1 K. 3:7; cf. 1 K. 11:14-22) must be understood in the context of a notion of an ordered world that reflects Egyptian provenience. It confesses a total inability to understand *mišpāṭ,* the meaning and order of the world, as well as a radical dependence on the divine gift of knowledge without which the king will always remain a *naʿar qāṭōn* and a *pᵉṯî.* It is an expression of humility and self-abasement that shows Solomon to be truly *ḥāḵām.*

Jeremiah's self-predication, *naʿar ʾānōḵî* (Jer. 1:6), may be interpreted similarly as resistance to God's call to be a prophet. It has nothing to do with age but acknowledges total lack of experience and of ability for a preaching mandate of such magnitude, while asking implicitly for God's assistance and support.

b. *Military.* As in some Ugaritic texts, *naʿar* can refer to a specific military function. When fleeing from Saul, David is accompanied by *nᵉʿārîm* (1 S. 21:2-10[1-9]). These are mercenaries in his service and under his command, adventurers and malcontents from all social classes whom he had engaged as irregulars (22:2; 25:13; cf. 27:2; 30:9) even before his break with Saul.[62] Ten of his *nᵉʿārîm* negotiate with Nabal over payment of protection (25:2ff.); they are identical with the *ʾᵃnāšîm* of vv. 13,20. At the suggestion of Abner, accepted by Joab, twelve of David's *nᵉʿārîm* and twelve of Ishbaal's fight a representative duel (2 S. 2:12-17; cf. 1 S. 17; 2 S. 21:15-22).[63] That a contest of such consequence would involve picked professional warriors goes without saying. In some cases *nᵉʿārîm* occupy the trusted position of armor-bearer, e.g., in the case of Jonathan (1 S. 14:1,6; 20:21f.,35ff.) and Joab (2 S. 18:15). As a rule they are already experienced fighters (but cf. Jgs. 8:20; 1 S. 20:35). The account of the war between Ahab and the Aramean Ben-hadad (1 K. 20) speaks of the *nᵉʿārîm* of the district governors used by Ahab as shock troops in a surprise attack on the camp of Ben-hadad, while the militia follows them. The text refers to units made up of experienced professional soldiers under the personal command of the district governors. Such units do not resurface until the time of Nehemiah, who in the process of rebuilding Jerusalem appoints his *nᵉʿārîm* both to protect against hostile incursions (Neh. 4:10[16]) — a task the militia, "something of a rabble,"[64] could not carry out by themselves — and to supervise and continue

60. K. Elliger, *Deuterojesaja. BK,* XI/1 (1978), 100.
61. See C. Westermann, *Isaiah 40–66. OTL* (Eng. trans. 1969), 406f.
62. A. Gunneweg, *Geschichte Israels bis Bar Kochba. TW,* II (^{4}1982), 73.
63. Cf. also *ANET,* 20; *AOT,* 57f.; Yadin, I, 266f.
64. W. Rudolph, *Esra und Nehemia. HAT,* XX (1949), 125.

the rebuilding of the walls (4:10[16]; 5:16). At other times they perform police functions and administrative duties (13:19; cf. 1 K. 11:28). As agents and representatives of the governor, they have considerable economic and social status (Neh. 5:1-10). This holds true in general also for the early period.

c. *Servant.* As servants, *n*[e]*'ārîm* form part of the sometimes extensive households of wealthy individuals (1 S. 9:1,3; 25:8; Ruth 2:9); they perform miscellaneous tasks (Gen. 18:7; 22:3,5,19) and are employed as field hands (2 K. 4:19,22; Ruth 2:9,15,21; Job 1:15) or shepherds (1 S. 25:8,14,19; Job 1:16f.). A *na'ar* occasionally accompanies his master on a journey (Nu. 22:22; Jgs. 19:3ff.; 2 K. 4:24). Sometimes he becomes a personal servant and confidant (Jgs. 7:10f.; 9:54; 1 S. 9:5ff.; 1 K. 18:43; 19:3; 2 K. 4:12,25; 5:20; 8:4). The *na'ar* of a member of the royal family or of the king himself is of high birth and his position is exalted (2 S. 13:17,23ff.; Est. 2:2; 6:3,5; cf. 2 K. 19:6f. par. Isa. 37:6f.).

d. *Steward.* The *na'ar* of Boaz (Ruth 2:5ff.) and Ziba, the *na'ar* of Saul (2 S. 9:9) or of Saul's house (2 S. 19:18), perform the functions of an estate manager or steward. Israelite and Ammonite seals in the form PN_1 *n'r* PN_2 suggest that *n'r* served as the title of the person administering the royal domains.[65]

e. *Cultic Functionary (?).* A few occurrences of *na'ar* appear in cultic contexts (Ex. 24:5; 33:11; Jgs. 17:7,11f.; 18:3,15; 1 S. 1:24; 2:11,18,21,26; 3:1,8). A *na'ar* can perform various services at a sanctuary. Nevertheless, the Canaanite parallels and OT passages are insufficient evidence to suggest that *na'ar* is a technical term for a cultic functionary.[66]

4. *na'*[a]*râ.* The semantics of the fem. *na'*[a]*râ* are, mutatis mutandis, similar to those of *na'ar,* albeit without equivalent usage in the military realm.

a. *Girl, Young Woman.* The noun *na'*[a]*râ* designates a young female (1 K. 1:2-4; 2 K. 5:2; Ruth 2:5,6; 4:12), more specifically a single but marriageable girl (Gen. 24:16,28,55,57; 34:3,12; Dt. 22:23-27,28f.; Jgs. 21:12; 1 S. 9:11; 1 K. 1:2ff.; Est. 2:2ff.,12f.). The noun *b*[e]*tûlâ* in apposition shows that she is still a virgin (Gen. 24:16; Dt. 22:23,28; Jgs. 21:12; 1 K. 1:2; Est. 2:2f.) who has not yet "known"[67] a man (Gen. 24:16; cf. Jgs. 21:12). She already has certain limited legal rights and can make a vow (Nu. 30:4; 11QTemple 53:17). A married woman can be called a *na'*[a]*râ* when the text addresses her continuing relationship with her former family or her father even after marriage (Jgs. 19:3-9; Dt. 22:13-21; Est. 2:20).

b. *Servant.* The plural with a suffix (Gen. 24:61; Ex. 2:5; 1 S. 25:42; Prov. 9:3; 27:27; 31:15; Ruth 2:8,22; 3:2; Est. 2:9; 4:16) or a genitive personal name (Ruth 2:23; Est. 4:4) refers to female servants with a variety of positions and functions. As maids

---

65. Stähli, 181. For the Israelite seals see F. Vattioni, "I sigilli ebraici," *Bibl,* 50 (1969), 357-388. For the Ammonite seals see N. Avigad, "Seals and Sealings," *IEJ,* 14 (1964), 190-94; M. F. Martin, "Six Palestinian Seals," *RSO,* 39 (1964), 203ff.

66. J. Becker, *BZ,* 26 (1982), 116, contra Stähli, 184-217. On the Canaanite parallels see II.2 above.

67. → ידע *yāḏa'* (V, 448-481).

they work in the field (Ruth 2:8,22f.), as ladies of the court they are of high birth and belong to the personal retinue of Pharaoh's daughter (Ex. 2:5), Abigail (1 S. 25:42), and Esther (Est. 2:9; cf. 4:4,16).

c. *Am. 2:7.* The *na'ᵃrâ* in Am. 2:7 is problematic. Citing Hittite laws, many scholars assume that the ancient Near Eastern institution of cultic prostitution was present in Israel (Hos. 4:14; cf. 1 K. 14:24; 15:12; 22:47; 2 K. 23:7; Dt. 23:18f.) and theorize that she was a cult prostitute.[68] A variant theory associates *na'ᵃrâ* with the sacral meal of a household congregation (Jer. 16:5; Am. 6:7) and thinks of her as "some sort of hostess attached to the *mrzḥ*."[69] More likely and more appropriate to the cultic context of Am. 2:6-8 is the interpretation of the text as referring to a social offense against a woman in a weak position because of her low social status. The theory that *na'ᵃrâ* here means "female slave"[70] encounters the problem that the presumed relationship to Ex. 21:7ff. is mostly unlikely; furthermore, *na'ar/na'ᵃrâ* never means "slave" (male or female). The text probably refers in general terms to a young virgin of marriageable age, who enjoys legal protection (Dt. 22:28f.; cf. Ex. 22:15; Dt. 22:13ff.; Jgs. 19:23f.; 20:6; 2 S. 13:12) but is insulted by the conduct excoriated in Am. 2:7.

5. *nō'ar, nᵉ'ûrîm, nᵉ'urôṯ.* The three abstract formations *nᵉ'ûrîm* (*qaṭûl* masc. pl.; 46 occurrences), *nᵉ'urôṯ* (*qaṭûl* fem. pl.; Jer. 32:30), and *nō'ar* (*quṭl;* Ps. 88:16[5]; Job 33:25; 36:14; Prov. 29:21) all refer to "youth" without distinction. In particular contexts, of course, specific attributes such as young, inexperienced, immature, unmarried, or fresh, radiant, vigorous can shape the semantics of the text in question.

The expression *minnᵉ'ûrîm* serves as a statement of time, e.g., "from [my] youth until this day" (1 S. 12:2; cf. 2 S. 19:8[7]). "From youth" is equivalent to "throughout an entire lifetime"; the expression may refer to an occupation (Gen. 46:34; 1 S. 17:33) or to religious conduct: the wicked nature of human beings (Gen. 8:21), the sinfulness of the people (Jer. 3:25; cf. 22:21), fear of God (1 K. 18:12), trust in God (Ps. 71:5), or avoidance of unclean things (Ezk. 4:14). The phrase *'ēšeṯ nᵉ'ûrîm,* "wife of one's youth," deserves special notice. A man's relationship to the wife of his youth is especially intimate; he should treat her with constant fidelity. This notion comes to symbolize the relationship with Yahweh (Mal. 2:14f.) or with wisdom (Prov. 5:18) or the constant love of God for his people (Isa. 54:6). Similar expressions refer to the "friend *('allûp̄)* of one's youth" (Jer. 3:4; Prov. 2:17), the "husband *(ba'al)* of one's youth" (Joel 1:8), and the "devotion *(ḥeseḏ)* of one's youth" (Jer. 2:2).

---

68. Comms. on Amos: K. Marti, *KHC,* XIII (1904), 167; E. Sellin, *KAT,* XII (^{2}1930), 170; A. Weiser, *ATD,* 24 (^{6}1974), 141f.; T. H. Robinson, *HAT,* XIV (^{3}1964), 79; H. E. W. Fosbroke, *IB,* VI, 787f. For Hittite laws see *AOT,* 430; *ANET,* 196.

69. Barstad, 35.

70. L. Dürr, "Altorientalisches Recht bei den Propheten Amos und Hosea," *BZ,* 23 (1935/36), 150-54; M. A. Beek, "The Religious Background of Amos II 6-8," *OTS,* 5 (1948), 132-141; Maag, 175f.; W. Rudolph, *KAT,* XIII/2.

IV. 1. *Dead Sea Scrolls.* To date, some 20 occurrences of *nʿr* and related terms have been found in the Dead Sea Scrolls; half are in 11QTemple 65,66. The midrash on Hab. 1:17 lists those who will perish by the sword: *neʿārîm ʾaššîm ûzeqēnîm nāšîm weṭap̱,* "youths, men and old men, women and children" — in a word, everyone (1QpHab 6:11). The camp of those armed for the final battle must not be entered by *naʿar zaʿaṭûṭ weʾiššâ,* "a boy, a youth, or a woman," or by anyone who is unclean (1QM 7:3; 4QMa [4Q491] fr. 1-3 6; cf. Nu. 5:1-4). All the occurrences in the Temple Scroll are in legal contexts. 11QTemple 53:17 speaks of the legal competence of a woman *binʿûrîyâ,* "during her youth in her father's house" (cf. Nu. 30:4). 11QTemple 65 (9,10,15) draws on Dt. 22:13-21 (a man's accusation that his wife was not a virgin when they married); 11QTemple 66 (2,6,8,10) combines Dt. 22:28 with Ex. 22:15f.(16f.),[71] modifying the laws governing violation of a *naʿarâ* and making them more precise. In a fragmentary marriage rite (4Q502), the term appears several times in a formula recalling Ps. 148:12 (4Q502 9:4; 19:3). In 11QPsa 21:11,13, a Hebrew text of Sir. 51:13,15, Sirach emphasizes his search for wisdom "from his youth." In 11QPsa 155:11 the psalmist prays, "Remove from me the sins of my youth" (cf. the similar expression in Ps. 103:12).

The texts 1QH 17:10; 4Q502 108:3; 6Q9 60:2 are too damaged to allow any conclusions.

2. *LXX.* The LXX uses a variety of words to translate *nʿr* and related terms. For *naʿar,* the most common are *paidárion* (140 times), *paidíon* (27 times), *país* (18 times), *neanískos* (25 times), *neós* (19 times), *neanías* (10 times), and *neánis* (8 times). The semantic nuance of "servant" is reflected correctly in *diákonos* and related terms. The 5 occurrences of *parthénos* are striking. For *naʿarâ* we find *neánis* (19 times), *korásion* (13 times), *país* (10 times), *parthénos* (6 times), and *hábra* (5 times). For *neʿûrîm* we generally find *neótēs* (35 times; also for *neʿurôṯ*), but also *nēpiótēs* (4 times). For *nōʿar* we find *neótēs, nḗpios,* and *país.*

Fuhs

71. For a synopsis see Yadin, I, 281ff.

נָפַח *nāpaḥ*

Contents: I. Semitic. II. OT Occurrences. III. Usage: 1. God's Breath; 2. *nāpaḥ nepeš;* 3. Fire; 4. Blow Away.

I. Semitic. Heb. *nāpaḥ* represents a common Semitic root with the basic meaning "blow"; the radicals *pḫ* are probably onomatopoeic; cf. the Hebrew by-form *pwḫ* (Arab.

fāḫa), "breathe, blow." The root has the secondary meaning "blow up, swell," hence (?) Heb. *tappûaḥ,* "apple" (Cant. 2:3,5; 7:9[Eng. v. 8]). Reflexes include Akk. *napāḫu,* Aram. and Syr. *n^epaḥ,* Arab. *nafaḫa* (cf. *nafaḥa,* "blow"), Eth. *nafḫa.* In Ugaritic the root appears only in the noun *mpḫm* (with instrumental *m-* preformative; cf. Heb. *mappûaḥ,* Jer. 6:29), "bellows." The meaning of the OSA noun (pl.?) *mnfḫt* is uncertain.[1]

II. OT Occurrences. The verb occurs 12 times in the OT; except for the earliest occurrence in Gen. 2:7 (J), it appears only in exilic or postexilic texts, mostly prophetic. There are 9 occurrences of the qal (Gen. 2:7; Isa. 54:16; Jer. 1:13; 15:9; Ezk. 22:20,21; 37:9; Hag. 1:9; Job 41:12[20]), two of the hiphil (Mal. 1:13; Job 31:39), and one of the pual (Job 20:26). Cf. also (with Jer. 15:9 and Job 31:39) the hapax legomenon *mappaḥ* in Job 11:20.

III. Usage. Even though the precise meaning of *nāpaḥ* in many passages is disputed, the notion of blowing (in, out, upon, away, with mouth or nose) is always present. In three texts God is the subject; elsewhere the subject is a human being, identified directly or indirectly.

1. *God's Breath.* In the first instance, human "blowing" consists by nature and necessity in breathing, a sign of life (cf. 1 K. 17:17). In the creation story of J (Gen. 2:7), therefore, Yahweh Elohim blows the breath of life *(nišmaṯ ḥayyîm)* into the nose of Adam (because human beings breathe through the nose; cf. Isa. 2:22), whom he has formed from clay, thus making him a living being (*nep̄eš ḥayyâ;* also of animals: Gen. 1:20,21,24,30, etc.). In contrast to the forming of human beings from dust or clay, this image is unique in the ancient Near East; the expression resembles Akk. *tanappaḫ ana naḫīrīšu,* describing the use of a reed to blow a drug into the nose of a sick man.[2] The vivifying breath of God appears also in Ezk. 37:9, where the spirit *(rûaḥ)* blowing through the whole world is summoned to blow on the dry bones of the slain to restore them to life (cf. Arab. *nafaḫa fī rūḥihī* and *nafaḫa fī ṣūratihī,* "revive someone"). In the OT view, all earthly life derives from the breath of God (cf. Isa. 42:5; Job 33:4); when this breath is taken away, they die (Ps. 104:29; Job 34:14f.; Isa. 57:16). Breath and life *(n^ešāmâ* and *nep̄eš)* are therefore synonymous (cf. Josh. 10:40 with 10:35 and Job 41:13[21]).

2. *nāp̄aḥ nep̄eš.* Against this background, we can analyze the expression *nāp̄aḥ nep̄eš.*

a. *Qal.* In Jeremiah's lament over Jerusalem (Jer. 15:9), the mother of seven sons languishes and blows out her *nep̄eš;* this is usually translated "breathes out her life" — i.e., she dies. There are other interpretations: *KBL*[2] interprets the phrase as "breathe

1. Biella, 309.
2. *CAD,* XI/1, 264.

heavily, sigh" (cf. Akk. *napāḫu* D, "snort" [nose]; "rattle" [windpipe]; "hiss" [snake]), *HAL* as "gasp, pant," *GesB* as "be despondent" (Luther: "sigh from the heart"; Wilhelm Rudolph: "lost her senses," i.e., "swooned" [also NRSV]).[3] But since *nepeš* also means "vitality," and in light of the antithetic expressions *šôḇēḇ nepeš* (Ps. 23:3) and *hēšîḇ nepeš* (Ruth 4:15; Lam. 1:11,16,19), "restore vitality," the text may equally well mean that when the body languishes the individual's vital energy expires; this may be the meaning of the LXX, which uses the hapax legomenon *apekákēsen*.

b. *Hiphil.* The hiphil appears in Job 31:39 in the image of the land crying out. The context suggests less causing the death of the owner ("if I blew the life out of its owners"[4]) than "causing anguished groans" on the part of exhausted individuals,[5] which also amounts to impairment of physical and psychical vitality (LXX: *elýpēsa;* Vulg.: *afflixi;* Luther: "made the life of the farmhands bitter"; Artur Weiser: "brought affliction to the souls of the farmhands"[6]).

c. *mappaḥ nepeš.* Interpreters have also treated the noun phrase *mappaḥ nepeš* in Job 11:20 quite variously. The hope of the wicked is either death ("their last breath"; "to breathe their last" [NRSV]), the gradual loss of vitality, or groans and sighs, i.e., sorrow of soul, heartache (Vulg. *abominatio animae;* cf. Sir. 30:12).[7]

3. *Fire.* Like the other Semitic languages, Hebrew sometimes uses *nāpaḥ* in the specialized sense of "fan or kindle a fire (*'ēš,* with or without *bᵉ-*)."

a. *Qal.* In Isa. 54:16 the smith (Akk. *nappāḫu!*) fans the fire of coals *(nōpēaḥ bᵉ'ēš peḥām).* In Jer. 1:13 a *sîr nāpûaḥ* appears in a vision — a kettle or pot under which a fire is blown, i.e., fanned so vigorously (LXX *hypokaiómenos*) that its contents bubble and steam (cf. Isa. 64:1).[8] In v. 14, noting the LXX translation *ekkauthḗsetai* and to achieve clearer assonance with *nāpûaḥ* (like *šāqēḏ/šōqēḏ* in vv. 11f.), many interpreters also introduce a form of *nāpaḥ,* such as *tuppaḥ* (disaster is "stoked" from the north), *nāpaḥtî* (a "blazing" pot — I will cause disaster to "blaze"), or *tāpûaḥ* (from the by-form *pwḥ;* cf. *hēpîaḥ* in Ps. 12:6[5]; Hab. 2:3 — a "seething pot," "it will steam, fume, flame up").[9] Weiser and others find emendation unnecessary.[10]

In a symbolic discourse, Ezk. 22:20 speaks of the fire of a smelting furnace blown on by Yahweh in his wrath (v. 21).

---

3. *KBL²*, 624; *HAL,* II, 709; *GesB,* 534; W. Rudolph, *Jeremia. HAT,* XII (³1968), 102.

4. B. Duhm, *Das Buch Hiob. KHC* (1897), 150.

5. F. Horst, *Hiob 1–19. BK,* XVI/1 (1968), 174.

6. A. Weiser, *Das Buch Hiob. ATD,* 13 (²1956), 211.

7. For death see *ibid.,* 82. For loss of vitality, G. Fohrer, *Das Buch Hiob. KAT,* XVI (1963), 222.

8. For a different interpretation see S. L. Harris, "The Second Vision of Jeremiah," *JBL,* 102 (1983), 281f.

9. Cf. *BHS* and G. R. Driver, *JQR,* 28 (1937-38), 98. For *tuppaḥ* see comms. by C. F. Houbigant (1753); K. H. Graf (Leipzig, 1862); B. Duhm, *KHC,* 11 (1901). For *nāpaḥtî* see P. Volz, *Jesaia, Kap. 40–66. KAT,* 9 (1922), 8. For *tāpûaḥ* see F. Hitzig, *Die zwölf kleinen Propheten. KEHAT,* 1 (²1866), 5f.

10. A. Weiser, *Der Prophet Jeremia. ATD,* 20/21 (⁶1969), 10.

b. *Pual.* Job 20:26 calls the fire of God's rage or judgment, which consumes the wicked (cf. 15:16; Dt. 32:22; Jer. 15:14; 17:4), an "unfanned fire" *('ēš lō'-nuppāḥ),* i.e., a fire not fanned by human hand, a figurative fire.

c. *Hiphil.* It is not clear from the context how to translate the hiphil *w^ehippaḥtem 'ôṯô* in Mal. 1:13. The EÜ translates: "and kindle the fire." Others suggest "you make me kindle (fire)," i.e., "thus you kindle my passion" (*'ôṯô* being a *tiqqûn sōp^erîm* for *'ôṯî*), or "you infuriate me."[11] Still others, citing *hēpîaḥ b^e* in Ps. 10:5 (likewise disputed), take *hippaḥ* in the sense of "blow on," "sniff at," i.e., "esteem lightly, despise," or ascribe to it the meaning it has when used with *nepeš* in Job 31:39: "cause to pant."[12]

4. *Blow Away.* The metaphorical use of the verb (qal) in Hag. 1:9 presents no problem: to punish the Israelites, who are interested only in their own houses and not in rebuilding the temple, Yahweh has "blown away" the harvest, i.e., he has somehow destroyed it or made it vanish (cf. Isa. 11:4: the Messiah kills the wicked with the breath of his lips; also 40:7,24; also Akk. *napāḫu* D: the south wind blows clouds away[13]). The interpretation of this blowing as a magical act intended to cause devastation (cf. *incantare*),[14] although possibly reflected already in Targ. Jonathan ("I send the curse"), is unlikely, because the OT considers all forms of magic an abomination to Yahweh (Dt. 18:9-14; Nu. 23:23).

Maiberger†

---

11. For the former see W. Rudolph, *Maleachi. KAT,* XIII/4 (1976), 258; for the latter see K. Elliger, *Maleachi. ATD,* 25 (⁷1975), 194.

12. For the former see *GesB,* 534; LXX *exephýsēsa autá;* NRSV; for the latter see *KBL*², 624.

13. *AHw,* II, 732.

14. J. C. Matthes, *ZAW,* 23 (1903), 123.

נָפַל nāpal; נֵפֶל nēpel; נְפִילִים n^epîlîm

Contents: I. Other Languages; Statistics. II. Neutral or Positive Meanings. III. Negative Meanings. IV. Isa. 26:18,19. V. 1. Nouns; 2. Later Development.

---

nāpal. H. A. Brongers, "Darum, wer fest zu stehen meint, der sehe zu, dass er nicht falle," *Symbolae biblicae et Mesopotamicae. Festschrift F. M. Th. de Liagre Böhl* (Leiden, 1973), 56-70; M. Delcor, "Quelques cas de survivances du vocabulaire nomade en Hébreu Biblique," *VT,* 25 (1975), 307-322, esp. 313ff.; K. Elliger, *Deuterojesaja in seinem Verhältnis zu Tritojesaja. BWANT,* 103 (1933); J. C. Greenfield, "Lexicographical Notes I," *HUCA,* 29 (1958), 203-228,

I. Other Languages; Statistics. The verb *nāp̄al* has its closest analogs in Ugaritic, Amarna Canaanite (impf. *nupul,* from the loanword *napālu* III[1]), Egyptian Aramaic, Nabatean, Palmyrene, Jewish Aramaic, and Samaritan. Middle Hebrew represents a further development. Also comparable are Arab. *nafala* II, "divide as booty," which recalls OT texts describing the casting of lots, and above all Akk. *napālu* I, which in the G stem has the causative meaning "break stones, tear, destroy (an eye, etc.)."[2] There is probably no OT equivalent to *napālu* II, "pay compensation."[3] Isa. 26:18 (qal) and 19 (hiphil) are philologically problematic.[4] The nouns *mappelet̠, mappālâ,* and *mappāl* are normal derivatives, but *nēp̄el* and *nᵉp̄îlîm* demand closer examination.[5]

The verb occurs 367 times in the qal, 61 times in the hiphil, and 5 times in the hithpael; the single occurrences of the pilpel (Ezk. 28:23) should probably be emended to the qal.[6] The occurrences are distributed evenly; there is no observable significance for narrower linguistic domains (including exceptional appearance as a technical term). As is often the case, the verbal root has so broad a semantic range that translation requires a variety of compounds besides the use of a simple equivalent. This explains why the LXX uses *píptein* only 250 times for the qal and just 4 times for the hiphil (plus once for *mappelet̠* [Prov. 29:16] and twice for *mappālâ* [Isa. 23:13; 25:2], translating the sense). It uses *empíptein* 25 times for the qal, and uses *epipíptein* 32 times for the qal and 3 times for the hiphil (Nu. 35:23; Job 6:27; Ps. 78:28).

It is possible, as Wolfram von Soden argues, that the initial *n* is a root augment analogous to the parallels he cites, and that the verb should be included among the onomatopoeic verbs ("make the sound *pul-pul*"; cf. Eng *plo*p, *plu*mp, *spla*sh).[7]

The verb is so universal that one can only be surprised at some of its highly specific nuances. The majority of its occurrences in the OT point to the realm of destruction — especially death, but also injury. We may therefore classify uses of the verb roughly within two broad categories: neutral or positive meanings and negative meanings.

II. Neutral or Positive Meanings.
1. When a fruit tree is shaken, its fruit falls (Nah. 3:12). When a sieve is shaken, pebbles fall through (Am. 9:9). An ax head fell into the water (2 K. 6:5f. [qal; someone accidentally caused it to fall, v. 6, hiphil]). Rebekah "fell" (i.e., dismounted; NRSV: "slipped quickly") from her camel (Gen. 24:64 [qal]). People cast (lit. "cause to fall,"

---

esp. 215ff.; W. Grundmann, "Stehen und Fallen im qumranischen und neutestamentlichen Schrifttum," *Qumrān-Probleme,* ed. H. Bardtke. *DAWB,* 42 (1963), 147-166; P. Hugger, *Jahwe meine Zuflucht. Münsterschwarzacher Studien,* 13 (1971); L. Prijs, "Ergänzungen zum talmudisch-aramäischen Wörterbuch," *ZDMG,* 117 (1967), 266-286, esp. 280; W. Wifall, "Gen 6,1-4, a Royal Davidic Myth?" *BTB,* 5 (1976), 294-301.

1. *AHw,* II, 734.
2. Cf. *HAL,* 709; *AHw,* II, 733; not cited by *HAL.*
3. *AHw,* II, 734; cf. *HAL,* II, 709; and IV below.
4. See IV below.
5. See V below.
6. *HAL,* II, 710.
7. *GaG,* 137.

hiphil) lots to determine God's will (1 S. 14:42; Jon. 1:7 [twice]; Neh. 10:35 [Eng. v. 34]; 11:1; 1 Ch. 24:31; 25:8; 26:13); in a more secular sense, the *pûr* lot is cast (Est. 3:7; 9:24); the lot fell on Jonah (Jon. 1:7). One may commit such abominable acts as casting lots over an orphan (Job 6:27) or over the clothing of a dying man while he is still alive (Ps. 22:19[18]). In a very different (and figurative) sense, Prov. 1:14 says: "Throw in your lot among us"; cf. 1QH 7:34: "You [God] did not cause my lot to fall among the congregation of the. . . ." Ezk. 24:6bα, a secondary addition not found in the LXX,[8] is obscure, since the image (rust on a pot) is not developed clearly.

2. In the five texts that speak of casting lots to apportion inherited land, we are dealing with a truly technical usage of the verb together with its prepositional extensions. The best starting point is Nu. 34:2: "This is the land that falls to you through inalienable inheritance *(lāḵem tippōl benaḥalâ).*" The concluding expression in particular suggests a legal formula. The formula appears more often in the hiphil, describing the act itself (Josh. 13:6; Ezk. 45:1; 47:22; 48:29 [conj.], all late texts). Josh. 23:4 and Isa. 34:17 probably reflect an abbreviated version of the formula (verb in hiphil with *le*); but they lead to a freer usage, in which one text (Ps. 78:55) can speak of Yahweh as apportioning the land. A late addition to the description of the boundary between Manasseh and Ephraim (Josh. 17:5) speaks of portions *(ḥaḇālîm)* falling to subdivisions of Manasseh; Ps. 16:6, a familiar text, exhibits an especially fine figurative usage: "Portions fell to me upon a pleasant land" — in an almost unique spiritualization of the idiom, the worshipers (temple singers) describe God as their portion. Such usage is reflected in the Dead Sea Scrolls: "they decide the lot of every living being" (1QS 4:26); "the man received his eternal lot" (1QH 2:29); "and casting the lot with the messengers of the countenance [angels]" (1QSb [1Q28b] 4:26).

3. Nu. 6:12 appears also to exhibit a technical usage: when a period of dedication as a nazirite is interrupted, the days already spent "drop away" (NRSV: "are void"). The verb is used in a similarly technical sense for the contact (accidental, of course) of an animal carcass with anything used in the cult, rendering it unclean (Lev. 11:32,33,35,37,38). Ruth 3:28 introduces an idiomatic usage: Ruth is to wait and see how Boaz's words "fall (out)," i.e., whether they actually come to pass. In a similar vein, Est. 6:10 says that Haman must not "cause to fall" (NRSV: "leave out") anything that he has mentioned. This idiom is used to say that Yahweh let none of Samuel's words fall to the ground (1 S. 3:19), none of Elijah's (2 K. 10:10), and of course none of his own (Josh. 21:45; 23:14 [twice]; 1 K. 8:56). It is a proverbial expression (always part of a promissory oath) that not a hair shall fall from someone's head (1 S. 14:45; 2 S. 14:11; 1 K. 1:52). Finally, a highly original and artful locution appears in Job 29:24, in Job's oath of purgation: those on whom Job smiled did not cause the light of his countenance to fall.

---

8. W. Zimmerli, *Ezekiel 1. Herm* (Eng. trans. 1979), 494.

4. The tone is totally different, albeit not negative, when *nāp̱al* is used to express humility. More than 25 passages speak of falling on one's face before someone of higher rank or status (including God); 2 passages speak of falling on one's nose (1 S. 20:41; 2 S. 14:4), 3 of falling on the ground (2 S. 1:2; Job 1:20; 2 Ch. 20:18), 4 of falling at the feet of the superior one (1 S. 25:24; 2 K. 4:37; Ps. 45:6[5]; Est. 8:3), 3 of falling before his face (Gen. 44:14; 50: 18; 2 S. 19:19[18]), and 1 of falling before his nose (1 S. 25:23). In 2 K. 5:21 Naaman's "falling" from his chariot before Elisha can hardly mean that he simply jumped down (NRSV) in the normal way; it is rather the act of a supplicant. The hithpael (Dt. 9:18,25 [twice]; Ezr. 10:1) is used only for falling before God. It is unclear whether Gen. 50:1 refers to a mourning ritual or merely a gesture of respect when it speaks of Joseph falling on his father's face.

5. We enter the liturgical realm with the statement (found primarily in the narrative of Jeremiah's persecution at the time of Jerusalem's fall) that someone causes a *t^eḥinnâ,* a plea for favor, to fall before Yahweh (hiphil: Jer. 38:26; 42:9) or that such a plea falls before Yahweh (qal: 36:7; 37:20; 42:2). The expression appears in the same situation in Dnl. 9:18,20. The idiom suggests an attitude of humility in prayer.

6. Just as the verb can express the notion of voluntarily recognized superiority, so too it can express an involuntary weakening of the self, without negative overtones. This took place when the hand or *rûaḥ* of Yahweh fell on a prophet (Ezk. 8:1; 11:5). In Balaam's oracles the seer describes himself as falling when he saw his visions (Nu. 24:4,16). For King Saul, however, it was embarrassing when he fell into a frenzy and lay naked (1 S. 19:24). But simple human joy can also be so overpowering that it causes someone to fall: Esau falls on Jacob's neck (Gen. 33:4), Joseph on Benjamin's (45:14) and on his father Israel's (46:29).

7. Also neutral is the Hebrew expression *nāp̱al ʿal/ʾel,* "fall to," "go over to." Jeremiah is brought to trial on the charge of desertion, a capital offense (Jer. 37:13-14) — in the final phase of the siege of Jerusalem, there is much talk of defecting or surrendering to the Babylonian army (2 K. 25:11 [Jer. 52:15]; Jer. 21:9; 38:19; 39:9). But the expression has distinctly positive overtones in 1 Ch. 12:20 (twice),21; 2 Ch. 15:9, where the North Israelites defect to David or Judah. According to 2 K. 7:4, four starving beggars desert to the Aramean camp, which they find deserted. A position of (blameless) weakness inducing a shift to the stronger side probably accounts for this idiom. There is no hint of reproach in 1 S. 29:3: Achish of Gath speaks on behalf of David, who had deserted Saul for the Philistines (qal inf. const. without *ʿal*).

Finally, *nāp̱al ʿal* appears in Isa. 54:15. Here the expression cannot mean, as the MT is usually interpreted,[9] "fall on account of Jerusalem." The parallels cited indicate that this text, too, must refer to a change of sides (cf. LXX).[10] As is well known, the

---

9. E.g., *HAL,* II, 709.
10. See also III.8 below.

MT appears to be corrupt, especially because *'ep̄eš* does not mean "not" and v. 15bα looks like a doublet of v. 15a. The text should be emended on the basis of the LXX and translated: "If anyone should attack you, should indeed attack you, at my instigation [1QIs[a]: *mē'ittî;* MT: *mē'ôṯî*] they will go over to you."[11] The motivation is the city so gloriously rebuilt by Yahweh (54:11f.,14-17aα; v. 13 MT is a gloss on the association with v. 10, based on Jer. 31:31-34).

III. Negative Meanings.

1. The transition from the positive group to the negative is not without a middle ground. For example, Jer. 8:4 asks quite generally: "When people fall, do they not get up again?" Eccl. 4:10 demonstrates that two are better than one by means of the help one gives when the other falls. Apropos the ordering of the world, Prov. 24:16 says that the righteous fall seven times but rise up again. Malice already makes itself heard in Mic. 7:8 when the enemy rejoices over the fall of the righteous; the latter rises again, however — the enemy has rejoiced too soon. Isa. 31:3 illustrates the chaos of battle by saying that when the helper stumbles, the one helped falls. By contrast, Ps. 145:14 extols Yahweh for upholding those who fall and raising up those who are bowed down; Ps. 37:24 is similar, as is 118:13, a narrative statement in a thanksgiving hymn. The possible consequences of a fall appear in 2 S. 4:4: an adult is lame because he fell when he was a child. According to 2 K. 1:2, Ahaziah of Israel was confined to bed as a result of falling through a roof lattice and could not be cured. Isa. 24:18,20 describe someone who falls into a pit from which there is no escape (cf. Jer. 48:44). Ex. 21:18 deals with the case of someone who is not killed in a fight but falls in such a way that he is confined to bed (cf. v. 33, which regulates compensation for an ox that has fallen to its death). In his oath of purgation, Job says: "Let my shoulder blade fall from my shoulder, if . . ." (Job 31:22). Jer. 25:34 uses "fall like a choice vessel" as a simile for the destruction of nations. Clearly it is universally human to rejoice when people fall into the pit they have dug for others (Prov. 26:27; 28:10; Ps. 7:16[15]; 35:8; 57:7[6]; cf. 141:10 [their own nets]). Eccl. 10:8 draws the opposite conclusion: it can happen that someone digs a pit for a good reason and then falls into it.

2. Several of the texts just cited are to be understood figuratively; the list is easily extended. The wicked fall on account of their own wickedness (Prov. 11:5). The perverse of tongue (17:20), those who follow crooked ways (28:18), those who trust in their riches (11:28) — they all fall. Indeed, a whole nation falls when there is no guidance (11:14,26; 1 Ch. 5:22; 10:1). The wise do not rejoice when their enemies fall (Prov. 24:17), but worshipers may pray that their enemies will stumble and fall (Ps. 27:6; 36:13[12]; cf. Est. 6:13; Dnl. 11:19). It is a particular horror that Yahweh makes those with whom he is angry fall into the mouth of a strange woman as into a pit that kills many (Prov. 7:26). Ps. 37:14 laments that the wicked bring down the poor and needy. In Prov. 13:17 we should probably read the hiphil instead of the qal, and translate:

11. Elliger; see *BHS*.

"A bad messenger causes people to fall into trouble."[12] Ps. 69:10(9) laments pointedly that insults meant for Yahweh have fallen on the psalmist; but the psalmist of Ps. 73:18 acknowledges that Yahweh makes the wicked fall into ruin. Hos. 7:7 speaks more figuratively than literally of the fall of kings. Two texts are noteworthy for their originality: in 1 S. 17:32, before his battle with the Philistine Goliath, David says that no one's heart should fall on anyone else (i.e., fear should not spread); in 1 S. 26:20 David asks that his blood not fall on foreign soil because of Saul — an expression with courtly overtones.

3. Hebrew has a very graphic sense of the forces that can cause a fall. In 1 S. 28:20 Saul falls to the ground in fear on account of a message spoken by the "shade" of Samuel. Even more vivid and entirely true to life are Gen. 15:12; Ex. 15:16; Josh. 2:9; Ps. 35:5; 105:38; Est. 8:13; 9:2f.; Dnl. 10:7, describing the terror that can befall people and render them incapable of acting. This is true particularly of dread of God: 1 S. 11:7; Job 13:11; Jer. 15:8 (hiphil), and with particular force, Jer. 3:13: Yahweh will not cause his face to fall "on/among you" in anger. In Gen. 2:21 God causes Adam to fall into a deep sleep, which merely renders him unconscious; in all other cases, however, a deep sleep entails great fear (Gen. 15:12; 1 S. 26:12 [danger more than fear]; Job 4:13; 33:15). In Prov. 19:15, too, there is more emphasis on danger: "Laziness brings on deep sleep," because those who are idle suffer hunger. Jgs. 2:19 makes the remarkable and unique statement that, when the Israelites relapsed into apostasy, "they did not cause any of their wicked deeds to fall away" — perhaps because these deeds were too strong. The context of prostrating oneself before other gods suggests passionate bondage. The curse formula pronounced over a *śôṭâ* (a woman accused of adultery) implies clearly that irresistible forces are at work: if she is guilty, her thigh will fall away and the flow of blood will not stop (Nu. 5:21,27; v. 22 is a secondary addition that uses the hiphil to make this an act of Yahweh).

4. Injury as a result of falling (in its widest range of meanings) can be expressed much more directly. Most of the occurrences are in the hiphil: knocking out a tooth (Ex. 21:27), causing a sword (Ezk. 30:22) or arrows (Ezk. 39:3) to drop from someone's (right) hand, unintentionally dropping a stone on someone (Nu. 35:23), breaking down a wall (2 S. 20:15). Many of these occurrences serve as images of total destruction[13] — the collapse of walls (Josh. 6:5,20; 1 K. 20:30; Ezk. 38:20), towers (Isa. 30:25), bulwarks (Jer. 50:15; Ezk. 13:11,12,14), even walls of rock (Ezk. 38:20; Job 14:18; cf. Hos. 10:8: people will appeal to the mountains and hills to fall on survivors, an image of chaos). It also signifies collapse when the arms of Pharaoh fall (Ezk. 30:25; the arm symbolizes military power). The mode of expression in Isa. 30:13 is quite remarkable: a break in a wall "falls," as though the observer were seeing the break itself come into being and expand. Jgs. 7:13 tells how the Midianites on whom Gideon was eavesdrop-

---

12. *HAL,* II, 710.
13. See III.7 below.

ping dreamed that their tents fell — likewise an obvious image. By contrast, Am. 9:11 (cited in CD 77:16; 4QFlor [4Q174] 1:12,13) promises restoration of the fallen booth of David. Without imagery, Isa. 47:11 speaks of disaster falling as an appropriate punishment for Babylon. Eccl. 9:12, however, says bluntly that times of disaster fall quite unpredictably and can strike the innocent instead of those who deserve disaster.

5. Falling that results in injury can also have a reflexive meaning. Job insists that he does not fall below his friends intellectually (12:3; 13:2). Neh. 6:16 states that Nehemiah's enemies fell in their own esteem on account of his successes. Similarly reflexive but very different in meaning are the texts that speak of miscarriage *(nēp̱el).* Ps. 8:9(8); Job 3:16; Eccl. 6:3 do not reflect injury to the family or parents but speak of the injury suffered by the stillborn child through never being able to behold the beautiful light of the sun. Arguing from this position, Eccl. 6:3 concludes characteristically that it is even worse vanity if a man has a hundred sons, lives a long life, possesses great wealth, is even enraptured, but does not know how to be content in his soul.

6. Some 115 out of 434 occurrences (about 105 of 367 in the qal), in other words more than one-fourth, refer to "falling" in death, as in English. We shall cite only a few of the more significant texts to indicate the range of meanings. Yahweh made the Israelites fall in the wilderness (Ps. 106:26); he caused their descendants to fall (NRSV: disperse) among the nations (v. 27).[14] The expression "fall by the sword" occurs 35 times, but the hiphil "cause to fall by the sword" is found only in 2 K. 19:7 par. Isa. 37:7; Jer. 19:7; Ezk. 6:4; 32:12; Dnl. 11:12; 2 Ch. 32:21; it is strikingly frequent in 1QM. Isa. 31:8 deserves special mention in this context: Assyria will fall by the sword of someone who is not a mortal (Yahweh, *mal'āḵ?*); cf. 1QM 19:11: they fall by the sword of El.

Collectives, too, can fall: Sisera's army (Jgs. 4:16), the Aramean army (1 K. 20:25), Judah (Isa. 3:8), Edom (Jer. 49:21: the earth trembles at its fall). Jer. 51:49 cites a parallel: just as many nations fell because of Babylon, so Babylon must fall because of Israel.

Falling into someone's hands has deadly results in Jgs. 15:18; Lam. 1:7; 1 Ch. 5:10; 20:8; hiphil: 1 S. 18:25 (Saul planned to make David fall into the hands of his enemies the Philistines). In 1 Ch. 21:13 it is deadly to fall into Yahweh's hand. In 2 S. 24:14, however, David would rather fall into the hand of Yahweh than into human hands.

The "fallen" (ptcp.) are mentioned in Josh. 8:25; Jgs. 8:10; 20:46; 1 S. 31:8; fallen warriors appear explicitly in 2 S. 1:19,25,27; 1 Ch. 10:8. Lev. 26:36 foretells that at God's judgment the Israelites will fall though sheer terror. To describe the carnage of battle, with rank upon rank falling, Jer. 46:16 says that a man falls beside his neighbor. Isa. 10:3f. are most vivid: when the day of punishment comes, those who perverted justice will seek refuge but will fall like corpses among the slain (cf. Nu. 14:32; Jer. 9:21[22]; 26:20,24).

---

14. *HAL,* II, 711, conj. *hēp̱îṣû,* graphically dubious in my opinion.

Eli, the chief priest of Shiloh, fell to his death from his seat upon hearing that his two sons were dead and that the ark, which had been entrusted to them, had been captured (1 S. 4:18). When a tiny poisonous snake by the wayside bites a horse, it rears up so that its rider or the charioteer falls backward and is killed: the speaker of the tribal oracle in Gen. 49:17 looks for the tiny tribe of Dan to have this effect on enormously superior forces.

Legal precision is probably the goal of Dt. 21:1,4. The text does not deal with murder by a person or persons unknown in general but with a murder victim discovered on fertile ground *(śāḏeh)*. The desecration of life in such a place demanded the ritual described, quite apart from the curse on the unknown murderer (27:24).

7. Relevant here are a series of images representing catastrophic destruction. For example, the fire from Yahweh upon Elijah's altar that consumed not only the sacrifice but the very stones of the altar (1 K. 18:38) signified a deadly threat to Israel, which had to be averted by the butchering of the 450 prophets of Baal. Among the calamities inflicted on Job is the fire of Yahweh that fell from heaven and consumed his sheep and servants (Job 1:16). Isaiah uses extraordinarily graphic language: Yahweh sent a word against Jacob, and it fell on Israel (Isa. 9:7[8]). Exalted Lebanon (par. "tall trees": Isa. 10:34) will fall — as will its cedars (Zec. 11:2) and the tall tree of Pharaoh (Ezk. 31:12). Egypt will fall like fish falling on an open field (Ezk. 29:5). Judah will fall like a peg falling with its load (Isa. 22:25).

8. Just as falling can be fatal, so can "falling upon" another party. When the subject is an army, *nāpal* is construed with b^e, as in Jgs. 7:12: Midian, Amalek, and the people of the East fell upon the plain (Jezreel). Josh. 11:7 tells how Joshua fell upon his enemies at the waters of Merom; 1QM 1:9 describes an attack on the Kittim. The verb without any preposition also has this meaning in Job 1:15.

The expression *nāpal ʿal* means something like "overwhelm"; the tactic is described in 1 S. 17:12: Hushai counsels that Absalom should assemble a mighty force, and then "we shall light on him as the dew upon the ground." The comparison to the dew must mean that David's forces can be totally overwhelmed; the meaning "inconspicuously" is out of the question. Isa. 16:9 and Jer. 48:32 foretell that Hedad, the destroyer, will fall upon the harvest of Sibmah (cf. NRSV). The hithpael with *ʿal* can be used for falling on a small number of people within a restricted space, like a house (Gen. 43:18). Joel 2:8 should probably be included in this group of texts, at least if we follow Wilhelm Rudolph in retaining *šelaḥ* and translating it "water conduit," so that the attack (of the locusts) invaded by way of the carefully protected water conduit. Isa. 54:15 has already been discussed.[15]

9. Uniquely and somewhat idiosyncratically, Gen. 4:5,6 describe a countenance as falling. Since v. 7 speaks of "lifting up" (presumably of the countenance) as the

15. See II.7 above.

opposite, implying a positive relationship with the circle surrounding the person in question, falling of the countenance probably refers to introverted alienation from others. In this case, "sin is lurking at the door like a crouching (demon)." Cain does not ask Yahweh why his offering was not accepted, but turns in on himself and becomes a murderer.

Dnl. 8:10 exhibits some unique religio-historical features. The context speaks of two constellations representing great powers: a ram (Persia) and a male goat (Greece); with its single horn, the goat throws the ram on the ground and tramples it. The imagery changes in v. 10. A little horn comes out of one of the four horns that grew up after the original horn (Alexander the Great) was broken off, becomes larger and larger, and casts down (hiphil) to the earth some of the starry host. The continuation of the text indicates that we should not envision battles between princes of heaven or the like (as in Dnl. 10), but an abomination committed by the little horn that affects the whole cosmos, not just the earthly powers. This echoes 7:25, which says the horn coming after the ten horns attempts to change the sacred seasons and *dāṯ* — the fundamental cultic ordinances reflecting the order of the universe, the ordinances prescribed by the heavens based on that order. Mythologically, 8:10 clearly reflects Isa. 14:12 (the fall of the morning star, i.e., the king of Babylon); but like the fall of the arrogant (Jer. 50:32; cf. Ps. 20:9[8]), in Isaiah this fall restores the cosmic order.

IV. Isa. 26:18,19. In the light of these observations, the use of the verb in Isa. 26:18,19 remains puzzling. The usual translation, "be born" (qal) and "give birth to" (hiphil), is not supported by *nēpel,* "miscarriage," or Middle Hebrew hiphil and Jewish Aramaic aphel (from *n^e^pal*), "let drop, have a miscarriage," since birth in the OT always represents a joyous occasion, while a miscarriage represents the opposite.[16] In v. 19 the simplest solution philologically is to assume that the metaphor of the "dew of Yahweh" is continued, and to translate: "and on the earth of the Rephaim you [Yahweh] cause [your dew] to fall" (cf. 2 S. 17:12: blanket totally). In Isa. 26:18bβ the LXX does not read the consonants *wbl* before *yplw;* they may therefore be a corrupt dittography, suggesting the reading: "and the inhabitants of the world fall (to ruin)." If this solution is not satisfactory, I believe one should posit a different root. A possible candidate is *napālu* II, "to make a support payment, to compensate,"[17] which recalls Heb. *šillēm.* In v. 19, then, the idea would be that the earth yields the Rephaim in compensation for Yahweh's dew (Arab. *nafilat,* "grandchildren,"[18] could suggest that they are a reimbursement to their grandparents). In v. 18 one would have to assume an ellipsis, since there would be no subject, and translate: "and the inhabitants of the world are not replaced." I nevertheless consider it questionable to posit a separate root or an idiosyncratic special meaning for just two occurrences (in v. 18b, contra C. F. Whitley, *bal* can hardly have two different meanings).

---

16. Cf. C. F. Whitley, *ZAW,* 84 (1982), 216; *HAL,* II, 711.
17. *CAD,* XI/1, 275.
18. *HAL,* II, 711.

V. 1. *Nouns.* The nouns *mappāl,* "what falls from the grain, refuse" (Am. 8:6), "flabby cheeks" (of Behemoth) (Job 41:15[23]); *mappālâ,* "heap of ruins" (Isa. 17:1), "ruin" (Isa. 23:13; 25:2); and *mappelet,* "carcass" (that which has fallen: Jgs. 14:8), "fallen trunk" (Ezk. 31:13), or "fall, downfall" (Ezk. 26:15-18; 27:27; 31:16; 32:10; Prov. 29:16), fill out the picture without qualification. In the case of *nēpel,* however, we must examine its usage carefully. The noun probably does not refer to the process of birth (the falling of the newborn infant) or the falling of a miscarriage. Its meaning derives from the primary meaning of the qal: an entity whose necessary property is to fall, a casualty. The Nephilim (Gen. 6:4; Nu. 13:33) should be interpreted analogously. The noun seems to embody the notion, so characteristic of ancient Israel, that something gigantic, something exalted, must necessarily fall.[19]

2. *Later Development.* To date, usage in the Dead Sea Scrolls appears to agree entirely with that of the OT. Ezr. 7:20 (Aramaic) adds a nuance to the semantic spectrum: it speaks of payments that "fall to someone's lot" (with l^e introducing both the person obliged to pay and the purpose).

Seebass

19. H. Gese, *Vom Sinai zum Zion. BevT,* 64 (1974), 110, n. 47: "those who have fallen heroically in battle"; L. Köhler, *Hebrew Man* (Eng. trans., New York, 1956), 44: "usually translated 'giants' "; both cited in *HAL,* II, 709.

נֶפֶשׁ *nepeš*

Contents: I. Comparative Linguistics. II. Ancient Near East: 1. Akkadian; 2. Ugaritic. III. Statistics, LXX, Fundamentals. IV. OT Usage: 1. Throat, Gullet; 2. Desire; 3. Vital Self, Reflexive Pronoun; 4. Individuated Life; 5. Living Creature, Person; 6. The *nepeš* of God. V. Postbiblical Usage: 1. Middle Hebrew; 2. Dead Sea Scrolls.

nepeš. S. Abir, " 'Denn im Bilde Gottes machte er den Menschen' (Gen 9,6 P)," *TGl,* 72 (1982), 79-88; J. H. Becker, *Het Begrip* nefesj *in het OT* (1942); N. P. Bratsiotis, "*Nepheš* — ψυχή," *Volume du Congrès, Genève 1965. SVT,* 15 (1966), 58-89; C. A. Briggs, "The Use of *npš* in the OT," *JBL,* 16 (1897), 17-30; H. A. Brongers, "Das Wort *'NPŠ'* in den Qumranschriften," *RevQ,* 4 (1963), 407-415; M. Dahood, "Hebrew-Ugaritic Lexicography VI," *Bibl,* 49 (1968), 355-369, esp. 368; A. Dihle, E. Jacob, E. Lohse, and E. Schweizer, "ψυχή," *TDNT,* IX, 608-666; R. Dussaud, "La notion d'âme chez les Israélites et les Phéniciens," *Syr,* 16 (1935), 267-277; L. Dürr, "Heb. נֶפֶשׁ = akk. *napištu* = Gurgel, Kehle," *ZAW,* 43 (1925), 262-69; J. Fichtner, "Seele oder Leben in der Bibel," *TZ,* 17 (1961), 305-318; W. Gottlieb, "The Term *'nepeš'* in the Bible: A Re-appraisal," *GUOST,* 25 (1973/74 [1976]), 71-84; E. Guimet, "Les âmes égyptiennes," *RHR,* 1913 B, 1-17; R. D. Haak, "A Study and New Interpretation of *QṢR NPŠ,*"

I. Comparative Linguistics. The word *nepeš* is part of the common Semitic vocabulary stock; it is probably a primitive noun that does not derive from a verbal root.[1] Since its meaning must be determined entirely on the basis of usage (even more than is generally the case),[2] I shall not present the comparative Semitic material in detail but shall mention only a few noteworthy points. Akkadian and Ugaritic usage will be explored at somewhat greater length in II below, because both languages cast light on Hebrew usage.

The noun *nepeš* is fem.; the masc. pl. *nᵉpāšîm* in Ezk. 13:20 is clearly an error.[3] Manfred Weippert believes that the Old Aramaic and Phoenician spelling *nbš* represents dialectal variation.[4] Eb. *nu-pu-uš-tu-um* deserves mention on account of its antiquity,

---

JBL, 101 (1982), 161-67; R. Haclili, "The *NEPEŠ:* The Jericho Column-Pyramid," *PEQ,* 113 (1981), 33-38; J. Halévy, "La croyance de l'immortalité de l'âme chez les peuples sémitiques," *Mélanges Halévy* (Paris, 1883), 365-380; *idem,* "L'immortalité de l'âme chez les peuples sémitiques," *RA,* 1882 B, 44-53; A. R. Johnson, *The Vitality of the Individual in the Thought of Ancient Israel* (Cardiff, ²1964); A. Kammenhuber, "Die hethitischen Vorstellungen von Seele und Leib, Herz und Leibesinnern, Kopf und Person," *ZA,* N.S. 22 (1964), 151-212; K. Lang, "Ka, Seele und Leib bei den alten Ägyptern," *Anthropos,* 20 (1925), 55-76; R. Lauha, *Psychophysischer Sprachgebrauch im AT* (Helsinki, 1983); R. Laurin, "The Concept of Man as Soul," *ExpT,* 72 (1960/61), 131-34; cf. 349-350; M. Lichtenstein, *Das Wort* נֶפֶשׁ *in der Bibel* (Berlin, 1920); D. Lys, "The Israelite Soul According to the LXX," *VT,* 16 (1966), 181-228; *idem, Nèphèsh: Histoire de l'âme dans la révélation d'Israël au sein des religions proche-orientales. Études d'histoire et de philosophie religieuses,* 50 (1958); R. Machlin, " 'הקוטביות במלה 'נפש (The Polarization in the Word נפש)," *BethM,* 19/3 (1974), 401-416; E. W. Marter, "The Hebrew Concept of 'Soul' in Pre-Exilic Writings," *AUSS,* 2 (1964), 97-108; E. Moreau, "La nourriture du monde-à-venir," *NRT,* 103 (1981), 567-570; A. Murtonen, *The Living Soul. StOr,* 23/1 (1958); M. Nishi, *The Usage of* נפש *in the OT and the Ancient Israelite View of Humans* (Tokyo, 1971); S. M. Paul, "An Unrecognized Medical Idiom in Canticles 6,12 and Iob 9,21," *Bibl,* 59 (1978), 545-47; H. F. Peacock, "Translating the Word for 'Soul' in the OT," *BT,* 27 (1976), 216-19; M. Philonenko, "L'âme à l'étroit," *Hommages à A. Dupont-Sommer* (Paris, 1971), 421-28; M. N. Pope, "A Little Soul-Searching," *Maarav,* 1 (1978/79), 25-31; F. C. Porter, "The Pre-existence of the Soul in the Book of Wisdom and in the Rabbinical Writings," *OT and Semitic Studies in Memory of W. R. Harper,* I (Chicago, 1908), 205-270; L. Sabourin, "Nefesh, sang et expiation (Lv 17,11.14)," *Sciences ecclésiatiques,* 18 (1966), 25-45; H. W. F. Saggs, " 'External Souls' in the OT," *JSS,* 19 (1974), 1-12; O. Sander, "Leib-Seele-Dualismus im AT?" *ZAW,* 77 (1965), 329-332; J. Scharbert, *Fleisch, Geist und Seele im Pentateuch. SBS,* 19 (1967); *idem,* "Fleisch, Geist und Seele in der Pentateuch-Septuaginta," *Wort, Lied und Gottesspruch. Festschrift J. Ziegler,* I. *FzB,* 1 (1972), 121-143; W. H. Schmidt, "Anthropologische Begriffe im AT," *EvT,* 24 (1964), 374-388; J. Schwab, *Der Begriff der nefeš in den heiligen Schriften des ATs* (1918); M. Seligson, *The Meaning of* npš mt *in the OT. StOr,* 16/2 (1951); D. Silber, "... נפש נשמה ורוח," *BethM,* 16/3 (1971), 312-325; W. von Soden, "Die Wörter für Leben und Tod im Akkadischen und Semitischen," *Vorträge gehalten auf der 28. Rencontre Assyriologique Internationale. BAfO,* 19 (1982), 1-7; W. E. Staples, "The 'Soul' in the OT," *AJSL,* 44 (1927/28), 145-176; C. Westermann, "נֶפֶשׁ *nepeš* 'soul,' " *TLOT,* II, 743-759; H. W. Wolff, *Anthropology of the OT* (Eng. trans., Philadelphia, 1974), esp. 10-25. Quotations from the last two works have been normalized with respect to transliteration.

1. *HAL,* II, 711f.; *AHw,* II, 738; *CAD,* XI/1, 296ff.

2. Cf. J. Barr, *Semantics of Biblical Language* (Oxford, 1961).

3. W. Zimmerli, *Ezekiel 1. Herm* (Eng. trans. 1979), 289.

4. M. Weippert, *The Settlement of the Israelite Tribes in Palestine. SBT,* 2/2 (Eng. trans. 1971), 78. Cf. also the Tel Arad potsherd (*HAL,* II, 711).

as does Old Akk. *napaštu.*[5] In Middle Hebrew, *nep̱eš* can denote the "soul" (inner portion) of a fabric.[6] Compared to OT usage, this application appears to be due to the influence of some other language. The same is true of the use of the noun in Aramaic, Old South Arabic, and Middle Hebrew in the sense of "tomb, monument," since a derivation from the sense "corpse" is probably out of the question.[7]

II. Ancient Near East. The Egyptian conceptions of the soul are highly complex. We must take at least three different terms into account. The *ka (kȝ)* is a person's double; the noun can also mean "vital energy" and "nourishment."[8] The *ba (bȝ),* often translated "soul," refers to the capacity to assume a form and can therefore mean "embodiment, manifestation," or more generally "capability, power." At the moment of death, the *ka* departs from the body in the form of a bird.[9] Finally, the *akh (ȝẖ)* represents the dead individual "transfigured": the departed becomes an *akh* through burial rites.[10] Despite the studies cited, Erik Hornung believes that these terms have not been explored completely;[11] nonetheless, it is reasonably clear that no comparable notions are found in ancient Israel.

It will be worthwhile, however, to examine the abundant Akkadian use of both *napištu* (many scribal variants; not derived from any verb) and *napāšu* I, *napīšu,* "breath, perfume, odor," as well as the adj. *napšu,* "abundant."[12] Their usage turns out to be extraordinarily similar to that of OT *nep̱eš,* even though their range of meanings is greater. The similarity is all the more striking in that the sumero- and akkadogram for *napištu* in Hittite represents totally different notions.[13] A few Ugaritic texts will be presented alongside the Akkadian material.

1. *Akkadian.* According to Wolfram von Soden, the distinction between the commonest Akkadian words for "life" is that "*balāṭu* denotes life primarily as extending over a long period of time, whereas *napištu* denotes a state the opposite of death."[14] Even though he makes the proviso that there is no complete corpus of occurrences and that these meanings in their narrow sense cannot be assigned without violence to all the known occurrences of the words, he has isolated a tendency that is illuminating for Hebrew.[15] He notes, for example, that *napištu* occurs only rarely with *arāku,* "to be long" (*balāṭu* only with one

---

5. On the former see G. Pettinato, *BA,* 39 (1976), 50. On the latter see *AHw,* II, 736.
6. G. Dalman, *AuS,* V, 102.
7. See *HAL,* II, 711-13; also IV.5 below.
8. L. Greven, *Der Ka in Theologie und Königskult der Ägypter des Alten Reiches. ÄF,* 17 (1952); U. Schweitzer, *Das Wesen des KA im Diesseits und Jenseits der alten Ägypter. ÄF,* 19 (1956).
9. E. M. Wolf-Brinkmann, *Versuch einer Deutung des Begriffes 'bȝ' anhand der Überlieferung der Frühzeit und des Alten Reiches* (Freiburg im Breisgau, 1968); L. V. Žabkar, *A Study of the BA Concept in Ancient Egyptian Texts. SAOC,* 34 (1968).
10. G. Englund, *Akh, une notion religieuse dans l'Égypte pharaonique. Boreas,* 11 (1978).
11. E. Hornung, *Einführung in die Ägyptologie* (Darmstadt, 1967), 64f.
12. *AHw,* II, 741.
13. Kammenhuber.
14. P. 4.
15. See below.

of the derivatives or in conjunction with *dāru,* "continue, endure"), while *balāṭu* is never associated with expressions referring to the shortness of life, where *napištu* is found.[16] If, as in Hebrew, vitality is one of the basic meanings of the Akkadian word, this usage is quite natural.[17] Expressions referring to the ending of life (even including *tabāku,* "pour out") similarly require *napištu;* "not be alive" is *lā balāṭu:* here *napištu* would be out of place.[18] It is also noteworthy that verbs meaning "save, protect, etc. someone's life" use *napištu;* cf. also the expression *ana napišti/napšāti muššuru,* "release alive, spare."[19] A *bēl napištim* is therefore a person responsible for someone's life (e.g., granting it) or (Middle Assyrian) having the right to avenge a homicide. But when gods or goddesses are called "lords of life," the phrase is *bēl/bēlet balāṭi:* "A totally fulfilled life, a preserved life, in mythology a life without death such as Gilgamesh seeks, is *balāṭu.*"[20] Finally, it is probably significant that *napištu* can mean "sustenance," especially in the expressions *napišti māti,* "sustenance of the land," and *napišti niši,* "sustenance of the people," while "food as nourishment and much more frequently as medicine" requires the phrases *mû balāṭi* and *akal balāṭi* ("water/food of life"), respectively.

Conversely, "there is no phrase using *balāṭu* . . . that corresponds to the common literary expression *šiknāt* (earlier *šaknāt*) *napišti(m),* 'living beings, creatures.'[21] The same holds true for *napšātu,* 'persons,'[22] common in later texts, and *napištum,* 'self,' which is used much less frequently in this sense than in West Semitic, because the normal Akkadian word for 'self' is *ramānu.*"[23]

A series of further observations will serve to round out the picture:

a. For the verb *napāšu* I, whose range of meanings is greater than in Hebrew, *AHw* and *CAD* give the following meanings: "to breathe freely, relax, to expand, to become abundant, to make a claim"; in the D stem: "to let respire, to make feel easy, to air [textiles], to put in good repair"; N stem: "to become expanded." The Hebrew niphal, "relax, breathe freely," thus corresponds to the Akkadian G stem. That the semantic associations in Akkadian differ from those in Hebrew can be seen, for example, from the use of the G stem with *libbu,* "heart": "let her mind be calmed, let her heart respire."[24] It can also denote increase of wealth *(mimmušu)* or the good condition of a house.[25]

b. While von Soden disputes that *napištu* means "breath,"[26] there is in any case a separate noun *napīšu* (Old Babylonian and Late Babylonian) meaning "breath, odor,

16. P. 5.

17. *CAD,* II, 296ff., deriving this sense from "breath," contra *AHw,* II, 738. See also G. Steiner, *Der Begriff "Leben" in den Vorstellungen des Alten Orients. BAfO,* 19 (1982), 149, who translates *napištu* "vital force," citing cogent texts.

18. Von Soden, *Vorträge.*

19. *Ibid.,* 5.

20. *Ibid.,* 5.

21. Cf. *AHw,* III, 1234b.

22. *CAD,* XI/1, 300f.

23. Von Soden, *Vorträge.*

24. *CAD,* XI/1, 289.

25. *CAD,* XI/1, 290.

26. Von Soden, *Vorträge,* contra *CAD,* XI/1, 302.

perfume." When associated with Enkidu, *CAD* claims that it means "virility" — or possibly even "desire," as in Hebrew.[27] There are, however, not many occurrences of this noun.

c. For *napištu, CAD* gives the following meanings, which agree with those given by *AHw:* "life, vigor, vitality, good health; living beings; person, somebody, (negated) nobody; capital case; personnel, persons of menial status, animals counted in a herd; body, self; sustenance, provisions; throat, neck."[28] Other meanings are disputed: "opening, air hole," and "neckerchief."[29] A few noteworthy texts cited by *CAD* follow:

(1) The phrase *mūtu napšatu* denotes a capital case; from the mouth of the king, we read: "I . . . released him alive *(ana napišti)*"; the same expression is used for "flee for one's life." The phrase *napištī uballiṭ* means "I escaped with my life," and a sick individual recounts: "I fell sick and barely escaped with (my) life *(ina napištim).*" Especially noteworthy is: "Do you not know that I love (you like my own) life *(kīma napištim)*?" i.e., like myself.

(2) Interesting on account of the legal notions embodied are the texts dealing with the principle of "a life for a life," e.g., "If they do not discover the one who murdered him, they will deliver 3 persons as a fine (*umallu,* 'make full')"; in the case of an unborn child: "He gives restitution as for a person *(napšāte umalla)*"; a pretrial settlement: "Do not go to court against me, I will replace your slave for you with a person *(napšāti ša qallika ūšallamka).*"

(3) Important for the light it throws on OT usage is the meaning "body, corpse" in: "The plain was too small for . . . their bodies (they ran out of land to bury them)."

(4) Like Heb. *nepeš,* Akk. *napištu* can serve as a first-person intensifier: *anāku napšātīa ana šarri lû paqdā,* "I, my *napištu,* is submissive to the king"; cf. analogous oath formulas: *ana lā nīš ilišu u napištišu,* "without an oath sworn by his god's life and by his own."

(5) The expression *bīt napištim* means "house of provisions"; the following text is illuminating: *nakkamtī ša rēši napištiya ukallu tākulā u napišti tattaksā,* "You have used up my storehouse where my provisions were ready for me and thus you have cut my throat." The Euphrates can be called *napišti māti.*

(6) Utnapishtim, the hero of the Flood Story, can no longer be cited in this context without qualification, since the reading *ú-ta-na-iš-tim* is now attested.[30]

In summary, we may note that neither *CAD* nor *AHw* cites the meaning "soul," which must be sought, if anywhere, in the Hittite use of the sumerogram ZI and the akkadogram NAPIŠTUM.[31] Despite the close relationship with Hebrew, Akkadian does not yield an anthropological term, as can be seen from the rarity with which the word is used in the sense of "self" and above all from the meanings "provisions, capital case, air hole (or bile duct)."

---

27. *CAD,* XI/1, 305.
28. *Ibid.,* 296.
29. "Opening, air hole," are from *CAD,* XI/1, 304; von Soden: "bile duct." He rejects "neckerchief."
30. *CAD,* XI/1, 297; Gilg. (Meissner fr., Old Babylonian version of tablet 10), iv. 6, 13.
31. A. Kammenhuber, *ZA,* N.S. 23 (1965), 183.

2. *Ugaritic.* We supplement this discussion of Akkadian with a few Ugaritic texts, cited from *WUS,* which lists the following meanings: "gullet, throat; appetite, desire(?); soul; living being, human person."[32] The meaning "soul," it should be noted, is far from certain. The following noteworthy texts may be cited with assurance: *bnpš bn ʒlm mt,* "into the maw of the divine son Mot"; cf. *npš ḫsrt bn nšm,* "my [Mot's] *npš* had a lack of [= hungered for] human beings."[33] We also find *yqr' mt bnpšh,* "Mot roars with his throat," and *ṣ't npšh,* "the screams that issue from her [Anat's] throat."[34] Finally, *npš mm* means "water maw, whirlpool."[35]

The noun *brlt* appears several times in parallelism with *npš.*[36] The etymology of this word is uncertain; *WUS* gives the meaning "vital spirit, appetite, desire."[37] The word thus lies within the sphere of meaning of Heb. *nepeš.*

III. Statistics, LXX, Fundamentals.

The noun occurs 754 times, the verb (in the niphal) 3 times (Ex. 23:12; 31:17; 2 S. 16:14). Claus Westermann gives the following list:

Gen.	43	Ezk.	42	Ps.	144
Ex.	17	Hos.	2	Job	35
Lev.	60	Jo.	—	Prov.	56
Nu.	50	Am.	3	Ruth	1
Dt.	35	Ob.	—	Cant.	7
Josh.	16	Jon.	5	Eccl.	7
Jgs.	10	Mic.	3	Lam.	12
1 S.	34	Nah.	—	Est.	6
2 S.	17	Hab.	3	Dnl.	—
1 K.	23	Zeph.	—	Ezr.	—
2 K.	15	Hag.	1	Neh.	—
Isa.	34	Zec.	2	1 Ch.	5
Jer.	62	Mal.	—	2 Ch.	4

The distribution appears quite uniform. A significant portion of the occurrences can be noted in the Psalms and their poetry (with ancillary texts). This comports best with the meaning of the noun, as will be shown below. A technical use of the noun appears in

32. No. 1826; cf. *UT,* no. 1681.
33. For the first see *KTU,* 1.5, I, 7; for the second, 1.6, II, 17.
34. For the former see *KTU,* 1.4, VII, 48; for the latter, 1.16, I, 35.
35. *KTU,* 1.3, VI, 9; M. Dahood, *JANES,* 5 (1973), 85f.
36. Nine instances are cited by B. Cutler and J. Macdonald, *UF,* 5 (1975), 68; and an additional one by M. Dietrich, et al., *UF,* 7 (1975), 537f.
37. No. 585. Cf. Dietrich, et al., *UF,* 7, 538: "longing, desire." On the etymology see J. C. de Moor, *JNES,* 24 (1965), 365: by dissimilation from **ballatu* (cf. Akk. *balāṭu,* "life"); B. Cutler and J. Macdonald, "An Akkadian Cognate to Ugaritic *brlt,*" *UF,* 5 (1973), 67-70: Akk. *mēreltu* < *mēreštu,* "desire"; M. Pope, *UF,* 13 (1981), 305f.: Arab. *burā'il, bur'ūlah,* "neck feathers."

P^G, P^S, and H in laws and personal narratives that seek to avoid the gender-specific word *'îš* (very rarely *'āḏām*) and refer explicitly to any individual at all. The poetry of the Psalms accounts for more than one-fifth of the occurrences, technical legal usage approximately one-fifth. There are also smaller groups, such as the carefully considered Deuteronom(ist)ic expression "with all your *lēḇ* and with all your *nep̱eš*" (18 occurrences) or the idiom "have one's soul as prize" (4 occurrences).

According to Daniel Lys, in some 680 of 740 instances (depending on the enumeration of the MSS.), the LXX uses *psychḗ* to translate *nep̱eš*.[38] It uses the plural substantially more often than the MT, but without misrepresenting the sense (see the discussion of individuation below). According to the complementary study by Nikolaus P. Bratsiotis, it is no longer possible to say without qualification that the translation *psychḗ* is totally inappropriate, since pre-Platonic usage of *psychḗ* exhibits striking similarities to OT usage.[39] "The basic meaning of *psychḗ* is 'breath'; it often occurs in the meaning 'life' and can indicate the seat of desire, of emotions, and the 'center of religious expression; . . . it can also stand for 'person' or in place of a pronoun."[40] Lys cites 62 passages of the LXX where *psychḗ* translates some word other than *nep̱eš*. "But this very phenomenon indicates, however, that for the LXX translators *psychḗ* has more of an OT than a specifically Gk. meaning."[41] Since, however, the linguistic development of Greek led to the Platonic and post-Platonic usage of *psychḗ,* the translation of the LXX must be labeled significant, insofar as in the lingua franca it provided biblical tradition with a counterpoise. In any case, the *psychḗ* of the LXX shares the variety of the Hebrew noun. It would be better, however, not to follow the lead of this translation.[42]

Since the excellent studies of Aubrey Johnson, Hans Walter Wolff, W. H. Schmidt, and Westermann, description of OT usage presents no fundamental problems. In the Greek translation we may detect a circumstance that is universally present but whose full implications may not be sufficiently appreciated: more than other OT words, *nep̱eš* is truly anthropological,[43] probably comparable in this respect only to *bāśār* (cf. the merism used in Isa. 10:18: "from *nep̱eš* to *bāśār*"). Anthropologically, we are dealing with a synthetic-stereometric noun, well suited to making the OT interpretation of human nature fundamentally accessible.[44] Following an observation by Søren Kierkegaard, we can interpret human beings as creatures related to themselves. If we understand the language of this definition prephilosophically, it catches the essence of the OT noun *nep̱eš* extraordinarily well. But human beings in the OT do not think of themselves in a subject-object relationship (spirit and soul); the subject in particular is not thematic. On the basis of being alive, of individuation within life, of perceiving life as an in-and-out rhythm (breathing?), they find themselves to be living quanta with

38. *VT,* 16, 181-228.
39. *SVT,* 15, 58-89; see Westermann, 759. But cf. *HAL,* II, 711, 713.
40. Westermann, 759.
41. *Ibid.*
42. *HAL,* II, 711, 713; see the excursus in IV.2 below.
43. Cf. Wolff, whose list of such terms may be too inclusive.
44. Wolff, 10f.; cf. also Johnson.

respect to *ḥayyîm,* life. The word *nep̱eš* does not refer to spirit, intellect, thought; these do not have anthropological status in the OT. It means joy of life (expressed through need[45]) as a force against death and the longing for death. With its translation *psychḗ,* the LXX recognized *nep̱eš* as a key term of OT anthropology. That is an enduring achievement, even if we rightly abandon this translation.

IV. OT Usage. As the sections to follow cite the particular meanings of *nep̱eš,* we must always keep in mind that the concrete meanings discussed at the beginning do not have a semantic preponderance. Much more typical of OT usage is the global understanding, which requires stereometrically a harmonization of all the meanings.

1. *Throat, Gullet.* The concrete primary meaning of *nep̱eš* is usually assumed to be "maw, throat, gullet," as the organ used for eating and breathing. Like certain Ugaritic texts,[46] Isa. 5:14 speaks of the mouth of Sheol: "Sheol enlarges its *nep̱eš,* opens its mouth beyond measure." Hab. 2:5 transfers the image to the rapacious individual, who "is like Death and never has enough." The topos clearly centers on the throat, but it applies to the whole person. The same is true in Prov. 10:3: "Yahweh does not let the *nep̱eš* of the righteous go hungry, but he thwarts the craving *(hawwâ)* of the wicked"; 13:25: "The righteous have enough to satisfy their *nep̱eš,* but the belly *(beṭen)* of the wicked is empty"; 25:25: "Cool water to a thirsty *nep̱eš* is good news from a far country." Instances of the topos could easily be multiplied, but I must agree with Westermann that the concrete sense of "throat" as an organ for nourishment is rather uncommon.[47] It is clearly present in Prov. 28:25: "The *r^eḥaḇ-nep̱eš* stirs up strife, but whoever trusts in Yahweh will be well nourished" — the subject is someone with a gaping throat, a greedy-guts.[48] Textual uncertainty makes Prov. 23:1f. obscure, but *baʿal nep̱eš* seems to make sense only with the meaning "possessor of a throat, guzzler." In v. 2, in my opinion, one should not postulate *śakkîn,* "knife," and *lōaʿ,* "throat," but read *śakkôn* and *b^elōaʿ* and translate: "You [the guzzler] should provide a cover for your swallowing."

Equally uncommon is the meaning "breath" or "organ of breathing." It is clearly present only in some occurrences of the verb. According to 2 S. 16:4, after strenuous flight from Absalom, David was able to "breathe easily" (NRSV: rest) by the Jordan. Ex. 23:12 requires that the homeborn slave and the resident alien "breathe easily" (NRSV: be refreshed) on the seventh day. Ex. 31:17 applies this usage to Yahweh, who "breathed easily" (NRSV: was refreshed) after the six days of creation, thus establishing the basis for the vital rhythm of creation. In a similar vein, Gen. 1:30 speaks of all the creatures that can move about, in which there is *nep̱eš ḥayyâ.* Jer. 2:24 probably belongs here as well: "In the heat of her *nep̱eš* she gasps for air";[49] cf. Job 41:13(Eng. v. 21):

---

45. Wolff, 24f.
46. See II above.
47. Pp. 745f.
48. Wolff, 12.
49. Westermann (p. 747) interprets differently.

the *nepeš* of the crocodile kindles coals. A number of metaphors show, however, that the language was well aware of the connection between breath and the life of the individual: "the *nepeš* departed" from Rachel when she died (Gen. 35:18); the *nepeš* of the child in whom there was no breath *(nešāmâ)* returned (1 K. 17:21f.); the mother who bore seven exhaled her *nepeš* (Jer. 15:9); Jerusalem gasps for breath like a woman in labor and says: "My *nepeš* is faint before killers" (Jer. 4:31). There is also the wonderful statement, fundamental to the thought of J and probably a new idea, that the man became (not "received") a *nepeš ḥayyâ* when Yahweh Elohim breathed his breath into him. The expression *bātê nepeš* in Isa. 3:20 is obscure; the context does not help. The best translation appears to be that of the Vulg., "scent-bottles,"[50] lit. "little houses [containers] of vital energy [life]," made use of by breathing.

"In this archaic anatomy, therefore, the throat stands without terminological distinction for both the windpipe and the esophagus. When 'the floods rise to the *nepeš*,' there is danger of drowning (Jon. 2:6[5]; Ps. 69:2[1]; cf. Ps. 124:4f.)."[51] "The only weakly attested meaning 'breath' easily combines with the meaning 'throat, gullet' reflecting the various functions of the throat. . . . That various categories of the use of *nepeš* still evidence the effects of both functions of the throat, swallowing and breathing, confirms this relationship. One function echoes in the meaning 'desire, wish, craving' . . . and in a series of expressions associated with *nepeš* that presume the original meaning 'throat, jaws, gullet' (e.g., *śbʿ* hi. 'to sate,' Isa 58:11; *mlʾ* pi. 'to fill,' Prov 6:30; *rēq* 'empty,' Isa 29:8; *šôqēq* 'thirsty,' Isa 29:8; Psa 107:9]; par. to *peh* 'mouth,' Eccl. 6:7; par. to *gargārôṯ* 'neck,' Prov 3:22; cf. also Num 21:5; 1 Sam 2:33; Jer 4:10; Psa 105:18; Prov 23:7 txt?), the other in the three instances of the verb and in association with *qṣr* and *ʾrk*."[52]

Contra Wolff, it is better not to see *nepeš* as referring to the (outward) neck.[53] In all cases the imagery suggests strangulation, e.g., Ps. 105:18, a text central to Wolff's argument: "His feet were hurt with fetters, his *nepeš* came 'into' iron" (cf. 1 S. 28:9 [the medium to Saul]: "Why are you laying a snare for my *nepeš* to bring about my death?"). In particular, it would be quite wrong to cite in support of this meaning such expressions as "smite someone's *nepeš*," used for precision in describing homicide.[54]

2. *Desire*. The meaning "desire, appetite" is obviously closely related to the meaning "throat." Thus *nepeš* can denote simple hunger, as in Hos. 9:4: "Their bread is only for their *nepeš*." Dt. 23:25(24) allows grapes to be eaten for one's *nepeš* in a vineyard, but they must not be carried away. Isa. 29:8 uses the image of a hungry person who dreams of eating but wakes up with empty *nepeš* and dreams of drinking but wakes up with thirsty *nepeš*. Prov. 27:7 says that to a ravenous appetite even the bitter is sweet; the contrasting line shows that the whole person is intended: "A sated appetite

50. Also *HAL*, II, 124, s.v. *bayit* I.2.
51. Wolff, 13.
52. Westermann, 745f.
53. Pp. 14f.; also Westermann, 745f.
54. See 4 below.

treads down [NRSV: spurns] honey" — the whole person does the treading. Prov. 16:26, a very dense maxim, is probably best translated concretely: "The *nep̱eš* (appetite) of the worker works for him; his mouth drives him on." Isa. 56:11 may reflect observation of animals: dogs are *ʿazzê nep̱eš,* "strong [by virtue] of hunger," and must not be disturbed while they are eating. Isa. 55:2 refers to finer fare: "Delight your *nep̱eš* with rich food" (cf. Jer. 31:12,24f.: "Their *nep̱eš* will be like a watered garden").

The OT considers simple sexual craving, which can be satisfied by prostitution, to be blind and therefore repulsive (Jer. 2:24), but erotic desire has positive significance as part of the joy of living. Westermann rightly emphasizes that the meaning "desire, appetite" is not secondary (contra Eichrodt) but denotes something inherently human and does not view desire *(epithymía)* in a negative light; this understanding has much in common with "modern psychology and sociology."[55] The synthetic view of life always thinks of desire as involving the whole person. Thus Gen. 34:3 says that Shechem's *nep̱eš* "was drawn to" *(dāḇaq)* Dinah; 34:8 goes on to say that his *nep̱eš* loved her. Ezk. 23:17f. states the opposite: after her prostitution, Oholibah's *nep̱eš* turned away from her lovers; in like fashion Yahweh will turn away from Oholibah, just as he turned away from the *nep̱eš* of Oholah (cf. 23:22,28). Erotic desire, however, is only one form of passionate attachment and love. For example, Gen. 44:30 records that Israel's *nep̱eš* was bound up *(qᵉšûrâ)* with Benjamin, Joseph's only full brother. The same is said of Jonathan in 1 S. 18:1: his *nep̱eš* was so bound up with David that he came into conflict with his father's enmity toward David. But the most passionate attachment known is that between man and woman, so that in Cant. 1:7; 3:1-4 it is hardly possible to distinguish between the individual and the longing *nep̱eš.*

Not unrelated to this sense is the usage that speaks of enemies' thirst for vengeance, as in Ex. 15:9: "I [Egypt] will satisfy my *nep̱eš*"; Ezk. 16:27: "I gave you up to the *nep̱eš* of your enemies"; cf. Ps. 27:12: "Do not give me up to the *nep̱eš* of my enemies" (similarly 41:3[2]). Especially vivid is 35:25, which recalls the greedy cry of the psalmist's enemies': "How wonderful for our *nep̱eš;* we have swallowed him up." In these cases *nep̱eš* may have a weakened sense, something like "wish";[56] cf. the expression *'im-yēš 'eṯ-napšᵉḵem,* "if it accords with your wish" (Gen. 23:8; cf. 2 K. 9:15). Dt. 21:14, usually assigned to this group of meanings, is quite obscure to me: if a man wishes to separate from a wife acquired as a prisoner of war, he shall let her go *lᵉnapšāh* (similarly Jer. 34:16). The wording has the feel of technical legal terminology, suggesting that the *nep̱eš* of the divorced wife is not to be burdened with public or private obligations imposed during the period of her dependency. This interpretation is supported by Jer. 34:16 as well as Ex. 23:9: "You shall not oppress a resident alien, for you know the *nep̱eš* [desire, longing; NRSV: heart] of a resident alien." Does *nep̱eš* here refer to something like the longing for an independent and self-sufficient way of life, without the restrictions imposed by the native population? Comparing the *nep̱eš* to someone who moves too hurriedly, Prov. 19:2 seems to have

55. P. 747.
56. Westermann, 746.

in mind something more like excessive zeal, desire without knowledge as a legitimate aspiration.

This brings us naturally to the use of *nepeš* with the qal or piel of *nś'*, "lift up," with the meaning "crave, desire," "cause someone to desire." Dt. 24:15 states that the laborer must be paid his wages, "because he is poor and lifts up his *nepeš* for them." Jer. 22:27; 44:14 (piel) speak eloquently of the people's lifting up their *nepeš* for the land to which they cannot return (cf. Ezk. 24:25 [v. 21: *maḥmāl* in the sense of *maśśā'*[57]). Of course, the object of such longing may also be something evil or worthless (Ps. 24:4 conj.). Hos. 4:8 describes the depravity of the priests: "They feed on the sin of my people, they lift up their *nepeš* for their iniquity," i.e., to profit from it. Prov. 19:18 appears to envision the same blind passion as 19:2: "Discipline your son while there is hope; do not lift up your *nepeš* for [NRSV: set your heart on] his destruction." We can almost hear the parent's fit of rage. Ps. 25:1; 86:4 (piel) speak of lifting up the *nepeš* to God, 143:8 (qal) of the *nepeš* being lifted up. In 25:1, it parallels "trust": it represents a particularly fervent prayer in the proper setting. In Ps. 25 the psalmist prays not to be put to shame; in 143:8 the psalmist prays for instruction in the right way to go; and in 86:4, for renewal of joy in poverty and need.

The *nepeš* appears somewhat more dissociated when used with *'wh* piel or hithpael, *'awwâ*, or *ta'ᵃwâ*, since both the verb and the nouns already express desire. "This association of *nepeš* with *'wh* implies a specific aspect of its meaning. . . . *nepeš*, then, is not fundamentally a passive state of being but an active pursuit of something."[58] "When the craving of the *nepeš* is for early figs (Micah 7:1), the eating of meat (Deut. 12:15, 20; I Sam. 2:16), or, beyond that, the drinking of wine (Deut. 14:26), then the throat may still be meant as well as the seat of the desire. But when evil (Prov. 21:10), the kingdom (II Sam. 3:21; I Kings 11:37) or God (Isa. 26:9) becomes the object of the wishes, or when there is no object at all (Prov. 13:4, 19), then *nepeš* means longing *per se,* the human urge of desire as the author of longing *('wh).*"[59] The common translation "what your *heart* desires" already shows that the idiom aims to express a greater concealment or indirectness than simple human craving would lead us to expect. In Mic. 7:1 a detached judgment indicates that there are no more of the desired figs. In 2 S. 3:21 the speaker (Abner) would be in some danger if he imputed an unbridled lust for power *(nepeš)* to David; the expression refers rather to the calculated desire of a masterful politician. In 1 K. 11:37 Jeroboam I is assured that his desire to rule over Yahweh's kingdom was quite legitimate in Yahweh's eyes. In 1 S. 20:4 (conj.), in a similar vein, Jonathan asks David to explain his unstated intentions. The worshipers offering sacrifice at Shiloh told Eli's sons that they should wait until the fat had been burned for Yahweh and then take whatever portions they found desirable (1 S. 2:16). Dt. 12:20; 14:26 state that it is reasonable in Yahweh's eyes for worshipers at the sanctuary carefully to search out meat and wine so as to be able to be joyful before

57. Zimmerli.
58. Westermann, 747.
59. Wolff, 15f.

"the Lord your God." Especially in association with words that mean "desire," then, *nepeš* appears to mean to establish the judicious nature of this desire. Therefore Westermann discusses these texts under the heading "soul," even though he does not consider this translation entirely appropriate. It suffices to note here that *nepeš* presupposes and expresses the characteristically human distance that human beings can observe in relationship to themselves. The word "soul" strikes a false note, unless it is taken as meaning *inward* suspension of judgment, indirect desire.

This is the place, therefore, to include such texts as Nu. 21:5: "Our *nepeš* detests this manna"; Jer. 50:19: "Israel shall satisfy its *nepeš* on the hills of Ephraim"; Isa. 66:3: "The *nepeš* of the Israelites takes delight in their abominations"; and Prov. 25:25: "Good news is like cold water to a thirsty *nepeš*." In such contexts a variety of verbs denote the satisfaction of desire: *śbʿ*, "be satisfied" (qal: Jer. 31:14; 50:19; Ps. 63:6[5]; 88:4[3]; 123:4; Eccl. 6:3; piel: Ezk. 7:19; hiphil: Isa. 58:10; *śāḇēaʿ*: Prov. 27:7; *śōḇaʿ*, "satisfaction": Prov. 13:25); *ʿng* hithpael, "delight oneself" (Isa. 55:2); *rwh* piel, "be satiated" (Jer. 31:14; hiphil: Jer. 31:25 [par. *mlʾ* piel]); *dšn* pual, "be made fat" (Prov. 11:25; 13:4). To this category belong also texts with negative import: Ps. 88:4(3) (be filled with troubles); 123:4 (have more than one's fill of scorn).[60]

This section concludes with two contrasting but important usages. It may well be considered characteristic that the *nepeš* should thirst and long for God (Ps. 42:2f.[3f.]; 63:2[1]; 119:20,81; 143:6 [*nepeš* thirsts like a parched land]) or for the courts of God's house (84:3[2]). This desire does not fall victim to sublimation; instead, vitality[61] is expressed in this fashion, because Yahweh is life itself and the psalmists never forget that human beings are *nepeš* (against death). Isa. 26:8f. convey the same meaning. In an entirely different vein, in Eccl. 6:1-12 (a difficult text) the skeptical philosopher examines unsatisfied desire. His musings are probably directed against unguarded glorification of desire as a principle of life.[62]

Excursus: The Translation "Soul"

As is well known, it is quite possible to translate *nepeš* as "soul." The more vaguely and naively this word is used, the more correct and appropriate this translation becomes. This excursus deals solely with the question whether it is appropriate to posit for *nepeš* a meaning "soul" alongside such other meanings as "throat" and "desire"; for it has become clear that to use the translation "soul" in every instance, as Johannes Pedersen does,[63] does not do justice to the textual evidence. Because of its exegetical precision, I will take Westermann's analysis as the point of departure.[64]

Westermann rightly notes several times that the specialized meaning "soul" can be

---

60. Westermann, 748.
61. Johnson.
62. D. Michel.
63. J. Pedersen, *ILC,* I-II, 99ff.
64. Pp. 747-752; cf. also Wolff, 17f.

considered only in a relatively small number of passages.[65] The nucleus comprises a group of texts that speak of the grief and sadness (less often the joy and consolation) of someone's *nepeš*. They also speak of placing hope in Yahweh.[66] Wolff introduces his discussion with the following statement: "It is only a short step from the *nepeš* as specific organ and act of desire to the extended meaning, whereby the *nepeš* is the seat and action of other spiritual experiences and emotions."[67] But a survey of the texts that Westermann in particular has attempted to identify with certainty cannot help raising doubts; it appears more accurate to identify the ego or the self as the subject of grief, sadness, and so on, especially in poetry.

Westermann begins with the texts that speak of an embittered *nepeš*.[68] He ascribes a surprising overimportance to this group: "By no means accidentally, the fixed expression *mar nepeš* indicates a typical element of the OT understanding of *nepeš:* melancholy, desperation, and bitterness demonstrate the humanity of the individual with particular clarity; these very elements constitute the 'uniqueness' (M. Heidegger) of humanity." But the phrase occurs much too seldom in proportion to the other characterizations to justify such emphasis. Westermann bases his argument on the fact that *nepeš* is associated much more often with grief, and so on, than with such terms as joy.[69] But the wealth of textual evidence demonstrates rather that the meaning of *nepeš* inherently suggests a defiant affirmation of life. Johnson is correct in pointing to vitality as the defining characteristic of *nepeš* — impassioned, abounding vital energy. The phrase *mar nepeš* therefore denotes human existential inauthenticity.

The asymmetry between suffering and pain on the one hand and feelings of joy on the other means therefore that *nepeš* inherently expresses joy in life, vitality. We read accordingly much more often of the *nepeš* praising and even calling on itself to offer praise than of its experiencing joy, the opposite of grief.[70] One's *nepeš* can be "fattened" (*dšn:* Prov. 11:25; 13:4) — that is characteristic of it. It is by nature so affirmative of life that any additional expression of joy has the nature of a supplement — e.g., that knowledge is pleasant (*nʿm:* Prov. 2:10) to the *nepeš,* or that a disciplined son "gives delight (*maʿᵃdannîm:* 29:17) to your *nepeš*." Ps. 138:3 is almost definitive: "On the day I called, you answered me, since you gave great strength to my *nepeš*." Ps. 116:7 is classic: "Return, O my *nepeš,* to your rest (*mᵉnûḥâ),* for Yahweh has dealt bountifully with you."

In this context we may also cite the lovely idiom "pour out one's *nepeš*" (1 S. 1:15; Ps. 42:5[4]; Job 30:16). By way of explanation, Westermann cites Ps. 102:1(superscription), which speaks of the psalmist's pouring out his *lament* to Yahweh.[71] It is accordingly the "lamenting self" that pours itself out; it is immediately clear that the psalmist's

65. Last on p. 752.
66. P. 750.
67. P. 17.
68. Pp. 748-750.
69. P. 750.
70. *Ibid.* But cf. Lauha, 81ff., citing Isa. 61:10; Ps. 35:9; 71:23; 86:4.
71. Westermann, 750.

vital energy has been able to lay down its burden of grief and torment before Yahweh — the relief is immediately apparent in English. We may also cite Lam. 2:12: babies and infants "pour out their *nepeš* on their mothers' bosom."

One last point remains. Just as *nepeš* does not mean simply "life," but rather the individuation of life, as which it effectively appears,[72] so too *nepeš* does not denote the soul as one nuance among others — it refers rather to psychic power, abounding personality, energy that exorcises all gloominess. This basic sense of *nepeš* is reflected perfectly in the fact that hoping and waiting for Yahweh have *nepeš* as their subject (Ps. 33:20; 130:5f.; Lam. 3:25). Following Westermann,[73] I also cite here the texts that use *nepeš* with the hiphil or polel of *šûḇ:* Ps. 23:3; Ruth 4:15; Lam. 1:11,16. Ps. 19:8(7) may stand as an example: "The law of Yahweh . . . revives vital energy"; in Ruth 4:15, similarly, Naomi's *nepeš* is restored following the birth of Ruth's son, after her son's childlessness had left her drained of energy. Quite appropriately, there is a penitential rite called *ʿinnâ nepeš* (Isa. 58:3,5; Ps. 35:13) that is specifically associated with the Day of Atonement (Lev. 16:29,31; 23:27,32; Nu. 29:7; 30:14[13]). In concrete form this rite represents a repression of vital energy through hunger and thirst (fasting) as expressions of repentance, itself most likely an *ʿinnâ nepeš.* It is not simply the soul in general and the need for nourishment that are involved, but the whole person as *nepeš,* a figure of joy in life and vitality.

3. *Vital Self, Reflexive Pronoun.* Many texts suggest that humans have a relationship with themselves as individuals; this is unmistakably the case when *nepeš* denotes the vital self. There are an unusual number of examples, not all of which need to be cited; it suffices to note a few of the most telling. In Gen. 12:13 Abram says to Sarai: "Say you are my sister, so that it may go well with me because of you and my *nepeš* may be spared on your account." Gen. 19:19f. — a lovely passage — is strikingly nuanced (Lot speaking to Yahweh): "You have shown me great kindness in keeping my *nepeš* alive. . . . Look, that city there is nearby; . . . let me take refuge there, . . . that my *nepeš* may be saved." "It is not by chance that the plea 'let me live!' is in Hebrew 'Let my *nepeš* live!' (I Kings 20:32)."[74] Balaam cannot help speaking God's word, and so he cries out: "Let my *nepeš* die the death of the upright" (Nu. 23:10). The summons to one's *nepeš* to praise Yahweh speaks for itself (Ps. 103:1,2,22; 104:1,35; cf. Isa. 61:10; Ps. 34:3[2]; 35:9; 71:23; 146:1).

Westermann lists 86 passages where *nepeš* is translated by means of the reflexive pronoun; Johnson cites between 123 and 233 passages, depending on interpretation.[75] The *nepeš* is "the precise subject of the psalms of lamentation; it is frightened (6:3), it despairs and is disquieted (42:5f.,11; 43:5), it feels itself weak and despondent (Jonah 2:7), it is exhausted and feels defenseless (Jer. 4:31), it is afflicted (Ps. 31:7; cf. Gen.

---

72. See 4 below.
73. P. 748.
74. Wolff, 23.
75. Westermann, 755f.; Johnson, 15.

42:21) and suffers misery (Isa. 53:11). The *nep̱eš* is often described as being bitter *(mar),* that is to say embittered through childlessness (I Sam. 1:10), troubled because of illness (II Kings 4:27), enraged because it has been injured (Judg. 18:25; II Sam. 17:8)."[76] The expression "man/men of bitter *nep̱eš*" (Jgs. 18:25; 1 S. 22:2; 2 S. 17:8) is a stock phrase meaning "outcasts,"[77] extremely dangerous fighters ready for anything. It is not their soul but their whole being that displays their bitterness. In Gen. 42:21 it must be understood as an intensification when Joseph's brothers say that they saw the anguish of his *nep̱eš* (not simply *his* anguish). The same is true in the case of the servant of Yahweh: Isa. 53:11 speaks of "the anguish of his *nep̱eš*" — consider the context describing his torments! Among archaic texts, the poetic "I" appears already in Jgs. 5:21b: "March on, my *nep̱eš,* with might."

Here belongs also the Deuteronomic and Deuteronomistic expression "love with all one's *nep̱eš.*" Only rarely can we read the language as suggesting that *nep̱eš* refers directly to the relationship between God and an individual (e.g., Ps. 63:9[8]: "My *nep̱eš* clings to Yahweh; his right hand upholds it"). For "God is in heaven, and you upon earth" (Eccl. 5:1[2]), i.e., a direct relationship would obscure the distance between profoundly ephemeral mortals and God, whose word endures forever. Therefore the expression does not require the *nep̱eš* to love God with all its might. Instead, people are required to love God *with* all their *nep̱eš* and all their might. Westermann rightly emphasizes that the word *lēḇ,* "heart, as the seat of intellect and reason," lends the expression a certain reflective character that clearly emphasizes the sense of distance.[78] "With all your *nep̱eš*" elevates the intensity of involvement of the entire being (Dt. 4:29; 6:5; 10:12; 11:13; 26:16; 30:2,6,10; Josh. 22:5; 23:14; 1 K. 2:4; 8:48 [par. 2 Ch. 6:38]; 2 K. 23:5; cf. 1 Ch. 22:19; 28:9: "with willing *nep̱eš*"). Highly audacious is the application of this expression to Yahweh in Jer. 32:41: "I will plant them in this land with all my heart and with all my *nep̱eš*" — hardly an empty formula,[79] but suggestive of an oath. "The expression has become formulaic in association with the observance of the commandments (2 Kgs 23:3 = 2 Chron 34:31). . . . Deut 11:18 . . . also evidences this formulaic diction: 'write these my words in the heart and in the soul.' Here *nep̱eš* has become something present in the person."[80]

Awareness that *nep̱eš* means the vital self makes expressions denoting repulsion appear even more vivid:[81] *śn',* "hate" (Prov. 29:24); *g'l,* "abhor" (Lev. 26:11,15,30,43; = "loathe," Jer. 14:19); *qûṣ,* "detest" (Nu. 21:5; Ps. 106:15 conj.?); *t'b* piel, "abhor" (Ps. 107:18; Prov. 6:16); *qûṭ* niphal, "loathe" (Job 10:1); *y/nq',* "be disgusted" (Ezk. 23:17,18,22,28); *šᵉ'āṭ,* "abhorrence" (Ezk. 25:6,15; 36:5).

In conclusion, we recall that according to Gen. 2:7 a person does not *have* a vital

---

76. Wolff, 17.
77. Westermann, 749.
78. Pp. 750f.
79. Contra Westermann, 751.
80. Westermann, 751.
81. *Ibid.*

self but *is* a vital self.[82] It is therefore not a good idea to assume that any of the meanings of *nepeš* involve "having,"[83] since such an interpretation would lead to a misunderstanding of the anthropological nature of *nepeš.*

4. *Individuated Life.* That *nepeš* can mean "life" is generally accepted. Here I merely refine the conclusions of previous studies by pointing out that the word denotes not life in general but life instantiated in individuals, animal or human. "An essential distinction from the prior categories . . . consists in the fact that *nepeš* is usually the subj. in the former; by contrast, in the latter it is usually the obj."[84] Prov. 8:35f. could well be cited as an introductory motto: "Whoever finds me [Wisdom] finds life *(ḥayyîm)* and obtains favor from Yahweh; but whoever misses me does violence *(ḥms)* to his *nepeš;* all who hate me love death."

In 2 S. 23:17 (par. 1 Ch. 11:19) we read of David's unwillingness to drink water brought by his followers at the risk of their lives *(nepeš);* similarly in Lam. 5:9 *śîm b^e^kap* with *nepeš* means "risk one's life" (Jgs. 12:3; 1 S. 19:5; 28:21; Job 13:14; [Ps. 119:109?]). Even more drastic is the very archaic Jgs. 5:18: scorning death (*nepeš!* cf. Jgs. 9:17: Gideon *hišlîk napšô*), Zebulun and Naphtali fought their enemies. That something is a matter of life and death is stated in Gen. 19:17; Dt. 4:15; Josh. 23:11; 1 K. 19:3; 2 K. 7:7; Jer. 17:21; Prov. 7:23; Lam. 2:19; Est. 7:7; 8:11; 9:16 (with *'el, 'al, l^e^,* or *b^e^*). That the life is that of an individual is especially clear in 1 S. 26:21: Saul's *nepeš* was precious to David and he preserved it; cf. 2 K. 1:13,14; 1 S. 26:24 *(gdl).* "Because the *nepeš* is dear and precious, it requires attention (*drš* Psa 142:5; *yd'* Psa 31:8; Job 9:21; *nṣr* Prov 24:12; cf. also Ezek 16:5 with *gô'al,* 'disregard,' 'because no one attended to your life')."[85]

Many texts have to do with saving life. Almost all the verbs of saving can have *nepeš* as an object: *nṣl* piel (Ezk. 14:14), hiphil (Josh. 2:13; Isa. 44:20; 47:14; Ezk. 3:19,21; 14:20; 33:9; Prov. 14:25; 23:14; with God as subj.: Jer. 20:13; Ps. 22:21[20]; 33:19; 56:14[13]; 86:13; 116:8; 120:2), and niphal (Gen. 32:31); *mlṭ* piel (1 S. 19:11; 2 S. 19:6[5]; 1 K. 1:12; Jer. 48:6; 51:6,45; Ezk. 33:5; Am. 2:14,15; Ps. 89:49[48]; with God as subj.: 116:4) and niphal (124:7). The following appear only with God as subj.: *ḥlṣ* piel (6:5[4]); *plṭ* piel (17:13); *yš'* hiphil (72:13); *pāḏâ* (2 S. 4:9; 1 K. 1:29; Ps. 34:23[22]; 49:16[15]; 55:19;18]; 71:23; Job 33:28); *gā'al* (Ps. 69:19[18]; 72:14); *šûḇ* hiphil, "restore" (Ps. 35:17; Job 33:30); *šlḥ,* piel, "release" (Ezk. 13:20); *yṣ'* hiphil (Ps. 142:8[7]; 143:11); *'lh* hiphil (30:4[3]: from the realm of the dead); *rp'* (41:5); *ḥśk,* "hold back" (78:50; Isa. 38:17 conj?).[86] Especially noteworthy is the lovely language of 1 S. 25:29: "May the life of my lord be bound in the bundle of the living under the care of Yahweh your God; but may he sling out the lives of your enemies as from the hollow of a sling."[87]

---

82. L. Köhler, *OT Theology* (Eng. trans., Philadelphia, 1957), 142.
83. Wolff, 10; Scharbert.
84. Westermann, 752.
85. Westermann, 753.
86. Westermann, 752.
87. See O. Eissfeldt, *Der Beutel der Lebendigen. BSAW,* 105/6 (1960).

Such texts are matched by a remarkably large number that speak of threats to life. It would be impossible and unnecessary to cite them all. One significant element is the formula *bqš* piel plus *nep̱eš*, "seek after someone's life," which appears already in early texts (1 S. 20:1; 22:23 [twice]; 23:15; 25:29; 2 S. 4:8; 16:11; 1 K. 19:10,14; Jer. 4:30; 11:21; 19:7,9; 21:7; 22:25; 34:20f.; 38:16; 44:30 [twice]; 46:26; 49:37; Ps. 35:4; 38:13[12]; 40:15[14]; 54:5[3]; 63:10[9]; 70:3[2]; 86:14; Ex. 4:19). Fear for one's life is mentioned in Josh. 9:24; Isa. 15:4; Ezk. 32:10. When deliverance from such threats becomes precarious, we find the idiom "have/give one's life as a prize of war" (Jer. 21:9; 38:2; 39:18; 45:5).[88]

The texts dealing with homicide deserve rather closer examination. The best starting point is the *talion* formula in Ex. 21:23f., probably its earliest version: "If any harm follows, then you shall give *nep̱eš* for *nep̱eš*, eye for eye, tooth for tooth, hand for hand, foot for foot." Since the harm is accidental and the statement appears in the context of indemnity regulations, it presumably deals also with indemnification.[89] "*nep̱eš* here abstractly mean 'life' but only the individual 'I.' "[90] It is not restitution but death that is at stake when one is responsible for another *nep̱eš*, for example, as a guard (2 K. 10:24; cf. Josh. 2:14). A case involving a determination based on the principle of *nep̱eš* for *nep̱eš* is described in 2 S. 14:7, albeit with a plea for a decision taking account of the special circumstance.

While ransom is allowed in cases of accidental killing of the *nep̱eš*, it is explicitly forbidden in cases of negligent homicide or murder (Nu. 35:31). If the owner of an ox knows that the ox is accustomed to gore and it kills a *nep̱eš*, ransom as imposed by the victim's family is permitted only if they do not demand the death penalty (Nu. 35:31). Lev. 24:17f. states a general norm: "If a man kills a *nep̱eš*, he shall be put to death. Whoever kills the *nep̱eš* of an animal shall make restitution for it." The particular circumstances are not discussed, so that the text appears to enunciate a norm.

Dt. 19:1-10 discusses in detail the asylum system in cases of accidental homicide (cf. also Josh. 20:3,9). Dt. 19:6 prescribes that the avenger of blood must not wrongly kill the *nep̱eš* of the unfortunate perpetrator simply because he has caught up with him. V. 11 goes on to discuss the question of murder: in this case, the one who has taken the life of another is to be taken from the city of asylum and handed over. Mention of the *nep̱eš* appears to lend precision and signal the intentional nature of the act. Reuben saw this clearly when he prevented the murder of Joseph (Gen. 37:21).

Dt. 19:21 prescribes that the principle of *nep̱eš* for *nep̱eš* should apply also in cases of false witness, and 1 K. 19:2 has Jezebel say that she will make Elijah's life like that of one of the prophets of Baal: life for life. Job 2:4 notes sententiously that people will give all they have to save their lives, and Prov. 13:8 observes that the rich have always sought to use their wealth to ransom their lives.

Similar but probably not quite identical is the notion that a census or registration

88. → II, 68.
89. M. Noth, *Exodus. OTL* (Eng. trans. 1962), 181f.
90. Westermann, 753.

involves the threat of danger from the Deity (who does not want to have life quantified?): a *kōper* (ransom) must therefore be offered (Ex. 30:12). Nu. 31:50 mentions a similar *kōper* as a tribute to Yahweh for captured spoils. Isa. 43:4 exceeds all limits: Yahweh says that he gives nations for Israel's *nepeš*. Clearly this does not refer to a judicial act but to historical events of such magnitude that Israel's redemption stands in correlation with the destruction of many nations — an idea that is certainly not fantastic with respect to Israel's mighty enemy Babylon. In the opposite vein, the sailors accompanying Jonah prayed that Yahweh would not let them perish on account of the *nepeš* of Jonah, whose life they had to take because of his offense (Jon. 1:14). Concluding his audience with Satan, God orders him not to take Job's *nepeš*, his life (Job 2:6). Only twice (1 K. 19:4; Jon. 4:3) does someone pray that Yahweh will take his life — in both cases a prophet.

To explain why the blood of both sacrificial victims and animals slaughtered for food must not be eaten, Dt. 12:23 states: "The blood, that is, the *nepeš*"; but life belongs to Yahweh alone. Gen. 37:21f. likewise appears to presuppose a connection between blood and *nepeš*, since Reuben's intervention to prevent the taking of Joseph's *nepeš* continues: "Shed no blood; throw him instead into an empty cistern." The identification of blood with *nepeš* as well as the application of this identification to the prohibition against eating blood appears to be the new feature in Dt. 12.[91] Lev. 17:11 states more precisely: "The *nepeš* of the flesh is in the blood." But here the function is different: "I give it [the blood] to you upon the altar to make atonement for your *n*ᵉ*pāšôṯ*; for it is the blood that makes atonement through the *nepeš*." Not until v. 14 is the principle of Dt. 12:23 cited: "For the life *(nepeš)* of all flesh — its blood is its life; therefore I have said to the people of Israel: You shall not eat the blood of all flesh, for the life *(nepeš)* of all flesh is its blood."[92] As Wolff suggests,[93] the pouring out of the servant's *nepeš* to death (Isa. 53:12; cf. Ps. 141:8) may be related to the blood ritual, especially since v. 10 incorporates another sacrificial image: "When his *nepeš* makes an offering for sin *('āšām)*." The text clearly speaks of bearing the guilt of others vicariously. Gen. 9:4f. extends to the whole human race the prohibition against eating flesh together with its *nepeš*. In the light of present-day reality, it would be impossible to exaggerate the extent to which *nepeš*, life, rests exclusively in God's hands, so that even the killing of animals must respect the fact that life belongs to God. Thus, as v. 5 states, God "will require your lifeblood from the hand of every living creature" when an animal has been killed.

I am not entirely sure where to list the oath formula "As Yahweh lives and your *nepeš*" (1 S. 1:26; 20:3; 25:26; 2 S. 11:11; 14:19; 2 K. 2:2,4,6; 4:30). Since an oath envisions something like the working of a heavenly hand, we may ask whether this formulation may not comprehend the meaning under discussion, the preceding meaning, and the meaning to be discussed next.

---

91. → דם *dām* (III, 234-250).

92. See B. Janowski, *Sühne als Heilsgeschehen. WMANT,* 55 (1982); → כפר *kipper* (VII, 288-303).

93. P. 19.

5. *Living Creature, Person.* In the previous section we discussed *nepeš* as individuated life; it is clearly easy for the emphasis to shift to "living individual," a human person. This usage has the advantage of including both males and females. It is therefore the usage found in lists of persons and in the most precise Priestly legislation. The language draws on ancient legal conceptions like the *talion* formula "*nepeš* for *nepeš*" (Ex. 21:23) and generalizes the terminology to include other situations involving all living creatures.

"If casuistic law seeks to designate the given actor as generally as possible, both in the determination of the circumstance and in the determination of the consequence, the original collective *'āḏām* (the formula *'āḏām kî* . . . 'if someone . . .' occurs in the OT in Lev 1:2; 13:2; Num 19:14; see Elliger, HAT 4, 34) or the gender-exclusive *'îš* (cf. Lev 17:4,9) is not very suitable; *nepeš* 'human, person, someone' serves here as a more abstract, juristic term."[94] Such texts include Gen. 17:14; Ex. 12:15,16,19; 31:14; Lev. 2:1; 4:2; 5:1,2,4,15,17,21[6:2]; 7:18,20-21,25,27; 17:12,15; 18:29 (pl.); 19:8; 20:6; 22:3,4,6; 23:29,30; Nu. 5:6; 9:13; 15:27,28,30,31; 19:13,20,22; 30:3-13[2-12]; also Ezk. 18:4,20. We find a similar use of *nepeš* in lists of persons; this usage begins very early (Josh. 10:28,30,32,35,37,39; 11:11; 1 S. 22:22; Jer. 43:6; 52:30; but cf. also Gen. 46:15-27; Ex. 1:5; 16:16; Nu. 31:28-46). In Gen. 36:6 *nepeš* refers to members of the immediate family; by contrast, in 12:5 it refers to the family's dependents, i.e., those for whom the head of the family was responsible.

In recent scholarship it has become common to find the meaning "corpse," derived from the meaning "person, individual."[95] Since the characteristic feature of *nepeš* is vitality, such a usage would be very surprising. Diethelm Michel points out that Lev. 21:11 speaks of *napšôṯ mēṯ:* the dead body is in the genitive following *nepeš*.[96] Furthermore, since *nepeš* is used as a feminine, in Nu. 6:6 *nepeš mēṯ* cannot mean "dead *nepeš*" but only "*nepeš* of a dead body." All the passages in this semantic group (Lev. 19:28; 21:1; 22:4; Nu. 5:2; 6:11; 9:6,7,10,11,13; Hag. 2:13) deal with an act that renders a person unclean. Nu. 19:11,13 are more precise: whoever touches a dead body *l^eḵol-nepeš 'āḏām* or *b^ekol-nepeš hā'āḏām '^ašer yāmûṯ* becomes unclean. Therefore *nepeš* cannot refer to the corpse itself, but only to something associated with it. Michel recalls Nu. 19:14f.: when someone dies in a tent, everyone who is in the tent or enters it becomes unclean for seven days; "and every open vessel with no cover fastened to it is unclean." The example of the open vessel shows that *nepeš* certainly does not refer to the dead body. Since *nepeš* means "vital force," it is reasonable to ask what happens to it after death. "Rich and abundant though this use of *nepeš* for life is, we must not fail to observe that the *nepeš* is never given the meaning of an indestructible core of being, in contradistinction to the physical life, and even capable of living when cut off from that life."[97] We may therefore assume that even in death the vital force is something uncanny, belonging solely to God, which God's people should not come

94. Westermann, 755.
95. Wolff, 22; Westermann, 756; *HAL,* II, 713.
96. D. Michel, "*nepeš* als Leichnam?" *Zeitschrift für Althebräistik,* 7 (1994), 81-84.
97. Wolff, 20.

near. The suggestion that the word means "shade" should probably be rejected, since there is a different word with that meaning.[98] The assumption that in these texts *nep̱eš* refers to the vital force of someone who has just died, which no longer finds expression in life and is therefore dangerous, easily explains Lev. 19:28 (prohibition against gashing the flesh of the dead); 22:4; Nu. 5:2; 6:6,11; 9:6f.,10; Hag. 2:13. Lev. 21:1 is a kind of superscription, to be understood on the basis of the texts that interpret it.

Priestly precision probably also gave rise to the expression *nep̱eš ḥayyâ* (Gen. 1:20; 2:19 [gloss]; 9:10,12,15,16 [*b*ᵉ*rîṯ*]; Lev. 11:10,46; Ezk. 47:9): it refers to the animal world, characterizing it in its association with human existence, conveying the sense of both individuation and life — recall the prohibition against eating blood. Most of the texts reflect joyful, teeming life, albeit probably not without overtones of imperiled human life (as perceived during or after the catastrophe of the exile). The Creator desires life, not death.

6. *The nep̱eš of God.* It is striking how rarely the OT speaks of the *nep̱eš* of God (and never of the *nep̱eš* of Yahweh); the word was not suitable for forming a standard expression like "the countenance/arm/glory of Yahweh." All that was possible was sporadic use in the sense that God, too, has a relationship with himself. In Am. 6:8; Jer. 51:14, he swears by his *nep̱eš* (i.e., by his own self).[99] The lovely phrase describing the appointment of the servant of God springs from the same root: "in whom my *nep̱eš* delights" (Isa. 42:1). These words express intense favor. The same idea appears in 1 S. 2:35: instead of the sons of Eli, Yahweh will "raise up a faithful priest, who shall do according to my *lēḇ* and according to my *nep̱eš*." As in the Deuteronomist, the merism expresses a totality of concord.

It may have been easier to use *nep̱eš* to evoke the impassioned anger of God, who was not unjust but stood in total solidarity with his people. In Isa. 1:14 *nep̱eš* expresses God's utter rejection of Jerusalem's festivals and prayers, extending to the utmost depths of God's living being. In Jer. 6:8 God warns Jerusalem "lest my *nep̱eš* turn from you"; this rejection is confirmed by Jer. 15:1 (cf. also 5:9,29; 9:8; Ezk. 23:18; Zec. 11:8; Lev. 26:11,30). These texts all articulate disgust, the rejection following impassioned favor: "*nep̱eš* is the intensely purposive 'I.'"[100] *nep̱eš* can clearly be attributed only very rarely to God and only in this restricted sense.

If we now inquire into the human correlate and do not devote too much attention to the generalities of OT religion (God's acts to save, punish, bless human beings, etc.[101]), only one further observation is worth making. When God acts upon a human *nep̱eš,* the latter always has the meaning "life"; when the human *nep̱eš* acts with respect to God, it always has the meaning "desire."[102] It accords with the reserve with which the OT uses *nep̱eš* for the relationship between human beings and God that such desire

98. Cf. K. Elliger, *Leviticus. HAT,* IV (1966), 288; Michel.
99. → שׁבע *šbʿ*.
100. Westermann, 757.
101. Westermann, 757f.
102. Westermann, 758f.

never aims at grasping and controlling God but rather at embodying true humanity in the eyes of God. The *nepeš* is clearly healthy only in such desire for God. Therefore it does not reveal human existence as "progress toward death" (Heidegger), because *nepeš* is utterly antithetical to the power of death.[103] It reveals human existence as being in relationship to itself in the guise of vital energy, which cannot exist without a relationship to God. Thus the note struck by the highly spiritual Ps. 16, although late, is highly significant: "You will not give my *nepeš* up to death" (v. 10).

V. Postbiblical Usage.

1. *Middle Hebrew.* Turning to later developments, I must note that in Postbiblical Hebrew a significant change must have taken place vis-à-vis the usage attested in the OT. In Middle Hebrew it is no longer possible to speak of an anthropological term. We still find the meanings "life, person, desire, appetite, and wish in the sense of intention." Neither is it surprising that *dînê nᵉpāšôṯ* means "trials for capital offenses," even if the expression reflects foreign influence.[104] But now *nepeš* also has such meanings as "attention, idea"; in other words, it appears to have shifted meaning in the direction of Biblical Heb. *lēḇ,* a phenomenon already noted (exceptionally) in Dt. 11:18.[105] Middle Heb. *baʿal nepeš* accordingly means "attentive." Especially surprising vis-à-vis OT usage, I find, is the phrase *nepeš rāʿâ* (Aram. *nᵉpaš bîšā'*), "(ill-will), jealousy." With time, *nepeš* must have lost its original OT sense "joy in life." The same holds true for the meaning "(funerary) monument," already attested in 3Q15 1:5, more precisely "memorial tomb" in contrast to Aram. *qᵉḇûrā',* "tomb."[106] This meaning probably did not develop from the anthropological senses "breath / throat — desire — person," but from something like the survival of a personality for the sake of remembrance. The noun exhibits an unmistakable tendency to take on a more abstract meaning.

2. *Dead Sea Scrolls.* The contrast with the situation in the Dead Sea Scrolls can only be called surprising. There are more than 150 occurrences in the texts published to date (including occurrences in problematic contexts). Usage remains relatively close to that found in the OT, even if there have been changes and extensions of meaning at some points.[107] I shall sketch the findings in a few strokes.

a. As far as I can see, there is only one occurrence with the meaning "throat," namely 11QPs^{a} 19:8: "My *nepeš* roars [*šā'ag:* like a lion] to extol your [God's] name."

b. "Desire, wish, craving, etc." Greed *(rᵉḥaḇ nepeš)* appears in 1QS 4:9, in a catalog of vices. I doubt whether 1QH 12:1 (context mutilated) should really be read *tirḥa(ḇ) nepeš,* "far off is my desire"; the supplied *b* can hardly be correct. In 1QS 10:19, in a vow, the *nepeš* of the speaker "does not crave wealth by violence." Alluding to Dt.

---

103. See the discussion of Akkadian in II.1 above.

104. See II above.

105. *ANH,* 275; on Dt. 11:18 see IV.3 above.

106. *HAL,* II, 713, citing Nabatean and Palmyrene usage; cf. also the Middle Hebrew expression *nepeš 'ᵃṭûmâ,* "cenotaph."

107. See "funerary monument" above.

12, 11QTemple 53:2 speaks of the desire of the *nepeš* for flesh; 60:13 speaks of the longing of the Levitical priests to be in the sanctuary. Unfortunately the text of 4Q499 47:1 is damaged: all that is clear is some relationship between *npš* and *dbq.* Very common is the Deuteronomistic expression "with whole *lēḇ* and with whole *nepeš*"; it appears primarily in Deuteronomic or Deuteronomistic contexts (1QS 5:9; CD 15:9f.,12; 11QTemple 54:13; 59:10), but twice it is quite independent (1QH 15:10: "with whole *lēḇ* and with whole *nepeš* I bless/praise you"; 4QDibHam[a] (4Q504) fr. 1-2 2:13 along with the expression "to implant your *tôrâ* in our hearts").

Bitterness *(mrr)* is mentioned by laments in the style of the Psalms (1QpHab 9:11; 1QH 5:12; cf. 1QH 5:34: the *nepeš* is blinded by the bitterness of the day). Borrowing from P[S], 11QTemple 25:11 requires that on the Day of Atonement "you shall humble your *n[e]pāšôṯ.*" Also relatively common is the language of loathing (1QS 3:11; 15:18 [*tʿb* piel]; CD 1:21; 11QTemple 59:9 [*gāʿal*]); especially noteworthy is 4QDibHam[a] (4Q504) fr. 1-2 6:7: "We have not rejected *(māʾas)* your trials, and our *nepeš* has not despised *(gāʿal)* your punishments, to the point of breaking your *b[e]rîṯ,* in spite of all the anguish of our *nepeš.*"

c. *Vital Self, Reflexive Pronoun.* This sense occurs almost exclusively in texts that use the language of the Psalms; the two exceptions will be noted first. Alluding to Dt. 13, 11QTemple 54:20 forbids mercy toward even a "friend who is like your *nepeš.*" Elsewhere the word appears only in prohibitions against uncleanness (1QS 11:13; CD 12:11f.; 11QTemple 51:19) and the directive that "anyone who is unclean *lānepeš* [in life? as a person?]" must not enter the sanctuary. The extent to which *nepeš* refers to the whole person is illustrated once more by 1QH 2:7: "you support my *nepeš* by strengthening my loins."

The use of the language of the Psalms is so strikingly original that a few examples must be cited. In laments we find 1QH 2:24, "With your permission they attack my *nepeš* so that you may be glorified," and 5:17f.: "The whole day they [the wicked] crushed my *nepeš;* but you, my God, change the storm to a calm and have saved the *nepeš* ["life"] of the poor." The shift to praise is even clearer in 2:28: "When my *lēḇ* turned to water, my *nepeš* was confirmed in your *b[e]rîṯ.*" More likely traditional are 1QH 2:29; 5:39; 8:29,32; 10:31; 11:7. I do not find 1QH 3:25 entirely clear: "The *nepeš* of the poor person lived in aberrations of greatness *(m[e]hûmôṯ rabbâ).*" In an "apostrophe to Zion" (11QPs[a] 22:15) we read: "Let my *nepeš* rejoice in your [Zion's] glory." Finally, we may cite the typical words of 1QH 11:30: "Gladden the *nepeš* of your servant with your truth."

d. *Individuated Life.* There is one mention of the *lex talionis,* more detailed than the passage in Exodus (11QTemple 61:12): "*nepeš* for *nepeš,* eye for eye, tooth for tooth, hand for hand, foot for foot. . . ." Here belong also the texts that speak of tribulation and deliverance, as well as a series of expressions that sound like quotations, e.g., "blood is the *nepeš*" (53:6); "murder with respect to life [*nepeš*]" (66:7); "seek his life" (59:19); and the religio-historically interesting text 1QH 2:20: "I give you thanks, Lord, because you put my *nepeš* in the bag of life and have protected me from all the traps of the pit" (no expressed hope for resurrection). "Tribulation of my/his *nepeš*" appears in 1QH 9:28; 15:16; 4QDibHam[a] (4Q504) fr. 1-2 6:8. Ransom for one's *nepeš* is mentioned in 4QOrd[a] (4Q159) fr. 1 2:6. Several verbs express deliverance: *yšʿ* hiphil (1QH 2:23), *nṣl* hiphil (11QPs[a] 18:15 [Syr. Ps. 2]), *plṭ* piel (1QH 9:33), *ʿzr* (1QH 7:23 [par. "exalted my horn"!], and *pdh* (1QH 3:19). Highly original, finally, are the words of 1QH 3:6: "[My enemies] made my *nep̱eš* like a ship upon the depths *(m[e]ṣôlôṯ).*"

e. *Living Creature, Person.* No examples of this usage are attested to date.

f. *The nep̱eš of God.* One text speaks of God's *nep̱eš,* clearly as an intensifier: "in harmony with your *nep̱eš*" (1QH 4:21).

g. *ʿal nep̱eš.* Finally we come to a usage not attested in the OT: the distinctly formulaic use of *ʿal nep̱eš,* which may well be connected with contractual obligations.[108] It appears in the important text 1QS 5:8-10 ("he shall take it upon himself *(yāqēm ʿal nap̱šô)* to return to the law"); cf. also the allusion in 7:3. In a psalmodic prayer, 1QH 14:17 says: "But I, I am familiar with *(ydʿ)* the wealth of your goodness, and with an oath I have enjoined *ʿal nap̱šî* not to sin against you" (cf. also CD 16:4-10; 16:1; 11QTemple 53:15-21; 54:4). With the same sense of legal obligation we find *ʿl npšh* in the schematic passages Mur 24 C 19; D 20; 36 fr. 1-2 6; 42:10; and with reference to a woman in 29 vo. 3.[109] By contrast, 11QTemple 48:9 prohibits tattoos (Lev. 21:5) for the *nep̱eš* (in the context of superstitious mortuary rituals).

Seebass

108. K. Beyer, *Die aramäischen Texte vom Toten Meer* (Göttingen, 1984), 640, l. 5.
109. See P. Benoit, et al., *Les Grottes de Murabbaʿât. DJD,* II (1961), in loc.

יצב/נצב *nṣb/yṣb;* נִצָּב *niṣṣāḇ;* נְצִיב *n[e]ṣîḇ;* מַצָּב *maṣṣāḇ;* מִ/מַצָּבָה *mi/maṣṣāḇâ;* מֻצָּב *muṣṣāḇ*

I. Occurrences: 1. The Double Root *nṣb/yṣb* in Hebrew; 2. Other Semitic Languages; 3. Ancient Versions. II. Verb: 1. Causative Stems; 2. Niphal; 3. Hithpael. III. Nouns. IV. Theological Aspects: 1. God Stands; 2. God Sets; 3. Human Subjects. V. Dead Sea Scrolls.

nṣb/yṣb. Y. Aharoni, *"n[e]ṣîḇ, n[e]ṣîḇîm, niṣṣāḇ, niṣṣāḇîm," EMiqr,* V, 914-966; D. R. Ap-Thomas, "Notes on Some Terms Relating to Prayer," *VT,* 6 (1956), 225-241, esp. 227f.; A. Caquot, "Préfets," *DBS,* VIII, 273-286; A. Deissler, *Psalm 119(118) und seine Theologie. MTS,* I/11 (1955), 188-190; G. R. Driver, "Farewell to Queen Hussab," *JTS,* 15 (1964), 296-98; T. N. D. Mettinger, *Solomonic State Officials. CB,* 5 (1971); F. Pintore, "I dodici intendenti di Salomone (1 Re 4,7-19)," *RSO,* 45 (1970), 177-207.

I. Occurrences.

1. *The Double Root nṣb/yṣb in Hebrew.* The root *nṣb,* found throughout the entire Semitic language group (except in Akkadian[1]), appears in Hebrew only in the causative stems (hiphil: 21 times; hophal: 2 times) and the niphal (50 times). The hithpael uses the variant form *yṣb.* This alternation between *nṣb* and *yṣb* is unique to Hebrew and has never been explained satisfactorily. The prevalence of *nṣb* in the other Semitic languages suggests that it is also the primary semantic vehicle in Hebrew. Some grammarians therefore treat *hiṯyaṣṣēḇ* as a formation analogical to פ״י verbs having *ṣ* as their second radical, which arose because of homographic confusion with פ״ן verbs.[2] But the existence of the root *yṣb* in Aramaic and possibly also in Arabic[3] supports the theory that *yṣb* is an independent variant of *nṣb* in Hebrew as well. The opposite explanation (that *yṣb* is the true root, since apart from *yāṣā'* all verbs beginning with *yṣ-* exhibit forms in which the *y* is assimilated[4]) is out of the question, since the existence of the root *nṣb* is confirmed by the noun *n^eṣîḇ,* and would be expected from its wide distribution in the other Semitic languages.

2. *Other Semitic Languages.* For the root *nṣb, HAL* cites parallels in almost all representatives of Northwest, West, and South Semitic.[5] To these should be added Old South Arabic, with the verb *nṣb* ("set up") and the nouns *nṣb* ("funerary stela") and *mnṣbt* (pl.: "pillars").[6] The lexeme *naṣābu* II is attested in Akkadian,[7] but it is a loanword from West Semitic.

In all occurrences of the root, we can derive the meaning from a basic meaning "assume an upright position." Most similar to Hebrew is Ugaritic, where the G stem means "set up" and the N stem "place oneself"; cf. also the root's appearance in the Amarna letters.[8] In Aramaic and Syr. an independent semantic development took place: the *nṣb* peal and pael mean "plant," and the corresponding nominal derivatives mean "plantation," "sapling," and the like; it is possible nevertheless to derive this meaning from the common Semitic basic meaning. Other semantic variations, especially in Syr.,[9] can be understood as figurative usages of the meaning "plant."

The root *yṣb* appears in Aramaic as well as Hebrew: in Biblical Aramaic we find the pael *yaṣṣāḇā'* (Dnl. 7:19) and the adv. *yaṣṣîḇ* (Dnl. 2:8,54; 3:24; 6:13[Eng. v. 12]; 7:16); in the Targ. of Ex. 12:19 we find the noun *yaṣṣîḇā'* (for Heb. *'ezrāḥ*). *HAL* cites an Arab. *waṣaba.*[10]

---

1. See below.
2. *VG,* I, 601; *BLe,* §55t.
3. See below.
4. *GK,* §71l; cf. A. Even-Shoshan, *A New Concordance of the Bible* (Jerusalem, [2]1989), 485,
5. II, 714.
6. Biella, 311.
7. *AHw,* II, 755a.
8. For Ugaritic see *UT,* no. 1685; *WUS,* no. 1831. For Amarna see *AHw,* II, 755.
9. *LexSyr,* 442.
10. *HAL,* II, 427.

3. *Ancient Versions.* The ancient versions agree substantially in translating the verbs, but the nouns present difficulties. The LXX consistently uses *hístēmi* and its compounds for the verbs; the only other translation used with any frequency is *stēloún.* The occasional use of other verbs almost always serves to make the meaning clearer, e.g., when *niṣṣāḇ* in Ps. 119:89 is translated *(ho lógos sou) diaménei.* Since the root *nṣb* has a different meaning in Aramaic and Syr. than in Hebrew, the Syr. version and the Targ. use the root *qwm* (peal and pael; causative aphel for the hiphil). The Targ. consistently uses *ʿtd* ethpeal for *hiṯyaṣṣēḇ.* The LXX has the most difficulty with the derived nouns: the translators were clearly no longer acquainted with the semantic distinctions among *n^eṣîḇ, niṣṣāḇ,* and *maṣṣāḇ,* and therefore exhibit inconsistencies of translation within the same text (e.g., 1 S. 14:1ff.). Sometimes they leave the Hebrew terms untranslated or treat them as proper names (1 S. 10:5; 13:3f.: *Nasib ho allóphylos*). The Targ. settled on *ʾisṭarṭêḡāʾ* (= *stratēgós*) as a standard translation for all three nouns, using it indiscriminately except in texts conveying a different meaning (as in Gen. 19:26; Josh. 4:3,9; Isa. 22:19; Jgs. 3:22). The Syr. exhibits the best understanding, using *qāy^emāʾ* for *maṣṣāḇ* and *n^eṣîḇ* when the translators thought the latter refers to a military outpost, and *qāyûmāʾ* when it refers to a person. In the latter case, *šallîṭāʾ* is also used (1 Ch. 18:6,13; 2 Ch. 17:2).

II. Verb. As the survey of the ancient versions has shown, little semantic variation is to be expected in the verbal realm. Since the qal of neither *nṣb* nor *yṣb* is attested, the semantic analysis best begins with the causative and factitive hiphil.

1. *Causative Stems.* The hiphil is represented by only 21 occurrences, but they are quite homogeneous in their semantic substance. With good justification, *HAL* suggests only the single meaning "set (up)."[11] This meaning is well illustrated by Gen. 21:28f.: when Abraham makes a covenant with Abimelech and gives him the agreed-upon animals, he sets seven ewe lambs apart *(l^eḇadd^ehen)* for himself. The verb thus means "set something (in a specific place)." It is not necessary that the place be mentioned explicitly; it may be omitted as being obvious or not worth mentioning (it is obvious, e.g., that the ox-goad in 1 S. 13:21 is set [*haṣṣîḇ*] on a stick). The object that is set does not necessarily stand upright. Therefore the hiphil of *nṣb* can be used not only for the setting up of a pillar (Gen. 35:14,20; 2 S. 18:18; 2 K. 17:10), a monument (*yāḏ:* 1 S. 15:12), or a road marker (Jer. 31:21), but also for the erecting of an altar (Gen. 33:20; the emendation of *mizbēaḥ* to *maṣṣēḇâ,* still suggested by *BHS,* is not required by linguistic consideration), the raising of a heap of stones (2 S. 18:17), or the setting of a trap (Jer. 5:26). Finally, the hiphil of *nṣb* can be used in a weakened sense, without reference to "setting," to mean simply "attach" (an ox-goad: 1 S. 13:21; gates: Josh. 6:26; 1 K. 16:34). The phrase *haṣṣîḇ g^eḇûl(ôṯ),* "fix a boundary (boundaries)," is virtually a technical term (Dt. 32:8; Ps. 74:17; Prov. 15:25). Only twice is a human being the object of *nṣb* hiphil; in both cases Yahweh is the subject. Lam. 3:12 uses a

---

11. *HAL,* II, 715.

simile: the lamenting speaker feels set before Yahweh "like a mark for an arrow." Ps. 41:13(12), too, speaks of "setting" only in a figurative sense.

The hophal as the passive of the hiphil is attested with certainty only in Gen. 28:12. In Jgs. 9:6 the hophal participle serves to define the *'ēlôn* tree by which Abimelech is to be made king. The ancient versions were already unable to determine the meaning of this expression; the common emendation to *maṣṣēḇâ* is attractive but finds no support there. A "*crux interpretum* of the first class" appears in the opening words of Nah. 2:8(7); to the many proposed emendations, Wilhelm Rudolph has added another, which retains the hophal of *nṣb* but is unconvincing because it presumes an otherwise unattested meaning ("set in order").[12] The text remains a puzzle.

2. *Niphal.* Of the 50 occurrences of the niphal, 43 involve forms of the participle. In the niphal, therefore, the verb serves primarily to describe a state or condition; it is often preceded by a verb of seeing or *hinnēh* (Gen. 18:2; 24:13,43; Ex. 18:14; etc.). "[Abraham] looked up and, behold, three men were standing before him *(hinnēh . . . niṣṣāḇîm).*" The state is not permanent; what is described is what can be seen now, at this very moment: someone has set himself in place and is now standing there. The niphal seeks to emphasize this semantic nuance. The "standing" can imply a preceding movement or action, especially when a finite form of the verb is used (an impv. or optative): "Stand on the rock" (Ex. 33:21; 34:2); "Go to Pharaoh . . . and stand by to meet him" (Ex. 7:15).

Even more frequently, *niṣṣāḇ* expresses anxious expectation of something about to happen:[13] Abraham's servant stands *(niṣṣāḇ)* by the spring expecting Yahweh to give him a sign (Gen. 24:13,43; cf. also Jgs. 18:16; Am. 9:1; Prov. 8:2). Therefore *niṣṣāḇ* is not really suited to expressing a static condition; there is no trace of the nuance of "standing fast" in these texts. This is true even in Ps. 119:89, "Forever, O LORD, your word stands in heaven." The continuation of the ל strophe speaks of the dynamic effect of Yahweh's *dāḇār,* an aspect that fits with the meaning of *niṣṣāḇ:* Yahweh's word — pronounced and thus "set forth" — is ready to display its effectual power.[14] Apart from this passage, *niṣṣāḇ* appears only once with a nonpersonal subject: "[Joseph's] sheaf rose *(qāmâ)* and stood upright *(w^{e}gam-niṣṣāḇâ)*" (Gen. 37:7). The passage does describe a steady state, but the emphasis is on the act of rising.

Of course *nṣb* niphal does not always invoke all the semantic possibilities. In Ex. 18:14, for example, *niṣṣāḇ 'al* serves to emphasize the contrast between the seated Moses and the standing people. Elsewhere it can simply denote the people standing around (1 S. 4:20; Gen. 45:1: all those present) or (almost like a technical term) the constant attendants of King Saul (1 S. 22:6f.; in v. 17, contrariwise, it is only an attributive ptcp. modifying *rāṣîm*).

In some contexts, however, the niphal of *nṣb* can also fulfill a passive function. The

---

12. *Nahum. KAT,* XIII/3 (1975), 168.
13. Ap-Thomas, 227.
14. Deissler, 188ff.

passage just mentioned speaks of the Edomite Doeg *niṣṣāḇ ʿal-ʿaḇḏê-šāʾûl* (v. 9). If *niṣṣāḇ ʿal* is taken here in the same sense as in vv. 6f., then Doeg is only a subordinate servant of Saul who is present by chance.[15] As Ruth 2:5 shows, however, the same *niṣṣāḇ ʿal* can also denote a status of superiority, e.g., that of the foreman in relationship to the reapers. It should be noted that *niṣṣāḇ ʿal* in the former sense ("the people standing around") is always plural and expresses a relationship to a single individual *(ʿālāyw);* in the latter sense, it describes the relationship of an individual to a group. Here the niphal has passive meaning: "someone who is placed in charge of others"; the expression implies that he owes this position to someone else and is not exercising his own authority. In this semantic variant the ptcp. *niṣṣāḇ* has become a term denoting an office. In the list of the highest officials of Solomon's court (1 K. 4:2-6), v. 5 refers to Azariah ben Nathan as *ʿal-hanniṣṣāḇîm.* This expression does not denote the permanent retinue of the king in the sense of 1 S. 22:6f. (as the Vulg. interprets the text) but rather the government officials called *niṣṣāḇîm* in 1 K. 4:7; 5:7, whose office corresponds roughly to that of provincial governor (cf. the definition of their function and the list of names in 4:7,8-19a).[16]

We also find *niṣṣāḇîm* in 1 K. 5:30(16); 9:23; 22:48. The organization of the works carried out at the king's behest is discussed in 1 K. 9:23 (5:30[16] is dependent on this passage[17]); they are supervised by 550 *śārê hanniṣṣāḇîm.* This phrase admits two interpretations: it can mean "superintendent," or the *śārîm* can be interpreted as subordinate officials of the provincial governors *(niṣṣāḇîm).*[18] Since *niṣṣāḇîm* is a general term and both meanings are attested, it is very difficult to make a convincing choice between the two possibilities. The ancient versions do not help; they avoided the problem either by translating only one of the two words or by interpreting *niṣṣāḇîm* as an attributive participle modifying *śārîm* (LXX^{Or} and Vulg. for 9:23; Syr. and LXX^{A} for 5:30[16]). Except for the Syr. of 9:23 *(qāyûmāʾ),* none of the ancient versions chose to see in the *niṣṣāḇîm* the previously mentioned provincial governors. Interpretations based on the numbers given are pointless, since the number of laborers assigned to the individual *śārîm* is unknown.[19]

In 1 K. 22:48 the Masoretic pointing of *ûmeleḵ ʾên beʾeḏôm niṣṣāḇ meleḵ* means "there was no king in Edom; a *niṣṣāḇ* was king," a clear reference to a governor. The Syr., LXX^{Or}, and Vulg., however, interpreted *niṣṣāḇ* as a predicative participle and either linked the second *meleḵ* to the following verse or omitted it. The LXX of 16:28e (= MT 22:48) reads *ʾarām* for *ʾeḏôm* and uses νασιβ (representing *neṣîḇ*); it is unclear whether it took νασιβ as part of the name Συρια or left it untranslated (or not understood) as a technical term. It is not inherently unlikely that the ambiguous word *niṣṣāḇ* was used here, in contrast to normal usage, for the governor of a defeated and dependent

15. H. J. Stoebe, *Das erste Buch Samuelis. KAT,* VIII/1 (1973), 409.
16. Caquot, 273ff.
17. M. Noth, *Könige, I. BK,* IX/1 (1968), 93.
18. For the first see A. Šanda, *Die Bücher der Könige. EHAT,* 9/I-II (1911-12), I, 109; for the second see Noth, *BK,* IX/1, 93, 219.
19. Contra Šanda.

territory; but the text-critical problems should caution against basing far-reaching conclusions about the political situation of Edom on this passage. We must be content with observing that *niṣṣāḇ* is not a clearly defined official title.

Quite problematic is the meaning of *hanniṣṣāḇâ* in Zec. 11:16. If it does not derive from another root, *nṣb* II,[20] we must find a positive meaning ("the one who stands upright, the healthy one") in the verb, following the Syr., Targ., and Vulg. ("that which stands"), and above all the LXX *(holóklēron)*. Rudolph, who has once again supported this translation, is probably correct in treating the expression as a metaphor based on human experience.[21]

3. *Hithpael.* There are 47 occurrences of the hithpael of *yṣb,* to which should be added Ezk. 26:20, emended on the basis of LXX *anastathḗs: wᵉlô' ṯēšēḇî* [or *tāšûḇî*] *wᵉṯiṯyaṣṣᵉḇî* for *wᵉnaṯattî ṣᵉḇî.* Conversely, Job 38:14 should be emended to *wᵉṯiṣṭabbaʿ*.[22] In Ex. 2:4, *tēṯaṣṣaḇ* is probably a scribal error for *tiṯyaṣṣaḇ* (Sam.; cf. Syr., Targ.); Josua Blau, however, proposes to find here an obsolete *t*-form of the hiphil.[23]

Semantically, *hiṯyaṣṣēḇ* is very close to *niṣṣāḇ,* though not identical. The similarity is illustrated by the alternation between the two verbs in the story of the plagues (J) (Ex. 7:15 [niphal]; 8:16; 9:13 [hiphil]). In the story of Balaam (Nu. 22), likewise, there is alternation between the two verbs; here, however, the semantic distinction is palpable. The messenger of God "took his stand on the road as his adversary" (hithpael, describing an action, v. 22); but the donkey saw the messenger "standing in the road" (niphal, describing a situation, v. 23; cf. vv. 31, 34). The same difference appears in Nu. 23:3,15 (hithpael) and 23:6,17 (niphal). This observation is confirmed by the fact that the commonest form of the niphal is the participle, whereas the participle of the hithpael is never used; instead, there are 15 occurrences of the imperative and almost as many of the narrative and consecutive imperfect. There can be no doubt that the hithpael of *yṣb,* in contrast to the niphal of *nṣb,* expresses not the state of "standing" but the action of "taking up a position." There is no evidence, however, for the first meaning given by *HAL,* "take one's stand (firmly)."[24]

Sometimes *yṣb* hithpael parallels *ʿmd* (2 S. 18:30; Hab. 2:1; 2 Ch. 20:17). The same distinction is found: *hiṯyaṣṣēḇ* denotes the act of taking up a position, while *ʿmd* expresses the state: "The king said, 'Turn aside, and stand there *(hiṯyaṣṣēḇ)*'; so he turned aside and stood still *(wayyaʿᵃmōḏ).*"

When *yṣb* hithpael is used, the place where the subject stands is often stated; but one has the impression that the localization of the action is less important than the relationship of the persons involved to the action. Moses' sister stands at a distance (Ex. 2:4, naturally to see without being seen); Moses, however, has to stand *lipnê parʿōh,* because he must negotiate with him (8:16[20]; 9:13). The people take their

---

20. *HAL,* II, 715; cf. *GesB,* 539, citing Arab. *naṣiba.*
21. *KAT,* XIII/4, 203.
22. *BHS; HAL,* II, 427; G. Fohrer, *Das Buch Hiob. KAT,* XVI (1963), 492.
23. J. Blau, *VT,* 7 (1957), 387.
24. *HAL,* II, 427.

stand at the foot of the mountain because they are to meet with God while still keeping the necessary distance (e.g., 19:17). This group of texts also includes 2 S. 18:13, where *tiṯyaṣṣēb minneḡeḏ* means "you will stand aloof (from the matter)."

The hithpael of *yṣb* can also express the nuance of "assemble," especially when the subject is a group or collective. This usage is associated with the notion of an organized assembly (Ex. 19:17; 1 S. 10:29 ["by your tribes and by your clans"]; cf. Nu. 11:16; Josh. 24:1; Jgs. 20:2; 2 Ch. 11:13).

This nuance leads to the use of *hiṯyaṣṣēḇ* in military contexts. The Philistine Goliath came every morning and evening and took his stand (ready to fight) (*wayyiṯyaṣṣēḇ:* 1 S. 17:16). Jer. 46:4 uses *hiṯyaṣṣēḇ* in conjunction with other words that are clearly military; it means something like "take up a position" (Jer. 46:14; Hab. 2:1) and is a technical term belonging to the language of military orders. Interpreted in this context, *yiṯyaṣṣᵉḇû* in Ps. 2:2 makes perfect sense and does not require emendation.[25] In Ps. 94:16 the cry *mî-yiṯyaṣṣēḇ lî* conveys the same meaning, but in a metaphorical sense with respect to the conflict between the psalmist and the *pōʿᵃlê ʾāwen.*

The same semantic variant "take up a position" explains the use of *hiṯyaṣṣēḇ* in Zec. 6:5; Job 1:6; 2:1; Prov. 22:29. This meaning is expressed elsewhere by *ʿmd lip̄nê:* "stand before someone ready to serve, stand in someone's service" (Prov. 22:29).

Especially in Deuteronomistic usage (Dt. 7:24; 9:2; 11:25; Josh. 1:5) but also in Job 41:2; 2 Ch. 20:6, *hiṯyaṣṣēḇ* can mean "withstand *(lip̄nê/bip̄nê).*" Here too it is reasonable to assume that the language reflects the technical military usage of *hiṯyaṣṣēḇ* (cf. 2 S. 23:12; 1 Ch. 11:14). In a figurative sense the Gibeonites can describe their situation as being such that they cannot hold out anywhere in the territory of Israel (*mēhiṯyaṣṣēḇ bᵉḵol-gᵉḇul yiśrāʾēl:* 2 S. 21:5). A similar usage is found in Ps. 5:6(5); Ezk. 26:20 (emended).

III. Nouns. In Hebrew, derivative nouns are formed only from the root *nṣb.*

1. *niṣṣāḇ.* The noun *niṣṣāḇ* is a *qiṭāl* form with secondary gemination.[26] It is a hapax legomenon (Jgs. 3:22) denoting the hilt of a sword or dagger, into which the blade is inserted.[27] In all other texts, *niṣṣāḇ* is the niphal participle.[28]

2. *maṣṣāḇ.* The noun *maṣṣāḇ* is a *maqṭāl* form. It occurs 10 times and has a synonymous feminine counterpart, *maṣṣāḇâ* (1 S. 14:12), if the latter is not a scribal error for *maṣṣāḇ* (cf. LXX *messab*). It denotes the location where something stands or is placed, i.e., a place or position. Josh. 4:3,9 refer to the place where the priests stood as *maṣṣaḇ raglê ḵōhᵃnîm.* Isa. 22:19 uses the noun figuratively (as in Eng.) for the "post" of Shebna the steward (par. *maʿᵃmāḏ*). Everywhere else it refers to the garrisons

---

25. H.-J. Kraus, *Psalms 1–59* (Eng. trans., Minneapolis, 1988), 124.
26. *BLe,* §61iβ, 474.
27. H. Peucker, *BHHW,* I, 347f.; *BRL*², 57ff.
28. See above.

the Philistines established in the land (1 S. 13:23; 14:1,4,6,11,15; 2 S. 23:14; *maṣṣāḇâ:* 1 S. 14:12). More precisely, the word denotes a military unit: people can show themselves to the garrison (14:11); it can go out (*yāṣā':* 13:23) and tremble (14:15). If *maṣṣāḇâ* in 14:12 is not an error, it may refer to the garrison as an institution rather than the troops manning it.

In Zec. 9:8 the Masoretic vocalization *miṣṣāḇâ* represents the reading *miṣṣāḇā',* "before the army [that marches to and fro]"; cf. Vulg. "ex his qui militant mihi." Both LXX *anástēma* and Syr. *qāyûmā',* however, suggest a derivation from *nṣb.* As in 1 S. 14:12, this interpretation presents Yahweh as a protective garrison encamped about his sanctuary. Despite the reservations expressed by Nowack, there is no other convincing interpretation.[29]

3. *muṣṣāḇ.* If *muṣṣāḇ* in Jgs. 9:6 is taken as a verbal form,[30] then Isa. 29:3 is the only text that uses the hophal participle of *nṣb* as a noun. The versions (LXX *chárax,* Vulg. *agger,* Targ. *karkôm* [= Gk. *charákōma*]) and the parallel terms *dûr* ("rampart"; the emendation *dwd* based on the LXX and still supported by *HAL* is unnecessary[31]) and *m^e^ṣurōṯ* indicate that *muṣṣāḇ* is a technical term of siege warfare, even though we do not know its precise meaning.

4. *n^e^ṣîḇ.* The noun *n^e^ṣîḇ* is particularly problematical. It is a *qaṭīl* form (the vocalization of the absolute in 1 K. 4:19 is "probably to be considered an aramaism introduced by the Masoretic editor"[32]) occurring 11 times (sg. and pl.). Some of these occurrences, however, present text-critical problems. In 1 S. 10:5 the LXX, Syr., and Vulg. have the singular, like the usual singular in the construct phrase with *p^e^lištîm* (1 S. 13:3,4; 1 Ch. 11:16); the sense also argues for the singular. In 2 Ch. 8:10 *niṣṣāḇîm* should be read, following the *qere* and several manuscripts, and corresponding to the parallel text 1 K. 9:23. In 1 Ch. 18:6 an object is lacking in the MT; *n^e^ṣiḇîm* should be supplied, with 2 S. 8:6 and the ancient versions. I shall discuss 1 K. 4:19 below.

The literal meaning of *n^e^ṣîḇ* is clear from Gen. 19:26: "pillar" or "stela."[33] It is found, however, only in this passage. The translation "victory pillar" sometimes proposed[34] for 1 S. 10:5 is a mistake based on the LXX and Syr. (neither *anástēma* nor *qāyemtā'* points persuasively to "pillar") and should be rejected. Except in Gen. 19:26, the noun is always used figuratively: "pillar" in the sense of support provided by a foreign power. In the individual texts it is almost always unclear whether the reference is to an individual ("prefect," military commander) or a military entity ("post," gar-

29. W. Rudolph, *Sacharja 9–14. KAT,* XIII/4 (1976), 169.

30. See II.1 above.

31. *HAL,* I, 217; cf. O. Kaiser, *Isaiah 13–39. OTL* (Eng. trans. 1974), 263, n. d.

32. *VG,* I, 357; cf. LXX *nasiph/naseib.*

33. G. Ryckmans, *Mus,* 71 (1957), 130-32; J. A. Fitzmyer, *JAOS,* 81 (1961), 190.

34. J. Wellhausen, *Der Text der Bücher Samuelis untersucht* (Göttingen, 1971), in loc.; A. Schulz, *Die Bücher Samuel. EHAT,* 8/I (1919), in loc.; R. de Vaux, *Les livres de Samuel. La Bible de Jérusalem* ([2]1961), in loc.

rison). Unfortunately, the ancient versions do not help decide the question; in fact, they display obvious uncertainty in translating *n*ᵉ*ṣîḇ*, alternating apparently at random between terms denoting persons and terms denoting institutions. The close relationship of *n*ᵉ*ṣîḇ* to *niṣṣāḇ* (in the sense of "overseer") and *maṣṣāḇ* (in the sense of "garrison") is illustrated by occasional alternation (or confusion) with these words (cf. 1 Ch. 11:16 and 2 S. 23:14; 2 Ch. 8:10 *K* and *Q*).

In 8 out of 10 texts, the *n*ᵉ*ṣîḇîm* clearly serve as agents of foreign domination: they represent the Philistines in Benjamin (1 S. 10:5; 13:3f.) and Judah (1 Ch. 11:16), David's dominion over Aram-Damascus (2 S. 8:6) and Edom (2 S. 18:14; 1 Ch. 18:13), and Jehoshaphat's dominion over "the cities of Ephraim that his father Asa had taken" (2 Ch. 17:2). Such dominion is exercised by garrisons commanded by a military commander ("overseer" — a somewhat unfortunate translation,[35] since the individual in question is not an administrative official). But garrison and commander go hand in hand and can therefore be represented by the same term. Since the word *maṣṣāḇ*, "garrison," was readily available, it is reasonable to assume that *n*ᵉ*ṣîḇ* originally denoted the military commander in charge of the occupying forces and was later extended to refer to the garrison under his command. Since later ages were not familiar with the precise distinction between the two terms (cf. the versions), it is hardly possible today to determine whether a particular text refers to the garrison or its commander. In 1 S. 13:3f., for example, Jonathan's heroic deed could be either the assassination of the Philistine commander (so read by the LXX, which treats "Nasib" as a proper name) or a surprise attack on the garrison stationed in Gibeah. An instance of imprecise usage occurs in 2 Ch. 17:2, which describes Jehoshaphat as installing *n*ᵉ*ṣîḇîm* not only in the former cities of the northern kingdom but also "in the land of Judah." Of course this cannot refer to garrisons of an army of occupation; probably the text records the establishment of additional military posts.

Totally different and unique is the usage in 1 K. 4:19b. The list of *niṣṣāḇîm* and their territories concludes with the fragmentary clause *ûn*ᵉ*ṣîḇ 'eḥāḏ 'ᵃšer bā'āreṣ*, clearly a secondary addition.[36] The LXX with its *en gḗ Iouda* bears witness to the incompleteness of the text; "Judah" must have been omitted by haplography (beginning of v. 20). We have here an expansion adding the administration of Judah, not included in the list itself. The gloss eschews *niṣṣāḇ*, the usual word in such contexts, in order to emphasize the special status of Judah.[37] Its author, however, reveals that he was no longer familiar with the exact meaning of *n*ᵉ*ṣîḇ*.

IV. Theological Aspects. The verbs and nouns derived from the root *nṣb/yṣb* do not belong to the domain of religious language; neither are they theological terms. The verbs, however, may have a theological aspect when used with a divine subject or to frame theological statements.

---

35. Contra *HAL*, II, 716.
36. Noth, *BK*, IX/1, 74.
37. M. Rehm, *Das erste Buch der Könige* (Würzburg, 1979), 54.

1. *God Stands.* In 8 texts Yahweh or Elohim is the subject of a niphal or hiphil form; there are also 4 passages in Nu. 22:22ff. with *mal'aḵ YHWH* as subject.[38] Taken in the literal sense, this usage presupposes that God appears anthropomorphically. This usage appears therefore in accounts of a revelation or theophany (Gen. 28:13; Ex. 34:5; 1 S. 3:10), where it emphasizes the reality of God's presence as experienced by the recipient of the revelation. In two visions Amos sees Yahweh "standing" (niphal ptcp.); both texts (7:7; 9:1) are associated with a proclamation of judgment. (In 7:7 *niṣṣāḇ* refers to Yahweh even if we follow the reading of the LXX, contra Weiser,[39] who considers *'ᵃnāḵ* the subj.) The elliptical statement in Lam. 2:4 has roughly the same meaning (again, the subj. is Yahweh, not *yᵉmînô*): Yahweh stands with his right hand (outstretched menacingly) like an enemy. Yahweh's standing to judge (Isa. 3:13; Ps. 82:1: niphal ptcp.) is also menacing. This stance appears contradictory to general forensic practice, according to which the judge is seated.[40] But the expression can hardly be meant to reflect a specific forensic situation; its purport is that God the judge stands ready to enforce his judgment (cf. the frequent exhortation *qûmâ* in the same context). The meaning of the unique text that speaks of the divine *dāḇār* as "standing" (Ps. 119:89) has already been discussed; it is similar to other examples of personification.[41]

2. *God Sets.* Only metaphorically is Yahweh said to "set" something (*nṣb* hiphil). Besides figurative similes (Ps. 78:13, borrowing from Ex. 15:8; Lam. 3:12) and texts with the specialized meaning "fix boundaries" (Dt. 32:8; Ps. 74:17; Prov. 15:25), Ps. 41:13(12) is noteworthy: *wattaṣṣîḇēnî lᵉpāneyḵā lᵉʿôlām;* there are no parallels (not even Ps. 16:11, which therefore does not cast any light on 41:13[12][42]). This text does not refer to the psalmist's dwelling "in the place of God's presence"; as vv. 9(8) *(šāḵaḇ lō'-yōsîp̱ lāqûm)* and 11(10) *(wahᵃqîmēnî)* show, it speaks of the restoration or "raising" of the psalmist lying on his sickbed (*lip̱nê* has causal force[43]).

3. *Human Subjects.* There are also aspects of religious significance when a human being is the subject of the verb. In the case of the hiphil, such cases include "erecting" an altar (Gen. 33:20) or a pillar (Gen. 35:14,20) in the sense of instituting a cultic observance. A standing posture is required for some religious or cultic acts (1 S. 1:26; Nu. 23:3,6; Ex. 17:9). Here also belongs the assembling of the people (or their representatives) *lip̱nê YHWH* to select a king (1 S. 10:19), to make (Dt. 29:9) or renew (Josh. 24:1) a covenant, or formally to discharge someone from office (1 S. 12:7,16). The adverbial modifier *lip̱nê YHWH* merely points to the divine presence without defining

38. See II.3 above.
39. A. Weiser, *Die zwölf kleinen Propheten. ATD,* 24 (^{6}1974), 184f.
40. H. J. Boecker, *Redeformen des Rechtslebens im AT. WMANT,* 14 (^{2}1970), 85.
41. See II.2 above; Deissler, 299f.
42. Contra Kraus, *Psalms 1–59,* 433; and A. Deissler, *Die Psalmen,* 3 vols. (Düsseldorf, 1965-69), in loc.
43. J. Reindl, *Das Angesicht Gottes im Sprachgebrauch des ATs. ETS,* 25 (1970), 30.

its nature in detail.[44] Such "assembling" of the people, however, is always associated with the expectation that a demonstration of God's power or a revelation of God's will is to be manifested (cf. Ex. 14:13; 19:17; Dt. 31:14; Jgs. 20:2; 2 Ch. 20:17). The hithpael of *yṣb* (like the more common *ʿāmaḏ lip̱nê*) can denote the reverent attendance of subordinate heavenly beings (Zec. 6:5; Job 1:6; 2:1), without any apparent difference in usage. It is a mark of Moses' special status, however, that he is told to stand (niphal) in the immediate present of Yahweh (Ex. 33:21; 34:2) — he alone receives such a command.

V. Dead Sea Scrolls. Only the verb appears in the Dead Sea Scrolls; there are 25 occurrences of *yṣb* hithpael, but only 2 clear occurrences of the hiphil (CD 2:3, also the only text with God as subj.; 4Qtestim [4Q175] 23, a quotation from Josh. 6:26). The usage resembles that of the niphal and hithpael in the OT, but exhibits a preference for figurative language. In the literal sense, *hiṯyaṣṣēḇ ʿal maʿamāḏô* is a technical military expression referring to the arrangement of lines of battle (1QM 8:3,17, etc.; cf. 4QM[a] [4Q491] fr. 1-3 11; fr. 11 2:20). The same idiom is used figuratively for incorporation into the spiritual community (1QH 3:21; 11:13). The verb *hiṯyaṣṣēḇ* also denotes the acceptance of specific obligations and function within the community (1QSa 1:11,12, etc.).

Reindl

44. *Ibid.*, 35f.

נֶצַח *neṣaḥ*; לַמְנַצֵּחַ *lamᵉnaṣṣēaḥ*

Contents: I. Philology and Semantics. II. Occurrences in the OT and Dead Sea Scrolls: 1. Noun; 2. Verb; 3. *lamᵉnaṣṣēaḥ*. III. LXX.

neṣaḥ. P. R. Ackroyd, "נצח — εἰς τέλος," *ExpT,* 80 (1968), 126; W. F. Albright, "The Early Alphabetic Inscriptions from Sinai and Their Decipherment," *BASOR,* 11 (1948), 6-22; A. A. Bevan, review of S. Schechter and C. Taylor, *Portions of the Book of Ecclesiasticus* (Cambridge, 1899), *JTS,* 1 (1899/1900), 135-143, esp. 142; E. R. Dalglish, *Psalm Fifty-One in the Light of Ancient Near Eastern Patternism* (Leiden, 1962); G. R. Driver, "Problems in 'Proverbs,'" *ZAW,* 50 (1932), 141-48, esp. 144f.; S. R. Driver, *Notes on the Hebrew Text and the Topography of the Books of Samuel* (Oxford, ²1913), 128f.; B. D. Eerdmans, *The Hebrew Book of Psalms. OTS,* 4 (1947), 54-61; I. Engnell, "Psaltaren," *Svenskt bibliskt uppslagsverk,* ed. Engnell and A. Fridrichsen, 2 vols. (Gävle, 1948-52), II, 787-832, esp. 801f.; J. A. Grindel, "Another Characteristic of the *KAIGE*-Recension: נצח/νῖκος," *CBQ,* 31 (1969), 499-513; L. Kopf, "Arabische Etymologien und Parallelen zum Bibelwörterbuch," *VT,* 8 (1958), 161-215, esp. 184-86; S. Mowinckel, *Psalmenstudien,* IV (repr. Amsterdam, ²1961), 17-22; J. J. Scullion, "Some Difficult Texts in

I. Philology and Semantics. Two roots *nṣḥ* occur in the OT. In Hebrew and cognate languages *nṣḥ* I is associated with five principal meanings; philologists are uncertain as to their relationship. (1) According to A. A. Bevan,[1] the basic meaning is "gleam," as in Syr. *neṣaḥ* (cf. Arab. *naṣaḥa,* Eth. *naṣḥa,* "be clear"); the common meaning "conquer" is therefore secondary. This meaning is found in Sir. 32:9f.; 43:5,13.[2] From it derives (2) the second meaning, "distinguish oneself" (hithpael), found in Biblical Aramaic (Dnl. 6:4[Eng. v. 3]) and Egyptian Aramaic. (3) The meaning "conquer, overcome," appears in the Dead Sea Scrolls, Aramaic, and Phoenician. (4) The meaning "be permanent" is often considered primary.[3] (5) The final meaning is "supervise, lead" (piel), also found in the Dead Sea Scrolls.

The root *nṣḥ* II is associated with Arab. *naḍaḥ/ḫa* "sprinkle." William F. Albright derives Heb. *neṣaḥ* from this root and deduces the meaning "vital force, permanence."[4] The two occurrences of *neṣaḥ* in Isa. 63:3,6 are usually connected with *neṣaḥ* II and interpreted as "juice" (of grapes), i.e., in this context, "blood." John J. Scullion, however, derives the noun from *nṣḥ* I and translates it "glory" (the second meaning cited above).[5]

II. Occurrences in the OT and Dead Sea Scrolls.

1. *Noun.* The noun has its first meaning in 1 S. 15:29, "Glory of Israel" (used as a divine appellative). Here the Syr. sees the second or third meaning, while the Vulg. *(triumphator)* translates with the third meaning.[6] Citing Arab. *naṣaḥa,* "be clear, reliable," Lothar Kopf proposes "the Faithful One of Israel," which is consonant with the following *lōʾ yešaqqēr.*[7] Kopf goes on to argue a semantic relationship between *nṣḥ* and *ʾmn* and proposes a similar meaning for *niṣḥî* in Lam. 3:18: "my faithful one."[8] In 1 Ch. 29:11, as the context shows, we have a further example of the first meaning: "Glory of God."

The third meaning appears in a juristic or quasi-juristic sense in two passages: Hab. 1:4, *welōʾ yēṣēʾ lāneṣaḥ mišpāṭ,* "justice does not go forth effectively, persuasively" (cf. NRSV: "never prevails"); and Prov. 21:28, *lāneṣaḥ yeḏabbēr,* "speaks persuasively" (cf. Aram. *tešûḇaṯ niṣṣeḥat,* "a persuasive answer."[9] In 1QM 4:13 *neṣaḥ* occurs with the meaning "victory."[10]

Isaiah cc. 56–66 in the Light of Modern Scholarship," *UF,* 4 (1972), 105-128, esp. 122; D. Winton Thomas, "Some Further Remarks on Unusual Ways of Expressing the Superlative in Hebrew," *VT,* 18 (1968), 120-124, esp. 124; *idem,* "The Use of נֵצַח as a Superlative in Hebrew," *JSS,* 1 (1956), 106-9; H. Torczyner (Tur-Sinai), *Leš,* 6 (1935), 120-26.

1. P. 142.
2. See also Driver, 128f., on 1 S. 15:29.
3. Torczyner.
4. P. 18, n. 63; cf. *GesB,* 517: "eternity."
5. P. 122.
6. See also Driver, 128f.
7. P. 184.
8. → אמן *ʾāman* (I, 292-323). But cf. W. Rudolph's conj., *Die Klagelieder. KAT,* XVII/1-3 (1962), 231.
9. Driver, 144f.
10. Y. Yadin, *The Scroll of the War of the Sons of Light Against the Sons of Darkness* (Eng. trans., Oxford, 1962), 277.

The fourth meaning is found in Lam. 3:18, but here *niṣḥî* could also mean "my glory" (cf. NRSV: "gone is my glory and all that I had hoped for from the LORD"). It is also found in the many texts where *neṣaḥ* or *lāneṣaḥ* has the meaning "forever" or, when negated, "never." In these cases it belongs to the same semantic field as → דור *dôr,* → עד *ʿaḏ,* and → עולם *ʿôlām,* although it occurs only rarely in parallelism with them: twice with *lāʿaḏ* (Am. 1:11; Ps. 9:19[Eng. v. 18]), 3 times with *leʿôlām* (Isa. 57:16; Jer. 3:5; Ps. 103:9), once with *leʿôlāmîm* (Ps. 77:8f.[7f.]), and 4 times with *dôr* (Isa. 13:20; Jer. 50:39 [*ʿaḏ dôr wāḏôr*]; Isa. 34:10 [*middôr lāḏôr*]; Ps. 77:9[8] [*leḏôr wāḏôr*]). Once (Lam. 5:2) it parallels *leʾōreḵ yāmîm.*

The span of time expressed by *neṣaḥ* always refers to the future, never to the past (in contrast to the double reference of *ʿôlām* to both past and future in Ps. 90:2 and possibly the similar reference of *dôr* in 90:1). No more than *dôr* and *ʿôlām* does *neṣaḥ* involve the concept of "eternity." Neither does it denote a specific period, although the LXX occasionally uses *aiṓn* to translate it; it means rather "duration, permanence." The plural in Isa. 34:10 *(leneṣaḥ neṣāḥîm)* is merely an emphatic expression emphasizing permanence; it has nothing to do with a succession of ages. The frequent adverbial use of *neṣaḥ,* with or without *le,* often obscures the substantival character of the word.

Most examples of *neṣaḥ* with temporal meaning are in contexts that describe how God has turned away or inflicted punishment, or how the people beg for deliverance from such a situation: Isa. 13:20 (never again will Babylon be inhabited; cf. also Jer. 50:39); Isa. 34:10 ("its smoke shall go up forever"); Jer. 15:18 ("why is my pain unceasing?" par. "incurable"); Am. 1:11 (Edom kept his wrath forever); Ps. 9:7(6) (the enemies have been defeated forever); 44:24(23) ("do not cast us off forever"); 49:20(19) (no one can live forever); 74:10 ("how long . . . is the enemy to revile your name forever?"); 74:19 ("do not forget the poor forever"); 77:9(8) (God's *ḥeseḏ* forever); Job 4:20 ("they perish forever"); 14:20 ("you prevail forever against them [human beings] and they pass away"); 20:7 (the wicked perish forever); 34:36 ("let Job be tried continually"; but see below).

The majority of examples of this negative meaning occur in laments. Although they express recognition of the finality of God's punishment or the reality of God's absence, they spring from trust in his faithfulness, out of which God will grant the plea.

Contrariwise, a minority of the occurrences are in contexts with a positive meaning; these suggest the passing of God's anger or the assurance of God's constant care and presence: Isa. 33:20 (the tent stakes of Jerusalem will never again be pulled up); 57:16 (God will not always be angry; cf. Jer. 3:5 [→ נטר *nāṭar*]; Ps. 103:9); Ps. 9:19(18) (the needy will not be forgotten forever); 16:11 (in God's hand are "pleasures forevermore"); 68:17(16) (Yahweh will dwell on Mt. Zion forever). Especially important in this connection is Isa. 25:8, although both the genuineness and the meaning of the passage are disputed. According to the traditional interpretation, the verse says that in a final victory God has destroyed (or will destroy) the archenemy death (*māweṯ;* → מות *mûṯ*) "forever" (*lāneṣaḥ;* LXX *ischýsas;* 1 Cor. 15:54: *eis níkos*).

In a few passages where *neṣaḥ* was formerly interpreted temporally, the view that it occasionally has superlative force suggests the translation "totally" or the like: Isa. 28:28; Ps. 13:2(1); 52:7(5); 74:1,3 (*maššuʾôṯ neṣaḥ,* "total ruins"); 79:5; 89:47(46);

Job 14:20; 20:7; Lam. 5:20.[11] In Job 34:36 *ʿaḏ neṣaḥ* could have this same superlative meaning: "to the limit."

It is noteworthy that the LXX and other Greek versions often use *níkē, níkos,* and related expressions to translate *neṣaḥ,* although this meaning is rare in the Hebrew OT: Hab. 1:4; Prov. 21:28;[12] and possibly Job 23:7, which probably says that Job's appeal to his judge will be successful (although it is also possible that Job means that the verdict will be "forever," i.e., final). The meaning of "victory" here is forensic, in contrast to the military meaning in 1QM.

In 1 Ch. 29:11 *nēṣaḥ,* "radiance," appears in a liturgical context that ascribes to God power and glory *(geḏullâ, geḇûrâ, tip'ereṯ, nēṣaḥ, hôḏ),* in a certain sense a parallel but also a contrast to the words on the banners of the returning army in 1QM 4:13, where *neṣaḥ 'ēl* means "God's victory." For 1 S. 15:29 see above.

2. *Verb.* The verb *nṣḥ* occurs only 7 times (plus once in Sirach). The fourth meaning appears in Jer. 8:5: *mešuḇâ niṣṣaḥaṯ* (niphal ptcp.), "perpetual backsliding." This meaning may also be present in the hithpael participle in 1QM 16:8; 17:13, "while the war with the Kittim goes on"; Yigael Yadin translates: "is fought to a victorious end." The fifth meaning appears in the piel (inf. const.: 1 Ch. 15:21; 23:4; 2 Ch. 34:12; ptcp.: 2 Ch. 2:1; 34:13), "lead, superintend" (work or music). This meaning appears also in the Dead Sea Scrolls, especially in the sense of military leadership (1QM 8:1,6,8,9,12; 9:2; 16:6). In Ezr. 3:8f. it refers to oversight of the rebuilding; in 2 Ch. 34:12f. it probably refers to the music accompanying the work.

3. *lamenaṣṣēaḥ.* The expression *lamenaṣṣēaḥ* presents a special problem. It appears in Hab. 3:9 and the superscription of 55 psalms, sometimes in conjunction with *leḏāwiḏ, mizmôr leḏāwiḏ, leḏāwiḏ mizmôr, leʿeḇeḏ YHWY leḏāwiḏ,* or *liḇnê qōraḥ mizmôr.* The difficulty is due in part to uncertainty over the meaning of *le* ("written by," "belonging to the collection of songs by," "for the use of," or simply "for" in a sense to be determined by the interpretation of *mnṣḥ?*). Most interpreters have taken *menaṣṣēaḥ* as a piel participle of *nṣḥ* with the fifth meaning and referring to the leader of the music (or of the choir?), and have assumed that the psalms in question belonged to the collection of this leader. In 1 Ch. 15:19ff. *lenaṣṣēaḥ* refers to the playing of stringed instruments and *lehašmîaʿ* to the sounding of cymbals. Association with the cult is possible. The term has also been interpreted as a reference to the king in his cultic role and an alternative North Israelite form of *leḏāwiḏ.*[13] Sigmund Mowinckel understood the word as a *nomen actionis* meaning "to cause [God's countenance] to shine," i.e., "to appease," "to make atonement" (presupposing that the Hebrew form has an assimilated *n*).[14] On the basis of these and other theories, it is impossible to draw any

11. Winton Thomas.
12. See above.
13. I. Engnell, *A Rigid Scrutiny* (Eng. trans., Nashville, 1969), 86.
14. Mowinckel, 17-22.

sure conclusion concerning the meaning of the expression. The various translations of the versions do not give us any guidance.[15]

III. LXX. The LXX offers a bewildering variety of translations of *nṣḥ.* In Jer. 8:5 *m^eššûḇâ niṣṣaḥaṯ* is translated *apostrophḗn anaidḗ;* the piel infinitive is represented by *ischýein* or *enischýein* (twice), *episkopeín* (once), and *ergodiṓktēs* (once), the participle by *ergodiṓktēs* and *epistátēs* (once each). In Hab. 3:19 *lam^enaṣṣēaḥ* is translated *toú nikḗsai,* but in the superscriptions of the psalms always *eis (tó) télos,* as though the word were *lāneṣaḥ* (cf. Vulg. *in finem*). Aquila, however, has *tǭ nikopoiǭ,* "for the victor," Symmachus *epiníkios,* "a victory song," and Theodotion *eis tó níkos,* "for the victory" (cf. Jerome *victori*).

Variation between "duration" and "victory" appears also in the translation of *neṣaḥ.* In Lam. 3:18 *niṣḥî* is translated *níkós mou;* in 1 Ch. 29:11 *hanneṣaḥ* is translated *hē níkē.* For *ʿaḏ neṣaḥ, neṣaḥ,* and *lāneṣaḥ* we find *ek toú aiṓnos* (once), *eis tón aiṓna chrónon* (twice), *eis tón aiṓna* (twice), *diá pantós* (3 times), *eis chrónon polýn* (once), *ischýsas* (once), *eis níkos* (6 times), and *eis télos* (21 times). In Isa. 63:3,6, we find *haíma.* The meaning "be victorious, mighty" predominates, but the common translation *eis tó télos* in the psalm superscriptions gives a certain quantitative precedence to the meaning "endure."

With few exceptions, the various translations of the LXX reflect the several meanings of the word and are not based on technical considerations of translation. In 1 S. 15:29 the translation of *neṣaḥ yiśrāʾēl* as *diairethḗsetai Israḗl eis dýo* probably arose through confusion between *nṣḥ* and *ḥṣh;* alternatively it may reflect a variant reading.

Anderson

15. See below.

נצל *nṣl;* הַצָּלָה *haṣṣālâ*

Contents: I. 1. Etymology; 2. Occurrences and Distribution; 3. LXX. II. Meaning in the OT: 1. Basic Meaning and Development; 2. Semantic Field; 3. Special Problems. III. Dead Sea Scrolls.

nṣl. C. Barth, *Die Errettung vom Tode in den individuellen Klage- und Dankliedern des AT* (Zurich, 1947); U. Bergmann, "נצל *nṣl* hi. 'to rescue,' " *TLOT,* II, 760-62; *idem,* "Rettung und Befreiung" (diss., Heidelberg, 1968); G. R. Driver, "Hebrew Homonyms," *Hebräische Wortforschung. Festschrift W. Baumgartner. SVT,* 16 (1963), 50-65; *idem,* "Plurima Mortis Imago,"

I. 1. *Etymology.* The root *nṣl* is not widely represented in Semitic. For East Semitic there are no certain occurrences in Akkadian.[1] The same is true for the few West Semitic occurrences in Ugaritic, Syriac, and Ethiopic.[2] The root is distributed more broadly in Northwest Semitic. It is found in various dialects of Aramaic: (1) "save, deliver" + accusative object; (2) "retain"; (3) "take, take back" + accusative object + *min.*[3] Klaus Beyer cites the basic meaning as "take away" (haphel), differentiated into "take away again" (+ acc. + *min*) and (usually) "deliver" (+ acc.).[4] It also appears in Hebrew.[5] For Southwest Semitic it appears in Arabic.[6]

The occurrences in Northwest and Southwest Semitic clearly are closely related semantically, so that for *nṣl* in Hebrew we would expect a meaning ranging from neutral "separate" to positive "deliver."

2. *Occurrences and Distribution.* The niphal occurs 15 times: Gen. 32:31(Eng. v. 30); Dt. 23:16(15); 2 K. 19:11; Ps. 33:16; 69:15(14); Prov. 6:3,5; Isa. 20:6; 37:11; Jer. 7:10; Ezk. 14:16,18; Am. 3:12; Mic. 4:10; Hab. 2:9; in Ezk. 14:14 the niphal should also be read instead of the piel.[7] The subject is always a person or persons, delivered from *(min, mippᵉnê, mēʿim)* a situation, sometimes with the help of *(bᵉ)* something and to *('el)* a place of refuge. The verb may be used absolutely or with an object; additional qualifications *(bᵉ, 'el)* are not obligatory.

The piel occurs 4 times: Ex. 3:22; 12:36; 2 Ch. 20:25; Ezk. 14:14 (where the niphal should be read instead[8]). The subject is the people, who take something away from Egypt (Ex. 3:22; 12:36) or take something for themselves (2 Ch. 20:25). Ex. 33:6 is the only use of the hithpael (as reflexive of the piel) in the OT: the Israelites strip themselves of their own ornaments.

The root occurs 191 times in the hiphil; in addition, 3 Aramaic forms appear in Dnl. 3:29; 6:15,28(14,27). In about 65 percent of the instances the subject is a divine being, in about 30 percent the subject is human, and in the remaining 5 percent it is something

---

Studies and Essays in Honor of A. A. Neumann (Leiden, 1962), 128-143; W. Förster, "σῴζω," *TDNT,* VII, 980-998; P. Hugger, *Jahwe, meine Zuflucht* (Münsterschwarzach, 1971), 94ff.; E. Jenni, *HP,* 240, 258; W. Kasch, "ῥύομαι," *TDNT,* VI, 998-1003; J. F. A. Sawyer, *Semantics in Biblical Research. SBT,* 2/24 (1972); I. L. Seeligmann, "Zur Terminologie für das Gerichtsverfahren im Wortschatz des biblischen Hebräisch," *SVT,* 16 (1967), 254; P. Weimar, *Die Berufung des Mose. OBO,* 32 (1980); H. W. Wolff, *GSAT. ThB,* 22 (²1973).

1. *AHw* (II, 755; III, 1579) derives 2 occurrences from the root *naṣālu; CAD* (XI/2, 33, 125) registers only a single occurrence, which it derives from *natālu.*

2. For Ugaritic a single occurrence is cited by *UT,* no. 1688: "to get gifts from [someone]." For Syriac see *LexSyr,* 443a. For Ethiopic, W. Leslau, *Hebrew Cognates in Amharic* (Wiesbaden, 1969), 98: "detach, make single, unfold."

3. *DISO,* 185.

4. K. Beyer, *Die aramäischen Texte vom Toten Meer* (Göttingen, 1984), 640f.; cf. also *LexLingAram,* 114f.

5. *HAL,* II, 717.

6. Wehr, 971: "to fall out, . . . to free."

7. See below.

8. See below.

such as righteousness. In about 85 percent of the instances the verb governs an accusative object with or without *'eṯ,* frequently in the form of a pronominal suffix. When a person (divine or human) is the subject, the accusative object may be either a person or a thing; in the other cases the accusative object denotes a person. About 60 percent of the time the verb has an additional object introduced by *min* (or *mittaḥaṯ;* only Ex. 18:10). Further syntactic additions may designate the reason for the action (*kᵉ:* Neh. 9:28; Ps. 119:170; *bᵉ:* Ps. 71:2; Ezk. 14:20; *lᵉma'an:* Ps. 79:9; no prep.: Ps. 109:21) or its time (*bᵉ:* Jgs. 11:26; Job 5:19; Isa. 57:13; Jer. 39:17; Ezk. 7:19 par. Zeph. 1:18; Ezk. 33:12; no prep.: Jgs. 10:15; Neh. 9:28; Ps. 106:43). The expression *maṣṣîl bên* in 2 S. 14:6 and the simile *(kᵉ)* "like a gazelle" in Prov. 6:5 are discussed below. Also frequent (15 times) is the adversative expression *wᵉ'ên maṣṣîl;* it may or may not have an object.

The hophal appears in two almost parallel texts, Am. 4:11 and Zec. 3:2: "a brand snatched from the fire." Its conjectured use in Job 21:30 is rejected by *HAL* and *BHK.*[9]

The noun *haṣṣālâ* occurs only in Est. 4:14.

3. *LXX.* The LXX translates *nṣl* variously. The piel forms (including Ezk. 14:14) are represented by *skyleúō,* "take the armor of a defeated enemy, despoil," the hithpael in Ex. 33:6 by *periairéomai,* "take off something encircling, lay aside."[10] Five texts use *aphairéomai,* "take something from someone for one's own use" (Gen. 31:9,16; 1 S. 7:14; 30:18; Hos. 2:11[9]), and six use the verb *ekspáō,* "draw out" (1 S. 17:35; Am. 3:12 [twice]; Hab. 2:9; and the two hophals in Am. 4:11; Zec. 3:2). The verb *sṓzō,* "keep safe or healthy," is used 24 times. The most frequent LXX translations of *nṣl,* however, are *exairéomai,* "take for oneself, take away" (80 occurrences plus Dnl. 6:15[14] [Aramaic]), and *rhýomai,* "avert, protect, deliver" (85 occurrences plus Dnl. 3:19; 6:28[27] [Aramaic]; very frequent in the Psalms). In Prov. 2:16; 19:19, the LXX represents a different text; in 2 S. 20:6; Jon. 4:6, it clearly reads a form of *ṣll* III, which it translates with *skiázō,* "cast a shadow, shroud in darkness." Jer. 7:10 uses *apéchomai,* "receive what one deserves"; Ezk. 14:20 uses *hypoleípomai,* "be left behind"; and Ezk. 34:12 uses *apelaúnō,* "drive away."

In Ex. 5:23; Isa. 36:15, the use of the infinitive absolute in conjunction with the finite form is not distinguished. The noun in Est. 4:14 is translated *sképē,* "cover, refuge." The expression *wᵉ'ên maṣṣîl* is represented in the LXX by *kaí ouk éstin ho exairoúmenos/rhyómenos* (Ps. 7:3[2]: *sṓzontos*). Dt. 32:39 and Prov. 14:25 use finite forms of the verb.

II. Meaning in the OT.

1. *Basic Meaning and Development.* I start with the hiphil because of its frequency. Occurrences with a nonpersonal accusative object suggest "take away" as the basic meaning of *nṣl* hiphil (Gen. 31:9,16 [livestock]; Hos. 2:11[9] [wool and flax]; Ps. 119:43 [the word of truth]). The LXX's use of *aphairéomai* in some passages also associates

9. *HAL,* II, 717.

10. H. Frisk, *Griechisches etymologisches Wörterbuch,* 2 vols. (repr. Heidelberg, 1960-70).

this meaning with *nṣl:* besides the four passages with nonpersonal objects, in 1 S. 30:18 the object is David's abducted wives. In Hebrew the place or condition from which something is removed is fundamentally neutral. If the accusative object is personal, the verb has positive valence because the condition from which the object is taken is negative for the object. The same holds true for the expression "save/spare someone's *nep̱eš* (life)" (e.g., Josh. 2:13; Isa. 44:20; 47:14; Ezk. 3:19,21; 14:20; 33:9; Ps. 22:21 [20]; 33:19; 86:13). The circumstances can be differentiated further. On the one hand, there are situations from which escape is still possible: from the hand *(yāḏ)* or fist *(kap̱)* of enemies (in general: Jgs. 8:34; 1 S. 12:10f.; 2 K. 17:39; Ps. 31:16[15]; cf. also Jer. 15:21; Ps. 82:4; 97:10; 144:11; mentioned by name: Ex. 3:8; Jgs. 6:9; 9:17; 1 S. 7:3,14; Jer. 42:11; Mic. 5:5; with *kap̱:* 2 S. 19:10[9]; 22:1 par. Ps. 18:1[superscription]; Ezr. 8:31; 2 K. 20:6 par. Isa. 38:6 par. 2 Ch. 32:11), forced labor (*ʿaḇōḏâ:* Ex. 6:6), or tribulation (*ṣārâ:* 1 S. 26:24; Ps. 54:9[7]); here the verb can be translated "deliver from." On the other hand, there are situations from which escape would usually be inconceivable: death (Ps. 33:19; 56:14[13]; Prov. 10:2; 11:4), Sheol (Ps. 86:13; Prov. 23:14), the sword (Ex. 18:4; Ps. 22:21[20]), the strange woman (Prov. 2:16); here a better translation would be "protect from." The LXX also recognizes this distinction, albeit in different passages: sometimes it uses *sṓzō* or *rhýomai,* which express the sense of "protection"; at other times it uses *exairéomai,* which graphically pictures removal from danger.

At root *nṣl* clearly denotes an act of separation;[11] constructed with *min,* it takes on the sense of "take out, rescue." Even in passages where *nṣl* takes on the meaning "protect," a perceptible notion of "rescuing" still hovers in the background (cf. Prov. 23:14 and the notion of the "nether" world). The use of *nṣl* in the Dead Sea Scrolls agrees with this line of development: there too the verb means to "take out, rescue," while the neutral sense of "take away" no longer appears.

The niphal clearly provides the passive or reflexive of the abstract meaning "rescue, deliver" conveyed by the hiphil; the two occurrences of the hophal refer to "being taken out."

The piel denotes an intensification of the act of "taking away": "take away for one's own use, despoil";[12] this is also the interpretation of the LXX. The hithpael correspondingly means "take oneself away, separate oneself from something, lay aside."

2. *Semantic Field.* The following terms constitute the central semantic field of *hiṣṣîl: hôšîaʿ* (→ ישׁע *yšʿ*), → עזר *ʿāzar,* → חלץ *ḥillēṣ, millēṭ,* → פלט *pillēṭ, pāṣâ,* and *pāraq.*[13] Among these, *hiṣṣîl* is exceptional in having no derived nouns (except for the hapax legomenon in Est. 4:14) and not being found to date in proper names. Since it appears in construct phrases less often than *hôšîaʿ, ʿāzar,* or *pillēṭ,* it can be used only in contexts

11. *TLOT,* II, 760; Driver, "Homonyms," 63.
12. *HP,* 240.
13. Sawyer, 35.

where nominalization is not needed. Thus on purely grammatical grounds *hiṣṣîl* has a more restricted semantic field than the synonyms listed above. The use of *min* with *hiṣṣîl* (128 times) in contrast to *hôšîaʿ* (7 times) clearly brings out the sense of spatial separation.[14]

Again in contrast to *hôšîaʿ,* which is used intransitively some 9 times, *hiṣṣîl* can be used only transitively. Whereas in practice *hôšîaʿ* appears only with Yahweh as subject and is a technical theological term for Yahweh's deliverance of Israel (37 times in the Deuteronomistic history), *hiṣṣîl* is not restricted to theological usage. It can be used of gods in general as well as for human objects (of 46 occurrences of *hiṣṣîl* in the Deuteronomistic history, only 14 refer to deliverance by Yahweh). Thus *hiṣṣîl* occupies a position between *hôšîaʿ* and *ʿāzar,* which is used only in secular contexts. The difference is especially clear in 2 K. 19: in v. 11 *nṣl* refers to "infidel" deliverance, while in vv. 19,34 *yšʿ* refers to deliverance by Yahweh. The same is true in Jer. 15:20.

Along with *heʿᵉlâ* (→ עלה *ʿālâ*), *hôšîaʿ,* and → גאל *gāʾal, hiṣṣîl* refers to the deliverance of the exodus. While *yšʿ* signifies removal of the oppressor and *pillēṭ* suggests "escape," *nṣl* and → פדה *pāḏâ* denote deliverance from oppression.[15] In the exodus narrative of the Yahwist, *hiṣṣîl* functions as a key word (Ex. 3:8; 5:23; 18:10a); it is not able to dominate, however, and is also widely distributed among the various source strata (D: Ex. 18:8; Jgs. 6:9; P^G: Ex. 6:6; R^P: Ex. 18:4,10b).

3. *Special Problems.* a. *wᵉʾên maṣṣîl.* The formulaic expression *wᵉʾên maṣṣîl,* "there is no deliverer," not always translated literally in the LXX, appears in Jgs. 18:28; 2 S. 14:6; Isa. 5:29; 42:22; Hos. 5:14; Mic. 5:7(8); Ps. 7:3(2); 50:22; 71:11; Job 5:4; with *mîyaḏ* in Dt. 32:39; Isa. 43:13; Job 10:7. It occurs also in the Dead Sea Scrolls (1QM 14:11). The hiphil participle is used positively in Prov. 14:25, where it refers to a truthful witness as a lifesaver, and in Ps. 35:10; Jgs. 8:34 with Yahweh as subject. Jgs. 8:34 even describes Yahweh as *hammaṣṣîl.* Hos. 2:12(10) is noteworthy: in contrast to 5:14, the expression is rephrased with a finite verb: "no one shall deliver her."

The theory that *maṣṣîl* is a word reserved for Yahweh is further supported by the observation that in Prov. 14:25, the only passage where the participle does not refer to Yahweh, the LXX paraphrases with a finite verb. In the Dead Sea Scrolls, too, *maṣṣîl* occurs only with Yahweh as subject (1QM 14:11; $11QPs^a$ 18 [Ps. 154, Syr. II]:16).

b. *Miscellaneous.* Only in Ex. 18:10b is *nṣl* used with *mittaḥaṯ.* Earlier in the same verse we find the normal construction with *min.* The repetition in v. 10b does not appear in the LXX. Umberto Cassuto is probably correct in asserting that the repetition is intended for emphasis; it derives from the design of R^P to emphasize Israel's liberation.[16]

Only in Dt. 23:16(15) is *nṣl* used with *mēʿim* instead of *min.* The meaning of *mēʿim* is specified further by the directional *ʾeleyḵā* and in the following verse by *bᵉqirbᵉḵā.*

---

14. Sawyer, 71.

15. → VI, 445.

16. U. Cassuto, *A Commentary on the Book of Exodus* (Eng. trans., Jerusalem, 1967, repr. 1974), 216.

In Jgs. 11:26, since the object to be separated (land) is immovable, G. R. Driver suggests confusion of *ṣll* III with *nṣl;* he must, however, assume a meaning of *ṣll* ("purify") that is attested otherwise only in Postbiblical Hebrew.[17] I. L. Seeligmann sees here as in Am. 3:12 and Ex. 22:12 a technical term of pastoral law.[18] His translation, "seize for one's own use," is the simplest and most sensible suggestion, and need not even reflect a technical term.

In 2 S. 14:6 *nṣl* clearly means "tear apart." The translation "settle a quarrel" fits the context,[19] but "tear apart" is preferable because it reflects the text more closely.

The meaning of *nṣl* in 2 S. 20:6 is obscure and controverted. Frank Crüsemann argues for a literal interpretation.[20] He maintains that "tearing out the eyes," as the Syr. also translates, describes a common way of rendering someone totally helpless. "Tearing out the eyes" was a common form of punishment and subjugation primarily in Mesopotamia. This verse would, however, represent the only use of *nṣl* for this act.[21] Karl Budde arrives at a different interpretation on the basis of the LXX *(skiázō):* he proposes *hēṣal* from *ṣll* III, "darken."[22] But this interpretation does not clarify the meaning of the text. Retaining the vocalization *hēṣal,* Driver therefore suggests the meaning "escape," which makes sense in the context and agrees with the Vulg.: "and escape from us" (also NRSV).[23] Driver supports this interpretation by citing Arab. *ḍalla,* which appears quite often with this meaning.

In 2 Ch. 20:25 the prep. *l*ᵉ, which seems odd in this context, is used twice. A substantive introduced by *l*ᵉ*'ên* with consecutive meaning is not uncommon in the Chronicler's history (cf. Ezr. 9:14; Neh. 8:10; 1 Ch. 22:4; 2 Ch. 14:10[11],12[13]; 21:18; 36:16). The expression *l*ᵉ*'ên* should therefore not be read as an accusative object with aramaizing *l*ᵉ instead of *'eṯ*.[24] The text should be translated: "They took for themselves until they could carry no more."[25]

In the book of Proverbs we find two difficult texts that use *nṣl.* In Prov. 6:5 the meaning of *hinnāṣēl mîyaḏ* is obscure. Hermann Strack therefore transposes the words and reads: "Save yourself from the hand."[26] Preferable, however, is the interpretation of Otto Plöger, who cites v. 5b and reads *miṣṣayyāḏ:* "Save yourself like a gazelle from the hunter."[27] The meaning of Prov. 19:19 is very difficult to determine: *g*ᵉ*ḏol-ḥēmâ*

17. *SVT,* 16, 63.
18. P. 354.
19. *GesB,* 518.
20. F. Crüsemann, *Der Widerstand gegen das Königtum. WMANT,* 49 (1978), 109.
21. *Ibid.,* 109.
22. K. Budde, *Die Bücher Samuel. KHC,* VIII (1902), 298.
23. Driver, *Festschrift Neumann,* 135.
24. Cf. the translators of JB; K. Galling, *Die Bücher der Chronik. ATD,* 12 (1954), 124; J. Goettsberger, *Die Bücher der Chronik. HSAT,* IV/1 (1939), 291; P. Welten (*Geschichte und Geschichtsdarstellung im Chronikbüchern. WMANT,* 42 [1973], 141) leaves it untranslated.
25. NRSV; cf. W. Rudolph, *Chronikbücher. HAT,* XXI (1955), 262; E. Kautzsch, *HSAT,* II (^{4}1923), 647.
26. H. Strack, *Kurzgefasster Kommentar zu den heiligen Schriften Alten und Neuen Testaments,* A, 6, 2 (^{2}1899).
27. O. Plöger, *Sprüche Salomos. BK,* XVII (1984), 61. Cf. *BHS,* NRSV.

(Q) is preferable. The verse says in effect that anyone who tries to calm a violent-tempered person will only increase that person's wrath.

In Job 21:30 several scholars without convincing reason emend *yûḇālû,* "be brought," to *yuṣṣal.*[28] Others read *yuḵal.*[29] Alfred Guillaume simply uses an Arabic meaning of *ybl* and translates: "that they are smitten with disease on the day of wrath."[30] The most attractive approach is still Eduard König's observation that they text is to be understood ironically: "that the wicked are spared for the day of catastrophe, for the day of great wrath they are rescued."[31]

Isa. 20:6 is the only passage in the OT where *nṣl* is constructed with *mipp*ᵉ*nê* instead of *min.* Hans Wildberger thinks the verse is secondary; F. Huber disagrees.[32] In any case, the preposition here emphasizes that the hoped-for coalition was intended to be a defensive alliance against Assyria (cf. LXX: *sṓzō*).

Jer. 7:10 is the only passage in which the LXX translates *nṣl* with *apéchein,* "to have received something by right." This translation reveals the theological impossibility of the statement in the Hebrew text: the verb expresses an extraordinary commitment on the part of God, who delivers his people from any conceivable disaster; it is used here to show how the people rely on this assurance while refusing to react appropriately. God's deliverance is naturally not an action that people can claim by right simply by virtue of being Israelites (possibly in exile[33]), while oppressing the alien, the orphan, and the widow (vv. 5ff.).

The piel in Ezk. 14:14 should be read as a niphal, with the LXX, not as a hiphil.[34]

Ezk. 14:20 is the only passage where the LXX uses *hypoleípomai* to translate *nṣl.* In the context of vv. 16,18, it is noteworthy that even in Hebrew the phrase "they save neither sons nor daughters" is not simply repeated; it is varied in each occurrence. The LXX extends this variation by using three different verbs to translate *nṣl: sṓzō, rhýomai,* and *hypoleípomai.* The LXX thus interprets the passage to mean that the righteousness of individuals cannot be communicated to others in any way — not even as being "left, spared," not to mention being actively "delivered."

In the context of the flock of Israel and its shepherds, *nṣl* appears in Ezk. 34:10 (LXX: *exairéomai*) and 34:12 (LXX: *apelaúnō* [only here]). Thus the LXX uses words appropriate to the pastoral imagery. If Seeligmann is correct in considering *nṣl* a technical term of pastoral law, then in this passage Heb. *nṣl* should be understood strictly in this sense.[35] But even if we are not dealing with a technical term, the passage

28. G. Fohrer, *Das Buch Hiob. KAT,* XVI (1963), 338; *BHK; HAL,* II, 717.

29. G. Hölscher, *Das Buch Hiob. HAT,* XVII (^{2}1952), 54; et al.

30. A. Guillaume, *Studies in the Book of Job* (Leiden, 1968), 45, 105.

31. E. König, *Das Buch Hiob* (Gütersloh, 1929), 220f.

32. H. Wildberger, *Isaiah 13–27* (Eng. trans., Minneapolis, 1997), 286, 297; F. Huber, *Jahwe, Juda und die anderen Völker beim Propheten Jesaja. BZAW,* 137 (1976), 107-113.

33. Cf. Wolff, 66.

34. See I.2.a above; W. Zimmerli, *Ezekiel 1. Herm* (Eng. trans. 1979), 310; contra A. Bertholet, *Hesekiel. HAT,* XIII (1936), in loc.; G. Fohrer, *Ezechiel. HAT,* XIII (^{2}1955), 77.

35. P. 254, n. 1.

makes good sense, especially if v. 10 uses *nṣl* to compare the shepherds, who should be protecting the sheep, to beasts of prey from whose mouths the sheep must be pulled (cf. 1 S. 17:35,37; Am. 3:12). Because *nṣl* in the sense of "deliver, preserve" also has overtones of "pull out," the passage can be read on three levels: that of the shepherd, who frees the sheep from the mouth of a beast of prey; that of the leaders of the people, whom Yahweh deprives of their position; and that of the people, God's flock brought together from all over. The passage also says that *hammaṣṣîl* is at work both in the catastrophe of the exile (because he saves the people from false shepherds) and in the regathering of the people after the exile. A similar formulation appears in 4QDibHam[a] (4Q504), fr. 1-2 6:12 ("save your people Israel out of all lands"), so that this language is not exceptional.

In Jon. 4:6 it is noteworthy that the prep. *l[e]* appears to be used instead of *'eṯ,* although this usage would be unique. Here the LXX read a form of *ṣll* III, influenced on the one hand by the "shade" mentioned in the preceding verse and on the other by *l[e]yônâ.* Wilhelm Rudolph notes that in the LXX the verse is completely tautologous.[36] To solve the problem, he proposes either *l[e]haṣṣilô,* with a dittography of *l,* or (following König[37]) an aramaizing use of *l[e]* instead of *'eṯ.*[38] The latter is probably the most likely solution, since the book of Jonah as a whole is a relatively late work.

III. Dead Sea Scrolls. The verb is relatively infrequent in the Dead Sea Scrolls in comparison with *yšʻ.* The hiphil occurs 16 times (1QpHab 8:2; 12:14; 1QM 14:11; [4QM[a] (4Q491) fr. 8-10 1:9]; 1QH 2:31; 3:5; 5:13; 11QPs[a] 18 [Ps. 154, Syr. II]:15,16; 19 [Plea]:10; 4QDibHam[a] [4Q504] fr. 1-2 2:16; 6:12; 7:2; 4QpPs[a] [4Q171] fr. 3-10 4:21; 4Q158 1-2:8; 4QFlor 9-10, 6; 185, 1-2, II, 3), the niphal 5 times (1QH 7:17; 4QpPs[a] fr. 1-2 2:9; CD 4:18; 14:2; 1Q14 [1QpMic] fr. 10 8), and the hophal once (1Q38 4:5) (4Q498 4:1?). This list includes two passages using the hiphil participle: 1QM 14:11 (the commonplace *'ên maṣṣîl*) and 11QPs[a] 18 (Ps. 154, Syr. II):16 (Yahweh the deliverer of the upright from the hand of the wicked).

The usage of *nṣl* does not vary significantly from OT usage but is somewhat narrower: only the Deity is the active subject (a single possible exception being CD 14:2, where God's covenant serves as guarantor of deliverance), and the accusative object is always personal. As eschatological hopes might lead us to expect, the conditions and situations from which people may be taken or delivered now even include time itself (11QPs[a] 18 [Ps. 154, Syr. II]:15).

Hossfeld–Kalthoff

---

36. W. Rudolph, *KAT,* XIII/2, 361.

37. E. König, *Historisch-kritisches Lehrgebäude der hebräischen Sprache,* 2 vols. printed in 3 (Leipzig, 1881-97), II/2, §289h.

38. The latter possibility is supported by *HAL,* II, 717; and H. W. Wolff, *Obadiah and Jonah* (Eng. trans., Minneapolis, 1986), 160f.

נָצַר nāṣar

Contents: I. Etymology and Meaning. II. Occurrences and Usage. III. Wisdom Literature. IV. Psalms. V. Prophets. VI. Miscellaneous. VII. Theological Considerations. VIII. *nṭr.* IX. LXX.

I. Etymology and Meaning. The root *nṣr* is common to all the classic Semitic languages, occurring in both their earlier and later stages.[1] Important for our discussion is that, besides being found in Mesopotamia (Akk. *naṣāru,* "keep") and Arabia (*naẓara,* "perceive with one's eyes"), it is firmly rooted in Syria and Palestine (Ugar. *nǵr,* "protect, keep, beware"; Aram. *nṣr,* "guard, protect, keep"; later form *nṭr*).[2] From the earliest to the latest traditions it retains the meaning "keep" (par. to *šmr*), "observe" through close (visual) attention issuing in action. If visual observation is the primary meaning of *nṣr,*[3] it must be added that this sensory perception is actively engaged and has certain consequences. The verb appears in both active and passive expressions. Both deities and human beings can be the subject of the action expressed by *nṣr.*

II. Occurrences and Usage. In view of the broad distribution of the common Semitic root, the modest number of occurrences in the OT is surprising. Apart from a few texts using the Hebrew by-form → נטר *nāṭar* and the single occurrence in Biblical Aramaic in Dnl. 7:28, we find only 64 instances of the root. The derivatives *n^eṣûrîm* and *māṣôr* hardly deserve our attention, since their derivation from *nṣr* is not beyond question.[4] Noteworthy is the exclusively verbal development of the root, found in the OT only in the qal (the pass. being represented by the pass. ptcp.).

The root appears in both theological and secular contexts, and in both early and late texts, although one must confess that the late texts dominate. It is impossible to overlook a concentration of usage in Proverbs and Psalms (some two-thirds of all occurrences: 19 in Proverbs, 2 in Job, and 24 in Psalms). There are 14 occurrences in the prophetic literature (1 in Proto-Isaiah, 3 in the Apocalypse of Isaiah, 4 in Deutero-Isaiah, 1 in

---

nāṣar. A. Díez Macho, "Jesús 'ho nazoraios,'" *Quaere Paulum. Festschrift L. Turrado* (Salamanca, 1981), 9-26; B. Hartmann, "Mögen die Götter dich behüten und unversehrt bewahren," *Hebräische Wortforschung. Festschrift W. Baumgartner. SVT,* 16 (1967), 102-5; J. F. Healey, "Syriac *nṣr,* Ugaritic *nṣr,* Hebrew *nṣr* II, Akkadian *nṣr* II," *VT,* 26 (1976), 429-437; S. E. Loewenstamm, "Ugaritic Formulas of Greeting," *BASOR,* 194 (1969), 52-54; W. J. Odendaal, "A Comparative Study of the Protosemitic Root *nṭr*" (diss., Stellenbosch, 1966); H. P. Rüger, "ΝΑΖΑΡΕΘ/ΝΑΖΑΡΑ ΝΑΖΑΡΗΝΟΣ/ΝΑΖΩΡΑΙΟΣ," *ZNW,* 72 (1981), 257-263; J. Sanmartín, "Zur ug. Basis *NṢR,*" *UF,* 10 (1978), 451f.; G. Sauer, "נצר *nṣr* 'to guard,'" *TLOT,* II, 762f.

1. The individual languages are cited in *HAL,* II, 718.

2. For Akkadian see *AHw,* II, 755. For Ugaritic, *WUS,* no. 1811. For Aramaic, *KAI,* 222 B 8, C 15,17; 225, 12,13; 240, 1; 266, 8; as a PN in 254. For the later Aramaic form see S. Segert, *Altaramäische Grammatik* (Leipzig, 1975), §§3.2.6.6; 3.2.7.5.5; *DISO,* 178, 185.

3. *HAL,* II, 718.

4. See VII below.

Trito-Isaiah, 3 in Jeremiah, 1 in Ezekiel, and 1 in Nahum). The remaining 5 are in formulaic expressions in Exodus (once), Deuteronomy, and Kings (twice each). The verb does not appear at all in narrative sections of the OT.

III. Wisdom Literature. We find a whole series of *nṣr* texts in Prov. 1–9, a collection of didactic and hortatory admonitions generally considered to be postexilic. The instructor typically addresses the disciple as *b^e^nî* ("my son": 3:1,11; 6:20; pl.: 4:1, etc.) while he himself is called *'āḇ* ("father": 4:1). On the evidence of 6:20, there may also have been female wisdom instructors, analogously called *'ēm* ("mother"). An astonishing variety of language using the imperative or jussive exhorts the one being instructed or admonished to hear, accept, observe, keep, not forget, trust in the teaching, instruction, discipline, commandments, prudence, understanding, wisdom, and the like (*tôrâ, miṣwâ, b^e^rîṯ, mûsār, t^e^ḇûnâ, m^e^zimmâ, da'aṯ,* etc.; also *tôrāṯî,* with pronominal suf.), in order to have life, happiness, prosperity, health, and divine and human favor. The manifold rewards promised substantiate the exhortation and motivate the disciple to act and behave as admonished. The content of this substantiation is always a promise, stated in a *kî* clause or a consecutive clause linked with the copula (cf. 3:1-2 and 3:3-4). The person addressed may also be represented by a synecdoche such as lips (5:2) or heart (3:1); the latter is the center of the entire personality.

The verb *nṣr* is one of several used to express the exhortation to take to heart and observe the admonition or instruction. Observance of the commandments must be such as to take on decisive significance for all of life — indeed, it must be the guiding principle for action and conduct. In this context *nṣr* refers not simply to sensory perception (including "hearing") of the commandments to be kept but also to doing what they require. The meaning of *nṣr* demands that the injunction be observed effectually (3:1,21; 4:13,23; 5:2; 6:20). In short, everything that wisdom urges be observed and kept can be subsumed under the concept of "heart."[5] It is within the heart that one decides for or against the exhortations of the wisdom instructor. If they are taken to heart, there flow from the heart the "springs of life" (*tôṣ^e^'ôṯ ḥayyîm:* 4:23 and context, esp. v. 21).[6]

Also in this context belongs Prov. 23:26, a maxim from one of the minor collections that contain preexilic proverbial material. If one follows the *qere,*[7] what is to be observed (and of course done) are *d^e^rāḵay,* the ways (conduct) advised and taught by the wisdom teacher (i.e., father). The "son" must choose these ways by giving his heart to his "father." The *kethibh* uses *rṣh,* "take pleasure in" (with the "ways" as its obj.).[8] Conversely, woe, sorrow, and diminution of life pursue those who disdain and reject warnings, admonitions, and wisdom, who refuse advice. This train of thought will identify wisdom with salvation and folly with perdition (cf. 4:19; 6:12ff.; etc.).

---

5. → לב *lēḇ* (VII, 399-437).
6. O. Plöger, *Sprüche Salomos. BK,* XVII (1984), 49; M. Dahood, *Bibl,* 49 (1968), 368f.
7. See *BHS.*
8. H. Ringgren, *Sprüche. ATD,* 16/1 (1962), 94; Plöger, *BK,* XVII, 260, 263.

The benefits associated with the "reward" that comes to those who obey the exhortation include the remarkable coincidence that those who keep the commandments are themselves kept, guarded, and protected by what they keep (Prov. 4:6): *ḥoḵmâ* and *bînâ* (identified with the teaching of the wisdom instructor) guard and protect those who observe, love, and do not forsake them (4:1-9). The same is true of prudence and understanding (2:11). As everywhere in the ancient Near East, it is ulṭimately God who gives wisdom, knowledge, and understanding (2:11). Therefore God also guards the upright *(yāšār),* the faithful who live blameless lives, who accept and live according to wisdom, counsel, and discipline (2:8). All these passages use *nṣr* (2:8,11; 4:6); its meaning in this context is certainly no less complex than in the exhortations. These texts focus not on engaged perception but on care, protection, and felicity. We must not ignore the marked theologization of a notion of conduct belonging by nature to the realm of pragmatic wisdom, a development that is a central feature of this late collection of didactic wisdom.

Prov. 10:1–22:16, a collection of aphorisms that are generally dated in the preexilic period, is dominated by short, bipartite maxims contrasting the wise and the foolish, the upright and the wicked, the faithful and the godless. The fruits of experience in the secular realm are handed on, as in 13:3: those who know how to restrain their flow of talk will go unmolested (*nōṣēr pîw šōmēr napšô,* "those who guard their mouths preserve their lives"), but those who "open wide their mouths (lips)" come to ruin (cf. also Ps. 34:14[Eng. v. 13]). A faithful individual who might be too weak to bridle mouth and lips prays that Yahweh will set a "guard" (*šmrh*[9]) for the mouth and a "watch" *(nṣrh)* over the door of the lips (Ps. 141:3).[10] The same contrast can be made between the antonyms *ṣ^{e}ḏāqâ* and *riš'â* (loyalty and disloyalty); again, it is emphasized that righteousness issuing in action "guards" the upright (Prov. 13:6). Like *lēḇ, dereḵ* is a collective term for the way of life governed by wisdom, which alone affords and preserves life (16:17: *šōmēr napšô nōṣēr darḵô;* v. 17a points the way clearly: *sûr mērā';* for *lēḇ,* cf. 4:23).

Naturally what applies to people in general holds true also for the king (20:28): *ḥeseḏ we'^{e}meṯ yiṣṣ^{e}rû meleḵ;* it is tacitly assumed that the king in turn "preserves" loyalty and truth (cf. v. 28b). The same protective function of faithfulness and truth is also prayed for on the king's behalf in Ps. 61:8(7).

Like the wisdom tradition of Israel's neighbors, Israelite wisdom teaches that reward and punishment for human conduct come ultimately from Yahweh. The verb *nṣr* is used to express this notion (Prov. 22:12): Yahweh's eyes keep watch over *(nṣr) da'aṯ* (this can refer only to human knowledge and probably ultimately implied divine knowledge of human beings[11]), whereas he overthrows *(y^{e}sallēp̄)* the affairs (words and deeds) of the faithless *(diḇrê bōḡēḏ).* The verb covers all aspects of protecting, preserving, and enhancing life. This watchfulness over human life *(napš^{e}ḵā)* means

9. See *BHS* and the comms.
10. See also M. Dahood, *Bibl,* 43 (1968), 368f.
11. Contra Plöger, *BK,* XVII, 255f., with LXX.

that Yahweh — not mentioned here by name — understands *(byn, yd')* human beings totally, so that they cannot excuse or conceal themselves before God (24:12: *tōkēn libbôṯ hû' yāḇîn wᵉnōṣēr napšᵉḵā hû' yēḏa'*; cf. 20:27 conj.[12]). Job (7:20) calls Yahweh the watcher of humanity *(nōṣēr hā'āḏām),* but in his lament expresses astonishment that Yahweh is not more generous, but persecutes the insignificant individual.

Finally, the proverbs of Solomon collected by the officials of Hezekiah (Prov. 25–29, dating from the middle period of the monarchy) record secular wisdom based on experience. According to 27:18, anyone who tends *(nṣr)* a fig tree will eat its fruit.[13] This passage clearly illustrates the range of activities covered by *nṣr* (hard work, cultivation, care). The one who is *nōṣēr tôrâ* (i.e., who keeps the law, observing it and putting it into practice, a complex process) earns the honorific *bēn mēḇîn* (the goal of wisdom instruction has been attained! 28:7).

In the language of piety (e.g., prayer), "keeping" God's will (commandments, laws, instructions, etc.) is often a prerequisite for anticipated prosperity or deliverance from affliction. What witnesses to OT spirituality (e.g., in the Psalms) as an expression of piety parallels the conduct inculcated by wisdom in Wisdom Literature. Ps. 119, which contains 10 of the 24 occurrences of *nṣr* in the Psalms, occasionally exhibits clear wisdom features in its description of devotion to the law. We see this at the very outset (vv. 1-8), where in the style of wisdom those are called happy who keep Yahweh's decrees *('ašrê nôṣᵉrê 'ēḏōṯāyw),* which they have been given to learn *(lmd)* (vv. 2,7). Vv. 33-34,100 actually pray that Yahweh as a wisdom teacher will teach (*yrh* hiphil, *byn* hiphil) the psalmist *dereḵ ḥuqqeyḵā* and *tôrâ,* "that I may keep *(nṣr)* them." This psalm describes in great variety the rewards (prosperity, comfort, etc.) that accompany ready observance of the law; but fulfillment of God's will can itself be happiness and well-being. "I understand more than the aged, for I keep your precepts" (v. 100). Even more — God's "decrees" are so wonderful in nature that the devout keeper of the law cannot help keeping them (v. 129).

Ps. 34, an individual thanksgiving, includes a typical wisdom passage (vv. 12-17[11-16]). The instructions that, if followed, bring life and days to enjoy good include keeping (impv. *nᵉṣōr,* v. 14[13]) tongue and lips from evil and from speaking deceit. Wisdom aphorisms may become confessions of faith, as in Ps. 25, a hymn of trust: Yahweh's paths are steadfast love and truth *(ḥeseḏ we'ᵉmeṯ)* for those who keep *(lᵉnōṣᵉrê)* his covenant and his decrees (v. 10). This interdependence of keeping and being kept also finds expression in the devout life. The psalmist is confident that integrity and uprightness (which he is called on constantly to observe, a requirement not stated explicitly but tacitly presumed) will preserve him (with overtones of a prayer that they may), for he places his hope and trust in this correlation, guaranteed by God (v. 21).

IV. Psalms. The preceding discussion makes clear that constitutive elements of piety such as find expression in prayers are intimately associated with the fundamental tenets

12. See *BHS.*
13. C. Amoz, "*nṣr* of Fig-Tree Will Eat Its Fruits," *BethM,* 25 (1979/80), 81f.

of wisdom thought. This is especially noteworthy in devotion to the law.[14] The joyous psalmist can declare that worth, reward, and meaning rest solely in the fact of keeping Yahweh's *piqqûḏîm* (laws, statutes, ordinances, etc.), in refusal to forsake, forget, deride, and turn away from God's instruction, as the arrogant and wicked do (Ps. 119:56, with context). He will not be led astray by persecution (v. 69) but meets evildoers head on, dismissing them, firmly resolved to keep the *miṣwôṯ ᵓᵉlōhay* (v. 115: *wᵉᵓeṣṣᵉrâ* [cohortative]). This declared situation justifies (is the reason for, *kî*) his prayer to be protected from scorn and contempt (v. 22) — even more: the cohortative suggests that he can expect God to answer his urgent prayer. He can even pester God: *ʿᵃnēnî YHWH* (v. 145).

Conversely, God's gift of the laws and commandments entails the expectation that the people of God will observe and keep them, as the historical summaries in the Psalter state (Ps. 78:7; 105:45). There is an interesting difference in viewpoint between these two texts: keeping the commandments is both a prerequisite for Yahweh's bestowal of divine gifts on his people and a consequence of Yahweh's favor already bestowed on them.

In some of the *nṣr* passages in hymns of lamentation or thanksgiving, the functional domain of *nṣr* is restricted exclusively to Yahweh, whether the text uses Yahweh directly as the subject of *nṣr* or expresses a plea that Yahweh will *nṣr.* As a motif of confidence, the prayer of the oppressed includes a declaration of faith that Yahweh always preserves *(nōṣēr)* the faithful *(ᵓᵉmûnîm)* (Ps. 31:24[23]). Texts in hymns of thanksgiving express the same idea (32:7; 40:12[11]). This confession of faith predicates Yahweh's protection from tribulation and the trustworthy tutelary function of Yahweh's steadfast love and truth. Wisdom aphorisms[15] use this pair of terms as the subject of *nṣr* (Prov. 20:28; Ps. 61:8[7]). In Ps. 40:12(11) we find the basic theological foundation of this notable rhetorical figure.

The lamenting psalmist trusts in the fundamental promises of God (Ps. 12:7[6]) to intervene on behalf of the oppressed (v. 6[5]), expressing confidence that Yahweh will guard *(nṣr)* the wrongfully accused from persecutors (v. 8[7]). In Ps. 64:2(1); 140:2,5(1,4), this notion takes the form of a petition (64:2[1]: *mippaḥaḏ ᵓôyēḇ tiṣṣōr ḥayyay;* 140:2[1]: *mēᵓîš ḥᵃmāsîm tinṣᵉrēnî*). In both texts the situation is the same, even though Ps. 140 appears to include physical as well as verbal (v. 4[3]) violence against the oppressed psalmist. But such vivid language can also stand for violence in the form of false accusations and charges. The foregoing predications and precautions are all confessional in nature. Yahweh is both able and willing to deliver and protect the oppressed person who turns to him.

V. Prophets. Analysis of the *nṣr* texts in the prophetic literature must confront the difficulty that, while this literature uses *nṣr* for a wide range of concepts, the palette of occurrences is not very extensive. (Jer. 1:5 will be excluded from the outset, because

14. See the references to Ps. 119 in III above.
15. See above.

the form here actually derives from *yṣr;* this familiar term associated with creation also fits the context better than *nṣr.*)

Two passages in Jeremiah speak of *nōṣerîm,* but in very different ways. In Jer. 4:16, in the context of the prophet's announcement of disaster, the *nōṣerîm* are "guardians" who come from a distant land to raise their accusatory voices in and against (*ʿal* in a hostile sense) Jerusalem; in anticipation of v. 17, they are foreigners who already set out to accomplish Yahweh's punitive judgment. (Wilhelm Rudolph proposes emending *nōṣerîm* to *ṣārîm,* but this reading conflicts with the par. *šōmerîm* in v. 17.)[16] These *nōṣerîm* focus their attention on deliberate actions. In Jer. 31:6, in a familiar collection of assurances of salvation, the *nōṣerîm* are "sentinels" who stand like audible signposts on the hills of Ephraim, pointing the way for those "returning" (from the north and the farthest parts of the earth: v. 8) to Yahweh in Jerusalem upon Mt. Zion. They, too, are engaged in an activity that demands their undivided attention.[17] Since they speak of Yahweh as "our God," in this case they cannot be foreigners, but must belong to Israel or Judah (prophets of salvation?).

There are more examples of a single rhetorical figure being used to describe antithetical phenomena. One who has been spared *(nāṣûr)* is strictly speaking a positive figure. But when he survives universal judgment (which in various ways has already struck down those both far off and near) only finally to perish himself, he is a tragic figure (Ezk. 6:12, in the context of vv. 11-13). By contrast, the Servant of God in Deutero-Isaiah (49:6) comes to restore the *neṣûrê yiśrāʾēl* (following *Q*), the "survivors of Israel," who have been preserved in the Diaspora after deportation; part of his mission is to bring them home. In other words, the *neṣûrîm* are the members of the people of God who have been protected and preserved in their identity. The Servant himself could be called a *nāṣûr,* since he is the object of Yahweh's keeping and protection. Of course Isa. 42:6; 49:8, the texts to which this observation applies, appear in passages that are supplementary to the actual Servant Songs (42:1-4,5-9; 49:1-6,7-12). They are no longer understood to be integral parts of the songs. Karl Elliger thinks 42:5-9 is addressed to Cyrus; Claus Westermann thinks it is addressed to the "Servant," to be understood here collectively as representing Israel (added epexegetically to the Servant song 42:1-4).[18] Both derive the form in v. 6 from *yṣr* rather than *nṣr,* but this interpretation is unnecessary. The interpretation of the passage is still disputed (cf. the uncertainty over tense [completed act or intention?] in the ancient versions and *BHS*). Neither is there any compelling reason not to see these verses as referring still to the Servant. Vv. 6f., in an oracle of Yahweh, speak in the 1st person of the calling of the Servant, his mission, and favor shown him by Yahweh, which includes "keeping" him *(weʾeṣṣorḵā).* The same theme is sounded in 49:8 (in some phrases identical with 42:6;

16. W. Rudolph, *Jeremia. HAT,* XII (²1958), 30.

17. On the authenticity of these passages see W. Thiel, *Die deuteronomistischen Redaktion von Jeremia. WMANT,* 41, 52 (1973-81), in loc., who is much more favorable to 4:16 than to 31:6; but see the discussion.

18. K. Elliger, *Deuterojesaja. BK,* XI/1 (1978), 229-231; C. Westermann, *Isaiah 40–66. OTL* (Eng. trans. 1969), 97-101.

here, too, Westermann proposes to read a form of *yṣr*[19]). In both passages it appears to be important that Yahweh himself speaks of his protective activity.

In the "Song of the Vineyard" in the Apocalypse of Isaiah (27:2-5), Yahweh describes himself as the "keeper" (*nōṣ^erâ,* suffixed ptcp.) of the vineyard, who keeps his eye on it (v. 3: *'eṣṣ^orennâ*) day and night so that no one can harm it. As in ch. 5, the "vineyard" is the people of God. A hymn to the strong city (surely Jerusalem) calls on it to open its gates so that the *gôy ṣaddîq* may enter in; the latter is said to "keep faith" in Yahweh (26:2; cf. vv. 3,4), by whom it is kept *(nṣr)* in peace *(šālôm)* (v. 3). Here Yahweh is not speaking in the 1st person; instead the hymn describes what he does. Once again, however, there is a causal relationship between the conduct of the people toward Yahweh and Yahweh's actions. Trust on the people's part meets with favor on Yahweh's part.[20]

In Hab. 2:1 the prophet stands at his watchtower *(mišmereṯ)* and watchpost (*maṣṣôrî,* with 1QpHab), probably a technical term for the place where oracles are received.[21]

VI. Miscellaneous. A series of other OT passages use *nṣr* in highly diverse ways. For example, the term can be used for the siege of a city or stronghold (Isa. 1:8; Nah. 2:2[1]). Many scholars have proposed emending Isa. 1:8, on the grounds that "besieged city" does not fit the context of vv. 4-9. Hans Wildberger's "restoration" of the text is not convincing; Otto Kaiser's interpretation also remains obscure.[22] All the versions read "besieged city; *BHS* adopts August Dillmann's reading: *n^eṣôrâ,* from *ṣwr.*[23] If it is truly quite impossible to make sense of this expression from its context (which is not a settled conclusion), *'îr n^eṣûrâ* could be understood as a "protected [by Yahweh] city." But the point of v. 8 appears to be that, despite the survival of the *baṯ-ṣîyôn,* protection and security are (still) not guaranteed and final (cf. v. 5).

Opinions differ also about the interpretation of Nah. 2:2(1). In this prophetic description of the fall of Nineveh (2:2-14[1-13], without v. 3[2]), one might see the account as beginning with the statement that the "destroyer"[24] has come up against the city and has besieged the stronghold (*nāṣôr m^eṣurâ;* here the Masoretes place the *athnach*). Then follow the (ironic) demands (masc. impvs.) to redouble the (futile) defensive struggle. On these grounds some exegetes propose including the first phrase in these demands: Friedrich Horst translates "reinforce the watches," repointing *m^eṣurâ* as *maṣṣārâ* ("watch," from *nṣr*); Elliger treats the phrase similarly but keeps *m^eṣurâ* ("rampart"): "Guard the rampart" (cf. NRSV).[25]

---

19. Westermann, *Isaiah 40–66,* 212.

20. Both passages present problems of interpretation; see H. Wildberger, *Isaiah 13–27* (Eng. trans., Minneapolis, 1997), in loc.

21. J. Jeremias, *Kultprophetie und Gerichtsverkündigung in der späten Königszeit Israels. WMANT,* 35 (1970), 104ff.

22. *Isaiah 1–12* (Eng. trans., Minneapolis, 1991), 19f., following F. X. Wutz; O. Kaiser, *Isaiah 1–12. OTL* (Eng. trans. ²1983), 17, n. 9 (differing from the 1st ed. [and Ger. eds. 1-4]).

23. Dillmann, *Der Prophet Jesaja. KEHAT* (⁵1890), in loc.

24. Elliger, *Das Buch der zwölf kleinen Propheten. ATD,* 25 (⁸1982), in loc.

25. F. Horst, *Die zwölf kleinen Propheten. HAT,* XIV (²1954), 160; Elliger, *ATD,* 25, 10.

In a prophecy of disaster in Trito-Isaiah (65:1-7), v. 4 uses the form *neṣûrîm,* usually translated (following the LXX) as "caves,"[26] in which those who are threatened by Yahweh spend the night (possibly to perform incubation rites[27]); the context associates these caves with idolatry. Bernhard Duhm thought that the obscure term meant "guard booths";[28] *BHS* analyzes the form as two words, *bên ṣûrîm,* "between rocks." But v. 4b exhibits parallel structure; if the principle of parallelism applies to v. 4a, the second line might have a meaning similar to that of the first: those who sit inside tombs spend the night among the "preserved," i.e., the dead.

A fixed idiom is used in 2 K. 17:9; 18:8 to describe the totality of a fortified site: *mimmigdal nōṣerîm ʿaḏ-ʿîr miḇṣār,* "from watchtower to fortified city [citadel]." Job 27:18 refers to a sentinel who makes a booth (e.g., in a field or vineyard at harvest time), which clearly is meant to provide only temporary protection. Job uses this simile *(ke)* to describe the enterprises of the wicked — superficially splendid and successful but actually feeble and frail.

In two passages the qal pass. ptcp. of *nṣr* means "be hidden." The prostitute who entices the callow youth (Prov. 7:10) is described as *neṣuraṯ lēḇ,* "hidden, uncommunicative with respect to her heart" — i.e., she does not reveal her true intentions. The expression can hardly convey the active meaning "with observant heart";[29] it must be a negative characterization. In Isa. 48:6 Deutero-Isaiah conveys Yahweh's intention to have unprecedented, hitherto unknown salvation declared and then to accomplish it. God's words are spoken in the 1st person. The salvation to come is described as new *(ḥadāšôṯ)* and hidden *(neṣurôṯ).*

VII. Theological Considerations. Our discussion has already referred repeatedly to theological usage of the root *nṣr.* Wisdom Literature, documents of OT spirituality (Psalms), and finally prophetic texts (esp. Deutero-Isaiah) speak of Yahweh's favor that protects and preserves the people of God. The upright, those who strive to keep God's commandments (as enshrined both in the law [Ps. 119] and in the rules of conduct laid down by wisdom [Proverbs]), can be assured of Yahweh's attentive protection.

In Ex. 34:6,7, a confessional statement has been added to the traditional material of J; clearly drawing on formulaic language, it is extremely concentrated theologically. V. 7 acknowledges Yahweh as *nōṣēr ḥeseḏ lāʾalāpîm;* the context shows that this *ḥeseḏ* manifests itself as mercy, pity, patience, and readiness to forgive. This God who maintains benevolence is *raḇ-ḥeseḏ weʾemeṯ* (v. 6). A similar formulation appears in the Decalog (Ex. 20:6). Here the *ʾalāpîm* are described more specifically as the *ʾōhaḇay* and the *šōmerê miṣwôṯay* (the suf. refers to Yahweh). Here again *nṣr* describes God's beneficent treatment of human beings.

Even more pregnant theologically is the election tradition recorded in the Song of Moses, which traces Israel's beginnings to Yahweh's finding his people in the desert

---

26. *HAL,* II, 716.
27. Westermann, *Isaiah 40–66,* 401.
28. Duhm, *Das Buch Jesaja* (Tübingen, ⁹1968), in loc.
29. Plöger, *BK,* XVII, 73, 74.

(Dt. 32:10; cf. Hos. 9:10; Jer. 31:2-3). God's care for the (helpless) people he found necessarily included shielding and guarding them (like the apple of the eye). Here Yahweh's tutelary activity is described with particular intensity and sensitivity. The root *nṣr* conveys almost emotional overtones.

The Blessing of Moses contains a highly characteristic example of the theologico-anthropological aspect of *nṣr* (Dt. 33:9). Within the blessing of Levi (vv. 8-11), vv. 9b,10 play a special role: these verses speak of Levi in the plural, whereas the other verses use only the singular. This "interpolation" may be considered secondary: the transition from v. 9a to v. 11 would be easy, and the change to the singular in v. 9b in the LXX and the Dead Sea Scrolls is clearly not original, but an attempt at harmonization. If these verses are not secondary, they are meant to explain why the members of the tribe of Levi turned their backs on family ties: because *(kî)* they observed *(šāmar)* Moses' word and strictly kept *(nāṣar)* his covenant. Thus they should (and will) fulfill their mission described in v. 10. These two verses present the tribe of Levi as preserving and handing on the laws and ordinances given through Moses. It is interesting that keeping the ordinances given by God not only brings personal well-being but also results in (or should we even say: qualifies for?) service to the community.

VIII. *nṭr*. A few passages in the Hebrew OT use → נטר *nāṭar* in the sense of "guard, keep, observe."

IX. LXX. The verb clearly created difficulties for the translators of the LXX, since they used a total of 26 words to translate it, some only once. The predominant translations are *ekzēteín* (11 times), *phylássein* (10 times), *tēreín* (6 times), and *exereunán* (5 times).

Wagner

נֵצֶר *nēṣer*

The noun *nēṣer* derives from a root that is not represented by a verb in the Hebrew OT. The same root also appears as a noun in Middle Hebrew, Judeo-Aramaic, and Arabic (Arab. *naḍura* means "gleam, blossom").[1] The meaning of the noun is constant: "shoot, blossom, branch, scion." In extension of this basic botanical meaning, the word is applied to historical situations: branch or shoot of a clan, offshoot of the rootstock of a family. This meaning appears in the well-known oracle of salvation Isa. 11:1-11

---

nēṣer. I. F. M. Brayley, " 'Yahweh Is the Guardian of His Plantation': A Note on Is. 60,21," *Bibl,* 41 (1960), 275-286; L. Moraldi, "Qumrania: *nēṣer* e *ṣemaḥ,*" *RSO,* 45 (1970), 209-216.

1. *HAL,* II, 718.

(the authenticity of which is disputed by Otto Kaiser but affirmed by many others),[2] which declares that a shoot *(nēṣer)* shall come out from the stump of Jesse (reading *yiprah* with the versions).

The image of a new king as *nēṣer* may be compared to the similar usage of → צמח *ṣemaḥ,* "branch" (Jer. 23:5; Zec. 3:8; 6:12). Geo Widengren finds here an allusion to the idea of the king as tree of life or the scepter as a branch of this tree.[3] One can hardly doubt that there are overtones of royal ideology in these texts. The basis is probably the notion (found among many Semitic peoples) that the family is like a tree, its vital force residing in its roots.[4]

A similar passage occurs in the Deir ʿAlla inscription (II, 5, 14), which speaks of a *nqr* (Old Aramaic = *nṣr*) who, after the time of tribulation, will inaugurate a new age of prosperity.[5]

In Trito-Isaiah's great prophecy of salvation, which goes into great detail concerning its nature, Isa. 60:21 calls the people *nēṣer maṭṭāʿê YHWH,* the shoot or scion of Yahweh's plantations (cf. 1QIs[a]); on them rests the glorious future.[6]

Daniel's extended historical vision, which sketches the course of history under the Persians and Alexander the Great from the perspective of the conflicts between the Ptolemies and the Seleucids, speaks of the successful campaigns of Ptolemy III Euergetes against Seleucis II Callinicus, calling him a shoot from (his father's) roots (Dnl. 11:7; the LXX reads *nēṣer miššorāšāyw*[7]).

In a song of triumph celebrating the fall of the king of Babylon, Isa. 14:19 uses *nēṣer* in its literal sense, albeit in a simile. The king's fall is depicted graphically by the image of his corpse, cast out of its grave, lying like a trampled branch (*k^enēṣer niṯʿāḇ* [*niṯʿāḇ* must have undergone an analogous extension of meaning]). Many exegetes emend *nēṣer* to *nēpel,* "miscarriage,"[8] but the point of comparison is not being buried but being cast off in contempt.

The *Hodayoth* of Qumran use *nēṣer* in 5 passages, with emphasis on its metaphorical meaning. In 1QH 6:15 the imagery has preserved many details of the word's botanical background: shoot, foliage, planting. In 6:16 the planting is pictured as a tree with branches and roots.[9] The "everlasting planting" is probably the Qumran community itself; the branches are its individual members or a particular messianic figure.[10] In 7:19 the "I" of the hymns (= the Teacher of Righteousness) appears to be empowered

---

2. Kaiser, *Isaiah 1–12. OTL* (Eng. trans. [2]1983), 253f.; cf. H. Wildberger, *Isaiah 1–12* (Eng. trans., Minneapolis, 1991), 465-69.

3. G. Widengren, *Sakrales Königtum im AT und im Judentum* (Stuttgart, 1955), 56; *idem, The King and the Tree of Life in Ancient Near Eastern Religion. UUÅ,* 1951/4, 50.

4. Kaiser, *Isaiah 1–12,* 255.

5. H. Ringgren, *RoB,* 36 (1977), 88.

6. Brayley, 275ff.

7. See *BHS* and O. Plöger, *Das Buch Daniel. KAT,* XVIII (1965), 155.

8. H. Wildberger, *Isaiah 13–27* (Eng. trans., Minneapolis, 1997), 42, 46.

9. → נטע *nāṭaʿ.*

10. A. Dupont-Sommer, *The Essene Writings from Qumran* (Eng. trans., repr. Gloucester, Mass., 1973), 219, n. 2.

by God to make a planting *(maṭṭaʿ)* flourish and cause the shoot to wax in strength *(lᵉgaddēl nēṣer)*. The point of this passage is surely the growth and security of the community. The same idea lies behind the differentiated use of *nēṣer* in 8:6,8,10. First trees of life belong to the plantation, which are to bring forth *nēṣer* for the eternal plantation (v. 6). The offshoot of its foliage (the subj. having shifted casually to the tree belonging to the plantation) is to serve as food for the animals dwelling in the forest (v. 8). But the one who brings forth the *nēṣer qōḏeš* for the plantation of truth remains hidden (v. 10). As in 6:15, "holy offshoot" can be understood both collectively and individually.

The LXX uses *ánthos, phytón,* and *ékgonos* to translate *nēṣer*.

Wagner

נָקַב *nāqaḇ;* נֶקֶב *neqeḇ;* נְקֵבָה *nᵉqēḇâ;* מַקֶּבֶת *maqqeḇet*

I. Etymology. II. 1. The Verb in the OT; 2. The Nouns in the OT; 3. LXX.

I. Etymology. Modern lexicons generally distinguish the root *nqb* from → קבב *qbb.*[1] The root *nqb* is attested in most Semitic languages. In Arabic the verb means "pierce, make a hole," but also "single out" and hence "make (someone) a leader" (cf. *naqīb,* "leader"). In Nabatean *nqb* means "(perforate >) appoint."[2] Akk. *naqâbu* means "deflower";[3] it occurs also in Gilgamesh: "whose skull pierces the heavens." The Siloam inscription uses the verb to mean "break through (rock)" and the noun *nqbh* to mean "breach" or "tunnel."[4] The basic meaning of *nāqaḇ* is therefore probably "make a hole, pierce." The noun *nᵉqēḇâ,* "female creature, woman," is likely related. Whether Ugar. *nqbn,* "part of the harness of a saddle animal," is related is unclear.[5]

II. 1. *The Verb in the OT.* For the verb, the meaning "pierce, bore" is attested unambiguously in 2 K. 12:10(Eng. v. 9) (boring a hole [*ḥōr*] in the lid of a chest), 18:21

nāqaḇ. H. C. Brichto, *The Problem of "Curse" in the Hebrew Bible. JBLMS,* 13 (1963); M. Dahood, "The Ugaritic Parallel Pair *qra* ǁ *qba* in Isa. 62:2," *Bibl,* 58 (1972), 527f.; E. Lipiński, "Les conceptions et couches merveilleuses de ʿAnath," *Syr,* 42 (1965), 45-73; J. J. Rabinowitz, "A Clue to the Nabatean Contract from the Dead Sea Region," *BASOR,* 139 (1955), 11-14; J. Scharbert, "'Fluchen' und 'Segnen' im AT," *Bibl,* 39 (1958), 1-26; H. Schult, "Leviticus 24,15b und 16a," *Dielheimer Blätter zum AT,* 7 (1974), 31f.; J. Starcky, "Un contrat nabatéen sur papyrus," *RB,* 61 (1954), 161-181; E. Ullendorff, "Job III 8," *VT,* 11 (1961), 350f.; J. Weingreen, "The Case of the Blasphemer," *VT,* 22 (1972), 118-123.

1. But see Scharbert, 14f.
2. *DISO,* 185; cf. also Rabinowitz, 14; and Starcky, 179.
3. *AHw,* II, 743; *CAD,* XI/1, 328.
4. *KAI,* 189, 1,2,4.
5. *WUS,* no. 1839.

par. Isa. 36:6 (a broken reed pierces someone's hand), and Job 40:24,26(41:2) (pierce the nose or jaw of a wild beast with a hook in order to tame it). In Hag. 1:6 the *ṣᵉrôr nāqûḇ* is a "bag with holes." In Hab. 3:14 the verb can hardly mean "bore through"; it must mean "strike a hole" (in the head, with sticks). Gen. 30:28 (*noqḇâ śᵉḵārᵉḵā,* "name your wages" [i.e., from the animals in the flock]) reflects the practice of identifying an animal by means of a hole in its ear.

From "mark, identify" it is not a long way to the meaning "distinguish, honor" (a human being). The *nᵉquḇê rē'šîṯ haggôyim* in Am. 6:1 are "the most distinguished among the first of the nations," i.e., the most aristocratic;[6] derivation from *qbh,* "pronounce (a name)," is unnecessary.[7] In the case of human beings, identification by a name replaces identification by a hole in the ear. In lists of persons, therefore, the niphal in conjunction with *bᵉšēmôṯ* means "designated by name" (Nu. 1:17; Ezr. 8:20; 1 Ch. 12:32[31]; 16:41; 2 Ch. 28:15; 31:19). The text always refers to appointment to a particular high office, in other words, a distinction. According to Isa. 62:2, vindicated Israel will be called "by a new name that the mouth of Yahweh will give" (reading *yiqqᵉḇennû*); here *nāqaḇ* has the nuance of "giving a (new) name as a mark of distinction."

In Lev. 24:11,15f. *nāqaḇ* takes on a different nuance in conjunction with the name of Yahweh. Because the verb parallels the piel of *qll,* it is usually translated "blaspheme (the name of Yahweh)." The different legal consequences ("bear the sin" in the sense of "have to live with the curse conjured up by the act" vs. "be put to death") show that *nqb* denotes a more serious offense than *qillēl.* "Cursing" refers to careless derogatory speech concerning God; "blaspheming" refers to deliberate slanderous speech concerning Yahweh, with explicit emphasis on Yahweh's name.[8] It is unlikely that this passage already interprets the prohibition against wrongful use of Yahweh's name (Ex. 20:7; Dt. 5:11) as an absolute prohibition against any use whatever of the name. The text refers rather to a negative "branding" of the name of Yahweh.

2. *The Nouns in the OT.* The meaning of the nouns developed from the basic meaning of the verbal root. The noun → מקבת *maqqeḇeṯ* has two meanings: "hole, opening (of a well)" (Isa. 51:1) and "hammer" (Jgs. 4:21; 1 K. 6:7; Isa. 44:12; Jer. 10:4). The meaning of *neqeḇ* in Ezk. 28:13 is unclear. Ancient and modern translators can only venture conjectures ("cavities" in the body of the king of Tyre?). Edward Lipiński suggests the sexual orifice of the female body;[9] this is quite unlikely, since the subject of discourse is a male (whom Lipiński pictures as a hermaphrodite).

The noun *nᵉqēḇâ,* "female," may be associated with the meaning "deflower." It appears almost always in conjunction with → זכר *zākhār,* "male."[10]

---

6. H. W. Wolff, *Joel and Amos. Herm* (Eng. trans. 1974), 274f.; W. Rudolph, *Amos. KAT,* XIII/2 (1971), 215f.

7. Contra Dahood.

8. See Schult.

9. Pp. 49-52.

10. On Jer. 31:22 → IV, 237f.

3. *LXX.* Only in the passages where *nqb* means "pierce" does the LXX remain close to the Hebrew meaning: *tetraínein* (2 K. 12:10; 18:21; Isa. 36:6; Job 40:19,24), *trypán* (Job 40:26[41:2]; Hag. 1:6), *diakóptein* (Hab. 3:14). Elsewhere it translates freely, depending on the context: *(ep)onomázein* (Lev. 24:11,16), *ana/epikaleín, synágein* (Ezr. 8:20), *diastéllein* (Gen. 30:28). For *n^eqēḇâ* it uses *thēly* (once *thēlykós*). Jer. 31:22 is interpreted in a different sense.

The noun *maqqeḇeṯ* is rended by *sphýra* and *téretron* ("drill"), and in Isa. 51:1 by *bóthynos.*

Scharbert

נָקָה *nāqâ;* נָקִי *nāqî;* נִקָּיוֹן *niqqāyôn*

I. 1. Etymology; 2. Occurrences. II. Verb: 1. Niphal; 2. Piel. III. *nāqî.* IV. *niqqāyôn.* V. LXX.

I. 1. *Etymology.* The central etymological problem is the relationship between Heb. *nqh (nqy)* and Akk. *naqû,* "pour a libation, offer." If they do not share a common root,[1] we are dealing with two homophonic but distinct forms, with the meanings "be free from punishment" (Hebrew) and "pour a libation, offer" (Akkadian), each with its own derivatives and Semitic parallels. If the two words derive from a common root, we can assume its original meaning to be "empty, be emptied." It is quite possible to connect Akk. "pour out a libation" with this meaning.[2] On the other side, in both Hebrew and Aramaic the meaning "empty" probably still appears as a polysemic variant (see Am. 4:6; Joel 4:21[Eng. 3:21]; Isa. 3:26 below; and esp. the Targ. of Isa. 3:26 ["empty"] and *CIS,* 146 ["libation"][3]). Furthermore, the Isaiah Scroll from Qumran has a form of *nqh* in Isa. 65:3; the only appropriate translation is "empty."[4]

Depending on which theory one accepts, one must assign the following material to

---

nāqâ. F. C. Fensham, "Das Nicht-haftbar-Sein im Bundesbuch im Lichte der altorientalischen Rechtstexte," *JNSL,* 8 (1980), 17-34; C. van Leeuwen, "נקה *nqh* ni. 'to be innocent,'" *TLOT,* II, 763-67; G. Liedke, *Gestalt und Bezeichnung alttestamentlicher Rechtssätze. WMANT,* 39 (1971), 47f.; G. Many, *Der Rechtsstreit mit Gott (RIB) im Hiobbuch* (Munich, 1971); W. Paschen, *Rein und Unrein. SANT,* 24 (1970); W. Rudolph, "Ein Beitrag zum hebräischen Lexikon aus dem Joelbuch," *Hebräische Wortforschung. Festschrift W. Baumgartner. SVT,* 16 (1967), 244-250, esp. 250; L. A. Snijders, "Psaume 26 et l'innocence," *OTS,* 13 (1963), 112-130, esp. 112ff.; I. Willi-Plein, *Vorformen der Schriftexegese innerhalb des ATs. BZAW,* 123 (1971), 27, 165.

1. Von Soden notes that Heb. *nqy* is stative, whereas Akk. *naqû* is fientic.

2. Cf. the Hittite equivalent: J. Friedrich, *Hethitisches Wörterbuch* (Heidelberg, 1952), I, 193; and Erg. (1965), 3, 29; equivalence, 311.

3. But cf. *AP,* 72, 15,16, p. 183: "purification."

4. M. Tsevat, *HUCA,* 24 (1952/53), 109f.; cf. also *ANH,* 277, which cites *nāqî* with the meaning "empty."

two roots or to a single root: Hebrew (including extrabiblical material);[5] Akk. *naqû,* "offer a libation," and its derivatives;[6] Aram. *nqy,* pael "purify," ithpael "be purified," *naqyā' (n^e^qê),* "pure, free";[7] Syr. *nq',* pael "offer"; Mand. *niqia,* "gifts" (?), *naqia,* "pure, clean";[8] Phoen. *nqt,* probably "release";[9] OSA *nqy,* "be pure";[10] modern South Arabic (Soq.) *néqe,* "is pure."[11] In Arabic we find among other forms: *naqiya,* "be pure," II "purify," and *naqīy,* "pure, clean."

In the Dead Sea Scrolls *nqh* appears in CD 5:14f. ("without punishment"); 5Q19 2:2; 11QTemple 63:7,8. In Postbiblical Hebrew the piel of *nqh* means "purify, make guiltless"; *nāqî* means "pure, clear, bright, innocent, empty" (Bab. *Pes.* 22b on Ex. 21:28: "free, with loss of his property"); *niqqāyôn* means "purity, clarity, innocence"; cf. *n^e^qîyûṯ,* (1) "purity, cleanness" (with "cleanness" signifying something distinct from the Levitical notion of "purity,"[12] (2) "purity of life, guiltlessness."

2. *Occurrences.* The verb occurs 44 times: once in the qal (Jer. 49:12), 25 times in the niphal (Prov. 6:29; 11:21; 16:5; 17:5; 19:5,9; 28:20; Jer. 2:35; 25:29 [3 times]; 49:12 [twice]; Nu. 5:19,28,31; Gen. 24:8,41; Zec. 5:3 [twice]; Ex. 21:19; Jgs. 15:3; 1 S. 26:9; Isa. 3:26; Ps. 19:14[13]), and 18 times in the piel (Ex. 20:7; 34:7 [twice]; Jer. 30:11; [twice]; 46:28 [twice]; Job 9:28; 10:14; Nu. 14:18 [twice]; Nah. 1:3 [twice]; Joel 4:21[3:21] [twice]; Dt. 5:11; 1 K. 2:9; Ps. 19:13[12]).

The adjective occurs 43 times, 21 of which are in combination with *dām* (Dt. 19:10,13; 21:8,9; 27:25; 1 S. 19:5; 2 K. 21:16; 24:4 [twice]; Isa. 59:7; Jer. 2:34; 7:6; 19:4; 22:3,17; 26:15; Joel 4:19[3:19]; Jon. 1:14; Ps. 94:21; 106:38; Prov. 6:17); 22 occurrences are in other contexts (Gen. 24:41; 44:10; Ex. 21:28; 23:7; Nu. 32:22; Dt. 24:5; Josh. 2:17,19,20; 2 S. 3:28; 14:9; 1 K. 15:22; Ps. 10:8; 15:5; 24:4; Job 4:7; 9:23; 17:8; 22:19,30; 27:17; Prov. 1:11).

The noun *niqqāyôn* is found in Gen. 20:5; Hos. 8:5; Am. 4:6; Ps. 26:6; 73:13. Charles F. Whitley has proposed emending *w^e^nōqēm* in Ps. 99:8 to *w^e^nōqām;*[13] he also proposes emending the niphal in Jer. 49:12 to the qal infinitive absolute.

II. Verb. Isa. 3:26 (niphal) and probably Joel 4:21(3:21) (piel) are special cases. In Isa. 3:25f. Jerusalem is told that her men will fall in battle and she will sit on the ground like a woman in mourning, "bereft" in the sense of "emptied."[14] The context, too,

---

5. *KAI,* 200, 11: "be free (of guilt)"; F. M. Cross, "The Cave Inscriptions from Khirbet Beit Lei," *Near Eastern Archaeology in the Twentieth Century. Festschrift N. Glueck* (Garden City, N.Y., 1970), 302, 306, n. 16.
6. *AHw,* II, 744f.
7. See also *DISO,* 186.
8. *MdD,* 299b, 286a.
9. *KAI,* 50, 6.
10. Biella, 316.
11. W. Leslau, *Lexique Soqoṭri* (Paris, 1938).
12. Levy, *WTM,* III, 438.
13. C. F. Whitley, "Psalm 99,8," *ZAW,* 85 (1973), 177-230.
14. E.g., Tsevat, *HUCA,* 24 (1952/53), 110: "and she sits emptied upon the ground."

makes likely an association with a basic meaning "empty" in this passage.[15] In Joel 4:21(3:21) many read *niqqamtî* for the first occurrence of *niqqêṯî,* but without any textual evidence.[16] Here, too, the possible meaning "empty" suggests translating the passage "and I will pour out their own blood, which I have not (yet) poured out."[17] Those who do not find sufficient evidence for the meaning "empty" take the piel of *nqh* as meaning "leave unpunished"[18] and read v. 21a as a question ("And will I leave their blood guilt unpunished? I will not leave it unpunished") or as a gloss referring to v. 19 ("And I declare their blood exempt from punishment, which I had not wished to declare so").[19]

1. *Niphal.* The niphal means primarily "be free, exempt from punishment." This meaning appears in all the passages where the context provides no further details. If *nqh* means "be free" from something else, the "something else" is introduced by *min.* In such cases an element of punishment is usually implicit. The verb takes on a technical sense as a legal term indicating that, pursuant to some act, a person is exempt from responsibility and consequences, especially punishment. There is also a broader sense that applies to the ethical realm in general. The assailant in Ex. 21:19 is exempt from punishment (albeit required to indemnify the victim for consequent damages), as are the malefactors in Zec. 5:3 (being punished instead by Yahweh's curse).[20] Immunity to the effects of "the water of bitterness that brings the curse" demonstrates the innocence of a wife unjustly accused of adultery (Nu. 5:19,28). In oracles of judgment the niphal of *nqh* means "escape judgment, go unpunished" (Jer. 25:29; 49:12). In Jer. 2:35 *nqh* is always translated "be innocent," as the second half of the verse requires, but Israel deduces its innocence from its having gone unpunished; otherwise the second clause would make no sense: "I have gone unpunished (and am therefore innocent); surely his anger has turned from me." "Because Yahweh did not punish Israel for its deeds, . . . Israel treated them lightly; but Yahweh will call Israel to account for this lack of responsibility."[21]

The many passages in Proverbs where *nqh* appears (6:29; 11:21; 16:5; 17:5; 19:5,9; 28:20) all have the same form: ". . . shall not go unpunished." The verb is always negated; the punishment is never named but is certain to be inflicted (cf. 6:28 in relation to v. 29). The offense often involves ethical conduct rather than violation of an actual law. When this is the case, the logical consequence is an analogous punishment, ultimately inflicted by Yahweh (11:21; 16:5; 17:5).

---

15. Contra H. Wildberger, *Isaiah 1–12* (Eng. trans., Minneapolis, 1991), 157, 159, who translates "all alone" but takes the basic meaning "bare, clean, be pure," as his point of departure and understands the verb as referring primarily to the woman.

16. Including LXX; see *BHS; HAL,* II, 720.

17. G. R. Driver, *JTS,* 39 (1938), 402.

18. See below.

19. For the former see Rudolph, 250. For the latter see H. W. Wolff, *Joel and Amos. Herm* (Eng. trans. 1977), 73, 84.

20. Rudolph, *Sacharja 1–8. KAT,* XIII/4 (1976), 116.

21. Rudolph, *Jeremia. HAT,* XII (^{3}1968), 23.

In 5 passages *nqh* is constructed with *min.* In Gen. 24:8,41, the niphal means "be free" of an obligation assumed under oath (v. 8: *miššᵉḇuʿāṯî;* v. 11: *mēʾālāṯî*) and probably also from the conditional self-curse associated with an oath — in other words, punishment. The qualifiers *mippešaʿ* in Ps. 19:14(13) (free of great transgression) and *mēʿāwōn* in Nu. 5:31 (free from iniquity) refer to offenses, but the connection of punishment with offense is maintained; indeed, it may be the use of *nqh* that retains the element of punishment. In Ps. 19:14(13), a late text, "be blameless" refers to the psalmist's entire way of life, in particular "be free from offense and punishment" occasioned by unconscious transgressions; cf. the relationship of this psalm to *tôrâ* liturgies and descriptions of the *ṣaddîq,* including Pss. 24 and 15, discussed below.[22] An understanding of the phrase *niqqêṯî mippᵉlištîm* in Jgs. 15:3 likewise requires the connection between offense and punishment; or the verb may be taken here in the sense of the adjective (with *min*) in Nu. 32:22 ("free of obligation to . . .").

2. *Piel.* Analogously to the niphal, the piel means "let go unpunished, make or declare exempt from punishment." Again, this applies to all the passages were the verb appears alone, i.e., without a prepositional construction. Two passages introduce a particular qualifier with *min:* Job 10:14 (*mēʿāwōnî,* "acquit me of my iniquity") and Ps. 19:13(12) (*minnistārôṯ,* "clear me from hidden faults"). But the punitive aspect of *nqh* is still present: if Job sins (10:14), God will apprehend him and "not let him go unpunished for his sin."[23] The same is true in Ps. 19:13(12) (cf. also what was said above concerning v. 14[13]). Among the other passages where the piel of *nqh* appears without a preposition, meaning "let go unpunished," Job 9:28 alone is often treated as an exception, referring only to guilt (on account of vv. 29ff.). But vv. 25-28 deal with the consequences of Job's guilt in the eyes of God. V. 28a mentions these consequences ("I become afraid of all my suffering"), so that 28b must be understood as meaning "I know that you will not declare me exempt from punishment."[24] Of course, Job's punishment and guilt go together — "God does not declare him innocent, as one can see from God's treating him as guilty."[25]

In 1 K. 2:9 David charges Solomon not to "leave unpunished" the man who cursed him. Elsewhere it is always Yahweh who does not leave the sinner unpunished (Ex. 20:7; Dt. 5:11; the remaining 5 passages exhibit the pattern "God shows mercy, but does not leave the guilty totally unpunished": Jer. 30:11; 46:28; Ex. 34:7; Nu. 14:18; Nah. 1:3).

The use of the piel of *nqh* is thus quite uniform. Except in Ps. 19:13(12), all its occurrences are negated. The nature of the punishment is never described; in 1 K. 2:9 at least its execution is left open. Except in 1 K. 2:9, the subject is always Yahweh; according to Ex. 20:7; Dt. 5:11, he will not "leave unpunished" anyone who misuses

---

22. See also H. J. Kraus, *Psalms 1–59* (Eng. trans., Minneapolis, 1988), 275.
23. G. Fohrer, *Das Buch Hiob. KAT,* XVI (1963), 197.
24. *Ibid.,* 196.
25. F. Hesse, *Hiob. ZBK* (1978), 84.

his name. In texts that begin by praising God's goodness and mercy, there follows the phrase *w^e^naqqēh lō' y^e^naqqeh* ("but he does not leave totally unpunished") to attest to his retribution for the iniquity of the fathers (Ex. 34:7; Nu. 14:18; cf. Nah. 1:3). The formula is also addressed to Israel in Jer. 30:11; 46:28: "I will not leave you totally unpunished" — in other words, God will not destroy Israel, but will discipline Israel equitably.

III. *nāqî.* The adjective covers a broader semantic range than the verb. In the first instance, however, we observe an analogous usage in the sense "free of obligation" or "free of punishment/offense." Like the verb, *nāqî* can also mean "free" of an oath (Gen. 24:41; Josh. 2:17,20; always with *min*) or an obligation to someone (Nu. 32:22, with *min* and the person; cf. *nqh* niphal in Jgs. 15:3).

Ex. 21:28 uses *nāqî* as a legal term for "exempt from punishment," in contrast to the death penalty and expiation. Gen. 44:10 should also be interpreted in this sense: punishment for an offense is not exacted. In such contexts, *nqh* and *nāqî* are technical terms of exoneration; *nqh* "declares that liability for a situation deemed to be an offense is denied."[26] "The man who is exonerated has in fact struck his victim (Ex. 21:19); the ox whose owner is exonerated has in fact gored (Ex. 21:28). In both cases the נָקִי of judgment at the gate saves the accused from death, in Ex. 21:19 more precisely from blood vengeance." Gen. 44:10 shows "that the formulation of the decision is by no means limited to a law court," and Ex. 21:19 shows how decisions embodying minor self-contradictions come into being "by combining the proposals of both parties."[27]

Dt. 24:5; 1 K. 15:22 are also to be understood in a technical (probably legal) sense: exemption from compulsory public service (military service, labor service). The text states an exception to an otherwise binding obligation. The context first states the nature of the obligation, so that *nāqî* can be used without further qualification. Uniquely, Dt. 24:5 indicates the purpose of the exemption: *l^e^b̲ēṯô,* "for his house."

In 2 S. 3:28; 14:9; Josh. 2:19, in mutually comparable contexts, *nāqî* is used in the sense "free of liability for an offense and its consequences" ("just as עון can mean guilt and punishment, so can נקי mean blameless, not guilty"[28]), "free of bloodguilt." Thus *nāqî* means "guiltless" (2 S. 14:9, where the context implies "free from *'āwôn,*" since the opposite is "*he'āwōn* be on me and on my father's house") and "free of guilt" (and punishment) for a homicide for which the individual is not responsible (Josh. 2:19; opposite: his blood be upon our heads) or a murder that was not ordered (2 S. 3:28, where *nāqî* is used twice with *min:* "guiltless before Yahweh for the blood").

In addition, *nāqî* can mean "innocent" (one who has committed no offense or is in the right) without reference to a specific act. The legal element is still present: Ex. 23:7 (par. to *ṣaddîq* and in contrast with *rāšā'*); Ps. 10:8 (par. to *'ānî*); 15:5; Prov. 1:11 (in an extended sense). The poor in particular are considered innocent (Jer. 2:34; Ps. 10:8).

---

26. Liedke, 47, citing F. Horst, *Hiob. BK,* XVI/1 (1968), 152, on Job 9:28; cf. above.
27. Liedke, 48.
28. C. Westermann, *Genesis 37–50* (Eng. trans., Minneapolis, 1982), 133.

In the context of a liturgy, Ps. 24:4 speaks of "clean hands" (among other things) as a requirement for entering the sanctuary. The ethical nature of this requirement is clear from the parallel "pure heart," the two concrete examples (esp. "does not swear deceitfully"), and the detailed parallel in Ps. 15:2-5, where all the requirements "refer to proper conduct in the everyday life of the community"[29] — the portrait of an "exemplary" *ṣaddîq*.[30] In the case of Job, too, *nāqî* means "innocent," although here the concept is extended and generalized, so as to encompass a total way of life: one who is innocent keeps far from sin (cf. 22:23), lives devoutly, has clean hands unspotted by guilt (22:30). It is claimed that such a person will never perish (4:7, in the language of wisdom, par. *yāšār*). God nevertheless — Job says — destroys the innocent like the guilty (9:23, par. *tām* and in contrast with *rāšā'*). The ultimate triumph of the innocent over the wicked is the subject of 27:17 (wisdom language; cf. 17:8, par. *yāšār;* 22:19, par. *ṣaddîqîm*). In Job *nāqî* also appears as the subject of various verbs (17:8; 22:19; 27:17).

The obvious question whether the various semantic aspects of *nqh* and *nāqî* can be accounted for in terms of conceptual development can be answered only with great caution. Is the narrowly defined meaning "(be) guiltless, exempt from punishment," a secondary development of the legal term, preceded by the more general meaning "(be) free, exempt" (which was still preserved)? But even the meaning "(be) free, exempt" is confined to certain contexts and associated with specific complements (obligation, responsibility, guilt, punishment). If the basic meaning is "empty, be empty," the meaning "(be) free" can probably be accommodated, even in its specialized senses. In the OT an understanding of *nqh* and *nāqî* as meaning "(be) clean" — unless this simply means "innocent" — must evolve from a usage that has been extended to the general ethical realm (including use in certain cultic texts). Matitiahu Tsevat says of *nqh:* "Its original meaning [was] 'to empty' from which the common 'to cleanse' is derived."[31] The meaning "(be) clean" can be extended figuratively to "(be) free from guilt or obligation."[32]

The phrase *dām nāqî,* "innocent blood," refers to the blood of someone wrongfully killed; shedding such blood incurs bloodguilt (Dt. 19:10) and must be expiated. This does not include killing in battle, a just death sentence, blood vengeance, the blood of an intruder, or the like. Bloody deeds were categorized variously,[33] and distinctions were made as to the guilt incurred (Dt. 19:1-13; Josh. 20:1ff.). When innocent blood is shed, bloodguilt *(dāmîm)* rests on the culprit (Dt. 19:10) or the culprit's entire family (2 S. 14:9), or even the whole land (Ps. 106:38) and nation (cf. Josh. 2:19). The nation and the land are particularly affected when an unknown culprit (Dt. 21:8) or the king (2 K. 24:3f.) has shed innocent blood. When blood vengeance (or some other form of

---

29. Kraus, *Psalms 1–59,* 227.

30. G. von Rad, " 'Righteousness' and 'Life' in the Cultic Language of the Psalms," *The Problem of the Hexateuch and Other Essays* (Eng. trans., New York, 1966), 246.

31. M. Tsevat, *HUCA,* 24 (1953/54), 109f.

32. D. R. Hillers, *JBL,* 97 (1978), 179.

33. → דם *dām,* III, 243f.

the death penalty) was exacted, the blood of the culprit "purged" from Israel the blood of the innocent victim with its fateful power (Dt. 19:13).[34] If the culprit remained unknown, an expiatory rite had to be performed (Dt. 21:8f.).

In the legal texts Dt. 19:10,13; 21:8f.; 27:25, *nāqî* means "innocent"; it can be used of any person, and its specific force is determined by the case at hand. In Dt. 19:10 someone who has inadvertently killed a person is not subject to blood vengeance: that would be shedding innocent blood; 27:25, where bribery precipitates the shedding of innocent blood, condemns primarily clandestine acts rather than those that are a matter of record. The word is also used in this sense in Jer. 7:6; Isa. 59:7 (probably referring to the helpless[35]).

Certain classes of persons are described as innocent:

1. Those unjustly condemned to death, an act that is often a royal transgression: Ps. 94:21; 106:38 (emended: "Reference is made to the bloody verdicts and judicial murders which an unjust judicial system conjured up. . . . Because of the later gloss . . . v. 38 was interpreted incorrectly together with v. 37"[36]); 2 K. 21:16; 24:4 (charged to Manasseh); Jer. 22:3 (Deuteronomistic), 17 (possibly Deuteronomistic). Since the king is addressed in the Jeremiah texts, both the context and the reference to 2 K. 21:16 suggest judicial murders or murders left unpunished.

2. Sacrificed children (Ps. 106:38 MT). This is probably a secondary interpretation: "A gloss to דם נקי has been interpolated here. It clearly breaks up the meter and interprets דם נקי incorrectly."[37] Without the gloss, the text refers to bloody verdicts.[38] In Jer. 19:4 the interpretation of *n^eqîyîm* as children remains uncertain; it depends on the meaning of *hammāqôm hazzeh*. If the latter phrase refers to Tophet, "the reference is not to 2 K. 21:16 but to child sacrifices, for which the kings led the way by setting bad examples (2 K. 16:3; 21:6)."[39] If *hammāqôm* means Jerusalem, as it does elsewhere, the "blood of innocent victims" probably refers again to evils in the administration of justice, for which a king would once more be responsible.[40] Possibly Jer. 19:4 comprehends both cases.[41]

3. Judahites whose blood was shed (Joel 4:19[3:19]). Interpretation of this expression depends on to whom the suffix in *b^eʾarṣām* refers. The text may reflect "the slaying of innocent and defenseless people in the land of Egypt and Edom," i.e., colonists or refugees and political émigrés,[42] or it may refer to Judahites slain in their own land by Egypt and Edom. In the latter case, the events of 2 K. 23:29 (Megiddo) or Ob. 9-14 must be meant.[43]

---

34. → III, 242f.
35. Cf. *TLOT,* II, 765; and Prov. 6:17.
36. H.-J. Kraus, *Psalms 60–150* (Eng. trans., Minneapolis, 1989), 316, 321.
37. *Ibid.,* 316.
38. See above.
39. Rudolph, *HAT,* XII^3, 126.
40. F. Giesebrecht, *Das Buch Jeremia. HKAT,* III/2 (^{2}1907), 110.
41. A. Weiser, *Das Buch Jeremia. ATD,* 20/21 (^{6}1969), 163.
42. W. Rudolph, *Joel. KAT,* XIII/2 (1971), 87.
43. Cf. Wolff, *Joel and Amos,* 84.

4. Prophets, who were probably the victims of some of the judicial murders. Wilhelm Rudolph, emending the text of Jer. 2:34, finds a reference to the prophets: "Since mention of the poor is inappropriate to the context, we should at least follow the LXX in deleting אביונים."[44] V. 34b, which can apply only to adults, rules out child sacrifice; neither can the text refer simply to judicial murders in general. The most likely targets were the prophets of Yahweh, "who paid with their lives for protesting against the cult of foreign deities."[45] "Jeremiah is probably thinking especially of the age of Manasseh, when 'innocent blood was shed in streams' (2 K. 21:16)."[46]

5. Private individuals like David, persecuted by Saul (1 S. 19:5); Jeremiah, threatened by the authorities (Jer. 26:15); and Jonah, thrown overboard (Jon. 1:14). On the interpretation of *dām nāqî* in Jon. 1:14, see Hans Walter Wolff:

> Here formal Israelite legal terminology has been taken over; cf. the wording of Deut. 21:8; Jer. 26:15. . . . "Innocent blood" always refers to the (shedding of the) blood of a slain person or of someone who is about to be slain (cf. Deut. 21:8) — in this case, that is to say, Jonah's blood, not the blood of the sailors. . . . Uncertainty can only arise because it is called "innocent." For Jonah has finally, in v. 12, himself admitted his guilt, which has been known to the sailors ever since the lots were cast (v. 7). . . . This being so, נקיא can only refer to the behavior of the men with regard to (the shedding of) Jonah's blood. What worries them is that the nature of the slaying which Jonah expects, according to v. 12, is not a punishment that accords with his guilt — that is to say, they are afraid that Yahweh might expect a different kind of expiation, rather than that they should throw Jonah into the sea. In this case Yahweh would lay an irresponsible shedding of blood to their charge, as guilt (irresponsible because not really appropriate to Jonah's guilt). דם נקיא therefore means "unjustly shed blood."[47]

Innocent blood is mentioned in a variety of contexts: legal regulations (Dt. 19:10,13; 21:8f.; 27:25), narrative texts (1 S. 19:5: Saul seeks to kill David; 2 K. 21:16; 24:4: royal annals; Jon. 1:14), prophetic indictments (against the people: Jer. 2:34; 19:4 [Deuteronomistic]; cf. Isa. 59:7; against Jehoiakim: 22:17 [Deuteronomistic]; against foreign nations: Joel 4:19[3:19]), laments and poetic reviews of history (Ps. 94:21; 106:38), admonitions (Jer. 22:3 [Deuteronomistic]; cf. 7:6 [Deuteronomistic]), and threats (Jer. 26:15).

The phrase "innocent blood" appears in two basic forms: *dam (han)nāqî,* "(the) blood of the/an innocent person," and *dām nāqî,* "innocent blood."[48] The concept may have belonged to the language from early on (Dt. 19:10),[49] but it did not become frequent until the period of Deuteronomy and Jeremiah. It becomes a stereotyped term in the legal traditions of Deuteronomy and appears at the same time (more fluidly) in Jeremiah (2:34; 26:15). It then becomes a commonplace as a Deuteronomic and Deuter-

---

44. *HAT,* XII, 22.
45. *Ibid.,* 23.
46. P. 22.
47. Wolff, *Obadiah and Jonah* (Eng. trans., Minneapolis, 1986), 119f. See also J. Magonet, *Form and Meaning. BBET,* 2 (1976), 69-73.
48. On the relationship between the two, → III, 243.
49. See R. P. Merendino, *Das deuteronomistische Gesetz. BBB,* 31 (1969), 206ff.

onomistic concept. Both 2 K. 24:4 and 21:16 are Deuteronomistic; except for 2:34; 26:25, so are the texts in Jeremiah:[50] 7:6; 19:4; 22:3; 22:17. Ps. 94:21; 106:38 are postexilic (cf. the Deuteronomistic structure of Ps. 106). The usage was borrowed in the late texts Isa. 59:7; Joel 4:19(18); Jon. 1:14; Prov. 6:17. Still problematic is 1 S. 19:5. The other occurrences in Deuteronomy (19:10,13; 27:25; 21:8f.) are in the context of the ritual for expiating a murder at the hands of an unknown assailant; here *dām nāqî* is a legal term that has nothing to do with the Levitical cult (the phrase does not occur in Leviticus).

The blood of the innocent is protected by Yahweh's commandment (Dt. 19:1-3; cf. Jer. 22:3). To shed such blood is therefore a heinous offense (Isa. 59:7; Ps. 94:21; 106:38; Prov. 6:17; etc.), which Yahweh will not pardon (2 K. 24:4). He declares his judgment against such transgressions (Jer. 19:4 against Israel [cf. Ps. 106:38]; Joel 4:19[3:19] against Egypt and Edom; Jer. 22:17f. and 2 K. 24:3f. against the king). He hates "hands that shed innocent blood" (Prov. 6:17); he repays them for their iniquity and wipes them out (Ps. 94:21ff.). Therefore people beseech him not to take account of innocent blood (Jon. 1:14; Dt. 21:8f.).

Parallel to *nāqî* we find *ṣaddîq,* "righteous" (Ex. 23:7; Ps. 94:21; Job 22:19; 27:17); *yāšār,* "upright" (Job 4:7; 17:8); *ʿānî,* "poor" (Ps. 10:8f.); and *tām,* "blameless." Antonyms are: *rāšāʿ,* "wicked" (Ex. 23:7; Job 9:22f.; 22:18f.); *ḥānēp,* "godless" (Job 17:8); and *ʿeḇeḏ,* "servant" (Gen. 44:10). In 2 S. 14:9 we find the expression *ʿālay heʿāwōn wᵉʿal-bêṯ ʾāḇî.*

IV. *niqqāyôn.* The noun *niqqāyôn* occurs in Am. 4:6; Hos. 8:5; Gen. 20:5; Ps. 26:6; 73:13; in the last three it is used with *kappay* (Gen. 20:5 in a const. phrase; Ps. 26:6 and 73:13 in the expression *ʾerḥaṣ bᵉniqqāyôn kappay*). Different interpretations must be weighed, especially in the case of Am. 4:6; Hos. 8:5. Ina Willi-Plein proposes "cultic purity and innocence" as a single translation acceptable for all occurrences.[51] If so, in Am. 4:6 this "expression borrowed from the language of the cult . . . denoting the purity given by Yahweh is used ironically to describe the privation sent by Yahweh."[52] In Hos. 8:5b, too, usually considered a gloss, the word "hardly fits the Hoseanic context."[53] As a further emendation, in the meaningless כי מ of v. 6a Willi-Plein proposes supplying a פ (omitted by haplography) after the כ; the resulting כפים establishes a connection like that in Gen. 20:5. The reader's gloss then asks: "How long will Israel not maintain innocence of hands?" — in other words, how long will it continue to sin in the eyes of Yahweh?[54]

This uniform translation of *niqqāyôn* as "cultic purity and innocence" (which also obtains for the other passages) is directed against the theory of special meanings in Am. 4:6; Hos. 8:5. "Here [Hos. 8:5] נקיון means neither impunity nor innocence, but

---

50. Thiel, *Die deuteronomistischen Redaktion von Jeremia. WMANT,* 41, 52 (1973-81).
51. P. 165.
52. P. 27.
53. P. 165.
54. P. 165.

cleanness in the physical sense as in Am. 4:6."[55] For Am. 4:6 Wolff proposes "cleanness of teeth" or "shining teeth."[56] This meaning is also found in Postbiblical Hebrew.[57] The view that *niqqāyôn* is a cultic term might be supported by Ps. 26:6;[58] 73:13, but the word always refers to ethical innocence, which in turn establishes cultic purity. (The usage of *nqh* and *nāqî* likewise does not support a cultic interpretation.) In Gen. 20:5 there is no cultic context; *b^e niqyōn kappay,* "in innocence of hands" (par. to *ṣaddîq* in v. 4) has ethical force. Neither is there a cultic context in Ps. 73:13, which deals with the *ṣaddîq* whose obedience to God's law remains unrewarded despite proper conduct. He appeals to the handwashing of the oath of purification, which has demonstrated his (ethical) innocence: "The psalmist has obviously demonstrated by means of an oath of cleansing that his oppressive suffering (v. 14) is not to be attributed to a failure on his part. He is suffering in innocence."[59] In the cultic and ritual usage of Ps. 26:6, too, *niqqāyôn* denotes an ethical status, summarizing the preceding verses; vv. 9f. similarly characterize ethically the antithesis to the "innocence" of the supplicant: murderers whose hands are full of evil and bribes.[60] Here also belongs the parallel usage (in the context of an entrance liturgy) of *n^e qî kappayim* in Ps. 24:4 (cf. the discussion of Ps. 24:4 and Ps. 15 above) in the pair "clean hands and pure heart."[61] Whether the influence of prophetic ideas led to the linking of cult and ethics in the psalms or worship and God's law were interwoven from the beginning does not affect the ethical aspect of *niqqāyôn.*[62] In either case, though, the expression "I wash my hands in innocence" may well have become independent of its cultic context so as to be used more metaphorically (Gen. 20:5; also Ps. 73:13; the expression is already stereotyped;[63] cf. also the tendency of late texts like Job and Proverbs to spiritualize the meaning of the adj.).

Nevertheless, the semantics of Am. 4:6; Hos. 8:5 remains difficult. We must again understand Am. 4:6 ironically (unless a special meaning is involved[64]) or, on the basis of the possible root meaning "empty," treat it as referring to "empty" teeth.[65] In any case, the context (par. to lack of bread) makes the situation clear. For Hos. 8:5 we

---

55. W. Rudolph, *Hosea. KAT,* XIII/1 (1966), 158.

56. Wolff, *Joel and Amos,* 209.

57. Cf. the discussion of *n^e qîyûṯ* above; also Aram. "clean" in contrast to "dirty"; most recently *HAL,* II, 721: "cleanness, whiteness," citing C. M. Doughty, *Travels in Arabia Deserta,* 2 vols. (Cambridge, 1936), I, 366.

58. I. L. Seeligmann, "Zur Terminololgie für das Gerichtsverfahren im Wortschatz der biblischen Hebräisch," *Hebräische Wortforschung. Festschrift W. Baumgartner. SVT,* 16 (1967), 258; N. Ridderbos, *GTT,* 50 (1950), 92.

59. Kraus, *Psalms 60–150,* 88.

60. Snijders.

61. → לֵב *lēḇ,* VII, 430; Kraus, *Psalms 1–59,* 314: "here purity and cleanness of external acts and the innermost movements of the heart are demanded."

62. For the former see H. Gunkel, et al.; for the latter, Kraus, *BK,* XV/1⁵, 226f.

63. C. Westermann, *Genesis 12–36* (Eng. trans., Minneapolis, 1985), 323.

64. See above.

65. See the discussion of the root's etymology above.

should probably have recourse to the most secure meaning, "innocence," and "purity," understood in the same sense. This interpretation rules out both idolatry and ethical misconduct:[66] "How long can Israel continue to be incapable of innocence?"

V. LXX. The LXX most often uses *athǭ́os/athǭoún* to represent *nqh/nāqî;* also worth mentioning are *atimṓrētos* (Prov. 11:21; 19:5; 28:10), *ekdikeín* (Zec. 5:3), *díkaios* (Job 9:23; 17:8; Joel 4:19[3:19]; Jon. 1:14; Prov. 6:17), *anaítios* (Dt. 19:10,13; 21:8), and *katharós/katharízein* (the latter not in the sense "be/make pure," as the context shows [Ex. 20:7; Dt. 5:11; Ex. 34:7; Nu. 14:18; Gen. 44:10; 24:8; also Job 4:7; Ps. 19:13f.[12f.]). The LXX translation of *nqh/nāqî* thus supports the meaning "unpunished, innocent," in both the legal and the more general ethical sense.

Warmuth

66. Cf. Kraus, *Psalms 1–59,* 314, on Ps. 24:4: Clean hands and a pure heart manifest themselves in two specific ways — no idolatry and no perjury.